THE CONSTRUCTION LAW LIBRARY FROM WILEY LAW PUBLICATIONS

CONSTRUCTION LITIGATION: STRATEGIES AND TECHNIQUES
Barry B. Bramble and Albert E. Phillips, Editors

CONSTRUCTION RENOVATION FORMBOOK
Robert F. Cushman and John W. DiNicola, Editors

CONSTRUCTION SCHEDULING: PREPARATION, LIABILITY, AND CLAIMS
Jon M. Wickwire, Thomas J. Driscoll, and Stephen B. Hurlbut

CONSTRUCTION SUBCONTRACTING: A LEGAL GUIDE FOR INDUSTRY PROFESSIONALS
Overton A. Currie, Neal J. Sweeney, and Randall F. Hafer, Editors

CONTRACTOR'S HANDBOOK OF BUSINESS AND LAW
Robert F. Cushman, G. Christian Hedemann, and Peter J. King, Editors

DESIGN PROFESSIONAL'S HANDBOOK OF BUSINESS AND LAW
Robert F. Cushman and James C. Dobbs, Editors

DRAFTING CONSTRUCTION CONTRACTS: STRATEGY AND FORMS FOR CONTRACTORS
Samuel F. Schoninger

FEDERAL CONSTRUCTION CONTRACTING
James F. Nagle

HANDLING FIDELITY, SURETY, AND FINANCIAL RISK CLAIMS (SECOND EDITION)
Robert F. Cushman, George L. Blick, and Charles A. Meeker, Editors

HAZARDOUS WASTE DISPOSAL AND UNDERGROUND CONSTRUCTION LAW
Robert F. Cushman and Bruce W. Ficken, Editors

LEGAL GUIDE TO AIA DOCUMENTS (THIRD EDITION)
Werner Sabo

1992 DIRECTORY OF CONSTRUCTION INDUSTRY CONSULTANTS
Wiley Law Publications, Editors

1992 WILEY CONSTRUCTION LAW UPDATE
Overton A. Currie and Neal J. Sweeney, Editors

PROVING AND PRICING CONSTRUCTION CLAIMS
Robert F. Cushman and David A. Carpenter, Editors

SWEET ON CONSTRUCTION INDUSTRY CONTRACTS (SECOND EDITION)
Justin Sweet

TROUBLED CONSTRUCTION LOANS: LAW AND PRACTICE
Stanley P. Sklar, Editor

SUBSCRIPTION NOTICE

This Wiley product is updated on a periodic basis with supplements to reflect important changes in the subject matter. If you purchased this product directly from John Wiley & Sons, Inc., we have already recorded your subscription for this update service.

If, however, you purchased this product from a bookstore and wish to receive (1) the current update at no additional charge, and (2) future updates and revised or related volumes billed separately with a 30-day examination review, please send your name, company name (if applicable), address, and the title of the product to:

Supplement Department
John Wiley & Sons, Inc.
One Wiley Drive
Somerset, NJ 08875
1-800-225-5945

CONSTRUCTION LITIGATION: REPRESENTING THE CONTRACTOR

SECOND EDITION

JOHN D. CARTER

ROBERT F. CUSHMAN

WILLIAM J. PALMER

Editors

Wiley Law Publications

JOHN WILEY & SONS, INC.

New York • Chichester • Brisbane • Toronto • Singapore

In recognition of the importance of preserving what has been written, it is a policy of John Wiley & Sons, Inc., to have books of enduring value published in the United States printed on acid-free paper, and we exert our best efforts to that end.

This publication is designed to provide accurate and authoritative information in regard to the subject matter covered. It is sold with the understanding that the publisher is not engaged in rendering legal, accounting, or other professional services. If legal advice or other expert assistance is required, the services of a competent professional person should be sought. *From a Declaration of Principles jointly adopted by a Committee of the American Bar Association and a Committee of Publishers.*

Library of Congress Cataloging-in-Publication Data

Construction litigation : representing the contractor / John D. Carter, Robert F. Cushman, William J. Palmer, editors. — 2nd ed.
p. cm. — (Construction law library)
Includes index.
ISBN 0-471-53586-9
1. Construction contracts—United States. 2. Construction industry—Law and legislation—United States. 3. Liability (Law)—United States. 4. Actions and defenses—United States. I. Carter, John D., 1946– . II. Cushman, Robert Frank, 1931– III. Palmer, William J., 1934– . IV. Series.
KF902.C626 1992
343.73'078624—dc20
[347.30378624] 91-37499
CIP

Printed in the United States of America

10 9 8 7 6 5 4 3 2 1

PREFACE

Representing the contractor in construction litigation calls for a team effort to bring together the essential elements in all successful litigation: credentials and experience in all areas pertinent to the dispute and the collective knowledge and expertise necessary to prove entitlement and present a clear and convincing case of contractor damages. Success comes from litigators who understand the issues and requirements specific to construction disputes and from functional experts and accountants familiar with proof methods and techniques required to link causal events to quantifiable damages in a construction setting.

Like patent infringement, trade secrets, or a host of other types of disputes, construction litigation is an animal unique unto itself. Those who spend their careers working with construction cases tend to be a separate and distinct breed. In compiling the second and entirely revised edition of *Construction Litigation: Representing the Contractor,* the editors have sought out as members of our team precisely such individuals: contributing authors who are not only experienced in resolving construction disputes but also known and respected for their expertise in specific critical areas commonly encountered in construction litigation.

Although intended primarily to assist attorneys, this book also provides a useful desk reference for anyone whose activities touch on long-term contract matters and gives individual contractors a better understanding of how their actions may affect this increasingly important part of operations.

December 1991

JOHN D. CARTER
San Francisco, California

ROBERT F. CUSHMAN
Philadelphia, Pennsylvania

WILLIAM J. PALMER
San Francisco, California

ABOUT THE EDITORS

John D. Carter is general counsel, senior vice president, and director of Bechtel Group, Inc., in San Francisco, California. He joined Bechtel Power Corporation's Legal Department in 1982 as chief counsel for the litigation, labor, and legislation group, managing all major claims and litigation. Mr. Carter previously was a partner with the San Francisco law firm of Thelen, Marrin, Johnson & Bridges, where his experience included several major construction and engineering trials for leading firms in the industry. He received his law degree from Harvard Law School and is admitted to practice before the U.S. Supreme Court, the United States Court of Appeals (Ninth Circuit), Court of Claims, District Courts (Northern California and Oregon), and Tax Court. He is active in a variety of professional groups and is a member of the bars of California, the United States Supreme Court, San Francisco, and the American Bar Association.

Robert F. Cushman is a partner in the international law firm of Pepper, Hamilton & Scheetz in Philadelphia, Pennsylvania, and is a recognized specialist and lecturer on all phases of construction and real estate law. He serves as legal counsel to numerous trade associations and construction, development, and bonding companies. Mr. Cushman is the editor and coauthor of numerous books pertaining to construction, real estate, and fidelity and surety laws, including the following John Wiley & Sons publications: *Construction Litigation: Representing the Owner* (2d ed.); *Construction Defaults: Rights, Duties, and Liabilities; Construction Failures; Proving and Pricing Construction Claims;* and *Alternative Dispute Resolution in the Construction Industry.* A member of the Pennsylvania bar, he is admitted to practice before the United States Supreme Court and the United States Claims Court. Mr. Cushman has served as executive vice president and general counsel to the Construction Industry Foundation, as counsel to the American Construction Owners Association, and as regional chairman of the Public Contract Law Section of the American Bar Association. He is permanent co-chairman with John D. Carter of the Andrews Conference Group's Construction Litigation and Hazardous Waste superconferences and is a charter member of the American College of Construction Lawyers.

William J. Palmer is chairman of Ernst & Young's National Construction Industry Group in San Francisco, California, and in that role coordinates his firm's services to over 1,000 construction companies. He is a graduate of the University of California at Berkeley and a is member of the American Institute of Certified Public Accountants and the Associated General Contractors of America. Because of Mr. Palmer's reputation and expertise in the areas of construction and contract accounting and his numerous publications on construction accounting and construction litigation, he frequently testifies as an expert witness in long-term contract disputes and related litigation.

SUMMARY CONTENTS

Short Reference List		xxvii
PART I	PRELIMINARY ISSUES	
Chapter 1	Factors Affecting Project Results	3
Chapter 2	Contemplating Litigation and Its Alternatives	21
Chapter 3	Organizing and Selecting the Litigation Team	53
Chapter 4	Bid Protests and Bid Mistakes	65
PART II	PARTIES TO LITIGATION	
Chapter 5	Suing the Private Owner	97
Chapter 6	Suing a Government: Special Considerations	125
Chapter 7	Suing the Construction Manager	149
Chapter 8	Suing the Design Professional	199
Chapter 9	Suing the Construction Lender	223
Chapter 10	Suing the Subcontractor and Material Supplier	247
Chapter 11	Contractor's Insurance Coverage under Its Liability and Builder's Risk Policies	269
Chapter 12	Contractors and Their Sureties	323
Chapter 13	Prosecuting and Defending Payment Bond Claims	361
PART III	LITIGATION ISSUES	
Chapter 14	Effective Preparation for a Construction Arbitration	389
Chapter 15	Preparing the Case for Litigation	413
Chapter 16	Proving Liability to Allow Contractor to Recover Damages	443
Chapter 17	Using Critical Path Network Analysis to Prove Delay	479
Chapter 18	Pricing Damages	493
Chapter 19	Labor Productivity in Construction Claims	521
Chapter 20	Defending Against Owner Claims	559
Chapter 21	Tax Considerations of Construction Litigation	601
Chapter 22	Trial and Appeal	625
Table of Cases		655
Index		715

DETAILED CONTENTS

Short Reference List

PART I PRELIMINARY ISSUES

Chapter 1 Factors Affecting Project Results

Mark A. Smith
Ernst & Young
San Francisco, California

§ 1.1 Introduction
§ 1.2 Early Decisions
§ 1.3 Project Life Cycle
§ 1.4 —Phases I and II
§ 1.5 Factors Influencing Early Decisions
§ 1.6 Industrial Construction: A Case Study
§ 1.7 Construction Project Scope Changes
§ 1.8 Major Influences on Construction Projects
§ 1.9 —Typical Project Problems
§ 1.10 Ever-changing Scope
§ 1.11 —Managing Change Control
§ 1.12 —Change Order System

Chapter 2 Contemplating Litigation and Its Alternatives

Overton A. Currie, Esquire
James E. Stephenson, Esquire
Philip E. Beck, Esquire
Smith, Currie & Hancock
Atlanta, Georgia

CONSTRUCTION RISKS AND REWARDS

§ 2.1 Not for the Timid
§ 2.2 —Inherent Risk Factors
§ 2.3 —Legislated Risks
§ 2.4 —Risk Management
§ 2.5 Construction Disputes
§ 2.6 —Complexity
§ 2.7 —Contract Structures
§ 2.8 —Sources of Disputes
§ 2.9 Need for Effective Risk, Dispute, and Litigation Management

RISK MANAGEMENT
§ 2.10 Parties and Relationships
§ 2.11 —Owners: Public and Private
§ 2.12 —Architect/Engineers
§ 2.13 —Construction Managers
§ 2.14 —General Contractors, Subcontractors, and Suppliers
§ 2.15 —Sureties
§ 2.16 —Construction Lenders
§ 2.17 Legal Parameters
§ 2.18 —Building Codes, Ordinances, and Regulations
§ 2.19 —Trade Usage and Implied Obligations
§ 2.20 Contract Documents: A Beginning
§ 2.21 —Uniform Commercial Code Applicability
§ 2.22 —Basic Provisions
§ 2.23 —Exculpatory and Special Clauses
§ 2.24 —Modifications

DISPUTE MANAGEMENT
§ 2.25 Types of Disputes and Their Causes
§ 2.26 —Bid Disputes
§ 2.27 —Performance Disputes
§ 2.28 Dispute Recognition and Reaction
§ 2.29 —Preservation of Evidence and Claims
§ 2.30 —Early Use of Experts
§ 2.31 Settling Disputes
§ 2.32 —Settlement Techniques
§ 2.33 —Negotiation Strategies
§ 2.34 —Arbitration versus Litigation
§ 2.35 —Other Alternatives

LITIGATION MANAGEMENT
§ 2.36 Litigation Objectives
§ 2.37 Selection of Parties, Remedies, and Forum
§ 2.38 Effective Litigation Strategy
§ 2.39 Effective Trial Presentation
§ 2.40 Appeal

Chapter 3 Organizing and Selecting the Litigation Team

William J. Palmer
Ernst & Young
San Francisco, California

§ 3.1 Preliminary Considerations
§ 3.2 Planning

§ 3.3 Organizing the Team
§ 3.4 —Fixing Internal Responsibility
§ 3.5 —Choosing the Lawyer
§ 3.6 —Selecting Other Members of the Team
§ 3.7 Characteristics of Expert Witnesses
§ 3.8 —Selecting the Damages Expert
§ 3.9 —Claim Consultant
§ 3.10 —Critical Path Consultant
§ 3.11 —Consulting Engineer
§ 3.12 —Construction Consultant
§ 3.13 Coordinating Consultants and Experts
§ 3.14 Locating Witnesses and Consultants

Chapter 4 Bid Protests and Bid Mistakes

David Buoncristiani, Esquire
Thelen, Marrin, Johnson & Bridges
San Francisco, California

§ 4.1 Introduction

BACKGROUND

§ 4.2 Overview
§ 4.3 Competitive Bidding
§ 4.4 General Considerations for Bid Protests
§ 4.5 General Requirements of Bids
§ 4.6 Contract Award Criteria
§ 4.7 —Responsiveness
§ 4.8 —Responsibility
§ 4.9 —Subcontractor Listing Requirements
§ 4.10 —Minority Business Enterprise Requirements
§ 4.11 General Grounds for Protest

FEDERAL CONTRACTS

§ 4.12 General
§ 4.13 Grounds for Protests
§ 4.14 Standing to Protest
§ 4.15 Protest Procedure
§ 4.16 Relief Available

FEDERALLY FUNDED GRANT PROJECTS

§ 4.17 General
§ 4.18 Grounds for Protests
§ 4.19 Standing to Protest
§ 4.20 Protest Procedure
§ 4.21 Relief Available

STATE AND LOCAL CONTRACTS
§ 4.22 General
§ 4.23 Grounds for Protests
§ 4.24 Standing to Protest
§ 4.25 Protest Procedure
§ 4.26 Relief Available

PRIVATE CONTRACTS
§ 4.27 Bidding on Private Contracts

BID MISTAKES
§ 4.28 General
§ 4.29 State Law Remedies for Bid Mistakes
§ 4.30 —Jurisdictions Following Equitable Principles
§ 4.31 Federal Law on Bid Mistakes
§ 4.32 Private Owners

PART II PARTIES TO LITIGATION

Chapter 5 Suing the Private Owner

Robert B. Flaig, Esquire
Lisa Schwartz Tudzin, Esquire
Thelen, Marrin, Johnson & Bridges
Los Angeles, California

Jesse B. Grove III, Esquire
Thelen, Marrin, Johnson & Bridges
San Francisco, California

§ 5.1 Introduction

BREACHES OF CONTRACT BY OWNER
§ 5.2 Changes
§ 5.3 —Scope of Work
§ 5.4 —Notice of Changes
§ 5.5 —Changed Physical Conditions
§ 5.6 —Constructive Changes
§ 5.7 Delay
§ 5.8 —No Damage for Delay Clauses
§ 5.9 Nonpayment
§ 5.10 Disputes Involving Subcontractors

REMEDIES
§ 5.11 Damages
§ 5.12 —Prevention of Completion
§ 5.13 —Extra Work
§ 5.14 Rescission and Restitution

§ 5.15 Reformation
§ 5.16 Termination
§ 5.17 Liens
§ 5.18 Exculpatory Clauses

Chapter 6 Suing a Government: Special Considerations

Scott E. Ransick, Esquire
Robert D. Wallick, Esquire
Steptoe & Johnson
Washington, D.C.

§ 6.1 Introduction
§ 6.2 Some Special Perils
§ 6.3 Sovereign Immunity and Its Waiver
§ 6.4 Waivers by the Federal Government
§ 6.5 —Federal Waiver for Contract Controversies
§ 6.6 —Judicial Review of Bid Protests
§ 6.7 —Administrative Forum for Bid Protests
§ 6.8 Waiver by States and State Agencies
§ 6.9 Funding and Fiscal Restrictions
§ 6.10 —Federal Fiscal Restrictions
§ 6.11 —Fiscal Restrictions on State and Other Governmental Bodies
§ 6.12 Authority to Act
§ 6.13 Ratification by Contracting Officer
§ 6.14 Authority to Act for the State

Chapter 7 Suing the Construction Manager

Julian F. Hoffar, Esquire
John B. Tieder, Jr., Esquire
Watt, Tieder, Killian & Hoffar
McLean, Virginia

INTRODUCTION
§ 7.1 Role of Construction Manager
§ 7.2 Construction Management Defined

FORMS OF CONSTRUCTION MANAGEMENT PRACTICE
§ 7.3 Agency Construction Management
§ 7.4 Guaranteed Maximum Price Construction Management
§ 7.5 Extended Service Construction Management

STANDARD OF CARE
§ 7.6 Professional or Contractor?
§ 7.7 Licensing Requirements
§ 7.8 Bond and Insurance Considerations
§ 7.9 Bidding Requirements

DUTY OWED BY CONSTRUCTION MANAGER
§ 7.10 Generally
§ 7.11 Contract Obligations
§ 7.12 Procurement Codes
§ 7.13 Building Codes and Industry Standards
§ 7.14 Construction Manager De Facto Rule
§ 7.15 Parties to Whom Duty Is Owed

THEORIES OF RECOVERY
§ 7.16 Negligence
§ 7.17 Third-Party Beneficiary
§ 7.18 Interference with Contract
§ 7.19 Implied Warranty

BASES FOR LIABILITY
§ 7.20 Generally
§ 7.21 Interference with Bids
§ 7.22 Design Defects
§ 7.23 Delayed Site Access
§ 7.24 Administration of Drawings
§ 7.25 Failure to Provide Timely Information
§ 7.26 Failure to Provide Construction Support Services
§ 7.27 Failure to Schedule and Coordinate

CONSTRUCTION MANAGER DEFENSES
§ 7.28 Owner/Construction Manager Contract
§ 7.29 Owner/Prime Contract
§ 7.30 Duty to Review Drawings and Prior Work
§ 7.31 No Damages for Delay Clauses
§ 7.32 Delay Not Contemplated by the Parties
§ 7.33 Unreasonable Delay
§ 7.34 Bad Faith or Fraud
§ 7.35 Active Interference
§ 7.36 Statutory Exceptions
§ 7.37 Delegation of Scheduling Functions to Contractors
§ 7.38 Forum Selection
§ 7.39 Owner's Agent
§ 7.40 Contributory and Comparative Negligence
§ 7.41 No Recovery for Economic Loss
§ 7.42 Statutes of Limitations
§ 7.43 Accrual
§ 7.44 Tolling

Chapter 8 **Suing the Design Professional**

Kenneth I. Levin, Esquire
Pepper, Hamilton & Scheetz
Philadelphia, Pennsylvania

§ 8.1 Bases for Contractor's Right of Action
§ 8.2 —Economic Loss Limitation
§ 8.3 Design Professional's Liability to the Owner for Indemnity
§ 8.4 Negligence
§ 8.5 —Proof of Negligence
§ 8.6 —Conduct Constituting Negligence
§ 8.7 Liability to Contractor Generally
§ 8.8 —Defective Design
§ 8.9 —Negligence in Supervision and Inspection
§ 8.10 —Negligence or Intentional Interference in Contract Administration
§ 8.11 —Scheduling and Coordination

Chapter 9 **Suing the Construction Lender**

Richard E. Alexander, Esquire
Stoel Rives Boley Jones & Grey
Portland, Oregon

§ 9.1 Introduction

STATUTORY REMEDIES
§ 9.2 Importance of Statutory Remedies
§ 9.3 —Mechanics' Lien Statutes
§ 9.4 —Stop-Notice Provisions
§ 9.5 —Requirements that Loan Agreement Be Recorded

CONTRACT THEORIES
§ 9.6 Introduction
§ 9.7 Treating Lender and Borrower as Single Entity
§ 9.8 Third-Party Beneficiary Status
§ 9.9 —Establishing Third-Party Beneficiary Status
§ 9.10 —Enforcing Third-Party Rights

RIGHTS BASED ON ESTOPPEL
§ 9.11 Introduction
§ 9.12 Estoppel Theories
§ 9.13 Elements of Successful Estoppel Claims
§ 9.14 —Actionable Representations
§ 9.15 —Reliance

UNJUST ENRICHMENT THEORIES

§ 9.16 Generally
§ 9.17 Defining Unjust Enrichment in Construction
§ 9.18 —When Does Unjust Enrichment Occur?
§ 9.19 —Measuring Unjust Enrichment
§ 9.20 Potential Limitations on Use of Unjust Enrichment Theories

TORT THEORIES

§ 9.21 Negligence
§ 9.22 Misrepresentation
§ 9.23 Other Tort Theories

Chapter 10 Suing the Subcontractor and Material Supplier

Robert J. Hoffman, Esquire
David L. Simmons, Esquire
Lowe Gray Steele & Hoffman
Indianapolis, Indiana

§ 10.1 Introduction
§ 10.2 Bidding and Contract Formation
§ 10.3 Bid Mistakes
§ 10.4 Flow-Down Clause
§ 10.5 Description of Work and Materials
§ 10.6 Coordinated and Timely Performance
§ 10.7 Remedies for Delayed Performance
§ 10.8 Warranties Relating to Defective Work and Materials
§ 10.9 Correcting Defective Work
§ 10.10 Indemnification
§ 10.11 Pass-Through Claims
§ 10.12 Default and Termination
§ 10.13 Documenting the Contractor's Claim

Chapter 11 Contractor's Insurance Coverage under Its Liability and Builder's Risk Policies

Barry L. Bunshoft, Esquire
Richard L. Seabolt, Esquire
Hancock, Rothert & Bunshoft
San Francisco, California

§ 11.1 Introduction
§ 11.2 Contra Proferentem and the Reasonable Expectations Doctrine

LIABILITY POLICY

§ 11.3 Introduction
§ 11.4 Insuring Agreement
§ 11.5 —Occurrence Requirement

§ 11.6 —Trigger of Coverage under Occurrence-Based Policies
§ 11.7 —Claims-Made Policies
§ 11.8 —Definition of Property Damage
§ 11.9 Exclusions
§ 11.10 —Contractually Assumed Liability
§ 11.11 —Care, Custody, or Control
§ 11.12 —Premises Alienated
§ 11.13 —Performance or Business Risk
§ 11.14 —Damage to Insured's Product or Work
§ 11.15 —Sistership or Recall
§ 11.16 —Explosion, Collapse, or Underground Property Damage
§ 11.17 —Completed Operations Hazard

BUILDER'S RISK POLICY

§ 11.18 Introduction
§ 11.19 Period of Coverage
§ 11.20 Limitations on Coverage: Fortuitous Losses
§ 11.21 —External Causes
§ 11.22 —Exclusions
§ 11.23 Burden of Proof
§ 11.24 Sue and Labor Clause
§ 11.25 Subrogation
§ 11.26 Future Practice

Chapter 12 Contractors and Their Sureties

Harvey C. Koch, Esquire
Koch & Rouse
New Orleans, Louisiana

James J. Myers, Esquire
Gadsby & Hannah
Boston, Massachusetts

SURETY BONDS GENERALLY

§ 12.1 Introduction
§ 12.2 Parties to Surety Bonds

SURETY BONDS ON PUBLIC AND PRIVATE PROJECTS

§ 12.3 Private (Common Law) Surety Bonds
§ 12.4 Statutory Payment Bonds

TYPES OF SURETY BONDS

§ 12.5 Bid Bond
§ 12.6 —Voiding the Bid Bond
§ 12.7 —Excuses
§ 12.8 —Form of Bid or Proposal Bond

§ 12.9 Completion Bond
§ 12.10 Payment Bond
§ 12.11 Lien Bond
§ 12.12 Subcontractor's Bond

ROLE OF THE SURETY
§ 12.13 Generally
§ 12.14 Performance Bond
§ 12.15 Who Is Covered?
§ 12.16 When the Principal Defaults
§ 12.17 Surety's Rights and Obligations upon Default
§ 12.18 —Events of Default
§ 12.19 —Notice and Investigation
§ 12.20 —Available Defenses
§ 12.21 —Obligee's Conduct
§ 12.22 Surety's Options upon Default of Performance Bond Principal
§ 12.23 Damages Recoverable from Performance Bond Surety
§ 12.24 Surety's Right to Contract Funds
§ 12.25 Subrogation

PARTIES AND CAUSES OF ACTION
§ 12.26 Introduction
§ 12.27 Contractor versus Surety
§ 12.28 Contractor versus Owner
§ 12.29 Contractor versus Miscellaneous Parties
§ 12.30 Surety versus Contractor
§ 12.31 Surety versus Bank
§ 12.32 Surety versus Owner
§ 12.33 Surety versus Miscellaneous Parties
§ 12.34 Owner versus Contractor and/or Surety

NOTICE AND LIMITATION OF ACTIONS
§ 12.35 Notice Periods
§ 12.36 Limitation Periods

CONSTRUCTION OF DOCUMENTS AND PAROL EVIDENCE
§ 12.37 Construction of Contracts
§ 12.38 Parol Evidence

Chapter 13 Prosecuting and Defending Payment Bond Claims

Edward G. Gallagher, Esquire
Whiteford, Taylor & Preston
Washington, D.C.

§ 13.1 Introduction
§ 13.2 Purpose of Payment Bond

§ 13.3 Typical Payment Bond Provisions
§ 13.4 Statutory Requirements
§ 13.5 Resolving Conflicts Between Bond and Statute
§ 13.6 Parties Making a Bond Claim
§ 13.7 Covered Bond Claims
§ 13.8 —Taxes, Contributions, and Insurance
§ 13.9 —Delay Damages and Lost Profits
§ 13.10 —Attorneys' Fees and Interest
§ 13.11 Notice Requirements
§ 13.12 —Time Period Allowed
§ 13.13 Suit Limitations
§ 13.14 —Commencement of Limitation Period
§ 13.15 —Estoppel
§ 13.16 Jurisdiction and Venue Requirements
§ 13.17 Arbitration and the Surety
§ 13.18 Possible Remedies if Payment Bond Claim Is Unavailable
§ 13.19 Practice Notes

PART III LITIGATION ISSUES

Chapter 14 Effective Preparation for a Construction Arbitration

Robert S. Peckar, Esquire
Peckar & Abramson
River Edge, New Jersey

§ 14.1 Introduction

ARBITRATION VERSUS LITIGATION
§ 14.2 Overview
§ 14.3 Informality
§ 14.4 Role of Law
§ 14.5 Role of Lawyers
§ 14.6 Prehearing Discovery
§ 14.7 Selection of Arbitrators
§ 14.8 Arbitration Awards

METHOD OF PREPARATION
§ 14.9 Scheduling the Hearing
§ 14.10 Knowledge of Adversary's Claim
§ 14.11 Application to the American Arbitration Association
§ 14.12 Application to Court
§ 14.13 Initial Presentation
§ 14.14 Description of Project
§ 14.15 Description of Project Time Frame
§ 14.16 Contract Price/Payment Analysis

§ 14.17 Scope of Work
§ 14.18 Schedule
§ 14.19 Overview of Claims
§ 14.20 Prehearing Written Submission
§ 14.21 Preparing for Hearings
§ 14.22 Who Will Tell the Story?
§ 14.23 Use of Experts
§ 14.24 Preparing Exhibits
§ 14.25 Use of Affidavits
§ 14.26 Creative Evidence
§ 14.27 Mediation

Chapter 15 Preparing the Case for Litigation

Philip R. Placier, Esquire
Thelen, Marrin, Johnson & Bridges
San Francisco, California

Laurence M. Scoville, Jr., Esquire
Clark, Klein and Beaumont
Detroit, Michigan

§ 15.1 Introduction

INITIAL INVESTIGATION AND PLANNING

§ 15.2 Start the Investigation Early
§ 15.3 —Contractor's Representatives
§ 15.4 Develop a Theory of the Case and a Litigation Plan
§ 15.5 —Litigation Plan and Trial Book

COLLECTING INFORMATION

§ 15.6 Initial Plan
§ 15.7 Documents
§ 15.8 —Selection, Form, and Numbering
§ 15.9 —Review
§ 15.10 Witnesses
§ 15.11 Experts

DISCOVERY

§ 15.12 Developing the Discovery Plan
§ 15.13 Litigation Support Group
§ 15.14 Written Discovery Requests
§ 15.15 —Drafting Discovery Requests
§ 15.16 —Interrogatories
§ 15.17 —Requests for Production of Documents
§ 15.18 —Requests for Admission
§ 15.19 Obtaining Responses to Discovery Requests

§ 15.20 Responding to Discovery Requests
§ 15.21 Depositions
§ 15.22 —Conducting the Deposition
§ 15.23 Other Discovery Devices
§ 15.24 Final Discovery Review

Chapter 16 Proving Liability to Allow Contractor to Recover Damages

Peter Goetz, Esquire
Goetz, Fitzpatrick & Flynn
New York, New York

§ 16.1 Introduction

DELAY CLAIMS

§ 16.2 General
§ 16.3 Owner's Failure to Perform an Affirmative Act
§ 16.4 Defective Plans and Specifications
§ 16.5 Owner's Failure to Provide Access to the Site
§ 16.6 Unforeseeable Subsurface Conditions
§ 16.7 Substantial Changes in Scope of Contract
§ 16.8 Extension of Time Clauses
§ 16.9 Changes
§ 16.10 —Directed Changes
§ 16.11 —Changes Clause Strictly Construed
§ 16.12 —Constructive Changes
§ 16.13 Restrictions on Contractor's Recovery
§ 16.14 —Delays Contemplated by the Parties
§ 16.15 Exceptions to No Damage for Delay Clauses
§ 16.16 —Active Interference
§ 16.17 —Active Interference Not Sufficient
§ 16.18 —Delays Not Contemplated by the Parties
§ 16.19 —Unreasonable or Excessive Period of Delay
§ 16.20 —Bad Faith or Fraud
§ 16.21 —Concurrent Delays Attributable to Both Parties
§ 16.22 Excusable Delays of the Contractor
§ 16.23 —Unforeseeability
§ 16.24 —Unusually Severe Weather
§ 16.25 —Labor Disputes

ACCELERATION CLAIMS

§ 16.26 Acceleration Defined
§ 16.27 Actual and Constructive Acceleration
§ 16.28 Disallowance of Acceleration Damage Claims

OTHER DAMAGE CLAIMS
§ 16.29 Changed Conditions
§ 16.30 Low Bidder Claims

ASSERTING DAMAGE CLAIMS
§ 16.31 Strict Adherence to Contract Provisions
§ 16.32 Delay and Time Extension Clauses
§ 16.33 Notice and Deadline Clauses
§ 16.34 When Time Is of the Essence

PROOF OF DAMAGES
§ 16.35 Actual Damages
§ 16.36 Total Cost Method
§ 16.37 —Labor Costs
§ 16.38 —Material Costs
§ 16.39 —Jobsite Indirect Costs
§ 16.40 —Home Office Overhead
§ 16.41 —Finance Costs
§ 16.42 Disruption Damages
§ 16.43 Lost Profits

Chapter 17 Using Critical Path Network Analysis to Prove Delay

Mark A. Smith
Ernst & Young
San Francisco, California

§ 17.1 Introduction
§ 17.2 Elements of Proof
§ 17.3 Common Techniques to Prove Delay
§ 17.4 —Owner-Caused Events
§ 17.5 —Comparing Manpower Schedules to Revenue Received
§ 17.6 —Critical Path Method
§ 17.7 Overview of Critical Path Method
§ 17.8 Using CPM in Proving Delay
§ 17.9 —Strengthening the CPM Proof Strategy

Chapter 18 Pricing Damages

William J. Palmer
Ernst & Young
San Francisco, California

§ 18.1 Introduction
§ 18.2 Categories of Contract Damages
§ 18.3 —Delay Damages
§ 18.4 —Disruption
§ 18.5 —Changed Conditions
§ 18.6 —Changes in Scope

§ 18.7 —Termination
§ 18.8 Pricing Damages
§ 18.9 Total Cost Approach
§ 18.10 —Four-Way Test
§ 18.11 Discrete Approach
§ 18.12 Cost Schedules
§ 18.13 Contract Audit
§ 18.14 Calculating Damages
§ 18.15 —Delay
§ 18.16 —Disruption
§ 18.17 —Changed Conditions
§ 18.18 —Changes in Scope
§ 18.19 —Termination
§ 18.20 Cost of Capital
§ 18.21 Claim Preparation Costs
§ 18.22 Home Office Overhead
§ 18.23 —*Eichleay* Formula
§ 18.24 —Total Direct Cost Allocation
§ 18.25 —Specific Base Allocation Method
§ 18.26 —Occupancy
§ 18.27 Profit Recovery

Chapter 19 **Labor Productivity in Construction Claims**

Roger Hewitt
Ernst & Young
San Francisco, California

§ 19.1 Introduction
§ 19.2 Productivity and Estimating
§ 19.3 —Expectations of the Contractor and Owner
§ 19.4 —Factors Affecting Construction Productivity
§ 19.5 —Reasonable Proof of Damages from Lost Productivity
§ 19.6 —Other Factors Affecting Labor Costs and Entitlement
§ 19.7 Selecting a General Approach
§ 19.8 —Top-down Approach
§ 19.9 —Problems with Top-down Approach
§ 19.10 —Bottom-up Analysis
§ 19.11 Developing the Claim: Variance Analysis
§ 19.12 Quantifying Productivity Losses
§ 19.13 Documenting Disruption
§ 19.14 Measured Mile Approach
§ 19.15 Dallavia Method
§ 19.16 —Modified Dallavia

§ 19.17 Using Productivity Curves to Calculate Damages
§ 19.18 —Productivity Losses from Acceleration
§ 19.19 —Acceleration Requirements
§ 19.20 —Inefficiency from Crew Increases and Overmanning
§ 19.21 —Productivity Loss from Increased Crewing (Without Crowding)
§ 19.22 —Overmanning/Crowding
§ 19.23 —Extended Overtime Inefficiency
§ 19.24 Calculating Lost Productivity from Inclement Weather
§ 19.25 Calculating Compounding Impacts
§ 19.26 Learning Curve Claims
§ 19.27 Ratio Delay Studies

Chapter 20 Defending Against Owner Claims

Mark L. Fleder, Esquire
Peter J. Smith, Esquire
Connell, Foley & Geiser
Roseland, New Jersey

§ 20.1 Available Defenses
§ 20.2 Compliance with Plans and Specifications
§ 20.3 Waiver
§ 20.4 Statutes of Limitations
§ 20.5 Supervening Impracticability
§ 20.6 Pre-existing Impracticability
§ 20.7 Warranties and their Limitations
§ 20.8 Damages
§ 20.9 When Owner Retains Duty to Coordinate
§ 20.10 Liquidated Damages
§ 20.11 Substantial Performance
§ 20.12 Accord and Satisfaction
§ 20.13 Arbitration Defense
§ 20.14 Termination Defense
§ 20.15 Other Contractual Remedy Limitations
§ 20.16 Other Owner Claims and Contractor Defenses

Chapter 21 Tax Considerations of Construction Litigation

Richard Hawkins, Esquire
Arthur Andersen & Co.
Portland, Oregon

James R. Puetz, Esquire
Price Waterhouse
Portland, Oregon

§ 21.1 Introduction

HOW PROCEEDS FROM SETTLEMENTS OR JUDGMENTS ARE TAXED

§ 21.2 Treatment of Proceeds
§ 21.3 —Proceeds Treated as Ordinary Income
§ 21.4 —Proceeds Treated as Return of Capital
§ 21.5 —Proceeds Treated as Nontaxable

HOW PAYMENT OF SETTLEMENTS AND JUDGMENTS IS TREATED FOR TAX PURPOSES

§ 21.6 Introduction
§ 21.7 General Principles
§ 21.8 Payments Treated as Deductible Expenses
§ 21.9 Payments Treated as Capital Expenditures
§ 21.10 Expenses That May Not Be Deducted or Capitalized

TIMING OF INCOME RECOGNITION AND EXPENSE DEDUCTION

§ 21.11 Introduction
§ 21.12 Cash and Accrual Methods
§ 21.13 Long-Term Contract Methods of Accounting
§ 21.14 —Percentage-of-Completion
§ 21.15 —Completed Contract Method

SUBSTANTIATING THE DESIRED TAX TREATMENT

§ 21.16 Introduction
§ 21.17 Written Documentation
§ 21.18 Actions of the Parties

TAX PLANNING

§ 21.19 Timing of Tax Planning
§ 21.20 Choice of Claims

Chapter 22 Trial and Appeal

William G. Schaefer, Esquire
Langley R. Shook, Esquire
Sidley & Austin
Washington, D.C.

§ 22.1 Overview

INITIAL ASSESSMENT

§ 22.2 Why an Assessment?
§ 22.3 What Facts Are Most Important to the Case?
§ 22.4 What Are the Parties' Key Legal Arguments?
§ 22.5 What Are the Equities of the Case?
§ 22.6 What Are the Client's Objectives?
§ 22.7 How Can Damages Be Measured?

§ 22.8 What Are the Potential Conflicts of Interest?
§ 22.9 What Is the Purpose of a Trial Plan?
§ 22.10 Should Alternatives to Litigation Be Pursued?

TRIAL PREPARATION

§ 22.11 What Constitutes Trial Preparation?
§ 22.12 What Picture Should the Judge and Jury See?
§ 22.13 Can a Jury Handle a Complex Construction Case?
§ 22.14 How Can Documents Be Managed Effectively?
§ 22.15 How Should Witnesses for Trial Be Selected?
§ 22.16 When and How Should Expert Witnesses Be Used?

MOTIONS AND FILINGS BEFORE TRIAL

§ 22.17 Pretrial Motions
§ 22.18 Pretrial Conferences
§ 22.19 Pretrial Filings

TRIAL

§ 22.20 Opening Statement
§ 22.21 Presentation of Evidence
§ 22.22 Cross-Examination
§ 22.23 Closing Argument

APPEAL

§ 22.24 Planning an Appeal
§ 22.25 Reassessment of the Case
§ 22.26 Appellate Brief
§ 22.27 Oral Argument

Table of Cases

Index

SHORT REFERENCE LIST

Short Reference	*Full Reference*
AIA	American Institute of Architects
CM	construction manager
FAR	Federal Acquisition Regulation
GAO	General Accounting Office
SOW	scope of work
UCC	Uniform Commercial Code (1989)

PART I

PRELIMINARY ISSUES

CHAPTER 1

FACTORS AFFECTING PROJECT RESULTS

Mark A. Smith

Mark A. Smith is a senior manager in the construction consulting and litigation practice of Ernst & Young's San Francisco, California, office. He has an extensive background in analyzing construction productivity and quantifying construction delay and disruption claims. Dr. Smith holds both undergraduate and graduate degrees in civil engineering and is a registered professional engineer. He has written and presented over forty papers and speeches on a variety of construction management issues.

§ 1.1 **Introduction**
§ 1.2 **Early Decisions**
§ 1.3 **Project Life Cycle**
§ 1.4 **—Phases I and II**
§ 1.5 **Factors Influencing Early Decisions**
§ 1.6 **Industrial Construction: A Case Study**
§ 1.7 **Construction Project Scope Changes**
§ 1.8 **Major Influences on Construction Projects**
§ 1.9 **—Typical Project Problems**
§ 1.10 **Ever-changing Scope**
§ 1.11 **—Managing Change Control**
§ 1.12 **—Change Order System**

§ 1.1 Introduction

Construction is a diverse industry that requires enormous amounts of capital and resources in order to function efficiently. Due to the size and diversity of the construction industry, the major industry players—owners, designers, and contractors—frequently appear to be in conflict. These conflicts can be brought on by any number of situations, but usually result from a lack of communication about the real needs of the construction project.

Construction problems are exacerbated by the fact that the construction industry is so fragmented. The Business Roundtable determined through its landmark *Construction Industry Cost Effectiveness Study*[1] that construction is a $445 billion industry made up of nearly 1 million contractors, over 70 national contractor associations, more than 10,000 local and national labor organizations, over 6.5 million workers, and an undeterminable number of owners. Without a single group to unite the various fragments, it is no wonder that construction disputes arise on almost every project.

This chapter is designed to develop an understanding of the various stages of evolution that most construction projects undergo. This ranges from the initial project development budgets and preliminary design activities through construction fieldwork and final closeout. Understanding these stages is important because it allows the reader to appreciate the complexities of construction decisionmaking and the subsequent problems that arise from this management process.

Although major construction problems frequently occur on so many projects and result in significant cost and schedule overruns, many of them can be avoided. Knowledge of the construction management process is essential in order to control the many factors that influence project results.

Both the owner and the contractor should recognize that the likelihood of a disputed claim on most major projects is likely. The principal objectives of both parties should be to avoid the problems and related litigation altogether. Failing to prevent and mitigate such damage, both parties should carefully track and document the impact of specific problems. In all cases, both parties should work toward an equitable disposition of all problems.

§ 1.2 Early Decisions

Decisions made at the outset of a proposed construction project have the greatest impact on its success or failure. The Construction Industry Institute has found that poor scope definition at the budget stage and losing

[1] A collection of 23 reports by study teams sponsored by the Business Roundtable's Construction Industry Cost Effectiveness (CICE) Task Force (Jan. 1983). The Business Roundtable can be reached at 200 Park Ave., New York, NY 10166.

control of the project scope rank as the most frequent contributing factors to cost overruns.[2]

Early scope definition is the most critical element in setting the proper course for a successful project. Recent studies[3] have concluded that about 80 percent of all project costs are determined in the initial 20 percent of the project's life cycle. These early decisions, unfortunately, must be made when the least amount of definite technical and financial information is available.

To establish the most important and critical information needs, high priority scope decisions must be evaluated in relation to their respective influence factors. *Influence factors* are defined as certain outside factors that influence the construction manager's major decisions. By identifying the factors that impact a project's scope, the entire decision-making process can be properly managed to achieve a well-defined project that meets time, cost, and quality constraints.

The concept that early decisions have the greatest impact on the final project results can be illustrated by **Figure 1–1**, which shows the increasing rate of project cost as compared to decreasing rate of cost influence versus project time. The figure represents activity phases for a large, industrial project and shows major cost components, which are placed so as to represent the approximate time interval and total cost percentage.

The greatest influence on the cost of a project occurs at its conception, that is, project definition. It seems reasonable to imply not only that the greatest impact on the final cost occurs at the project's beginning but that early activities also have the greatest influence on the overall project success, which is measured by cost, time, and operability constraints. Thus, the early decisions, which define the entire breadth of a construction project, must be critically examined before establishing a list of significant influence factors that affect project results.

§ 1.3 Project Life Cycle

A project can be separated into phases, each of which includes activities grouped together to define an overall objective for that phase, for example, scope definition, issuance of design drawings, or construction closeout. Even though a project can be divided into so-called independent phases,

---

[2] Construction Industry Institute, Scope Definition and Control, No. 6-2 (July 1986). The Construction Industry Institute is an organization of owners and contractors that works with the academic community to conduct research relating to the construction industry and to aid in the implementation of the results of that research.

[3] M. Smith, *Establishing Influence Factors to Determine Scope in the Definition Phase, in* Project Management Institute Symposium Proceedings (Calgary, Oct. 1990); Construction Industry Institute, Project Control for Construction, No. 6-5 (Sept. 1987); Construction Industry Institute, Constructability: A Primer, No. 3-1 (July 1986).

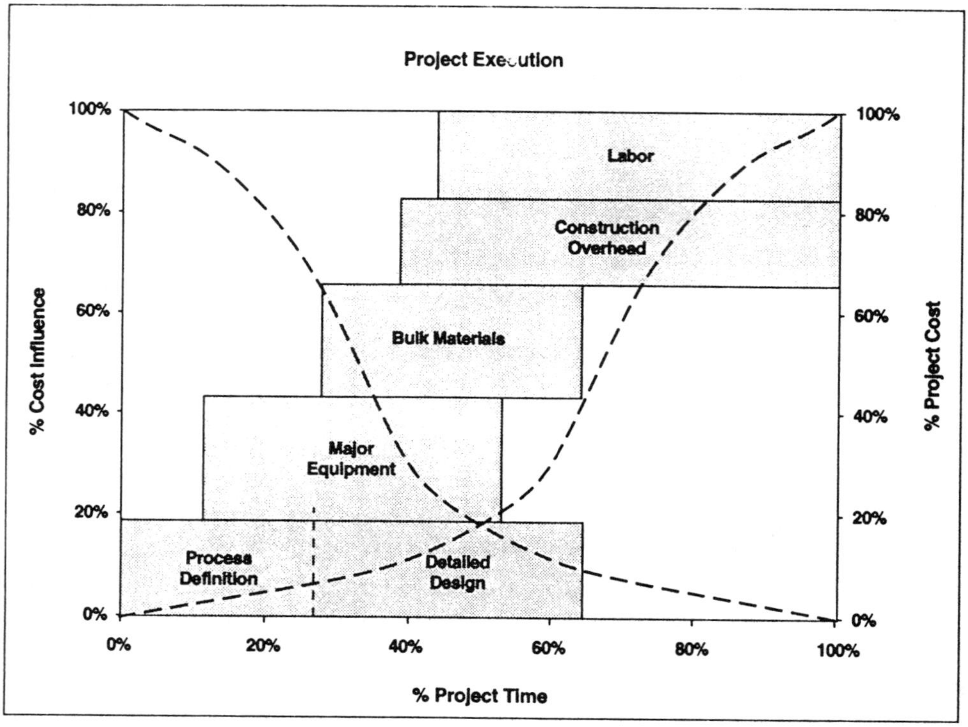

Figure 1–1. Cost influence and project cost versus project time.

this does not mean there is no overlap among phases. On typical fast-track projects, phases can overlap by as much as 60 percent, implying that when a phase is 40 percent complete, the next phase can begin. That is, a preceding phase need not be fully completed before the next phase can begin.

The breakdown of a large, industrial project into phases is shown in **Figure 1–2**. The project life cycle is separated into six phases: preliminary

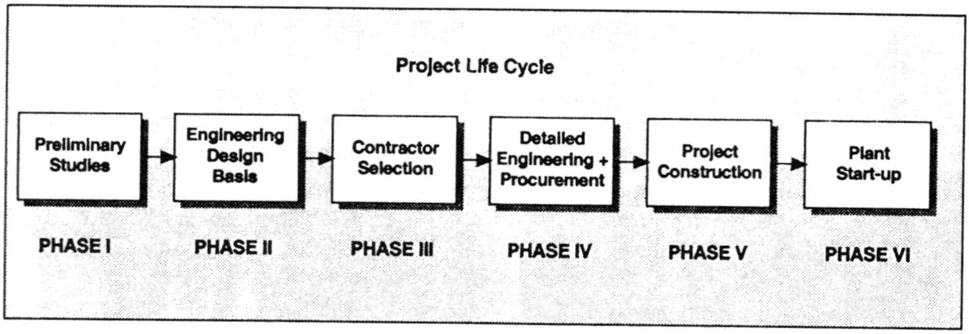

Figure 1–2. Life cycle of an industrial project.

studies, engineering design basis, contractor selection, detailed engineering and procurement, project construction, and plant start-up. Although the phases are illustrated to be performed in sequence, individual activities within each phase can and will overlap with activities in other phases.

Phase I of the project life cycle, preliminary studies, is concerned with activities that determine the technical and financial feasibility of the proposed project. Many conceptual ideas for projects get to this phase but never proceed any farther because they are not sound either technically or financially.

Preliminary Engineering Design Tasks

After it is determined that a proposed project is feasible, Phase II, engineering design basis, begins. On industrial projects, Phase II includes preliminary engineering tasks that define the type and general size of different process equipment that will produce the required output product. During this phase, detailed time schedules and cost estimates are developed for later phases.

Phase III, contractor selection, involves the procedures for evaluating contractors' proposals for performing detailed design and/or construction work as well as selecting the most qualified contractor(s). This particular phase can occur at a number of different times in the project life cycle.

If the project is extremely large or technically complex, an engineering design contractor will be selected to aid the owner's engineering staff in developing the project's scope, which occurs during the engineering design basis phase. In this case, the design contractor will be selected immediately after the preliminary studies phase. If separate contractors are to carry out the detailed design and construction activities, the design contractor will probably be selected before the construction contractor.

Developing Information for Construction

Detailed engineering and procurement occur during Phase IV, when the contractor uses the scopes of work defined in Phase II to develop the information required for construction. Detailed drawings and specifications must be produced for all parts of the project, and the purchase of major equipment and material to construct the project must be initiated during this phase.

Phase IV also represents the initial intensification of financial and manpower resources, which will continue to escalate until the project is complete. Consequently, the planning that is set forth during this phase as well as earlier phases is crucial in determining the successful completion of the project.

Phase V represents the actual field construction of a project. Prior to Phase V, only about 20 percent of the total project cost is expended. The financial resources needed for Phase V are much greater because of the magnitude of manpower and equipment needed. It is imperative that the overall project plan be complete at this stage because once the phase begins it will be extremely costly to correct any mistakes due to improper planning or scheduling procedures.

The final phase of the project is Phase VI, plant start-up, which establishes certain safety and operability checks for initial operation of the plant as well as demobilization of the construction contractor. This phase represents the culmination of all the previous phase activities; nevertheless, Phase VI is very important because the ongoing operating of a plant must produce the required output—within certain efficiency and safety requirements—for which it was designed and constructed.

§ 1.4 —Phases I and II

Because the activities at the beginning of a project have the greatest influence on the successful completion of the project, the first two phases of the project life cycle should be examined more carefully. These two phases, preliminary studies and engineering design basis, involve interrelated activities that define the objectives for each phase.

Each phase involves making decisions that initiate the activities defining the constraints for the phase. These constraints include project policies, organizational relationships, engineering requirements, and cost/schedule control. Construction managers must be able to work within these organizational and project constraints, because of the detailed contractual obligations agreed to between the owner and contractor.

Preliminary Studies Phase

The project decision flow for the preliminary studies phase is represented in **Figure 1–3**. The initial input into the decision network is a request by the client (owner) that the engineering consulting firm assist in determining the technical feasibility of a particular idea. The output from the decision network is a preliminary project scope of work (SOW), which will be analyzed to determine whether it is financially feasible.

In **Figure 1–3**, input and output information is represented by circles and the actual decisions are represented by squares. Interdependent decisions are enclosed by a rectangle, which symbolizes the information interaction between the decisions. The direction of the arrow represents the flow of the decisions; if an arrow is double-ended, the interconnecting decisions are made together.

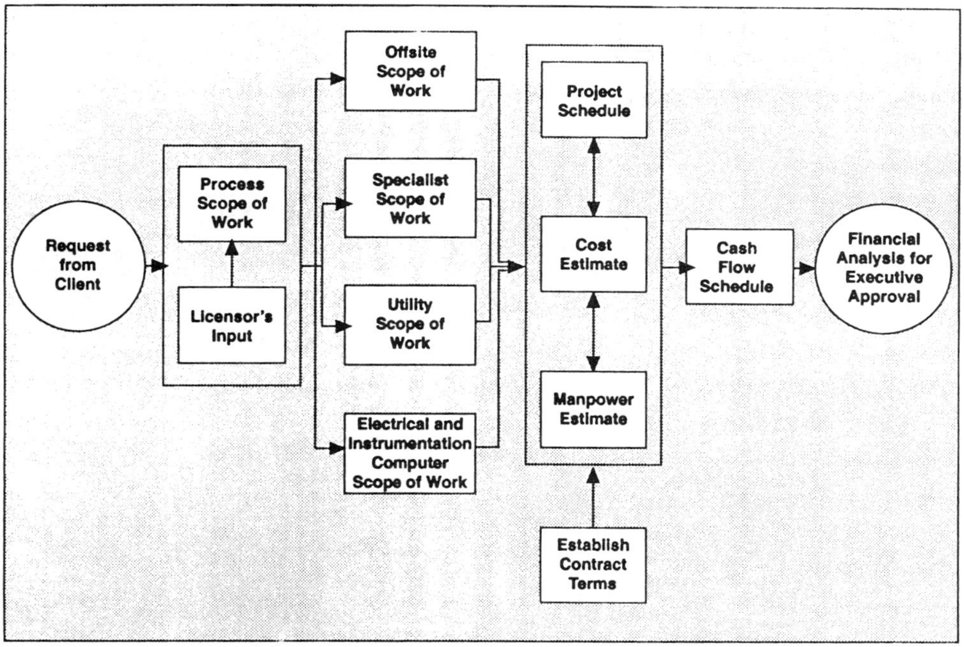

Figure 1–3. Decision flow for the preliminary study phase.

Each decision initiates several activities that are necessary in order to realize the final output; thus, an extremely important decision can be separated into subdecisions for further evaluation if needed. After the owner has given approval for the preliminary project to proceed, the next phase of the project life cycle begins.

Engineering Design Basis Phase

The engineering design basis phase (Phase II) is the next development phase of the project life cycle. **Figure 1–4** shows its decision network. As in **Figure 1–3**, the circles contain information that is an input or an output from the network, and the squares represent the decisions that initiate actions within the phase.

All the information input into the Phase II decision network is generated in the preliminary studies phase, as is the owner's executive approval to proceed with project development. The final output from the phase is the completed engineering design basis or the definition of all process units and supporting off-site areas. This output includes all detailed scopes of work for the process units as well as organizational policies and procedures for both the engineering and construction phases.

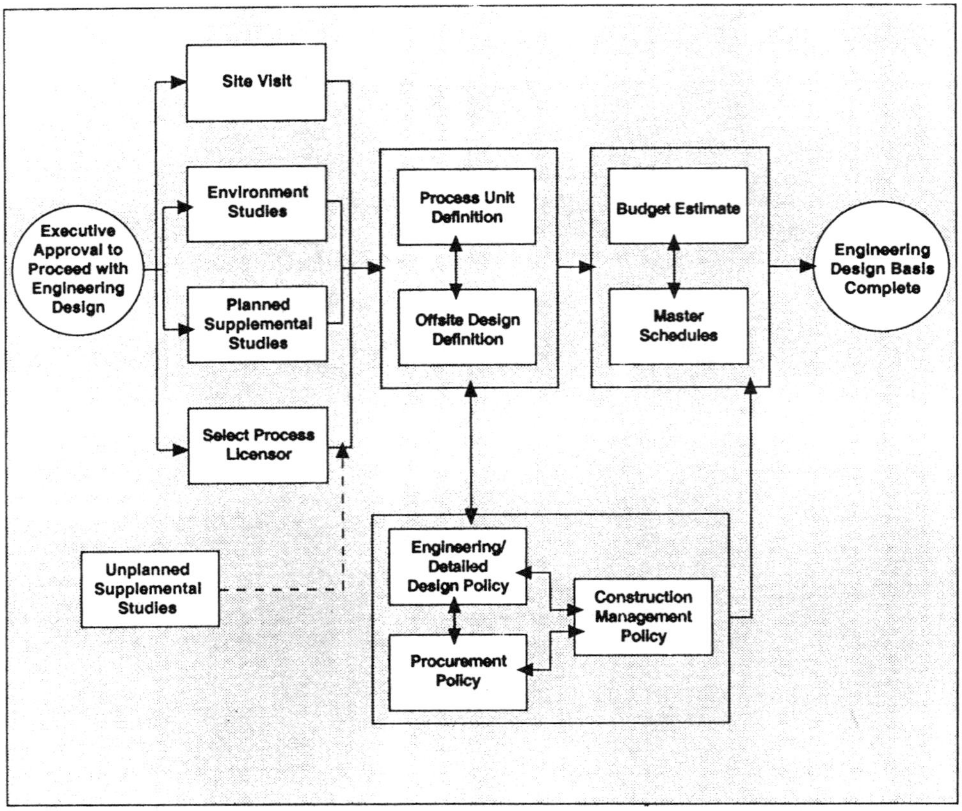

Figure 1–4. Decision flow for the engineering design basis phase.

After process unit specifications and supporting estimates for the budget and schedule are determined, the project is ready to move into the detailed engineering and procurement phase and then into the final phase of project construction. Thus, decisions made in Phases I and II have an enormous influence on the success of future project results.

§ 1.5 Factors Influencing Early Decisions

There are a number of factors that ultimately influence the end results of a construction project. These factors originate and are controlled by various parties involved with the project, such as the owner, the designer, and the contractor. For the most part, these so-called influence factors are the constraints imposed on the project. For example, the design and construction of a similar type of wastewater treatment plant will vary from project to project depending on such factors as engineering expertise, plant layout, past project experience, contract type, and so on.

Because almost all construction projects involve numerous organizational groups, it is important to identify which group has the most responsibility and control over a given set of influence factors. If the link between a project group and a set of influence factors can be established, the impact on final project results can be better managed.

Significant factors influencing the decisions made during a project's development are shown in **Figure 1–5**. These factors are categorized according to the particular group that is most responsible for controlling the factor. All of these groups play significant roles in any construction project of particular importance. For instance, the project management group can be represented by a variety of parties, such as the owner's staff, the construction manager, or the design-build contractor, depending on the nature of the particular project.

CLIENT

- Corporate Planning
- Intracorporate Communcation

OUTSIDE VENDORS

- Equipment Availability
- Equipment Vendor Quantity

PROJECT MANAGEMENT

- Technology Expertise
- Manpower Availability
- Time Availability
- Historical Information
- Past Project Procedures
- Company Specifications
- Contract Type
- Manpower Experience

OPERATING PLANT

- Operating Plant Preference
- Plant Layout
- Site Conditions
- Environmental Conditions
- Utilities Availability
- Output Guarantees
- Pollution Control Limits

OTHER

- Market Conditions
- Escalation Rate
- Technology Development

Figure 1–5. Factors influencing decisions in the scope definition phase.

The owner (client) is primarily responsible for providing guidance on the degree of project flexibility that is required for any long-range planning needs. Project management personnel are delegated the authority, by the owner, to control the project phases to assure that the project will be completed within time, cost, and quality constraints. If a new technological process is desired for the project, outside vendors will usually supply the needed design information and/or process equipment.

The operating plant is the group that specifies factors that will facilitate project operability as well as maintain environmental controls. Other factors are usually completely outside the control of any project group and include future market conditions and the economic inflation rate.

As can be seen from **Figure 1–5**, the project management group is influenced by a relatively large number of factors. Many of the influence factors relate to past experiences of project management in undertaking similar types of construction jobs. These factors include previous historical information, project procedures, contract type, and manpower experience. This points out a critical need for proper definition of project control systems before undertaking any major construction project.

Likewise, many critical influence factors impact the operating plant. Unlike the project management group, however, these factors are more technically oriented toward constraints on scope definition. These factors primarily relate to the plant site conditions, utilities availability, and pollution control limits.

Although the client has only two influence factors associated with its group, these two factors, corporate planning and intracorporate communication, are the most significant of all the various influence factors.

§ 1.6 Industrial Construction: A Case Study

A recent study of the design and construction of a large petroleum refinery plant revealed that the lack of scope definition was the most significant problem affecting both its cost and schedule.[4] The project had a total cost of approximately $1.1 billion and required 15 million worker-hours for design and construction over a five-year period.

Figure 1–6 illustrates the range of significant problems that occurred on this project, including their respective frequencies and impact values. The problems were identified from a review of the project's weekly progress reports, and their values were assigned by using a normalized weighting technique.

[4] M. Smith, *Managing Construction Scope Changes—Making the Best of the Situation, in* Project Management Institute Symposium Proceedings (Atlanta, Oct. 1989).

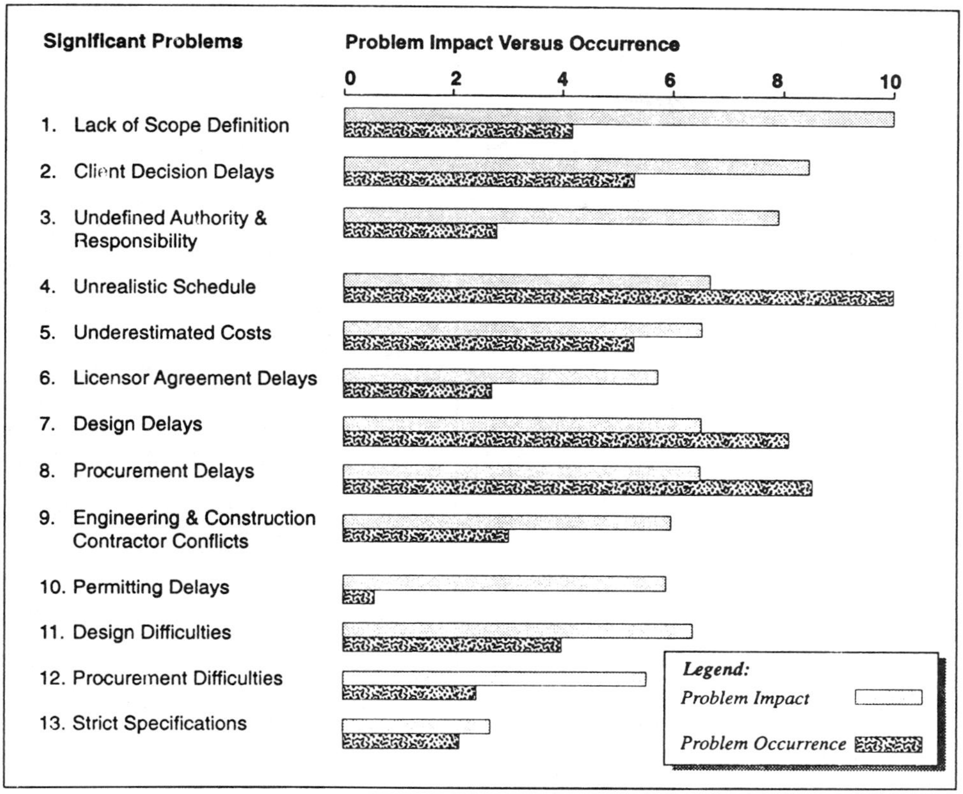

Figure 1–6. Significant problem impact versus occurrence.

Lack of scope definition on the project turned out to have the most significant impact in terms of cost and time, even though it did not occur as frequently as other problems. This suggests that the most frequently recurring problems should not always absorb a construction manager's attention. Moreover, the problem of client decision delays, ranking second in impact values, is closely related to the effort of reaching a proper scope definition.

In order to determine why there was a lack of scope definition in its early stages, information was gathered from the petrochemical project to measure the impact and controllability of various factors. A factor with a high impact rating was one that was identified as a leading cause of the problem. *Controllability* was defined as the relative degree of influence the project management team had in modifying a particular factor. Thus, a factor with a high degree of impact and controllability would be of vital importance to the construction manager.

Figure 1–7 illustrates the major influence factors for the petrochemical project's problem area, lack of scope definition. The most significant factors—corporate planning, intracorporate communications, technology

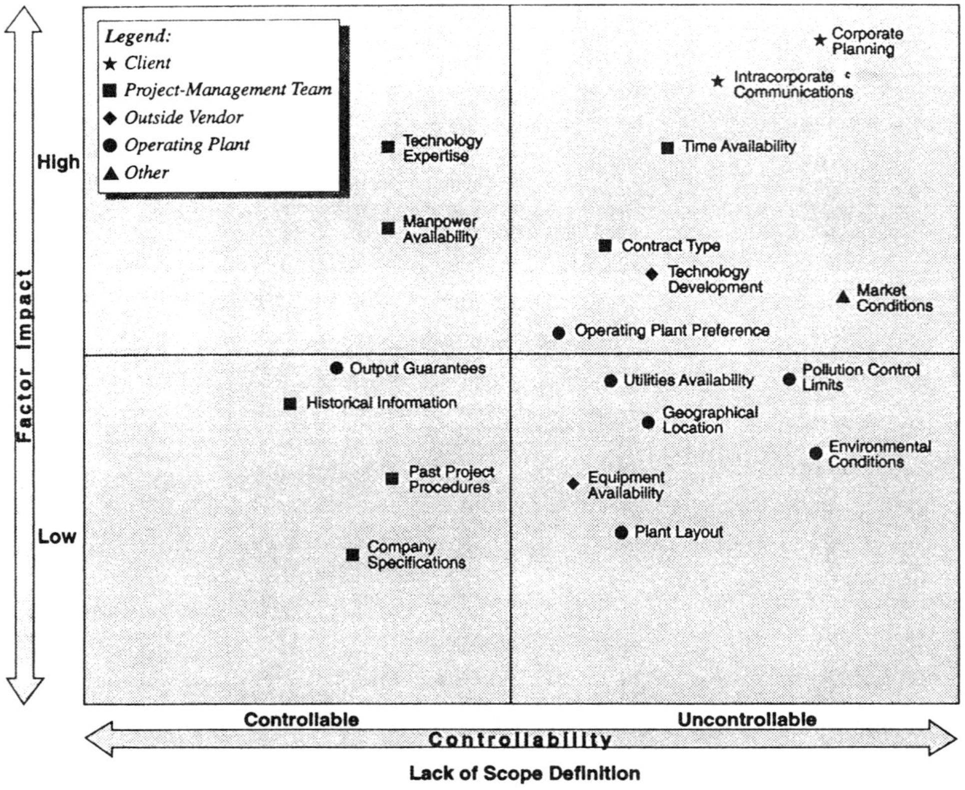

Figure 1–7. Reasons for lack of scope definition.

expertise, and time availability—are the highest-rated influences on this particular problem. Unfortunately, the construction manager has control over only one of these factors, technology expertise. The by-products of any poorly defined project are the numerous construction scope changes that will undoubtedly occur throughout the entire field construction phase. These changes can create significant tension between the project owner and construction contractor.

§ 1.7 Construction Project Scope Changes

If there is one constant in any construction project, it is the construction manager's success in dealing with the three primary project constraints—schedule, costs, and quality. Unfortunately, any evaluation is unlikely to take into consideration the almost inevitable changes that occur in the scope of any project, whether the construction of a major facility or a minor renovation undertaking. Such changes in scope occur so frequently because of a lack of communication between the project owner and the organizations designated to carry out the construction.

Construction managers must accept the fact that a well-defined scope—if one ever comes into being—will probably not emerge until the project is well into its advanced stages. Therefore, it is critical for the manager to monitor the issues that lead to changes in a project's scope and to implement techniques that can control the impact of such changes effectively.

Owner's Decision to Modify

An owner almost always initiates a project in response to the need for a particular product. This need becomes apparent from a long-range planning process that takes into account the economics of the marketplace. The need must usually be satisfied within a limited amount of time or the feasibility of the product itself will be diminished.

Market pressure is the single most important factor that drives an owner to modify the parameters of the project. Demand for a product, although intense, may be short-lived. Perceived changes in market demand will produce a change in the product and consequently in the project's scope. Similarly, increased competition, threatening to shut a company out of a market if it does not react quickly enough, may effect a change in scope.

Sometimes the change in a project's scope will come well into the advanced stages of construction and seem prohibitively expensive. But, if the expected profits outweigh the increased construction costs, the owner will still want to modify the scope. For example, the cost of constructing the Alaska oil pipeline rose from $900 million to more than $7 billion. Most of this increase was caused by poor scope definition. Although a cost overrun of that magnitude is staggering to a construction manager, the Alaska pipeline is considered an unarguable success because the profits, over the long term, have far exceeded the cost overruns.

The lesson is that the owner's needs must be balanced with the realities of designing and constructing a project within an expected amount of time and cost. Unfortunately, this balancing act never seems to flow smoothly from initial project conception to the final completion of construction.

§ 1.8 Major Influences on Construction Projects

Many factors influence how a construction project changes and evolves, even after the initial scope development. Some of the major influences are:

1. Multi-agency/-organization involvement
2. Long realization period
3. Labor intensity

4. Differing organizational objectives
5. Excessive litigation
6. Inescapable conflicting requirements
7. Political pressures.

The involvement by a myriad of external organizations and groups,—material suppliers, labor unions, regulatory agencies, attorneys, and consultants—has a tremendous influence on the complexity of every construction project. However, the owner's priority is to comply with the planned project schedule. This means recognizing that the time period from conception of a project to positive cash flow is usually measured in years. On the other hand, it also means dealing with a construction labor force that may number in the hundreds that is involved for only a short, but intense, period.

Because it is necessary to resolve disputes involving the myriad of parties working on a construction project, excessive litigation is likely to occur before, during, and after almost all major projects. To compound this problem, construction managers are constantly confronted with the task of completing a project despite increasing demands from labor organizations, environmental standards, and political/social priorities.

All of these influences play a major role in changing a project's scope over a period of time. In addition, these same influences create many of the significant problems that occur on almost every construction project.

§ 1.9 —Typical Project Problems

Although any number of problems can occur on construction projects, they can usually be classified under one of the following areas:

1. Poorly defined management controls
2. Insufficient work definition
3. Unrealistic schedules
4. Underestimated costs
5. Inadequate cost control and accounting.

Project management controls. Control areas that cause the greatest concern include: lack of meaningful cost control information, project decisions that are not made in a timely manner or not promptly implemented, decisions affecting the total project that are made by one group unilaterally, confusion regarding the authority and responsibility of project personnel, and an apparent lack of integrated planning.

Insufficient work definition. This has a far-reaching effect because a project's scope must be defined in enough detail for comprehensive scheduling, estimating, and resource allocation to be reasonably accomplished. Whenever the owner is unwilling to make a concerted effort to define the construction project in the early stages, problems will undoubtedly occur throughout the entire project life cycle.

Unrealistic schedules and underestimated costs. Whenever time schedules and/or project costs are based on optimistic predictions, the project will be burdened with missed milestone dates, costs overruns, and even low morale among project personnel. Sufficient time must be allocated in the planning stage of a project to realistically estimate time and cost requirements.

Inadequate cost control and accounting practices. This problem is associated with imperfect management planning and control. Possible explanations for why estimated costs for project activities are so inaccurate when compared to actual costs include: lack of planned information systems, poor correlation of work definitions, improper control of schedules and cost segregation, and inaccurate cost allocation methods.

§ 1.10 Ever-changing Scope

The owner is ultimately responsible for defining the scope of a project. During the conceptual phase of the project, the scope will probably change quite frequently without causing any undue hardship. However, changes that occur during the construction phase or even the detailed design phase of a project inevitably make life difficult for the construction manager.

Once a project moves beyond the conceptual phase, most construction managers want the scope to be finalized, set in concrete. Such a best-case scenario would enable the project to proceed to a timely completion with the least number of obstacles. Unfortunately, in the real world, this seldom happens. The project's scope will probably have to be altered several times during the detailed design and construction phases.

Scope changes result from a number of unavoidable factors for which no single group bears all responsibility. Some of the major factors contributing to scope modifications are:

1. Project owner desires
2. Design reviews
3. Constructability issues

4. Safety concerns
5. Operations and maintenance concerns.

Project Owner Desires

Owners initiate major changes in the scope throughout the project's life cycle. Most owners will continually perform and update feasibility studies to ensure that the project will yield the expected financial benefits. If the market changes, technical changes to the project will be necessary.

Particularly on cost-reimbursable contracts, owners will make changes for operating, maintenance, and marketing requirements without realizing the impact on construction costs. In such cases the construction manager should inform the owner of the significant cost ramifications of those changes. Once the owner is aware of the cost impacts, he can make an informed choice as to whether change is necessary.

Design Reviews

Design changes are another major cause of modifying a project's scope. Because multiple design disciplines are working, sometimes independently of each other, toward a fully integrated design, areas of confusion are bound to arise.

A change made in one area will probably cause changes in closely related areas. For example, a shift from a structural steel to a concrete support will usually cause a modification of the foundation type and probably result in some change in the mechanical/electrical work.

Constructability Issues

The concept of constructability—taking into account how a project can be constructed more efficiently—is being utilized extensively to reduce construction costs. Unfortunately, the constructability issues are usually not addressed until the design efforts are well under way. As with design changes, constructability changes affect design plans in many ways and sometimes sow discontent among design professionals.

Safety Concerns

Safety concerns cause scope modification more frequently on industrial and power projects than on other types of construction. Of course, these changes are usually mandatory in order to comply with health, safety, and environmental regulations.

Operations and Maintenance Concerns

Operations and maintenance staff members should have substantial input on the facility design because they will be responsible for the operational output of the completed facility. Changes they suggest generally incorporate human factors into the planned facility. The later into the design phase that these important suggestions are introduced, the more costly the construction changes will be. It is the construction manager's responsibility to ensure that all such considerations are brought forth early in the conceptual phase of the project.

§ 1.11 —-Managing Change Control

If a project is to be considered a success in the view of its ultimate critic, the owner, the construction manager must be able to manage and control the ever-changing definition of the project's scope. Ideally, owners would not want to proceed with a project until the scope is fully defined. In the real world, however, construction managers should expect that owners will continue with design and construction efforts even if the scope is not yet fully developed or is subject to change. Therefore, if time does not permit the full definition of the project's scope, the risks of cost and schedule overruns should be included in the project's feasibility analysis.

§ 1.12 —Change Order System

A construction manager must anticipate that changes will occur on every project and throughout every project's life cycle. Using a formal system to control the change order process can lessen many of the undesirable effects of the changes. A good system includes the following steps:

1. Identification of changes
2. Evaluation of benefits and costs
3. Proper approval by the owner
4. Incorporation of changes into the contract
5. Payment according to agreed-upon terms.

Either the owner or the contractor can identify proposed changes and should notify all project participants as soon as possible. This notification is not a formal change order, but only a request for information. The most essential information is the impact of the proposed change on the budget and schedule of the project.

The owner, or a representative of the owner, must properly evaluate the proposed changes through a quantitative assessment that ensures that the benefits of the change exceed the estimated cost.

Negotiation is usually required to arrive at a fair price for the modified work. The agreed-upon change should be formally approved by the owner. If the change is denied, appropriate documentation should be recorded in the control system.

A formal change order with the approval signature of the owner must then be issued to a contractor. The contractor should also sign the change order to indicate his acceptance. A change order may consolidate several changes that have a collective impact on a specific area of the project.

Finally, the change order should be paid according to the terms of the contract. It is important to identify paid change orders separately in the cost control system. This procedure will guard against future claims or litigation after the job is completed.

CHAPTER 2

CONTEMPLATING LITIGATION AND ITS ALTERNATIVES

Overton A. Currie
James E. Stephenson
Philip E. Beck

Overton A. Currie, senior partner of the Atlanta, Georgia, law firm of Smith, Currie & Hancock, founded and heads the firm's 50-lawyer construction law department. He earned an LL.M. from Yale University and remained on the Yale Law School faculty as a research associate until returning to private practice in 1959. Mr. Currie served the American Bar Association as national chairman of the Public Contract Section, national chairman of the Committee on Subcontracts, and national chairman of the Construction Litigation Committee of the Litigation Section. His experience includes both private and public projects across the nation and overseas. He is active in the Construction Law Network and is a member of the International Bar Association. He currently serves as a national director of the American Arbitration Association and is a founding fellow and president of the American College of Construction Lawyers.

James E. Stephenson is a partner in the Atlanta, Georgia, law firm of Smith, Currie & Hancock, where he has practiced law since 1976. He graduated from Yale University and Duke University School of Law. Mr. Stephenson has advised and counseled all of the major participants in the construction process including owners, general contractors, developers, subcontractors, architects, sureties, and construction managers. He devotes his practice to presenting cases for such clients to judges, juries, arbitrators, and administrative agencies and tribunals. He has written extensively on construction law and rights, has contributed chapters to several other Wiley Law Publications books, and edited *Alternative Clauses to Standard Construction Contracts* (John Wiley & Sons, 1990) and Wiley's newsletter, *Construction Contracting Alert*.

Philip E. Beck is a partner in the Atlanta, Georgia, law firm of Smith, Currie & Hancock and is a member of the firm's construction law department. He is a 1981 honors graduate of the University of Tennessee College of Law and holds a B.S. and an M.B.A. from the University of Tennessee. Mr. Beck has experience with a broad range of construction issues and different types of construction projects, both public and private, throughout the United States. He has written and lectured on a number of topics related to the construction industry and construction law, having spoken on programs sponsored by the University of Tennessee, the Georgia Institute of Technology, and the National Society of Professional Engineers.

CONSTRUCTION RISKS AND REWARDS

§ 2.1 Not for the Timid

§ 2.2 —Inherent Risk Factors

§ 2.3 —Legislated Risks

§ 2.4 —Risk Management

§ 2.5 Construction Disputes

§ 2.6 —Complexity

§ 2.7 —Contract Structures

§ 2.8 —Sources of Disputes

§ 2.9 Need for Effective Risk, Dispute, and Litigation Management

RISK MANAGEMENT

§ 2.10 Parties and Relationships

§ 2.11 —Owners: Public and Private

§ 2.12 —Architect/Engineers

§ 2.13 —Construction Managers

§ 2.14 —General Contractors, Subcontractors, and Suppliers

§ 2.15 —Sureties

§ 2.16 —Construction Lenders

§ 2.17 Legal Parameters

§ 2.18 —Building Codes, Ordinances, and Regulations

§ 2.19 —Trade Usage and Implied Obligations

§ 2.20 Contract Documents: A Beginning

§ 2.21 —Uniform Commercial Code Applicability

§ 2.22 —Basic Provisions

§ 2.23 —Exculpatory and Special Clauses

§ 2.24 —Modifications

DISPUTE MANAGEMENT
§ 2.25 Types of Disputes and Their Causes
§ 2.26 —Bid Disputes
§ 2.27 —Performance Disputes
§ 2.28 Dispute Recognition and Reaction
§ 2.29 —Preservation of Evidence and Claims
§ 2.30 —Early Use of Experts
§ 2.31 Settling Disputes
§ 2.32 —Settlement Techniques
§ 2.33 —Negotiation Strategies
§ 2.34 —Arbitration versus Litigation
§ 2.35 —Other Alternatives
LITIGATION MANAGEMENT
§ 2.36 Litigation Objectives
§ 2.37 Selection of Parties, Remedies, and Forum
§ 2.38 Effective Litigation Strategy
§ 2.39 Effective Trial Presentation
§ 2.40 Appeal

CONSTRUCTION RISKS AND REWARDS

§ 2.1 Not for the Timid

Most people are risk-averse. Given a choice of receiving either 50 cents or an opportunity to flip a coin for a chance at a dollar, most people will take the 50 cents. The popularity of the gambling industry (from state-run lotteries to private casinos) suggests that our propensity to take risks increases when the possible rewards are great in comparison to the cost, even though the odds against success also increase proportionately. The prospect of receiving something for nothing—or nearly nothing—will always be attractive to many. But when the possible rewards do not significantly outweigh the costs, most people prefer not to gamble. Contractors are not most people.

The typical contractor's profit margin—the percentage difference between revenues and costs—is very small in comparison to its risk exposure. Good business and money managers analyze investments in terms of a natural tradeoff between risk and return. The construction industry as a whole has a much lower dollars-for-profit per dollars-at-risk than almost any other type of business. The construction business requires large capital outlays, but is also labor-intensive. On almost every construction project, it is possible to lose much more money than it is possible to make. It is not unusual for a job that constitutes only five percent of a large contractor's business to have the potential to destroy 50 percent or more of the company's net worth.

A contractor has been defined as a card player who never gets to deal, cut the deck, or shuffle. One could add that contractors also are required to bet $10 just to make one. The construction business is truly not a business for the timid or the faint-hearted.

§ 2.2 —Inherent Risk Factors

The time-sensitivity of construction costs is one factor contributing to the business's risk. Time is money, especially in the construction industry. Construction projects typically extend over long periods of time and there are many time-related costs that increase in proportion to any increases in the performance period. If a 10-month job is stretched to 12 months, costs are likely to increase even though the quantity of work has remained constant. Ironically, if that same 10-month job is accelerated to eight months, that too will likely increase costs if the 10-month schedule represented the optimum allocation of resources.

The cyclical nature of the construction business also increases risk. Many costs are variable and can be avoided during periods of low construction activity, but many capital costs are not, and must be met even though the amount of available work is insufficient to support them.

Risks are also inherent in the construction process because of something no one can completely control or accurately predict: Mother Nature. Construction time and costs are very vulnerable to natural phenomena such as adverse weather and unanticipated subsurface conditions. Construction is not performed in a controlled, laboratory environment. Rather, it is performed in the dynamic, ever-changing, and often surprising real world of nature. This increases the risks involved.

The predominance of performance and payment surety bonds in the construction industry is evidence of the high-risk nature of the industry, and distinguishes it from most others. The construction business is undoubtedly exciting, but it is truly an excitement born of risk.

§ 2.3 —Legislated Risks

In recent years, the construction process has been made more risky by the creation of a number of new laws governing contractors. For reasons of public policy and the general welfare, legislators have created more contractor responsibilities while limiting their ability to control their risks. Although this is not a new development, it has accelerated in the 1970s, 1980s, and 1990s.

Federal environmental laws have created virtually unlimited and perpetual liability for contractors that innocently and unknowingly disturb or relocate hazardous waste or asbestos. Disadvantaged, minority, and small business utilization requirements, local preference laws, affirmative action hiring requirements, and other programs designed to further societal goals create additional requirements, and possibly less control and freedom-of-choice, and more risks for contractors. Still other new laws place greater responsibilities and liability on contractors for the sake of combatting everything from illegal aliens to illegal drugs. Whether one supports or opposes these and similar laws, one must agree that they have made an already complex and risky business even more complex and riskier.

§ 2.4 —Risk Management

There are profits to be realized in the construction business, but to be successful over the long term requires effective management skills and techniques. Management has been defined as "the function of getting things done through people and directing the efforts of individuals towards a common objective."[1] Only through good, sound management can a contractor marshal the integration of labor, materials, and expertise to construct a building or structure so as to accomplish the business's objective: realization of a profit.

§ 2.5 Construction Disputes

Most writings and programs on the topic of construction law and litigation begin with a discussion of the various factors that combine to make the construction industry the arena for a great many disputes. If high risk is the salt of the construction industry, controversy and disputes are the pepper. This is true for a number of reasons. First, the construction industry is the largest industry in the United States. However, the construction industry breeds a large number of disputes even for its size, not because the participants are unusually disagreeable or litigious by nature, but rather because of inherent characteristics of the industry.

---

[1] Haimann, Professional Management Theory and Practice 1 (1962).

§ 2.6 —Complexity

One of the principal factors leading to construction disputes is the unavoidable complexity of the industry. A multitude of factors affect the respective rights, responsibilities, and liabilities of the various parties involved in the construction process. The technical and changing nature of the construction itself adds to this complexity.

The large number of separate, yet interdependent, parties involved in a typical construction project is also a factor in the generation of disputes. Unlike many businesses that are characterized by two-party transactions, a construction project will likely involve an owner, one or more prime contractors, a number of different subcontractors and suppliers, an architect, one or more engineers, a number of sureties and insurance carriers, a construction lender, and perhaps a construction manager or various other consultants. The complex nature of construction and the number of parties involved also create communication difficulties that can themselves lead to disputes.

§ 2.7 —Contract Structures

The many different contract structures by which the various parties may align themselves create disputes by altering the rights and liabilities of the parties, often without their realization. For example, an owner may:

1. Employ a single general contractor, who in turn employs and coordinates various subcontractors
2. Contract directly with the various trade contractors, establishing multiple prime contracts, and expressly or implicitly assume the right and responsibility to coordinate the work of these various prime contractors
3. Employ multiple prime contractors and, in addition, employ a construction manager to assist in the coordination of their work
4. Enter into a design-build contract, contracting with a single entity to perform design and construction services, rather than employing a separate architect/engineer
5. Devise some hybrid of the foregoing, or fashion some different role, relationship, and contract structure.

§ 2.8 —Sources of Disputes

Most construction disputes that arise can be grouped into three broad categories:

1. Disputes pertaining to the quantity of the work
2. Disputes pertaining to the quality of the work
3. Disputes pertaining to the method (including the time frame) of performing the work.

Construction disputes, like other types of disputes, generally arise because the parties have different and conflicting interests and expectations. When an owner provides a construction design to a contractor, he imposes certain quantity, quality, method, scheduling, and sequencing restraints upon the contractor. Many owners, conscious of their substantial cash investment in the project, view these guidelines as minimum standards below which the contractor cannot trespass, but above which the contractor should aspire. The natural trade-off between cost and time on the one hand and quality on the other breeds disputes.

The architect is established under many contracts as the neutral referee of disputes between the owner and contractor. However, the architect's own set of interests and expectations may conflict with those of the owner and/or the contractor. The architect who designed the building and who is supervising its construction is often charged with the responsibility of insuring adherence to the design, but not with the responsibility for the timely completion of the project. The architect, therefore, has a natural tendency to demand quality, often at the expense of time and cost. Skyrocketing insurance premiums in recent years and the natural tendency toward risk aversion have caused architects, who are often in the enviable position of drafting the contract documents that define the respective rights and responsibilities of the various parties, to allocate less and less risk to themselves. This generally places greater risk on the contractor as well as the owner.[2]

§ 2.9 Need for Effective Risk, Dispute, and Litigation Management

The demanding nature of the construction business and the prevalence of disputes in the industry require a contractor to be a successful dispute manager. This entails being an effective manager of risk, to prevent and minimize disputes; an effective manager of disputes, once they arise; and an effective manager of the various instrumentalities of dispute resolution, including negotiation, arbitration, and litigation.

[2] *Compare* American Institute of Architects (AIA) Doc. A201 (1987) to AIA Doc. A201 (1976). *See generally* J. Sweet, Sweet on Construction Industry Contracts (John Wiley & Sons, Inc. 1991); J. Stephenson, Alternative Clauses to Standard Construction Contracts (John Wiley & Sons, Inc. 1990).

An old proverb states, "Agree, for the law is costly."[3] The potential costs of disputes are enormous. Through effective contract negotiation and administration, a contractor can minimize the likelihood of disputes and save itself enormous costs. When disputes do arise, as they inevitably will, the contractor must effectively manage the resolution of the dispute, whether by litigation, arbitration or negotiation, to ensure that the cure is not worse than the ailment. Any experienced lawyer can cite examples of litigation costs exceeding the amount in controversy. This is usually due to poor dispute resolution management.

Litigation and its alternatives should be viewed as means of accomplishing a certain objective, and should be subjected to the same type of cost-benefit analysis as any other business undertaking. If the anticipated benefits to be derived from litigation do not exceed the anticipated costs of litigation, it should not be undertaken. Benefits can, of course, include noneconomic and nonimmediate benefits. Sometimes a litigant will consciously choose to pursue a cause, with little regard for the cost, on principle. Most construction disputes, however, are purely economic disputes, and should be evaluated in solely economic terms.

In evaluating the costs of litigation and its alternatives, one should not lose sight of a number of indirect or hidden costs. One is the *time value of money.* It is a rudimentary concept of finance that a dollar today is worth more than a dollar tomorrow. It is the reason banks are willing to pay interest on deposits and can charge interest on loans. When litigation takes years to complete, the opportunity costs of not having capital to invest in other projects and ventures can become enormous. Another sometimes overlooked cost of litigation is the management time and resources that must be devoted to the matter rather than to the pursuit of other profit-generating endeavors.

The numerous parties and long time periods involved, the volume of paper generated, the necessity of using experts, the necessity of protracted discovery, and the length of trials and appeals (due to the complexity and size of construction disputes) all combine to make construction disputes more costly to litigate, both in terms of time and of money, than many other types of disputes. The best way to streamline, minimize, or avoid litigation and arbitration is to implement a management system that avoids many potential disputes, identifies and documents them when they occur, and generates and preserves documentation and evidence of the supporting facts. By doing this, the contractor not only minimizes the possibility of disputes, but enhances its position for a favorable resolution of disputes when they do occur. Recognition, preparation, presentation, defense, and resolution of construction claims should all be performed in accordance with the same management standards applied to operational decisions.

---

[3] Herbert, Jacula Prudentum (1651).

RISK MANAGEMENT

§ 2.10 Parties and Relationships

This chapter has touched upon the numerous parties involved in the construction process, and subsequent chapters of this book address in greater detail the contractor's relationship to these various parties. A brief introduction to these parties and relationships follows in **§§ 2.11** to **2.16**.

§ 2.11 —Owners: Public and Private

The *owner* is primarily a purchaser of materials and services: it pays for the construction and derives the benefit of the product. It is important for the contractor both to know the owner it is dealing with and looking to for payment, and specifically to determine the owner's ability to pay, its expertise, and its reputation. Much of the construction work performed, even in the United States, is performed for the benefit of public owners such as the federal government or state and local governments. A prudent contractor adjusts its construction administration methods depending upon the nature of the owner. In addition to differences in the contract documents, there are varying interests, philosophies, and legal rights and responsibilities.

Dispute resolution mechanisms also vary for the different types of owners. Disputes under private contracts are generally resolved, if not by agreement, either through arbitration, if the contract so provides, or otherwise through litigation. Construction contracts with public bodies, on the other hand, frequently refer disputes to special tribunals and procedures. For example, under the Contract Disputes Act of 1978,[4] disputes arising under federal government construction contracts are to be resolved through proceedings before one of the various agency boards of contract appeals or the United States Claims Court. Some states and municipalities also have special disputes procedures or requirements.

Contracting with governmental bodies also raises the issue of sovereign immunity, which is an ancient doctrine prohibiting or limiting suits against the government. Today, sovereign immunity is not a bar to most contract suits against governmental bodies, but it can in some cases bar or limit recovery, and, therefore, should not be ignored.

In short, the nature of the owner must be taken into account by both the contractor and the contractor's attorney, and both contractor and attorney must recognize and respond to the distinctions.

---

[4] 41 U.S.C. §§ 601–613 (1988).

§ 2.12 —Architect/Engineers

Under most contract structures, the *architect/engineer* is a design professional who is not in contractual privity (does not have a direct contractual relationship) with either the prime contractor(s) or the subcontractors. This limits the ability of a contractor to seek recourse against the architect/engineer for damages flowing from improper design, inspection, contract interpretation, or contract administration. The *Spearin* doctrine[5] is applied in federal government construction contract disputes and under the law of many states to provide the contractor a remedy for defective design against the owner, with whom it is in contractual privity. The *Spearin* doctrine specifies that the owner, in providing the contractor the construction design, impliedly warrants that the plans and specifications are reasonably free from defects.

In addition, although the contractor may not have a direct contractual cause of action against the architect/engineer, it may be able to recover directly against the design professional under one or more of the following legal theories:

1. Negligence on the part of the design professional
2. The commission of an intentional tort by the design professional
3. The existence of a third-party beneficiary relationship whereby the contractor can recover damages resulting from the design professional's breach of its contract with the owner.

The contractor's decision as to whether to seek recovery from the owner or directly from the design professional is an extremely important one and should depend on a number of factors. These include the law governing the dispute, the nature of the claim, the solvency of the owner and the design professional, whether the design professional is insured and if so the terms of the policy, the terms of the construction contract, the terms of the design professional's contract, and the forum in which the contractor would prefer to resolve the dispute.

§ 2.13 —Construction Managers

In recent years, it has become popular with many owners to contract directly with the various trade contractors and employ a *construction manager* to fulfill many of the functions traditionally performed by the general

[5] The *Spearin* doctrine originates from the 1918 United States Supreme Court decision in United States v. Spearin, 248 U.S. 132, 136 (1918).

contractor. Contractually, this entails using multiple prime contractors who may or may not be in contractual privity with the construction manager who is charged with the duty to coordinate and schedule their work. In the pure construction management scenario, when the prime contractors are not in contractual privity with the construction manager, their ability to seek recourse directly against the construction manager for the construction manager's failure to properly schedule or coordinate the work is limited in the same way as the contractor's ability to proceed directly against the architect (discussed in **§ 2.12**). Generally speaking, when an owner chooses to contract directly with multiple trade contractors, the owner assumes the obligation to coordinate the work of the various contractors, and cannot divest itself of that responsibility by employing a construction manager.[6]

The decision of whether to bring an action directly against the construction manager on a negligence, intentional tort, or third-party beneficiary contract theory, or to seek recovery from the owner, is an important strategic decision and should depend on several factors. Construction managers are sometimes grouped into two categories, distinguished by the background and experience of the firm providing the construction management services. First, the *professional construction manager* is a design professional by background and training. The *contractor-construction manager,* however, is usually a general contractor performing in this role. Which of these two categories applies to the construction manager in question should have a bearing on the contractor's litigation strategies; for instance, the professional construction manager is more likely to carry insurance and, therefore, be capable of paying a large judgment.

Other factors to consider regarding the contractor's litigation plan include the nature and origin of the action; the relative financial strength of the construction manager and the owner; the relative experience of the construction manager and the owner; whether the contractor desires to do business in the future with either the construction manager or the owner, or otherwise maintain a good relationship with one or the other; the relative culpability of the construction manager and the owner; and the specific facts of the particular situation, such as contract terms.

---

[6] *See* Eric A. Carlstrom Constr. Co. v. Independence Sch. Dist. No. 77, 256 N.W.2d 479 (Minn. 1977); Stehlin-Muller-Henes Co. v. City of Bridgeport, 97 Conn. 657, 117 A. 811 (1922). This obligation is analogous to the general contractor's obligation to coordinate subcontractors. *See* Johnson v. Fenestra, Inc., 305 F.2d 179 (3d Cir. 1962); United States v. Citizens & S. Nat'l Bank, 367 F.2d 473 (4th Cir. 1966); Great Lakes Constr. Co. v. Republic Creosoting Co., 139 F.2d 456 (8th Cir. 1943); Melwin Constr. v. Stonewall Constr. Co., 113 A.2d 108 (D.C. 1955).

§ 2.14 —General Contractors, Subcontractors, and Suppliers

The relationship between a general contractor and its subcontractors and suppliers is a very important one, and in many ways analogous to the owner-general contractor relationship. The general contractor and its subcontractors are often either powerful allies or powerful adversaries. The general contractor must not lose sight of the fact that the owner is contractually looking to it for timely and proper performance of the entire contract.

General contractors often make the mistake of building a case against a subcontractor that the owner can then use against the general contractor. Correspondence between the general contractor and its subcontractors containing accusations against each other often provides powerful ammunition for a capable construction litigator representing the owner when disputes between the owner and the contractor develop. This is not to say that a subcontractor should never be critical of its general contractor or that a general contractor should never be critical of its subcontractors; sometimes a critical or demanding letter may be necessary to force another party to adhere to its obligations. Rather, the parties should be aware of the legal ramifications of their actions and weigh those in making their decisions.

§ 2.15 —Sureties

On a construction project, both the general contractor and the various subcontractors will often be required to provide payment and performance bonds. This introduces another group of parties, with their own rights and obligations, to the project: the *construction sureties.*

Only in rare situations is it in the best interest of the contractor (the principal) to initiate litigation against its own surety. This is because the surety will in most cases have indemnity rights against the contractor, and in the case of small corporations, against the owners of the corporation. Thus, suing one's surety may constitute, in effect, suing oneself. More frequently, it may be in the best interest of a general contractor to bring suit against a subcontractor's surety, or in the interest of a subcontractor or supplier to bring suit against the general contractor's surety. This typically occurs when the principal defaults on its contract and is insolvent.

On federal construction projects and most other public work, the general contractor is required to provide performance and payment bonds to serve as a substitute for the lien rights that subcontractors and suppliers would normally have on a private project but do not have on public work.[7]

---

[7] The Miller Act, 40 U.S.C. § 270(a)–(f) (1988), imposes such requirements on federal work. A number of states have enacted Little Miller Acts; *see* Lifschitz, *Little Miller Acts,* Construction Briefings No. 8 (Aug. 1984).

A general contractor often has the option, however, of requiring subcontractors to provide performance and payment bonds, and should carefully evaluate whether the cost of doing so is warranted under the particular circumstances.

§ 2.16 —Construction Lenders

In some situations, a contractor may be entitled to seek legal recourse directly against the construction lender financing the project. Such action should be seriously considered if there is concern about the solvency of the owner. With regard to construction financing, the contractor must remember that it will lose important leverage if it allows progress payments to fall behind performance progress to such a point that it would be cheaper for the owner and lender to terminate it and employ another contractor than to pay the existing contractor to complete.

§ 2.17 Legal Parameters

There are a number of legal rights and obligations that exist separately and independently of those expressly created and assumed in the contract documents. Some of these can be altered or shifted in the contract documents; some cannot. The contractor must be aware of these and take them into account in bidding and performing its work.

§ 2.18 —Building Codes, Ordinances, and Regulations

Even though not specifically referenced in the contract documents, contractors are generally required to comply with the local laws of the jurisdiction in which the project is performed. One issue that commonly arises is who is responsible when a building is constructed in accordance with the design but does not conform to local building and safety codes. The question usually boils down to whether the contractor acted reasonably in relying upon the design professional to take local building and safety codes into account. As a rule of thumb, if the contractor has substantial experience in the area where the project is being built, it is not reasonable for it to rely entirely on the design professional in this regard. If the contractor is not familiar with the area, such reliance may be deemed reasonable. A contractor should, however, fully apprise itself of local codes in order to avoid disputes of this type.

In addition to local building and safety codes, a number of other laws and ordinances may affect the contractor and require its attention and compliance. Among these are licensing requirements, registration requirements, and tax requirements. The failure of a contractor to comply with these can result in substantial penalties and may even bar its ability to enforce the obligations of others.[8]

When a contractor contracts with a federal, state, or local governmental body to provide construction services, it impliedly submits itself to a myriad of public regulations and requirements. These can include safety regulations, wage standards, minority and female employment requirements, reporting and record-keeping requirements, notice requirements, and others. These, too, should be taken into account by the contractor and should govern its actions and decisions.

§ 2.19 —Trade Usage and Implied Obligations

When the express language of a contract does not unambiguously resolve a given dispute or controversy, courts, boards, and arbitration panels often look to trade custom and usage and the parties' prior dealings to interpret the intent of the contract.[9] Although the parties are free to establish by contract any rights and obligations totally different from prior dealings and trade custom, they must be careful to do so expressly and unambiguously.

There are a number of legal rights and obligations that arise from a contract even though not expressly stated therein. For example, a party to a contract impliedly promises not to do anything to hinder or impede the other party's performance.[10] This basic principle becomes the basis of the contractor's right, under appropriate circumstances, to recover delay damages and other forms of damages. The *Spearin* doctrine, referred to in **§ 2.12**, is another example of an implied obligation that arises from the contract without being expressed in words. The owner's obligation to coordinate multiple prime contractors and the general contractor's obligation to coordinate the various subcontractors are other examples of important implied rights and obligations. Finally, there are various implied warranties that may arise to impose obligations on the contractor, including implied warranties regarding the quality of materials and workmanship, and, in the

---

[8] *See, e.g.,* Ga. Code Ann. §§ 48-13-30 to 48-13-38; Department of Transportation, State of Ga. v. Moseman Constr. Co., 260 Ga. 369, 393 S.E.2d 258 (1990) (and prior decisions in this line of cases interpreting and applying the Georgia Nonresident Contractors Act); Sample v. Morgan, 311 N.C. 717, 319 S.E.2d 607 (1984); Allan S. Meade & Assocs., Inc. v. McGarry, 68 N.C. App. 467, 315 S.E.2d 69 (1984).

[9] *See, e.g.,* Frischhertz Elec. Co. v. Housing Auth., 534 So. 2d 1310 (La. Ct. App. 1988).

[10] *See* Weaver-Bailey Contractors, Inc. v. United States, 19 Cl. Ct. 474 (1990); Gulf M.&O. Ry. v. Illinois Cent. R.R., 128 F. Supp. 311 (N.D. Ala. 1954), *aff'd,* 225 F.2d 816 (5th Cir. 1955); S. Williston, A Treatise on the Law of Contracts §§ 1296, 1316 (3d ed. 1961).

case of residential construction in some states, the implied warranty of habitability.

Aside from express and implied contractual rights and obligations, the contractor has certain other rights and obligations, the breach of which can give rise to a right of recovery in tort. A contractor has an obligation to exercise reasonable care in the performance of the work and, in many states, has a right to expect the exercise of reasonable care by the architect, the construction manager, the owner, and others. The contractor has an obligation to refrain from committing various intentional torts and a right to be free from intentional torts of others. These tort rights and obligations arise independently of any contract and are fundamentally similar to those imposed on anyone driving a car or walking down the street.

§ 2.20 Contract Documents: A Beginning

Like a marriage license, the contract documents are essential, but only a beginning. The goal of the contract documents should be to define as clearly and unambiguously as possible the various rights and obligations of the parties. Some contractors bemoan the fact that the day of the handshake agreement is past. This is true, however, not solely due to any lack of trustworthiness on the part of modern-day participants, but because of the increased complexity of construction.

In the contract documents, the parties should strive to anticipate potential problems, to allocate the risks of such problems, and to provide for the efficient resolution of any disputes that may arise. This applies not only to the owner/general contractor contract but also to the general contractor/subcontractor contract. Moreover, the contractor must be careful to coordinate its subcontracts with the general contract to ensure consistency and the desired result.

§ 2.21 —Uniform Commercial Code Applicability

The Uniform Commercial Code (UCC) was devised as a recommended code of laws governing commercial conduct. Its substantial adoption by all 50 states except Louisiana resulted in a system of relatively uniform state laws governing frequently recurring forms of business transactions, including the sale of goods, the use of negotiable instruments and investment securities, bulk transfers, and financing arrangements involving security interests.

Article 2 of the UCC's nine articles governs transactions involving the sale of movable goods. Since the creation of the UCC, a debate has raged as to whether construction contracts, which typically involve the sale of services primarily and goods only secondarily, are covered by Article 2. The various states addressing the issue are split, with some holding that Article 2 of the UCC does apply to construction contracts.[11] In addition, a number of other decisions have held that the principles of the UCC should be applied to construction contracts by analogy, thus yielding the same result.[12] In addition, supply contracts involving solely the sale of movable goods fall squarely within the scope of UCC Article 2.

The application of UCC Article 2, directly or by analogy, has several ramifications. Section 2-204(1) provides that a contract "may be made in any manner sufficient to show agreement, including conduct by both parties which recognizes the existence of such a contract." Section 2-204(3) provides that a contract may be enforceable "even though one or more terms are left open." Both of these provisions represent major modifications of common law.

Perhaps the most significant effect of applying the UCC results from § 2-207, commonly referred to as the "battle of forms." Under traditional contract law, a *mirror image* rule was applied requiring, as a prerequisite to contract formation, an acceptance strictly conforming to the terms of the offer. Under UCC § 2-207, an expression of acceptance can operate as an acceptance of a contract "even though it states terms additional to or different from those offered or agreed upon, unless acceptance is expressly made conditional on assent to the additional or different terms." Section 2-207 goes on to describe when those additional or changed terms become part of the contract and when they do not.

§ 2.22 —Basic Provisions

A number of contract provisions are basic, if not essential, to all construction contracts. These include payment provisions, provisions defining the scope of the work, provisions governing changes in the scope of the work, provisions establishing requirements and procedures for termination of the contract, and provisions establishing procedures for the resolution of disputes arising under the contract.

The *changes clause* is unique, but essential, to construction contracts. Unlike most contracts, in which the scope of the undertaking can be firmly

---

[11] *See, e.g.,* Pittsburgh-Des Moines Steel Co. v. Brookhaven Manor Water Co., 532 F.2d 572 (7th Cir. 1976); Bonebrake v. Corx, 499 F.2d 951 (8th Cir. 1974); Omaha Pollution Control Corp. v. Carver-Greenfield Corp., 413 F. Supp. 1069 (D. Nev. 1976); Port City Constr. Co. v. Henderson, 266 So. 2d 896 (Ala. Ct. App. 1972).

[12] *See, e.g.,* Padbloc Co. v. United States, 161 Ct. Cl. 369 (1963); Redman Dev. Corp. v. Piedmont Heating & Air Conditioning Co., 128 Ga. App. 447, 197 S.E.2d 167 (1974); Aced v. Hobbs-Sesack Plumbing Co., 55 Cal. 2d 573, 360 P.2d 897, 12 Cal. Rptr. 257 (1961).

established at the outset, most construction owners desire the flexibility to make changes in the scope of the work as it progresses. In the absence of a changes clause, the scope of the work could be changed only by mutual modification of the contract if agreed to by both parties. Under the changes clause, a procedure is established whereby the owner may unilaterally order a change in the work, with the contractor's compensation and performance time adjusted accordingly.

A general contractor, in establishing the terms for its subcontracts, must incorporate *flow-down* provisions, binding the subcontractors to the same obligations, liabilities, and procedures to which the general contractor has bound itself in its contract with the owner. Critical provisions to be addressed in this way include:

1. Payment provisions (so that the general contractor is not bound to pay the subcontractor before the general contractor has been paid for that work)
2. Provisions for changes to the scope of the work (so that the general contractor is not obligated to grant the subcontractor a change order and additional compensation for which the general contractor is not compensated by the owner, unless the change merely involves shifting work within the original scope of the general contract from one subcontractor to another)
3. Default and termination provisions (so that, in the event the general contractor is terminated, the general contractor has the power to terminate the subcontractor)
4. Quality standards provisions
5. Suspension of work provisions
6. Special damages provisions (for example, no damages for delay clauses)
7. Provisions establishing dispute resolution procedures.

The general contractor should also be careful to ensure that all the work included within the scope of the general contract is also included within the scope of the subcontractors' work, unless the general contractor intends to perform and incur the costs of that work itself.

§ 2.23 —Exculpatory and Special Clauses

In addition to the basic contract provisions, an owner or general contractor may desire to include one or more exculpatory or special provisions in the contract. An *exculpatory clause* is a clause barring or limiting some type of liability.

A common example of an exculpatory clause (which may appear either in a general contract or in a subcontract) is the *no damages for delay* clause. Such a clause attempts to limit the owner's or general contractor's liability to the general contractor or subcontractor for damages resulting from construction delays. Such a clause may be broadly worded to apply to all delays, or may apply only to delays of a specific nature. It may purport to deny any relief for delays or may only limit the liability in some fashion. As a general rule, such provisions, when agreed to by both parties to the contract, are enforceable. However, the courts construe such provisions very narrowly and have developed many exceptions to the general rule of enforceability.[13] Although the contractor may often recover delay damages despite the presence of such a clause, the contractor should weigh very carefully the consequences of such a clause before entering a contract containing one. Exculpatory clauses are basically a means of shifting risk allocation and, presumably, there is a cost associated with that risk. The contractor should, therefore, demand a higher contract price when such a clause is included.

Another type of risk-allocation provision is one pertaining to unanticipated subsurface or latent conditions. Modern federal government construction contracts include a clause making the owner liable for the costs of any unanticipated and unusual subsurface conditions. In the absence of such a clause, the owner would be responsible for the costs of unanticipated conditions if the conditions were misrepresented in the contract documents, but the contractor might bear the cost of any conditions that were merely unanticipated. The federal government's *differing site conditions* clause places responsibility for both types of unanticipated conditions on the owner. By doing this the government, in theory, encourages lower bids by eliminating this risk factor. A third possible type of provision pertaining to such conditions is an exculpatory clause expressly making the contractor liable for any unanticipated or unexpected subsurface or latent conditions. Again, such exculpatory clauses are narrowly construed, but may bar contractor recovery.[14]

§ 2.24 —Modifications

As discussed in § **2.22**, the presence of a changes clause eliminates the need for a mutual contract modification to effect changes in the scope of the

[13] *See* 74 A.L.R.3d 187 (1976); *Gontar, The Enforceability of "No Damage for Delay" Clauses in Construction Contracts,* 28 Loy. L. Rev. 129 (1982). No damages for delay clauses may also be waived by the conduct of the parties. Findlen v. Winchendon Hous. Auth., 28 Mass. App. Ct. 977, 553 N.E.2d 554 (1990).

[14] *See, e.g.,* Green Constr. Co. v. Kansas Power & Light Co., 717 F. Supp. 738 (D. Kan. 1989).

work. The changes clause does not, however, prevent the parties from modifying the terms of the contract by mutual agreement. Contractors should not lose sight of the fact that a postcontract modification has the same power and effect as the preprinted contract form signed at the execution of the contract and, in fact, overrides any conflicting provisions in the original contract. In addition, contractual rights and obligations can sometimes be modified or waived by the parties' actions or course of conduct.[15]

DISPUTE MANAGEMENT

§ 2.25 Types of Disputes and Their Causes

Disputes may arise before, during, or after construction, for a variety of reasons. Contractors who are aware of areas of potential disputes and the usual causes of such disagreements will be better able to recognize, avoid, and resolve them.

§ 2.26 —Bid Disputes

It is not unusual for disputes to arise at the very outset of the construction process: the bidding stage. Most public construction work is required by law to be awarded on the basis of secret, competitive bidding to the lowest responsive and responsible bidder. Often disputes arise as to who is the lowest responsive and responsible bidder, resulting in a *bid protest.* The two most important words of advice to be offered to a bidder desiring to protest a proposed award are: act quickly. After the contract award is announced, a bidder desiring to protest a proposed award has roughly 10 percent of the rights and likelihood of success that it had before the announcement.

Bid mistakes can lead to another type of dispute. Such disputes usually result when the low bidder realizes that it made an error in compiling its bid and desires to modify or withdraw the bid.

A final type of dispute that may arise during the bidding process is when a subcontractor, on whose bid the general contractor relied in preparing and submitting its bid to the owner, refuses to honor the bid. Under appropriate circumstances, many states hold that a general contractor can recover

---

[15] *See* 74 A.L.R.3d 187 (1976); *Gontar, The Enforceability of "No Damage for Delay" Clauses in Construction Contracts,* 28 Loy. L. Rev. 129 (1982). No damages for delay clauses may also be waived by the conduct of the parties. Findlen v. Winchendon Hous. Auth., 28 Mass. App. Ct. 977, 553 N.E.2d 554 (1990).

damages from the prospective subcontractor on the theory of promissory estoppel, but other states refuse to impose liability in such situations.[16]

§ 2.27 —Performance Disputes

Of the disputes arising during performance of a construction contract, without question the most common are disputes involving (1) extra work and (2) delays and disruption.

Whether a contractor has performed extra work beyond the original scope of the contract, entitling it to additional compensation under the changes clause, depends on a comparison of the scope and nature of work specified in the contract and the work actually performed. Extra work may result from:

1. Changes needed to remedy defects in the design documents
2. Directives by the owner or the owner's architect or representative
3. Instructions, explanations, or interpretations of the contract by the owner or architect, requiring work beyond the reasonable contemplation of the contract documents
4. Unanticipated subsurface conditions
5. Improper rejection or unreasonable inspection of the work
6. Other acts and omissions of the owner or its representative.

Delays and disruptions may arise from any number of causes. As mentioned previously, the basis of the right to recover delay damages is the implied obligation on the part of the owner not to hinder or impede the contractor's performance. For the contractor to recover the costs associated with a delay from the owner, the delay must be both excusable and compensable under the terms of the contract.

An *excusable delay* is a delay for which the contractor is entitled to an extension of the contract performance time. Under the American Institute of Architects (AIA) Form Contract Document A201, delay resulting from "an act or neglect of the Owner or Architect, or of an employee of either, or of a separate contractor employed by the Owner, or by changes ordered in

---

[16] For cases allowing an action against the subcontractor in such circumstances, see Allen M. Campbell Co. v. Virginia Metal Indus., 708 F.2d 930 (4th Cir. 1983); Montgomery Indus. Int'l, Inc. v. Thomas Constr. Co., 620 F.2d 91 (5th Cir. 1980); Drennan v. Star Paving Co., 51 Cal. 2d 409, 333 P.2d 757 (1958); C.E. Frazier Constr. Co. v. Campbell Roofing & Metal Works, Inc., 373 So. 2d 1036 (Miss. 1979); E.A. Coronis Assocs. v. M. Gordon Constr. Co., 90 N.J. 69, 216 A.2d 246 (1966). *Contra* Home Elec. Co. v. Hall & Underdown Heating & Air Conditioning Co. 86 N.C. App. 540, 358 S.E.2d 539 (1987); Southeastern Sales & Serv. Co. v. T.T. Watson, Inc., 172 So. 2d 239 (Fla. Dist. Ct. App. 1965).

the Work, or by labor disputes, fire, unusual delay in deliveries, unavoidable casualties or other causes beyond the Contractor's control" constitutes excusable delay.[17] Generally speaking, nonexcusable delays are those that the contractor could and should have avoided, and those resulting from risks assumed by the contractor, such as anticipated conditions like normal bad weather.

Compensable delays, a subset of excusable delays, are those delays resulting from unanticipated acts or omissions chargeable to the owner or someone for whom the owner is responsible. This generally includes the architect, separate contractors, and employees and agents of the owner. Delay claims are probably the most litigated of all construction-related claims because of the prevalence of construction delays, the difficulty in precisely assessing and allocating responsibility for those delays, and the enormous economic impact of construction delays due to the highly time-sensitive nature of construction costs. To understand, evaluate, and present construction delay claims requires a high level of expertise, often including the use of sophisticated scheduling and analysis techniques.

Compensable construction delays may arise from a number of different causes, including:

1. The owner's failure to timely deliver owner-furnished materials[18]
2. The owner's failure to have the construction site prepared on time for the contractor's performance[19]
3. The owner's failure to provide timely and sufficient access to the construction site[20]
4. The owner's furnishing of defective contract documents prepared by the architect[21]
5. The owner's failure to make timely payment[22]
6. The owner's failure to coordinate properly the work of parallel prime contractors[23]

---

[17] AIA Doc. A201, General Conditions, ¶ 8.3.1 (1987).

[18] *See* Brown v. East Carolina R.R., 154 N.C. 300, 70 S.E. 625 (1911).

[19] *See* D.W. Segars v. Reaves, 567 So. 2d 249 (Ala. 1990); *In re* Roberts Constr. Co., 172 Neb. 819, 111 N.W.2d 767 (1961).

[20] *See* Blinderman Constr. Co. v. United States, 695 F.2d 552 (Fed. Cir. 1982); Higgins v. City of Fillmore, 639 P.2d 192 (Utah 1981).

[21] *See* Pathman Constr. Co., ASBCA No. 22,343, 81-1 B.C.A. (CCH) ¶ 15,010 (1981); Dewey Jordan, Inc. v. Maryland-National Capitol Park & Planning Comm'n, 258 Md. 490, 265 A.2d 892 (Ct. Spec. App. 1970).

[22] *See* Seretto v. Rockland, S.T.&O.H. Ry., 101 Me. 140, 63 A. 651 (1906).

[23] *See* Eric A. Carlstrom Constr. Co. v. Independence Sch. Dist. No. 77, 256 N.W.2d 479 (Minn. 1977); Stehlin-Muller-Henes Co. v. City of Bridgeport, 97 Conn. 657, 117 A. 811 (1922).

7. The owner's failure to give written orders for extra work[24] and
8. The owner's failure, through its architect, to approve shop drawings within a reasonable period of time.[25]

§ 2.28 Dispute Recognition and Reaction

Early recognition of potential claims and disputes is extremely important. It allows the contractor to comply with any contract prerequisites for relief; involve experts, including attorneys, at an early stage when they can often be of the most assistance; and begin documentation and preservation of important facts and evidence. Most construction-related disputes are controlled by the facts and by the contract. Therefore, in order to recognize potential claims and disputes early on, the contractor's key contract administration personnel, the people closest to the facts, must be intimately familiar with the contract documents.

For example, only by knowing the scope of the original contract can the contractor assess whether it is performing work beyond the scope of the contract, entitling it to additional compensation. A lack of familiarity with the contract documents can result in the contractor's losing entitlement to additional compensation for extra work because of:

1. The failure to give timely notice as required by the contract
2. The failure to preserve evidence necessary to prove the facts or
3. Being considered to have performed the work as a "volunteer" or under an implied or express agreement to perform it without additional compensation.

The necessity for informed decisions extends beyond just the contract documents and requires an understanding of the legal principles not expressed in the contract. For example, the authors are aware of projects in which the contractor or construction manager consciously failed to submit or revise construction schedules in the mistaken belief that to do so would either forgive the other party to the contract for past delays or otherwise adversely impact certain rights and obligations.This can result in a failure to administer the project effectively and can delay its completion. The contractor can usually read and understand the express provisions of the contract, but to understand and appreciate many of the legal and technical ramifications of the contractor's actions and decisions requires consultation with experts.

[24] *See* Baltimore v. Clarke, 97 A. 911 (Md. Ct. Spec. App. 1916).

[25] *See* Langvin v. United States, 100 Ct. Cl. 15 (1943).

§ 2.29 —Preservation of Evidence and Claims

It is imperative that the contractor, once it recognizes the potential for a claim or dispute, begin to document, and thereby preserve a written or tangible record of, the facts necessary to prevail. For one thing, the contractor should endeavor to comply with any contractual, statutory, or other notice requirements. Most construction contracts purport to require written directives or notice as a prerequisite to any recovery for extra work, delays, unanticipated subsurface conditions, and other types of potential claims. It is a good idea for a contractor to maintain a checklist of all notice requirements to ensure compliance. Although contractors can often prevail despite noncompliance with written notice requirements, such noncompliance is an unnecessary hurdle that sometimes cannot be overcome.[26]

In addition to satisfying contractual and statutory prerequisites to the submission of claims and disputes, the contractor should thoroughly document the facts from which the claim or dispute arose. Among the most common and useful types of project documentation are jobsite logs or diaries, photographs, conversation memoranda, cost accounting records, contract correspondence, superintendents' and foremen's daily reports, and internal memoranda, including memoranda to the file. It is possible to implement a routine reporting and record-keeping system utilizing fairly simple standard forms and procedures. A good construction documentation system actually serves a two-fold purpose: to ensure adequate project monitoring and control, and to ensure a complete and accurate record of job conditions, problems, and disputes and their effects. It is extremely difficult, especially in litigation years after an event has occurred, to re-create and prove the facts supporting the contractor's position without good documentation. Often, the most important piece of documentation is the construction schedule. A good project schedule serves both as a very useful project-monitoring and control tool and as a strong measure to prevent, preserve, present, defend, and prove claims.

§ 2.30 —Early Use of Experts

Contractors often do not consider employing expert engineers, attorneys, or consultants until long after the facts giving rise to their involvement occur. In so doing, these contractors fail to make the most effective use of

[26] *See, e.g.,* Westates Constr. Co. v. City of Cheyenne, 775 P.2d 502 (Wyo. 1989) (claim barred); Consolidated Fed. Corp. v. Cain, 195 Ga. App. 671, 394 S.E.2d 605 (1990) (claim not barred); Acquisition Corp. v. American Cast Iron Pipe Co., 543 So. 2d 878 (Fla. Dist. Ct. App. 1989) (some claims barred, some not).

these resources. Experts, when employed during the construction project, can:

1. Assist in identifying the resolving technical and complex problems and disputes
2. Suggest ways of mitigating damages
3. Recommend ways of preserving evidence
4. Advise the contractor as to how to optimize its legal and factual position
5. Through contributing to an informed decision-making atmosphere, increase the chances of early resolution and decrease the need for litigation.

§ 2.31 Settling Disputes

Quick and satisfactory settlement of claims and disputes is often essential to the continued success, and sometimes the survival, of a contractor. Devoting management time to the pursuit of claims while profitable business opportunities languish compounds the red ink flowing from the original claim. In short, the contractor should settle or resolve disputes by agreement whenever it offers a fair and reasonable result. Thus, it is important that the contractor utilize effective settlement and negotiation techniques and be able to appraise the costs and benefits of the dispute resolution alternatives.

§ 2.32 —Settlement Techniques

The best way to achieve a successful settlement is through early and thorough preparation. A well-prepared, well-documented, accurate, and thorough claim presentation goes a long way toward contributing to resolution of the claim or dispute. Such a presentation usually should be written and should contain a discussion of the factual basis of the claim, the costs associated with the claim, and the legal principles and contract provisions upon which the claim is based. A well-prepared claim document is an indication to the other side that the contractor is serious about the claim, that it believes in the merits of the claim, and that it is willing, if necessary, to go to trial. A successful negotiated settlement of the claim is far more likely if the other party is persuaded that the contractor is prepared to, and will, try the case if necessary. In addition, the chances of inconsistent positions or statements being asserted are diminished when the contractor prepares thoroughly and early.

In presenting a claim, the contractor should not lose sight of the human dynamics involved. The role of the experienced construction litigator is to make the complex appear simple and the dry, interesting. The case should be reduced to its common denominator and the best theory of the case should be emphasized, in lieu of using a shotgun approach. It is important that the contractor also maintain credibility by not overstating the case or by "crying wolf" when no claims exist. Many seek to overstate a claim grossly in the hope of achieving settlement somewhere in the middle. Such a strategy, at best, only destroys credibility and in some cases may subject the contractor to liability.

§ 2.33 —Negotiation Strategies

Once the well-prepared claim or defense has been effectively presented to the other party, the stage is set for effective negotiation. Negotiation is both an art and a science, requiring skill and experience. There have been many books and articles written on the subject, some of which are quite useful.[27] First of all, it should be noted that the well-prepared claim or defense takes into account the necessity for negotiation by providing bargaining room. In preparing the claim, the contractor should exercise sound judgment, but that judgment should be as favorable to the contractor as reasonableness, truth, and fair dealing allow.

This limited space cannot cover all of the rules and suggestions regarding negotiation that have been developed from years of experience and analysis. A few basic principles, however, deserve mention. Modern-day thinking favors a win/win approach to negotiation: the negotiator should strive for a resolution that both sides will view as at least a partial victory. A skillful negotiator will never try to embarrass or belittle the opponent, but will allow the adversary to save face and feel good about the resolution. A good negotiator will define the objectives prior to entering negotiations, and be cognizant of the points on which he must prevail to be successful and the points on which he can concede or compromise. The good negotiator will identify the other party's objectives and needs and will, in fact, restate their objectives and positions to them to convey an understanding and appreciation of their position and to identify common ground.

A claim or defense should be expressed in human terms that everyone can understand and appreciate. The way points are expressed can be very

---

[27] *See, e.g.,* Nierenberg, The Art of Negotiating (1968); Hermann, Better Settlements Through Leverage (1965); Coffin, The Negotiator (1976); McDonald, Principles and Techniques of Negotiation (1963); Armed Services Procurement Regulations Manual for Contract Pricing 13-18 (ASMP No. 1, 1969); Currie, House, Abernathy & Kelleher, *Preparing and Settling Construction Claims,* Construction Briefings No. 12 (Dec. 1983).

important. For example, the contractor is more likely to persuade the other party of the justness of its claim if its costs are expressed in terms of benefits received by the other party rather than damages incurred by the contractor. Finally, the successful negotiator must be innovative, up to and including devising an easy method for the other party to pay the contractor money or otherwise do what needs to be done.

The United States Army Corps of Engineers has published a manual for use by its own representatives in negotiating contract claims. That book is helpful and insightful with regard to negotiation techniques:

> *Establishing Negotiation Strategy.* Before entering into formal negotiations with the contractor, the negotiator must establish exactly what his objectives are and how they may best be attained. Clear-cut decisions must be made beforehand as to which objectives (i) cannot be compromised under any circumstances, (ii) can be compromised and to what extent and in exchange for what, and (iii) merely represent an antidote to anticipated "pie-in-the-sky" demands by the contractor. The latter, of course, can be quickly and easily jettisoned as soon as the contractor shows a reciprocal willingness to abandon his extreme demands. Whenever possible, alternative objectives should also be established.[28]
>
> * * *
>
> As a general rule, the counteroffer should be a total offer. It should also be the lowest possible offer that is justifiable and one that will permit logical and orderly negotiations of a mutually acceptable price.[29]
>
> * * *
>
> Within certain limits, at least, negotiation is a matter of "horse trading." The extent to which the negotiator or the contractor makes concessions without getting anything in return depends upon the relative bargaining positions of the parties.[30] The negotiator should emphasize the case's strong points, yet acknowledge its problems and weaknesses, explaining them forthrightly. A good negotiator will also carefully consider the location of the negotiating sessions, the timing of the sessions, and the composition of the negotiating team.

§ 2.34 —Arbitration versus Litigation

When settlement negotiations fail to accomplish complete resolution of a claim or dispute, the parties must turn to third parties to resolve them. The

---

[28] Department of the Army, Office of the Chief of Engineers, Construction Contract Negotiation ch. 3 at 26 (1966).

[29] *Id.* at 38.

[30] *Id.* at 42.

traditional means of dispute resolution is litigation before a court of law. There are, however, alternatives to litigation. As one alternative, the parties can usually contract to submit disputes and claims to arbitration for resolution. Today, arbitration is the rule rather than the exception for construction industry contract disputes. Arbitration has come to be viewed by many as preferable to litigation for construction-related disputes for a number of reasons.

Arbitration is often thought to yield a quicker and less expensive resolution of disputes. Although this can be true, it is not always so. Because arbitrators and tribunal administrators often do not have or do not exercise the same power as a judge regarding scheduling, time restraints, evidentiary limitations, and other matters, arbitration often requires the parties to exercise more self-control and mutual restraint.

Arbitration normally provides a more technically knowledgeable decisionmaker than would be the case with a judge and jury. A popular arbitration panel composition is one attorney, one contractor, and one architect/engineer. Such a panel provides expertise in each of these three disciplines and is equipped to grasp more readily than a judge or jury the often technical and complex facts arising in a construction dispute.

Normally, arbitration provides a much more private forum for the resolution of disputes than a court of law. This may be an important consideration for governmental bodies and many contractors who do not desire to air their grievances and problems publicly.

Arbitration proceedings are usually more informal than a courtroom trial. This can make the contractor more comfortable and contribute to a full and relaxed presentation of the facts. This informality is manifested in the arbitrator's ability to question the witnesses, a right a juror does not have. This ensures that the decisionmakers understand the presentation and that the parties address the points the decisionmakers feel are significant.

Arbitration provides more flexibility than litigation with regard to scheduling the time and location of the hearings. Generally, in arbitration, the parties are free to agree to the most mutually convenient location and time for hearings, and hearings can be conducted outside normal court hours and days, if desired.

The Greek philosopher Aristotle said, "The arbitrator looks to what is equitable, the judge to what is law; and it was for this purpose that arbitration was introduced, namely, that equity might avail."[31] It is doubtful that Aristotle foresaw modern-day construction arbitration, but this statement is still applicable. If a party has a very strong case equitably but is impaired by legal technicalities, it is more likely to prevail in an arbitration proceeding than in a court of law. The converse is, of course, also true.

---

[31] Aristotle, Rhetoric, Book 1, ch. 13.

Although the parties are free to agree otherwise either in their arbitration agreement or subsequently, arbitration generally does not afford the parties the same broad discovery rights that they would have in litigation proceedings. This can reduce costs, but can also lead to "trial by ambush," which existed in the court system before modern-day discovery practice. Whether this lack of discovery is a net benefit or a net detriment depends upon the circumstances of the particular case.

One limitation of arbitration arises when multiple parties are involved in a given dispute. Because of the contractual prerequisite to arbitration, arbitrators normally do not have the power to join in one arbitration all the parties that are involved. For example, the AIA General Conditions Document A201 precludes the contractor from joining the architect as a party to an arbitration between the contractor and the owner without the architect's permission.[32] The contractor also may be unable to include in one proceeding subcontractors, suppliers, sureties, lenders, and other parties with potential liability in the matter, as could be done in a court of law.[33]

Although a procedure does exist for petitioning a court of law to set aside an arbitration award, a party unhappy with an arbitration decision is much less likely to have that decision overturned than it would to have a court decision reversed. To vacate an arbitration award, the complaining party usually must be able to demonstrate that there was fraud on the part of the arbitrators, that the arbitrators failed to follow proper procedures, or that the decision was beyond the scope of the arbitrators' power. A disappointed party usually may not complain that the arbitrators failed to understand and apply the correct legal principles. This increases the risk of arbitration, but decreases the time and cost associated with achieving a final resolution of the dispute.

§ 2.35 —Other Alternatives

Court congestion, the high cost of litigation, and a number of other factors have caused parties in recent years to look for alternative means of dispute resolution in addition to arbitration. These methods include nonbinding mediation, binding mediation, and mini-trials. Some companies have even implemented a system whereby they try their case before a jury of their own employees prior to an actual trial, as a means of evaluating their case and the desirability of settlement. One or more of these alternative dispute resolution procedures may be appropriate, and more desirable than litigation or arbitration, for a given set of circumstances.

---

[32] AIA Doc. A201, General Conditions, ¶ 4.5.5 (1987).

[33] *See generally* Slutsky-Peltz v. Vincennes Community Sch., 556 N.E.2d 344 (Ind. Ct. App. 1990); Hoover Groups, Inc. v. Probala & Assocs. 710 F. Supp. 677 (N.D. Ohio 1989).

LITIGATION MANAGEMENT

§ 2.36 Litigation Objectives

Litigation of a construction case is perhaps the most challenging of all forms of litigation, because of the complexity of most construction disputes. Unlike personal injury cases, which may involve a traffic accident that occurred at one specific time at one location, construction disputes often involve a mass of details and a number of wrongs that occurred over an extended period of time. In addition, any one given act or omission is likely to have a ripple effect across time, upon many different activities and events. The large number of parties, facts, documents, and time involved make construction cases perhaps most analogous to complex antitrust cases, but nevertheless unique.

Trial lawyers are often taught to begin preparation for trial by writing their closing argument, and then working backward from there. This may seem strange until one remembers that an efficient traveler does not embark upon a journey until he knows where he wants the journey to end. This same advice is also useful throughout the construction process. Decisions such as what to include in the contract documents, what types of job records and documentation to maintain, and what experts and consultants to engage should all be governed, in part, by what the contractor will need in the event disputes arise. A solid strategy is essential both to construction administration and in litigation management: the contractor should define its objectives and then identify the means of achieving those objectives.

§ 2.37 Selection of Parties, Remedies, and Forum

Subsequent chapters of this book discuss the various avenues of recovery a contractor can pursue when it finds itself contemplating a claim. The choice of which avenue to pursue should receive careful consideration, with the assistance of expert advice. A contractor should be discriminating in its selection of allies and adversaries, remedies to be pursued, and the forum in which to pursue them. Factors such as the role played by each of the various parties, the terms of their contracts, their financial solvency, their reputation, the presence or absence of insurance or bonding, the personalities involved, the procedural, evidentiary, and discovery implications, the governing legal principles, and other disputes dynamics should all be considered before the contractor commits itself by forming alliances and declaring war. A defense unique to a particular owner, such as sovereign immunity, may make it advisable to institute an action directly against the architect or construction manager. Under other circumstances, it may be more profitable to sue the owner and seek the assistance of the construction manager or architect. As mentioned in **§ 2.14**, litigation with a subcontractor can jeopardize the general contractor's position with the owner, but may be appropriate under a given set of circumstances.

In addition to making decisions concerning the parties, and as a part of that process, the contractor must also choose the remedies and legal theories to be pursued and the forum in which to pursue them. Harsh contract terms limiting or barring recovery, or failure to comply with notice requirements, may make it desirable to seek rescission of the contract and recovery under the theory of quantum meruit (unjust enrichment) for the reasonable value of the work performed. The facts of a particular case may make it desirable to seek injunctive relief. The circumstances may cause the choice of parties to control the choice of remedy and forum, or a strong preference for a particular forum may control the other decisions.

§ 2.38 Effective Litigation Strategy

When a contractor finds itself in litigation, it should apply the same sound management techniques and standards that it applies in making other decisions regarding investments of the company's time and money. No step or action should be taken in litigation merely because it seems the next logical step. The contractor and its attorney must avoid tunnel vision and should at each step evaluate all options, weighing the costs and benefits of each.

The need for sound managerial decisionmaking begins at the initial pleading stage. Pleadings can usually be as vague and general or as specific as the pleader likes. Different circumstances call for different actions. A well-prepared, specific complaint, accompanied by a request for production of relevant documents and detailed interrogatories can have the same effect on a defendant as a well-prepared claim brief; it shows that the plaintiff is serious and prepared to pursue aggressively the resolution of the dispute. Effective use of various pretrial motions and procedures can reduce the cost of litigation and enhance the chances of success.

Pretrial discovery procedures can be immensely beneficial or wastefully expensive, depending upon whether they are effectively employed. The most common discovery techniques used in construction litigation are requests for production of documents, interrogatories, and depositions. A lesser-used tool, but one that can be extremely useful, is the request for admissions of fact. The large volume of documents, facts, people, and locations involved in any given construction dispute makes construction discovery very expensive, but also very important. Effective discovery increases the possibility of an acceptable settlement while at the same time preparing the contractor for a persuasive and successful trial presentation.

In addition to the construction attorney, it is usually necessary to engage other experts to assist in the preparation and presentation of a construction claim. The selection, management, preparation, and presentation of expert opinion testimony and associated demonstrative evidence is perhaps the most important aspect of effective construction litigation. The quality most needed in an expert witness is the ability to persuasively present the facts and opinions supporting the contractors's case. To be persuasive, the expert witness must be able to gather and analyze vast quantities of details and present them in a clear, simple, and understandable fashion. For most cases, this requires technical expertise, analytical ability, communicative skills, and a mastery of demonstrative evidence, visual aids, and other means of persuasive presentation. An expert can be the most knowledgeable person in the world on a given subject, but if he cannot persuade the fact finder of the correctness of the position, that expert is of little value as a witness. Such an expert may be very useful in a consulting or advisory role during construction and litigation, but the role of testifying should be assigned to experts with strong communication skills.

§ 2.39 Effective Trial Presentation

There is an adage that knowing the truth and proving it are two different things. The construction trial lawyer must be able to marshal a multitude of facts and present them in a simple, coherent fashion that will persuade the fact finder that the claimant is entitled to the relief sought. The most effective evidence that can be introduced at trial is the live testimony of a good witness. Nonlawyers often speak of whether there is "proof" or "evidence" of a particular fact, referring to documentation or other tangible evidence. The observations and recollections of a witness, stated in court, are themselves legal evidence and proof of the existence of facts. But in construction cases, probably more so than almost any other type of litigation, job documentation, prepared at the time of the facts and events it records, is almost essential to a persuasive case presentation.

Demonstrative evidence is a very effective means of simplifying and assisting the fact finder in comprehending complex construction issues. Demonstrative evidence can take the form of graphs, charts, models, diagrams, photographs, slides, movies, material samples, or virtually anything that helps the fact finder understand the facts. The use of demonstrative evidence in personal injury cases has gained much fame or notoriety (depending on one's perspective) in recent years. Such evidence can, if properly prepared and presented, be even more useful in complex construction litigation.

Finally, effective litigation preparation and presentation include calculation and proof of damages. Many construction cases are lost when it comes to proving damages; pricing the loss and presenting it in a persuasive fashion are essential elements of the construction case. A contractor can present a compelling case for entitlement, but if it cannot quantify and prove its damages, it has accomplished nothing more than a moral victory. Because of the complex nature of construction costs, proof of construction damages normally requires evaluation of extensive cost documentation maintained during the project.

To recover its costs, the contractor must establish that it actually incurred the costs, that the costs bear a legally sufficient cause/effect relationship to the act or omission of which it is complaining, and that it has acted reasonably to mitigate the damages. The required relationship between the cause and the cost varies depending on the legal theory under which the contractor is seeking to recover. In an action in contract, the damages must flow from the act or omission and be of such a nature that it was reasonably foreseeable at the time of entering the contract that such damages would result from any such breach. When recovery is sought under negligence or a tort theory, the test applied is whether the act or omission was the proximate cause of the damages. Obviously, the measure of damages to be applied, and the contractor's ability to prove the requisite facts, are additional factors to be taken into consideration at the outset in determining whom to sue and on what theory.

§ 2.40 Appeal

Without belaboring the point, most construction cases are decided on the facts. Trying a construction case does not normally involve complex, esoteric legal issues, but rather an organized, persuasive presentation of complex facts to fit a limited number of fairly basic legal principles. Because of this, construction cases are rarely reversed on appeal. Appellate courts generally accept the trial court's findings of fact and explore only whether there has been an error of law. The typical length and complexity of construction cases also make their appeals less fruitful than in other areas of the law. It is not unusual, however, for the losing party to appeal a construction decision because of the enormous amount of money that may be at stake. The main effect of such appeals is usually to delay the ultimate resolution of the dispute and payment of the money found due. It is sometimes in the contractor's interest to compromise a favorable judgment to avoid an appeal and the time associated with it; however, when available, postjudgment interest largely diminishes the leverage of the losing party in this regard.

Although it is usually in the contractor's best interest to avoid litigation, sometimes the costs associated with avoiding litigation are greater than the costs of pursuing it. Skillful and conscientious management, prior to and during construction, as well as during litigation, are necessary to minimize the costs of litigation and optimize its benefits.

CHAPTER 3

ORGANIZING AND SELECTING THE LITIGATION TEAM

William J. Palmer

William J. Palmer is chairman of Ernest & Young's National Construction Industry Group in San Francisco, California, and in that role coordinates his firm's services to over 1,000 construction companies. He is a graduate of the University of California at Berkeley and is a member of the American Institute of Certified Public Accountants and the Associated General Contractors of America. Because of Mr. Palmer's reputation and expertise in the areas of construction and contract accounting and his numerous publications on construction accounting and construction litigation, he frequently testifies as expert witness in long-term contract disputes and related litigation.

§ 3.1 **Preliminary Considerations**

§ 3.2 **Planning**

§ 3.3 **Organizing the Team**

§ 3.4 **—Fixing Internal Responsibility**

§ 3.5 **—Choosing the Lawyer**

§ 3.6 **—Selecting Other Members of the Team**

§ 3.7 **Characteristics of Expert Witnesses**

§ 3.8 **—Selecting the Damages Expert**

§ 3.9 **—Claim Consultant**

§ 3.10 **—Critical Path Consultant**

§ 3.11 **—Consulting Engineer**

§ 3.12 **—Construction Consultant**

§ 3.13 **Coordinating Consultants and Experts**

§ 3.14 **Locating Witnesses and Consultants**

§ 3.1 Preliminary Considerations

Experience and teamwork are key factors that can make the difference between winning and losing in construction litigation. Of the many considerations facing a contractor that is contemplating litigation, none is more important than carefully organizing and selecting the litigation team.

Contractors should approach the team organization just as though they were analyzing requirements for a construction project. Factors of prime consideration include:

1. Nature of the dispute (type of job)
2. Proof required for entitlement (construction methods)
3. Ability of the contractor's organization to prepare the claim for entitlement and damages (experienced superintendent and foreman)
4. Experience and credentials of the lawyer handling the litigation (joint venture partner)
5. Types of expert witnesses required (subcontractors)
6. Strategies of the opposing party (owner's behavior)
7. Size of the potential damages (contract price)
8. Projected litigation costs (job cost budget).

§ 3.2 Planning

As with any major construction project, most long-term contract disputes heading toward litigation require a formal master plan. A plan in writing supported with critical path schedules is not necessary, but a conceptual framework for the overall process is a must. Playing it by ear in a highly complex construction litigation invites disaster.

Because most law firms have systematized the legal aspects of the litigation process, this part of the litigation plan will already have been put in place. However, the legal portion of the plan must be augmented to take into account all the other members of the litigation team who will join the process. Some of the things to consider when developing a plan are—

1. Organization of the team: what types of work and functional skills are needed
2. Who on the team has what responsibilities
3. Discovery dates
4. Progress and milestone meeting dates
5. Completion dates for the various consultants and experts

6. Exchange of information among team members who need the results of other's efforts
7. Whether written reports will be required of experts, and their due dates.

In short, any key dates or interrelationships that will affect the timing or work of other members on the litigation team should be addressed in the plan.

Once the plan has been developed, a budget for the total cost of the litigation should be prepared. Except for the cost of preparing for deposition and the trial itself, costs for most members of the team can be estimated within a reasonable range. In addition to the lawyer's estimated fees, court costs, arbitrators' fees, contractor employee costs, and the potential costs of expert witnesses and consultants should be included in the budget. It should be updated on a prescheduled basis (such as monthly or quarterly) with explanations by the various team members as to any variances.

The completed plan should be discussed with all members of the litigation team as well as with the contractor who will bear the ultimate cost of the effort and will want to weigh (taking into account the lawyer's advice) the anticipated cost with possible or proposed settlement amounts.

§ 3.3 Organizing the Team

The organization of the team must be an early consideration. Key members are useful in helping to prepare the plan, can identify potential problems early, and should be in place or on hold when the master plan or conceptual framework is prepared. Although many team members may not be needed until later, getting the case underway will be difficult unless the administrative and planning groundwork have been carefully thought out. Another reason for identifying and planning the work of consultants and potential expert witnesses is to develop a budget so that the potential cost of the litigation can be estimated. Also, the attorney may want to enlist potential consultants and experts before the opposition does.

In smaller and less complex litigation, the economics of the situation usually dictate that most of the work be carried out by the contractor's personnel and attorney. In large, complex disputes, the litigation team is made up of outside experts working in consort with the contractor's key personnel.

The contractor should first determine two things: who inside the company will be responsible for overseeing the process, and the lawyer who will manage the process on a hands-on basis. Selection of the lawyer should be done with care because complex litigation in the construction industry requires unique skills.

§ 3.4 —Fixing Internal Responsibility

Quite often, the individual in charge of the contractor's in-house litigation team is either the job superintendent who had responsibility for the disputed contract or a superintendent who is between projects. This individual must be at a level high enough to have substantial power. These superintendents generally have complete authority and responsibility for project-level decisions, but have no authority over chief operating officers, chief financial officers, and other executives in the contractor's organization. There is a tendency in larger contractor organizations to avoid being involved with contract litigation. In fact, a mid-level or semi-senior executive may feel there is nothing to be gained and everything to lose by being associated with contract litigation. In reality, taking on such a responsibility would remove executives from the well-organized, normal daily routines and steer them into unfamiliar terrain, causing added stress and tension.

A carefully chosen internal team leader will help to keep turnaround time to a minimum. Delays in making decisions, having data prepared, and ensuring that progress meetings are attended can be costly. Opportunities for settlement and obtaining information necessary to prove entitlement and/or compute damages can be lost during the process.

§ 3.5 —Choosing the Lawyer

The lawyer selected to head the litigation team should be a highly skilled manager and administrator with considerable construction litigation experience and good business skills to evaluate the cost benefit aspects of decisions made during the litigation process.

The lawyer's personality and style are also important considerations. Because every contracting firm has a different approach, it is imperative that the lawyer make a good fit with the contractor's executive and employees.

Many contractors use law firms that are very good at handling the everyday aspects of their business, but one attorney must be the team leader. It is critical that the team leader be experienced in the important tasks of selecting and working with entitlement and damage experts. Many general practice firms lack personnel with the requisite experience in pursuing large and complex contract disputes. Contractors should discuss this matter openly with their regular law firm and if the firm lacks the necessary experience, they should obtain recommendations for experienced construction litigation firms. There are many law firms of all sizes throughout the United States that specialize in litigating complex construction matters. It may be necessary for contractors to seek representation outside their local community.

§ 3.6 —Selecting Other Members of the Team

Once a lawyer has been chosen to serve as team leader and work closely with the company's designated internal manager, the process of selecting the other members of the team can begin. **Figure 3–1** sets forth the typical organization for large, complex litigation.

Although **Figure 3–1** and the following discussions indicate a number of functional skills the team requires, some expert witnesses can handle several of those responsibilities. For example, a consulting engineer with an engineering claims consulting firm can usually testify as to critical path schedule analysis, fixing responsibility for delays as well as testifying to inadequate drawings and construction methods. This individual, however, usually has not been involved in the direct preparation of the critical path schedule, documentation of delay events, analysis of drawings, and so forth. Therefore, key members of the consulting engineer's organization who have responsibility for these aspects of the litigation should be included in the team and in progress meetings and distribution of information. The same is true with many of the damage expert firms, usually medium- to larger-sized certified public accounting firms. Many of these firms now have on their staffs civil engineers, industrial engineers, mechanical engineers, and others capable of carrying out some of the technical skills required in putting the claim entitlement and the damages together. In selecting experts lawyers will want to consider how credible an engineering consulting firm is in presenting damages. Likewise lawyers

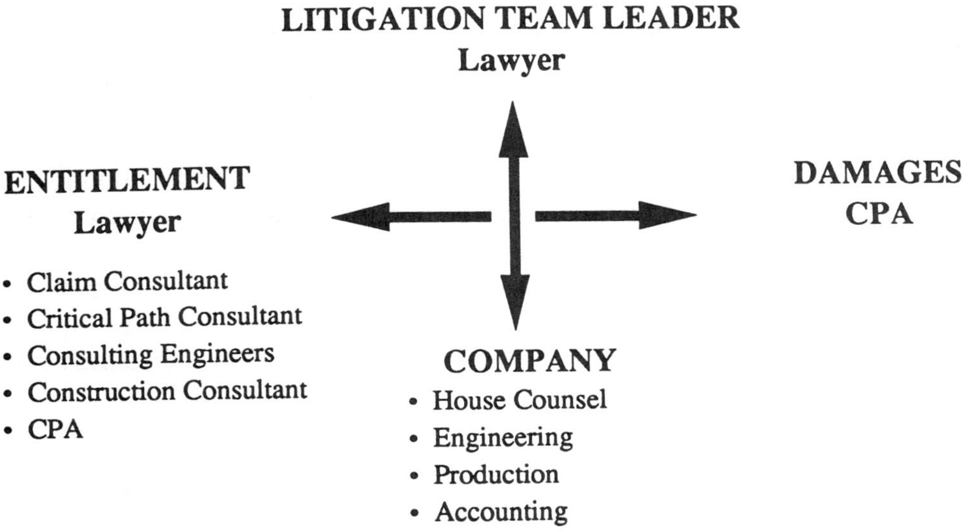

Figure 3–1. Team structure.

must consider how credible an accounting firm would be in providing expert testimony on engineering and construction matters.

§ 3.7 Characteristics of Expert Witnesses

Experienced attorneys will know what type of traits and characteristics to look for in potential expert witnesses. The desired characteristics may vary depending on whether the litigation will be before a judge, jury, arbitrator, or special master. The experienced attorney who has worked with expert witnesses and has seen firsthand how individuals handle themselves under fire often will maintain a list of favorite candidates. The attorney's client usually will have some say regarding which experts will be chosen, taking into account economic factors and experts the contractor may have worked with previously.

A number of things should be considered when selecting the expert witness, in addition to the witness's experience. Some of these considerations are:

1. Physical presence. Does the potential witness use mannerisms that convey objectivity and believability?
2. Do the individual's personal traits fit the audience for his opinions?
3. Can the potential witness present complex information in a simple and understandable fashion?
4. Does the expert have the artistic ability to conceptualize visual aids, making the testimony more understandable?
5. Can the expert think fast on his feet? On cross-examination will she be able to field questions that might not have been contemplated?
6. Does the expert put herself on the opposing team's side, anticipating the attack on the direct testimony?
7. Does the expert have the resources needed to support his opinion?
8. Is the expert creative in coming up with damage presentation strategies?
9. Is the expert's location convenient to the attorney, the contractor's records, and the site of the trial?
10. What are the hourly rates for the expert as well as any assistants who may work on the matter?

Typically, people with engineering, accounting, and other technical backgrounds are not well trained or exceptionally talented in presenting their viewpoints to others. However, these skills are a must for the expert.

Many seasoned construction litigation lawyers use psychological consulting firms to help in the expert witness selection process. These firms also counsel the lawyer on the types of graphics used at trial, selection of the jury, and evaluation of witness testimony as the trial progresses. They quite often impanel "shadow juries" with similar characteristics and background as the actual jury, then have expert witnesses testify and get the shadow jury's reactions. Dry runs are often videotaped to sharpen the expert's presentation skills.

§ 3.8 —Selecting the Damages Expert

The primary role of the damages expert in contract disputes is to serve as a consultant in pricing entitlement events and presenting them as a expert witness. Typically, lawyers will want a CPA as the damage consultant and trial expert. In choosing the damages expert, the lawyer will be looking for experience, credentials, and credibility.

To prepare effectively and present damages at trial, the damages expert should have documented accounting experience for long-term contracts, significant construction industry experience, and should be able to speak the language of the industry. Previous experience in contract claims will make the expert an invaluable member of the litigation team and also a key consultant for the lawyer. The damages expert can help in developing sound strategies, interpreting relative accounting and cost accounting principles and practices, and in determining certain regulatory requirements that may have an impact on the success of the litigation.

Quite often, an individual in the contractor's regular auditing firm will have experience in pricing damages and testifying at trial. In this situation lawyers must determine the advisability of using the existing firm's auditors at trial. Many lawyers bypass the existing accounting firm under the theory that there is more objectivity in engaging consultants and experts who have had nothing to do with the contractor. If one is not familiar with experts who have experience, credentials and credibility, a place to start in locating experts is with the existing accounting firm, particularly if they are extensively involved in the construction industry.

The damages expert and consultant should be selected as early as possible, almost in tandem with selecting the lawyer. In many cases the damages expert is chosen first and can make recommendations as to lawyers with a proven track record in winning contract disputes. Typically, the damages expert will:

1. Assist the attorney in identifying key issues, information needs, claim strategies, and approaches to presenting damages, and may participate in the litigation strategies themselves.
2. Assist in selecting and locating other experts who may be needed as consultants or to present testimony at trial. Larger accounting firms

have clients in all industries and can assist the lawyer in locating and engaging individuals with documented expertise in the particular subject matter.

3. Provide assistance to the lawyer in preparing briefs, interrogatories, depositions, and rebuttal of the opposing attorney's arguments.
4. Advise on the need or appropriate use of automated data retrieval systems. In complex cases that stretch over long periods of time, how data is stored and retrieved can be critical.
5. Calculate damages and present alternative approaches for the presentation of damages.
6. Help prepare litigation cost budgets and monitor progress.
7. Present testimony, which usually includes the use of visual aids and other materials, in support of the plaintiff's case. Here, the ability to present complex data in a simple and understandable fashion before a jury or arbitrators is critical. A documented track record is imperative.

§ 3.9 —Claim Consultant

Having developed in concert with the lawyer and CPA the entitlement strategies and basic claim documents, the claim consultant usually prepares the narrative that accompanies the claim document. The narrative includes an overview of the project, the parties involved, and the activities that occurred during the project and have led to the dispute. For example, the document describes delays imposed upon the contractor, required changes in construction methods, lack of access, defective materials, late drawings, and other conditions that may have caused economic damage to the contractor. In subsequent sections, the claim document addresses each problem in detail. For example, it provides dates of each delay and the names of those involved in them, specific examples of late drawings and defective materials, and details concerning other events that caused problems for the contractor.

§ 3.10 —Critical Path Consultant

Whenever there are delay and related labor disruption claims, it is possible that prices for labor, materials, equipment, and other items necessary for the project may have escalated. Typically, the critical path consultant develops two graphic presentations that are usually referred to as a *network analysis*. If not already prepared by the contractor, the consultant will first devise an as-planned schedule, using the contractor's bid and other planning documents. Next, she will prepare an as-built critical path schedule that details how the actual work was completed. It is not unusual to see major differences between these two schedules. See **Chapter 17** for more on the critical path method.

The two schedules are then compared in order to isolate and identify the delays to the contractor's schedule. Many of the delays that were thought to have caused an overall slippage in the project schedule will be found to be *noncontrolling* delays. These delays are not on the critical path, or in other words involve parallel processes with enough float or slack built in not to affect the project schedule.

Obviously, if the contractor has already prepared as-planned and as-built critical path schedules, the consultant will audit them to ensure they are correct. If the contractor has not prepared the schedules but has the capability to do so, it may be wise to have the contractor prepare them under the direction of the critical path consultant who will testify at trial. Both approaches will lower the contractor's expense because having the consultant prepare the schedules can be a costly effort.

The next step is to identify the events that caused the delays, usually related to the owner's instructions to cease work until a drawing is clarified, late drawings, lack of access or right of way, re-work, or similar problems. The critical path consultant works with foremen's diaries, correspondence files, contractor employees, and other litigation team consultants to fix responsibility for the events leading to or causing the delay. The delays are then summarized by type of cause and the overall effect on the critical path schedule is determined in terms of days, weeks, or months of delay. The damages expert will then price the delay that has been determined by the critical path consultant.

§ 3.11 —Consulting Engineer

Quite often, delays and disruption of labor productivity are related to the interpretation of plans and drawings. If the original plans or drawings do not appear to fit the scope of work upon which the contractor prepared his bid, contain errors, or do not tie in with drawings for other portions of the project and all these have led to delays or disruption of labor productivity, then the consulting engineer may be brought in as a potential expert witness. She can testify as to whether the plans would enable the contractor to build the project in accordance with the drawings and may also testify as to whether owner-furnished materials were defective.

The consulting engineer is also useful in disputes involving changed conditions. Changed conditions are usually found in earth-moving projects—highways, dams, tunnels, and so forth. Most earthwork projects contain specifications as to the type of subsurface materials the contractor will encounter. These specifications are usually based upon test bore samples or other statistical data. As the contractor begins its work, it may find that such specifications are incorrect and must devise a completely different approach to carrying out the work. In changed condition situations, the consulting engineer can play a major role in proving the changed condition entitlement.

Some changed conditions claims allege that because there are so many change orders, in pricing any single change order it is impossible to take into account its effect on the total project and that therefore a *cardinal change* has occurred. In other words, the final project bears no relationship to the original scope upon which the contractor prepared the bid.

§ 3.12 —Construction Consultant

Construction consultants are usually brought in to assist in proving that owner-directed construction methods were unworkable in the given situation. A change in construction methods (equipment mix, shoring, crew size, crew sequencing) can result in delays, lower labor productivity, more costly equipment, and added materials.

§ 3.13 Coordinating Consultants and Experts

It is not uncommon that the work of many consultants and experts in complex litigation will overlap or need to be sequenced because of the necessary exchange of information among them. The team leader should hold regular meetings during the course of preparing for litigation and include the outside experts as well as in-house personnel. All personnel involved on the team should present progress reports, summarizing the scope of their work and the information they have generated to date. Such meetings serve to keep the team leader informed and better able to keep litigation costs under control and also provide information documenting current strategies.

Progress meetings also keep consultants and experts informed as to what information is being or can be generated by other members of the litigation team that might be helpful in carrying out their work or forming opinions.

The contractor's employees are the most familiar with the facts and can generate much of the basic data. Obviously, the more work the contractor's own employees can perform, the lower the cost in carrying out the claims and litigation process. When the contractor is a large organization, almost all the detailed work can be carried out by its employees under the direction of the consultants and experts. For example, to price delay the damages expert will need to identify increases in time-related costs that were caused by the delay. The contractor's own accountants are much more familiar with such costs and can make the preliminary determination as to which of the project costs are time-related versus volume-related. If the delay has caused "stop, start, and leap frog," the contractor's accountants can analyze the payroll records, time cards, and foreman's diaries to document the shifting of crews among work areas in the project because of delays.

§ 3.14 Locating Witnesses and Consultants

It is clear that the litigation process as a whole and specifically the management of a team of outside consultants and experts, their coordination with in-house contractor employees, and the sequencing of the team's work require lawyers who are as much experts in management as they are in the law. In addition to legal, business, and management skills, these lawyers must have a successful track record and personal knowledge of the people who will make the best team members to win the dispute. In practical terms, they must be good at managing people with enormous egos and unusual personalities and must have a good understanding of the nature, type, and characteristics of each team member's work.

There are a number of sources available for contractors that are seeking a team leader/lawyer with a proven track record. For example, the American Bar Association's Forum on Construction and construction industry trade associations such as the Associated General Contractors, Associated Builders and Contractors, Mechanical Contractors, and National Electrical Contractors Association are all good sources for recommendations. Most have rosters listing lawyer members, a good indication of those lawyers with experience and an interest in the construction industry.

Similar sources exist for the selection of expert witnesses. Associations made up of lawyers can provide recommendations for consultants and expert witnesses and their backgrounds. Additionally, many national and local associations such as the American Bar Association and state bar associations publish expert witness directories.

CHAPTER 4

BID PROTESTS AND BID MISTAKES

David Buoncristiani

David Buoncristiani is a partner in the San Francisco, California, office of Thelen, Marrin, Johnson & Bridges. He is a graduate of Hastings College of the Law and has been primarily involved in construction industry related problems, including all facets of the competitive bidding process. He has handled numerous bid protest proceedings, both on the federal and state level. He is a member of the ABA sections on Public Contracts and Litigation and the California AGC Legal Advisory Committee.

§ 4.1 Introduction

BACKGROUND

§ 4.2 Overview

§ 4.3 Competitive Bidding

§ 4.4 General Considerations for Bid Protests

§ 4.5 General Requirements of Bids

§ 4.6 Contract Award Criteria

§ 4.7 —Responsiveness

§ 4.8 —Responsibility

§ 4.9 —Subcontractor Listing Requirements

§ 4.10 —Minority Business Enterprise Requirements

§ 4.11 General Grounds for Protest

FEDERAL CONTRACTS

§ 4.12 General

§ 4.13 Grounds for Protests

§ 4.14 Standing to Protest

§ 4.15 Protest Procedure

§ 4.16 Relief Available

FEDERALLY FUNDED GRANT PROJECTS

§ 4.17 General

§ 4.18 Grounds for Protests

§ 4.19 Standing to Protest

§ 4.20 Protest Procedure

§ 4.21 Relief Available

STATE AND LOCAL CONTRACTS

§ 4.22 General

§ 4.23 Grounds for Protests

§ 4.24 Standing to Protest

§ 4.25 Protest Procedure

§ 4.26 Relief Available

PRIVATE CONTRACTS

§ 4.27 Bidding on Private Contracts

BID MISTAKES

§ 4.28 General

§ 4.29 State Law Remedies for Bid Mistakes

§ 4.30 —Jurisdictions Following Equitable Principles

§ 4.31 Federal Law on Bid Mistakes

§ 4.32 Private Owners

§ 4.1 Introduction

With the present level of competition in the construction industry, all contractors should be aware of the procedures available to challenge a proposed award to another bidder or to defend against such a challenge if one is the apparent low bidder. This chapter outlines generally the procedures available and the rules applying to the award of competitively bid construction work for federal, state, and local contracts. The rules are in many cases informal and subject to constant change. Care should be taken to consult appropriate sources and to determine the applicable law.

Because the apparent low bidder may sometimes desire to be relieved of the obligations of performing the work in accordance with its bid, this chapter also briefly discusses the criteria for a material mistake in a bid and the available relief.

BACKGROUND

§ 4.2 Overview

In the United States, most contracts for the construction of public facilities are awarded through competitive bidding. Federal, state, and local agencies typically require competitive bidding for public projects because these public owners desire an objective and impartial method of selecting a contractor to construct the project at the lowest possible price. The statutes and regulations dealing with competitive bidding on public construction contracts are intended to implement this goal.

To insure that the awards will be based on objective criteria, the laws governing public contracting typically provide that "interested persons" who believe a government agency has acted to frustrate the bidding process may obtain a determination of the propriety of the award by means of a *bid protest.* Although competitive bidding is common throughout the United States, these protest procedures are established by different government agencies and vary considerably. This chapter presents an overview of the competitive bidding process in the United States and describes the basic concepts and rules applicable to bid protests. Because California has codified the rules for many of the subjects encountered in protests, some of its procedures have been used as representative examples.

One preliminary word of caution: Of necessity, this discussion cannot be an exhaustive treatise on all legal principles applicable to the award of competitively bid construction contracts. Specific protests are dependent on the terms of the contract documents, the controlling statutes and case law, and the nature of the awarding authority. Our intent is to provide the reader with a general familiarity with the applicable legal concepts. Such an overview is needed because, except for direct federal government contracts regulated by the General Accounting Office (GAO), there is no clearly defined set of procedures or rules common to the various levels of government. As a result, the procedures for pursuing bid protests depend to a great extent on the rules enforced by the particular awarding agency and, in many cases, the source of the funding. Consequently, the analysis is divided into four sections, addressing the procedures and rules employed by various types of public awarding authorities, and briefly addressing the rules applicable to private owners. **Sections 2.3** through **2.11** provide the necessary background for this analysis with a general discussion of the fundamental concepts of competitive bidding.

§ 4.3 Competitive Bidding

Despite the variety of bid protest procedures, the general competitive bidding process does not vary greatly. The public owner must first advertise the work to be undertaken. This solicitation, often referred to as an *invitation for bids* (IFB), describes the work to be accomplished and establishes a specific date and time by which all the bids are to be received and subsequently opened at a public opening. The bids are opened and reviewed, and the contract is then awarded to the "lowest responsive, responsible bidder." Every public agency is subject to rules and regulations governing each of these activities for its major contracts.

The bidder who is awarded the contact must have submitted the lowest dollar bid, have been determined to be responsive to the IFB, and be a responsible bidder. As discussed in more detail in **§ 4.7**, *responsive* refers to the bidder's conformance with the material elements of the solicitation and is determined at the time of bid opening. The requirement for a *responsible* bidder addresses the trustworthiness, quality, fitness, and capacity of the bidder to perform the work and is often determined after bid opening.

Once the awarding agency announces an intent to award the contract to the bidder it determines to be the lowest responsive, responsible bidder, bid protests commonly arise in two situations. The first involves the bidder who submits a lower total price for completion of the contract work (*apparent low bidder*) but who is determined by the owner to be nonresponsive because of a failure to comply with a material portion of the solicitation. The apparent low bidder may protest any award to a higher bidder on the ground that any deviation from the solicitation was a minor irregularity that did not disqualify the bid nor justify awarding the contract to the next highest bidder.

The more common situation arises when a higher bidder seeks to disqualify one or more bidders whose proposals are lower than the protestor's on the grounds that the lower bidders are either not responsive or not responsible. In this situation, the protestor requests an award of the contact although other bids are lower.

§ 4.4 General Considerations for Bid Protests

Before submitting a bid protest to the awarding authority, a potential protestor should consider the following factors. The first and most obvious consideration is that the protesting party must have sufficient legal grounds for challenging the award. This requires the protestor to analyze the IFB, the applicable statutory rules, and substantive case law in the jurisdiction and to satisfy itself that there are material violations of the competitive bidding process. All protests result in some disruption of the contracting process, and frivolous protests without substantive grounds may result in the protestor's being penalized.[1]

Second, the would-be protestor must determine whether it has standing to challenge the action of the awarding agency; that is, whether it is a proper party to pursue a protest.

Third (and contemporaneously with the first two determinations), the protestor must consider the appropriate procedure for filing the bid protest. In all jurisdictions, immediate written notice is critical to preserving the right to protest the decision of the awarding agency.[2] In many cases, the statutory deadlines provided for bid protests are extremely short and, if not met, preclude even a meritorious protest.

Once these determinations are made, it is essential that the protestor examine the specific relief available if the bid protest is successful. In some instances, even though the protestor's position is legally sound, the expenditure of considerable time and effort may not be justified if the potential result is limited to merely a reprimand of the awarding agency by the responsible authority. For example, on the federal level, the GAO is reluctant to overturn an award already made despite the ability of the protestor to establish an impropriety.

§ 4.5 General Requirements of Bids

The competitive bidding statutes are designed to allow maximum competition for the award of public works contracts and to prevent collusion and fraud. The competitive bidding process achieves these goals by allowing all those parties interested in performing a given construction project to evaluate the requirements of the project and to submit the lowest price for which they are willing to undertake the described work. From these bids, the government agency or owner is, theoretically, able to select the proper low bid on any given project.

In selecting the lowest bid, the owner does not look solely at the dollar amount of the bid. Both state and federal regulations require that the awarding agency evaluate the bids within certain designated parameters to determine the *low bidder*. The process of employing these parameters to

---

[1] *See* 40 C.F.R. § 35.939(a) (1990).

[2] *See* 4 C.F.R § 21.2(a) (1991), limiting bid protests filed with the GAO after bid opening to within 10 days of actual or constructive knowledge of the basis of the protest.

determine which bidder receives the contract requires that the bidders and the owner fulfill their respective obligations. These obligations are established by the rules and regulations applicable in each jurisdiction, but certain rules regarding the respective obligations of the owner and bidder are common to all jurisdictions.

The owner must prepare a complete and accurate set of contract documents, fully descriptive of the work to be performed, and must make them available to all parties responding to the IFB. The clarity and accuracy of the contract documents are of utmost importance. If material portions of the documents are vague or susceptible of more than one rational interpretation, the owner will receive bids that are not comparable, thereby frustrating the purpose of competitive bidding and forcing rejection of all bids. The owner must also disclose the specific procedure it intends to use in evaluating the submitted bids. Any such procedure must be fair and objective.

The contractor must also follow general procedural requirements in order to have its bid considered. Some of the requirements concern the form of the bid and are seemingly routine, for example, the contractor's signature on all the necessary forms. However, such requirements are strictly enforced. Although the omission of a signature may be merely an oversight and the bid might otherwise be acceptable, failure to sign the bid documents where required generally renders the entire bid void.

The contractor's bid must further address all material aspects of the owner's solicitation, including all addenda issued prior to bid. The bidders may not make any material omissions or include any qualifications except where specifically requested to do so. The bidder is also required to state clearly the dollar value of the bid and to indicate correctly all pricing, whether it be lump-sum, unit price, or some other specific mechanism prescribed by the bid documents.

The contractor should also consider any specialized statutes or provisions in the solicitation that could affect the responsiveness of the bid or the owner's determination of responsibility. These provisions include, but are not limited to:

1. Specialized licensing requirements
2. Subcontractor listing requirements
3. Subcontractor or supplier qualification requirements (for example, five years' minimum experience)
4. Minority business enterprise goals or commitments.

Once the owner has prepared an IFB that is sufficient and the contractors have submitted completed bids, the owner opens and examines each of the bids. The contract must then be awarded to the lowest responsive, responsible bidder.

§ 4.6 Contract Award Criteria

Determination of the lowest bid is normally an arithmetical computation based on the indicated pricing. The more complicated concepts are the responsiveness of the bid and the responsibility of the bidder. Responsiveness is determined at bid opening; a nonresponsive bid cannot legally be accepted by the owner. However, a bidder can establish responsibility after bid opening and be awarded the contract, even though questions of responsibility existed at bid opening.

§ 4.7 —Responsiveness

The goal of the competitive bidding process is to obtain from each bidder a complete, definitive, unqualified offer that the awarding authority need only accept to create a binding contract to perform all work described in the solicitation. For a bid to be responsive, it must conform to the material terms of the solicitation at the time of the bid opening and permit the owner simply to accept the offer. Thus, the contractor's bid may not contain omissions or ambiguities regarding price, quality, quantity, or time of performance, nor will the contractor be permitted to modify its bid to cure such deficiencies after bid opening. Omissions or ambiguities of this type afford the contractor a competitive advantage over other bidders because the owner cannot simply accept the bid and create a binding contract for all material elements of the bid. If an owner is required to deviate from the terms of the solicitation, the contractor has the option of accepting or refusing an award, an advantage not shared by other bidders whose offers are unqualified. All rules and regulations on competitive bidding require that nonresponsive bids be disregarded.

However, minor irregularities in a bid may not render it nonresponsive. A *minor irregularity* is a deviation from the solicitation requirements that can be waived by the owner because it does not affect price, quality, quantity, or time, and does not afford the bidder a competitive advantage. The basic test of whether a deviation is a minor irregularity or a fatal defect is whether the bidder would be required to perform all the work described in the solicitation or whether it could escape performance because the bid omits a material element, and thus does not constitute an unqualified offer. For example, a bidder's failure to sign the bid or commit to a precise dollar value for the work could prevent the owner from compelling the bidder's performance on the terms mandated by the IFB.

However, failure to include in a bid certain information requested by the bid documents, such as the identity of equipment suppliers, will normally be considered either a minor irregularity or a condition of responsibility that can be cured after the bid opening, and will not disqualify the bid unless the IFB clearly makes such information a condition of responsiveness. This is because the owner can accept the bid even without such information, and require the contractor to meet all material conditions of the bid; the bidder obtains no competitive advantage over others who included such information.

§ 4.8 —Responsibility

The requirement that the award must be made to the lowest responsible bidder mandates that the contractor whose bid is accepted be capable of performing the work. Commonly, the test of contractor responsibility is measured by such factors as the trustworthiness, quality, fitness, and capacity of the contracting entity.[3] This evaluation is often undertaken after the opening of the bids and the contractor may furnish post-bid-opening information to facilitate a favorable determination.

As the foregoing demonstrates, it is often difficult to determine whether the failure to include requested information renders a bid nonresponsive and therefore void, or simply constitutes a minor irregularity or condition of responsibility, which can be waived by the awarding authority or addressed after bid opening. For this reason, the terms of the IFB must be carefully examined in any protests. The language of an IFB may make certain information required for the bid a condition of responsiveness, even though, without such language, the failure to supply such information would merely be considered an irregularity that would not prevent award of the contract. Subcontractor or supplier listing laws and minority business enterprise requirements provide good examples of IFB conditions that can be either conditions of responsiveness or conditions of responsibility.

§ 4.9 —Subcontractor Listing Requirements

Subcontractor listing laws are codified in several states for the purpose of precluding bid shopping.[4] *Bid shopping* occurs when the contractor, who based its bid on quotations from certain subcontractors or suppliers and who has been awarded the contract, is allowed to disregard those subcontractors and suppliers and obtain lower pricing from different

---

[3] City of Inglewood-Los Angeles County Civic Ctr. Auth. v. Superior Court, 7 Cal. 3d 861, 500 P.2d 601, 103 Cal. Rptr. 689 (1972).

[4] Cal. Gov't Code § 4100 (West 1990).

subcontractors. The practice is perceived to be detrimental to the public interest because, although the contractor obtains the benefit of a price reduction, the public obtains no similar benefit and potentially receives a lower quality product. IFBs sometimes require contracts to identify material suppliers for the same reason.

Some states seek to prevent bid shopping by statute. For example, California has enacted legislation to preclude bid shopping, requiring that subcontractors whose bids are in excess of one-half of one percent of the total bid price be identified by each general contractor in its bid.[5] The applicable statutes further prescribe an exclusive method for substituting subcontractors which, if not followed, authorizes the owner to assess certain penalties and cancel the contract, and entitles the subcontractor to legal redress against the offending contractor. Failure to comply with such listing requirements can provide a basis for a bid protest either on the grounds of nonresponsiveness or on the basis that the bidder is not responsible.

Even in the absence of anti-bid-shopping statutes, IFBs frequently include mandatory language such as "the contractor 'shall' [or 'must'] comply with prescribed subcontractor or supplier listing requirements." When an IFB contains this language, the bidder must determine whether the failure to list subcontractors will render the bid nonresponsive and lead to rejection of the bid. Although the use of mandatory language seems to indicate that a failure to list will void the bid, it is not always the case.

In fact, the effect of an IFB's inclusion of specific listing requirements has been the source of a substantial number of bid protests on Environmental Protection Agency-funded projects. As discussed further in §§ **2.17** through **2.21**, the EPA has developed a sophisticated set of protest procedures and has a reported body of bid protest precedents applicable to EPA-funded projects.

In the course of administering its projects, the EPA found that many subcontractor or supplier listing requirements were being improperly used by the recipients of the funds (grantees) to select or reject bidders. The EPA determined that when the use of terms such as "must" and "shall" in the language of the IFB made it appear that such listing requirements were mandatory, grantees did not uniformly enforce such requirements. If the grantee was satisfied with a low bidder who failed to comply with the listing requirements, the grantee would simply decide that such requirements were a condition of responsibility that did not render the bid void. In other cases, if the grantee favored the second low bidder, and the low bidder failed to comply with the listing requirements, the grantee would interpret the listing requirements as conditions of responsiveness and invalidate the low bid.

---

[5] *Id.* § 4104.

Because rejection of the low bidder necessarily meant that the project would require higher funding levels, the EPA adopted a regulation that provided that a grantee could disqualify an otherwise low bid because of a failure to comply with a subcontractor or supplier listing law only if the IFB was clear and unequivocal on two points: first, that the subcontractor or supplier listing requirement was a condition of responsiveness, and second, that a failure to comply with such a condition would render the bid nonresponsive and result in rejection.[6] After the adoption of this rule, the EPA promulgated regulations simplifying the evaluation of the procurement processes of the grantee agencies.[7] Although these regulations did not include the rule requiring clear and unequivocal notice of the condition of responsiveness, EPA administrative decisions have consistently held that the standards reflected in this requirement are matters of EPA policy that apply to EPA-funded projects regardless of whether the protest arises under 40 C.F.R. Part 33 or 40 C.F.R. Part 35.[8]

There are a number of cases where, although the IFB utilized terms such as "shall" and "must," the EPA determined that the grantee had failed to comply with its regulation and refused to disqualify a low bidder who had not fully complied with the terms of the listing requirements.[9] The EPA administration determinations on these and other issues provide an excellent source of information regarding the proper considerations in evaluating bid protests.

§ 4.10 —Minority Business Enterprise Requirements

A second area that has generated a significant number of protests on the federal, federally funded, and state and local levels has been the determination of whether a bidder has fully complied with the minority business enterprise (MBE) requirements of an IFB. More specifically, because many federal and state contracts have MBE requirements, it is incumbent upon the bidder to determine whether the information submitted at the time of bid regarding such programs constitutes conditions of responsiveness or of responsibility. Again, the issue hinges largely on the language of the IFB. The Environmental Protection Agency (EPA) follows essentially the same standard for determining whether the grantee agency has made the MBE

[6] 40 C.F.R. § 35.938-4(h)(6) (1990).

[7] *Id.* § 33.00.

[8] City of Los Angeles, Project No. C-06-1205-110 (Protest of Advanco Contractors, Inc.) (EPA Region IX, June 6, 1983).

[9] *See* City of Statesville, N.C., Grant No. C370395-02 (Protest of DPS Contractors, Inc.) (EPA Region IV, Nov. 17, 1982).

requirements of an IFB a matter of responsiveness as it has done for listing requirements. In order for a grantee agency to make the MBE requirements a matter of responsiveness, the IFB must clearly establish that compliance with the MBE requirements to be included with the bid documents is a matter of responsiveness.[10] When bidding on an EPA-funded grant project, it is important to pay particular attention to the terms in the solicitation describing the MBE requirements and to determine whether the MBE requirements of the bid are a matter of responsiveness.

Suffice it to say that there are both administrative determinations and federal case law establishing that the MBE requirements of a particular IFB can be either conditions of responsiveness, which render a nonconforming bid invalid, or conditions of responsibility, which permit a bidder to submit post-opening information to substantiate compliance.

§ 4.11 General Grounds for Protest

Although an owner retains the right to reject all bids, this right is infrequently exercised unless the bid protests are so numerous or the solicitation is so confusing that the only reasonable option is to rebid the project. However, it can also be invoked for other legitimate reasons, such as when even the lowest bid exceeds the amount of funding awarded the project.

If the owner does not reject all bids, but proposes an award of the contract to the bidder determined to be the lowest responsive, responsible bidder, a proper party may protest the award of the contract. **Sections 2.12** through **2.27** examine the general rules for bid protests in four contexts: direct federal contracts, federally funded grant projects, state and local contracts, and private contracts. Regardless of the category of owner or the source of funding, bid protests are normally based on one or more of the following grounds:

1. Improprieties in the solicitation procedure, including the failure to advertise properly the solicitation or providing bid information to one bidder but not others[11]
2. Defects in the specifications
3. Material deviations from the IFB in the bid of the contractor to whom the award is proposed and made
4. Deficiencies in the bid evaluation process.

---

[10] *See* Albert Lea, (Protest of Orvedahl Constr., Inc.) (EPA Region V, Sept. 18, 1980); City of Fort Wayne, (Protest of Davis Excavating, Inc.) (EPA Region V, Mar. 24, 1981).

[11] 48 C.F.R. § 14.201 (1990); Comp. Gen. Dec. B-167382 (Oct. 16, 1969).

FEDERAL CONTRACTS

§ 4.12 General

The rules governing bid protests of federal contact awards are well defined and differ from those applicable to federally funded grant projects. Protests of federally funded grant projects awarded through state and local government agencies are addressed in §§ **2.22** through **2.26**.

§ 4.13 Grounds for Protests

If the construction project is funded directly by an appropriation from the federal government, protest procedures are the responsibility of the General Accounting Office (GAO) and are contained in Title 4 of the Code of Federal Regulations.[12] Virtually any deficiency in the specifications or proposed award is a proper subject for a bid protest. When the protest is directed to the proposed award, it can encompass any material failure to comply with the provisions of the solicitation. In general, this type of protest will necessarily be determined on a case-by-case basis only after review of the bids of other contractors following bid opening.

Deficiencies in the evaluation process may also be sufficient grounds for sustaining a bid protest. For example, the improper determination of responsiveness or responsibility by the federal government has been held to be sufficient grounds for maintaining a successful bid protest.[13]In addition, if a federal agency improperly rejects all bids, interested parties may successfully protest.[14]

Despite numerous attempts in Congress to include listing requirements on federal projects, none have passed. Consequently, on the federal level at least, subcontractor listing is not a protest issue. At one time, the General Services Administration (GSA) required a listing of subcontractors on contracts that met certain minimum requirements. These requirements were eliminated in 1984 and replaced with a rule providing that all GSA solicitations are to contain language instructing bidders that they must subcontract only with firms not listed on the Consolidated List of Debarred, Suspended, and Ineligible Contractors without specific authorization.[15]

---

[12] 4 C.F.R. § 21 (1991).

[13] Brown & Son Elec. Co. v. United States, 163 Ct. Cl. 465 (1963).

[14] FAR § 14.404-1(c) (Sept. 19, 1983); 48 C.F.R. § 14.401-1(c) (1990). The Federal Acquisition Regulations contain the policy and procedure guidance for acquisitions by federal agencies, and are codified at 48 C.F.R. pt. 1.

[15] 49 Fed. Reg. 5755 (Feb. 15, 1984). As of July 1, 1985, the Federal Procurement Regulation's system was replaced by the Federal Acquisition Regulations.

§ 4.14 Standing to Protest

Under federal statute and regulations, any "interested party" may protest the award or proposed award of a federal contract. An *interested party* is defined by statute as "an actual or prospective bidder or offeror whose direct economic interest would be affected by the award of the contract or by failure to award the contract."[16] This definition has been interpreted quite narrowly by a series of recent decisions. To be an interested party, the protester must have bid as a prime contractor. Thus, the interested party rule eliminates subcontractors,[17] suppliers,[18] unions,[19] and trade associations[20] because they do not have the requisite direct economic interest to file bid protests. Further, in a sealed-bid context, only the second-lowest bidder is an interested party unless the protester has challenged the solicitation itself or the eligibility of all lower bidders.[21] For example, the fourth-lowest bidder can file a bid protest only by making allegations that the first-, second- and third-lowest bidders are all ineligible,[22] or by asserting that the solicitation should be cancelled and rebid.[23] It is unclear whether this rule applies in the negotiated procurement context. The GAO always limits interested parties to the next-lowest bidder.[24] However, at least two GSA Board of Contract Appeals decisions have found that because further rounds of competition are possible after a protest to a negotiated procurement, the next-lowest bidder rule does not apply.[25]

Because an award can be made only to a responsive bidder, a preliminary matter for the protest forum to resolve is whether the *protester's* bid is responsive. If it is not responsive, the protest fails for lack of standing.[26]

---

[16] 40 U.S.C. § 759(f)(9)(B) (1988).

[17] Comp. Gen. Dec. B-226185 (5 Jan. 1988), 88-1 CPD ¶ 2; Comp. Gen. Dec. B-228373 (26 Jan. 1988), 88-1 CPD ¶ 76.

[18] Comp. Gen. Dec. B-225525.2 (14 Jan. 1987), 87-1 CPD ¶ 58.

[19] Comp. Gen. Dec. B-225335.2 (5 Feb. 1987), 87-1 CPD ¶ 124.

[20] Comp. Gen. Dec. B-223820 (7 Aug. 1986), 86-2 CPD ¶ 169.

[21] United States v. International Business Machs. Corp., 892 F.2d 1006, 1011 (Fed. Cir. 1989), *reh'g denied,* (Jan. 17, 1990).

[22] Comp. Gen. Dec. B-229642 (29 Mar. 1988), 88-1 CPD ¶ 316.

[23] Comp. Gen. Dec. B-225326, B-225327, B-225879 (6 Mar 1987), 87-1 CPD ¶ 260.

[24] Thermal Reduction Co., B-236724, 89-2 CPD ¶ 527 (1989); *see* CFS Air Cargo, Inc., B-238698.4, 90-1 CPD ¶ 315 (1990).

[25] Sysorex Info. Sys., GSBCA Nos. 10642-P, 10644-P, 10656-P, 1990 BPD ¶ 153 (1990); Planning Research Corp., GSBCA No. 10697-P, 1990 BPD ¶ 224 (1990). *But see* Unit Data Serv. Corp., GSBCA No. 10775-P, 1990 BPD ¶ 281 (1990) (reaching the opposite conclusion).

[26] United States v. International Business Machs. Corp., 892 F.2d 1006, 1012.

§ 4.15 Protest Procedure

Presently, there are five forums in which bid protests can be filed:

1. The contracting officer
2. The General Accounting Office (GAO)
3. Federal district courts
4. The United States Claims Court
5. The General Services Administration Board of Contract Appeals (GSBCA).

Although the GAO encourages initial review by the awarding agency, it may be strategically wise to submit a bid protest directly to the GAO because an awarding agency may be particularly defensive of its award decision. Accordingly, GAO is the most frequently used forum, receiving approximately 3,000 bid protests annually.

Protests to the GAO must be received within 10 days of either the denial of a protest submitted to the contracting officer or the date on which the protestors knew or should have known of the basis for the protest. This deadline is crucial for obtaining review of the proposed award by the GAO, although it may consider a late protest for good cause or when the protest raises a significant issue.[27] A protest directed to the contracting officer should be made pursuant to the awarding agency's specific regulations governing bid protests.

The protest should be in writing and should set forth all relevant facts supporting the protest. No specific form is required, but the initial protest must include the name and address of the protestor, contract number, a statement of the grounds, and a specific request for ruling, and must in general be concise, logical, and direct.[28]

The federal protest procedures were modified in 1984 pursuant to the Competition in Contracting Act of 1984.[29] The Act required the GAO to promulgate new rules for bid protests. The new rules are published at 4 C.F.R. part 21, and are designed to provide the framework for the consideration of bid protests by the GAO.[30]

The present rules require an awarding agency to file a complete report on the protest with the GAO within 25 days of the date of the notice of the

---

[27] 4 C.F.R. § 21.2(b) (1991).

[28] *Id.* § 21.1(c); *Bid Protests at GAO; A Descriptive Guide* 10 (4th ed. 1991).

[29] 31 U.S.C. §§ 3551–3556 (1984).

[30] 4 C.F.R. § 21 (1991).

protest.[31] The protestor is required to respond to the agency's report within seven days after receipt. This response is mandatory: a protestor's failure to file comments, a statement requesting that the decision be based on the existing record, or a request for an extension will result in dismissal of the protest. This seven-day limit may be extended if the circumstances warrant, but the rules provide that extensions are to be considered "exceptional" and are to be granted only sparingly.[32]

Several new rules have also have promulgated with respect to withholding an award or suspension of contract performance pending a resolution of a protest filed with the GAO. Section 3553(c) and (d) of the Act provide that, when the GAO receives a protest, it is to provide notice of the protest to the contracting agency. The contracting agency may not award a contract in the protested matter while the protest is pending unless the awarding agency determines that there are "urgent and compelling circumstances significantly affecting interests of the United States [that] will not permit waiting for the General Accounting Office decision."[33] A new section has been added to the regulations, providing that the GAO will not consider subcontractor protests unless the subcontract is "by or for the government."[34]

Parties to a bid protest often desire a hearing or conference for the purpose of confronting other parties to the protest. The GAO has the discretion to grant such a request by a protesting or interested party.[35] In addition, the GAO itself may request that a conference be held at any time during the protest proceedings if it determines that such a conference is needed to clarify material issues.[36]

Pursuant to a relatively new procedure, GAO may hold a fact-finding conference to resolve a specific factual dispute that is essential to deciding the protest.[37] In a fact-finding conference, witnesses testify under oath and can be examined by any party. The admissibility of evidence is determined by the presiding GAO official, with the Federal Rules of Evidence as a guide.[38] The parties may request such a conference or GAO may hold one of its own accord; however, GAO has been granting them very infrequently.[39]

---

[31] *Id.* § 21.3(c).

[32] *Id.* § 21.3(e).

[33] *Id.* § 21.4(a).

[34] *Id.* § 21.3(m)(10).

[35] *Id.* § 21.5(a).

[36] 4 C.F.R. § 21.5(a)(3) (1991).

[37] *Id.* § 21.5(b).

[38] *Id.* § 21.5(b)(2), (3).

[39] In the eight months after the fact-finding regulations became effective in 1988, only three conferences had been held. Ackley, *Remedies of Unsuccessful Offerors: GAO Bid Protests,* 27-50-190 Army L. 48 (1988).

As of January 1988, bid protesters may request in writing specific documents relevant to their protests.[40] The GAO has stated that it will apply Freedom of Information Act standards to discovery requests in determining what documents it will produce to protesters.[41]

Normally, the GAO is required to issue a decision on the protest within 90 days from the date the protest is filed.[42] The new rules also provide for an "express option" whereby the protest procedure time is shortened. The express option may be requested by a protestor, the contracting agency, or an interested party, and must be filed in writing and received by the GAO no later than three days after the protest is filed. The GAO has the sole discretion to employ the express option in those cases suitable for resolution within 45 days. Use of the express option reduces the contracting agency's time to file a report with the GAO to 10 days from the receipt of notice that the express option will be used, and limits the comment period on the agency report to five days after receipt of the report. Under this option, the GAO retains its discretion to arrange a conference on any material issue, but it is required to issue its decision on the bid protest within 45 days from the date the protest is filed.[43]

§ 4.16 Relief Available

The relief available to a protestor depends upon whether the award has been made. On occasion, all bids may be rejected. Rejection of all bids is not favored but may occur under certain circumstances. For example, the Federal Acquisition Regulations provide that all bids may be rejected and the IFB cancelled when the contracting officer determines that the solicitation is somehow defective.[44] Rejection of bids is justified when:

1. Specifications are inadequate or ambiguous
2. The supplies or services procured are no longer needed
3. All acceptable bids received are at unreasonable prices
4. The bids received were not arrived at independently, were collusive, or were submitted in bad faith
5. Cancellation is clearly in the best interest of the government.

---

[40] 4 C.F.R. § 21.3(c) (1991).

[41] 52 Fed. Reg. 46,445 (1987).

[42] 4 C.F.R. § 21.7(a) (1991).

[43] *Id.* § 21.8.

[44] FAR 14.404-1(b) (Sept. 19, 1983, as amended Jan. 11, 1985, and Dec. 23, 1985).

The GAO may overrule a contracting officer's decision to reject all bids.[45] Normally, however, the GAO will not interfere when the contacting officer exercises that authority, absent a clear showing of abuse of discretion.[46]

If the protest is determined favorably to the protestor prior to award, the protestor may be awarded the contract. However, even if the contract was initially awarded to an improper party, the GAO retains the power to direct cancellation of the contract. This remedy is rarely employed because the awardee who is the subject of the cancellation may seek breach of contract damages in claims court.[47] Instead of cancellation, the GAO will often terminate the contract for convenience. The GAO's refusal to cancel the contract or terminate the award does not prevent the frustrated bidder from recovering bid preparation costs.[48] Bidders can recover bid preparation costs only if the contracting agency has unreasonably excluded the protestor from the procurement. The recovery of these costs is subject to the exception that, if the GAO recommends that the contract be awarded to the protestor and the protestor receives the award, costs are not recoverable.

Relief is also available through the courts. One method for protesting a contract award to another bidder is the writ of mandamus. Although not frequently employed in this context, it has been held that mandamus may issue to prevent an award if the plaintiff can establish that the proposed award is improper and will cause grave and irreparable injury.[49]

Injunctive relief may be obtained when the contracting officer's award is found to be without any rational basis. However, the burden of the protesting party is substantial and, in the absence of a showing that the award is clearly arbitrary and capricious or in violation of the statute or regulation, injunctive relief is not available in the federal courts.[50]

The rules governing selection of the proper forum for bringing a suit for injunctive relief have recently changed. The Federal Court Improvement Act of 1982 (FCIA) created the United States Claims Court and vested it with the trial jurisdiction of the former Court of Claims.[51] The FCIA also expanded the jurisdiction of the new court over that of the former Court of Claims by giving it exclusive jurisdiction to grant declaratory judgments and equitable relief on contract claims.[52] The United States Claims Court's

---

[45] 39 Comp. Gen. 396 (Nov. 25, 1959).

[46] Comp. Gen. Dec. B-159287 (Jul. 26, 1966).

[47] Warren Bros. Rds. Co. v. United States, 173 Ct. Cl. 714 (1965).

[48] *See* Keco Indus., Inc. v. United States, 428 F.2d 1233 (Ct. Cl. 1970).

[49] Noce v. Morgan, 106 F.2d 746 (8th Cir. 1939); *see In re* Smith & Wesson, 757 F.2d 431 (1st Cir. 1985).

[50] Wheelabrator Corp. v. Chafee, 455 F.2d 1306 (D.C. Cir. 1971).

[51] 28 U.S.C. § 1491 (1988).

[52] *Id.* § 1491(a)(3). For an extensive discussion of the legislative history of the FCIA, see United States v. John C. Grimberg Co., 702 F.2d 1362, 1369–72 (Fed. Cir. 1983).

equitable jurisdiction is limited by the Act to claims brought before the contract is awarded.[53]

A party desiring to protest the solicitation procedures of a contracting agency and enjoin award of the contract must file a claim with the Claims Court prior to the contract award. The fact that the protesting party has filed a protest with the contracting agency prior to award does not satisfy the requirement for filing a claim with the Court before an award is made.[54] When the protesting party desires to bring a suit for equitable relief after the award of a contract, it must bring the action in the federal district court. The FCIA does not disturb the district courts' jurisdiction to consider both pre- and post-award government contract disputes.[55]

According to the provisions of the Contract Disputes Act of 1978,[56] the former Court of Claims and the Board of Contract Appeals for each agency had concurrent jurisdiction to review appeals from decisions of a contracting officer. The FCIA explicitly eliminates the equitable jurisdiction of the boards of contract appeals over bid protests, a significant change in the prior law.

Under the present statutory scheme, a protestor desiring to obtain equitable or declaratory relief may bring an action prior to award of the contract in either the Claims Court or the federal district court. If the contract has been awarded, the protestor is limited to bringing the action in the federal district court. If the protestor's appeal is not equitable in nature, then it may be brought either to the district court, the Claims Court, or the board of contract appeals.

During the last decade, a significant number of government contracts have been in the area of automated data processing equipment (ADPE). Under the Brooks Act,[57] the Administrator of General Services has the authority to coordinate the procurement of ADPE for all agencies. The Competition in Contracting Act of 1984 (CICA), an amendment to the Brooks Act, made the General Services Administration Board of Contract Appeals (GSBCA) a bid protest forum and gave it jurisdiction to hear bid protests from ADPE procurement awards.[58] Since 1985, the GSBCA has interpreted its bid protest jurisdiction as equal to that of the GSA Administrator under

---

[53] 28 U.S.C. § 1491(a)(3) (19).

[54] United States v. John C. Grimberg Co., 702 F.2d 1362 (Fed. Cir. 1983); *see also* Santa Fe, Inc. v. United States, 13 Cl. Ct. 464 (1987).

[55] Coco Bros., Inc. v. Pierce, 741 F.2d 675 (3d Cir. 1984).

[56] 41 U.S.C. §§ 601–613 (Supp. 1987).

[57] 40 U.S.C. § 759 (1988).

[58] Pub. L. No. 98-369, § 2713, 98 Stat. 1175, 1182 (1984) (codified at 40 U.S.C. § 759(f) (1988)).

the Brooks Act.[59] However, in a series of cases, the United States Court of Appeals for the Federal Circuit, which has appellate jurisdiction over the GSBCA, has consistently limited the Board's authority to hear bid protests.[60]

FEDERALLY FUNDED GRANT PROJECTS

§ 4.17 General

The rules governing federally funded grant projects differ from those applicable to direct federal contracts. The distinction is founded on the differences in the two procurement processes. Direct *federal public works contracts* originate in a federal agency and are awarded by that agency directly to the contractor. In contrast, *federally funded grant projects* involve federal monies given as a grant to a local or state agency (grantee) that is then responsible for awarding the contract. Channeling the funds through a grantee subjects the protestor to additional legal rules governing the bidding process.

The substantive and procedural rules of the state or local jurisdiction are normally applied in conjunction with applicable federal regulations. The result is that not only must the contractor act pursuant to the regulations promulgated to govern the award of contracts by the grantor (the federal agency), it must also follow the state and local regulations applicable to the grantee.

Although many federal agencies fund grants to state and local entities for the construction of public works projects, in the 1970s and early 1980s a substantial number of public works construction projects were funded by grants from the EPA. Not surprisingly, the EPA has developed elaborate bid protest procedures, which are often employed by other federal agencies and

---

[59] SMC Info. Sys., Inc., 85-3 B.C.A. (CCH) ¶ 18,889 at 92,231 (GSBCA 1985). *See* Murphy, *The Federal Circuit and the GSBCA: Review of Protest Decisions*, 40 Am. U.L. Rev. 1065, 1066 (1991).

[60] *See, e.g.,* Data Gen. Corp v. United States, 915 F.2d 1544 (Fed. Cir. 1990) (finding that GSBCA cannot review agency's assessment of its own ADPE needs); United States v. Citizens & S. Nat'l Bank, 889 F.2d 1067 (Fed. Cir. 1989) (GSBCA has no authority to hear protests concerning Treasury Department's choice of financial agent although it involves use of ADPE); United States v. Electronic Data Sys. Fed. Corp., 857 F.2d 1444 (Fed. Cir. 1988) (GSBCA jurisdiction does not include Postal Service ADPE procurements); Electronic Data Sys. Fed. Corp. v. General Servs. Admin. Bd. of Contract Appeals, 792 F.2d 1569 (Fed. Cir. 1986) (only ADPE procurements actually conducted under Brooks Act can be protested to GSBCA, not those that should have been).

therefore serve as a model for this discussion of the legal requirements of bid protests on federally funded grant projects. These legal requirements are applied through decisions of the EPA regional administrators, which are published and collected in annual volumes. The published decisions have significant value as legal precedent and are available for review at all 10 EPA regional offices. For these reasons, this discussion focuses on the EPA protest procedures.

§ 4.18 Grounds for Protests

A contractor may look either to the state and local competitive bidding law or to the federal agencies' regulations to determine if sufficient grounds exist for a bid protest regarding a federally funded grant project. The EPA grant regulations[61] incorporate state and local law into the rules governing bid protests on EPA grants. The contractor desiring to protest must first determine if there has been a violation of a state or local regulation. If no such violation is found, the contractor may still have sufficient grounds to protest under the EPA regulations. When state and local criteria do not provide for fair treatment of bidders or do not provide for basic principles of fairness employed in the federal procurement system, the federal rules will be followed in a bid protest.[62]

§ 4.19 Standing to Protest

Any party with a "direct financial interest adversely affected" by a procurement action has standing to file a protest with the EPA. This may include subcontractors or manufacturers of proprietary products, which are excluded from the solicitation. The criterion is similar to the federal standing requirements for interested parties used on direct federal contracts.[63]

§ 4.20 Protest Procedure

A bid protest on a federal grant project must initially be presented to the grantee agency and may be reviewed on appeal by the grantor agency. In general, the grantee agency is the proper authority to hear protests over awards for public works projects supported by federal grants. The protest procedures are generally the same as the bid protest procedures required by

---

[61] 40 C.F.R. § 33.

[62] Comp. Gen. Dec. B-180278 (Oct. 17, 1975).

[63] See § **4.14**.

the state or local agency for nonfederal contract protests. The grantee is initially charged with the responsibility for determination of the bid protest. Normally, it is also the proper authority to conduct a hearing or otherwise to allow the interested parties to submit documents outlining their respective positions. The grantee agency must also decide questions of local law such as subcontractor or supplier listing requirements. Such determinations based on local law will not be disturbed by the EPA on appeal unless they are contrary to established EPA policies.

The EPA regulations establish definite time limits for filing of a bid protest.[64] A protest relating to an allegedly deficient specification must be brought prior to bid opening and within one week after the protesting party should have been aware of the basis of the protest. Protests against the award of a bid must be in writing, directed to the grantee within seven days of the bid opening.

If the grantee agency rules unfavorably on the protest, a protest appeal may be taken to the appropriate EPA official within seven days of receipt of the decision. This initial appeal should be in the form of a written complaint, filed with the assistant general counsel for grants or the office of regional counsel,[65] or in the form of a petition for review by the regional administrator.[66]

The EPA award official will permit all interested parties to present written submissions outlining their respective positions on the subject protest. This submission must include all legal and factual contentions relevant to the appeal. The award official also may hold a hearing or telephone conference on the protest appeal and will generally issue a decision within a two-week period. The award official's determination constitutes final agency action.[67]

§ 4.21 Relief Available

Judicial review of the regional administrator's decision is available. However, in most cases it is unlikely to result in cancellation of the project or award of the contract to the protesting party. The grantee agency's decision and the determination of the EPA regional administrator will be overturned only if the protestor can establish that it is arbitrary, capricious, an abuse of discretion, or otherwise in violation of the law.[68]

---

[64] *See, e.g.,* 40 C.F.R. § 35.939(b)(1) (1990).

[65] *Id.* § 33.1105.

[66] *Id.* § 35.939, for grants subject to these rules.

[67] *Id.* §§ 33.1145(g), 35.939(e)(3).

[68] *See* Gruman Ecosys. Corp. v. Gainesville-Alachua, 402 F. Supp. 582 (N.D. Fla. 1975).

Although review of the regional administrator's decision by the GAO was previously available, the GAO will no longer review the propriety of contract awards made by grantee agencies upon the request of contract bidders. The general standard of review of the grantee agency's decision was whether it had a "rational basis" in light of the fundamental principles of competitive bidding, but as of January 17, 1985, the GAO no longer considers such protests.[69] As with direct federal contracts, bid protestors whose protests are determined favorably can generally recover bid preparation costs.

STATE AND LOCAL CONTRACTS

§ 4.22 General

Although states and most local public entities are subject to competitive bidding statutes, they are not typically required for formal adoption of a protest procedure. In some states, such as Oregon and Montana, the state chapters of the Associated General Contractors have formally published uniform guidelines for protest procedures, but most states do not have uniform protest procedures. As a result, a potential protestor must contact the state or individual agency to determine whether any formalized protest procedures exist.

Even if no formalized procedure has been adopted, applicable statutes and case law will normally require that some procedure by available to test fairly an owner's award of a contract. Although the procedures may vary, they will generally be required to comply with a fundamental fairness standard. The decision of the awarding authority will usually be reviewable by some judicial procedure on a relatively narrow standard of review to ensure, at a minimum, that the hearing procedure and the ultimate award were appropriate.

§ 4.23 Grounds for Protests

The grounds for protests to state and local agencies are substantially the same as those for federal and federally funded contracts.[70] The concepts of low, responsive, and responsible bidders remain essentially the same and are tested by the same standards.[71]

---

[69] *See* Comp. Gen. Dec. B-185790 (July 9, 1976).

[70] See §§ **4.12–4.21**.

[71] *See, e.g.,* Cal. Pub. Cont. Code §§ 20111, 20128, 20405 (West Supp. 1985–1991). The California statute does not use the term "responsive," but the courts have accepted a responsiveness test.

Although some states employ the concept of "best bidder," which vests the awarding authority with substantial discretion in determining the entity to whom the contract will be awarded,[72] most states have rejected any kind of "relative superiority" test. That is, the agency may not compare the qualifications of a low bidder with those of other bidders unless the comparison is done in accordance with a disclosed standard that is itself fair and impartial. In California, the governing board of any school district may contract with any of the three lowest responsible bidders for the procurement or maintenance of electronic data processing systems and supporting software.[73]

4.24 Standing to Protest

The requirements for standing to protest the award of a competitively bid project may vary considerably from state to state. The interested party requirement employed in federal bid protest procedures does not necessarily apply to the state and local government agencies hearing bid protests. For example, the California statute provides that any bidder who submitted a bid on a project may initiate a protest on the grounds that it is the lowest responsible bidder meeting the specifications.[74] This requirement differs significantly from the federal requirement because a bidder who is not the next-lowest bidder may still have standing to bring a protest of the proposed award. Conceivably, the highest bidder has standing to protest if it establishes that the other bidders are not responsible or not responsible.

A person seeking relief from a proposed award by a writ of mandamus to restrain a public official's award of a contract is subject to a different standing requirement in most states. Frequently, standing to oppose the award of a contract through a mandamus action is much broader, because the mandamus action to restrain a public official's discretion is available to any taxpayer who is a citizen of the state.[75] In those jurisdictions where this broad standing requirement exists, persons without an economic interest in the award of the contract may still be able to challenge the proposed award with a mandamus proceeding.

---

[72] *See* State *ex rel.* Fisher Constr. Co. v. Linzell Constr. Co., 101 Ohio App. 219, 137 N.E.2d 427 (1955).

[73] Cal. Pub. Cont. Code § 20118.1 (West Supp. 1991).

[74] Cal. Pub. Cont. Code § 10306. (West 1990).

[75] *See* Baldwin-Lima-Hamilton Corp. v. Superior Court, 208 Cal. App. 2d 803, 25 Cal. Rptr. 798 (1962).

§ 4.25 Protest Procedure

If no specific protest procedure has been adopted by the awarding authority, a contractor should follow a procedure similar to that outlined for more formalized bid protests. That is, to commence a protest, a contractor should do the following:

1. Upon determination that a protest should be pursued, the contractor should initiate the protest in writing as soon as reasonably possible after the grounds for the protest have been determined. In all instances, a contractor should not wait more than seven days from the date of bid opening to notify the awarding authority of its intent to pursue a protest.
2. The contractor should request a hearing or some method of presenting its position regarding the protest. In this regard, counsel or the entity involved should be contacted to determine what rules have been adopted by the entity for such hearings.
3. The contractor should prepare and deliver to the awarding authority a written memorandum outlining the basis of its protest and the reason its protest should be sustained. This memorandum should be delivered either with the original protest letter or as soon as reasonably practical thereafter.

§ 4.26 Relief Available

If the protest is favorably determined prior to award of the contract, the protesting party can successfully obtain an award of the contract. If however, an award is made prior to determination of the protest, or the determination is unfavorable, most states will permit a protestor to file a suit for declaratory relief and may allow the court to entertain a request to restrain the award or, after award, the performance of the contract. Actions of this type often require the posting of a bond to cover damages sustained by the awarding authority as a result of the delay, and normally require the protestor to sustain a heavy burden of proof that performance of the contract by the apparent low bidder will result in irreparable injury or was an abuse of discretion on the part of the awarding authority.

In California and in other states, a protestor who receives an unfavorable determination from the awarding authority may also file for a writ of administrative mandamus. If the awarding authority conducts the hearing in accordance with certain requirements, an unsuccessful protestor may challenge the decision on the grounds that it was improper and unlawful. Significantly, the reviewing court will consider only whether there is some support in the record for the agency's determination rather than deciding whether the court would have reached the same decision. However, the remedy has the benefit of being relatively quick and normally does not require posting of a bond. Some authority exists at the state level for allowing recovery of bid preparation costs if the bid protest is determined favorably.

PRIVATE CONTRACTS

§ 4.27 Bidding on Private Contracts

Although a bidder under a public contract can, in proper cases, require the awarding authority to award it the contract because the controlling statutes mandate an award to the lowest responsive, responsible bidder, no such right exists in the private sector. A private owner's IFB for construction projects normally reserves the owner's right to accept *any* of the bids. This reservation allows the private owner to reject the low bid and contract with a higher bidder for the construction. The basic principles of contract law establish that no contractual relationship exists until the bid is accepted. Consequently, a disappointed low bidder usually has no remedy against the private owner for rejection of its low bid.[76]

If the private owner fails to reserve the right of rejection in the IFB for bids and uses language in the solicitation establishing a commitment to award the contract to the lowest responsible bidder, then the disappointed bidder may have a remedy in contract law founded on the theory of promissory estoppel.[77] If the owner rejects the low bidder, or all bids, in bad faith or in furtherance of a scheme to obtain estimates from the bidders at no cost, the disappointed bidder may recover bidding expenses.[78]

BID MISTAKES

§ 4.28 General

There may be occasions when a bidder desires to be relieved of the obligation to perform the work. Protest procedures are not available for this

---

[76] Universal By-Prods., Inc. v. City of Modesto, 43 Cal. App. 3d 145, 117 Cal. Rptr. 525 (1974).

[77] *See* Swinerton & Walberg Co. v. Inglewood, 40 Cal. App. 3d 98, 114 Cal. Rptr. 834 (1974).

[78] *See id.;* Milton v. Hudson Sales Corp., 152 Cal. App. 2d 418, 313 P.2d 936 (1957).

purpose, but other actions are appropriate. A bidder may obtain relief in some circumstances if the bid submitted in response to the solicitation contains a material mistake. The type of relief available and the particular circumstances in which relief may be granted will first depend upon whether the bidding procedures are subject to state or federal law and whether the owner is public or private. Accordingly, this analysis of bid mistakes is divided into two separate discussions of the particular rules applicable in state and federal jurisdictions.

However, before examining particular rules governing bid mistakes, it is important at the outset to classify the kind of mistake. The following outline suggests a method to evaluate different types of bid mistakes:

1. Unilateral versus bilateral or mutual
2. Clerical (mistake of fact, mistake in filling out the bid) versus judgmental (error in judgment, carelessness in inspecting the site or in reading the plans or specifications)
3. Material versus inconsequential
4. Non-negligent (excusable; honest; caused by ordinary negligence) versus culpable (caused by gross negligence or neglect of legal duty).

In general, relief is available only for material, excusable mistakes that are clerical rather than judgmental.

§ 4.29 State Law Remedies for Bid Mistakes

Several states have statutes governing bid mistake remedies. California's statutes have evolved over the last 75 years and provide a good example of the principles affecting bid mistakes for other jurisdictions.[79]

If a bid contains a mistake that is a product of a clerical error and is material, a bidder may obtain a release from the mistaken bid by following the statutory procedures. Written notice specifying the mistake in detail must be given to the awarding authority within five days after bid opening. The statutes also require that, in any suit brought for a bid mistake, the summons must be served on the state or public entity within 90 days after bid opening.

The mistaken bidder has the burden of proving that the mistake was material, clerical in nature, and not the result of an error of judgment. A mistake is *material* if it is significant in contrast to the total value of the contract and would lead a reasonable person to conclude that the contractor would not willingly perform the work at the price.

---

[79] The procedures governing bid mistakes in California appear in Cal. Pub. Cont. Code § 5100.

California law does not fully recognize relief for a mistaken bid founded on general equitable principles. However, remedies for mistakes at common law may apply if the owner is not one of several state entities expressly covered under the statutes. In these situations, relief from a mistaken bid may be obtained under a contract theory of rescission or reformation. According to a well-established line of authority, when a mutual mistake of the parties is the basis for the formation of a contract, rescission of the contract is allowed.[80] Thus, if both bidder and owner are mistaken as to a material element of the work, a bid can be rescinded.

Rescission may also be available for unilateral mistakes. Equitable principles may support an action for rescission of a mistaken bid submitted because of a clerical mistake when the circumstances make the enforcement of the mistaken bid unconscionable.[81] Circumstances important to such a determination include:

1. The inadvertence of the error
2. The owner's knowledge of the error
3. The owner's opportunity to re-advertise
4. Equitable considerations based on the differential in bid price and contract cost.[82]

A contractor seeking to rescind an erroneous low bid that is the result of a unilateral mistake of fact must meet certain conditions.[83] In general, the bidder must provide prompt notice of the material mistake of fact and its desire to rescind the bid. In addition, the bidder must establish that it has not neglected any legal duty and must provide proof to the awarding agency that enforcement of the contract based upon the erroneous bid would be unconscionable. The bidder will be required to reimburse the agency for any value received so that the agency's position is the same as it would have been had the bid not been withdrawn.

A contractor submitting an erroneous bid may recover the bidder's security that would normally be forfeited due to the bidder's failure to execute the contract. In order to recover the security, the bidder must establish:

1. That the mistake made was material to the intended amount of the bid
2. That it provided notice to the agency within five days of bid opening, describing in detail how the bid mistake occurred

---

[80] *See* C. Kaufman, 3 Corbin on Contracts § 608 (Supp. 1991).

[81] M.F. Kemper Constr. v. City of Los Angeles, 37 Cal. 2d 696, 235 P.2d 7 (1951).

[82] *Id.* at 702, 703.

[83] *See id.;* White v. Berenda Mesa Water Dist., 7 Cal. App. 3d 894, 87 Cal. Rptr. 338 (1970).

3. That it was a mistake in the preparation of the bid not due to an error in judgment or carelessness.

Reformation is available only for mutual mistakes. If the bidder makes a bid mistake and eventually performs the contract after notifying the owner of the error, the bidder may not later reform the contract after performance to secure the higher payment amount.[84]

In California the statutory provisions of the state's Public Contract Code and other applicable statutes are the exclusive remedies for mistakes in bids submitted to agencies covered by the bidding statutes.[85] Failure to comply with the statutory notice requirements is sufficient grounds for denial of recovery. All the California statutes governing bid mistakes expressly provide that no change shall be made in a bid because of mistake. This contrasts with federal law, which allows corrections. If the bidder is not relieved of the bid, it will be held to the bid if selected as the lowest bidder. The statutes uniformly provide that a bidder who obtains relief for a bid mistake cannot rebid in response to the same solicitation.

§ 4.30 —Jurisdictions Following Equitable Principles

Absent a specific statute for relief for material mistakes, a contractor must rely on traditional theories available in the jurisdiction for such relief. Many state courts that have addressed the problem of bid mistakes follow the rule that equity can allow withdrawal of a material clerical mistake if the bidder acts promptly to seek relief.[86] Several courts deny relief for any kind of mistake, citing various theories such as avoiding possible fraud or preserving the sanctity of competitive bidding; other courts rely on statutes providing that bids may not be withdrawn after opening. Some rely on provisions in the IFBs to establish that no relief will be granted for mistakes. No matter what procedure is available, it is vital to determine the nature of the error and to advise the owner as early as possible.[87]

---

[84] Lemoge Elec. v. County of San Mateo, 46 Cal. 2d 659, 297 P.2d 638 (1956).

[85] A&A Elec., Inc. v. City of King, 54 Cal. App. 3d 457, 126 Cal Rptr. 585 (1976).

[86] *See* Boise Jr. College Dist. v. Mattefs Constr. Co., 92 Idaho 757, 450 P.2d 604 (1969); Smith & Lowe Constr. Co. v. Herrera, 79 N.M. 239, 442 P.2d 197 (1968); Rushlight Auto Sprinkler Co. v. City of Portland, 189 Or. 194, 219 P.2d 732 (1950); cases collected in Annotation, 52 A.L.R.2d 792–814 (1957); Annotation, 70 A.L.R.2d 1370, 1375–77 (1960).

[87] *See* Triple A Contractors, Inc. v. Rural Water Dist., 226 Kan. 626, 603 P.2d 184 (1979); Board of Educ. v. Sever-Williams Co., 22 Ohio St. 2d 107, 258 N.E.2d 605, *cert. denied,* 400 U.S. 916 (1970); Modany v. State Pub. Sch. Bldg. Auth., 417 Pa. 39, 208 A.2d 276 (1965); A.J. Colella, Inc. v. County of Allegheny, 391 Pa. 103, 137 A.2d 265 (1957); City of Newport News v. Doyle & Russell, Inc., 211 Va. 603, 179 S.E.2d 493 (1971).

§ 4.31 Federal Law on Bid Mistakes

Federal law requires the contracting officer to examine all bids submitted in response to an IFB to determine if mistakes are present.[88] Two types of mistakes are most frequently identified by the contracting officer: clerical mistakes that are apparent from the face of the bid; and mistakes that are errors of assumption or judgment not readily apparent from examining the bid. The basis for the contracting officer's examination is often the appearance of a large discrepancy between the mistaken bid and either the other bids or the government's estimate.

When a contracting officer discovers what it believes to be a mistaken bid, it must request verification.[89] The contracting officer is obligated to notify the bidder of the information leading the officer to believe the bid is suspect and must allow sufficient time for the bidder to respond to the request for verification.[90]

Additional federal rules for bid mistakes apply depending on when the mistake is discovered. If the mistake is discovered prior to the award, the contracting officer may allow withdrawal of the bid for an honest mistake. That is, to qualify for withdrawal, the bidder must establish that reasonable grounds exist for the mistake. This principle is based on the theory that a contracting officer cannot accept a bid if it knows or should have known the bid contains an error.

In exceptional cases the contracting officer may allow correction of a bid. If a bidder can establish the manner in which the error occurred and the actual intended price, the bid may be corrected, provided that the correction does not displace another bidder. The contracting officer may allow correction of a bid even if it displaces another bidder if both the mistake and what the contractor intended to bid are obvious on the face of the bid documents.

After an award of a contract, reformation of the contract is available to correct mutual mistakes. Reformation is not available for unilateral mistakes unless the contracting officer, prior to acceptance of the bid, had actual or constructive notice of the probability that an error existed in the bid. If this occurs, the GAO or the court may allow cancellation of the contract or adjustment of the contract price, but may not adjust the price so that it exceeds the price of the next lowest bidder. If the contract has been substantially performed, the bidder may be able to obtain a quantum meruit or quantum valebant recovery, subject to the limitation that it may not exceed the price of the next lowest bidder.

---

[88] *See* Comp. Gen. Dec. B-180329 (Oct. 1, 1974); Comp. Gen. Dec. B-182700 (Dec. 23, 1974).

[89] *See* 43 Comp. Gen. 327 (1963).

[90] *See* 44 Comp. Gen. 383 (1965); 54 Comp. Gen. 545 (1974).

§ 4.32 Private Owners

The rules governing mistakes in bids submitted to private owners vary greatly from those applicable to government contracts. For example, a bidder may withdraw the bid at any time prior to acceptance. A bid may be also withdrawn after the opening of the bids unless the doctrine of promissory estoppel applies. Consequently, a bidder may withdraw its bid before acceptance for any kind of mistake or for any reason (or for no reason at all). This rule clearly differs from that applicable to public contracts, which allows withdrawal for any reason or without reason prior to bid opening, but does not allow withdrawal once the bids are open unless it is able to establish that relief should be available because of a mistake in the bid.

Once a private owner has accepted the bid, rescission of the contract is ordinarily not available due to unilateral mistake. However, even in the private sector, some courts have allowed bidders on private contract to rescind their bids if a clerical error was not discovered until after the contract was signed.[91]

---

[91] *See* Geremia v. Boyarsky, 107 Conn. 387, 140 A. 749 (1928).

PART II

PARTIES TO LITIGATION

CHAPTER 5

SUING THE PRIVATE OWNER

Robert B. Flaig
Jesse B. Grove III
Lisa Schwartz Tudzin

Robert B. Flaig is the managing partner of the Los Angeles, California, office of the law firm of Thelen, Marrin, Johnson & Bridges. He received his B.A. degree from the University of Southern California, cum laude, and his J.D. from the University of Southern California School of Law. His practice emphasizes construction law and litigation. Mr. Flaig is a member of the California, Los Angeles, and American Bar Associations. He is a frequent speaker for California Continuing Education of the bar programs and is a noted lecturer on construction law, claims, and litigation matters. He has also authored and coauthored numerous articles on construction law and litigation topics.

Jesse B. Grove III is a trial lawyer with Thelen, Marrin, Johnson & Bridges in San Francisco, California. He has substantial experience in all phases of construction claims on major projects such as dams, tunnels, powerhouses, wastewater treatment plants, highways, bridges, and municipal, industrial, and highrise buildings; antitrust claims involving predatory pricing, tying, attempted monopolization, price discrimination, and mergers; and insurance disputes, including builder's risk and computer lease indemnity claims.

Lisa Schwartz Tudzin is an associate at Thelen, Marrin, Johnson & Bridges in Los Angeles, California, specializing in litigation, with emphasis on construction industry matters. She has handled construction cases involving representation of contractors, engineers, manufacturers, and material suppliers in a wide range of litigation and arbitration disputes, including extra-work claims, delay claims, mechanic's lien foreclosures, and breaches of contracts for supply of materials and equipment.

---

§ 5.1 Introduction

BREACHES OF CONTRACT BY OWNER

§ 5.2 Changes

§ 5.3 —Scope of Work

§ 5.4 —Notice of Changes

§ 5.5 —Changed Physical Conditions

§ 5.6 —Constructive Changes

§ 5.7 Delay

§ 5.8 —No Damage for Delay Clauses

§ 5.9 Nonpayment

§ 5.10 Disputes Involving Subcontractors

REMEDIES

§ 5.11 Damages

§ 5.12 —Prevention of Completion

§ 5.13 —Extra Work

§ 5.14 Rescission and Restitution

§ 5.15 Reformation

§ 5.16 Termination

§ 5.17 Liens

§ 5.18 Exculpatory Clauses

§ 5.1 Introduction

In any given construction contract relationship, either the owner or the contractor can breach the contract. Generally, the types of breach for which an owner is sued fall into one of the following three categories:

1. Changes, including changes due to defective plans and specifications or unexpected contingencies
2. Delay, including delay due to interference with contractor's performance, failure to approve and process change orders, failure to grant jobsite access, and failure to approve drawings or provide owner-furnished equipment
3. Nonpayment, including failure to make progress payments.

The courtroom is the most familiar forum for dispute resolution, but quite often construction disputes are resolved by arbitration, mediation, or another proceeding agreed upon by the parties to the dispute either prior to or after the dispute arises. According to the American Arbitration Association, 2,675 construction arbitration claims with a value of $447.7 million were filed with the Association nationwide in 1983. In 1990 the number of claims rose to 5,440 with a value of $800 million.

This chapter discusses areas of dispute between contractors and owners in the context of a private works contract. In many situations, the courts apply the same or similar rules to construction contracts between private parties as they do to public works contracts between a private contractor and a governmental body. Accordingly, cases in which the owner is a public entity have been cited when the rule followed is equally applicable to both types of owners.

BREACHES OF CONTRACT BY OWNER

§ 5.2 Changes

The construction contract is an anomaly in the law of contracts because it usually contains a changes clause permitting one party to change unilaterally the other party's obligations. This detour around the normal requirement of mutual agreement for an effective modification of a contract has a long history and is now commonplace.

The earliest approach to a changes clause in this country appears in an 1818 United States Army contract with Asa Waters for 10,000 muskets: "Should any alterations . . . be decreed by the Ordinance Department, the said Asa Waters will be entitled to compensation for any extra expenses occasioned by such alterations."[1] That contract did not give the Ordinance Department the right to decree alterations in the musket specifications;

---

[1] R. Nash, Jr., Government Contract Changes 12 (1975).

apparently the parties assumed that this was an inherent right of the government.

There are probably more disputes arising from the changes clause than from any other provision of the construction contract. Litigation relating to the changes clause in government contracts has been more frequent than that relating to any other clause.[2] It appears that in 1984 only cases involving the default clause exceeded in number those relating to the changes clause.[3]

A typical changes clause can be found in the 1987 AIA Document A201, Article 7.

A change order increases or decreases the contract price by the difference between what it would have cost to perform the unchanged work and what it cost to perform the changed work. Typically, the changes clause limits the owner's right to make changes to those within the scope of the work required under the contract. Changes beyond the scope of the work that are characterized as "cardinal changes" in the government contracts setting have been held to be breaches of contract.[4]

In *Daugherty Co. v. Kimberly-Clark Corp.*,[5] the court held that an excessive number of changes imposed by the owner on a contractor such that the original contract's scope of work has been significantly altered is sufficient to finding that the contract has been abandoned. Although the contract may be abandoned, the work is not necessarily so and the court in *Daugherty Co.* allowed the contractor to recover in quantum meruit.

In *Hensler v. City of Los Angeles*,[6] the court observed that a "contract entered into by a governmental body and an individual is governed by the same rules which apply to the construction of contracts between private persons." The contract in that case gave the owner (the city) the right to make changes "as may be considered necessary or desirable to complete fully and acceptably the proposed construction in a satisfactory manner."[7] The owner issued a change order deleting portions of the work. As a result of the deletions, the project was unusable and the deleted work was not performed until several months later when the owner let a contract for the deleted work to another contractor.

---

[2] "In fiscal year 1974, over 31% of the cases before the [Armed Services Board of Contract Appeals] were based on the Changes clause." *Id.* at 4.

[3] There were 253 default clause cases as opposed to 243 changes clause cases. 26 Gov't Contractor ¶ 324 (Nov. 12, 1984).

[4] Saddler v. United States, 287 F.2d 411 (Ct. Cl. 1961); General Contracting Co. v. United States, 84 Ct. Cl. 570 (1937); Boomer v. Abbett, 121 Cal. App. 2d 449, 263 P.2d 476 (1953).

[5] 14 Cal. App. 3d 151, 156, 92 Cal. Rptr. 120 (1971).

[6] 124 Cal. App. 2d 71, 268 P.2d 12 (1954).

[7] *Id.*

The court affirmed a judgment for the contractor on the ground that the deletion of work constituted a breach of contract. The court said that the right to make changes "cannot be used . . . for the purpose of legitimatizing the deletion of so integral a part of the work as to leave the improvement in an unfinished condition and still insulate the city from liability.[8]

§ 5.3 —Scope of Work

Most disputes about the scope of the work occur because of inaccurate, incomplete, or ambiguous contract provisions and details in the specifications and plans. For example, in *Ronald Adams, Contractor, Inc. v. Louisiana,*[9] the contractor performed a unit price contract in accordance with the original plans and specifications, but the quantity of excavation work performed was 79.9 percent less than estimated and the embankment work was 31.58 percent less than estimated. The contract provided that when there was a difference between the final and estimated quantities, the contractor was to be paid the original unit price "except as provided in Section 40," which read:

> The owner reserves and shall have the right to make such alterations in the work . . . as may increase or decrease the originally awarded contract quantities, provided that the aggregate of such alterations does not change the total contract cost or the total cost of any major contract item by more than 25 percent. . . . Should the aggregate amount of altered work exceed the 25 percent limitation . . . such excess altered work shall be covered by supplemental agreement.[10]

In affirming a judgment for the contractor, the court rejected the state's contention that "alterations in the work" meant merely alterations in the plans or design.

The court also rejected the state's argument that the contractor was entitled to additional compensation for only the portion of the alterations that exceeded the 25 percent limitation. Construing any ambiguity as to the applicable provisions' meaning against the party who drafted the contract, the court said: "These provisions were obviously made in recognition that an over-run or under-run exceeding 25 percent . . . constitutes a substantial change in the contract and the basis upon which the parties entered into it."[11]

---

[8] *Id.* at 80, 268 P.2d at 19.

[9] 457 So. 2d 778 (La. Ct. App. 1984).

[10] *Id.* at 780.

[11] *Id.* at 781.

The contractor in *Acchione & Canuso, Inc. v. Commonwealth*[12] entered into a contract to perform 13,131 lineal feet of trenching at a unit price per lineal foot. The trenching was to be performed on earth, sidewalk, and highway and the contractor estimated the respective costs per lineal foot for the three types of trenching as $13, $23, and $52. Based on estimated quantities, the contractor's composite bid price was $24 per lineal foot. After the contract was entered into, the state added 17,433 lineal feet of trenching. The quantity of the least expensive trenching rose about 50 percent and the quantity of the most expensive trenching rose over 300 percent.

Prior to bid the contractor had questioned the estimated quantities and had been directed by the owner's engineers to assume that 50 percent of the existing conduit would be reusable and thus would require no new trenching. The 17,433 lineal feet of trenching were

> required due to the omission by the designer and the consultant in the plans and in the Contract of a contingency item . . . to cover the installation of conduit where reusable conduit does not check out to be usable. The corresponding trenching item was also not revised accordingly. The complete item for trenching on the interconnect system was also omitted by the designer and the consultant.[13]

The court in *Acchione & Canuso* held that the increased expenses incurred by the contractor were a direct result of the contractor's reliance on the misrepresentation of the owner's engineers. The representation was arbitrary and/or a gross mistake and was therefore actionable. Similarly, it has been held that when an owner imposes an excessive number of changes on the contractor, the magnitude of which is of such that they materially change the scope of work initially contemplated, an abandonment of contract may properly be found and the contractor is entitled to recover the reasonable value of work performed on a *quantum meruit* basis (without being limited by the original contract amount).[14]

§ 5.4 —Notice of Changes

Many construction contracts contain one or more provisions that make the giving of notice of a change that is not the subject of a written change order a condition precedent to the contractor's right to payment for performing the changed work. This requirement may be expressly or impliedly waived

---

[12] 501 Pa. 337, 461 A.2d 765 (1983).

[13] *Id.* at 767.

[14] C. Norman Peterson Co. v. Container Corp., 172 Cal. App. 3d 628, 640, 218 Cal. Rptr. 592, 598 (1985). *See* Daugherty Co. v. Kimberly-Clark Corp., 14 Cal. App. 3d 151, 92 Cal. Rptr. 120 (1971).

by the owner. Implied waivers have been found when the owner considers and acts on the claim for additional compensation on its merits,[15] when the owner had actual knowledge of the change so that notice would have served no useful purpose,[16] and when the owner was not prejudiced by the absence of notice from the subcontractor.[17] However, absent proof of express or implied waiver, notice provisions normally will be enforced.[18]

Most changes clauses require that change orders be in writing. This requirement may be waived but the waiver must be clearly established, particularly in public contracts. Generally, an owner is said to have waived a written change orders clause when the owner's acts are inconsistent with a desire to enforce it, that is, when the owner knows of the extra work but does not object to its completion without a writing.

In *Nether Providence Township School Authority v. Thomas M. Durkin & Sons, Inc.,*[19] the contract to construct a school building provided, "No change in the contract shall be made without the written approval of the Board. A request for any change must be in writing."[20] The contractor brought an assumpsit action for extra work performed during the course of construction. When, during the course of construction, a discrepancy between the site plans and the topographical conditions arose, the School Authority authorized its secretary to write a letter to the contractor acknowledging the disagreement as to who should bear the cost of added work and recommending continuation of the work with resolution of any problem at a later time. The contractor completed the job and billed the School Authority for the extra work.

The trial court held that the secretary's letter was a waiver of the requirement of writing. The supreme court reversed, however, saying that waiver could be accomplished only by formal written action of the School Authority's board or ratification of the extra work claim by resolution of the board. The secretary's letter was not the action of the full board and thus there was no waiver of the requirement for written change orders. The Supreme Court in *Nether Providence* thus denied the contractor's claim for additional compensation from the owner on the grounds that the contractor's change orders for additional site development were not submitted in strict compliance with the contract provisions.

When there is no explicit contract provision requiring change orders to be in writing, but when changes are subject to the owner's approval, it has

---

[15] George A. Fuller Co. v. United States, 104 Ct. Cl. 176, 218 (1945).

[16] General Ins. Co. v. Commerce Hyatt House, 5 Cal. App. 3d 460, 85 Cal. Rptr. 317 (1970).

[17] Charles H. Siever, PSBCA No. 460, 80-2 B.C.A. (CCH) ¶ 14,740 (1980).

[18] Indiana v. Omega Painting, Inc., 463 N.E.2d 287 (Ind. Ct. App. 1984).

[19] 505 Pa. 42, 476 A.2d 904 (1984).

[20] *Id.* at 906.

been held that the contractor should be compensated for work performed pursuant to unwritten change orders.[21] "The (owners) made many changes and additions to the written contract in an informal fashion . . . . They cannot be permitted to retain the benefits of the oral change orders without compensating (the contractor)."[22] In *Davenport & Co. v. Spieker* the court found that the owner had the opportunity to insist on written change orders if so desired, but did not. The doctrine of estoppel, involving a contractor's reliance on the owner's words and actions, further operates to allow the contractor to recover for changes that are not the subject of a writing.

§ 5.5 —Changed Physical Conditions

Many of today's construction contracts contain clauses dealing with the rights and obligations of the parties if unforeseen physical conditions are encountered. The federal government's clause is entitled "Differing Site Conditions" and covers "(1) subsurface or latent physical conditions . . . differing materially from those indicated in this contract, or (2) unknown physical conditions . . . of an unusual nature, differing materially from those ordinarily encountered and generally recognized as inhering in work of the character provided for in this contract."

The corresponding clause in the AIA Document A201 is called "Claims for Concealed or Unknown Conditions." Its language is essentially identical to that found in the federal government's clause.

The Engineers Joint Contract Documents Committee 1910-8 has a clause entitled "Report of Differing Conditions," which relates to "any physical condition uncovered or revealed at the site [that] differs materially from that indicated, reflected or referred to in the Contract Documents.[23]

The Court of Claims has said that the purpose of a changed or concealed conditions clause is to take at least some of the gamble of discovering unexpected subsurface conditions out of bidding. The clause shifts the risk of encountering an adverse subsurface condition to the owner and encourages the contractor not to include contingency amounts therefor in its bid.[24]

In *Empire Construction Co.,*[25] after award of the contract the government supplied as-built drawings that did not show a two-inch lateral line coming off the main gas line and continuing below a concrete slab that had

---

[21] Davenport & Co. v. Spieker, 197 Cal. App. 3d 566, 242 Cal. Rptr. 911 (1988) (certified for partial publication).

[22] *Id.* at 571, 242 Cal. Rptr. at 914.

[23] NSPE Form 1910-8 (1983).

[24] Foster Constr. C.A. v. United States, 435 F.2d 873, 887 (Ct. Cl. 1970).

[25] ASBCA No. 27540, 84-3 B.C.A. (CCH) ¶ 17,531 (1984).

to be removed by Empire. During removal of the slab, the two-inch line was ruptured. In sustaining the contractor's appeal, the board said:

> Although the as-built drawings relied upon by appellant to give the locations of existing gas, steam and heat lines were not a part of the original contract drawing package, they were Government drawings furnished to appellant in the course of its performance by the Government representatives at Mather Air Force Base. As such they related to conditions "indicated in the contract" as contemplated by the "Differing Site Conditions" clause. . . . [A]ppellant has demonstrated that a latent condition existed, that it was not shown on the drawings, and that the failure to so show it was the proximate cause of the gas line rupture.[26]

In *Wunderlich v. State,*[27] the State provided certain test samples to bidding highway contractors of the location, quality, and quantity of materials needed to perform the contract. The State explicitly set forth in the standard specifications section of the contract that the test samples are "furnished for the Contractor's or the bidder's convenience only and the State does not guarantee such tests and assumes no responsibility whatsoever as to the accuracy thereof or the interpretation thereof stated in the test record."[28] The State also provided that it "will be assumed that the bidder has investigated and is satisfied as to the conditions to be encountered, as to the character, quality and quantities of the work to be performed and materials to be furnished . . . ."[29] The language was included in the contract documents to make clear the fact that the contractor assumed the risk of relying on the samples provided by the State.

The contractor relied on the State's samples in choosing the source of its base material and fill. Several weeks into the project the contractor learned that the source contained too much sand and could not be used. The contractor sued the State on a breach of warranty theory, claiming that misinformation provided by the State unexpectedly caused the contractor to have to rely on remote materials sources, resulting in increased construction costs. The California Supreme Court reversed a judgment for the contractor, holding that:

> When there is no misrepresentation of factual matters within the state's knowledge or withholding of material information, and when both parties have equal access to information as to the nature of the tests which resulted in the state's findings, the contractor may not claim in the face of a pertinent disclaimer that the presentation of the information, or a reasonable

---

[26] *Id.* at 87,309.

[27] 65 Cal. 2d 777, 423 P.2d 545, 56 Cal. Rptr. 473 (1967).

[28] *Id.* at 546, 56 Cal. Rptr. at 478.

[29] *Id.*

summary thereof, amounts to a warranty of the conditions that will actually be found.[30]

In the companion case of *E.H. Morrill Co. v. State,*[31] however, the California Supreme Court allowed the contractor to recover damages for differing subsurface conditions despite the usual disclaimer clause because the State was found to have misled the contractor concerning concealed conditions. The court held that when the State made positive factual misrepresentations about subsurface obstacles, the State would be liable for damages resulting from the misinformation despite an attempt to shift the burden of such unforeseen conditions onto the contractor.[32]

Consistent with the California court's analysis, in a New Jersey case,[33] the court considered a clause entitled "Article 1.2.12 Subsurface Conditions," which read as follows:

> It is obligation of the Bidder to make his own investigations of subsurface conditions prior to submitting his Proposal. Borings, test excavations and other subsurface investigations, if any, made by the Engineer prior to the construction of the project, the records of which may be available to bidders, are made for use as a guide for design. Said borings, test excavations and other subsurface investigations are not warranted to show the actual subsurface conditions. The Contractor agrees that he will make no claims against the State, if in carrying out the Project he finds that the actual conditions encountered to not conform to those indicated by said borings, test excavations and other subsurface investigations.
>
> Any estimate or estimates of quantities shown on the Plan or in the form of proposal, based on said borings, test excavations and other subsurface investigations, are in no way warranted to indicate the true quantities. The Contractor agrees that he will make no claims against the State, if the actual quantity or quantities do not conform to the estimated quantity or quantities . . . .[34]

The court said:

> In *Sasso* . . . we found that article 1.2.12 was a specific exculpatory clause focusing directly on subsurface conditions and the contract language was ". . . straightforward, unambiguous and categorical . . . in placing responsibility for subsurface investigations on the contractor." Id. at 489, 414 A.2d 603. Thus we concluded that under the terms of the contract the State's

[30] *Id.* at 550, 56 Cal. Rptr. at 478.

[31] 65 Cal. 2d 787, 423 P.2d 551, 56 Cal. Rptr. 479 (1967).

[32] 423 P.2d at 554, 56 Cal. Rptr. at 482.

[33] Ell-Dorer Contracting Co. v. State, 197 N.J. Super. 175, 484 A.2d 356 (App. Div. 1984).

[34] 484 A.2d at 360.

representations were merely gratuitous and the reliance by the contractor was at his own peril.

* * *

Golomore and *Sasso* stand for the proposition that when the State makes false representations it will be liable for damages resulting from them despite a general disclaimer of liability for inaccurate representations. However, if the disclaimer is sufficiently specific or if the statements only purport to be the results of tests rather than being actual conditions or descriptions of actual conditions, then the contractor cannot recover.[35]

§ 5.6 —Constructive Changes

The legal fiction of constructive change developed in federal government construction contracts in order to permit contractors to be paid under the changes clause even though no change order had been issued. The Boards of Contract Appeals and later the Court of Claims held that when a contractor's performance requirements were changed by some action or inaction by the government that amounted to a direction to the contractor, there had been a constructive change compensable under the changes clause.

Constructive changes generally arise from an owner's direction to the contractor to perform additional work that the owner does not consider to be a change in the contract. Owners are frequently guilty of imposing constructive acceleration orders. If a contractor experiences an excusable delay that effectively extends the contract completion date, but the owner insists on completion in accordance with the original schedule, the owner's conduct amounts to a constructive acceleration order.

The constructive change doctrine has gained wide acceptance and has been applied in cases between state or local governments and private contractors. In *Weeshoff Construction Co. v. Los Angeles County Flood Control District,*[36] the court said:

> Although . . . the district refused to explicitly name the procedure it was ordering, it clarified, by example, the material it was then requiring when it [used] temporary pavement. Since this procedure has been found to constitute a change in the original contract, it is clear that the district, by its conduct, exerted an intentional attempt to affect [sic] a contractual change without complying with the change order provision . . . . [T]he district's performance . . . itself, affected [sic] a change of contractual terms.[37]

---

[35] *Id.* (citing Sasso Contracting Co. v. State, 173 N.J. Super. 486, 414 A.2d 603 (1980); Golomore Assocs. v. New Jersey State Highway Auth., 173 N.J. Super. 55, 413 A.2d 361 (1980)).

[36] 88 Cal. App. 3d 579, 152 Cal. Rptr. 19 (1979).

[37] *Id.* at 590, 591, 152 Cal. Rptr. at 24, 25.

Some other examples of constructive changes are:

1. The owner requires performance of work that is beyond the scope of the work required by the contract but that the owner does not recognize as a change.
2. The owner supplies defective design specifications or contract drawings that necessitate extra work on the part of the contractor.
3. The owner requires performance in accordance with only one of two or more optional methods of performance specified in the contract. The increase in cost of performance over the cost of performance pursuant to the least expensive option is compensable.
4. The owner demands higher standards of inspection or workmanship or applies tests different from those specified in the contract. Increases in the contractor's performance costs because of such standards are compensable.
5. The owner requires work in accordance with an incorrect interpretation of the specifications. The increase in cost over the cost of the work done in accordance with the correct interpretation is compensable.

§ 5.7 Delay

Most construction contracts have provisions dealing with delays in the work. **Section 5.8** discusses *no damage for delay clauses,* which provide that a contractor's only remedy for delay is an extension of the contract completion date. *Termination clauses,* which give one or both parties the right to terminate performance of the work in the event of certain delays, are discussed in **§ 5.16**. Other types of delay clauses and delay situations are dealt with in this section.

Examples of owner-caused delays include:

1. The owner's delay in investigating a contractor's request for a change order or time extension
2. The owner's unreasonable delay in making the site available to the contractor
3. The owner's failure to furnish materials on a timely basis, or
4. The owner's failure to make timely inspections of the project.

Some contract provisions relating to delay claims require that the owner be given reasonable notice of such upcoming claims. For instance, in *Eagle's Nest, Ltd. Partnership v. Brunzell,*[38] the contract provided that:

---

[38] 99 Nev. 710, 669 P.2d 714 (1983).

> If the contractor wishes to make a claim for an increase in the Guaranteed Maximum Price, . . . he shall give the Owner written notice thereof within a reasonable time after the occurrence of the event giving rise to such claim . . . . Claims arising from the delay shall be made within a reasonable time after delay . . . .[39]

The contractor, Brunzell, sued the owner for additional costs and expenses incurred because of construction delay in the building of a condominium complex.[40] The contractor argued that the owner's failure to provide the appropriate number of large precast concrete forms (a responsibility assigned by the contract to the owner) resulted in substantial construction delays. The owner countered that insufficient notice of the delay claim was given. On appeal to the Nevada Supreme Court, the judgment for $544,386.78 in favor of the contractor was affirmed, reimbursing the contractor for its costs and expenses related to the several-month delay. The court held that a letter from Brunzell consisting of notice that (1) difficulties had arisen for which Brunzell was disclaiming any liability, and (2) Brunzell expected to be compensated for any resulting delay, was sufficient although at the time the notice was sent the amount of the claim was not yet determined.[41]

In *Continental Heller Corp.,*[42] the government was late in furnishing an environmental report that was a prerequisite to the issuance of a building permit. The lack of a building permit forced the contractor to adopt unanticipated construction procedures, creating inefficiencies in and delays to the work. The board held that the government's conduct constituted a constructive change entitling the contractor to an equitable adjustment.

Delay damages that are ordinarily recoverable by a contractor include increased material and other expenses resulting from escalating prices, extended duration costs, and standby costs of contractor-owned equipment. When the delay is attributable in part to the contractor and in part to the owner, the delay and consequent damages can be shared between the two parties.[43]

Some delays in construction work are the result of the owner's suspension of all or part of the work under a *suspension of work clause.* These clauses give the owner the right to halt the contractor's work, an act that would otherwise be a breach of contract, and provide contractually for the payment of any increased costs. Such a clause is found in ¶ 14.3 of the AIA Document A201 *General Conditions,* allowing an owner to suspend, delay, or interrupt the work without cause for the desired period of time. Of

---

[39] *Id.* at 713, 669 P.2d at 715.

[40] *Id.* at 712, 669 P.2d at 715.

[41] *Id.* at 715, 669 P.2d at 716.

[42] GSBCA No. 6812, 84-2 B.C.A. (CCH) ¶ 17,275 (1984).

[43] Pathman Constr. Co. v. Hi-Way Elec. Co., 65 Ill. 3d 480, 382 N.E.2d 453 (1978).

course, the owner is thereafter expected to adjust accordingly the cost of performing the contract.

§ 5.8 —No Damage for Delay Clauses

A typical no damage for delay clause is similar to the following:

> The contractor agrees to make no claim for damages for delay in the performance of this contract occasioned by any act or omission of the [owner] or any of its representatives and agrees that any such claim shall be fully compensated for by an extension of time to complete performance of the work as provided herein.[44]

This clause has been the subject of much litigation with varied results from state to state. Some courts generally enforce such a clause unless the delay:

1. Is not contemplated by the parties
2. Amounts to an abandonment of the contract
3. Is caused by bad faith of the owner
4. Amounts to active interference by the owner.[45]

Other jurisdictions either do not recognize the active interference exception,[46] or they construe the no damage for delay clause broadly, which favors the owner. Courts in other jurisdictions construe the clause narrowly,[47]

---

[44] Kalisch-Jarcho, Inc. v. City of N.Y., 58 N.Y.2d 377, 448 N.E.2d 413, 461 N.Y.S.2d 746 (1983).

[45] Blake Constr. Co. v. C.J. Coakley Co., 431 A.2d 569, 579 (D.C. 1981). The court stated:

> [D]elays . . . resulted from conduct amounting to active interference, largely due to Blake's improper work sequencing. Specifically, we refer to the trial court's findings of Blake's failure, after receiving notice from Coakley, to take effective steps to prevent further installation of pipes, ducts and electrical conduits contrary to the subcontract's terms; to provide heat for tarp-enclosed spaces; to assure that Coakley would have a reasonably clear work area; and to assure that fireproofing in place would not be damaged by other subcontractors or the elements.

[46] Chicago College of Osteopathic Medicine v. George A. Fuller Co., 719 F.2d 1335 (7th Cir. 1983); Kalisch-Jarcho, Inc. v. City of N.Y., 58 N.Y.2d 377, 448 N.E.2d 413, 461 N.Y.S.2d 746 (1983).

[47] U.S. Indus., Inc. v. Blake Constr. Co., 671 F.2d 539 (D.C. Cir. 1982); Giammetta Assocs., Inc. v. J.J. White, Inc., 573 F. Supp. 112 (E.D. Pa. 1983). Neither of the clauses mentioned delays caused by suppliers, although the clause in *Blake* referred to delays due to the furnishing of materials. It was held that the clauses do not apply to supplier-caused delays.

thus favoring the contractor by limiting the types of delay to which the clause will apply.

In California, state law significantly limits the use of a no damage for delay clause in the public contracts context.[48]

§ 5.9 Nonpayment

Because payment of the contract price is probably the most important of the owner's few obligations under construction contracts, it is not surprising that most nonpayments by owners constitute breaches of contract. The nonpayments arise in many different contexts.

A Minnesota Supreme Court case[49] arose out of an owner's refusal to make the final payment to a house builder of $7,500, out of a total contract price of $75,000, until all defects were repaired and the builder gave up its lien rights. The builder refused to release its lien rights and did not make the repairs. The court found that the owner had breached the contract with the builder and awarded the builder damages in the full amount of the final payment, less the amount saved by not repairing the defects.

In another case,[50] an owner who was dissatisfied with the quality and timeliness of a house builder's work notified the builder that he wanted to change the weekly payments to a single payment after the owner was satisfied that all the work was completed. When the builder objected, the owner said that no more payments would be made until the house was completely finished. The builder walked off the job and sued the owner. The Indiana Court of Appeals held that the owner had repudiated the contract by refusing to make further payments and that the builder was justified in stopping performance and treating the contract as terminated.

By adopting an arbitrary performance evaluation system, the government in one case determined certain work to be unsatisfactory and deducted some $4,035 from the first monthly progress payment of about $11,095 owed to a refuse removal and cleaning contractor.[51] The contractor then abandoned the job. The Board of Contract Appeals held that the substantial underpayment was a breach of contract justifying the contractor's abandonment of the work.

Progress or installment payments are the usual method of paying a contractor under construction contracts. The failure to make progress payments because of a legitimate dispute is usually not such a material breach as to authorize a contractor to abandon the work and sue for damages.

---

[48] Cal. Pub. Cont. Code § 7102 (West).

[49] Zobel & Dahl Constr. v. Crotty, 356 N.W.2d 42 (Minn. 1984).

[50] Burras v. Canal Constr. & Design Co., 470 N.E.2d 1362 (Ind. Ct. App. 1984).

[51] Building Maintenance Co., ENGBCA No. 4115, 83-2 B.C.A. (CCH) ¶ 16,629 (1983).

However, an unjustified material failure by the owner to make progress payments or an outright refusal to pay may entitle the contractor to rescind and recover the reasonable value of the labor and materials furnished.[52]

§ 5.10 Disputes Involving Subcontractors

Subcontractors have successfully sued owners in a variety of cases despite the lack of privity of contract. For instance, in *Berkel & Co. Contractors, Inc. v. Providence Hospital,*[53] the subcontractor, Berkel, sued the owner and its architect on tort theories to recover what it had expended on unaccepted piles, alleging a breach of duty in directing pile installation. The owner's defense of lack of privity was disposed of when the court cited cases holding that a duty may arise from a social relationship as well as from a contractual relationship. The court quoted Professor Prosser: "[B]y entering into contract with A, the defendant may place himself in such a relation toward B that the law will impose upon him an obligation, sounding in tort and not in contract, to act in such way that B will not be injured."[54]

The hospital argued that even if privity were not a defense, the facts showed that no duty was owed to Berkel. The court said:

> In deciding whether to impose a duty in a construction contract, the trial court should analyze six factors:
>
> "(1) [T]he extent to which the transaction was intended to affect the other person; (2) the foreseeability of harm to him; (3) the degree of certainty that he suffered injury; (4) the closeness of the connection between the defendant's conduct and the injury; (5) the moral blame attached to such conduct; and (6) the policy of preventing future harm."
>
> . . . Under this standard, Providence clearly owes Berkel a duty to act reasonably in directing and approving pile construction work.[55]

Other courts, however, are reluctant to dispose of the privity requirement. For instance, the Third Circuit ruled that an owner could not recover from a subcontractor under Delaware law in negligence for economic loss, absent privity of contract.[56] That court further held that the owner could not maintain an action for breach of contract against a subcontractor on a third-party beneficiary theory.

---

[52] Integrated, Inc. v. Alec Fergusson Elec. Contractor, 250 Cal. App. 2d 287, 58 Cal. Rptr. 503 (1967).

[53] 454 So. 2d 496 (Ala. 1984).

[54] *Id.* at 502.

[55] *Id.* at 502–03 (citations omitted).

[56] Pierce Assocs., Inc. v. Nemours Found., 865 F.2d 530 (3d Cir. 1989).

This stance is more consistent with the intent of the language used in AIA Document A201, *General Conditions,* in which ¶ 1.1.2 reads in relevant part, "The Contract Documents shall not be construed to create a contractual relationship of any kind . . . between the Owner and the Subcontractor or Subsubcontractor . . . ." The *General Conditions* are usually incorporated into subcontracts between the contractor and subcontractor to avoid any misunderstanding as to each party's proper role.

REMEDIES

§ 5.11 Damages

A contractor's damage remedy will vary according to the situation giving rise to the claim. There are two main types of claims for which recovery may be sought: (1) claims for damages when the owner's breach prevents the contractor from completing the project; and (2) claims for extra costs incurred by the contractor because of extra work or delays.

§ 5.12 —Prevention of Completion

Generally, "contract performance is excused when it is hindered or rendered impossible by the other party . . . . Stated differently, every contract contains an implied condition that each party will not unjustifiably hinder the other from performing."[57]

If the owner's breach prevents the contractor from completing work on the project, the contractor usually claims a damage remedy in the amount of the profit the contractor could have expected had it been allowed to complete the work. The expected profit is usually measured as the contract price less the actual or estimated cost to the contractor of completing the work.[58] Some courts hold that the contractor may additionally recover amounts already spent for material and labor, but must deduct prepayments or progress payments made by the owner.[59] In addition, a contractor

[57] Zobel & Dahl Constr. v. Crotty, 356 N.W.2d 42, 45 (Minn. 1984).

[58] Della Ratta, Inc. v. American Better Community Developers, Inc., 38 Md. App. 119, 380 A.2d 627, 639 (1977); Holman v. Sorenson, 556 P.2d 499, 500 (Utah 1976); Williams v. Kerns, 153 Ga. App. 259, 265 S.E.2d 605, 606 (1980).

[59] Williams v. Kerns, 153 Ga. App. 259, 265 S.E.2d 605, 606, 609 (1980); First Atl. Bldg. Corp. v. Neubauer Constr. Co., 352 So. 2d 103, 104–05 (Fla. Dist. Ct. App. 1977) (contractor allowed to recover lost profit plus reasonable cost of labor and materials incurred in good faith in partial performance).

may normally recover incidental and consequential damages arising from the owner's breach.[60]

Damage awards for lost profits plus consequential and incidental damages give expression to the general principle of contract law that damages normally fulfill a party's expectation interest. In awarding damages, the court tries to place the complaining party in the position it could have expected to be had the contract been carried out.[61] A contractor's damage award is further subject to the general requirement, originating in the celebrated case of *Hadley v. Baxendale,*[62] that recovery for breach of contract includes only foreseeable damages.[63]

Damages may be *foreseeable* either because they are likely to follow from the breach in the ordinary course of events, or because they are likely to result from special circumstances the breaching party had reason to know of at the time the contract was formed.[64] A contractor in construction cases must establish three elements to recover lost profits due to a breach of contract by the owner:

1. That breach by the owner was the cause of the loss
2. That when the contract was executed, the owner could reasonably foresee that lost profits would result from a breach
3. That lost profits can be proved with reasonable certainty.[65]

---

[60] *Consequential damages* include losses resulting from the breaching party's defective performance. *See* Restatement (Second) of Contracts § 347B and cmt. c (1981). In Tull v. Gundersons, Inc., 707 P.2d 940, 946 (Colo. 1985), for example, the court held that consequential damages relating to the cost of equipment leases when the equipment remained idle due to the owner's breach were recoverable. *Incidental damages* include costs incurred in a reasonable effort to mitigate losses. Restatement (Second) of Contracts § 347B and cmt. c (1981). In Spang Indus., Inc., Fort Pitt Bridge Div. v. Aetna Casualty & Sur. Co., 512 F.2d 365, 367, 370 (2d Cir. 1975), for example, the court upheld an allowance of damages covering extra costs incurred when the contractor, in a good faith effort to mitigate damages, embarked on a crash program to pour concrete before the onset of winter.

[61] Gundersons, Inc. v. Tull, 678 P.2d 1061, 1064 (Colo. Ct. App. 1984), *modified on other grounds,* 709 P.2d 940 (Colo. 1985); Williams v. Kerns, 153 Ga. App. 259, 265 S.E.2d 605, 606 (1980); Restatement (Second) of Contracts §§ 344, 347 (1981).

[62] 9 Ex. Ch. 341, 156 Eng. Rep. 145 (1854).

[63] Ely v. Bottini, 179 Cal. App. 2d 287, 293–94, 3 Cal. Rptr. 756, 760 (1960); Della Ratta, Inc. v. American Better Community Developers, Inc., 38 Md. App. 119, 380 A.2d 627, 639 (1977). In *Ely,* a contractor sued a subcontractor rather than an owner. When cases cited here involve suits other than between contractors and owners, the principles they illustrate are of general application.

[64] Restatement (Second) of Contracts § 351(2) (1981).

[65] Della Ratta, Inc. v. American Better Community Developers, Inc., 38 Md. App. 119, 380 A.2d 627, 639 (1977).

In construction cases, the courts are likely to have little difficulty finding lost profits to have been a foreseeable element of damages following from an owner's breach. In *Della Ratta, Inc. v. American Better Community Developers, Inc.,*[66] for example, the court found that the contractor's lost profits were foreseeable (although not recoverable for lack of certainty) because the owner should have known that the contractor entered into the building contract to make a profit.

The contractor may have more difficulty proving the foreseeability of consequential damages. To establish such damages, the contractor must prove that they follow from particular circumstances of which the owner had reason to know at the time the contract was formed. In *Traylor v. Henkels & McCoy, Inc.,*[67] the court denied the contractor's claim for damages arising from the liquidation of the contractor's business, because the contractor failed to show that the owner had been aware that the contractor was depending on the owner's payments to stay in business.

All actual damages recovered by a contractor are subject to another general contract law principle requiring that damages be certain. Unlike the foreseeability requirement, the certainty requirement may prevent recovery of lost profits as well as consequential damages. In *Della Ratta* the court held that lost profits were foreseeable, but it denied the contractor's claim for lost profits because the contractor had failed to prove them with sufficient certainty.[68] Although contractors need prove the amount of their damages only with reasonable certainty, and not with absolute certainty, the contractor must provide "a reasonable basis for computation and the best evidence obtainable under the circumstances of the case that will enable the trier of fact to arrive at a fairly approximate estimate of the loss."[69] The court in *Della Ratta,* however, found that the contractor had not proved lost profits beyond mere speculation.[70]

A final contract law principle affecting a contractor's recovery of consequential damages is the general requirement of *mitigation:* consequential damages that a claimant could have avoided are not recoverable. In *Gundersons, Inc. v. James H. Tull,*[71] for example, a contractor was denied recovery of the cost of retaining its superintendent after the owner terminated the project, because the contractor could have avoided this cost by temporarily laying off the superintendent. The court held, however, that the cost of

---

[66] *Id.*

[67] 99 Idaho 560, 585 P.2d 970, 972–73 (1979).

[68] 38 Md. App. 119, 380 A.2d 627, 639 (1977).

[69] Tull v. Gundersons, Inc., 709 P.2d 940, 945 (Colo. 1985) (citations omitted).

[70] 38 Md. App. 119, 380 A.2d 627, 641 (1977).

[71] 678 P.2d 1061, 1064–65 (Colo. Ct. App. 1984), *modified on other grounds,* 709 P.2d 940 (Colo. 1985).

maintaining long-term equipment leases was unavoidable and therefore recoverable.

§ 5.13 —Extra Work

A different measure of damages determines the amount of a contractor's recovery for extra work. A contractor who incurs extra expense as a result of changes ordered after a project has begun may generally recover those extra costs as damages. The contractor's recovery may be based on a provision in the contract providing for equitable adjustments, or if the extra work was not covered by a specific contract clause, on a quantum meruit theory, allowing the contractor to obtain the reasonable value of services and material benefits conferred on the owner.[72] Some courts may under certain circumstances allow quantum meruit recovery for extra costs even when an express contract exists.[73] Under either an equitable adjustments clause or a quantum meruit theory, recoverable extra costs include the costs of materials, labor, subcontracts, overtime, and additional equipment.[74]

In contractors' suits against private owners, as in suits under government contracts, the acceptable methods of proving the extra costs resulting from a breach are a matter of some controversy. Most courts would prefer the contractor to give evidence showing the actual costs caused by each change or breach.[75] Such precision in proving causation and damages may be difficult, however, and contractors may resort to the total cost method to prove damages. Under the total cost method, the extra costs resulting from a change or breach are computed by deducting the bid estimate from the actual cost incurred by the contractor.[76]

---

[72] Affholder, Inc. v. Southern Rock, Inc., 736 F.2d 1007, 1011, 1014 (5th Cir. 1984) (recovery under specific contract provision); C. Norman Peterson Co. v. Container Corp., 172 Cal. App. 3d 628, 218 Cal. Rptr. 592 (1985) (recovery on quantum meruit theory).

[73] *E.g.*, Southern Bell Tel. & Tel. Co. v. Acme Elec. Contractors, Inc., 418 So. 2d 1187 (Fla. 1983).

[74] *See, e.g.*, Affholder, Inc. v. Southern Rock, Inc., 736 F.2d 1007, 1014 (5th Cir. 1984) (cost of materials); *In re* King Enters., 678 F.2d 73, 77 (8th Cir. 1982) (cost of materials and labor); General Ins. Co. of Am. v. Hercules Constr. Co., 385 F.2d 13, 21 (8th Cir. 1967) (overtime costs; suit by contractor against subcontractor's surety); Natkin & Co. v. George A. Fuller Co., 347 F. Supp. 17, 35 (W.D. Mo. 1972) (overtime costs and additional equipment costs); Union Bldg. Corp. v. J&J Bldg. & Maintenance Contractors, Inc., 578 S.W.2d 519, 520 (Tex. Civ. App. 1979) (subcontractors' extra costs).

[75] *See, e.g.*, Highland Constr. Co. v. Union Pac. R.R., 683 P.2d 1042, 1046–47 (Utah 1984).

[76] *Id.* at 1046.

The inadequacies of the total cost theory have long been recognized by the courts. The method may produce an inaccurate figure for the extra costs caused by a change or breach either if the bid was unrealistically low or if factors other than the change or breach in question contributed to the added costs.[77] Some courts, however, may allow a contractor to prove extra costs using the total cost method under certain restricted circumstances that minimize its potential inaccuracies. The Utah Supreme Court, for example, has listed four conditions under which the total cost method is acceptable for determining damages for extra work:

1. If the nature of the particular losses makes it impossible or impracticable to determine the losses accurately
2. If the bid or estimate was realistic
3. If the actual costs incurred were reasonable, and
4. If the plaintiff was not itself responsible for the added costs.[78]

Principal elements of damages recoverable by a contractor for owner-caused delay include extended overhead and equipment rental costs and escalation costs.[79] Overhead and equipment rental costs are recoverable as delay damages only if incurred for an extended period of time. Extended overhead costs may be of two types: home-office overhead, including general and administrative expenses at the central office, such as rents and salaries; and field or jobsite overhead, including on-site expenses such as telephones, field payroll, electricity, and rents.[80]

Further controversy surrounds the method of calculating the home-office overhead expenses attributable to a contract.[81] For government

---

[77] *E.g.,* John F. Harkins Co. v. School Dist., 313 Pa. Super. 425, 460 A.2d 260, 265 (1983) (suit by contractor against public entity).

[78] Highland Constr. Co. v. Union Pac. R.R., 683 P.2d 1042, 1047 (Utah 1984).

[79] Guy James Constr. Co. v. Trinity Indus., Inc., 644 F.2d 525, 532–33 (5th Cir. 1981) (extended overhead; contractor sued supplier); Arcon Constr. Co. v. South Dakota Cement Plant, 349 N.W.2d 407, 413–15 (S.D. 1984) (extended equipment rental; contractor sued supplier); Higgins v. City of Fillmore, 639 P.2d 192, 194 (Utah 1981) (escalation; contractor sued public owner).

[80] *E.g.,* District Concrete Co. v. Bernstein Concrete Corp., 418 A.2d 1030, 1038 (D.C. 1980) (field overhead).

[81] Some courts require the contractor to prove that the extended home-office overhead costs claimed were additional to the overhead expenses the contractor would have experienced without the delay; that is, but for the delay, other jobs would have been obtained to absorb the overhead. *See, e.g.,* Guy James Constr. Co. v. Trinity Indus., 644 F.2d 525, 532–33 (5th Cir. 1981). Other courts reject this strict requirement of proof and allow recovery of home-office expenses if they are merely allocated to the company's various jobs on some fair basis. *See, e.g.,* General Ins. Co. v. Hercules Constr. Co., 385 F.2d 13, 23 (8th Cir. 1967).

contract cases, the board of contract appeals developed the *Eichleay formula* for determining home-office overhead costs. Under this formula, the amount of overhead allocable to a particular job is calculated based on the ratio of billings for the particular job to the total billings by the company for that period.[82] The acceptability of the Eichleay formula is somewhat uncertain at present because several decisions have rejected its use.[83] The Federal Circuit, however, upheld the use of the formula,[84] and a contractor may be able to persuade a court to accept the formula in computing damages against a private owner.[85]

§ 5.14 Rescission and Restitution

In some suits equitable remedies rather than damages may be available to the contractor against the owner. The contractor may be able to rescind the contract and restore the precontract conditions through restitution of any benefits conferred by one side on the other. If the contract as drafted fails to reflect the agreement reached by the parties, the contractor may be able to reform the contract to bring it into conformance with the agreement. See § **5.15**.

Under general principles of contract law, rescission is available to a party if the contract is based on a mutual mistake of fact. The mistake must be material or concern a basic assumption underlying the contract. The *Restatement (Second) of Contracts* accordingly recognizes that rescission is available to the adversely affected party if the mutual mistake goes to a basic assumption on which the contract was made and has a material effect on the agreed exchange of performances.[86]

In construction cases, a number of courts have stated a four-part test for rescission based on mutual mistake:

1. The mistake must go to a material feature of the contract
2. The mistake must be of grave consequence so that enforcement of the contract would be unconscionable
3. The mistake must have occurred despite the exercise of reasonable care

[82] Eichleay Corp., ASBCA No. 5183, 60-2 B.C.A. (CCH) ¶ 2688 (1960).

[83] *E.g.*, Berley Indus., Inc. v. City of N.Y., 45 N.Y.2d 683, 385 N.E.2d 281, 412 N.Y.S.2d 589 (1978).

[84] Capital Elec. Co. v. United States, 729 F.2d 743, 747 (Fed. Cir. 1984).

[85] *E.g.*, PDM Plumbing & Heating, Inc. v. Findlan, 13 Mass. App. 950, 431 N.E.2d 594, 595 (1982) (subcontractor sued both contractor and owner).

[86] Restatement (Second) of Contracts § 1521 (1981).

4. It must be possible to restore the other party to its precontract condition.[87]

In *John Burns Construction Co.,* the court granted rescission of the contract because subsoil conditions were concededly a material feature of the contract to construct a sewer pipeline, and the problems encountered with subsoil conditions were beyond the contemplation of the parties so it would have been unconscionable to enforce a predetermined price schedule for extra work.[88] The court further found that the contractor had exercised reasonable care.[89] The court held, however, that restoration of the status quo ante in that case was not a prerequisite for rescission if restoration has been made impossible through no fault of the party seeking rescission.[90]

When a court allows rescission of a contract, any benefits conferred by either party on the other generally must be restored to the party possessing them before the contract was made.[91] If a contractor has performed some work under the rescinded contract, restitution of benefits conferred takes the form of the recovery of the reasonable value of services rendered and material furnished.[92]

Under certain circumstances, rescission may be available to a contractor for unilateral mistakes in bidding. See **Chapter 4**. When the contractor discovers its bid mistake and seeks to withdraw its bid before acceptance by the owner, some courts have allowed rescission under conditions similar to those enumerated by the *John Burns* court for mutual mistake.[93] After a bid has been accepted and a contract formed, however, courts may be more

---

[87] *E.g.,* John Burns Constr. Co. v. Interlake, Inc., 105 Ill. App. 3d 19, 433 N.E.2d 1126 (1982).

[88] *Id.* at 1130.

[89] *Id.* at 1131.

[90] *Id.*

[91] Restatement (Second) of Contracts § 376 (1981).

[92] Carnicle v. Swann, 314 N.W.2d 311 (S.D. 1982).

[93] *E.g.,* Smith & Lowe Constr. Co. v. Herrera, 79 N.M. 239, 442 P.2d 197, 198 (1968). In *Smith* the court permitted withdrawal of the bid because:

1. The mistake was of such grave consequence that to enforce the contract would have been unconscionable
2. The mistake concerned a material and fundamental feature of the contract
3. The bidder acted in good faith and its mistake did not arise from the violation of a legal duty or from gross negligence
4. The bidder was reasonably prompt in giving notice of the error
5. The offeree's status had not changed or the offeree had been restored to the status quo so that it suffered no serious hardship or prejudice other than the loss of the bargain.

See also City of Baltimore v. De Luca-Davis Constr. Co., 210 Md. 518, 124 A.2d 557, 562 (1956).

reluctant to allow withdrawal of the bid and rescission of the contract due to unilateral mistake.[94] Rescission is more readily allowed if the owner knew or should have known of the bid mistake.[95]

In addition to mutual and unilateral mistake, material breach by the owner may be grounds for rescission of a contract by a contractor. The most commonly litigated material breach is the owner's failure to make progress payments.[96] In *Brady Brick & Supply Co. v. Lotito*[97] the contract provided for payments to be made to the contractor as the job progressed. The owner refused the contractor's second request for payment and the trial court held that this was a material breach justifying rescission.[98] The court of appeals upheld the trial court's award of rescission and restitution of the value of labor and materials already furnished under the contract, finding that the court's verdict was not manifestly against the weight of the evidence.[99]

§ 5.15 Reformation

The remedy of reformation is generally available only if a contract as drafted fails to reflect the agreement actually reached by the parties because of mutual mistake as to the contents or effect of a writing. Under such circumstances, the instrument may be reformed so as to reflect the agreement accurately.[100]

In construction contracts, a contractor may seek reformation based on claims that the scope of the work agreed to by the parties is not accurately expressed in the contract document.[101] Alternatively, the contractor may dispute whether the bid price contained in the document accurately reflects

---

[94] *See* Bruner, *Mistakes in Bids,* 4 Construction Briefings 5 (Sept. 1978), in Construction Briefings Collection 43, 47 (1982) (after bid has been accepted, rescission will be allowed for unilateral mistake only if contractee knew or should have known of error). Some courts, however, allow rescission after acceptance of the bid on basically the same grounds as before acceptance. *See, e.g.,* John J. Calnan Co. v. Talsma Builders, Inc., 67 Ill. 2d 213, 367 N.E.2d 695, 698 (1977).

[95] City of Baltimore v. De Luca-Davis Constr. Co., 210 Md. 518, 124 A.2d 557, 562 (1956) (citing Black, Rescission and Cancellation § 130 (2d ed. 1929)).

[96] See § **5.9**.

[97] 43 Ill. App. 3d 62, 356 N.E.2d 1126, 1130–31 (1976).

[98] *Id.*

[99] *Id. See also* Integrated, Inc. v. Alec Fergusson Elec. Contractor, 250 Cal. App. 2d 287, 295–97, 58 Cal. Rptr. 503, 509–10 (1967) (substantial failure to make progress payments constitutes substantial breach justifying rescission).

[100] Restatement (Second) of Contracts § 155 (1981).

[101] Ed Sparks & Sons v. Joe Campbell Constr. Co., 99 Idaho 139, 578 P.2d 681, 682–84 (1978).

the agreed price.[102] In *Paterson,* for example, both the contractor and the owner suspected a mistake in the bid at the time the bids were opened.[103] After the bid was accepted and the contract was formed, the contractor discovered the error. The trial court granted reformation of the contract, but the court of appeals reversed on the grounds that the defendant-owner at no time agreed to any price other than the price contained in the contract document.[104] Because the error was not a mutual mistake about the contents of the instrument, reformation was unavailable.[105]

§ 5.16 Termination

A termination clause allows the owner to terminate a contract either by reason of a default by the contractor or at the convenience of the owner.

If a contractor believes that it has been improperly or wrongfully terminated by the owner, the contractor may have a suit against the owner for breach of contract. In *Allen Engineering Corp. v. Lattimore*[106] a cement contractor sued a builder for breach after the builder terminated the contract. The contract's termination clause allowed the builder to terminate if the cement contractor caused undue delay or violated any condition in the contract.[107] The builder alleged that the cement contractor had violated the terms of the contract by not obtaining the required worker's compensation insurance, but the court of appeals upheld the trial court's finding that no violation had occurred.[108] The court affirmed the lower court's verdict for the cement contractor for breach of contract.[109]

Termination for convenience clauses allow owners to terminate a contract without cause and therefore can give rise to no such breach of contract actions.[110] These clauses are most often found in government contracts or

---

[102] Paterson v. Board of Trustees, 157 Cal. App. 2d 811, 321 P.2d 825 (1958).

[103] *Id.* at 814, 321 P.2d at 826.

[104] *Id.* at 814–15, 321 P.2d at 828.

[105] *Id.* at 817, 321 P.2d at 828. The court also found that the defendant, a public body, was not estopped from refusing to reform. *Id.* at 819, 321 P.2d at 829.

[106] 201 A.2d 13, 13–15 (Md. Ct. Spec. App. 1964).

[107] *Id.* at 14.

[108] *Id.* at 15.

[109] *Id.* at 16. *See also, e.g.,* Pathman Elec. Co. v. Hi-way Elec. Co., 65 Ill. App. 3d 480, 382 N.E.2d 453, 455–56, 458 (1978) (contractor's termination of subcontractor for cause was claimed to be improper because contractor failed to comply with notice requirements, but court upheld verdict for contractor because subcontractor had raised issue for first time on appeal).

[110] *See, e.g.,* Nolan Bros., Inc. v. United States, 405 F.2d 1250, 1253 (Ct. Cl. 1969) (termination for convenience clause gave fullest discretion to contracting officer to terminate work according to best interests of government).

subcontracts under government contracts, but may appear in private contracts as well.[111] Although AIA Document A201, *General Conditions,* provides only for termination for cause, it does allow suspension for convenience. A contractor terminated for convenience may, however, have an action to recover costs incurred plus profits already earned.[112]

§ 5.17 Liens

The laws of every state provide a remedy in the form of a mechanic's lien for anyone contributing labor or materials to a construction project, including a contractor.[113] Because the mechanic's lien is entirely a creature of state statute, a contractor seeking to foreclose such a lien must look to the particular details of the statute in force in the jurisdiction in which the project is located.[114] Different states' mechanic's lien statutes vary in many specific respects, including, for example, the date from which the mechanic's lien exists[115] and the notice requirements imposed on the claimant under the lien.[116]

---

[111] *E.g., id.;* United States Propellers v. Zenith Plastics Co., 187 Cal. App. 2d 780, 10 Cal. Rptr. 137 (1960) (government contracts or subcontracts thereunder); Arc Elec. Constr. Co. v. George A. Fuller Co., 24 N.Y.2d 99, 247 N.E.2d 111, 299 N.Y.S.2d 129, 131 (1969) (private contract; clause allowed intermediate contractor to terminate subcontract at any time prior to completion).

[112] *See* Nolan Bros., Inc. v. United States, 405 F.2d 1250, 1253 (Ct. Cl. 1969) (government contract).

[113] *See, e.g.,* Cal. Civ. Code § 3110 (Deering 1991); *see also* Lifschitz & Little, *Mechanics' Liens: Basic Principles and Guidelines,* 5 Construction Briefings 1, 1 (Sept. 1982). Because stop notices are similar to mechanic's liens, this section does not discuss stop notices directly. Those interested in differences between stop notices and mechanic's liens should consult the applicable state's statutes. For a discussion of the stop notice remedy in California, see J. Acret, Attorney's Guide to California Construction Contracts and Disputes 151–52 (1976).

[114] *See, e.g.,* Wingler v. Niblack, 58 Ill. App. 3d 287, 374 N.E.2d 252, 253 (1978).

[115] In most states, the lien is deemed to exist from a date prior to the filing of the lien claim; that is, the lien relates back to a period predating the lien claim. *See, e.g.,* Hodgins v. Marquette Iron Mining Co., 503 F. Supp. 88, 90 (W.D. Mich. 1980) (under Michigan law, liens attach at time of commencement of work). In some states, however, the lien does not relate back to a time before filing of the claim. *See, e.g.,* Mervin L. Blades & Son, Inc. v. Lighthouse Sound Marina & Country Club, 37 Md. App. 265, 377 A.2d 523, 526 (1977) (under Maryland law, lien attaches only after claimant prevails on lien claim in court).

[116] *See, e.g.,* Peninsular Supply Co. v. C.B. Day Realty, 423 So. 2d 500, 501 (Fla. Dist. Ct. App. 1982) (notice to owner required within 45 days of first furnishing materials); William Moors, Inc. v. Pine Lake Shopping Ctr., Inc., 74 Mich. App. 12, 253 N.W.2d 658, 659 (1977) (notice required within 90 days of first furnishing material or supplying labor); Cal. Civ. Code § 3114 (West) (preliminary 20-day notice required in order to enforce lien rights).

The amount the contractor may recover under a mechanic's lien generally depends on the nature of the contract and claim as well as the applicable state statutes. Under a fixed-price contract, the contractor may recover the contract price less amounts already paid by the owner or credits due the owner.[117] If the contract is not a fixed-price contract, or if recovery is sought for extra work, the amount of the contractor's recovery will be the reasonable value of labor and materials.[118] In a cost-plus contract, the contractor's recovery may include profit and overhead if specified in the contract.[119]

Unless the mechanic's lien statute provides that the statutory lien is the exclusive remedy, an equitable lien may in some instances be available if the claimant fails to perfect the mechanic's lien. A case in point is *Peninsular Supply Co. v. C.B. Day Realty.*[120] In this case, a supplier not in privity with the owner failed to comply with the 45-day notice requirement to perfect a mechanic's lien.[121] The court nevertheless held that the supplier had an equitable lien claim because the mechanic's lien statute explicitly provided that the statutory lien was not the exclusive remedy.[122]

§ 5.18 Exculpatory Clauses

Section 5.5 discussed the exculpatory clause in *Ell-Dorer Contracting Co. v. State.*[123] That type of specific disclaimer of responsibility for test results is rather common, particularly in public contracts.[124] However, such exculpatory clauses do not relieve the owner of responsibility for positive representations in the contract. In *E.H. Morrill Co. v. State,*[125] § 1A-12 of the contract in question provided:

> The site is situated on a terminal moraine. The soil is composed of granite boulders, cobbles, pebbles, and granite sand. Boulders which may be

---

[117] *See, e.g.,* Knoell Constr. Co. v. Hanson, 205 Neb. 305, 287 N.W.2d 435, 436, 438 (1980).

[118] *See, e.g.,* Wingler v. Niblack, 58 Ill. App. 3d 287, 374 N.E.2d 252, 253–54 (1978) (extra work); Maxwell v. Anderson, 18 Mont. 215, 593 P.2d 29, 30, 32–33 (1979) (when "estimated cost ceiling" in contract was not firm limit, contractor could recover value of labor and materials).

[119] *See, e.g.,* Sloane v. Malcolm Price, Inc., 339 A.2d 43, 45 n.1 (D.C. 1975). *See generally* Lifschitz & Little, *Mechanic's Liens: Basic Principles and Guidelines,* 5 Construction Briefings 1, 3 (Sept. 1982).

[120] 423 So. 2d 500 (Fla. Dist. Ct. App. 1982).

[121] *Id.* at 501–02.

[122] *Id.*

[123] 197 N.J. Super. 175, 484 A.2d 356 (App. Div. 1984).

[124] *See, e.g.,* Wunderlich v. State, 65 Cal. 2d 777, 423 P.2d 545, 56 Cal. Rptr. 473 (1967).

[125] 65 Cal. 2d 787, 789–90, 423 P.2d 551, 553, 56 Cal. Rptr. 479 (1967).

> encountered in the site grading and other excavation work on the site vary in size from one foot to four feet in diameter. The dispersion of boulders varies from approximately six feet to twelve feet in all directions, including the vertical.

In its ruling the court stated:

> Section 1A-12 did not purport merely to present the results of the state's own tests and investigations . . . but flatly asserts that the bidders could expect to confront only specified site conditions. It is clearly a "positive and material representation as to a condition presumably within the knowledge of the government. . . ."
>
> . . . The responsibility of a governmental agency for positive representations it is deemed to have made through defective plans and specifications "is not overcome by the general clauses requiring the contractor to examine the site, to check up the plans, and to assume responsibility for the work . . . ." (United States v. Spearin, 248 U.S. 132, 137, 39 S. Ct. 59, 61, 63 L. Ed. 166). Accordingly, the language in section 4 requiring the bidder to "satisfy himself as to the character . . . of surface and subsurface materials or obstacles to be encountered" cannot be relied upon to overcome those representations as to materials and obstacles which the state positively affirms in section 1A-12 not to exist, and plaintiff was entitled to rely and act thereon.[126]

In *Stenerson v. City of Kalispell,*[127] a lump-sum contract for rough grading of a golf course provided that the calculations on the "Rough Grading Plan" were "approximate" and that the contractors "shall make [their] own determination as to the amount of topsoil and grading work to be done before submitting a bid."[128] The contractors sued to recover the cost of moving an extra 27,477 cubic yards of earth that had not been included in the rough grading plan calculations. The owner argued that by reason of the language quoted above, the contractors had assumed the risk of extra quantities of earth. Nevertheless, in affirming the judgment awarding the contractors the total cost of the overrun, the Supreme Court of Montana said that contractors have the right to rely on plans and specifications furnished to them in bidding on and contracting a job. Further, the court stated:

> We affirmed the district judge in that decision but noted: "We are not here holding that such exculpatory clauses may not be enforced in other situations, that detrimental reliance may be assumed in all cases, or that parties to such contracts are bound to exercise anything less than reasonable and prudent judgment. In other words we look to 'justifiable reliance.'"[129]

---

[126] *Id.* at 792–93, 423 P.2d at 553–54.

[127] 629 P.2d 773 (Mont. 1981).

[128] *Id.* at 774.

[129] *Id.* at 776.

CHAPTER 6

SUING A GOVERNMENT: SPECIAL CONSIDERATIONS

Scott E. Ransick
Robert D. Wallick

Scott E. Ransick is an associate at Steptoe & Johnson in Washington, D.C. He holds a B.A. degree from Rice University, a J.D. with high honors from the University of Arkansas at Fayetteville, and an L.L.M. from the Judge Advocate General's School for the Army. He is licensed to practice law in the District of Columbia, Arkansas, and various federal courts and agencies. Mr. Ransick's primary practice has been government contract law and related litigation.

Robert D. Wallick has been a partner at Steptoe & Johnson in Washington, D.C., since 1963. He holds a B.S. degree in electrical engineering and one in business administration from Lehigh University, Bethlehim, Pennsylvania, and also an L.L.B. degree from George Washington University. He is licensed to practice in the District of Columbia, Maryland, and before various federal courts and agencies. Mr. Wallick is a member of a special panel created by the Congress in 1991 to streamline acquisition statutes, a member of the Council of the U.S. Court of Claims, and an active participant on various bar associations and other committees. He lectures and writes frequently on government contract issues.

§ 6.1 Introduction

§ 6.2 Some Special Perils

§ 6.3 Sovereign Immunity and Its Waiver

§ 6.4 Waivers by the Federal Government

§ 6.5 —Federal Waiver for Contract Controversies

§ 6.6 —Judicial Review of Bid Protests
§ 6.7 —Administrative Forum for Bid Protests
§ 6.8 Waiver by States and State Agencies
§ 6.9 Funding and Fiscal Restrictions
§ 6.10 —Federal Fiscal Restrictions
§ 6.11 —Fiscal Restrictions on State and Other Governmental Bodies
§ 6.12 Authority to Act
§ 6.13 Ratification by Contracting Officer
§ 6.14 Authority to Act for the State

§ 6.1 Introduction

Governments and governmental bodies—federal, state, and local—account for much of today's construction work. Because of inherent government complexities and their special legal status, contracting with them is different from contracting with private owners. Special pitfalls and hurdles await the aggrieved contractor who contemplates a claim against a government body.

§ 6.2 Some Special Perils

Over the past decade, the federal government has become increasingly concerned about what it and the public perceive to be fraud and waste in federal procurement. New statutes and regulations have been enacted and old ones revised. New enforcement organizations and procedures have been created and old ones instilled with an increased vigor. Our experience is that generally, state and local governments are on similar tracks.

Construction contractors seeking or performing federal contracts should have in place vigorous ethics, compliance, and training programs. The federal government believes responsible contractors do just that. And there is great risk that any deviation from a statutory, regulatory, or contractual requirement might be viewed by the government as a basis for seeking civil or criminal penalties and for suspending and debarring a contractor from further federal contracts.

The following list, although far from complete, identifies some of the initiatives and processes for contractors to consider in fashioning ethics, compliance, and training programs:

1. The Truth in Negotiation Act and related provisions in the Federal Acquisition Regulation (FAR)[1] mandate that when cost or pricing

[1] 10 U.S.C. § 2306(a) (1988); FAR § 15.804 (1991).

information is to be provided to the contracting officer, the data must be accurate, complete, and current.

2. The FAR system specifies cost principles and cost accounting standards that may govern how a contractor is to account for its costs when necessary.[2]
3. A relatively new "procurement integrity" statute and related regulations[3] potentially penalize, inter alia, unauthorized receipt or disclosure of proprietary and source selection information.
4. Federal criminal statutes, such as 18 U.S.C. § 287, which sanctions, inter alia, certain false statements to the federal government, and civil statutes, such as 31 U.S.C. § 3730, which penalizes certain false claims to the federal government, have potentially broad reaches and are being vigorously enforced.
5. Under FAR § 9.4, federal agencies have the authority to suspend or debar a contractor government-wide, if they determine the contractor is not presently responsible. The FAR provision provides guidance as to when and why this action should occur.
6. The federal government has created inspector generals (IGs) at its principal departments and agencies. One of their primary missions is to investigate possible procurement misconduct. The IGs have broad power to subpoena documents and are seeking power to subpoena testimony.
7. Areas of primary focus by the IGs have included possibilities of labor mischarging, defective pricing, product substitution (providing something other than what the government specified), and misconduct by government or contractor personnel.
8. Formal certifications are being required of contractors for a host of reasons.

§ 6.3 Sovereign Immunity and Its Waiver

The doctrine of sovereign immunity, which holds that a government may not be sued without its consent, is ancient but not universally hallowed. Part 9 of the American Bar Association's Model Procurement Code for State and Local Governments (ABA Model Code) calls for waiver of sovereign immunity for contracts.[4] The federal government and many state governments have enacted waivers in various forms and degrees.

Nevertheless, considerable vitality remains in the old doctrine. In fact, a few states have not waived immunity on construction contracts. Moreover,

---

[2] FAR pt. 30.

[3] 41 U.S.C. § 423 (1988); FAR § 3.104.

[4] *See* § 9-401, Waiver of sovereign immunity in connection with contracts.

waivers are often limited to special tribunals and coupled with rigid temporal, procedural, and definitional strictures. The immunity doctrine and prejudices in favor of the doctrine may weigh heavily in judicial interpretations of unclear legislative grants of authority or relief.

§ 6.4 Waivers by the Federal Government

The federal government's sovereign immunity in contract actions has been waived by four statutes—the Contract Disputes Act of 1978,[5] the Federal Courts Improvement Act of 1982,[6] the Competition in Contracting Act of 1984,[7] and the Administrative Procedure Act[8]—and by the progeny of a landmark decision, *Scanwell Laboratories, Inc. v. Shaffer.*[9] The federal waivers are broad, extending to pre-award and post-award controversies; but, as explained in **§§ 6.9** and **6.12**, the waivers are not unlimited.

§ 6.5 —Federal Waiver for Contract Controversies

The Contract Disputes Act[10] governs controversies arising after a procurement contract is formed. It applies to any express or implied-in-fact contract for procurement of property (other than real property in being) or services, or construction, alteration, repair, or maintenance of real property.[11] Jurisdiction under the Act is initiated as follows:

> All claims by a contractor against the government relating to a contract shall be in writing and shall be submitted to the contracting officer for a decision. All claims by the government against a contractor relating to a contract shall be the subject of a decision by the contracting officer.[12]

---

[5] 41 U.S.C. §§ 601–613 (1988).

[6] 28 U.S.C. §§ 1295, 1491 (1988).

[7] 31 U.S.C. §§ 3551–3556 (1988).

[8] 5 U.S.C. § 702 (1988).

[9] 424 F.2d 859 (D.C. Cir. 1970).

[10] 41 U.S.C. §§ 601–613 (1988).

[11] *Id.* § 602(a).

[12] *Id.* § 605(a). In addition to its jurisdiction under the Contract Disputes Act over appeals of contracting officer decisions, the United States Claims Court has jurisdiction

> to render judgment upon any claim against the United States founded either upon the Constitution, or any Act of Congress or any regulation of an executive department or upon any express or implied contract with the United States, or for liquidated or unliquidated damages in cases not sounding in tort.

28 U.S.C. § 1491(a)(1) (1988).

This parallels a provision in the now-superseded Tucker Act, 28 U.S.C. § 1491 (1970 & Supp. V 1975). Prior to March 1, 1979, the effective date of the Contract Disputes

The contractor may appeal the contracting officer's decision either to an agency board of contract appeals (within 90 days of receipt of the decision) or to the United States Claims Court (at the present time within 12 months of the decision, but this may be reduced by the Congress to 90 days). The time limitations are jurisdictional and strictly construed.[13]

In either tribunal, the contractor is entitled, in effect, to de novo hearing and determination on its claim.[14] Both forums have subpoena power and allow discovery. Decisions by the agency boards and their pre-Contract Disputes Act progenitors and by the United States Claims Court are reported by private legal publishing services.[15]

The agency boards and the Claims Court are generally well respected and viewed by the private and government bars as professional and independent. Board membership is governed by 41 U.S.C. § 607(b)(1). The United States Claims Court is an Article 1 (executive department) court. Its 16 judges are appointed by the president, with approval by the Senate, to renewable 15-year terms.

The procedures followed by the boards and the Claims Court differ considerably. These differences may be of significance for a particular case in terms of time and cost of litigation. For example, pursuant to statutory requirements, the agency boards provide expedited procedures for claims of $10,000 or less and accelerated procedures for those of $50,000 or less.[16] It should also be noted that the Claims Court appears to be stricter than the boards in enforcing its rules of procedure.[17]

Judgments by the boards and the United States Claims Court under the Contract Disputes Act are payable "promptly" and ab initio from funds appropriated for the payment of judgments.[18] Appeals of both board and Claims Court decisions rendered since October 1, 1982, are to the United

---

Act, waiver of federal sovereign immunity over post-award procurement contract controversies had been under the counterpart general grant of jurisdiction to the United States Court of Claims under the Tucker Act, *id.* § 1491(a)(1), which continues to have vitality for actions not covered by the Contract Disputes Act, that is, other than procurement contract actions. *See, e.g.,* Chevron Chem. Corp. v. United States, 5 Cl. Ct. 807 (1984) (partial summary judgment was issued for breach of settlement and disposition agreement covering disposal of silvex products).

[13] 41 U.S.C. §§ 606, 609(a) (1988). *See* Cosmic Constr. Co. v. United States, 697 F.2d 1389 (Fed. Cir. 1982).

[14] 41 U.S.C. § 605(b) (1988).

[15] Agency board decisions are reported by Commerce Clearing House in *Board of Contract Appeals Decisions* (B.C.A.); Claims Court decisions appear in West Publishing Company's *Claims Court Reporter.*

[16] 41 U.S.C. §§ 605(c)(1), 608 (1988).

[17] *See, e.g.,* Claude E. Atkins Enters. v. United States, 899 F.2d 1180 (Fed. Cir. 1990) (Claims Court sua sponte dismissal of appeal for contractor failure to file status reports on time upheld).

[18] 41 U.S.C. § 612 (1988).

States Court of Appeals for the Federal Circuit.[19] The standard of review of agency board decisions is prescribed by statute as follows:

> [T]he decision of the agency board on any question of law shall not be final or conclusive, but the decision on any question of fact shall be final and conclusive and shall not be set aside unless the decision is fraudulent, or arbitrary, or capricious, or so grossly erroneous as to necessarily imply bad faith, or if such decision is not supported by substantial evidence.[20]

The standard of review of Claims Court decisions is the *clearly erroneous* standard applicable generally to federal circuit court reviews of lower court decisions.[21]

There are significant limitations upon the waiver of immunity granted by the Contract Disputes Act. First, it extends only to the types of procurement contracts described in 41 U.S.C. § 602. These include express or implied contracts whereby an executive agency procures:

1. Property other than real property in being
2. Services
3. Construction, maintenance, or repair of real property or
4. Disposal of property.[22]

The Contract Disputes Act also applies to contracts of those nonappropriated fund activities described in 28 U.S.C. §§ 1346 and 1491.[23] The Contract Disputes Act does not apply to, inter alia:

1. Grant contracts[24]
2. Service contracts involving the judiciary[25]
3. Contracts in which the government provides services rather than procures them[26]
4. Forward pricing rate agreements.[27]

---

[19] 28 U.S.C. § 1295(a)(3), (10) (1988); 41 U.S.C. § 607(g)(1)(A) (1988).

[20] 41 U.S.C. § 609(b) (1988).

[21] *See* Atlas Corp. v. United States, 895 F.2d 745, 749 (Fed. Cir.), *cert. denied,* 111 S. Ct. 46 (1990); Alger v. United States, 741 F.2d 391, 393 (Fed. Cir. 1984).

[22] 41 U.S.C. § 602 (1978).

[23] *Id.* The Contract Disputes Act may also apply to a claim arising out of a nonappropriated fund contract containing a clause giving the right to appeal to a board of contract appeals. *See, e.g.,* COVCO Haw. Corp., 83-2 B.C.A. (CCH) ¶ 16,554 (ASBCA 1983).

[24] *See, e.g.,* Busby Sch. of N. Cheyenne Tribe v. United States, 8 Cl. Ct. 596 (1985).

[25] *See, e.g.,* Erwin v. United States, 19 Cl. Ct. 47 (1989).

[26] *See* Rider v. United States, 7 Cl. Ct. 770 (1985).

[27] *See* Dillingham Shipyard, 84-1 B.C.A. (CCH) ¶ 16,984 (ASBCA 1983).

In addition, claims over $50,000 must be certified before they are presented to the contracting officer.[28] Under the Federal Acquisition Regulation (FAR) 33.207, the contractor is required to certify that its claim is "made in good faith," supported by data that is "accurate and complete to the best of the contractor's knowledge and belief," and that the claimed amount "accurately reflects the contract adjustment for which the contractor believes the Government is liable."[29] Further, FAR 33.207 provides that if the contractor is an individual, that individual must certify the claim.[30] If a contractor is not an individual, the claim may be certified by either "(i) a senior company official in charge at the contractor's plant or location involved; or (ii) an officer or general partner of the contractor having overall responsibility for the conduct of the contractor's affairs."[31] Concerning the first type of representative authorized to certify the claim, a project manager who is also a senior company official satisfies the FAR requirement.[32] Regarding the second type of representative, a president or a vice president with authority to direct the affairs of the contractor meets the FAR standard.[33] Examples of individuals who are not authorized to certify a contractor's claim include a chief cost engineer,[34] and a project manager who is not a senior company officer.[35] Both the elements of the certification and the requirements of the individual authorized to certify the claim are strictly construed and considered jurisdictional.

Interest does not start to accumulate until the claim has been received by the contracting officer, and, for claims over $50,000, interest does not start until after receipt of a certified claim.[36]

Moreover, equitable and declaratory relief,[37] and punitive damages against the government plainly appear to be outside the reach of the Contract Disputes Act's jurisdictional grant. Under the predecessor Tucker Act,[38] relief granted by the United States Court of Claims was limited to

---

[28] 41 U.S.C. § 605(c)(2) (1978). *See* W.M. Schlosser Co. v. United States, 705 F.2d 1336 (Fed. Cir. 1983).

[29] FAR 33.207(a) (1991).

[30] *Id.* 33.207(c)(1).

[31] *Id.* 33.207(c)(2).

[32] *See* Western Empire Constructors, Inc. v. United States, 20 Cl. Ct. 668 (1990).

[33] *See* Triax Co. v. United States, 20 Cl. Ct. 507 (1990).

[34] *See* Ball, Ball & Brosamer, Inc. v. United States, 878 F.2d 1426 (Fed. Cir. 1989).

[35] *See* Al Johnson Constr. Co. v. United States, 19 Cl. Ct. 732 (1990).

[36] *See* 41 U.S.C. §§ 611, 605 (1988). *See* ReCon Paving, Inc. v. United States, 745 F.2d 34, 40 (Fed. Cir. 1984); Dawco Constr., Inc. v. United States, 18 Cl. Ct. 682, 701–04 (1989), *aff'd,* 930 F.2d 872 (Fed. Cir. 1991).

[37] *See* Continental Heller Constr. v. United States, 21 Cl. Ct. 471, 473–74 (1990); Alan J. Haynes Constr. v. United States, 10 Cl. Ct. 526 (1986).

[38] 28 U.S.C. § 1491 (1970 & Supp. V 1975), discussed earlier in this section.

compensatory monetary damages,[39] and the agency boards exercised a similarly limited jurisdiction. The Contract Disputes Act was grafted onto that existing process and the Act's procedures are triggered by the filing of a claim (or certified claim). The Federal Circuit has concluded that by this and other language in the Act, Congress intended to limit relief to compensatory money damages.[40]

Before the Contract Disputes Act, the Tucker Act's grant of jurisdiction over federal contract disputes was held to be exclusive and adequate.[41] Procurement contractors could not, for example, seek equitable or declaratory relief in United States district courts under the Administrative Procedure Act.[42]

§ 6.6 —Judicial Review of Bid Protests

In a 1970 case, *Scanwell Laboratories, Inc. v. Shaffer,*[43] the United States Court of Appeals for the District of Columbia Circuit first established that an aggrieved bidder for a federal contract had "standing to sue," that is, had a right to judicial review. Thirty years earlier, in *Perkins v. Lukens Steel Co.,*[44] the Supreme Court had held to the contrary. In *Scanwell,* the District of Columbia Circuit based its conclusion that bidders had standing to sue on § 10(a) of the Administrative Procedure Act,[45] which was enacted in 1946, subsequent to *Lukens Steel.*[46]

Following the District of Columbia's decision, the other circuit courts split. Thus, in *GF Business Equipment, Inc. v. Tennessee Valley Authority,*[47] the Sixth Circuit affirmed a district court decision that an aggrieved bidder

---

[39] *See* United States v. King, 395 U.S. 1 (1969).

[40] *See* Overall Roofing & Constr., Inc. v. United States, 929 F.2d 687 (Fed. Cir. 1991), in which the Federal Circuit stated that "[i]t would be singularly inappropriate of us to invest the Claims Court with the authority Congress has specifically, intentionally, and repeatedly withheld." *Id.* at 690. Continental Heller Constr. v. United States, 21 Cl. Ct. 471, 474; Alan J. Haynes Constr. v. United States, 10 Cl. Ct. 526, 528.

[41] International Eng'g Co. v. Richardson, 512 F.2d 573, 578 (D.C. Cir. 1975), *cert. denied,* 423 U.S. 1048 (1976); Warner v. Cox, 487 F.2d 1301 (5th Cir. 1974). In *Warner,* the court noted that "the APA [Administrative Procedure Act] does not provide for review under such circumstances. Specifically exempted from review is agency action for which there is some 'other adequate remedy in a court.' 5 U.S.C. § 704. Suit under the Tucker Act in the Court of Claims has been held such an adequate remedy." *Id.* at 1304.

[42] 5 U.S.C. § 702 (1988).

[43] 424 F.2d 859 (D.C. Cir. 1970).

[44] 310 U.S. 113 (1940).

[45] 5 U.S.C. § 702 (1988).

[46] Scanwell Lab., Inc. v. Shaffer, 424 F.2d 859, 866–67.

[47] 430 F. Supp. 699 (E.D. Tenn. 1975), *aff'd mem.,* 556 F.2d 581 (6th Cir. 1977).

on a direct federal procurement contract did not have standing to sue because the bidder was not within the protected "zone of interest."[48] However, the majority of the federal circuits followed *Scanwell.*[49]

In *M. Steinthal & Co. v. Seamans*[50] the District of Columbia Circuit set out what has become the standard for judicial review of procurement solicitation and award decisions, concluding that:

> (1) courts should not overturn any procurement determination unless the aggrieved bidder demonstrates that there was no rational basis for the agency's decision; and (2) even in instances where such a determination is made, there is room for sound judicial discretion, in the presence of overriding public interest considerations, to refuse to entertain declaratory or injunctive actions in a pre-procurement context.[51]

Under the *Steinthal* standard of review, aggrieved bidders on federal procurements have had little success on the merits. Moreover, with the enactment of the Competition in Contracting Act (CICA) and its stay of contract award or performance in a Government Accounting Office (GAO) protest, the number of *Scanwell* actions has substantially decreased.[52] Nonetheless, *Scanwell* and *Steinthal* opened up the possibility of judicial review to an aggrieved bidder with a strong case.

The Court Reform Act of 1982 added complexity to this area. The jurisdictional grant to the United States Claims Court under that Act includes the following:

> (3) To afford complete relief on any contract claim brought before the contract is awarded, the court shall have exclusive jurisdiction to grant declaratory judgments and such equitable and extraordinary relief as it

---

[48] *See also* Cincinnati Elecs. Corp. v. Kleppe, 509 F.2d 1080 (6th Cir. 1975).

[49] *See, e.g.,* B.K. Instrument, Inc. v. United States, 715 F.2d 713 (2d Cir. 1983); Merriam v. Kunzig, 476 F.2d 1233 (3d Cir.), *cert. denied,* 414 U.S. 911 (1973); William F. Wilke, Inc. v. Department of Army, 485 F.2d 180 (4th Cir. 1973); Hayes Int'l Corp. v. McLucas, 509 F.2d 247 (5th Cir.), *cert. denied,* 423 U.S. 864 (1975); Armstrong & Armstrong, Inc. v. United States, 514 F.2d 402 (9th Cir. 1975); Airco, Inc. v. Energy Research & Dev. Admin., 528 F.2d 1294 (7th Cir. 1975); *but see* People's Gas, Light & Coke Co. v. United States Postal Serv., 658 F.2d 1182 (7th Cir. 1981).

[50] 455 F.2d 1289 (D.C. Cir. 1971).

[51] *Id.* at 1301.

[52] It should be noted that CICA specifically refrained from giving the GAO exclusive jurisdiction over bid protests. CICA does not affect the interested party's right to protest to the agency, or file an action in federal district court or Claims Court. *See* 31 U.S.C. § 3556 (1988). However, with the injunctive relief available in a GAO protest, courts are becoming more reluctant to grant this remedy so long as the protestor can go to the GAO. *See, e.g.,* Diverco, Inc. v. Cheney, 745 F. Supp. 739, 741 (D.D.C. 1990) (preliminary injunction denied because relief available in GAO protest prevents finding of irreparable injury if court refused to grant injunction).

> deems proper, including but not limited to injunctive relief. In exercising this jurisdiction, the court shall give due regard to the interests of national defense and national security.[53]

The government argued that, as a result of the Court Reform Act, federal district courts had no *Scanwell* jurisdiction (that is, the Claims Court jurisdiction is exclusive) and that the Claims Court's jurisdiction is limited to legal actions initiated prior to award. On the first point—exclusive jurisdiction in the Claims Court—the government's argument has not been successful. As noted above, not all circuits follow *Scanwell.* In those that do, jurisdiction generally is recognized when the suits are initiated after award under the solicitation.[54] Two circuits went further and found pre-award jurisdiction concurrent with that of the Claims Court.[55]

On the second point, that the Claims Court's jurisdiction under 28 U.S.C. § 1491(a)(3) was limited to pre-award controversies, the government was more successful. In *United States v. John C. Grimberg Co.,*[56] the plaintiffs were disappointed bidders under two government procurements and sought injunctive and declaratory relief from the Claims Court. Before award, the plaintiffs had filed protests with the contracting officer. The latter had acknowledged the protests and had advised, "[t]he bids are being evaluated and you will be advised of our decision before award is made."[57] However, the contracting officer made awards to another a few days later, without advising the plaintiffs. The disappointed bidders petitioned the Claims Court shortly thereafter. Sitting en banc, a divided Federal Circuit affirmed a Claims Court decision that concluded that the Claims Court lacked jurisdiction because suit had been initiated after award. The case was transferred to a federal district court.

In 28 U.S.C. § 1491(a)(3) the pre-award bid protest jurisdiction was created in the Claims Court, giving it jurisdiction over "any contract claim

---

[53] 28 U.S.C. § 1491(a)(3) (1988).

[54] *See, e.g.,* B.K. Instrument, Inc. v. United States, 715 F.2d 713 (2d Cir. 1983); Merriam v. Kunzig, 476 F.2d 1233 (3d Cir.), *cert. denied,* 414 U.S. 911 (1973); William F. Wilke, Inc. v. Department of Army, 485 F.2d 180 (4th Cir. 1973); Hayes Int'l Corp. v. McLucas, 509 F.2d 247 (5th Cir.), *cert. denied,* 423 U.S. 864 (1975); Rex Systems, Inc. v. Holiday, 814 F.2d 994, 997–98 (4th Cir. 1987); Armstrong & Armstrong, Inc. v. United States, 514 F.2d 402 (9th Cir. 1975); Airco, Inc. v. Energy Research & Dev. Admin., 528 F.2d 1294 (7th Cir. 1975); *but see* People's Gas, Light & Coke Co. v. United States Postal Serv., 658 F.2d 1182 (7th Cir. 1981).

[55] *See* Ulstein Maritime, Ltd. v. United States, 833 F.2d 1052, 1057–58 (1st Cir. 1987); *see, e.g.,* Coco Bros., Inc. v. Pierce, 741 F.2d 675 (3d Cir. 1984); *In re* Smith & Wesson, Inc., 757 F.2d 431 (1st Cir. 1985) (Federal Courts Improvement Act did not eliminate district court jurisdiction in pre-award cases).

[56] 702 F.2d 1362 (Fed. Cir. 1983).

[57] *Id.* at 1364.

brought before the contract is awarded." The precise reach of that jurisdiction is still being resolved judicially.

§ 6.7 —Administrative Forum for Bid Protests

Traditionally, the GAO has functioned as the administrative bid protest forum where an aggrieved federal contract bidder sought relief outside the contracting agency itself. Prior to 1984, although federal contractors and government agencies generally followed the GAO recommendations for resolving a protest, the executive branch questioned the GAO's legal authority over it on bid protest matters.[58]

The GAO's authority to resolve bid protests submitted to it was expressly established in 1984 by the Competition in Contracting Act (CICA).[59] The GAO has implemented CICA by promulgating bid protest rules detailing the extent to which the statute waived sovereign immunity in this area.[60]

Under the GAO rules "[a]n interested party may protest to the General Accounting Office a solicitation issued by or for a federal agency for the procurement of property or services, or the proposed award or the award of such a contract."[61] When filing a protest at GAO, *interested party* means "an actual or prospective bidder or offeror whose direct economic interest would be affected by the award of a contract or by the failure to award a contract."[62]

The time for filing the protest depends upon the nature of the basis for protest. If the grounds for protest are apparent upon examination of the agency solicitation or request for bid, the protestor must file before bid opening or when the contractor's proposals are initially due. Otherwise, protests are due within 10 days after the basis of the protest "is known or should have been known, whichever is earlier."[63] Untimely protests will be denied.[64] The GAO is required to issue its decision within 90 days from the date the protest is filed. However, if one of the parties requests the express

---

[58] *See, e.g.,* Scanwell Lab., Inc. v. Shaffer, 424 F.2d 859 (D.C. Cir. 1970).

[59] 31 U.S.C. §§ 3551–3556. CICA also established a jurisdiction in the General Services Administration Board of Contract Appeals to hear bid protests concerning automatic data processing contracts.

[60] 4 C.F.R. pt. 21 (1991).

[61] *Id.* § 21.1 (Filing a Protest). Although not discussed here, it should be noted that protests involving automated data processing equipment and services are not filed with the GAO, but with the General Services Administration Board of Contract Appeals. 40 U.S.C. § 759(a)-(h) (1988); 41 C.F.R. § 6101 (1991).

[62] 4 C.F.R. § 21.0(a) (1991).

[63] *Id.* § 21.2(a)(1-2).

[64] Under *id.* § 21.2(c), the GAO may consider untimely protests for good cause or if significant new issues are raised.

or accelerated option, which streamlines the process, the decision must be rendered within 45 days.[65]

The parties may request that a hearing be conducted and testimony taken.[66] However, the decision whether to allow a hearing is left to the discretion of the GAO. Should a hearing be ordered, prehearing conferences may be convened to resolve procedural matters prior to the hearing.

Under the CICA, the filing of a timely and serious protest stays the award or performance of the affected contract, unless the agency formally finds that "urgent and compelling circumstances significantly affecting interests of the United States will not permit waiting for the General Accounting Office decision."[67]

The remedies available to the protester include GAO recommendations to the contracting agency on how to proceed on the protested contract or solicitation. Examples include recommendations not to exercise contract options, terminate the contract if already awarded, and issue a new solicitation to cure a defective one.[68] Should the agency decline to follow the GAO decision, it must report this action to Congress. The GAO can also award the successful protestor its costs of pursuing the protest (including attorneys' fees) as well as bid and proposal preparation costs.[69]

§ 6.8 Waiver by States and State Agencies

A contractor wishing to sue a state may find itself faced with sovereign immunity issues that may or may not have been expressly waived. This is a changing area of law. For example, in 1976 the State of Maryland waived sovereign immunity in contract actions.[70] Original jurisdiction over contract controversies and bid protests with the state and its agencies was ceded to a special three-member Board of Contract Appeals.[71] Previously, in *Charles E. Brohawn & Bros., Inc. v. Board of Trustees,*[72] the Maryland

---

[65] *Id.* §§ 21.7, 21.8.

[66] *Id.* § 21.5.

[67] *Id.* §§ 21.4(a), 21.4(b); 31 U.S.C. § 3553(c)-(d) (1988). It should be also be noted that FAR § 33.104(d) requires the agency to give written notice to the protester if there is any decision to proceed with award or contract performance.

[68] 4 C.F.R. § 21.6(a) (1991).

[69] *Id.* § 21.6(d).

[70] Law of May 4, 1976, ch. 450, 1976 Md. Laws 1180 (codified as amended at Md. State Gov't Code Ann. §§ 12-201 to 12-204 (1984 & Supp. 1990)).

[71] Md. Ann. Code art. 21, §§ 15-205, 15-207 (Supp. 1984).

[72] 269 Md. 164, 304 A.2d 819 (1973).

Court of Appeals had reaffirmed that sovereign immunity applied generally in breach of contract actions against a state agency,[73] explaining that:

> a litigant is precluded from asserting an otherwise meritorious cause of action against this sovereign State or one of its agencies which has inherited its sovereign attributes, unless expressly waived by statute or by a necessary inference from such a legislative enactment. And in the absence of statutory authorization, neither counsel for the State nor any of its agencies may, "either by affirmative action or by failure to plead the defense, waive the defense of governmental immunity. . . ." *Bd. of Education v. Alcrymat Corp.*, 258 Md. 508, 266 A.2d 349 (1970).[74]

If the contracting party is a local government or an entity created by the state or local government, the doctrine of sovereign immunity may not apply. In *Charles E. Brohawn,*[75] the Maryland Court of Appeals phrased the issue as whether the agency is one that "inherited" the state's sovereign attributes.[76] A good example of this is *In re Dormitory Authority,*[77] in which the Court of Appeals of New York considered the obligation of the Authority to arbitrate a dispute pursuant to an arbitration provision in a contract. The Authority sought a stay of that arbitration on the grounds of sovereign immunity but was rebuffed in a lower court. On appeal, the court held that the Authority was obligated to arbitrate the dispute. The principal basis for sustaining the refusal to stay arbitration was the conclusion that the Authority was not the alter ego of the state and could not, therefore, avail itself of the defense of sovereign immunity. The court stated:

> A reading of section 1678 discloses that the Authority has been given power: to sue and be sued; to have its own seal; to make its own by-laws; to appoint officers, agents and employees as well as fix their compensation; to acquire real property in the name of the State; to acquire personal property for its own corporate purposes; to enter contracts and execute instruments necessary for its purposes, subject only to the State Budget Director's approval as to cost; to fix and collect rentals for the use of the dormitories;

---

[73] Because *Brohawn* was a state court action, the Eleventh Amendment, which deprives the federal courts of jurisdiction, was not, as such, applicable. As an academic proposition, there should be no significant distinction between the state's rights under the Eleventh Amendment and the state common law right of sovereign immunity. *See* Jones v. Scofield Bros., Inc., 73 F. Supp. 395, 396 (D. Md. 1947).

[74] 269 Md. 164, 165–66, 304 A.2d 819, 820 (1973) (footnote & citation omitted).

[75] Charles E. Brohawn & Bros., Inc. v. Board of Trustees, 269 Md. 164, 304 A.2d 819 (1973).

[76] The court there concluded that the contracting agency, Chesapeake College, was such a state agency and therefore was immune from suit for breach of contract. *Id.*

[77] 218 N.Y.2d 114, 218 N.E.2d 693, 271 N.Y.S.2d 983 (1966).

> and to borrow money and issue negotiable bonds. In addition, section 1678 bestows upon the Authority a broad grant of power to do all things necessary and convenient to carry out its purposes. . . .
>
> Considering and weighing all the above powers, functions, and obligations, it is clear that this Authority, enjoying a separate existence, transacting its own business, hiring and compensating its own personnel, is not identical with the State.[78]

An unresolved question remains: are agreements to arbitrate by state governmental agencies enforceable? It was decided early on that federal officials have no authority to commit the federal government to arbitration.[79] However, *Dormitory Authority* and other decisions have concluded that such agreements are enforceable against state agencies.[80]

§ 6.9 Funding and Fiscal Restrictions

Government bodies seeking to contract must operate within their enabling and limiting fiscal rules—constitutional, legislative, charter, regulatory, and funding. These restrictions, grafted as they are onto vestiges of sovereign immunity plus judicial concern for the taxpayer's purse, and implemented often by exculpatory, excusatory, and limiting contract language, can have a considerable effect. Whether or not at fault, a contractor may find itself in considerable financial jeopardy if fiscal rules are not satisfied.

§ 6.10 —Federal Fiscal Restrictions

Fiscal restrictions imposed by Congress, and implemented by the GAO may cause cancellation of a solicitation, impede a settlement, furnish a defense to a claim, delay the award, or cause a termination. These restrictions arise under the Anti-Deficiency Act and related federal fiscal statutes. They limit the federal government's ability to obligate itself, under

---

[78] 218 N.E.2d at 695, 271 N.Y.S.2d at 985–86 (citation omitted).

[79] *See* United States v. Ames, 24 F. Cas. 784, 789 (C.C.D. Mass. 1845) (No. 14,441); Braucher, *Arbitration under Government Contracts,* 17 L. & Contemp. Probs. 473 (1952). *But see* United States v. Farragut, 89 U.S. (22 Wall.) 406 (1875) (when pending case is referred by order of court to arbitrators, final award made by arbitral tribunal could be adopted as decree of court).

[80] *See In re* Dormitory Auth., 218 N.Y.2d 114, 218 N.E.2d 693, 271 N.Y.S.2d 983 (1966); Minton Constr. Corp. v. Commonwealth, 397 Mass. 879, 494 N.E.2d 1031 (1986); Minnesota v. McGuire Architects-Planners, 245 N.W.2d 218 (Minn. 1976); Commonwealth v. Eastern Paving Co., 288 Pa. 571, 136 A. 853 (1927); City of Auburn v. Nash, 34 A.D.2d 345, 312 N.Y.S.2d 700 (1970); Pytko v. Connecticut, 28 Conn. Supp. 173, 255 A.2d 640 (1969).

contract, beyond statutory authority and available appropriations. In enacting these statutes, Congress intended "to prevent executive officers from involving the Government in expenditures or liabilities beyond those contemplated or authorized by the lawmaking power."[81]

The statutes establish several relevant fiscal principles. The first, embodied in the Adequacy of Appropriation Act,[82] prohibits an agency from making a commitment that existing appropriations are inadequate to fulfill[83] "unless otherwise authorized by law." If a contract violates this prohibition, it is void ab initio.[84]

The second rule, the Anti-Deficiency Act,[85] enjoins agency officials from creating obligations "under any appropriation or fund in excess of the amount available therein" or "in advance of an appropriation made for such purpose." This second rule builds on the first.[86] If there is enough money in an appropriation at the time a contract is made, there is no violation of 41 U.S.C. § 11 and the contract is valid and enforceable. If the applicable appropriation is exhausted sometime after the contract is executed, 31 U.S.C. § 1341(a) is activated and forbids the involved agency to make payments otherwise due to the contractor or to create any other additional monetary obligations.[87]

A third rule, established by 31 U.S.C. § 1301, provides that appropriations can be used only for the purpose for which they were appropriated. Under a *necessary expenses* concept developed by the GAO, this purpose-restriction rule may be extended to permit expenses to be charged against an appropriation for a particular object so long as the expenses are necessary to the proper execution of the object.[88] However, the necessary expenses concept cannot be used to justify the transfer of funds appropriated for a specific purpose to another appropriation account for which the funds would not have been available originally.[89] Similarly, the availability of an

---

[81] 21 Op. Att'y Gen. 244, 248 (1895). *See* 42 Comp. Gen. 272, 275 (1962). *See generally* Hopkins & Nutt, *The Anti-Deficiency Act (Revised Statutes 3679) and Funding Federal Contracts: An Analysis,* 80 Mil. L. Rev. 51 (1978); Efros, *Statutory Restrictions on Funding of Government Contracts,* 10 Pub. Cont. L.J. 254 (1978) [hereinafter Efros].

[82] 41 U.S.C. § 11 (1988).

[83] *See* 42 Comp. Gen. 272 (1962); Efros at 262.

[84] Efros at 262. Excepted from these funding restrictions are certain defense contracts for necessities, such as clothing, fuel, and hospital supplies for the current year. *See* 41 U.S.C. § 11(a) (1988).

[85] 31 U.S.C. § 1341(a) (1982).

[86] *See* 42 Comp. Gen. 272, 275 (1962).

[87] *See* Efros at 262.

[88] *See id.* at 260–61.

[89] *See id.* at 261–62. *See generally* Hopkins & Nutt, *The Anti-Deficiency Act (Revised Statutes 3679) and Funding Federal Contracts: An Analysis,* 80 Mil. L. Rev. 51, 105–15 (1978).

appropriation for a specific object precludes the use of a general appropriation to fund the object, even if the specific appropriation becomes exhausted.[90]

The last two rules are complementary. The first principle, loosely known as the *one-year rule,* states, "The balance of an appropriation or fund limited for obligation to a definite period is available only for payment of expenses properly incurred during the period of availability or to complete contracts properly made within that period of availability . . . ."[91] To enable this fiscal year limitation to work in practice, the GAO has evolved the *bona fide needs rule.*[92] This rule allows the government to obligate one fiscal year's appropriation for goods or services to be paid in a succeeding fiscal year, if the obligation is for a purpose that satisfies a genuine agency need arising during the year in which the obligation is incurred.[93]

The second principle, embodied in the Advance Payment Statute,[94] furthers the same purposes as the one-year rule, in a more practical context, by placing explicit limitations on the government's ability to pay money out of the treasury to fulfill contractual obligations.[95] This rule prohibits the advancement of public money unless the payment is authorized by "specific appropriation or other law."[96] The rule also forbids payment in excess of the value of the services rendered or goods delivered prior to the payment.[97]

These funding limitation principles appear deceptively simple. They establish the present availability and amount of appropriations as the general fundamental controls on the government's power to contract. An agency or contracting officer is explicitly prohibited from creating an obligation in the absence or in advance of an appropriation legally available therefor, allocating a current appropriation to liquidate over-obligations of prior years, or using an appropriation to pay for bona fide needs of future years.

However, by incorporation of the phrase "unless [otherwise] authorized by law," these statutory provisions permit deviations from their apparently strict fiscal accountability if there is statutory support for the departure. Thus, the ultimate requirement is in fact that there be an adequate

---

[90] *See, e.g.,* 36 Comp. Gen. 526 (1957); 19 Comp. Gen. 892 (1940).

[91] 31 U.S.C. § 1502(a) (1988).

[92] *See* 78-2 CPD ¶ 380 (1978); *In re* Burroughs Corp., 56 Comp. Gen. 142 (1976); 55 Comp. Gen. 768 (1976); 42 Comp. Gen. 272 (1962); 36 Comp. Gen. 683 (1957); Efros at 267–69.

[93] However, certain statutory exceptions to the bona fide needs rule exist. *See, e.g.,* Pub. L. No. 99-190, § 8005, 99 Stat. 1203 (1987) (appropriations available for 12-month tool maintenance contracts beginning anytime during fiscal year).

[94] 31 U.S.C. § 3324 (1988).

[95] *See In re* General Tel. Co., 57 Comp. Gen. 89 (1977).

[96] 31 U.S.C. § 3324(b)(1) (1988).

[97] *Id.* § 3324(a).

appropriate or statutory authority for any deviation from these strict fiscal limitations.

Moreover, in applying them to specific situations, these rules prove to be complicated and controversial. Must an agency allow prospectively for changes and other potential charges against an appropriation? Will a contractor be reimbursed for costs incurred or effort expended before award and obligation? When does an authorizing statute qualify as a grant of authority to exceed appropriations? What activities fall within the legislative purpose for an appropriation? To what extent may appropriated funds be transferred?

In deciding such questions, basic philosophical and interpretive differences arise between the GAO, which is charged by Congress with the responsibility of enforcing the statutes, and executive agencies, which must exercise the government's contractual power in conformity with them. Such differences have often been resolved in particular cases by practical accommodations. However, more than once, divergent opinions on interpretation have resulted in the GAO's nullification of an agency's apparent contractual obligation.[98]

§ 6.11 —Fiscal Restrictions on State and Other Governmental Bodies

Fiscal restrictions on contracting by the states and other nonfederal governmental bodies have their roots in the doctrine of sovereign immunity and in questions of authority. Prior to its statutory waiver of sovereign immunity,[99] Maryland was an example of the former. Thus, in a decision made obsolete by the statutory change, *Charles E. Brohawn & Bros., Inc. v. Board of Trustees,*[100] the Maryland Court of Appeals had aptly explained:

> "[I]t is established that neither in contract nor tort can a suit be maintained against a governmental agency, first, where specific legislative authority has not been given, second, even though such authority is given, if there are no funds available for the satisfaction of the judgment, or no power reposed in the agency for the raising of funds necessary to satisfy a recovery against it."[101]

---

[98] Efros at 267–69. *See, e.g.,* Leiter v. United States, 271 U.S. 204 (1926); *In re* Burroughs Corp., 56 Comp. Gen. 142 (1976); 42 Comp. Gen. 272 (1962); 36 Comp. Gen. 683 (1957).

[99] Law of May 4, 1976, ch. 450, 1976 Md. Laws 1180 (codified as amended at Md. State Gov't Code Ann. §§ 12-201 to 12-204 (1984 & Supp. 1990)).

[100] 269 Md. 164, 304 A.2d 819 (1973).

[101] *Id.* at 166, 304 A.2d at 820 (quoting University of Md. v. Maas, 173 Md. 554, 559, 197 A. 123, 125 (1938)).

The availability of authorized funds has been critical to any contractor seeking to enforce contract rights against a state or its agencies. For example, in *Fisher & Carozza Bros. Co. v. Mackall,*[102] the court of appeals considered a case involving a contractor's breach of contract action against the Maryland State Roads Commission. The State Roads Commission claimed that it was immune from suit after the repeal of an authorizing statute. The court of appeals dismissed the action for damages, not because the statute had been repealed, but because there was no fund from which the plaintiff could have been paid.

On the other hand, the courts may infer authority for an expenditure from the fact that funds are available. In *State ex rel. Lane v. Dashiell,*[103] Maryland brought a declaratory judgment action to determine whether it was liable to the defendant contractor for additional costs incurred by reason of delays while the contractor was constructing a hospital for the state. The legislature had appropriated an amount not to exceed $250,000 to satisfy this defendant's claim for additional compensation if it were determined there was a legal obligation to pay. The legislature thereby sanctioned the suit and the court of appeals determined that the state was liable.

In another case[104] the Maryland Court of Appeals considered a declaratory judgment suit claiming that the State Roads Commission should bear the cost of removal, relocation, and construction of gas and electric utility facilities necessitated by some construction work. Under the common law, the costs to the utility company would have been an expense without a remedy (damnum absque injuria) because the action of the state did not amount to a taking. A statute, however, provided that all private property damaged or destroyed in the course of activities thereby authorized would be restored or repaired, or adequate compensation would be paid. The court of appeals held that the statute *did* change the common law. The court had emphasized that, upon examining the legislative scheme, it became clear that the cost of the project was to be paid out of bond revenues and that the users of the project were to bear all costs ultimately by the payment of tolls.[105]

In *Comptroller of Treasury v. Panitz,*[106] the court of appeals held that a plaintiff who had contracted with the University of Maryland for the printing of a magazine could recover the amount owed under the contract if there were funds available that had not been allocated for other purposes.

---

[102] 138 Md. 586, 114 A. 580 (1921).

[103] 195 Md. 667, 75 A.2d 348 (1950).

[104] Baltimore Gas & Elec. Co. v. State Roads Comm'n, 214 Md. 266, 134 A.2d 312 (1957).

[105] *Id. See also* Masson v. Reindollar, 193 Md. 683, 69 A.2d 482 (1949), in which the court assumed that the cost overruns on the first Chesapeake Bay bridge would be financed by additional bonds.

[106] 267 Md. 296, 297 A.2d 289 (1972).

Similarly, the nonavailability of funds was determinative in *University of Maryland v. Maas,*[107] a suit brought by a contractor claiming damages from breach of contract in connection with a construction contract for buildings at the University of Maryland.

§ 6.12 Authority to Act

The general rule is that ordinary principles of estoppel and apparent authority, which might under similar circumstances bind a private party, cannot be used to bind the government.[108] There must be actual authority. This principle was best articulated by the United States Supreme Court in the historic case of *Federal Crop Insurance Corp. v. Merrill,*[109] in which the Court explained:

> Whatever the form in which the Government functions, anyone entering into an arrangement with the Government takes the risk of having accurately ascertained that he who purports to act for the Government stays within the bounds of his authority. The scope of this authority may be explicitly defined by Congress or be limited by delegated legislation, properly exercised through the rule-making power. And this is so even though, as here, the agent himself may have been unaware of the limitations upon his authority.[110]

The obvious question is: Who may bind the government? Clearly, the warranted contracting officer (CO) may do so, but what about other government representatives with whom the contractor must deal on a more regular basis? Do they have authority and if so, to what extent? These questions are significant because the contractor assumes the risk that the person representing the government possesses the requisite authority to bind the government.[111]

By definition, the term *contracting officer* includes "certain authorized representatives of the contracting officer acting within the limits of their authority."[112] Courts and boards finding authority in representatives other than the contracting officer have based their decisions on this definition.

---

[107] 173 Md. 554, 197 A. 123 (1938).

[108] *See* Office of Personnel Management v. Richmond, 110 S. Ct. 2465, 2469, 2471 (1990). For a general discussion of the authority of government employees to bind the government, *see* Essen Mall Properties v. United States, 21 Cl. Ct. 430, 439–45 (1990); C. Anticau & M. Mecham, Tort Liability of Government Officers and Employees (John Wiley & Sons 1990).

[109] 332 U.S. 380 (1947).

[110] *Id.* at 384.

[111] *Id.; see* Eliel v. United States, 18 Cl. Ct. 461 (1989).

[112] 48 C.F.R. § 2.101 (1990).

These cases primarily focus on the duties, responsibilities, and relationships of the representatives involved. The broader the duties and responsibilities of a representative, the wider his discretion becomes and the more likely that the officer will be deemed to have acted within his authority.

For example, very few decisions involving inspectors have found an inspector to have the authority to bind the government, because inspectors are ordinarily no more than the government's observers.[113] They have very little contact with COs. On the other hand, cases finding a field representative to be the authorized representative of the CO, and thus capable of binding the government, are numerous. This result is not surprising when one considers the broader duties and correspondingly broader scope of authority inherent in the field representative's function. This reasoning is best explained by the Board of Contract Appeals in *Industrial Research Associates,* in which the board stated:

> [A] contracting officer can and sometimes does delegate his authority to technical representatives. And in these circumstances, the Government is bound by the directives given by the representative. . . . Similarly, an engineer or some other kind of technical advisor whose function is the giving of technical guidance to a contract may also order a change in work. Thus, it seems clear to us that what is at issue here are the actual functions of the Government's engineer.[114]

Increased responsibility translates into increased authority. This concept is illustrated by *Lillards,*[115] a 1961 Armed Services Board of Contract Appeals (ASBCA) case involving a construction contract. In *Lillards* the government's installation engineer ordered the contractor to provide manhole covers not required by the contract. The government argued that the engineer lacked authority to do so and consequently the government was not bound by the changes that he directed. Holding for the contractor, the board found that the engineer did in fact have authority. The board stated, "He was in *direct control of the job,* the covers were obviously needed . . . it is inconceivable that he lacked authority to do what he did."[116]

---

[113] *See, e.g.,* DeKonty Corp., ASBCA No. 32140, 89-2 B.C.A. ¶ 21,586. *But see* Gonzales Custom Painting, Inc., ASBCA Nos. 39527, 39529, 39547, 39812, 90-3 B.C.A. ¶ 22,950, in which the Board held that an inspector who had authority to accept or reject performance could direct the contractor to change its method of performance in correcting inadequate work.

[114] Industrial Research Assocs., Inc., DCAB No. WB-5, 68-1 B.C.A. (CCH) ¶ 7069 at 32,685 (footnotes omitted). *See also* Stephenson Assocs., Inc., GSBCA Nos. 6573, 6815, 86-3 B.C.A. ¶ 19,071.

[115] ASBCA No. 6630, 61-1 B.C.A. (CCH) ¶ 3053 (1961).

[116] *Id.* at 15,801 (emphasis added).

In a similar example, the General Services Administration Board of Contract Appeals (GSBCA) held that a Social Security physical security specialist who managed and supervised one part of a guard services contract had authority to bind the government when he directed changes in performance of that portion of the contract.[117]

Inspectors and field representatives are not the only representatives who may, under appropriate circumstances, bind the government. Several court and board decisions have found procurement personnel authorized to act on behalf of the CO and thus capable of binding the government. As with the field representative, and to a lesser extent the inspector, the actual job function controls; that is, circumstances, not job title, dictate the outcome. For example, in *Morrison-Knudsen Co.,*[118] a 1972 ASBCA decision, the board determined that a contracting officer's assistant who gave guidance at a prebid conference was, in this limited situation, the CO's authorized representative and had authority equivalent to the CO.

In another ASBCA decision, *Wickham Contracting Co.,*[119] an estimator was found to have authority. The controversy in *Wickham* centered on an error in one of the drawings in the invitation for bids for an underground electrical cable replacement. Apparently, the government's estimator knew of the error but failed to report it. The ASBCA stated, "[W]e find that the Government's estimator was the authorized representative of the contracting officer for the purpose of preparing the Government's estimate of the cost of the work, and for the purpose of initiating drawings corrections."[120]

§ 6.13 Ratification by Contracting Officer

In cases involving contract language clearly restricting the authority of the government's representatives, courts and boards have often circumvented the authorized representative issue by finding authority in the related concepts of contracting officer (CO) ratification, acquiescence, and imputation of knowledge.[121] A typical decision binding the government on the basis of imputed knowledge is *United States Federal Engineering & Manufacturing.*[122] In *Federal Engineering* the CO was not informed that the project manager had approved certain additions correcting defective

---

[117] *See* Gricoski Detective Agency, GSBCA Nos. 8901, 8922, 8923, 8924, 8925, 8926, 90-3 B.C.A. (CCH) ¶ 23,131.

[118] ASBCA No. 16483, 72-2 B.C.A. (CCH) ¶ 9733.

[119] ASBCA No. 19069, 75-1 B.C.A. (CCH) ¶ 11,248.

[120] *Id.* at 53,576.

[121] Tepfer, *Authority and the Contracting Officer's Representatives,* 24 A.F. L. Rev. 1.3 (1984).

[122] ASBCA No. 19909, 75-2 B.C.A. (CCH) ¶ 11,578.

specifications. The board nevertheless allowed the contractor to be compensated for the extra work, holding:

> The fact that the contracting officer did not have actual knowledge of the additions to be made to the device does not insulate the Government from the consequences that actual knowledge would impose. His various representatives are his eyes and ears (if not his voice) and their knowledge is treated for all intents and purposes as his.[123]

The closer the working relationship of the representative with the CO, the more likely the representative's knowledge will be presumed to be the knowledge of the CO.[124] Consequently, inspector decisions rarely find the type of imputed knowledge found in *Federal Engineering.*

Decisions based on contracting officer acquiescence hold that when the CO was or should have been aware of the changes proposed by its representative, the CO will be held to have approved them. A typical example is found in *W. Southward Jones, Inc.,*[125] a case in which the contractor, the government technical personnel, and the contracting officer were all operating on the same military base. In finding that the CO had acquiesced to a change ordered by technical personnel, the ASBCA stated:

> Performance proceeded almost from the outset under the eyes of assigned supervisory personnel in a manner patently at variance with the contract drawings. . . . The digging of the conduit in question continued in plain view along the taxiway at the Base every day for almost a month. Base technical personnel clearly knew what was going on and as clearly intended that the original drawings should not be followed. . . .
>
> Conceding therefor that the contracting officer was the only one empowered to authorize changes in the contract and that a special clause was included to emphasize the limitations in authority of the technical personnel, we must hold under the peculiar circumstances of this case that he had timely notice of changes, if not actually, then certainly constructively.[126]

Whether contractor recovery in a particular case is based upon a finding that the representative was the authorized representative of the contracting officer or, alternatively, that there was CO ratification, acquiescence, or constructive knowledge, thus depends on the circumstances of each case.

---

[123] *Id.* at 55,298.

[124] Tepfer, *Authority and the Contracting Officer's Representatives,* 24 A.F. L. Rev. 1.3 (1984).

[125] ASBCA No. 6321, 61-2 B.C.A. (CCH) ¶ 3182.

[126] *Id.* at 16,498. *See* Gricoski Detective Agency, GSBCA Nos. 8901, 8922, 8923, 8924, 8925, 8926, 90-3 B.C.A. (CCH) ¶ 23,131; Coalition for United Community Action, Inc., 88-1 B.C.A. (CCH) ¶ 20,290 (LBCA 1987).

§ 6.14 Authority to Act for the State

Court and board decisions involving the authority for state and local contract actions have been couched in terms of the liability of a state or local governmental body on contracts entered into by unauthorized representatives. The decisions finding liability rely on theories of implied contract, ratification, and estoppel. Presumably, courts and boards would apply the same theories in determining a government's liability for unauthorized changes.

Courts finding liability based on ratification hold that ratification or affirmance can create an implied promise of payment if the unauthorized contract is one that the state or local government may lawfully make.[127] Other cases have reached the same result by utilizing the concept of estoppel. These cases hold that a municipality or other government body may be estopped from asserting that its agents lacked contracting authority when the contract was one that the government could lawfully make and the government has accepted the contract's benefits. Although this estoppel theory has been applied to local governments, its applicability (if any) to states is unclear. As the New York Court of Appeals explained in *Parsa v. State,* "[T]he State's acceptance of benefits furnished under a contract made without authority does not estop it from challenging the validity of the contract or from denying liability pursuant to it."[128]

The cases that find liability based on quasi-contract/quantum meruit theories hold that the state or other political subdivision must pay the reasonable value of the services rendered by the contractor although the services were rendered pursuant to an unauthorized contract. For example, in *Ridley v. Pipe Maintenance Services, Inc.,*[129] the Pennsylvania Commonwealth Court allowed contractor recovery for the cost of maintenance and repair work performed pursuant to an unauthorized contract. The court reasoned that when a municipality has voluntarily accepted and retained the benefits of a contract that (1) it had the power to make, but (2) was

---

[127] *See, e.g.,* Township of Ridley v. Haulaway Trash Removal, Inc., 68 Pa. Commw. 16, 448 A.2d 654 (1982) (partial payment tantamount to ratification of unauthorized contract). *See generally Liability of municipality or other governmental body on implied or quasi contract for value of property or work,* 154 A.L.R. 354, 373 (1945); J. Director, *Liability of Municipality on Quasi Contract for Value of Property or Work Furnished without compliance with Bidding Requirements,* 33 A.L.R.3d 1164 (1970).

[128] 64 N.Y.2d 143, 145, 474 N.E.2d 235, 237, 485 N.Y.S.2d 27, 29 (1984). *See also* 21 N.Y. Jur. *Estoppel, Ratification and Waiver* § 77 (1982).

> [T]here can be no estoppel against the state which will impede the exercise of sovereign powers for the protection of the people, [although] in a proper case, the state may be estopped, the same as an individual, by representations and conduct, provided its officers and agents . . . were acting with authority. *Id.*

[129] 68 Pa. Commw. 16, 477 A.2d 610 (1984).

defective in its making, and (3) thus was invalid, the party who has conferred those benefits may recover compensation therefor, not on the invalid contract itself, but in quantum meruit.

An equal, if not greater, number of decisions, however, have denied contractor recovery in cases involving contracts entered into by unauthorized representatives. These cases deny that a governmental body must pay for the benefits derived from an unauthorized contract.[130]

[130] *See, e.g.,* Sorenson v. City of N.Y., 202 F.2d 857 (2d Cir. 1953), *cert. denied,* 347 U.S. 951 (1954); Parsa v. State, 64 N.Y.2d 143, 474 N.E.2d 235, 485 N.Y.S.2d 27 (1984); Dour v. Village of Port Jefferson, 89 Misc. 2d 146, 390 N.Y.S.2d 965 (Sup. Ct. 1976); Seif v. Long Beach, 286 N.Y. 382, 36 N.E.2d 630 (1941).

CHAPTER 7

SUING THE CONSTRUCTION MANAGER

Julian F. Hoffar
John B. Tieder, Jr.

Julian F. Hoffar, senior partner in the Washington, D.C., law firm of Watt, Tieder, Killian & Hoffar, specializes in national and international contract law. Mr. Hoffar earned his undergraduate degree from Wittenberg University and is an honor graduate of the National Law Center, George Washington University, where he was a member of the Law Review. Mr. Hoffar has written articles on construction contracting, and has lectured before several industry groups on the subject of construction law.

John B. Tieder, Jr., is a senior partner in the Washington, D.C., law firm of Watt, Tieder, Killian & Hoffar. He specializes in the representation of owners, architects, engineers, contractors, and subcontractors in construction matters. Mr. Tieder received his A.B. degree from the Johns Hopkins University in 1968 and his J.D. from the American University Washington College of Law in 1971. Mr. Tieder is the author and coauthor of a variety of publications on construction matters, and is currently a visiting lecturer in government contracts law at Marshall-Wythe School of Law, College of William and Mary.

INTRODUCTION

§ 7.1 Role of Construction Manager

§ 7.2 Construction Management Defined

FORMS OF CONSTRUCTION MANAGEMENT PRACTICE

§ 7.3 Agency Construction Management

§ 7.4 Guaranteed Maximum Price Construction Management

§ 7.5 Extended Service Construction Management

STANDARD OF CARE

§ 7.6 Professional or Contractor?

§ 7.7 Licensing Requirements

§ 7.8 Bond and Insurance Considerations

§ 7.9 Bidding Requirements

DUTY OWED BY CONSTRUCTION MANAGER

§ 7.10 Generally

§ 7.11 Contract Obligations

§ 7.12 Procurement Codes

§ 7.13 Building Codes and Industry Standards

§ 7.14 Construction Manager De Facto Rule

§ 7.15 Parties to Whom Duty Is Owed

THEORIES OF RECOVERY

§ 7.16 Negligence

§ 7.17 Third-Party Beneficiary

§ 7.18 Interference with Contract

§ 7.19 Implied Warranty

BASES FOR LIABILITY

§ 7.20 Generally

§ 7.21 Interference with Bids

§ 7.22 Design Defects

§ 7.23 Delayed Site Access

§ 7.24 Administration of Drawings

§ 7.25 Failure to Provide Timely Information

§ 7.26 Failure to Provide Construction Support Services

§ 7.27 Failure to Schedule and Coordinate

CONSTRUCTION MANAGER DEFENSES

§ 7.28 Owner/Construction Manager Contract

§ 7.29 Owner/Prime Contract

§ 7.30 Duty to Review Drawings and Prior Work

§ 7.31 No Damages for Delay Clauses

§ 7.32 Delay Not Contemplated by the Parties

§ 7.33 Unreasonable Delay

§ 7.34 Bad Faith or Fraud
§ 7.35 Active Interference
§ 7.36 Statutory Exceptions
§ 7.37 Delegation of Scheduling Functions to Contractors
§ 7.38 Forum Selection
§ 7.39 Owner's Agent
§ 7.40 Contributory and Comparative Negligence
§ 7.41 No Recovery for Economic Loss
§ 7.42 Statutes of Limitations
§ 7.43 Accrual
§ 7.44 Tolling

INTRODUCTION

§ 7.1 Role of Construction Manager

As more owners rely on fast-track[1] and/or multi-prime construction or simply wish to withdraw from the active management of their construction projects, construction management has evolved as a separate field of construction practice. The *construction manager* (CM) is employed by the owner to perform some or all of the services traditionally provided by a design architect, a supervisory engineer, a quality control inspector, or a general contractor. These services can include all or portions of the design, preparation of bidding documents, review and evaluation of bids, inspection, scheduling, and coordination. Usually, the CM does not perform any actual construction work, although it is not uncommon for the CM to provide and maintain basic project services such as temporary power and sanitary facilities. Typically, the CM does not have any contractual relationship with the actual prime contractors, although this is not always the case.[2]

The concept of the construction manager is relatively new. Thus, to date there are not many reported cases dealing specifically with the liability of the CM to the contractors on the project. Because the CM's duties encompass many of the traditional duties of an architect/engineer and a general contractor, it is possible to rely on cases discussing the obligations of these parties in order to determine the CM's liability to the contractor.

---

[1] See § 7.2.

[2] On some projects denominated as construction management projects, the CM does have direct contracts with the several prime contractors. *See, e.g.,* United States v. Johnson Controls, Inc., 2 FPD ¶ 15 (Fed. Cir. 1983).

§ 7.2 Construction Management Defined

The term *construction management* has two similar but distinct meanings. First, it is a method of construction; second, it is an emerging separate discipline or profession. In these two contexts, the term "construction management" refers to a system whereby each of the construction subcontractors on a particular project has a direct contract with the owner, and the work is administratively controlled by a separate entity that performs little or no direct construction work—the construction manager.[3] It differs from a traditional single-prime contractor project in that the parties that typically performed as subcontractors now perform as primes. Although it is possible to have a construction management project with very few or even one contractor, the typical construction management project has several primes; it can be as many as 50 or more.[4]

Although it is not an inherent part of construction management, many projects using this method have some element of *fast-tracking* or *phased* construction. This means that certain portions of the project are designed and let for construction while other portions are still being designed.[5] Although this process can reduce overall project time[6] because the start of construction is not restrained by the completion of the design, it is virtually impossible to award a single overall prime contract. Thus, individual contracts are awarded as various portions of the design are completed.

The concept of construction management, almost of necessity, had to give rise to the discipline of a construction manager. Although the role of the CM is fairly clear (to administer the construction for the owner), the status of the CM is a subject of considerable controversy. Is the CM a professional and thus susceptible to the liability of other professionals (architects and engineers), or is the CM a general contractor?[7] On most projects, the CM enters into a contract with the owner for administration of all or some portion of the overall construction project.

The relationship between owners and construction managers may take various forms, making it difficult to characterize it completely as either one of principal-agent, owner-independent contractor, or employer-employee. The issue is not settled between the courts and the determination often depends heavily on the facts of the particular case. In *Brady v.*

---

[3] Conner, *Contracting for Construction Management Services,* 46 Law & Contemp. Probs. 5 (Winter 1983).

[4] Tieder & Cox, *Construction Management & the Specialty Trade (Prime) Contractors,* 46 Law & Contemp. Probs. 39 (Winter 1983).

[5] *Id.* at 44.

[6] *Overall project time* means the time between the start of design by the architect/engineer and the completion of the project such that it is available for use by the owner.

[7] This issue is discussed in detail in **§ 7.6**.

Ralph Parsons Co.,[8] a Maryland court discussed several factors in determining whether a construction manager is an agent of the owner or simply an independent contractor. The crucial distinction, according to the court, is the degree of control the CM maintained over the day-to-day construction operations. When the owner maintained strict control and the CM was charged merely to carry out the owner's wishes, the CM was properly classified as an agent of the owner and the owner might be subject to vicarious liability. When the CM is not subject to the direct control of the owner, but must instead see to the implementation of broader goals set forth by the owner, she is an independent contractor and the doctrine of respondeat superior will not ordinarily apply.[9]

A New Jersey appellate court has found that when a construction manager's contract renders it solely responsible for the performance and payment of its subcontractors, it is in the same relationship to the subcontractors and suppliers as a general contractor and will be treated as a general contractor.[10] Thus, the filing of a construction management agreement will bar the filing of a subsequent mechanic's notice of intention.

In *Guarantee Electric Co. v. Big Rivers Electric Corp.,*[11] a federal court characterized the CM's relationship with the owner as that of an independent contractor rather than an agent. The CM rendered service in the course of an independent occupation at the site and followed the will of the owner only as to the end result and not as to the means and methods by which that result was to be accomplished. Thus, the owner could not be liable for the alleged negligent failure of the CM to notify the subcontractor that construction of a particular unit was to be put on hold prior to the subcontractor's commencement of work.

On the other hand, an Illinois court has characterized a construction manager as an agent of the owner.[12] A contractor brought a claim for delay damages against a CM despite a no damage clause in the owner/contractor agreement. The court determined that, because of the extensive responsibilities placed on the CM by the owner, the CM must be treated as the agent of the owner and would therefore receive the same protection under the clause.

In *Paterson-Leitch Co. v. Massachusetts Wholesale Electric Co.,*[13] a federal court held that a contractor could not sue the CM for a breach of contract claim because there was no privity of contract. The court

[8] 308 Md. 486, 520 A.2d 717 (1987), *aff'd,* 82 Md. App. 519, 572 A.2d 1115 (1990).

[9] 520 A.2d at 729–31.

[10] Port Liberty Partnership v. Strober Bros., 228 N.J. Super. 155, 549 A.2d 72 (1988).

[11] 669 F. Supp. 1371 (W.D. Ky. 1987).

[12] L.K. Comstock & Co. v. Morse/UBM Joint Venture, 153 Ill. App. 3d 475, 505 N.E.2d 1253 (1987).

[13] 840 F.2d 985 (1st Cir. 1988).

characterized the CM as an agent of the owner and not a party to the owner-contractor agreement. Thus, because the CM was acting as an agent of a fully disclosed principal, the breach of contract claim against the CM was barred.

In *Wellons v. T.E. Ibberson Co.,*[14] a contractor sued a CM for damages caused by the CM's negligent provision of test results, which resulted in the contractor's improper design. The court characterized the CM as an agent of the owner, a finding that was not challenged by the contractor. Furthermore, because the owner and contractor had previously settled their claim, the court ruled that the settlement had res judicata effect on the contractor's suit against the CM, considering the CM's position as an agent of the owner.

A South Carolina court has found that when the owner/CM contract is ambiguous regarding the CM's compensation, the CM may be characterized as an employee of the owner and hence may recover her compensation independent of the contract sum.[15]

FORMS OF CONSTRUCTION MANAGEMENT PRACTICE

§ 7.3 Agency Construction Management

The agency form of construction management practice is similar to the owner-architect relationship, in that the CM is an agent of the owner, managing the project for a fixed or cost-plus fee.[16]

Agency construction management is typically performed by architects or engineers familiar with the rights and responsibilities owed by a design professional to an owner. The owner's cost savings, if any, result directly from the CM's success in reducing the cost and time of completion of the building. When the CM assumes both design and management roles (often called an A/CM), the construction management services can be viewed as an extension of the architect's duties because there is no independent design review function. When the CM is also acting as a general contractor by letting contracts, performing some of the work, or guaranteeing a maximum price, the identity of interests necessary to support the "relationship of trust and confidence" of an agency usually does not exist because the CM-contractor has a financial interest in all or part of the work.

---

[14] 896 F.2d 1166 (8th Cir. 1989).

[15] Ringer v. Graham, 293 S.C. 238, 359 S.E.2d 523 (Ct. App. 1987).

[16] AIA Doc. B801, Standard Form of Agreement Between Owner and Construction Manager, Art. 1 (1980).

§ 7.4 Guaranteed Maximum Price Construction Management

Guaranteed maximum price (GMP) construction management retains the most important characteristic of a general contractor/owner relationship: it offers a form of cost security to the owner. In this arrangement, the construction manager (CM) assumes control over the performance of the work and contractually guarantees a price ceiling, with all overruns deducted from the CM's fee. In some cases, there is also a cost-saving incentive that nets the CM a percentage of the owner's savings if the job is completed under budget. The GMP format appears in an Associated General Contractors (AGC) form stating that "[c]osts in excess of the Guaranteed Maximum Price" come out of the CM's fee.[17]

The GMP format creates a potential conflict of interest between the CM and the owner by establishing financial incentives for the CM to keep construction costs low. This is one owner goal, but another is reducing long-term operating costs, which can often be achieved by using higher quality material at a slight increase in construction costs. The incentive to cut costs may adversely influence the CM's decision whether to install more durable material or implement other changes that may benefit the owner in the long run.

§ 7.5 Extended Service Construction Management

Construction management services, although normally limited to activities related to construction and design, are sometimes extended to include a complete line of ancillary services. For example, some construction management contracts provide for the standard design and construction services, as well as claims resolution, tenant solicitation and space planning, and occupancy scheduling. An extended service agreement is similar to the design-build relationship in that the owner delegates all but the most general duties concerning the project to the CM.

Guaranteed maximum price construction management is sometimes combined with design services to create a professional design-build package. In this format, the architect/CM/contractor offers an integrated building concept to the owner, relieving the owner of all supervisory and coordination responsibilities. The disadvantage of this system is that the owner often has no independent representative on the project, because both the architect/engineer and the CM are allied with the contractor.

---

[17] Associated General Contractors of America, AGC Doc. No. 500, Standard Form of Agreement Between Owner and Construction Manager (Guaranteed Maximum Price Option), Art. 7.3.5 (1980).

STANDARD OF CARE

§ 7.6 Professional or Contractor?

Unlike the traditional positions of design architect or supervisory engineer, the role of the CM to date has not been clearly defined by statute, case law, or industry practice. Thus, to identify the standard of care owed by the CM to the contractor, it must first be determined if the CM is functioning as a professional or as a general contractor. This distinction is important because it establishes the basic standard of care to which the CM will be held.

An architect/engineer or other engineering professional owes a duty of ordinary skill and competence of members of that profession.[18] This standard applies to both the design and administration of the project.[19] If that duty is not met, the engineering professional may be liable to the owner or third parties for negligence. In the absence of a specific contractual agreement to the contrary, a professional is not required to provide a perfect design nor to perform other engineering services to perfection, but is liable only for a failure to exercise reasonable care and skill in the design or supervision of the work.[20] The standard by which the professional is judged varies, depending upon the nature and location of the work.[21] A professional in charge of a large, complex industrial plant will be held to a higher degree of care than the professional in charge of a small office building. Likewise, a professional holding itself out as a specialist in a particular industrial application will be held to a higher degree of care. Finally, a professional working in a large metropolitan area will be subject to closer scrutiny than one working in a small, rural area.[22]

---

[18] *See, e.g.,* Gravely v. Providence Partners, 549 F.2d 958 (4th Cir. 1977); La Rossa v. Scientific Design Co., 402 F.2d 937 (3d Cir. 1968); Allied Properties v. John A. Blume & Assocs., Eng'rs, 25 Cal. App. 3d 848, 102 Cal. Rptr. 259 (1972); Borman's, Inc. v. Lake State Dev. Co., 60 Mich. App. 175, 230 N.W.2d 363 (1975); Queensbury Union v. Jim Walter Corp., 91 Misc. 2d 804, 398 N.Y.S.2d 832 (1977); Ryan v. Morgan Spear Assocs., Inc., 546 S.W.2d 678 (Tex. Ct. App. 1977). Some jurisdictions apply a stricter standard and hold that the architect/engineer is deemed to have warranted the adequacy of its plans and specifications. *See, e.g.,* Broyles v. Brown Eng'g Co., 275 Ala. 35, 151 So. 2d 767 (1963); Bloomsburg Mills, Inc. v. Sordoni Constr. Co., 401 Pa. 337, 164 A.2d 201 (1960); Hill v. Polar Pantries, 219 S.C. 263, 64 S.E.2d 885 (S.C. 1951); Prier v. Refrigeration Eng'g Co., 74 Wash. 2d 25, 442 P.2d 621 (1968).

[19] Normoyle-Berg Assocs. v. Village of Deer Creek, 39 Ill. App. 3d 744, 350 N.E.2d 559 (1976).

[20] AIA Doc. B801, Standard Form of Agreement Between Owner and Construction Manager, Art. 1 (1980).

[21] Mounds View v. Walijarvi, 263 N.W.2d 420, 424 (Minn. 1978).

[22] Bondumin-McClure, Inc. v. Snow, 183 Cal. App. 2d 58, 6 Cal. Rptr. 52 (1960); *but see* Carroll-Boone Water Dist. v. M.&P. Equip. Co., 280 Ark. 560, 661 S.W.2d 560 (1984),

Proving that the standard was not met in a particular case invariably requires expert testimony. A general contractor's duty to third parties is one of ordinary and reasonable care.[23] It should be noted, however, that some jurisdictions hold that the duty of care owed by a contractor, or any other party possessing special knowledge or skill, is commensurate with the circumstances.[24] In these jurisdictions, a CM, even if regarded as a general contractor, will be held to a higher standard than ordinary care. The standard of care will depend on such matters as the complexity of the project, the skill and expertise needed to effect the work, and similar surrounding circumstances.

Thus, the determination of whether a CM is acting as a professional or a general contractor establishes the standard of care owed to third parties. **Sections 5.7** through **5.9** set forth several factors the courts examine in making this determination: licensing requirements, bond and insurance requirements, and bidding requirements for public projects.

§ 7.7 Licensing Requirements

All states require professionals such as architects and engineers to obtain licenses. Many states require contractors to obtain some type of license or registration.[25] Although no states have specific licensing requirements for CMs, a construction manager may be required to be licensed either under a contractor's licensing statute or under a design professional's licensing statute. Some architectural licensing statutes specifically including the administration of construction contracts in the definition of architectural services might be construed to prohibit anyone but a licensed architect from supervising construction.[26] States that do not specifically include construction management in their definition of architectural services, but do refer to "supervision of construction" or "administration of construction," might still require a construction manager to be licensed as an

in which the court held that the "same locality" rule applied only to medical professionals, not architect/engineers.

[23] Green Constr. Co. v. William Form Eng'g Corp., 506 F. Supp. 173, 177 (W.D. Mich. 1980); Hawthorne v. Kober Constr. Co., 196 Mont. 519, 640 P.2d 467, 470 (1982).

[24] *See* La Vine v. Clear Creek Skiing Corp., 557 F.2d 730 (10th Cir. 1977), which discusses the standard of reasonable prudence as it is affected by the special skills of the actor charged with negligence. The court stated that "a person having special knowledge must exercise a quantum of care which is commensurate with the circumstances, one of which is his or her special skill and training." *Id.* at 734.

[25] Associated General Contractors of America, *Legal Trends—Does the CM Need a License?,* 1982 CM Bulletin.

[26] *See, e.g.,* Ill. Ann. Stat. ch. 111, ¶ 1204 (Smith-Hurd 1991); N.Y. Educ. Law § 7301 (McKinney 1985); Okla. Stat. Ann. tit. 59, § 46.3(A)1 (1989).

architect.[27] Some states specifically include construction management in their definitions of general contracting services,[28] but others include the functions of a construction manager within their definitions of a general contractor.[29] In states such as Virginia and Nevada, in which the functions of a construction manager are included in both definitions, both licensing requirements might well apply. When a CM must be licensed as either an architect or a contractor, the standard of care should be the same as for any other licensee of that category.

A CM who fails to obtain the required license is subject to a variety of criminal and civil sanctions. For example, the Utah licensing statute provides that anyone "acting in the capacity of contractor . . . without a license as herein provided shall be guilty of a misdemeanor."[30] In addition, a CM who fails to obtain the proper license may be prohibited from instituting a lawsuit against the owner for collection of a fee or even from asserting a counterclaim or setoff if sued by another party.[31]

Although a construction manager may need to be licensed in most states as an architect or as a contractor, at least one state, Indiana, has restricted the CM from performing either of those duties while acting as the manager of the same project.[32] However, the Indiana code requires that a construction manager be specifically designated as such by the contract.[33] As a result, it might be possible for an owner to procure the services of architect, contractor, and CM from the same firm under Indiana law, so long as that

---

[27] Colo. Rev. Stat. Ann. § 20-288(3) (West 1989); Fla. Stat. Ann. § 481.203(6) (West Supp. 1990); Haw. Rev. Stat. § 464-1(6) (1985); Idaho Code § 54-309(c) (Supp. 1989); Ind. Code Ann. § 25-4-1-17 (West 1982); Neb. Rev. Stat. § 81-840(2) (1987); Nev. Rev. Stat. Ann. § 523.015(4) (Michie 1986); N.J. Stat. Ann. § 45.3-1.1(k) (West Supp. 1989); N.C. Gen. Stat. § 83A-1(7) (1985); Or. Rev. Stat. § 671.010(5) (1989); Va. Code Ann. § 54.1-400 (Michie 1988); Vt. Stat. Ann. tit. 26, § 121(5) (1989); Wash. Rev. Code Ann. § 18.080320(10) (West 1989); Wis. Stat. Ann. § 443.01(5) (West 1988).

[28] Nev. Rev. Stat. Ann. § 624.020(4) (Michie 1986) (definition of contractor includes a "construction manager who performs management and counseling services on a construction project for a fee"); N.M. Stat. Ann. § 60-13-3(c) (Michie Supp. 1989) (definition of contractor includes "a construction manager who coordinates and manages the building process").

[29] Ala. Code § 34-8-1 (Supp. 1989); Ark. Code Ann. § 17-22-101(a) (Michie Supp. 1989); N.C. Gen. Stat. § 87-1 (1989); Tenn. Code Ann. § 62-6-102 (Supp. 1989); Wash. Rev. Code Ann. § 18.27.020 (West 1989); Va. Code Ann. § 54.1-1100 (Michie Supp. 1990).

[30] Utah Code Ann. §§ 58-23-3(3), 58-23-18 (1953). *See* Meridian Corp. v. McGlynn/Garmaker Co., 567 P.2d 1110 (Utah 1977).

[31] Cochran v. Ozark County Club, Inc., 339 So. 2d 1023 (Ala. 1976); Bird v. Pan W. Corp., 261 Ark. 56, 546 S.W.2d 417 (1977); Gorrell v. Fowler, 248 Ga. 801, 286 S.E.2d 13 (1982); United Stage Equip., Inc. v. Charles Carter & Co., 342 So. 2d 1153 (La. Ct. App. 1977); Meridian Corp. v. McGlynn/Garmaker Co., 567 P.2d 1110 (Utah 1977).

[32] Ind. Code Ann. § 5-16-10-2 (West 1989).

[33] *Id.* § 5-16-10-1.

firm is not employed under a separate contract designating it as a construction manager.

§ 7.8 Bond and Insurance Considerations

Contractors are routinely required to obtain bonds guaranteeing performance of the contract and proper payment to all subcontractors and suppliers.[34] Architects and engineers are typically exempt from bonding requirements. In *Mongiovi v. Doerner,* the Oregon Court of Appeals explained the rationale behind this exception: "[S]ince performance of a contract involving esthetic judgment cannot be measured objectively, it would not be reasonable to require an architect to post a performance bond."[35] In that case, a county contracted with an architect, a space-use planner, and a CM during the design and fast-track construction of a courthouse annex. The contracts were challenged as violating state procurement laws requiring bids and bonds of public contractors. The court held that all three contracts were properly let under the professional services exemption of the bid and bond laws.

The design professional's closest counterpart to the contractor's performance bond is its errors and omissions (E&O) or malpractice insurance. These policies typically indemnify the owner for damages caused by the negligence of the design professional, such as drafting errors in the plans and specifications or failure to make required inspections during construction. A typical E&O policy covers "liability arising out of any negligent act, error, mistake, or omission in rendering or failing to render professional services."[36] A requirement for E&O insurance in a CM contract[37] would indicate that the CM must meet the design professional's standard of care. Thus, the type of bond or insurance coverage maintained by a CM should assist in determining the classification of a CM as a design professional or general contractor.

---

[34] C. Foster, Challenges for Suretyship: Bonding the CM and Design-Build/Fast Track Construction 10 (1982) (unpublished manuscript presented at Duke Univ. Symposium on Construction Management and Design/Build "Fast Track" Construction, Jan. 21–22, 1983).

[35] Mongiovi v. Doerner, 24 Or. App. 639, 546 P.2d 1110, 1113 (1976).

[36] C. Foster, Challenges for Suretyship: Bonding the CM and Design-Build/Fast Track Construction 10 (1982) (unpublished manuscript presented at Duke Univ. Symposium on Construction Management and Design/Build "Fast Track" Construction, Jan. 21–22, 1983).

[37] *E.g.,* AIA Doc. B801, Standard Form of Agreement Between Owner and Construction Manager, Art. 10 (1973).

§ 7.9 Bidding Requirements

On public contracts, the issue of the CM's classification and the resultant standard of care can at least be narrowed, if not resolved, by reference to the procurement codes and building requirements of the particular public body soliciting the contract. These codes frequently limit the types of services for which a public body can contract or, at least, they categorize the CM as either a design professional or a contractor.

Most public agencies are required to procure construction services by public competitive bidding. They are also allowed, however, to procure professional services by negotiation. Thus, the question of whether a CM is performing as a design professional or as a contractor can be resolved, in part, by examining the method used to procure the services.

Approximately eight states have specific statutes providing for the procurement of construction management services and define the procedure by which these services will be procured. In most states, however, the method of procuring construction management services is not specifically set forth. The courts have, therefore, taken a pragmatic view in determining whether a contract should be competitively bid as a construction contract or negotiated as a design professional contract. In California, for example, the supreme court held that a construction management contract guaranteeing the maximum contract price was "too closely akin to traditional lump sum general construction contracting to be held exempt from the statutory competitive bidding requirements."[38] The court reasoned that the purpose behind the statutory exemption was that professional service contracts cannot be evaluated by objective criteria, but that the same rationale does not apply to a guaranteed maximum price contract, which can be judged on the basis of price.

The Indiana Court of Appeals reached a different conclusion in the case of an agency construction management contract, holding that the contract at issue was for a professional service. The court held that the contract did not involve any duties or responsibilities that would not otherwise be required of a licensed engineer, and stated, "Significantly, [the contract] did not guarantee that the total cost of each addition would be at or below the total value of the bids. A decision that implies exemption of all CM contracts from public bidding was reached in Oregon in 1976."[39] The Oregon Court of Appeals had held that a construction management contract was exempt, stating that "when making a contract involving professional or

[38] City of Inglewood-Los Angeles County Civic Ctr. Auth. v. Superior Court, 7 Cal. 3d 861, 500 P.2d 601, 103 Cal. Rptr. 689 (1972).

[39] Attlin Constr., Inc. v. Muncie Community Sch., 413 N.E.2d 281 (Ind. Ct. App. 1980).

esthetic judgment, the legislature could not have intended lowest price to be the ultimate determining factor."[40]

A Kansas appellate court recently held that a school district's hiring of a construction manager was not subject to the state's competitive bidding laws.[41] The case involved a school district entering into a construction management agreement without following competitive bidding procedures. The CM's duties included the supervision of other contractors, work scheduling, bid solicitation, and the development of detailed construction plans. The court held that these functions did not qualify as either construction or the procurement of goods, but were simply services to which the competitive bidding laws did not apply. The management firm was not allowed to bid on the project itself, however.

A similar result was reached in a Texas attorney general's opinion holding that a construction management consultant was exempt from competitive bidding requirements, so long as it did not bid on the project for which it served as CM.[42] In his opinion, the attorney general treated construction management as a "professional service," which was exempt by statute from competitive bidding requirements.[43] To do otherwise would defeat the purpose of obtaining professional consultation by forcing the school district to go with the lowest, and perhaps least qualified, bidder.

DUTY OWED BY CONSTRUCTION MANAGER

§ 7.10 Generally

The standard of care owed by a CM is determined first by its classification as either a professional or a general contractor and then by the degree of care owed by that category, depending on the nature and locale of the project.[44] The contractual duty owed by the CM depends primarily on the CM's specific undertaking on a project.[45] A CM cannot be held liable to a third

---

[40] Mongiovi v. Doerner, 24 Or. App. 639, 546 P.2d 1110, 1113 (1976).

[41] D-1 Constructors, Ltd. v. Unified Sch. Dist., 14 Kan. App. 2d 245, 788 P.2d 289 (1990).

[42] Tex. Att'y Gen. Op. JM-940 (Aug. 17, 1988).

[43] Tex. Educ. Code Ann. § 21.901 (West).

[44] See **§ 7.6**.

[45] Plan-Tec v. Wiggins, 443 N.E.2d 1212 (Ind. 1983). The paperwork surrounding negotiations for the services of CMs and design professionals, with glossy brochures and expansive-sounding correspondence, can, in conjunction with other activity, give the appearance that the parties have a deal for CM services. In W.E. Gilbert & Assocs. v. South Carolina Nat'l Bank, 285 S.C. 421, 330 S.E.2d 307 (1985), the owner terminated

party for its failure to perform tasks it has no obligation to perform. For the most part, the CM's obligations are set forth in its contract with the owner.[46] These contractual obligations, however, can be either extended or limited by specific statutes or regulations applicable to a project and by the tasks undertaken *in fact* by the CM, regardless of its contractual obligation to perform such work. Each of these matters used to determine the duty owed by the CM, is discussed in §§ **7.11** to **7.15**.[47]

§ 7.11 Contract Obligations

Even though the contractor does not typically enter into a contract with the CM, and is not a party to the owner/CM contract, the scope of duty owed by the CM to the contractor is defined by the owner/CM contract. Thus, a construction manager's contractual duties will not extend beyond those obligations specified within the owner/CM contract, and contract damages will be recovered only if a breach of those duties is found.[48] In *Bates & Rogers Construction Corp. v. North Shore Sanitary District,*[49] the court held, "[A] duty runs from the architect or engineer who engaged in a tortious action which hinders and damages the contractor. The scope of that duty, although based upon tort rather than contract, is nevertheless defined by the architect and engineer's contract with the owner."[50]

Virtually all jurisdictions addressing the issue have taken a similar approach.[51] Thus, before initiating an action against a CM, the contractor must know what contractual obligations were owed by the CM to the owner. For example, a contractor cannot sue the CM for a failure to schedule the work properly unless the CM's contract with the owner required it to prepare, monitor, and maintain the construction schedule.

---

its CM after two jobs. The CM sued for breach of contract and prevailed in the trial court. The court of appeals reversed, holding that until specific agreement had been reached with respect to future projects, no contract for them had been formed. Because there was no contract, no breach was possible.

[46] Krieger v. S.E. Griner Co., 282 Md. 50, 832 A.2d 1069 (1978).

[47] For another discussion of this topic, see Note, *Professional Construction Management: Developments in Legal Liability,* 32 Loy. L. Rev. 447 (1986).

[48] *See, e.g.,* Guarantee Elec. Co. v. Big Rivers Elec. Co., 669 F. Supp. 1371, 1382 (W.D. Ky. 1987).

[49] 92 Ill. App. 3d 90, 414 N.E.2d 1274 (1980).

[50] 414 N.E.2d at 1280. *See generally* Flinn & Stone, *Construction Manager Liability to Contractors,* Construction Briefings No. 84-5 (1984).

[51] Krieger v. S.E. Griner Co., 282 Md. 50, 832 A.2d 1069 (1978); Craig v. Everett M. Brooks Co., 351 Mass. 497, 222 N.E.2d 752 (1967); Vanasik v. Hirsch & Stevens, 65 Wis. 2d 1, 221 N.W.2d 815 (1974).

In order to recover damages in tort, the CM must also be guilty of a breach of a duty of care. The Fifth Circuit has held that, at least for economic damages, liability depends on a breach of the duty of care owed to the owner, not merely to the contractor.[52] In *Bagwell Coatings,* a fireproofing contractor sued an owner and his CM for increased cost in applying fireproofing material because of obstructed access to the worksite. The CM had refused to clear several worksites at the contractor's request, stating that it would not be in the owner's best interests to do so because of excessive cost. The contractor conceded that the CM was not liable under contract as an agent for a disclosed principal, but claimed that there was liability in tort.[53] The court found that the CM's actions were not only justified, but were in fact compelled by his duty to the owner to reduce costs.[54] Because the evidence did not support a finding that the CM had breached any duty owed to the owner, the contractor could not recover in tort from the agent. The court rejected the contractor's argument that the CM had assumed the separate roles of A/E and contractor, and thus owed a distinct duty to third parties to perform those functions in a non-negligent manner.

With noneconomic damages, that is, damages to persons and property, a design professional or CM may owe a duty to third parties that is not specifically described in the scope of its contract with the owner. This is particularly the case when safety responsibilities have been performed by the CM. Thus, when a jury could reasonably determine that the injuries sustained by a contractor's employees resulted from the CM's breach of his contractual obligation to provide a safe workplace, the employee was allowed to bring a personal injury claim against the CM for that breach despite a lack of privity.[55]

Similarly, the Massachusetts Supreme Judicial Court has held that a claim in tort against a CM may arise from his contractual relationship with the owner, and may be available to persons not a party to the owner/CM contract.[56] The case involved a worker injured by a defective electrical distribution panel worked on by an engineering and construction management firm in 1982. The CM contract had stated that the CM was responsible for the design and procurement of safety features on the electrical system. The court held that the CM's contractual obligations raised a potential jury question regarding whether the CM breached his duty of reasonable care to the subsequently injured employee.[57]

[52] Bagwell Coatings, Inc. v. Middle S. Energy, Inc., 797 F.2d 1298 (5th Cir. 1986).

[53] *Id.* at 1309.

[54] *Id.* at 1312.

[55] Riggins v. Bechtel Power Corp., 44 Wash. App. 244, 722 P.2d 819 (1986).

[56] Parent v. Stone & Webster Eng'g, 408 Mass. 108, 556 N.E.2d 1009, 1012 (1990).

[57] 556 N.E.2d at 1012, 1013.

§ 7.12 Procurement Codes

Even though the owner/CM contract is the primary source for determining the scope of the CM's duty, a secondary source is the statutes, regulations, and standards applicable to a given contract. The procurement codes of various public agencies frequently define the types of services on which public funds can be expended. In New York, for example, the state is prohibited from delegating its duty to coordinate construction projects.[58] This legislative prohibition against the delegation of coordination responsibilities has been interpreted so strictly that a contract clause requiring a prime contractor to submit a progress schedule was held invalid.[59] Thus, a construction management contract to coordinate the work of several prime contractors would be illegal and the CM could not be held responsible for its failure to perform a duty which, by statute, it is not permitted to perform.

The federal government is also prohibited from delegating certain duties to a CM:

> Notwithstanding any other provision of this section the Administrator shall be responsible for all construction authorized by this chapter, including the interpretation of construction contracts, the approval of materials and workmanship supplied pursuant to a construction contract, approval of changes in the construction contract, certification of vouchers for payment due the contractor, and final settlement of the contract.[60]

Several states have adopted procurement codes that might be interpreted to prohibit fast-track construction projects, which often use construction managers. For example, Kansas requires that, before any bids are taken, the project architect provide all construction plans and specifications to the secretary of administration and the state agency for which the project is being constructed.[61] Wisconsin requires that the plans for any construction project greater than $30,000 be completed before the project itself is begun.[62] California requires public owners to "prepare full, complete, and

---

[58] N.Y. Gen. Mun. Law § 101 (McKinney 1977). *See also* B. Gladstone & D. Hartzog, Allocation of Risk in the Construction Industry: The Nonprofessional Owner and His Construction Manager 8 (1982) (unpublished manuscript presented at the Duke Univ. Symposium on Construction Management and Design/Build "Fast Track" Construction, Jan. 21–22, 1983).

[59] General Bldg. Contractors v. County of Oneida, 54 Misc. 2d 260, 282 N.Y.S.2d 385 (1967).

[60] 40 U.S.C. § 609(c) (1976).

[61] Kan. Stat. Ann. § 75-1259 (1989).

[62] Wis. Stat. Ann. § 13.48(10) (West 1986).

accurate plans" before the public offering of a fixed-price, competitively bid contract.[63]

§ 7.13 Building Codes and Industry Standards

Virtually all construction, public or private, must be designed and erected in accordance with various codes and standards. These include building and safety codes mandated by federal, state, and local governments and industry standards. Compliance with these codes is either required by contract or mandated by law, regardless of contract. All construction professionals are charged with knowledge of and a duty to comply with these codes and standards.

Design professionals and contractors must comply with applicable building, safety, and fire codes. A CM who is serving the function of either a design professional or a contractor must also comply with these codes. Even the CM serving in the most limited role as overall project coordinator may be held responsible to a contractor for a failure of the designer or another contractor to comply with an applicable code. For example, in an Illinois case, an architect/engineer was held liable to an owner for damages resulting from a subcontractor's failure to comply with the local electrical code in designing a telephone cable encasement.[64]

Most construction contracts require work to be "of good quality" and "performed in a good and workmanlike manner." These phrases are given meaning by industry standards, which are often codified and endorsed by industry councils or associations. The methods of calculating minimum steel dimensions prescribed by the American Institute of Steel Construction (AISC), the concrete reinforcing formulas specified by the American Concrete Institute (ACI), and the ductile iron pipe connections recommended by the American Water Works Association (AWWA) are only a small sample of the industry standards available to design professionals and contractors. The CM should be held responsible for either complying with these standards or assuring that others comply with them.

§ 7.14 Construction Manager De Facto Rule

Even though the owner/CM contract and the applicable statutes, regulations, and standards define the scope of the CM's duties, a CM can be liable to third parties for tasks it undertakes *in fact.* Some jurisdictions will not

---

[63] Cal. Pub. Cont. Code § 10120 (West).

[64] Himmel Corp. v. Stade, 52 Ill. App. 3d 294, 367 N.E.2d 411 (1977).

hold a CM or similarly situated party liable for an action unless there is a clear contractual obligation to perform such an action.[65] Other jurisdictions, however, have taken a more expansive view.[66] In *Plan-tec v. Wiggins*[67] the court held:

> A duty of care may also arise where one party assumes such a duty, either gratuitously or voluntarily . . . . The assumption of such a duty creates a special relationship between the parties and a corresponding duty to act in the manner of a reasonably prudent person . . . . Failure to act in a reasonable manner will give rise to an action for negligence.[68]

A number of decisions have held the CM's duties to third parties to include those responsibilities assumed by the CM although not expressly described in the owner/CM contract. The critical considerations are the extent of the CM's supervisory responsibilities, her authority to stop work in response to a perceived safety threat, and her actual or constructive knowledge of the hazard.[69] Although the CM's duties may be expressly contained in her contract with the owner, the *Riggins* court held that the affirmative assumption of responsibilities outside the contract may establish a duty as well.[70]

An Indiana court has held that when a CM assumes a duty of care with respect to jobsite safety, a third party may bring an action in negligence for a failure to act in a reasonable manner.[71] The CM in *Phillips* had not contracted for the specific duty to provide for safety at the jobsite. However, it did employ a "safety coordinator" whose duties included general inspection and the responsibility to "govern the safety of the contractors." The safety coordinator did not seek to correct any violations, nor did he have actual knowledge of the hazard responsible for the particular injury suffered by the plaintiff. Nevertheless, the court held that the mere presence of the safety director was sufficient to present a jury question as to whether or not the CM assumed responsibility for jobsite safety.[72]

---

[65] Wheeler & Lewis v. Slifer, 195 Colo. 291, 577 P.2d 1092 (1978).

[66] Swarthaut v. Beard, 33 Mich. App. 395, 90 N.W.2d 373 (1971), *rev'd on other grounds,* 388 Mich. 637, 202 N.W.2d 300 (1972); Miller v. DeWitt, 37 Ill. 2d 273, 226 N.E.2d 630 (1967).

[67] 443 N.E.2d 1212 (Ind. 1983).

[68] *Id.* at 1219 (citations omitted).

[69] Riggins v. Bechtel Power Corp., 44 Wash. App. 244, 722 P.2d 819, 822–23 (1986) (although involving duties of A/E, court indicated that treatment would be similar for construction manager).

[70] 722 P.2d at 823.

[71] Phillips v. United Eng'rs & Constructors, Inc., 500 N.E.2d 1265, 1268–69 (Ind. Ct. App. 1986).

[72] *Id.* at 1269.

A Maryland court has similarly held that a duty of care may be imposed on a CM who assumes responsibility for jobsite safety either by contract or by conduct.[73] In *Brady* a CM expressly assumed a contractual obligation to the owner to maintain a safe workplace conforming to Occupational Safety and Health Administration (OSHA) and state standards. Although the CM contended that this duty did not run to the benefit of a contractor's employees, the court disagreed. It held that the duty to provide a safe workplace may run to third parties outside the contract when that duty was assumed for their indirect benefit.[74] According to the court, the CM would not be liable as a result of statutory violations, because it was not the statutory employer to whom the safety regulations applied. Rather, liability to third parties resulted from the CM's duty to exercise reasonable care in the performance of its obligations to the owner, thus justifying an action in ordinary negligence.[75]

A CM not in privity with an injured employee's contractor will probably not be treated as that employee's statutory employer under a state's labor laws. However, statutory liability for safety violations may still be extended to a CM under certain circumstances. For example, in *Nowak v. Smith & Mahoney*[76] a New York court held that a CM was subject to state labor regulations applying to contractors because the targets of those regulations were those in control of the jobsite and capable of enforcing safety standards, not simply "contractors." Because the relevant question was the ability to control, rather than the actual exercise of that control, the court reasoned that the regulations should apply to CMs as well as to contractors.[77]

The courts have so far refused to extend the duty of a CM or A/E to include third parties in the absence of an explicit contractual agreement or conduct indicating voluntary assumption of the duty. In *Young v. Eastern Engineering*[78] a subcontractor's employee was injured when he fell into an elevator shaft. The court granted summary judgment in the architect's favor, noting that he had neither contracted to make extensive on-site inspections nor had he voluntarily assumed such a duty.

The Pennsylvania Supreme Court recently affirmed this approach to a design professional's liability in *Marshall v. Port Authority,*[79] holding that an engineer's power to stop the work did not create a duty to an injured

---

[73] Brady v. Parsons, 82 Md. App. 519, 572 A.2d 1115, 1120 (1990).

[74] 572 A.2d at 1119–20.

[75] *Id.* at 1123.

[76] 110 A.D.2d 288, 494 N.Y.S.2d 449 (1985).

[77] 494 N.Y.S.2d at 450–51.

[78] 381 Pa. Super. 428, 554 A.2d 77 (1989).

[79] 524 Pa. 1, 568 A.2d 931 (1990).

worker.[80] Although the engineer was permitted to halt work on the site for safety reasons, the court held that such a power should not be converted into an affirmative duty to do so. To extend the engineer's monitoring duties to include safety precautions would undermine the contractor's sole responsibility for construction means. Furthermore, the engineer's role was essentially passive in nature and did not involve a continual duty to seek out safety hazards.

It is important to note that the majority of the cases dealing with the liability of the CM for de facto duties deal with safety on the jobsite.[81] There is, however, nothing in the reasoning of these cases to make them inapplicable to a contractor's claim against the CM. Thus, a contractor should look to the CM's actual role or course of conduct on a given project, as well as the responsibilities set forth in the contract, to determine the scope of CM's duties.

§ 7.15 Parties to Whom Duty Is Owed

The majority of the cases addressing the issue of CM or architect/engineer liability to third-party contractors involve prime contractors. Because the CM's liability to the prime contractor in most cases is based in tort, and not on the existence of a contract agreement between them, the duty can be owed to subcontractors and suppliers as well as primes. At least one court has found that a CM can be liable to a subcontractor in negligence.[82] Likewise, in *Waldinger Corp. v. Ashbrook-Simon-Hartley, Inc.*,[83] a supervisory architect/engineer has been found liable to a supplier for interference with contract.

The Seventh Circuit later modified the holding in *Waldinger Corp. v. Ashbrook-Simon-Hartley, Inc.*, and found that an architect/engineer is conditionally privileged to interfere in a contract between a subcontractor and a supplier.[84] The privilege is not absolute, however, and may be overcome by a showing that the A/E was not acting within the obligations of her own contract when the interference was made. For example, when an A/E enforces literal compliance with contract specifications in order to further her own goals rather than to protect her principal's interests, the

[80] *But see* Moore v. PRC Eng'g, Inc., 565 So. 2d 817 (Fla. Dist. Ct. App. 1990), which held that a contractor's injured employee could sue the project engineer for negligent supervision of instruction, based on the engineer's contractual power to halt the work in response to any perceived safety threats.

[81] Caldwell v. Bechtel, 631 F.2d 989 (D.C. Cir. 1980).

[82] Case Prestressing Corp. v. Chicago College of Osteopathic Medicine, 118 Ill. App. 3d 782, 455 N.E.2d 811 (1983).

[83] 564 F. Supp. 970 (C.D. Ill. 1983).

[84] Waldinger Corp. v. CRS Group Eng'rs, Inc., 775 F.2d 781, 790–91 (7th Cir. 1985).

privilege will be overcome and the A/E will be liable for tortious interference with contract.

In *Mobil Chemical Co. v. Blount Bros.,*[85] a hybrid contract-tort case, the Fifth Circuit held that a construction manager may be liable to subcontractors for any damages caused by a negligent decision to accelerate work. The owner and CM had entered into a fixed-price, best efforts contract to complete the project by January 1983. Because of a failure by both the owner and the CM to effectively schedule the work, the project fell behind. The owner and the CM jointly decided to accelerate the work in order to meet the deadline. Due to the fixed-price nature of his contract, and because he undertook no actual construction, the CM stood only to gain as a result of the acceleration of work. The court held that both were liable to subcontractors for increased costs, although the owner was not entitled to indemnification from the CM for those damages caused by his own "negligent" breaches of contract.[86]

A North Carolina appellate court has held a construction manager liable to a co-prime and its subcontractor for delay damages.[87] Under North Carolina law[88] a construction project in excess of $50,000 must involve a multiprime contract. The general contractor for a project to build a university library building was also designated as the "project expediter," and was granted much the same authority as a construction manager. A co-prime and its subcontractor claimed delay damages as the result of the CM's mismanagement. The court held that the CM could not be liable to the coprimes or their subcontractors in negligence, but liability was possible under the state statute, which specified that each prime must be financially responsible for undue delay it caused its co-primes. Furthermore, because the CM was contractually obligated to schedule and coordinate the work program, it could be liable for a breach of both its statutory and contractual duties.

New York courts have apparently been unwilling to find A/E liability to subcontractors in negligence, however. In *Widett v. U.S. Fidelity & Guaranty Co.*[89] a subcontractor could not maintain a negligence action against an architectural firm because there was no contractual relationship between the A/E and the subcontractor. Citing a substantial line of New York cases, the court concluded that absent privity of contract, the architect owes no duty to the subcontractor.[90] As a result, the subcontractor may not recover damages from the architect under either contract or tort.

[85] 809 F.2d 1175 (5th Cir. 1987).

[86] *Id.* at 1181–82.

[87] Bolton Corp. v. T.A. Loving Co., 94 N.C. App. 392, 380 S.E.2d 796 (1989).

[88] N.C. Gen. Stat. § 143-128.

[89] 815 F.2d 885 (2d Cir. 1987).

[90] *Id.* at 887.

THEORIES OF RECOVERY

§ 7.16 Negligence

There are four potential theories of recovery in an action by a contractor against a CM:

1. Negligence
2. Third-party beneficiary
3. Interference with contract and
4. Implied warranty.

Of these four theories, negligence is the most common.

To establish a cause of action in negligence against a CM, the contractor must prove three things:

1. That the contractor was owed a duty by the CM
2. That the CM failed to carry out that duty in accordance with the applicable standard of care
3. That the contractor was damaged as a result of the CM's breach of its duty.[91]

As set forth in **§ 7.11**, the issue of whether a particular duty was owed to the contractor by the CM is established primarily by the contract between the CM and the owner, along with the obligations imposed by any applicable statutes, regulations, or standards, plus the tasks the CM has in fact undertaken on a project. There is no requirement that there be a direct contractual relationship or privity of contract between the contractor and the CM.[92]

As set forth in **§ 7.6**, the standard of care is determined by whether the CM is regarded as a professional or a general contractor on a particular project. The issue of whether the CM breached the applicable standard of care is determined by comparing the CM's performance on the project in

---

[91] *See, e.g.*, Sides v. Richard Mach. Works, Inc., 406 F.2d 445 (4th Cir. 1969); Morrison v. MacNamara, 407 A.2d 555, 560 (D.C. 1979).

[92] Arizona seems to have been the last to abandon the "privity" rule. *See* Donnelly Constr. Co. v. Oberg/Hunt/Gilleland, 136 Ariz. 579, 667 P.2d 1298 (1984). *See also* A.R. Moyer, Inc. v. Graham, 295 So. 2d 397 (Fla. 1973); Conforti & Eisele, Inc. v. John C. Morris Assocs., 175 N.J. Super. 341, 418 A.2d 1290 (1981).

dispute to the standard of performance applicable to that CM.[93] This comparison typically requires expert testimony.[94]

Although in many situations a court requires expert testimony in an action against a design professional or CM, there are times when such testimony is not necessary. For example, a Pennsylvania court has held that when a professional's negligence is within the comprehension of an ordinary layman, expert testimony will not be required.[95] The case involved an engineer who approved a cable company's excavation plans without warning of an underground pipeline. The engineer was found liable under negligence rather than malpractice.

When the issues in the case are complicated, however, a court is likely to require expert testimony before negligence may be established. In *Nelson v. Commonwealth*[96] the Virginia Supreme Court held that expert testimony was necessary to establish a claim of negligent administration of construction against a design professional unless the alleged breach was within ordinary knowledge and experience.

In order to establish that it was damaged by the CM, the contractor must show that it incurred additional costs as a direct result of the CM's negligence. Otherwise stated, the negligence must be the *proximate cause* of the contractor's damages.[97]

§ 7.17 Third-Party Beneficiary

A contractor can recover from the CM under a third-party beneficiary theory only if it can establish that it was an *intended,* as compared to an *incidental,* beneficiary of the owner/CM contract. This means that the contractor must prove that the owner and the CM specifically intended that the contractor be benefited by the CM's performance of its contract for the owner. Because owner/CM contracts rarely identify third-party beneficiaries, the proof of this intent is difficult. In the absence of any contract language clearly designating the contractor as a beneficiary of the owner/CM contract, the contractor will most likely not be deemed a third-party beneficiary. In *Gateway Erectors v. Lutheran General Hospital*[98] an Illinois

[93] *E.g.,* Gateway Erectors v. Lutheran Gen. Hosp., 102 Ill. App. 3d 300, 430 N.E.2d 20 (1981); James McKinney & Son, Inc. v. Lake Placid 1980 Olympic Games, Inc., 92 A.D.2d 991, 461 N.Y.S.2d 483 (1983).

[94] *See, e.g.,* Dillon Properties, Inc. v. Minmar Builders, Inc., 257 Md. 274, 262 A.2d 740 (1970); Alfieri v. Butler, 38 A.D.2d 672, 327 N.Y.S.2d 108 (1971).

[95] Cipriani v. Sun Pipe Line Co., 393 Pa. Super. 471, 574 A.2d 706 (1990).

[96] 235 Va. 228, 368 S.E.2d 239 (1988).

[97] Sides v. Richard Mach. Works, Inc., 406 F.2d 445 (4th Cir. 1969); Morrison v. MacNamara, 407 A.2d 555 (D.C. 1979).

[98] 102 Ill. App. 3d 300, 430 N.E.2d 20 (1981).

court allowed an action in tort against a CM although specifically denying an alternative count on a third-party beneficiary theory, holding, "Morse/Diesel [Project Manager] was the agent of a disclosed principal and did not agree to become personally liable under the contract. Consequently, it is not personally liable on a contract theory."[99] Likewise, most courts have denied a third-party beneficiary approach in traditional architect/engineer and owner contracts or owner/prime contracts.[100]

In *Guarantee Electric Co. v. Big Rivers Electric Corp.*[101] a federal court held that the contractor had established neither an intent on the part of the owner or CM to confer a benefit on the contractor, nor had it shown that the performance of the owner/CM contract would satisfy any existing duty owed to the contractor, which would make it a creditor beneficiary. Similarly, an Illinois court has held that, although a contractor may be an incidental beneficiary of a clause in an owner/CM contract mandating prompt payments to contractors, this is not a sufficient direct benefit to allow the contractor to sue directly on the contract as a third-party beneficiary.[102]

In at least one case, however, a third-party beneficiary action has been allowed. In *Broadway Maintenance Corp. v. Rutgers*[103] a contractor sued the owner for its alleged failure to schedule and coordinate the work on a project properly. The court denied the action and held that, pursuant to the terms of the owner's contract with its construction manager, the CM[104] had specifically agreed to schedule and coordinate the work for the benefit of the contractors. In addition, each contractor's prime contracts with the owner stated that the CM would be responsible for the scheduling and coordination. Absent such explicit language making the CM responsible to other contractors for scheduling and coordination, however, it is unlikely that a contractor can succeed on a third-party beneficiary cause of action.

§ 7.18 Interference with Contract

A contractor can also sue the CM for interference with contract. An interference with contract action specifically against a CM was attempted in

---

[99] 430 N.E.2d at 23.

[100] A.R. Moyer, Inc. v. Graham, 285 So. 2d 397 (Fla. 1977); Buchman Plumbing Co. v. Regents of Univ. of Minn., 298 Minn. 328, 215 N.W.2d 479 (1974); Valley Landscape Co. v. Rollader, 218 Va. 257, 237 S.E.2d 120 (1977).

[101] 669 F. Supp. 1371 (W.D. Ky. 1987).

[102] Santucci Constr. Co. v. Baxter & Woodman, Inc., 151 Ill. App. 3d 547, 502 N.E.2d 1134 (1986).

[103] 108 N.J. Super. 350, 434 A.2d 1125 (1981).

[104] In *Broadway Maintenance,* the CM was also the general contractor on the project.

John E. Green Plumbing & Heating Co. v. Turner Construction Co.[105] Although the contractor did not meet its burden of proof, the cause of action was allowed. A New York court dismissed a similar cause of action, however, holding that the CM was acting in the owner's interests when he gave his advice and was not solely motivated by an intent to harm the plaintiff.[106]

In order to establish a cause of action for interference with the contract, the contractor must establish five elements:

1. The existence of a valid contract
2. The defendant's knowledge of the contract
3. Malicious interference by the defendant
4. A causal relationship between the defendant's interference and the breach for nonperformance of the contract
5. Resulting damages.[107]

Obviously, the most difficult element of this cause of action is to prove that the interference was malicious. This was the element on which the *John E. Green Plumbing & Heating* case foundered.

Similar causes of action have been allowed against architect/engineers. For example, in *Waldinger Corp. v. Ashbrook-Simon-Hartley, Inc.*,[108] a supplier of equipment was able to recover from an engineer on the grounds that the engineer unreasonably failed to approve its shop drawings. The court held that this was an intentional interference with the supplier's contract with its contractor. In a similar vein, a contractor successfully sued an architect/engineer for interference with a potentially beneficial financial relationship; the architect/engineer had interfered with the contractor's bid to the owner.[109]

An Illinois appellate court has allowed a third-party contractor to recover economic damages from a project engineer for tortious interference with contractual relations and prospective advantage.[110] The claim involved allegations that the engineer had both negligently and intentionally

---

[105] 500 F. Supp. 910 (E.D. Mich. 1980).

[106] N.S. Elec. Corp. v. Procida Constr. Corp., N.Y.L.J., Dec. 13, 1989, at 24 (N.Y. Sup. Ct. Kings County) (Shaw, J.), 11 CLR 78. The CM had advised the owner to terminate the contractor for his failure to unionize and to supply a work schedule. When the owner did so, the contractor brought an action for interference with contract and slander. The CM was entitled to summary judgment in the contractor's interference action.

[107] Downey v. United Weatherproofing, Inc., 363 Mo. 852, 253 S.W.2d 976 (1953).

[108] 564 F. Supp. 970 (C.D. Ill. 1983).

[109] Joba Constr. Co. v. Burns & Roe, Inc., 121 Mich. App. 615, 329 N.W.2d 760 (1982).

[110] Santucci Constr. Co. v. Baxter & Woodman, Inc., 151 Ill. App. 3d 547, 502 N.E.2d 1134 (1986).

encouraged the contractor's suppliers to terminate their accounts, and subsequently advised the owner to terminate the contractor's performance on the basis of the suppliers' actions. The contractor alleged that the engineer had acted both with malice and with the deliberate intent to inflict economic harm. The court held that the counts alleging negligent interference with contractual relations were properly dismissed because they sought economic damages in an action for negligence. The counts alleging intentional interference were allowed, however, because the economic loss doctrine was not a bar to such a claim. The tort of contractual interference is intended to protect a party's economic interest in contractual relations, therefore economic losses must be recoverable.

In *Waldinger Corp. v. CRS Group Engineers*[111] the Seventh Circuit, applying Illinois law, made a similar finding with respect to tortious interference with a contract. The court held that a design professional is conditionally privileged to interfere in the contractual relations of its principal, and that this conditional privilege extends to subcontracts as well. However, the court found that liability may be imposed if the professional has acted intentionally and without just cause. In particular, if the plaintiff can show that the professional was not acting within her contractual obligations to the principal, tortious interference will almost certainly result in liability.

In *Dehnert v. Arrow Sprinklers, Inc.*,[112] a subcontractor brought an action against a project engineer for intentional interference based on the engineer's recommendation that the contractor be terminated. The court held that when design professionals act within the scope of their contractual obligation to the owner, they will not be liable for advising the owner to terminate a contractual relationship absent bad faith or malice.[113]

§ 7.19 Implied Warranty

It may be possible to have a cause of action against a CM on the theory of implied warranty. In *Taramac Development Co. v. Delamater Fround & Associates, P.A.*,[114] the Supreme Court of Kansas held:

> It can be said that certain professionals, such as doctors and lawyers, are not subject to such an implied warranty. However, an architect and an engineer stand in much different posture as to insuring a given result than does a doctor or a lawyer. The work performed by architects and engineers is an exact science: that performed by doctors and lawyers is not. A person who

[111] 775 F.2d 781 (7th Cir. 1985).

[112] 705 P.2d 846 (Wyo. 1985).

[113] *Id.*

[114] 234 Kan. 618, 675 P.2d 361 (1984).

contracts with an architect or engineer for a building of a certain size and elevation has a right to expect an exact result.[115]

A few other jurisdictions have also taken an implied warranty approach as relates to an architect/engineer.[116] Although to date there have been no similar causes of action by a contractor against a CM, there is no reason why such a theory could not be maintained if there was in fact a warranty, express or implied, running from the CM to the owner. Because the scope of the CM's duty to the owner is defined by the owner/CM contract,[117] a breach of warranty action could be allowed under either a negligence or a third-party beneficiary theory.[118]

BASES FOR LIABILITY

§ 7.20 Generally

As set forth in **§ 7.11**, the grounds upon which a contractor can sue the CM are determined by the scope of the duties owed by the CM to the owner. Thus, the breach of any obligation owed by the CM to the owner can form the basis of a contractor's action. Because there is still limited case law specifically referring to a CM by name, in several situations analogies must be made to architect and/or engineer cases. The various bases for liability are presented here in the general chronological order of a construction project.

§ 7.21 Interference with Bids

Construction managers are frequently charged with reviewing and evaluating the bids of the various potential contractors on a project and recommending to the owner which bid to accept. In the case of *John Green Plumbing v. Turner Construction,*[119] the plaintiff was a bidder on a contract for an agency of the City of Detroit. The defendant was a consulting

---

[115] *Id.* at 364.

[116] *See, e.g.,* Broyles v. Brown Eng'g Co., 275 Ala. 35, 151 So. 2d 767 (1963); Bloomburg Mills, Inc. v. Sordoni Constr. Co., 401 Pa. 337, 164 A.2d 201 (1960).

[117] See **§ 7.11**.

[118] At least one court, however, has refused to allow a warranty action by a contractor because of the lack of privity between the contractor and the CM. James McKinney & Son, Inc. v. Lake Placid 1980 Olympic Games, Inc., 92 A.D.2d 991, 461 N.Y.S.2d 483 (1983).

[119] 500 F. Supp. 910 (E.D. Mich. 1980).

engineer who advised the city not to accept the plaintiff's bid. Plaintiff sued the defendant on the grounds that the defendant did not have adequate justification for recommending that the owner reject its bid. The court agreed and awarded the contractor its probable lost profits for the contract plus punitive damages on the theory that the defendant had interfered with a beneficial economic relationship. Thus, a contractor can sue a CM or similarly situated party if it improperly interferes with the contractor's bid to the owner.

§ 7.22 Design Defects

The CM is not generally responsible for the overall design of a construction project. It may, however, participate in design reviews and make recommendations to the owner for changes or improvements. Although there have been no cases to date in which a contractor has sued a CM for design defects, it is clear that such a cause of action would be allowed. This conclusion is based on two lines of cases that have already been fully developed: (1) contractor claims against design architect/engineers;[120] and (2) owner claims against CMs for their participation in the design process.[121]

The board of contract appeals has held that when the owner or designer is responsible for serious errors in a project's design, a construction manager will not be liable.[122] The case involved project designs that did not properly take into account the interstitial spaces to be built into a structure. The board held that the contractor hired by the government was a construction manager and not a general contractor, and therefore had no duty to discover the design errors.

A contractor is clearly entitled to recover from an architect if design defects cause the contractor to incur increased performance costs. Thus, when a contractor incurred additional costs to overcome an allegedly defective concrete design, it was entitled to seek recovery of those costs from the architect who designed the project.[123] In a similar vein, an owner has been able to recover from its CM when the CM contributed to a defective design.[124] Thus, there seems to be no reason why a contractor cannot recover from a CM for a defective design.

---

[120] *See, e.g.,* A.R. Moyer, Inc. v. Graham, 285 So. 2d 397 (Fla. 1973); Detweiler Bros., Inc. v. John Graham Co., 412 F. Supp. 416 (E.D. Wash. 1976); Conforti & Eisele, Inc. v. John C. Morris Assocs., 175 N.J. Super. 341, 418 A.2d 1290 (1981).

[121] Construction Litigation: Representing the Owner (R. Cushman, K. Cushman, L. Peters, eds., 2d ed., John Wiley & Sons 1990).

[122] Turner Constr. Co., ASBCA Nos. 25447, 29472, 29591, 29592, 29593, 29830, 29851, 29852, 90-2 BCA (CCH) ¶ 22,649.

[123] United States v. Rogers & Rogers, 161 F. Supp. 132 (S.D. Cal. 1958).

[124] First Nat'l Bank v. William F. Cann, 503 F. Supp. 419 (W.D. Ohio 1980).

§ 7.23 Delayed Site Access

One of the characteristics of a CM-directed project is the large number of prime contractors involved.[125] One of the CM's standard duties is to schedule the access of the several prime contractors to their portions of the overall work. If the CM fails to provide adequate or timely access, it can be liable to the contractor adversely affected. In one case, the CM and the owner were both found liable to a prime contractor for failure to provide adequate site access because they allowed other contractors on the site to drain water into the plaintiff's work area.[126] On another project, it was held that a subcontractor could maintain an action against the CM because the CM directed the subcontractor to commence its work before there was adequate site access.[127]

§ 7.24 Administration of Drawings

One of the CM's duties on most projects is to review and approve the shop drawings submitted by the contractor. This activity can result in CM liability to the contractor in two situations: (1) when the CM rejects drawings that should have been approved; and (2) when the CM delays the approval of drawings. In the case of *Waldinger Corp. v. Ashbrook-Simon-Hartley, Inc.*,[128] a contractor and its supplier sued the owner's project engineer for its failure to approve certain equipment proffered by the supplier. As a result of this failure, the equipment had to be obtained from another source. The court, applying Illinois law, found the engineer liable under both negligence and interference with contract theories, because there was no justification for the failure to approve the drawings.[129]

With regard to delays and approval of shop drawings, most owner/prime contracts set forth a time within which the shop drawings will be reviewed and returned by the CM. If the CM fails to return the drawings within the stated time, there is a possible cause of action for negligence.[130] It is unlikely, however, that occasional short delays in the approval of shop drawings will provide the basis for a cause of action. It is only when there have been considerable delays on several occasions that the requisite standard of care could be deemed to have been breached.

---

[125] See § **7.2**.

[126] R.S. Noonan, Inc. v. Morrison-Knudsen Co., 522 F. Supp. 1186 (E.D. La. 1981).

[127] Gateway Erectors v. Lutheran Gen. Hosp., 102 Ill. App. 3d 300, 430 N.E.2d 20 (1981).

[128] 564 F. Supp. 970 (C.D. Ill. 1983).

[129] *Id.* at 980–81.

[130] John E. Green Plumbing & Heating Co. v. Turner Constr. Co., 500 F. Supp. 910 (E.D. Mich. 1980).

§ 7.25 Failure to Provide Timely Information

The CM is typically required to provide the contractors on a project with the information necessary to carry out the work. This includes such items as clarification of drawings, schedules of other contractors, advance notice of proposed changes to the work, and similar items. In one Illinois case, the contractor sued the project engineer for its failure to provide timely responses to requests for instructions and complete details to the plans.[131] The court held that "the supervising engineer owes a duty to a general contractor to avoid negligently causing extra expenses for the contractor in the completion of the construction project."[132] In another case, the court allowed an action in negligence for the CM's failure to approve change orders in a timely fashion, although the CM eventually prevailed on other grounds.[133]

§ 7.26 Failure to Provide Construction Support Services

The CM is frequently required to provide basic construction support services—heat, light, power, and sanitary facilities—to the contractors on a project. The CM's failure to provide these items can be the basis of liability. For example, in an Illinois case, a contractor was allowed to bring an action both for the CM's failure to survey and stake the project properly and for its failure to provide electrical power.[134] In another case, the failure of the CM to provide heat to the project during the winter season was the basis for a cause of action by one of the project contractors.[135] The contractor's action can be based on both the inadequacy of the services provided and any delay or interruption in the service.

---

[131] Normoyle-Berg Assocs. v. Village of Deer Creek, 39 Ill. App. 3d 744, 350 N.E.2d 559 (1976).

[132] 350 N.E.2d at 561.

[133] John E. Green Plumbing & Heating Co. v. Turner Constr. Co., 742 F.2d 965 (6th Cir. 1984).

[134] Bates & Rogers Constr. Corp. v. North Shore Sanitary Dist., 92 Ill. App. 3d 90, 414 N.E.2d 1274 (1980).

[135] John E. Green Plumbing & Heating Co. v. Turner Constr. Co., 742 F.2d 965 (6th Cir. 1984).

§ 7.27 Failure to Schedule and Coordinate

On most projects, the CM's primary duty is to schedule and coordinate the work of the various contractors.[136] Provisions to this effect appear in most owner/CM and owner/contractor contracts.[137]

Under such provisions, the CM is required to create and implement a reasonable construction schedule. Such a schedule must accommodate the site access, concurrent usage, shop drawing reviews, material and equipment deliveries, and critical path needs of the owner and all the project contractors. In addition, the CM must monitor that schedule throughout the course of the project, assure that all parties meet their deadlines, take corrective action when a party is behind schedule, and modify the schedule if necessary. Failure to perform any of these activities can result in the CM's liability.

In Illinois, the court held that an engineer fulfilling the role of the CM was liable for improper supervision:

> A supervising engineer owes a duty to a general contractor to avoid negligently causing extra expenses for the contractor in the completion of a construction project. A supervising engineer must be held to know that a general contractor will be involved in a project and will be directly affected by the conduct of the engineer. This relationship, supervising engineer and general contractor, gives rise to a duty of care on the part of each party to the other. Such a duty exists even in the absence of a direct contractual relationship. We do not express an opinion as to the duty owed by the supervising engineer to parties connected with the construction project other than the general contractor.[138]

It should be noted that although the above case referred only to the CM's duty to a prime contractor, a subsequent Illinois case extended that duty to include subcontractors.[139]

In *Magnolia Construction v. Mississippi Gulf South Engineers, Inc.*,[140] the Supreme Court of Mississippi held that a project engineer may assume a

---

[136] AIA Doc. B801, Standard Form of Agreement Between Owner and Construction Manager, Art. 1 (1980). *See* AIA Doc. A201/CM, General Conditions of the Contract for Construction—Construction Management Edition, Art. 2.3.7 (1980).

[137] *E.g.*, Associated General Contractors of America, AGC Doc. No. 510, Standard Form of Agreement Between Owner and Construction Manager (Owner Awards All Trade Contracts), Arts. 2.1.1, 2.2.1.5 (1979).

[138] Normoyle-Berg Assocs. v. Village of Deer Creek, 39 Ill. App. 3d 744, 350 N.E.2d 559, 561 (1976).

[139] Case Prestressing Corp. v. Chicago College of Osteopathic Medicine, 118 Ill. App. 3d 782, 455 N.E.2d 811 (1983).

[140] 518 So. 2d 1194 (Miss. 1988).

duty to protect a contractor from economic loss, and that duty may be breached by the engineer's own negligent supervision. The case involved a contractor who relied on the engineer to ensure that the project was proceeding according to specifications. When it became clear that several lines had been laid off-grade, the contractor brought an action against the engineer, claiming negligent supervision and approval of work. The court held that such a cause of action may lie, and that the engineer may be liable to the contractor for economic damages incurred as the result of the contractor's own work.

However, a federal court has held that a claim for negligent supervision may not be brought in the absence of a duty. Thus, a third-party contractor may not bring an action in negligence against a CM whose "negligence" consists solely of a breach of the owner/CM contract.[141] Similarly, the Fifth Circuit has held that when a CM has made a change in scheduling in accordance with its duty to the owner, a contractor may not bring a claim of negligent supervision.[142] An Illinois court has likewise held that when there is no contractual obligation to the contractor, a CM may not be sued in negligence for economic damages resulting from changes in scheduling.[143]

Another case addressing the issue of a CM's liability for delay was *Casson Construction, Inc.*[144] In that case, a CM was hired by the government to coordinate 21 separate contractors. One contractor's late completion forced acceleration of a follow-on contractor, for which the government sued the late contractor. The General Services Administration (GSA) Board of Contract Appeals disallowed the GSA's claim, stating that the delay was actually caused by the CM's improper project coordination.[145]

After a finding that the owner has liability to a contractor because of a breach of the contract's scheduling requirements committed in the owner's name by the CM, the owner is likely to look to the CM for indemnity. However, the owner's recovery is not automatic. In *Bagwell Coatings, Inc. v. Middle South Energy, Inc.,*[146] the owner was held liable to the fireproofer when the CM ordered obstructing work installed before the fireproofer's work began, violating a clause in the contract guaranteeing the fireproofer unobstructed access. The owner was not entitled to indemnity from the CM, however, because, as the court noted, it was possible that the savings to the owner gained by the breach exceeded the damages owed to the fireproofer.

---

[141] Guarantee Elec. Co. v. Big Rivers Elec. Co., 669 F. Supp. 1371 (W.D. Ky. 1987).

[142] Bagwell Coatings, Inc. v. Middle S. Energy, Inc., 797 F.2d 1298 (5th Cir. 1986).

[143] Santucci Constr. Co. v. Baxter & Woodman, Inc., 151 Ill. App. 3d 547, 502 N.E.2d 1134 (1986).

[144] GSBCA Nos. 4884 *et al.,* 83-1 B.C.A. (CCH) ¶ 16,523.

[145] *Id.*

[146] 797 F.2d 1298 (5th Cir. 1986).

CONSTRUCTION MANAGER DEFENSES

§ 7.28 Owner/Construction Manager Contract

Because the CM's duties to the contractor are defined in large part by the owner/CM contract,[147] the CM may be able to rely on other provisions of the same contract to defend against a contractor's claims. If the owner/CM contract does not require the CM to perform a certain function, or provides that the CM is not responsible for a specific function, then the CM should not be liable to a contractor for a failure to perform that function. If, however, a CM actually does undertake a function, it may well be liable for a failure to perform that function properly, regardless of the provisions of its contract with the owner.[148]

In some cases the owner/CM contract may state that the contractor cannot rely on provisions of that contract.[149] Such language has been held to defeat a contractor's action based on a third-party beneficiary theory, but not a negligence action.[150]

§ 7.29 Owner/Prime Contract

On many construction management projects, the owner/prime contract specifically refers to the functions that will be performed by the CM.[151] The courts have held that, because the contractor can rely on such provisions in bringing an action against a CM, the CM can rely on other provisions of the owner/prime contract in defending against claims by a contractor. One court stated:

> We believe it would be manifestly inequitable to permit [the contractor] to both claim that [the CM] is liable to it for its failure to perform the contractual duties described in the [Owner-Contractor] agreement and at the same time deny that [the CM] is a party to that agreement in order to avoid arbitration of claims clearly within the ambit of the arbitration clause. "In short, the

---

[147] See § **7.11**.

[148] See § **7.14**.

[149] AIA Doc. B801, Standard Form of Agreement Between Owner and Construction Manager ¶ 13.2 (1980).

[150] Gateway Erectors v. Lutheran Gen. Hosp., 102 Ill. App. 3d 300, 430 N.E.2d 20 (1981).

[151] AIA Doc. A201/CM, General Conditions of the Contract for Construction—Construction Management Edition, Arts. 2.3.1, 2.3.2 (1980).

> plaintiff cannot have it both ways. It cannot rely on the contract when it works to its advantage and repudiate it when it works to [its] disadvantage."[152]

Owner/prime contracts contain a variety of provisions that may be used by a CM in defending against contractor claims. The most common of such provisions are discussed in §§ **7.30** through **7.44**.

§ 7.30 Duty to Review Drawings and Prior Work

Many contracts attempt to shift the burden of reviewing the drawings to the contractor.[153] Although contract language may not shift the total responsibility for the plans and specifications to the contractors, it can attempt to shift to them at least a portion of the duty to verify the accuracy of the plans and specifications.

An even more troublesome provision from a contractor's viewpoint is one making it responsible for conformance to plans and specifications of a prior contractor's work.[154] Although the effectiveness of such clauses has not been ruled on in the context of contractor/CM litigation, similar provisions have been held to bar a contractor's claims against an owner.[155] At the very least, it seems that such provisions shift at least a portion of the obligation to discover design defects or prior nonconforming work to the contractor, and its failure to discover such items could at least constitute contributory negligence.[156]

§ 7.31 No Damages for Delay Clauses

A *no damages for delay* clause typically provides that, in the event of a delay, a contractor will be entitled only to a time extension. Alternatively, it will provide that the contractor cannot recover damages for delay or interference. A typical clause reads as follows:

> Should the Contractor be delayed in the commencement, prosecution or completion of the Work by the act, omission, neglect or default of the Owner, Construction Manager, or of anyone employed by them, or of any

---

[152] Hughes Masonry v. Greater Clark County Sch. Bldg. Corp., 659 F.2d 836 (7th Cir. 1981) (citations omitted).

[153] AIA Doc. A201/CM, General Conditions of the Contract for Construction—Construction Management Edition, Art. 4.2.1 (1980).

[154] AIA Doc. A201/CM, General Conditions of the Contract for Construction—Construction Management Edition, Art. 6.2.2 (1980).

[155] Granite Constr. Co., IBCA No. 1-1442-3-81, 82-2 B.C.A. (CCH) ¶ 15,975.

[156] See § **7.40**.

> other Contractor or Subcontractor on the Project, or by any other cause beyond the Contractor's control, none of which are due to any fault, neglect, act or omission on its part, then the Contractor shall be entitled to an extension of time only, such extension to be for a period equivalent to the time lost by reason of any and all of the aforesaid causes, as determined by the Construction Manager. The Contractor shall not be entitled to any such time, however, unless a claim therefor is presented in writing to the Construction Manager within twenty-four (24) hours of the commencement of such claimed delay. Such extension of time, as determined by the Construction Manager, shall release and discharge the Owner and Construction Manager from any and all claims of whatever character by the Contractor on account of said delay.[157]

This clause even purports to absolve the owner and CM of liability for their own negligence.

As a general rule, courts will uphold no damages for delay clauses. They will, however, strictly construe such clauses and apply them only when the allocation of risk is clear and unambiguous.[158] Moreover, any ambiguities in such clauses will be resolved against the author of the contract. Thus, in *John E. Green Plumbing & Heating Co. v. Turner Construction Co.,*[159] the court (applying Michigan law) held that a no damages for delay clause would not bar a contractor's claim against a CM for damages for extra labor due to interference because the clause referred only to "delay damages."[160]

However, an Illinois appellate court held that a contractor not in privity with the project's CM was barred from suing the CM on a no damage for delay clause in the owner/contractor agreement.[161] The contractor had brought an action against the CM to recover for delay damages, claiming that the CM breached his duty to the contractor to run the project properly. Because the owner/CM contract specifically designated the CM as the owner's agent, the court reasoned that the no damage clause must apply to the CM as well as the owner in order to ensure that the CM's activities in the service of the owner not be hindered. To hold otherwise might create a situation in which the CM could seek indemnification from the owner for a contractor's successful claim, thus defeating the original purpose of the no damage clause.[162]

---

[157] This provision is a composite from several private contracts.

[158] City of Seattle v. Dyad Constr., Inc., 17 Wash. App. 501, 565 P.2d 423 (1972).

[159] 500 F. Supp. 910 (E.D. Mich. 1980).

[160] *Id.*

[161] L.K. Comstock & Co. v. Morse/UBM Joint Venture, 153 Ill. App. 3d 475, 505 N.E.2d 1253 (1987).

[162] 505 N.E.2d at 1255. As in Bates & Rogers Constr. Corp. v. North Short Sanitary Dist., 92 Ill. App. 3d 90, 414 N.E.2d 1274 (1980), the court treats the CM as a third-party beneficiary of the owner/contractor agreement.

Notwithstanding the fact that most courts will give effect to no damages for delay clauses, four judicial exceptions to the application of the clause have developed. These were summarized in *Peter Kiewit Sons' Co. v. Iowa Southern Utilities Co.*:[163]

1. When the delay was not of a kind contemplated by the parties
2. When the length of the delay was unreasonable
3. When there was evidence of bad faith
4. When the delay was caused by the active interference of the owner.[164]

These exceptions are applied differently in the various jurisdictions.

§ 7.32 Delay Not Contemplated by the Parties

Despite a no damages for delay clause, many jurisdictions award delay damages when the delay was not of a kind contemplated by the parties. The typical approach is to treat the clause as exculpatory in nature and construe it strictly against the drafter. Thus, although the owner has failed to provide the necessary rights-of-way for the completion of a highway project, a no damages clause will be defeated when it contemplates only court-ordered injunctions as a potential delay.[165]

In *Franklin Contracting Co. v. State,*[166] a New Jersey court allowed recovery for delay caused by lack of access to the jobsite. The contract specified that the contractor would become familiar with the means of access and would assume the costs of providing access. When Franklin requested proof of the availability of a right-of-way, the state's representatives gave assurances of access. However, there was no such right-of-way and construction was delayed for six months. The court held that this situation was not within the contemplation of the parties at the time of contracting:

> In a case where inquiry of the Director has disclosed that the status of one or more rights-of-way is such that they have not been obtained, it would be clear that in such circumstances this [no damages] clause would be operative in foreclosing the contractor from making any claim for delay. But where, as here, inquiry as to the status brought forth a representation that there was no problem with respect to same, it can hardly be claimed that this clause was

---

[163] 355 F. Supp. 376 (S.D. Iowa 1973).

[164] *Id.* at 397.

[165] Department of Transp. v. Arapaho Constr., Inc., 257 Ga. 269, 357 S.E.2d 593, 595 (1987).

[166] 144 N.J. Super. 402, 365 A.2d 952 (1976).

> intended to render the State immune from liability or that the parties contemplated delay because the State did not have a valid right-of-way.[167]

The same result has been reached by other courts.[168]

When the delay has been addressed in the contract, a no damages clause will defeat a contractor's attempt at recovery. In *Corinno Civetta Construction Corp. v. City of New York,*[169] the court agreed that a no damages clause in a public works contract applied only to those delays that were reasonably foreseeable, arose from the contractor's own work during performance, or were mentioned specifically in the contract. Damages could be recovered for:

1. Delays caused by bad faith and willful or grossly negligent conduct
2. Uncontemplated delays
3. Unreasonable delays amounting to intentional abandonment, and
4. Breach of a fundamental affirmative obligation by the owner, such as the one occurring in *Arapaho Construction.*[170]

In *Civetta,* however, the court found that because the delays caused by a city moratorium on street openings and unexpected subsurface conditions at the jobsite were specifically addressed within the contract, they were not compensable.[171]

The Ohio Supreme Court has held that when a contract specifically provides that no claim for damages may be made when a delay is caused by government act or regulation, a contractor will be unable to recover damages for a delay in procuring conditional zoning necessary for a building permit from the city of Akron.[172] Similarly, an Illinois court has held that when the contract between the contractor and the state expressly indicated that it would not be liable to the contractor for damages caused by a failure to acquire a right-of-way absent bad faith or gross negligence, the contractor will be precluded from recovering delay damages.[173]

Some state courts, however, view a no damages for delay clause as extending to unforeseeable causes, reasoning that such clauses are sufficiently

---

[167] 365 A.2d at 956.

[168] Buckley & Co. v. State, 140 N.J. Super. 289, 356 A.2d 56 (1975); McGuire & Hester v. City & County of S.F., 113 Cal. App. 186, 247 P.2d 934 (1952).

[169] 67 N.Y.2d 297, 493 N.E.2d 905, 502 N.Y.S.2d 681 (1986).

[170] 493 N.E.2d at 910.

[171] *Id.* at 913–14.

[172] Carrabine Constr. Co. v. Chrysler Realty Corp., 25 Ohio St. 3d 222, 495 N.E.2d 952 (1986).

[173] Newberg v. Illinois State Toll Highway Auth., 153 Ill. App. 3d 918, 506 N.E.2d 658 (1987).

unambiguous to survive even a strict interpretation. The Texas Court of Appeals explained this position in *City of Houston v. R.F. Ball Construction Co.*:[174]

> The clause does not limit its application to those delays and hindrances that were foreseen by the parties when they entered into the contract. Instead, it embraces all delays and hindrances which may occur during the course of the work, foreseen and unforeseen. Indeed, it is the unforeseen events which occasion the broad language of the clause since foreseeable ones could be readily provided for by specific language.[175]

Similar results were reached in Washington[176] and Utah.[177] In *John E. Gregory & Son, Inc. v. A. Guenther & Sons Co.*,[178] the Supreme Court of Wisconsin held that there were only three, rather than four, exceptions to a no damage clause: fraud, bad faith, and unnecessary orders resulting from ignorance or incompetence. The court reasoned that a no damage clause is unnecessary in the case of contemplated delays because the parties may simply negotiate around such circumstances. An uncontemplated delay is thus the only situation in which a no damage clause will be necessary, and to refuse to enforce it then would render it completely useless. A literal reading of such a clause is therefore appropriate and a claim for delay damages will be barred.[179]

A Maryland court has likewise extended the coverage of a no damage clause to include uncontemplated delays, at least in the absence of intentional wrongdoing, gross negligence, fraud, or misrepresentation by the party asserting the clause.[180] In *Greiner* a contractor sought delay damages against the state despite a no damage clause in its contract, claiming that the delays that occurred were not foreseen by either party. The court considered the two distinct lines of cases, as represented by *Civetta* on the one hand and *Gregory* on the other, and concluded that no damage clauses are sufficiently unambiguous to be afforded literal enforcement. The court thus refused to award the contractor delay damages, holding that the "uncontemplated delay" exception is not recognized in Maryland.[181]

---

[174] 570 S.W.2d 75 (Tex. Ct. App. 1978).

[175] *Id.* at 78.

[176] Nelse Mortensen v. Group Health, Inc., 17 Wash. App. 703, 566 P.2d 560 (1977).

[177] Western Eng'rs, Inc. v. State Rd. Comm'n, 20 Utah 2d 294, 437 P.2d 216 (1968).

[178] 147 Wis. 2d 298, 432 N.W.2d 584, 586–87 (1988).

[179] 432 N.W.2d at 587.

[180] State Highway Admin. v. Greiner Eng'g Sciences, Inc., 83 Md. App. 621, 577 A.2d 363 (1990).

[181] 577 A.2d at 372.

§ 7.33 Unreasonable Delay

An unreasonable or excessive delay on the part of the owner may also override a no damages for delay clause, especially when the delay is close to an abandonment of the project. In a leading New York case,[182] damages for a three-year suspension of performance were awarded despite a limitation of liability clause:

> The contract in question, Clause J, does not admit of a construction that the board of education could be the exercise of arbitrary power extend the time of realtor's work and delay the same for 3 years or longer. The clause must be construed as inapplicable to delays so great or so unreasonable that they may fairly be deemed equivalent to an abandonment of the contract and thus interpreted was not a bar to realtor's claim.[183]

A delay of eight months in the performance of a 350-day contract was considered "sufficiently unreasonable to strike at the heart of the contract and justify the contractor in abandoning it," notwithstanding a no damages for delay clause.[184] In another New York case, although the court found that the State had actively interfered with construction, it indicated that the no damages for delay clause would probably be inapplicable to a 21-month delay.[185] However, in another case, the New York Court of Appeals ruled that the no damages for delay clause was intended to cover a range of unreasonable delays and that active interference, absent bad faith or deliberate intent, would not make such a clause unenforceable. A strongly worded dissent would have upheld the right of the contractor to recover upon a finding of active interference for an extraordinarily long delay—28 months.[186]

One court has held that extensive delay without actions showing actual abandonment of the contract is not enough to make the no damages for delay clause unenforceable.[187] Other courts have found the specific delay in question not excessive.[188]

---

182 People v. Craig City, 232 N.Y. 125, 133 N.E. 419 (1921).

183 133 N.E. at 426.

184 Brady v. Board of Educ., 222 A.D. 504, 506, 226 N.Y.S. 707, 709 (1926).

185 American Bridge Co. v. State, 245 A.D. 535, 283 N.Y.S. 577 (1935).

186 Kalisch-Jarcho, Inc. v. City of N.Y., 58 N.Y.2d 377, 448 N.E.2d 413, 461 N.Y.S.2d 746 (1983).

187 F.D. Rich Co. v. Wilmington Hous. Auth., 392 F.2d 841 (3d Cir. 1968).

188 E.C. Ernst, Inc. v. Manhattan Constr. Co., 551 F.2d 1026 (5th Cir. 1977) (two-month delay); Dickerson Co. v. Iowa State Dep't of Transp., 300 N.W.2d 112 (Iowa 1981) (two-year delay); Endres Plumbing Corp. v. State, 198 Misc. 546, 95 N.Y.S.2d 574 (1950) (six-month delay).

§ 7.34 Bad Faith or Fraud

If an owner's delay is found to be a result of bad faith, fraud, concealment, or willful misrepresentation, a no damages for delay clause can be set aside.[189] Because every contract implies fair dealing between the parties, bad faith or tortious intent can withdraw the benefit of a bargain from the party abusing it.[190] In *Housing Authority v. Hubbell,*[191] bad faith was found when an owner caused delays willfully by "unreasoning action." In that case the delays were caused by the arbitrary and capricious requirements of the owner's architect, and recovery was allowed despite the no damages for delay clause.

Extreme negligence can also supersede a damages disclaimer. In *Ozark Dam Constructors v. United States*[192] the government delayed delivery of cement to a construction site because the cement plant was closed by a strike. Although the government was aware of the likelihood of a strike, it failed to warn bidders or to procure cement through other channels.

> The possible consequences were so serious, and the action necessary to prevent those consequences was so slight, that the neglect was almost willful. It showed a complete lack of consideration for the interest of the Plaintiffs. If the Plaintiffs really included in their bid an amount to cover the contingency of such inconsiderate conduct on the part of the Government's representatives, the Government was buying and the public was paying for things that were worth less than nothing.[193]

Similarly, a city's failure to obtain a right-of-way was termed a "knowing delay of the public authority, which transcends lethargy or bureaucratic bungling," and therefore a no damages for delay clause was held inapplicable.[194]

§ 7.35 Active Interference

A no damages for delay clause will not protect the owner from liability for delay caused by *active interference.* The standard for active interference was defined in *Peter Kiewit Sons' Co. v. Iowa Southern Utilities Co.*[195] as:

---

[189] *See* Annotation, *Validity and Construction of "No Damage" clause with respect to delay in Building or Construction Contract,* 74 A.L.R.3d 187, 215 n.38 (1976).

[190] Psaty & Fuhrman, Inc. v. Housing Auth., 76 R.I. 87, 68 A.2d 32, 36 (1949).

[191] 325 S.W.2d 880 (Tex. Ct. App. 1959).

[192] 127 F. Supp. 187 (Ct. Cl. 1955).

[193] *Id.* at 191.

[194] Southern Gulf Utils., Inc. v. Boca Ciega Sanitary Dist., 238 So. 2d 458 (Fla. Dist. Ct. App. 1970).

[195] 355 F. Supp. 376 (S.D. Iowa 1973).

> [s]ome affirmative, willful act, in bad faith, to unreasonably interfere with plaintiff's compliance with the terms of the construction contract. . . . The use of the term "active" to modify interference . . . is significant and clearly implies that more than a simple mistake, error in judgment, lack of total effort is needed for plaintiff to prove the "active interference" necessary to render unenforceable an otherwise clear and unambiguous "no damages" clause.[196]

Although there have been numerous cases on the issue of active interference, one case has specifically addressed the owner's responsibility on a multi-prime project. In *United States Steel Corp. v. Missouri Pacific Railroad,*[197] the court, applying Arkansas law, decided that an owner's directive to a follow-on prime to commence performance, even though a prior prime's work had not been completed, constituted active interference. Specifically, the owner directed a steel erector on a bridge project to commence performance before the preceding concrete piers had been completed. In *Blake Construction Co. v. C.J. Coakley Co.,*[198] a case with significant potential for application in the construction manager context, the court found that a prime had actively interfered with one of its subcontractors by failing to schedule and sequence properly the work of other subcontractors. Thus, a subcontractor was allowed to recover delay damages in spite of a comprehensive no damages for delay clause.

Delays within the contemplation of the parties are not, of course, interference.[199] Likewise, mere negligence will not override a no damages for delay clause.[200] In *Dobson v. State*[201] a New Jersey appellate court held that an exception to the no damage clause may exist when the delay is the result of active interference by the owner. The contractor's claim arose out of delays in a public works project caused by the owner's refusal to allow the contractor to obtain material from a substitute supplier. The court held that active interference connotes more than simple negligence, and must amount to some affirmative, willful conduct by the owner that unreasonably interferes with the contractor's performance.[202] The court found that the contractor had failed to show conduct sufficiently outrageous to constitute active interference, and refused to allow delay damages under the no damage clause. In *Kalisch-Jarcho, Inc. v. City of New York*[203] the New York

---

[196] *Id.* at 399.

[197] 668 F.2d 435 (8th Cir.), *cert. denied,* 459 U.S. 836 (1982).

[198] 431 A.2d 569 (D.C. 1981).

[199] Gherardi v. Board of Educ., 53 N.J. Super. 349, 147 A.2d 535 (1958).

[200] Cunningham Bros., Inc. v. City of Waterloo, 254 Iowa 659, 117 N.W.2d 46 (1962).

[201] 218 N.J. Super. 123, 526 A.2d 1150 (1987).

[202] 526 A.2d at 1153.

[203] 58 N.Y.2d 377, 448 N.E.2d 413, 461 N.Y.S.2d 746 (1983).

Court of Appeals ruled that the active interference exception would not apply unless such interference was "actuated by bad faith and deliberate intent."[204] This is, however, a dramatic departure from prior New York decisions.

§ 7.36 Statutory Exceptions

A growing number of states are showing their reluctance to enforce no damage clauses in the form of statutory exceptions. California prohibits the use of no damage clauses in public contracts when the delays are "unreasonable under the circumstances involved, and not within the contemplation of the parties."[205] Oregon and Colorado prohibit their use in any public contract, regardless of the nature of the delay.[206] Washington prohibits their use in both public and private contracts.[207]

Thus, owners and construction managers cannot protect themselves from delays they cause.

§ 7.37 Delegation of Scheduling Functions to Contractors

Many owner/prime contracts attempt to delegate the duty to schedule and coordinate the overall project work to the several prime contractors, regardless of whether there is a CM on the project. In a similar vein, some owner/prime contracts attempt to shift the liability for delay directly to the individual contractor causing the delay.

One of the earliest cases to address directly the obligations of the various parties on a CM project was *Pierce Associates, Inc.*[208] This was a GSA contract containing a provision that the contractors were to coordinate with each other and that, if one prime was delayed by another, it should seek recovery from that other contractor.[209]

One of the contractors was delayed approximately five months and brought its claim directly against the GSA. The GSA defended on the grounds that the contract limited the contractor's recovery to actions

---

[204] *Id.* at 380.

[205] Cal. Pub. Cont. Code § 7102 (West Supp. 1990).

[206] Colo. Rev. Stat. § 24-91-103.5(2) (Cum. Supp. 1989); Or. Rev. Stat. § 279.063 (1989).

[207] Wash. Rev. Code Ann. § 4.24.360 (West 1988).

[208] GSBCA No. 4163, 77-2 B.C.A. (CCH) ¶ 12,746.

[209] *Id.* at 61,939.

against other contractors. The GSA Board of Contract Appeals denied the GSA's defense and held that the GSA contracting officer still had an affirmative duty to coordinate the work.[210] A similar result was reached in *Jacobson & Co.,*[211] in which the GSA Board of Contract Appeals held:

> The Government can decide on whatever method of construction and contracting it chooses, but, in doing so, it also assumes the responsibilities inherent in its choice. With phased construction, it is obvious that the contracting officer has the obligation and duty to demand that the various contractors cooperate with the construction schedule and not interfere with the work of any other contractor.[212]

Although these cases deal with the owner's obligations, they would be equally applicable to the CM.

In a series of cases arising out of the construction of the University of New Jersey Medical Facilities at Rutgers, a different conclusion was reached. On that project, the owner entered into six separate prime contracts but designated one of the contractors to be responsible for overall scheduling and coordination. Each of the other contractors was directed to comply with the directives of this single contractor.[213]

Disregarding this language, at least two of the primes elected to file suit directly against the owner. In both cases, the court ruled that because the duty of coordination was clearly delegated to a party other than the owner, the owner was not liable for delays and lack of coordination.[214] In reaching this overall decision, the trial court seemed to rely heavily on its determination that each contractor was a third-party beneficiary of each of the other contractor contracts and had a right to sue one another. It also appears that one of the contractors was fulfilling the role of a CM.

The difference between the GSBCA's decision in *Pierce Associates, Inc.*, and the New Jersey decisions in *Dobson* and *Broadway Maintenance* seems to be that in the former, no one party was clearly responsible for scheduling and coordination, but in the latter two cases, the duty was clearly assigned to a prime contractor who was fulfilling the role of a CM. Thus, it seems that a general delegation of the duty to schedule and coordinate to several contractors will not relieve the CM of responsibility.

---

[210] *Id.* at 61,943.

[211] GSBCA No. 5605, 80-2 B.C.A. (CCH) ¶ 14,521.

[212] *Id.* at 71,565.

[213] Broadway Maintenance Corp. v. Rutgers, 108 N.J. Super. 350, 434 A.2d 1125, 1127–28 (1981).

[214] Edwin J. Dobson, Jr., Inc. v. Rutgers State Univ., 157 N.J. Super. 357, 384 A.2d 1121 (1978).

§ 7.38 Forum Selection

Many owner/prime contracts designate a particular forum for resolving disputes between the parties. In at least one case, a court has held that a contractor with a negligence claim against the CM was required to submit the matter to arbitration because its contract with the owner required that all owner/contractor disputes be arbitrated.[215] The court ruled that it would be "manifestly inequitable" to permit the prime to bring a negligence suit against the CM based on the CM's duties as defined in the owner/CM contract and not require the contractor to be bound by other terms of that contract.[216]

In another case, when the owner/contractor agreement specifies handling claims disputes with a "dual notice mechanism," that is, notice will be made first to the CM and then to the owner, the First Circuit has held that failure to follow that procedure will bar the contractor's breach of contract action against both the CM and the owner.[217] The court reasoned that when the parties to the contract are sophisticated businesses, the language of the contract regulating their behavior should not be rewritten.

§ 7.39 Owner's Agent

It may be possible for a CM to argue that because it is performing as an agent of an owner, it is not independently liable for its negligence. The general test for the existence of an agency relationship is whether the owner has the right to control and direct the work, not only as to the result of the accomplished work but also as to the manner and means by which that result is accomplished.[218] The CM who is the owner's agent is obligated to obey the owner's reasonable orders and carry out all duties in the owner's interest.[219] An independent contractor, on the other hand, is not required to comply with these duties; it is responsible only for carrying out the terms of its contract with the owner.

The Fifth Circuit has held that when a CM is acting as an agent on the owner's behalf, a contractor may not bring an action in negligence against the CM if there has been no breach of duty to the owner.[220] The CM in this

---

[215] Hughes Masonry v. Greater Clark County Sch. Bldg. Corp., 659 F.2d 838 (7th Cir. 1981).

[216] *Id.* at 838–39.

[217] Paterson-Leitch Co. v. Massachusetts Mun. Wholesale Elec. Co., 840 F.2d 985 (1st Cir. 1988).

[218] S. Williston, A Treatise on the Law of Contracts § 1012A (3d ed. 1967).

[219] *Id.* § 1012B.

[220] Bagwell Coatings, Inc. v. Middle S. Energy, Inc., 797 F.2d 1298 (5th Cir. 1986).

case refused to clear a jobsite for the contractor on the grounds that the added expense to the owner was not justified. The court held that, rather than committing a breach of duty, the CM was actually compelled by his obligation to the owner to undertake such a measure. Because the contractor had shown no breach of a duty owed by the CM, the CM could not be negligent. The action in tort was therefore rejected.

In *Parkway Windows, Inc. v. River Tower Associates*[221] a New York appellate division held that an agent was personally responsible for affirmative wrongdoing, as opposed to omissions. Although an agent was not liable for a failure to act, those actions undertaken by the agent imposed a duty of reasonable care. Thus, when a CM acting as an "agent" for the owner intentionally interferes with a contractor's work, denies site access, and willfully terminates the contractor, then seeks to wrongfully convert the contractor's property following termination, the contractor may state a claim against the CM despite his agency status with the owner.

§ 7.40 Contributory and Comparative Negligence

Under general principles of tort law (that is, negligence), a plaintiff who is negligent in a particular situation cannot recover in negligence from another party. Called the doctrine of *contributory negligence,* this is applied in many jurisdictions.[222] In other jurisdictions, a concept of *comparative negligence* has evolved. This means that the courts will compare the negligence of the plaintiff and the defendant and apportion damages based on the degree of negligence of each party.[223] For example, if the court finds that a plaintiff and a defendant are each 50 percent responsible for a situation, the plaintiff's damages could be reduced by 50 percent.

In *Brady v. Ralph M. Parsons Co.*[224] a Maryland appellate court held that a CM sued by an injured worker's estate may assert the defenses of contributory negligence and assumption of risk. The plaintiff argued that such a defense was inappropriate under the statutory regulations for jobsite safety. The court disagreed, however, holding that although OSHA regulations did impose a duty on the CM to monitor jobsite safety,[225] the CM was not a statutory employer. As a result, the plaintiff's claim was based on common law negligence rather than a statutory violation, and the defenses of contributory negligence and assumption of risk were available. Thus, a contractor suing a CM for project delays could lose its case under the doctrine of

---

[221] 108 A.D.2d 660, 485 N.Y.S.2d 755 (1985).

[222] Prager v. City of N.Y. Hous. Auth., 112 Misc. 2d 1034, 447 N.Y.S.2d 1013 (1982).

[223] Sprayregen v. American Airlines, Inc., 570 F. Supp. 16 (S.D.N.Y. 1983).

[224] 82 Md. App. 519, 572 A.2d 1115 (1990).

[225] See § **7.14**.

contributory negligence or have its damages reduced under the doctrine of comparative negligence if the CM could establish that the contractor contributed to or caused part of the delay.

§ 7.41 No Recovery for Economic Loss

Although there is little doubt that a contractor can sue a CM for negligence, there is considerable controversy as to whether the CM will be liable for the contractor's economic loss. Although the term *economic loss* is not precisely defined, it generally means any money damages other than compensation for direct damage to a person or property.[226]

Some jurisdictions hold that a design professional is liable for economic loss only to its client, that is, the owner or the other party with whom it has a contract. For example, in *Local Joint Executive Board v. Stern*[227] the court held as follows:

> The well established common-law rule is that absent privity of contract or an injury to person or property, a plaintiff may not recover in negligence for economic loss. . . . The primary purpose of the rule is to shield a defendant from unlimited liability for all of the economic consequences of a negligent act, particularly in a commercial or professional setting, and thus to keep the risk of liability reasonably calculable.[228]

New York courts have recently limited an A/E's or other design professional's use of the economic loss doctrine when the parties are either in privity or in a relationship approaching that of privity.[229] An architect hired by the plaintiff school district subsequently hired two engineers who erroneously advised the district that it had to shut down one of its buildings because of inadequate support. The district subsequently filed a claim against the engineers for economic damages suffered as a result of the unnecessary closing of the building. The New York Court of Appeals held that, although privity is not absolutely required for recovery of economic loss against a design professional, there must be a relationship so close as to approximate privity. In order to bring a claim for economic damages, the court held that the plaintiff needs to establish: (1) awareness by the professional that his work would be used for a particular purpose; (2) reliance by

---

[226] Steckmar Nat'l Realty & Inv. Corp., Ltd. v. J.I. Case Co., 99 Misc. 2d 212, 415 N.Y.S.2d 946 (1979).

[227] 98 Nev. 409, 651 P.2d 637 (1982).

[228] 651 P.2d at 638.

[229] Ossining Union Free Sch. Dist. v. Anderson LaRocca Anderson, 73 N.Y.2d 417, 539 N.E.2d 91, 541 N.Y.S.2d 335 (1989).

a known party on the professional's work for that particular purpose; and (3) some conduct by the professional linking it to the plaintiff.[230] The court held that the school district had in fact established all three elements, so that the A/E was subject to suit in negligent misrepresentation for economic losses by the district.

The Supreme Court of Illinois has extended the economic loss defense to third-party claims against design professionals.[231] Plaintiff homeowners sued the A/E for negligence, citing numerous flaws in the design of their building. The court held that because the plaintiffs had no privity with the A/E and were suing under tort, they may not claim purely economic damages resulting from the poor quality of the services provided to the building's developer.

In Illinois the economic loss doctrine applies to construction professionals whether or not alternate means of recovery are available.[232] In *Anderson* the plaintiff subcontractor sought to recover economic losses incurred as a result of the owner's improper demand that completed work be redone. The court held that the subcontractor's complaint alleged damages appropriate to a contract action, and were not recoverable under tort. It was irrelevant that the subcontractor had no other recourse because of lack of privity.

A few other states have followed Illinois by applying the economic loss doctrine to design professionals. The Supreme Court of Ohio has held that, absent privity of contract, a contractor may not sue an A/E for economic losses resulting from a negligent design.[233] The plaintiff contractor had sought recovery of increased costs suffered as the result of a design error by the architect. Although economic actions had previously been allowed against accountants in the absence of privity, the court held that there is no duty to exercise reasonable care to prevent economic injury to others absent privity. Furthermore, the court held that there was no relationship between the architect and the subcontractors to serve as a reasonable substitute for privity. Because the number of parties who might rely on the A/E's design were potentially quite large and unforeseeable, the court reasoned that liability for economic losses should not be extended in the context of a construction contract.

---

[230] 539 N.E.2d at 95. (This is the New York standard for financial professionals, adopted in Credit Alliance Corp. v. Andersen & Co., 65 N.Y.2d 536, 483 N.E.2d 110, 493 N.Y.S.2d 435 (1985). The court reasoned that there was no reason it should not also apply to other professionals, such as A/E's and CM's.)

[231] 2314 Lincoln Park W. Condominium Ass'n v. Mann, Gin, Ebel & Frazier, Ltd., 136 Ill. 2d 302, 555 N.E.2d 346 (1990).

[232] Anderson Elec., Inc. v. Ledbetter Erection Corp., 115 Ill. 2d 146, 503 N.E.2d 246 (1986).

[233] Floor Craft Floor Covering, Inc. v. Parma Community Gen. Hosp., 54 Ohio St. 3d 1, 560 N.E.2d 206 (1990).

Virginia has similarly disallowed recovery of economic losses from design professionals absent privity.[234] The case involved a contractor who sued for economic losses resulting from the project architect's negligent failure to provide plans in a timely manner, as specified in the owner-A/E contract. The court narrowly interpreted a statute specifying that lack of privity is no longer a defense in actions for personal or property damage, and held that the statute was not intended to apply to purely economic harm. Because the architect was under no contractual or statutory duty to protect the contractor from economic loss, the contractor's tort claim was barred. The court's language was particularly broad, indicating that a similar result would almost certainly apply to a CM.[235]

In those jurisdictions applying the economic loss doctrine to construction managers and other design professionals, a claim for economic damages may still be made by altering the pleading. For instance, in *Santucci Construction Co. v. Baxter & Woodman, Inc.,*[236] the court denied recovery for economic losses to a contractor under a negligence claim, but allowed the action to proceed as a claim of intentional interference with contractual relations and intentional interference with prospective economic advantage. Similarly, the Eleventh Circuit disallowed a contractor's claim for economic damages under a negligent supervision theory due to a lack of privity, but it did allow a claim for negligent misrepresentation of subsurface conditions.[237]

Despite the growing application of the economic loss doctrine in the construction context, the majority of states allow an action for purely economic damages against a design professional in the absence of privity. A Florida appellate court has allowed a claim for the recovery of economic damages under a theory of negligence when there is no alternative theory of recovery available.[238] The Minnesota Supreme Court has held that the economic loss doctrine is not intended to apply to service transactions such as design and construction management.[239] As a result, a contractor may sue an architect for negligence and bad faith to recover economic damages even in the absence of privity.[240]

---

[234] Blake Constr. Co. v. Alley, 233 Va. 31, 353 S.E.2d 724 (1987).

[235] 353 S.E.2d at 727.

[236] 151 Ill. App. 3d 547, 502 N.E.2d 1134 (1987). *See also* Waldinger v. CRS Groups, 775 F.2d 781 (7th Cir. 1985).

[237] Gulf Contracting v. Bibb County, 795 F.2d 980 (11th Cir. 1986).

[238] Latite Roofing Co. v. Urbanek, 528 So. 2d 1381 (Fla. Dist. Ct. App. 1988).

[239] Prichard Bros., Inc. v. Grady Co., 428 N.W.2d 391 (Minn. 1988).

[240] *Id. See* Bacco Constr. Co. v. American Colloid Co., 148 Mich. App. 397, 384 N.W.2d 427 (1986); Waldor Pump & Equip. Co. v. Orr-Schelen-Mayeron & Assocs., 386 N.W.2d 375 (Minn. Ct. App. 1986).

§ 7.42 Statutes of Limitations

All legal actions are governed by statutes of limitations, which establish time limits within which a cause of action may be brought. These statutes vary from state to state, and generally apply different time limits to contract and negligence actions.[241] As a general rule, the statutes of limitations for negligence actions are shorter than those for written contracts; they range from two to five years from the date of accrual of the cause of action. However, they vary widely from state to state.[242] Some states also have special statutes applying to any improvements to real property.[243] A contractor should be sure to verify the statute of limitations in its jurisdiction.

§ 7.43 Accrual

A statute of limitations for negligence starts to run when the tort occurs.[244] The determination of when the tort occurs requires an evaluation of all the facts and circumstances of the particular case, but some generalizations are possible. For actions arising during the course of construction, the statute of limitations usually does not begin to run until substantial completion of the construction.[245] Similarly, actions originating from defective design usually do not accrue until the design is completed.[246]

For those jurisdictions with special statutes of limitations for improvements to real property, the statute typically starts to run from the date the project was substantially complete.[247] *Substantial completion* is that stage of completion when the project is ready for its intended purpose.[248]

---

[241] Construction Litigation: Representing the Owner (R. Cushman, K. Cushman & L. Peters, eds., 2d ed., John Wiley & Sons 1990).

[242] *Id.*

[243] A. Kornblut, Statutory Trends: Statutes of Limitations and Repose and Anti-Indemnification Statutes, Paper for ABA Forum Comm. on the Constr. Indus. (Oct. 19–20, 1984).

[244] Construction Litigation: Representing the Owner (R. Cushman, K. Cushman & L. Peters, eds., 2d ed., John Wiley & Sons 1990).

[245] *See, e.g.,* President & Directors v. Madden, 660 F.2d 91 (4th Cir. 1981).

[246] *See, e.g.,* McCloskey & Co. v. Wright, 363 F. Supp. 223 (E.D. Va. 1973).

[247] A. Kornblut, Statutory Trends: Statutes of Limitations and Repose and Anti-Indemnification Statutes, Paper for ABA Forum Comm. on the Constr. Indus. (Oct. 19–20, 1984).

[248] Liptak v. Diane Apartments, Inc., 109 Cal. App. 3d 762, 167 Cal. Rptr. 440 (1980).

§ 7.44 Tolling

There are several exceptions to the rule that the statute of limitations begins to run when the tort occurs. These circumstances are said to *toll* or delay the start of the running of the statutory time limit.

The most significant exception that tolls the limitation is the discovery rule, which holds that certain causes of action do not accrue until the plaintiff knew or reasonably should have known about the harm. The discovery rule has been widely applied to tort claims but is not generally accepted for breach of contract actions.[249] As a general precept, however, the discovery rule would not apply to contractor claims against the construction manager. The contractor should know of its harm by the time of project completion.

Evasive or deceptive tactics by the defendant to frustrate or mislead a plaintiff can also toll the statute. For example, a contractor was not allowed to plead the statute of limitations when it avoided the plaintiff's attempt to sue it by lying about its residence.[250]

---

[249] *See* Board of Directors v. Regency Tower Venture, 2 Haw. App. 506, 635 P.2d 224 (1981).

[250] Kessler v. Peck, 266 Ala. 669, 98 So. 2d 606 (1957).

CHAPTER 8

SUING THE DESIGN PROFESSIONAL

Kenneth I. Levin

Kenneth I. Levin is a partner in the law firm of Pepper, Hamilton & Scheetz, Philadelphia, Pennsylvania, specializing in construction litigation. He received his undergraduate degree from Cornell University and graduated *magna cum laude* from Villanova Law School. He is vice chair of the American Bar Association's Section of Public Contract Law's State and Local Contract Claims and Remedies Committee, and vice chair of Region II of its Regional Division. He is also a member of the ABA's Section of Litigation, Section of Torts and Insurance Practice, Fidelity and Surety Committee, and the Forum Committee on the Construction Industry. He is a contributing author of several chapters in construction law books, including *Architect and Engineer Liability: Claims Against Design Professionals* (John Wiley & Sons, Inc., 1987), *Construction Failures* (John Wiley & Sons, Inc., 1989), and *Design Professionals Handbook of Business and Law.* Mr. Levin has spoken before bar associations and construction industry groups, and also has taught at Villanova Law School on construction contracts.

§ 8.1 Bases for Contractor's Right of Action

§ 8.2 —Economic Loss Limitation

§ 8.3 Design Professional's Liability to the Owner for Indemnity

§ 8.4 Negligence

§ 8.5 —Proof of Negligence

§ 8.6 —Conduct Constituting Negligence

§ 8.7 Liability to Contractor Generally

§ 8.8 —Defective Design

§ 8.9 —Negligence in Supervision and Inspection

§ 8.10 —Negligence or Intentional Interference in Contract Administration

§ 8.11 —Scheduling and Coordination

§ 8.1 Bases for Contractor's Right of Action

The recognition of the contractor's right of action against the design professional, though no longer a novelty, is still a development of relatively recent origin. Moreover, although it appears that the right has been sanctioned by the many jurisdictions, acceptance has been neither universal nor unqualified.

The 1958 decision in *United States ex rel. Los Angeles Testing Laboratory v. Rogers & Rogers*[1] marked the beginning of a new era in the law of architectural malpractice. Before *Rogers,* the defense of privity had effectively insulated the design professional from direct malpractice liability for economic losses to all members of the contracting group except its client, the owner.[2] In *Rogers* a prime contractor sued a project architect. The architect had, after reviewing tests performed on concrete supplied by the plaintiff's subcontractor, authorized the incorporation of the concrete in the building under construction. The owner-architect agreement required the architect to review the test reports. Upon later inspection, a state agency refused to pass the structural members in which the concrete had been incorporated and the architect stopped the work while corrective measures were taken. The prime contractor sued the architect to recover costs incurred in compensating for the defects and resulting from the ensuing delay, on the theory that the architect had been negligent in interpreting the test reports.

The architect moved for summary judgment, asserting that because he was not in contractual privity with the contractor, he owed no duty of care to the contractor (as opposed to the owner) in interpreting the test reports. However, the court held that the architect owed a duty to the contractor to supervise the project with due care under the circumstances alleged, notwithstanding that his sole contractual relationship was with the owner. Regarding the question of whether the absence of privity should bar a right of action, the court said:

> The determination whether in a specific case the defendant will be held liable to a third person not in privity is a matter of policy and involves the balancing of various factors, among which are the extent to which the transaction was intended to affect the plaintiff, the foreseeability of harm to him, the degree of certainty that the plaintiff suffered injury, the closeness of the connection between the defendant's conduct and the injury suffered, the moral blame attached to the defendant's conduct, and the policy of preventing future harm.[3]

---

[1] 161 F. Supp. 132 (S.D. Cal. 1958).

[2] The design professional had always faced indirect exposure to contractor claims by way of owner claims for indemnity. See **§ 8.3**.

[3] United States v. Rogers & Rogers, 161 F. Supp. 132, 135 (citations omitted).

Weighing these factors, the court concluded that a right of action should exist, stating:

> Considerations of reason and policy impel the conclusion that the position and authority of a supervising architect are such that he ought to labor under a duty to the prime contractor to supervise the project with due care under the circumstances, even though his sole contractual relationship is with the owner, here the United States. Altogether too much control over the contractor necessarily rests in the hands of the supervising architect for him not to be placed under a duty imposed by law to perform without negligence his functions as they affect the contractor. The power of the architect to stop the work alone is tantamount to a power of economic life or death over the contractor. . . . It is only just that such authority, exercised in such a relationship, carry commensurate legal responsibility.[4]

The *Rogers* decision has been criticized, not so much because it rejected the defense of privity as an absolute bar to a contractor's right of action for professional negligence, but because of the way in which it stated the test for liability. One commentator observed that the characterization of the design professional as an all-powerful "master builder" with independent authority to stop the work is no longer accurate. The language of the standard form owner-professional agreements has over time been modified to divest the design professional of the independent authority to stop the work. Further, the design professional's supervisory, quality control, administrative, and coordination functions are now often shared with a separate construction manager. Therefore, the commentator argued, it is inappropriate to impose a liability upon the professional simply on the basis of assumptions regarding his status and powers. Rather, whether a duty is owed by a professional to a contractor should depend upon (1) the scope of the professional's

---

[4] *Id.* at 135–36. The court also held that the contractor's claim against the architect was actionable on an alternative theory of negligent misrepresentation. The court stated:

> Additionally, it should be noted that insofar as the counterclaim alleges that the architect negligently interpreted and construed reports of tests on the concrete and then authorized the incorporation of the bents into the building, the contractor in effect asserts a claim of negligent misrepresentation by the architect, with reasonably foreseeable reliance thereon by the contractor to the latter's detriment. This is so because authorization to incorporate the bents into the building, given by the architect, who is admittedly responsible for overseeing the work of the testing laboratories and for supervising construction to assure conformity with specifications, must be taken to imply a representation, first, that the architect has inspected the bents and reviewed the tests performed on the concrete of which they were made, and second, that both the bents and the concrete therein conform to specifications.
>
> The later cases indicate that the California courts would impose liability for such a negligent representation . . . .

Id. at 136 (citations omitted).

obligation under the owner-professional agreement (or otherwise assumed by the professional apart from that agreement) and (2) whether the contractor's reliance upon the professional's careful performance of such obligations was reasonably foreseeable.[5] In fact, it appears that considerations of scope of duty and foreseeability of reliance have been implicitly, if not explicitly, operative in the cases following *Rogers.* Thus, it seems appropriate that such considerations should be the primary focus of inquiry.[6]

§ 8.2 —Economic Loss Limitation

In *Rogers'* wake, many decisions recognized the existence of a contractor's right of action in negligence against the design professional.[7] However, the cases have not been unanimous in their recognition of the contractor's right

---

[5] *See* Note, 92 Harv. L. Rev. 1076, 1084–85 (1979).

[6] It is important to note, however, that a design professional may, by its conduct, assume liabilities to a contractor in excess of the scope of its duties as defined in the contract with the owner. *See* Seattle W. Indus., Inc. v. David A. Mowat Co., 110 Wash. 2d 1, 750 P.2d 245 (1988) (holding refusal to instruct jury that written contract limited scope of duty not error).

[7] *See, e.g.,* E.C. Ernst v. Manhattan Constr. Co., 551 F.2d 1026 (5th Cir. 1977) (applying Alabama law); Donnelly Constr. Co. v. Oberg/Hunt/Gilleland, 139 Ariz. 184, 667 P.2d 1298 (1984); Guardian Constr. Co. v. Tetra Tech Richardon, Inc., 583 A.2d 1378 (Del. Super. Ct. 1990); A.R. Moyer, Inc. v. Graham, 285 So. 2d 397 (Fla. 1973); United States *ex rel.* Seminole Sheet Metal Co., 828 F.2d 671 (11th Cir. 1987) (applying Florida law); Peter Kiewit Sons' Co. v. Iowa S. Utils. Co., 355 F. Supp. 376 (S.D. Iowa 1973); S.K. Whitty & Co. v. Laurence L. Lambert & Assoc., 576 So. 2d 599 (La. Ct. App. 1991); Milton J. Womack, Inc. v. House of Representatives, 509 So. 2d 62 (La. Ct. App. 1987); Gurtler, Hebert & Co. v. Weyland Mach. Shop, Inc., 450 So. 2d 660 (La. Ct. App. 1981); National Sand, Inc. v. Nagel Constr., Inc., 182 Mich. App. 327, 451 N.W.2d 618 (1990); Pritchard Bros., Inc. v. Grady, 428 N.W.2d 391 (Minn. 1988); City of Columbus v. Clark-Dietz & Assocs.-Eng'rs, Inc., 550 F. Supp. 610 (N.D. Miss. 1982); Owen v. Dodd, 431 F. Supp. 1239 (N.D. Miss. 1977); Lane v. Geiger-Berger Assocs., P.C., 608 F.2d 1148 (8th Cir. 1979) (applying Missouri law); Conforti & Eisele, Inc. v. John C. Morris Assocs., 175 N.J. Super. 341, 418 A.2d 1290 (Law Div. 1981), *aff'd,* 199 N.J. Super. 498, 489 A.2d 1233 (1985); Shoffner Indus. v. W.B. Lloyd Constr. Co., 42 N.C. App. 259, 257 S.E.2d 50 (1979); Davidson & Jones, Inc. v. County of New Hanover, 41 N.C. App. 661, 255 S.E.2d 580 (1979); Forte Bros., Inc. v. National Amusements, Inc., 525 A.2d 1301 (R.I. 1987); Seattle W. Indus., Inc. v. David A. Mowat Co., 110 Wash. 2d 1, 750 P.2d 245 (1988); Detweiler Bros., Inc. v. John Graham & Co., 412 F. Supp. 416 (E.D. Wash. 1976). *See also* COAC, Inc. v. Kennedy Eng'rs, 67 Cal. App. 3d 916, 136 Cal. Rptr. 890 (1977) (holding contractor to be third-party beneficiary of engineer's duty under owner-engineer agreement); John E. Green Plumbing & Heating Co. v. Turner Constr. Co., 742 F.2d 965 (6th Cir. 1984) (applying Michigan law; holding that construction manager owes duty to contractor on third-party beneficiary theory); James McKinney & Son, Inc. v. Lake Placid 1980 Olympic Games, Inc., 92 A.D.2d 991, 461 N.Y.S.2d 483 (1983), *modified on other grounds,* 61 N.Y.2d, 462 N.E.2d 137, 473 N.Y.S.2d 960 (1984) (holding that responsibilities of project/construction manager were such as to establish duty in tort to subcontractor).

of action,[8] nor have all those refusing to permit a right of action turned upon the bar of privity. More recently, those denying a right of action have questioned a contractor's ability to recover in tort for purely economic losses.[9]

One of the principal arguments presented by design professionals for the economic loss defense is that it is consistent with a general rule applied in the law of torts that recovery may not be had in actions for negligence when a plaintiff's losses are entirely economic in character. The professionals also argue that the allocation of liabilities among members of the contracting group should be purely a matter of contract.

Contractors, on the other hand, present the following counterarguments. To be sure, courts often recognize the general tort law rule holding that recovery may not be had for purely economic losses in an action based solely upon negligence.[10] The rationale for requiring physical injury to property or person as a predicate to recovery for economic losses is that a bright-line rule is necessary to protect against an otherwise virtually limitless scope of liability for negligence in terms of dollar magnitude and number of potential plaintiffs.[11] For example, as a matter of policy, it would be inappropriate for an individual who negligently caused an automobile collision during the morning rush hour to be held liable for lost wages to all commuters who were delayed on their way to work. As a matter of policy, the law has drawn lines short of the broader limits of foreseeability in such circumstances.

However, contractors argue that the rationale for the economic loss limitation should be inoperative when it is possible to confine the right of action to a narrow and readily identifiable group, whose reliance upon the performance of a duty with care is reasonably foreseeable. For example, the *Restatement (Second) of Torts* notes that the general bar to an action for

---

[8] *See, e.g.,* Bryant Elec. Co. v. City of Fredericksburg, 762 F.2d 1192 (4th Cir. 1985) (applying Virginia law); Peyronnin Constr. Co. v. Weiss, 208 N.E.2d 489 (Ind. Ct. App. 1965); Hogan v. Postin, 695 P.2d 1042 (Wyo. 1985); Bernard Johnson, Inc. v. Continental Constructors, Inc., 630 S.W.2d 365 (Tex. Ct. App. 1982).

[9] *See, e.g.,* Floor Craft Floor Covering, Inc. v. Parma Community Gen. Hosp. Ass'n, 54 Ohio St. 3d 1, 560 N.E.2d 206 (1990); Bernard Johnson, Inc. v. Continental Constructors, Inc., 630 S.W.2d 365 (Tex. Ct. App. 1982); Bryant Elec. Co. v. City of Fredericksburg, 762 F.2d 1192 (4th Cir. 1985); Bates & Rogers Constr. Corp. v. North Shore Sanitary Dist., 128 Ill. App. 3d 962, 471 N.E.2d 915 (1984), *aff'd on other grounds sub nom.* Bates & Rogers Constr. Corp. v. Greeley & Hansen, 109 Ill. 2d 225, 486 N.E.2d 902 (1985); Waldinger Corp. v. CRS Group Eng'rs, Inc., 775 F.2d 781 (7th Cir. 1985) (applying Illinois law). *Cf.* Briar Contracting Corp. v. City of New York, 156 A.D.2d 628, 550 N.Y.S.2d 717 (1989).

[10] *See, e.g.,* Restatement (Second) of Torts § 766C (providing, among other things, that as a general rule there is no liability in tort for negligence interfering with another's performance of his contract or making the performance more expensive or burdensome).

[11] *See, e.g.,* East River S.S. Corp. v. Transamerica Delaval, 106 S. Ct. 2295 (1986).

negligent interference with contract does not apply when the plaintiff stands in a special relationship to the tortfeasor:

> e. Duty of care to prevent pecuniary loss. Outside the scope of this Section are certain cases in which the actor renders a service or has some other contractual relationship in which he owes a duty to use reasonable care to avoid a risk of pecuniary loss to the person with whom he is directly dealing, and that same duty is held to extend to another person whom he knows to be pecuniarily affected by the service rendered. Most of the cases coming within this category are covered by § 552, involving information negligently supplied for the guidance of others. Other cases, involving other services than the supplying of information, may not fall within the exact provisions of § 552 but are covered by the general principle underlying it . . . .[12]

Similarly, the section of the *Restatement* dealing with the scope of liability for negligent misrepresentation could support an argument that members of the contracting group are a sufficiently confined group as to invest in them a right to be free of economic loss resulting from a design professional's malpractice. That section provides:

> 9. The City of A is about to ask for bids for work on a sewer tunnel. It hires B Company, a firm of engineers, to make boring tests and provide a report showing the rock and soil conditions to be encountered. It notifies B Company that the report will be made available to bidders as a basis for their bids and that it is expected to be used by the successful bidder in doing the work. Without knowing the identity of any of the contractors bidding on the work, B Company negligently prepares and delivers to the City an inaccurate report, containing false and misleading information. On the basis of the report C makes a successful bid, and also on the basis of the report D, a subcontractor, contracts with C to do a part of the work. By reason of the inaccuracy of the report, C and D suffer pecuniary loss in performing their contracts. B Company is subject to liability to B [sic C] and to D.[13]

In short, there are arguments both for and against the application of the economic loss defense as applied to contractors' claims against design professionals.[14]

---

[12] Restatement (Second) of Torts § 766C cmt. e, at 26.

[13] *Id.* § 552 illus. 9, at 135.

[14] Claims by contractors grounded on third-party beneficiary theories appear not as common as tort claims, probably because most of the standard forms of agreements expressly negate an intent to create third-party beneficiary rights against design professionals. *See, e.g.*, AIA Doc. B141 ¶ 9.7 (1987).

However, in COAC, Inc. v. Kennedy Eng'rs, 67 Cal. App. 3d 916, 136 Cal. Rptr. 890 (1977), a contractor was permitted to pursue a third-party beneficiary claim against a design professional. The claim arose in connection with a water treatment plant. The contractor's claim, it appears, was not against the designer of the plant, but rather

This is not, however, to say that the imposition of such a limitation is inappropriate when claims are brought by members of the public outside the contracting group who do not stand in any special relationship to the professional.[15]

§ 8.3 Design Professional's Liability to the Owner for Indemnity

Even when a contractor may not sue a design professional directly, there remains an indirect exposure by way of an owner's claim for indemnity. For example, in the *United States v. Skidmore, Owings & Merrill*[16] the government's contract with the architect for the construction of the Hirshhorn Museum included an express indemnity term stating that the architect would be liable to the government "for all costs incurred as a result of

---

against the firm engaged by the owner to prepare an environmental impact report. Construction of the project was delayed by the engineer's late preparation of the report, a rejection by the state Department of Environmental Resources, and the subsequent need to resubmit the report. The court held that the contractor could maintain an action against the engineering firm as a third-party beneficiary. It held that the contractor was a creditor beneficiary of the owner-engineer agreement under Restatement (Second) of Contracts § 133.

In another case, John E. Green Plumbing & Heating Co. v. Turner Constr. Co., 742 F.2d 965 (6th Cir. 1984), *cert. denied,* 471 U.S. 1102 (1985), although the analysis is less than clear, the court appears to have assumed a right of action by a prime plumbing contractor against a construction manager on a third-party beneficiary theory.

[15] *Cf.* Moore v. Pavex, Inc., No. 2843 S 1984, slip op. (C.P. Dauphin County, Pa., Oct. 4, 1985) (owner and contractors on construction project could not be held liable to class consisting of entire business community of City of Harrisburg for purely economic losses resulting from puncture of water main).

The courts are divided on whether design professionals are liable for economic losses claimed to have been suffered by tenants or subsequent purchasers of facilities they have designed. Cooper v. Jevne, 56 Cal. App. 3d 860, 129 Cal. Rptr. 724 (1976) (purchasers of condominium units may sue for economic losses); Bay Garden Manor Condominium Assoc., Inc. v. James D. Marks Assocs., Inc., 576 So. 2d 744 (Fla. Dist. Ct. App. 1991) (condominium association may sue engineers who inspected building and issued structural report prior to conversion to condominium); San Francisco Real Estate Investors v. J.A. Jones Constr. Co., 524 F. Supp. 768 (S.D. Ohio 1981), *aff'd,* 703 F.2d 976 (6th Cir. 1983) (subsequent purchaser of structure may not sue architect).

In A.E. Inv. Corp. v. Link Builders, Inc., 214 N.W.2d 764 (Wis. 1974), the court held that a tenant, the operator of a supermarket, could sue an architect for damages consisting of loss of profits, loss of fixtures, equipment, and merchandise, and loss of reputation and good will, where it claimed that the architect's design negligence had resulted in floor subsidence which made the leased structure untenantable. Id. 766. The court, however, ruled that the architect would, at trial, be permitted to present evidence on whether public policy considerations should in the particular case preclude an award of damages for such economic losses. Id. 770.

[16] 505 F. Supp. 1101 (S.D.N.Y. 1981).

[Skidmore's] negligent performance of any of the services furnished under this contract." The contractor sued the government for delay damages when the architect improperly rejected a scale model and refused to approve any shop drawings before a second model was accepted. After settling the contractor's claim, the government sued the architectural firm for indemnity. The tribunal denied the architect's motion for summary judgment, holding that the architect could be liable for the delay damages under the indemnity claim even though the statute of limitations had run on direct negligence and breach of contract causes of action.

A common law claim for indemnity may also be implied in a contract between the owner and the design professional although an express provision does not exist. In *Miller v. City of Broken Arrow*[17] the contractor sued the city for withheld retainage, lost profits, and delay damages when muddy soil conditions made it impossible for him to lay a pipeline. The contractor had consulted the engineer who was under contract to the city in an attempt to find a solution to the problem. The engineer refused to respond to further requests by the contractor for a design solution after his original suggestion failed. The court held that the engineer was negligent in refusing to respond to the contractor and awarded judgment against the city "over against" the engineer under an implied indemnity theory.[18]

In *Fairbanks North Star Borough v. Roen Design Associates*[19] a design firm was liable to the borough under a theory of common law indemnification even though a contractor's claim for economic loss against the owner was outside the scope of an express indemnity provision. The court held:

> A contractual indemnity clause is interpreted so as to effectuate the intent of the parties. It is accorded a certain preemptive effect, displacing rights of common law indemnity within its intended scope of coverage. While by its terms it might also evidence an intent to preclude common law indemnification altogether, we see no indication of such intent here. The provision protects the Borough from liability for claims for tangible property damage or personal injury as a result of Roen's acts, whether or not Roen acted negligently. It provides the Borough greater protection than it would have under principles of common law but it does not suggest an intent to exonerate Roen from other losses suffered by the Borough as a result of Roen's negligence. The Borough therefore is not precluded from maintaining a claim for common law indemnity.[20]

---

[17] 660 F.2d 450 (10th Cir. 1981), *cert. denied,* 455 U.S. 1020 (1982).

[18] *Id.* at 458–59.

[19] 727 P.2d 758 (Alaska 1986).

[20] *Id.* at 761 (citations omitted).

§ 8.4 Negligence

Before proceeding to a review of the scope and nature of the design professional's direct obligations to contractors, it is appropriate to consider the legal standard by which a design professional's liability is measured.

In the absence of express contractual warranties or stipulations imposing a different standard of care, proof of negligence has traditionally been required as a basis for the imposition of liability in damages upon design professionals. The basic rule has been stated as follows:

> Plaintiff was an engineer and was employed as such. In performing the work which he undertook, it was his duty to exercise such care, skill and diligence as men engaged in that profession ordinarily exercise under like circumstances. He was not an insurer that the contractors would perform their work properly in all respects; but it was his duty to exercise reasonable care to see that they did so.[21]

Although the doctrines of implied warranty and strict liability (liability without fault) are widely applied as a basis for imposing liability upon manufacturers of defective products, the courts, for the most part, have rejected these doctrines in assessing the liability of design professionals.[22]

The rationale for refusing to impose strict liability upon design professionals are articulated in *City of Mounds View v. Walijarvi,*[23] in which the court observed:

> Architects, doctors, engineers, attorneys, and others deal in somewhat inexact sciences and are continually called upon to exercise their skilled judgment in order to anticipate and provide for random factors which are

---

[21] Pastorelli v. Associated Eng'rs, Inc., 176 F. Supp. 159, 166 (D.R.I. 1959) (quoting Cowles v. City of Minneapolis, 128 Minn. 452, 151 N.W. 184, 185 (1915)).

[22] Del Mar Beach Club Owners Ass'n v. Imperial Contracting Co., 123 Cal. App. 3d 898, 176 Cal. Rptr. 886 (1981); Castaldo v. Pittsburgh-Des Moines Steel Co., 376 A.2d 88 (Del. 1977); Borman's, Inc. v. Lake State Dev. Co., 60 Mich. App. 175, 230 N.W.2d 363 (1975); City of Mounds View v. Walijarvi, 263 N.W.2d 420 (Minn. 1978); Board of Trustees v. Kennerly, Slomanson & Smith, 167 N.J. Super. 311, 400 A.2d 850 (Law Div. 1979); Sears, Roebuck & Co. v. Enco Assocs., Inc., 43 N.Y.2d 389, 372 N.E.2d 555, 401 N.Y.S.2d 767 (1977). *Contra* Federal Mogul Corp. v. Universal Constr. Co., 376 So. 2d 716 (Ala. Civ. App. 1979) (dicta); Broyles v. Brown Eng'g Co., 275 Ala. 35, 151 So. 2d 767 (1963) (limited to provision of routine services); Bloomsburg Mills, Inc. v. Sordoni Constr. Co., 401 Pa. 358, 164 A.2d 201 (1960) (warranty of fitness). *See also* Doundoulakis v. Town of Hempstead, 42 N.Y.2d 440, 368 N.E.2d 24, 398 N.Y.S.2d 401 (1977) (holding that strict liability could apply when design was for project that in itself constituted an abnormally dangerous activity as defined in Restatement (Second) of Torts § 520 (1976)).

[23] 263 N.W.2d 420 (Minn. 1978).

> incapable of precise measurement. The indeterminate nature of these factors makes it impossible for professional service people to gauge them with complete accuracy in every instance. Thus, doctors cannot promise that every operation will be successful; a lawyer can never be certain that a contract he drafts is without latent ambiguity; and an architect cannot be certain that a structural design will interact with natural forces as anticipated. Because of the inescapable possibility of error which inheres in these services, the law has traditionally required, not perfect results, but rather the exercise of that skill and judgment which can be reasonably expected from similarly situated professionals.
>
> * * *
>
> [Further], while it is undoubtedly fair to impose strict liability on manufacturers who have had ample opportunity to test their products for defects before marketing them, the same cannot be said of architects. Normally, an architect has but a single chance to create a design for a client which will produce a defect free structure. Accordingly, we do not think it just that architects should be forced the bear the same burden of liability for their products as that which has been imposed on manufacturers generally.[24]

It is, however, possible for a design professional to contract to a different standard of care, as illustrated by *Arkansas Rice Growers Cooperative Association v. Alchemy Industries, Inc.,*[25] which arose out of a project to construct an experimental plant for the combustion of rice hulls. When the plant did not perform as anticipated, the owner sued the designer.

The designer had agreed to provide

> the necessary engineering plant layout and equipment design and the on-site engineering supervision and start-up engineering services necessary for the construction of a hull by-product facility capable of reducing a minimum of seven and one-half tons of rice hulls per hour to ash and producing a minimum of 48 million BTUs per hour of steam at 200 lbs. pressure.[26]

Both the trial and appellate courts concluded that this provision amounted to an express warranty of the design. Accordingly, proof that the plant

---

[24] *Id.* at 424, 425. This formulation is consistent with the Restatement (Second) of Torts in its general articulation of a professional standard of care:

> Unless he represents that he has greater or less skill or knowledge, one who undertakes to render services in the practice of a profession or trade is required to exercise the skill and knowledge normally possessed by members of that profession or trade in good standing in similar situation.

Restatement (Second) of Torts § 299A (1965).

[25] 797 F.2d 565 (8th Cir. 1986).

[26] *Id.* at 566.

failed to perform as anticipated was sufficient to establish the owner's case. Additional proof of professional negligence was not required.[27]

Although, as *Arkansas Rice* demonstrates, a professional may by contract agree to a more rigorous standard of care, it has been held that the benefit of such higher standard will run solely to those in privity and not to contract or tort claimants.[28]

§ 8.5 —Proof of Negligence

To establish an architect or engineer's liability for professional negligence, a claimant must present evidence

1. Establishing the applicable standard of care
2. Demonstrating a violation of the standard and
3. Demonstrating the causal relationship between the violation and the harm complained of.[29]

Ordinarily, proof of professional negligence must be established by expert testimony. The standard of care must be determined from the testimony of experts unless the conduct involved is within the common knowledge of laymen.[30] Depending upon the jurisdiction in which the claim arises, the design professional's conduct may be measured by a national, rather than a local or regional, standard of care.[31] Although the standard of care is determined with reference to ordinary practices, it has nevertheless been urged that a failure to adopt new and available technology might constitute professional negligence even though its utilization was not yet customary in the profession.[32]

---

[27] Although it might be tempting for an owner to hold a professional to a warranty of results as in *Arkansas Rice,* such a provision might impair or exceed the scope of coverage afforded by the professional's errors and omissions insurance policy. Such policies usually afford coverage only as to professional negligence.

[28] *See* Peter Kiewit Sons' Co. v. Iowa S. Utils. Co., 355 F. Supp. 376, 394 (S.D. Iowa 1973).

[29] Bell v. Jones, 523 A.2d 982, 987 (D.C. 1986).

[30] *See* Allied Properties v. John A. Blume & Assocs., Eng'rs, 25 Cal. App. 3d 848, 102 Cal. Rptr. 259 (1972); Paxton v. County of Alameda, 119 Cal. App. 2d 393, 259 P.2d 934 (1953); Overland Constructors, Inc. v. Millard Sch. Dist., 220 Neb. 220, 369 N.W.2d 69, 76 (1985); R.G. Wood & Assocs. Ltd., 85-1 B.C.A. (CCH) ¶ 17,898 (PSBCA 1985) *See generally* Annotation, 3 A.L.R.4th 1023 (1981). *See also* Milton J. Womack, Inc. v. House of Representatives, 509 So. 2d 62, 67 (La. Ct. App. 1987), discussed in **§ 8.8**.

[31] *See* Bell v. Jones, 523 A.2d 982, 988 (D.C. 1987).

[32] *See* Peck & Hoch, *Engineer's Liability: State of the Art Consideration in Defining Standard of Care,* 30 Vill. L. Rev. 403 (1985). The authors cite, inter alia, The T.J. Hooper, 60

It has been held that proof of a violation of a municipal building code will constitute evidence of negligence,[33] as may violation of private safety standards.[34] It has also been held that the *Architect's Handbook of Professional Practice* could be considered as evidence of a standard of care, although a violation of its standards would not constitute negligence per se.[35]

§ 8.6 —Conduct Constituting Negligence

Reasonable precision is required in the drafting of plans and specifications for the construction project. In *Eggers Partnership*[36] an architect was held negligent for specifying that installation of a particular roofing material should be in accordance with the manufacturer's installation manual, although project conditions, in fact, required a special application technique. It was improper for the architect to rely upon the contractor to ascertain that special application techniques were required.

A design professional is not entitled simply to rely upon the assurances of manufacturers or the advice of its consultants. In *Scott v. Potomac Insurance Co.*[37] an architect was held to be negligent in substituting tin-plated steel tubing for copper tubing in a radiant heating system without changing the method or manner of installation to allow for the different expansion characteristics of the steel tubing. Reliance upon the manufacturer's statement that the steel tubing would be a suitable substitute and a heating consultant's approval of the substitution was not sufficient to satisfy the architect's duty of care. The court held that the architect had an obligation to ascertain independently the true suitability of the substitute material and

---

F.2d 737, 739–40 (2d Cir.), *cert. denied,* 287 U.S. 662 (1932), in which Judge Learned Hand stated:

> There are, no doubt, cases where courts seem to make the general practice of the calling the standard of proper diligence. . . . Indeed in most cases reasonable prudence is in fact common prudence; but strictly it is never its measure; a whole calling may have unduly lagged in the adoption of new and available devices. . . . There are precautions so imperative that even their universal disregard will not excuse their omission.

[33] Johnson v. Salem Title Co., 246 Or. 409, 425 P.2d 519 (1967) (uniform building code). Indeed, in Burran v. Dambold, 422 F.2d 133, 135 (10th Cir. 1970), it was held that a failure to design in accordance with a state building code constituted negligence per se.

[34] Evans v. Howard R. Green Co., 231 N.W.2d 907 (Iowa 1975) (Ten-State Standards promulgated by Great Lakes-Upper Mississippi River Board of State Sanitary Engineers). *But see* Hackley v. Waldorf-Hoerner Paper Prods. Co., 149 Mont. 286, 425 P.2d 712 (1967) (advisory codes or standards of safety without force of law not admissible in evidence).

[35] Taylor, Thon, Thompson & Peterson v. Cannaday, 749 P.2d 63 (Mont. 1987).

[36] 82-1 B.C.A. (CCH) ¶ 15,630 (IBCA 1982).

[37] 217 Or. 323, 341 P.2d 1083 (1959).

to determine if it could be safely installed in the manner originally prescribed for the copper tubing. The court stated, "It ill-behooves a man professing professional skill to say I know nothing of an article which I am called upon to use in the practice of my profession. . . ."[38]

The professional's duty of care and design also extends to the development of solutions to problems arising during the course of construction. In *Clemens v. Benzinger*[39] the original plans for the erection of steel columns called for the columns to be attached to anchor bolts embedded in concrete floors. However, the concrete contractor neglected to embed the anchor bolts in several locations when the floor was originally poured. The engineer directed the contractor therefore to drill holes for the installation of the omitted anchors and then to grout around the bolts with cement. Although the strength of those bolts as supports for the columns was then entirely dependent on the resistance of the cement around the bolts, the engineer thereafter failed to warn the steel erector that the grout was not fully cured. An employee of the erection contractor was killed when anchor bolts to which columns were then attached pulled up out of the floors because the cement grout had not fully hardened. The court stated:

> When the [concrete contractor] deviated from the original plans, a new situation arose which required a new plan, or at least a new direction to the contractors in place of the original plan. The duty to take care of the situation which had then arisen rested on the defendant [engineer], and it recognized such duty and took steps in accordance with it. The superintendent of that company gave direction as to how the problem was to be met. Negligence in this act is the same as negligence in respect to the original plans, and gives rise similarly to a cause of action in favor of one who receives injury therefrom.[40]

In general, the courts have rejected efforts to impose "clerk of the works"-type supervisory or inspection responsibilities upon design professionals, which would, in effect, make them guarantors of the quality of construction. In *Weill Construction Co. v. Thibodeaux*[41] an architectural firm was sued by the owner of an ice-skating facility. After completion of the facility, water seeped through the concrete slab and damaged the hardwood floor of the rink. The trial court found that the general contractor for the project had poured the slab improperly so as to create a horizontal cold joint through which the seepage had occurred.

The owner's claim for negligent supervision of the construction by the architectural firm was rejected by both the trial and appellate courts,

---

[38] 341 P.2d at 1088.

[39] 211 A.D. 586, 207 N.Y.S. 539 (1925).

[40] 207 N.Y.S. at 543.

[41] 491 So. 2d 166 (La. Ct. App. 1986).

which held that the architect had no duty to supervise the construction of the slab floors. The appeals court relied on the testimony that the architect's fee for the project was 5 percent of the construction costs, when a fee of 6 percent or 7 percent would have been required if it had contracted to supervise the work of the general contractor. Similarly, the court concluded that the language of the general conditions of the contract for construction tended to negate, rather than create a duty of supervision.

Even though, as in *Thibodeaux,* an architect has not contracted to provide continuous on-site inspection, the cases nevertheless demonstrate that he still owes a duty of care in making such periodic observations or inspections as agreed to.[42] In making those inspections or observations, it has been held that an architect has a duty specifically to inspect those aspects of the construction likely to create safety hazards if installation is improper.

In *Pastorelli v. Associated Engineers, Inc.,*[43] after completion of construction, an employee of the owner was injured by a falling heating duct. The duct, which was 20 feet long and weighed 500 pounds, was suspended from hangers attached by nails to a ceiling of 7/8-inch sheathing. Considering the weight of the duct, good installation practice would have required securing the hangers to the roof joists or to the roof itself with lag screws. The evidence showed that the architect was not aware of the defective manner of installation of the hangers. He had not been present while the duct was being installed and had made no effort afterward to determine how the duct was installed. The court held that because it was apparent that the safety of persons in the structure required that the ducts be securely fastened, the architect's failure to take steps to ascertain how they were attached constituted negligence.

§ 8.7 Liability to Contractor Generally

Against this background, it is appropriate to consider in more detail representative cases that have considered the design professional's liabilities and duties to contractors. The courts have evaluated the liabilities of design professionals to contractors for errors or omissions in the following areas:

---

[42] *See* Dickerson Constr. Co. v. Process Eng'g Co., 341 So. 2d 646 (Miss. 1977). *But cf.* Moundsview Indep. Sch. Dist. No. 621 v. Buetow & Assocs., Inc., 253 N.W.2d 836 (Minn. 1977) (when architect did not observe deficiencies in installation of roof on its periodic visits, summary judgment in favor of architect was appropriate; court will not give owner benefit of clerk-of-the-works-type inspection if owner paid for less).

[43] 176 F. Supp. 159 (D.R.I. 1959).

1. Design
2. Supervision and inspection
3. Administration (including review of submittals, consideration of substitutes, and reaction to unanticipated conditions)
4. Scheduling and coordination.

The cases demonstrate that, in assessing such liabilities, the courts have been attentive to the scope of the design professional's responsibilities as set forth in the owner-professional agreement or as otherwise established by the professional's conduct during the project, to the foreseeability of the contractor's reliance on the professional's performance of such duties, and to evidence of the professional's compliance or noncompliance with prevailing standards of care.[44]

§ 8.8 —Defective Design

City of Columbus v. Clark-Dietz & Associates—Engineers, Inc.,[45] arose out of the construction of a wastewater treatment plant, and more particularly, the failure of a protective levee surrounding the construction site when the project was nearly complete. As a result of the failure, the site was inundated, causing extensive damage and delay in the completion of the facility. The owner brought suit against the contractor and the engineer for damages resulting from the failure, and the contractor both counterclaimed against

---

[44] Claims by contractors grounded on third-party beneficiary theories appear not as common as tort claims, probably because most of the standard forms of agreements expressly negate an intent to create third-party beneficiary rights against design professionals. *See, e.g.,* AIA Doc. B141 ¶ 9.7 (1987).

However, in COAC, Inc. v. Kennedy Eng'rs, 67 Cal. App. 3d 916, 136 Cal. Rptr. 890 (1977), a contractor was permitted to pursue a third-party beneficiary claim against a design professional. The claim arose in connection with a water treatment plant. The contractor's claim, it appears, was not against the designer of the plant, but rather against the firm engaged by the owner to prepare an environmental impact report. Construction of the project was delayed by the engineer's late preparation of the report, a rejection by the state Department of Environmental Resources, and the subsequent need to resubmit the report. The court held that the contractor could maintain an action against the engineering firm as a third-party beneficiary. It held that the contractor was a creditor beneficiary of the owner-engineer agreement under the Restatement (Second) of Contracts § 133.

In another case, John E. Green Plumbing & Heating Co. v. Turner Constr. Co., 742 F.2d 965 (6th Cir. 1984), *cert. denied,* 471 U.S. 1102 (1985), although the analysis is less than clear, the court appears to have assumed a right of action by a prime plumbing contractor against a construction manager on a third-party beneficiary theory.

[45] 550 F. Supp. 610 (N.D. Miss. 1982).

the City and crossclaimed against the engineer to recover for extra construction expenses resulting from negligent design. The court concluded that the failure of the levee was due to negligent design on the part of the engineer, that the contractor had a right of action in tort against the engineer for negligence, and that the owner and the engineer were therefore jointly and severally liable to the contractor for the damages resulting from the failure.

In *Columbus* the parties agreed that the levee failures had occurred where pipes encased by concrete seepage collars penetrated a slurry wall. They also agreed that the failure occurred as a result of water seepage and consequent "piping" through the wall at the level of the pipes, which eventually permitted the water to surge through and cause the wall to collapse. The contractor claimed that the failure was due to professional negligence and defective design. The engineer claimed that the failure was a result of defective construction.

The original design had called for pipes to be placed through the levee with a slurry wall then to be placed around the pipes. When the necessary pipes were unavailable at the outset of the slurry wall construction, the engineer decided that the slurry wall construction could proceed without the pipes in place and that cuts could be made in the wall for later installation of pipe. The engineer's representatives determined that seepage collars would be adequate to restore the cuts in the slurry wall necessitated by the delayed pipe installation.

During the course of installing the pipes and collars, a disagreement arose as to the method of installing the collars. The contractor maintained that the collars should be encased with clay to seal the concrete, thus eliminating direct contact between the slurry and the collar itself. The engineer, however, insisted that the collar be keyed directly into the slurry.

Based upon expert testimony presented by the contractor, the court ultimately concluded that vastly differing deformability characteristics of the concrete collar and the cement-bentonite slurry in the wall constituted the primary cause of the seepage and piping that led to the failure of the levee. The court also concluded that the engineer's conduct with respect to the placement of the collars constituted professional negligence in that the engineering personnel who made the design decisions:

1. Did not have sufficient prior experience with cement-bentonite slurry to evaluate the sufficiency of the collar design
2. Did not consult a report available to them, from which the compressive strength of the slurry could have been computed
3. Did not run tests to compute the strength of the slurry and
4. Made no effort to determine the suitability of the collar design either through consultation with slurry experts or with specialty engineers in-house at their own firm.

The court therefore concluded that the engineer was liable to the contractor for the losses resulting from the levee failure.[46]

Similarly, in *Milton J. Womack, Inc. v. House of Representatives*[47] the court held that when an architect that had devised plans for the renovation of a state capitol building failed to discover a metal x-brace within an interior basement wall scheduled for demolition, it was an omission from which laymen could infer negligence without the necessity of expert testimony. The existence of the x-brace was shown in the original blueprints for the capitol, which were available on microfilm. The court stated:

> It is 'common sense' to conclude that it is the duty of an architect to use reasonable skill and care to determine the location of important structural elements before he completes his plans and authorizes work to begin in accordance with those plans.[48]

In *Seattle Western Industries, Inc. v. David A. Mowat Co.*[49] a subcontractor responsible for steel fabrication and erection in the construction of a bridge sued an engineer for negligence. The engineer's design inaccurately assumed that the vertical members of the existing tresses of a bridge were plumb rather than perpendicular to the bridge roadway. The discrepancy was not noted until after fabrication of new trusses was under way. The subcontractor could not get a change order from the owner for the change in orientation because of an exculpatory provision of the contract stating that the dimensions were not guaranteed. The subcontractor was held entitled to recover from the engineer on the basis of a total cost calculation for its increased costs of fabrication under the contract. *Mowat* illustrates one of the reasons contractors may sue design professionals, which is that they may be barred from suing the owner under exculpatory clauses in the owner-contractor agreement.

---

[46] Closely related to the concept of liability for negligent design is liability for negligent misrepresentation. For example, in Davidson & Jones, Inc. v. County of New Hanover, 41 N.C. App. 661, 255 S.E.2d 580 (1979), the court held that a contractor could maintain an action against the owner's soils consultant for negligent misrepresentation of subsurface conditions. This right in tort was held to exist notwithstanding provisions of an exculpatory character contained in the owner-contractor agreement. Similarly, in Lane v. Geiger-Berger Assocs., P.C., 608 F.2d 1148 (8th Cir. 1979), the court held that a subcontractor's reliance upon the professional's representation as to the character of fill that would be permitted on a project would provide a basis for a claim by the subcontractor against the professional. *See also* Gulf Contracting v. Bibb County, 795 F.2d 980 (11th Cir. 1986) (applying Georgia law).

[47] 509 So. 2d 62, 67 (La. Ct. App. 1987).

[48] *Id.* at 67.

[49] 110 Wash. 2d 1, 750 P.2d 245 (1988).

Similarly, in *Guardian Construction Co. v. Tetra Tech Richardson, Inc.*,[50] a contractor was held entitled to pursue a claim on a theory of negligent misrepresentation against a design engineer for alleged miscalculations as to tidal heights and project benchmarks, which the contractor claimed to have relied upon in the preparation of its bid.

§ 8.9 —Negligence in Supervision and Inspection

Also at issue in *City of Columbus v. Clark-Dietz & Associates—Engineers, Inc.*,[51] were the relative responsibilities of the contractor and the engineer for deficiencies in other areas of the levee that had not failed, but nevertheless required correction. Although these deficiencies were found, in part, to be a result of deficiencies in construction work, as opposed to design, the contractor argued that the engineer should bear full responsibility because of its supervisory responsibilities on the project. Considering that the owner-architect agreement, however, did not impose a duty of continuous and exhaustive inspection upon the engineer, the court held that the engineer owed no duty of supervision to the contractor other than to exercise reasonable care when it provided instructions and test results at the jobsite. Upon examining the design professional's contract with the owner, the court concluded:

> These paragraphs unambiguously limit Clark-Dietz' duty for supervising construction to an obligation to observe the general progress of the work, and not to make continuous and exhaustive inspections. We hold that Clark-Dietz performed this contractual duty by generally overseeing construction and conducting soil tests with reasonable care. . . .
>
> The language in the Clark-Dietz-City contract clearly does not create a requirement for Clark-Dietz to inspect and verify every step of [the contractor's] work. In the absence of an active undertaking to guarantee the contractor's work, courts have ordinarily held that similar language absolves the architect of any liability for the contractor's poor workmanship. . . . Thus, we hold that Clark-Dietz owed no duty of supervision to [the contractor] other than to exercise reasonable care when it provided instructions and test results at the job site. Having found that Clark-Dietz was not negligent in these respects, [the contractor] must bear responsibility for the unacceptable soil material found in the embankment except for sand seams directly above the slurry wall, and is liable to the City for damages resulting therefrom.[52]

---

[50] 583 A.2d 1378 (Del. Super. Ct. 1990).

[51] 550 F. Supp. 610 (N.D. Miss. 1982).

[52] *Id.* at 627.

Although *Columbus* absolves the professional of a duty of continuous inspection, it does reaffirm the professional's responsibilities for specific approvals.[53] In *Shoffner Industries, Inc. v. W.B. Lloyd Construction Co.,*[54] the court held that a contractor had a right of action against the design professional for negligence in approving the work of its supplier. The case arose out of the collapse of a roof structure, as a result of defective trusses supplied by the contractor's supplier. The contractor claimed that the architect had inspected and approved the trusses before they were incorporated in the roof structure, and that the contractor had relied on that approval. The allegations were held adequate to state a cause of action against the professional.[55]

Similarly, in *Magnolia Construction Co. v. Mississippi Gulf South Engineers, Inc.,*[56] the Mississippi Supreme Court reversed a summary judgment in favor of an engineer. A contractor sued to recover the expense of correcting defective work: a sewer pipe that had been laid off-grade and not discovered by the engineer until final inspection of the project. The engineering firm had provided a inspector during the course of the project and had certified the contractor's periodic payment requisitions without identifying any deficiencies. The court held that whether the contractor could reasonably rely upon the engineer to inspect its work on a consistent basis was a triable issue of fact as was the issue of the scope of the engineer's inspection responsibilities owed to the contractor.

§ 8.10 —Negligence or Intentional Interference in Contract Administration

E.C. Ernst, Inc. v. Manhattan Construction Co.[57] deals primarily with the issue of the design professional's liability to the contractor for negligence in the performance of its obligations of project administration. In *Ernst* an electrical subcontractor on a hospital construction project sued to recover damages for delays from the owner, the general contractor, the architect, and one of its suppliers. Following a lengthy bench trial, the district court denied the subcontractor's claims for damages. The subcontractor appealed.

On appeal, the court of appeals concluded that a no damage for delay clause in the subcontract barred Ernst's claims against the general

---

[53] *See* United States *ex rel.* Los Angeles Testing Lab. v. Rogers & Rogers, 161 F. Supp. 132 (S.D. Cal. 1958).

[54] 42 N.C. App. 259, 257 S.E.2d 50 (1979).

[55] *Cf.* Lutz Eng'g Co. v. Industrial Louvers, Inc., 585 A.2d 631 (R.I. 1991) (holding that engineer owed no duty of care to contractor in reviewing submittals of contractor).

[56] 518 So. 2d 1194 (Miss. 1988).

[57] 551 F.2d 1026 (5th Cir. 1977), *cert. denied,* 434 U.S. 1067 (1978).

contractor. The court also concluded that the subcontractor could not recover directly from the owner because it was not a third-party beneficiary of the owner/general contractor agreement. Nevertheless, the court concluded that the subcontractor did have a viable right of action in tort against the architect.

Ernst's claims against the architect were predicated upon the architect's alleged negligence in refusing to approve a particular bed light fixture application and, with respect to an emergency generator system, in drawing faulty specifications and failing to act promptly on submittals. The court of appeals held that the architect's procrastination and inconsistency in acting on generator submittals constituted negligence as a matter of law, for which the subcontractor could recover damages. It also remanded to the district court for further consideration the issues of whether the architect had been negligent in its actions upon the bed light submittals and in drafting the plans and specifications for the emergency generator system.

The pattern of action with respect to the emergency generator submittals (which the court concluded amounted to professional negligence as a matter of law) revealed an initial approval ("providing that the requirements of the plans and specifications [would be] met"), followed by a series of criticisms based initially upon claims of foreign manufacture, and later upon claims that the submitted generator was not a standard product and failed to meet horsepower requirements. The architect initially urged resubmittals, then suggested that it would accept the generator subject to tests, and then refused to permit tests and ultimately disapproved the system. During the process, which spanned more than a year, the professional consistently failed to list its reasons for disapprovals in a manner that might have resolved the impasse. Reviewing the history of this process, the court concluded:

> [The architect's] activities regarding its arbitral responsibilities on the emergency generator submittals constituted negligence as a matter of law. They represent a pattern of procrastination which, in view of the interdependence of effort so vital on a construction project, falls below the standard of care required in this situation for professional architects.[58]

In *Waldor Pump & Equipment Co. v. Orr-Schelen-Mayeron & Associates, Inc.,*[59] a subcontractor on a wastewater treatment plant sued the owner's engineer for negligence in preparing and drafting the plans and specifications.

---

[58] *Id.* at 1032. Significant, also, was the court of appeals' conclusion that the professional could not avail itself of the traditional defense of arbitral immunity based upon its status under the owner-contractor agreement as resolver of disputes between owner and contractor and as interpreter of the contract documents. The court concluded that the architect's pattern of delay and of tentative, incongruous, and inconsistent action deprived it of the benefit of this defense. *Id.* at 1033–34.

[59] 386 N.W.2d 375 (Minn. Ct. App. 1986).

The subcontractor had agreed to supply eight Wilden sludge pumps to the successful bidder for the prime contract. The subcontract provided that if the engineer should reject the Wilden pumps, the subcontractor would provide conforming pumps at no additional cost. When the engineer rejected the Wilden pumps, the subcontractor was required to supply more expensive Dorr-Oliver pumps. The subcontractor sued the engineer on a variety of theories, including negligence in drafting and interpreting the specifications. The subcontractor presented evidence at the trial to show that the Wilden pumps satisfied the salient performance requirements of the specifications and that the engineer had unreasonably relied on a design, rather than performance, feature in rejecting the pumps. The jury found that the engineer had been negligent and awarded the subcontractor the increased costs of supplying the replacement pumps.

On appeal, the engineer argued that it could have no liability for negligence to the subcontractor, because the subcontractor was not in privity of contract with it. The court, however, held that "[t]he reasonable skill and judgment expected of professionals must be rendered to those who foreseeably rely upon the services."[60]

Relying on decisions in other jurisdictions, the court further held it foreseeable that the subcontractor and other subcontractors who were bound to follow the specifications prepared by the engineer could be harmed by the engineer's negligent drafting or interpretation of the specifications, and that the engineer therefore owed a duty to the subcontractor to reasonably draft and interpret the specifications. The appellate court also rejected the engineer's contention that the subcontractor could not recover for its losses because they were purely economic losses for which recovery would not apply under a negligence theory. The court held, "economic losses are those resulting from the failure of a product to perform to the level expected by the buyer. . . . We do not read [the rule limiting recovery for economic losses] to limit the legal remedies of individuals economically injured by the negligent rendition of professional services."[61]

Other cases concerning the conduct of design professionals in their administrative functions, conduct that may give rise to liability to a contractor on tort theories, have been considered. For example, in *Detweiler Bros., Inc. v. John Graham & Co.,*[62] the court held that an engineer could incur liability to a contractor for reversal of a decision upon which the contractor had relied to its detriment. In *Detweiler,* which involved allegations that an

---

[60] *Id.* at 377.

[61] *Id.* at 377–78. *See also* Waldinger Corp. v. Ashbrook-Simon-Hartley, Inc., 564 F. Supp. 970 (C.D. Ill. 1983), *aff'd in part and remanded in part sub nom.* Waldinger Corp. v. CRS Group Eng'rs, Inc., 775 F.2d 781 (7th Cir. 1985); Craviolini v. Scholer & Fuller Associated Architects, 89 Ariz. 24, 357 P.2d 611 (1961) (imposing liability upon professional for intentional interference with contract).

[62] 412 F. Supp. 416 (E.D. Wash. 1976).

engineer had first approved a mechanical subcontractor's submittal to substitute grooved piping for welded or threaded pipe and then later ordered the contractor to stop work and replace the grooved pipe with welded pipe, a cause of action in negligence was stated.

Similarly, in *W.H. Lyman Construction Co. v. Village of Gurnee*[63] the court held that although an engineer had no liability to a contractor for an alleged failure to disclose a subsurface water condition, the engineer could be liable in tort to the contractor for delay in devising a design solution to the problem. In *Gurtler, Hebert & Co. v. Weyland Machine Shop, Inc.*,[64] the court held that allegations that an architect had delayed in the approval of shop drawing submittals were adequate to support a claim in tort against the architect.

§ 8.11 —Scheduling and Coordination

Peter Kiewit Sons' Co. v. Iowa Southern Utilities Co.[65] involved a contractor's claim against an engineer for alleged negligence in scheduling and coordinating the construction of a power plant project. Although the contractor's claim was ultimately denied, the decision is significant because (1) it holds that an engineer with scheduling and coordination functions does owe a duty of care to a contractor in the performance of those functions, and (2) it illustrates the manner in which the performance of those functions will be evaluated.

The construction of the project was let on a multi-prime, modified fast-track basis. Both the contract for engineering services and the various prime contracts contained provisions requiring completion by May 1, 1968. Completion by that date was essential because the utility/owner's contracts for outside power were to expire then. The engineer's contract with the owner required the engineer to coordinate and expedite the work on the project, and the various prime contracts also contained provisions pertaining to the engineer's authority in coordination and scheduling.

The claim in *Kiewit* was brought by the prime contractor for general construction. Delays (which were determined to have occurred essentially without the fault of either contractor) in precedent work under the structural steel fabrication and erection contract and the boiler fabrication and erection contract considerably impacted the general construction contractor in its ability to proceed with its work in a productive fashion. In particular, the delays affected the contractor's sequencing and scheduling of concrete slab pours. The contractor's work was further adversely impacted when efforts to bring the project back on schedule after the initial delays

[63] 84 Ill. App. 3d 28, 403 N.E.2d 1325 (1980).

[64] 405 So. 2d 660 (La. Ct. App. 1981).

[65] 355 F. Supp. 376 (S.D. Iowa 1973).

led to congestion and further disruption of its activities. The general contractor sought to recover from the engineer damages resulting from the disruption and loss of productivity on a theory of negligent scheduling and coordination.

Initially, the court held that, despite provisions in the owner-contractor agreement giving the engineer broad discretion in the planning and management of the project, the engineer's discretion was tempered by a duty of care owed to the contractor.[66]

Ultimately, however, the court concluded that the engineer did not breach the duty of care owed to contractor, stating:

> There is no evidence that Black & Veatch failed to provide adequate and competent personnel to administer the contract documents on the job site. . . . [T]he evidence is that Black & Veatch handled the site supervision very efficiently, by coping with potentially disastrous setbacks and yet completing the job substantially on time. In fact, the Engineer's efficiency in this regard is one of the matters about which Kiewit most bitterly complains. Black & Veatch certainly was not negligent in this respect.
>
> There is no evidence that Black & Veatch administered the contract in any manner other than that accepted by the trade. In the first place, Kiewit put on no evidence but its own self-serving declarations as to how a supervising engineer should function. In the larger respect, however, the Court cannot fathom how Black & Veatch could have operated any differently than it did, considering the circumstances, and still have performed its obligations to the Owner.
>
> . . . The circumstances on the site caused the Engineer to order substantial deviations, in some instances, from [the original schedule]. The Engineer's actions in this regard, however, were reasonable and were within the contemplation of the contracts of all parties involved.
>
> * * *
>
> Kiewit alleges that the Engineer required Plaintiff to work under costly and inefficient circumstances not contemplated by the contract documents. Kiewit did have to work under less than ideal circumstances, but all other contractors also suffered from the same problem. . . . This job had more than its share of difficulties, but the contracts clearly allowed Black & Veatch to do what it did. Black & Veatch would have breached its contract with the Owner, had it done differently. Kiewit was the victim of those circumstances that sometimes construction contractors experience. The fault here was not with the Engineer.[67]

The findings of fact that appeared to lend support to the conclusion that the engineer had not breached its duty of care to the contractor included:

1. When it appeared that the project might be delayed by default in the preparation of shop drawings by the structural steel contractor,

---

[66] *Id.* at 394.

[67] *Id.* at 395–96.

the engineer actively worked to assist the contractor in the preparation of shop drawings and assigned additional staff to the review of such drawings, thus avoiding a delay in that regard.

2. When delays did unavoidably occur in the steel erection work due to delays in material deliveries, the engineer required the erection contractor to run longer day shifts at premium time in order to speed up the work. Other alternatives, such as night-shift work, were considered, but rejected because of concerns about safety and the lack of sufficient qualified iron workers to man such a shift.
3. The engineer relaxed specifications and sequencing requirements affecting the general construction contractor's work in order to assist it in maintaining productivity.
4. The engineer actively worked to alleviate safety hazards to the general contractor's performance created by other contractors and also to mitigate damage by other contractors to the general contractor's work.
5. When it became apparent that the project was falling behind, the engineer adopted a monthly CPM update process (not called for in the original contract documents), and often made daily field scheduling adjustments to accommodate events as they occurred on the project.
6. The engineer provided adequate and competent staffing on-site, and the project was never delayed for want of such staffing.
7. There was no hindrance of the general construction contractor's work because of defects in plans and specifications.
8. The general construction contractor conceded that there had been no favoritism in scheduling decisions by the engineer, and it appeared that the engineer had considered the economic impact upon various contractors and the overall goal of the May 1, 1968, completion date as prime considerations in making its scheduling decisions.

Therefore, although *Kiewit* denied a recovery to the contractor, the case also stands for the proposition that an engineer with scheduling and coordination responsibilities can be held liable to a contractor on a negligence theory if the engineer:

1. Fails promptly to address, acknowledge, or respond to delays occurring on the project
2. Fails to consider available alternatives for bringing the project on schedule
3. Fails properly to update or adjust schedules
4. Shows favoritism in its scheduling or coordination decisions or
5. Provides inadequate or incompetent staffing to perform the scheduling and coordination functions.

CHAPTER 9

SUING THE CONSTRUCTION LENDER

Richard E. Alexander*

Richard E. Alexander is a partner in the Portland, Oregon, office of Stoel Rives Boley Jones & Grey. He specializes in the area of construction and design law, representing prime contractors, subcontractors and suppliers, architects and engineers, and owners of construction projects. Mr. Alexander is an associate member of the Associated General Contractors of America, Inc., member of the Public Contracts Section of the American Bar Association, and associate member of the Construction Specifications Institute and American Institute of Architects. A contributing author to the first edition of *Construction Litigation, Representing the Contractor* (John Wiley & Sons, 1985), he is also an arbitrator appointed by the American Arbitration Association for construction disputes, and a member of the American College of Construction Lawyers.

§ 9.1 Introduction

STATUTORY REMEDIES

§ 9.2 Importance of Statutory Remedies

§ 9.3 —Mechanics' Lien Statutes

§ 9.4 —Stop-Notice Provisions

§ 9.5 —Requirements that Loan Agreement Be Recorded

CONTRACT THEORIES

§ 9.6 Introduction

§ 9.7 Treating Lender and Borrower as Single Entity

§ 9.8 Third-Party Beneficiary Status

*The author would like to acknowledge the major contribution of Keith M. Garza a summer associate of Stoel Rives Boley Jones & Grey, and David S. Barlow, with Donaldson, Kiel & McKenzie, who was a contributor to the first edition of this book.

§ 9.9 —Establishing Third-Party Beneficiary Status

§ 9.10 —Enforcing Third-Party Rights

RIGHTS BASED ON ESTOPPEL

§ 9.11 Introduction

§ 9.12 Estoppel Theories

§ 9.13 Elements of Successful Estoppel Claims

§ 9.14 —Actionable Representations

§ 9.15 —Reliance

UNJUST ENRICHMENT THEORIES

§ 9.16 Generally

§ 9.17 Defining Unjust Enrichment in Construction

§ 9.18 —When Does Unjust Enrichment Occur?

§ 9.19 —Measuring Unjust Enrichment

§ 9.20 Potential Limitations on Use of Unjust Enrichment Theories

TORT THEORIES

§ 9.21 Negligence

§ 9.22 Misrepresentation

§ 9.23 Other Tort Theories

§ 9.1 Introduction

Actions against construction lenders are a relatively uncommon remedy for contractors, subcontractors, and suppliers. The existence of more accessible defendants, statutory remedies, built-in limitations in the legal theories available for such suits, and judicial assumptions about who should bear the risk in a construction project all account for this slow development.

Although claims against a lender are generally not the preferred remedy for an unpaid contractor, subcontractor, or supplier, a contractor[1] will often encounter situations where it must make a claim against a construction lender. For example, a lender may be the only remaining solvent party, or the contractor, because of its contract, its own error, or the nature of a particular jurisdiction's lien laws, may have no other potential source of recovery.

This chapter explores the theories available to a contractor, subcontractor, or supplier seeking to recover from a construction lender. It reviews the

[1] The term "contractor" refers in this chapter to prime contractors, subcontractors, and suppliers, unless otherwise noted.

ways a contractor can bring an action against a lender, the requirements and limitations of the various theoretical approaches, and how these theories have fared in contractor-construction lender litigation to date. **Sections 7.2** through **7.5** discuss potential statutory remedies. When available, these may well be the contractor's best remedy. **Sections 7.7** through **7.11** explore means to establish and enforce contractual rights against the lender and discuss possible arguments for establishing privity and third-party beneficiary theories. The remaining sections discuss estoppel theories, equitable remedies, and possible tort theories.

STATUTORY REMEDIES

§ 9.2 Importance of Statutory Remedies

A contractor considering making a claim against a construction lender should initially review the particular jurisdiction's available statutory remedies. Statutory schemes may provide the contractor with various remedies against a lender. They also may dictate what theories are available for the contractor attempting to sue a lender.[2]

§ 9.3 —Mechanics' Lien Statutes

A contractor should first consider the relative priority between the lender and the contractor pursuant to the applicable mechanics' lien law. Though most jurisdictions will treat a construction lender's properly recorded security interest as superior to any lien filed by a contractor, this is not the case in all jurisdictions.[3] When a contractor enjoys priority over a lender, resorting to more exotic remedies may not be necessary. When the secured lender enjoys priority over the contractor or subcontractor, the need for alternative approaches will be greater.

---

[2] California, for instance, has statutorily abolished the equitable lien. Cal. Civ. Code § 3264 (West 1974). *See also* Pankow Constr. Co. v. Advance Mortgage Corp., 618 F.2d 611, 616–17 (9th Cir. 1980) (holding that § 3264 bars recovery under third-party beneficiary theory). Alaska has judicially abolished the equitable lien through interpretation of a stop-notice statute. Donnybrook Bldg. Supply Co. v. Alaska Nat'l Bank, 736 P.2d 1147, 1153–54 (Alaska 1987); Great W. Sav. Bank v. George W. Easley Co., 778 P.2d 569, 577 (Alaska 1989).

[3] *E.g.*, Or. Rev. Stat. § 87.025(1), (2), (6) (1989).

§ 9.4 —Stop-Notice Provisions

Some states provide a statutory mechanism to inform a lender that a subcontractor or supplier has not been paid on a project.[4] Once notice of nonpayment is given, the lender either is barred from making further payments or bears the risk of proceeding.[5] These statutes, however, protect only subcontractors and suppliers.[6]

Each statute has its idiosyncrasies. As with lien remedies, stop-notice statutes generally have short time periods in which to file. The subcontractor or supplier also must meet various statutory requirements. Moreover, the courts generally construe stop-notice statutes narrowly.[7] Therefore, these statutes should be checked promptly and their specific requirements carefully followed.[8] When such a statutory remedy exists, it provides a useful mechanism to freeze assets sufficient to pay for labor and materials provided on a project.

§ 9.5 —Requirements that Loan Agreement Be Recorded

Other states require the construction lender to record the loan agreement to protect its statutory lien priority.[9] Such public recording statutes can be a useful tool for the contractor, because public recording allows the contractor to review the loan agreement before deciding to proceed. The recording statutes can also be used as a weapon in litigation with lenders. A lender can also lose its priority for knowingly filing a contract that misrepresents

---

[4] At least nine states have enacted stop-notice statutes: Ala. Code § 35-11-227(b) (1977); Alaska Stat. § 34.35.062 (1985 & Supp. 1989); Cal. Civ. Code §§ 3158–75 (West 1974 & Supp. 1991); Ind. Code Ann. § 32-8-3-9 (West 1980); Miss. Code Ann. § 85-7-181 (1973 & Supp. 1990); N.J. Stat. Ann. §§ 1A:44-77 to -78 (West 1987); N.C. Gen. Stat. § 44A-20 (1990); Tex. Rev. Civ. Stat. Ann. § 53.081 (Vernon 1989 & Supp. 1991); Wash. Rev. Code Ann. § 60.04.210 (1990). *See generally* Reitz, *Construction Lenders' Liability to Contractors, Subcontractors, and Materialmen,* 130 U. Pa. L. Rev. 416, 432–34 (1981); Sweet, Legal Aspects of Architecture and Engineering 471–72 (2d ed. 1977). Note, *Mechanics' Liens: The Stop Notice Comes to Washington,* 49 Wash. L. Rev. 689 (1974).

[5] *E.g.,* Cal. Civ. Code §§ 3161–3162 (West 1974 & Supp. 1991); Wash. Rev. Code Ann. § 60.04.210(4) (1990).

[6] *See, e.g.,* Sofias v. Bank of Am. Nat'l Trust & Sav. Ass'n, 172 Cal. App. 3d 583, 218 Cal. Rptr. 388, 389 n.4 (1985).

[7] Town Concrete Pipe, Inc. v. Redford, 43 Wash. App. 493, 717 P.2d 1384, 1386 (1986); *cf.* Donnybrook Bldg. Supply Co. v. Alaska Nat'l Bank, 736 P.2d 1147, 1151 (Alaska 1987).

[8] *See, e.g.,* Manos v. Degen, 203 Cal. App. 3d 1237, 250 Cal. Rptr. 493 (1988).

[9] *E.g.,* N.Y. Lien Law §§ 13, 22 (McKinney 1966).

the loan funds available or by modifying the agreement without recording the change.[10] Again, the recording statutes generally protect only subcontractors and suppliers.

CONTRACT THEORIES

§ 9.6 Introduction

If statutory remedies are not available or not practical, a contractor should next consider any rights it might have under the construction loan agreement.

Although a contractor can occasionally negotiate with the lender and provide itself with protection, a lender normally has no express contractual relationship with a project's contractors, because only the borrower has dealt directly with the lender. Therefore, the contractor seeking to enforce rights pursuant to the construction agreement must establish that it is in privity or otherwise has a right to enforce the agreement's terms.

In asserting contractual rights, contractors should consider several approaches. They may argue that the formal contractual separation between the owner and lender should be ignored, for example, or that they are third-party beneficiaries of the agreement between the lender and borrower. Contractors can also argue that estoppel requires the lender to perform certain obligations or not to take certain actions.

§ 9.7 Treating Lender and Borrower as Single Entity

One approach is to argue that the lender and contractor in fact should be treated as being in privity despite the parties' formal contractual separation. Essentially, the contractor argues that the lender's involvement in the project extends beyond simply supplying funds, and that its role in the project justifies treating the lender and borrower as one party. If the contractor has privity with the borrower, treating the lender and borrower as one creates the possibility of direct contractual claims against the lender.

This view has not been widely adopted. Most courts view the lender only as a supplier of capital and not as an active participant in the construction project. Cases suggest that this would not be so if the lender's activities on

---

[10] *See, e.g.,* Nanuet Nat'l Bank v. Eckerson Terrance, Inc., 47 N.Y.2d 243, 391 N.E.2d 983, 417 N.Y.S.2d 901 (1979).

a project clearly exceed those of a normal lender, but do little to define what those activities might be.[11]

One area in which courts have been willing to treat the owner and lender as a unit has been in litigation involving projects financed by the government through the National Housing Act.[12] On these projects, otherwise assetless nonprofit entities contract with the contractors to build housing. The owner receives its financing completely from a lender. The lenders are willing to make these loans because they are insured by the government; when a project fails, the government steps in for the lender. In cases arising from these projects, the courts have found that prime contractors can assert rights against the government.[13] The courts have recognized that the government's role in financing and controlling the project makes it an active participant in the project and thus subject to suit by the contractor.

Similar arguments could probably be made in the private sector where the lender, by exercise of control, sharing of profits, of other direct participation in the project, becomes in effect a joint venturer.[14] One commentator suggests that the lender and borrower could be compressed into a single entity for privity purposes using partnership, limited partnership, or joint venture theories.[15] These theories, however, have met with little success to date.[16]

An alternative approach, accepted by at least one court, is contractual integration. In *Gilmore v. Century Bank & Trust Co.*[17] a Massachusetts appellate court integrated separate lender-borrower and borrower-subcontractor workout agreements, thereby creating privity between the subcontractors and the lender. *Gilmore* involved the renegotiation of a

---

[11] *E.g.,* Wierzbicki v. Alaska Mut. Sav. Bank, 630 P.2d 998 (Alaska 1981); Mortgage Assocs., Inc. v. Monona Shores, Inc., 47 Wis. 2d 171, 177 N.W.2d 340, 349–50 (1970); Connor v. Great W. Sav. & Loan Ass'n, 69 Cal. 2d 850, 73 Cal. Rptr. 369 (1969).

[12] 12 U.S.C.A. §§ 1715Z-1 to 17152-20 (West 1989 & Supp. 1991).

[13] C.H. Sanders Co. v. BHAP Hous. Dev. Fund Co., 903 F.2d 114, 121 (2d Cir. 1990); Niagara Mohawk Power Corp. v. Bankers Trust Co., 791 F.2d 242, 244–45 (2d Cir. 1986); S.S. Silberblatt, Inc. v. East Harlem Pilot Block, 608 F.2d 28 (2d Cir. 1979); Trans-Bay Eng'rs & Builders, Inc. v. Hills, 551 F.2d 370, 381–82 (D.C. Cir. 1976). *C.f.* Korea Dev. Corp. v. United States, 9 Cl. Ct. 167 (1985); Penne Towne Builders, Inc. v. United States, 4 Cl. Ct. 677 (1984).

[14] See Reitz, *Construction Lenders' Liability to Contractors, Subcontractors, and Materialmen,* 130 U. Pa. L. Rev. 416, 453–59 (1981), for an excellent discussion on the idea of treating the lender and borrower as a single unit.

[15] *Id.* at 457.

[16] *See, e.g.,* the California Supreme Court's rejection of a joint venture argument involving an owner and lender in Connor v. Great W. Sav. & Loan Ass'n, 69 Cal. 2d 850, 477 P.2d 609, 73 Cal. Rptr. 369, 375 (1969). As with other theories discussed in this chapter, it is often difficult to meet the legal requirements to establish that a joint venture exists.

[17] 20 Mass. App. 49, 477 N.E.2d 1069 (1985).

condominium construction loan. Prior to completion of the project, the loan funds were exhausted and the subcontractors were left unpaid. Separate workout agreements were then executed between lender-borrower and borrower-contractor. The lender subsequently breached its contract.

The court held that similarities between the workout agreements, that is, simultaneity of execution, identity of subject matter and parties, cross-referencing, and interdependency of provisions, coupled with the degree of control exercised by the lender over the workout,[18] required the court to read the agreements together.[19] This allowed the subcontractors to maintain a breach of contract action against the lender.

Contractual integration offers a contractor the ability to establish privity while avoiding the difficulties of proving joint venture. A contractor considering this approach should carefully evaluate both formal and informal relationships between the loan agreement and the construction or supply contract.

These theories offer a potential basis for providing the privity needed for a contractually based claim against the lender. As one commentator summarized;

> There may be sound basis in many projects to characterize the construction lender as part of the developer's team rather than as an independent entity merely supplying secured credit. This may be the most principled path toward establishing the normative standards for construction lender liability, and would meld well with the growing body of contract law that is extending the bounds of traditional privity concepts.[20]

§ 9.8 Third-Party Beneficiary Status

A more tested theory for asserting contractual rights is to argue that the contractor is a third-party beneficiary of agreements between the lender and borrower. As such, the contractor can enforce obligations created in the construction loan agreement.

The basic limitation on any third-party beneficiary argument is the need to show that the lender and borrower intended to make the contractor a third-party beneficiary of their agreement. Under the *Restatement (Second)*

---

[18] The court noted that the lender maintained a list of subcontractors who were hesitant to participate in the workout, and counseled the borrower as to tactics for generating compliance: mentioning the possibility of foreclosure and encouraging particularly willing subcontractors to convince the others. *Id.* at 1071. As a result, the hesitant subcontractors extinguished mechanics' liens and accepted the workout. *Id.* at 1072.

[19] *Id.* at 1073–74.

[20] Reitz, *Construction Lenders' Liability to Contractors, Subcontractors, and Materialmen,* 130 U. Pa. L. Rev. 416, 459 (1981).

of Contracts[21] there are two basic ways to make a party a third-party beneficiary: the third party can establish that the promisor's performance under the contract discharges a duty otherwise owed the third party by the promisee; or the third party can show an intent to benefit. Other courts continue to analyze third-party beneficiary issues using the donee, creditor, and incidental beneficiary language of the first *Restatement of Contracts.*[22] Under either approach, the court must also determine that the beneficiary's enforcement of the agreement would be appropriate. If the contractor cannot satisfy these tests, it has no right as a third-party beneficiary to enforce the lender's obligations in its contract with the borrower.[23]

What is sufficient to establish the necessary intent to create a third-party beneficiary varies among the different jurisdictions. Some courts require that the intent to benefit third parties affirmatively appear in the contract.[24] Other courts vary on whether both parties must manifest an intent to benefit, or only the promisee.[25]

A fairly standard formulation of the necessary intent is set forth below:

> Though the third party beneficiary need not be named in the contract, the terms of the contract must express directly and clearly an intent to benefit the specific party or an identifiable class of which the party asserting rights as a third party beneficiary is a member. Inasmuch as people usually contract and stipulate for themselves and not for third persons, a strong presumption arises that such was their intention, and the implication to overcome that presumption must be so strong as to amount to an express declaration.[26]

---

[21] Restatement (Second) of the Law of Contracts § 302 (1981):

§ 302. Intended and Incidental Beneficiaries.

(1) Unless otherwise agreed between promisor and promisee, a beneficiary of a promise is an intended beneficiary if recognition of a right to performance in the beneficiary is appropriate to effectuate the intention of the parties and either

(a) the performance of the promise will satisfy an obligation of the promisee to pay money to the beneficiary; or

(b) the circumstances indicate that the promisee intends to give the beneficiary the benefit of the promised performance.

(2) An incidental beneficiary is a beneficiary who is not an intended beneficiary.

[22] Restatement of Contracts § 133 (1932).

[23] Gee v. Eberle, 279 Pa. Super. 101, 420 A.2d 1050, 1056 n.4 (1980); Knight Constr. Co. v. Barnett Mortgage Trust, 572 S.W.2d 381, 382–83 (Tex. Ct. App. 1978), *writ refused, n.r.e.*

[24] *Compare* Knight Constr. Co. v. Barnett Mortgage Trust, 572 S.W.2d 381, 382–83 (Tex. Ct. App. 1978), *writ refused, n.r.e. with In re* Gebco Inv. Corp., 641 F.2d 143 (3d Cir. 1981).

[25] Khabbaz v. Swartz, 319 N.W.2d 279, 285 n.9 (Iowa 1982); Gee v. Eberle, 279 Pa. Super. 101, 420 A.2d 1050, 1056 (1980).

[26] Laclede Inv. Corp. v. Kaiser, 596 S.W.2d 36, 42 (Mo. Ct. App. 1980).

§ 9.9 —Establishing Third-Party Beneficiary Status

In attempting to establish rights as a third-party beneficiary, contractors have relied on various factors, including the terms of the construction loan agreement, industry custom, and the contractor's direct dealings with the parties to the loan agreement.

Construction loan agreements often include an express disclaimer of any intent to create third-party rights. These clauses may announce in general terms that no third party is entitled to rely on the agreement's provisions, or may specifically state that the lender owes no obligation and has no relationship with the project's contractors. The presence of such a clause will normally negate any attempt to establish third-party beneficiary rights.[27]

Some courts have indicated that such an express disclaimer would prevent a third-party beneficiary claim even if other evidence suggested such an intent.[28] In *Silverdale Hotel v. Lomas & Nettleton Co.,*[29] a Washington appellate court held that the trial court's finding that the lender promised to pay the contractor through an escrow account in the face of such a clause violated the parol evidence rule. The court found that the oral agreement was inconsistent with a contract term denying lender liability to any contractor or supplier.[30] Thus, a contractor considering suing on a third-party

---

[27] Volpe Constr. v. First Nat'l Bank, 30 Mass. App. Ct. 249, 567 N.E.2d 1244, 1249 (1991); Sofias v. Bank of America Nat'l Trust & Sav. Ass'n, 172 Cal. App. 3d 583, 218 Cal. Rptr. 388, 390 (1985); Gee v. Eberle, 279 Pa. Super. 101, 420 A.2d 1050, 1055 n.4 (1980); Pioneer Plumbing Supply Co. v. Southwest Sav. & Loan Ass'n, 102 Ariz. 258, 428 P.2d 115, 122 (1967). *But see* Twin City Constr. Co. v. ITT Indus. Credit Co., 358 N.W.2d 716 (Minn. Ct. App. 1984). In *Twin City* the contractor performed approximately $600,000 worth of work on a project. When the borrower failed to pay, the contractor filed liens. The borrower then sought an additional loan to rescue the project. As a condition of the new loan, the lender required the contractor to release its lien, subordinate its interest, and waive any lien rights. The agreement between the lender and borrower for the new loan expressly stated that no third party could rely on it. Subsequently, the lender did not make a final payment to the contractor.

The Minnesota court found that the contractor could establish third-party beneficiary status either by showing that the lender assumed the duty owed by the promisee or by showing an intent to benefit. The court found that the "duty owed" test had been met, stating that the lender assumed the duty to pay for the work when it committed itself to making the loan and making progress payments. It found an intent to benefit the contractor from the documents as a whole. The court particularly emphasized the lender's requirement that the contractor forgo its statutory remedies in exchange for the lender's additional loan for the project.

[28] Knight Constr. Co. v. Barnett Mortgage Trust, 572 S.W.2d 381, 383 (Tex. Ct. App. 1978), *writ refused, n.r.e.*

[29] 36 Wash. App. 762, 677 P.2d 773, 779, *review denied,* 101 Wash. 2d 1021 (1984).

[30] The contractor, though, was able to enforce the agreement on a promissory estoppel theory.

beneficiary theory should review the construction loan agreement for any disclaimer of intent to benefit third parties.

In other situations, contractors have argued that the construction loan agreement's provisions show an intent to make the contractor a third-party beneficiary. Pennsylvania courts in particular have been active in determining if a construction loan agreement creates third-party rights for a contractor.[31]

The Pennsylvania cases show, though, that often the contract language alone is not determinative. The parties' conduct during a project is also an important factor in determining the contracting parties' intent.[32] For instance, in *Clardy v. Barco Construction Co.*[33] and *Demharter v. First Federal Savings & Loan Association,*[34] Pennsylvania courts construed identical payout provisions in two construction loan agreements. In *Clardy* the court found that a subcontractor suing on the prime's rights was a third-party beneficiary.[35] In *Demharter* the court had held that no third-party beneficiary status existed for subcontractors and suppliers.[36]

The Pennsylvania Superior Court distinguished the cases based on the *Demharter* lender's ability to choose to pay either the subcontractors or the contractor-owner. In *Clardy* the superior court found that other portions

---

[31] For a detailed analysis of the Pennsylvania cases discussed in this section, see Reitz, *Construction Lenders' Liability to Contractors, Subcontractors, and Materialmen,* 130 U. Pa. L. Rev. 416, 424–26 (1981); *see also In re* Gebco Inv. Corp., 641 F.2d 143 (3d Cir. 1981); R.P. Russo Contractors v. C.J. Pettinato Realty, 334 Pa. Super. 72, 482 A.2d 1086, 1091–92 (1984).

[32] *See also* Gilmore v. Century Bank & Trust Co., 20 Mass. App. 49, 477 N.E.2d 1069 (1985). In *Gilmore,* discussed at **§ 9.7**, the court held that cooperation between lender, borrower, and subcontractors in an attempt to rescue a stalled construction project created "interdependencies signified by reciprocal rights and duties," making the subcontractors intended third-party beneficiaries of the lender-borrower agreement. *Id.* at 1074–75.

[33] 205 Pa. Super. 218, 208 A.2d 793, 795–96 (1965).

[34] 412 Pa. 142, 194 A.2d 214 (1963).

[35] ". . . [I]t is mutually agreed between the parties hereto that the Association *shall:*

* * *

> 6. Pay out of the funds to contractors, subcontractors or materialmen, as the Association may elect, for work performed, services rendered, and materials furnished in and about the construction of the building. Such payments shall be made at such times and in whatever amounts the Association may deem expedient, and shall be made according to requisitions approved by a building inspector designated by the Association, which requisition shall be in such form and shall contain such information as the Association may require; it being the intention of the parties hereto that the Association shall be free to make the payments heretofore mentioned in such manner that the Association's security shall at all times be protected.

Clardy v. Barco Constr. Co., 205 Pa. Super. 218, 208 A.2d 793, 795 n.1 (1965) (emphasis in original).

[36] Demharter v. First Fed. Sav. & Loan Ass'n, 412 Pa. 142, 194 A.2d 214, 221.

of the contract obligated the lender to pay the contractor directly. The court emphasized that the contract provided that the contractor would be paid in full before the owner was entitled to any return of the money, that the contractor was named in the contract, and that the contractor was a signatory to it. The superior court also emphasized the parties' conduct, pointing out that payments under the loan agreement had been made directly to the contractor.[37]

Contractors have also tried unsuccessfully to establish themselves as third-party beneficiaries based on industry practice. In one New Jersey case, subcontractors sought to rely in part on a lender's policy manual to establish how the lender should have conducted its affairs.[38] The subcontractors argued—unsuccessfully—that a manual suggesting that a lender make payment only after obtaining affidavits from the contractor establishing that it paid subcontractors and suppliers and a contract clause requiring such affidavits created third-party rights.

Plaintiffs in some of the cases noted in **§ 9.24**, which discusses negligent disbursement of loan funds, have also attempted to use industry custom to establish lender liability. Though plaintiffs have not succeeded with this argument, industry custom and practice is a potential source of an implied obligation to pay.

Contractors have also sued as third-party beneficiaries when the contractor led an owner/borrower to a lender and the lender did not make the loan or stopped payment,[39] but these arguments receive short shrift. The courts have noted the lack of intent to benefit the contractor and the failure of the owner/borrower to perform obligations that were conditions precedent to the lender's duty to pay.

In other cases, plaintiffs have sought to impose liability based on facts similar to those used to support equitable estoppel arguments.[40] In these cases, the contractor has contended that the lender somehow induced it to provide additional services or material. Even when the court has found the facts sufficient to support an equitable estoppel argument, it also has found the contractor unable to show any intent by the contracting party to make it a third-party beneficiary.

---

[37] Clardy v. Barco Constr. Co., 208 A.2d 793, 795–96. *See also In re* Gebco Inv. Corp., 641 F.2d 143 (3d Cir. 1981); Kreimer v. Second Fed. Sav. & Loan Ass'n, 196 Pa. Super. 644, 176 A.2d 132, 133–34 (1961).

[38] First Nat'l State Bank v. Carlyle House, Inc., 102 N.J. Super. 300, 246 A.2d 22, 31–34 (1968), *aff'd,* 107 N.J. Super. 389, 258 A.2d 545 (1969).

[39] Burns v. Washington Sav., 251 Miss. 789, 171 So. 2d 322 (1965); Stephens v. Great S. Sav. & Loan Ass'n, 421 S.W.2d 332, 335–37 (Mo. Ct. App. 1967); Winnebago Homes, Inc. v. Sheldon, 29 Wis. 2d 292, 139 N.W.2d 606, 609 (1966).

[40] Apex Siding & Roofing Co. v. First Fed. Sav. & Loan Ass'n, 301 P.2d 352, 354–55 (Okla. 1956); Silverdale Hotel v. Lomas & Nettleton Co., 36 Wash. App. 762, 677 P.2d 773, *review denied,* 101 Wash. 2d 1021 (1984); Winnebago Homes, Inc. v. Sheldon, 29 Wis. 2d 692, 139 N.W.2d 606, 609 (1966).

§ 9.10 —Enforcing Third-Party Rights

Even if the contractor establishes third-party beneficiary status, it must still establish its right to be paid. The party alleging third-party status has no greater rights under the contract than those of the party through which it claims.[41] The owner's failure to provide an assignment of rents or evidence of clear title or to perform other conditions precedent to the lender's obligation to pay can prevent a contractor's enforcement of contract rights.[42] Similarly, the contractor's own material failure of performance can prevent it from asserting third-party beneficiary rights.[43]

Establishing a third-party beneficiary status is a way for the contractor to enforce the terms of the loan agreement. However, the requirements of this approach are difficult to meet because a contractor must establish both its third-party status and the fact that the lender's performance is due. Though courts have shown flexibility when the equities favor the contractor, the criteria discussed in **§§ 9.8** through **9.10** limit the widespread use of a third-party beneficiary theory.

RIGHTS BASED ON ESTOPPEL

§ 9.11 Introduction

Another approach to suing a construction lender rests on the concept of estoppel. Contractors may argue that a lender is estopped from either not paying the contractor for work or from asserting a lien priority because of representations or promises made by the lender on which the contractor relied to its detriment.[44]

§ 9.12 Estoppel Theories

Different forms of estoppel exist. Plaintiffs in cases involving construction lenders have argued theories of promissory estoppel, equitable estoppel,

---

[41] Stephens v. Great S. Sav. & Loan Ass'n, 421 S.W.2d 332, 337 (Mo. Ct. App. 1967).

[42] *Id.* at 335–37; L.B. Herbst Corp. v. Northern Ill. Corp., 99 Ill. App. 2d 101, 241 N.E.2d 125 (1968).

[43] R.P. Russo Contractors v. C.J. Pettinato Realty, 334 Pa. Super. 72, 482 A.2d 1086, 1091–92 (1984).

[44] Strouss v. Simmons, 66 Haw. 32, 657 P.2d 1004 (1982); Fretz Constr. Co. v. Southern Nat'l Bank, 626 S.W.2d 478 (Tex. 1982).

and even quasi-estoppel. According to the *Restatement (Second) of Contracts, promissory estoppel* requires showing

> [a] promise which the promisor should reasonably expect to induce action or forbearance on the part of the promisee or a third person and which does induce such action or forbearance is binding if injustice can be avoided only by enforcement of the promise. The remedy granted for breach may be limited as justice requires.[45]

Equitable estoppel requires assertion of a position by conduct or word, reasonable reliance, and prejudice.[46] It differs from promissory estoppel in requiring only a representation, and not a promise, to the relying party. *Quasi-estoppel* does not require reliance, but looks for a showing that facts and circumstances make the assertion of a contrary or inconsistent position unconscionable. Though reliance is not a necessary element, the courts will consider whether the party asserting the inconsistent position has gained an advantage or produced some disadvantage to the other party.[47]

§ 9.13 Elements of Successful Estoppel Claims

Regardless of the precise estoppel theory articulated, reported cases involving contractor suits against lenders focus on two factors: first, that a promise or representation was made to the contractor; and second, that the contractor reasonably relied on the representation to its detriment.

Promissory and equitable estoppel are helpful theories when the contractor has had independent contact with the lender. Unlike a third-party beneficiary claim, the contractor need not show that any contracting parties intended to benefit it. Demonstrated reliance on the lender's representations or promises is all that is needed. Reliance is usually based on continuing work or foregoing statutory remedies, although the contractor must show that its reliance was reasonable.

§ 9.14 —Actionable Representations

As a rule, the contractor must show more than that the lender promised to make funds available to the borrower. California cases, for a period prior to the statutory death of the equitable lien in that state, found that knowledge of the existence of the loan fund was a sufficient basis to establish the

---

[45] Restatement (Second) of Contracts § 90 (1981).

[46] *E.g.,* Alaska Statebank v. Kirschbaum, 662 P.2d 939, 942 (Alaska 1983).

[47] *Id.* at 943.

reliance necessary for an equitable lien.[48] Other courts, however, require a showing that the lender made some type of separate representation or enforceable promise to the contractor beyond indicating the existence of a loan.[49]

In *Apex Siding & Roof Co. v. First Federal Savings & Loan Association,*[50] the court found that estoppel applied when a contractor specifically inquired about whether a loan was made and relied on the lender's affirmative reply.[51] Similarly, in *Silverdale Hotel v. Lomas & Nettleton Co.,*[52] the court found that a lender's statement to a contractor that the borrower was not in default and that it would pay according to the loan agreement established promissory estoppel. Representations that money would be set aside to pay for work on a project also have been found sufficient evidence to support a promissory estoppel argument.[53]

In *Gee v. Eberle,*[54] the court held that lender representations that sufficient financing existed and that the owners were "strong" and "everything seems okay" were sufficient evidence to support a reliance argument. Other jurisdictions, however, have found similar representations insufficient to establish the basis for an equitable lien.[55]

The courts have found that lenders have no duty to inform contractors that a borrower is in default or faces financial difficulties.[56] Accordingly, reliance based on a lender's failure to warn will normally not result in estoppel.

However, a lender that changes its loan disbursement pattern in such a way as to lure a contractor into believing that it will be paid can be subject to estoppel. In *Great Western Savings Bank v. George W. Easley Co.,*[57] a contractor, without its knowledge, was periodically paid for completed

---

[48] *E.g.,* Doud Lumber Co. v. Guaranty Sav. & Loan Ass'n, 254 Cal. App. 2d 585, 60 Cal. Rptr. 94, 96–97 (1967).

[49] Pioneer Plumbing Supply Co. v. Southwest Sav. & Loan Ass'n, 102 Ariz. 258, 428 P.2d 115, 122 (1967); Strouss v. Simmons, 66 Haw. 32, 657 P.2d 1004, 1012–13 (1982); Gee v. Eberle, 279 Pa. Super. 101, 420 A.2d 1050, 1063–64 (1980); Silverdale Hotel v. Lomas & Nettleton Co., 36 Wash. App. 762, 677 P.2d 773, *review denied,* 101 Wash. 2d 1021 (1984).

[50] 301 P.2d 352 (Okla. 1956).

[51] *See also* H.O. Bragg Roofing, Inc. v. First Fed. Sav. & Loan Ass'n, 226 Cal. App. 2d 24, 37 Cal. Rptr. 775 (1964).

[52] 36 Wash. App. 762, 677 P.2d 773, 779, *review denied,* 101 Wash. 2d 1021 (1984).

[53] Fretz Constr. Co. v. Southern Nat'l Bank, 626 S.W.2d 478, 482–83 (Tex. 1982).

[54] 279 Pa. Super. 101, 420 A.2d 1050, 1062–64 (1980).

[55] *E.g.,* Indiana Mortgage & Realty Inv. v. Peacock Constr., 348 So. 2d 59 (Fla. Dist. Ct. App.), *cert. denied,* 353 So. 2d 677 (Fla. Dist. Ct. App. 1977).

[56] *E.g.,* L.B. Herbst Corp. v. Northern Ill. Corp., 99 Ill. App. 2d 101, 241 N.E.2d 125, 126 (1968); Mortgage Assocs., Inc. v. Monona Shores, Inc., 47 Wis. 2d 171, 177 N.W.2d 340, 349 (1970).

[57] 778 P.2d 569 (Alaska 1989).

work from funds set aside for later construction costs. This practice led the contractor to incorrectly believe that sufficient funds existed for completion of the project. The Alaska Supreme Court upheld a jury finding that the lender was equitably estopped from denying that it had approved the change in disbursement.[58]

In short, there must be a showing that the lender, either by word or conduct, made independent representations or promises to the contractors. Neither silence nor representations that a loan was made are normally enough to estop the lender. Generally, before allowing estoppel the courts require independent assurances either that adequate funding exists, that funds will be set aside, or that the borrower is financially sound.

§ 9.15 —Reliance

The second essential element of an estoppel claim is reliance. Contractors usually establish their reliance by showing either that they continued work based on the lender's representation or promise or that they forewent use of their statutory rights.[59] Estoppel theory, however, could be expanded to fit other types of detrimental reliance.

Furthermore, the reliance must be reasonable. An argument that a contractor relied on representations that a loan would be made, for instance, was found unreasonable in the face of clauses specifically conditioning how the loan would be paid.[60] However, in *Great Western Savings Bank v. George W. Easley Co.*[61] (see § **9.14**) the court held that a contractor's continued work, despite questionable loan disbursement practices, constituted reasonable reliance even though a phone call to the lender would have revealed insufficient funds to complete the project.

UNJUST ENRICHMENT THEORIES

§ 9.16 Generally

Because of the difficulties in establishing privity or the right to otherwise enforce loan agreements, contractors have turned with increasing frequency

---

[58] *Id.*

[59] H.O. Bragg Roofing, Inc. v. First Fed. Sav. & Loan Ass'n, 226 Cal. App. 2d 24, 37 Cal. Rptr. 775 (1964); Strouss v. Simmons, 66 Haw. 32, 657 P.2d 1004, 1012–14 (1982); First Nat'l State Bank v. Carlyle House, Inc., 246 A.2d 22 (N.J. Super. Ct. 1968), *aff'd,* 258 A.2d 545 (1969).

[60] Strouss v. Simmons, 66 Haw. 32, 657 P.2d 1004, 1012–14 (1982).

[61] 778 P.2d 569, 579 (Alaska 1989).

to various equitable theories of recovery. These theories, however, have met with limited success.

Chief among equitable theories is unjust enrichment, which involves the basic principle that allowing a person to retain the money or property of another is inequitable. Some courts proceed under the general rubric of unjust enrichment without specifying the exact nature of the equitable remedy involved,[62] but others attempt to fit the contractor-lender relationship into a traditional equitable remedy, such as the equitable lien, constructive trust, or subordination.[63]

Equitable liens, constructive trusts, and subordination are equitable remedies based on property concepts. There is no contractual relationship requirement. The *equitable lien* essentially grants a security interest in specific property. The *constructive trust* theory finds that a person holding identifiable property inequitably is the trustee to the person actually entitled to possession. *Subordination* is an equitable remedy that places a losing party's proprietary interest behind that of the prevailing party. These theories overlap; hence, §§ **9.17** through **9.20** discuss unjust enrichment in generic terms.

§ 9.17 Defining Unjust Enrichment in Construction

Defining unjust enrichment has been a problem in construction contractor-construction lender litigation, and the courts vary considerably in how they approach, define, and measure the enrichment. Although the courts are generally unreceptive to contractor claims of unjust enrichment, they wrestle with issues such as when a lender has been unjustly enriched, how the amount of unjust enrichment is measured, and what conditions precedent, if any, must be satisfied before a claim of unjust enrichment exists.

§ 9.18 —When Does Unjust Enrichment Occur?

The courts disagree on when unjust enrichment can occur between a construction lender and contractors. Florida, for example, allows a claim for unjust enrichment only when the construction project has been completed.[64] The rationale for this rule is that completion of a project leaves a

[62] S.S. Silberblatt, Inc. v. East Harlem Pilot Block, 608 F.2d 28, 38 (2d Cir. 1979); Twin City Constr. Co. v. ITT Indus. Credit Co., 358 N.W.2d 716, 719 (Minn. Ct. App. 1984).

[63] Great W. Sav. Bank v. George W. Easley Co., 778 P.2d 569 (Alaska 1989); Gee v. Eberle, 279 Pa. Super. 101, 420 A.2d 1050 (1980); Ralph C. Sutro Co. v. Paramount Plastering, Inc., 216 Cal. App. 2d 433, 31 Cal. Rptr. 174 (1963).

[64] Edd Helms Elec. Contracting, Inc. v. Barnett Bank, 531 So. 2d 238 (Fla. Dist. Ct. App. 1988); Blosam Constr., Inc. v. Republic Mortgage Inv., 353 So. 2d 1225 (Fla. Dist. Ct.

lender with both the finished improvement as security and the undistributed construction loan funds. Allowing a lender to retain both the improvement and the loan funds meant to pay for the improvement is inequitable. Therefore, Florida courts have granted contractors an equitable lien on the undisbursed loan funds. On uncompleted projects, however, they indicate that the value of the labor and material provided will likely exceed the structure's market value and thus will not allow an equitable lien.[65]

Other courts have not drawn such a sharp distinction between completed and uncompleted projects, indicating that unjust enrichment should be determined on a case-by-case basis. Most courts require the contractor to show some element of wrongdoing by the lender. Once this is proven, unjust enrichment is generally available if a contractor can show that its work in some manner enhanced the lender's return from its security. Some courts have found no need for the claiming contractor to have finished its work on the project if it has not materially breached the contract.[66]

§ 9.19 —Measuring Unjust Enrichment

Case law is not explicit about the proper measure of a lender's unjust enrichment. Generally, the courts require evidence of undistributed construction loan funds and evidence that the claimant increased the value of the improvement for the lender.[67] Even in such cases, the courts have had difficulty evaluating the extent to which a particular party has been enriched.[68] Using the contractor's own loss, that is, the value of labor and materials provided, gives an inaccurate measure because this figure will not necessarily equal the value of the uncompleted improvement.[69] In trying to value

---

App. 1977), *cert. denied,* 359 So. 2d 1218 (Fla. Dist. Ct. App. 1978); J.G. Plumbing Serv., Inc. v. Coastal Mortgage Co., 329 So. 2d 393 (Fla. Dist. Ct. App.), *cert. denied,* 339 So. 2d 1169 (Fla. Dist. Ct. App. 1976). *See also* Meyers Plumbing & Heating v. West End Fed. Sav. & Loan, 345 Pa. Super. 559, 498 A.2d 966, 969 (1985); Town Concrete Pipe, Inc. v. Redford, 43 Wash. App. 493, 717 P.2d 1384, 1388 (1986).

[65] J.G. Plumbing Serv., Inc. v. Coastal Mortgage Co., 329 So. 2d 393, 395 (Fla. Dist. Ct. App.), *cert. denied,* 339 So. 2d 1169 (Fla. Dist. Ct. App. 1976).

[66] S.S. Silberblatt, Inc. v. East Harlem Pilot Block, 608 F.2d 28, 37 (2d Cir. 1979); Miller v. Mountain View Sav. & Loan Ass'n, 238 Cal. App. 2d 644, 48 Cal. Rptr. 278, 292 (1965) (prior to statutory end of equitable lien doctrine in California); Gee v. Eberle, 279 Pa. Super. 101, 420 A.2d 1050, 1057 n.5, 1059 (1980).

[67] Trans-Bay Eng'rs & Builders, Inc. v. Hills, 551 F.2d 370, 382–83 (D.C. Cir. 1976); Gee v. Eberle, 279 Pa. Super. 101, 420 A.2d 1050, 1061 n.9 (1980).

[68] Reitz, *Construction Lenders' Liability to Contractors, Subcontractors, and Materialmen,* 130 U. Pa. L. Rev. 416, 445–46 (1981); *cf.* Miller v. Mountain View Sav. & Loan Ass'n, 238 Cal. App. 2d 644, 48 Cal. Rptr. 278, 288–89 (1965).

[69] D.A. Hill Co. v. Clevetrust Realty Investors, 524 Pa. 425, 573 A.2d 1005, 1009 (1990).

the contractor's improvement, courts have occasionally looked to the resale value of the improvement involved.[70]

If the lender has paid out all the money in the fund or has paid for the specific work in question, the courts reason that the lender may retain the work as part of its security interest in the improvement, because it has paid the intended amount for the work. In such cases, the courts find that no unjust enrichment exists.[71]

§ 9.20 Potential Limitations on Use of Unjust Enrichment Theories

In Gee v. Eberle[72] the Pennsylvania Superior Court, in attempting to identify a lender's liability to subcontractors under an equitable lien theory, analogized that relationship to the more frequently discussed owner-subcontractor relationship. The court observed that the weight of authority was against finding owner liability when the subcontractor lacked privity with the owner, noting that previous court decisions generally advanced three reasons therefor:

1. The subcontractor must show wrongdoing by the lender
2. The subcontractor must exhaust its statutory or contractual remedies and
3. A direct contractual relationship must exist.

The *Gee* court, however, suggested that none of these reasons should prevent recovery in either the owner-subcontractor or contractor-construction lender situation.

With regard to intent, the court indicated that it is the result of unjust enrichment, not the wrongful intent, that should be the court's concern.[73] Most courts, however, including the Pennsylvania Supreme Court, have failed to follow this approach.[74] They require wrongful conduct by a lender,

---

[70] Miller v. Mountain View Sav. & Loan Ass'n, 238 Cal. App. 2d 644, 48 Cal. Rptr. 278 (1965); Gee v. Eberle, 279 Pa. Super. 101, 420 A.2d 1050 (1980).

[71] Volpe Constr. v. First Nat'l Bank, 567 N.E.2d 1244, 1252 (Mass. App. Ct. 1991); Gee v. Eberle, 279 Pa. Super. 101, 420 A.2d 1050 (1980).

[72] 279 Pa. Super. 101, 420 A.2d 1050 (1980).

[73] *Id.* at 1059. *See also* Embree Constr. Group v. Rafcor, Inc., 97 N.C. App. 418, 388 S.E.2d 604, 606–07 (1990). For a case that might be read to support this proposition, see Town Concrete Pipe, Inc. v. Redford, 43 Wash. App. 493, 717 P.2d 1384 (1986).

[74] *See, e.g.,* D.A. Hill Co. v. Clevetrust Realty Investors, 524 Pa. 425, 573 A.2d 1005, 1010 (1990).

or at least a request for the benefit conferred, before allowing a contractor to use an equitable remedy against a lender.[75]

As to requiring the contractor to exhaust statutory remedies, the *Gee* court stated that the mechanics' lien would generally be the preferred remedy. Depriving the subcontractor of the advantage associated with lien laws was penalty enough. The court indicated further that denying relief for failure to utilize other remedies when unjust enrichment existed was inconsistent with equitable principles.[76] This would not be applicable, though, when the statutory remedies were intended to stop use of equitable remedies.[77]

Finally, the court rejected a requirement imposed by some other courts that a finding of unjust enrichment required a contractual relationship between the parties. The court argued that the essence of an unjust enrichment is that no direct contractual remedy exists.[78]

In *Gee v. Eberle* the court anticipated and rejected many arguments that a contractor may face in bringing an unjust enrichment argument against a lender. Particularly in jurisdictions where the law is unsettled or hostile, the *Gee* decision may serve as a helpful guide to a contractor trying to sue a lender on unjust enrichment theories.

When there are undistributed loan proceeds for a completed project, some courts recognize the right of the contractor to impose an equitable lien on the undisbursed fund. In other factual settings, such as an incomplete project or where loan funds have been disbursed, the availability of an equitable lien is more disputed. It is an area where creative reliance on decisions involving HUD-financed projects and analogies to suits involving other relationships in the construction process can be effective.[79]

---

[75] Volpe Constr. v. First Nat'l Bank, 567 N.E.2d 1244, 1251 (Mass. App. Ct. 1991); D.A. Hill Co. v. Clevetrust Realty Investors, 524 Pa. 425, 573 A.2d 1005, 1010 (1990); *cf.* Superior Glass Co. v. First Bristol County Nat'l Bank, 8 Mass. App. 356, 394 N.E.2d 972 (1979), *aff'd,* 380 Mass. 829, 406 N.E.2d 672 (1980).

[76] This argument is different from the principle that equity is unavailable if legal remedies are adequate. Town Concrete Pipe, Inc. v. Redford, 43 Wash. App. 493, 717 P.2d 1384, 1387 (1986). Thus, a subcontractor with both contract and quasi-contract actions against the contractor and a surety was unable to assert a claim in equity against the lender. Ed Helms Elec. Contracting, Inc. v. Barnett Bank, 531 So. 2d 238 (Fla. Dist. Ct. App. 1988).

[77] Pankow Constr. Co. v. Advance Mortgage Corp., 618 F.2d 611, 616 (9th Cir. 1980); Gee v. Eberle, 279 Pa. Super. 101, 420 A.2d 1050, 1060 (1980); Cal. Civ. Code § 3264 (West 1974).

[78] Gee v. Eberle, 279 Pa. Super. 101, 420 A.2d 1050, 1060 (1980).

[79] *Cf.* Volpe Constr. Co. v. First Nat'l Bank, 567 N.E.2d 1244, 1250–51 (Mass. App. Ct. 1991) (rejecting HUD analogy in private construction field).

TORT THEORIES

§ 9.21 Negligence

Contractors have also tried various tort theories to reach a construction lender. To date, these theories have not met with significant success. Negligence, however, appears to be an area susceptible to development. Arguments could be made that a lender was negligent in making a loan, in administering construction payments, or in disbursing loan proceeds. Another potential area for attack is the lender's failure to observe accepted banking practices, such as failing to require signed releases or necessary bonds.

At least one contractor was successful in a suit against a lender on a negligent disbursement of loan funds theory. In *Cook v. Citizens Savings & Loan Association*[80] the contractor requested payment from the lender after completing work. The lender paid money directly to the owner without receiving any account of its use, which resulted in the contractor's not being paid. The court concluded that the lender owed the contractor a duty of reasonable diligence to see that the funds were actually used for paying the construction costs. Nevertheless, subsequent courts have read *Cook* narrowly, tying it to the particulars of Mississippi law.[81]

In California a surety successfully sued a lender for negligent disbursement in *Commercial Standard Insurance Co. v. Bank of America.*[82] The suit arose when the owner sued the contractor and the contractor's surety. The surety alleged that the bank had made disbursements exceeding the value of the work done. The court specifically rejected the bank's contention that it owed no duty to the surety. It stated that the question of duty was "question begging" and that it was reasonably foreseeable that the surety would be injured by the bank's failure to exercise care.[83]

Negligence theories, though, usually meet defeat on the issue of duty. Although the courts have at times recognized that lenders owe a duty to other parties involved in the construction project, they generally do not extend this duty to include contractors.[84] To succeed in this area, a contractor will want to analogize to other construction lender relationships.

---

[80] 346 So. 2d 370 (Miss. 1977).

[81] *E.g.,* Rockhill v. United States, 288 Md. 237, 418 A.2d 197, 202 (1980).

[82] 57 Cal. App. 3d 241, 129 Cal. Rptr. 91, 95 (1976).

[83] 129 Cal. Rptr. at 94–95. *See also* R.A. Peck, Inc. v. Liberty Fed. Sav. Bank, 108 N.M. 84, 766 P.2d 928 (Ct. App. 1988).

[84] First Fed. Sav. Bank v. Fretthold, 195 Ga. App. 482, 394 S.E.2d 128 (1990); Bescor, Inc. v. Chicago Title & Trust Co., 113 Ill. App. 3d 65, 446 N.E.2d 1209 (1983); Rockhill v. United States, 288 Md. 237, 418 A.2d 197, 199–205 (1980); Superior Glass Co. v. First

Additionally, a contractor will need to establish what the duty is. Industry custom, internal policy manuals, and other documents can be helpful in this regard.[85]

§ 9.22 Misrepresentation

Another possible tort theory is *negligent misrepresentation.* The *Restatement (Second) of Torts* recognizes that liability can exist for information negligently supplied for the guidance of others:

> (1) One who, in the course of his business, profession or employment, or in any other transaction in which he has a pecuniary interest, supplies false information for the guidance of others in their business transactions, is subject to liability for pecuniary loss caused to them, by their justifiable reliance upon the information, if he fails to exercise reasonable care or competence in obtaining or communicating the information.[86]

The *Restatement* limits this liability to cases in which the loss is suffered by a person for whose benefit or guidance the information was given and involves a transaction (or one substantially similar) that the maker intends to influence or knows that the recipient of the information intends to influence.[87]

In a Wisconsin case[88] a trial court allowed a subcontractor to allege negligent misrepresentation when a lender informed the subcontractor that $46,000 was available for construction when in fact $20,000 of that amount had been withdrawn. The appellate court affirmed on another theory and did not address the negligent misrepresentation issue. Similarly, in *R.A. Peck, Inc. v. Liberty Federal Savings Bank,*[89] a New Mexico appellate court reinstated a contractor's negligent misrepresentation claim where, after instructing the contractor to submit bills directly to it for payment, the lender

---

Bristol County Nat'l Bank, 8 Mass. App. 356, 294 N.E.2d 972, 975–76 (1979), *aff'd,* 380 Mass. 829, 406 N.E.2d 672 (1980); Riley Bldg. Supplies, Inc. v. First Citizens Nat'l Bank, 510 So. 2d 506 (Miss. 1987); Daniels v. Big Horn Fed. Sav. & Loan Ass'n, 604 P.2d 1046, 1048–50 (Wyo. 1980).

[85] Commercial Standard Ins. Co. v. Bank of Am., 57 Cal. App. 3d 241, 129 Cal. Rptr. 91 (1976); First Nat'l State Bank v. Carlyle House, Inc., 102 N.J. Super. 300, 246 A.2d 22 (1968), *aff'd,* 107 N.J. Super. 389, 258 A.2d 545 (1969); Daniels v. Big Horn Fed. Sav. & Loan Ass'n, 604 P.2d 1046 (Wyo. 1980).

[86] Restatement (Second) of Torts § 552 (1977).

[87] *Id.* § 522(2).

[88] Klein-Dickert Oshkosh, Inc. v. Frontier Mortgage Corp., 93 Wis. 2d 660, 287 N.W.2d 742 (1980).

[89] 108 N.M. 84, 766 P.2d 928 (Ct. App. 1988).

allowed the contractor to continue working after the depletion of construction funds.

Other courts find, however, that a mistaken representation about the amount of undisbursed loan funds is not an "affirmative deception" similar to fraud and misrepresentation that would justify equitable relief.[90] Nevertheless, a negligent misrepresentation theory may be available in other factual situations. A lender's representation, for instance, that an adequate bond existed or that the owner had unencumbered title could be actionable in the right factual setting.

§ 9.23 Other Tort Theories

Only the facts and one's imagination limit the development of other tort theories. One possibility is *intentional interference with contract.*[91]

In *Lincor Contractors, Ltd. v. Hyskell*[92] a contractor successfully sued a lender on an intentional interference with contract theory. The lender insisted that the contractor be removed from a project and told the owner that no more loan proceeds would be made available until the owner removed the contractor. The Washington court found that the lender had no right equal or superior to the contractor's right to perform that justified this interference, and awarded the contractor its anticipated profit.

A similar claim may exist when a lender in bad faith diverts loan funds to the detriment of contractors and subcontractors. A principal issue in these intentional interference with contract cases is whether the lender's own interests justified its interference with the contractor.[93]

A contractor can meet more egregious lender behavior with causes of action sounding in fraud.[94] In certain situations punitive damages may be

---

[90] Indiana Mortgage & Realty Inv. v. Peacock Constr., 348 So. 2d 59, 61 (Fla. Dist. Ct. App.), *cert. denied,* 353 So. 2d 677 (Fla. Dist. Ct. App. 1977); J.G. Plumbing Serv., Inc. v. Coastal Mortgage Co., 329 So. 2d 393 (Fla. Dist. Ct. App.), *cert. denied,* 339 So. 2d 1169 (Fla. Dist. Ct. App. 1976).

In Nibbi Bros., Inc. v. Brannan St. Investors, 205 Cal. App. 3d 1415, 253 Cal. Rptr. 289, 295 (1988), the court denied a contractor's misrepresentation claim, but stated that the lender "skirted closely this area of liability" by representing that it had set aside funds sufficient to cover the cost of work and that the contractor would be paid.

[91] Koppers Co. v. Garling & Langlois, 594 F.2d 1094, 1100 (6th Cir. 1979); Pankow Constr. Co. v. Advance Mortgage Corp., 618 F.2d 611, 617 (9th Cir. 1980); Embree Constr. Group v. Rafcor, Inc., 97 N.C. App. 418, 388 S.E.2d 604, 607–08 (1990); R.P. Russo Contractors v. C.J. Pettinato Realty, 334 Pa. Super. 72, 482 A.2d 1086, 1091 (1984).

[92] 39 Wash. App. 317, 692 P.2d 903, 908 (1984), *review denied,* 103 Wash. 2d 1036 (1985).

[93] *Id.*

[94] Cal-West Nat'l Bank v. Superior Court, 185 Cal. App. 3d 96, 229 Cal. Rptr. 431 (1986). *See also* Nibbi Bros. v. Brannan St. Investors, 205 Cal. App. 3d 1415, 253 Cal. Rptr. 289

appropriate.[95] Another possible theory is *outrageous conduct.* The contours of this tort vary between jurisdictions, but its hallmark is that the conduct in question must be beyond the bounds tolerated by society.[96] When no other remedy seems available, outrageous conduct may be a possible approach. Although there do not appear to be any cases on point, a jury issue could exist if a lender used excessive or illegal means to protect its interests at the expense of contractors.

(1988); R.A. Peck, Inc. v. Liberty Fed. Sav. Bank, 108 N.M. 84, 766 P.2d 928 (Ct. App. 1988).

[95] *See, e.g.,* Great W. Sav. Bank v. George W. Easley Co., 778 P.2d 569, 580 (Alaska 1989).

[96] *See generally* Turman v. Central Billing Bureau, 279 Or. 443, 568 P.2d 1382 (1977); W. Prosser, Prosser on Torts 57–58 (4th ed. 1971).

CHAPTER 10

SUING THE SUBCONTRACTOR AND MATERIAL SUPPLIER

Robert J. Hoffman
David L. Simmons

Robert J. Hoffman is a partner in the Indianapolis, Indiana, law firm of Lowe Gray Steele & Hoffman, and concentrates his legal practice in the area of construction and public works law. He received his B.A. degree and J.D., summa cum laude, from Indiana University. Mr. Hoffman is a member of the Indianapolis, Indiana, and American Bar Associations, and serves on the Public Contracts Section and Forum Committee on the Construction Industry of the ABA. He serves as general counsel for the Associated General Contractors of Indiana, is a frequent lecturer, and is the author of numerous publications and articles on construction law.

David L. Simmons is a partner in the Indianapolis, Indiana, law firm of Lowe Gray Steele & Hoffman and concentrates his legal practice on construction law, public contract law, and commercial litigation. He received his B.A., M.B.A., and J.D. degrees from Indiana University. Mr. Simmons is a member of the Indianapolis, Indiana, and American Bar Associations, and is a member of the ABA's Public Contracts Section and Forum Committee on the Construction Industry. He is a frequent lecturer and author on construction law.

§ 10.1 Introduction

§ 10.2 Bidding and Contract Formation

§ 10.3 Bid Mistakes
§ 10.4 Flow-Down Clause
§ 10.5 Description of Work and Materials
§ 10.6 Coordinated and Timely Performance
§ 10.7 Remedies for Delayed Performance
§ 10.8 Warranties Relating to Defective Work and Materials
§ 10.9 Correcting Defective Work
§ 10.10 Indemnification
§ 10.11 Pass-Through Claims
§ 10.12 Default and Termination
§ 10.13 Documenting the Contractor's Claim

§ 10.1 Introduction

In earlier times, when construction became discernible as a semi-distinct trade or enterprise, all the talent, materials, and manpower involved in the building process were furnished and controlled by the master builder. The prospects of the master builder's economic success on a project (and in some cases the ability to keep his head) depended only on his ability to manage and control his own talent and resources, not upon the performance and quality of work furnished by people who were not ultimately subject to his control. The master builder proved to be the ancestor of the modern general contractor, one who contracts directly with an owner to perform all work and furnish all material and equipment necessary to transform a design into a finished product ready for use and occupancy.

The modern contractor's links to those remote origins have been all but severed. No longer does a contractor perform all the work with its own forces. Instead, he has become more of a broker or middleman. He contracts with an owner to construct a project; but to fulfill his commitments, he must retain and rely upon a host of *subcontractors* (those who are to perform some portion of work on the project) and *material suppliers* (those who are primarily expected to sell and furnish material and equipment to be used in construction). Thus, to a significant extent, the modern contractor's contractual reliance on lower tiers has replaced the master builder's physical or economic control over his own forces.

The contractor's ability to fulfill his promise to the owner is, from the bidding stage to project completion and subsequent warranty periods, subject to and governed by the qualitative and timely performance of lower-tier elements. Today's prime contractor is much like an orchestra conductor: the owner sitting in the audience, expects him to produce a coordinated, well-rehearsed presentation of the advertised masterpiece; to meet his obligation and give an acceptable performance, the conductor must rely on the ability of the musicians to play their instruments properly and in harmony with the others. When the contractor steps up on the podium, he is entering an uncertain and risk-filled environment.

It is not at all surprising that disputes involving subcontractors and material suppliers have become so prevalent. A contractor faces a continual risk of liability to an owner for the failure of his subcontractors and suppliers to perform as they must if he is to meet the demands placed on him by his contract with the owner. Disputes involving subcontractors and suppliers can arise during any phase of construction and, in some instances, long after the project is completed. Subcontractor-contractor controversies occur under the same circumstances that arise between the owner and contractor, and normally are governed by the same legal principles. Hence, a contractor who is the subject of a claim by the owner will likely pass the claim down to his subcontractor responsible for the work; this represents the contractor's attempt, as middleman, to pass on all of its first-tier liabilities to the ultimately responsible lower-tier party. A claim by the contractor against a subcontractor may also arise separately when the contractor incurs his own distinct damages as a result of the subcontractor's failure to perform. The outcome of the contractor's claim, whether independent of or corollary to the owner's claim, will frequently depend upon the contractor's ability to shift or allocate liabilities and duties to his subcontractors and suppliers, at least to the same extent that risks have been allocated to it by the terms of its prime contract with the owner.

This chapter describes general principles governing a contractor's relationship with its subcontractors and material suppliers and discusses the more prevalent remedies, theories of recovery, and (most importantly) protective subcontract terminology, which will all enhance the contractor's most fundamental objective: assuring that the risk of loss because of the conduct of a lower-tier party is ultimately borne by that party and not by the contractor who engaged him.

Contractor claims against subcontractors and material suppliers can develop from a wide variety of circumstances and may involve literally hundreds of different expressions found in the written subcontract, purchase order, or one or more of the contract documents that form the integrated contract between the contractor and owner and that may (and should) be incorporated into the subcontract by reference. It is impossible to discuss each factual or contractually derived dispute within the confines of one chapter. Instead, this chapter focuses on some of the more common dispute categories, together with general principles and contract language that enhance a contractor's chances of either winning disputes with subcontractors or avoiding them altogether.

For purposes of brevity, the term "subcontractor" is used throughout this chapter without necessarily being accompanied by the term "material supplier"; however, in most cases the discussion applies equally to both types of lower-tier participants on a project. Note, though, that a dispute involving a material supplier (as opposed to a subcontractor) may be subject to additional, and in some situations conflicting, rules and standards as provided by the Uniform Commercial Code, specifically Article 2 dealing with the sale of goods.

§ 10.2 Bidding and Contract Formation

The construction bidding process, viewed from the contractor's perspective, is one involving numerous parties; it is at this stage that the contractor must, in order to submit its own bid commitment to an owner, assemble, through a sub-bidding process, a subcontractor and material supplier team to perform the job in the event the prime bid is accepted by the owner.

Traditional concepts of contract law govern the bidding process as well as the subsequent stages of construction. A contract between two or more parties creates a legally enforceable relationship and defines the obligations and reciprocal rights of the contracting parties. In a traditional sense, contracts for construction are formed by the making of an offer (bid) by one party and the acceptance (award) of that offer by the other party, thereby resulting in a meeting of the minds, which serves as an enforceable system of reciprocal promises and commitments.

Before submitting a bid to the owner, the contractor must define to a high degree of certainty his costs of performance. To this end, the contractor solicits and receives bid proposals from subcontractors for certain assigned portions of the work (or certain items of material or equipment). The contractor should assure that a subcontractor's bid proposal is in fact a *definite offer to perform,* which will become an enforceable contract if the bid is accepted, as opposed to a naked price quotation, which courts have frequently viewed as mere preliminary negotiations.[1]

Without contrary language appearing in the bid or invitation to bid, or some enforceable type of reliance by the contractor upon the subcontractor's bid, the subcontractor may, under traditional contract formation rules, withdraw its bid at any time before communication of acceptance by the contractor. The amount of the subcontractor's proposal and the scope of work and other conditions to which the subcontractor commits are indispensable ingredients in the contractor's formulation of his bid and bid price to the owner. Consequently, a contractor who receives and acts upon subcontractor quotations and proposals is in a predicament: he has no need or desire to accept the proposal until he knows whether or not his prime bid has been accepted. The time lapse between submission and

[1] Mitchell v. Siqueiros, 99 Idaho 396, 582 P.2d 1074 (1978).

owner acceptance (or nonacceptance) creates the risk, under traditional contract law principles, that the subcontractor will withdraw his bid in the meantime. In an effort to deal with this risk and avoid disputes when a subcontractor withdraws a bid in such a manner, contractors frequently require subcontractor offers to be firm and nonrevocable for a definite period of time after submission. A firm offer may be stated so on the face of the bid or may be required by a formal solicitation for bids.

Contractors are usually required to make the same type of firm offer bids to owners; likewise, they should extract the same commitment from potential subcontractors and suppliers so that all subcontractors will be bound to hold their bids open for as long as the contractor is bound on his bid to the owner. A firm, nonrevocable offer is a contractual commitment and legally enforceable. A subcontractor who fails to honor such a bid may be liable to the contractor for the resulting damages.[2]

The Uniform Commercial Code (UCC) provides additional protection for the contractor who has received a bid regarding the purchase of materials. Under this statute, a written bid assuring its continued validity is not revocable during the time stated. If no specific period of time is stated, the bid cannot be withdrawn for a "reasonable period" of time, not to exceed three months.[3] What constitutes a reasonable period depends on the circumstances of each case.[4] It is important to note, however, that the UCC applies only to the sale of goods and movable equipment, and to contracts under which the sale of goods is the dominant transaction.[5] Application of UCC provisions pertaining to sale of goods is therefore useful in the material supplier context, but will rarely control in a dispute arising from a subcontract for installation, labor, or services.[6]

Although a bidding contractor will not always be able to extract formal irrevocable proposals from subcontractors, it must still rely upon subcontractor proposals in pricing his bid to the owner. Problems arise when a subcontractor withdraws his bid after it was relied upon by the contractor and the contractor receives the award from the owner.

Courts in many jurisdictions have, with near complete uniformity, recognized a contractor's peculiar vulnerability in this situation and have afforded contractors relief under the theory of *promissory estoppel.* This doctrine essentially permits a court to transform the subcontractor's bid

---

[2] Illinois Valley Asphalt, Inc. v. J.F. Edwards Constr. Co., 90 Ill. App. 3d 768, 413 N.E.2d 209 (1980).

[3] U.C.C. § 2-205.

[4] Scarano v. Board of Regents of Univ., 57 A.D.2d 991, 394 N.Y.S.2d 322 (1977).

[5] U.C.C. Art. 2.

[6] Gateway Co. v. Charlotte Theatres, Inc., 297 F.2d 483 (1st Cir. 1961); J&R Elec. Div. of J.O. Mory Stores, Inc. v. Skoog Constr. Co., 38 Ill. App. 3d 747, 348 N.E.2d 474 (1976). *But see* Mingledorff's, Inc. v. Hicks, 13 Ga. App. 27, 209 S.E.2d 661 (1974).

into a firm, irrevocable offer even though the bid itself does not express such irrevocability, based upon the contractor's justifiable reliance. To avoid the inequities that would otherwise result in such a situation, the courts have held that a subcontractor's bid cannot be withdrawn if the subcontractor knew, or had reason to know, that the contractor would rely on the bid in preparing and submitting his bid to the owner, and if the contractor would be damaged if the bid was withdrawn before acceptance.[7] Some courts have applied the theory of promissory estoppel to enforce a prospective subcontractor's bid even though it was oral.[8] The mere use, however, of a subcontractor's bid by a prime in submitting a bid to the owner does not, without more, constitute an acceptance of the subcontractor's offer by the prime, resulting in a contract upon award of the prime contract.[9]

The UCC contains a potential trap for a contractor who receives an oral proposal from a supplier involving the sale of goods or equipment. The UCC statute of frauds provides that, subject to defined exceptions, a party cannot enforce a contract for the sale of goods of $500 or more unless the contract is in writing and signed by the party against whom enforcement is sought.[10] The question then arises as to whether a transaction is removed from the statute of frauds based on a theory of promissory estoppel, thus enabling the contractor-buyer to enforce an oral agreement based on its detrimental reliance.

The courts have split on this issue. Some courts have held that the statute of frauds must be enforced despite the existence of justifiable reliance, which in other cases could bring the promissory estoppel doctrine into play.[11] Other courts recognize promissory estoppel as a device to avoid the UCC statute of frauds provisions and have held that oral bids for the sale of goods will be enforceable when there was justifiable reliance.[12]

§ 10.3 Bid Mistakes

Bidding mistakes are another source of subcontract disputes. Subcontractors, like the contractors who engage them, can make mistakes in preparing

---

[7] Montgomery Indus. Int'l, Inc. v. Thomas Constr. Co., 620 F.2d 91 (5th Cir. 1980); C&K Eng'g Contractors v. Amber Steel Co., 23 Cal. 3d 1, 587 P.2d 1136, 151 Cal. Rptr. 323 (1978); Harry Harris, Inc. v. Quality Constr. Co., 593 S.W.2d 872 (Ky. Ct. App. 1979); C.E. Frazier Constr. Co. v. Campbell Roofing & Metal Works, Inc., 373 So. 2d 1036 (Miss. 1979); James King & Son, Inc. v. DeSantis Constr. No. 2 Corp., 97 Misc. 2d 1063, 413 N.Y.S.2d 78 (1977).

[8] Montgomery Indus. Int'l, Inc. v. Thomas Constr. Co., 620 F.2d 91 (5th Cir. 1980); Hooks v. Southeast Constr. Corp., 538 F.2d 431 (D.C. Cir. 1976).

[9] Mitchell v. Siqueiros, 99 Idaho 396, 582 P.2d 1074 (1978).

[10] U.C.C. § 2-201.

[11] Anderson Constr. Co. v. Lyon Metal Prods., Inc., 370 So. 2d 935 (Miss. 1979).

[12] Edward Joy Co. v. Noise Control Prods., Inc., 111 Misc. 2d 64, 443 N.Y.S.2d 361 (1981).

bids, often because of the hurried conditions under which they must submit their bids. If the mistake is significant, the bidder may attempt to withdraw his proposal or refuse to go forward with performance, thereby incurring the risk of liability. Courts have fashioned various theories for resolving bid mistakes, depending on the size of the mistake and the reasonableness of the contractor's reliance.

As a general principle, a bid mistake will relieve the bidder of his obligation to perform if his bid is at such a variance from other bids that the contractor should reasonably have concluded or suspected that a mistake had been made.[13] In such a situation, given the obviousness of the error, there has not been the meeting of the minds necessary for the formation of a contract. Contractors therefore should review subcontractor bids to ascertain their reasonableness before assuming that the subcontractor will be bound. A contractor should verify any questions about the amount of a subcontractor's bid before submitting his own bid.

Subcontractors have been allowed to withdraw their bids and escape performance obligation when the contractor purported to accept the bid but added terms that were not made known to the subcontractor prior to submission of the bid.[14] This commonly occurs when a contractor submits to the subcontractor an agreement containing terms that were never part of the proposal. To avoid this problem, the contractor's invitation to bid should expressly state that "the subcontractor shall perform its work according to the terms and provisions of all relevant contract documents, including plans and specifications, which are available for inspection at [the contractor's office]."

§ 10.4 Flow-Down Clause

A prime contractor who obtains a contract award from the bidding process rather than negotiation normally has little bargaining leverage with the owner. He usually takes the contract as he finds it. The owner will draft the contract documents to shift a wide range of risks and obligations to the prime contractor and away from himself. It is therefore imperative that no gaps exist between the obligations expressed in the subcontract and those in the primary contract with the owner. A well-drafted subcontract should consequently contain a clause placing the contractor on exactly the same footing with his subcontractor as the owner occupies against the contractor.

The protective language in the subcontract's *flow-down* or *conduit* clause is an express statement that the subcontractor is obligated to the contractor to the same extent as the contractor, under the provisions of the contract

---

[13] Robert Gordon, Inc. v. Ingersoll-Rand Co., 117 F.2d 654 (7th Cir. 1941); Southeastern Sales & Serv. Co. v. T.T. Watson, Inc., 172 So. 2d 239 (Fla. Dist. Ct. App. 1965).

[14] C.H. Leavell & Co. v. Grafe & Assocs., Inc., 90 Idaho 502, 414 P.2d 873 (1966).

documents, is obligated to the owner. Such a clause should contain a proviso permitting conflicting provisions within the subcontract instrument itself to take precedence over other contract obligations that are incorporated by reference. Some courts have held that a subcontract requiring the subcontractor to perform pursuant to the prime's plans and specifications was sufficient to incorporate by reference the prime's contract for all purposes.[15]

Ultimately, an effectively drafted flow-down clause assures the contractor that he may step into the shoes of the owner and thereby employ all the risk-shifting terminology in the prime contract against a nonperforming subcontractor or material supplier.

§ 10.5 Description of Work and Materials

A flow-down clause is not helpful in describing the scope of a subcontractor's work or materials because the prime contract includes all work, whereas the subcontract or material supply purchase order is intended to cover only a portion of the whole. A great number of disputes between contractors and their subcontractors arise when a subcontractor refuses to perform some item of work because "it wasn't in my price," thereby forcing the contractor to have the work performed with his own crew, or through others, with the resulting additional expense charged back against the subcontractor. The contractor's recovery of these additional expenses, usually as damages arising from the subcontractor's breach of contract, rests upon the contractor's ability to point to a specific description of the scope of the subcontractor's work contained in the subcontract agreement. Remember, it is the description of work in the final agreement, not the subcontractor's bid, that governs.

The subcontract should at a minimum refer to the section of the prime contract specifications that is to be performed by the subcontractor, so that the description of the quality and quantity of work is exactly the same as that defining the contractor's obligation to the owner. However, this may not always be enough. Frequently, supplementary terminology is needed to broaden the subcontractor's obligations beyond those set forth in the specifications, to encompass additional work (found in other sections or contract documents) normally performed by the trade to which the subcontractor belongs.

Good draftsmanship alone will not solve all disputes between contractors and subcontractors concerning scope of work. When such disputes develop, the contractor must have the means to assure that the disputed work

---

[15] Lincoln Welding Works, Inc. v. Ramirez, 98 Nev. 342, 647 P.2d 381 (1982).

will be performed without undue disruption of the project schedule. Therefore, a subcontractor should be obligated to perform the disputed work upon the unilateral directive of the contractor or face termination of the subcontract. Such a clause should be coupled with language imposing time limits within which the subcontractor must make or reserve a claim for additional compensation, in the event that the subcontractor prevails and the disputed work was not included in the original scope. The contractor thus receives a measure of assurance that work will continue at an uninterrupted pace without having to hire a replacement subcontractor or incur expense to perform the work with his own resources.

Virtually every prime contract contains a provision whereby the owner may unilaterally make changes, additions, deletions, or other modifications in the scope of work by written change order. The contractor must use appropriate language to reserve the same right to make unilateral changes in the subcontract work, thus obligating the subcontractor to perform the changed work. Typically, a subcontract deals with the subject of changed and extra work by providing that the subcontractor shall have no right to claim or receive extra compensation for such work unless it is authorized and directed in writing by the contractor. Some subcontracts add terminology limiting the subcontractor's recovery to the amount collected by the contractor from the owner for that work.

§ 10.6 Coordinated and Timely Performance

Project delay and disruption caused by a subcontractor can have devastating results to a prime contractor on at least three fronts. First, disruptions and delays significantly expose the contractor to liability for economic damages suffered by the owner. The prime contract frequently contains a liquidated damage provision imposing hundreds or even thousands of dollars in damages against the contractor for each day that project completion is delayed. Second, the contractor may be subject to delay damage claims asserted by other subcontractors or material suppliers. Third, the contractor can expect to incur losses and expenses within its own organization because of the delay.

The subcontract should expressly confirm the subcontractor's liability for all such loss and damages incurred by the contractor. A subcontract agreement merely requiring a subcontractor to complete his work by a certain date is not sufficient for this purpose. Additional contract language should be included that obligates the subcontractor to coordinate and schedule its work in cooperation with the contractor and with other subcontractors. In the drafting and administration of the subcontract, the contractor should explicitly tie the subcontractor to the construction schedule governing the interrelated performance of work by all trades.

If a dispute or lawsuit develops concerning a significant delay, the contractor and his attorney can expect that everyone affected by the delay, including subcontractors, the contractor, and the owner, will blame the other parties involved. In litigation that focuses upon project delays, a contractor will be forced to assume a defensive posture as much as an offensive one. It has become common for contractors to attempt to insulate themselves from delay damage claims asserted by subcontractors by employing *no damage for delay* clauses in their subcontract forms. Such clauses limit a subcontractor's remedy for delay to an extension of time and prohibit the recovery of delay damages against the contractor. Some contractors adopt a milder version permitting a subcontractor to recover delay-related damages, but only to the extent that the contractor recovers and collects damages from the owner or some other party. Some jurisdictions construe no damage for delay clauses strictly against the contractor, and do not apply them when the contractor has caused the delay by actively interfering with the subcontractor's work[16] or when the delay was brought about by circumstances totally beyond the contemplation of the parties.[17]

§ 10.7 Remedies for Delayed Performance

A subcontractor who fails to complete his work within the specified time or according to the project schedule without excuse or justification may be liable to the contractor for the resulting damages.[18] A subcontractor's failure to understand the contractor's construction schedule will not excuse its failure to perform timely in accordance with the schedule.[19] A contractor's damages resulting from the subcontractor's delay may include liquidated damages assessed by the owner or other delay damages resulting from the subcontractor's performance.[20] However, if the subcontractor can show that the delay was caused by events outside his control, the delay is excusable, and the subcontractor may not be liable to the contractor for damages.[21] The contractor should be aware, however, of the risk of inconsistent

[16] Blake Constr. Co. v. C.J. Coakley Co., 431 A.2d 569 (D.C. 1981). See also **Chs. 5, 7.**

[17] Phoenix Contractors, Inc. v. General Motors Corp., 135 Mich. App. 787, 355 N.W.2d 673 (1984). See also **Ch. 7.**

[18] Robberson Steel, Inc. v. J.D. Abrams, Inc., 582 S.W.2d 558 (Tex. Civ. App. 1979).

[19] Carrington v. W.A. Soefker & Sons, Inc., 624 S.W.2d 894 (Tenn. Ct. App. 1981).

[20] Concrete Sys., Inc. v. Florida Elec. Co., 425 So. 2d 632 (Fla. Dist. Ct. App. 1983); Usemco, Inc. v. Marbro Co., 60 Md. App. 351, 483 A.2d 88 (1984).

[21] United States v. John Kerns Constr. Co., 140 F.2d 792 (8th Cir. 1944); Structural Sales, Inc. v. Vavrus, 132 Ill. App. 3d 718, 477 N.E.2d 745 (1985).

results relating to the assessment of delay damages by the owner for untimely performance of the subcontractor's work.[22]

Delay may not be the sole responsibility of the subcontractor, however. Rather, both the contractor and subcontractor may have contributed to the delayed performance. When a contractor has attempted to impose liquidated damages under a situation of mutual delay, the courts will generally not attempt to apportion the damages, but will simply hold that the provisions of the contract with reference to liquidated damages will be annulled.[23] The courts have adopted such a rule to avoid speculation regarding the relative delay caused by the parties.[24]

However, the courts have not been reluctant to allocate responsibility for actual damages resulting from mutual delay among the parties if supported by sufficient evidence.[25] The apportionment of damages in a case of mutual delay is a question of fact and the burden of proof is on the party claiming such damages to prove the damages were caused by default of the party to be charged, separate from any damages that may have resulted from the acts of the claimant.[26] When there is sufficient evidence to allow the court to make a reasonably certain division of responsibility for delay, the assessment of damages may be allocated among several parties, even though the performance of work is sequential and the delay is the result of multiple causes.[27] However, the courts have generally refused to apply principles of comparative negligence to allocate responsibility in construction disputes involving damages for pure economic loss.[28]

§ 10.8 Warranties Relating to Defective Work and Materials

A subcontractor will usually be subject to both express and implied warranties in performing its work for the contractor, just as the contractor is governed by similar warranties in its contract with the owner. A subcontract should, therefore, require that the subcontractor assume all warranty obligations of the general contract relating to the subcontractor's work.[29]

---

[22] See § **10.11**.

[23] Acme Process Equip. Co. v. United States, 347 F.2d 509, 171 Ct. Cl. 324 (1965).

[24] Pathman Constr. Co. v. Hi-Way Elec. Co., 65 Ill. App. 2d 480, 382 N.E.2d 453 (1978).

[25] *Id.*

[26] *Id.*

[27] *Id.*

[28] Broce-O'Dell Concrete Prods., Inc. v. Mel Jarvis Constr. Co., 6 Kan. App. 2d 757, 634 P.2d 1142 (1981).

[29] AIA Doc. A401, Contractor-Subcontractor Agreement Form ¶ 4.5.1 (1987).

For example, a subcontract agreement normally requires the subcontractor to warrant that he has used new materials and equipment, that his work complies with the plans and specifications for the project, and that the work is free of any defect because of faulty materials or workmanship. In addition, the subcontractor normally warrants that his work and materials are of good quality. In the event the general contract requires the contractor to provide work and materials of the "best" quality or some higher standard, all such warranty obligations should be assumed by the subcontractor as well.

A subcontract often requires a subcontractor to warrant his work or materials for one year from the date of either substantial completion or final acceptance of the project. Such a provision may require a subcontractor to warrant his work for a substantially longer period than one year because final acceptance of the project may be subject to substantial delays. Consistent with other responsibilities of the contractor, the subcontract agreement shall incorporate the warranty obligation of the general contract, including relevant time limitations.

A material supplier will also be subject to implied warranties imposed by the Uniform Commercial Code (UCC). The "implied warranty of merchantability" described in U.C.C. § 2-314 requires that the materials or equipment supplied by merchantable, of at least average or medium quality. The "implied warranty of fitness" described in § 2-315 requires that the equipment or materials supplied be fit for the particular use for which they are required, providing the customer relied on the vendor's skill or judgment in selecting or furnishing the specific equipment or materials supplied. These warranties can be modified or excluded altogether pursuant to U.C.C. § 2-316. Provisions may create several express warranties in favor of the owner, architect, and contractor that will be subject to the appropriate statutes of limitation for contract breach. Such warranties generally are not waived by final payment.[30]

A subcontractor, like a contractor, may be subject to the implied warranty of workmanship, which requires that work be performed in a good and workmanlike manner and free from defects.[31] Likewise, a manufacturer

[30] *See, e.g.,* AIA Doc. A201, General Conditions of the Contract for Construction ¶ 4.3.5 (1987). *See* AIA Doc. A201 ¶ 12.2.2, imposing obligations on the subcontractor to correct work based on incorporation into AIA Doc. A401. This warranty of correction is separate and distinct from the express warranties contained in A401 ¶ 4.5.1 and does not limit the express warranties of the subcontractor or the implied warranty of good workmanship. Burton-Dixie Corp. v. Timothy McCarthy Constr. Co., 436 F.2d 405 (5th Cir. 1971); Houston Fire & Casualty Ins. Co. v. Riesel Indep. Sch. Dist., 375 S.W.2d 323 (Tex. Civ. App. 1964).

[31] Insurance Co. of N. Am. v. Radiant Elec. Co., 55 Mich. App. 410, 222 N.W.2d 323 (1974).

providing both products and installation impliedly warrants to its customer that the product and installation will be workmanlike and free of defects.[32] Some jurisdictions, however, do not recognize the implied warranty of workmanship.[33]

§ 10.9 Correcting Defective Work

The contract documents typically require the contractor to correct or replace any work that is rejected or found by the owner's architect or engineer to be defective or otherwise not in accordance with the specifications. Arguably, a well-drafted flow-down clause[34] will impose a similar obligation upon a subcontractor who performed the rejected work. Nevertheless, a contractor should include a clause within the subcontract agreement specifically requiring the subcontractor to replace or correct any work which, in the opinion of the architect or contractor, is deficient or not in accordance with the applicable contract documents. Such provisions are enforceable and the contractor's judgment in making such an evaluation will be upheld if made in good faith.[35] The subcontract should include a procedure for notification regarding such deficiencies and impose deadlines for the subcontractor to take appropriate corrective action.

When work is rejected by the owner's architect, the contractor should immediately notify the subcontractor of the rejection according to the procedure outlined in the subcontract agreement. If the subcontractor fails to cure the deficient work as requested, the contractor cannot afford to disrupt his construction schedule while the dispute is resolved. The subcontract should therefore enable the contractor to declare the subcontractor in default and terminate the subcontract accordingly.[36] Whether or not the subcontract is terminated, the subcontract should authorize the contractor to hire others to perform corrective work and charge the expense against the subcontractor.

Apart from such contractual language, a contractor's case against a material supplier may be enhanced by important implied warranties. The Uniform Commercial Code establishes an implied warranty that the materials and equipment furnished will be "merchantable," meaning that they will "pass without objection in the trade under the contract description" and

---

[32] Paint Prods. Co. v. AA-1 Stell Equip. Co., 35 Conn. Supp. 52, 393 A.2d 1317 (1977).

[33] National Hills Shopping Ctr., Inc. v. Insurance Co. of N. Am., 320 F. Supp. 1146 (S.D. Ga. 1970).

[34] See § **10.4**.

[35] Anahuac, Inc. v. Wilkes, 622 S.W.2d 634 (Tex. Ct. App. 1981).

[36] See § **10.9**.

will be "of fair average quality as required by the contract."[37] Under the UCC, a material supplier impliedly warrants that the goods will be fit for the purchaser's (contractor's) particular purpose, if the supplier has reason to know the purpose to which the goods will be used at the time they are sold and that the purchaser is relying upon the supplier's superior skill and judgment.[38] These implied warranties can provide an important foundation for recovery of damages by a contractor against a defaulting supplier, but, in appropriate circumstances, they may be contractually disclaimed. The contractor will no doubt avoid such disclaimer language in its own subcontract or purchase order forms; however, other documents included in the contract with the subcontractor or supplier should be scrutinized carefully to uncover disclaimer language that could eliminate the contractor's implied warranty remedies.

§ 10.10 Indemnification

Occasionally, a contractor will find itself subjected to claims for bodily injury, death, or loss or damage to property arising out of a subcontractor's performance of work on a project. A contractor needs to transfer the risk of liability for such claims to his subcontractor by express contractual language. To this end, contractors regularly employ an indemnification clause in their subcontract forms, under which the subcontractor agrees to indemnify the contractor and hold him harmless from claims, demands, liabilities, and losses, including attorneys' fees, that may be incurred by the contractor in defending the claim. Such clauses fall within three general categories, according to the scope of protection offered:

1. Narrow coverage, subjecting the subcontractor to liability only for claims resulting from its own acts or omissions, and not the negligence of others
2. Intermediate coverage, subjecting the subcontractor to liability for claims caused in whole or in part by any negligent act of the subcontractor
3. Broad indemnity, subjecting the subcontractor to liability for claims caused by the contractor's own negligence, without negligence on the part of the subcontractor.

Regardless of the scope of protection afforded by an indemnification clause, a subcontractor is liable to the contractor only after he has sustained

---

[37] U.C.C. § 2-314.

[38] *Id.* § 2-315.

the loss.[39] A subcontractor may also be required to indemnify the contractor for liability he incurs under his indemnity clause with the owner.[40]

A subcontractor will likely be held within the grip of the first two categories of indemnification clauses. The enforceability of the third type, the broad-form clause, however, is far more questionable. Several states have enacted so-called anti-indemnity statutes that severely limit or prohibit the enforcement of a contractual clause indemnifying one against one's own negligence.[41] In other states, nonenforceability has become the rule by judicial decree. Those jurisdictions upholding the validity of such clauses require that the contract language be clear and explicit, or that such an intention be clearly expressed in unequivocal terms.[42] Even if the subcontractor is not liable to the contractor under the indemnification clause, he may still be obligated to provide liability insurance that would protect the prime against his own negligence.[43] Therefore, in drafting a subcontract indemnity clause, a contractor would be well advised to consult the law of the jurisdiction where the work will be performed in order to determine whether the proposed indemnity will be enforceable. Contractors who regularly engage in work in numerous states would be well advised to employ the intermediate form of indemnity clause.

In some instances, a subcontractor may be liable to a contractor under a theory of implied indemnification, even in the absence of express indemnification language in the subcontract instrument. *Implied indemnification* arises when a contractor is exposed to liability because of the subcontractor's negligence or breach of contract. The contractor who is held liable and incurs damages as a result of such negligence or breach may seek indemnification against the subcontractor for its losses.[44]

§ 10.11 Pass-Through Claims

Disputes inevitably arise on today's complex construction projects because of the vast number of parties involved and a variety of competing interests and liabilities. It is not uncommon for a project to involve an owner, one or

---

[39] Hooks v. Southeast Constr. Corp., 538 F.2d 431 (D.C. Cir. 1976); Montgomery Indus. Int'l, Inc. v. Thomas Constr. Co., 620 F.2d 91 (5th Cir. 1980).

[40] Vey v. Port Auth., 54 N.Y.2d 221, 429 N.E.2d 762, 445 N.Y.S.2d 84 (1981).

[41] Cal. Civ. Code § 2782, 2782.5 (West); Ga. Code Ann. § 13-8-2(b); Idaho Code § 29-114 (Michie); Ind. Code Ann. § 26-2-5-1 (West); Tenn. Code Ann. § 62-6-123 (Michie).

[42] Johnson v. McGough Constr. Co., 294 N.W.2d 286 (Minn. 1980); Howard S. Wright Constr. Co. v. F.E. DeBeer Mechanical Constr. Co., 185 Mont. 47, 604 P.2d 323 (1979).

[43] Hooks v. Southeast Constr. Corp., 538 F.2d 431 (D.C. Cir. 1976).

[44] Leaseway Warehouses, Inc. v. Carlton, 568 F. Supp. 1041 (N.D. Ill. 1983); Maxfield v. Simmons, 96 Ill. 2d 81, 449 N.E.2d 110 (1983).

more prime contractors, subcontractors, suppliers, insurance carriers and sureties, a construction lender, and a construction manager. Owner claims resulting from the defective performance or other failures of a subcontractor pose special problems for the contractor, who may find himself caught in the middle of the battle. The courts generally require a party to be in privity with another in order to recover economic damages. Due to these restrictions of privity, a construction owner that has been damaged by the acts or omissions of a subcontractor may be required to pursue its action against the contractor. A contractor must then decide whether to litigate or arbitrate the dispute against the owner on behalf of the subcontractor, or whether to function as a conduit by passing through to the subcontractor the owner's claim and bring the subcontractor into the proceedings in a consolidated multi-party case.

The joinder of arbitration proceedings in the construction industry may be facilitated by contractual language permitting multi-party arbitration.[45] For example, a clause which permits the consolidation of arbitration proceedings between persons involved in a common question of fact or law could be included in the contract documents and incorporated by reference into the subcontract agreement. To avoid unnecessarily complicated proceedings, consolidation of arbitration proceedings should be limited to those parties having a substantial involvement in the transaction.

Although a provision may permit the contractor to join his subcontractor in consolidated arbitration proceedings, it does not allow the joinder of arbitration proceedings against the architect except by written consent. Without such clauses, consolidation of arbitration becomes difficult because the courts generally lack authority to order the consolidation of separate arbitration proceedings, even though they concern common issues of fact and contract interpretation, and even though separate arbitrations could lead to inconsistent results.[46] Some courts have recently held, however, that consolidated arbitration could be judicially ordered if there was a threat of inconsistent results.[47]

Consolidation of common issues of law and fact may be accomplished in litigation by virtue of *third-party practice.*[48] Under this procedure, a contractor who has been sued by an owner as a result of a subcontractor's breach may name its subcontractor as a third-party defendant, asserting that the subcontractor may be liable to him for all or part of the owner's claim. Likewise, a subcontractor can name as a third-party defendant other

---

[45] AIA Doc. A201 ¶ 4.5.5 (1987).

[46] Stop & Shop Cos. v. Gilbane Bldg. Co., 364 Mass. 325, 304 N.E.2d 429 (1973).

[47] Episcopal Hous. Corp. v. Federal Ins. Co., 273 S.C. 181, 255 S.E.2d 451 (1979); Chariot Textiles Corp. v. Wannalancit Textile Co., 18 N.Y.2d 793, 221 N.E.2d 913, 275 N.Y.S.2d 382 (1966).

[48] Fed. R. Civ. P. 14.

contracting parties liable to him for all or part of the claim asserted. Federal and state rules of procedure also provide for consolidation of cases or trials involving common questions of law or fact.[49]

Consolidation of arbitration or litigation avoids the risk of inconsistent results and the unnecessary expense of duplicate proceedings. Consider, for example, the claim of an owner against a contractor for damages caused by the defective work of a subcontractor. If the contractor is found liable to the owner for the breach, the contractor may pursue the subcontractor for the damages imposed in the earlier proceeding. There is no guarantee that a different arbitration panel or trial court would reach the same result, thereby leaving the contractor faced with the risk of inconsistent results. To avoid such an unjust result, several federal courts have construed the AIA standard form arbitration clause and subcontract flow-down clause to compel multi-party arbitration, even if the subcontract clause contains an arbitration clause materially different from the contractor's arbitration clause.[50]

The consolidation of arbitration proceedings and third-party practice in litigation may reduce the risk of inconsistent results, but will likely result in a less expeditious and more expensive dispute resolution. Consequently, a contractor may consider the use of a liquidation agreement, whereby it agrees to prosecute the claim of an owner against the subcontractor, or the claim of a subcontractor against an owner, in exchange for a stipulation of contingent liability. Such a stipulation might, for example, limit the contractor's liability to the owner to the extent that an award is made in arbitration or litigation, and allocate the costs associated with the dispute as well as any award of damages.

A contractor involved in a construction dispute normally aligns itself with his subcontractors, and the owner aligns with its architect or engineer. However, these parties may reach a different alignment depending on the culpability of the parties involved in a default and the terms and provisions of the contract documents. The Third Circuit Court of Appeals recently reviewed the alignment of a contractor and owner against a mechanical subcontractor that abandoned its performance.[51] The owner and contractor reached a settlement after litigation was commenced. The owner decided to pursue the mechanical subcontractor for damages relating to defective work, completion, and delays. The settlement provided that the owner and contractor would share any damages recovered by the owner, who asserted claims against the subcontractor based on third-party beneficiary, negligence, and indemnification grounds.

---

[49] *Id.* 42; T.R. 42 of Ind. P.R.

[50] Gavlik Constr. Co. v. H.F. Campbell Co., 526 F.2d 777 (3d Cir. 1975).

[51] Pierce Ass'n, Inc. v. Nemours Found., 865 F.2d 530 (3d Cir. 1989).

The court concluded that the subcontractor was not liable to the owner on a theory of third-party beneficiary because the contract documents clearly stated that the subcontractor would be liable only to the prime contractor, not to the owner. Nor was the subcontractor liable to the owner under a theory of negligence because the owner's damages were purely economic and its claims against the contractor were released pursuant to the settlement agreement. The court also rejected the owner's claim for indemnification against the subcontractor for damages incurred as a result of its delay. The court found that there was no express provision imposing liability on the owner for the subcontractor's delay and therefore there was no right of indemnification.

This case is instructive to contractors considering liquidation agreements in multi-party litigation or arbitration. Such agreements should avoid a final release of claims against the party sponsoring the claim. Instead, the sponsoring party should remain conditionally liable for the claim. A contractor must also be aware of the rules of privity that may effectively preclude actions between noncontracting parties for economic damages relating to negligence, third-party beneficiary, and contract breach. Such an agreement should detail the responsibilities for prosecuting the claim and the allocation of costs associated with the proceedings. If the parties decide to share in a recovery, a precise formula for distribution of an award should be included. The agreement should specify which party has control over the terms of any settlement reached, particularly the amount of any settlement. The issue of control should ultimately be decided in accordance with the claim at stake. For example, if the contractor merely passes through the owner's claim for damages against the subcontractor, it may be appropriate for the owner to maintain primary control over decisions regarding settlement of the claim. Conversely, if the claim contains elements of damages incurred by both the contractor and owner, control of the settlement should be allocated accordingly.

§ 10.12 Default and Termination

Occasionally, a subcontractor's presence and involvement (or perhaps lack thereof) on a job generates such discord that the contractor may be required to hire a replacement subcontractor to complete the work. Consider a subcontractor who, because of some dispute involving the work or because of sheer lack of economic resources to complete, walks off the job and abandons the project. Subcontractors frequently see the threat of "closing down the job" as giving them a substantial amount of leverage during a dispute. A subcontractor who contemplates such action often feels that it is a superior form of leverage for extracting concessions from the contractor, but fails to realize that abandoning the project will almost assuredly result in a court decision that renders him liable for all expenses incurred by the contractor to retain a replacement and complete the work.

If the subcontractor's abandonment is necessitated by its economic inability to perform, then the contractor unhappily has a hollow remedy against the subcontractor for damages that will no doubt be uncollectible. A contractor may consider providing financial support to the subcontractor as a less expensive and more pragmatic alternative to termination. In these uncertain economic times, the prospect of default has led many contractors to require major subcontractors to furnish labor and material payment bonds permitting the contractor, in the event of default, to recover damages against the contract surety.

A more complex scenario exists when the subcontractor remains on the job and professes his willingness and ability to complete the agreement, but the contractor considers the subcontractor to be in default under the contract. A contractor normally desires to terminate the subcontractor and procure a replacement to finish the work under such circumstances.

Many contractors, faced with severe subcontractor-caused problems on a project, go through the process of terminating the defaulting the subcontractor without fully appreciating the legal consequences that could flow from the termination. A defaulting subcontractor whose breach goes to the heart of his ability to contractually perform may be terminated, in which case the contractor may implement the default and termination clauses of the subcontract agreement and recover all excess costs and related damages incurred in retaining a new subcontractor to finish the work. Occasionally, the courts have even allowed the recovery of attorneys' fees as part of contract damages, when a wrongful act necessitates the incurrence of legal fees and such fees are the legal consequences of the original wrongful act.[52]

However, significant factual and legal issues may exist regarding whether the subcontractor's default constituted a material breach of the subcontract, as opposed to a lesser form of breach entitling the contractor to recover damages, but not terminate. In short, if the contractor is unable to establish that the subcontract permits the action that was taken, he may not recover his excess costs to complete through a replacement subcontractor. In addition, he may be liable to the defaulting subcontractor for the profits he would have earned had he been permitted to complete. A contractor who makes the wrong decision, or who has a subcontract agreement that inadequately treats the subject of termination, will be unable to pass these combined losses on to the owner.

In cases of subcontractor default, it is essential for the contractor to (1) maximize his chances of recovering completion-related damages, and (2) avoid potential liability to the subcontractor because of wrongful termination. This can be accomplished by employing a default and termination

---

[52] Murray First Thrift & Loan Co. v. N-C Paving, 576 P.2d 455 (Wyo. 1978).

clause in the subcontract that endorses the contractor's right to terminate the subcontractor. The default clause in the subcontract should explicitly define the types of occurrences constituting an event of default warranting termination, such as:

1. Failure on the part of the subcontractor to pay his sub-subcontractors and suppliers
2. Failure to prosecute the work diligently as directed by the contractor or as required by the agreed project schedule
3. Failure to perform any term or condition set forth in the subcontract agreement or other contract document incorporated by reference
4. Refusal to perform corrective work as directed
5. Violation of applicable laws and regulations
6. Bankruptcy.

A well-drafted default and termination provision in a subcontract should also establish a defined procedure for termination. Such a provision should require that a notice be sent to the subcontractor describing the default and establishing a period of time during which the subcontractor must cure the event of default and thereby retain its entitlement to continue on the job. The default clause should require that a second, follow-up notice be sent to the subcontractor after the expiration of the initial grace period. This second notice should describe the subcontractor's failure to cure the deficiencies as requested and explain the contractor's intention to terminate.

The default clause should also describe the remedies available to the contractor upon termination. Frequently, termination clauses provide that the contractor may take possession of the subcontractor's materials, tools, and equipment and finish the subcontractor's work by whatever means the contractor may determine to be appropriate. The contractor should be entitled to recover all monies expended and all other damages and extra expense (including overhead and attorneys' fees) that result from the subcontractor's default, termination, and completion of work. The subcontractor should not be entitled to any additional payment under the contract until the contractor's damages are ascertained, that is, after the subcontractor's work is completed by the replacement or by the contractor's own forces.

A contractor should consider using a separate, additional clause permitting termination of the subcontract "for convenience." Federal government contracts and many state and local public works contracts employ such clauses in the prime contract, allowing the owner to terminate the contract even in the absence of breach. Upon such termination, the contractor's recovery is limited to the work completed, without additional profit on uncompleted work. Such a clause, if employed by the contractor in its subcontract agreements, gives it similar protection. The contractor may also limit its exposure to a defaulting subcontractor by providing that a termination for default, if determined to be incorrect, will constitute a termination for convenience, thereby limiting the subcontractor's recovery and preventing the subcontractor from recovering lost profits on unperformed work.

§ 10.13 Documenting the Contractor's Claim

As already suggested, a variety of legal rules and theories exist which, when combined with a comprehensive, well-drafted subcontract agreement, provide a sound and formidable foundation to support a contractor's suit against a subcontractor. However, it is only a foundation; the contractor must still prove its case against the subcontractor. To accomplish this ultimate objective, it is imperative that the contractor's claim be supported by sufficient documentary and other evidence to establish his right to relief.

It is indeed paradoxical that many contractors go to great lengths to use subcontract forms giving them every possible legal and economic leverage and then, when it comes time to implement the boilerplate and prove their case against a subcontractor, utterly fail to furnish the factual documentation necessary to persuade a court or jury that the facts entitle them to the remedy being sought. A contractor who has been damaged by a subcontractor's actions must ultimately convince the trier of fact of the relationship of the parties, the conduct relating to the dispute, and the monetary damages resulting from the subcontractor's breach of his obligations. It is therefore critical for the contractor to document and maintain sufficient proof to substantiate its position.

A more detailed discussion of the types and items of documentation a contractor should maintain as a matter of course on a construction project is set forth in other chapters.[53] These suggested means of documentation apply with equal force to the contractor-subcontractor relationship. At the first hint of dispute between contractor and subcontractor, the contractor's staff and frontline personnel should institute immediate steps to build an evidentiary record focusing on the specific problem involved and following it through to the point of full and complete resolution.

In the area of subcontract relations and dispute handling, as with other areas of construction law, the legal and economic environment that now surrounds modern construction serves as a warning to contractors that times have changed and the construction industry must change accordingly. Handshake agreements, which served as the backbone and theme of construction in the past, have now lost their appeal. The use of a blank purchase order as a means of engaging a subcontractor to perform work on a

---

[53] See **Chs. 15, 16**.

project serves today as a potential shortcut to business failure. Reliance on a telephone conversation rather than a written confirmation is no longer prudent.

Legal rules and theories are available to protect the contractor and enable him to formulate a claim for relief against a defaulting subcontractor. Good draftsmanship can arm the contractor with the contractual basis for administering and enforcing its expectations and reliance. Effective documentation, recordkeeping, and evidence preservation constitute the third indispensable member of the triumvirate. Together, they furnish the contractor with the means to assert a claim against a subcontractor and recover on that claim, thereby fulfilling the legitimate objective of allowing liability to flow to the party at fault.

CHAPTER 11

CONTRACTOR'S INSURANCE COVERAGE UNDER ITS LIABILITY AND BUILDER'S RISK POLICIES

Barry L. Bunshoft
Richard L. Seabolt*

Barry L. Bunshoft is the managing partner of Hancock, Rothert & Bunshoft, San Francisco, California. He received his undergraduate degree from the University of Massachusetts and his law degree from Harvard University. Mr. Bunshoft has extensive experience in litigation and arbitration involving international and domestic construction and insurance coverage disputes. He has represented contractors in proceedings under the International Chamber of Commerce Rules and in hearings before the United States—Iran International Claims Tribunal at The Hague.

*The authors gratefully acknowledge William J. Baron, who is associated with Hancock, Rothert & Bunshoft, for the preparation of the updated and revised version of this chapter.

Richard L. Seabolt is a partner in the San Francisco, California, law firm of Hancock, Rothert & Bunshoft. He received his undergraduate degree from the University of Michigan and his law degree from the University of California, Hastings College of the Law. He devotes a major portion of his general litigation practice to construction litigation and insurance coverage litigation. Mr. Seabolt is a member of the American Bar Association Forum Committee on the Construction Industry and an affiliate member of the Associated General Contractors of America.

---

§ 11.1 Introduction

§ 11.2 Contra Proferentem and the Reasonable Expectations Doctrine

LIABILITY POLICY

§ 11.3 Introduction

§ 11.4 Insuring Agreement

§ 11.5 —Occurrence Requirement

§ 11.6 —Trigger of Coverage under Occurrence-Based Policies

§ 11.7 —Claims-Made Policies

§ 11.8 —Definition of Property Damage

§ 11.9 Exclusions

§ 11.10 —Contractually Assumed Liability

§ 11.11 —Care, Custody, or Control

§ 11.12 —Premises Alienated

§ 11.13 —Performance or Business Risk

§ 11.14 —Damage to Insured's Product or Work

§ 11.15 —Sistership or Recall

§ 11.16 —Explosion, Collapse, or Underground Property Damage

§ 11.17 —Completed Operations Hazard

BUILDER'S RISK POLICY

§ 11.18 Introduction

§ 11.19 Period of Coverage

§ 11.20 Limitations on Coverage: Fortuitous Losses

§ 11.21 —External Causes

§ 11.22 —Exclusions

§ 11.23 Burden of Proof

§ 11.24 Sue and Labor Clause

§ 11.25 Subrogation
§ 11.26 Future Practice

§ 11.1 Introduction

The most productive time and energy a lawyer can expend to benefit a contractor client faced with a claim is to recognize that the claim may be covered by insurance, to identify all potentially applicable insurance policies, and to tender the claim to the insurers. From the client's financial perspective, full insurance coverage is a result only slightly less favorable than a defense verdict.

A lawyer representing a contractor should review the client's insurance coverage as soon as a potentially insured claim is brought to the lawyer's attention. Defending a contractor without notifying all potentially involved insurers may jeopardize the client's insurance coverage.[1]

If there is some arguable basis for even partial coverage of the claims made against the client, most jurisdictions require the insurer to provide a defense as a separate obligation under a comprehensive general liability policy.[2] In some states the existence of a coverage issue and a reservation of rights by the insurer may require the insurer to pay the attorneys' fees of an independent defense attorney selected by the insured client.[3] Because of the

---

[1] A. Windt, Insurance Claims and Disputes: Representation of Insurance Companies and Insureds ch. 1 (2d ed. 1988) [hereinafter Windt], provides a thorough discussion of issues related to insurance notice requirements, and includes a breakdown of those jurisdictions in which (1) late notice without prejudice is a sufficient policy defense; (2) late notice is a defense if the insured can prove no prejudice to the insurer; and (3) late notice is not a defense unless the insurer can prove prejudice. *Id.* at 10–16.

[2] St. Paul Fire & Marine Ins. Co. v. Sears, Roebuck & Co., 603 F.2d 780, 786 (9th Cir. 1979) (following Gray v. Zurich Ins. Co., 65 Cal. 2d 263, 275, 419 P.2d 168, 54 Cal. Rptr. 104 (1966)); *see also* Windt at 159–61.

In Central Mut. Ins. Co. v. Del Mar Beach Club Owners Ass'n, 123 Cal. App. 3d 916, 930–31, 176 Cal. Rptr. 895 (1981), the court indicated that the insurers of various construction entities could not use a declaratory relief action to terminate their duty to defend because the court found that the applicability of the various exclusions had to await the outcome of the underlying litigation against the insureds.

[3] Prashker v. United States Guar. Co., 1 N.Y.2d 584, 136 N.E.2d 871, 876, 154 N.Y.S.2d 910 (1956); Executive Aviation, Inc. v. National Ins. Underwriters, 16 Cal. App. 3d 799, 809, 94 Cal. Rptr. 347 (1971); San Diego Navy Fed. Credit Union v. Cumis Ins. Soc'y, Inc., 162 Cal. App. 3d 358, 361, 208 Cal. Rptr. 494 (1984). A few years after *Cumis,* the California legislature enacted Cal. Civ. Code § 2860, which details the insured's right to independent counsel in a potential conflict situation. *See generally* Windt at 169–74; Berg, *Losing Control of the Defense—The Insured's Right to Select His Own Counsel,* For the Defense 11 (July 1984); Berg, *After Cumis: Regaining Control of the Defense,* For the Defense 13 (Aug. 1985).

high cost of defending most construction disputes, an insurer-provided defense can result in substantial savings for the client.[4]

There is a distinction between a duty to defend and an obligation merely to pay defense costs. The former refers to a duty to hire, supervise, and pay attorneys for insureds who otherwise might be defenseless. Sophisticated insureds often self-insure for losses up to a certain amount, and purchase excess coverage that does not entail a duty to defend, because such coverage is less expensive and gives the insured greater control over claims handling. For example, in *Gribaldo, Jacobs, Jones & Associates v. Agrippina Versicherunges, A.G.,*[5] the court found that the insurer had no duty to defend under a policy stating that the insurer "shall be entitled at any time to take over and conduct in the name of the insured the defense of any claim." In a recent case, a California court of appeal reached the same conclusion when the policy stated that the insurer "shall have the right and shall be given the opportunity to associate with the Insured . . . in the defense of any claim, suit, or proceeding."[6]

In *Gon v. First State Insurance Co.,*[7] in which the policy stated that the insurer would pay defense expenses actually incurred, but did not otherwise provide a general duty to defend, the court ruled that defense costs should be apportioned between covered and uncovered claims. The court required the insurer to advance all the insured's defense costs because apportionment was difficult before coverage issues were litigated, but stated that the insured had to reimburse advanced costs related to items eventually found not covered. Furthermore, the court suggested that the trial court use a special master to monitor ongoing defense expenditures and to hasten any possible apportionment of covered and uncovered costs as the litigation progressed. *Id.*

Although lawyers often are not in a position to advise their contractor clients on insurance matters until after a liability-producing event has occurred, they should encourage their clients to have a close working relationship with an insurance broker who is experienced with construction insurance issues. The broker can provide the contractor client with advice on its insurance needs, including compliance with contract insurance requirements.[8] The contractor client should supplement the insurance

---

[4] A lawyer may wish to consult with the client contractor's insurance broker before taking an extremely aggressive position on coverage or defense obligations. A poor claims history could have an adverse impact on a client's future premiums or even insurability in a tight insurance market.

[5] 3 Cal. 3d 434, 476 P.2d 406, 91 Cal. Rptr. 6 (1970).

[6] Harbor Ins. Co. v. City of Ontario; 231 Cal. App. 3d 927, 282 Cal. Rptr. 701 (1991), *review denied* (Sept. 19, 1991).

[7] 871 F.2d 863, 868–69 (9th Cir. 1989).

[8] *See generally* W. Derk, Insurance for Contractors 3–5 (1981).

broker's advice by consulting a lawyer to review areas in which case law may affect the client's insurance needs. Preventative legal advice is critical to securing the coverage desired by the insured. As one author has stated:

> There is still, however, no substitute for familiarizing oneself with the details of a particular policy. This is most crucial in preventative law practice so that the client can be assured of receiving the protection he needs prior to a loss rather than searching the policy afterwards in an attempt to find coverage.[9]

The moment of truth arrives when a claim arises. If the contractor client failed to purchase an appropriate insurance policy or if the insurer denies coverage in arguable circumstances, it is essential that the contractor's lawyer be familiar with the most significant coverage issues facing construction contractors.

§ 11.2 Contra Proferentem and the Reasonable Expectations Doctrine

All insurance coverage disputes result from the conflict between the conscious intent of the insurance underwriter to leave certain risks uninsured and the reasonable (or unreasonable) expectation of the insured that the particular claim is covered. Historically, the insurance industry has had mixed success in drafting standard policy language that achieves this intent to leave certain risks uninsured. Before discussing judicial treatment of specific policy provisions, this chapter briefly sets out the general rules of contract interpretation as applied to insurance policies.

In addressing all contracts, the courts are required to construe the contract language solely according to its own terms, if possible, and must consider the specific wording in its ordinary and popular sense.[10] The contract is also to be viewed as a whole and interpreted so as to give meaning to

---

[9] Henderson, *Insurance Protection for Products Liability and Completed Operations—What Every Lawyer Should Know,* 50 Neb. L. Rev. 415, 446 (1971).

[10] Windt at 279–80. *See, e.g.,* Cal. Civ. Code §§ 1638–1639, 1644 (West). The latter rule is qualified, however, in § 1644:

> The words of a contract are to be understood in their ordinary and popular sense, rather than according to their strict legal meaning; unless used by the parties in a technical sense, or unless a special meaning is given to them by usage, in which case the latter must be followed.

The second clause of this statute indicates that insurance policy language should be construed according to its technical meaning within insurance industry practice. The United States Supreme Court has supported this view: "The Court, moreover, has long emphasized that in interpreting insurance contracts reference should be made to considerations of insurance and business practices." Standard Oil Co. v. United States, 340 U.S. 54, 60 (1950).

every part.[11] When contract language permits conflicting interpretations, each jurisdiction provides particular rules of construction to resolve the ambiguity.[12] Generally, the courts try to determine the intended meaning of ambiguous provisions by considering extrinsic evidence, such as the parties' actions and expressions after the contract was formed and before the dispute arose.[13] If extrinsic evidence cannot resolve the dispute, the courts, as a last resort, generally will interpret the contract language against the party who created the ambiguity, that is, against the party who drafted the relevant provision, normally, the insurer.[14] This rule is known as the doctrine of *contra proferentem,* from the Latin phrase meaning "against the party who proffers or puts forward a thing."[15]

However, in the insurance context, some courts have simply resolved ambiguities in a policy against the insurer, without first considering extrinsic evidence of the parties' intent.[16] As one commentator observed, such holdings "[c]an, of course, result in the creation of coverage when neither party expected or intended such coverage. This should not, therefore, be the law."[17]

The contra proferentem doctrine properly applies to construction of insurance contracts, as in all other contract actions, only if the policy language is found to be ambiguous, and even then only if the parties' actual intent concerning the policy's meaning cannot be determined through extrinsic evidence.[18] Thus, the insured's statements and actions relating to his

---

[11] Windt at 280; Cal. Civ. Code § 1641.

[12] *See, e.g.,* Cal. Civ. Code §§ 1635–1656.

[13] *E.g.,* Kennecott Corp. v. Union Oil, 196 Cal. App. 3d 1179, 1189, 242 Cal. Rptr. 403 (1987): "The conduct of the parties after execution of the contract and before any controversy has arisen as to its effect affords the most reliable evidence of the parties' intentions"; Meadows v. Lee, 175 Cal. App. 3d 475, 483, 221 Cal. Rptr. 22 (1985), *review denied* (1986): "The interpretation of a contract is often shown by the acts and conduct of the parties subsequent to the execution of the contract and prior to its controversy."

[14] For example, Cal. Civ. Code § 1654 states that this rule may be applied only when an uncertainty is not clarified by all the other rules of contract interpretation.

[15] Black's Law Dictionary 327 (6th ed. 1990).

[16] Windt at 282–83, n.7.

[17] *Id.* at 282–83.

[18] *See id.* at 283 and cases cited at 283–84 n.8. This is the rule in California. *See, e.g.,* Producers Dairy Delivery Co. v. Sentry Ins. Co., 41 Cal. 3d 903, 912, 718 P.2d 920, 226 Cal. Rptr. 558 (1986); Ranier Credit Co. v. Western Alliance Corp., 171 Cal. App. 3d 255, 263–64, 217 Cal. Rptr. 291 (1985). It is also the rule in New York. American Home Prods. v. Liberty Mut. Ins. Co., 565 F. Supp. 1485, 1492 (S.D.N.Y. 1983), *modified,* 748 F.2d 760 (2d Cir. 1984).

or her understanding of the policy, made after the policy was formed, should be considered in construing ambiguous language.[19]

As applied to insurance policies, the contra proferentem doctrine is intended to protect insureds who have little or no bargaining leverage in negotiating their policies. Therefore, some courts have refused to apply this rule when the insured is sophisticated and has equal bargaining power with the insurer.[20] Furthermore, there is no reason to construe a policy against the insurer when the insured or its brokers themselves drafted the policy language in question.[21] In such cases, ambiguities not clarified by extrinsic evidence arguably should be resolved against the insured.[22]

---

[19] Scott Elec. Co. v. Industrial Indem. Co., 30 Cal. App. 3d 797, 808, 106 Cal. Rptr. 710 (1973); Zito v. Fireman's Ins. Co., 36 Cal. App. 3d 277, 285, 111 Cal. Rptr. 392 (1973). *See also* Northwestern Mut. Life Ins. Co. v. Bland, Cave & Dew, 345 Mo. 391, 189 S.W.2d 542, 549 (1945):

> Any uncertainty or doubt about the policy provision has been settled by the conduct of the parties. . . . [W]here an ambiguity in an insurance policy has been removed by the construction of the parties there is no room for the application of the rule a policy must be constructed strictly against the insurer.

In AIU Ins. Co. v. Superior Court (FMC Corp.), 51 Cal. 3d 807, 823–24 n.9, 799 P.2d 1253, 274 Cal. Rptr. 820 (1990), the California Supreme Court stated that the parties' actions—including the insured's assertions regarding the same policies in unrelated litigation—were irrelevant in determining their intent when the policies were created. The court did not comment upon, or question the validity of, the numerous prior cases that had held that the parties' subsequent actions are the most reliable evidence of their intent at the time of contracting. *See* Kennecott Corp. v. Union Oil Co., 196 Cal. App. 3d 1179, 1189, 242 Cal. Rptr. 403 (1987), and cases cited therein.

[20] Garcia v. Truck Ins. Exch., 36 Cal. 3d 426, 438, 682 P.2d 1100, 204 Cal. Rptr. 435 (1984); Fireman's Fund Ins. Co. v. Fibreboard Corp., 182 Cal. App. 3d 462, 468, 227 Cal. Rptr. 203 (1986); Ostrager & Ichel, *The Role of Bargaining Power Evidence in the Construction of the Business Insurance Policy: An Update,* 18 Forum 577–90 (Summary 1983).

[21] Windt at 285. In AIU Ins. Co. v. Superior Court (FMC Corp.), 51 Cal. 3d 807, 823, 799 P.2d 1253, 274 Cal. Rptr. 820 (1990), the California Supreme Court noted:

> [W]here the policyholder does not suffer from lack of legal sophistication, or a relative lack of bargaining power, and where it is clear that an insurance policy was actually negotiated and jointly drafted, we need not go so far in protecting the insured from ambiguous or highly technical drafting.

[22] In *FMC Corp.,* although the insured was sophisticated and enjoyed great bargaining power, the court held that ambiguities would be resolved "against the party responsible for their inclusion in the policies." 51 Cal. 3d 807, 823, 799 P.2d 1253, 274 Cal. Rptr. 820. The court deemed that party to be the insurers, which had presented no evidence that the specific provisions at issue were actually negotiated. *Id.* This language suggests that uncertainties not clarified by extrinsic evidence should be resolved against the insured when it drafted the policy and thus is responsible for the ambiguity's inclusion in the policy. Similarly, in Fireman's Fund v. Fibreboard, 182 Cal. App. 3d 462, 468, 227 Cal. Rptr. 203 (1986), the court observed that because the insured had proposed the policy language in

Where the courts find ambiguity, they may also apply the *reasonable expectations doctrine* to protect the objectively reasonable expectations of the group of policyholders in the position of the particular insured. This doctrine prevents insurers from enforcing provisions that are unclear, inconspicuous, misleading, or unfair.[23] Like the contra proferentem rule, the reasonable expectations doctrine should be applied only if particular policy wording is found to be ambiguous[24] and if the insurer forced policy language on an insured lacking sophistication and an equal bargaining position.[25] However, some courts have pushed this doctrine so far as to abandon the fundamental contract principle that both parties are bound by the unambiguous terms of the insurance contract. These courts require the insurer to meet an almost impossible burden of proving that the insured was aware of and understood the effect of the particular provision or exclusion upon which the insurer relied.[26] What emerges is a sui generis body of insurance law that construes standard policy language to maximize the insured's recovery from the insurer in the particular case, at the expense of general certainty of interpretation.[27]

---

question, "to the extent that any ambiguity exists, ordinarily it would be interpreted against Fibreboard [the insured], the party who caused the ambiguity to exist."

[23] Windt at 291–92.

[24] Producers Dairy Delivery Co. v. Sentry Ins. Co., 41 Cal. 3d 903, 912, 718 P.2d 920, 226 Cal. Rptr. 558 (1986); Hallmark Ins. Co. v. Superior Court, 201 Cal. App. 3d 1014, 1019, 247 Cal. Rptr. 638, *review denied,* (1988); American Home Prods. v. Liberty Mut. Ins. Co., 565 F. Supp. 1485, 1511 (S.D.N.Y. 1983), *modified,* 748 F.2d 760 (2d Cir. 1984). Of course, the insured cannot rely on the reasonable expectations doctrine to create coverage when extrinsic evidence indicates that the insured subjectively knew that coverage did not exist. Stewart v. Estate of Bohnert, 101 Cal. App. 3d 978, 989–90, 162 Cal. Rptr. 126 (1980).

[25] Reserve Ins. Co. v. Pisciotta, 30 Cal. 3d 800, 807–08, 640 P.2d 764, 180 Cal. Rptr. 628 (1982).

[26] *See generally* Windt at 291–94. According to Windt, *id.,* this expansion of the reasonable expectations doctrine was first expressly adopted in a Pennsylvania lower court decision, Hionis v. Northern Mut. Ins. Co., 230 Pa. Super. 511, 327 A.2d 363, 365–66 (1974). Although other courts have endorsed this rule, the Pennsylvania Supreme Court subsequently rejected *Hionis* and held that the reasonable expectations doctrine should not be applied when the policy language is clear and unambiguous. Standard Venetian Blind Co. v. American Empire Ins. Co., 503 Pa. 300, 469 A.2d 563, 567 (1983), *reh'g denied* (1985).

[27] An extreme example of judicial reaching comes from several pollution coverage cases in which the courts have twisted the word "sudden" to encompass gradual seepage. *See, e.g.,* Claussen v. Aetna Casualty, 259 Ga. 333, 380 S.E.2d 686, 687 (1989); Jackson Township v. Hartford Accident & Indem. Co., 186 N.J. Super. 156, 451 A.2d 990, 994 (1982).

The lawyer's ability to stretch a contractor's insurance coverage beyond the insurance underwriter's intent at the time the policy was drafted or issued depends on the particular jurisdiction's view of insurance policies. Some courts sympathetic to the complex language of insurance policies have stated that "[i]t is widely recognized that language of insurance policies is often necessarily complicated and difficult for the layman to fully understand."[28] Other courts hostile to insurers have characterized some insurance policies as "an inexplicable riddle, a mere flood of darkness and profusion . . . printed in such small type, and in lines so long and crowded, that the perusal of it was made physically difficult, painful and injurious."[29]

Such wide-ranging attitudes among various jurisdictions about insurance policies tend to promote forum shopping by lawyers familiar with these judicial attitudes. However, some courts may take steps to limit such practices. One California court dismissed a coverage case brought by an East Coast insured on an East Coast claim against an East Coast insurer, stating that "California courts do not throw their doors wide open to forum shopping."[30] Alternatively, a court may retain jurisdiction over an action but refuse to apply that state's substantive laws. In another California case, the relevant policy was written in Oklahoma, the decision to deny coverage was made in Oklahoma, and the insured was an Oklahoma resident who had moved to California after coverage was denied. The California court resolved the dispute under Oklahoma law, specifically stating that application of California law in such circumstances would encourage forum shopping.[31]

In sum, the contra proferentem rule reflects the predisposition of various courts to find the language of insurance policies ambiguous, and the reasonable expectations doctrine in practice can mean open season on insurers. The history of the development of the standard liability policy forms reflects the efforts of the insurance industry to tighten the policy language that courts have found ambiguous or unenforceable. To understand the current liability policy form, it is necessary to review the development of the form that resulted from this tug of the courts and pull of the insurance industry.

---

[28] McGann v. Hobbs Lumber Co., 150 W. Va. 364, 145 S.E.2d 476, 481 (1965).

[29] Delancey v. Insurance Co., 52 N.H. 581, 587–88 (1873) (*quoted in* Storms v. United States Fid. & Guar. Co., 388 A.2d 578, 580 (N.H. 1978).

[30] Appalachian Ins. Co. v. Superior Court (Union Carbide Corp.), 162 Cal. App. 3d 427, 438, 208 Cal. Rptr. 627 (1984).

[31] Zimmerman v. Allstate Ins. Co., 179 Cal. App. 3d 840, 847, 224 Cal. Rptr. 917 (1986).

LIABILITY POLICY

§ 11.3 Introduction

The insurance industry first prepared a standard general liability policy in 1940, with revisions in 1943, 1955, 1966, 1973, 1986, and 1988.[32] The basic format of the *comprehensive* general liability (CGL) policy was set in the 1966 version. The 1973 revisions clarified and refined the 1966 policy language. However, the Insurance Services Office (ISO) issued an entirely new form of liability policy for use after January 1, 1986, called the *commercial* general liability policy (1986 CGL policy). The ISO subsequently introduced further revisions in its most recent CGL form, dated November 1988.

This chapter focuses on the 1973 CGL language and discusses and compares the 1986 and 1988 policy forms. Coverage issues under the pre-1986 CGL policy will continue to arise for some years. In addition, the courts will no doubt interpret the most recent policy, as they did its predecessors, with consideration of the earlier forms of the CGL policy as historical background.

Because the most difficult coverage issues faced by contractors under CGL policies involve property damage claims, not bodily injury claims, this chapter deals primarily with property damage issues. Most bodily injury claims are covered either by the contractor's CGL policy or under other policies or endorsements (for example, automobile, mobile equipment, aircraft, watercraft, workers' compensation, or completed operations). In contrast, many property damage claims against contractors are not covered by either the standard CGL policy or any other commonly available standard insurance policy.[33]

The coverage provided by a CGL policy is "not intended to indemnify the contractor for direct damages resulting because the contractor furnished

---

[32] Tinker, *Comprehensive General Liability Insurance—Perspective and Overview,* FIC Q. 217 (Spring 1975). *Underlying Coverage, in* 1 The Attorney's Umbrella Book 69 (P. Ligeros ed., 1991).

[33] One insurer representative explained in a 1959 article that: "Because the world at large takes less precautions for property damage, the insurance man must take more precautions. There is a greater moral hazard here than in the case of bodily injury." He explained: "The idea that one person's gain may be someone else's loss does not shock us, but to gain by someone else's bodily injury, however, does shock us." Bean, *The Accident Versus the Occurrence Concept,* Ins. L. J. 550–58 (Sept. 1959).

defective materials or workmanship,"[34] nor does it purport to provide coverage for all liability that can result from a contractor's errors and omissions.[35]

The ISO and its predecessors drafted the CGL policy with the intent of avoiding coverage for business risks within the effective control of the insured. Meeting contract requirements for quantity, quality, and timeliness of the work creates business risks that can be reduced by competent business management. The CGL policy is not intended to serve as a warranty or performance bond.[36]

The significant negative risks of cost overruns, contractual penalties for failure to complete on time, and costs for correction of defective work are undertaken by the contractor for the positive expectation of a substantial profit. Insurance underwriters traditionally have been unwilling to insure these business risks.[37] If an insured could maximize its profits by performing defective work and passing on the costs of correction to the insurer, such a policy would be a type of financial guaranty not contemplated by the relatively modest premium structure of the CGL policy. What the CGL policy does intend to cover are *fortuities,* that is, unexpected and unintended occurrences.

§ 11.4 Insuring Agreement

The insuring agreement states the insurer's obligation to indemnify and defend the insured, subject to the definitions, exclusions, and conditions contained elsewhere in the policy. Although the insuring agreement of the 1973 comprehensive general liability policy was reworded significantly in

---

[34] Maryland Casualty v. Reeder, 221 Cal. App. 3d 961, 967, 270 Cal. Rptr. 719, *review denied* (1990); Rafeiro v. American Employers' Ins. Co., 5 Cal. App. 3d 799, 808, 85 Cal. Rptr. 701 (1970).

[35] Many major construction contractors have insurance programs that provide professional liability coverage in addition to general liability coverage. Such professional liability insurance is particularly important to a contractor who performs design services or construction management services, because any liability for construction delays would not be covered by a CGL policy. Construction delay claims do not involve an occurrence or property damage as defined by those policies, and also may be excluded by the performance exclusion. This chapter does not discuss the question of whether, under a policy that provides professional liability coverage, a contractor may be covered for damage to others caused by its delay in performance of the work.

[36] *See generally* Tinker, *Comprehensive General Liability Insurance—Perspective and Overview,* FIC Q. 217, 223–24 (Spring 1975).

[37] Sandridge, *Professional Liability Coverage for the CM, in* Liability in Construction Management 38–39 (D. Lee ed. 1983). The author also points out that a performance bond surety does not insure against these risks; the surety acts only as a guarantor to protect the owner and the surety retains the right to proceed against the contractor in the event of default.

the 1986 commercial general liability form, the earlier language is still the subject of most ongoing litigation.

> The 1973 insuring agreement states:
>
> The company will *pay on behalf of* the insured all sums which the insured shall become legally obligated to pay as damages because of
>
> Coverage A. bodily injury or
> Coverage B. *property damage*
>
> to which this insurance applies, caused by an *occurrence,* and the company shall have the right and duty to defend any suit against the insured seeking damages on account of such bodily injury or property damage, even if any of the allegations of the suit are groundless, false, or fraudulent (emphasis added).

The agreement to "pay on behalf of" distinguishes the liability policy from an agreement to indemnify against loss. The obligation is to pay third parties on behalf of the insured, not simply to reimburse the insured.[38]

The ISO attempted to introduce certain vital changes with the 1986 CGL form. Most significantly, the 1986 revisions provided for alternative policies offered on either an occurrence or claims-made basis (but otherwise identical).[39] This chapter discusses both the occurrence definition and the claims-made format.

Aside from the changes regarding trigger of coverage, the 1986 form deletes potentially important language from the 1973 policy. The 1986 policy omits the language stating that the insurer agrees to defend the insured against "groundless, false, or fraudulent" allegations. Instead, it indicates that the insurer assumes the duty to defend only against claims for damages that are covered by the policy.[40] Of course, the ultimate effect of this wording change will remain unclear until courts pass on its meaning. Many courts might simply ignore this revision and uphold the current rule that the duty to defend encompasses all claims in an action as long as some covered damages are alleged. But under the new wording "this can no longer be taken for granted."[41] Insurers can reasonably argue that because many courts have emphasized the "groundless, false, or fraudulent" language in

---

[38] This distinction is important, for instance, to a general contractor with an insurance-covered claim against a bankrupt subcontractor or supplier. A liability insurer must "pay on behalf" of the insured all claims covered under the policy, whether or not the insured is bankrupt. *See* 11 Couch on Insurance 2d §§ 44:250–44:252 at 386–89 (rev. ed. 1982).

[39] *Underlying Coverage, in* 1 The Attorney's Umbrella Book 151 (P. Ligeros ed., 1991).

[40] The 1986 ISO insuring agreement indicates that the insurer is bound to defend only actions seeking "those damages" that turn out to be covered.

[41] *Underlying Coverage, in* 1 The Attorney's Umbrella Book 80 (P. Ligeros ed., 1991).

justifying the current rule,[42] and because this language has been deliberately omitted from the recent CGL policy, the new wording intends that defense costs be apportioned between covered and uncovered items.

§ 11.5 —Occurrence Requirement

The word "occurrence" is a central term in each version of the ISO policy from 1966 to the present. The term has two critical functions. First, it encompasses the fortuity requirement, which is basic to all contracts of insurance. Second, it determines the trigger of coverage under occurrence-based policies, and is part of the coverage trigger formulation in claims-made policies.

Fortuity

The 1966 and 1973 CGL policies define *occurrence* as follows:

> "Occurrence" means an accident, including continuous or repeated exposure to conditions, which results in bodily injury or property damage neither expected nor intended from the standpoint of the insured.[43]

---

[42] *E.g.,* in Gray v. Zurich Ins. Co., 65 Cal. 2d 363, 373, 419 P.2d 168, 54 Cal. Rptr. 104 (1966), the court quoted the applicable duty to defend clause, including the "groundless, false, or fraudulent" phrase, and concluded: "This language, in its broad sweep, would lead the insured reasonably to expect defense of any suit regardless of merit or cause." In deciding that the duty to defend is broader than the duty to indemnify, the *Gray* court mentioned the "groundless, false, or fraudulent" clause six times. *Id.* at 267, 272–74. *See also* Lowell v. Maryland Casualty Co., 65 Cal. 2d 298, 301, 419 P.2d 180, 54 Cal. Rptr. 116 (1966). Similarly, in CNA Casualty v. Seaboard Sur. Co., 176 Cal. App. 3d 598, 606, 222 Cal. Rptr. 276 (1986), the court stated:

> [E]ach of the insurance policies at issue required the insurer to defend [the insured] in any suit alleging an injury under the respective policy even if the suit is " . . . groundless, false, or fraudulent." *Under such a clause* it is the duty of the insurer to defend the insured when sued in any action where the facts alleged in the complaint support a recovery . . . covered by the policy, regardless of the fact that . . . the injury is not in fact covered (emphasis added).

[43] The 1986 and 1988 ISO CGL forms (both the occurrence and claims-made versions) restate this wording, placing the "accident," "property damage," and "expected and intended" requirements in distinct parts of the policy. In these policy forms, the insuring agreement states that "[t]his insurance . . . applies to 'property damage' caused by an 'occurrence.'" The shortened occurrence definition reads in full: "'Occurrence' means an accident, including continuous or repeated exposure to substantially the same conditions." Finally, these policies express the "expected or intended" requirement as an exclusion to coverage rather than a condition of the insuring agreement. When these reworked clauses are taken together, coverage under the new forms is still contingent on "an accident . . . which results in property damage . . . neither expected nor intended from the standpoint of the insured."

The "accident" and "neither expected nor intended" language emphasizes the essential nature of insurance: an insurer, in exchange for the payment of a premium, accepts the risk that the insured will become legally obligated to pay damages covered by the policy. If the element of risk has been eliminated so that the bodily injury or property damage is either expected or intended, there is no coverage.[44]

This requirement of fortuity is an essential part of every insurance agreement, whether or not a specific policy contains the phrase, "damage neither expected nor intended from the standpoint of the insured." When this language is absent from a particular policy, the courts imply a fortuity requirement as a matter of law.[45]

Whether express or implied, the fortuity requirement precludes coverage for harm expected or intended from the insured's point of view. In determining whether a loss was "fortuitous," the courts do not ask simply whether the specific insured had an actual subjective expectation that the damage in question would occur. That is only the first step in the analysis. Even if the insured did not in fact anticipate the damage, most courts make an objective determination of whether a reasonable person would

---

[44] In Bartholomew v. Appalachian Ins. Co., 655 F.2d 27, 29 (1st Cir. 1981), the court stated, "The concept of insurance is that the parties, in effect, wager against the occurrence or non-occurrence of a specified event: the carrier insures against a risk, not a certainty."

[45] Professors Keaton and Widiss have explained this basic principle:

> The implied exceptions that apply to insurance transactions almost always are predicated on an application of one of two concepts . . . . The [second] concept, which is widely viewed as a fundamental principle of insurance law, is that insurance contracts should not provide coverage when a loss is not fortuitous.

R. Keaton & A. Widiss, Insurance Law—A Guide to Fundamental Principles, Legal Doctrines, and Commercial Practices § 5.3(a) at 475, § 5.4(a) at 497–98 (Practitioner's ed. 1988).

In Chu v. Canadian Indem. Co., 224 Cal. App. 3d 86, 94–95, 274 Cal. Rptr. 20, *review denied* (1990), the court observed: "The concept of 'fortuity' is basic to insurance law. Insurance is designed to protect contingent or unknown risks of harm . . . , not to protect against harm which is certain or expected." Cal. Ins. Code § 22 (West) has codified this fortuity requirement: "Insurance is a contract whereby one undertakes to indemnify another against loss, damage, or liability arising from a contingent or unknown event." Black's Law Dictionary 802 (6th ed. 1990) defines "insurance" as a "contract whereby one undertakes to indemnify another against loss, damage, or liability arising from an unknown or contingent event."

have expected the result.[46] There is generally no coverage if the insured "should have known" that the harm was substantially probable.[47]

Trigger of Coverage

The ISO policy language regarding trigger of coverage has been rewritten several times since 1955, both to reflect and respond to judicial trends in interpretation. In the pre-1966 versions, the policy covers damages caused by "accidents." Early decisions held that the term "accident" required a

---

[46] Wickman v. Northwestern Nat'l Life, 908 F.2d 1077, 1088–89 (1st Cir.), *cert. denied,* 111 S. Ct. 581 (1990). The *Wickman* court held:

> If the fact-finder determines that the insured did not expect an injury similar in type to that suffered, the fact-finder must then examine whether the suppositions which underlay that expectation were reasonable. . . . This analysis will prevent unrealistic expectations from undermining the purpose of accident insurance. If the fact-finder determines that the suppositions were unreasonable, then the injuries shall be deemed not accidental.

Id. at 1088. The court concluded that if the insured's subjective expectation cannot be determined, the jury should engage in an objective analysis of the insured's expectations, asking whether a reasonable person "would have viewed the injury as highly likely to occur as a result of the insured's intentional conduct." *Id.*

Numerous other courts have adopted this objective expectation standard. *See, e.g.,* City of Carter Lake v. Aetna Casualty & Sur. Co., 604 F.2d 1052, 1058–59 (8th Cir. 1979); Aetna v. Sheft, 756 F. Supp. 449, 451–52 (C.D. Cal. 1990); County of Broome v. Aetna Casualty & Sur., 146 A.D.2d 337, 540 N.Y.S.2d 620, 622 (1989); Bay State Ins. Co. v. Wilson, 96 Ill. 2d 487, 71 Ill. Dec. 726, 451 N.E.2d 880, 882 (1983).

This conclusion is consistent with the manner in which corporate insureds understood the "neither expected nor intended from the standpoint of the insured" language when it was included in the 1966 revisions. The 100-page booklet published by the American Society of Insurance Management (now the Risk Insurance Management Society (RIMS)), entitled Customer Analysis of the Comprehensive General Liability Policy adopted in October, 1966, acknowledged the objective expectation standard by stating: "There should be cover when the injury is an unintended result of an intentional act *provided such result was not reasonably foreseeable"* (emphasis in original). *Id.* at viii.

[47] However, a few courts apply the "expected or intended" limitation only to damage subjectively intended by the issued. *See, e.g.,* City of Johnstown v. Bankers Standard Ins., 877 F.2d 1146, 1150 (2d Cir. 1989). This position leaves the entire question of coverage contingent on the insured's forthrightness, which creates great room for deceit. *See* Mogil v. California Physicians Corp., 218 Cal. App. 3d 1030, 1040, 267 Cal. Rptr. 487 (1990) (adopting an objective standard regarding a pre-existing condition exclusion). Moreover, sole reliance on the insured's intent effectively deletes the word "expected" from the "expected or intended" clause, and thus violates the basic rule that meaning should be given to each part of a contract. As explained in Farm Bureau Town & Country Ins. Co. v. Turnbo, 740 S.W.2d 232, 236 (Mo. Ct. App. 1987):

> "Intend" means the insured desires to cause the consequences of his act or believes that the consequences are substantially certain to result. "Expect" means

sudden event and precluded coverage for damages resulting from gradually developing causes.[48] Other decisions abandoned this temporal requirement, thus fostering uncertainty of interpretation.[49]

Because some courts interpreted "accident" to include gradually occurring situations, ISO's predecessors resolved the conflict by replacing the term "accident" with "occurrence" in the 1966 general liability policy. *Occurrence* was defined as "an accident, including injurious exposure to conditions."[50] In addition to expanding the temporal requirement, this language was intended to limit a series of related events to one occurrence and, therefore, to one limit of liability. However, some courts construed the new policy to intend that each incident in a series constituted a separate occurrence, and multiplied the applicable policy limits accordingly.[51]

§ 11.6 —Trigger of Coverage under Occurrence-Based Policies

The trigger of coverage under the 1973 CGL policy, which is written only on an occurrence basis, is "physical injury to or destruction of tangible property which occurs *during the policy period.*" The date of the negligent act causing the property damage generally is unimportant in determining

---

that the insured realized or should have realized there was a strong probability the consequences in question would result from his acts.

[48] *See, e.g.,* Arthur A. Johnson Corp. v. Indemnity Ins., 6 A.D.2d 97, 175 N.Y.S.2d 414 (1958), *aff'd,* 7 N.Y.2d 222, 164 N.E.2d 704, 196 N.Y.S.2d 678 (1959); Hutchens v. McClure, 176 Kan. 43, 296 P.2d 473 (1954); Adams v. Bryant, 274 S.W.2d 791 (Ky. 1954); Forman v. Jordan, 131 So. 2d 796 (La. Ct. App. 1961).

[49] *See, e.g.,* Canadian Radium Uranium Corp. v. Indemnity Ins. Co., 411 Ill. 325, 104 N.E.2d 250 (1952); Baker v. American Ins. Co., 324 F.2d 748 (4th Cir. 1963); Travelers v. Humming Bird Coal Co., 371 S.W.2d 35 (Ky. Ct. App. 1963).

[50] Defense Research Institute (DRI), General Liability Insurance—1973 Revisions at 1974(1):10.

[51] *Id.; see* Maurice Pincoffs Co. v. St. Paul Fire & Marine Ins. Co., 447 F.2d 204, 206 (5th Cir. 1971).

whether there is coverage.[52] The date on which a claim was first made is also unimportant in determining whether there is coverage.[53]

The trigger of coverage when there is continuing damage is one of the most controversial issues in insurance law. Continuing damage issues can arise in many construction-related contexts, including roof leaks, foundation settlement cracks, pipeline leakage, and spalling concrete. Continuing damage may have the effect of broadening a contractor's coverage by permitting a stacking of policy limits so that, for example, two consecutive policies with $100,000 limits provide coverage totaling $200,000.

Much of the recent litigation on trigger issues has concerned coverage for bodily injury resulting from continuing exposure to asbestos. Although property damage cases are distinguishable from asbestos bodily injury matters and different rules properly apply in each situation,[54] the terms of reference between insurers and insureds regarding trigger of coverage have been defined in the asbestos coverage actions.

The various litigants in those actions take several different positions, which are reflected in judicial decisions addressing the question of continuous bodily injury. Some courts have found that every single exposure to asbestos fibers constitutes a separate occurrence, thus triggering each liability policy in force during the entire period that the underlying claimant

---

[52] Remmer v. Glens Falls Indem. Co., 140 Cal. App. 2d 84, 88, 295 P.2d 19 (1956); Home Mut. Fire Ins. Co. v. Hosfelt, 233 F. Supp. 360 (D. Conn. 1962). *See generally* Berg, *Occurrence: An Elusive Description, in* 1982 DRI Monograph No. 2; "Occurrence" and Other Insurance Coverage Issues (DRI 1982). In INA v. Sam Harris Constr. Co., 22 Cal. 3d 409, 411–12, 583 P.2d 1335, 149 Cal. Rptr. 292 (1978), and Sylla v. United States Fid. & Guar. Co., 54 Cal. App. 3d 895, 900–01, 127 Cal. Rptr. 38 (1978), the courts used the reasonable expectations doctrine to rationalize expanding the definition of "occurrence" to include the acts that caused the damage, and found coverage although the damage resulted after the relevant policy had expired or was cancelled. However, subsequent cases have rejected the result in *Sylla* as inconsistent with the prevailing rule, and distinguished *Sam Harris Construction Co.* based on the specific policy language at issue. *See* Hallmark Ins. Co. v. Superior Court, 201 Cal. App. 3d 1014, 1018–19, 247 Cal. Rptr. 638, *review denied* (1988); State Farm Mut. Auto. Ins. Co. v. Longden, 197 Cal. App. 3d 226, 230–31, 242 Cal. Rptr. 726 (1987), and cases cited therein.

[53] The 1986 and 1988 CGL forms include an option for claims-made coverage, which is triggered when a claim is first made against the insured, subject to certain other requirements.

[54] For example, in Home Ins. Co. v. Landmark Ins. Co., 205 Cal. App. 3d 1388, 1395, 253 Cal. Rptr. 277 (1988), the court stated:

> Common sense tells us that property damage cases, even those involving continuous damage such as the one before us, differ from asbestos bodily injury cases. . . . [T]he rationale for apportioning liability in the asbestos cases is not a basis to deviate from settled principles of law applicable to this [property damage] case.

was exposed to asbestos products.[55] Other courts have rejected this exposure theory and, referring to the policy requirement that physical injury, sickness, or disease must occur during the policy period, held that CGL policies are triggered only in the year that asbestos-related disease first manifests itself.[56] A few courts have adopted a *continuous trigger* position, finding coverage under all policies in effect from the initial exposure until manifestation, on the theory that asbestos fibers cause worsening lung damage even after exposure ceases.[57]

In *American Home Products v. Liberty Mutual Insurance Co. (AHP)*[58] the court undertook an extensive review of the above theories, and rejected each of them. The *AHP* court determined that all three theories are inconsistent with the CGL policy language and drafting history, and concluded that the various positions had resulted from earlier courts' result-oriented efforts to find coverage for the specific claims before them.[59] After criticizing such efforts as misguided on public policy grounds, the *AHP* decision adopted an *injury in fact* test, under which policies are triggered if the insured proves that "injury, sickness, or disease" first occurred during the policy period.[60] Under this rule, multiple occurrences could be found "from exposure to manifestation," but to achieve this result the insured would have to demonstrate that new injuries had actually occurred in different policy terms.[61] Thus, this approach is potentially much less inclusive than the exposure or continuous trigger theories, yet potentially broader than the manifestation view.

As these asbestos-related coverage cases were being decided, insureds began to assert that the broad trigger rules from the asbestos bodily injury context should apply in property damage cases. Some courts accepted this position. In *California Union Insurance Co. v. Landmark Insurance Co.*[62] the court held that where there had been one occurrence involving continuous, progressive, and deteriorating property damage, such as earth

[55] *E.g.,* Insurance Co. of N. Am. (INA) v. Forty-Eight Insulations, 633 F.2d 1212, 1222 (6th Cir. 1980), *reh'g granted in part and denied in part,* 657 F.2d 814 (6th Cir.) *cert. denied,* 454 U.S. 1109 (1981).

[56] *E.g.,* Eagle-Picher Indus., Inc. v. Liberty Mut. Ins. Co., 682 F.2d 12, 17 (1st Cir. 1982), *cert. denied sub nom.* Froude v. Eagle-Picher Indus., 460 U.S. 1028 (1983) ("it is the resulting injury, *not* the exposure, which must take place 'during the policy period' in order to trigger coverage" (emphasis added)).

[57] *E.g.,* Keene Corp. v. INA, 667 F.2d 1034, 1048 (D.C. Cir. 1981), *cert. denied,* 455 U.S. 1007 (1982).

[58] 565 F. Supp. 1485 (S.D.N.Y. 1983), *modified,* 748 F.2d 760 (2d Cir. 1984).

[59] *Id.* at 1497–1511.

[60] *Id.* at 1511–13.

[61] *Id.* at 1498.

[62] 145 Cal. App. 3d 462, 469, 193 Cal. Rptr. 461 (1983).

movement caused by leakage from a defectively constructed swimming pool, "the carrier in whose policy period the damage first becomes apparent remains on the risk until the damage is finally and totally complete." Citing *INA v. Forty-Eight Insulations*[63] and *Keene Corp. v. INA,*[64] the court found coverage under a second policy that was in force between the time the damage was caused and the time it became manifest.[65]

More recent decisions have recognized that the development of asbestos-related disease is not analogous to ongoing property damage and thus rejected the exposure and continuous trigger in property damage cases. For example, the *Home Insurance Co. v. Landmark Insurance Co.* decision cited the longstanding general rule that an "occurrence" arises when the complaining party was actually injured, and held that injury to property occurs when actual damage becomes apparent.[66] The *Home* court criticized the *California Union v. Landmark* decision for accepting a coverage theory developed in an inapplicable bodily injury context:

> To apportion damage and hold an insurer liable for damage manifested in another insurer's policy period also violates the loss in progress rule, i.e., that an insurance company may insure only against contingent or unknown risks. . . . [footnote omitted]. Liability will not be imposed . . . where damages occur and are apparent before the date the policy takes effect . . . . *California Union* misapplied three pre-manifestation cases to hold a post manifestation carrier jointly and severally liable.[67]

The result in *Home* was subsequently confirmed by the California Supreme Court in *Prudential-LMI Commercial Insurance v. Superior Court.*[68]

---

[63] 633 F.2d 1212 (6th Cir. 1980), *cert. denied,* 454 U.S. 1109 (1981).

[64] Keene Corp. v. INA, 667 F.2d 1034 (D.C. Cir. 1981); *cert. denied,* 445 U.S. 1007 (1982); INA v. Forty-Eight Insulations, 633 F.2d 1212 (6th Cir.), *reh'g granted in part and denied in part,* 657 F.2d 814 (6th Cir. 1980), *cert. denied,* 454 U.S. 1109 (1981).

[65] This later damage, even though resulting from the same damage-causing forces, was unexpected and unintended when the insurer came on the risk, because the latter damage had not yet manifested itself. 145 Cal. App. 3d at 477. The *California Union v. Landmark* apportionment formula, in which earlier insurers have greater liability than later insurers, was rejected by the *Forty-Eight Insulations* court in favor of an apportionment based on the number of years each insurer was on the risk. INA v. Forty-Eight Insulations, 633 F.2d 1212, 1226.

[66] 205 Cal. App. 3d 1388, 1392, 253 Cal. Rptr. 277 (1988).

[67] *Id.* at 1395.

[68] 51 Cal. 3d 674, 728 P.2d 1230, 274 Cal. Rptr. 387, *modified,* 52 Cal. 3d 517a (1990). The *Prudential-LMI* court explained:

> [P]rior to the manifestation of damage, the loss is still a contingency under the policy and the insured has not suffered a compensable loss. Once the loss has manifested, however, the risk is no longer contingent.

Id. at 699.

Both *Home* and *Prudential-LMI* concerned first-party insurance and expressly deferred consideration of coverage triggers under third-party liability policies.[69] A recent California decision extended the manifestation trigger to property damage claims under third-party insurance, stating that "the distinction between first and third party coverage is not legally significant" in determining trigger of coverage.[70]

In sum, the courts have required that there be actual property damage during the policy period for a particular policy to be triggered. But whether under occurrence policies undiscovered damage triggers coverage has been the subject of diverse and inconsistent positions by the courts.[71]

When confronted with a continuing damage case, it is prudent for the contractor's lawyer to notify all insurers on the risk for all periods during which there is evidence of actual damage. As a practical matter, because the facts frequently are unclear, it is wise to notify all insurers from the period the work was performed to the period the claim was made against the contractor. CGL insurers insuring a general contractor before the completion of construction probably would not accept even partial coverage because damage occurring before completion usually would be excluded entirely by the care, custody, and control exclusion. See **§ 11.11**. CGL insurers coming on the risk after the insured reasonably could expect that damage would continue (and, certainly, those coming on the risk after the insured received a demand or complaint) would not accept coverage because the damage by that time had become expected from the standpoint of the insured. Within these parameters, however, the determination of the periods in which continuing damage claims are covered seems limited only by the imagination of the lawyer and the mood of the judge.

§ 11.7 —Claims-Made Policies

In response to the battering it has taken in the courts over the trigger of coverage, the insurance industry attempted to change from an occurrence

---

[69] Home Ins. Co. v. Landmark Ins. Co., 205 Cal. App. 3d 1388, 1393; Prudential-LMI Commercial Ins. v. Superior Court, 51 Cal. 3d 674, 698.

[70] Fireman's Fund Ins. Co. v. Aetna Casualty & Sur. Co., 223 Cal. App. 3d 1621, 1626–28, 273 Cal. Rptr. 431 (1990).

[71] *Compare* New Castle County v. Continental Casualty Co., 725 F. Supp. 800, 813 (D. Del.), *motion for reconsideration denied,* 728 F. Supp. 340 (D. Del. 1989), *aff'd in part and rev'd in part,* 1991 U.S. App. LEXIS 7849 (3d Cir. Apr. 30, 1991) (continuous trigger in property case) *with* Mraz v. Canadian Universal Ins. Co., 804 F.2d 1325, 1328 (4th Cir. 1986) (manifestation trigger in property case).

to a claims-made format in the mid-1980s.[72] The ISO issued a 1986 claims-made policy form, which was subsequently modified by a 1988 version. The claims-made policy provides coverage only when the occurrence, the property damage, and the claim all happen during the same policy term. This restrictive trigger provision was designed to counter the courts' tendency to stack limits under occurrence policies, and to ensure that "only one insurance policy with its single set of limits applies to each injury or damage-causing event."[73]

However, the claims-made form ran into trouble before it was put into effect. Numerous state insurance commissions rejected the claims-made policy as first proposed by ISO because the limited proposed reporting period would have led to potential coverage gaps and policy cancellations after known occurrences.[74] The state insurance commissions dropped their objections after ISO agreed to certain revisions, such as lengthening the claims reporting period and guaranteeing the availability of an optional supplemental reporting tail.[75]

The claims-made policy initially received a hostile reception from certain courts. For example, in *Sparks v. St. Paul Insurance Co.*[76] the New Jersey Supreme Court voided a policy clause that required the occurrence and the claim to occur within the policy period. The *Sparks* court ruled that because the policy lacked an adequate extended reporting period, the insured's reasonable expectation required the court to find coverage under an occurrence trigger.[77] In *Merrill & Seeley v. Admiral Insurance Co.,*[78] however, the court stated that although claims-made policies offer limited coverage, "an insurer has a right to limit the policy coverage in plain and understandable language, and is at liberty to limit the character and extent of the risk it undertakes to assume." The *Merrill & Seeley* court specifically rejected the *Sparks* holding; because the policy was unambiguous,

---

[72] In one commentator's view, the introduction of claims-made coverage was motivated by insurance industry losses of $20 billion in 1984 and $20-plus billion in 1985. Krizan, *Insurers Tighten Policies Further,* 216 ENR 50 (Feb. 6, 1986).

[73] *Id.*

[74] Finlayson, *New Changes May Ease Claims-Made Approval,* Bus. Ins. 1, 37 (Jan. 20, 1986); Finlayson, *RIMS Drops Its Opposition to Claims-Made,* Bus. Ins. 1, 66 (Jan. 27, 1986).

[75] Finlayson, *New Changes May Ease Claims-Made Approval,* Bus. Ins. 1, 37 (Jan. 20, 1986); Finlayson, *RIMS Drops Its Opposition to Claims-Made,* Bus. Ins. 1, 66 (Jan. 27, 1986).

[76] 495 A.2d 406, 414–15, 100 N.J. 325 (1985).

[77] *Id.*

[78] 225 Cal. App. 3d 624, 630, 275 Cal. Rptr. 280 (1990).

the reasonable expectations doctrine was irrelevant and the claims-made reporting requirements were valid.[79]

Notwithstanding these difficulties with courts and regulatory bodies, the ultimate problem facing the claims-made policy is that market acceptance has been limited.[80] The claims-made form would resolve future trigger of coverage disputes in favor of manifestation, discovery, and prompt notification of claims. But because of the market's hesitation regarding claims-made coverage, future judicial decisions will have to address the meaning of the occurrence language under the 1986 and 1988 ISO policies.

§ 11.8 —Definition of Property Damage

The term *property damage* is defined in the 1973 CGL policy, in part, as "the *physical* injury to or destruction of tangible property." The significance of this definition is best understood by reviewing its evolution in response to earlier court decisions.

CGL insurers historically have attempted to avoid coverage for pure warranty-type claims—defective products or work not causing other damage—by using narrowly defined terms in the insuring agreement and specific exclusions. Despite the efforts of the insurance industry to avoid coverage for the cost of repair or replacement of defective products or work of the insured, the courts usually granted coverage when the defective product or work was a component integrated into the whole. In the leading case in this area, *Hauenstein v. Saint Paul-Mercury Indemnity Co.,*[81] the Minnesota Supreme Court held that a plaster distributor was covered under its liability policy for a warranty claim made because the plaster shrunk and cracked after it was used in the construction of a hospital. The court found that the claim satisfied the policy requirement of "injury to or destruction of property" because the presence of the defective plaster

[79] *Id.* at 629–31. *See also* Slater v. Lawyers' Mut. Ins. Co., 227 Cal. App. 3d 1415, 1424, 278 Cal. Rptr. 479 (1991); Pacific Employers Ins. Co. v. Superior Court, 221 Cal. App. 3d 1348, 1357–61, 270 Cal. Rptr. 179, *review denied* (1990).

[80] While ISO was developing the claims-made CGL form, it intended that most coverage would be written under the new format. Teff, *Alarm from London,* The Brief 20 (Fall 1985). In early 1986, one broker predicted: "It is safe to say that by Jan. 1, 1987 the world will be claims made." Krizan, *Insurers Tighten Policies Further,* 216 ENR 50 (Feb. 6, 1986). But market resistance to the anticipated claims-made policy prompted ISO to bill the 1986 claims-made and occurrence forms as co-equal alternatives before they were even implemented, and the status of the claims-made CGL form continued to decline. Teff, *Alarm from London,* ENR 20 (Fall 1985).

[81] 242 Minn. 354, 65 N.W.2d 122 (1954).

diminished the value of the building. The *Hauenstein* decision was widely followed.[82]

In response to such decisions, the 1966 revisions to the standard liability policy added the requirement that there be "injury or destruction to tangible property," probably on the theory that the diminution in value caused to a structure by incorporation of a defective product was an intangible loss.[83] The addition of the word "tangible" seems to have had little effect. The Nevada Supreme Court found that property damage existed under the 1966 language when the insured cement company incurred shoring expenses to strengthen a structure weakened by the insured's defective concrete.[84] The court relied on *Hauenstein* and its progeny without discussing the effect of the changed definition of property damage.

The 1973 revisions attempted to reverse the trend begun by *Hauenstein* by changing to the current definition of property damage. This change achieved the desired result in at least some states. In *Wyoming Sawmills v. Halis Transportation Insurance Co.*[85] the Supreme Court of Oregon distinguished the *Hauenstein* line of cases as decided before "property damage" was defined to require "*physical* injury to tangible property." The court stated, "[T]he inclusion of this word ['physical'] negates any possibility that the policy was intended to include 'consequential or intangible damage,' such as depreciation in value, within the term 'property damage.'"[86] Subsequently, in *Federated Mutual Insurance Co. v. Concrete Units, Inc.,* the Minnesota Supreme Court, the very court that had decided *Hauenstein,* rejected application of the *Hauenstein* rationale to the 1973 policy and held that "diminution in value" did not satisfy the 1973 definition of property damage.[87] In a later federal case involving primary policies containing the 1966 language and excess policies with the 1973 wording, the court cited *Hauenstein, Federated Mutual,* and *Wyoming Sawmills* and held that the primary policies covered diminution of value but the excess policies did not.[88]

---

[82] *See, e.g.,* Geddes & Smith, Inc. v. St. Paul-Mercury Indem. Co., 51 Cal. 2d 558, 344 P.2d 881 (1959); Dakota Block Co. v. Western Casualty & Sur. Co., 81 S.D. 213, 132 N.W.2d 826, 826–29, *reh'g denied* (1965).

[83] Bowers, *General Liability Insurance Coverage for Defective Materials and Workmanship, in* Construction Litigation 181 (B.C. Hart ed., 1979).

[84] United States Fid. & Guar. v. Nevada Cement Co., 93 Nev. 179, 561 P.2d 1335, 1337–38 (1977).

[85] 282 Or. 401, 578 P.2d 1253, 1256 (1978); *see also* St. Paul Fire & Marine Ins. Co. v. Coss, 80 Cal. App. 3d 888, 892–93, 145 Cal. Rptr. 836 (1978).

[86] Wyoming Sawmills v. Halis, 578 P.2d 1253, 1256.

[87] 363 N.W.2d 751, 756–57 (Minn. 1985).

[88] Hartford Accident & Indem. Co. v. Pacific Mut. Life Ins. Co., 861 F.2d 250, 253–54 (10th Cir. 1988).

Other cases construing the 1973 policy language, such as the California *Economy Lumber* case,[89] have continued to follow *Hauenstein* and its progeny, holding that there is coverage for subcontractors who perform defective component work or for suppliers of defective components if the component work or the components reduce the value of the entire structure. However, a recent federal decision sharply criticized *Economy Lumber* and refused to apply it as reflective of California law.[90] Noting that *Economy Lumber* had involved the 1973 property damage definition but that the court simply followed *Hauenstein* and ignored the revisions in the 1966 wording, a Ninth Circuit panel concluded, "In light of the Minnesota Supreme Court's explicit repudiation of its previous holding in *Hauenstein* due to these modifications, it would be suspect to rely on *Economy Lumber* to support a more expansive interpretation of the [1973] property damage definition."[91] Thus, the federal court held that under California law diminution in value is not "property damage" as defined in the 1973 CGL form. In another recent case, a California court held that mere faulty work or installation of defective components is not property damage as defined by the 1973 policy form.[92]

The 1986 revision to the CGL policy makes no substantive change in the definition of property damage. Although the 1973 revisions, *Wyoming Sawmills,* and other cases would seem to end the diminution in value trick, the *Economy Lumber* decision indicates that this issue may survive the 1986 revision.[93]

---

[89] Economy Lumber Co. v. Insurance Co. of N. Am., 157 Cal. App. 3d 641, 203 Cal. Rptr. 135 (1984) (court quoted but did not discuss post-1973 property damage definition; court limited its discussion to whether there was an "occurrence" and whether various exclusions were applicable).

[90] New Hampshire Ins. Co. v. Vieira, 930 F.2d 696, 700 (9th Cir. 1991).

[91] *Id.* The *New Hampshire Insurance Co.* court recognized that the Ninth Circuit is normally bound by a California appellate decision construing California law, unless it is persuaded that the California Supreme Court would disagree with the court of appeal decision. Because the California Supreme Court had followed the Minnesota high court's *Hauenstein* decision regarding the 1966 property damage definition, the *New Hampshire Insurance Co.* panel believed that the California Supreme Court would also follow the Minnesota decision in *Federated Mutual* concerning the meaning of the 1973 language. 930 F.2d 696, 701.

[92] Maryland Casualty Co. v. Reeder, 221 Cal. App. 3d 961, 969–70, 270 Cal. Rptr. 719 (1990). Unfortunately, the decision is unclear on the distinction between the 1966 and the 1973 property damage definition. The case holds that the underlying claimants alleged damages within the policy language because the defective construction caused damage to the contents of the subject condominiums. *Id.* at 971. However, the opinion cites *Hauenstein* approvingly, and indicates that the court considered "property damage" to include harm to the contractor's own work caused by the faulty construction. *Id.* at 970.

[93] In the 1988 ISO policy form, the definition of property damage also addresses trigger of coverage. The 1988 definition states that loss of use of damaged tangible property "shall

§ 11.9 Exclusions

The standard comprehensive general liability (CGL) policy contains exclusions that narrow the scope of the insuring agreement. As the saying goes, "What the insuring agreement giveth, the exclusions taketh away." There are several purposes for the exclusions:

1. To avoid duplication of coverage typically provided in other liability insurance policies (for example, automobile, mobile equipment, watercraft, pollution, war risk, liquor liability, employer's liability, and worker's compensation)
2. To identify specific risk the contractor can buy back or modify for an additional premium (for example, contractually assumed liability; care, custody, and control; damage to the work performed on behalf of the insured; product recall; and explosion, collapse, or underground hazard)
3. To eliminate risks inherent in the contractor's business, which the contractor cannot buy back or modify for an additional premium (for example, delay in or lack or performance of the contract, and failure of products or work performed to meet the level warranted).

Endorsements are available to provide coverage for many of the exclusions identified in item 2. The most important endorsement for a contractor is the Broad Form Property Damage endorsement, which narrows the care, custody, and control and the damage to work exclusions. The version of this endorsement that includes completed operations is highly recommended for all contractors.[94]

This chapter does not deal with exclusions designed to avoid duplication of coverage available in other liability policies or with other limitations on coverage, such as the controversial issue of whether public policy prohibits

---

be deemed to occur at the time of the physical injury that caused it," and that "loss of use of tangible property that is not physically injured . . . shall be deemed to occur at the time of the 'occurrence' that caused it." Although this language indicates a clear intent to avoid stacking and limit coverage to one policy period, future insureds will no doubt argue otherwise, and the ultimate effect of this language will be decided in the courts.

[94] The Broad Form Property Damage (BFPD) (including completed operations) endorsement replaces and narrows exclusion (k), the care, custody, and control exclusion, and exclusion (o), the damage to work exclusion. During the course of construction, BFPD coverage generally narrows the application of these exclusions to the particular part of any property upon which operations are being performed by the insured or its subcontractors at the time of the property damage. After completion of operations, BFPD coverage generally narrows the application of exclusions (k) and (o) so that damage to work arising out of a subcontractor's work would be covered. *See* II General Liability Manual IV.B. 18–20 (International Risk Management Institute 1983).

coverage of punitive damages.[95] Instead, it focuses on the exclusions most troublesome for contractors.

§ 11.10 —Contractually Assumed Liability

Exclusion (a), the contractually assumed liability exclusion, of the 1973 CGL policy states:

> This insurance does not apply:
>
> (a) to liability assumed by the insured under any contract or agreement except an incidental contract; but this exclusion does not apply to a warranty of fitness or quality of the named insured's products or a warranty that work performed by or on behalf of the named insured will be done in a workmanlike manner . . . .

This exclusion is intended to emphasize the rule that liability insurance covers only tort liability for negligence, and does not cover liability in contract actions for breach of contractual promises.[96] The CGL insurer does not underwrite the insured's contractual undertakings.[97] The exception for the defined term "incidental contract" rarely will effect coverage for the contractor.

The classic example of an excluded contractually assumed liability is an indemnity agreement that requires the insured to indemnify another for losses not caused by the insured's own negligence. The rationale is that the insurer has accepted a premium in exchange for indemnifying the insured from the consequences of the insured's own negligence. The premium, which is set at the beginning of the policy, is not intended to cover risks later undertaken by the insured through indemnity agreements.

---

[95] This issue of coverage for punitive damages is discussed in Annotation, *Insurance Coverage—Punitive Damages,* 17 A.L.R.4th 11 (1982); Ghiardi & Kucher, *Insurance Against Punitive Damages, in* 1982 DRI Monograph No. 2. A list of cases addressing this issue appears in *Policy Terms, in* 1 The Attorney's Umbrella Book (P. Ligeros ed., 1991).

[96] The phrase "legally obligated to pay as damages" in the insuring agreement is held to refer to tort damages and not to liability for breach of contract. Home Indem. Co. v. Avol, 706 F. Supp. 728, 729–30 (C.D. Cal. 1989), *aff'd,* 912 F.2d 469 (9th Cir. 1990); Fireman's Fund Ins. Co. v. City of Turlock, 170 Cal. App. 3d 988, 998, 216 Cal. Rptr. 796 (1985); International Surplus Lines, Inc. v. Devonshire Coverage Corp., 93 Cal. App. 3d 601, 610–11, 155 Cal. Rptr. 654 (1979). Thus, purely contractual obligations are not covered by insurance policies, even without this exclusion.

[97] 12 Couch on Insurance 2d § 44A: 36 (1981); Haugan v. Home Indem. Co., 86 S.D. 406, 197 N.W.2d 18, 21–23 (1972).

The exclusion applies only when the liability is based solely upon contract.[98] Under the exception to the exclusion—"but this exclusion does not apply to a warranty of fitness or quality of the named insured's products or a warranty that work performed by or on behalf of the named insured will be done in a workmanlike manner"—this exclusion does not apply if the insured would be "legally obligated to pay" even absent any express contractual assumption of liability. The exception clarifies the fact that express warranties that simply reiterate warranties implied by law are not contractually assumed liabilities. Although liability for damage to the insured's work or products is excluded under other exclusions, the exception to the contractually assumed liability exclusion means that coverage for damage to other property resulting from a breach of the described warranties is not barred by this exclusion.[99]

For example, some indemnity and other contract provisions obligate the contractor to be responsible only for the contractor's own negligence. Such provisions do not add any obligation to the contractor's general duty to perform work with reasonable care. If a contractor negligently causes damage that also qualifies as a breach of such a provision, the contractually assumed liability exclusion will not preclude coverage. In *American Casualty Co. v. Timmons*[100] the contractor expressly agreed in its contract to be responsible for all damages that resulted from his fault or negligence. The court found that the contractually assumed liability exclusion did not exclude coverage, because the liability was imposed by law and the contractor "would have been liable for negligence even in the absence of contractual liability." The court commented that the very purpose of the insurance policy was to protect against liability for such negligence.[101] The test is whether that particular contract enlarged the obligations that would be imposed by law.[102]

---

[98] 12 Couch on Insurance 2d §§ 44A:37 to :38 (1981); Colonial Refrigerated Transp., Inc. v. Worsham, 705 F.2d 821, 827 (6th Cir. 1983).

[99] Oliver B. Cannon & Son, Inc. v. Fidelity & Casualty Co., 484 F. Supp. 1375, 1384 n.35 (D. Del. 1980):

> Exclusion (a) is obviously intended to exclude liability assumed under a contract but is not meant to exclude the types of liability subsumed under the category "products liability." This is the reason for the proviso to (a). This proviso is thus much broader than the exclusion[s] . . . which apply only to exclude the costs of replacing the insured's own defective products or parts of products.

[100] 352 F.2d 563, 568 (6th Cir. 1968).

[101] *Id.* at 568; *see also* Lumbermen's Mut. Casualty Co. v. Town of Pound Ridge, 362 F.2d 430, 434 (2d Cir. 1966); United States Fidelity & Guar. Co. v. Virginia Eng'g Co., 213 F.2d 109, 112 (4th Cir. 1954).

[102] Drechsler, *Scope and effect of clause in liability policy excluding from coverage liability assumed by insured under contract not defined in policy, such as one of indemnity,* 63 A.L.R.2d 1122, 1123 (1959).

The insurance industry anticipated and attempted to avoid court decisions that would use the exception to the contractually assumed liability exclusion to undercut the effectiveness of other exclusions, by finding a grant of coverage in an exception to an exclusion. The post-1966 language, "but this exclusion does not apply to," was intended to make clear that the exception affected only the exclusion in which it was contained. One well-respected commentator predicted in 1969 that "this unambiguous language avoids any inference that another exclusion may not apply."[103] Despite this prediction, the exception to the contractually assumed liability exclusion has spawned extensive litigation and a major split of opinion among various jurisdictions. The issue is whether the language is ambiguous and thus, although couched as an exception to an exclusion, can be read to create coverage for the insured's warranty-type obligations associated with the insured's defective products or faulty workmanship.

Other exclusions in the CGL policy exclude coverage for "property damage to the named insured's products arising out of such products or any part of such products" or "property damage to work performed by or on behalf of the named insured arising out of the work or any portion thereof, or out of materials, parts or equipment furnished in connection therewith." Courts in several jurisdictions have held that these exclusions do not apply if the liability of an insured is premised on the warranties described in the exception to the contractually assumed liability exclusion.[104] However, the vast majority of courts have enforced the policy language as written and held that the exception to the contractually assumed liability exclusion applies only to that exclusion and not to any others. These courts hold

[103] 3 R. Long, The Law of Liability Insurance app. 4, app. B, § 10 (1969).

[104] This view has been taken by courts in Arizona, Colorado, Missouri, New Hampshire and North Dakota. Federal Ins. Co. v. P.A.T. Homes, Inc., 113 Ariz. 135, 139, 547 P.2d 1050 (1976), *overruled in part by* State Farm Mut. Ins. Co. v. Wilson, 162 Ariz. 251, 782 P.2d 727 (1989); Worsham Constr. Co. v. Reliance Ins. Co., 687 P.2d 988 (Colo. Ct. App. 1984); McRaven v. F-Stop Photo Labs, Inc., 660 S.W.2d 459, 462 (Mo. Ct. App. 1983); Commercial Union Assurance Cos. v. Gollan, 118 N.H. 744, 748, 394 A.2d 839 (1978) (3–2 decision); Aid Ins. Servs., Inc. v. Geiger, 294 N.W.2d 411, 414 (N.D. 1980).

However, this interpretation is now subject to doubt in Arizona. The *Federal Insurance Co.* court based its holding on a determination that ambiguities are always to be resolved against the insurer. 547 P.2d 1050, 1053. The Arizona Supreme Court subsequently overruled *Federal Insurance Co.* regarding this rule of construction. State Farm Ins. Co. v. Wilson, 162 Ariz. 251, 782 P.2d 727 (1989). The court held that ambiguities must be resolved through a consideration of legislative goals, public policy, and the insurance transaction in its entirety, and that the contra proferentum rule should not be automatically applied. 782 P.2d at 734. This holding undercuts the rationale for the *Federal Insurance Co.* result. Thus, in recently rejecting the minority rule that the exception to this exclusion extends coverage, the Vermont Supreme Court mentioned the fact that the basis of the *Federal Insurance Co.* holding had been overturned. Peerless Ins. Co. v. Wells, 580 A.2d 485, 488 (Vt. 1990).

that claims based on the warranties described in this exception are subject to the other exclusions of the policy.[105] Such decisions have generally been based on the principle that exclusion clauses subtract from coverage rather

[105] This view has been adopted in almost 30 jurisdictions, including three that formerly took the minority position. The weight of recent judicial authority in this area heavily favors this majority position. Peerless Ins. Co. v. Wells, 580 A.2d 485, 488 (Vt. 1990); T.C. Bateson Constr. Co. v. Lumberman's Mut. Ins. Co., 784 S.W.2d 692, 699 (Tex. Ct. App.), *writ denied* (1989); Peerless Ins. Co. v. Brennon, 654 A.2d 383, 386–87 (Me. 1989), *overruling* Baybutt Constr. Co. v. Commercial Union Ins. Co., 455 A.2d 914 (Me. 1983); St. Paul Surplus Lines v. Diversified Athletic Servs., 707 F. Supp. 1506, 1510–11 (N.D. Ill. 1989) (applying Pennsylvania law); McCorkle v. Fireman's Ins. Co., 678 F. Supp. 562, 564 (W.D. Pa. 1988) (applying Pennsylvania law); Engineered Prods., Inc. v. Aetna Casualty & Sur. Co., 295 S.C. 375, 368 S.E.2d 674, 675–76 (1988); Gary L. Shaw Builders, Inc. v. State Auto. Mut. Ins. Co., 182 Ga. App. 220, 355 S.E.2d 130, 133 (1987); Taylor-McDonnell Constr. Co. v. Commercial Union Ins. Co., 229 Mont. 34, 744 P.2d 892, 894–95 (1987) (specifically approving the federal court's interpretation of Montana law in Stillwater Condominium Ass'n v. American Home Assurance Co., 508 F. Supp. 1075, 1079 (D. Mont. 1981), *aff'd,* 688 F.2d 848 (9th Cir. 1982), *cert. denied,* 460 U.S. 1038 (1983)); Vari Builders, Inc. v. USF&G, 523 A.2d 549 (Del. Super. Ct. 1986); Taylor-Morley-Simons, Inc. v. Michigan Mut. Ins. Co., 645 F. Supp. 596, 601 (E.D. Mo. 1986), *aff'd,* 822 F.2d 1093 (8th Cir. 1987) (applying Missouri law, but expressly rejecting the minority rule holding of McRaven v. F-Stop Photo Labs, 660 S.W.2d 459 (Mo. Ct. App. 1983), on the grounds that McRaven was poorly reasoned and contradicted Transport Indem. Co. v. Teter, 575 S.W.2d 780, 784 (Mo. Ct. App. 1978), an earlier Missouri appellate case holding that exceptions to exclusions do not create coverage); Owings v. Western Casualty & Sur. Co., 237 Kan. 89, 697 P.2d 865, 869–70 (1985); Bulen v. West Bend Mut. Ins. Co., 125 Wis. 259, 371 N.W.2d 392, 393–94 (1985); Century I Joint Venture v. USF&G, 63 Md. App. 545, 493 A.2d 370, 377–78, *cert. denied,* 304 Md. 297, 488 A.2d 1183 (1985); Bond Bros., Inc. v. Robinson, 393 Mass. 546, 471 N.E.2d 1332, 1334–36 (1984); Qualls v. Country Mut. Ins. Co., 123 Ill. App. 3d 831, 834, 78 Ill. Dec. 934, 462 N.E.2d 1288, 1291 (1984); Sturla, Inc. v. Fireman's Fund Ins. Co., 67 Haw. 203, 684 P.2d 960, 964 (1984); Turner v. USF&G, 440 So. 2d 1026, 1028 (Ala. Civ. App. 1983); Fresand v. Michigan Millers Mut. Ins. Co., 414 Mich. 686, 327 N.W.2d 286, 290, *aff'g but overruling as to this issue* 97 Mich. App. 584, 590, 296 N.W.2d 112 (1982); Helfeldt v. Robinson, 20 S.E.2d 896, 901 (W. Va. 1981); Nationwide Mut. Ins. Co. v. Wenger, 222 Va. 263, 267, 278 S.E.2d 874, 876 (1981); Zanii Constr. Co. v. Fireman's Ins. Co., 81 A.D.2d 106, 109, 440 N.Y.S.2d 353, *aff'd,* 54 N.Y.2d 999, 430 N.E.2d 922, 446 N.Y.S.2d 45 (1981); Indiana Ins. Co. v. DeZutti, 408 N.E.2d 1275, 1278–79 (Ind. 1980); LaMarche v. Shelby Mut. Ins. Co., 390 So. 2d 325, 326–27 (Fla. 1980) (disapproving Fontainebleau Hotel Corp. v. United Filigree Corp., 298 So. 2d 455 (Fla. Dist. Ct. App. 1974)); Vernon Williams & Sons Constr., Inc. v. Continental Ins. Co., 591 S.W.2d 760, 763–65 (Tenn. 1979); United States Fire Ins. Co. v. Colver, 600 P.2d 1, 3–4 (Alaska 1979); Weedo v. Stone-E-Brick, Inc., 81 N.J. 233, 247, 405 A.2d 788, 795–96 (1979); St. Paul Fire & Marine v. Coss, 80 Cal. App. 3d 888, 896, 145 Cal. Rptr. 836 (1978); Biebel Bros. v. USF&G, 522 F.2d 1207, 1212 (8th Cir. 1975) (applying Missouri law); Haugan v. Home Indem. Ins. Co., 86 S.D. 406, 413, 197 N.W.2d 18, 22 (1972).

Ironically, the Florida appellate court decision that first held that the exception granted coverage and became a direct or indirect basis for all the other minority view decisions, was subsequently overruled by the Florida Supreme Court.

than extend it,[106] and that claims coming within an exception to an exclusion remain subject to all other policy exclusions.[107]

Contractual liability insurance can be obtained by paying an additional premium. In the insurance context, "contractual liability" refers only to the assumption of another party's tort liability for negligence. Contractual liability insurance does not provide coverage for an insured's breach of its own contractual obligations.[108]

The 1986 ISO CGL form substantially changes standard coverage for contractually assumed liability. It attempts to eliminate the exception to the exclusion problem, as one court had suggested,[109] by defining contractual liability in the definitions section and removing the exception from the text of the exclusion. The definition of *insured contract* includes contracts pertaining to the insured's business under which the insured assumes the tort liability of another. This change has the effect of narrowing the applicability of the contractually assumed liability exclusion. Business-related contracts assuming the tort liability of another constitute a much broader exception to the exclusion than the warranty exception used in the current CGL policy.

The 1986 form specifically states that the exclusion does not apply to liability that the insured would have in the absence of the contract. This is consistent with judicial decisions interpreting the current CGL policy.[110]

§ 11.11 —Care, Custody, or Control

Exclusion (k), the care, custody, or control exclusion, of the 1973 CGL policy states:

> This insurance does not apply:
>
> (k) to property damage to
>
> (1) property owned or occupied by or rented to the insured,
>
> (2) property used by the insured, or

---

[106] *See, e.g.,* Weedo v. Stone-E-Brick, Inc., 81 N.J. 233, 405 A.2d 788, 795 (1979).

[107] *See, e.g.,* St. Paul Fire & Marine Ins. Co. v. Coss, 80 Cal. App. 3d 888, 896, 145 Cal. Rptr. 836 (1978).

[108] See § **11.8**.

[109] Oliver B. Cannon & Sons, Inc. v. Fidelity & Casualty Co., 482 F. Supp. 1375, 1384 n.35 (D. Del. 1980).

[110] See § **11.8**. In the 1988 ISO CGL form, subpart (1) specifies that the exclusion does not apply to liability for damages "[a]ssumed in a contract or agreement that is an 'insured contract,' *provided the 'bodily injury' or 'property damage' occurs subsequent to the execution of the contract or agreement*" (emphasis added). II General Liability Manual V.A.2—V.A.5 (International Risk Management Institute 1983).

> (3) property in the care, custody or control of the insured or as to which the insured is for any purpose exercising physical control;
>
> but parts (2) and (3) of this exclusion do not apply with respect to liability under a written sidetrack agreement and part (3) of this exclusion does not apply with respect to property damage (other than to elevators) arising out of the use of an elevator at premises owned by, rented to or controlled by the named insured . . . .

This exclusion substantially narrows the coverage under the CGL policy for occurrences during the course of construction. It typically eliminates coverage for damage to any property owned, occupied, or rented by the insured or under the care, custody, or control of the insured.[111] It avoids potential overlap between coverage under the standard CGL policy and the builder's risk policy.[112]

By contractual agreement, general contractors assume control of an entire project. Subcontractors do not assume that degree of responsibility and are not afforded that degree of control.[113] The difference between their roles is crucial to the interpretation of this exclusion: courts enforce the exclusion very broadly against general contractors and very narrowly against subcontractors. Because the general contractor normally has the contractual duty to supervise the entire job and to protect the property during construction, most courts have held that the entire project is in the general contractor's "care, custody, or control" for the purposes of this exclusion, and that general contractors are not covered for damage resulting from their own work or that of a subcontractor.[114]

---

[111] *See generally* Annotation, *Scope of Clause Excluding from Contractor's or Similar Liability Policy Damage to Property in Care, Custody, or Control of Insured,* 8 A.L.R.4th 563 (1979); 12 Couch on Insurance 2d §§ 44A:13–44A:22 (rev. vol. 1984); 1A R. Long, The Law of Liability Insurance § 10.09 (1991).

[112] Hart, *The Comprehensive General Liability Insurer: Claims By and Against, in* Construction Contract Claims 394, 399 (B.C. Hart ed., ABA 1978); Estrin Constr. Co. v. Aetna Casualty & Sur. Co., 612 S.W.2d 413, 425–27 (Mo. Ct. App. 1981). *See* North Am. Iron & Steel Co. v. Isaacson Steel Erectors, Inc., 36 A.D.2d 770, 321 N.Y.S.2d 254, 256 (1971), *aff'd mem.,* 30 N.Y.2d 640, 282 N.E.2d 621, 331 N.Y.S.2d 667 (1972) (general contractor bought builder's risk policy). See also §§ **11.18–11.25**.

[113] This discussion treats all contractors either as general contractors, who have general responsibility for and control over an entire project, or as subcontractors, who have limited responsibility for an aspect of a project. For coverage purposes, a prime contractor on a project with multiple primes would be analogous to a subcontractor.

[114] L.L. Jarrell Constr. Co. v. Columbia Casualty Co., 130 F. Supp. 436, 437 (S.D. Ala. 1955) (quoting provisions of the contract specifications). *See* Hartford Accident & Indem. Co. v. Shelby Mut. Ins. Co., 208 So. 2d 465, 467–68 (Fla. Dist. Ct. App. 1968) (interpreting general conditions and specifications of the contract); Bor-Son Bldg. Corp. v. Employees Commercial Union Ins. Co., 323 N.W.2d 58 (Minn. 1982) (contractor's control determined by reference to contract documents); Estrin Constr. Co. v. Aetna Casualty & Sur. Co., 612 S.W.2d 413, 427 (Mo. Ct. App. 1981); Maryland Casualty Co. v. Farmers

A few courts have found coverage for the general contractor on the theory that it did not have control over work performed by a subcontractor. In one case, when the general contractor hired a crane operator, the court ruled that damage caused by the crane was not excluded because it had remained under the subcontractor's control.[115] In a similar vein, a lone commentator has argued that the general contractor "regains custody and control over the property within the meaning of the exclusion clause [only] after the termination of the work by the subcontractor."[116] However, in the 33 years since this annotation appeared, only one published decision (by a Pennsylvania lower court) has cited it to support a holding that the general contractor relinquished care, custody, and control over work performed by subcontractors.[117]

The care, custody, or control exclusion in the 1973 policy form could be narrowed by the Broad Form Comprehensive General Liability (BFCGL) Endorsement for an additional premium.[118] This endorsement to exclusion

---

Alliance Mut. Ins. Co., 566 P.2d 168, 170 (Okla. Ct. App. 1977); McCord, Conderon & McDonald, Inc. v. Twin City Fire Ins. Co., 607 S.W.2d 956, 958 (Tex. Ct. App. 1980) (general contractor in possession until contract completed).

[115] Dubay v. Trans-America Ins. Co., 75 A.D.2d 312, 429 N.Y.S.2d 449, 452–53 (1980).

[116] Annotation, *Scope of Clause Excluding Contractor's or Similar Liability Policy Damage to Property in Care, Custody or Control of Insured,* 62 A.L.R.2d 1242, 1254 (1958), superseded by article of the same title, 8 A.L.R.4th 563 (1981). This comment was based solely on a misreading of L.L. Jarrell Constr. Co. v. Columbia Casualty Co., 130 F. Supp. 436 (S.D. Ala. 1955). In *Jarrell* the court held that exclusion (k) precluded coverage for damage caused by the general contractor's employee, because the project remained under the general contractor's care, custody, or control. *Id.* at 438. The court based this conclusion on three factors: (1) the contract documents specified that all work was under the general contractor's "custody . . . charge and care," (2) the general contractor had a watchman at the jobsite at all times, and (3) the subcontractor had finished most of its work at the time of the accident." *Id.* at 437–38. Although the 1958 annotation mentioned each of these factors (62 A.L.R.2d 1242, 1254), it implicitly reached the unwarranted conclusion that the *Jarrell* court would have disregarded the first two factors and held that the general contractor had relinquished control, if the accident had occurred before the subcontractor completed its work. The 1981 annotation gives a fuller explanation of the three factors underlying the *Jarrell* court's ruling, and does not repeat the inference that the general contractor had yielded control while the subcontractor performed its work. 8 A.L.R.4th 563, 630.

[117] Slate Constr. Co. v. Bituminous Casualty Corp., 228 Pa. Super. 1, 323 A.2d 141, 145 (1973). After citing this annotation, the *Slate* court held that application of exclusion (k) was "not free from doubt" when the general contractor's employee damaged portions of a bridge on which a subcontractor was working. *Id.* Given this "doubt," the court found coverage under the contra proferentem doctrine. *Id.* at 145–46.

[118] Hart, *The Comprehensive General Liability Insurer: Claims By and Against,* in B.C. Hart, Construction Contract Claims, 394, 399 (ABA 1978); *see* Estrin Constr. Co. v. Aetna Casualty & Sur. Co., 612 S.W.2d 413, 425 (Mo. Ct. App. 1981). Another method of extending coverage, particularly to subcontractors, is to obtain a wrap-up policy endorsed to provide coverage "as if separate policies had been issued to each insured." Continental Casualty Co. v. Gilborne Bldg. Co., 391 Mass. 143, 461 N.E.2d 209 (1984).

(k) replaces the care, custody, or control and the insured's work exclusions so that only the following is excluded:

> (1) . . . property owned or occupied by or rented to the insured, or, except with respect to the use of elevators, to property held by the insured for sale or entrusted to the insured for storage or safekeeping;
>
> (2) except with respect to liability under a written sidetrack agreement or the use of elevators
>
> (a) . . . property while on premises owned by or rented to the insured for the purpose of having operations performed on such property by or on behalf of the insured,
>
> (b) . . . tools or equipment while being used by the insured in performing his operations,
>
> (c) . . . property in the custody of the insured which is to be installed, erected or used in construction by the insured,
>
> (d) . . . that particular part of any property, not on premises owned by or rented to the insured,
>
> (i) upon which operations are being performed by or on behalf of the insured at the time of the property damage arising out of such operations, or
>
> (ii) out of which any property damage arises, or
>
> (iii) the restoration, repair or replacement of which has been made or is necessary by reason of faulty workmanship thereon by or on behalf of the insured;
>
> (3) with respect to the completed operations hazard and with respect to any classification stated in the policy or in the company's manual as "including completed operations," . . . property damage to work performed by the named insured arising out of such work or any portion thereof, or out of such materials, parts or equipment, furnished in connection therewith.

Without the BFCGL Endorsement, exclusion (k) denies the general contractor completed operations coverage for damage arising from its own work or that of its subcontractors. The Endorsement narrows that coverage restriction so that, although the general contractor is not covered for damage caused by its work, it is covered for damage caused by its subcontractor's performance.[119]

The availability of the BFCGL Endorsement may support an insurer's argument that the care, custody, and control exclusion should be strictly applied when the Endorsement is not included in a particular policy. In *Estrin Construction Co. v. Aetna Insurance Co.* the court enforced the exclusion and found no duty to indemnify or defend.[120] In reviewing the

---

[119] *See* Mid-United Contractors, Inc. v. Providence Lloyd's Ins. Co., 754 S.W.2d 824 (Tex. Ct. App. 1988). *See also* discussion of the insured's work exclusion in **§ 11.14**.

[120] 612 S.W.2d 413, 429 (Mo. Ct. App. 1981).

terms of the exclusion and the general contractor's relative sophistication in insurance matters, the court noted that the contractor had not opted to obtain the available broad form property damage endorsement.[121]

In contrast to general contractors, subcontractors regularly avoid this exclusion, under a number of theories.[122] For instance, the courts enforce it against subcontractors only when the damaged property was under the supervision of the subcontractor and it was a necessary element of the subcontractor's work.[123] In one case a New Jersey court applied the exclusion to a boiler explosion because the insured was responsible for completely dismantling and refurbishing the boiler.[124] In another a Connecticut court barred a tile installer from coverage for damage arising from improper use of acid to remove grout from the face of tiles.[125]

Subcontractors have successfully narrowed the application of this exclusion with a variety of arguments:

1. Injury to items that are "merely incidental" to the subcontractor's work is not excluded[126]
2. Damage arising out of the subcontractor's access to its work area may not be excluded[127]
3. Diminution in the overall value of realty resulting from the subcontractor's work on a portion of the realty may not be excluded[128]

---

[121] *Id.* at 425–26.

[122] *See generally* Elcar Mobil Home, Inc. v. D.K. Baxter, Inc., 66 N.J. Super. 478, 169 A.2d 509 (1961); 12 Couch on Insurance 2d §§ 44A:15–44A:22 (rev. vol. 1984).

[123] *See* Herbison v. Employers Ins. Co., 593 S.W.2d 923 (Tenn. Ct. App. 1979) (painter has care of sprinkler heads in ceiling that was painted); *but compare* Haerens v. Commercial Casualty Ins. Co., 30 Cal. App. 2d Supp. 892, 279 P.2d 211 (1955) (windowpanes not in care of subcontractor painting metal framing between panes). *See also* Hartford Accident & Indem. Co. v. Shelby Mut. Ins. Co., 208 So. 2d 465, 469 (Fla. Dist. Ct. App. 1968) (subcontractor had joint control under contract).

[124] Condenser Serv. & Eng'g Co. v. American Mut. Liab. Ins. Co., 58 N.J. Super. 179, 155 A.2d 789 (1959); *see* H.E. Wiese, Inc. v. Western Stress, Inc., 407 So. 2d 464, 466 (La. Ct. App. 1981) (stress relief contractor had control of boiler tube sheet).

[125] Ceramic Tiles, Inc. v. Aetna Casualty & Sur. Co., 39 Conn. Supp. 477, 466 A.2d 348 (1983).

[126] Royal Indem. Co. v. T.B. Smith, 121 Ga. App. 272, 173 S.E.2d 738, 739–40 (1970) (damage to boom tank because of repositioning was merely incidental to sandblasting); Thomas W. Hooley & Sons v. Zurich Gen. Accident & Liab. Ins. Co., 235 La. 289, 103 So. 2d 449, 450–51 (1958) (ornamental urn at base of statute); Meiser v. Aetna Casualty & Sur. Co., 8 Wis. 2d 233, 98 N.W.2d 919, 923 (1959) (damage to windows by plastering subcontractor during cleanup was merely incidental).

[127] McCreary Roofing Co., Inc. v. Northern Ins. Co., 218 Pa. Super. 193, 275 A.2d 388, 389 (1971) (roofing installation).

[128] Petrol Indus., Inc. v. Gearhart-Owen Indus., Inc., 424 So. 2d 1059, 1064 (La. Ct. App. 1982) (oil well).

4. Injury to items over which the subcontractor shares control with the general contractor is not excluded in some states[129]
5. Injury to items to which the subcontractor is given "temporary or limited access" is not excluded in some states[130]
6. Injury to realty not in the overall control of the subcontractor usually is not excluded.[131]

These cases have produced substantial inconsistencies among courts of different states and even among courts of a single state at different times. As a result, practically indistinguishable situations have produced diametrically opposed results.[132]

---

[129] Home Indem. Co. v. Leo L. Davis, Inc., 79 Cal. App. 3d 863, 872, 145 Cal. Rptr. 158 (1978) (crane operator could not see object being lifted); Dubay v. Trans-America Ins. Co., 74 A.D.2d 312, 429 N.Y.S.2d 449, 453 (1980) (general contractor did not have exclusive control); General Mut. Ins. Co. v. Wright, 7 Misc. 2d 331, 161 N.Y.S.2d 974, 976 (Sup. Ct. 1957) (steel erector did not have custody or control of steel supplied by general contractor); *see* Bor-Son Bldg. Corp. v. Employees Commercial Union Ins. Co., 323 N.W.2d 58 n.9 (Minn. 1982) (mentioning, but not applying, exclusive care and control test); Applegren v. Milbank Mut. Ins. Co., 268 N.W.2d 114, 118 (N.D. 1978) (duty to defend based on allegations in complaint); McCreary Roofing Co. v. Northern Ins. Co., 218 Pa. Super. 193, 275 A.2d 388, 389 (1971) (concurring opinion).

[130] Boston Ins. Co. v. Grable, 352 F.2d 368 (5th Cir. 1965) (Georgia law) (subcontractor's workers were only occupants of house when fire started, but did not have control). *See* Bigelow-Liptak Corp. v. Continental Ins. Co., 417 F. Supp. 1276, 1286–87 (E.D. Mich. 1976) (boiler lining repair contractor); Baldwin v. Auto-Owners Ins. Co., 5 Ill. App. 3d 300, 282 N.E.2d 204, 206 (1972) (tenant did not have custody of building during construction of improvements by landlord); Krichner v. Hartford Accident & Indem. Co., 440 S.W.2d 751, 756–57 (Mo. Ct. App. 1969) (swimming pool repair contractor did not have access to pool during night when groundwater pressure raised bottom of pool).

[131] Bigelow-Liptak Corp. v. Continental Ins. Co., 417 F. Supp. 1276, 1286–87 (E.D. Mich. 1976) (boiler lining repair contractor); Leiter Elec. Co. v. Bituminous Casualty Corp., 99 Ill. App. 2d 386, 241 N.E.2d 325 (1968) (welding contractor who attached cables linking pipe sections); Klapper v. Hanover Ins. Co., 39 Misc. 2d 215, 240 N.Y.S.2d 284 (1963) (window washer).

[132] 1A R. Long, The Law of Liability Insurance § 10.09, at 10-50 to 10-57 (1991). *See* Bigelow-Liptak Corp. v. Continental Ins. Co., 417 F. Supp. 1276, 1288 (E.D. Mich. 1976) (genuine split of authority); Estrin Constr. Co. v. Aetna Casualty & Sur. Co., 612 S.W.2d 413, 417–18 (Mo. Ct. App. 1981) (harmonizing local cases). *Compare* General Mut. Ins. Co. v. Wright, 7 Misc. 2d 331, 161 N.Y.S.2d 974 (Sup. Ct. 1957) (steel erection contractor did not have control over work) *with* North Am. Iron & Steel Co. v. Isaacson Steel Erectors, Inc., 35 A.D.2d 770, 321 N.Y.S.2d 254, 256 (1971), *aff'd mem.*, 30 N.Y.2d 640, 282 N.E.2d 621, 331 N.Y.S.2d 667 (1972) (steel erection contractor had control of beams that collapsed). *Compare* McLouth Steel Corp. v. Mesta Mach. Co., 214 F.2d 608 (3d Cir. 1954) (Illinois law; machine installation contractor did not have control over machine it was installing) *with* International Derrick & Equip. Co. v. Buxbaum, 240 F.2d 536, 538–39 (3d Cir. 1956) (Pennsylvania law) (criticizing *McLouth;* antenna mast erector had control over mast). *Compare* Glen Falls Ins. Co. v. Fields, 181 So. 2d 187, 189 (Fla. Dist. Ct. App. 1965) (crane operator did not have control over silo it was moving) *with* Phoenix

The ISO 1986 revision changes the language of the exclusion substantially. Exclusion (j) would specifically limit the care, custody, and control exclusion to personal property. The purpose of the change generally is to incorporate the coverage of the current broad form property damage endorsement into the coverage of the standard policy. The new exclusion applies only to the particular work on which either the contractor or its subcontractor was performing operations.

§ 11.12 —Premises Alienated

Exclusion (*l*) of the 1973 CGL policy states:

> This insurance does not apply:
>
> (1) to property damage to premises alienated by the named insured arising out of such premises or any part thereof.

The application of this exclusion in a construction setting generally is limited to owners and developers that have sold real property with structures and other improvements that cause property damage. Since the typical construction contractor does not own and later sell the real property on which the construction work is performed, this exclusion ordinarily does not affect the coverage provided to a contractor. However, it would arguably affect contractor-developers that perform turnkey construction or build on speculation. Although the exclusion was not meant to apply when the insured contractor-developer builds a self-owned project for sale, the 1973 language does not state this intent clearly.[133] Thus, it is possible to interpret this provision as excluding coverage for builder-developers.[134]

The 1986 ISO form includes the alienated premises exclusion with the care, custody, or control exclusion (j). The 1986 form also clarifies the intent to cover the work of builder-developers.

---

of Hartford v. Holloway Corp., 268 So. 2d 195, 199 (Fla. Dist. Ct. App. 1972) (crane operator had physical control over reactor head it was moving). *Compare* Hendrix Elec. Co. v. Casualty Reciprocal Exch., 297 So. 2d 470 (La. Ct. App. 1974) (electrical contractor had only temporary access to fuse box) *with* Visant Elec. Contractors v. Aetna Casualty & Sur. Co., 530 S.W.2d 76 (Tenn. 1975) (electrical contractor had control of switchboard in which it attempted to install circuit breakers). *Compare* Goldberry Operating Co. v. Cassity, Inc., 367 So. 2d 133, 135 (La. Ct. App. 1979) (oil well contractor hired to perforate lower section of oil well had control over entire well) *with* Petrol Indus., Inc. v. Gearhart-Owen Indus., Inc., 424 So. 2d 1059, 1964 (La. Ct. App. 1982) (oil well contractor hired to patch middle section of well did not have control over entire well; opinion did not cite *Goldberry*).

[133] II General Liability Manual II.C.11 (International Risk Management Institute 1983).

[134] This is the position stated in the Fire Casualty & Surety Bulletin Ba-9, Ba-10 (National Underwriters Ass'n 1982). *See* Maryland Casualty Co. v. Reeder, 221 Cal. App. 3d 961, 976–77, 270 Cal. Rptr. 719, *review denied* (1990).

In a recent case dealing with the 1973 language, the court accepted the insured developer's argument that the 1986 revisions were meant to clarify rather than change the earlier version of the exclusion, and held that the 1973 wording was not intended to exclude coverage for builder-developers.[135] The court expressly based this finding on the fact that the insured had paid for broad form CGL coverage, implying that coverage would have been denied under the 1973 alienated premises exclusion without the broad form endorsement.[136]

§ 11.13 —Performance or Business Risk

Exclusion (m), the performance or business risk exclusion, of the 1973 CGL policy states:

> This insurance does not apply:
>
> (m) to loss of use of tangible property which has not been physically injured or destroyed resulting from
>
> (1) a delay in or lack of performance by or on behalf of the named insured of any contract or agreement, or
>
> (2) the failure of the named insured's products or work performed by or on behalf of the named insured to meet the level of performance, quality, fitness or durability warranted or represented by the named insured;
>
> but this exclusion does not apply to loss of use of other tangible property resulting from the sudden and accidental physical injury to or destruction of the named insured's products or work performed by or on behalf of the named insured after such products or work have been put to use by any person or organization other than an insured . . . .

This exclusion thus precludes coverage for loss of use claims resulting from the insured's delay, nonperformance, or faulty performance, or from certain defects in the insured's products.[137] For example, subsection (1) would exclude coverage for the owner's delayed occupancy of a building caused by the insured contractor's performance delays, and subsection (2)

---

[135] Maryland Casualty Co. v. Reeder, 221 Cal. App. 3d 961, 978, 270 Cal. Rptr. 719, *review denied* (1990).

[136] *Id.*

[137] Given this purpose, the performance exclusion is also called the business risk exclusion. However, exclusions (n) and (o), discussed in **§ 11.14**, are sometimes also referred to as business risk exclusions. *See, e.g.,* Gary L. Shaw Builders, Inc. v. State Auto. Mut. Ins. Co., 182 Ga. App. 220, 355 S.E.2d 130 (1987); Century I Joint Venture v. USF&G, 63 Md. App. 545, 493 A.2d 370, 374 (1985). To avoid confusion, this section refers to exclusion (m) as the performance exclusion.

would exclude coverage for delayed occupancy due to the insured's defective performance or use of defective products.[138] The performance exclusion in the 1966 and 1973 policies is essential to exclude coverage for such risks, because the 1966 revisions broadened the definition of property damage to include loss of use of tangible property caused by an occurrence, and occurrence was redefined to eliminate the element of suddenness.[139] Under the 1973 wording, this exclusion applies only to limit coverage for claims for loss of use of tangible property not physically injured or destroyed; it does not limit coverage for third-party property damage claims arising from an occurrence.[140]

The exception to this exclusion is intended to be narrow. It is meant to reintroduce the requirement that the property damage be "sudden and accidental," which otherwise would have been eliminated in the 1966 revisions, when the term "accident" was replaced with the term "occurrence" in the insuring agreement, and *occurrence* was defined to include "continuous and repeated exposure to conditions." However, several courts have broadened the exception to the exclusion beyond its intended meaning. In one case, the court held that re-work costs and delay damages resulting from defective concrete that had failed to harden properly and had to be replaced were caused by "sudden and accidental" physical injury to the concrete.[141] Other decisions have concluded that this "sudden and accidental" exception is meant to distinguish "between a physical breakdown of the insured's product and a mere failure of the product to perform as well as warranted," and that the former event remains covered but the latter is excluded as an uninsurable business risk.[142] This conclusion ignores the distinction between a *sudden* physical breakdown of the insured's product and gradual deterioration of that product. The latter event is properly excluded under this language.[143]

---

[138] Meng v. Bituminous Casualty Corp., 626 F. Supp. 1237, 1239 (S.D. Miss. 1986).

[139] Tinker, *Comprehensive General Liability Insurance—Perspective and Overview,* FIC Q. 217, 279 (Spring 1975).

[140] The 1973 revisions narrowed the scope of the exclusion, reduced the complexity of the wording, and eliminated an "active malfunctioning" exception that had proved difficult to apply to specific fact situations. Hart, *The Comprehensive General Liability Insurer: Claims By and Against, in* B.C. Hart, Construction Contract Claims 404–05 (ABA 1978).

[141] Federated Mut. Ins. Co. v. Concrete Units, 363 N.W.2d 75 (Minn. 1985). The court did not explain its reasoning, but it is difficult to imagine that the process of concrete's drying could be considered "sudden." But see **§ 11.2**.

[142] Honeycomb Sys., Inc. v. Admiral Ins. Co., 567 F. Supp. 1400, 1407 (D. Me. 1983); Sterilite Corp. v. Continental Casualty Co., 17 Mass. App. Ct. 316, 458 N.E.2d 338 (1983).

[143] The court's reliance on this misguided distinction in *Honeycomb v. Admiral* was perhaps unimportant given the facts of the case. There, the relevant damages resulted when a paper machine built by the insured suddenly cracked. 567 F. Supp. 1400, 1402.

The 1986 ISO revision, although worded differently, makes no substantive changes in exclusion (m) as modified by the broad form endorsement.

§ 11.14 —Damage to Insured's Product or Work

The 1973 CGL policy contains two similar exclusions, (n) and (o), that are intended to exclude coverage for damage to the insured's own products or damage to the insured's own work that arises out of such product or such work. The exclusions state:

> This insurance does not apply:
>
> (n) to property damage to the named insured's products arising out of such products or any part of such products;
>
> (o) to property damage to work performed by or on behalf of the named insured arising out of the work or any portion thereof, or out of materials, parts or equipment furnished in connection therewith . . . .

Because contractors usually provide services and not products, they are generally concerned primarily with the insured's work exclusion. However, the two exclusions are so similar that there is considerable crossover in court decisions interpreting these exclusions.[144]

The work and product exclusions are the heart and soul of the insurance industry's intent to avoid assuming the insured's business risks in the CGL

However, in *Sterilite v. Continental Casualty* there was only bare mention of physical breakdown of the insured's product, and no hint that any such breakdown occurred suddenly. 458 N.E.2d 338, 343. By ignoring the "sudden and accidental" requirement in the exception, the *Sterilite* court found coverage for a warranty-type claim within the intended meaning of this exclusion.

The *Honeycomb* court also stated, without deciding, that "[s]everal courts have held this exclusion inapplicable where the insured's product had been incorporated into another structure." 567 F. Supp. at 1407 (citing International Hormones, Inc. v. Safeco, Inc., 57 A.D.2d 857, 394 N.Y.S.2d 260 (1977)). This holding in *International Hormones* was based on that court's misreading of Sturges Mfg. Co. v. Utica Mut. Ins. Co., 37 N.Y.2d 69, 332 N.E.2d 319, 371 N.Y.S.2d 444 (1975). In *Sturges* the court determined that the insured's product exclusion did not apply because the insured's component had been incorporated into a larger product. *Id.* at 72–73, 332 N.E.2d at 322. The court then ruled that the 1966 performance exclusion was ambiguous and therefore did not bar coverage. *Id.* at 73–74, 332 N.E.2d at 322, 323. The *International Hormones* court confused these distinct rulings in *Sturges* and held that incorporation of the insured's product into another product vitiated the performance exclusion. 394 N.Y.S.2d 260, 261. Furthermore, both *Sturges* and *International Hormones* addressed the 1966 policy wording. The *Honeycomb* court compounded the mistaken holding in *International Hormones* by hinting that that ruling might apply to the 1973 wording of the performance exclusion.

[144] There is a discussion of the distinction between these exclusions in Maryland Casualty Co. v. Reeder, 221 Cal. App. 3d 961, 270 Cal. Rptr. 719, *review denied* (1990).

policy. These exclusions are designed to exclude the insured's warranty-type obligations to repair or replace its own defective work or defective products.[145]

The intent of these exclusions was illustrated in an early decision that stated:

> [I]f a contractor builds a house and as a result of an improper mixture of the stucco, water is absorbed into the walls and the stucco cracks and falls off and a child is injured by the falling stucco, the injury to the child would not be excluded . . . but the replacement cost of the stucco would be excluded. Also, if the water absorbed into the walls should reach the interior walls and injure a valuable painting hanging there the damage to the painting would be recoverable under the policy while the damage to the walls would not.[146]

The pre-1966 standard work product exclusion language excluded injury to products or "work completed by or for the named insured, out of which the accident arises."[147] Some courts held that this language excluded coverage only for the cost of repairing or replacing the component part that failed.[148] The 1966 revisions added the language, "or any part of such products" and "or any portion thereof," to clarify the insurance industry's intent that even nondefective portions of the insured's work product were excluded if they were damaged by defective components of the insured's work product. Two subsequent cases concluded that courts interpreting the post-1966 policy language had "consistently held that this

---

[145] Fresno Economy Import Used Cars, Inc. v. USF&G, 76 Cal. App. 3d 272, 284, 142 Cal. Rptr. 681 (1977); Geddes & Smith, Inc. v. St. Paul Mercury Indem. Co., 63 Cal. 2d 602, 604, 47 Cal. Rptr. 564, 407 P.2d 868 (1965); Geddes & Smith, Inc. v. St. Paul Mercury Indem. Co., 51 Cal. 2d 558, 566, 334 P.2d 881 (1959).

[146] Liberty Bldg. Co. v. Royal Indem. Co., 177 Cal. App. 2d 583, 587, 2 Cal. Rptr. 329 (1960). *See also* Volf v. Ocean Accident & Guar. Corp., 50 Cal. 2d 373, 376, 325 P.2d 987 (1958):

> This exclusion means that the policy will not protect the insured if he has to repair or replace some product or work which proved defective and caused an accident. The exclusion has no reference to liability for damage to other property or personal injury arising out of such accident . . . . In the instant case, the plaintiffs seek protection for the very thing that is specifically excluded by [this exclusion], i.e., the cost to the plaintiffs of replacing the stucco that proved to be defective.

[147] Henderson, *Insurance Protection for Products Liability and Completed Operations—What Every Lawyer Should Know,* 50 Neb. L. Rev. 415, 441–42 (1971).

[148] *See, e.g.,* Pittsburgh Bridge & Iron Works v. Liberty Mut. Ins. Co., 444 F.2d 1286 (3d Cir. 1971); Ownes Pac. Marine, Inc. v. Insurance Co. of N. Am., 12 Cal. App. 3d 661, 90 Cal. Rptr. 826 (1970); Blackfield v. Underwriters at Lloyd's London, 245 Cal. App. 2d 271, 53 Cal. Rptr. 838 (1966); Eichler Homes, Inc. v. Underwriters at Lloyd's, London, 238 Cal. App. 2d 532, 47 Cal. Rptr. 843 (1965); S.L. Rowland Constr. Co. v. St. Paul Fire & Marine Ins. Co., 72 Wash. 2d 682, 434 P.2d 725 (1967).

language unambiguously excludes coverage for the cost of repairing or replacing non-defective as well as defective components of the insured's work product."[149]

These exclusions have a much greater effect on a general contractor than on a subcontractor. The work exclusion excludes "property damage to work performed by or on behalf of the named insured." From the general contractor's standpoint, this excludes damage to all work performed at a construction project, because subcontractors perform their work "on behalf of" the general contractor.[150] This is consistent with an intent to provide the general contractor with an incentive to exercise care in supervising the workmanship of its subcontractors and thus reduce the risk of covered losses involving personal injury and damage to property of others. In contrast, a subcontractor that performs defective work that damages the work of another subcontractor will have coverage for the damage to the other subcontractor's work, even though the insured subcontractor will not have coverage for damage to its own work.

The general contractor can eliminate the "on behalf of" problem, however, by paying an additional premium for the Broad Form Property Damage endorsement. The BFPD endorsement eliminates the words "on behalf of the named insured" from exclusion (o). This modification intends that the general contractor "would have coverage for damage to his work arising out of a subcontractor's work [and] for damage to a subcontractor's work arising out of the subcontractor's work."[151] Accordingly, several courts have upheld the intended narrowing of this exclusion under the BFPD endorsement.[152] However, the Minnesota Supreme Court has twice taken the opposite position and determined that the omission of the "on behalf of" language did not allow coverage for subcontractors' defective work, stating

---

[149] Todd Shipyards Corp. v. Turbine Serv., Inc., 674 F.2d 401, 422 (5th Cir.), *cert. denied, sub nom.* Sentry Ins. v. Todd Shipyards Corp., 459 U.S. 1036 (1982); Western Employers Ins. Co. v. Arciero & Sons, 145 Cal. App. 3d 1027, 1031, 194 Cal. Rptr. 688 (1983). *See also* Maryland Casualty Co. v. Imperial Contracting Co., 212 Cal. App. 3d 712, 723–24, 260 Cal. Rptr. 797 (1989); T.C. Bateson Constr. Co. v. Lumbermens Mut. Casualty Co., 784 S.W.2d 692, 696 (Tex. Ct. App. 1989), *writ denied* (1990).

[150] T.C. Bateson Constr. Co. v. Lumbermens Mut. Casualty Co., 784 S.W.2d 692, 695–96 (Tex. Ct. App. 1989), *writ denied* (1990). Of course, if the particular insurance policy contains the standard exception to the contractually assumed liability exclusion, and the policy is governed by the laws of a minority-view jurisdiction, a claim based on warranty theory will be covered despite the work product exclusion. See **§ 11.10**.

[151] *See* Maryland Casualty Co. v. Reeder, 221 Cal. App. 3d 961, 971–72, 260 Cal. Rptr. 797, *review denied* (1990), which discusses several insurance industry publications that express this intention.

[152] *Id.* at 973–74; Fireguard Sprinkler Sys., Inc. v. Scottsdale Ins. Co., 864 F.2d 648, 653–55 (9th Cir. 1988).

that such events were a business risk of the general contractor that could not be absolved by the BFPD endorsement.[153]

The 1986 ISO revision broadens the standard coverage to provide substantially the same coverage as that under the BFPD endorsement.

§ 11.15 —Sistership or Recall

Exclusion (p), the sistership or recall exclusion of the 1973 CGL policy states:

> This insurance does not apply:
>
> (p) to damages claimed for the withdrawal, inspection, repair, replacement, or loss of use of the named insured's products or work completed by or for the named insured or of any property of which such products or work form a part, if such products, work or property are withdrawn from the market or from use because of any known or suspected defect or deficiency therein.

This exclusion bars coverage for damages associated with products or work withdrawn from the market because of a known or suspected deficiency. It is referred to as the sistership exclusion because it was first used in connection with the recall of aircraft (sister ships) similar to an aircraft known to have a defect.[154] This exclusion refers to costs of recalling other similar products or other similar work, not damage to the product itself or the work itself (which are excluded by other exclusions). As one court stated:

> While the insurance [covered] damages for bodily injuries and property damage caused by the product that failed, it was never intended that the insurer would be saddled with the cost of preventing other failures, any more than it was intended that the insurer would pay the cost of preventing

---

[153] Knutson Constr. Co. v. St. Paul Fire & Marine Ins. Co., 396 N.W.2d 229, 237 (Minn. 1986); Bor-Son Bldg. Corp. v. Commercial Union Ins. Co., 323 N.W.2d 58 (Minn. 1982). The BFPD endorsement was not addressed in the *Bor-Son* opinion, and the insured in *Knutson* argued that the endorsement in its policy thus distinguished the two cases. However, the *Knutson* opinion stated that the issue had been briefed in *Bor-Son,* and that the *Bor-Son* court had rejected the insured's argument. Knutson Constr. Co. v. St. Paul Fire & Marine Ins. Co., 396 N.W.2d 229, 237.

Knutson and *Bor-Son* were specifically rejected in Maryland Casualty Co. v. Reeder, 221 Cal. App. 3d 961, 972–73, and Fireguard Sprinkler Sys., Inc. v. Scottsdale Ins. Co., 864 F.2d 648, 653–54.

[154] Yakima Cement Prods. Co. v. Great Am. Ins. Co., 22 Wash. App. 536, 590 P.2d 371, 374 (1979), *rev'd on other grounds,* 93 Wash. 2d 210, 608 P.2d 254, *reconsideration denied* (1980).

> the first failure if the product had been discovered to be in a dangerous condition before the occurrence.[155]

Because this exclusion applies almost exclusively to product or material suppliers, it does not affect significantly a construction contractor's coverage.

The 1986 ISO revision makes no substantive changes to this exclusion.

§ 11.16 —Explosion, Collapse, or Underground Property Damage

The standard CGL policy contains an exclusion that excludes property damage, but not bodily injury, claims for explosion, collapse, or underground (XCU) property damage. Because the language defining these hazards is quite specific, the exclusion has created few legal issues.[156] Contractors engaging in operations that involve these risks currently may buy back the applicable coverage by endorsement. This exclusion would disappear altogether in the proposed 1986 revision, but endorsements that would exclude such coverage are available.

§ 11.17 —Completed Operations Hazard

The 1973 standard CGL policy does not contain a completed operations exclusion. However, it does include the following definition of the completed operations hazard:

> "*completed operations hazard*" includes *bodily injury* and *property damage* arising out of operations or reliance upon a representation or warranty made at any time with respect thereto, but only if the *bodily injury* or *property damage* occurs after such operations have been completed or abandoned and occurs away from premises owned by or rented to the *named insured.* "Operations" include materials, parts or equipment furnished in connection therewith. Operations shall be deemed completed at the earliest of the following times:
>
> (1) when all operations to be performed by or on behalf of the *named insured* under the contract have been completed,

---

[155] Ohio Casualty Ins. Co. v. Terrace Enters., Inc., 260 N.W.2d 450, 455 (Minn. 1977) (citations omitted).

[156] In one of the few cases to consider this exclusion, the trial court had contrived an ambiguity in order to find coverage, but the appellate court found that the exclusion was clear. Tennessee Corp. v. Lamb Bros. Constr. Co., 265 So. 2d 533 (Fla. Dist. Ct. App. 1972), *questioned on other grounds by* Baron Oil Co. v. National Mut. Fire Ins. Co., 470 So. 2d 810, 815 (Fla. Dist. Ct. App. 1985). The *Tennessee Corp.* court sent the action back to the trial court for factual findings in light of its interpretation of the exclusion. *Id.*

(2) when all operations to be performed by or on behalf of the *named insured* at the site of the operations have been completed, or

(3) when the portion of the work out of which the injury or damage arises has been put to its intended use by any person or organization other than another contractor or subcontractor engaged in performing operations for a principal as a part of the same project.

Operations which may require further service or maintenance work, or correction, repair or replacement because of any defect or deficiency, but which are otherwise complete, shall be deemed completed.

The *completed operations hazard* does not include *bodily injury* or *property damage* arising out of

(a) operations in connection with the transportation of property, unless the *bodily injury* or *property damage* arises out of a condition in or on a vehicle created by the loading or unloading thereof,

(b) the existence of tools, uninstalled equipment or abandoned or unused materials, or

(c) operations for which the classification stated in the policy or in the company's manual specifies "including completed operations" . . . (emphasis in original).

The completed operations hazard is significant to contractors in several ways. First, the exclusion is contained in the Manufacturers and Contractors liability insurance form, which some insurers still require. It states: "This insurance does not apply: to bodily injury or property damage included within the completed operations hazard or the products hazard."[157]

Second, the standard CGL policy includes completed operations in its list of hazards for rating purposes and in its list of hazards subject to aggregate limits of liability.

Third, the Broad Form Property Damage endorsement replaces exclusion (o) with an exclusion stating that with respect to the completed operations hazard, the insurance will not apply to "property damage to work performed by the named insured arising out of the work or any portion thereof or out of materials, parts or equipment furnished in connection therewith." This eliminates an exclusion for damage to work performed by a subcontractor on behalf of an insured contractor that occurred after the operation was completed.

The completed operations hazard and the products hazard are somewhat parallel in the way they affect the coverage provided by the standard CGL policy to providers of services and manufacturers, respectively. Because

---

[157] Additional discussion of the completed operations exclusion can be found in Landis & Rahdert, *The Completed Operations Hazard,* 19 Forum 570-90 (Summer 1984); Annotation, *Liability Insurance—"Completed Operations,"* 58 A.L.R.3d 12 (1974).

contractors generally are viewed as providing services, a contractor's concerns focus primarily on the completed operations hazard.[158]

Before 1966 the standard policy language treated the completed operations hazard as a subclassification of the products hazard exclusion. Because the pre-1966 policies combined the service and product aspects into one Product-Completed Operations Hazard, the majority of courts found that there was no coverage only if the work performed principally involved a product. As one court has pointed out, the effect of this majority view was that the completed operations hazard in pre-1966 policies was "superfluous."[159] Because the 1966 revisions clarified this ambiguity, courts in recent decisions have commented that earlier decisions involving pre-1966 language have "little precedential value."[160]

The post-1966 language separates the completed operations hazard from the products hazard and focuses on the principal issue surrounding the completed operations exclusion by defining when operations are deemed completed. The line between an uncompleted operation and a completed operation can be rather elusive. The Nebraska Supreme Court found that a welder's operations were completed, and held the exclusion applicable, when a fire damaged equipment within 20 minutes after the welder left the scene.[161] In contrast, a North Carolina court affirmed a jury finding that an electrician had not completed his operations and that the exclusion was inapplicable when a fire was observed an hour and a half after the electrician's departure. The court disposed of the issue by commenting that the electrician's obligation "was not 'completed' until the light fixtures were put in a *safe* working condition."[162]

Operations are considered complete as soon as the particular portion of the work is put to its intended use by a third party, even though further service or maintenance work is required. Even this language, however,

---

[158] Friestad v. Travelers Indem. Co., 260 Pa. Super. 178, 393 A.2d 1212 (1978), provides a well-reasoned decision that an installer of a product requires completed operation, but not products hazard, coverage.

[159] 393 A.2d at 1214.

[160] Martinez v. Hawkeye-Security Ins. Co., 196 Colo. 184, 576 P.2d 1017, 1018 n.1 (1978); *see also* Tiano v. Aetna Casualty & Sur. Co., 102 Mich. App. 177, 301 N.W.2d 476 (1980) ("cases decided before 1966 are of scant use"); Abco Tank & Mfg. Co. v. Federal Ins. Co., 550 S.W.2d 193, 194 n.1 (Mo. 1977). An excellent discussion of the history of this exclusion is found in Henderson, *Insurance Protection for Products Liability and Completed Operations—What Every Lawyer Should Know,* 50 Neb. L. Rev. 415–46 (1971). Unfortunately, as the author notes in his conclusion, because no cases involving post-1966 language had been decided at the time the article was written, the principle value of the article is to provide historical perspective. Pre-1966 interpretations have precedential value, of course, in continuing damage cases construing pre-1966 policies.

[161] Lavalleur v. State Auto. & Casualty, 208 Neb. 82, 302 N.W.2d 362 (1981).

[162] Woodard v. North Carolina Farm Bureau Mut. Ins. Co., 44 N.C. App. 282, 261 S.E.2d 43 (1979), *cert. denied,* 299 N.C. 546, 265 S.E.2d 406 (1980) (emphasis added).

continues to lead to difficulties. The Colorado Supreme Court held that a contractor did not have coverage for injuries to a two-year-old who was badly burned by gasoline after entering a basement with a defective door latch. It reasoned that the door on which the contractor had not yet repaired the latch mechanism was complete because its intended use was to provide access rather than to act as a barrier.[163] In contrast, the South Carolina Supreme Court held that a stairway was not an excluded completed operation because it had not been put to its intended use, even though it had been used temporarily by the occupants of a new house. The court reasoned that the intended purpose was to afford passage to and from the attic "indefinitely."[164]

Although historically the completed operations exclusion had a dramatic effect on the comprehensive coverage afforded to a contractor under a CGL policy, the courts generally seemed willing to enforce the exclusion.[165] Pragmatically, the courts were influenced by the fact that completed operations coverage was available to those contractors who agreed to pay the increased premium.

Even though the 1973 CGL policy provides completed operations coverage, it is important that the contractor understand that the policy is written on an occurrence basis. There are a number of cases in which insureds had coverage for the period in which they were performing their operations, but failed to renew their coverage after operations were completed.[166] As discussed in **§ 11.5**, the trigger of coverage for policies written on an occurrence basis is the resulting damage or injuries, rather than the earlier negligent acts.

The ISO's 1986 revision simplified the definition of products-completed operations, but made no substantive changes in it. Exclusion (*l*) would exclude:

> "Property damage" to "your work" arising out of it or any part of it and included in the "products-completed operations hazard." This exclusion

---

[163] Martinez v. Hawkeye-Security Ins. Co., 196 Colo. 184, 576 P.2d 1017, 1020 (1978).

[164] W.N. Leslie, Inc. v. Travelers Ins. Co., 264 S.C. 408, 215 S.E.2d 448, 451 (1975).

[165] *See, e.g.,* Prieto v. Continental Ins. Co., 358 So. 2d 851 (Fla. Dist. Ct. App. 1978) (building completed before collapse); Adkins v. La Terre Dev. Corp., 387 So. 2d 652 (La. Ct. App. 1980) (insured failed to fill hole 11 months before claimant's injury); Meier v. Hardware Mut. Casualty Co., 281 So. 2d 793 (La. Ct. App. 1973) (construction of gin pole completed before collapse); Tiano v. Aetna Casualty & Sur. Co., 102 Mich. App. 177, 301 N.W.2d 476 (1980) (exploding heating system considered completed); Security Ins. Co. v. Kaye Milling Supply, Inc., 297 Minn. 348, 211 N.W.2d 519 (1973) (emergency use of unfinished silo considered completed when put to intended use); Casey v. Employers Nat'l Ins. Co., 539 S.W.2d 181 (Tex. Ct. App. 1976) (affected area completed even though building only 75% complete).

[166] Singsaas v. Diederich, 307 Minn. 153, 238 N.W.2d 878 (1976); Williams v. Aetna Casualty & Sur. Co., 151 N.J. Super. 68, 376 A.2d 562 (App. Div. 1977); Storms v. United States Fid. & Guar. Co., 118 N.H. 427, 388 A.2d 578 (1978).

> does not apply if the damaged work or the work out of which the damage arises was performed on your behalf by a subcontractor.

This exclusion, in substance, tracks the current Broad Form Property Damage endorsement.

BUILDER'S RISK POLICY

§ 11.18 Introduction

Because the comprehensive general liability policy does not provide coverage for damage to the contractor's own work, the contractor can obtain additional coverage in the form of a first-party builder's risk policy.[167] A *builder's risk policy* covers loss of or damage to the work the contractor has contracted to perform. The name of the policy comes from the common law rule that the damage or destruction of work in progress is a risk borne by the builder.[168] The policy insures against this risk. For example, the policy may cover damage to a building under construction, materials, and tools and equipment on the project site.

Depending on the language of the policy, the amount the contractor may recover for loss or damage under the builder's risk policy is either the actual value of the property at the time of loss or damage, or the cost of repair or reconstruction.[169] The insurer's responsibility to the insured is also subject to the particular policy limits.

§ 11.19 Period of Coverage

Coverage under a builder's risk policy may commence on a specified date, but in many cases coverage attaches upon the commencement of construction and extends throughout the period of construction. Under a policy providing coverage "during construction," there is no coverage for losses occurring prior to actual physical commencement of construction. In one leading case, the court held that there was no coverage for damage to an old building, the component parts of which were to be used in constructing a

---

[167] Coverage under builder's risk policies is discussed in: Braude & Patin, *"All Risk" Insurance,* Construction Briefings 1–12 (Nov. 1981); Annotation, *Builder's Coverage under Builder's Risk Insurance Policy,* 97 A.L.R.3d 1270 (1980); Seabolt & Baron, *Builder's Risk Insurance, in* Insuring Real Property (S. Cozen, ed., 1991).

[168] *See, e.g.,* Ingle v. Jones, 69 U.S. (2 Wall.) 762 (1865); *see also* Annotation, *Builder's Risk Insurance Policy,* 97 A.L.R.3d 1270, 1274 n.5 (1980).

[169] Teeples v. Tolson, 207 F. Supp. 212, 215–16 (D. Or. 1962); Essex House v. St. Paul Fire & Marine Ins. Co., 404 F. Supp. 978 (S.D. Ohio 1975).

new building, when the damage to the old building occurred prior to commencement of construction of the new building.[170]

Coverage may terminate on a specified date or upon some other occurrence specified in the policy. The ISO 1990 builder's risk policy applies to buildings "in the course of construction"; it lists several occurrences that can cause coverage termination.

Termination of coverage under many builder's risk policies is dependent on completion of construction. "Completion" usually means whatever the parties intend the term to mean, pursuant to the provisions of the construction contract itself.[171] When the policy has not set forth a definition of "completion of the building," the courts have construed that term in a variety of ways. Some courts have held that coverage terminates when a building is ready to be put to the *full* use for which it was intended.[172] Other courts have held that the duration of coverage must be determined with reference to the object to be accomplished by the completed structure.[173]

The courts are divided on the question of whether a building has been completed, and coverage thus terminated, when minor repair work remains to be performed. In *Scottish Union & National Insurance Co. v. Encampment Smelting Co.*[174] a builder's risk policy provided coverage for the building and machinery of an ore mill. The court held that, although the loss occurred after the building had been completed, the insured was allowed a reasonable amount of time "to test the composite structure, adjust its parts to each other and ascertain whether it [would] perform its function before construction can be said to be completed and occupancy begun. . . ."[175] The Eighth Circuit panel ordered the trial court to determine whether the insured's "reasonable amount of time" for testing had passed.[176] However, other courts have denied coverage when construction was largely, but not entirely, completed when a loss occurred.[177]

---

[170] Newman v. National Fire Ins. Co., 152 Miss. 344, 118 So. 295, 297 (1928). In Patton v. Aetna Ins. Co., 595 F. Supp. 533, 535 (N.D. Miss. 1984), the court expressed doubts regarding the *Newman* decision, but merely distinguished *Newman* based on its specific facts.

[171] Philadelphia Facilities Management Corp. v. St. Paul Fire & Marine Ins. Co., 379 F. Supp. 780, 784 (E.D. Pa. 1974).

[172] Cuthrell v. Milwaukee Mechanics Ins. Co., 234 N.C. 137, 66 S.E.2d 649, 651 (1951).

[173] Scottish Union & Nat'l Ins. Co. v. Encampment Smelting Co., 166 F. 231, 237 (8th Cir. 1908), *disapproved on other grounds by* Concordia Ins. Co. v. School Dist. No. 98, 282 U.S. 545, 551 (1931).

[174] 166 F. 231, 237–38 (8th Cir. 1908).

[175] *Id.* at 237.

[176] *Id.* at 238. *See also* Cuthrell v. Milwaukee Mechanics Ins. Co., 234 N.C. 137, 66 S.E.2d 649, 651 (1951) (loss covered when structure completed, but plumbing, wiring, and painting unfinished).

[177] Fireman's Fund Ins. Co. v. Millers' Mut. Ins. Ass'n, 451 F.2d 1140, 1141 (10th Cir. 1971); Hendrix v. New Amsterdam Casualty Co., 390 F.2d 299, 304 (10th Cir. 1968).

Some policies provide for termination of coverage on the date a building becomes occupied or when the building is occupied for a certain period of time. When termination of coverage is dependent on occupancy of the building, the building will not be deemed to be occupied until it is put to a "practical and substantial use for the purpose for which it was designed."[178] "Transient" or "trivial" use will not terminate coverage.[179]

§ 11.20 Limitations on Coverage: Fortuitous Losses

Coverage under a builder's risk policy is subject to some important limitations in the form of implied conditions and specified exclusions. As with all insurance policies, one fundamental implied limitation on builder's risk coverage is that only fortuitous losses are covered.[180] A *fortuitous loss* generally is one that is dependent on chance, is beyond human control, and is not certain to occur.[181] Accordingly, loss or damage resulting from depreciation or ordinary wear and tear would not be covered because such events are usually certain to occur.[182] Many courts have held that negligence is a fortuitous event and have allowed contractors to recover for damage and loss caused by their own negligence and negligence of their agents.[183] However, a recent decision distinguished such rulings as involving fortuitous accidents caused by defective workmanship, and held that the fortuity requirement precludes coverage for the cost of merely repairing or replacing mistakes in construction.[184]

§ 11.21 —External Causes

Some policies limit coverage to losses resulting from an external cause, and courts sometimes read this requirement into builder's risk policies by implication.[185] Courts distinguish between external cause and external damage: an *external cause* is one with an external origin; *external damage* refers to

---

[178] Reliance Ins. Co. v. Jones, 296 F.2d 71, 73–74 (10th Cir. 1961).

[179] Cuthrell v. Milwaukee Mechanics Ins. Co., 234 N.C. 137, 66 S.E.2d 649, 651 (1951).

[180] Texas E. Transmission Corp. v. Marine Office—Appleton & Cox Corp., 579 F.2d 561, 564 (10th Cir. 1978); Avis v. Hartford Fire Ins. Co., 283 N.C. 142, 195 S.E.2d 545, 548 (1973).

[181] Texas E. Transmission Corp. v. Marine Office—Appleton & Cox Corp., 579 F.2d 561, 564 (10th Cir. 1978).

[182] Avis v. Hartford Fire Ins. Co., 283 N.C. 142, 195 S.E.2d 545, 548 (1973).

[183] C.H. Leavell & Co. v. Fireman's Fund Ins. Co., 372 F.2d 784, 789 (9th Cir. 1967); General Am. Transp. Corp. v. Sun Ins. Office Ltd., 369 F.2d 906, 908 (6th Cir. 1966).

[184] Trinity Indus., Inc. v. INA, 916 F.2d 267, 269 (5th Cir. 1990), *reh'g denied,* 923 F.2d 851 (5th Cir. 1991).

[185] *See* Avis v. Hartford Fire Ins. Co., 283 N.C. 142, 195 S.E.2d 545, 549 (1973).

the condition of the exterior part of an object. There is coverage only for a structure's damage caused by a force of external origin, and not for losses caused by damage inherent in the exterior of the structure.[186] Some courts have read the fortuity and external cause requirements together, finding the required element of fortuity in the chance introduction of an external force without which the loss would not have happened.[187]

Under policies containing an external cause requirement, when the cause of a loss cannot for some reason be explained or traced (for example, collapse of building), the courts generally do not require the insured to prove that the loss resulted from an external cause and are willing to find coverage.[188]

§ 11.22 —Exclusions

Coverage also may be limited by specific exclusions. Some of the more typical exclusions preclude coverage for loss or damage caused by:

1. Faulty workmanship and materials
2. Design defects, errors, and omissions
3. Latent defects
4. Inherent vice
5. Equipment breakdown
6. Earth movement and subsidence.

Damage resulting from fire, acts of nature, and war may also be excluded.

A dispute may arise when several factors contributed to a loss and some of the causes are excluded but others are not. If the specific policy language does not resolve the question, some courts adopt a *concurrent cause* approach, under which coverage is found if any one contributing cause is not subject to an exclusion.[189] Other courts look for the efficient proximate cause of the loss, and decide coverage by determining whether that cause is excluded.[190] In 1983 the ISO amended its form builder's risk policy in an attempt to clarify coverage in cases of multiple causation. The ISO policy states that "loss or damage is excluded regardless of any other cause or event

---

[186] Dubuque Fire & Marine Ins. Co. v. Caylor, 249 F.2d 162, 164–65 (10th Cir. 1957); Connie's Constr. Co. v. Continental Ins. Co., 227 N.W.2d 204 (Iowa 1975); City of Barre v. New Hampshire Ins. Co., 136 Vt. 484, 396 A.2d 121, 122 (1978).

[187] *See* Standard Structural Steel Co. v. Bethlehem Steel Corp., 597 F. Supp. 164 (D. Conn. 1984), and cases cited therein.

[188] *See, e.g.*, Morrison Grain Co. v. Utica Mut. Ins. Co., 632 F.2d 424, 430 (5th Cir. 1980).

[189] Texas E. Transmission Corp. v. Marine Office—Appleton & Cox Corp., 579 F.2d 561, 565 (10th Cir. 1979).

[190] Sabella v. Wisler, 59 Cal. 2d 21, 31–32, 377 P.2d 889, 27 Cal. Rptr. 689 (1963). The California Supreme Court subsequently ruled that the efficient proximate cause test

that contributes concurrently or in any sequence to the loss."[191] A federal court, construing California law, enforced this limitation on coverage.[192] However, a subsequent California decision found that this limitation could apply only when several causes acted concurrently to produce a loss, but could not bar coverage when an excluded risk was the efficient proximate cause of a loss.[193]

Unless otherwise specified, exclusions in builder's risk policies apply to subcontractors not named as insureds.[194] In one noteworthy case a subcontractor was named as an insured and a loss occurred as a result of the subcontractor's faulty workmanship.[195] Even though the general contractor was not at fault, the court applied a workmanship and materials exclusion that made no distinction as to the source of the defective workmanship and denied coverage.

Contractors have been quite successful in avoiding the workmanship and materials exclusion. Most courts have held that the exclusion is limited to errors in the structure itself and not to errors in the methods of construction. These courts reason that "workmanship" refers only to work that affects the quality of materials used in the construction project and does not necessarily refer to the defective construction work itself.[196] Thus, a contractor may avoid the exclusion by showing that the damage or loss was caused by its own negligence.

Contractors have avoided the defective design exclusion by showing:

1. That the design was used successfully in other projects
2. That the structure was successfully rebuilt using the same design and
3. That an omitted element alleged to have caused damage or loss was not one customarily required for the particular design.[197]

---

applies in first-party insurance cases, and that the concurrent cause test governs with respect to third-party liability insurance. Garvey v. State Farm Fire & Casualty Co., 48 Cal. 3d 395, 405, 770 P.2d 704, 257 Cal. Rptr. 292 (1989).

[191] This provision is included in the exclusions section of the ISO form, "Causes of Loss—Basic Form," which is incorporated into the ISO builder's risk policy.

[192] State Farm Fire & Casualty Co. v. Martin, 872 F.2d 319 (9th Cir. 1989).

[193] Howell v. State Farm Fire & Casualty Co., 218 Cal. App. 3d 1446, 267 Cal. Rptr. 708 (1990), *reh'g denied* (1991).

[194] Kraemer Bros., Inc. v. United States Fire Ins. Co., 89 Wis. 2d 555, 278 N.W.2d 857 (1979).

[195] St. Paul Fire & Marine Ins. Co. v. Murray Plumbing & Heating Corp., 65 Cal. App. 3d 66, 135 Cal. Rptr. 120 (1976).

[196] Equitable Fire & Marine Ins. Co. v. Allied Steel Constr. Co., 421 F.2d 512, 514 (10th Cir. 1970); City of Barre v. New Hampshire Ins. Co., 136 Vt. 484, 396 A.2d 121, 122 (1978). *But see* U.S. Indus., Inc. v. Aetna Casualty & Sur. Co., 690 F.2d 459, 462–63 (5th Cir. 1982).

[197] Dow Chem. Co. v. Royal Indem. Co., 635 F.2d 379 (5th Cir. 1981).

In construing latent defect exclusions, the courts have developed a general rule that a defect is latent if (1) it cannot be discovered by any known and customary test, or (2) it could not have been discovered by a proper or reasonable inspection.[198] In many cases, contractors have avoided the latent defect exclusion by showing that a particular loss or damage was caused by the contractor's own negligence.

An inherent vice exclusion excludes coverage for damage or loss caused by phenomena occurring over time because of the nature of the property itself (for example, the rotting of wood or the fading of paint). Thus, the exclusion precludes coverage for losses caused entirely from the internal decomposition of the property that brings about its own injury or destruction.[199] Once again, however, the exclusion can be avoided by showing that the damage or loss was caused by the contractor's own negligence.

The equipment breakdown exclusion excludes coverage for loss or damage caused by *mechanical breakdown,* which is defined as a failure in the working mechanism of the machinery, that is, a functional defect in the moving parts of the equipment causing it to cease functioning or to function improperly.[200] This exclusion applies only when the loss results from a breakdown caused by the inherent malfunctioning of the equipment, including instances when the mechanical failure is caused by negligence in the assembly or repair of the equipment.[201]

An earth movement exclusion precludes coverage for loss or damage caused by such things as earthquakes, volcanic eruptions, and landslides. To come within the exclusion, the insurer must show that the earth movement involved forces operating within the earth itself. Unless otherwise specified in the policy, superficial effects of external forces, such as erosion by runoff rainwater, do not come within the exclusion.[202]

Closely related to the earth movement exclusion is the subsidence exclusion. This exclusion applies when damage or loss is caused by a gradual settling that is the primary cause of collapse or other damage.[203]

---

[198] General Am. Transp. Corp. v. Sun Ins. Office, Ltd., 369 F.2d 906, 908 (6th Cir. 1966); Essex House v. St. Paul Fire & Marine Ins. Co., 404 F. Supp. 978, 992 (S.D. Ohio 1975).

[199] Equitable Fire & Marine Ins. Co. v. Allied Steel Constr. Co., 421 F.2d 512 (10th Cir. 1965); Employers Casualty Co. v. Holm, 393 S.W.2d 363 (Tex. Ct. App. 1965).

[200] National Investors Fire & Casualty Co. v. Preddy, 248 Ark. 320, 451 S.W.2d 457 (1970).

[201] Little Judy Indus., Inc. v. Federal Ins. Co., 280 So. 2d 14, 14–15 (Fla. Dist. Ct. App.), *cert. denied,* 284 So. 2d 220 (Fla. 1973).

[202] Peach State Uniform Serv., Inc. v. American Ins. Co., 507 F.2d 996, 1000 (5th Cir. 1975).

[203] Dow Chem. Co. v. Royal Indem. Co., 635 F.2d 379, 388–89 (5th Cir. 1981).

§ 11.23 Burden of Proof

The builder's risk policy has a significant advantage over other forms of insurance policies with respect to burden of proof requirements. Under a CGL policy the insured must prove the policy terms and demonstrate that the loss is covered by the insuring provisions, and the insurer then has the burden of proving that the loss is somehow excluded.[204] However, in the majority of jurisdictions, under an all-risk builder's risk policy the insurer must prove that the policy does not cover a particular loss or damage.[205] Although the contractor usually must prove that a particular loss or damage was caused by a fortuitous event, once this is shown the insurer must prove that the loss is not covered.[206] Moreover, the insured's "burden of demonstrating fortuity is not a particularly onerous one."[207] Various courts have held that the insured is not required to demonstrate the exact cause of a loss in order to meet the fortuity requirement under an all-risk policy.[208]

§ 11.24 Sue and Labor Clause

Many builder's risk policies also contain *sue and labor clauses* imposing upon the insured a duty to "sue and labor" to safeguard the insured's property from actual or imminent loss or to minimize the loss once it occurs by taking immediate protective measures. Under a sue and labor clause, the insurer reimburses the insured for the expenses incurred in suing and laboring with respect to covered damages.[209]

§ 11.25 Subrogation

Under builder's risk policies an owner's insurer may not subrogate to the owner's rights and sue either the general contractor[210] or a subcontractor[211]

---

[204] Executive Aviation, Inc. v. National Ins. Underwriters, 16 Cal. App. 3d 799, 806, 94 Cal. Rptr. 347 (1971).

[205] Redna Marine Corp. v. Poland, 46 F.R.D. 81, 86 (S.D.N.Y. 1969).

[206] Texas E. Transmission Corp. v. Marine Office—Appleton & Cox Corp., 579 F.2d 561, 564 (10th Cir. 1978); Strubble v. United Servs. Auto. Assocs., 35 Cal. App. 3d 498, 504, 110 Cal. Rptr. 828 (1973).

[207] Morrison Grain Co. v. Utica Mut. Ins. Co., 632 F.2d 424, 430 (5th Cir. 1980).

[208] *Id.* at 431; Texas E. Transmission Corp. v. Marine Office—Appleton & Cox Corp., 579 F.2d 561, 564 (10th Cir. 1978).

[209] Southern Cal. Edison Co. v. Harbor Ins. Co., 83 Cal. App. 3d 747, 757, 148 Cal. Rptr. 106 (1978).

[210] Glen Falls Ins. Co. v. Globe Indem. Co., 214 La. 467, 38 So. 2d 139 (1948).

[211] Transamerica Ins. Co. v. Gage Plumbing & Heating Co., 433 F.2d 1051, 1055 (10th Cir. 1970).

for causing damage to insured property when they are co-insureds of the owner under the policy.[212] When a subcontractor is not named as a co-insured of the general contractor or the owner, the courts have held that even though the subcontractor is not specifically excluded from coverage, it still is a co-insured immune from subrogation claims by the insurer.[213] One line of authority has rejected this rule, holding that the immunity of a subcontractor not named as an insured extends only to subrogation claims by the insurer for damage to the subcontractor's property, and does not protect the subcontractor against liability to others caused by its own negligence.[214]

§ 11.26 Future Practice

Although the world of insurance may appear at first glance to be mysterious, there is logic to it. If the contractor, its insurance broker, and its lawyer take the time to understand the rationale and buy the right insurance package, they can avoid most of the problems that have set insureds against insurers in recent years.

The history of the standard form CGL policy is like the history of Holland: where the insureds have breached the dike, the insurers have shored it up. For every court decision that damaged the insurance industry, there is now a policy exclusion. This practice continues today, primarily in the sensitive areas of toxic torts and pollution liability which can span many years of alleged continuing damage.

Despite the changes in the 1986 and 1988 CGL forms, it seems inevitable that the tension between insureds and their insurers will continue as long as the plaintiffs' lawyers use their creativity to devise new areas of contractor liability. As their exposures to liability grow, contractors will continue to test the elasticity of the language of their policies. As they succeed, the insurance industry will respond by tightening its policy language.

---

[212] Frank Briscoe Co. v. Georgia Sprinkler Co., 713 F.2d 1500, 1504 (11th Cir. 1983); Harvey's Wagon Wheel, Inc. v. MacSween, 96 Nev. 215, 606 P.2d 1095, 1097–98 (1980).

[213] Louisiana Fire Ins. Co. v. Royal Indem. Co., 38 So. 2d 807 (La. 1949) (the so-called Louisiana Rule).

[214] Turner Constr. Co. v. John B. Kelly Co., 442 F. Supp. 551, 553 (E.D. Pa. 1976).

CHAPTER 12

CONTRACTORS AND THEIR SURETIES

Harvey C. Koch
James J. Myers*

Harvey C. Koch is the senior partner of the New Orleans, Louisiana, law firm of Koch & Rouse. He is a graduate of Tulane University and its School of Law, and was admitted to the Louisiana bar in 1961. He has devoted a major portion of his practice to litigation arising from all aspects of the construction process. Mr. Koch has authored numerous articles, lectured extensively, and served as chairman and cochairman of various national programs on construction law on the relationship between contractors and sureties. He is currently the chair of the Fidelity & Surety Law Committee of the American Bar Association, is a member of the Committee on International Construction Contracts of the International Bar Association, and is a member of the Forum on the Construction Industry of the American Bar Association.

James J. Myers is a senior partner in the Boston, Massachusetts, and Washington, D.C., law firm of Gadsby & Hannah. He heads the firm's construction division, and for more than 25 years has specialized in national and international construction law. His work covers both public and private contracts and representation of employers, contractors, subcontractors, architects, engineers, industry associations, suppliers and managers doing business in the Middle East, Far East, and Europe and Africa. He is a graduate of the University of Pennsylvania and Boston University School of Law, where he later served as a lecturer of law. He is a member of the Massachusetts bar, the District of Columbia bar, and the bar of the federal courts in those jurisdictions of the United States Supreme Court. Mr. Myers has published numerous papers, and he regularly lectures throughout the Middle East, Far East, Europe and Africa.

*Sincere thanks are extended to R.D. Kuehnle, Of Counsel to Mr. Koch's firm, for his expert assistance in the preparation of this chapter.

SURETY BONDS GENERALLY

§ 12.1 Introduction

§ 12.2 Parties to Surety Bonds

SURETY BONDS ON PUBLIC AND PRIVATE PROJECTS

§ 12.3 Private (Common Law) Surety Bonds

§ 12.4 Statutory Payment Bonds

TYPES OF SURETY BONDS

§ 12.5 Bid Bond

§ 12.6 —Voiding the Bid Bond

§ 12.7 —Excuses

§ 12.8 —Form of Bid or Proposal Bond

§ 12.9 Completion Bond

§ 12.10 Payment Bond

§ 12.11 Lien Bond

§ 12.12 Subcontractor's Bond

ROLE OF THE SURETY

§ 12.13 Generally

§ 12.14 Performance Bond

§ 12.15 Who Is Covered?

§ 12.16 When the Principal Defaults

§ 12.17 Surety's Rights and Obligations upon Default

§ 12.18 —Events of Default

§ 12.19 —Notice and Investigation

§ 12.20 —Available Defenses

§ 12.21 —Obligee's Conduct

§ 12.22 Surety's Options upon Default of Performance Bond Principal

§ 12.23 Damages Recoverable from Performance Bond Surety

§ 12.24 Surety's Right to Contract Funds

§ 12.25 Subrogation

PARTIES AND CAUSES OF ACTION

§ 12.26 Introduction

§ 12.27 Contractor versus Surety

§ 12.28 Contractor versus Owner

§ 12.29 Contractor versus Miscellaneous Parties

§ 12.30 Surety versus Contractor

§ 12.31 Surety versus Bank

§ 12.32 Surety versus Owner

§ 12.33 Surety versus Miscellaneous Parties

§ 12.34 Owner versus Contractor and/or Surety

NOTICE AND LIMITATION OF ACTIONS

§ 12.35 Notice Periods

§ 12.36 Limitation Periods

CONSTRUCTION OF DOCUMENTS AND PAROL EVIDENCE

§ 12.37 Construction of Contracts

§ 12.38 Parol Evidence

SURETY BONDS GENERALLY

§ 12.1 Introduction

The customary way of obtaining security for the performance of public construction contracts is to require surety bonds issued by a qualified surety corporation. Surety bonds are a form of assurance to the owner that the contractor will perform its work according to the contract and will pay for the labor and materials it uses in performing the contract. To an established maximum amount, the surety guarantees to pay the cost of completing the work if the contractor defaults in its performance, and guarantees to pay for labor and materials for which the contractor does not pay.

Bonds are customarily required in private construction contracts, and are uniformly required by statute in federal and most state and municipal projects. The rationale for requiring payment bonds on public projects is that as a matter of public policy, liens cannot be filed upon public property. This is so because public policy opposes the sale of public property to satisfy liens, especially when such property is not available for sale under an execution following a judgment against a state or municipality.[1] Consequently, surety bonds have evolved as a substitute in public projects for the lien protection afforded to laborers and material suppliers on private projects.

§ 12.2 Parties to Surety Bonds

The *surety,* an insurance company, is the party that obligates itself directly to an obligee (owner) by agreeing to perform the undertakings of the principal (contractor) under its contract with the obligee. The bond is conditioned

[1] *See, e.g.,* Friedman v. Hampden County, 204 Mass. 494, 90 N.E. 851 (1910).

upon performance by the principal. In the event of failure or default of the principal, the obligee has a direct right against the surety to remedy the failure or default by performing or by responding in money damages.

The *obligee* is the party that receives the benefit, protection, and security of the surety bond. In essence, it receives the guarantee, by contract, of the surety that the obligations of the principal will be performed in accordance with the terms and provisions of the agreement between the obligee and the principal.

The *principal* is the party who enters into an agreement with the obligee and who has been required by the obligee to furnish bonds under which the contractual undertakings of the principal are guaranteed or bonded by a surety.

The payment bond involves the principal, the obligee, the surety, and the beneficiaries of the bond, the claimants. *Claimants* are that class of persons defined in the bond who are effectively third-party beneficiaries of the bond and are entitled to enforce its terms.

SURETY BONDS ON PUBLIC AND PRIVATE PROJECTS

§ 12.3 Private (Common Law) Surety Bonds

There is no statutory requirement that private contracts be bonded either for performance or for payment of labor and materials. Parties to a private contract are at liberty to limit or condition their liability as long as they do not violate statutes or public policy. Considerable variety exists in form, type, and extent of protection afforded by private bonds. These private bonds are often referred to as *common law bonds.*

A common law bond is a contract for suretyship. The bond usually provides for joint and several liability of the principal and surety to pay up to the penalty sum of the bond in the event the obligee is damaged because of a default. The penalty sum is a fixed maximum sum for the surety's liability specified in the bond. Payment on the bond is subject to the condition that if the principal performs the obligation or undertaking for which the bond is given, the bond or obligation will be void. If the principal fails to perform, the bond is enforceable.

§ 12.4 Statutory Payment Bonds

Every state, as well as the federal government, requires that construction contractors for certain government contracts furnish bonds for the protection of laborers and material suppliers. In general, these statutes follow the same suretyship principles as common law bonds, but require that certain procedural conditions precedent be met before a cause of action can be valid under their coverage. Because many of these statutes were modeled to a greater or lesser extent after the federal Miller Act,[2] these statutes have become known as "little Miller Acts."

A public contractor's bond offered pursuant to such a statute includes the provisions of the statute by operation of law, whether or not such provisions are recited in the bond. This has come to be known as the *Christian doctrine,* established by the Court of Claims decision in *G.L. Christian & Associates v. United States.*[3] According to this doctrine, the statutory provisions are, by law, read into the bond. Failure to include specific reference to the statute has been held to have no effect on the statutory validity of the bond. In *Martin Fireproofing Corp. v. Aetna Insurance Co.*[4] the payment bond given to satisfy state law requirements contained no requirement for notice (which *was* required by the statute).[5] The court held, (because notice was not given) that there could be no recovery based solely on the provisions in the bond and that the notice requirement in the statute governed.[6]

TYPES OF SURETY BONDS

§ 12.5 Bid Bond

Public agencies usually require bidders for public construction contracts to furnish surety bonds as a requisite to any final award of the contract. A contractor for public building or public work construction is ordinarily required to furnish bid security by a *bid bond.* The successful bidder is also usually required to furnish a *performance bond* for the performance of the contract and a *payment bond* for indemnification of the obligee against liability for the claims of laborers, material suppliers, and subcontractors in the prosecution of the work.

A bid bond is a surety contract between the principal (bidding contractor), the obligee public authority, and the surety. The bond provides that if the contractor is awarded the contract, it will, according to the contract

---

[2] 40 U.S.C. §§ 270a–270d (1986).

[3] 312 F.2d 418 (Ct. Cl.), *cert. denied,* 375 U.S. 954 (1963).

[4] 346 Mass. 498, 194 N.E.2d 1010 (1963).

[5] Mass. Gen. Laws Ann. ch. 149, § 29 (West 1985).

[6] *See also* Metropolitan Pipe & Supply Co. v. D'Amore Constr. Co., 309 Mass. 380, 35 N.E.2d 211 (1941).

provisions (which may include a specified time limit), enter into a formal contract with the obligee/owner to perform the contract and also provide all required bonds for the property performance of the contract.

§ 12.6 —Voiding the Bid Bond

Although the contractor's compliance with the provisions upon award of the contract will render the bid bond void, the contractor's failure to enter into the contract or to provide the required surety bonds will cause the principal and the surety to become liable to the obligee. The obligee (owner) is therefore secured against the default of the bidder for the contract, although the surety will be liable to indemnify the owner only up to the penal sum of the bond.[7]

§ 12.7 —Excuses

The bidder's refusal to enter into the contract may be based on one of two grounds: change in condition, or mistake in the bid. When mistake results from an honest error, the contractor is usually excused from its bid. When the contractor is so excused, the bid bond surety is also relieved. For example, in *M.J. McGough Co. v. Jane Lamb Memorial Hospital*[8] a contractor and its surety were found entitled to have the bid rescinded (and the surety therefore released from liability on the bond) when a clerical error caused the bid to be low by 10 percent of the total bid, and notification of the error, which was not caused by gross negligence, was received before the bid was accepted.

§ 12.8 —Form of Bid or Proposal Bond

Standard forms for bid or proposal bonds, such as American Institute of Architects (AIA) Document A310 (1970), are available from most insurance agencies. Such bonds require that the principal, if it is the successful bidder, execute a contract within a certain number of days after notice of award. Should the principal, after award, fail to execute the contract or fail to furnish a performance bond as required, then the condition of the obligation has not been met and the surety will be liable for the difference

---

[7] United States *ex rel.* Empire Plastics Corp. v. Western Casualty & Sur. Co., 429 F.2d 905 (10th Cir. 1970).

[8] 302 F. Supp. 482 (S.D. Iowa 1969).

between the amount of the principal's bond and the amount of the bid selected, but not to exceed the penal sum of the bond.

§ 12.9 Completion Bond

Completion bonds are not frequently used today. Completion bonds were once commonly required of contractors who were developing real estate. The bond was conditioned upon the completion of the project within a specified time, free from liens.

§ 12.10 Payment Bond

A *payment bond* is a contract between a surety and the owner for the benefit of third-party laborers and material suppliers. The payment bond insures that persons furnishing labor and materials will be paid in full. This insulates the owner and insures payment to subcontractors and suppliers, regardless of what may be due to the prime contractor under its contract with the owner. Also, the payment bond is independent of the performance bond, under which additional monies may be owed to the owner. A payment bond may be a standard form, such as AIA Document A311 (1970), or (for public contracts) may be as prescribed by state statutes and regulations.

The payment bond and the performance bond are usually two separate bonds. Note, however, that a combination of payment and performance bond form in one instrument may involve a single penal sum. That single penal sum constitutes the limit of the surety's liability on both payment and performance obligations. Combination payment and performance bond forms, as well as straight payment bond forms, are available from most insurance agencies.

§ 12.11 Lien Bond

The contractor provides a *lien bond* to guarantee that it or its surety will indemnify the owner of the realty against losses resulting from the filing of liens against the owner's property. Lien bonds serve two purposes: (1) to discharge a mechanics' lien; and (2) to indemnify against the filing of a mechanics' lien.

Bonds to discharge mechanics' liens are characterized by the undertaking of the prime contractor, with a surety, to assure that the obligee will not be encumbered by any mechanics' lien caused by debts to the contractor and/or the contractor's defaults in payment to third parties. An indemnity bond is given by the surety to provide that no lien will be filed. The bond substitutes the security of the bond for lien rights on the title to real estate. Forms for such a lien bond are available from most insurance agencies.

§ 12.12 Subcontractor's Bond

The *subcontractor's bond* is given by the subcontractor as principal, and its surety, to the general contractor; the general contractor and its surety are thus the obligees of the subcontractor's bond. Subcontractor's surety bonds do not run to other subcontractors or suppliers of the principal. Material supplier's of the subcontractor ordinarily cannot recover on a subcontractor's bond.[9]

Subcontractor's bonds are similar to the bonds furnished by the prime contractor (principal) to the owner (obligee). Payment and performance bonds furnished by the subcontractor guarantee that the subcontractor's surety will pay to the general contractor and its surety up to the amount of the penal sum of the bond if the subcontractor defaults on its contract obligations. Forms of subcontractor payment and performance bonds are available from most insurance agencies.

ROLE OF THE SURETY

§ 12.13 Generally

Payment and performance bonds in construction serve the purpose of assuring owners that contracts will be properly completed in accordance with the plans and specifications and that monies owed for labor and materials used in satisfaction of the contract will be paid. Issuance of contract performance and payment bonds by the surety signifies to the owners that the surety has prequalified—in effect, guaranteed—the contractor's ability to complete the contract successfully. In other words, the surety has impliedly informed the owner that it has thoroughly investigated the contractor's ability to complete the contract successfully and has determined that the contractor is capable of doing so.

The product of the surety is the surety bond. Sureties, by assuming certain risks in their bonds, play an important and major role in assuring performance by their principals and in paying for losses resulting form nonperformance. One must recognize that surety companies are businesses

---

[9] Treasure State Indus., Inc. v. Welsh, 173 Mont. 403, 567 P.2d 947 (1977); McGrath v. American Sur. Co., 307 N.Y. 552, 122 N.E.2d 906 (1954).

with the objective to be profitable. Consequently, unless a tribunal finds the surety to be legally responsible for a loss, or concludes that it has substantial risk of liability, the surety is rarely a willing contributor to construction loss situations.

The most important principle to remember is that a bond is a contract. Just as contract provisions can differ and establish different rights between the parties, so too can bond provisions be written differently. Such provisions are enforceable in accordance with their terms.

§ 12.14 Performance Bond

There are generally three parties to a performance surety bond. They are properly defined as the surety, the obligee, and the principal. The form of the performance bond may be AIA Document A311 (1970) or one prescribed by state statutes and regulations. Such forms are available from most insurance agencies.

§ 12.15 Who Is Covered?

Under the performance bond, the obligations run solely between the prime contractor (principal), the owner (obligee), and the surety to insure proper compliance with and completion of the contract. Subcontractors or suppliers have no protection thereunder.[10]

Note that the relief available to the obligee of a performance bond is limited to a much narrower class of persons than under the payment bond. If a court finds, however, as it did in *Amelco Window Corp. v. Federal Insurance Co.,*[11] that the parties intended the performance bond to operate for the benefit of third parties, a subcontractor can maintain an action on the bond for payments due. Attempts have been made, usually unsuccessfully, by subcontractors and suppliers to recover from performance bond sureties as third-party beneficiaries.[12] To avoid any unintended interpretations, performance bonds commonly include the provision that "no right of action shall accrue under this bond to or for the use of any person other than the obligee named herein."

---

[10] *See* United States *ex rel.* Warren v. Kimrey, 489 F.2d 339 (8th Cir. 1974), in which a subcontractor sought to recover against the contractor and its surety on a performance bond. The court of appeals ruled that a performance bond, furnished by the contractor's surety to the government, could not be converted into a payment bond for the benefit of labor and material suppliers.

[11] 127 N.J. Super. 342, 317 A.2d 398 (1974).

[12] Continental Casualty Co. v. Hartford Accident & Indem. Co., 243 Cal. App. 2d 565, 52 Cal. Rptr. 533 (1966).

§ 12.16 When the Principal Defaults

When a construction loss occurs on a project in which the surety is notified that the contractor defaulted or that the contractor was terminated, the performance bond surety must first conduct an investigation of the facts as to whether or not its principal is responsible in whole or in part for the alleged default. The surety must ascertain whether its principal, the contractor, is in default in order to determine whether it, as surety, has any obligations.

Unless the contractor has failed to perform because it ran out of money, the surety's principal vigorously (and most often, genuinely) asserts that it is not in default of its contract, that the owner's notice of termination was wrongful, and that the failure was not caused by the contractor's work but rather resulted from design errors, owner-caused problems, and/or subcontractor errors. In large loss situations resulting in termination of its principal, a prudent surety will conduct an independent investigation to try to untangle the conflicting allegations of the parties with respect to responsibility for the failures that ultimately result in contract termination. When a surety's exposure is relatively small, in an effort to economize, the surety will often make only a token investigation and accept the assertions of its principal.

A major consideration for the surety is the financial strength of its principal. If the principal is a financially strong contractor, with ample assets to satisfy a judgment if the principal is found to be in default, the surety will often accept the principal's denial of responsibility and permit the principal to defend the matter with its own resources, while the surety only monitors developments.

However, when the surety's principal is financially weak or questionable and the risk involved is sizable, thereby exposing the surety's assets if a judgment is rendered against its principal, then the surety will normally assume a more active role. In this situation the surety's position tends to be more objective and may not necessarily coincide with the position taken by its principal.

Sureties, like people, have different philosophies as to how to manage their obligations. Some sureties take a more active, positive, and dynamic role along with (and sometimes instead of) their principal when that principal is alleged to be in default of its contract. Other sureties are more passive, do little, and merely stay abreast of events as they occur.

In considering the financial strength of its principal, the surety often has the comfort of relying upon an indemnity agreement it obtained as a condition to furnishing the surety bond. In this way the principal (contractor) and the individual owners of the construction firm agree in a separate instrument with the surety that they will indemnify and hold the surety harmless should the surety sustain any costs, losses, or expenses, including attorneys' fees, in connection with the bond. Although a corporate principal's resources may be weak or questionable, often the resources of the individual indemnitors are substantial, and the surety must then move to secure the indemnitor's assets so that they will be available to pay for such loss should a judgment be rendered against the principal. A surety will often take such action even before it is called upon to utilize its assets under the usual exoneration provisions of the indemnity agreement.

In order to gain insight into the legal principles that guide the surety's conduct, a basic understanding of the rights and obligations of the parties to the performance bond is necessary. When a performance bond surety is faced with the agonizing decision as to what course to pursue after default of its principal, the surety must consider the number and amount of subcontractors and suppliers that have not been paid and may have valid claims against the surety's payment bond. There is one entire risk: part in the performance bond and part in the payment bond. The surety must assess both.

§ 12.17 Surety's Rights and Obligations upon Default

No obligation arises on the part of the surety until occurrence of the event upon which liability is conditioned. This is commonly referred to as the *default* of the principal. Under a performance bond, a default occurs when the contractor/principal fails to perform its contract obligations to the obligee under the construction contract. Under a payment bond, a default occurs when the principal fails to pay its debts to its subcontractors and suppliers.

When a default or claimed default of the contractor/principal occurs, then and only then does any obligation of the performance bond surety arise. The surety must be satisfied that its principal has in fact defaulted before it will undertake any obligations. If the owner claims that the contractor/principal is in default and the contract requires positive action to terminate, the owner must place the contractor in default in accordance with the procedures set forth in the construction contract. It is highly unusual that a surety would proceed to take over a completed job without determining that its principal is in default of the contract, because the surety would suffer serious negative consequences for making the wrong decision.[13]

---

[13] See § **12.22**.

§ 12.18 —Events of Default

The contract between the obligee (owner) and the principal (contractor) usually defines those events that constitute a default. Common *events of default* in construction contracts include:

1. Substantial violation of the contract
2. Failure to proceed with or abandonment of the work
3. Persistent refusal to supply workers to the job
4. Permitting liens to be filed against the real estate on which the work is being performed or against the contract funds
5. Insolvency proceedings
6. Failure to pay for labor or material obligations incurred in the performance of the contract.

AIA Document A201 (1987) offers a typical termination for default provision.

§ 12.19 —Notice and Investigation

The surety will normally receive notice of the principal's default from the obligee after the obligee declares the principal in default. This is usually because the obligee seeks the surety's participation to complete the contract. Unless the bond expressly provides otherwise, however, notice to the surety is not a condition of the surety's liability. Often, a financially troubled principal voluntarily informs the surety of its inability to continue performance or to pay bills.

Upon receipt of notice the surety normally investigates the status of the contract work and financial condition of the principal. Assuming that the surety ascertains that the principal is in default, it must then determine whether any defenses exist that would discharge its obligations under the bond. If no such defenses exist, the surety must select one of several options to meet its bond obligation. Should the surety make the wrong decision, however, and take over its principal's contract even though the principal is not in default, the surety is considered a volunteer and cannot recover its losses or expenses.[14]

---

[14] Seaboard Sur. Co. v. Dale Constr. Co., 230 F.2d 625 (1st Cir. 1956).

§ 12.20 —Available Defenses

The surety may assert any defense that the principal could have asserted under the construction contract, and also any defense the surety may have as a result of the bond terms and conditions or the obligee's conduct. The principal's most common defense asserted by a surety defending against claimed liability is that the principal did not default or breach its contract with the obligee. Other less commonly available defenses of the principal the surety might assert are:

1. Illegality of the construction contract
2. Impossibility of performance of the construction contract
3. Fraud or duress on the part of the obligee in obtaining the consent of the principal to the construction contract
4. The obligee's prior breach of its obligations under the construction contract
5. Failure of consideration to support the construction contract
6. Material change in the principal's contract obligation without notice to or approval by the surety.

Defenses arising as a result of the bond terms and conditions generally relate to the failure of the obligee to perform some condition precedent. Examples include the obligee's failure to bring an action within the time set forth in the bond, and its failure to take any action required of it in the construction contract, such as making payments to the principal in the manner and at the times specified in the construction contract.

§ 12.21 —Obligee's Conduct

Surety bonds normally contain conditions precedent to the enforceability of the bond. These conditions precedent must be satisfied in order for the obligee to recover on the bond.[15] A surety's defenses arising from the conduct of the obligee include: (1) fraud or misrepresentation of the obligee in inducing the surety to execute the bond; and (2) material alteration of the construction contract's terms with respect to the scope of the work or the time and method of payment (not waived by an express provision in the bond itself).

---

[15] Kanters v. Kotick, 102 Wash. 523, 173 P.2d 329 (1918).

A condition precedent to the surety's obligation on the bond is that the obligee/owner perform all its obligations to the principal/contractor under the construction contract. The owner's primary obligation is to pay the contractor for its work in accordance with the contract. The surety normally has a defense if the obligee/owner pays the contractor too little, thereby causing the default, or pays the contractor too much, thereby reducing the contract balance available to the surety to complete and thus prejudicing the surety's rights. In this latter instance, however, the surety's defense is limited to the extent that the surety is monetarily prejudiced.

§ 12.22 Surety's Options upon Default of Performance Bond Principal

Assuming that the principal is in default and that no substantial defenses exist, the surety must decide how to meet its performance bond obligation.

Payment of damages. The surety on the common form of performance bond may rest on its contract of suretyship by responding in damages to the consequences of the contractor's default, within the *penal sum* (limit) on the bond.[16] The surety may thus require the obligee to determine how to complete the project. Upon completion of the project, the obligee will be entitled to submit its claims to the surety for costs incurred in excess of the contract amount. The surety will thereafter be required to pay those claims as damages for the default, within the penal sum of its bond.

Takeover agreement. The surety may enter into a takeover agreement with the obligee, whereby the surety agrees to complete the principal's contract and the obligee agrees to pay all retainages and contract proceeds, without reduction or setoff, to the surety. The surety then engages another contractor (one acceptable to the obligee) to complete the project. Sometimes the surety contracts with its own principal to complete, but conceptually it then becomes the surety's contract. When the surety takes over and completes the contract, it loses its position as surety and assumes all the principal's contract obligations, thereby waiving the penal sum of the bond.[17] That is, when the surety takes over and assumes the obligation to complete, the surety must complete at any cost. By assuming the obligation to complete, unless the bond form expressly provides otherwise, the surety's obligation is not limited by the penal sum of the bond.

---

[16] Caron v. Andrews, 133 Cal. App. 2d 402, 284 P.2d 544 (1955).

[17] McWaters & Bartlett v. United States *ex rel.* Wilson, 272 F.2d 291 (10th Cir. 1959).

New contractor and contract. The surety may select another contractor and persuade the obligee to enter into a contract with that new contractor for completion of the project. The surety will then pay (and its loss is generally limited in such agreements to) the difference between the remaining original contract funds and the contract price at which the substitute contractor has consented to complete the work.

Financing existing contractor. The surety may elect to finance the principal for the purpose of completing bonded work. This choice requires the surety's close supervision of the principal and joint control of all funds used for completion of the contract. Here again, the penal sum of the bond does not limit the surety's liability, and the surety's payments for or on behalf of its principal are not credited toward the bond penal sum.[18]

On rare occasions the surety will be able, by negotiating payment of a stipulated sum, to buy back its bond. Although done infrequently, this may occur when work has not yet commenced or other unusual circumstances exist.

§ 12.23 Damages Recoverable from Performance Bond Surety

Unless the bond itself places restrictions on the surety's liability, the surety's liability is coextensive with that of the principal.[19] Normally, however, the surety's liability is limited to the penalty or penal sum of the bond.[20] Note, however, that when the surety undertakes to complete the contract following a default, the surety is generally deemed to have waived the penal sum limitation on its liability.[21]

If, however, the surety breaches its contract with the obligee to perform its obligations under the bond itself, then the penal sum of the bond still may not limit the liability of the surety. In *Continental Realty Corp. v. Andrew J. Crevolin Co.*,[22] involving a bond that required the surety to make payments to the obligee or complete the work upon default, the surety did neither and the court found it liable for sums substantially in excess of the penal sum of the bond. These damages were assessed after the

---

[18] Caron v. Andrews, 133 Cal. App. 2d 402, 284 P.2d 544.

[19] American Sur. Co. v. Wheeling Structural Steel Co., 114 F.2d 237 (4th Cir. 1940).

[20] Chicago Bonding & Sur. Co. v. Augusta Savannah Navigation Co., 250 F. 616 (7th Cir.), *cert. denied,* 247 U.S. 509 (1918).

[21] McWaters & Bartlett v. United States *ex rel.* Wilson, 272 F.2d 291 (10th Cir. 1959).

[22] 380 F. Supp. 246 (S.D. W. Va. 1974).

cost of completion had been determined. The surety totally failed in its contract obligation to the obligee, and thereby became liable to the obligee for a breach of contract separate from the bond's obligation to indemnify the owner against the principal's default (recovery for which would be limited by the penal sum).

When the obligee completes the project, its recovery includes the amount in excess of the contract price actually and reasonably expended in completion. Special damages may be recoverable if they are within the contemplation of the parties to the contract.[23] Interest, although recoverable within the penal sum of the bond, is permitted to be recovered in excess of the penal sum of the bond only when there is an independent default of the surety.[24] Also, the surety will be liable for the obligee's attorneys' fees only when the contract or a statute requires such payment.[25] Loss of profits and other consequential damages to the obligee resulting from the principal's refusal to complete its contract are not recoverable from the surety.[26]

§ 12.24 Surety's Right to Contract Funds

Controversy frequently arises between the completing surety of a defaulted contractor and the contractor's creditors (usually banks or lending institutions that have taken the contractor's receivables as security for a loan) as to who is entitled to the earned contract balance on the project. The courts have uniformly held that upon default of the principal, the surety is entitled to such contract balances and retainages, provided the surety undertakes performance of the construction contract. This is so even though the surety has not perfected any security interest in the principal's receivables, because the surety's rights are based upon the theory that an assignee takes no greater rights than its assignor.[27]

Thus, the courts generally hold that a completing surety is entitled to the contract balance after a default, even though other creditors, such as banks, may have perfected a security interest under the Uniform Commercial Code (UCC).[28] The legal relationship of a surety in this situation is governed not by the UCC, but by equitable principles complementary to and

---

[23] Miracle Mile Shopping Center v. National Union Indem. Co., 299 F.2d 780 (7th Cir. 1962).

[24] Cunningham v. Cunningham, 157 F.2d 859 (D.C. Cir. 1946).

[25] Maryland Casualty Co. v. Cunningham, 234 Ala. 80, 173 So. 2d 506 (1937).

[26] Terry v. United States Fid. & Guar. Co., 196 Wash. 206, 82 P.2d 532 (1938).

[27] Travelers Indem. Co. v. Western Ga. Nat'l Bank, 387 F. Supp. 1090 (N.D. Ga. 1974); Deer Park Bank v. Aetna Ins. Co., 493 S.W.2d 305 (Tex. 1973).

[28] U.C.C. Art. 9.

not superseded by the UCC.[29] The surety's right to the unpaid balance of the principal's contract with the owner relates back to the time of the suretyship agreement, and is superior to any rights of the contractor or its assignees.[30] The surety does not, however, have priority, over other creditors of the principal, to obtain receivables from any project on which the principal is not in default and the surety is not completing the contract.

Note that progress payments or retainages already paid to the contractor or to other creditors can almost never be recovered by the surety. However, in *American Fidelity Fire Insurance Co. v. Pavia-Byrne Engineering Corp.*[31] the court allowed recovery by a surety against a third-party engineer whose negligent issuance of payment certificates resulted in the owner's improper, but good faith, disbursement of retainage to the contractor.

§ 12.25 Subrogation

The prevailing rule of equitable subrogation is that a surety that pays its principal's debt is thereby entitled to use all the rights of the person it paid to enforce the surety's right to be reimbursed. Thus, in one case, the rights of a surety that had paid the laborers and material suppliers of its bankrupt principal and thus stood in the shoes of those laborers and material suppliers, were held to be superior to the rights of general creditors, which rights the receiver in bankruptcy represented.[32]

PARTIES AND CAUSES OF ACTION

§ 12.26 Introduction

Sections 12.26 through **12.34** cover those matters most frequently litigated between contractors and their sureties and related parties, with one exception. Litigation initiated by subcontractors and material suppliers to enforce their claims against contractors and their sureties is the subject of **Chapter 13**.

---

[29] National Shawmut Bank v. New Amsterdam Casualty Co., 411 F.2d 843 (1st Cir. 1969); Canter v. Schlager, 358 Mass. 789, 267 N.E.2d 492 (1971).

[30] Uptagraff v. United States, 315 F.2d 200 (4th Cir.), *cert. denied,* 375 U.S. 818 (1963); American Casualty Co. v. Shattuck, 228 F. Supp. 834 (W.D. Okla. 1964).

[31] 393 So. 2d 830 (La. Ct. App.), *cert. denied,* 397 So. 2d 1362 (La. 1981).

[32] Segovia Dev. Corp. v. Constructora Maza, Inc., 628 F.2d 724 (1st Cir. 1980).

§ 12.27 Contractor versus Surety

The causes of action most frequently brought by contractors against their sureties are breach of contract, interference with performance of the contract, and breach of good faith. A contractor's charge that the surety breached its contract usually involves the surety's failure or refusal to pay the claims of subcontractors and material suppliers against the contractor and/or to discharge liens against the project. (Litigation of this nature is also discussed in **Chapter 13**, but with regard to actions brought against contractors by sureties.) The elements of such surety claims, however, are being investigated as possible weapons for contractors in their surety-targeted attacks.

Interference with contract performance and breach of good faith also used to be raised mostly as defenses, but are now being seen as offensive weapons.[33] An action for contract interference in construction cases usually arises after the surety notifies the owner that the contractor is in default and that no further contract funds should be released. This normally occurs when the contractor has not formally admitted default. The owner then usually holds the funds, depriving the contractor of the cash flow attributable to that specific contract. Subsequently, contractor sues surety for tortious interference with the prime contract.

This approach applies only to alleged intentional contract interference and is to be distinguished from negligent interference with a contract. Recovery for the latter is uniformly denied.[34] However, recovery for intentional interference with contractual relations is allowed in every jurisdiction except Louisiana.[35] The five elements of the tort are:

1. An enforceable contract (in Wyoming it applies also to an unenforceable contract)[36]

---

[33] Federal Ins. Co. v. Community State Bank, 905 F.2d (5th Cir. 1990); Lamberg v. Maryland Casualty Co., 418 So. 2d 553 (La. 1982). For a detailed analysis of *Lamberg* and its significance, see Koch, *The Surety's General Indemnity Agreement: Current or Out of Date?*, Proceedings of ABA Fidelity & Sur. L. Comm., ABA Midwinter Meeting (New York 1984). Copies of ABA and IAIC seminar materials mentioned throughout this chapter are available from Stradley, Ronon, Stevens & Young, 2600 One Commerce Square, Philadelphia, PA 19103.

[34] Restatement (Second) of Torts § 766c cmt. a (1977).

[35] Robins Dry Dock & Repair Co. v. Flint, 275 U.S. 303 (1927); Consolidated Aluminum Corp. v. C.F. Bean Corp., 639 F. Supp. 1173 (W.D. La. 1986), *aff'd,* 833 F.2d 65 (5th Cir. 1987) *reh'g denied en banc,* 837 F.2d 1090 (5th Cir.), *cert. denied,* 486 U.S. 1055 (1988); P.P.G. Indus., Inc. v. Bean Dredging Corp., 447 So. 2d 1058, 1059 (La. 1984); Professional Answering Serv., Inc. v. Central La. Elec. Co., 521 So. 2d 549 (La. Ct. App. 1988).

[36] Kvenild v. Taylor, 594 P.2d 972 (Wyo. 1979). In Fidelity Dep't Stores v. Moite, 452 U.S. 392, 403 (1981), the Supreme Court noted the holding in *Kvenild* but held it inapplicable to the case being decided.

2. Knowledge of the contract's existence
3. Intentional inducement of a breach
4. Absence of justification
5. Resultant damages.[37]

However, one who in good faith asserts a legally protected, presently existing interest that may be impaired by performance of another contract is privileged to prevent that performance, and ill will toward the plaintiff will not defeat the privilege.[38]

Tortious interference with business expectancy or relations is a different cause of action.[39] A contractor's expectancy of good faith and fair dealing from its surety arises from the implied covenant of good faith and fair dealing inherent in any contract.[40] The breach of that implied covenant involves more than bad judgment, negligence, or insufficient zeal on the surety's part; it carries an implication of a dishonest purpose, conscious wrong, or breach of duty through motive of self-interest or ill will.[41]

Although the covenant of good faith and fair dealing is couched in contractual terms, it is largely a creation of tort law. Punitive damages will lie

---

[37] Dougherty v. Parsec, Inc., 872 F.2d 766 (6th Cir. 1989); Flintridge Station Assoc. v. American Fletcher Mortgage Co., 761 F.2d 434 (7th Cir. 1985); Heheman v. E.W. Scripps Co., 661 F.2d 1115 (6th Cir. 1981), *cert. denied,* 456 U.S. 991 (1982); Phil Crowley Steel Corp. v. Sharon Steel Corp., 536 F. Supp. 429, 432 (E.D. Mo. 1982), *rev'd on other grounds and remanded,* 702 F.2d 719 (8th Cir. 1983); Hurst v. Town of Shelburn, 422 N.E.2d 322 (Ind. Ct. App. 1981).

[38] Wright v. Heizer Corp., 560 F.2d 236 (7th Cir. 1977); Bailey v. Meister Brau, Inc., 535 F.2d 982 (7th Cir. 1976); Ollice v. Alyeska Pipeline Serv., 659 P.2d 1182 (Alaska 1983); Alyeska Pipeline Serv. v. Aurora Air Serv., Inc., 604 P.2d 1090 (Alaska 1979); Wyatt v. Ruck Constr. Co., 117 Ariz. 186, 571 P.2d 683 (1977); Brown v. Safeway Stores, Inc., 94 Wash. 2d 359, 617 P.2d 704 (1980). *See* Annotation, 44 A.L.R.4th 1078 (1986).

[39] Rickel v. Schwinn Bicycle Co., 144 Cal. App. 3d 648, 192 Cal. Rptr. 732 (1983); Sandolph v. P&L Hauling Contractors, Inc., 430 So. 2d 102 (La. Ct. App. 1983); Joba Constr. Co. v. Burns & Roe, Inc., 121 Mich. App. 615, 329 N.W.2d 760 (1982); Friedman v. Edward L. Bakewell, Inc., 654 S.W.2d 367 (Mo. Ct. App. 1983); Leigh Furniture & Carpet Co. v. Isom, 657 P.2d 293 (Utah 1982).

[40] Filner v. Shapiro, 633 F.2d 139 (2d Cir. 1980); Reinharcz v. Chrysler Motors Corp., 514 F. Supp. 1141 (C.D. Cal. 1981); Carol C. Gelardi Corp. v. Miller Brewing Co., 502 F. Supp. 637 (D.N.J. 1980); Manchester Bank v. Connecticut Bank & Trust Co., 497 F. Supp. 1304 (D.N.H. 1980). *See* 3 Corbin on Contracts § 570, at 341 (1960); 17A C.J.S. Contracts § 328 n.40.5 (1963) citing cases from Maryland, Massachusetts, Oklahoma, Rhode Island, South Carolina, Utah, Vermont, and Washington. *See also* Miller, *Overview of the Problem of Bad Faith and Punitive Damages,* 15 Forum 194 (Fall 1979); Reinert, *The Duty of the Performing Surety to Its Bond Principal and Indemnitors; Good Faith,* 15 Forum 1005 (Summer 1980).

[41] Hartford Accident & Indem. Co. v. Millis Roofing & Sheet Metal, Inc., 11 Mass. App. Ct. 998, 418 N.E.2d 645 (1981).

only if the insurer breaches the implied covenant and, in addition, acts with oppression, fraud, or malice.[42]

In 1983, one commentator suggested that, although sureties have not yet been successfully attacked on the breach of good faith theory, by 1990 "all forms of insurance relationships . . . [including] insured versus surety . . . will be vulnerable to some form of extra contract claim."[43]

The very next year, two cases fulfilled this prediction. An Illinois appellate court found that the performance bond surety's actions did not "demonstrate the good faith expected of a surety," and affirmed a judgment for more than double the face amount of the bond.[44] And the Ohio Supreme Court held that, having acted in bad faith as to claims handling and payment, the surety on a financial responsibility bond was liable to the third-party plaintiff for compensatory and punitive damages beyond the amount of the bond.[45]

California state and federal courts subsequently have held construction bond sureties liable for punitive damages for unfair claims settlement practices,[46] and have awarded $5 million punitive damages against a blanket bond surety.[47]

Although the Alabama Supreme Court reversed, on factual grounds, a judgment against a bankers blanket bond surety for bad faith denial of claim, the clear thrust of the opinion was that a surety is subject to the same bad faith rules as any other insurer.[48] A Connecticut court affirmed both compensatory and punitive damages, holding that provisions of the general agreement of indemnity did not insulate a bid bond surety from a bad faith refusal to issue the contractor performance and payment bonds.[49] The Supreme Court of North Dakota held that a contractor's surety was subject to a bad faith action brought by an unpaid subcontractor.[50] On a question certified from the Ninth Circuit Court of Appeals, the Montana Supreme Court held that a surety violating Montana's unfair claims settlement laws

---

[42] Los Angeles Memorial Coliseum Comm. v. NFL, 791 F.2d 1356 (9th Cir. 1986); San Jose Prod. Credit Ass'n v. Old Republic Life Ins. Co., 723 F.2d 700, 703 (9th Cir. 1984).

[43] Kornblum, *Extra-Contract Actions Against Insurers: What's Ahead in the Eighties?* 19 Forum 58, 60–61 (Fall 1983).

[44] Fisher v. Fidelity & Deposit Co., 125 Ill. App. 3d 362, 466 N.E.2d 332, 339 (1984).

[45] Suver v. Personal Serv. Ins. Co., 11 Ohio St. 3d 6, 462 N.E.2d 415 (1984).

[46] Alvarez v. Insurance Co. of No. Am., 667 F. Supp. 689 (N.D. Cal. 1987); General Ins. Co. of Am. v. Mammoth Vista Owners Ass'n, Inc., 174 Cal. App. 3d 810, 220 Cal. Rptr. 291 (1985).

[47] Downey Sav. & Loan Ass'n v. Ohio Casualty Ins. Co., 189 Cal. App. 3d 1072, 234 Cal. Rptr. 835 (1987), *cert. denied,* 486 U.S. 1036 (1988).

[48] Insurance Co. of No. Am. v. Citizenbank, 491 So. 2d 880 (Ala. 1986).

[49] L.F. Pace & Co. v. Travelers Ins. Co., 9 Conn. App. 30, 514 A.2d 766 (1986).

[50] Szarkowski v. Reliance Ins. Co., 404 N.W.2d 502 (N.D. 1987).

is liable for tort damages independent of, and in excess of, any breach of contract damages.[51] An Oregon court, despite a general indemnity agreement provision giving the performance bond surety "sole discretion" in compromising claims against the contractor, held that failure of the surety to make a reasonable investigation of the claims and of the contractor's defenses and counterclaims, subjected it to bad faith damages.[52] In addition, a federal district court explained that, under Illinois law, when the insured is obligated to indemnify its construction bond surety, all that is necessary to establish the surety's bad faith is a showing of negligence.[53]

§ 12.28 Contractor versus Owner

The possible actions a contractor might have against an owner, beginning from the bid process to the termination or completion of a project, are myriad.[54] Two of the more common actions, however, are quantum meruit and damages for delay.

The expression *quantum meruit* means literally "as much as he deserves." It describes the extent of liability implied by law on a contract. This liability is predicated on the reasonable value of services performed.[55] The elements of this action are:

1. Valuable services were rendered or materials furnished
2. Such services or materials were accepted, used, and enjoyed by defendant
3. Circumstances exist charging the defendant with notice that the plaintiff expected to be paid for those services or materials.[56]

In the construction contract scenario, an action for quantum meruit usually arises after the formal contract has been terminated prior to completion[57] or when the required performance falls outside the terms of the

[51] K-W Indus. v. National Sur. Corp., 231 Mont. 461, 754 P.2d 502 (1988).

[52] City of Portland v. G.D. Ward & Assocs., Inc., 89 Or. App. 452, 750 P.2d 171, *review denied,* 305 Or. 672, 757 P.2d 422 (1988).

[53] Rush Presbyterian St. Luke's Medical Ctr. v. Safeco Ins. Co., 712 F. Supp. 1344 (N.D. Ill. 1989).

[54] *See* R. Carrigan, Claims Against the Owner (Public and Private) (ABA Nat'l Inst. on Construction Cont. Claims 1977) [hereinafter Carrigan].

[55] Nardi & Co. v. Allabastro, 20 Ill. App. 3d 323, 314 N.E.2d 367, 370 (1974).

[56] Montes v. Naismith & Trevino Const. Co., 459 S.W.2d 691, 694 (Tex. Ct. App. 1970).

[57] Kinchen v. Gilworth, 454 So. 2d 1130 (La. Ct. App. 1984).

original agreement and no supplemental agreement is evidenced.[58] A prerequisite for its application is that the plaintiff have no remedy at law.[59]

The other common action arises from the theory that owner-caused delays resulting in increased costs to the contractor or preventing the contractor from completing the job on time can be held compensable by the owner.[60] As a direct reaction to a chain of large judgments in favor of contractors against owners, it is now routine for owners to insert a no damage for delay clause in the construction contract.

This clause waives recovery for any damages arising from delays caused by the owner or another contractor.[61] Although the clause is a harsh measure that must be strictly construed, it is enforceable when it is free from ambiguity, reflects the intent of the parties, and is reasonably interpreted.[62]

Exceptions not affected by the clause are delays not contemplated at the time the agreement is executed, unreasonably long delays, and delays resulting from fraud, bad faith, or active interference by owner.[63] Among events not considered exceptions are violation of scheduling provisions; inadequate storage space; labor problems; congestion at the jobsite; delay in arrival of equipment; weather delays; danger from falling objects; or rivalry among subcontractors.[64]

With these actions (and many others) available as recourse, many contractors, having dealt with public owners, tend to forget the basic requirement in dealing with a private owner, that is, making certain that the party appearing to be the owner is the true owner of the property. A private owner in satisfactory financial condition at the start of a project may be insolvent before it is finished. Thus, the contractor's only security is its ability to place liens on the property, and liens are granted only to secure the obligations of the property owner.

When the contractor is to work for a lessee, it is essential that the lease be scrutinized closely. Generally, an unpaid contractor can place a valid lien against the lessor's property if the lease requires such work to be done, if the lessor requests the work to be done, or if the lessor ratifies the work by its actions.[65] However, in Louisiana, for example, when a lessee builds at its

---

[58] Brookhaven Landscape & Grading Co. v. J.F. Barton Contracting Co., 676 F.2d 516 (11th Cir. 1982).

[59] Creely v. Leisure Living, Inc., 437 So. 2d 816 (La. 1983); Harrington v. Oliver, 459 So. 2d 111, 114 (La. Ct. App.), *cert. denied,* 462 So. 2d 198 (La. 1984).

[60] *See* Carrigan.

[61] *See* Gontar, *The Enforceability of "No Damage for Delay" Clauses in Construction Contracts,* 28 Loy. L. Rev. 129 (1982) [hereinafter Gontar]. See also **Ch. 5**.

[62] Annotation, *Validity and Construction of "No Damage" Clause with Respect to Delay in Building or Construction Contract,* 74 A.L.R.3d 187, 207–13 (1950).

[63] *Id.* 214–15 n.21.

[64] *See* Gontar at 132–33 n.53.

[65] Christensen v. Idaho Land Developers, Inc., 104 Idaho 458, 660 P.2d 70 (1983).

expense and for its own use, even with the owner's consent, only the structure (not the land) can be encumbered with a lien.[66]

Private construction contracts may contain litigation traps not found in public works contracts. For example, one contract provided that the contractor had a "relationship of trust and confidence" with the owner. The court held that such a relationship required the contractor to inform the owner of incipient cost overruns, and failure to do so was a breach of contract.[67]

In another case, the owner was damaged through no fault of the contractor. The basic contract provided that the contractor would indemnify the owner for all damages regardless of negligence. The AIA indemnity provision, incorporated by reference, required indemnity only if the contractor was negligent, but also provided that in any conflict between the two, the basic contract would prevail. The contractor escaped that trap by convincing the court that the difference between the two was not a conflict but merely a modification.[68]

§ 12.29 Contractor versus Miscellaneous Parties

A contractor possesses a cause of action against a subcontractor and its surety for breach of contract in the event of a default. It also has actions against a subcontractor on the same grounds that the owner has against the contractor, because the flow-down clause included in most subcontracts creates the same legal relationship between the subcontractor and the contractor as that existing between the contractor and the owner.[69] Most subcontracts also contain an indemnity agreement holding the prime contractor harmless from damages.[70]

Contractors may also have causes of action against architects, engineers, and others involved in the construction process for breach of their professional duties.[71] In a rather unusual case, a contractor also prevailed against its liability insurer for some $148,000 in attorneys' fees incurred by itself and its performance bond surety in defending a third-party demand in a negligence action.[72]

---

[66] La. Civ. Code Ann. arts. 464, 493 (West); P.H.A.C. Servs. v. Seaways Int'l, Inc., 403 So. 2d 1199 (La. 1981).

[67] Jones v. J.H. Hiser Constr., Inc., 60 Md. App. 671, 484 A.2d 302 (1984), *cert. denied,* 303 Md. 114, 492 A.2d 616 (1985).

[68] Sears, Roebuck & Co. v. Shamrock Constr. Co., 441 So. 2d 379 (La. Ct. App. 1983).

[69] See **Ch. 10**.

[70] *See id.*

[71] See **§ 12.33**.

[72] Merrick Constr. Co. v. Hartford Fire Ins. Co., 449 So. 2d 85 (La. Ct. App.), *writ denied,* 450 So. 2d 958 (La. 1984).

§ 12.30 Surety versus Contractor

Actions by a construction bond surety against its contractor/principal may be conveniently divided by reference to whether the surety's liability has become established and whether the surety has performed in accordance with its bond obligations. If the contractor has not defaulted, but has given the surety reason to be concerned about such matters as, for example, progress payments being applied to other, nonbonded projects, contract funds being diverted to the contractor's personal use, and amounts due subcontractors and material suppliers being understated, an action in quia timet is appropriate.[73]

A legal concept developed under Roman law, *quia timet* means "because he fears," and it may be effectively used to protect the surety against a variety of reasonably anticipated future injuries. The action may be brought before the surety's liability has matured,[74] but the surety may not actually receive payments from the contract funds. Such an action is appropriate, for example, for requiring specific performance of the contractor's duty under an indemnity agreement to deposit funds equal to any loss reserve established by the surety.[75]

A secondary benefit from the quia timet suit is that all the surety's actions against the contractor are taken in accordance with court orders. Thus, later claims by the contractor for domination, interference with contract, or breach of the implied covenant of good faith are prevented.

If the surety's liability has become absolute, it has available the remedy of *exoneration*. That remedy allows the surety to require the contractor to discharge the primary obligation before the surety has made any payments.[76] When the contractor is financially unable to discharge its obligations, this equitable right to exoneration may be used to have any contract funds in the hands of the owner applied to the payment of material suppliers or subcontractors.[77]

Occasionally, a project will be completed and accepted, with claims of material suppliers and subcontractors still outstanding, when a contractor refuses to execute the close-out papers necessary to release the contract balances. In such a case, a surety can, under its exoneration right, have a receiver appointed to execute the necessary documents, thus releasing the funds for application by the surety to outstanding claims.[78]

---

[73] *See* Mann & Jennings, *Quia Timet: A Remedy for the Fearful Surety,* Proceedings of ABA Fidelity & Sur. L. Comm., ABA Annual Meeting (Chicago 1984).

[74] 2 Story Equity Jurisprudence §§ 825, 826 (1972).

[75] United Bonding Ins. Co. v. Stein, 273 F. Supp. 929 (E.D. Pa. 1967).

[76] Admiral Oriental Lines, Inc. v. United States, 86 F.2d 201, 204 (2d Cir. 1936).

[77] Glades County v. Detroit Fid. & Sur. Co., 57 F.2d 449, 451–52 (5th Cir. 1932).

[78] Western Casualty & Sur. Co. v. Biggs, 217 F.2d 163 (7th Cir. 1954). *See generally* Downs, *A Surety's Basic Rights and Remedies,* 15 Def. L.J. 139 (1966); Auerbach, *Quia*

After a surety has performed its bond obligations, the most frequent action brought against the defaulted contractor is for reimbursement of the surety's losses incurred in completing the job and/or paying the claims of subcontractors and material suppliers. Such an action is usually brought under the provisions of a general indemnity agreement[79] executed by the contractor and individual indemnitors as part of the consideration for the surety's issuance of the bonds. However, a performing surety is also entitled to indemnity from its contractor/principal by operation of law, its right of equitable subrogation.[80] The surety may bring this suit against one or more of the indemnitors without releasing those not joined as defendants, because the indemnity agreement specifies that their obligation is joint and several.[81] Usually, all indemnitors are joined.

Most suits against bond indemnitors are good candidates for summary judgment. Basically, the surety has only to attach copies of the indemnity agreements to its complaint and exhibit a personal-knowledge affidavit of loss with the motion for summary judgment. Prayers for declaratory judgment fixing the ripening of the surety's right of subrogation as of the bond date and declaring the indemnity agreement assignments to be in effect as of the indemnity agreement date, are useful protection should subsequent third-party actions develop.

The indemnitors' answers will frequently deny the allegations of the complaint. In such cases, use of the request for admissions[82] will quickly establish the necessary undisputed facts.

The surety, of course, owes an indemnitor the duty of good faith, a duty that cannot be waived. The surety must also notify an indemnitor of its intention before using any assets available to reduce the indemnitor's liability, and must communicate to indemnitors all settlement offers.[83] Regardless of legal requirements, it is good practice promptly to notify all indemnitors of anything that might conceivably affect them, and invite their written objections, if any. Such practice can avoid obscure legal pitfalls. For example, if the surety has issued a statutory bond and the

---

Timet: Relief by Summary Judgment on Indemnity Agreement, 39 Ins. Couns. J. 536 (Oct. 1972); Babcock, *An Update—Suits for Exoneration and Other Special Relief,* 17 Forum 344 (Fall 1981).

[79] *See generally* Koch, *The Surety's General Indemnity Agreement: Current or Out of Date?,* Proceedings of ABA Fidelity & Sur. L. Comm., ABA Midwinter Meeting (New York 1984); McNamara & Mungall, Construction Contract Bond Indemnity Agreement Provisions (Defense Research Inst. Monograph No. 3, 1975).

[80] United States v. Bellard, 674 F.2d 330, 335 (5th Cir. 1982); Merrick Constr. Co. v. Hartford Fire Ins. Co., 449 So. 2d 85 (La. Ct. App.), *writ denied,* 450 So. 2d 958 (La. 1984); Hollabaugh, *Surety's Right to Equitable Subrogation: Overture for an Arrow,* 51 Ins. Couns. J. 547 (Oct. 1984).

[81] T.P.M.P.T. Employees Credit Union v. Charpentier, 376 So. 2d 592 (La. Ct. App. 1979).

[82] Fed. R. Civ. P. 36, or comparable state rule.

[83] New Amsterdam Casualty Co. v. Lundquist, 293 Minn. 274, 198 N.W.2d 543 (1972).

statutes specify the jurisdiction and venue of suits, settlement of a suit brought elsewhere may preclude recovery from an indemnitor.[84]

§ 12.31 Surety versus Bank

Conflicts between a construction bond surety and the contractor's bank frequently arise after the contractor defaults. Both assert claims to the contract funds remaining in the owner's hands: the bank, by reason of assignment of all funds due or to become due the contractor that was executed as security for interim financing; the surety, by its right of subrogation and also through the assignments in the indemnity agreement.

The bank nearly always has its security interest perfected under the Uniform Commercial Code (UCC); the surety seldom has anything publicly recorded. However, the courts have uniformly held that the surety's right of subrogation is superior to the rights of the contractor/principal, its assigns, or a trustee in bankruptcy,[85] and relates back to the date of issuance of the bond.[86] This superiority applies to a financing bank's perfected security interest,[87] and that is so even if the security interest is perfected before the bond is issued.[88]

In the 1960s, some courts apparently felt that Article 9 of the UCC superseded the construction bond surety's right of subrogation.[89] However, that contest was settled in the surety's favor by a 1969 decision.[90]

---

[84] Safeco Ins. Co. v. J.L. Henson, Inc., 601 S.W.2d 183 (Tex. Ct. App. 1980).

[85] Prairie State Bank v. United States, 164 U.S. 227 (1869); Henningsen v. United States Fidelity & Guar. Co., 208 U.S. 404 (1908); Pearlman v. Reliance Ins. Co., 371 U.S. 132 (1962).

[86] Home Indem. Co. v. United States, 313 F. Supp. 212 (W.D. Mo. 1970); Division of Employment Sec. v. Trice Constr. Co., 555 S.W.2d 65 (Mo. Ct. App. 1977); Finance Co. of Am. v. United States Fidelity & Guar. Co., 277 Md. 177, 353 A.2d 249 (1976); Third Nat'l Bank v. Highlands Ins. Co., 603 S.W.2d 730 (Tenn. 1980). *See generally* Hallenbeck, *Surety's Remedies—Enforcing Rights to Contract Funds,* Proceedings of International Ass'n of Ins. Counsel (I.A.I.C.) Fidelity & Sur. Comm., I.A.I.C. Meeting (New York 1984) [hereinafter Hallenbeck].

[87] Alaska State Bank v. General Ins. Co., 579 P.2d 1362 (Alaska 1978); First Fed. State Bank v. Town of Malvern, 270 N.W.2d 818 (Iowa 1978); Schneider Fuel & Supply Co. v. West Allis State Bank, 70 Wis. 2d 1041 236 N.W.2d 266 (Wis. 1975)(superseded by statute as stated in Kraemer Bros., Inc. v. Pulaski State Bank, 138 Wis. 2d 395, 406 N.W.2d 379 (1987)).

[88] Fidelity & Casualty Co. v. Central Bank, 409 So. 2d 788 (Ala. 1982).

[89] Whitney, Rubin & Stabbe, *Twenty Years of the Uniform Commercial Code and Fidelity and Surety Bonding—Some Random Observations,* 18 Forum 670, 676–80 (Summer 1983).

[90] National Shawmut Bank v. New Amsterdam Casualty Co., 411 F.2d 843 (1st Cir. 1969). *See also* Hallenbeck.

The subrogation rights of the surety as to a defaulted contractor's materials are not as clear, but it has been held that an owner's right to such material is superior to that of the financing bank.[91] Consequently, because a performing surety is subrogated to the owner's rights,[92] and the owner would normally prevail in this scenario, so should the surety. Persuasive arguments in proper cases can also be made, by way of a surety's subrogation to the rights of the contractor, subcontractors, and material suppliers, that it has first claim to such materials.[93]

A bank cannot set off a debt against a contractor's account when it has information indicating that the contractor is de facto in default, even though no formal default has been declared. The bank is charged with knowledge that construction bond sureties routinely take indemnity agreements from their contractors.[94]

§ 12.32 Surety versus Owner

Most suits by sureties against owners involve the rights to contract funds after the contractor has defaulted. These funds, depending on whether the default arises from nonperformance or nonpayment by the contractor, may be earned by unpaid progress payments, unearned contract funds, or the percentage of retained funds in the owner's hands after the job is completed.

Other claimants to such funds may be a financing bank, a contractor's trustee in bankruptcy, and the government. The performing surety's superior right as against the bank or trustee is well established, whether a performance or payment bond is involved.[95] However, when the government is the owner, the situation is more complex. The government cannot set off unpaid taxes against retained funds when the surety is acting under a performance bond,[96] but it can do so when the surety is acting under a payment bond.[97] Liquidated damages can be set off against retained funds

---

[91] Howard Dodge & Sons, Inc. v. Finn, 391 N.E.2d 638 (Ind. Ct. App. 1979); Graves Constr. Co. v. Rockingham Nat'l Bank, 220 Va. 844, 263 S.E.2d 408 (1980).

[92] First Fed. State Bank v. Town of Malvern, 270 N.W.2d 818.

[93] *See* Sutton, *Contractor's Default: Can the Surety Take the Construction Materials?,* 4 Construction Law. 5 n.3 (Summer 1983).

[94] INA v. Northhampton Nat'l Bank, 708 F.2d 13 (1st Cir. 1983).

[95] *See* Prairie State Bank v. United States, 164 U.S. 227 (1869); Henningsen v. United States Fid. & Guar. Co., 208 U.S. 484 (1908); Pearlman v. Reliance Ins. Co., 371 U.S. 132 (1962).

[96] Trinity Universal Ins. Co. v. United States, 382 F.2d 317 (5th Cir.), *cert. denied,* 390 U.S. 906 (1967).

[97] Royal Indem. Co. v. United States, 371 F.2d 462 (Ct. Cl.), *cert. denied,* 389 U.S. 833 (1967).

regardless of the nature of the bond issued.[98] A performing surety is subrogated to the government's right of setoff, even against unbonded jobs.[99]

When, in a suit for possession of the retainage, the court indicates it will grant the surety's motion for summary judgment, but the owner's counterclaim remains to be tried, there is a useful mechanism for putting the retained funds to work: ask the court to certify a summary judgment under Federal Rule of Civil Procedure 54(b), but to stay it under Rule 62(h) until the counterclaim is decided. Meanwhile, the owner deposits the funds with the court, where they are invested in short-term, high-yield government obligations. The result is a better return than legal prejudgment interest would have provided.[100]

Another fairly common action against the owner is an action to recover contract funds paid to the contractor after default. This situation arises when the contractor is completing or has completed the job satisfactorily but subcontractors and material suppliers remain unpaid. Some owners do not realize that failure to pay for labor and materials is as much a default as abandoning the job.[101] Consequently, even though the surety has formally notified the owner of the default and requested that no further payments be made, the owner may still release the funds to the contractor.

Such a payment constitutes an unlawful conversion of funds to which the performing surety is entitled.[102] The surety's rights in this situation apply to the United States as well as to state or private owners, and to progress payments as well as retainage.[103] However, a government contracting officer is allowed considerable discretion with respect to progress payments, and it is essential for the surety to be able to establish when notice of default was actually received.[104] Like the suit against indemnitors, this action is usually a good candidate for summary judgment.

The Bankruptcy Reform Act of 1978 (Bankruptcy Code)[105] substantially affected surety rights and must be considered in any litigation involving

---

[98] Great Am. Ins. Co. v. United States, 492 F.2d 821 (Ct. Cl. 1974). *See generally* American Fid. Fire Ins. Co. v. Construcciones Werl, 407 F. Supp. 164, 191 (V.I. 1975) (Supplementary Analysis No. 1).

[99] District of Columbia v. Aetna Ins. Co., 462 A.2d 428, 432 (D.C. 1983).

[100] Hartford Accident & Indem. Co. v. Boise Cascade Corp., 489 F. Supp. 855 (N.D. Ill. 1980).

[101] Martin v. National Sur. Co., 300 U.S. 588 (1937); United States Fid. & Guar. Co. v. Triborough Bridge Auth., 297 N.Y. 31, 74 N.E.2d 226, 228, *reh'g denied,* 297 N.Y. 694, 77 N.E.2d 9 (1947).

[102] Claiborne Parish Sch. Bd. v. Fidelity & Deposit Co., 40 F.2d 577, 578–79 (5th Cir. 1980).

[103] National Sur. Corp. v. United States, 319 F. Supp. 45, 48–49 (N.D. Ala. 1970).

[104] *See* United States Fid. & Guar. Co. v. Orlando Utils. Comm'n, 564 F. Supp. 962 (M.D. Fla. 1983); **§ 12.35**.

[105] 11 U.S.C. § 101.

sureties.[106] A prefiling analysis of the Bankruptcy Code's possible effects may be important even though the contemplated suit's defendant cannot take bankruptcy.

For example, assume suit is to be filed against a state to recover retained funds released to a defaulted contractor after notice and request to stop payment, and another suit is to be filed against that contractor and its individual indemnitors for reimbursement of the surety's losses in paying subcontractors and material suppliers. The contractor is in precarious financial condition and might well file for bankruptcy as soon as the indemnity suit is served. State law provides that all parties to a contract are indispensable parties in a suit arising from that contract.

In such a situation, the strategy must be to bring suit against the state first. If the reverse order is used and the contractor files for bankruptcy, the surety may be left without a forum in which to recover the released retainage. This is so because the Bankruptcy Code's automatic stay would prevent the surety from joining the contractor as a defendant in the state suit, failing which the state court would dismiss. The surety cannot alternatively pursue its claim for the retainage in the bankruptcy court because the Constitution's sovereignty clause does not allow a state to be sued in a federal court.[107]

§ 12.33 Surety versus Miscellaneous Parties

Professionals whose services are involved in a construction project owe a duty to others involved in the same project without regard to privity of contract.[108] This duty has been expressed as that "which rests upon any one to another where such person pretends to possess some skill and ability in some special employment, and offers his fitness to act in the line of business for which he may be employed."[109] It is also expressed as the duty "of

---

[106] *See* Haug & Haug, *Bankruptcy 1984 v. The Surety's Right to Contract Proceeds,* Proceedings of ABA Fidelity & Sur. L. Comm., ABA Annual Meeting (New York 1985); Griffin, *General Contractor in Proceedings under the Bankruptcy Code: A Surety's Perspective, in* ABA Joint Program on Bankruptcy, Crisis in the Construction Industry (New York 1983); Cushman & Miller, *Effect of the New Bankruptcy Law on Traditional Surety Rights,* 16 Forum 1011 (Summer 1981); Duree, *The Effect on the Surety of Bankruptcy Reorganizations of Bond Principals, Obligees and Claimants under the Bankruptcy Reform Act of 1978,* Proc. ABA Fid. & Sur. L. Comm. (New Orleans 1981).

[107] U.S. Const. amend. XI; Hans v. Louisiana, 134 U.S. 1 (1890); Governor v. Madrazo, 26 U.S. (1 Pet.) 110, 122–23 (1828).

[108] *See generally* Chapman, *The Liability of Design Professionals to the Surety,* Proceedings of ABA Fid. & Sur. L. Comm., ABA Midwinter Meeting (New York 1985); Hirsch & Karpowitz, Liability of Architects and Engineers (Defense Research Inst. No. 1, 1982).

[109] Coombs v. Beede, 89 Me. 187, 36 A. 104, 104–05 (1896).

exercising that degree of professional care and skill customarily employed by others of the same profession in the same general area."[110]

This duty is owed by architects,[111] engineers,[112] appraisers/inspectors,[113] and surveyors.[114] The duty is owed not only to owners but also to contractors,[115] subcontractors,[116] sureties,[117] users of the project,[118] and the guarantor of the bank loan financing the construction.[119] Thus, a performing surety may have a right of action against those parties either through its right of subrogation[120] or by a direct action for negligent breach of that duty to perform professionally.[121] Among the breaches for which damages have been held recoverable by the surety are:

1. Negligent release of retainage[122]
2. Negligent certification of progress estimates[123]
3. Failure to detect improper construction techniques[124]
4. Failure to detect misuse of contract funds[125]
5. False certification of work performed[126]
6. Negligent interpretation of plans and specifications[127]
7. Negligent inspection of the work.[128]

---

[110] Calandro Dev., Inc. v. R.M. Butler Contractors, Inc., 249 So. 2d 254, 265 (La. Ct. App. 1971).

[111] General Trading Corp. v. Burnup & Sims, Inc., 523 F.2d 98, 101 (3d Cir. 1975).

[112] American Fid. Fire Ins. Co. v. Pavia-Byrne Eng'g Corp., 393 So. 2d 830 (La. Ct. App. 1981).

[113] Alley v. Courtney, 448 So. 2d 858 (La. Ct. App. 1984).

[114] Jenkins v. Krebs & Sons, Inc., 322 So. 2d 426 (La. Ct. App. 1975).

[115] United States v. Rogers & Rogers, 161 F. Supp. 132 (S.D. Cal. 1958).

[116] E.H. Leavell & Co. v. Glantz Contracting Corp., 322 F. Supp. 779 (E.D. La. 1971); Gurtler, Hebert & Co. v. Weyland Mach. Shop, Inc., 405 So. 2d 660 (La. Ct. App. 1981).

[117] American Fid. Fire Ins. Co. v. Pavia-Byrne Eng'g Corp., 393 So. 2d 830.

[118] Emond v. Tyler Bldg. & Constr. Co., 438 So. 2d 681, 685 (La. Ct. App. 1983).

[119] Alley v. Courtney, 448 So. 2d 858.

[120] Peerless Ins. Co. v. Cerny & Assocs., Inc., 199 F. Supp. 951, 954 (D. Minn. 1961).

[121] Unity Tel. Co. v. Design Serv. Co., 160 Me. 188, 201 A.2d 177 (1964); State *ex rel.* National Sur. Corp. v. Malvaney, 221 Miss. 190, 72 So. 2d 424 (1954).

[122] State *ex rel.* National Sur. Corp. v. Malvaney, 72 So. 2d 424.

[123] Peerless Ins. Co. v. Cerny & Assocs., Inc., 199 F. Supp. 951.

[124] Aetna Ins. Co. v. Hellmuth, Obata & Kassabaum, Inc., 392 F.2d 472 (8th Cir. 1968).

[125] *Id.*

[126] Westerhold v. Carroll, 419 S.W.2d 73 (Mo. 1967).

[127] Givoh Assocs. v. American Druggist Ins. Co., 562 F. Supp. 1346 (E.D.N.Y. 1983).

[128] Calandro Dev., Inc. v. R.M. Butler Contractors, Inc., 249 So. 2d 254.

Through its right of subrogation, the prime contractor's surety can also reach a subcontractor's surety, despite a clause in the subcontractor's bond declaring that it "is one of indemnity only and does not inure to the benefit of or confer any right of action upon any person other than [the general contractor]."[129] The crucial distinction leading to that result is that the prime's surety is not "another person" but is the successor to the general contractor.[130] Under proper factual conditions, a surety can also recover from its principal's liability insurer either by subrogation, directly as the real party in interest, or as a third-party beneficiary of the liability policy.[131]

§ 12.34 Owner versus Contractor and/or Surety

Just as the other participants in the construction project have direct rights of action against the owner for any breach of a contractual or other duty owed them, so the owner has similar rights. Upon default of the contractor, the owner can proceed against both the contractor and the surety guaranteeing the performance of the work and payment to those furnishing labor or material to the project. For breaches of contract short of default, such as defective workmanship,[132] the owner has a similar right.

In theory, the owner is also entitled to delay damages from a contractor. In practice, however, the owner, being in the stronger bargaining position, is able to insist on including a liquidated damages clause in the contract. This clause usually provides for a fixed sum per day to be paid the owner by the contractor for each day the project remains unfinished beyond the time period or date specified in the contract.

Such a clause is valid and enforceable if the stipulated amount represents a reasonable estimate, at the time the contract was executed, of actual damages.[133] On the other hand, if the amount is excessive considering the terms, nature, and purpose of the contract, it will be treated as a penalty, regardless of how it is named.[134] Whether the clause is a legitimate attempt to

---

[129] Financial Indem. Co. v. Steele & Sons, Inc., 403 So. 2d 600 (Fla. Dist. Ct. App. 1981).

[130] Argonaut Ins. Co. v. Commercial Standard Ins. Co., 380 So. 2d 1066 (Fla. Dist. Ct. App.), *review denied,* 389 So. 2d 1108 (Fla. 1980).

[131] *See* Crowder, *Surety's Remedies—Rights Other than Those to Contract Funds,* Proceedings of I.A.I.C. Fidelity & Sur. Comm., I.A.I.C. Midwinter Meeting (New York 1984). For a nonconstruction case, *see* Western World Ins. Co. v. Travelers Indem. Co., 358 So. 2d 602 (Fla. Dist. Ct. App. 1978).

[132] Pickeys v. Brown, 431 So. 2d 880 (La. Ct. App. 1983).

[133] National Coop. Refinery Ass'n v. Northern Ordnance, Inc., 238 F.2d 803 (10th Cir. 1956).

[134] Hyman v. Cohen, 73 So. 2d 393 (Fla. 1954).

assess liquidated damages or the imposition of a penalty is a question of law for the court.[135] A liquidated damages clause will not be enforced when:

1. It is held to impose a penalty[136]
2. No actual damages have been sustained[137]
3. The delay was caused in part by the owner[138] or
4. The owner's acts or silence constitute an election not to invoke the clause.[139]

An owner may also include in the prime contract an indemnification agreement requiring the contractor to hold the owner harmless from all injuries and damages, however caused. Such a clause has been held valid, even to indemnify the indemnitee against its own negligence.[140] However, in some jurisdictions, a contract to indemnify another against his or her own negligence is against public policy.[141]

In seeking indemnification from the contractor's surety, the owner must be particularly cautious. A performance bond cannot be substituted for liability insurance.[142] Thus, when an owner incurred attorneys' fees in defending against a subcontractor's suit and subsequently sued the prime contractor's performance bond surety to recover those fees, its failure to allege and prove that the prime contractor was the owner's indemnitor barred recovery.[143]

A troublesome source of litigation between these parties is when the owner discovers defects in the project after it has been certified complete, accepted, and paid for. The contractor and surety then refuse either to remedy the defects or to pay damages. Their reasons might be that acceptance and occupancy of the project waives any claims for defective work and/or that applicable guaranty periods or statutes of limitation periods have expired. The owner then files suit.

---

[135] Yarborough Realty Co. v. Barar, 37 Ala. App. 342, 67 So. 2d 853 (1953).

[136] National Coop. Refinery Ass'n v. Northern Ordnance, Inc., 238 F.2d 803.

[137] Northwest Fixture Co. v. Kilbourne & Clark Co., 128 F. 256, 261 (9th Cir. 1904).

[138] United States v. United Eng'g & Contracting Co., 234 U.S. 236 (1913).

[139] 5 S. Williston, A Treatise on the Law of Contracts § 688 (3d ed. 1961); Autrey v. Williams & Dunlap, 343 F.2d 730 (5th Cir. 1965).

[140] Employer Ins. v. Cajun Contractors & Eng'rs, Inc., 459 So. 2d 610 (La. Ct. App. 1984); Frank Corrente v. Conforti & Eisele Co., 468 A.2d 920 (R.I. 1984); Framington Plumbing & Heating Co. v. Fischer Sand & Aggregate, Inc., 281 N.W.2d 838 (Minn. 1980); Dorothy L. Draper v. Airco, Inc., 580 F.2d 91 (3d Cir. 1979).

[141] Cal. Civ. Code § 1782 (West 1972); Ga. Code Ann. § 13-8-2 (Harrison 1982); Ill. Rev. Stat. ch. 29, § 61 (1985); Mich. Comp. Laws Ann. § 691.991 (West 1968); N.Y. Gen. Oblig. Law § 5-324 (McKinney 1978).

[142] Long v. City of Midway, 169 Ga. App. 72, 311 S.E.2d 508 (1983).

[143] State Sur. Co. v. Lamb Constr. Co., 625 P.2d 184 (Wyo. 1981).

The key determination in such litigation is whether the defects were patent or latent, that is, whether they were discoverable upon a reasonable inspection (*patent defects*)[144] or whether they were not so discoverable (*latent defects*).[145] Acceptance, payment, and occupancy waive any action for patent defects,[146] but the owner still has recourse against the contractor and surety for latent defects.[147] Because applicable statutes of limitation do not begin to run until the latent defect is discovered, contractors and sureties have been subjected to what amounts to open-ended liability.[148]

To counteract this situation, some 40 states have passed special statutes of limitations to cover participants in the construction industry.[149] Some of these statutes provide for minimum and maximum periods within which actions for latent defects may be brought; others set only the outer limits. In either case, they provide some relief to contractors and sureties, and indirect incentives to those professionals employed to supervise and inspect construction projects for giving increased attention to the building process.[150]

NOTICE AND LIMITATION OF ACTIONS

§ 12.35 Notice Periods

The notice and limitation periods most often raised in construction litigation are those controlling claims and suits by subcontractors and material

[144] Renown, Inc. v. Hensel Phelps Constr. Co., 154 Cal. App. 3d 413, 201 Cal. Rptr. 242 (1984); Mattingly v. Anthony Indus., Inc., 109 Cal. App. 3d 506, 167 Cal. Rptr. 292 (1980).

[145] City of Osceola v. Gjellefald Constr. Co., 225 Iowa 215, 279 N.W. 590 (1938); Town of Tonawanda v. Stapell, Mumm & Beals Corp., 240 A.D. 472, 270 N.Y.S. 377, *aff'd,* 265 N.Y. 630, 193 N.E. 419 (1934). *See* Warin, *The Surety's Liability for Latent Defects,* Proc. ABA Fid. & Sur. L. Comm. (New York 1985).

[146] Salem Towne Apartments, Inc. v. McDaniel & Sons Roofing Co., 330 F. Supp. 906 (E.D.N.C. 1970); Stearns Constr. Corp. v. Carolina Corp., 63 Wis. 2d 342, 217 N.W.2d 291 (1974).

[147] Aubrey v. Helton, 276 Ala. 134, 159 So. 2d 837 (1964).

[148] School Bd. v. St. Paul Fire & Marine Ins. Co., 449 So. 2d 872 (Fla. Dist. Ct. App. 1984) (citing authorities from Iowa, New Jersey, New York, North Carolina, Oregon, and Texas); Milana, *The Performance Bond and the Underlying Contract,* 12 Forum 187 (Fall 1976).

[149] *See* Witherwax, *Special Statutes of Limitations Against the Contractor—A Defense to the Surety,* 16 Forum 1057 (1980).

[150] *See* Hinchey & Lord, *Liability of Surety, Contractor and Subcontractor after Final Completion and Acceptance,* ABA Joint Program on Trouble Areas in Construction (New York 1985).

suppliers against the contractor and/or its surety. These matters are covered in **Chapter 13**.

There are, however, less well-known matters of notice and limitations that can seriously affect the contractor, owner, and surety when litigation arises. For example, the language of a performance bond creates an implied duty in the bond obligee/owner to notify the surety of the contractor's delays. Failure to do so releases the surety from liability for resulting damages to the extent that the surety could have remedied those delays.[151] Nevertheless, if an owner's late notice is not shown to prejudice the surety, no release is effected.[152] Although the foregoing is the generally accepted rule, one recent case holds that actual prejudice is not required for an insurer to disclaim liability when notice was not timely given.[153]

A detailed discussion of the Miller Act[154] and its jurisprudence is beyond the scope of this chapter. However, it should be noted that the only safe way to serve notices such as letters of default, direction, and stop payment on the government is by hand delivery to and personal receipt by the contracting officer of copies of the documents. Otherwise, that officer may later testify that he did not actually see those notices. Such testimony, coupled with the broad discretion granted a contracting officer in making progress payments, can result in a substantial portion of contract funds, which should have been available to the surety for payment of subcontractors and material suppliers, disappearing into the defaulted contractor's pocket.[155]

§ 12.36 Limitation Periods

In a suit by the owner against the contractor and surety, different limitation periods may apply. Such was the holding in a suit for defective work brought 11 years after final certification and delivery of the job. Because the bond was under seal but the contract was not, a 12-year limitation applied to the surety, whereas a three-year period applied to the contractor. The court held that although a valid cause of action existed against the surety, the surety was entitled to indemnification and exoneration from the contractor because the contractor's defense of the statute of limitations was a personal defense not available to the surety.[156]

---

[151] Blackhawk Heating & Plumbing Co. v. Seaboard Sur. Co., 534 F. Supp. 309 (N.D. Ill. 1982).

[152] United States Fid. & Guar. Co. v. Orlando Utils. Comm'n, 564 F. Supp. 962 (M.D. Fla. 1983).

[153] Kosanovich v. Meade, 463 N.E.2d 257 (Ind. 1984).

[154] 40 U.S.C. §§ 270a–270d.

[155] United States Fid. & Guar. Co. v. United States, 676 F.2d 622 (Ct. Cl. 1982).

[156] President & Directors v. Madden, 660 F.2d 91 (4th Cir. 1981).

Carelessness in filling in blank spaces in contracts can be costly, particularly when that space sets the period for limitation of actions. Such a failure may create open-ended liability for the surety.[157] Sureties issuing construction bonds to subcontractors on government projects should also be aware that their exposure to suit may be for a much longer period than they expect—longer than the periods provided for by the Miller Act,[158] longer than those provided for by states' public and private works acts, and longer than those specified in the bonds.

Regarding the Miller Act, this possibility of longer exposure arises because the Act does not require a subcontractor's bond and, therefore, such a bond does not automatically incorporate the notice and limitation periods of the Act.[159] Similarly, because a government project does not belong to a state or any agency or subdivision thereof, a state's public works law limitation periods would not apply. A state's private works statutes would also not apply because they are predicated on the assumption that the bonded work is lienable, but government property is not lienable. Finally, in states that do not allow general statutory limitation periods to be shortened by contract, but only by specific statutory limitation periods, a shorter period provided for in the bond would have no legal effect. Thus, what is left is the limitation period for actions on a contract, which is usually longer than that for claims arising out of construction projects. In Louisiana, for example, the period is 10 years.[160]

The automatic stay provisions of the Bankruptcy Code[161] do not toll the bond limitation period for an action by a Chapter 11 debtor/contractor against a subcontractor and its surety. The reason is that those stay provisions apply only to actions brought against the debtor, not by the debtor.[162]

Is all lost for the surety when it files suit against the owner beyond the two-year limitation period provided for in the bond? Not necessarily. Why not argue that the suit was brought, not under the bond, but under the indemnity agreement's assignment from the contractor, to whose rights the surety is subrogated? At least one court has agreed.[163]

---

[157] Peters Township Sch. Auth. v. United States Fid. & Guar. Co., 78 Pa. Commw. 365, 467 A.2d 904 (1983).

[158] 40 U.S.C. §§ 270a–270d.

[159] United States *ex rel.* Wheeling-Pittsburgh Steel Corp. v. Algernon Blair, Inc., 329 F. Supp. 1360 (D.S.C. 1971).

[160] La. Civ. Code Ann. art. 3499 (West 1985).

[161] 11 U.S.C. § 362, Rules 11-44(a) and 12-33(a).

[162] 1616 Remine Ltd. Partnership v. Atchinson & Keller Co., 14 Bankr. 484 (E.D. Va. 1981).

[163] Balboa Ins. Co. v. W.C.B. Assocs., Inc., 390 So. 2d 172 (Fla. Dist. Ct. App. 1980).

CONSTRUCTION OF DOCUMENTS AND PAROL EVIDENCE

§ 12.37 Construction of Contracts

Generally, public works statutes are construed liberally to effect the intent of the legislative body to protect those whose labor and materials go into public projects.[164] Contracts, if they contain ambiguities, are construed against the drafter. Compensated surety bonds are construed by most courts as requiring the use of both rules.[165] Obviously, such construction rules strongly affect litigation involving contractors and sureties, usually adversely to the surety. Only occasionally will a court apply the rules even-handedly and, for example, hold that if the surety bond follows statutory language and contains an ambiguity it must be strictly construed against the state.[166]

Further complicating surety bond construction is the fact that at least one court has specifically declared such a bond to be an insurance contract,[167] and most others treat it as such. Consequently, the doctrines of reasonable expectations[168] and unconscionability could be applied to such bonds.[169]

The Arizona Supreme Court may have provided some light at the end of this tunnel. The *four corners rule* of contract interpretation states that the intentions of the parties are to be elicited from the instrument as a whole, that is, the "four corners" of the instrument, and not from any isolated parts.[170] According to the Arizona Supreme Court, applying the four corners rule to standardized contracts has such mischievous consequences that the courts are required to invent ambiguities and then construe those ambiguities against the drafter to reach a just result. Declaring that "the time has

---

[164] Clifford F. MacEvoy Co. v. United States *ex rel.* Calvin Tomkins Co., 332 U.S. 102 (1944).

[165] *See* Frederick v. Electro-Coal Transfer Corp., 548 F. Supp. 83 (E.D. La. 1982), and cases cited therein.

[166] Florida *ex rel.* Consolidated Pipe & Supply Co. v. Houdaille Indus., 372 So. 2d 1177 (Fla. Dist. Ct. App. 1979).

[167] Austin v. Parker, 672 F.2d 508, 519 (5th Cir. 1982).

[168] R. Keeton, Basic Text on Insurance Law 360 (1971); Carpenter v. Suffolk Franklin Sav. Bank, 370 Mass. 314, 346 N.E.2d 892 (1976).

[169] *See* Mittelman, *Reasonable Expectations and Bad Faith in the Settlement of a Health Insurance Claim,* 19 Forum 340 (Winter 1984); Koch, *The Surety's General Indemnity Agreement: Current or Out of Date?,* Proc. ABA Fid. & Sur. L. Comm. (1984).

[170] Black's Law Dictionary 591 (5th ed. 1979).

come to remove insurance law from the land of make-believe," the court proceeded to revise the entire body of Arizona insurance law.[171]

The rules that *Darner* propounds are fair and recognize the realities of modern business practices. The boilerplate language in a contract is held unenforceable when it conflicts with the express agreement between the parties or the reasonable expectations of the insured.[172] The rules of *Darner* apply not only to situations in which the insured's reasonable expectations are induced by the insurer's promises or misrepresentations but also to certain situations in which no express representations are made and the boilerplate terms are unambiguous.[173] When the boilerplate terms cannot be understood by "the reasonably intelligent consumer who might check on his or her rights," the boilerplate terms, albeit unambiguous, are unenforceable.[174] The rules of *Darner,* consequently, have become the cutting edge of a new trend in the construction of standardized contracts, which of course include surety bonds and indemnity agreements.

§ 12.38 Parol Evidence

Oral change orders are a source of frequent dispute among owners, contractors, and subcontractors, and some of these disputes result in litigation.

When a contractor follows an oral change order, it is not liable for resulting damage.[175] The rationale in most jurisdictions is that a written contract may be waived or modified by a subsequent parol agreement.[176] This is so even though the contract contains a capitalized provision stating, "No extra work shall be paid for unless authorized in writing from owner's office. Verbal authorization shall not be recognized."[177] Louisiana law allows parol evidence of a subsequent agreement to modify or revoke a written

---

[171] Darner Motor Sales, Inc. v. Universal Underwriters Ins. Co., 140 Ariz. 383, 682 P.2d 388 (1984).

[172] *Id.* at 394, 682 P.2d at 399.

[173] State Farm Mut. Auto. Ins. Co. v. Dimmer, 160 Ariz. 453, 773 P.2d 1012 (1989); State Farm Mut. Auto. Ins. Co. v. Bogart, 149 Ariz. 145, 717 P.2d 449 (1986).

[174] Gordinier v. Aetna Casualty & Sur. Co., 154 Ariz. 266, 272, 742 P.2d 277, 283 (1987).

[175] Mannella v. Pittsburgh, 334 Pa. 396, 6 A.2d 70 (1939).

[176] 30 Am. Jur. 2d *Evidence* § 1063 (1967).

[177] Son-Shone Grading, Inc. v. ADC Constr. Co., 68 N.C. App. 417, 315 S.E.2d 346, *review denied,* 312 N.C. 85, 321 S.E.2d 900 (1984); W.E. Garrison Grading Co. v. Piracci Constr. Co., 27 N.C. App. 725, 221 S.E.2d 512 (1975), *cert. denied,* 289 N.C. 296, 222 S.E.2d 695 (1976). *See also* D.K. Meyer Corp. v. Bevco, Inc., 206 Neb. 318, 292 N.W.2d 773 (1980); Ekco Enters., Inc. v. Remi Fortin Constr., Inc., 118 N.H. 37, 382 A.2d 368 (1978).

agreement unless that written agreement is one required by law to be in writing.[178]

The problem, of course, is proving the oral agreement. Immediately sending a confirmation letter containing one's understanding of the agreement to the other party is recommended.

---

[178] Torrey v. Simon-Torrey, Inc., 307 So. 2d 569 (La. 1974).

CHAPTER 13

PROSECUTING AND DEFENDING PAYMENT BOND CLAIMS

Edward G. Gallagher*

Edward G. Gallagher is a partner in the Washington, D.C., office of Whiteford, Taylor & Preston, he specializes in fidelity and surety law. He is a graduate of William College and George Washington University Law School. Mr. Gallagher is active in the Fidelity and Surety Law Committee of the American Bar Association and the International Association of Insurance Counsel, and has been a speaker at numerous programs on surety law. His articles on surety topics have been published by the Tort and Insurance Practice Section of the ABA.

§ 13.1 Introduction

§ 13.2 Purpose of Payment Bond

§ 13.3 Typical Payment Bond Provisions

§ 13.4 Statutory Requirements

§ 13.5 Resolving Conflicts Between Bond and Statute

§ 13.6 Parties Making a Bond Claim

§ 13.7 Covered Bond Claims

§ 13.8 —Taxes, Contributions, and Insurance

§ 13.9 —Delay Damages and Lost Profits

§ 13.10 —Attorneys' Fees and Interest

§ 13.11 Notice Requirements

*Portions of this chapter are reprinted from the 1991 Supplement by Loren W. Peters, Esquire.

§ 13.12 —Time Period Allowed
§ 13.13 Suit Limitations
§ 13.14 —Commencement of Limitation Period
§ 13.15 —Estoppel
§ 13.16 Jurisdiction and Venue Requirements
§ 13.17 Arbitration and the Surety
§ 13.18 Possible Remedies if Payment Bond Claim Is Unavailable
§ 13.19 Practice Notes

§ 13.1 Introduction

Suretyship is a contractual relationship in which one party agrees in writing to answer for the debt or default of another.[1] Every surety contract involves three parties: a principal, a surety, and an obligee. The *obligee* is the party for whose benefit and protection the surety contract is written. The *principal* is the party primarily liable to the obligee, and the surety is secondarily liable to the obligee if the principal fails to pay the debt or perform the obligation that underlies the surety contract.

In a modern labor and material payment bond, the principal is the contractor or subcontractor providing the bond, the surety is usually an insurance company, and the named obligee is the owner, lender, or prime contractor requiring the bond. Although not named as obligees, those furnishing labor or material to the principal for use in the performance of the contract work are explicitly or implicitly additional obligees entitled to sue on the bond.[2]

§ 13.2 Purpose of Payment Bond

On a private (that is, nongovernment) construction project, those furnishing labor or material for use in the performance of the work may file a mechanics' lien against the property. In order to protect its property from such liens, an owner can require the contractor to provide a bond conditioned on payment of those furnishing such labor or material.[3] If the

---

[1] Stearns, Law of Suretyship § 1.1, at 1 (5th ed. 1951); 74 Am. Jur. 2d Suretyship § 1, at 2 (1974).

[2] *See, e.g.,* 40 U.S.C. § 270b(a) (1988); American Institute of Architects (AIA) Doc. A311, Performance Bond and Labor and Material Bond (1970), and Doc. A312, Performance Bond and Labor and Material Payment Bond (1984).

[3] There are also *no lien bonds* requiring only that the surety protect the owner's property from mechanics' liens.

contractor fails to make payment, the surety will have to do so, and the owner's property will be protected.

Although government property is usually exempt from mechanics' liens,[4] the government has a moral obligation to see that those whose work has gone into a public construction project are paid. In order to meet this moral obligation,[5] and to make it easier for public contractors to obtain material on credit, Congress and the state legislatures have enacted statutes requiring public works contractors to post payment bonds.[6]

In light of these purposes, it follows that the owner has no right to make a claim on the payment bond.[7] Nor will a waiver in advance of the right to assert a mechanics' lien claim by a subcontractor be construed to waive the right to make a claim against the payment bond.[8] Similarly, a provision in a subcontract whereby the subcontractor waives claims against the contractor's payment bond is void as against public policy and will not be enforced.[9]

§ 13.3 Typical Payment Bond Provisions

The basic condition of a payment bond is that the principal promptly make payment for labor and material furnished for use on the project. Each bond form, however, has slightly different phrasing and may impose conditions or restrictions on the surety's obligation. Anyone concerned with prosecuting or defending a bond claim should first read the bond.

The United States requires use of a standard form payment bond[10] on all federal projects. The most common form on private jobs has been American Institute of Architects (AIA) Document A311.[11] Although a more recent

---

[4] F.D. Rich Co. v. United States *ex rel.* Industrial Lumber Co., 417 U.S. 116 (1974); Stauffer Constr. Co. v. Tate Eng'g, Inc., 44 Md. App. 240, 407 A.2d 1191 (1979); United States *ex rel.* Eastern Gulf, Inc. v. Metzger Towing, Inc., 910 F.2d 775 (11th Cir. 1990).

[5] United States *ex rel.* Mississippi Rd. Supply Co. v. H.R. Morgan, Inc., 542 F.2d 262 (5th Cir. 1976), *cert. denied,* 434 U.S. 828 (1977); R.C. Stanhope, Inc. v. Roanoke Constr. Co., 539 F.2d 992 (4th Cir. 1976).

[6] *See, e.g.,* 40 U.S.C. § 270a; Cal. Pub. Cont. Code § 7103 (West); Tex. Rev. Civ. Stat. Ann. art. 5160 (West). Each state's payment bond statute is printed in an appendix to Payment Bond Manual (E. Gallagher, Ed., ABA 1991).

[7] Board of Educ. v. Hartford Accident & Indem. Co., 152 Ill. App. 3d 745, 504 N.E.2d 1000 (1987).

[8] Western Waterproofing, Inc. v. Springfield Hous. Auth., 669 F. Supp. 901 (C.D. Ill. 1987).

[9] American Casualty Co. v. Coastal Caisson Drill Co., 542 So. 2d 957 (Fla. 1989).

[10] 48 C.F.R. § 53.301-25-A (1990).

[11] Performance Bond and Labor and Material Payment Bond (1970). This form, and all AIA documents referred to in this chapter, are available from the American Institute of Architects, 1735 New York Avenue, NW, Washington, DC 20006.

AIA form, Document A312,[12] has been issued, it has been largely ignored by the construction and surety industries.

Some state agencies draft their own form, which is usually patterned after the federal one, but most will accept any reasonable payment bond. Most surety companies have printed bond forms their agents will use if the obligee has not required a specific form. Many of these company forms are merely the AIA bond reprinted on the company's letterhead, but others vary from company to company.

The coverage, notice, and suit limitations commonly included in payment bonds are discussed in subsequent sections of this chapter. It is important to remember that a surety is not an insurer of its principal[13] and is liable only if a claimant has strictly complied with the conditions of the bond, unless, of course, a restriction in the bond is itself contrary to law.

§ 13.4 Statutory Requirements

At common law there was no requirement of a payment bond. When Congress and the various state legislatures enacted laws compelling government contractors to provide such bonds, they also specified certain terms and conditions the bond would have to incorporate. These terms and conditions are read into the bond by operation of law, whether or not they are actually stated in the bond.[14]

For example, the federal Miller Act[15] provides that a claimant must file suit within one year of last furnishing labor or material for use in the performance of the contract. Although the bond itself contains no such provision, the one-year limitation of the statute is read into the bond, and a claimant who lets the one-year period run without filing suit will lose its right to collect on the payment bond.

In order to construe a bond given by a public works contractor, therefore, it is essential to read the statute requiring the posting of the bond as well as the bond itself. Almost all state bond statutes are patterned after the Miller Act and, in the absence of controlling state decisions, the state courts will look to Miller Act precedents for guidance.[16]

---

[12] Performance Bond and Payment Bond (1984).

[13] Pearlman v. Reliance Ins. Co., 371 U.S. 132 (1962); United States *ex rel.* Getz Bros. & Co. v. Markowitz Bros. (Del.), Inc., 383 F.2d 595 (9th Cir. 1967); State Highway Admin. v. Transamerica Ins. Co., 278 Md. 690, 367 A.2d 509 (1976).

[14] Mayor of Baltimore v. Fidelity & Deposit Co., 282 Md. 431, 386 A.2d 749 (1978).

[15] 40 U.S.C. §§ 270a–270c.

[16] Solite Masonry Units Corp. v. Piland Constr. Co., 217 Va. 727, 232 S.E.2d 759 (1977); Montgomery County Bd. of Educ. v. Glassman Constr. Co., 245 Md. 192, 225 A.2d 448 (1967). See also **Ch. 12**.

The results, however, are by no means uniform and state bond statutes and the decisions interpreting them vary from state to state. One should never assume that the rights of a claimant on a state bond are identical to those of a claimant under the Miller Act. There is simply no substitute for reading the bond itself and the statute, if any, requiring that it be furnished.

§ 13.5 Resolving Conflicts Between Bond and Statute

In an ideal world there would be no conflict between a public works contractor's bond and the statute requiring that it be posted. The contractor and its surety's agent would be sure that the bond form they used conformed to the statutory requirements, and if they failed to do so, the government's contracting officer would reject the bond and require that a proper one be furnished. In the real world, however, mistakes are made and the resolution of a conflict between the bond and statute occasionally determines the validity of a claim.

If the bond purports to provide less than the minimum coverage required by the statute, the statute will be read into the bond on the theories that the surety entered into its contract with knowledge of the law and private parties cannot reduce the protection the statute provided to claimants. The surety will be held to have provided the minimum coverage specified by law.[17] On the other hand, most courts hold that the surety is free to contract to provide more than the required coverage, and if a claim is valid under the bond the claimant will usually prevail even though the minimum requirements of the statute would not have covered the claim.[18]

Many bond forms, including the AIA bonds, provide that if the suit limitation provided in the bond is prohibited by law, then the limitation shall be deemed amended to the minimum period permitted by the statute. At least one court has interpreted its state payment bond statute to "prohibit" a limitations period different from that specified in the statute, and so construed the bond to provide only the statutory period for suit even though the period stated in the bond was longer. The court recognized that the surety could contract to provide greater coverage than required by the statute, but held that it had not done so because of the savings clause in the bond.[19]

---

[17] Mayor of Baltimore v. Fidelity & Deposit Co., 282 Md. 431, 386 A.2d 749 (1978). *Accord* Pyco Supply Co. v. American Centennial Ins. Co., 85 N.C. App. 253, 354 S.E.2d 360 (1987).

[18] American Casualty Co. v. Irvin, 426 F.2d 647 (5th Cir. 1970); Barreto Granite Corp. v. State, 147 Vt. 148, 513 A.2d 608 (1986).

[19] Joseph F. Hughes & Co. v. George H. Robinson Corp., 211 Va. 4, 175 S.E.2d 413 (1970).

§ 13.6 Parties Making a Bond Claim

On any construction project a great many persons will play some part, directly or indirectly, in the performance of the work. Employees of the contractor perform some of the work using material purchased from distributors or manufacturers. Other parts of the work will be subcontracted to firms that in turn purchase materials, hire laborers, and, possibly, re-subcontract parts of their portion of the work. Tools and equipment to be used on the project will be purchased or rented. Consumables such as electric power, fuel, telephone service, and portable sanitation facilities are necessary even though they are not incorporated into the building, and even intangibles such as insurance and working capital will be necessary to the successful completion of the work.

Potentially, an almost unlimited number of parties could claim to have contributed something to the performance of the contract. That does not mean, however, that each of them can make a claim under the contractor's payment bond. The surety is not an insurer of the principal's obligations.

Employees of the contractor who actually worked on the project are certainly within the coverage of the bond, but it is almost never necessary for them to resort to the surety for payment. If a contractor does not pay his employees one week, they are unlikely to continue to work. A significant arrearage of back wages almost never accrues.

A building cannot be constructed with labor alone, however; the contractor must also acquire materials. These are normally supplied on credit and sold by a material supplier.[20] A material supplier who sells directly to the bond principal is covered by the bond,[21] but a material supplier who sells to another material supplier, such as to a wholesaler or distributor, is not covered under the Miller Act bond or under most other bonds.[22]

A material supplier who sells to a subcontractor may be covered if he gives written notice as required by the terms of the bond. Most bonds require notice to the bond principal,[23] but some provide for notice to any two

---

[20] A subcontractor is one who actually takes over a specific portion of the contract work.

[21] Such a material supplier, of course, has a direct contractual relationship with the bond principal. *See* 40 U.S.C. § 270(b); AIA Doc. A311 (1970); AIA Doc. A312 (1984).

[22] Clifford F. MacEvoy Co. v. United States *ex rel.* Calvin Tomkins Co., 322 U.S. 102 (1944); United States *ex rel.* Hasco Elec. Corp. v. Reliance Ins. Co., 390 F. Supp. 158 (E.D.N.Y. 1975); United States *ex rel.* Bryant v. Lembke Constr. Co., 370 F.2d 293 (10th Cir. 1966); United States *ex rel.* Wellman Eng'g Co. v. MSI Corp., 350 F.2d 285 (2d Cir. 1965). *Accord* West Bank Oil, Inc. v. Hartford Accident & Indem. Co., 205 N.J. Super. 56, 500 A.2d 32 (1985).

[23] *E.g.*, the Miller Act (40 U.S.C. §§ 270a–270f); AIA Doc. A312 (1984); and most state statutes. *See* J.W. Cooper Constr. Co. v. Public Hous. Admin. *ex rel.* Rio Grande Steel Prods. Co., 390 F.2d 175 (10th Cir. 1968); Travelers Indem. Co. v. United States *ex rel.* Western Steel Co., 362 F.2d 896 (9th Cir. 1966); F.D. Rich Co. v. United States *ex rel.* Industrial Lumber Co., 417 U.S. 116 (1974).

of the principal, owner, or surety.[24] A material supplier who sells to a sub-subcontractor or more remote subcontractor is usually not covered.[25]

A *subcontractor* is generally defined as one who takes over performance of a specific part of the work from the prime contractor.[26] A subcontractor must be distinguished from a material supplier, who supplies material but does not have responsibility for a specific part of the work, and from a sub-subcontractor (or second-tier subcontractor), who performs a specific part of the work but does not have a direct contractual relationship with the prime contractor. Confusion can result if a definition of subcontractor in a case addressing the distinction between a subcontractor and a material supplier is applied in a case involving a sub-subcontractor.[27]

An unpaid subcontractor (as just defined) is covered under the prime contractor's payment bond. A sub-subcontractor can be within the coverage of the prime contractor's bond if it gives the required notice.[28] A third tier or lower subcontractor is not within the coverage of the Miller Act bond[29] or AIA bonds,[30] but may be covered by some state statutory bonds.[31]

Anyone providing materials to a material supplier of any tier, including a material supplier who has a direct contractual relationship with the prime contractor, is not normally covered by the prime contractor's bond.[32]

---

[24] *See* AIA Doc. A311, ¶ 3(a).

[25] J.W. Bateson Co. v. United States *ex rel.* Board of Trustees, 434 U.S. 586 (1978). *But cf.* Md. Ann. Code SF § 17-108, which requires such coverage.

[26] Clifford F. MacEvoy Co. v. United States *ex rel.* Calvin Tomkins Co., 322 U.S. 102 (1944); F.D. Rich Co. v. United States *ex rel.* Industrial Lumber Co., 417 U.S. 116 (1974); J.W. Bateson Co. v. United States *ex rel.* Board of Trustees, 434 U.S. 586 (1978).

[27] *See, e.g.*, the decision of the United States Court of Appeals for the District of Columbia Circuit in United States *ex rel.* Board of Trustees v. J.W. Bateson Co., 551 F.2d 1284 (D.C. Cir. 1977), which was reversed by the Supreme Court in J.W. Bateson Co. v. United States *ex rel.* Board of Trustees, 434 U.S. 586 (1978).

[28] *See* Clifford F. MacEvoy Co. v. United States *ex rel.* Calvin Tomkins Co., 322 U.S. 102 (1944); F.D. Rich Co. v. United States *ex rel.* Industrial Lumber Co., 417 U.S. 116 (1974); J.W. Bateson Co. v. United States *ex rel.* Board of Trustees, 434 U.S. 586 (1978); United States *ex rel.* Benkart Co. v. John A. Johnson & Sons, Inc., 236 F.2d 864 (3d Cir. 1956). *But see* Wichita Sheet Metal Supply, Inc. v. Dahlstrom & Ferrell Constr. Co., 792 P.2d 1043 (Kan. 1990). The court held that, inasmuch as contractors' bonds on public works projects are substitutes for mechanics' liens, a supplier's rights on the bond are no greater than its rights to a mechanics' lien on a private project. Because Kansas statutes do not provide lien coverage for suppliers to sub-subcontractors, those suppliers have no rights under a public works payment bond.

[29] United States *ex rel.* Powers Regulator Co. v. Hartford Accident & Indem. Co., 376 F.2d 811 (1st Cir. 1967).

[30] *See* AIA Doc. A311 ¶ 1 (1970); AIA Doc. A312 ¶ 15.1 (1984).

[31] *See, e.g.*, Md. Ann. Code SF § 17-108; Yellow Pine Lumber Co. v. Insurance Co. of N. Am., 882 F.2d 470 (10th Cir. 1989).

[32] *See* Clifford F. MacEvoy Co. v. United States *ex rel.* Calvin Tomkins Co., 322 U.S. 102 (1944); United States *ex rel.* Hasco Elec. Corp. v. Reliance Ins. Co., 390 F. Supp. 1958 (E.D.N.Y. 1975); United States *ex rel.* Bryant v. Lembke Constr. Co., 370 F.2d 293 (10th

§ 13.7 Covered Bond Claims

A payment bond is conditioned on the payment for labor or material furnished for use in the prosecution of the contract work.[33] Labor performed on the jobsite in connection with the contract is covered and usually causes no difficulty. Similarly, there is usually no contest over coverage of material actually incorporated into the finished project.

A more difficult question is presented by a claim for material ordered for use on the bonded job but diverted by the contractor to some other use. The claimant can still recover by showing a reasonable, good faith belief that the material was intended for use on the bonded job.[34] The material need not have been delivered to the jobsite.[35] Furthermore, even material sold on open account, with the supplier having no information at the time of sale whether it was to be used on a bonded project, may be covered if the supplier can later prove that it was purchased for use in the project.[36]

The open-account sale of materials also gives rise to another problem. The contractor may, in fact, pay from job proceeds for all the material purchased and used on the project. However, if the contractor fails to direct the supplier to apply the payments to the project bills, the supplier is free to apply them to older purchases (which may be time-barred), purchases of materials used in nonbonded jobs, or other bills that by themselves could not have been valid claims against a payment bond. Contractors experiencing financial difficulty will frequently send in partial payments on account to keep their suppliers happy without directing how the payments are to be applied. The result: nonbond claims are converted by the accounting method used by the supplier into claims on the payment bond.[37]

Some tangible items consumed during the prosecution of the contract work are not actually incorporated into the job. At one time there was considerable litigation over whether such consumables were covered by the

---

Cir. 1966); United States *ex rel.* Wellman Eng'g Co. v. MSI Corp., 350 F.2d 285 (2d Cir. 1965).

[33] 40 U.S.C § 270b; AIA Doc. A311 (1970); AIA Doc. A312 (1984). In the rare case when a bond by its terms does not provide protection for payment bond claims, but has been issued in that form by mistake, it may be reformed to provide the appropriate coverage. River Valley, Inc. v. American States Ins. Co., 297 Ark. 386, 699 S.W.2d 745 (1985).

[34] Glassell-Taylor Co. v. Magnolia Petroleum Co., 153 F.2d 527 (5th Cir. 1946); United States *ex rel.* Westinghouse Elec. Supply Co. v. Endebrock-White Co., 275 F.2d 57 (4th Cir. 1960); United States *ex rel.* Krupp Steel Prod., Inc. v. Aetna Ins. Co., 831 F.2d 938 (11th Cir. 1987); United States *ex rel.* Balzer Pac. Equip. Co. v. Fidelity & Deposit Co., 895 F.2d 546 (9th Cir. 1990).

[35] United States *ex rel.* Carlson v. Continental Casualty Co., 414 F.2d 431 (5th Cir. 1969).

[36] Balboa Ins. Co. v. Southern Distribs. Corp., 710 P.2d 725 (Nev. 1985).

[37] *See, e.g.*, Waukesha Concrete Prods. Corp. v. Capitol Indem. Co., 127 Wis. 2d 332, 379 N.W.2d 333 (Ct. App. 1985).

bond, but now, either by statute, explicit bond language,[38] or court decision, they are generally covered. Thus, claimants who supplied fuel,[39] groceries (if they are not otherwise generally available in the area of the job site),[40] utilities,[41] transportation,[42] and tires[43] have all been held to have valid payment bond claims on the theory that the items supplied were used or consumed during the performance of the work.

If a contractor purchases equipment and happens to use it on a bonded job, the seller of the equipment does not thereby acquire a claim against the surety for any unpaid part of the purchase price.[44] Because the equipment can be used on many jobs, the surety should not be held liable for its cost. If the contractor rents equipment for use on a particular job, however, its payment bond surety will be liable for any unpaid obligations under the rental contract. This liability would include the cost of maintaining or repairing the equipment, if the rental contract puts these obligations on the contractor, as well as the unpaid rent.[45]

§ 13.8 —Taxes, Contributions, and Insurance

Contractors encountering financial difficulty often fail to pay withheld payroll taxes to the Internal Revenue Service (IRS). The employees still get credit on their tax returns for the withheld monies and the IRS has to try to

---

[38] *See, e.g.,* AIA Doc. A311 (1970); AIA Doc. A312 (1984).

[39] Glassell-Taylor Co. v. Magnolia Petroleum Co., 153 F.2d 527 (5th Cir. 1946).

[40] Brogan v. National Sur. Co., 246 U.S. 257 (1918); Equitable Casualty & Sur. Co. v. Helena Wholesale Grocery Co., 60 F.2d 380 (8th Cir. 1932). *But cf.* Delaware Dredging Co. v. Tucker Stevedoring Co., 25 F.2d 44 (3d Cir. 1928).

[41] AIA Doc. A311 (1970); AIA Doc. A312 (1984); Va. Code Ann. § 11-58 (Michie).

[42] Standard Accident Ins. Co. v. United States *ex rel.* Powell, 302 U.S. 442 (1938); United States *ex rel.* Mid Seven Transp. v. Blinderman Constr. Co., 735 F. Supp. 272 (N.D. Ill. 1990).

[43] United States *ex rel.* J.P. Byrne & Co. v. Fire Ass'n, 260 F.2d 541 (2d Cir. 1958).

[44] United States *ex rel.* Eddie's Sales & Leasing, Inc. v. Federal Ins. Co., 634 F.2d 1050 (10th Cir. 1980); Ibex Indus., Inc. v. Coastline Waterproofing, 563 F. Supp. 1142 (D.D.C. 1983); United States *ex rel.* Bros. Builders Supply Co. v. Old World Artisans, Inc., 702 F. Supp. 1561 (N.D. Ga. 1988); United States *ex rel.* Sunbelt Pipe Corp. v. United States Fid. & Guar. Co., 785 F.2d 468 (4th Cir. 1986); United States *ex rel.* Carlisle Constr. Co., v. Coastal Structures, Inc., 689 F. Supp. 1092 (M.D. Fla. 1988).

[45] Illinois Sur. Co. v. John Davis Co., 244 U.S. 276 (1917); United States *ex rel.* Mississippi Rd. Supply Co. v. H.R. Morgan, Inc., 542 F.2d 262 (5th Cir. 1976), *cert. denied,* 434 U.S. 828 (1977); Public Water Supply Dist. No. 3 v. Reliance Ins. Co., 708 S.W.2d 190 (Mo. Ct. App. 1986); Symons Corp. v. Insurance Co. of N. Am., 94 N.C. App. 541, 380 S.E.2d 550 (1989). *But see* Garco Indus. Equip. Co. v. Mallory, 485 N.E.2d 652 (Ind. Ct. App. 1985), holding that the owner of equipment repossessed from the lessor could not claim on the lessee contractor's bond. The court's analysis suggests that it will treat long-term leases much as though the claim is for equipment being sold.

collect from the delinquent employer. The IRS would often look to the payment bond and claim that withholding taxes for employees on the bonded job were monies due for labor furnished in the prosecution of the work. The sureties argued that the employees had been paid in full and that IRS was simply a general creditor of the contractor and had not supplied labor or material for use on the bonded job.

On federal jobs this controversy was decided by a 1966 amendment to the Miller Act making the performance bond liable for withheld payroll taxes if the government gives the surety written notice of its claim within certain time limits. On non-Miller Act projects, unless an applicable statute or the bond explicitly provides coverage for withheld taxes, the surety should not be liable for such tax claims.[46]

If the contractor has failed to pay wage-based contributions to a union trust fund, the surety will be liable for that portion of the delinquent payment attributable to the bonded job and, in a suit by the trustees of the fund, the surety will also be liable for auditing fees, interest, and attorneys' fees to the extent they are provided for in the union contract signed by the principal. The courts have accepted the unions' argument that such benefit payments are part of the amount due for work performed on the job by the contractor's employees.[47] If the employee does not receive credit for the contribution until it is actually paid, then this result seems to be defensible. If the employee receives credit anyway, then the situation would be analogous to withholding taxes and the union trustees should be viewed as mere creditors who did not furnish labor or material.

Insurance premiums are not labor or material and thus are not within the coverage of the payment bond even though insurance is necessary to the performance of the contract. This is true even for worker's compensation insurance, for which the premium is based on wages paid by the contractor.[48]

§ 13.9 —Delay Damages and Lost Profits

Payment bonds typically give a right of action for sums "justly due." Claimants argue that they are justly due an amount that will make them

---

[46] United States v. Commonwealth of Pa. Dep't of Highways, 349 F. Supp. 1370 (E.D. Pa. 1972); United States v. Maryland Casualty Co., 323 F.2d 473 (5th Cir. 1963); United States v. Crosland Constr. Co., 217 F.2d 275 (4th Cir. 1954).

[47] United States *ex rel.* Sherman v. Carter, 353 U.S. 210 (1957); J.W. Bateson Co. v. United States *ex rel.* Board of Trustees, 434 U.S. 586 (1978).

[48] United States *ex rel.* West v. Peter Kiewit & Sons' Co., 235 F. Supp. 500 (D. Alaska 1964); United States *ex rel.* Bordallo Consol., Inc. v. Markowitz Bros. (Del.), Inc., 249 F. Supp. 610 (D. Guam 1966); Cobb-Strecker-Dumphy & Zimmerman v. M.A. Mortenson Co., 706 F. Supp. 685 (D. Minn. 1989).

whole for the contractor's default, including delay damages, lost profits, interest, and attorneys' fees. They want to be in the same financial position as if the contractor had never defaulted. The surety, on the other hand, argues that it is liable only for the actual cost of labor or material furnished for use on the bonded job, and that such breach of contract damages are neither labor nor material.

There is a split of authority as to whether the surety is liable for delay damages. Some courts accept the argument that at least some delay costs are part of the sum justly due for the labor or material furnished.[49]

Other courts, however, reject such arguments and hold that a claimant's recovery is limited to the price stated in the original contract with the surety's principal. These courts reason that the parties themselves set the price of the labor and material and that delay damages are, as the name implies, due to the subcontractor to compensate for delay rather than for supplying labor or material. Thus, there are cases holding that the surety is not liable for delay damages.[50]

The trend in the law, however, seems to be toward finding liability for some categories of delay damages. The payment bond statutes are universally admitted to be a remedial legislation designed to protect those whose work goes into government construction projects, and they are liberally construed to effect this legislative intent. To the extent that delay damages quantify the actual increased costs incurred by a contractor or subcontractor as a consequence of a wrongful act of another party, they can be recovered. If the bond claimant's contract entitles it to a price increase because of a compensable delay, then the surety logically should be liable for that increase as an amount justly due in return for the labor or material the claimant has furnished.[51] On the other hand, if the damages claimed are for breach of contract rather than the actual increased cost of furnishing the labor or material, this should not be recoverable from the surety.

At one time sureties argued that they should not be liable for a claimant's profit because profit is neither labor nor material, but now it is accepted

---

[49] United States *ex rel.* Mariana v. Piracci Constr. Co., 405 F. Supp. 904 (D.D.C. 1975); United States *ex rel.* Heller Elec. Co. v. William F. Klingensmith, Inc., 670 F.2d 1227 (D.C. Cir. 1982); General Fed. Constr., Inc. v. D.R. Thomas, Inc., 52 Md. App. 700, 451 A.2d 1250 (1982); United States *ex rel.* Pertun Constr. Co. v. Harvesters Group, Inc., 918 F.2d 915 (11th Cir. 1990).

[50] McDaniel v. Ashton-Mardian Co., 357 F.2d 511 (9th Cir. 1966); United States *ex rel.* Pittsburgh-Des Moines Steel Co. v. MacDonald Constr. Co., 281 F. Supp. 1010 (E.D. Mo. 1968); United States *ex rel.* E&R Constr. Co. v. Guy H. James Constr. Co., 390 F. Supp. 1193 (M.D. Tenn. 1972), *aff'd,* 489 F.2d 756 (6th Cir. 1974).

[51] United States *ex rel.* Mariana v. Piracci Constr. Co., 405 F. Supp. 904 (D.D.C. 1975); United States *ex rel.* Heller Elec. Co. v. William F. Klingensmith, Inc., 670 F.2d 1227 (D.C. Cir. 1982); General Fed. Constr., Inc. v. D.R. Thomas, Inc., 52 Md. App. 700, 451 A.2d 1250 (1982). *See generally* Sobel, *Owner Delay Damages Chargeable to Performance Bond Surety,* 21 Cal. West. L. Rev. 128 (1984).

that a reasonable profit is part of the amount justly due for the labor or material furnished to the principal (but not, of course, lost profit not earned because of the principal's breach of contract).[52] Similarly, it would seem that in the future actual increased costs due to compensable delays may be recognized as a proper part of the surety's liability.

§ 13.10 —Attorneys' Fees and Interest

Claimants routinely demand interest and attorneys' fees, but seldom receive them. This poor record of success is partly because claimants usually make the wrong arguments to bolster their position. If a claimant's only argument in support of an award of interest or attorneys' fees is that they are necessary to make it whole for the principal's default, then it is unlikely to prevail because the surety did not insure it against damage from its mistake in contracting with the insolvent principal. The surety is liable for the amount justly due for labor or material furnished for use on the bonded job, but interest and attorneys' fees are not labor or material. In order to have a chance to recover attorneys' fees, the claimant must point to a statute, a contract provision, or an action by the surety itself to justify their award. The mere fact that the principal did not pay will not be sufficient.

The *American Rule* is that a prevailing party is not entitled to attorneys' fees as an item of damages. The Supreme Court has explicitly applied this general rule to Miller Act bonds,[53] and the logic of the Court's holding would be equally relevant to other bonds if there is no controlling state statute or decision. There are four recognized exceptions to the American Rule. One allows attorneys' fees to a prevailing plaintiff acting in the public interest. This so-called *private attorney general exception* would not seem to be relevant to a payment bond claim.

A second exception allows attorneys' fees if a statute authorizes them to be awarded. The Freedom of Information Act, for example, provides that a plaintiff who substantially prevails shall be awarded reasonable attorneys' fees. The Miller Act and most state bond statutes are silent on the question of attorneys' fees. Some state statutes, however, do provide for fees and a prevailing claimant on a bond under such a statute can recover them. A claimant on a Miller Act bond, however, cannot recover attorneys' fees even if the state within which the project is located has such a provision in its statute.[54]

A third exception applies if the surety's conduct in handling the claim violates an applicable statute authorizing attorneys' fees or if the court finds

[52] Arthur N. Olive Co. v. United States *ex rel.* Marino, 297 F.2d 70 (1st Cir. 1961).

[53] F.D. Rich Co. v. United States *ex rel.* Industrial Lumber Co., 417 U.S. 116 (1974).

[54] *Id.*

the surety's conduct to have been so outrageous that attorneys' fees should be awarded as, in effect, punitive damages.[55]

A claimant's best chance of recovering attorneys' fees is under the fourth exception: fees authorized by contract. If the bond itself (either explicitly or by incorporating the contract by reference)[56] or the claimant's contract with the surety's principal[57] provides that the prevailing party will be entitled to attorneys' fees, then the claimant can argue that attorneys' fees are part of the bargained-for price of the labor and material furnished and are justly due under the bond.

Interest is awarded to compensate one party for another party's delay in payment. If the claimant's contract with the bond principal calls for interest, it can argue that such interest is part of the amount justly due for labor or material.[58] If the contract does not provide for interest, the claimant can still obtain it by claiming entitlement under state law. Many states, by statute or court decision, provide for interest if payment of a liquidated amount is delayed.[59]

If interest is proper, it will run from the date the payment should have been made.[60] Virtually all bonds provide that the surety is liable only if the principal has failed to make payment within 90 days of the date upon which the claimant last furnished labor or material, and interest should not commence to run against the surety until that 90-day period expires. In addition,

---

[55] United States *ex rel.* General Elec. Supply Co. v. Minority Elec. Co., 537 F. Supp. 1018 (S.D. Ga. 1982); K-W Indus. v. National Sur. Corp., 855 F.2d 640 (9th Cir. 1988); United States *ex rel.* Mid Seven Transp. v. Blinderman Constr. Co., 735 F. Supp. 272 (N.D. Ill. 1990).

[56] Dale Benz, Inc., Contractors v. American Casualty Co., 303 F.2d 80 (9th Cir.), *reh'g denied,* 305 F.2d 641 (9th Cir. 1962).

[57] Travelers Indem. Co. v. United States *ex rel.* Western Steel Co., 362 F.2d 896 (9th Cir. 1966); United States *ex rel.* Sherman v. Carter, 353 U.S. 210 (1957); United States *ex rel.* Carter Equip. Co. v. H.R. Morgan, Inc., 544 F.2d 1271 (5th Cir.), *reh'g granted,* 554 F.2d 164 (5th Cir. 1977); Ibex Indus., Inc. v. Coast Line Waterproofing, 563 F. Supp. 1142 (D.D.C. 1983); United States *ex rel.* C.J.I., Inc. v. Western States Mechanical Contractors, Inc., 834 F.2d 1534 (10th Cir. 1987).

[58] D&L Constr. Co. v. Triangle Elec. Supply Co., 332 F.2d 1009 (8th Cir. 1964); United States *ex rel.* Billows Elec. Supply Co. v. E.J.T. Constr. Co., 517 F. Supp. 1178 (E.D. Pa. 1981), *aff'd,* 688 F.2d 827 (3d Cir.), *cert. denied,* 103 S. Ct. 126 (1982); Ibex Indus., Inc. v. Coast Line Waterproofing, 563 F. Supp. 1142 (D.D.C. 1983).

[59] Arnold v. United States *ex rel.* Bowman Mechanical Contractors, 470 F.2d 243 (10th Cir. 1972); United States *ex rel.* A.V. DeBlasio Constr., Inc. v. Mountain States Constr. Co., 588 F.2d 259 (9th Cir. 1978); United States *ex rel.* Astro Cleaning & Packaging Corp. v. Jamison Co., 425 F.2d 1281 (6th Cir. 1970). Note that such interest may be collectible at the *legal rate,* which will not necessarily be the same as the rate specified in the contract. Waukesha Concrete Prods. Corp. v. Capitol Indem. Co., 127 Wis. 2d 332, 379 N.W.2d 333 (Ct. App. 1985).

[60] United States *ex rel.* Schaefer Elec., Inc. v. O. Frank Heinz Constr. Co., 300 F. Supp. 396 (S.D. Ill. 1969).

the surety cannot be expected to pay until a demand is made against it.[61] Some courts, however, have awarded prejudgment interest against the surety from the date its principal should have made payment.[62]

§ 13.11 Notice Requirements

Virtually all bonds require a claimant with no direct contractual relationship with the bond principal to give written notice of the claim. Because one supplying a material supplier is not covered by most bonds,[63] the practical effect of the notice requirement is that a sub-subcontractor or a supplier to a subcontractor must give written notice of its claim or lose its rights against the prime contractor's bond.

The purpose of this notice requirement is to enable the prime contractor to protect itself by withholding payments otherwise due the subcontractor until the subcontractor pays its debt.[64] It must be remembered that a prime contractor and its surety can be liable on the payment bond to such a supplier or sub-subcontractor even though the prime contractor has paid the subcontractor in full for the work or material for which the claim is being made. The notice requirement is designed to mitigate the unfairness of imposing such double liability on the prime contractor while still giving the supplier or sub-subcontractor an opportunity to be paid under the bond.

There is no reason to require notice by a material supplier or subcontractor in a direct contractual relationship with the bond principal, because the principal already knows such a material supplier or subcontractor is, or claims to be, unpaid. Such a notice requirement would serve no purpose and could be a trap for the unwary or unsophisticated.

Under the Miller Act, AIA Document A312,[65] and most state bond statutes, notice must be given to the prime contractor. Under AIA Document A311, however, notice must be given to any two out of three among the owner, the contractor, and the surety.[66] If notice is given to the owner or

---

[61] American Auto Ins. Co. v. United States *ex rel.* Luce, 269 F.2d 406 (1st Cir. 1959); United States *ex rel.* Caldwell Foundry & Mach. Co. v. Texas Constr. Co., 237 F.2d 705 (5th Cir. 1955).

[62] *See, e.g.,* Baker & Ford Co. v. United States *ex rel.* Urban Plumbing & Heating Co., 363 F.2d 605 (9th Cir. 1966); J.F. White Eng'g Corp. v. United States *ex rel.* Pittsburgh Plate Glass Co., 311 F.2d 410 (10th Cir. 1962); United States *ex rel.* Astro Cleaning & Packaging Corp. v. Jamison Co., 425 F.2d 1281 (6th Cir. 1970).

[63] See **§ 13.6**.

[64] United States *ex rel.* Honeywell v. A&L Mechanical Contractors, Inc., 677 F.2d 383 (4th Cir. 1982); United States *ex rel.* Kinlau Sheet Metal Works, Inc. v. Great Am. Ins. Co., 537 F.2d 222 (5th Cir. 1976); United States *ex rel.* Jinks Lumber Co. v. Federal Ins. Co., 452 F.2d 485 (5th Cir. 1971).

[65] AIA Doc. A312 (1984).

[66] AIA Doc. A311 ¶ 3(a) (1970).

surety, they will presumably inform the contractor, but because the purpose of requiring notice is to alert the contractor to a default by its subcontractor, it does not seem logical to rely on such indirect notification.

The Miller Act and both AIA bonds require that the notice be in writing and that it "state with substantial accuracy the amount claimed and the name of the party to whom" the labor or material was furnished. At least part of the notice must be in writing, but it can be supplemented by information communicated orally. Thus, once some written communication is established, the court will consider other contacts to decide whether all the elements of notice have been furnished.[67]

The courts also give a liberal interpretation to a requirement that notice be sent by registered or certified mail. The general rule is that such a requirement is merely to provide proof that the notice was received; if receipt is admitted or otherwise proven, notice will not fail because it was not sent in the prescribed manner.[68]

In judging the required contents of the notice, however, the courts are only slightly less liberal. The contractor should be informed of the approximate amount owed[69] and the subcontractor for whom the work was performed.[70] Most importantly, the notice must tell the contractor that the unpaid supplier or sub-subcontractor is looking to the contractor for payment.[71] The sufficiency of any given notice will be judged in light of the purpose of the notice requirement, and the prime contractor must be advised that the claimant is looking to it for payment so that it can withhold the amount claimed from any payments otherwise due the defaulting subcontractor.

§ 13.12 —Time Period Allowed

The courts strictly enforce the requirement that notice must be given within 90 days of the last date upon which the claimant furnished labor or material for which a claim is made. The determination of that date is

---

[67] United States *ex rel.* Kelly-Mohrhusen Co. v. Merle A. Patnode Co., 457 F.2d 116 (7th Cir. 1972).

[68] United States *ex rel.* Hillsdale Rock Co. v. Cortelyou & Cole, Inc., 581 F.2d 239 (9th Cir. 1978); Fleisher Eng'g & Constr. Co. v. United States *ex rel.* Hallenbeck, 311 U.S. 15 (1940).

[69] United States *ex rel.* Pool Constr. Co. v. Smith Rd. Constr. Co., 227 F. Supp. 315 (D. Okla. 1964).

[70] Apache Powder Co. v. Ashton Co., 264 F.2d 417 (9th Cir. 1959).

[71] United States *ex rel.* Charles R. Joyce & Son, Inc. v. F.A. Baehner, Inc., 326 F.2d 556 (2d Cir. 1964); United States *ex rel.* Jinks Lumber Co. v. Federal Ins. Co., 452 F.2d 485 (5th Cir. 1971); Bowden v. United States *ex rel.* Malloy, 239 F.2d 572 (9th Cir. 1956), *cert. denied,* 353 U.S. 957 (1957); United States *ex rel.* Bailey v. Freethy, 469 F.2d 1348 (9th Cir. 1972).

complex, and the criteria to be considered are discussed at some length in connection with the commencement date of the suit limitations period in **§ 13.13**.

One problem unique to the 90-day notice requirement, however, is this: what happens if 90 days elapse following delivery of material, with no notice being given, and then additional material is delivered, followed by timely notice? The claimant will argue that the timely notice resurrects the barred claim, but the prime contractor and surety will argue that they can be liable for only the additional material.

The Miller Act provides that the notice must be given within 90 days of the last delivery for which claim is made.[72] Thus, if the additional material is not included in the claim (if it was delivered C.O.D. or delivered directly to and paid for by the prime contractor, for example), then it will not resurrect the barred claim.[73] There is also authority holding that notice given within 90 days of delivery of material under a separate purchase order or contract on the same project will not revive a barred claim.[74]

On the other hand, if the claimant has a single contract with a subcontractor to supply material on the bonded job, a 90-day gap in deliveries will not prevent the date of the later delivery from being the last date upon which material for which claim is being made was supplied, and the additional delivery triggers a new 90-day period during which notice can be given for the entire claim.[75]

If a claimant finds that its right of action on the payment bond is or may be barred by the 90-day notice requirement, it can do one of two things. It can try to convince the court that it was a subcontractor or material supplier with a direct contractual relationship with the bond principal (and thus not required to give the notice), or it can argue that the principal waived the notice requirement or is estopped to assert it.

One way of establishing a direct contractual relationship with the prime contractor is to show that the purported subcontractor with whom the claimant dealt was really an alter ego of the prime. The courts will not permit a contractor to reduce the protection afforded to the subcontractor under the Miller Act by creating a "straw" or dummy subcontractor and

---

[72] 40 U.S.C. § 270b(a).

[73] United States *ex rel.* Harris Paint Co. v. Seaboard Sur. Co., 437 F.2d 37 (5th Cir. 1971); United States *ex rel.* Olmsted Elec., Inc. v. Neosho Constr. Co., 599 F.2d 930 (10th Cir. 1979).

[74] United States *ex rel.* J.A. Edwards & Co. v. Peter Reiss Constr. Co., 273 F.2d 880 (2d Cir. 1959), *cert. denied,* 362 U.S. 951 (1960); United States *ex rel.* I. Burack, Inc. v. Sovereign Constr. Co., 338 F. Supp. 657 (S.D.N.Y. 1972); United States *ex rel.* A&M Petroleum, Inc. v. Santa Fe Eng'rs, Inc., 660 F. Supp. 1111 (S.D. Miss. 1987). *But cf.* Noland Co. v. Allied Contractors, Inc., 273 F.2d 917 (4th Cir. 1959).

[75] United States *ex rel.* J.A. Edwards & Co. v. Peter Reiss Constr. Co., 273 F.2d 880 (2d Cir. 1959), *cert. denied,* 362 U.S. 951 (1960).

then arguing that persons who have dealt with this subcontractor must give the 90-day notice.[76] That is not to say that a prime contractor cannot subcontract work to a related but separate entity. The courts will consider factors such as whether the prime and purported subcontractor have separate facilities, equipment, and employees, and whether they work on separate jobs. In the final analysis, the claimant will have to convince the court that in reality, if not on paper, the prime and purported subcontractor are one and the same.

If a subcontractor encounters financial difficulties, the prime contractor will often take steps to assure a smooth flow of material to the job. If the prime merely issues joint checks payable to the subcontractor and the supplier, it should not be found to have entered into a direct contractual relationship with the supplier.[77] On the other hand, if the prime contractor makes a separate agreement with the supplier, such as by guaranteeing payment or agreeing to pay the supplier directly or by taking over the subcontract work itself and requesting that the supplier of sub-subcontractor continue to work, then the court will find a direct contractual relationship and no 90-day notice will be required.[78]

If a subcontractor is in financial difficulty, the prime contractor should be very careful in any dealings with the suppliers or sub-subcontractors. There is no reason to risk incurring liability for a past-due debt barred by the supplier's failure to give the 90-day notice if an item is readily available from another source or can just as well be purchased by a replacement subcontractor.

The prime contractor should also be very careful not to waive the 90-day notice requirement or estop itself from asserting it. Anything the prime does that would reasonably lead an unpaid supplier or sub-subcontractor to believe it will be paid without having to give the 90-day notice invites a court to find that notice has been waived or that the prime contractor is estopped from asserting the defense of failure to give the notice.[79] Vague assurances that the matter is being taken care of or promises of future payments are especially dangerous. Prime contractors can avoid handing claimants such waiver or estoppel arguments if they make no promises about past-due

---

[76] National Sur. Corp. v. United States *ex rel.* Way Panama, S.A., 378 F.2d 294 (5th Cir.), *cert. denied,* 389 U.S. 1004 (1967).

[77] United States *ex rel.* State Elec. Supply Co. v. Hesselden Constr. Co., 404 F.2d 774 (10th Cir. 1968); United States *ex rel.* Fordham v. P.W. Parker, Inc., 504 F. Supp. 1066 (D. Md. 1980).

[78] United States *ex rel.* Billows Elec. Supply Co. v. E.J.T. Constr. Co., 517 F. Supp. 1178 (E.D. Pa. 1981), *aff'd,* 688 F.2d 827 (3d Cir.), *cert. denied,* 103 S. Ct. 126 (1982); United States *ex rel.* Greenwald-Supon, Inc. v. Gramercy Contractors, Inc., 433 F. Supp. 156 (S.D.N.Y. 1977); American Casualty Co. v. Southern Materials Co., 261 F.2d 197 (4th Cir. 1958).

[79] United States *ex rel.* Franklin Paint Co. v. Kagan, 129 F. Supp. 331 (D. Mass. 1955).

accounts and explicitly reserve all rights under the payment bond and applicable statutes. Contact with potential claimants should be in writing or, at least, followed promptly by a letter confirming the reservation of rights.

§ 13.13 Suit Limitations

The most common, serious, and easily avoided mistake committed by payment bond claimants is the failure to file suit against the surety within the time limits set by the bond or statute. Virtually all bonds require that suit be filed within one year, but the event with which that one-year period commences varies from bond to bond. Normally, there is no requirement that the claimant first sue the contractor/principal or even join him in the action in order to sue the surety directly.[80]

The Miller Act and most state payment bond statutes require that suit be filed within one year of the last date upon which the claimant furnished labor or materials for use in the prosecution of the contract work.[81] AIA Document A311 sets the one-year period as running from the date upon which the principal ceased work on the bonded project, unless such a limitation is prohibited by law, in which event the limitation shall be the minimum permitted by law.[82] Under AIA Document A312 the one-year period commences on the earlier of the dates on which the claimant gave the contractor written notice of the claim or the last date upon which anyone furnished labor or material under the construction contract.[83] Other bonds start the one-year period from final completion or final acceptance of the contract work, or from the making of final payment to the contractor.

Because the various payment bond statutes, including the Miller Act, create a remedy unknown at common law, the courts hold that suit within the one-year period is a condition precedent to an action on the bond: it is a limitation on the right itself, not merely on the remedy. That is, the one-year limitation is not merely a statute of limitations that will be waived if not properly pled, but a jurisdictional prerequisite that can be raised at any time, even on appeal.[84] In most cases this distinction is one of semantics, with no practical consequences. In Miller Act cases, however, the surety can argue that a United States district court has no subject matter jurisdiction because of the claimant's failure to file within the one-year period.

---

[80] Play Sys., Inc. v. American Druggists Ins. Co., 176 Ga. App. 372, 336 S.E.2d 308 (1985).

[81] 40 U.S.C. § 270b(b).

[82] AIA Doc. A311 ¶ 3(b) (1970).

[83] AIA Doc. A312 ¶ 11 (1984).

[84] United States *ex rel.* Celanese Coatings Co. v. Gullard, 504 F.2d 466 (9th Cir. 1974); United States *ex rel.* Soda v. Montgomery, 253 F.2d 509 (3d Cir. 1958); United States *ex rel.* Statham Instruments, Inc. v. Western Casualty & Sur. Co., 359 F.2d 521 (6th Cir. 1966).

§ 13.14 —Commencement of Limitation Period

Because construction projects often take a long time to complete even if the contractor is not in financial difficulty, a limitation period commencing upon completion of the project gives such an extended period within which to file suit that few claimants find themselves barred. Those that do typically argue that the contract is not complete (or the principal has not ceased work, or the project is not accepted) until final payment is made or even until all warranties have expired.

Many claimants, however, run afoul of the one-year limitation if it commences on the last date they furnished labor or material. Although a year would seem to be plenty of time in which to sue, many claimants are unaware of their bond rights and delay seeking legal advice. For whatever reason, a great deal of litigation has been devoted to determining the last date upon which a claimant furnished labor or material.

There is no minimum amount of work that must be done to qualify as furnishing labor or material, but the work must have been required under the prime contract.[85] A visit to the job by the claimant's employees for inspection purposes or to prepare a final estimate of labor and material supplied or to correct work previously performed but found to be defective will not count as furnishing labor or material.[86] Work performed or material delivered as a sham to gain coverage under the bond will not be considered.[87]

If the claimant is a material supplier, delivery slips will almost always establish the date upon which material was furnished. If the claimant is a subcontractor, certified payrolls, daily reports, inspectors' reports, and invoices are useful in determining the nature of the work performed. A surety will often find that the subcontractor's own invoices show its work to be 100 percent complete long before the date it now claims to have furnished labor or material. If the claimant rented equipment, the last day upon which the equipment was available for use on the job (rather than the last day it

---

[85] United States *ex rel.* Joseph I. Richardson, Inc. v. E.J.T. Constr. Co., 453 F. Supp. 435 (D. Del. 1978).

[86] United States *ex rel.* Billows Elec. Supply Co. v. E.J.T. Constr. Co., 517 F. Supp. 1178 (E.D. Pa. 1981), *aff'd,* 688 F.2d 827 (3d Cir.), *cert. denied,* 103 S. Ct. 126 (1982); United States *ex rel.* H.T. Sweeney & Son, Inc. v. E.J.T. Constr. Co., 415 F. Supp. 1328 (D. Del. 1976); General Ins. Co. of Am. v. United States *ex rel.* Audley Moore & Son, 406 F.2d 442 (5th Cir.), *on reh'g,* 409 F.2d 1326 (5th Cir.), *cert. denied,* 396 U.S. 902 (1969); United States *ex rel.* Greenwald-Supon, Inc. v. Gramercy Contractors, Inc., 433 F. Supp. 156 (S.D.N.Y. 1977); United States *ex rel.* Altman v. Young Lumber Co., 376 F. Supp. 1290 (D.S.C. 1974); United States *ex rel.* T. Square Equip. Corp. v. Gregor J. Schaefer Sons, Inc., 272 F. Supp. 962 (E.D.N.Y. 1967); Kuchenski v. Kramer Sheet Metal, Inc., 377 N.W.2d 133 (N.D. 1985).

[87] United States *ex rel.* First Nat'l Bank v. United States Fid. & Guar. Co., 240 F. Supp. 316 (N.D. Okla. 1965).

was actually used) will start the one year running, but the claimant cannot extend the period by leaving unused equipment on the jobsite after a request to remove it.[88]

The most common dispute is over labor or material supplied after substantial completion of the claimant's work. The surety will argue that any additional items are maintenance or guaranty work, but the claimant will say it is original contract work that was not done previously.

The crucial question is whether the item was never supplied, or was furnished but proved defective. If it was omitted entirely, then it constitutes original work when furnished for the first time.[89] If a defective item was furnished and is later corrected or replaced, the corrective or warranty work is not considered in computing the one-year period.

Once the commencement date of the one-year period is determined, the one year is usually computed according to Rule 6(a) of the Federal Rules of Civil Procedure or the "policy" underlying Rule 6(a). The day upon which the last work was performed is not included, but the final day of the one-year period is included. Thus, if August 2, 1991, is the last day upon which labor or material was furnished, suit must be filed on or before August 2, 1992 unless the court is closed on August 2, 1991, in which event the suit can be filed on the next day the court is open.[90]

For the first 90 days of the one year following the date upon which the claimant last furnished labor or material, the surety cannot be sued. The surety's liability commences if the claimant has not been paid within this 90-day period and, theoretically, premature suits should be dismissed. If such a dismissal takes place after the year has expired, the claimant loses its bond rights.

Under modern pleading, however, the complaint can be amended, or a supplemental complaint filed, to allege that the 90-day period has expired, and the amended complaint should relate back to the date of the original filing. No modern court is going to let a surety escape liability because of a premature suit or pleading mistake, as long as the claimant acts promptly to correct its error.[91] Although a more difficult case is presented if a claimant

---

[88] Mike Bradford & Co. v. F.A. Chastain Constr., Inc., 387 F.2d 942 (5th Cir. 1968).

[89] United States *ex rel.* Lank Woodwork Co. v. CSH Contractors, Inc., 452 F. Supp. 922 (D.D.C. 1978).

[90] United States *ex rel.* Pre-Fab Erectors, Inc. v. A.B.C. Roofing & Siding, Inc., 193 F. Supp. 465 (S.D. Cal. 1961); Bailey v. Faux, 704 F. Supp. 1051 (D. Utah 1989). *But cf.* United States *ex rel.* Magna Masonry v. R.T. Woodfield, 709 F.2d 249 (4th Cir. 1983), rejecting the use of Rule 6(a) and United States *ex rel.* Altman v. Young Lumber Co., 376 F. Supp. 1290 (D.S.C. 1974), which applied Rule 6(a) and, in effect, made the period a year and a day.

[91] United States *ex rel.* Capitol Elec. Supply Co. v. C.J. Elec. Contractors, Inc., 535 F.2d 1326 (1st Cir. 1976); Security Ins. Co. v. United States *ex rel.* Haydis, 338 F.2d 444 (9th Cir. 1964); United States *ex rel.* Pittsburgh-Des Moines Steel Co. v. Dauphin Steel & Eng'g Co., 53 F.R.D. 382 (S.D.N.Y. 1971).

files a timely suit but names the wrong surety, it can probably save itself after the one-year period has expired by amending its complaint to name the proper defendant and arguing that the amended complaint relates back to the date of the filing of the original complaint, if the requirements of Rule 15(c) of the Federal Rules of Civil Procedure are met.[92] Because Rule 15(c) requires that the proper surety have notice of the commencement of the action within the one year period, however, such an argument will often fail.

§ 13.15 —Estoppel

Whatever the outcome of the unusual cases in which a timely suit is filed against the wrong defendant or a premature suit is filed, the one-year limitation is a very powerful defense that time and time again allows sureties to defeat otherwise valid claims. If the one-year period has expired, a claimant loses its rights against the payment bond unless it can convince the court that the surety should be estopped from asserting the limitations defense.

Although rare, such an estoppel has been found when the surety misled the claimant into reasonably believing that its claim would be paid without the necessity of filing suit.[93] If the surety represents to a claimant that it will be paid, it is inviting an estoppel argument. For this reason anyone defending against a claim should make no promises and reserve all rights under the bond and any applicable statute. Because such a reservation should always be made or confirmed in writing, many sureties make it a standard practice to write each claimant suggesting that the claimant take whatever steps it deems necessary to protect its position.

§ 13.16 Jurisdiction and Venue Requirements

The Miller Act provides that suit must be brought "in the United States District Court for any district in which the contract was to be performed

---

[92] United States *ex rel.* Statham Instruments, Inc. v. Western Casualty & Sur. Co., 359 F.2d 521 (6th Cir. 1966) (dissenting opinion); Travelers Indem. Co. v. United States *ex rel.* Construction Specialities Co., 382 F.2d 103 (10th Cir. 1967); 3 Moore's Federal Practice ¶ 15.15 [4.-2] (1991).

[93] McWaters & Bartlett v. United States *ex rel.* Wilson, 272 F.2d 291 (10th Cir. 1959); United States *ex rel.* B&B Welding, Inc. v. Reliance Ins. Co., 743 F. Supp. 129 (E.D.N.Y. 1990); United States *ex rel.* Nelson v. Reliance Ins. Co., 436 F.2d 1366 (10th Cir. 1971); United States *ex rel.* E.E. Black, Ltd. v. Price-McNemar Constr. Co., 320 F.2d 663 (9th Cir. 1963); United States *ex rel.* Humble Oil & Ref. Co. v. Fidelity & Casualty Co., 402 F.2d 893 (4th Cir. 1968); Annotation, *Fraud, Misrepresentation or Deception as Estopping Reliance on Statute of Limitations,* 43 A.L.R.3d 429 (1972); Terrell, *How to Prevent Loss of a Contract Surety's Rights by Waiver and Estoppel,* 10 Forum 878 (1975). *Cf.* United States *ex rel.* Witt v. JP, Inc., 655 F. Supp. 480 (D. Alaska 1987).

and executed and not elsewhere . . . "[94] Almost all other bonds require that suit be filed in the state court for the political subdivision in which the project is located or in the federal court for the district in which the project is located. The Miller Act gives exclusive jurisdiction to the federal courts without regard to the amount in controversy or the citizenship of the parties.[95] In a Miller Act suit, the parties cannot confer jurisdiction on a state court by contract or subsequent agreement, and a suit filed in a state court is ineffective even to toll the running of the one-year limitation period.[96]

The federal court in which the suit is filed, however, is only a venue requirement that can be waived by the parties.[97] If suit is erroneously filed in a federal district other than one in which the contract is to be performed, the defendants may waive the improper venue by failing to make a timely objection; if objection is made, the suit may be transferred to the proper district[98] under 28 U.S.C. § 1406(a). Some courts have even held that the bond principal may contract to establish venue in another district and that the surety is bound by the principal's contract.[99]

If a Miller Act bond is given for a contract to be performed outside the United States, a claimant will not be deprived of a remedy for lack of proper venue. Even over the objection of the defendants, the suit will be heard.[100]

---

[94] 40 U.S.C. § 270b(b).

[95] *Id.*

[96] United States *ex rel.* Harvey Gulf Int'l Marine, Inc. v. Maryland Casualty Co., 573 F.2d 245 (5th Cir. 1978).

[97] United States *ex rel.* Caswell Equip. Co. v. Fidelity & Deposit Co., 494 F. Supp. 354 (D. Minn. 1980); United States *ex rel.* Capolino Sons, Inc. v. Electronic & Missile Facilities, Inc., 364 F.2d 705 (2d Cir.), *cert. denied,* 385 U.S. 924 (1966); United States *ex rel.* Angell Bros., Inc. v. Cave Constr., Inc., 250 F. Supp. 873 (D. Mont. 1966). *But cf.* United States *ex rel.* Coffey v. William R. Austin Constr. Co., 436 F. Supp. 626 (W.D. Okla. 1977).

[98] 28 U.S.C. § 1406(a). *See* Griners & Shaw, Inc. v. Federal Ins. Co., 234 F. Supp. 753 (D.S.C. 1964); United States *ex rel.* Caswell Equip. Co. v. Fidelity & Deposit Co., 494 F. Supp. 354 (D. Minn. 1980); United States *ex rel.* Essex Mach. Works, Inc. v. Rondout Marine, Inc., 312 F. Supp. 846 (S.D.N.Y. 1970); United States *ex rel.* Harvey Gulf Int'l Marine, Inc. v. Maryland Casualty Co., 573 F.2d 245 (5th Cir. 1978).

[99] United States *ex rel.* Fireman's Fund Ins. Co. v. Frank Briscoe Co., 462 F. Supp. 114 (E.D. La. 1978); United States *ex rel.* Caswell Equip. Co. v. Fidelity & Deposit Co., 494 F. Supp. 354 (D. Minn. 1980). *But cf.* United States *ex rel.* Vermont Marble Co. v. Roscoe-Ajax Constr. Co., 246 F. Supp. 439 (N.D. Cal. 1965); *In re* Fireman's Fund Ins. Co., 588 F.2d 93 (5th Cir. 1979).

[100] United States *ex rel.* Bryant Elec. Co. v. Aetna Casualty & Sur. Co., 297 F.2d 665 (2d Cir. 1962); United States *ex rel.* Bailey-Lewis-Williams, Inc. v. Peter Kiewit Sons Co., 195 F. Supp. 752 (D.D.C. 1961), *aff'd,* 299 F.2d 930 (D.C. Cir. 1962).

§ 13.17 Arbitration and the Surety

Arbitration clauses are often included in subcontracts, and the claimant may have an obligation to arbitrate with the bond principal. The payment bond, however, will almost never contain an arbitration clause.

If the claimant's arbitration award against the principal is reduced to judgment, collateral estoppel will arguably bind the surety to this determination of its principal's liability. In a non-Miller Act case, the normal rules of issue preclusion should apply and the surety is unlikely to be allowed to relitigate the question of its principal's debt.[101] The surety, of course, would remain free to assert any defense not available to its principal in connection with the underlying claim, such as failure to file suit within the limitation period applicable to a suit on the bond,or the inclusion of claims outside the coverage of the bond.

A Miller Act bond surety can argue that any preclusive effect given to an arbitration award (or confirming judgment) against its principal would deprive it of its statutory right to have its liability determined by the United States district court. The reported cases are split on this question.[102]

A related question is the surety's right or obligation to participate in the arbitration between the claimant and its principal. If both the payment bond and the claimant's subcontract incorporate the prime contract by reference and the prime contract contains the arbitration clause, there is an argument that the surety and the claimant are bound to arbitrate their dispute. Otherwise, it would seem to be in the claimant's interest to try to "vouch in" the surety by offering it the opportunity to participate in the arbitration proceeding. Certainly a court is more likely to give preclusive effect to the arbitration award in a subsequent action against the surety if the surety had notice of and an opportunity to participate in the arbitration proceeding between the claimant and the bond principal.

Finally, a claimant should remember that the arbitration proceeding does not toll the running of the limitation period in which to sue the surety. If necessary, a protective suit should be filed against the surety and then stayed pending the conclusion of the arbitration proceeding.

---

[101] Fidelity & Deposit Co. v. Parsons & Whittemore Contracting Corp., 48 N.Y.2d 127, 397 N.E.2d 380, 421 N.Y.S.2d 869 (1979); Powers Regulator Co. v. United States Fid. & Guar. Co., 7 Mass. App. Ct. 913, 388 N.E.2d 1205 (1978).

[102] *Compare* United States Fid. & Guar. Co. v. Hendry Corp., 391 F.2d 13 (5th Cir. 1968), and United States *ex rel.* Pensacola Constr. Co. v. St. Paul Fire & Marine Ins. Co., 705 F. Supp. 306 (W.D. La. 1988) (indicating the surety is not bound) *with* United States *ex rel.* Aurora Painting, Inc. v. Fireman's Fund Ins. Co., 832 F.2d 1150 (9th Cir. 1987).

§ 13.18 Possible Remedies if Payment Bond Claim Is Unavailable

Even though a statute or contract may have required a payment bond, it is possible for a person who has supplied labor or material to an insolvent contractor not to have bond protection. The surety might be insolvent, claims against the bond might exceed the bond penalty, or a claimant might lose its bond remedy by failing to file a timely suit against the surety. Although rare, there are even cases in which the required bond was never furnished.

A claimant with the dual misfortune of selling to an insolvent contractor and finding that its payment bond remedy is unavailable very likely will not be paid. In some circumstances, however, such a claimant can still recover all or part of what is owed.

The first possible source of payment is any contract balance still in the hands of the owner. Once the contract is complete, the owner is a stakeholder of any remaining contract funds, and those who supplied labor or material for use in the performance of the contract have an equitable claim to be paid out of the contract balance.[103] If the owner is not protected by sovereign immunity, the unpaid subcontractor or supplier can sue to recover the amount due.[104] If the owner is the United States, sovereign immunity will bar a direct suit,[105] but the unpaid claimant can prevent anyone else from obtaining the funds. The court may authorize the United States to pay the claimant, but cannot compel the government to do so.[106]

A second possible source of recovery is any other bond the contractor may have furnished. That is, if a payment bond was not written but a bid bond or performance bond was, the unpaid subcontractor or supplier can argue that it was a third-party beneficiary of the bid or performance bond.[107]

In particular, the contractor may have given a performance bond to the owner. If the unpaid material supplier is able to perfect a mechanics' lien

---

[103] American Sur. Co. v. Westinghouse Elec. Mfg. Co., 296 U.S. 133 (1935); Pearlman v. Reliance Ins. Co., 371 U.S. 132 (1962); United States Fid. & Guar. Co. v. United States, 475 F.2d 1377 (Ct. Cl. 1973); Gallagher, *Unpaid Subcontractor's or Supplier's Right to Payment out of Contract Funds,* 10 Construction Law. No. 1 (Jan. 1990).

[104] Kennedy Elec. Co. v. United States Postal Serv., 508 F.2d 954 (10th Cir. 1974); Active Fire Sprinkler Corp. v. United States Postal Serv., 811 F.2d 747 (2d Cir. 1987).

[105] United Elec. Corp. v. United States, 647 F.2d 1082 (Ct. Cl. 1981).

[106] United States Fid. & Guar. Co. v. United States, 475 F.2d 1377 (Ct. Cl. 1973); North Denver Bank v. United States, 432 F.2d 466 (Ct. Cl. 1970).

[107] United States *ex rel.* Empire Plastics Corp. v. Western Casualty & Sur. Co., 429 F.2d 905 (10th Cir. 1970); United States *ex rel.* Victor Elec. Corp. v. Maryland Casualty Co., 213 F. Supp. 800 (E.D.N.Y.), *further proceedings,* 215 F. Supp. 700 (E.D.N.Y. 1963); 17 Am. Jur. 2d *Contractors' Bonds* § 19 (1990). *Cf.* Johns-Manville Sales Corp. v. Reliance Ins. Co., 410 F.2d 277 (9th Cir. 1969).

successfully on the project, the performance bond surety will provide a source of funds from which the claim will be paid. That is because one requirement of the contractor's performance is likely to be its promise to deliver the project free from liens. The bond claim may be more valuable than the mechanics' lien by itself. The lien standing alone might have little economic value because, for example, it has a lower priority than a previously filed mortgage whose unpaid balance is large enough to leave no equity in the property. The low-priority lien claim that a surety is obliged to pay, on the other hand, represents a valuable right.

Another possibility to explore, as a last resort, is that the contractor had furnished a license bond to the state or a municipality. See **Ch. 12**.

Another last-ditch tactic is to determine whether the failure to furnish the bond was the fault of the contractor's insurance agent and to assert a tort of third-party beneficiary claim against the agent for failure to procure the necessary bond.[108]

Finally, there is a remote possibility that the owner was under some duty to require the contractor to furnish a bond. If no bond was in fact furnished, the owner's breach of that duty may provide the basis of a claim for relief directly against the persons responsible.[109]

One other cause of action might be maintained against the officers, directors, or agents of an owner, contractor, or subcontractor who directed diversion of construction loan funds or construction payments to purposes other than payment of lower-tier participants and project overhead. One can argue that the controlling individuals have a fiduciary duty to lower-tier participants or to their bonding companies to refrain from directing monies earmarked for a particular project to cover losses on unrelated projects or declaring such persons to be trustees for the benefit of lower-tier project participants and declaring misdirection of construction funds to be fraudulent as to those beneficiaries.[110] The same policy arguments that support such a statute should support common law imposition of similar liabilities.

§ 13.19 Practice Notes

If a contractor is solvent and generally appears to be meeting its obligations, its surety is very unlikely to become involved in a dispute between the contractor and its subcontractors or suppliers. The surety is a financial

---

[108] *See* Hainess-LaBar Ins. v. Julien Constr. Co., 743 P.2d 1262 (Wyo. 1987).

[109] *See, e.g.,* Warrior Hinkle, Inc. v. Andalusia City Sch. Bd., 469 So. 2d 1285 (Ala. 1985); Greenville Indep. Sch. Dist. v. B.&J. Excavating, Inc., 694 S.W.2d 410 (Tex. Civ. App. 1985).

[110] Tex. Prop. Code Ann. §§ 162.001–162.033 (West). The statute gives an aggrieved party a cause of action against the persons deemed to be fiduciaries. McCoy v. Nelson Utils. Servs., 736 S.W.2d 160 (Tex. Civ. App. 1987).

guarantor, not a judge or referee, and if the principal denies owing a claim the surety will normally support it. A claimant will do better to put its efforts into reaching an agreement with the contractor than into trying to use the surety to pressure the contractor into paying a disputed claim.

Once it becomes apparent that the contractor is in financial difficulty, however, the unpaid subcontractor or material supplier should immediately present a claim to the surety. The subcontractor's first step is to get a copy of the bond from the owner[111] and verify the identity of the surety. The bond and any applicable statute should be carefully studied for any notice or limitation requirements and a detailed, supported claim sent to the surety.

Most sureties will want to see delivery slips, invoices, copies of any purchase orders or subcontracts, and a summary of any running account showing purchases for and payments made on account of the bonded job. If the claimant has a written admission by the bond principal of the amount due, a copy should be sent to the surety along with an unequivocal demand for immediate payment.

Sureties are generally large, bureaucratic organizations and it is easy for letters to be filed away and forgotten. If a satisfactory response is not received promptly, the surety itself (not its local agent) should be telephoned. A claimant should, if necessary, call the bond claim department in the surety's home office and ask about the status of its claim. After determining the claim number and the name and mailing address of the person handling the file, any future correspondence should be addressed to that person. If the surety has not set up a claim file and assigned a claim number, a claimant should assume that it is not planning to take any action in the near future.

A surety will certainly need time to obtain information from its principal and consider its position, but if a commitment to pay an undisputed claim has not been made within a reasonable time, the claimant should write a letter threatening to file suit for the undisputed amount, plus interest and attorneys' fees, if a commitment to pay the claim is not made by a date certain in the near future. If the surety does not respond satisfactorily to the threatening letter, file suit. Some suits may be filed on claims the surety would have paid anyway, but it is better to file an unnecessary suit than to join the legion of claimants delaying so long that their claim was barred.

The surety is entitled to information and supporting documents, which should be supplied promptly, but once it has the facts the surety should be able to make a decision. In surety claims, as in much else in life, the squeaky wheel gets the grease.

---

[111] The Miller Act (40 U.S.C. § 270c) and most state bond statutes require the government to furnish a certified copy of the payment bond to any potential claimant.

PART III

LITIGATION ISSUES

CHAPTER 14

EFFECTIVE PREPARATION FOR A CONSTRUCTION ARBITRATION

Robert S. Peckar

Robert S. Peckar is a senior partner at Peckar & Abramson in River Edge, New Jersey. He is a graduate of Rutgers University and Columbia Law School. Mr. Peckar has gained recognition for formulating creative, multi-million dollar settlements to complex construction disputes and the implementation of alternative dispute resolutions. He serves as general counsel to the Building Contractors Association of New Jersey, the New York Building Congress, and the National Construction Financial Management Association. He is also a fellow of the American College of Construction Lawyers. He is a frequent lecturer, author of many articles on construction law topics, and is also a contributing author in several construction law textbooks.

§ 14.1 Introduction

ARBITRATION VERSUS LITIGATION

§ 14.2 Overview

§ 14.3 Informality

§ 14.4 Role of Law

§ 14.5 Role of Lawyers

§ 14.6 Prehearing Discovery

§ 14.7 Selection of Arbitrators

§ 14.8 Arbitration Awards

METHOD OF PREPARATION

§ 14.9 Scheduling the Hearing

§ 14.10 Knowledge of Adversary's Claim

§ 14.11 Application to the American Arbitration Association

§ 14.12 Application to Court

§ 14.13 Initial Presentation
§ 14.14 Description of Project
§ 14.15 Description of Project Time Frame
§ 14.16 Contract Price/Payment Analysis
§ 14.17 Scope of Work
§ 14.18 Schedule
§ 14.19 Overview of Claims
§ 14.20 Prehearing Written Submission
§ 14.21 Preparing for Hearings
§ 14.22 Who Will Tell the Story?
§ 14.23 Use of Experts
§ 14.24 Preparing Exhibits
§ 14.25 Use of Affidavits
§ 14.26 Creative Evidence
§ 14.27 Mediation

§ 14.1 Introduction

This chapter provides a practical guide for the unique preparation appropriate to a construction arbitration.

For the purposes of providing a meaningful context for this chapter, it is assumed that an arbitration has already been commenced in accordance with the filing of a demand for arbitration under the auspices of the American Arbitration Association, pursuant to the American Arbitration Association's (AAA) Construction Industry Arbitration Rules,[1] or pursuant to a submission by the parties to some other arbitration procedure. It is also assumed that the disputes involve substantially complex issues and/or substantial sums.

ARBITRATION VERSUS LITIGATION

§ 14.2 Overview

Those who have made the tactical error of coming before a panel of arbitrators inadequately prepared usually have common misperceptions and

[1] As amended and in effect Jan. 1, 1991 [hereinafter AAA Rules or Construction Industry Arbitration Rules]. For a more thorough discussion of construction arbitration, see M. Callahan, B. Bramble, & P. Lurie, Arbitration of Construction Disputes (John Wiley & Sons 1990); Alternative Dispute Resolution in the Construction Industry (R. Cushman, G. Hedemann & A. Tucker, eds., John Wiley & Sons 1990).

erroneous expectations concerning arbitration. Such attitudes include the following:

"Arbitration is informal."

"Arbitration is where I sit down and tell my story to my fellow industry members and they will recognize the validity of my case. That will be that."

"It does not matter what you do or say, the arbitrators are still going to split your demand in half."

"The law has nothing to do with arbitration."

"Why pay my lawyer to prepare for the case of my testimony? In arbitration I can say what I want without any judge to stop me."

Some of these misperceptions have been afforded respectability by inclusion in published works. For example, in one textbook for construction management students, the author states:

> The advantages of arbitration are the following:
>
> 2. Legal costs are reduced, both because the sessions are shorter and because the parties concerned can state their own case without the difficulties in admission of evidence they would encounter in Court. The lawyer, if used, spends less time in preparation of the case. In a technical [Court] case, an attorney must spend a great deal of time preparing the matter so it is apparent to a lay jury; this preparation is unnecessary in arbitration.[2]

It is worthwhile to review what the arbitration process is and why this process requires a high degree of preparation.

§ 14.3 Informality

Arbitration is not a formal court proceeding; however, most arbitrations are far from informal. The claimant presents its case first and the respondent usually has the opportunity to cross-examine the claimant's witness before presenting its own case.[3] Testimony is usually offered in the identical question-and-answer format as in a court trial. Because often at least one attorney sits as an arbitrator, reasonable objections will be tolerated by the panel of arbitrators. These objections will be heard, if not to apply court rule restrictions, then for the instructive value to the arbitrators of the explanations and arguments accompanying these objections. The practice of using court stenographers aids the arbitrators and parties in compensating for the time lapse between hearings,[4] and adds to the formality of the proceedings.

The inapplicability during arbitration of the rules of evidence is a major factor in the need for thorough preparation. The Construction Industry

[2] R. King, The Construction Manager (1974).

[3] AAA Rule 29, "Order of Proceedings and Communications with Arbitrator."

[4] See § **14.9**.

Arbitration Rules provide that: "The arbitrator shall be the judge of the relevance and the materiality of the evidence offered, and conformity to legal rules of evidence shall not be necessary."[5]

Although adherence to the rules of evidence in court imposes a somewhat cumbersome and time-consuming ritual, it also affords predictable protection against certain types of evidence that have proven to be unreliable. For example, a court would not permit testimony by a subcontractor's carpenter foreman that he knew the general contractor had used inadequate concrete because "one of the guys on the job mentioned a problem with concrete to a buddy of mine and then he told me." This statement would be inadmissible upon the grounds that it constitutes hearsay. In an arbitration, however, the statement would likely be heard by the arbitrators. Therefore, the attorney must be prepared to handle the unpredictable. To do so requires imaginative and thorough preparation.

§ 14.4 Role of Law

It is true that the body of court cases and the legal principles and doctrines that have developed from them are technically not binding upon arbitrators. However, this does not limit the right or prerogative of a lawyer or party in an arbitration to bring supportive court cases to the attention of the arbitrators as guidance in resolving the dispute.

There is a danger in this practice though. The value of contractor and architect/engineer arbitrators is their technical knowledge and familiarity with the construction industry; they are not trained to evaluate legal arguments formulated upon judicial decisions. Although most courts refuse to invade the realm of arbitrator discretion even upon a determination that the arbitrators ignored or misapplied a legal principle, there have been cases where courts vacated arbitration awards upon such grounds.[6]

§ 14.5 Role of Lawyers

In virtually every significant arbitration, the parties are represented by lawyers, and wisely so. Because lawyers are trained to present cases, their services in an arbitration are invaluable. However, the lawyer's approach

---

[5] AAA Rule 31.

[6] Under the Uniform Arbitration Act and most arbitration statutes, errors of law by arbitrators are not grounds to vacate or modify an arbitration award. However, in some reported and unreported court decisions, courts have in fact vacated awards on the grounds that the arbitrators misapplied the law. *See, e.g.*, Lewis v. Erie Ins. Exch., 281 Pa. Super. 193, 421 A.2d 1214 (1980).

must be in keeping with the tone and setting of a construction industry arbitration. Arbitrators respond favorably to attorneys who promote an orderly, expeditious, competent, and fair arbitration. On the other hand, they may express annoyance with attorneys who impose courtroom behavior and tactics upon the intimacy of the arbitration table.

§ 14.6 Prehearing Discovery

One of the features of arbitration that may be advantageous is the absence of automatic prehearing discovery,[7] although it may be permitted.[8] The statutes of some jurisdictions permit discovery in aid of an arbitration upon the direction of the arbitrators or upon application to a court.[9] There is compelling reason to permit prehearing discovery. Under the Construction Industry Arbitration Rules, the filing of a demand for arbitration is required to contain specified information: "a statement setting forth the nature of the dispute, the amount involved and the remedy sought . . . ."[10] In practice, however, some claimants and respondents, in filing their claims in arbitration, offer no more insight into the nature of the disputes to be arbitrated and the amount in controversy than the cryptic statements set forth in the following example:

Nature of Dispute:

Breach of Construction Contract.

The Amount Involved:

The amount in controversy has not yet been fully determined, but is greater than the amount $10,000.

---

[7] McDonald, *Major Construction Claims/Arbitration or Litigation,* Construction Specifier 62 (Oct. 1984).

[8] AAA Rule 10.

[9] The Uniform Arbitration Act of 1955, which has been adopted by a majority of states, specifically permits the arbitrators' issuance of subpoenas to compel the attendance of witnesses at hearings or depositions, as well as the production of documents and other evidence. However, the availability and issuance of subpoenas are not the equivalent of broad pretrial discovery available in the court action setting. In New York, for example, the civil practice rules specifically allow a court order request to provide a party with discovery in aid of an arbitration. N.Y. Civ. Prac. L. & R. Law § 3102 (McKinney). *See also* Willenhen, *Discovery in Aid of Arbitration,* 6 Litig. 16 (1980); Poppleton, *The Arbitrator's Role in Expediting the Large and Complex Commerical Case,* 36 Arb. J. 6 (Dec. 1981).

[10] AAA Rule 7, "Initiation Under a Submission."

Remedy Sought:

An award against the respondent for claimant's damages plus interest, costs of suit, and reasonable attorneys' fees.

As preposterous as it might sound, some parties actually attend the first hearing of arbitration knowing nothing more about the other party's case than these "one liners." The availability of limited discovery remedies this otherwise inexcusable approach.

Indeed, many complex arbitrations do have a discovery component to them, largely in response to the contention of the AAA that limited discovery sometimes enhances the value of hearing time by avoiding discovery on the stand. On the other hand, arbitration has no appropriate nor practical vehicle to respond to discovery abuses. Any recourse is up to the arbitrators. Although the AAA's regional director and tribunal administrators may be helpful and indeed persuasive in dealing with such problems, they are without authority, all of which is vested entirely in the panel of arbitrators. When abuse occurs, it is difficult to convene the arbitrators for a rapid response to the complaint; accordingly, one must weigh the benefits of limited discovery with the possible problems that may accompany the use of discovery techniques in the arbitration.

If discovery is to be allowed, it is best to complete it before hearings by stipulation between counsel and pursuant to agreement made with AAA's regional office. In this way, the likelihood of discovery abuse is lessened and the issues the arbitrator will hear with regard to discovery are more limited and defined.

§ 14.7 Selection of Arbitrators

The AAA rules provide three methods for the selection of arbitrators. The most commonly utilized is the appointment of arbitrators from the National Panel of Arbitrators maintained by the AAA.[11] The second method is the direct appointment by a party or the parties pursuant to their agreement.[12] The third method is the appointment of a neutral arbitrator by party appointed arbitrators.[13]

The selection of arbitrators is as critical to an arbitration as the selection of jurors is to a jury trial. Each arbitrator brings with him the perspective of his background, the sympathies of his occupational view and the qualities of his education and construction experience. Simply allowing the choice of arbitrators to be relegated to a young tribunal administrator because of the

---

[11] *Id.* Rule 13.

[12] *Id.* Rule 14.

[13] *Id.* Rule 15.

attorney's lack of attention to this critical issue is equivalent to depriving a client of the best possible forum for the resolution of the dispute.

Rule 14 permits attorneys to select a balanced panel of arbitrators cooperatively in order to assure the number of arbitrators, to assure that arbitrators with appropriate background are selected, and to assure the quality of the panel. This result is best achieved when the attorneys for all the parties to an arbitration confer and agree upon the appropriate character of the panel. For example, in a general contractor/subcontractor dispute, the attorneys for the two parties might agree that one arbitrator should be a contractor, one should be a subcontractor, and one should be an attorney or design professional without any significant commitment to the perspective of one side or the other. By making such an agreement in advance, the AAA is then able to generate separate lists for each of the categories.

Typically, Rule 13 appointments, which allow the parties simply to delete names from the AAA list, involve a difficult and sometimes prolonged process because the parties desire to eliminate every proposed arbitrator who would be understanding of the adversary's perspective. For this reason, subcontractors cross off all general contractors, general contractors cross off all subcontractors, and then they both complain that the AAA selected three arbitrators who were lawyers and engineers. By stipulating in advance the category of each arbitrator, the parties eliminate the possibility that the arbitrators may lack industry or technical knowledge, the primary advantage of construction industry arbitration. With an expectation of a balanced panel, the parties can easily agree that names will be crossed off the list of proposed arbitrators only if there is a genuine conflict of interest or other basis to believe that a proposed arbitrator would not be appropriate.

Too many arbitrations are delayed by confrontations over the selection of arbitrators. Although the selection process is certainly critical, it should be conducted with the goal of an early commencement of arbitration hearings.

Panel's Procedures

A typical three-member arbitration panel includes an attorney, a contractor, and an architect or engineer.[14] There is no rule or protocol to determine which member of the panel will serve as its chairman, but the attorney member almost always assumes the chairman's seat. Some chairmen are extremely deferential to their industry member co-arbitrators, but others

[14] The AAA Rules refer to a single "arbitrator" (AAA Rule 13, "Appointment from Panel"). However, they also provide that the AAA may, in its discretion, direct that a "greater number of arbitrators be appointed" if the arbitration agreement does not so specify (AAA Rule 17, "Number of Arbitrators"). Accordingly, a request for the appointment of a three-member panel must be made in the absence of a contractual requirement. The AAA usually appoints a three-member panel in complicated cases and in cases involving a sum exceeding a threshold set by the AAA.

preempt the meaningful participation of nonlawyer arbitrators. In those few instances when no attorney sits on a panel or when a nonattorney serves as chairman, hearings range from well-conducted business sessions to formless meetings in which abuse of arbitration's weaknesses runs rampant.[15]

Arbitrators often interrupt the parties and their attorneys with questions and think aloud about the issues before them. Arbitrators usually accept virtually every document placed before them as evidence, even if the document is obviously self-serving. However, they do so with the condition that in "admitting the document as evidence" (note the formality of this procedure), they will afford it "whatever weight it deserves." In any case, the arbitrators will read the document.

Unlike judges who have the benefit of pleadings, motions, and other proceedings before trial, all of which educate the court as to the nature of the case, arbitrators arrive at the first hearing with nothing more than the demand and the answering statement. Those documents are usually so cryptic as to be virtually useless as an information tool.[16] Therefore, arbitrators respond very favorably to a well-prepared and well-presented introduction at early sessions and continuation of that level throughout the hearings. The AAA promotes early presentation of an overview of the case to the arbitrators at procedural conferences held in advance of hearings.[17]

§ 14.8 Arbitration Awards

Despite the generalization that arbitrators "split the baby," it is more common for arbitrators to render a carefully considered award, following a study of the evidence and lengthy deliberation. A party entering an arbitration should expect a favorable award if its position is valid and effectively presented to the arbitrators.

It is a prudent assumption that the arbitration award rendered by the arbitrators will be final and binding. The grounds upon which most state and federal courts will vacate and arbitration award are very narrow.[18]

---

[15] McDonald, *Major Construction Claims/Arbitration or Litigation,* Construction Specifier 63 (Oct. 1984).

[16] See § **14.6**.

[17] Poppleton, *The Arbitrator's Role in Expediting the Large and Complex Commercial Case,* 36 Arb. J. 6, 7 (Dec. 1981).

[18] The grounds for vacating an arbitration award are limited to such circumstances as:

1. Egregious and prejudicial conduct by the arbitrators, exceeding the bounds of their authority
2. An undisclosed conflict of interest between an arbitrator and a party
3. Actual fraud by the arbitrator
4. The arbitrator's failure to follow the procedures under the applicable arbitration statute.

METHOD OF PREPARATION

§ 14.9 Scheduling the Hearing

Although arbitration hearings may convene many months or years before a trial would commence, the procedure may suffer because arbitrators are volunteers engaged in substantial other activity and are therefore available only on a limited basis. This fact, plus the acceptance within the industry and the legal profession that arbitration is a process with many interruptions, has led to the unfortunate result that an arbitration involving 20 days of hearing may indeed extend over a several year period with a hiatus of a month or more between hearings. When this occurs, arbitration is not perceived as an expeditious process. Too many practitioners accept this result without complaint (even gladly, on occasion) while their clients suffer the consequences of a prolonged proceeding. The two key elements to a speedy arbitration—scheduling hearings and maximizing substantive hearing time—are closely entwined.

There is nothing more tragically comical than watching three arbitrators, two attorneys, two clients, and two sets of consultants or experts try and establish a single date when they are all available to meet. Given such scheduling techniques, it is no wonder that hearings extend over many months with long intervals between them. Furthermore, interrupting the flow of a witness's testimony or the continuity of the case makes each hearing less effective and the overall arbitration procedure prolonged. The best way to avoid substantial intervals and discontinuity is to schedule consecutive days of hearing. Unfortunately, consecutive hearings may become an inconvenience or imposition on the arbitrators when they are asked to take off significant time from their regular business during any one week.

Once the parties have estimated the number of hearings that will likely be needed, they should meet with the AAA and the arbitrators to schedule the entirety of the case, planning on more hearings than necessary so that when an illness or some other conflict arises that necessitates the cancellation of a hearing, there is no need to spend weeks or months finding a new available date. By saving these dates in advance, well before other scheduled commitments are made, the likelihood of completing the arbitration within the schedule is enhanced.

The parties can agree to use a scheduling technique that allows both timely completion of the arbitration's hearing phase and consideration of the arbitrators' business. The author has used this technique, particularly when parties, experts, or arbitrators must travel and remain overnight for hearings. The system involves three days of hearing in one week as follows:

Day 1—Hearings convene at 1:00 P.M. and conclude at 6:00 P.M.

Day 2—Five hours of hearing without interruption as the parties may schedule.

Day 3—Hearings convene at 8:00 A.M. and conclude at 1:00 P.M.

Using this format, the arbitrators can spend a half-day in their office engaged in their regular business on each of the three days. Those traveling are able to arrive at the city of arbitration on the morning of Day 1, spend only two nights away from their home or office, and be home by the conclusion of Day 3. Just as important, however, is the fact that there will be 15 hours of consecutive hearing time in a particular week. By specifically scheduling five continuous hours of hearing on each of three consecutive days, the parties may be able to achieve in one week what otherwise might have taken four days of hearing to achieve over four to six months. By electing to conduct these three-day blocks on alternate weeks, a 20-day arbitration can be concluded within four months of hearings, as compared to the usual 18 months or more.

Although the scheduling of hearings can be enormously helpful in expediting the procedure, the parties themselves can do as much, if not more, to make the best use of the arbitrators' time. In that regard, the following devices have proven to be successful:

1. The parties should pre-mark all documents they expect to introduce as evidence in the proceeding. Those documents should be bound in a book, numbered sequentially, and a complete copy given to each arbitrator and the adverse party. After the book has been reviewed by the adverse party, all stipulated documents should be considered as evidence and referred to by identification numbers. Any problems regarding particular documents may be resolved with the arbitrators at a preliminary conference or at the first hearing. The parties can further agree that notwithstanding their stipulation of admissibility they are free to identify to the arbitrators any particularly significant feature of a document. For example, although a party may agree that a document containing hearsay may be admitted, that party should be able to remind the arbitrators that the included hearsay is less reliable than direct testimony and to urge the arbitrators to afford appropriate weight to the document.
2. All nonargumentative and documentary evidence should be submitted to the arbitrators by both parties with a joint designation number to speed the proceeding and create an appropriate atmosphere of cooperation with respect to undisputed documents or facts.
3. A stenographic record of lengthy arbitrations facilitates the hearings because the parties are confident of the record that has been

established and therefore not inclined to seek repetition of already established testimony.

§ 14.10 Knowledge of Adversary's Claim

A party may commence an arbitration or file a counterclaim in arbitration without affording the other party much information about the claims to be presented. There are several ways to compel the other party to disclose its claims, and using one or more of these methods is essential to the proper preparation of the case. Without knowing the magnitude of the claims and without a clear understanding of the matters in dispute, it is impossible to prepare properly for the arbitration. In fact, without this information, a party is deprived of a fair understanding of the seriousness of the impending arbitration.

§ 14.11 Application to the American Arbitration Association

In the event that the opposing party files a cryptic, nondisclosing demand or counterclaim that fails to comply with the obvious intent of AAA Rule 7 (that the nature and amount of the dispute and the remedy sought be reasonably described), the responding party should contact the AAA's regional director, describing the noncompliance and contending that, absent such compliance, the arbitration may not be administered by the AAA. The AAA is usually not inclined to direct a party to do anything; it serves merely as a valuable administrator in the arbitration process and not infringe on the role of the arbitrators.

However, there are some arguments that motivate the AAA to take action. One of those arguments is based upon the requirement that the appropriate filing fee (as provided in § 48 of the AAA Rules) be submitted to the AAA, together with the demand or answering statement. Those filing fees are set forth in a schedule contained within the AAA Rules.

The AAA's arbitration fees are computed upon a percentage of the amount of claim or counterclaim. Although the Rules do not clearly enable the AAA to avoid the administration of a case because a party refuses to disclose the amount of its claim and pay the required fee over and above the $200 initiation fee, in practice the AAA can be prodded to exert substantial pressure upon a party to express the dollar amount of the claim and to file an appropriate filing fee. In the event that the foregoing method is unsuccessful, a party can request a prehearing conference with the regional director pursuant to AAA Rule 10. At that conference the regional director will attempt to mediate between the parties and suggest that the amount in dispute and the nature of the dispute be more adequately disclosed. AAA Rule 10 specifically contemplates that "an exchange of information" will be accomplished as a result of the conference. If the opposing party purposely avoids the disclosure of its claim, the prehearing conference will be of no particular value because the AAA's case administrator has no authority to impose any sanctions or to involve himself in discussions with the arbitrators about its perceptions of the parties' behavior.

The ultimate step available within the context of the AAA is a conference with the arbitrators, at which time application can be made for an order compelling the other party to disclose its claims in a sufficient manner. Rule 52 of the Construction Industry Arbitration Rules provides that the "Arbitrator shall interpret and apply these Rules insofar as they relate to the arbitrator's powers and duties." Rule 31 requires that the parties produce "such evidence as the arbitrator may deem necessary to an understanding and determination of the controversy." It is clear that the arbitrators may compel, by the issuance of an order, one party to furnish information to enable the other party to understand the nature and scope of the claims asserted against it.

It is very likely that the arbitrators would compel such disclosure and that any attempts to avoid cooperating would be unsuccessful and severely prejudice the arbitrators' view of that party. However, it should be noted that the first time the Construction Industry Arbitration Rules provide an opportunity to compel the other party to come forward with a reasonable statement of the value and nature of its claims is in a prehearing conference with the arbitrators. By that time many months will likely have passed. Furthermore, once the arbitrators meet as a panel, they desire to expedite the commencement of evidentiary hearings. Therefore, waiting for a prehearing conference with the arbitrators to compel the other party to provide such basic information runs the risk of severely limiting the time within which a party will be able to prepare its own case in response to that information. Accordingly, access to the courts may be of value.

§ 14.12 Application to Court

It should be possible in virtually every jurisdiction to make an application to court to compel the other party to disclose the nature of its claims. Many judges will appropriately remind the complainant that the courts look favorably upon arbitration, in large part because it removes such specialized commercial disputes from the dockets. Those judges, therefore, are not delighted at the prospect of being involved in the procedural aspects of a contractually stipulated arbitration. However, when basic due process considerations, arising from a lack of awareness of the claims that a party is defending against, are at issue, the courts are more inclined to become involved and to compel a reasonable adherence to the arbitration rules (just as the court could compel the performance of any other contractual obligation).

There are several benefits of commencing a court proceeding in such an instance. First, access to the court may be accomplished on an expedited basis, thereby obtaining knowledge of the other party's claims earlier. Second, a party intending to abuse the arbitration process is less likely to continue those attempts once it has had to appear before a court that can hold that party in contempt for failure to comply with a court order. Third, the party complaining to the court will leave with a judicial determination in hand that says that the other party was not cooperating from the first moment. That judicial determination may be revealed to the arbitrators at an appropriate time if the other party continues to be uncooperative once the arbitration commences.

In determining to apply to a court, the attorney should evaluate the local arbitration statutes and compare them with the Federal Arbitration Act because there may be an available election to apply either to the United States district court or to the local courts, provided that jurisdiction is otherwise established. The attorney should also evaluate any time limitations applicable to such relief under prevailing statutes.[19]

§ 14.13 Initial Presentation

The attorney and his client come before the arbitrators with the purpose of convincing the panel of the appropriateness of the client's position. The other party arrives with the same goal. The arbitrators enter upon the arbitration process with the goal of reaching a fair, correct, and just result. The focus of the attorney and his client should be to convince the arbitrators of the validity of their position in a way that demonstrates that they share the arbitrators' goal and that they are doing everything possible to present fair and truthful evidence of what really happened.

Remembering that the arbitrators probably know absolutely nothing about the project, the dispute, or the parties, the first order of business is to educate the arbitrators about these critical facts. Arbitrators delight in a

[19] In addition to a concern about timing, the attorney should be careful to avoid filing a lawsuit upon the claims pending before the arbitrators in order to obtain the benefit of discovery, because such action may constitute a waiver of the right to arbitrate in some jurisdictions. *See* Burton-Dixie Corp. v. Timothy McCarthy Constr., Inc., 436 F.2d 405 (5th Cir. 1971) (waiver occurred); E.C. Ernst, Inc. v. City of Tallahassee, 527 F. Supp. 1141 (D. Fla. 1981) (no waiver occurred because the adverse party did not change its position by reason of the "waiving" conduct); Hudik-Ross, Inc. v. 1530 Palisades Corp., 131 N.J. Super. 159, 329 A.2d 70 (1974) (right to arbitrate was not waived when party in litigation preserved arbitration as pleaded defense).

party's obvious desire for the arbitrators to understand the case. In the process, a party offering such insight will find its credibility immediately enhanced. Such a presentation is best accomplished by a combination of:

1. Submitting a written, factual summary of the dispute's history that is accurate and essentially objective
2. Submitting a copy of all critical contract documents and other undisputed important documents for each arbitrator
3. Making an oral presentation of the important elements of the dispute, using graphic aids.

Aside from the good public relations value of this presentation, the arbitrators will benefit from an early understanding of the scope of the disputed issues and will therefore be better able to appreciate an effectively presented case.

Regardless of the particular format used for this presentation, several items should be addressed; these elements are separately discussed in §§ **14.7** through **14.21**.

§ 14.14 Description of Project

The presentation of the site plan and elevations is usually sufficient to describe the physical project. Too much detail at this early stage may be counterproductive. However, an overview of the structure's components and the identity of the contractor or other party responsible for each major portion of the work should be described. The attorney should make brief reference to areas of the project that are in dispute and explain their relevance.

§ 14.15 Description of Project Time Frame

A graphic representation of the time periods applicable to the project should be presented to each arbitrator. This chart will serve as a quick-reference tool for the arbitrators during the balance of the arbitration. The chart should include, at a minimum:

1. The bid date
2. The contract date
3. The date work commenced
4. The scheduled project completion date
5. The actual substantial completion date
6. The actual project completion date.

If the parties hold different positions regarding important dates, such as substantial completion, it may be advisable to indicate the dates contended by each party on the chart.

The benefit of demonstrating objectivity in this early presentation is enhanced credibility from the very start of the arbitration. However, in the absence of a formal, written, and demonstrable position by the adverse party, that party should be left to announce its own positions.

§ 14.16 Contract Price/Payment Analysis

If the dispute involves money, it is extremely helpful for the arbitrators to know from the first day of arbitration how the money damages sought, or sought to be voided, relate to the contract, change orders, backcharges, and payments. In preparing such a submission, each party should present this analysis from its own perspective. That is, the claimant seeking a money recovery should indicate those contract price adjustments that are bilateral and then simply list the other adjustments it seeks, without seeking to indicate its adversary's position. This presentation should be approached as if the arbitrators might simply convert the statement of account into the arbitrators' award. Therefore, a schedule similar to the example below should be presented to the arbitrators:

(a)	Original contract Price			$10,000,000
(b)	Change orders:			
	C.O.1 (5/19/90)	Add	1,000,000	
	C.O.2 (7/30/90)	Deduct	(500,000)	
	(list all change orders signed and recognized by both parties)			
(c)	Accepted backcharges			
	8/1/90 Electric bill	Deduct	(10,000)	
	10/1/90 Additional cleanup	Deduct	(50,000)	
(d)	Entitlement to additional compensation			
	(i) 8/10/90 claim for additional pumping	Add	100,000	
	(ii) 9/30/90 claim for additional cost of two-block wall system at east face of garage (list all claims intended to be proved)	Add	50,000	
(e)	Claimed adjusted contract price			10,590,000
(f)	Payments to date			(9,000,000)
(g)	Amount sought in this arbitration			1,590,000
(h)	Interest from 8/10/90 to date of award			
(i)	Costs of arbitration			
(j)	Reasonable attorneys' fees			

This chart can, of course, be modified as appropriate to the particular case. For the party defending a claim or seeking an affirmative award that the amount it owes to the other is less than claimed, item (d) could be called "Entitlement to credits." Under that category, matters such as backcharges, credits, claims, and other such price-reducing matters should be set forth. Additionally, if the retainage should be withheld, an item indicating withheld retainage should be inserted after item (f).

Many parties make the mistake of placing only those items they perceive as contested claims before the arbitrators, omitting items such as the contract balance when they believe it is not contested. An omission on that basis is dangerous and inappropriate. The contract balance and other uncontested matters should always be included in the claims before the arbitrators. The adversary's acknowledgment of such matters can always be graciously accepted.

It is customary for most parties in arbitration to include a demand for reasonable attorneys' fees. In item (j) in the example, reasonable attorneys' fee are included in the presentation of damages and claims. However, there is a risk in seeking and receiving an award for reasonable attorneys' fees. In most jurisdictions, attorneys' fees are not awarded as a matter of course to the prevailing party. Therefore, an arbitration award of attorneys' fees will not be recognized as consistent with the law unless a contractual provision in the underlying contract between the parties to arbitration permits one.

When such a contract clause exists, the arbitrators are merely fulfilling their responsibilities to carry out the terms of the contract. However, when there is no contract provision permitting the award of attorneys' fees, the arbitrators may be sufficiently moved by the egregious conduct of one party to award them anyway. Such an award may be an unfortunate victory, however, because including attorneys' fees in an award without a contract clause permitting them may jeopardize the validity of the entire award and may subject the prevailing party to a court challenge on the basis that the arbitrator's award, on its face, demonstrates that the arbitrators exceeded their authority. Accordingly, lacking contractual entitlement, the attorney should consider whether it is worth the risk to include a request for reasonable attorneys' fees.

§ 14.17 Scope of Work

Virtually every construction arbitration involves issues concerning the scope of work the contractor was required to perform. Before informing the arbitrators of the particular items of work in dispute,[20] it is wise to inform the arbitrators of the general scope of work of the contract in issue.

[20] See § **14.13**.

A simple and fast way to accomplish this is to present the arbitrators with copies of a highlighted table of contents from the technical specifications, in conjunction with an oral description of the items of the work that are part of the subject contract. In multiple prime contractor situations, this clarification, presented early in the arbitration, may avoid confusion in later hearings. At least one complete set of the specifications should be presented to the arbitrators as well. Every effort should be made to present a clean set of specifications that has been conformed to addenda, bulletins, and other amendments.

If at all possible, a clean set of the plans should also be presented to the arbitrators, together with an oral presentation as to which drawings (by category or list) are particularly relevant to the arbitration. Once the drawings are on the table, it is common for the arbitrators to leaf through them and ask questions, which the attorney and his client should be fully prepared to answer. This situation is precisely what was meant by the earlier statement that construction arbitration requires extraordinary preparation. The dividends from being able to demonstrate that level of preparation from the outset are self-evident, and the arbitrators will communicate their approval and appreciation accordingly.

§ 14.18 Schedule

If delay is an element of the dispute, the initial presentation should include an as-planned/as-built comparative chart. This chart may be in bar graph form or in network form. The extent of detail, the breakdown of trades and areas of work, and other such considerations should be determined after the case has been thoroughly prepared, so that the chart highlights the areas of strength in the case and provides a reference tool for the arbitrators that is consistent with the testimony and exhibits offered in the arbitration.

It is important to emphasize that the presentation of a well-thought-out comparative schedule in the preliminary phase also benefits the attorney in his closing arguments after producing testimony and documentary evidence consistent with the graphic presentation offered at the commencement of the hearings. However, this chart is not intended to be the evidentiary submission of the actual project critical path method (CPM), bar chart, or other such scheduling chart.

§ 14.19 Overview of Claims

The presentation of an overview of the claims is akin to the opening argument before a court. Many experienced trial attorneys would counsel their colleagues to offer as brief and nonspecific an opening as possible, so as not to commit to specific assertions of facts to be proven that may haunt that attorney at the end of the trial. There is merit to this position. However, arbitration is different from court litigation in important respects, and the author believes that those differences bespeak the advisability of fully explaining the claims to the arbitrators on the first day of hearings. The key reasons for such a presentation are:

1. The likely substantial time gaps between hearings
2. The arbitrator's lack of any knowledge of the case before the first hearing
3. The substantial possibility that the arbitrators may insist upon such a presentation if not voluntarily offered.

The presentation should take advantage of and build upon the submissions discussed in §§ **14.6** through **14.11**. However, there is a particular format that industry arbitrators will relate to and understand well. Indeed, the advocate, by using this presentation format, will come as close as he may to the ultimate dream of presenting the case without the risk of testimonial bloopers by his client.

Taking each major element of the claim in an appropriate order, the attorney should establish the following:

1. What does the contract require? (Cite the sections of the specifications and/or the drawings, details, and shop drawings.)
2. What work was actually performed or had to be performed?
3. How does the actual condition of the work differ from the contractual scope?
4. Why did the work have to be performed as it was?
5. Who is responsible for the need to perform the work differently from that set forth in the original contract scope?
6. That the work was performed (or that the performance of it is necessary).
7. The cost of the disputed work.
8. The impact of the disputed work on time, sequences, productivity, or other features of the project.

§ 14.20 Prehearing Written Submission

In some instances it may be both possible and advisable to present the arbitrators with a prehearing written submission that essentially provides the same information as the presentation outline in § **14.12**. One advantage of a prehearing written submission is that the arbitrators understand the case before the first meeting. If the other party does not provide a similar submission, the arbitrators may even arrive with a favorable bias. However, the attempt to furnish the arbitrators with a prehearing submission is not always successful, and in the process the other party may become motivated to prepare and submit its own presentation.

It is the AAA's practice to require that the other party both receive a copy of the proposed submission and consent to the submission before the AAA will send it on to the arbitrators. If the other party refuses, the Association asks the arbitrators if they wish to receive the submission before the hearings despite the objection. Even if the arbitrators decide to receive the submission (they will often decline to do so under such circumstances), the edge (the goal of the submission) may be lost and the other party receives a full education in the process. Therefore, planning for a presentation at the first arbitration session is most advisable and preferable.

§ 14.21 Preparing for Hearings

Having accomplished the education of the arbitrators, the prosecution of the claims must be properly thought out before preparation for testimonial and documentary evidence may proceed. The backdrop of this planning must include an awareness that industry arbitrators, not a judge, will decide the dispute. The other differences between arbitration and litigation must also be considered.

§ 14.22 Who Will Tell the Story?

Arbitrators prefer to hear a story from someone who was involved in the circumstances in dispute. They also enjoy a well-presented summary presentation by someone (attorney, client, consultant, or expert) who places the actual evidence in a perspective that is meaningful to experienced industry arbitrators. The attorney's determination of which witnesses will present the factual and summary evidence is critical to the arbitration strategy.

When an attorney is planning the witnesses in contemplation of a jury trial, he might well fear that a poorly spoken field superintendent will make an unfavorable impression before the jury, will be easily abused by a skilled adversary, and will do great harm to the case in the process. If arbitration has one particularly redeeming feature, it is the understanding of construction and construction projects that industry arbitrators bring to the hearing. That understanding and appreciation for people involved in construction provides a setting in which that very same field superintendent may feel rather comfortable and enjoy an increased level of credibility, notwithstanding his lack of finesse, as long as he is perceived as honest and sincere.

The arbitrators will often ensure that the attorney's questions are generally understandable and sensible in the context of the dispute. If there is an obvious attempt to confuse the witness with questions that the arbitrators readily recognize as being unfair, tricky, or ridiculous, the arbitrator will often caution the attorney to limit cross-examination to relevant questions concerning the issues in dispute. Consequently, there should be much less concern about utilizing a field worker before a panel of industry arbitrators. Indeed, it is often best to utilize such individuals because, given this industry setting, the field worker can present the most comprehensive and credible explanation of what actually occurred.

In contrast, many attorneys prefer to place the college-educated officer or supervisor on the stand to project a very credible, refined, and businesslike demeanor. Experienced arbitrators are capable of making insightful distinctions between the individual's personal knowledge and what he has learned from reading the documented records of those actually involved in the construction of the project.

Many arbitrators will confirm that some of the most effective testimony in arbitration is given by the field superintendent, the staff engineer, or the owner's clerk of the works. Any individual whose involvement in the disputed project permits that witness to speak definitively about matters from his own experience, rather than relying upon second- and third-hand references to letters and other documents, is helpful. The attorney should carefully consider the appropriate scope of the fact witness's testimony with the arbitration setting in mind.

The arbitrator's desire to get to the heart of a dispute is in part a foreseeable feature of their not being afraid to delve into very technical aspects of a construction dispute. This feature is a direct result of the arbitrators' construction industry background. Few judges would willingly embark upon a journey into highly technical matters, such as the inherent stresses in certain types of concrete structures, in order to evaluate the credibility of the witnesses. Arbitrators, on the other hand, who are engineers or architects by profession or who are contractors with substantial experience, will not only desire to get into such technical matters but will insist that those matters be evaluated. In that respect, a mere recitation of the self-serving positions taken in letter, telegrams, and memoranda to file will usually not suffice in an arbitration.

§ 14.23 Use of Experts

It is important to realize that the expert's role in an arbitration may be very different from its role in a court case. A clear distinction is the likelihood that a claims consultant will be permitted to present arbitration testimony that is little more than an interpretation of jobsite records, albeit in an organized and convincing fashion. Therefore, using a claims consultant as a witness is possible, but not always recommended. In planning the preparation and presentation of an arbitration case, the attorney should consider carefully the different perspective of arbitrators and judges before assuming that the testimony or report of a claims consultant or other expert will be given much weight in arbitration. There is a great danger in that assumption.

There is little question that in highly technical matters the testimony of an expert can be very helpful. If that expert is counselled to testify in a manner that demonstrates to the arbitrators that he is objective and fair, the testimony may have a far greater effect before industry arbitrators than might otherwise be achieved in court. The industry arbitrators will be able to recognize and independently conclude that the expert's testimony is correct, based upon their technical understanding of the subject matter. Accordingly, when expertise is important, the use of a qualified expert is recommended.

However, it is critical for the attorney to establish the factual predicates for the expert's testimony by using witnesses who were involved in the construction of the project. Although a claims consultant's testimony may be valuable, some attorneys make the mistake of believing that a claims consultant's testimony or an attractively bound report will serve as a substitute for the factual testimony of individuals involved in the project. To be certain, many claims consultants employ individuals who are experienced witnesses, offering the assurance that a very well-spoken person will present their claims. However, when the attorney uses the claims consultant as the client's spokesman, he runs substantial risk of implying that his client is cleverly trying to package a factually unsupportable claim. The greater value of claims consultants is their ability to assemble the documentation of a substantial dispute in a workable order and to call upon the expertise and experience of their colleagues to analyze those records and identify for the attorney the critical elements of the dispute for which testimony is needed.

Is the intended witness truly an expert, or is he just a consultant? If the proposed expert witness attempts to tell the arbitrators what occurred in a dispute by reciting what the parties said to one another in letters, by making characterizations of and judgments about the other party's behavior based on reading those letters, and by then graphically demonstrating how he has concluded from the written record that his client should be the prevailing party, then that expert is likely to cause a very unfavorable impression before the arbitrators. If, on the other hand, the expert has been brought in to render technical valuations on issues requiring expertise and if he is qualified and thoroughly prepared, it may help the arbitrators form their opinions.

§ 14.24 Preparing Exhibits

Once a determination has been made as to which documents will be used as exhibits, a sufficient number of copies should be prepared for each arbitrator and adverse party. The offering party should mark each exhibit with numbers. Having a sufficient quantity of premarked exhibits will expedite proceedings enormously. Any effort to streamline the procedure results in fewer interruptions and enables the attorney to present more testimony and evidence in each hearing.

With respect to exhibits, some practical considerations should be taken into account by the attorney. Because arbitration hearings are commonly held in hotel rooms, conference rooms, or other locations to which the arbitrators must travel, they must carry with them any relevant exhibits. Arbitrators do not appreciate having to transport voluminous documents and heavy packages of exhibits. Therefore, in planning the presentation of evidence, it is often wise to offer only certain pages from specification books and individual drawings or copies of details on drawings, while marking and retaining the complete specifications and drawings for use at each hearing.

§ 14.25 Use of Affidavits

Under the Construction Industry Arbitration Rules, a party may offer an affidavit in lieu of oral testimony before the arbitrators.[21] Such an offer is certain to result in the adversary's strenuous objection because it is impossible to cross-examine an affidavit. If a party intends to offer an affidavit, it is important to be prepared to explain the unique circumstances justifying the use of that affidavit, and to offer the adverse party an opportunity for examination or rebuttal testimony to demonstrate that the proposed use of an affidavit is not intended to obtain an unfair advantage. Before offering evidence by affidavit, the attorney should weigh the value of such an offer against the likely resistance by the adverse party and perhaps the arbitrators. It is not at all uncommon for arguments and discussion about the appropriateness of accepting the affidavit to consume far more time than the proposed affiant's testimony in the arbitration hearing. Additionally, the adverse party will almost always urge the arbitrators to believe that the motive behind using an affidavit was to avoid the witness's obvious embarrassment of being cross-examined. There are few instances in the complicated arbitration when testimony by affidavit accomplishes anything meaningful.

§ 14.26 Creative Evidence

The informality of the arbitration process offers the imaginative attorney any number of opportunities to communicate his client's case effectively to

[21] AAA Rule 32, "Evidence by Affidavits and Post-hearing Filing of Documents or Other Evidence."

the arbitrators. For example, the Construction Industry Arbitration Rules specifically allow the arbitrators to visit the construction site with the parties.[22] In an appropriate case, a party may gain a substantial advantage by having the arbitrators visit the site and inspect the work in dispute. The timing of that request and of the visit, the manner in which the visit should be handled, and the careful preparation to avoid unpleasant surprises are matters the attorney must fully address.

Photographs have long been a mainstay of construction dispute proceedings, and now the ability to communicate a situation photographically has been greatly enhanced by the advent of the videotape. A two- or three-hour video taped presentation could very well communicate circumstances that might take many days of testimony. The video tape presentation also allows the witness to narrate as it is made. By so doing, and by having that witness available for cross-examination at a hearing, it is possible for the witness to communicate effectively images and facts that may be extremely difficult to convey simply through testimony.

§ 14.27 Mediation

The AAA or the arbitrators may suggest that the parties consider referring the dispute to mediation. If this is done, it is important to remember the following distinctions. The arbitrator's role is to impose his judgment upon the parties after hearing all the evidence. However, the role of a mediator is to facilitate settlement discussions, so that the parties achieve their own solution. A mediator does not impose his judgment upon the parties. Accordingly, although arbitrators are encouraged by the AAA to ask the parties if they wish either to refer their matter to mediation or to conduct a mediation in parallel with the arbitration, the use of a specially trained mediator is critical when mediation is elected. Trained arbitrators are not necessarily trained mediators.

---

[22] AAA Rule 33, "Inspection or Investigation."

CHAPTER 15

PREPARING THE CASE FOR LITIGATION

Philip R. Placier
Laurence M. Scoville, Jr.*

Philip R. Placier is chairman of the Management Committee of Thelen, Marrin, Johnson & Bridges, which has offices in San Francisco, New York, Washington, D.C., Houston, Los Angeles, San Jose, Orange County and Hong Kong. A graduate of the University of Michigan Law School, he has had over 25 years of experience in handling trials and arbitrations on construction industry disputes. In recent years he has handled complex cases involving oil refineries, tunnels, and other large construction projects.

Laurence M. Scoville, Jr., is the chairman of the Executive Committee of Clark, Klein and Beaumont, a general practice firm in Detroit, Michigan, and head of its Litigation Department. He was graduated from Dartmouth College and the University of Michigan Law School. He has 30 years of experience in construction industry disputes. In the last several years he has had primary responsibility for handling complex engineering and construction matters both in litigation and in various forms of alternative dispute resolution.

*Appreciation is expressed to Edward J. Hood, Mark L. McAlpine and Kevin O'Brien for their invaluable assistance.

§ 15.1 Introduction

INITIAL INVESTIGATION AND PLANNING

§ 15.2 Start the Investigation Early

§ 15.3 —Contractor's Representatives

§ 15.4 Develop a Theory of the Case and a Litigation Plan

§ 15.5 —Litigation Plan and Trial Book

COLLECTING INFORMATION

§ 15.6 Initial Plan

§ 15.7 Documents

§ 15.8 —Selection, Form, and Numbering

§ 15.9 —Review

§ 15.10 Witnesses

§ 15.11 Experts

DISCOVERY

§ 15.12 Developing the Discovery Plan

§ 15.13 Litigation Support Group

§ 15.14 Written Discovery Requests

§ 15.15 —Drafting Discovery Requests

§ 15.16 —Interrogatories

§ 15.17 —Requests for Production of Documents

§ 15.18 —Requests for Admission

§ 15.19 Obtaining Responses to Discovery Requests

§ 15.20 Responding to Discovery Requests

§ 15.21 Depositions

§ 15.22 —Conducting the Deposition

§ 15.23 Other Discovery Devices

§ 15.24 Final Discovery Review

§ 15.1 Introduction

This chapter presents a number of guidelines for pretrial preparation of a contractor's claim in a typical construction litigation setting involving multiple claims and usually multiple parties. The attorney's effective pretrial preparation is important because contractor claims are almost always factually complex and based on subjective or judgmental assumptions. A successful claim or defense requires adequate investigation, thorough research, and presentation in a cogent, organized manner.

INITIAL INVESTIGATION AND PLANNING

§ 15.2 Start the Investigation Early

Whether the dispute casts the contractor defending against owner or subcontractor claims, or prosecuting its own claims, the initial approach is substantially the same. At the earliest opportunity, begin to familiarize yourself with the dispute and start your investigation to identify the legal and factual issues most relevant to the contractor, depending upon its role in the project and the nature of the dispute.

The first steps involve ascertaining the general substance of the dispute, the identity of major problem areas, and the damages and/or exposures involved. Try to assume as little as possible. If practical, arrange to talk to the people directly involved to get their first-hand perspective of the dispute.

Equally important is the need to begin marshalling the people and resources needed to resolve the dispute. It is not too early to begin developing basic litigation strategy and the decision-making process best suited for litigating this particular dispute. Establish the lines of communication for distribution of pertinent information and periodic litigation status reports, and the procedures for identifying and making important policy decisions regarding development, prosecution, and perhaps settlement of the action.

Establish an initial plan; this should be regularly reviewed and updated as the case is prepared for trial. The legal and factual complexities involved in today's construction litigation require planning to avoid duplication and wasted effort. A preliminary identification and outline of the major questions or issues involved in the dispute will determine how to organize the tremendous volume of incoming information, and how to extract that portion eventually needed for discovery or at trial.

Although the initial investigation is typically confined to in-house interviews, the overall inquiry into the factual circumstances underlying the dispute should cover three sources of available information: in-house investigation or interviews; outside investigation involving third parties or persons not directly involved in the litigation; and discovery proceedings in the litigation itself. Do not rely on any one of the three to the exclusion of any other. Each should be used to complement the overall investigation, because each has its own advantages and disadvantages.

Two questions must be answered promptly: Who is involved in the dispute? What work is involved? Because of the interlocking legal relationships among the various parties involved in a construction project, it is important to determine promptly the party or parties contributing to the cause or circumstances giving rise to the dispute. It is also important to get an early sense of the alignment and degree of responsibility of each of the parties already involved in the case and those likely to become involved in the case, so that decisions can be made regarding whether and which other parties need to be brought into the dispute.

If the contractor had only a peripheral role in the project, some prompt initial discovery should be considered to learn more about the roles and responsibilities of the various parties involved. A brief set of interrogatories and a simple request for documents may be all that is either required or desirable in order to accomplish such an inquiry.

There is little to be gained and much to be lost by waiting to start your investigation until you are responding to an opposing party's discovery. Memories fade, recollections become selective, and persons with pertinent information become unavailable. Moreover, it is human nature for people to lose interest as they become concerned with today's problems rather than yesterday's.

§ 15.3 —Contractor's Representatives

The initial investigation stage is also the time to select responsible management representatives of the contractor to assume an active and continuing role in the management of the litigation.[1] A team approach that combines the respective resources of legal counsel and knowledgeable contractor personnel is usually the most effective and mutually satisfactory approach for both the contractor and counsel.

The team approach has several distinct advantages that more than compensate for the modest extra demands it may place on the contractor. It promotes the best possible utilization of the resources of both legal counsel and the contractor, thereby maximizing the likelihood of success in the litigation. Counsel should not overlook the contractor's potential wealth of information and experience relevant to the dispute. By the same token, the contractor must not expect counsel alone simply to take care of the matter and then expect a cost-effective defense. Regular meetings should be scheduled between the contractor's management and counsel to monitor the progress of the case.

The contractor's active involvement with the litigation team and the decision-making process also insures that major decisions are consistent with the contractor's actual experience and in line with the company's general policies. As a less direct benefit, the contractor's responsible management will necessarily become educated regarding the advantages and

[1] See **§ 15.13** for a more detailed description of the suggested composition of the litigation team.

disadvantages of various practices and procedures and can begin shaping future policies to avoid repeating prior mistakes.

§ 15.4 Develop a Theory of the Case and a Litigation Plan

A convincing theory of the case and a well-thought-out litigation plan are necessary to litigate today's complex construction dispute effectively, with a satisfactory net result to the contractor. A theory of the case maximizes both the likelihood and degree of success, and a litigation plan helps minimize the costs of litigation in general and discovery proceedings in particular.

Keep in mind that litigation is ultimately a question of persuasion. A theory of the case should therefore strive to pull together all the necessary elements of the claim in a manner that is most persuasive to the trier of fact, whether it is an arbitrator, a contracting officer, a judge, or a jury. Regardless of the forum, the trier of fact will be called upon to decide, in the context of an adversarial proceeding, which side is right. It will reach its decision in the relatively abbreviated time period of a trial, on the basis of only a fraction of the evidence available to the parties.

It is unlikely that the trier of fact will have any intuitive sense as to the merits of the dispute. Its knowledge of the facts underlying the claim is confined to those presented by the parties to the dispute. Hence, the task of education is crucial. The trier of fact must be able to understand the claim to be persuaded of its merits.

In sifting through the facts and circumstances of the dispute to develop the theory best suited for the particular case, it is helpful to keep certain general guidelines in mind. To be persuasive, the evidence to be presented must be both understandable and believable. Therefore, whatever the theory, it must have a solid factual basis that can be put in evidence and, conversely, should not be flatly contradicted by other strong evidence. Any basic recurring themes in the litigation should be emphasized whenever possible.

Next, the theory should appeal to both common sense and reason. The trier of fact will have neither training, experience, nor familiarity with the general background of the dispute and, instead, will have to rely upon common sense in reaching a decision. Presenting the important facts and circumstances underlying the dispute by devising a theory of the case that ties together the unfamiliar facts and circumstances in a consistent and logical manner makes the critical task of persuasion easier to follow and ultimately more effective.

Last, the theory of the case will consequently determine the types of facts and evidence needed to prove the claims underlying the theory. To a large extent, therefore, the theory of the case dictates the foundation of the litigation plan in that it provides a framework for the facts and circumstances to be investigated and developed during the course of litigation. As information is developed, however, the theory of the case must always remain flexible to account for both the positive and negative points that surface during the course of the litigation.

§ 15.5 —Litigation Plan and Trial Book

As a general rule, at least a preliminary litigation plan should be prepared as soon as counsel has a general understanding of the dispute. The timetable will vary with each dispute and the particular needs of the contractor. The general rule is the earlier, the better.

The preparation of the litigation plan itself provides several benefits. It has the immediate effect of forcing counsel and the litigation team to take the time to organize their thoughts and gives the contractor's management a clear picture of what to expect ahead both in terms of activities and costs. A litigation plan should typically include provisions for all major aspects of the litigation, including:

1. Investigation and research
2. Pleadings
3. Motions
4. Experts
5. Discovery (including document requests, interrogatories, depositions, and other items)
6. Settlement
7. Pretrial
8. Trial.

An incidental benefit of developing and implementing a litigation plan is that it can promote settlement. Ideally, such a plan will provide the means for management to obtain a realistic assessment of either its claim or exposure, as well as the likely costs associated with the overall prosecution or defense of the litigation pursuant to the plan. Obviously, an early assessment of such information, tempered with the recognition that it is only as good as the current assumptions, will substantially improve the mechanisms for evaluation of settlement possibilities.

One effective tool in organizing and implementing your litigation plan is to prepare a trial book at an early stage of the litigation. The trial book is usually a looseleaf binder, subdivided into various categories. The categories should include:

1. Things to do
2. Issues
   —Factual
   —Legal
3. Pleadings
4. Discovery
5. Witnesses
6. Exhibits
7. Trial preparation.

The trial book should include a sufficient number of additional categories or subcategories to include all the important issues involved in the case. Note, in writing, everything you have done and insert your notes into your trial book as the litigation proceeds. If you do so, there will be no question later as to what you have previously done, and more importantly, you will be able to organize your ideas in a convenient way to manage the incoming information.

COLLECTING INFORMATION

§ 15.6 Initial Plan

One of the first tasks of a litigation plan should be to plot out the initial investigation to match previously identified general areas of inquiry with the sources of information available at the time. Relative priorities should be established in order to obtain the most important material promptly.

Certain types of files and other sources of information are almost always needed and should therefore be obtained promptly. The contract documents, the plans and specifications concerning all disputed items of work, the change orders file if extra work is at issue, the correspondence file, and other similar records are the types of documents generally needed to understand the circumstances underlying the dispute.

Because the documents generally take time to assemble, you should promptly begin to collect all the various records, files, documents, and other needed materials. Contract documents and those files and documents relating to the essence of the dispute should be critically reviewed as soon as possible. Similarly, key witnesses should be identified and initial contacts made at the earliest opportunity. Any experts needed should also be contacted at an early stage of the litigation in order to ensure their availability and to maximize the level of expert assistance.

§ 15.7 Documents

Project records, correspondence, and other contemporaneous documents often play a pivotal role in construction litigation, with both sides attempting to reconstruct their respective versions of the dispute using the existing documentation. A prompt initial compilation and review of the contractor's own documents provide a start toward understanding the core of the dispute. Despite their importance, however, both initial review and subsequent document production during discovery are all too often done routinely and hence not in a very efficient or cost-effective manner. It is therefore desirable to develop an efficient initial document review system that will not require duplication of effort during subsequent discovery proceedings.

To a large extent, the complexity of the case and the number of documents involved will determine both the level of effort and type of approach best suited to the particular case. A small mechanics' lien case will, of course, be treated much differently from a multi-party multi-million-dollar engineering/construction dispute. However, despite the range of differences, several general rules apply.

First, take the time to determine the identity of the documents available, their physical location, and the identity of the person(s) who maintain the documents or who are knowledgeable about their contents. Attempt to determine approximately how many documents are involved. Once a rough inventory is made, an initial inspection to identify the most important documents can begin.

It is generally useful to prepare a comprehensive index of the files or other documents that are, or may become, relevant to the dispute. See **Chapter 22**. If the indexing is done by or under the direction of counsel, the index will probably be protected from subsequent disclosure by the attorney work product privilege.

The time and effort saved through using the index during subsequent review or production will more than pay for its initial cost. There are also other indirect advantages to using a file index system approach. It permits a more orderly initial review and affords a way to keep track of the files that have been reviewed. Additionally, if a large number of documents is involved, an index system facilitates a staggered or phased production of documents to opposing counsel that is less burdensome to the contractor. For example, if part of the documents requested include current or working files, you can arrange to have them produced on nonbusiness hours or on scheduled days to minimize the inconvenience to the contractor's staff. Similarly, if bulky files are located in other places or offices, as is frequently the case with large contractors who have home, regional, and project offices as well as a field office, separate arrangements can be made. As long as the index is updated and file integrity is maintained, subsequent production, inspection, and copying may be done according to a prearranged schedule with minimum supervision by counsel and a minimum of disruption to the contractor.

§ 15.8 —Selection, Form, and Numbering

Once a rough inventory of the documents has been made, the next step is to develop a procedure for extracting the most important documents. One of the primary functions of the initial inspection is to determine which documents need to be copied, and in what form or format copies should be made. The economy of scale factors also apply to this second stage of initial document review. It is probably more efficient to copy the entire file of a small case than to sift through the file to decide what needs to be copied.

The big case presents a decidedly different situation. Unless there is a compelling reason to do so, do not routinely decide to copy all the documents. Copy only those documents reasonably needed, consistent with the necessary time frame. If an index exists, additional copies of files or documents can be obtained merely by designating the appropriate file title from the index.

If large numbers of copies are to be made, consider using microfilm. Hard copies of the most important documents will be needed, but not of the vast majority of the documents involved in the dispute. Some principal advantages of microfilm include ease of storage of the microfilm, reasonable cost per copy, a ready-made sequential numbering system of documents by reel and frame and an index of documents by document number, portability of microfilming equipment for on-site document copying, and subsequent ease of access to specific documents for the reviewer. Disadvantages of microfilm include the need for (and hence cost of) the microfilm reader, office space needed for the reader, decreased efficiency in reviewing documents, and generally less desirable quality hard copies. In many locales, independent litigation support service companies, including large copying services, can be used for this work and because of their experience they may be more cost effective than doing this work with contractor personnel.

If hard copies of all or substantially all the documents are to be made for a working file, consider having an extra set made at the same time for subsequent production during discovery. It is usually considerably easier to have two (or more) sets of copies made at the same time than it is to return to recopy all the documents later. Maintaining a master set from which all subsequent copies are made will cut down on unnecessary recopying, which usually results in deterioration of copy quality.

Sequential numbering of a master set of the pertinent documents may prove useful. The numbering system may be either continuous from any starting point or staggered by groups. For example, all document numbers preceded with a P might be produced by the plaintiff or all documents in the P10000 series might be job files. Additionally, the numbering provides a reliable system for keeping track of what has been produced and by whom.

The actual mechanics of affixing the document number to each of the documents presents an important logistical consideration. Defacing original documents in current working files by stamping numbers on them is generally not greeted with enthusiasm by contractors, although it does help to ensure file integrity. On the other hand, because it is desirable to retain a numbered set of the documents to be produced to opposing parties, copying the documents and then numbering a set of the copies introduces extra trouble and requires extra copying.

§ 15.9 —Review

Once the initial inventory and screening is accomplished, the review must commence. While often the sheer volume and technical nature of the documents require that an initial screening be done by others, any substantive review should be done by someone with an understanding of the issues, both legal and factual, involved in the litigation.

If separate and unrelated claims are involved, physical segregation of the documents by issue can be useful. If there are a large number of overlapping issues, however, it may require cross-indexing or duplicating copies of the same document. Placing some or all the documents in chronological order is another useful system.

If the litigation is exceptionally complex, consider the feasibility of utilizing a computerized document retrieval system. This approach is not appropriate for every case, primarily because of its sharply higher cost, but it can be invaluable in the right circumstances. Large numbers of documents can be cross-referenced by topic, author, witness, or any other issue and accessed at once. The system should be designed with a certain amount of flexibility so that developments in the nature of the case and the evidence can be assimilated. An outside litigation support service consultant can often provide the appropriate software and systems.

§ 15.10 Witnesses

It is important in construction litigation to identify promptly the witnesses with knowledge of the dispute, and to ascertain their future availability. Hourly personnel often change jobs or leave the area when the project is completed, making it more difficult to locate them later and making subsequent interviews inconvenient and expensive. Likewise, salaried personnel may be transferred to other projects in other areas, again making it inconvenient and more costly to interview them.

To the extent reasonably practical, keeping in mind that opposing parties may not be contacted by counsel after the litigation has commenced, attempt to interview all the witnesses who have knowledge of the dispute, whether friendly, neutral, or hostile. Start by identifying the contractor's personnel who know the most about the dispute. Usually, a small number or group of individuals will know the most about the dispute, either because of their position in project management, their tenure on the job, or a combination of both. It is advisable to contact these individuals first, and to make arrangements for continued access to them.

Because many construction disputes are complex, the desire for promptness in interviewing witnesses must be balanced with the need to conduct sufficient preparatory work to be able to identify the relevant issues and orient and refresh the witness's recollection, particularly when dealing with nonparty witnesses. At times only general observations and impressions may be desired; at other times a detailed reconstruction of a disputed sequence of events is critical. The particular need will determine both the timing and the level of preparatory work necessary.

Generally speaking, witness interviews are best conducted one-on-one in a comfortable setting. Let the witness do the talking and tell the story in her own words. Take notes as necessary in order to return to areas you want to cover in greater detail or want to ask further questions about. Write up your interview notes and your general impressions of the witness as soon as possible, and insert them in the trial book under the witness's name.

Consider whether it is advisable to obtain written or recorded witness statements from contractor employees or from neutral witnesses. If witness statements are desired, they should probably be obtained by counsel to preserve the attorney work product privilege.

§ 15.11 Experts

As the construction industry becomes increasingly specialized, so too do the nature and complexity of the technical issues underlying disputes within the industry. It is becoming increasingly common for experts to become involved early to assist in investigating, quantifying, and assembling the claim or the lawsuit, as well as in their more traditional roles of expert consultant and trial witness.

If the dispute involves technical issues or work of a specialized nature, it will often be desirable, if not necessary, to use one or more consulting experts to assist in preparation of the case. See **Chapter 22**. Consultants can educate counsel and other members of the litigation team, as well as help in identifying the critical issues in the case. Depending upon the contractor's expertise and level of sophistication, the technical nature and complexity of the problems, and the size, posture, and importance of the case, counsel may choose to rely on knowledgeable individuals already employed by the contractor or may instead decide to retain independent experts. Cost is obviously a significant factor to be considered.

Independent experts should be retained early. If the area of technical specialty needed is unique, locate and retain an expert as soon as possible. The opposition may also be seeking the best experts, particularly if there are multiple parties involved in the litigation. Retaining the best experts early, regardless of their ultimate opinion or whether they eventually testify or not, helps educate the entire litigation team to the strengths and weaknesses of the case and may also forestall highly damaging expert testimony against the contractor.

In order to preserve the attorney work product privilege, counsel, not the contractor, should retain the expert. It is also a good practice to insist that the expert sign a secrecy agreement preventing disclosure or subsequent use of the information provided or developed in connection with the case.

If it is anticipated that the expert will be used as a witness at trial, and hence deposed by an opposing party, several basic rules should be kept in mind when communicating with the expert. First, everything the expert receives or relies upon may have to be revealed to the opposition. Therefore, to the extent practical, the expert's basic background information about the dispute should be provided through pleadings or other documents already available to the opposition.

Second, once it has been decided to designate the expert to testify at trial, communicate with her primarily by telephone or in meetings and not in writing, because correspondence may be discoverable. Resist the temptation to ask for written reports. Reports in draft form and initial conclusions are not necessarily protected from disclosure and often provide a fertile source of impeachment material.

Last, make sure that the expert is timely provided with all the necessary underlying information, both favorable and adverse, to get a complete picture and to reach an informed opinion. If, on the basis of her initial review of material, the expert feels there is or may be any additional information relevant to the dispute or to her opinion, take steps to provide it in a timely manner.

Your expert will likely be asked during deposition, and perhaps at trial, to identify all the information she both reviewed and relied upon in forming her opinion. It reflects adversely on the expert's opinion if important material has not been reviewed and evaluated or if other information was requested or needed and not furnished. Furthermore, although the expert's opinion need not be based on admissible evidence, as long as it is based on the type of material reasonably relied upon by other experts in the field, the underlying material should be credible or it will undermine the validity of the expert's opinion.

DISCOVERY

§ 15.12 Developing the Discovery Plan

Proper planning is the key to effective discovery. Once a litigation plan has been developed, documents and witnesses located, and expert technical assistance secured, the next step is to formulate a discovery plan. This plan will be your road map through the discovery process.

The single most important rule of this and every other phase of discovery is to think through the problem thoroughly before taking any action. Review your theory of the case and litigation plan to determine what types of evidence will be needed, then decide how to go about obtaining that evidence. The initial investigation may already have produced much of the necessary proof, in which case discovery requires only filling in the gaps. Comprehensive discovery in such a case may serve only to tip your hand to opposing counsel. Conversely, it may be necessary in some cases to use discovery to elicit nearly all the relevant facts. In any event, the time spent thinking about how discovery should be utilized before actually beginning the process is invariably time well spent.

In addition to defining the client's discovery needs and determining the means by which to satisfy them, you should also consider whether taking or even responding to discovery will prejudice any substantive rights of the client. For example, if the client has a contractual right to insist upon arbitration of the controversy, you should consult the law of the jurisdiction to ascertain whether taking discovery is tantamount to a waiver of the arbitration right. Further, even before the case has been filed, you should contemplate whether information can be obtained from your adversary through informal means. Many contracts contain provisions affording unlimited access to the files of a general or subcontractor for auditing purposes. Obviously, your exercise of this right of audit will be met with greater receptivity by the other side if it is done before the suit is filed. As the foregoing illustrates, it is worthwhile to think not only about how to go about obtaining discoverable information, but also about what consequences the invocation of discovery will have on your client's substantive rights.

A thorough review of the applicable court rules should also be undertaken at the outset. This is especially important when the forum is an unfamiliar one, of course, but knowledge of the current rules is essential in any context. Do not assume that you have an adequate command of the rules simply because you have conducted discovery before. The federal *Manual for Complex Litigation*[2] can also be a valuable source of information on marshalling and conducting discovery in a complicated case.

Be sure you have made adequate provision for the processing, storage, and retrieval of information and documents to be produced during discovery. The indexing system established during the initial investigation phase should be expandable to include items disclosed by discovery. A system that permits cross-indexing between different types of information (for example, between deposition summaries and documents produced) is highly desirable. In a complex case you may wish to use a computer-based system of information storage and retrieval. See **§ 15.9**. Keep in mind, however, that such a system will be far more costly than simple manual storage.

Explore the possibilities of cooperation with opposing counsel. Discovery will proceed more smoothly and effectively if agreement can be reached as to discovery schedules or even limitations on discovery requests. If trade secrets or confidential or privileged documents are likely to be involved, it may be possible to stipulate to a reciprocal form of protective order without the necessity of intervention by the court. In fact, a more favorable protective order can usually be obtained through negotiation with the opposition than can be elicited from a court.

All these considerations apply with equal force to arrangements with counsel for any third parties or co-parties, including third parties not directly involved in the case. Your client may have claims, defenses, and strategies in common with co-parties. Do not let the opposition use the technique of divide and conquer. In the appropriate case, pool discovery plans and schedules with co-parties to take maximum advantage of common strengths.

Once you are on the verge of plunging into the formal discovery process, it is advisable to draw up an overall discovery plan. **Figure 15–1** is an example of a general discovery timeline and provides a useful overview of a case. Of course, any discovery plan must be flexible enough to adapt to inevitable contingencies; however, the extent of those contingencies will be significantly reduced if, at an early stage, you devote adequate time to plotting all your tasks through trial.

§ 15.13 Litigation Support Group

Anyone who has participated in significant construction litigation can attest to the simple truth that extensive client involvement is mandatory during the discovery stage. It is incumbent upon the attorney to mobilize the client's resources within the framework of a plan that streamlines client participation, keeps business disruption to a minimum and remains within

[2] Manual for Complex Litigation (Fed. Judicial Center 2d ed. 1982).

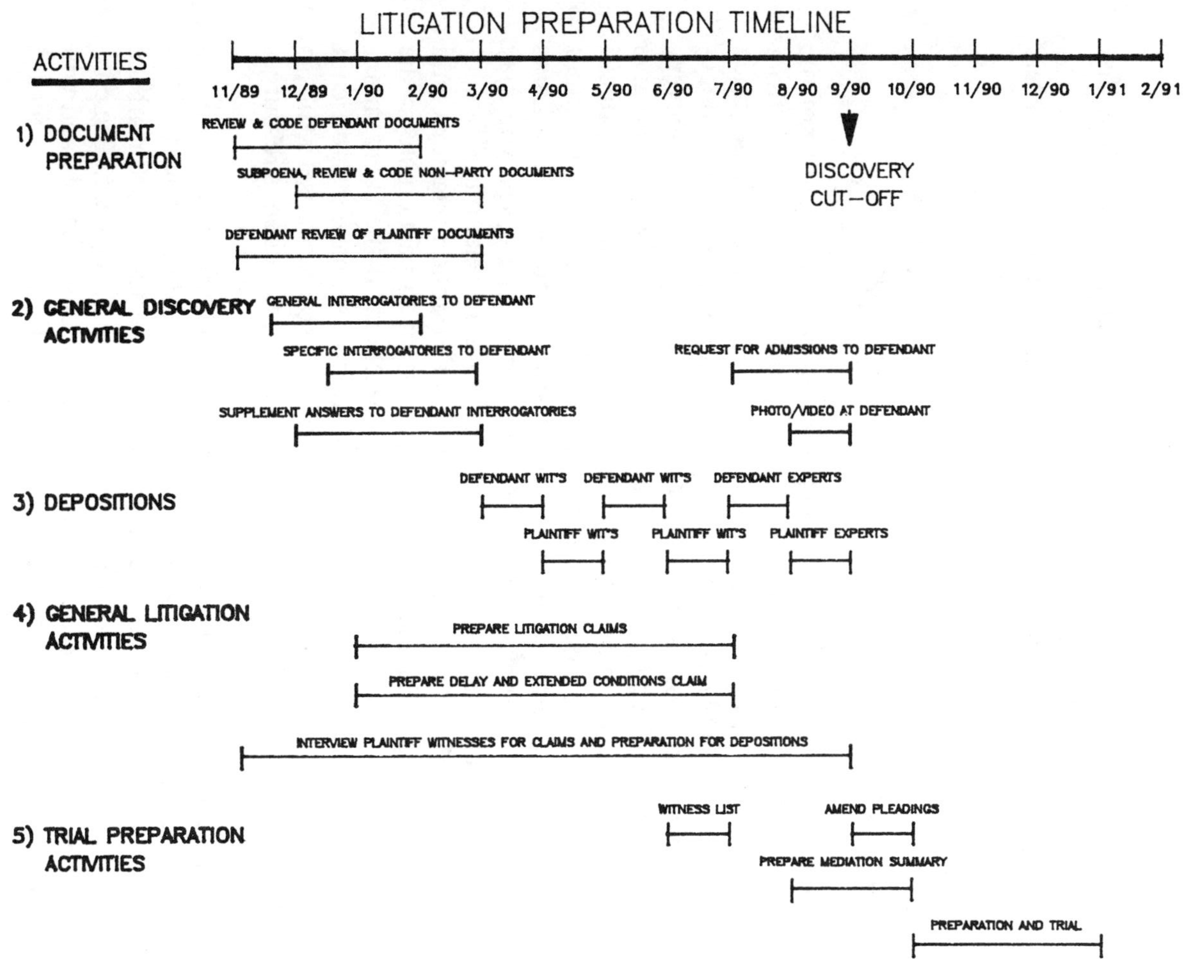

Figure 15–1. Litigation preparation timeline.

cost parameters defined by the client. These ends can be attained to a large extent through formation of a litigation support group (LSG) within the client's organization. A collection of individuals drawn from diverse levels of the client's hierarchy and having unique expertise, the LSG can be useful in such discovery areas as:

1. Determining the documents, witnesses, and technical know-how that are vital to the case
2. Educating the attorneys on the underlying facts and technical matters
3. Reviewing and compiling the other side's documents
4. Collecting the client's own documents
5. Making witnesses available for depositions and interviews
6. Searching for ex-employees with relevant knowledge.

The composition of the LSG will depend largely on the nature of the case. In general, the LSG should include at least one representative from each department of the company involved in the project at issue. Such individuals are particularly helpful with respect to identification of documents and witnesses, imparting relevant facts, and defining discovery needs. In cases involving highly technical issues, in-house experts can give the attorneys a crash course on the specialized knowledge needed to distill and resolve the issues at hand. Further, such individuals can provide input in the selection of independent expert witnesses and outside consultants who may later become part of the LSG. In high profile cases, you may consider enlisting an individual from the client's public relations office for the LSG; indeed, if the case threatens the client's public image or could cause internal discord, hiring an outside consultant to participate in the LSG could be a worthwhile investment for the client. If the client maintains in-house counsel, such individuals will, of course, have a significant role in determining the composition of the LSG. In-house counsel will also themselves serve as valuable conduits through which the client's resources are mobilized.

The LSG should include an individual who can make financial decisions regarding discovery. Although discovery is the most expensive part of litigation, the contractor will not intuitively understand the need for all the discovery deemed desirable for adequate preparation of the case. The contractor engages in cost-benefit analysis every day in doing its job, and will expect counsel to do the same. The LSG is a useful tool in this regard because LSG members will actively participate in formulating overall discovery strategy and in making specific cost-related decisions. Further, the LSG is a vehicle through which the client can observe the results of your combined efforts and of other services for which it is paying.

By using the LSG to keep the client involved in discovery, you automatically accomplish a number of objectives relating to keeping the client informed, making efficient use of the client's resources, and remaining cost-effective. Moreover, LSG participation will inevitably foster a client's positive psychological stake in the litigation.

§ 15.14 Written Discovery Requests

The three most widely used types of written discovery requests are interrogatories, requests for production of documents, and requests for admission. A construction case of any complexity is likely to require the use of at least one of these devices and perhaps all of them.

Written discovery devices are not only useful, they are indispensable in most cases. They are extremely flexible, and, with careful drafting, can perform a wide variety of useful functions. They can bring to light both the factual and legal contentions of the party to whom they are addressed. They can be broadly drafted to elicit the entire factual background of a case or directed narrowly at particular facts or issues; they can serve the ends of both investigation and advocacy.

Nevertheless, written discovery requests have a number of disadvantages. The most important of these is that preparation of the response to the request will undoubtedly be supervised by the attorney representing the responding party. Responses are thus likely to be carefully crafted, and there is no opportunity to cut through an incomplete or evasive answer with an immediate follow-up question. Also, written discovery procedures are slow. The responding party may be permitted as many as 30 days to answer and extensions are routinely sought. If answers are not timely filed, a motion to compel must be brought, which entails further delays. Moreover, written requests by definition are limited to a question-and-answer format, and as such are not designed to elicit narrative factual descriptions. Many of these disadvantages can be avoided or minimized, however, by thoughtful and careful preparation of discovery requests.

§ 15.15 —Drafting Discovery Requests

In the area of drafting, the guiding principle again is to think before you write. Consider precisely what you hope to elicit with your request. Boilerplate interrogatories, document requests, and requests for admissions developed in other cases or taken from the form file are no substitute for discovery requests tailored to the specific facts of the case. Form requests almost always produce too much of what is not needed and too little of what is needed. Of course, a form can be useful to outline and establish the basic structure of the discovery device, the logical order of questions or requests, and the like. Nevertheless, the actual interrogatories, document requests, or requests for admission should be as narrowly and thoughtfully directed to the particulars of the case at hand as possible.

A well-drafted discovery request should start with a preface that puts the party or person to whom it is directed on notice as to what is being requested and what the penalties are for noncompliance. The preface should also make it clear that information sought includes matters within the knowledge of not only the person addressed but also its attorneys,[3] agents, employees, officers, and representatives. The rules concerning supplementation of discovery requests[4] should also be alluded to.

Definitions and instructions are a second important feature of any written discovery device. Using a defined term to encompass a long list of details allows concise and efficient drafting of the actual discovery requests, and facilitates expansion of the scope of particular questions. For example, "document" can be defined to include all imaginable media through which information can be stored or transmitted; in the same way, "person" can include all conceivable legal entities. In interrogatories, the term "identify" often requires a listing of specified information concerning the person or thing identified. Terms such as "the project" or "the accident" can be used to refer to specific aspects of the case. Comprehensive definitions encompassing critical issues, such as which documents are included in the contract, help avoid evasive objections and allow for considerable economy of language in drafting broad-reaching questions.

The form of the questions or requests themselves depends upon the particular type of discovery device being used, but some basic rules apply to all of them. For example, it usually makes sense for the sequence of questions to track those pleadings that set forth the answering party's claims and defenses (for example, the complaint, answer, or affirmative defenses). Also, the litigation plan should be consulted to make sure that discovery requests cover all areas that should be explored at that particular stage of litigation.

Writing discovery requests in plain English should not be overlooked. If the opponent can rightfully claim that a request is ambiguous or otherwise unanswerable because of bad grammar, poor sentence structure, or

---

[3] A discovery request to include information in the hands of the responding party's attorneys is, of course, likely to be objected to on the grounds of privilege or work product. Do not automatically acquiesce to such an objection. Demand identification of any information withheld on the ground of privilege and a detailed statement of the basis for the claim. The courts have interpreted privilege and work product claims in a surprisingly narrow fashion in many cases. Not as much information can be protected on these grounds as many attorneys would like to think.

[4] Fed. R. Civ. P. 26(e).

typographical errors, it is unlikely that she will be required to respond to it. Make every effort to draft with both clarity and precision. Do not try to get too much out of any one question or request. Break the subject matter down into its elements and cover each element separately. The information elicited through this approach will be more useful and the responding party will find such requests more difficult to evade.

Always remember that discovery is a two-edged sword. It is common for opposing counsel to change the names on a discovery request from her client's to that of the party drafting it, and send it right back. If this can be done with your document, be sure you are in a position to respond to what is in essence your own discovery request. In that same vein, you should consider the leverage to be gained by being first. By initiating discovery requests, you force your opponent to set the tone for responses. The party first obliged to respond must determine the level of completeness of its responses and the quantity of its objections. Having the opposition's discovery responses in hand is a distinct advantage when drafting your client's. Because your opponent will have set precedent, it will be in a tenuous position to complain when you respond to its discovery requests with a like degree of completeness and similar objections.

§ 15.16 —Interrogatories

Interrogatories will undoubtedly be used in all but the simplest cases. They are relatively easy to prepare and, when well prepared, may be very difficult to answer in a way that avoids disclosing the information requested. Furthermore, under the Federal Rules of Civil Procedure and in the practice of most states, interrogatory answers must be signed under oath by the party or its representative. Thus, although prior inconsistencies in deposition testimony may sometimes be explained away as a result of faulty recollection or a failure to comprehend the question, a party's written interrogatory answers (which presumably it had the opportunity to investigate and contemplate) are much more likely to be viewed by the trier of fact as firmly binding.

Under the Federal Rules of Civil Procedure, and in most states, interrogatories may inquire into any discoverable matter. They are, however, most useful to elicit general and background information and to narrow issues. In a reasonably complex case, interrogatories should be divided into successive sets, each of which performs a distinct function. The first set should identify the entities, persons, and documents involved in the case, as well as their relationship in a general sense. The second set, perhaps in conjunction with witness depositions, should establish the basic facts that form the foundation of the case to be presented to the trier of fact. Additional sets, possibly in conjunction with requests for admission, should be used to fill in any holes in the evidence prior to trial. Keep in mind, however, that state or local court rules may limit the number of interrogatories (including subquestions) that may be propounded.

Interrogatories used to identify witnesses should inquire specifically about the identity of expert witnesses and the subject matter of expert testimony, and should request a summary of any expert testimony to be offered and the grounds therefor. Federal Rule of Civil Procedure 26(b)(4)(A) and some state rules expressly allow such discovery. Some states, however, have separate and distinct procedures for mutual disclosure and discovery of expert witnesses and their opinions.

Interrogatories should ask for the location and the identity of the custodian of the opponent's documents, and for identification of all documents the opponent intends to use to support every element of its claims or defenses. The manner in which the opponent keeps its records, the types of documents that are available, and the types of information they contain can also be learned through interrogatories. This information will make specific requests for document production much easier to draft.

Specific inquiry should always be made into the nature and amount of each element of any claimed damages. Establishing the parameters of the contractor's exposure in this manner is vital to an intelligent evaluation of the advisability of settlement as opposed to litigation.

Finally, interrogatories can also be used to explore a party's legal theories. Federal Rule of Civil Procedure 33(b) permits interrogatories to seek "an opinion or contention that relates to fact or the application of law to fact . . . ." Thus, to the extent possible within the written question format, the opponent may be compelled to disclose its legal, as well as factual, theories. This can in turn lay the groundwork for a motion for summary judgment or other pretrial disposition.

§ 15.17 —Requests for Production of Documents

Construction projects are often voluminously, if not meticulously, documented. This often makes a complete document review a practical impossibility in a construction case. Nevertheless, documents will nearly always be central to the issues involved in the litigation. See **Chapter 22**. Top priority must be given to identifying the documentary evidence the other side will rely upon, obtaining copies of those documents, and learning how to interpret them. Identification, inspection, and copying of documents in the possession of parties are accomplished under Federal Rule of Civil Procedure 34 and parallel state rules through a "request for production of documents." Documents of nonparties must be obtained through voluntary cooperation or a subpoena duces tecum. Some state rules provide that document production can be obtained only by court order after motion and hearing.

Document production efforts are most frequently derailed when, in response to an overly broad document request, the other side simply offers to open all of its files for inspection. The party requesting production is then put to the task of sorting through and attempting to understand immense amounts of material, much of which may be irrelevant to the case.

It is possible to avoid, or to at least minimize, this inundation. First of all, as with all other discovery requests, materials seeking document production should be precisely drafted. Do not mechanically request "all documents" relating to the dispute. To the extent possible, only specified types or categories of documents should be requested. Your consulting expert or members of the LSG will likely be able to assist in identifying the necessary documents.

It is possible that the opposing party has a file or document indexing system already in use. If the system was devised and put into use by the party, as opposed to counsel, this index should be discoverable. If so, it will make identification of relevant documents much simpler. It may also be advisable at an early point to schedule the deposition of the custodian of the opponent's documents to ascertain whether all available sources have been checked and prior document requests fully complied with.

It is also important to insist that all documents withheld under a claim of privilege or on some other basis be identified, with a full explanation of the basis of the claim. As noted in **§ 15.15**, the courts generally do not interpret the doctrine of privilege as broadly as most lawyers do, and a motion to compel may be warranted. Again, however, because discovery is a two-edged sword, you must be prepared to disclose and defend your own claims of privilege on the same basis.

The types of documents which should be requested will vary with the issues of each case. Nevertheless, in most construction litigation at least some of the following types of documents will be sought:

1. Contract documents, including documents on which the opposing party intends to rely (all copies bearing notes or interpretive markings) and any drafts, working papers, and notes or memos used in contract negotiations
2. Drawings and specifications
3. Change orders
4. Construction logs and foremen's diaries
5. Quality control/quality assurance reports
6. Reports to owners; progress and payment schedules
7. Reports to regulatory agencies and authorities

8. Accident or incident reports
9. Insurance policies and bonds
10. All correspondence, including interoffice memoranda.

These categories, and any other categories relevant to the particular case, should be reflected in the document indexing system previously devised during the investigatory phase. If a mechanized or computerized system is in use, be sure it can be expanded or adapted to accommodate new categories disclosed during discovery.

§ 15.18 —Requests for Admission

Requests for admission under Federal Rule of Civil Procedure 36 are a powerful discovery tool and an effective strategy device as well. They cast on the opponent the burden of taking a specific position on identified issues that may well go to the very heart of the case. Admissions elicited early in the case may lead to a motion for full or partial summary judgment or to a favorable settlement. Nevertheless, attorneys by and large do not make sufficient use of requests for admission in construction litigation.

The degree to which admissions obtained from an opposing party will be useful depends directly on the clarity and specificity of the requests themselves. The objective is to have the opponent admit exactly what it needed to prove or facilitate proof of the client's claim or defense, neither more nor less. Each individual request should deal with a single fact, and should be phrased so as to leave the other side with no practical alternative other than a yes or no answer or its equivalent. Vague terminology or incomplete descriptions that give the other side the opportunity to be nonresponsive should be avoided. Denial of requested admissions should always be followed up or coupled with interrogatories directed to the basis of the denial.

The subject matter of requests for admission will vary with the facts of the particular case. Nevertheless, there are recurring features of construction lawsuits that lend themselves particularly well to this discovery device:

Authentication of or foundation for documents. Because construction cases are often lengthy and complex, requests for admissions are frequently used to establish the authenticity of or evidentiary foundation for documents. This avoids tedious trial testimony on authenticity and allows counsel flexibility in witness scheduling. Generally, the opponent is simply asked to admit the authenticity of specified documents, copies of which are attached to the request.[5] Other bases for the evidentiary admissibility of

[5] Such copies must be attached, according to Fed. R. Civ. P. 36.

documents, such as elements of the business record exception to the hearsay rule, can also be established through this type of request for admission.

Basic facts. The factual building blocks of the case, such as dates, times, addresses, dollar amounts, the accuracy of numerical computations, and other basic matters are also well-suited for inclusion in requests for admission. Witnesses often display uncertainty on such subjects, particularly numbers, at trial. Obtaining admissions concerning hard-to-remember but basically uncontested details facilitates a smooth presentation of evidence.

Application of law to fact. Requests for admission concerning opinions or the application of law to fact are permitted under the Federal Rules, even if they involve questions of "ultimate" law or fact. This can be an extremely effective aspect of this discovery device in the proper case.

§ 15.19 Obtaining Responses to Discovery Requests

Service of a discovery request unfortunately does not automatically ensure that the information sought will be forthcoming. The party served with the request may try to avoid answering through delay, by objecting to a particular request, or by intentionally or negligently failing to provide all the information sought. Effective use of discovery requires conscientious follow-up and a swift reaction to any attempt to avoid or delay responding.

Frequently, opposing counsel will request an extension of the time given to respond. Whether to grant such a request depends on a variety of factors well known to most practitioners, including the degree to which professional courtesies exist or are honored in the locality. Any extension should, however, be memorialized in a written stipulation and order specifying the date on which discovery is to be forthcoming. This precludes any misunderstandings and facilitates a motion to compel if the extended deadline is not met.

Meritless objections to discovery requests should be addressed through a motion to compel. Some states require, in fact, that the party objecting to the discovery arrange to have the objections brought before the court. Most lawyers have found, however, that judges by and large dislike discovery motions and prefer that the parties work out their differences about discovery without the court's intervention. One manifestation of this reluctance to become involved in discovery disputes is that motions to compel are frequently the subject of local court rules and thus subject to special requirements and procedures. Become familiar with such rules so that the delay is not exacerbated by rejection of your motion on procedural grounds.

All possible efforts should be made to obtain compliance informally before bringing a motion to compel, even if such efforts are not strictly required by court rule. If a motion does in fact become necessary, the moving party will want to be able to demonstrate that the other party was given a fair chance to respond.

A corollary of this proposition is that motions to compel can be used to educate the court, both about the issues and about the parties. Choose your opportunity with care. Do not run to the court for relief from trifling omissions or on matters that can be obtained through other means. Do, however, ask the court to deal firmly with parties or counsel who are acting in palpable bad faith.

The range of valid grounds for objecting to discovery is actually fairly limited. For example, many courts construe relevance broadly for discovery purposes and will allow discovery in all but the most extreme circumstances. Burdensomeness is a frequent objection to discovery in construction litigation, and is best avoided by careful preparation of discovery requests in the first instance. The requesting party should be able to demonstrate that, even though the discovery request is extensive, everything sought is important to the parties' and the court's understanding of the case.

Confidentiality is another frequent objection to discovery in construction cases. Offering to submit to a protective order providing for either limited disclosure of information or in camera inspection limited to the court and attorneys for the parties is an effective response.

§ 15.20 Responding to Discovery Requests

Discovery, of course, works both ways in construction litigation as elsewhere. Many of the same general guidelines applicable to the preparation of discovery requests should also be followed in the preparation of responses. Interrogatory answers, answers to requests for admission, and the production of certain documents may be construed as admissions of the party at trial. Accordingly, careful analysis of the request and a thorough evaluation and understanding of the legal and tactical situation are essential. For example, if a party is asked to produce all documents upon which it intends to rely to prove a particular point, it may be precluded at trial from using other documents not brought forward in response to the requests. Similarly, counsel in receipt of discovery requests should keep in mind the duties of supplementation imposed by court rules such as Federal Rule of Civil Procedure 26(e).

Responding to interrogatories and requests for admission is much like preparing a witness for cross-examination. It is important to answer only what the question asks and not to build the other side's case. Objections to discovery requests should be carefully considered, keeping in mind the judicial attitude toward discovery disputes discussed in § **15.18**. The Federal

Rules of Civil Procedure permit interposition of an objection, in lieu of an answer to an interrogatory, so long as the grounds for the objection are clearly stated. In some cases, however, it may be preferable to state both the objection and the answer, thereby preserving both the objection and the court's good graces.

Promptness is also important; the indulgence of counsel should not be relied upon to excuse untimely responses. If an extension of time to respond is requested and granted, it should be confirmed in writing.

§ 15.21 Depositions

The oral deposition is one of the most flexible (and certainly one of the most expensive) forms of discovery available. Because of their flexibility, depositions are useful in following up on interrogatory answers and document productions and in framing requests for admission.

Persons with direct knowledge of the operative facts of the case should be identified as soon as possible. Witnesses who will testify for the opposing party should be deposed early in the discovery process, both to tie them to a particular version of the facts and to preserve their testimony for potential impeachment use at trial. Each witness should be asked in the course of the deposition to identify other persons who may have knowledge of the pertinent facts.

The depositions of experts and employees of the owner or subcontractors who do not have direct knowledge of the operative facts but who will have knowledge of the circumstances, procedures, methods of operation, and other relevant information may be deferred until the later phases of the discovery process. This allows time for adequate preparation and facilitates the authentication of documents needed for trial.

A strategic decision that is commonly overlooked relates to the order in which witnesses in the opposing party's organization are deposed. Typically, each party to a construction case is in effective control of numerous witnesses with wide-ranging roles in the events leading up to the controversy. At the outset of discovery, you should have a fair idea of which witnesses in the opponent's camp you wish to depose. It is a mistake to assume that the order in which you take the depositions does not matter, as long as you depose all of the witnesses at some point in the case. The organizational level at which you begin to take the depositions does make a difference, and the order should coincide with your overall goals in the litigation.

For instance, starting at the higher levels of the opponent's management hierarchy has distinct advantages and drawbacks. If you decide to start with such policy-making individuals, you are likely to gain a good understanding of the inner-workings of their organization, which could prove useful for purposes of other witnesses' depositions. Further, deposing the individuals clothed with broad decision-making powers may permit you to impress upon them the strengths of your case and the time and cost that protracted litigation is likely to exact upon their own business. In that way, beginning at the top of the organization could facilitate more rapid settlement of the matter.

Conversely, if your examination of the policy-making individuals is extensive, you are likely to reveal your themes on germane issues at an early stage but come away with only a general knowledge of what transpired in the field. In so doing, you also afford the other side more information with which to prepare subsequent witnesses. For that reason, it may be prudent to begin with the "hands-on" positions associated with the project. By initially attacking the bottom of the hierarchy with inquiries that are confined to discrete aspects of the project, you have a better chance of obtaining detailed testimony before it can be obscured or retouched. As with all facets of discovery strategy, the order of depositions should be dictated by the particular circumstances surrounding the action, not the least of which is what your client hopes to accomplish through the litigation.

It is not, however, always necessary to know in detail the management hierarchy of an organization from which discovery will be sought in order to begin taking depositions. Federal Rule of Civil Procedure 30(b)(6) permits the organization itself to be named as the deponent in a notice of taking deposition or subpoena that describes "with reasonable particularity" the matters to be inquired into. The organization must then itself designate one or more persons to testify in response to the notice or subpoena (a subpoena must notify a nonparty organization of this duty). This presents a useful way to get a foot in the door of an unfamiliar organization for discovery purposes.

Sometimes the court rules of the forum are insufficiently tailored to prevent disputes engendered by, or to otherwise facilitate, discovery in complex construction litigation cases. It is not uncommon for depositions in this area of litigation to number in the hundreds. Thus, any procedural disputes among the parties are likely to persist over a considerable amount of time and require repeated court intervention. However, foresight, creativity, and cooperation with opposing counsel can reduce the number of trips through the courthouse door.

Federal Rule of Civil Procedure 29 allows the parties to stipulate to more elaborate deposition protocol. A stipulated order may detail deposition procedure so as to obviate picayune disputes known to arise in connection with depositions. In fashioning the order, counsel may wish to address the following subjects:

1. Noticing of depositions
2. Subpoenas

3. Overall scheduling
4. Holidays
5. Time and place
6. Witness fees and expenses for party-deponents
7. Procedures for examinations
8. People who may attend depositions
9. Marking of deposition exhibits
10. Simultaneous depositions
11. Objections and instructions not to answer
12. Conduct of counsel
13. Telephone rulings by the court
14. Witness signatures of transcripts
15. Production of witnesses by parties with whom they are identified.

This list is offered by way of suggestion only, and you may wish to add or delete topics as the circumstances warrant. The stipulated discovery order device makes it possible to resolve anticipated problems in advance. Correlatively, the court is likely to welcome such an order because, if well crafted, it will cut down on the parties' appearances before the court on discovery disputes for the entire case.

Recent technological advances can make depositions more useful. If numerous depositions are contemplated and if evidence is compiled and stored in a computerized data base, locate and agree with opposing counsel upon the use of a court reporting service that has recording equipment to interface directly with your computer. Most court reporting services can now provide you with a computer disk containing the deposition transcript. With a compatible software package, you can use your computer to sort through the transcript by using key search terms, make side notes at critical points in the testimony, and compile a comprehensive digest of the witness's testimony by topic.

If key deponents will be unavailable for trial, videotape depositions are the best substitute for live testimony, especially if the demeanor of the witness is important. If videotape depositions are contemplated, local court rules relative to their taking and admissibility should be carefully analyzed and followed. Preparation for videotape depositions requires attention to a number of factors not pertinent to the normal transcribed deposition.[6]

---

[6] Especially careful preparation is required for videotape depositions because shuffling papers and long pauses can prove distracting and will detract from the effectiveness of the presentation. In many cases, hiring a reputable firm to produce the deposition is the best means of assuring a quality presentation. Different camera angles should be used to eliminate the "talking head" effect of one stationary camera focused on the witness.

§ 15.22 —Conducting the Deposition

No two depositions are quite alike and no two lawyers will conduct a deposition in quite the same way. Nevertheless, some guiding principles have universal applicability:

Thorough preparation. Prepare for the deposition as you would for the testimony of that witness at trial, even if you are not conducting the examination. After all, the witness may become unavailable, in which case the deposition testimony may actually become the witness's testimony. Moreover, if important questions go unasked or improper material is not objected to, the damage may be difficult (if not impossible) to repair later.

Goals. If you are taking the deposition, know what you want to accomplish. Is this merely an exploratory, fact-finding inquiry, or do you plan to elicit particular facts or admissions for use at trial? Are there documents that should be authenticated by this witness? If so, are your copies adequate and legible? Is there an applicable adverse witness statute that will let you proceed by leading questions?

Prepare your witness. If your witness is being deposed, make sure she is thoroughly prepared. The best preparation is for you to take the role of opposing counsel, conducting the deposition as if the witness were adverse. You will have done your job if opposing counsel asks no questions that you did not. Be every bit as hard on your witness as you expect opposing counsel to be. The witness will be better prepared and you will have an opportunity to assess the strengths and weaknesses of your own case.

Flexibility. Have a plan, but be flexible. You should almost always have a written list of subjects you want to cover with the witness, but be prepared to abandon the list temporarily to follow unexpected developments in the testimony. It is not advisable to rely on a written list of questions, except for particular critical points, because this practice often stifles spontaneity and creativity. However, if you utilize computerized disk transcripts and the appropriate software (see **§ 15.9**), it is helpful to develop a standard jargon for the case that may be used at the depositions. Injecting buzzwords into your questions will allow you to more efficiently and accurately sort through and digest the deposition transcripts with the aid of a computer.

Expert witnesses. Additional considerations apply to depositions of expert witnesses. Your consulting expert or the contractor's expert personnel should be involved in preparing for the deposition and in formulating hypothetical questions. Find out as much as you can about the deponent prior to the deposition. Review her curriculum vitae in advance and read any of her published works that may touch on the subject matter of the testimony; the expert may have taken a position in an article or publication that is at variance with the anticipated testimony. Answers to interrogatories relating to the expert's proposed testimony will also be helpful in planning the scope and direction of your examination. Do not allow the witness to use technical jargon without defining such terms for the trier of fact.

In a complex case it is likely that numerous depositions will be taken and that each deposition will be quite lengthy. This makes it essential that a system of transcript summarization be instituted. Actual preparation of summaries can often be delegated to a legal assistant, but the lawyer who attended the deposition should review the summary as soon as possible after it is prepared to be sure that essential points are not missed. If the attorney who took the deposition will not be conducting the actual trial, an early conference between the deposing attorney and the trial attorney is essential to discuss the witness's strengths, weaknesses, and overall demeanor before trial.

§ 15.23 Other Discovery Devices

Two other related discovery devices are most useful in construction cases: the request to inspect, test, or sample items in the possession of another party; and the request to go upon the land of another party to measure, survey, photograph, test, and the like. Both are governed by Federal Rule of Civil Procedure 34.

As a rule, if these devices are to be useful at all, they should be used early in the case. The physical condition of real and personal property relevant to the case may change dramatically over the course of discovery, which often takes several years. The admissibility of evidence relating to physical condition may turn directly on the amount of time that has elapsed between the events giving rise to the litigation and the inspection or testing of the item.

These devices can be useful in a number of ways. In a case involving failure of a building component, physical testing may reveal whether the failure resulted from faulty design, faulty materials, or faulty workmanship. Soil tests may reveal whether building subsidence resulted from subsoil conditions or from oversight by the architect.

If construction on the project continues during litigation, having photographs of the site as it existed at the time of the dispute may be invaluable. Likewise, measurements and surveys may be relevant to disputes involving claims of architectural malpractice.

§ 15.24 Final Discovery Review

As the trial date approaches, but before discovery cutoff, the litigation plan must be reevaluated to make sure it satisfactorily accounts for new or additional facts and contentions disclosed through discovery. Experts should have concluded their investigations and reached their opinions, and will probably have been deposed. The basic framework of the dispute has been set.

If permissible under the local rules of the forum, it is often useful to propound a last set of cleanup interrogatories to tie up any remaining loose ends. These should include an interrogatory asking if any previous interrogatory answers need to be updated or changed to reflect subsequently discovered information or documents.

At this juncture, attention should be devoted to the precise proof needed to present the case and how the proper foundation for its admissibility will be established. Agreeing to reasonable stipulations as to the foundation for or admissibility of routine documents will save time at trial.

Determine what demonstrative evidence is necessary or desirable to the presentation of the case. Photographs, models, or other tangible exhibits are usually necessary to tie together the testimony of various witnesses and aid in focusing the attention of the trier of fact. Graphs, charts, or summaries may help simplify, clarify, or explain otherwise unmanageable or overly complicated supporting documentation, such as cost accounting records.

To be admissible, demonstrative evidence must be a fair and accurate representation of what it purports to represent; it must be relevant and must help the trier of fact understand the evidence. Standards for admissibility vary from state to state, court to court, and even judge to judge. It is therefore prudent to inquire as to the local rules and practice before taking any substantial steps toward developing any particular form of demonstrative evidence.

The earlier efforts to organize the documents will pay handsome dividends during trial preparation. Determine which documents are needed and in which order. Unless the foundation has already been agreed to with the opposition, be sure all the foundational requirements are met for each exhibit, given the sequence of presentation of witnesses.

CHAPTER 16

PROVING LIABILITY TO ALLOW CONTRACTOR TO RECOVER DAMAGES

Peter Goetz

Peter Goetz is a founder and senior partner of the New York, New York, law firm of Goetz, Fitzpatrick & Flynn, specializing construction and engineering matters throughout the United States and abroad. He received his B.C.E. from Rensselaer Polytechnic Institute and his LL.B. from Brooklyn Law School. Mr. Goetz is a member of the Committee on Construction Law of the Association of the Bar of the City of New York, the Construction Arbitrator's Panel of the American Arbitration Association, as well as the New York and American Bar Associations' Construction Committee, Litigation Section, Forum Committee on Construction Contract Law, Public Contract Law Section, and Construction and Surety Section. He is a coauthor for several Wiley Law Publications, including *Alternative Dispute Resolution in the Construction Industry* (1991), and he has been a guest lecturer at numerous construction seminars.

§ 16.1 Introduction

DELAY CLAIMS

§ 16.2 General

§ 16.3 Owner's Failure to Perform an Affirmative Act

§ 16.4 Defective Plans and Specifications

§ 16.5 Owner's Failure to Provide Access to the Site

§ 16.6 Unforeseeable Subsurface Conditions

§ 16.7 Substantial Changes in Scope of Contract

§ 16.8 Extension of Time Clauses

§ 16.9 Changes

§ 16.10 —Directed Changes

§ 16.11 —Changes Clause Strictly Construed
§ 16.12 —Constructive Changes
§ 16.13 Restrictions on Contractor's Recovery
§ 16.14 —Delays Contemplated by the Parties
§ 16.15 Exceptions to No Damage for Delay Clauses
§ 16.16 —Active Interference
§ 16.17 —Active Interference Not Sufficient
§ 16.18 —Delays Not Contemplated by the Parties
§ 16.19 —Unreasonable or Excessive Period of Delay
§ 16.20 —Bad Faith or Fraud
§ 16.21 —Concurrent Delays Attributable to Both Parties
§ 16.22 Excusable Delays of the Contractor
§ 16.23 —Unforeseeability
§ 16.24 —Unusually Severe Weather
§ 16.25 —Labor Disputes

ACCELERATION CLAIMS

§ 16.26 Acceleration Defined
§ 16.27 Actual and Constructive Acceleration
§ 16.28 Disallowance of Acceleration Damage Claims

OTHER DAMAGE CLAIMS

§ 16.29 Changed Conditions
§ 16.30 Low Bidder Claims

ASSERTING DAMAGE CLAIMS

§ 16.31 Strict Adherence to Contract Provisions
§ 16.32 Delay and Time Extension Clauses
§ 16.33 Notice and Deadline Clauses
§ 16.34 When Time Is of the Essence

PROOF OF DAMAGES

§ 16.35 Actual Damages
§ 16.36 Total Cost Method
§ 16.37 —Labor Costs
§ 16.38 —Material Costs
§ 16.39 —Jobsite Indirect Costs
§ 16.40 —Home Office Overhead
§ 16.41 —Finance Costs
§ 16.42 Disruption Damages
§ 16.43 Lost Profits

§ 16.1 Introduction

On a factual basis, there are as many variations in the substantive nature of contractor claims as there are differences in the construction techniques used in erecting buildings, airports, bridges, and highways. Because there is so much diversity in the subject matter of this chapter, the author has chosen to cover the claim areas with the biggest economic impact on the contractor's costs. In terms of financial considerations, delay-related claims are the big money items in the field of litigated construction matters. Acceleration, suspension, and interference actions likewise are claims with significant financial repercussions.

As is shown in this chapter, a delay claim may involve a myriad of separate subsidiary claims that in and of themselves fall under separate and distinct categories. **Sections 16.3** through **16.12** contain examples of delay claims in terms of such subsidiary claim items as defective plans or specifications, failure to obtain site access, unforeseeable subsurface conditions, and so on. Each of these items gives the contractor the right to recover its extra costs, but each may also give rise to a more significant claim, that is, a delay claim.

This chapter focuses on time of performance claims and shows how these time-related claims are caused by (or at least frequently influenced by) various peripheral claims that surround the principal claim. In other words, the eventual sum proves to be greater than the total of the individual numbers. Delay, acceleration, and other time-related claims are emphasized because the success or failure of a project may hinge on the amount recovered by the contractor for these claims.

DELAY CLAIMS

§ 16.2 General

By far the most commonly and hotly litigated contractor claims involve delays caused by the owner or by persons for whom the owner is responsible. As a general rule, if a contractor agrees to do certain work within a specified time but is prevented from performing the contract by the act or default of another party, or by the acts of persons for whose conduct that other party is responsible, the contractor is entitled to the economic loss sustained as a result of the delay.[1] Of course, this is somewhat of a simplification because

---

[1] *See* 13 Am. Jur. 2d *Building and Construction Contracts* § 48 (1964).

the contract language in the owner-contractor documents controls the liabilities of these parties.

§ 16.3 Owner's Failure to Perform an Affirmative Act

When the owner is under a contractual obligation to perform an affirmative act, its failure to perform will give rise to a claim for damages caused by such failure. For example, in *Glassman Construction Co. v. Maryland City Plaza, Inc.,*[2] the owner's failure timely to obtain building permits and locate sewer lines (along with a continuous flow of revisions from the owner) prevented the contractor from performing its work. Consequently, the contractor was entitled to recover its losses due to delay.

Likewise, in *George A. Fuller Co. v. United States*[3] the government was held liable for the contractor's damages resulting from government delays in furnishing models as required by contract.

§ 16.4 Defective Plans and Specifications

If the furnishing of defective plans and specifications is the cause of delay, the contractor, in addition to recovering its extra costs, also has a viable cause of action against the owner for delay damages. Extra work costs were allowed for delay in *Jasper Construction v. Foothill Junior College District,*[4] which involved a claim by the contractor that inadequate and defective plans and specifications caused it to suffer delays and added expenses. The court reiterated the general rule that "a contractor of public work who, acting reasonably, is misled by incorrect plans and specifications issued by public authorities as the basis for bids and who, as a result, submits a bid which is lower than he would have otherwise made may recover in a contract action for extra work or expenses necessitated by the conditions being other than represented."[5] However, in qualifying this general rule, the court stated that the contractor must demonstrate an affirmative misrepresentation or concealment of material fact in the plans and specifications.

In *Laburnum Construction Corp. v. United States*[6] the delay was caused when deficient specifications were furnished to the contractor by the government. The court directed that the contractor could recover its increased

---

[2] 371 F. Supp. 1154 (D. Md. 1974), *aff'd,* 530 F.2d 968 (4th Cir. 1975).

[3] 69 F. Supp. 409 (Ct. Cl. 1947).

[4] 91 Cal. App. 3d 1, 153 Cal. Rptr. 767 (1979).

[5] *Id.* at 8, 153 Cal. Rptr. at 770.

[6] 325 F.2d 451 (Ct. Cl. 1963).

costs from the owner. Because the owner alone caused the delay, it was a compensable delay.

§ 16.5 Owner's Failure to Provide Access to the Site

Unfortunately, it is common for a contractor to be denied timely access to the project site. The courts have historically entertained contractors' claims for delay based on such access denial, because the law assumes that timely access was anticipated by the parties. For example, in *E.C. Ernst, Inc. v. Koppers Co.*[7] the follow-on contractor, which could perform its work only after other contractors had prepared the work area, was awarded damages as a result of being delayed in commencing its work.

However, in *Burgess Construction Co. v. M. Marrin & Son Co.*[8] the court found that a general contractor's failure to provide access to the site on the dates stated in the contract was not a breach of its implied promise not to hinder or delay its subcontractor's performance. After examining the contract language and surrounding circumstances, the court determined that the general contractor did not have an unconditional obligation to complete work necessary for the subcontractor's site access on the specified date. The court found dispositive the fact that the contract provided for an extension of the subcontractor's time in the event of a delay by the general contractor.[9]

§ 16.6 Unforeseeable Subsurface Conditions

As a general rule, the contractor can recover additional costs when it encounters unforeseeable subsurface conditions. In *L.G. DeFelice & Sons, Inc. v. State*[10] the court stated that delays in performance of contracts ordinarily are compensated only by an extension of time for completion; such extensions are routinely granted when site availability is delayed or there is interference between the contractor and other contractors or utility owners.[11] The court further held that for delays in contracts to be actionable, they must be more than ordinary delays and in fact should be "extraordinary" and not reasonably contemplated by the parties. The *DeFelice* court found that an increase of almost 400 percent in the amount of topsoil required constituted an extraordinary delay and was not reasonably contemplated by

---

[7] 626 F.2d 324 (3d Cir. 1980).

[8] 526 F.2d 108 (10th Cir. 1976).

[9] See §§ **16.13** and **16.22–16.25** for treatment of contract clauses that exculpate one party from its otherwise ordinary obligations.

[10] 63 Misc. 2d 357, 313 N.Y.S.2d 21 (Ct. Cl. 1962).

[11] See § **16.7**.

the parties at the time of entering into the contract. Thus, the contractor was entitled to recover additional sums expended.

§ 16.7 Substantial Changes in Scope of Contract

The courts have held that a contract may validly provide that a contractor shall be entitled to no relief for delay except an extension of time of performance, even though such delay does in fact increase the costs.[12] In most jurisdictions, though, when the increased costs result from a substantial change in the scope of the contract, such a disclaimer is ineffective.[13]

In *Peter Kiewit Sons' Co. v. Summit Construction Co.*[14] the prime contractor, instead of permitting the subcontractor to backfill unimpeded as agreed to by contract, required the backfilling to be done in three phases after pipe had been laid. This increased the difficulty of the backfill operation and resulted in a 300-percent increase in backfill costs. The court determined that the prime contractor's conduct constituted a substantial breach because it substantially changed the scope of the work. The court expressly found that a disclaimer providing for an extension of time but prohibiting additional costs was not applicable when the increase in the subcontractor's costs was caused primarily by a change in the scope of the contract.[15]

§ 16.8 Extension of Time Clauses

Customarily, a time extension provision neither bars nor allows per se the right to recover compensation for delays. In the strictest sense, a time extension clause simply provides that under general or specified circumstances, whichever the case, if a delay is beyond the control of the contractor, the owner is obligated to extend the time of completion by the amount of the excusable delay period.

Time extension clauses are not to be confused with other contract provisions relating to compensation for extra work or forfeiture of monies (liquidated damages) caused by delays in performance of the work. Their only function is to provide extended completion time in the event the contractor is delayed for causes either within or beyond the owner's control.

---

[12] Lichter v. Mellon-Stuart Co., 305 F.2d 216 (3d Cir. 1962).

[13] Peter Kiewit Sons' Co. v. Summit Constr. Co., 422 F.2d 242 (8th Cir. 1969).

[14] *Id.*

[15] *Id.* at 265.

§ 16.9 Changes

Virtually all current construction contracts contain a changes clause. In fact, without such a clause, the owner would be unable to alter or add work without being liable for breach of contract. A typical changes clause is found in Article 12 of American Institute of Architects (AIA) Document A201.[16]

The changes clause generally delineates in substantial detail the specific manner in which changes are to be effectuated. These clauses usually require that notice of changes be made in writing and specify the means for adjusting the contract price.

The courts have allowed contractors in some cases to recover costs of delays under the changes clause. The disputes that generally arise from these clauses, however, are whether the changes are within or beyond the contract scope of work.[17]

§ 16.10 —Directed Changes

If the owner directs the contractor to make changes and the subject changes are covered by the changes clause of the contract, the contractor may also be entitled to damages for delay. In *Brooks Towers Corp. v. Hunkin-Conkey Construction Co.*,[18] changes in the structural specifications were covered under the changes clause, caused changes in the sequence of work, and resulted in delays. The court allowed recovery of delay damages under the changes clause.

§ 16.11 —Changes Clause Strictly Construed

The courts will generally strictly construe the notice provisions of the changes clause, claiming that the owner should be made aware that the modification constitutes a change for which the contractor seeks extra compensation. In *Indiana v. Omega Painting, Inc.*,[19] a contractor's claim for delays under a changes clause was denied when it failed to adhere strictly to notice requirements found in that clause.[20]

Most changes clauses require the change to be issued to the contractor in writing, in the form of an extra work or change order. The contractor

---

[16] AIA Doc. A201, General Conditions, Art. 12, "Changes in the Work" (1976).

[17] See **§ 16.7**.

[18] 454 F.2d 1203 (10th Cir. 1973).

[19] 463 N.E.2d 287 (Ind. Ct. App. 1984).

[20] *See also* J.A. Ross & Co. v. United States, 115 F. Supp. 187 (Ct. Cl. 1953).

should insist on strict adherence by the owner to this provision. Typically, the changes clause will also provide for alternate methods of payment (for example, agreed or contract unit price, lump sum, or, in the absence of an agreement, a time and material basis).

Always check the language of the changes clause to see the extent to which the owner can authorize changes. In public works, by contract or by legislative enactment, the owner's representative may not have authority to issue change orders beyond a certain magnitude or make changes that are beyond the scope of the contract.

Similarly, when dealing with public contracts, the contractor should be extremely careful to determine who has authority to issue changes or change orders. Without contract authority, regardless of good faith reliance by the contractor acting on the directed changes, it is unlikely that recovery will be allowed for unauthorized changes. In one case[21] the contractor was denied payment for extra work although the owner's representative authorized the extra work. (The contractor also failed to adhere strictly to the written notice requirements.) The court reasoned that because only the entire school board could authorize changes, the representative's authorization was not controlling. Obviously, if delays are part of the change's extra cost, that claim will likewise be denied if the extra work claim fails to qualify.

§ 16.12 —Constructive Changes

Another source of change found under law is the *constructive change.* These are changes not acknowledged by the owner or its representative at the time they are issued, but treated by the courts as changes as if the owner had issued a formal order.

Various types of claims are allowed under the changes clause on the legal theory of constructive changes. When defective or incomplete plans and specifications required extra work to accomplish the intention of the contract, recovery by the contractor has been allowed on the theory that the owner warrants the sufficiency of the plans and specifications.[22] Also allowed are claims for extra work caused by:

1. Performance in a different manner due to impossibility of performance as specified or designed
2. Enforcement of extraordinarily rigid performance requirements

---

[21] Nether Providence Township Sch. Auth. v. Thomas M. Durkin & Sons, Inc., 505 Pa. 42, 476 A.2d 904 (1984).

[22] United States v. Spearin, 248 U.S. 132 (1918). See also § **16.4**.

3. Superior knowledge by the owner of work requirements requiring performance in a more costly manner
4. Ambiguous plans and specifications under which the contractor contemplated a less costly means of performance.[23]

§ 16.13 Restrictions on Contractor's Recovery

Owners commonly attempt to restrict a contractor's ability to recover for delay damages by inserting a no damage for delay clause into the contract. Essentially, the no damage clause is an exculpatory provision that provides that regardless of what one party does to delay the work of the other party, even if caused through neglect, fault, or omission, it will not be liable for delay suffered by the injured party. A typical no damage clause provides: "No payment or compensation of any kind shall be made to the contractor for damages because of the hindrance or delay from any cause in the progress of the work, whether such hindrance or delays be avoidable or unavoidable."[24]

As a general rule, such clauses are enforceable when they are clear and unambiguous and reflect the intent of the parties.[25] Due to the harsh results fostered by such clauses, they are strictly construed by the courts.[26] However, the mere fact that the result is a harsh one will not prevent the application of a no damage clause. They are effective to prevent liability for unreasonable delays as well. It is not the harshness of the results that is the touchstone of the effectiveness of such clause, but rather the scope of the delay contemplated by the parties at the time the contract was made.

§ 16.14 —Delays Contemplated by the Parties

If the delays encountered are found to be within the contemplation of the parties at the time they entered into the contract, the no damage clause will be enforced.

In *McDaniel v. Ashtown-Mardian Co.*[27] a subcontractor brought an action against the general contractor and its bonding company under the

---

[23] United States v. Spearin, 248 U.S. 132 (1918).

[24] Psaty & Fuhrman, Inc. v. Housing Auth., 76 R.I. 87, 68 A.2d 32 (1949) (cited in Annotation, 10 A.L.R.2d 789, 795 (1950)). *See* Annotation, *Delay in Building or construction contract,* 74 A.L.R.3d 187 (1976).

[25] Note, *The Enforceability of "No Damage for Delay Clauses" in Construction Contracts,* 28 Loy. L. Rev. 129 (1982); Cunningham Bros., Inc. v. City of Waterloo, 117 N.W.2d 46 (Iowa 1962).

[26] Cunningham Bros., Inc. v. City of Waterloo, 254 Iowa 659, 117 N.W.2d 46 (1962).

[27] 357 F.2d 511 (9th Cir. 1966).

Miller Act.[28] The subcontract was expressly made subject to the prime contract and the subcontract recognized within its own provisions that changes and additions might delay the work. The court held that the subcontractor could not recover damages from the general contractor for delays occasioned by proper change orders of the government because the general contractor and subcontractor both knew when they entered into the subcontract that it might very well not be completed within the time specified in the general contract. The court also held that the government might make changes that would necessarily extend the performance period, and that if any such changes authorized by the government should result in delay damages to the general contractor, no compensation for such damages could be recovered by the general contractor from the government.

In *Wes-Julian Construction Corp. v. Commonwealth*[29] a highway contractor petitioned to recover for extra work and increased costs and expenses from the State of Massachusetts. The court held that the contract provision giving the state power to delay commencement of the work "if it shall deem it best for its interests to do so" exculpated the state from liability for delay even if its actions were negligent, unreasonable, due to indecision, or arbitrary, willful, and capricious. In this case, the contractor had no claim for damages, but would have been entitled to an extension of time.

Western Engineers, Inc. v. State Road Commission[30] involved a situation in which the plaintiffs were to complete their performance in nine months, but did not complete until approximately 3½ years had elapsed. The court held that the no damage clause precluded recovery for damages. The contract clause provided that "no changes or claims for damages will be made by them for any delay or hindrances, of any cause whatsoever, during the progress of any portion of services specified in the agreement; such delays or hindrances, if any, shall be compensated for by an extension of time for such reasonable periods as the road commission may decide."[31]

§ 16.15 Exceptions to No Damage for Delay Clauses

Various exceptions have been held to preclude the application of the no damage for delay provisions found in construction contracts. They can be broadly classified as follows:

1. A delay that is the result of wrongful conduct, particularly fraud, bad faith, or active interference on the part of one seeking the benefit of the provision

---

[28] 40 U.S.C. § 270a.

[29] 351 Mass. 588, 223 N.E.2d 72 (1967).

[30] 20 Utah 2d 294, 437 P.2d 216 (1968).

[31] *Id.* at 296, 437 P.2d at 217.

2. A delay that has extended such an unreasonable length of time that the party delayed would have been justified in abandoning the contract
3. A delay not within the specifically enumerated delays to which the "no damage" clause is to apply and
4. A delay that, in light of the relationship of the parties and objective and attendant circumstances, was not intended or contemplated by the parties to be within the purview of the no damage provision.[32]

§ 16.16 —Active Interference

In *Peter Kiewit Sons' Co. v. Iowa Southern Utilities Co.*[33] the court, in addressing the concept of active interference, stated:

> It, therefore, would appear that to be guilty of "active interference" in the instant action, the defendants herein would have to have committed some affirmative, willful act, in bad faith to unreasonably interfere with plaintiffs' compliance with the terms of the construction contract. This court concludes that the use of the term "active" to modify "interference" by the Court in *Cunningham* was intentional, is significant, and clearly implies that more than a simple mistake, error in judgment, lack of total effort or lack of complete diligence is needed for plaintiff to prove the "active interference" necessary to render unenforceable an otherwise clear and unambiguous "no damage" clause.[34]

The *Peter Kiewit* court declined to find active interference when a general contractor engaged in an electric power plant construction brought suit against the owner and engineering contractor for expenses incurred because of interruptions in the construction. The court noted that in order for a plaintiff to recover due to construction delays of both a tortious and contractual nature, it must "prove that the delays charged in the complaint were the product of fraud, evil intent, improper motive or willfulness amounting to bad faith."[35]

In *Johnson v. State*[36] active interference was found. Over the protests of the contractor, the state opened the uncompleted roadway to traffic for the use of other contractors. It also actively interfered with the contractor's seeding and planting, which caused it to miss the planting season. The court found that the extra work and costs to which the contractor was subjected

---

[32] Annotation, *No Damage Clause-Delay,* 10 A.L.R.2d 801 (1950); Annotation, *Construction Delay-No Damage Clause,* 74 A.L.R.3d 187, 214–15 (1950); E.C. Ernst, Inc. v. Manhattan Constr. Co., 551 F.2d 1026 (5th Cir.), *cert. denied,* 434 U.S. 1067 (1977).

[33] 355 F. Supp. 376 (S.D. Iowa 1973).

[34] *Id.* at 399 (citations omitted).

[35] *Id.* at 398.

[36] 24 N.Y.2d 958, 250 N.E.2d 75, 302 N.Y.S.2d 489 (1969).

by reason of the state's action went far "beyond the cooperation required under the terms of the contract" and allowed recovery for damages by reason of the state's active and indirect interference with the performance of the work.

In *Grant Construction Co. v. Burns,*[37] because a contractor's work depended upon the removal of utility poles by third parties, the failure of the state highway department to schedule removal of the poles was held not to have been within the contemplation of the parties and thus constituted active interference. It is interesting to note that the court found the delay in the removal of the poles, once scheduled, *was* contemplated by the parties.

Bad faith was demonstrated in *United States Steel Corp. v. Missouri Pacific Railroad Co.,*[38] in which the court found active interference and held the railroad liable for damages suffered by a bridge builder that waited 120 days beyond its original start-up date to gain access to the jobsite. The court found that the railroad committed an affirmative, willful act in bad faith, which unreasonably interfered with the contractor's compliance with the terms of the contract, when it issued the contractor a notice to proceed, knowing that necessary substructure work would not be completed on time and knowing of the large numbers of commitments the contractor would make on the basis of the start-up order.

§ 16.17 —Active Interference Not Sufficient

New York's highest court has decided that active interference by the owner, standing alone, no longer warrants an exception to a no damage for delay clause. In *Kalisch-Jarcho, Inc. v. City of New York*[39] the heating, ventilating, and air conditioning (HVAC) contractor on a new police headquarters building sought damages because the job's completion was extended for an additional 28 months. The active interference alleged by the contractor included "endless" revisions of plans and drawings, the city's failure to coordinate the activities of the prime contractors, and other acts of omission or commission interfering with the sequence and timing of the work.

The court focused on the contract language, the intent of the parties, and the purported public policy surrounding no damage clauses. It found that the unambiguous contract language provided that the contractor was to make no claims for delay damages caused by any act or omission by the city. It determined that the clause's "unmistakable intent" was that the contractor was to absorb damages occasioned by contractee-caused delay, whether

[37] 92 Idaho 408, 443 P.2d 1005 (1968).

[38] 668 F.2d 435 (8th Cir.), *cert. denied,* 459 U.S. 836 (1982).

[39] 58 N.Y.2d 377, 448 N.E.2d 413, 461 N.Y.S.2d 746 (1983).

a reasonable or unreasonable delay.[40] Finally, the court acknowledged that such no damage clauses are commonly found in construction contracts and are enforced as a matter of public policy except in exceptional circumstances, such as fraud, malice, bad faith, or willful or gross negligence.

The court held that active interference alone was insufficient to show the gross negligence necessary to invalidate the no damage clause. The court found that, to meet that standard, the contractor would have to prove "the City acted in bad faith and with deliberate intent delayed the [contractor] in performance of his obligation."[41]

Kalisch-Jarcho is important because it indicates that the courts, at least in New York, will not make an exception to the no damage clause even when the fact finder determines that active interference caused the delays and caused the contractor unexpected additional costs.

Three interesting cases were decided after *Kalisch-Jarcho: Slattery Associates v. City of New York;*[42] *Bradley Environmental Contractors v. Village of Sylvan Beach;*[43] and *Corinno Civetta Construction Corp. v. City of New York.*[44] In *Slattery* the court failed to find an exception to a no damage clause when the contention that the city was guilty of intentional misconduct rested only on its alleged failure to provide adequate police protection for the jobsite.

In *Bradley* the contractor sued the Village for breach of contract in connection with a water pollution abatement project and water pollution control plant. The contractor sought damages resulting from the Village's delay in, among other things, approving shop drawings, materials, and vendors. The appellate division reversed the lower court's dismissal of these causes of action, which had been based on its finding that the actions were barred by a clause in the contract precluding recovery by the contractor for damages occasioned "by any delay on the part of the owner in doing the work or furnishing the material to be done or furnished by it." In reversing, the appeals court stated that "a no damage for delay clause must be strictly construed against the party seeking exemption from liability because of its own fault."[45]

In *Corinno* a sewer contractor sued the City for, among other things, delays resulting from the City's alleged interference with the contractor's work, failure to perform its own work in a punctual manner, and failure to coordinate the project properly, which forced the contractor to work

---

[40] *Id.* at 384, 448 N.E.2d at 416, 461 N.Y.S.2d at 749.

[41] *Id.* at 386, 448 N.E.2d at 418, 461 N.Y.S.2d at 751.

[42] 98 A.D.2d 686, 469 N.Y.S.2d 758 (1983).

[43] 98 A.D.2d 973, 470 N.Y.S.2d 214 (1983).

[44] 67 N.Y.2d 297, 493 N.E.2d 905, 502 N.Y.S.2d 681 (1986).

[45] Bradley Environmental Contractors v. Village of Sylvan Beach, 98 A.D.2d 973, 470 N.Y.S.2d 214, 215 (1983).

outside the normal sequence of construction. In deciding *Corinno,* the New York Court of Appeals limited the harsh *Kalisch-Jarcho* standard and held that the no damage for delay clauses in public work contracts encompassed only those delays that either were reasonably foreseeable, arose from the contractor's work during performance, or were mentioned in the contract. The *Corinno* court stated, "It can hardly be presumed, however, that the contractor bargained away his right to bring a claim for damages resulting from delays which the parties did not contemplate at the time."[46]

§ 16.18 —Delays Not Contemplated by the Parties

In most states, if the courts determine that the delay was caused by an occurrence not within the contemplation of the parties, the no damage for delay clause will be held inapplicable.

U.S. Industries, Inc. v. Blake Construction Co.[47] is a case in which the court, noting that exculpatory clauses generally are not favored, strictly construed a no damage clause to determine that the delay was neither intended nor contemplated by the parties to be within the purview of the no damage provision. The mechanical subcontract for construction of a hospital included a provision exculpating the contractor from liability for delay on the part of other contractors or subcontractors involved in the work or furnishing of materials. The court held that it did not immunize the prime contractor from damages for delay in erecting the steel structure of the building and its outer shell, which was allegedly caused by failure of the prime contractor's supplier to timely deliver the steel to the jobsite. The no damage clause in pertinent part stated that the "contractor shall not be liable for any damages that may occur from delays or other causes on the part of other contractors or subcontractors involved in work, or furnishing of materials pertaining to the project."[48] The court found that if the parties had intended to immunize the prime contractor from liability for delay caused by its suppliers and vendors, they easily could, and presumably would, have so provided.

In *Johnson v. City of New York*[49] the court determined that under a contract for sewer work (allowing the borough president to suspend work, without compensation to contractor, if he should deem it in the city's interest), the borough president was not authorized to suspend work because the city had made no appropriation to pay for the engineering and inspection it

[46] 67 N.Y.2d 297, 493 N.E.2d 905, 502 N.Y.S.2d 681, 686.

[47] 671 F.2d 539 (D.C. Cir. 1982).

[48] *Id.* at 543.

[49] 191 A.D. 205, 181 N.Y.S. 137 (1920).

was bound to furnish. The court found dispositive the fact that the city suspended the work because it failed in one of its obligations under the contract.

Corinno Civetta Construction v. City of New York[50] held that an exculpatory clause relieving the contractee from liability for delay damage will not bar claims resulting from delays caused by the contractee if the delays or their causes were not within the contemplation of the parties at the time they entered into the contract. The court in *Corinno* stated:

> The [no damage for delay] rule is not without its exceptions, however, and even exculpatory language which purports to preclude damages for *all* delays resulting from *any* cause whatsoever are not read literally . . . . Generally, even with such a clause, damages may be recovered for: (1) delays caused by the contractee's bad faith or its willful, malicious, or grossly negligent conduct, (2) uncontemplated delays, (3) delays so unreasonable that they constitute an intentional abandonment of the contract by the contractee, and (4) delays resulting from the contractee's breach of a fundamental obligation of the contract.[51]

In a recent case[52] citing *Corinno,* the court held that damages arising from delays caused by a contractee's bad faith or willful, malicious, or grossly negligent conduct are recoverable, irrespective of a clause generally exculpating the contractee from delay liability. The court noted that uncontemplated delays also give rise to a claim for damages despite the existence of an exculpatory clause.

§ 16.19 —Unreasonable or Excessive Period of Delay

If the period of delay is found to be unreasonable or excessive, the courts do not allow a no damage for delay clause to bar recovery, especially if the delay would have enabled the contractor to abandon the contract justifiably. In *John T. Brady & Co. v. Board of Education,*[53] a landmark case in New York prior to *Kalisch-Jarcho,* a contractor engaged to construct a public school in New York City within 350 days sued because of the city's unreasonable neglect in removing certain structures from the site of the proposed school. The court, despite the existence of a no damage clause,

---

[50] 67 N.Y.2d 297, 493 N.E.2d 905, 502 N.Y.S.2d 681 (1986).

[51] 502 N.Y.S.2d at 686.

[52] Spearin, Preston & Burrows, Inc. v. City of N.Y., 160 A.D.2d 263, 553 N.Y.S.2d 372 (1990).

[53] 222 A.D. 504, 226 N.Y.S. 707 (1928).

found the city's delay of eight months "sufficiently unreasonable to strike at the heart of the contract and justify the contractor in abandoning it."[54]

In *People ex rel. Wells & Newton Co. v. Craig*[55] a heating and ventilating contractor was delayed in excess of two years on a contract intended to be completed within 120 days. The court, notwithstanding a no damage clause, granted damages. The court ruled that such a clause "must be construed as inapplicable to delays so great or so unreasonable that they may fairly be deemed equivalent to an abandonment of the contract . . . ."[56]

§ 16.20 —Bad Faith or Fraud

If the delay is caused by the owner's misrepresentation, bad faith, or fraud, the resulting delay claims are not immunized by a no damage for delay clause.[57] The courts nullify the effects of a disclaimer when they find active misrepresentation on behalf of the party seeking the benefits of such clauses.[58] In *Warner Construction Corp. v. City of Los Angeles*[59] the court, in sustaining a claim for breach of warranty and fraudulent concealment, stated that a cause of action for nondisclosure of material facts arises when:

1. The defendant makes representations but does not disclose facts that materially qualify the facts disclosed or render the disclosure likely to mislead
2. The facts are known or accessible only to the defendant, and the defendant knows they are not known to or reasonably discoverable by the plaintiff or
3. The defendant actively conceals facts from discovery by the plaintiff.

The court found the city liable in all three instances.

An owner's extreme negligence, which the court found to approach willful negligence, has been held actionable by a contractor. In *Ozark Dam Constructors v. United States*[60] a joint venture contracted to build a dam for which the government was to supply the cement. The government, faced with a strike by the railroad transporting the cement, made absolutely no provisions for alternate transportation until three days after the strike had begun. The court found determinative that "the possible consequences

---

[54] 226 N.Y.S. at 709.

[55] 232 N.Y. 125, 133 N.E. 419 (1921).

[56] *Id.* at 143.

[57] *See* Annotation, *Construction Delay—No Damage Clause,* 74 A.L.R.3d 187 (1976).

[58] County Asphalt, Inc. v. State, 40 A.D.2d 26, 337 N.Y.S.2d 415 (1972).

[59] 2 Cal. 3d 285, 466 P.2d 996, 85 Cal. Rptr. 444 (1970).

[60] 127 F. Supp. 187 (Ct. Cl. 1955).

were so serious, and the action necessary was so slight, that the neglect was almost wilful. It showed a complete lack of consideration for the interest of the [contractor]."[61]

In *Edwin J. Dobson, Jr., Inc. v. State,*[62] the New Jersey appellate court held that the "active interference" exception to a no damage for delay clause was allowable only if the public agency acted in bad faith and evinced evil-mindedness. The plaintiff contractor in that case had requested a substitution for the piping called for in the contract. The state rejected the request for substitute piping, threatening to buy the pipe itself and charge the plaintiff with the price and a penalty. The contractor then ordered the pipe from the specified manufacturer, but it was delivered late. The contractor sued the state for delay damages and the state raised the defense of a no damage for delay clause. The trial court found that the state official had acted in bad faith and thereby interfered in the contract. The appellate division reversed this finding by requiring an incredibly high level of bad faith: the contractor must establish that the official acted with "evil-mindedness."

The court found that the no damage clause was a bar to recovery because the state had not acted intentionally, willfully, or in bad faith. Absent reprehensible behavior or an affirmative, willful act in bad faith, the clause would be enforced. The court used an almost impossibly high standard of bad faith, a subjective test equating "evil-mindedness" with bad faith.

In a recent New York case, *Earthbank Co. v. City of New York,*[63] the court held that the no damage for delay clause in a public contract did not bar a contractor's claim for payments above the unit price for additional work when the court found that the additional work resulted from the city's misrepresentation that it had secured an appropriate permit for the excavation of tidal wetlands.

§ 16.21 —Concurrent Delays Attributable to Both Parties

Frequently, the responsibility for the delay in a construction project cannot be attributed solely to either one of the parties, but rests in some measure with both. In some cases, if both the owner and the contractor proximately contribute to the same delay, neither party is allowed to recover. For example, in the case of *J.A. Jones Construction Co. v. Greenbriar Shopping Center*[64] the contractor contributed to the delay when its subcontractor failed to perform on time. The owner contributed to the delay with repetitive

---

[61] *Id.* at 189.

[62] 218 N.J. Super. 123, 526 A.2d 1150 (App. Div. 1987).

[63] 78 N.Y.2d 855, 598 N.E.2d 443, 549 N.Y.S.2d 314 (1989).

[64] 332 F. Supp. 1336 (N.D. Ga. 1971), *aff'd,* 461 F.2d 1269 (5th Cir. 1972).

design changes and late delivery of the architect's drawings. The court refused to allow the owner to collect liquidated damages and denied the contractor the delay costs.[65] This so-called *rule against apportionment* states that under a liquidated damages provision against delay, when the owner has contributed to delays on the project, it may not apportion the fault and forfeits all right to recovery under the provision.

This rule has been adopted by some jurisdictions but rejected by others.[66] For example, in *E.C. Ernst, Inc. v. Manhattan Construction Co.*[67] the Fifth Circuit, applying Alabama law, held that an owner was entitled to liquidated damages for delay in completion of a construction contract although it had contributed to such delays itself.

In a well-reasoned opinion presenting the modern trend, the court in *United States v. William F. Klingensmith, Inc.*,[68] apportioned damages between a subcontractor and a contractor when both were found to have contributed to the cause of the delay. The court determined that the general contractor had violated its contractual obligations to its subcontractor on a parking garage by failing to coordinate the work of a subcontractor adequately and failing to provide sufficient supervisory personnel on the job, although the subcontract contained no completion date. The court also determined that the subcontractor breached the subcontract by contributing to the delays.

The court held that "where each party delays the other, it follows that each should be able to recover to the extent of the injury caused by the other's delay."[69] The court felt that such a rule protects each party from losses caused by the delay of the other throughout the period of performance. It also induces each party to avoid imposing such losses on the other at any time during the period of delay.

Addressing itself to the rule against apportionment, the court stated:

> [A] rule precluding a party from recovering damages for delay, once the party itself delays, would leave the parties to a contract unnecessarily vulnerable to delay by the other. We see no wisdom in, nor authority for such a rule of preclusion. Therefore, when both parties to a contract breach their contractual obligations by delaying performance, a court must assess the losses attributable to each party's delay and apportion damages accordingly.[70]

---

[65] *See* 17A C.J.S. *Contracts* § 502 (1963).

[66] Annotation, *Building Contract-Liquidated Damages,* 152 A.L.R. 1349 (1944).

[67] 551 F.2d 1026 (5th Cir.), *cert. denied,* 434 U.S. 1067 (1977).

[68] 670 F.2d 1227 (D.C. Cir. 1982).

[69] The court noted that neither party claimed that its own delay was caused by the other party's delays. The court indicated that if such a claim were asserted, it would relate both to the claimant's responsibility for its own delay and the other party's responsibility for the delay. *Id.* at 1230. *See* 6A Corbin, Contracts § 1264 (2d ed. 1964).

[70] United States v. William F. Klingensmith, Inc., 670 F.2d 1227, 1231.

When there are concurrent delays by both owner and contractor, the latter is still entitled to a time extension.

§ 16.22 Excusable Delays of the Contractor

Excusable delays are those delays created by events beyond the control of either the contractor or the owner for which neither can be held responsible. When a delay is excusable, neither party can recover damages and the contractor may not be held in default. Examples of excusable delays would be those caused by unusually severe weather and acts of God such as tornadoes, floods, or earthquakes.

§ 16.23 —Unforeseeability

An essential element of all excusable delays is that they are caused by an unforeseen occurrence. In *United States v. Brooks-Calloway Co.*[71] the contractor sought to be relieved of liquidated damages based upon his defense that his work on a levee had been delayed by floods. The lower court found the contractor not at fault. However, the Supreme Court reversed and sent the case back to the lower court for further consideration, holding that there was no finding that the floods were unforeseeable (in fact, high water was found to have been predicted), which was necessary if the contractor was to be free of liability.

§ 16.24 —Unusually Severe Weather

In a government board of contract appeals case, *Herman H. Neumann,*[72] the board considered the question of a delay caused by weather and granted a time extension when it found that the delay was caused by unforeseeable and unusually severe weather.

The key to determining whether severe weather will give rise to a time extension is the unusual nature of the weather for the particular geographical area involved. Acts of God include unusually severe weather. By definition they are unforeseeable and beyond the control of the contractor. Therefore, the contractor cannot be held responsible for failing to perform because of such disturbances. Natural disasters such as earthquakes, unforeseeable floods, and tornadoes would all be classified as acts of God.

---

[71] 318 U.S. 120 (1943).

[72] 70-1 B.C.A. (CCH) ¶ 8216 (1970).

§ 16.25 —Labor Disputes

Labor disputes or strikes that are unforeseeable may excuse the delay, but usually only if the contract contains a provision protecting against a delay caused by a strike. If there is a *no strike* reference in the time extension clause, the contractor will be liable for delay damages to the owner.

In *Fritz Rumer Cooke Co. v. United States*[73] the court considered a "construction type" contract between the contractor and the United States, covering the removal and loading of railroad track from an area near a gaseous diffusion plant. The contract contained no provision protecting against delay caused by strike. The contractor was required to complete its undertaking without right of recovery against the United States for any damages that might be sustained by reason of a strike at the plant; during the course of that strike, a picket line was set up, which the contractors' employees observed. The government claimed that it provided the contractor with access to the jobsite, which remained available during the picketing. The court held: "It has long been a well-settled rule of law that if a party by his contract charges himself with an obligation possible to be performed, unforeseen difficulties, however great, will not excuse him, unless the performance is rendered impossible by Act of God, the law or the other party."[74]

ACCELERATION CLAIMS

§ 16.26 Acceleration Defined

Many contractors' claims are based upon the theory of *acceleration.* Although relatively dated, perhaps one of the clearest descriptions of these costs is found in a government report:[75]

> Acceleration costs are described as those additional costs incurred by a contractor to overcome excusable delays, including those caused by the addition of extensive modifications work, within the time limits originally established in the contract to meet the relatively inflexible completion dates set by the [owner]. Acceleration costs are paid for multiple shift operations, and other increased operating expenses related to the performance or the work on an accelerated time schedule.

---

[73] 279 F.2d 200 (6th Cir. 1960).

[74] *Id.* at 201.

[75] Controller General's Report to the Congress, *Review of the Administration of Construction of Certain Launch Facilities for the Atlas and Titan Intercontinental Ballistic Missile at Selected Air Force Bases* 31–32 (Jan. 1963).

Another good definition is provided by the court in *Contracting & Material Co. v. City of Chicago,*[76] which stated:

> Acceleration is the process by which the material or ordinary progress of events is quickened. In the case of a contract, acceleration occurs when the contractor speeds up his work so that he is performing the job at a faster rate than prescribed in the original contract. Commonly acceleration is achieved by working overtime or working double shifts. Acceleration costs, as claimed by plaintiff, are costs incurred by virtue of acceleration.

§ 16.27 Actual and Constructive Acceleration

There are basically two types of acceleration, *actual* and *constructive.* The former is easy to identify: it occurs when the contractor is directed to accelerate its work by adding workers, working weekends, evenings, and so on.

Constructive acceleration does not result from a direct order from the owner, but results from the owner's refusal to allow a rightfully entitled time extension. With constructive acceleration, no order or directive is given, but the contractor is required to accelerate its work in order to keep pace with the job or to complete its work by the contract completion date. A typical constructive acceleration claim situation arises when the contracting officer or architect refuses to act on the contractor's time extension request, requiring the contractor to accelerate, when in fact the contractor is entitled to the extension.

Another common scenario is when the owner's agent tells the contractor that it will consider the time extension request at the end of the job. This benevolent gesture places the contractor in the predicament of not knowing what to do. If it waits until job completion for the agent's decision, then it runs the risk of exposing itself to liquidated damages or other damage claims by the owner if the time extension request is rejected. If it chooses to accelerate, it will normally be entitled to recover its costs on a constructive acceleration claim, provided it notifies the owner it is accelerating the work.

In both these situations, however, the contractor's problem is the same. When a time extension request is rejected, the contractor has only two choices: it can finish its work late or it can accelerate to meet the schedule imposed upon it.

In *Wallace Process Piping Co. v. Martin-Marietta Corp.*[77] the court recognized acceleration costs while determining equitable adjustments in government contracts. The court was careful to state that acceleration costs are

---

[76] 20 Ill. App. 3d 684, 692, 314 N.E.2d 598, 604 (1974), *rev'd on other grounds,* 64 Ill. 2d 21, 349 N.E.2d 389 (1976).

[77] 251 F. Supp. 411 (E.D. Va. 1965).

allowable only for efforts to overcome excusable delays. However, in this case the court did not grant acceleration costs for Wallace's claim for its excess labor costs because Wallace did not establish by a preponderance of the evidence that its directions to accelerate were the sole cause, or even the primary cause, for costs in excess of those for which it had already received compensation.

The *Wallace* court then held that an order to complete additional work, without an extension of time, which made necessary a work week in excess of the 50 hours upon which the subcontract price was based, was a change within the meaning of the subcontract. Therefore, the subcontractor was entitled to be compensated for overtime or premium pay resulting from orders to accelerate the work.

Acceleration costs have been recognized by the courts in equitable adjustments of private contracts as well. In *Natkin & Co. v. George A. Fuller Co.*[78] the court held that the insistence by the owner and the prime contractor (implemented by threats and withholding of the subcontractor's progress payment) that the subcontractor either add workers or go on overtime to complete the work, including change order work at a time when certain delays were known to have occurred, constituted a change under the contract. Thus, the subcontractor was entitled to recover additional costs incurred for and as a result of such acceleration.

Acceleration claims were also allowed in *Nat Harrison Associates, Inc. v. Gulf States Utilities Co.*[79] The defendant indicated to the plaintiff-contractor that no extension of time for delay would be permitted and directed it to provide additional manpower and equipment to maintain the original work schedule. (Harrison had agreed to construct approximately 158 miles of transmission line in Louisiana for Gulf States Utilities). Although the contract allowed for time extensions for delays attributable to "strikes and other unavoidable casualties," and Harrison was delayed due to inclement weather, strikes, and other unavoidable causes, Harrison's requests for extensions were either ignored or refused by Gulf States. Thus, the court allowed Harrison's acceleration damages claim.

In *Contracting & Material Co. v. City of Chicago*[80] the contractor claimed it was forced into an abbreviated performance schedule resulting in overtime expenses when the owner wrongfully and inequitably refused to extend the contract performance date to reflect delays caused by a 46-day suspension order and a 51-day strike. The court held that the owner's refusal to recognize that an excusable delay had occurred, its refusal to grant a legitimate time extension, and its insistence that the contractor was

[78] 347 F. Supp. 17 (W.D. Mo. 1972).

[79] 491 F.2d 578 (5th Cir. 1974).

[80] 64 Ill. App. 2d 21, 349 N.E.2d 389 (1976).

obligated to complete the work on the original completion date constituted a constructive acceleration.

In *Mobil Chemical Co. v. Blount Bros. Corp.*[81] the United States Court of Appeals for the Fifth Circuit held that the general contractor was equally liable with the owner of the project for damages sustained by the subcontractors. The court found that unlike the typical general contractor, this general contractor undertook no actual construction. Under its fixed-price contract it acted as a construction manager and stood only to gain by acceleration and by rapid completion of the project.

In this case, the owner and the general contractor engaged in a joint effort to push the subcontractors to an early completion date by overmanning and by acceleration. The owner even threatened to blackball several contractors if they did not add workers. The court divided the liability equally between the owner and the general contractor. This case sends a warning to general contractors faced with acceleration pressures from the owner. Before taking sides with the owner and compelling the subcontractors to accelerate, the general contractor should realize that by doing so it may be imposing acceleration liability upon itself that perhaps can be avoided by negotiating the appropriate extensions of time.

§ 16.28 Disallowance of Acceleration Damage Claims

Acceleration claims are disallowed when contract performance is behind schedule because of the contractor's own action or delay. In *Tri-Cor, Inc. v. United States,*[82] although the contracting officer notified the contractor that contract performance was behind schedule, and directed the contractor to take whatever steps were necessary to meet the completion dates, the contractor was not entitled to a price adjustment based on additional acceleration costs because it was not entitled to a time extension. Likewise, in *Siefford v. Housing Authority,*[83] acceleration was denied when the contractor was substantially and continually behind schedule under the contract, and the delay was not caused by the owner's breach of contract or willful hindrance of the contractor's work.

In *Johnson Controls, Inc. v. National Valve & Manufacturing Co.,*[84] a case decided under Oklahoma law, a subcontractor was denied claims for additional expense it incurred for acceleration, because it failed to make written

---

[81] 809 F.2d 1175 (5th Cir. 1987).

[82] 458 F.2d 112 (Ct. Cl. 1972).

[83] 192 Neb. 643, 223 N.W.2d 816 (1974).

[84] 569 F. Supp. 758 (E.D. Okla. 1983).

application for an extension of time and for compensation due to acceleration, although such was required by the contract.

In this case, the subcontractor contracted with the prime contractor to provide certain instrumentation work on a power plant project located near Hugo, Oklahoma. The terms of the prime contract between owner and contractor were incorporated into the subcontract. The prime contract contained a rather common clause allowing the owner to make changes to the work and requiring the contractor to give the owner written notice of time extensions resulting from the changes, and estimates of any additional costs resulting therefrom. This clause also provided for a waiver of the contractor's right to additional compensation or a time extension if the contractor failed to give written notice in advance of performance of the changed work.

The prime contractor's actual performance fell substantially behind schedule, thus delaying the subcontractor's work. In order to meet the mandatory deadline, the subcontractor accelerated its performance by tripling its work force, working overtime and weekends, and adding a night shift. It then sought additional compensation for the acceleration and extra work it had performed. The contract provided and the parties had agreed that Oklahoma law would govern. The subcontractor argued, however, that because no existing Oklahoma cases dealt with acceleration of work claims, federal government contract law should be applied. Specifically, the subcontractor urged the court to follow *Norair Engineering Corp. v. United States,*[85] wherein a prima facie case for increased costs of acceleration under a changes clause was established when the contractor demonstrated: that any delays giving rise to the order of acceleration were excusable; that the contractor was ordered to accelerate; and that the contractor in fact accelerated performance and incurred extra costs. A specific advance request for an extension of time or for additional compensation was not required in *Norair,* however.

The court rejected the use of federal law in the matter, holding that Oklahoma indicated clearly its desire for strict compliance with the unambiguous terms of a contract, that the changes provision was not ambiguous, and that the parties had agreed that Oklahoma law would govern this contract. The court cited Oklahoma case law and concluded that: "If a contract unambiguously requires written application for additional compensation, then that requirement is a condition precedent to recovering additional compensation . . . . When a party makes a contract and reduces it to writing, he must abide by its plainly stated terms."[86]

---

[85] 666 F.2d 546 (Ct. Cl. 1981).

[86] Johnson Controls, Inc. v. National Valve & Mfg. Co., 569 F. Supp. 758, 761 (E.D. Okla. 1983).

Johnson Controls points out the necessity for a contractor to scrutinize its contract and follow the notice requirements contained in these provisions.

OTHER DAMAGE CLAIMS

§ 16.29 Changed Conditions

Another common ground for contractors' claims for damages is changed conditions, a problem that usually also involves delays. Changed condition clauses are common to many public and private contracts, and are intended to provide the contractor with a means of protecting itself against unexpected subsurface conditions while at the same time protecting the owner from inflated prices needed to cover the unexpected conditions. *Changed conditions clauses* provide for a price adjustment and time extension if the contractor encounters materially different subsurface or latent physical conditions than those anticipated. In the absence of a changed conditions clause or a quality variation clause,[87] most jurisdictions will deny the contractor a price adjustment for substantial quantity changes unless there has been fraud or misrepresentation by the owner.

In *Depot Construction Corp. v. State*[88] an excavation contractor had agreed to a unit price for the removal of what was expected to be 1,000 cubic yards of rock. When the job was finished, 3,000 cubic yards had been excavated, the work had stretched into winter, and additional as well as different equipment had been required. The court held that the contractor was limited to the contract unit price even in the face of a lower court's findings that the test borings were clearly adequate. The court reasoned that the existence of the unit price contract, with clear language stating that there were no representations as to the amount of work to be performed, conclusively demonstrated that the parties, each of whom had the same information at their disposal, considered all the contingencies.

In *P.J. Maffei Building Wrecking Corp. v. United States*[89] a demolition contractor prepared its bid on the demolition and removal of the United States Pavilion from the 1964 World's Fair site by relying on drawings referred to in the invitation to bid as "for information only," which were specifically not made part of the contract. The invitation to bid specifically stated: "The quantity, quality, completeness, accuracy and availability of

---

[87] A *quality variation clause* is generally provided in unit price contracts and acts to set percentage limits for both increases and decreases, beyond which percentage adjustments are not permitted.

[88] 19 N.Y.2d 109, 224 N.E.2d 866, 278 N.Y.S.2d 363 (1969).

[89] 732 F.2d 913 (Fed. Cir. 1984).

this drawing are not guaranteed." The court denied the contractor's claim under the changes provision of the contract, noting that the contractor's reliance on the documents was not reasonable when the invitation to bid was replete with caveats to the effect that documents in question were not in the possession of the federal government and would not be part of the contract documents.

In *Fattore Co. v. Metropolitan Sewerage Commission Co.*[90] the court awarded substantial damages of $1.5 million to a sewer contractor under a changed condition and equitable adjustment provision of the contract. The court reasoned that when a government entity seeks to reduce its contract costs by making borings and providing the information to bidders, it is deemed to warrant the adequacy of its plans and specifications to the extent that compliance therewith will result in satisfactory performance.

In *Borell v. Municipality of Metropolitan Seattle*[91] a contractor brought suit against a municipality for extra compensation for laying pipe at locations with unexpected soil conditions. The contract did not contain a changed conditions clause. In fact, it contained express disclaimers with respect to any representations concerning subsurface conditions. Moreover, it expressly provided that no payment would be made over contract price on account of differences between contract soil information and conditions disclosed at the site. The court denied recovery.

§ 16.30 Low Bidder Claims

In government contract cases, the unmistakable trend appears to be that a low bidder who was wrongfully denied the contract can recover its bid preparation costs. In *Scanwell Laboratories, Inc. v. Thomas*[92] the court reiterated that suits by disappointed bidders for bid preparation costs "are founded in an implied contract between the government and its bidders under which the government agrees to consider each bid fairly and honestly in return for the bidder's submission of an eligible bid."[93] Although noting that the court of claims consistently denies recovery of lost profits,[94] the *Scanwell* court, without accepting or rejecting the contractor's tort claim for lost profits, held that the claim fell within one of the exceptions to government liability of the Tort Claims Act.

In *Keco Industries, Inc. v. United States*[95] the court held that the ultimate standard in deciding whether an unsuccessful low bidder is entitled to be

---

[90] 505 F.2d 1 (7th Cir. 1974).

[91] 698 F.2d 1229 (9th Cir. 1983).

[92] 521 F.2d 941 (D.C. Cir. 1975), *cert. denied,* 425 U.S. 910 (1976).

[93] *Id.* at 946.

[94] *See, e.g.,* McCarty Corp. v. United States, 499 F.2d 633 (Ct. Cl. 1974).

[95] 492 F.2d 1200 (Ct. Cl. 1974).

compensated for the expense of undertaking the bidding process is whether the government conduct toward the bidder/claimant was arbitrary and capricious. In determining whether the government's behavior was arbitrary and capricious, the court addressed four general criteria:

> One is that subjective bad faith on the part of procuring officials, depriving a bidder of the fair and honest consideration of his proposal normally warrants recovery of bid preparation costs . . . . A second is that proof that there was "no reasonable basis" for the administrative decision will also suffice at least in many situations . . . . The third is that the degree of proof of error necessary for recovery is ordinarily related to the amount of discretion entrusted to the procurement officials by applicable statutes and regulations . . . . The fourth is that proven violation of pertinent statutes or regulations can but need not necessarily be a ground for recovery . . . . The application of these four general principles may well depend on (1) the type of error or dereliction committed by the government and (2) whether the error or dereliction occurred with respect to the claimant's own bid or that of its competition.[96]

ASSERTING DAMAGE CLAIMS

§ 16.31 Strict Adherence to Contract Provisions

A contractor or subcontractor should be extremely mindful of any and all contract provisions restricting its rights to pursue claims for damages. Such clauses, discussed in §§ **16.32** through **16.34**, must be strictly adhered to in order for a claim to be considered.

§ 16.32 Delay and Time Extension Clauses

All modern contracts spell out the time of commencement, contract calendar days allotted for performance of the work, and the dates for substantial and final completion. More sophisticated contracts will designate the method of scheduling to be used (for example, CPM). Generally, these contracts also provide for specific periodic updating and revisions to progress schedules. Failure to comply with these updating provisions can negate or void an otherwise viable delay claim.

Time extension clauses generally set out the causes for which the owner agrees to allow an extension of contract time. These causes are for acts and circumstances beyond the control of the contractor, that is, strikes, acts of

---

[96] *Id.* at 1204.

God, unusually severe weather, and so on.[97] When presenting a time extension request or delay claim, the contractor must be sure that it is cast in terms that track the contractual agreements.

§ 16.33 Notice and Deadline Clauses

Customarily, the changes, changed conditions, disputes, and time extension clauses all contain notice requirements. Because notice requirements are usually mandatory, failure to comply may result in a waiver of the claim. Frequently, in public contracts, there are also *follow-up notice clauses* that require even more; for instance, a detailed statement of all claims, to be submitted with the final payment requisitions, is often mandated.

A contractor should consider deadline clauses to be the same as contract limitations. As an example, in certain federal contracts containing a 30-day period to appeal from a contracting officer's final decision, the courts have held that failure to comply with this deadline provision was fatal to the contractor's claim, regardless of the merit of the appeal.

§ 16.34 When Time Is of the Essence

As a general rule, time is not of the essence in a construction contract in the absence of a provision in the contract making it such. When time is of the essence, the party not performing on time is liable for damages resulting from the delay. However, an express statement, using those exact words, is not really necessary to indicate that time is of the essence in a contract. As expressed by Professor Corbin:

> Again, the agreement may be in such terms that the first party promises performance by a stated time and the second party expressly makes its return promise conditional on the exact performance; in such a case, failure by the first to perform on time gives to the second a right to damages and also the legal privilege of not performing his own promise. And still further, although the second party's return promise may not be in terms conditional, it may be made so by construction of law because the first party's failure to perform on time will deprive the second of the substantial benefit for which he bargained.[98]

There is little doubt that time was of the essence in *General Insurance Co. of America v. Hercules Construction Co.*[99] Here, the general contractor

[97] See §§ **16.22–16.25**.

[98] 3A Corbin, Contracts § 713 (1951) (discussion of "When Is Time of the Essence").

[99] 385 F.2d 13 (8th Cir. 1967).

contracted with the owner to construct a parking structure in St. Louis, Missouri. That general contractor signed a subcontract whereby the subcontractor agreed to supply it with custom precast concrete components, which were to comprise a substantial portion of the parking structure. The subcontract specifically directed attention to the fact that the target date for completion of the entire project was August 1, 1962, and that completion of the project was contingent upon adherence to the progress schedule for the subcontractor's phase of the work. Delivery of the precast components was to commence approximately January 6, 1962, and be completed approximately April 15 of that year. The subcontractor was made aware by express provisions in the subcontract and by subsequent dealings with the general contractor that timely delivery in proper sequence of the precast components was an overriding feature of the agreement.

The subcontractor breached the subcontract. Delivery was one month late to start and almost five months late on final delivery. Furthermore, almost 25 percent of the precast units delivered were defective. The general contractor thereby incurred extra costs in the area of labor, erection equipment, costs, premium time, and additional construction costs. The court held that ultimate acceptance of the parking structure by the owner without penalty to the general contractor for a two-month delay in completion was irrelevant to whether the general contractor was entitled to recover on the subcontractor's bond for extra costs it incurred because of the breach, considering that time was of the essence.

This case is noteworthy because it refers to a surety's liability for delay damages and also because it clearly illustrates that a subcontractor can be liable for delay damages even though the general contractor is exonerated for delay damages by the owner.

PROOF OF DAMAGES

§ 16.35 Actual Damages

Once the contractor or subcontractor has established its claim, the next step is the proof of damages to sustain the claim. Various legal theories of damages are regularly sustained by the courts.

A contractor may recover damages for breach of contract only for such losses as were reasonably foreseeable at the time of execution of the contract.[100] In other words, the contractor must demonstrate either that such losses are those usually flowing from the type of contract that was breached

---

[100] Hadley v. Baxendale, 156 Eng. Rep. 145 (1854).

or that the breaching party had reason to know, through some form of communication or otherwise, that such special losses would occur.[101]

Generally, damages need not be proved with mathematical certainty but rather by "whatever degree of certainty the case permits."[102] Proof of damages may consist of reasonable possibilities and inferences[103] but cannot be based on "mere speculation, guess or conjecture."[104] There must be a logical nexus between the amount of damages demanded and the proof presented.[105] Basically, a contractor must prove its damages with a reasonable degree of certainty.

A concise and clear test on the law of proof of damages as it relates to the aspect of certainty is set forth in *M&R Contractors & Builders v. Michael.*[106] There, the court said:

> Courts have modified the "certainty" rule into a more flexible one of "reasonable certainty." In such instances, recovery may often be based on opinion evidence, in the legal sense of that term, from which liberal inferences may be drawn. Generally, proof of actual or even estimated costs is all that is required with certainty.
>
> Some of the modifications which have been aimed at avoiding the harsh requirements of the "certainty" rule include: (a) if the fact of damage is proven with certainty, the extent or the amount thereof may be left to reasonable inference; (b) where a defendant's wrong has caused the difficulty of proving damage, he cannot complain of the resulting uncertainty; (c) mere difficulty in ascertaining the amount of damage is not fatal; (d) mathematical precision in fixing the exact amount of damage is not required; (e) it is sufficient if the best evidence of the damage which is available is produced; and (f) the plaintiff is entitled to recover the value of his contract as measured by the value of his profits.[107]

§ 16.36 Total Cost Method

One method which has been used to calculate damages is the *total cost method,* whereby the contractor takes actual job costs less anticipated bid costs or contract price to arrive at actual damages. The courts have

---

[101] *See also* Restatement of Contracts § 330 (1932); Restatement (Second) of Contracts § 351 (1981).

[102] John E. Green Plumbing & Heating Co. v. Turner Constr., 742 F.2d 965 (6th Cir. 1984) (quoting Shakin v. Buskirk, 454 Mich. 490, 93 N.W.2d 293 (1958)).

[103] E.C. Ernst, Inc. v. Koppers Co., 626 F.2d 324 (3d Cir. 1980).

[104] Zirin Lab. Int'l v. Mead-Johnson & Co., 208 F. Supp. 633 (E.D. Mich. 1962).

[105] Manshul Constr. Co. v. Dormitory Auth., 79 A.D.2d 383, 436 N.Y.S.2d 724 (1981).

[106] 215 Md. 340, 138 A.2d 350 (1958).

[107] 138 A.2d at 335.

sanctioned the use of this method when they feel no other method is available;[108] however, they acknowledge that it is not the preferred method of calculating damages.[109]

Due to the unreliability of the total cost method, some courts permit its use only under the following circumstances:

1. If the nature of the particular losses makes it impossible or highly impractical to determine such costs with a reasonable degree of accuracy by any other means
2. If the contractor's bid or estimate is proven to be realistic
3. If the contractor's actual costs are reasonable and
4. If the contractor was not responsible for the additional expenses.[110]

The total cost method of proving delay damages is not an equal substitute for the well-accepted actual cost method. The burden of proving the four elements listed above can be as cumbersome as proving actual costs. Thus, when possible, the contractor should document the impact of the delays he encounters on any given project, as well as the costs he incurs because of those delays. In the end, it will be easier to prove delay damages under the actual cost method.

The majority view rejects this method because, to accept it, one must assume that the claimants' original bid estimate was reasonable, that the claimants' costs were reasonable, and that the claimants were not responsible for any of the increased costs.[111] The courts realize that such is not always the case, and there are too many unknowns that creep into this theory of damages.

Sections 16.37 through **16.42** cover various measures of damages recoverable when a contractor or subcontractor demonstrates that each is applicable to its particular theory of damages.

§ 16.37 —Labor Costs

The contractor may experience increased labor costs, both because of additional man-hours expended on the job and as a result of escalated wages needed for premium pay for overtime and/or increased union wages. Additionally, if out-of-sequence work is performed, and added workers or

[108] *See* Joseph Pickard's Sons Co. v. United States, 532 F.2d 739 (Ct. Cl. 1946).

[109] *See* Moorehead Constr. Co. v. City of Grand Fortis, 508 F.2d 1008 (8th Cir. 1973).

[110] U.S. Steel v. Construction Aggregates Corp., 559 F. Supp. 414 (E.D. Mich. 1983).

[111] F.H. McGraw & Co. v. United States, 130 F. Supp. 394 (Ct. Cl. 1955); Oliver-Finnie Co. v. United States, 279 F.2d 498 (Ct. Cl. 1960); Fattore Co. v. Metropolitan Sewerage Comm'n, 505 F.2d 1 (7th Cir. 1974).

overtime is used to accelerate the work, the contractor will most likely experience diminished productivity from its labor force.

§ 16.38 —Material Costs

When a contractor is delayed, more often than not its material costs increase, sometimes sharply, especially in inflationary periods. Three methods are used to demonstrate additional material costs:

1. Comparison of the material costs on the days it should have been purchased with actual costs
2. The use of indices
3. The cost of replacing vendors who have defaulted or refused to honor quoted prices.

If the contractor had materials on hand or specially fabricated for the project, it is entitled to demurrage and storage costs.

§ 16.39 —Jobsite Indirect Costs

Jobsite indirect costs are the costs of maintaining the jobsite, including supervisory and personnel costs, field engineer costs, field office costs, costs of rental equipment, and watchmen services. These costs usually can be allocated to a specific project without difficulty.

§ 16.40 —Home Office Overhead

Costs for extended home office overhead have been the subject of much litigation. Since it was first introduced in 1960, the *Eichleay*[112] formula and its variations have become very popular in construction contract litigation, but in the past few years the formula has drawn increasing criticism regarding its true usefulness as an exclusive and singular means for computing delay damages. Even though *Eichleay* has met its share of challenges in the last 10 years, no discussion of delay damages is complete without some explanation of the formula which, up to recent time, was used in almost all delay claims. Moreover, the appropriate use of an *Eichleay*-type formula, coupled with supplemental evidence of a relationship between home office expenses and the delay, should still prove effective in proving

---

[112] Eichleay Corp., 60-2 B.C.A. (CCH) ¶ 2688 (ASBCA 1960).

delay damages. The basic *Eichleay*-type approach can be reduced to three simple steps in equation form:

Step 1:

Contract billing (total company billing for original contract period)	×	Total home office overhead for contract period	=	Home office overhead allocable to contract

Step 2:

Allocable overhead (days of contract performance)	×	Daily home office overhead allocable to project

Step 3:

Daily overhead rate	×	Number of days of compensable project delay	=	Total compensable extended home office overhead

Over the years, the courts and the boards have criticized contractors' sole and exclusive reliance on the *Eichleay* formula on the grounds that it does not provide a logical nexus between what is proved and the damages the fact finder is requested to determine.

In *Berley Industries, Inc. v. City of New York*[113] the highest court in New York held that the *Eichleay* formula was insufficient, insofar as it was offered as a substitute for direct evidence, to establish that the plaintiff sustained delay damages for increased home office overhead expenses during the period it was unable to start on the project after receiving the notice to proceed. There was no showing that delay caused an increase in home office overhead activity or expense of any kind and no attempt was made to show that the formula was logically calculated to produce a fair estimate of actual damages.

In *Savoy Construction Co. v. United States*[114] the court, although applying the *Eichleay* formula, noted its shortcomings, that is, its lack of mathematical precision and the failure to relate compensable delay to alleged increased home office overhead.

Therefore, the contractor should use an approach that clearly demonstrates a direct cause/effect correlation between delay and home office overhead. In New York cases decided after *Berley,* the courts have approved of the use of various formulas if the plaintiff first demonstrates that: the

---

[113] 45 N.Y.2d 63, 385 N.E.2d 281, 412 N.Y.S.2d 589 (1978).

[114] 80-1 B.C.A. (CCH) ¶ 392 (ASBCA), *motion for reconsideration denied,* 80-1 B.C.A. (CCH) ¶ 14,724 (ASBCA 1980).

defendant was responsible for the delay; such delays caused delays in completion of the contract; and the plaintiff suffered damages because of such delays, resulting in increased home office overhead. In these cases the courts approved the use of the formulas because they were vital in furnishing some rational basis for the court to estimate such damages, considering that precise measure was not possible.[115]

§ 16.41 —Finance Costs

Finance costs are those costs the contractor encounters as a result of not receiving its money in a timely manner. If the contractor is forced to borrow money to finance construction, the interest costs of borrowing represent a finance cost. If the contractor is substantial and can prove it would have invested the monies withheld, the lost investment revenues or lost opportunity costs constitute another financing cost.

In a recent circuit court case,[116] applying Missouri law, the court held that appropriate damages for delays incurred by a contractor included the cost either of borrowing additional monies or of using its own money to finance the work. The issue decided by the court in that case was the right of a contractor who was the victim of a breach of contract to recover not only the cost of extra work and delays incurred on a project but also the cost of interest on borrowed funds used to perform the extra work and carry the work forward during the period of delay.

Generally, to recover such interest, the contractor must prove that he paid the interest and that the borrowing was necessitated by the delay caused by the owner. Recovery under this theory of damages is not limited to the cost of borrowing money, but may also include the interest that would have been earned on the contractor's own funds used to finance the work during the delay. In the case of *Havens Steel Co. v. Randolph Engineering Co.*,[117] Havens was awarded a contract to fabricate and erect certain steel components for use in the expansion of a cement plant. Havens entered into a subcontract with Randolph to perform the erection portion of Havens's base contract. A series of delays occurred during construction and a number of unresolved disputes remained after completion of the work. Havens sued Randolph for breach of contract and Randolph countersued, alleging that Havens interfered with its work, causing delays and extra work. After a trial without jury, the federal district court found in favor of Randolph on all liability claims and on the bulk of Randolph's

---

[115] *See* Fehlhaber Corp. v. State, 69 A.D.2d 362, 419 N.Y.S.2d 773 (1979); Manshul Constr. v. Dormitory Auth., 79 A.D.2d 383, 436 N.Y.S.2d 724 (1981).

[116] Havens Steel Co. v. Randolph Eng'g Co., 813 F.2d 186 (8th Cir. 1987).

[117] 813 F.2d 186 (8th Cir. 1987).

counterclaims for damages. On appeal, the central issue was the lower court's finding in favor of Randolph's damage claim for the cost of capital.

The issue in the appeal was whether Randolph could recover the interest on the capital Randolph used to finance the additional expenses associated with the delays and extra work caused by Havens. Randolph had borrowed under a continuing line of credit to finance its work on this and other projects and introduced evidence that the amount borrowed for any particular project could be ascertained from its records. The court found that because it was undisputed that Randolph paid over $188,000 as a result of Havens's breach, Randolph could recover whether it borrowed the additional money or used its own money.

The court in *Havens* followed the general rule that a contractor can recover damages for incurring the cost of acquiring capital because of delay when it proves that the additional cost was necessitated by the delay and that the contractor expended those costs. The court in *Havens,* however, refused to distinguish between the cost of borrowed funds and the cost of using one's own capital if the cost was in fact incurred by reason of the delay.

The court of appeals pointed out that under Missouri law, "a claim for the cost of money used to pay expenses necessitated by a breach of contract is a claim for damages, not prejudgment interest." This is a significant distinguishing point because in many jurisdictions the courts will not allow prejudgment interest on claims.

Note, though, that the federal government does not recognize interest as a cost of performing extra or delayed work.[118]

§ 16.42 Disruption Damages

Disruption damages are those suffered by the contractor as a result of the owner's breach of implied obligation not to hinder the contractor in its performance. The courts, depending on the cause, often distinguish between delay and disruption activities.

In *Gardner Displays Co. v. United States*[119] a manufacturer of rubber terrain maps sued for the increased cost of latex during a period of government-caused delay in inspection and approval of the preproduction model when, despite the delay, the contractor still managed to perform within the contract time limits. The court found the government unreasonable in its dilatory and inconclusive inspection and approval procedure,

[118] Dravo Corp. v. United States, 594 F.2d 842 (Ct. Cl. 1979); Framlau Corp. v. United States, 568 F.2d 687 (Ct. Cl. 1977); Bell v. United States, 404 F.2d 975 (Ct. Cl. 1968).

[119] 346 F.2d 585 (Ct. Cl. 1965).

which hindered the contractor's performance, and awarded money damages for the disruption.

In *Metropolitan Paving Co. v. United States*[120] the court stated that if the contractor suffered damages as a result of "deliberate harassment and dilatory tactics" employed by the government's employees, it could recover.

In *D'Angelo v. State*[121] the contractor sued the state on the grounds that it failed to provide the contractor with designs for culverts shown on the plans until it was too late to construct them during the winter season as planned. Despite the fact that the contractor finished the job within 19 days of the scheduled completion date, the court said that damages could be awarded, because the contract may have been completed within such a short time only as a result of costly overtime expense.

A contractor may also recover delay damages if it can prove that it planned on performing the work before the specified completion time but, because of interference by the owner, it completed its work only by the contract completion date.

§ 16.43 Lost Profits

When a contractor or a subcontractor is prevented from performing because of a breach by the owner or a person for whose action the owner is responsible, it is entitled to lost profits.[122] As the *Restatement of Contracts* provides, the builder is to be put "in as good a position as he would have been had the contract been fully performed."[123] In order to do this, the contractor should be entitled to the full contract price less any amount it saves as a result of the owner's breach.[124]

The courts generally refuse to award damages under the theory of lost profits for a contractor's alleged unearned profits on other jobs on which it was unable to bid because of the owner's breach. The courts apparently feel that it is far too speculative to grant recovery for such claims when it is not clear that the contractor would have bid on other jobs, would have been awarded the contracts, and, most importantly, would have earned any profits on the prospective jobs.[125]

---

[120] 325 F.2d 241 (Ct. Cl. 1963).

[121] 41 A.D.2d 77, 341 N.Y.S.2d 84 (1973), *modified,* 46 A.D.2d 983, 355 N.Y.S.2d 377 (1974).

[122] Restatement of Contracts § 346 comment G (1932).

[123] *Id.*

[124] *See also* Sampley Enters., Inc. v. Laurilla, 494 So. 2d 841 (Fla. Dist. Ct. App. 1981); Fostic v. United Home Improvement Co., 428 N.E.2d 1351 (Ind. Ct. App. 1981); Ferrell Constr. Co. v. Russell Creek Coal Co., 645 P.2d 1005 (Okla. 1982).

[125] Manshul Constr. Corp. v. Dormitory Auth., 111 Misc. 2d 209, 444 N.Y.S.2d 792 (1981).

CHAPTER 17

USING CRITICAL PATH NETWORK ANALYSIS TO PROVE DELAY

Mark A. Smith

Mark A. Smith is a senior manager in the construction consulting and litigation practice of Ernst & Young's San Francisco, California, office. He has an extensive background in analyzing construction productivity and quantifying construction delay and disruption claims. Dr. Smith holds both undergraduate and graduate degrees in civil engineering and is a registered professional engineer. He has written and presented over forty papers and speeches on a variety of construction management issues.

§ 17.1 Introduction
§ 17.2 Elements of Proof
§ 17.3 Common Techniques to Prove Delay
§ 17.4 —Owner-Caused Events
§ 17.5 —Comparing Manpower Schedules to Revenue Received
§ 17.6 —Critical Path Method
§ 17.7 Overview of Critical Path Method
§ 17.8 Using CPM in Proving Delay
§ 17.9 —Strengthening the CPM Proof Strategy

§ 17.1 Introduction

Construction delays are one of the most frequent causes of contract disputes between the owner and contractor. In general, a construction delay occurs when a project is extended beyond its anticipated completion date. The reasons for this extension of time can result from many factors, such as inefficiencies due to acceleration, inefficiencies due to disruption of scheduled work, and extended time on the site because of numerous change orders.[1]

If a contractor is delayed in completing a construction project, the contractor's organization will undoubtedly experience financial hardship. In most cases, contractors bid on and, if awarded the contract, undertake a job that is anticipated to be completed within a fixed time. Time-related costs, such as job supervision, field office costs, and home office overhead are normally estimated based on the planned duration of a project. If the project's completion date is extended, it follows that all or most of the contractor's time-related costs will continue.

In addition, delay costs can extend to other areas, such as reduced labor productivity that results when the contractor is forced to accelerate its efforts by adding additional labor crews and/or works overtime in an attempt to complete a project on time. Also, if certain job activities are forced out of a planned sequence because of numerous design changes or owner-caused disruptions, direct costs for labor and material can escalate.

If a construction delay occurs and the contractor experiences a *cost overrun,* which is the difference between the contractor's actual and estimated job expenditures, this does not necessarily entitle it to recover the entire cost overrun from another party. In order to recover the costs, the contractor must prove either that the delay was not its fault or that it was beyond the contractor's control. In addition, the contractor must prove that the delay period is of the type that allows for compensation and not just an extension of time.

§ 17.2 Elements of Proof

In general, a contractor must establish proof that the delay, or a culmination of delays, was caused by other parties or that they were beyond its control. In order for the contractor to recover any cost overruns due to the delay situation, the delay must be excusable and compensable. The two conditions, excusable and compensable, are separate and distinct and both must be established in order for the contractor to recover monetary damages.

A delay can be classified as *excusable* if the situation that caused the delay is beyond the control of the contractor or the situation was unforeseeable. Common examples of this type of delay category include owner-mandated

---

[1] *See* B. Bramble & M. Callahan, Construction Delay Claims (2d ed. John Wiley & Sons 1992); J. Wickwire, Construction Scheduling: Preparation, Liability, and Claims (John Wiley & Sons 1992).

scope changes, design errors and omissions, unanticipated weather, and labor disputes. Once a delay is found to be excusable, it can be further classified into the type of damages that may be compensable.

A *compensable* delay entitles the contractor to both an extension of contract time as well as any damages that resulted from the actions that created the delay. In most cases, the contract will govern the situations that constitute a compensable delay. In general, situations involving changes to the project's scope that create delays to the contractor's planned schedule—owner-initiated changes, design changes, or changed conditions—would be treated as compensable delays.

Proof of construction delay normally requires a five-step process:

1. Identification of the as-planned schedule of activities and project deliverables
2. Identification of the as-built schedule of activities and deliverables
3. Identification of delays and/or gains that occurred between the as-planned and as-built schedules
4. Identification of the specific causes for the delays
5. Assessing responsibility for the events that resulted in delays.

Assessing responsibility for delays is critical to establishing a solid claim. The mere fact that the delay has occurred does not, in itself, establish the entitlement to damages. The contractor can be certain that the owner will assert that all or part of the delays were the contractor's fault.

When two or more delay situations occur during the same time period, *concurrent* delay occurs. Concurrent delays become extremely important to the contractor seeking delay damages. For example, assume that a significant delay occurs during the construction of a highrise building because the owner has issued a major change order, but at the same time the contractor incurred a mechanical breakdown to its hoisting crane, resulting in a delay period of the same length. This concurrent delay allows no delay damages to either party.

Moreover, when there are concurrent causes for the delay and the contractor is unable to identify specific events and their impact on the schedule, the court or arbitrators may very well refuse to accept the claim as valid.[2] When developing a delay claim, it is extremely important that the contractor focus on individual events and their relationships to specific activities in the schedule.

---

[2] Commerce Int'l Co. v. United States, 167 Ct. Cl. 529 (1964); Minmar Builders, Inc., GSBCA No. 3430, 72-2 B.C.A. (CCH) ¶ 9599 (1972); Toombs & Co. v. United States, 4 Ct. Cl. 535 (1984).

§ 17.3 Common Techniques to Prove Delay

The types of quantitative analysis employed to prove a delay situation can be just as varied as the different categories of construction projects. The delay analysis can be either quite strong or weak, depending largely on the amount of reliable project documentation the contractor uses.

Three general proof strategies are normally encountered in delay claims:

1. The owner-caused list of events
2. The comparison of planned manpower percentages versus actual revenues and
3. The critical path method (CPM) comparison of the as-planned versus as-built schedule.

Of these three proof strategies, the CPM analysis is by far the strongest analytical method in determining the amount of delay attributable to the individual parties involved in a construction job. Although the CPM analysis method is strongly preferred, the first two methods are also used by contractors in an attempt to prove delay. Of course, the two approaches are more likely to be used when specific project documentation may be lacking. Before reviewing the CPM network analysis approach, the first two methods are discussed, highlighting their respective strengths and weaknesses.

§ 17.4 —Owner-Caused Events

The owner-caused list of events approach has several variations, usually related to a total cost-type claim and most often resulting from a lack of data necessary to support discrete analysis of delay. In its most simplest form, it is nothing more than a descriptive list of all the owner-caused problems experienced on the job. By producing this list and all the correspondence to the owner describing the effects of the various problems, the contractor hopes to sway the court or arbitrators with the sheer magnitude of the problems and their impact on the overall delays actually experienced.

A slightly more sophisticated variation of this approach records the delay caused by specific events and relates them to specific job activities. The individual delays are then combined to yield a total delay for the entire project. The resulting claim is a comprehensive, but usually very confusing, collection of activity data. Although an improvement over the first type of listing, this type of claim generally is subject to attack because it does not consider the float or slack time in many of the noncritical work activities. Without such an analysis and allowance, this type of delay claim most probably becomes inflated.

The contractor who uses the owner-caused list of events in an attempt to prove delay should be aware of the following typical defense strategies against this approach:

1. A mere listing of owner-caused problems does not establish a clear relationship to overall project delay
2. Delays for some individual activities are normal and part of the contingency allowance in the contractor's estimate
3. Most of the delay actually experienced resulted from the contractor's own inability to manage the job, as evidenced in part by its failure to keep adequate job records.

§ 17.5 —Comparing Manpower Schedules to Revenue Received

The strategy of comparing planned manpower schedules to actual revenue received usually is used to support a delay claim and, with slight variation, to illustrate the impact of acceleration.

Generally, the approach involves first establishing that contract payments are tied to the percentage of contract completion, which in turn is based on costs incurred by the contractor. A variation of this approach uses planned revenue schedules based on scheduled labor costs to complete specific schedule milestones. A graph is then devised to plot the planned percentages of worker-hours or revenues to be expended on the job versus the percentage of revenue payments actually received. This concept is illustrated in **Figure 17–1**.

The contractor will then attempt to establish delay be measuring the time lag between planned worker-hours and receipt of an equal percentage of payment. Typically, the focus will be on the later project months and will indicate a lag of three to five months. The intended suggestion is that delays in receipt of planned revenues are the result of claimed project delays.

Close examination of the technique reveals clearly that it is a somewhat weak attempt to mix worker-hours and percentage of completion. In fact, the suggested mathematical relationship between planned or actual worker-hours and contract payments does not exist as a hard rule in the construction industry. Although payments are often based on planned percentages of completion, the costs typically include many items other than labor, including materials, equipment, and mobilization. Moreover, the payment schedules are typically unbalanced, or *front-loaded,* to help the contractor finance project costs. The curve depicted in **Figure 17–1** is, most often, characteristic of the schedule anticipated by the contractor when the job budget was developed.

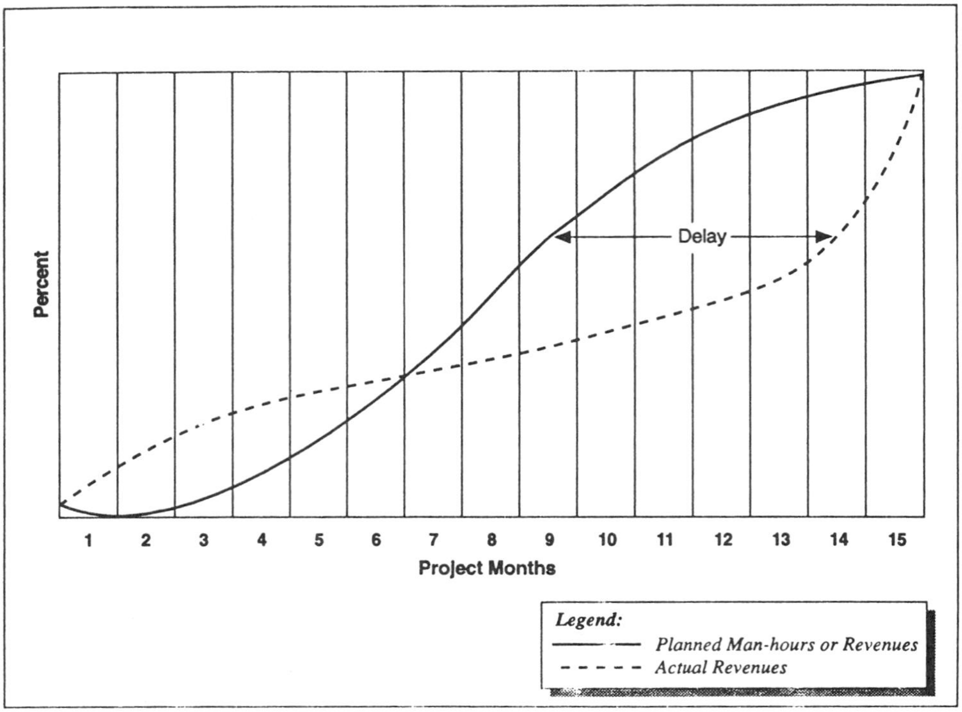

Figure 17–1. Delay analysis using planned man-hours versus revenues received.

Aside from understanding the fallacy of its premise, the worker-hours versus revenue approach is also weakened by analyzing its mathematical logic. This is accomplished best by discretely identifying and separating costs by type—labor, material, equipment, and so on—and by time period of occurrence so that relationships can be readily compared. Front-loading can then be approximated by identifying project revenues by time period and comparing early period profit margins to the profit margins bid on the entire job.

A simple check to determine whether a contractor should attempt to use the claimed worker-hours versus payments relationship can be best accomplished by drawing a comparison between worker-hours actually worked in a given period and payments made by the owner in the same period. **Figure 17–2** indicates this relationship. When substantial front-loading or other early costs are involved, the comparison will show substantially higher costs per hour of labor in the early periods. These early period costs will be well above average composite rates, but those in the later periods are well below actual average labor rates. A line graph, such as **Figure 17–3**, illustrates graphically the front-loading analysis method.

Before proceeding with the comparison of planned manpower to actual revenue received, contractors should verify to see whether any front-loading

Project Month	Amount Paid	Worker-hours Expended	Dollars per WH	Cumulative Paid	Cumulative Worker-hours	Cumulative $ per Hour
1	112,000	1550	72	112.000	1550	72
2	336,000	2200	153	448,000	3750	119
3	496,000	3460	143	944,000	7210	131
4	420,000	6350	66	1,364,000	13560	101
5	358,000	6850	52	1,722,000	20410	84
6	415,000	11300	37	2,137,000	31710	67
7	444,000	7650	58	2,581,000	39360	66
8	550,000	12750	43	3,131,000	52110	60
9	580,000	13250	44	3,711,000	65360	57
10	548,000	10350	53	4,259,000	75710	56
11	275,000	10950	25	4,534,000	86660	52
12	228,000	10000	23	4,762,000	96660	49
1	238,000	7600	31	5,000,000	104,260	48
2	106,000	7200	15	5,106,000	111,460	46
3	50,000	6100	8	5,156,000	117,560	44
4	100,000	3150	32	5,256,000	120,710	44
5	67,000	1450	46	5,323,000	122,160	44
6	0	0	0	0	0	0
7	0	0	0	0	0	0
8	0	0	0	0	0	0
9	0	0	0	0	0	0
10	0	0	0	0	0	0
11	0	0	0	0	0	0
12	0	0	0	0	0	0
1	0	0	0	0	0	0
2	0	0	0	0	0	0
3	0	0	0	0	0	0
4	0	0	0	0	0	0
5	0	0	0	0	0	0
6	0	0	0	0	0	0
7	0	0	0	0	0	0
8	0	0	0	0	0	0
9	0	0	0	0	0	0
10	0	0	0	0	0	0
11	0	0	0	0	0	0
12	0	0	0	0	0	0
Total	**5,323,000**	**122,160**	**44**	**5,323,000**	**122,160**	**44**

Figure 17–2. Front-loading analysis comparison of dollars paid versus man-hours expended.

of labor force was utilized in developing progress payments for the construction job. If front-loading methods were used, this defense will most likely be raised by the owner.

§ 17.6 —Critical Path Method

The most acceptable method of calculating the impact of delay is to use a critical path network analysis of the as-planned versus as-built project. This approach identifies specific events causing delay and the specific activity affected. In addition, the CPM approach utilizes network analysis to determine the net impact on the project schedule. Properly used, this technique can provide convincing evidence of delays and their impact on the overall schedule.

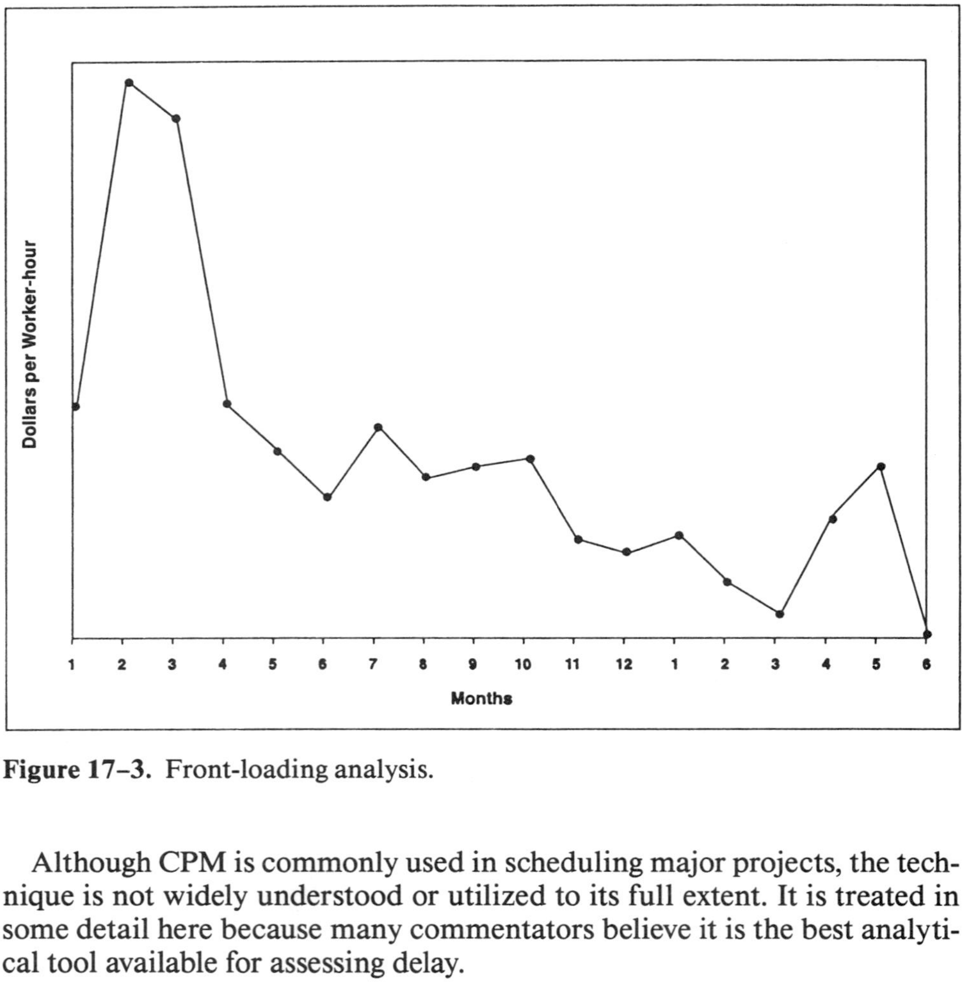

Figure 17–3. Front-loading analysis.

Although CPM is commonly used in scheduling major projects, the technique is not widely understood or utilized to its full extent. It is treated in some detail here because many commentators believe it is the best analytical tool available for assessing delay.

§ 17.7 Overview of Critical Path Method

Projects typically consist of a network of activities, some of which must be completed sequentially and others, concurrently. Every project has within it a *critical path,* that is, the longest, continuous path of sequential activities that represents the total elapsed duration of the project. The critical path sequence of work activities has no float or slack time; in other words, the activity on the critical path must be completed as scheduled or a delay will occur in finishing the project on time.

Critical path work activities are represented by arrows, the type of activity is described above the line, and the time duration is usually listed below the line. Each activity consists of two events—an initiating event (tail of the arrow) and a terminating event (point of the arrow). Events may consist of single activities or multiple activities. Dotted lines are sometimes included to show network logic restraints that do not constitute a work activity. Known as a *dummy* activity, it is necessary for the logic of the network to indicate an event that cannot be started without first completing a task that falls outside the activity sequence.

Generally, projects also consist of other tasks or series of sequential activities that can be conducted concurrently with critical path activities. These are displayed on a critical path network chart creating a visual network of all project activities and sequence logic. **Figure 17–4** contains a condensed CPM network diagram.

All activities and events must eventually link to a path that leads to completion of the project. Dangling events are forbidden, as are unending loops in which more than one activity starts from and ends in the same two events. Activities are identified in numerical terms by reference to their connecting event numbers, for example, Activity 10-20.

Be definition, work activities not on the critical path have a certain amount of flexibility or *float* with respect to their scheduled start or finish dates. Thus, some postponement is possible without affecting the overall project schedule. Although a delay to a critical path activity almost always will increase the overall schedule, a delay to a noncritical path item may simply reduce the overall float in a series of activities. In order to determine the impact of a delay on the project, it is first necessary to determine the total time required as scheduled, the project critical path, and the amount of float that exists for each project work activity.

Determining the time requirement for the entire project is a relatively simple process once the network activities have been established. The duration needed to complete any event is simply the longest time of any activity

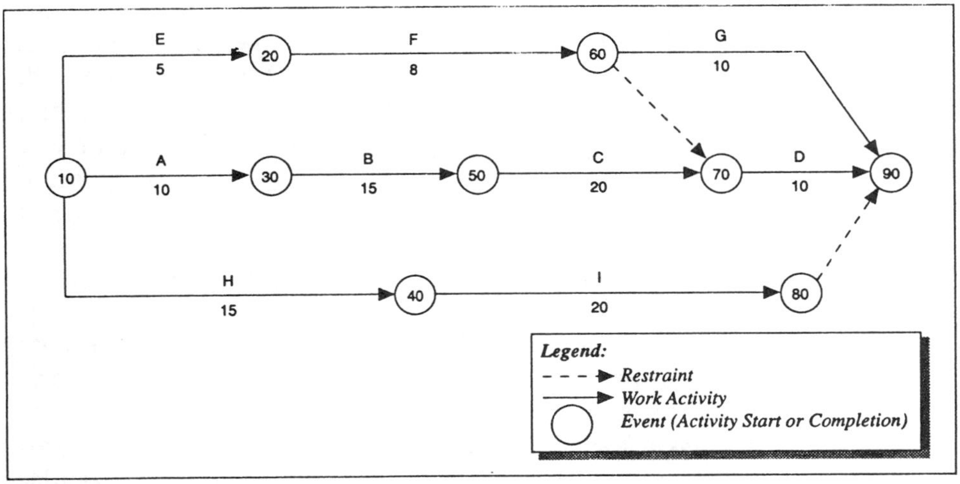

Figure 17–4. Critical path network.

sequence within the event. By working forward through the network, called a *forward pass,* the analyst can identify the earliest time that each event and the total project can be completed. The longest activity sequence through the network is the critical path.

Float can be determined by working backward through the path, called a *backward pass,* and subtracting from each event the time duration of each linking critical path event. This procedure establishes the latest time that an individual activity can be started without affecting the project's overall completion date. Generally, there are two different types of float that are recognized: total float and free float. *Total float* is the amount of time an activity can be delayed without impacting the overall project completion date. *Free float* is the amount of time an activity can be delayed without impacting the earliest starting time of the next preceding activity in the sequence.

This distinction between float terminology is important because once an activity's total float is used, the activity as well as the entire sequence of activities becomes a part of the critical path. In contrast, if an activity's free float is used, this does not necessarily mean that the activity becomes part of the critical path. In fact, when an activity's free float is exceeded, the only consequence is that the next activity in the sequence chain will be delayed in starting. Contractors should understand the difference between these types of floats in their attempts to accurately portray which events caused a project to be delayed.

§ 17.8 Using CPM in Proving Delay

Using CPM to prove delay in a claim involves two major steps. The first is to prepare an as-planned critical path schedule showing the logical relationships, dependencies, and time requirements for the project work activities according to the contractor's original plan. Undisputed use of the network in a claim requires agreement by both parties that the network does, in fact, represent the actual planned project schedule. If the network schedule was agreed upon when the project was initiated, there should be little problem in achieving this agreement. However, when the as-planned schedule is constructed after the fact and is really an "as-should-have-been" schedule, considerable disagreement between the owner and contractor is likely to occur.

The second step is to develop an as-built critical path. Specific events affecting the planned construction are isolated and documented and each is analyzed with respect to the specific work activity on which it occurred. The duration of the task affected is adjusted accordingly to reflect the impact of relevant events and the network is subjected to a complete recalculation to determine overall impact or delay on the project schedule.

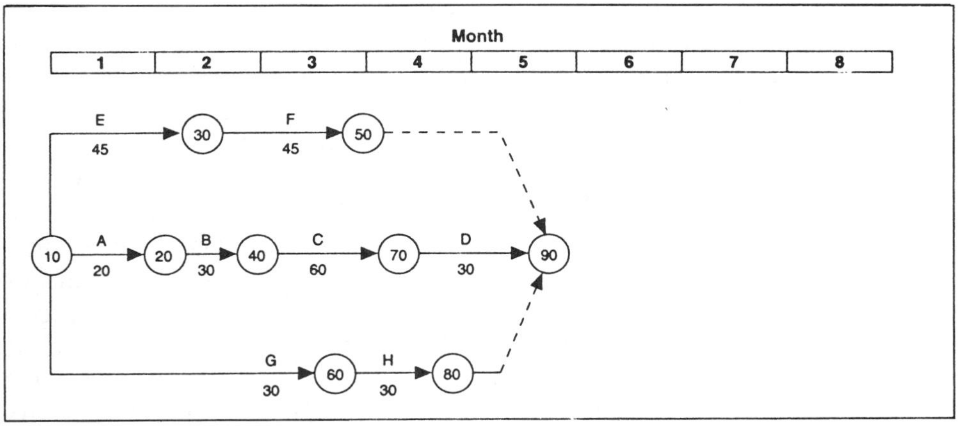

Figure 17–5. Planned critical path schedule.

Presentation of the CPM network analysis is usually best accomplished by laying out the diagram in a calendar time-phased manner. **Figure 17–5** is a simple example of an as-planned network diagram using this approach. In this example, the total project duration is 140 days, which is determined by adding the individual activity durations along the critical path activity sequence of A-B-C-D. Once the total duration is known, float times can be computed. For example, the total float for the activity sequence of E-F is 50 days, which is determined by subtracting its earliest finish time of 90 days from the latest finish time of 140 days.

Events impacting the project are then inserted in highly visible activity blocks on the activities affected, extending the scheduled activities in accordance with the documented impact. **Figure 17–6** illustrates the as-built

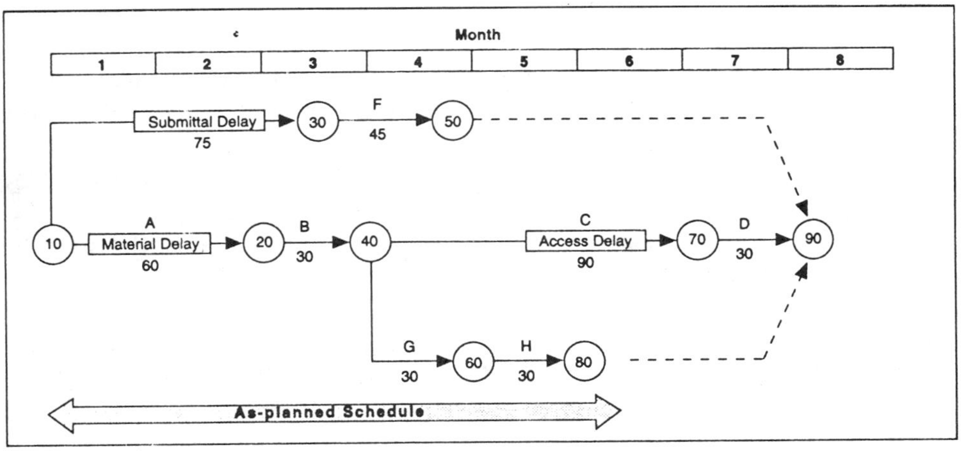

Figure 17–6. As-built critical path schedule.

diagram for the project example planned in **Figure 17–5**. Note the delay activities in this diagram contain narrative descriptions. This is sometimes more effective when multiple events are involved in causing the delays.

In **Figure 17–6**, the as-built example, the total duration of the project now becomes 210 days because of the associated delays that occurred on the job. This represents a total delay of 70 days. There were three delays that impacted the overall as-planned schedule: material delay of 40 days, submittal delay of 30 days, and an access delay of 30 days. The total of these individual delays accounts for 100 days of delay. The fallacy in simply adding all delays is clearly illustrated in this example. There is a need for a proper network analysis to determine both critical and noncritical delays because in this project the actual delay is only 70 days. In particular, the submittal delay of 30 days occurs in the activity sequence of E-F, an activity not on the critical path, with a total float time of 50 days. Because the submittal delay does not exceed the available float time, this particular delay does not impact the final completion date of the project.

Once the responsibility for the events that caused the overall project delay has been determined, the contractor can now proceed in the determination of associated time-related damages.

§ 17.9 —Strengthening the CPM Proof Strategy

Contractors should be aware that the defense will undoubtedly attack the use of CPM network analysis to prove delays. The contractor should develop a sound and documented approach so that the CPM analysis will withstand a detailed critique of the network logic, time estimates, and events causing the delay. In general, once its network analysis has been performed, the contractor should ensure that the CPM methodology meets the following standards:

Thorough preparation. Examine the logic presented in the CPM network to determine whether relationships actually exist as depicted. Often, the higher-level CPM diagrams may appear to be accurate in this respect. However, when subjected to a more detailed, lower-level activity analysis, they sometimes reveal concurrent activities that can mitigate delays. It is extremely important, therefore, that engineers knowledgeable in the specific type of construction provide assistance in preparing the CPM logic.

Accurate time estimates. Evaluate the reasonableness of the time estimates in the as-planned schedule. This requires an understanding of the work activities themselves, knowledge of reasonable labor productivity levels for the type of work being performed, and understanding of conditions that were known or should have been known when the job was initially planned. Again, these determinations require specific expertise in construction of the type under review.

Valid delay data. Ensure the validity of the data used in calculating the delays. The defense will attack casual relationships between specific events and delays that ultimately occurred or the inadequacy and unreliability of the project's records used to support the claim.

Documented delays. Develop sound documentation support for all project delays. The owner will typically argue that the contractor is responsible for some or all of the events that resulted in the project delays. The owner may assert that the contractor's inability to manage or to take reasonable steps to mitigate the effect of various occurrences was the major factor causing delays and increased costs. Owners will normally include counterclaims for increased costs as a result of the delayed project completion.

CHAPTER 18

PRICING DAMAGES

William J. Palmer

William J. Palmer is chairman of Ernst & Young's National Construction Industry Group in San Francisco, California, and in that role coordinates his firm's services to over 1,000 construction companies. He is a graduate of the University of California at Berkeley and is a member of the American Institute of Certified Public Accountants and the Associated General Contractors of America. Because of Mr. Palmer's reputation and expertise in the areas of construction and contract accounting and his numerous publications on construction accounting and construction litigation, he frequently testifies as an expert witness in long-term contract disputes and related litigation.

§ 18.1 Introduction
§ 18.2 Categories of Contract Damages
§ 18.3 —Delay Damages
§ 18.4 —Disruption
§ 18.5 —Changed Conditions
§ 18.6 —Changes in Scope
§ 18.7 —Termination
§ 18.8 Pricing Damages
§ 18.9 Total Cost Approach
§ 18.10 —Four-Way Test
§ 18.11 Discrete Approach
§ 18.12 Cost Schedules
§ 18.13 Contract Audit
§ 18.14 Calculating Damages
§ 18.15 —Delay
§ 18.16 —Disruption
§ 18.17 —Changed Conditions

§ 18.18 —Changes in Scope
§ 18.19 —Termination
§ 18.20 Cost of Capital
§ 18.21 Claim Preparation Costs
§ 18.22 Home Office Overhead
§ 18.23 —*Eichleay* Formula
§ 18.24 —Total Direct Cost Allocation
§ 18.25 —Specific Base Allocation Method
§ 18.26 —Occupancy
§ 18.27 Profit Recovery

§ 18.1 Introduction

Recent years have seen a significant growth in the complexity of construction contracts. This is in part due to the rapid expansion of infrastructure and commercial work as well as technological advances in refineries, power plants, and other complex projects. Other factors are increased government regulation and pressure from environmental and other special interest groups. As contracts have become more complex, they have also become more susceptible to contract disputes and often litigation is the result. Additionally, large sums of money are frequently involved in these disputes and settlement by handshake becomes difficult. Budgetary aspects of governmental agencies have also had their effect.

For most contracts, change orders and requests for additional compensation are a routine process. Generally these changes in the contract price are made without dispute or negotiation. When change orders and requests for additional compensation are rejected, the next step is usually a formal claim. When these claims are significant in terms of money, legal counsel and other consultants are usually brought to ensure proper preparation, documentation, and presentation of the claim. This adds more fuel to the fire and further complicates the settlement process. If this process fails, the dispute will most likely move into the litigation phase, which becomes very costly to all parties involved. At this stage, the contractor and its attorney need help not only in developing the best overall strategy but also in preparing the damages and subsequent expert testimony. The outside experts will also help in evaluating the soundness of testimony as to damages submitted by others.

§ 18.2 Categories of Contract Damages

Claims and resulting litigation arise for a myriad of reasons. Quite often, they involve such things as definition of contract scope, timing of the contract effort, pricing of change orders, defective or late drawings, lack of access or right-of-way, out-of-sequence work, and any other factors that might affect the contractor's schedule, labor productivity, or sequence of work. In short, any act by another party that has affected the economic results planned for by the contractor may result in a claim against that party.

Table 18–1 groups these types of events into five broad categories for purposes of computing damages:

1. Delay
2. Disruption
3. Changed conditions
4. Changes in scope
5. Termination.

Table 18–1

Events That Cause Claims

Event	Type of Claim Caused				
	Delay	Disruption	Changed Conditions	Scope Changes	Termination
Late drawings	x	x			
Changes in sequence	x	x	x		
Lack of decision	x	x			
Acceleration		x	x	x	
Deceleration	x	x			
Lack of access	x	x			
Lack of right-of-way	x	x	x		
Delays	x	x			
Interference	x	x			
Errors	x	x			
Differing site conditions	x	x	x		
Suspensions	x	x			x
Bankruptcy					x
Lack of funds					x
Impossibility			x	x	x
Weather	x	x	x		
Strikes	x	x			x
Lack of approvals	x	x		x	
Erroneous bid specs	x	x	x	x	

§ 18.3 —Delay Damages

When a contractor has been unable to maintain a predetermined schedule, a claim for delay may arise.[1] Even when a contractor finishes on a contractually determined date, a delay claim may be submitted if a contractor believes that it would have completed ahead of schedule but for acts of the other party. Delays can be caused by many events, but most frequently are caused by:

1. Owner-instructed delays
2. Late drawings
3. Defective drawings
4. Defective materials
5. Lack of access and right-of-way
6. Working out of sequence
7. Forced changes in approaches to the work
8. Numerous change orders, and other factors that cause a schedule slippage.

Delays directly affect a contractor's time-related costs. Time-related costs are those based on the passage of time rather than production volume. They include contract management, for which the planned cost is based on how long management will be in place on the project, management's annual monthly salary and benefits, and so on. Other examples of time-related costs are management vehicles such as pickup trucks, company cars, and jobsite trailer, guard service, telephone and utilities (excluding tolls and long-distance charges), owned and outside rental equipment, small tools, and any other costs associated with the passage of time.

Delays may indirectly give rise to claims for escalation in labor rates, material, and equipment cost. Claims for acceleration are most frequently associated with delay; the contractor may have increased crew size, gone to multiple shift work or extended overtime to attempt to maintain the original schedule or to mitigate the damages caused by delay. Delay also usually results in a claim for additional unrecovered home office overhead.

§ 18.4 —Disruption

As a result of the delays discussed in **§ 18.3**, most claims for delay will also include claims for lower labor productivity (see **Chapter 19**) or labor

[1] *See* B. Bramble & M. Callahan, Construction Delay Claims (2d ed., John Wiley & Sons 1992).

disruption. Frequent delays in the project may force contractors to "start, stop and leapfrog"; for example, construction crews that cannot continue on plan must alternate working on different portions of the contract in an attempt to keep the project moving on time. Increasing crew size, going to overtime, or multiple shift work will generally result in lower labor productivity as well.

§ 18.5 —Changed Conditions

When data furnished by the owner to the contractor for use in preparing a bid differ from the conditions that the contractor actually encounters, claims for additional compensation can be expected. For example, during excavation, the subsurface material actually encountered may differ from that indicated by the test borings supplied in requests for bid. Another example involves change orders that are so numerous that the final project bears no resemblance to what was planned.

Claims for changed conditions are not readily susceptible to discrete pricing. Typically, a total cost or jury verdict approach is used in these situations. Had the correct specifications been given at the time of bid or the original scope included the change orders, the theory is that the contractor's actual cost would have approximated its bid.

§ 18.6 —Changes in Scope

When a contractor considers its increased costs to be the result of changes in the original scope of works, change orders will usually be submitted. If the contractor is unsuccessful in negotiating a change in scope, a formal claim is the next step. When that approach fails, litigation results.

The argument generally centers on whether the alleged change is part of the original scope; it frequently involves the cost of the change rather than the fact that the change occurred. In many cases change orders are priced and submitted with the qualification that the price does not take into account schedule slippage and the resultant effect on time-related project costs and unrecovered home office overhead. Therefore, although the direct cost of change orders may have been recovered through executed documents during the project, a change order may be filed during or at the end of the project to recover the costs of schedule extension and unrecovered home office overhead.

Damages for unapproved change orders are usually presented in the claim or damage summary as a listing of such change orders that shows the direct cost, and the associated unrecovered home office overhead and profit.

§ 18.7 —Termination

When a contract is terminated before the work is completed, a termination claim usually results. Contractors file termination claims for a variety of reasons. For example, the contractor may have incurred significant costs at the front-end of the contract that were not covered by progress payments through the date of termination. This is quite common in earth-moving projects (highways, dams, tunnels), when the contract is priced on a unit price basis. For example, the contractor quotes a price per cubic yard of excavation, concrete poured, and so on, spreading front-end contract costs such as mobilization and batch plant setup over all the units expected to be performed. Therefore, if the contractor performs only half the anticipated units on the project, only half the front-end mobilization or batch plants setup costs will be recovered.

Other costs associated with demobilization are idle equipment time until such equipment can be removed from the project and demobilization costs, plus project superintendent, foreman, and other managerial costs to oversee the demobilization.

In termination claims the contractor will often seek lost profits due to unanticipated idle resources. This assumes that had the contractor known the original time frame of the terminated work, other bids would have been prepared and the resources would not have been idle.

§ 18.8 Pricing Damages

Although there may appear to be a variety of overall approaches to damages, in reality they fall into categories. These are the total cost approach and the discrete approach. Jury verdict and other similar descriptions are merely variations of the total cost approach.

§ 18.9 Total Cost Approach

As an overall approach to pricing damages, the *total cost approach* (shown in **Table 18–2**) is the simplest. It basically converts a fixed-priced contract into a cost-plus contract. In simple terms, it is the contractor's actual cost less some form of budget or contract price, to which are added the additional home office overhead recovery and profit. Quite often, interest on negative cash flow during the contract and prejudgment interest are also included.

The total cost approach assumes that the events proved on the entitlement/liability side can be shown to have resulted in the excess costs of actual versus budget. The total cost approach is not allowed in many jurisdictions

Table 18–2

Total Cost Approach—Claim Summary (Round to Nearest 1000)

Contract costs incurred		
Direct costs		
Labor	$100,000	
Materials	50,000	
Subcontracts	450,000	
Equipment	100,000	
Other	50,000	
		$750,000
Indirect costs		80,000
Total cost		830,000
Total revenue (contract price and change orders)		720,000
Contract overrun		110,000
Add:		
Unrecovered home office general and administrative costs (10% of total cost)		83,000
Profit (15% of total cost plus unrecovered overhead)		137,000
Cost of capital		20,000
Total claim		350,000
Claim preparation costs		50,000
Interest from date of notice through _____ (current date of claim)		15,000
Total due at _____ (date of claim)		$415,000

and therefore is in disfavor among most knowledgeable lawyers. It is a useful and allowable approach, however, if the plaintiff can show that because of the nature of the entitlement, no other approach is feasible. For example, because changed conditions claims are generally not susceptible to a discrete pricing approach, the total cost approach is usually acceptable.

§ 18.10 —Four-Way Test

In recent years and as a result of certain legal opinions, meeting the *four-way test* is usually the measure for making the total cost approach acceptable. The four tests that must be met and proven are:

1. The contractor's actual total costs incurred on the contract must be correct and reasonable. In other words, the costs charged to the contract must be in accordance with generally accepted accounting principles or other applicable requirements, and when allocation of costs among contracts is required, the method and base used for such allocations must be appropriate. "Reasonable" means that the costs do not include the contractor's own mismanagement, mistakes, or costs not necessary for the performance of the contract.
2. The overrun of actual versus original contract budget or price must be the result of the other party's acts and costs leading to portions or all of the overrun cannot be a result of the contractor's own inefficiencies, mistakes, mismanagement, or other unnecessary costs.
3. The budget or contract price must be reasonable and the original bid properly prepared. "Reasonable" means that the budget or price reflects what the marketplace would expect; "properly prepared" means that the original bid is free from errors and omissions. One way to determine whether the original price or budget is reasonable is to compare prices submitted by other bidders for the project. A cost estimating engineer can also be used to rebid the project and concur with the reasonableness of the contractor's bid. This consultant can also testify as to the bid being properly prepared and that there are no significant errors or omissions.
4. The nature of the dispute must be such that it is impossible or impractical to use any other approach. The failure of the contractor to keep records necessary for a discrete approach is generally not an acceptable excuse for using the total cost approach. Other than in changed conditions claims and certain termination situations, it is difficult to imagine contractors meeting this test. If the number of drawings in a late drawing situation is so voluminous and its impact on delay and labor so pervasive, it may be impractical to keep records on its effect other than the actual lateness of the drawings. The same is true for defective materials. If the number of defective materials is voluminous and pervades the entire project, it may be impractical to estimate the cost effect of these events. In most cases, however, because time sheets can be adjusted and additional cost codes set up to account for problems, not keeping proper records cannot be justified for a way of meeting this task.

The total cost approach is not favored by most attorneys or courts. It requires the contractor/plaintiff to be fault-free and that is rarely the case. Converting what was intended to be a fixed price contract to a cost-plus contract is difficult to justify.

§ 18.11 Discrete Approach

Although the *discrete approach* to pricing damages is considerably more difficult and much more complex than the total cost approach, in most cases it will be the best approach. In effect, each of the events or categories of events that caused cost overruns or deterioration of profits through excess costs is priced separately (discretely), as shown in **Table 18–3**. For example, the cost of delay is priced by determining project time-related costs and applying these to the delay period. Indirect results of the delay, such as higher labor or materials costs, are priced separately. Deterioration in labor productivity due to acceleration, increased crew sizes, multiple shift, or overtime work is priced separately. The discrete approach presents a linkage of entitlement with the damages.

Table 18–3

Discreet Approach—Claim Summary

Delay	
Extended field support due to late drawings (10 weeks at $12,000/week)	$120,000
Escalation of costs due to delay (materials)	8,000
Disruption	
Decline of 12% in labor productivity due to late drawings	83,000
Unpaid change orders	
Extended sewer excavation	13,000
Acceleration (premium on overtime to attempt to meet original schedule)	8,000
Cost of capital (negative cash flow due to delay, disruption, and unpaid change orders)	4,000
	236,000
Unrecovered home office general and administrative cost at 10% of costs, excluding cost of capital	23,200
	259,200
Profit at 15%, excluding cost of capital	25,520
Total claim	$284,720
Interest from date of notice through ______ (current date)	24,000
Total due at ______ (date of claim)	$308,720

§ 18.12 Cost Schedules

After carefully selecting the attorney who will be the team leader in the anticipated litigation, one of the first things the contractor should do for the attorney and ultimately the damage expert is to prepare a series of schedules that show in various forms the final results of the contract in dispute. These schedules will give the attorney a much better understanding of the situation and can serve as a starting point for determining damage strategies. After gaining an understanding of the economics of the potential litigation, the attorney may then advise the contractor to take an offered settlement rather than proceed with litigation. The schedules should include:

1. As much detail as possible concerning a bid versus actual comparison and the resulting variances (**Table 18–4**)
2. Reconciliation of the original contract price with the final price: a schedule of the original price plus change orders, and either a summary

Table 18–4

Comparison of Bid Versus Actual by Contract Work Item

Work	Cost		Over
Item	Bid	Actual	(Under)
1	$ 50,000	$ 40,000	$ (10,000)
2	85,000	100,000	15,000
3	85,000	110,000	25,000
4	160,000	200,000	40,000
5	185,000	300,000	115,000
	$565,000	$750,000	$185,000

Table 18–5

Reconciliation of Original Contract Price with Final Revenue

Original contract dated ______		$675,000
Change orders		
No. 1, ______	$10,000	
No. 2, ______	15,000	
No. 3, ______	40,000	
No. 4, ______	(20,000)	
		45,000
Total revenue		$720,000

Table 18–6

Project Cost Report
(Detail of Cost and Revenues by Contract Work Item and Cost Function)

Work Item	Costs					Revenue	Profit (Loss)
	Labor	Materials	Subcontract	Equipment	Total		
Actual							
1	$ 30,000	$ 10,000	$ 0	$10,000	$ 50,000	$ 65,000	$ 15,000
2	40,000	15,000	40,000	5,000	100,000	125,000	25,000
3	0	10,000	80,000	10,000	100,000	100,000	0
4	100,000	50,000	0	50,000	200,000	180,000	(20,000)
5	100,000	100,000	80,000	20,000	300,000	250,000	(50,000)
	270,000	185,000	200,000	95,000	750,000	720,000	(30,000)
Budget	220,000	175,000	200,000	70,000	565,000	675,000	110,000
Over/ (Under)	$ 50,000	$ 10,000	$ 0	$25,000	$185,000	$ 45,000	$(140,000)

of each change order with description, or copies of the change orders themselves (**Table 18–5**)

3. A copy of the original contract
4. A project cost report, sometimes referred to as a contract status report or cost ledger (**Table 18–6**)
5. Summary of overhead for the preceding five years compared with direct costs of all contracts performed and the resultant percent that overhead bears to direct contract costs (**Table 18–7**)
6. A five-year summary of gross profit as a percent of direct contract costs (**Table 18–8**)
7. If interest on negative cash flow (investment in the project) is contemplated, a schedule of bank borrowings during the contract period and related interest costs
8. A schedule of contractor claim preparation costs to date.

Table 18–7

Historical Overhead Analysis (Based on Audited Income Statement Data)

	Years				
	1	2	3	4	Total
Total cost (all jobs)	$800,000	$700,000	$900,000	$1,000,000	$3,400,000
General and administrative expense	120,000	100,000	145,000	150,000	515,000
Percentage	15%	14.3%	16.1%	15%	15.1%

Table 18–8

Historical Profit Analysis (Based on Audited Income Statement Data)

	Years				
	1	2	3	4	Total
Total cost (all profitable jobs)	$800,000	$700,000	$900,000	$1,000,000	$3,400,000
Gross profit (all profitable jobs)	85,000	88,000	89,000	95,000	357,000
Percentage	10.6%	12.7%	9.9%	9.5%	10.5%

It is usually best to prepare most of these schedules using a total cost approach when applicable. Even though the ultimate team leader may decide upon a discrete approach to the claim, it will give the attorney an idea of the maximum potential damage recovery that is needed to make his client whole and provide a fair overhead and profit. These schedules will also provide the starting point for carrying out a contract audit if required and may be of use to other team consultants and expert witnesses.

§ 18.13 Contract Audit

Once the damage specialist is selected, it is usually best to conduct an audit of the contract costs, revenues, and resulting cost overrun. The audit can be carried out either by the damage specialist if he is a certified public accountant, or by the contractor's accounting firm, and then presented as separate testimony at trial. The expense of having the existing accounting firm prepare the audit under the direction of a CPA/damage expert should result in efficiencies. At any rate, the contract audit is one of the key aspects of presenting damages at trial and provides the following benefits:

1. If the total cost approach is being used, the contract audit will help to meet the first step of the four-way test, that is, that costs are correct and reasonable.
2. The audit can help to identify the contractor's own mistakes, unneeded cost in performance of the contract, or embarrassing costs that would make a total cost approach overstated or indicate failure to mitigate damages.
3. If the discrete approach is used, costs associated with pricing the discrete events can be reconciled to the cost audit, thereby insuring that amounts are correct and giving such pricing added credibility.
4. The audit provides the damage expert with knowledge and understanding of the contractor's cost system, history of the contract, and related disputes so that he can provide valuable advice to the attorneys for interrogatories, depositions, and other aspects of his consulting role. The expert can also assist by suggesting effective approaches and strategies in presenting the damages.
5. The audit develops an important data base for the costs of labor, material, equipment, and miscellaneous and overhead costs. This information is necessary to price damages using the discrete approach. Such a documented data base also allows for last minute changes in approaches to pricing and presenting damages.
6. The audit's information may have an important bearing or impact on the entitlement aspects of the case. Information from the audit is

often useful or complements the work of the critical path consultant or other entitlement consultants and experts.

7. The audit provides for a cost-effective way of obtaining information. Actually, the audit usually pays for itself through the benefits already noted and results in more reliable information for use by other experts and for presentation of information at trial.

During or by the end of the audit phase, the attorney, in concert with the damage and other experts, will have decided on the overall approach to presenting and proving the damages. Under either the total cost or discrete approach, the audit will be extremely useful in proving the damages and adding credibility to damage approaches. For the discrete approach, the audit can be used to set out the key cost elements being used to price specific events. For example:

1. Labor rates being used to price disruption can be reconciled to audited figures
2. Time-related costs used to price delay can be identified and reconciled to the audit for use in pricing delay
3. Escalation in materials, equipment, labor, and other items can be shown to have been incurred and matched with planned material costs to identify the resulting overrun.

§ 18.14 Calculating Damages

During the audit phase and upon the completion of the audit, the team leader will have decided which overall approach to use in presenting the contractor's damages. The team will move forward under either the total cost or discrete approach. If the total cost approach is selected, then little further discussion is required except in the areas of overhead, profits, and other costs outside the direct cost of the contract that may need to be considered.

If the discrete approach is to be used, further discussions will be needed during the course of preparing for litigation because of the many different ways of pricing the discrete events. **Sections 18.15** through **18.19** discuss the approaches to pricing the major categories of discrete events.

§ 18.15 —Delay

During the audit phase, the CPA should identify all time-related costs. These costs generally include such things as job management salaries, job-site office, guards, accountants, timekeepers, and all other costs that are paid on a fixed charge basis over the life of the project. For example, if the cost of the project superintendent's salary and benefits is $5,000 per month, then every month the superintendent is on the job longer than planned, the project cost will increase by that amount. All such costs should be handled in this manner.

Once these costs have been identified (they are usually scheduled on an actual per-month basis during the life of the job), they can then be applied in the aggregate to the months of delay determined by the critical path consultant.

§ 18.16 —Disruption

Disruption is the decline in labor productivity resulting from acts of the other party. (See **Chapter 19**.) Of all discrete categories of damages, decline in labor productivity is the most difficult to prove and quantify. The following approaches can be used:

Past projects. Past production productivity for similar work in similar geographic and weather conditions can be used for comparative purposes. Larger contractors maintain detailed empirical data on the productivity of past performed projects. This information is used primarily for future bids, but is also relevant to proving declines in labor productivity.

Measured mile technique. If the contractor has experienced nondisruptive work on the project, the productivity achieved during that period can be compared with actual productivity in the disrupted period. Usually, the first 10 percent and the last 10 percent of the project are ignored because of the disruptions of mobilization and demobilization. In other words, focus on the productivity that is achieved during normal production.

Learning curve analysis. When repetitive work is performed by the contractor, learning curve techniques can be employed to determine what the average productivity per unit should have been. In most situations the 80 percent learning curve technique is used under the theory that each unit of work performed is 20 percent more efficient than the immediate previous unit performed. This technique evolved in the defense and aerospace industry during World War II, when it was found that repetitive work usually followed an 80 percent learning curve.

Experience curves. The Army Corps of Engineers and many trade associations have developed experience curves that attempt to quantify the effect of increasing crew sizes, going to overtime, or multiple shift work to accelerate work.

In addition to these analytical approaches to quantifying labor productivity problems, there should be a connection between specific events and the resultant impact on labor. If, for example, late drawings are believed to have caused labor productivity problems, then the team leader should consider having the engineering consultant compute the effect of several drawings on labor productivity. The percentage derived from this approach should then be compared with the analytical results obtained using the other methods.

It is recommended to use whatever approaches are applicable and cost beneficial to calculate and support the aggregate impact being claimed.

Once the percentage of decline in productivity can be determined, it is then a relatively simple process to apply the dollars to the event. During the audit phase, the CPA should schedule out all actual labor rates for each type of craft labor during the life of the contract. In summarizing the results of the audit during the trial, supplemental schedules reconcilable to the audit should be presented so that when the claim itself is presented these labor rates can be shown to have been audited and applied properly to the disruption portion of the claim.

§ 18.17 —Changed Conditions

Pricing changed conditions claims usually involves presenting a total cost approach. However, if only a portion of the total project were affected by changed conditions, then the actual cost for that portion of the job, less the budget or bid amount for that portion of the job, should be used.

Even though the total cost approach is being used for a discrete element of the project when changed conditions have occurred, the team leader should consider the effects of pricing the delay aspect of the changed conditions, and the effect on labor productivity following the change of conditions. These approaches are set forth in §§ **18.3** and **18.4**. Getting approximately the same answer using these techniques when compared with the total cost approach will lend credibility to the total cost approach presentation.

§ 18.18 —Changes in Scope

Two types of cost are presented in pricing changes in scope: the actual direct cost of the change (labor, materials, equipment, and subcontracts), plus the markup usually set forth in the contract's change order clause for home office overhead and profit. The altered schedule's effect on the cost of the balance of the work (ripple effect) should also be considered. If the change orders are numerous and can be shown to have caused delay to the contractor's overall schedule, then the delay should be calculated and the approach used in **18.22** should be applied.

§ 18.19 —Termination

Pricing of termination claims usually involves identifying and presenting the actual costs incurred that have not been recovered through progress payments at the date of termination. These costs include such items as demobilization, plant closing, extra equipment time, discontinued batch plant operations, and supervision.

During the contract audit the CPA should identify front-end contract costs that were scheduled to be recovered through subsequent progress payments. A careful analysis should be made to determine how much of these front-end costs have been recovered at the date of termination. For example, if all mobilization costs were incurred prior to the first progress payment at the point that 50 percent of the contract cost has been incurred for the total project, 50 percent of the revenue from the contract should have been received, leaving an uncollected balance of 50 percent of the mobilization costs. If, however, only 40 percent of the contract revenue has been received, then only 40 percent of the mobilization costs have been recovered, leaving 60 percent for the claim.

Unrecovered front-end contract costs are a difficult concept to explain to judges, juries, and arbitrators. Here, the CPA's ability to present complex accounting data in a simple, understandable form is all-important. Too often, accountants believe that their love for numbers is mirrored by others. To the extent possible, the CPA should avoid tables of numbers. The concepts will be more readily conveyed by using graphs, and the judging parties will be more enthusiastic about listening to the testimony.

§ 18.20 Cost of Capital

Negative cash flow during the progress of the work results in an investment in the project by the contractor. In these situations *negative cash flow* (actual cost incurred less payments received) should be scheduled on a monthly basis over the life of the project. The company's borrowing rate with its commercial bank should be the rate for computing the interest on the negative cash flow, and credit should be given for periods when the contractor is in a positive cash flow using the company's normal investment rate during the period (treasury bill rate or certificates of deposit). In most cases, it is difficult to collect the cost of capital unless the contractor can show borrowing from the banks or others to finance the investment in the project. In other words, the contractor must show that such costs were incurred and in fact paid. Proof of the borrowings coupled with the graphs showing that the borrowings parallel the investment in the project as it occurs over the life of the job are usually sufficient to prove cost of capital.

§ 18.21 Claim Preparation Costs

Upon initiation of the claim process, the contractor should set up cost accounts to capture and keep track of all costs related to preparation of the claim, litigation, and outside consultants and potential expert witnesses. Costs for the contractor's own employees should be segregated during this process, then presented as part of the damages along with attorneys' fees and other consultants' and experts' fees.

§ 18.22 Home Office Overhead

After presenting the direct costs of the discrete events or in total cost approach situations, the additional unrecovered home office overhead should be presented. Like labor disruption calculations, extended home office overhead is complex and difficult both from a proof and pricing point of view. Because it usually involves significant amounts of money, a CPA's presentation skills will be critical. **Sections 18.23** through **18.26** discuss the approaches to calculating extended home office overhead.

§ 18.23 —*Eichleay* Formula

The Eichleay method got its name from a successful court case involving the Eichleay Corporation.[2] In the *Eichleay* case, the contractor incurred a work suspension (delay claim) while waiting for change orders to the contract. Work could not be abandoned and replacement work was not feasible. To recover the cost of unabsorbed home office overhead (general and administrative expenses of the company) applicable to the delay, the contractor applied a daily rate method that was successful in the trial judgment.

---

[2] Eichleay Corp., 60-2 B.C.A. (CCH) ¶ 2688 (ASBCA 1960).

Eichleay Formula

$$\frac{\text{Disputed Contract Billings}}{\text{Total Contract Billings*}} \times \begin{array}{c}\text{Total}\\ \text{Overhead}\end{array} = \begin{array}{c}\text{Overhead Applicable}\\ \text{to Disputed Contract}\end{array}$$

$$\frac{\begin{array}{c}\text{Overhead Applicable}\\ \text{to Disputed Contract}\end{array}}{\begin{array}{c}\text{Days of Contract}\\ \text{Performance}\end{array}} = \text{Daily Overhead Rate}$$

$$\text{Daily Overhead Rate} \times \text{Days of Delay} = \text{Claimed Overhead}$$

*During contract period in dispute

Table 18–9 shows how the *Eichleay* method works.

Overhead Calculation

Overhead Applicable to Disputed Contract:

$\$10{,}000 \div \$30{,}000 \times \$3{,}000 = \$1{,}000$

Daily Overhead Rate:

$\$1{,}000 \div 300$ contract days $= \$3.33$/Day

Claimed Overhead:

$60 \times \$3.33 = \$199.80$

There are obvious weaknesses in the *Eichleay* method. For example, contract billings are included in the numerator of the formula to determine total home office overhead applicable to the disputed contract. In an overall loss situation on the contract, cost will always exceed billings and therefore the disputed contract naturally provides less than its fair share of the home office recovery overhead. Second, profit margins may vary depending on the type of contracts being performed. In general, there is less of a correlation between home office overhead and contract billings than with direct contract cost. Overhead does not support billings. It generally supports the cost of labor, materials, equipment, and other contract costs.

In the example set forth in **Table 18–9**, the disputed contract gets one-third of the overhead under the *Eichleay* formula because its billings are one-third of total billings during the same time frame. However, if the cost relationship is used, then the disputed contract would get approximately 43 percent of overhead ($12,000 ÷ $28,000), as opposed to the 33 percent under the *Eichleay* method using billings.

Table 18–9

Project Results

	Contract		
	Disputed	Others	Total
Billings	$10,000	$20,000	$30,000
Cost	12,000	16,000	28,000
Gross profit (loss)	$ (2,000)	$ 4,000	$ 2,000
General and administrative expense			$ 3,000
Days of delay			60
Contract days			300

Another problem with *Eichleay* is that "days of total contract performance" used to compute the "daily contract overhead rate" includes the "days of contract delay", which understates the rate and the resulting unabsorbed fixed overhead applicable to the contract.

The *Eichleay* method tends to fall in and out of favor in the legal community. Some years back the board of contract appeals disallowed it in *Capital Electric.*[3] Nevertheless, many lawyers are comfortable with this method because of its simplicity and its acceptance in many court cases. The method also enables relatively inexperienced accountants to make the computation of the unabsorbed overhead. Because the *Eichleay* method can also be explained to laymen, its acceptance in court makes the attorney and the contractor more comfortable when using it to compute damages.

§ 18.24 —Total Direct Cost Allocation

Another approach to applying overhead and contract claims is based on total direct costs. (See **Table 18–10**.) Although this method has drawbacks under certain circumstances, it is relatively easy to use and may be especially valuable when presenting the merits of a claim to a judge or jury.

Generally, the total direct cost method assigns overhead costs to individual contracts in proportion to the direct cost of the contract compared with the total direct costs of all contracts in the same time frame. The example in **Table 18–10** illustrates this method. It demonstrates how easy it is to compute an overhead rate and apply it to a disputed contract or any other contract. The overhead rate ($0.10 in this example) is computed by dividing

[3] 65 B.C.A. (CCH) Nos. 5313, 5316 (1965).

Table 18–10

Total Direct Cost Method

	Disputed Contract	All Other Contracts During Period of Performance	Total
Direct costs	$200,000	$800,000	$1,000,000
Total general and administrative/ overhead expenses			100,000
Overhead rate per dollar of direct cost:	$\frac{\$\ 100,000}{\$1,000,000}$ =	$0.10	
Overhead applied to disputed contract:	$0.10 ×	$200,000 =	$ 20,000
Loss, overhead in bid damages:			15,000
Overhead in damages calculation:			$ 5,000

total overhead ($100,000) by the total direct costs for all contracts ($1,000,000). Overhead is applied to each contract by multiplying the overhead rate ($0.10) to total direct cost for each contract ($200,000 for the disputed contract). Direct costs for contracts other than the disputed contract should include only costs incurred during the performance of the disputed contract.

In theory this method may not be suitable for many contractors because it does not allow for differences among various types of contracts. For example, some accountants may argue that contracts that consist mostly of subcontract work or materials costs should not be burdened with the same percentage of overhead costs as contracts that consist primarily of labor from the contractor's own staff.

In practice, this method is best applied to contractors that use approximately the same mix of labor, material, equipment, subcontract, and other costs for most contracts. If the cost of a major component changes significantly from job to job, direct cost allocation is probably not the best method to use.

Other allocation methods may be more useful when a significant time delay is experienced on a long-term contract. If a delay results in reducing the amount of work performed in a year (thereby reducing actual direct costs), direct cost allocation will not provide a contractor with a reasonable allocation of indirect overhead costs for contract claim purposes. In other words, if no direct job costs are incurred during the delay period, overhead will not be recovered during this period. This problem also occurs when overhead allocation is based upon direct labor hours or direct labor costs.

If replacement work is not available to use the excess capacity created by delay, the total allocation base used to distribute indirect overhead costs will be reduced. This in turn will increase the overhead rate used on other active contracts, resulting in a lower profit margin on those contracts. Overhead that should be allocated to the delayed contract will then be allocated to other active jobs, hence the reduction in profits.

In general, the total direct cost allocation method of assigning the overhead cost to individual contracts is best suited to companies that (1) typically maintain a relatively constant mix of inputs (labor, material, subcontract, and other costs) in relation to total contract costs, and (2) have not experienced significant shutdown periods on their contracts. The primary benefit of using this method is its simplicity. Judges and juries normally are able to understand its logic and application, which may aid the credibility of the claim, as will an expert who can present complex financial data simply and clearly.

§ 18.25 —Specific Base Allocation Method

The specific base allocation method (SBAM) is one of the most accurate approaches for distributing overhead costs among specific projects and/or work items within a contract. It also provides management with cost information that can be used to control costs on current jobs and help in estimating costs on future jobs. This method allocates overhead costs based on specific characteristics of each job and each overhead cost element.

SBAM requires that each overhead cost element be analyzed to determine the most appropriate allocation cost base for assigning it to an individual job. Breaking home office overhead into separate overhead pools and assigning them to a project on the cost base that most closely correlates with it will result in a more appropriate allocation to any specific project. For example, on a labor-intensive job, direct labor hours may be the most appropriate method for allocating home office payroll department costs. On a capital-intensive job that requires an unusually large amount of home office equipment maintenance and overhaul, then equipment hours may be the better allocation base for home office equipment yard expense.

Table 18–11 lists examples of home office overhead functional categories and the allocation base that most closely correlates with that cost.

If only a portion of the project is in dispute, it will be necessary to allocate certain jobsite costs among the work items. These are usually referred to as general conditions, pool, or distributable costs **Table 18–11** shows suitable allocation bases for these costs as well.

Table 18–11

Bases for Allocating Overhead

Pool Account	Allocation Base
Drill bits and steel	Cubic yards of excavation
Equipment, fuel, and supplies	Equipment hours by bid item
Concrete hauling	Cubic yards of concrete
Superintendents	Direct labor hours
Utilities	Direct labor hours
Procurement and purchasing	Direct material dollars
Accounting	Total direct cost
Interest income and expense	Total direct cost

SBAM alleviates many of the problems associated with arbitrary allocation methods, such as assigning overhead costs based on contract price, total job direct costs, direct labor costs, and so on. To illustrate the distortion of income reported for two jobs using an arbitrary allocation method, consider the example in **Table 18–12** in which overhead is allocated to two jobs on the basis of direct labor dollars. Both projects contribute the same amount toward overhead and operating profit ($100,000 per job), but in using direct labor dollars as a base, Job A, which used more direct labor than subcontract labor, is shown as a loss job. If the specific base allocation method is used, gross profits will be more uniform.

Although SBAM is, in theory, one of the soundest approaches to allocating overhead, practical drawbacks limits its use. Few contractors can justify

Table 18–12

Direct Labor Cost Method

	Job A	Job B
Contract revenue	$1,500,000	$1,500,000
Direct costs:		
Direct labor	300,000	100,000
Subcontracts	100,000	300,000
Materials	900,000	900,000
Equipment	100,000	100,000
	1,400,000	1,400,000
Variable margin	100,000	100,000
Overhead @ $.50 per labor dollar	150,000	50,000
Operating profit (loss)	$ (50,000)	$ 50,000

the cost of allocating overhead on multiple bases. Second, wide variations in the type and mix of jobs would require that formulas for allocating overhead cost elements be adjusted for each project. Although this task is not impossible, the cost of doing it is seldom justified.

SBAM is suitable primarily for large, high-risk projects with high potential for major claims. In certain claim situations, especially when distributable costs (pool, general conditions, and so on) are large, many professionals believe that the more specific the allocation method is, the more defensible the financial aspects of a claim will be. This consideration should be weighed against increased complexity (and costs) of this allocation method, and the likelihood that a judge and jury will be able to understand the complexities of the method.

§ 18.26 —Occupancy

In some contracts overhead cost is more a function of occupancy than contract dollars. If home office overhead costs are made up primarily of depreciation of fabrication facilities and equipment, then a standard method of determining contract occupancy should be determined. For example, assume that a contractor has a contract to manufacture heat exchangers and to install them in an electrical power plant. Assume that the contract is delayed and that most of the home office overhead is made up of facilities for the manufacture of the heat exchangers. In this situation floor space reserved for the manufacture of the heat exchangers on the disputed contract versus total available floor space can be used to determine the percentage of overhead applicable to the contract in dispute.

$$\frac{\text{Disputed Contract Reserved Flooring}}{\text{Total Contracts Flooring}} \times \text{Total Overhead} = \text{Overhead Allocated to Disputed Contract}$$

§ 18.27 Profit Recovery

After working with its claims and litigation team to determine additional costs as the result of claim entitlement, including recovery of additional home office overhead, it would seem obvious that the contractor should be entitled to a reasonable profit. This is not always the case, however. Questions constantly arise as to equity, profit percentages, and the base to which profit percentages should be applied. Should the profit percentage applied be the same as that in the original bid? Should it be the historic profit average on contracts performed by the company? Should it be the profit margin on contracts of a similar nature? Should there be any profit at all if costs are awarded and the contractor is made whole? A myriad of questions seem to arise when recovery of profit on a claim is sought. There have been cases in arbitrations in which the contractor has clearly proven its entitlement and the cost of the entitlement, but in attempting to please both parties, the arbitrators have not given the contractor overhead, profit, and interest. Also, the availability of profit may well depend on the legal theory counsel advances: damages for breach, quantum merit, or reliance on the contract change order clause provisions. The change order clause provisions are of course the simplest way to get profit in many cases, because the change order provisions usually include a built-in profit and overhead percentage.

It would seem clear to most businessmen, contractors, and others familiar with the moneymaking process and the other subjective aspects of the claim process that a contractor should be entitled to a fair and reasonable profit once entitlement has been established and damages presented.

In determining a profit percentage to apply in the damage calculations, it would seem that the contractor ought to use the profit percentage applied in its original bid for the same project. This will work well if the contractor can show that it routinely achieves that margin on other work. Attempting to collect a 10 percent profit margin when the best the company has been able to do on the average is 7 percent would seem to raise questions about the propriety of the claimed amount. To support the percentage used in arriving at the dollar amount of profit in the claim, the best approach usually is to present a schedule of profitable contracts completed in the past and a computation of the average percentage achieved. If a contractor performs jobs of a diverse nature with differing profit margins in differing marketplaces, then the schedule should be of similar jobs completed in recent years and the average profit margin for that type of work computed. Previous jobs resulting in losses should be excluded from the computations because the contract in the claim situation at issue would have been profitable but for acts of the other party. Therefore, the average profit margin on profitable jobs should be the base for the calculation.

Another approach to supporting the profit percentage is to prepare a compilation and summary of the contractor's total company income statements for several years preceding the disputed job, adjusted for lost contracts. It is best if these figures are derived from audited annual financial statements because the auditor's opinion will lend credibility to the numbers used in the calculations. This historical profit analysis coupled with an individual job listing approach is not difficult to prepare and the team leaders should consider using both approaches. If just the job listing approach is used, it should be reconciled to the audited financial statements on an annual basis.

Questions also arise as to what base should be used for applying the profit percentage. A schedule should be presented showing the contractor's actual final cost and overhead in the same format as the original bid. If in the bid the profit percentage is applied to direct contract cost plus home office overhead recovery, then that should be the manner in which the damage calculations are made for profit. The team leader should also consider having the damage expert present a summary of how the contractor will be made whole if the damages are awarded, thus revealing that the overhead and profit figures are equal to what was in the bid or some form of historic analysis.

Calculating damages in complex construction litigation requires careful thought and strategies. The extent to which the calculations will stand up at trial quite often depends on the consultant and expert witness selected by the team leader to prepare and present the damages. Many attorneys have no background in accounting. If their undergraduate degrees are in other fields, they require a damage expert who can quickly gain their confidence and function like a subcontractor to the attorney. This relieves the attorney of having to focus on the numbers and other areas he is ill-equipped to understand or question.

The ability to present damages to judges, juries, and others with little understanding of accounting principles or their application in a simple understandable fashion will go a long way toward collecting the damages if the entitlement aspect of the case can be proved.

Table 18–13 provides a handy checklist for the attorney to insure that all events impacting the contractor have been considered in the damage calculations.

Table 18–13

Damages Checklist*

	Additional Cost Yes	No
Delay		
Increase in time-related costs		
Escalation in material costs		
Escalation in labor costs		
Additional equipment time		
Effect on other contracts		
Rental versus owned equipment		
Ripple effect		
Increased bond premium		
Increased workers' compensation premiums		
Other insurance costs		
Subcontractor claims		
Lower labor productivity		
Lost alternative income		
Disruption		
Lower productivity/increased labor cost		
Costs of materials increased by mistakes		
Additional move-in/move-out		
Delay		
Higher workers' compensation premiums		
Higher performance bond premiums		
Changed Conditions		
Additional labor head count		
Change in mix of craft laborers		
Additional/different equipment		
Additional materials		
Extended schedule		
Additional supervision		
Change Orders		
Labor		
Materials		
Equipment		
Subcontracts		
Schedule delay		
Ripple effect		
Other		
Termination		
Demobilization		
Labor		
Equipment		
Materials		
Subcontracts		
Loss on forced sale of equipment		
Supervision		
Jobsite facilities		
Lost alternative income		

* There obviously are additional factors that can have an impact on damage calculation. Those listed here are helpful in providing general guidelines.

CHAPTER 19

LABOR PRODUCTIVITY IN CONSTRUCTION CLAIMS

Roger Hewitt

Roger Hewitt is a director in Ernst & Young's San Francisco, California, office, with over 29 years' experience in managing and conducting complex investigative and analytical engagements. He is a graduate of the University of California at Berkeley. Mr. Hewitt is a member of the firm's National Construction Industry Group and focuses his services on litigation support and consulting to the construction industry. His experience in analyzing damages includes over 30 major engagements involving construction contract disputes, antitrust, trade secrets violations, misappropriation of funds, and business interruption.

§ 19.1 Introduction

§ 19.2 Productivity and Estimating

§ 19.3 —Expectations of the Contractor and Owner

§ 19.4 —Factors Affecting Construction Productivity

§ 19.5 —Reasonable Proof of Damages from Lost Productivity

§ 19.6 —Other Factors Affecting Labor Costs and Entitlement

§ 19.7 Selecting a General Approach

§ 19.8 —Top-down Approach

§ 19.9 —Problems with Top-down Approach

§ 19.10 —Bottom-up Analysis

§ 19.11 Developing the Claim: Variance Analysis

§ 19.12 Quantifying Productivity Losses

§ 19.13 Documenting Disruption

§ 19.14 Measured Mile Approach

§ 19.15 Dallavia Method

§ 19.16 —Modified Dallavia
§ 19.17 Using Productivity Curves to Calculate Damages
§ 19.18 —Productivity Losses from Acceleration
§ 19.19 —Acceleration Requirements
§ 19.20 —Inefficiency from Crew Increases and Overmanning
§ 19.21 —Productivity Loss from Increased Crewing (Without Crowding)
§ 19.22 —Overmanning/Crowding
§ 19.23 —Extended Overtime Inefficiency
§ 19.24 Calculating Lost Productivity from Inclement Weather
§ 19.25 Calculating Compounding Impacts
§ 19.26 Learning Curve Claims
§ 19.27 Ratio Delay Studies

§ 19.1 Introduction

Quantifying construction labor productivity losses and linking them to events and conditions on the job are two of the more difficult and least understood aspects of discrete cost claims. Contractors, owners, and their attorneys and experts often fail to appreciate what constitutes reasonable determination of compensable productivity loss, that is, the bringing together of three proof elements: lost productivity, its cost, and compensable cause.

Certainly, a plaintiff contractor should be entitled to recover additional labor costs incurred because of and on behalf of the owner. On the other hand, an owner should not be expected to pay for added costs simply because a contractor failed to provide the productive work force promised or because the contractor failed to manage the labor force or to provide the support resources needed on the job.

Therein lies the basis for nearly every lost productivity cost claim, and the problem facing every expert or layman claim analyst as well: two points of view and two adamant and plausible positions. How does a contractor prove to a judge or jury who know little about construction that its position is right, especially with something as nebulous as lost productivity? And how can any nonconstruction person be expected to sort through the myriad of arguments and counterarguments to decide whether a contractor really suffered some sort of efficiency loss?

The author has observed that proof is basically whatever the triers of fact accept from the information presented them by either side of a dispute. What they see and think they understand is what you get. Whether they really understand may be a different matter entirely, as may be the reasonableness of the judgment or award. But, instead of complaining about their ignorance, it is better to focus on providing the judge or jury with clear and convincing evidence, that is, evidence they understand.

Understanding evidence is not terribly difficult when it comes to the cost of 100 extra yards of concrete. But productivity? Productivity is a real uphill fight. Not only must contractors prove that they incurred an added cost, but that cost now must be linked to an unseen, shadowy concept about which little is known or understood. Consequently, the contractor must become an educator as well as a plaintiff. In addition to understanding the costs incurred, the trier(s) must be led to understand concepts of productivity, how productivity affects contracting and construction costs, and what factors impact productivity. They must understand that efficiency losses are not "fluff," as the defense surely will contend, but are real and costly.

The claims analyst preparing the proof theories and supporting evidence should begin work with a basic assumption that those who will decide the outcome of the dispute lack construction or production knowledge. In addition to collecting and presenting factual evidence of impact, the analyst must develop a tutorial presentation that provides a basic familiarity with productivity, those factors that impact construction production, and the relevant issues important to deciding efficiency disputes. The analyst's presentation should start with ground-level basics, including:

1. Construction productivity and estimating concepts: how the reasonable expectations of contractors and owners affect anticipated productivity, how anticipated productivity affects costs and profits, and what factors affect productivity
2. What constitutes reasonable evidence of lost productivity damages (from an analyst's perspective)
3. What factors must be examined in analyzing lost productivity
4. Common methods for calculating productivity losses, their reasonableness, and their limitations.

This chapter begins with a discussion of these four issues. The chapter also discusses the characteristics and relative merits of the "top down" and "bottom up" approaches, then steps through the analysis of productivity losses, and examines some of the more common causes of lost productivity and alternative methods for quantifying their impact.

§ 19.2 Productivity and Estimating

Productivity can be defined as the amount of output for each time unit of resource applied. Labor production typically is measured in outputs for each worker hour, for example, square feet per hour, tons per hour, or cubic yards per hour. Construction job estimates, however, typically are calculated and measured using the reverse productivity measure—worker hours per unit.

Labor hours are planned for specific work activities and the job in aggregate, based on:

1. Estimated quantities of work to be performed (outputs)
2. The type and complexity of the work activities, the anticipated work schedule, contract specifications, and anticipated site conditions
3. The production rate anticipated for each unit comprising the whole job.

Once quantities, specifications, complexities, and work methods have been determined, work requirements can be estimated in detail by using historical productivity data developed internally from similar work, production data and adjustment factors from one or more industry research services, or some combination of similar data that, when quantities and rates are extended, provides a reasonable approximation of expected labor costs.

By combining all the data, the project schedule, and reasonable assumptions regarding site conditions and the work force, the contractor can develop manloading, equipment, and material schedules, and a final budget for the job. (Manloading refers to the number of workers needed for a job.)

Any errors made in estimating quantities, productivity rates, or unit costs will have an inverse impact on actual costs versus those budgeted. The same is true with respect to changes to the conditions and representations upon which the contractor has relied in preparing his estimate, bid, and budget.

§ 19.3 —Expectations of the Contractor and Owner

If the contractor has bid the job on a lump-sum basis, or any basis wherein profitability may be impacted by the owner or others, the contractor necessarily relies on certain expectations in putting together the cost estimate. Such expectations are critical to issues of productivity, both to the contractor planning the job and to the claims analyst concerned with lost productivity. The intent here is not to impart points of law regarding implied warranties or contractual reliances, but to emphasize that certain expectations are reasonable requisites to the construction planning and estimating process and are important considerations in establishing a foundation for lost productivity.

First in the area of reliance are the contract documents and representations made by the owner to the contractor regarding the nature and scope of the work, the specifications that must be met, the schedule, and, in some instances, the site conditions. In addition, the contractor's plan assumes that owner-furnished documents are accurate, that the owner will not interfere with the performance of the contractor's work, that the contractor will be given reasonable access to the jobsite in order to perform its work, and that the contractor will not be subjected to unreasonable delays or unreasonable interferences by other contractors. Absent information to the contrary, the contractor is assumed to have planned the job to optimize his profits (using optimum crewing levels) and expects a reasonable opportunity to work as efficiently as possible so long as the contractor does not impact the project schedule or disrupt the work of others.

To the extent the contractor's plan is in accordance with the contract documents and representations by the owner or the owner's representatives, and to the extent that the plan is free of determinable errors or unreasonable expectations, the contractor's plan, as represented in its bid, budget, and schedule, should be considered a reasonable basis from which all actual performance is measured. In other words, absent errors in the plan, optimum performance should be no worse than that planned by the contractor and accepted by the owner.

The owner also has certain expectations that bear on productivity. First is the expectation that the contractor has the ability to deliver the job on time and on budget as represented by the contractor. The owner expects a workmanlike performance from competent craftsmen working under the contractor's effective management and the owner expects contractors to coordinate their work so it will not disrupt efficient construction of the owner's project.

§ 19.4 —Factors Affecting Construction Productivity

Many events and conditions can affect construction productivity, ranging from something as seemingly minor as waiting for tools or information to unforeseen site conditions to blinding snowstorms. However, not all productivity losses are compensable. Losses resulting from inclement weather and other acts of God, for example, typically are not compensable except in unusual situations or when the owner caused a condition the contractor otherwise would not have experienced, for example, a delay resulting in work during inclement weather. Production losses are generally not compensable when they occur because of the contractor's own acts or omissions or failure to provide competent crews.

There are three primary steps in analyzing lost productivity:

1. Establishing that a labor overrun did, in fact, occur
2. Determining whether the cost overrun resulted from lost productivity or other changes and

3. Assessing whether the contractor's estimating errors or management actions may have contributed to any lost productivity.

Doubtless, some will question that an actual overrun is necessary to experience an impact on labor productivity. It is true that productivity could be affected without exceeding an estimate or budget. However, establishing such a claim will still require the same three primary steps, but with an additional step aimed at establishing a reasonable increase in the planned productivity rate. This would precede step 1 in order to assert a revised budget that would have been achieved but for the impacts actually experienced. Thereafter, the concepts and proof requirements remain the same.

The analyst, therefore, must be concerned not only with factors causing lost productivity but also with the underlying causes that brought about conditions resulting in lost productivity, that is, the *root cause* creating entitlement to compensation. Little purpose would be served in calculating the lost productivity resulting from extended overtime if, for example, that overtime had been worked only to recover production slippage because the contractor failed to man the job or supply needed equipment and materials according to the schedule. The analyst must recognize and prepare to prove occurrence both of the factors affecting productivity and the root causes bringing those factors into play.

Table 19–1 illustrates an analytical approach that is helpful in analyzing and developing productivity claims, specifically in focusing on potential impact factors, their causes, and issues that may constitute underlying proof requirements. The approach consists of separating impact factors into three categories: primary, secondary (or underlying), and root causes.

A *primary causal factor* is one that emerges as having the most apparent direct impact on productivity and cost. Extended overtime or out-of-sequence work could be examples. Typically, these factors provide the basis for quantifying the cost incurred.

The *secondary* and *root causes* relate more to issues of entitlement, that is, the underlying cause and responsibility for events and conditions leading to the visible impact factor. One example is delay resulting from late delivery of owner-furnished materials as opposed to delay from failure to man the job.

Table 19–1 depicts delay (a primary causal factor for time-related costs) as a secondary factor potentially impacting many productivity claims. When applicable, then, the delay itself must be established in order to pursue recovery of productivity costs ultimately flowing from it, such as acceleration costs. Why is delay a secondary cost rather than a root cause? The distinction is made here only to emphasize the myriad of potential root causes underlying a delay, only some of which are the owner's responsibility.

Consider that delay might be a related issue in claiming damages for lost efficiency in winter work or for productivity losses from overtime,

Table 19–1

Common Causes of Lost Productivity

Causal Factor	P = Primary S = Secondary	Root Cause
Delay Extended Term	S	• Poor crew qualification • Over-inspection • Regulatory/administrative holds • Weather • Failure to man/equip job; early quits, late starts • Late deliveries of materials and equipment • Defective drawings, holds placed on work • Access restrictions • Late approvals of submittals • Changes, changed conditions • Excessive absence, terminations
Crowding, Stacking Overmanning Overtime Second Shift	P	• Excessive changes, no extension • Directed expediting • Delay, no extension • Increased scope, no extension • Changed condition, no extension • Failure to coordinate schedule/trades • Rework/repair of damages
Rework/Repair to Completed Work	P	• Defective workmanship; inadequate supervision and training, QA, QC, turnover procedures • Over-inspection • Change in specifications • Damage by contractor, damage by others
Winter Work Extreme Heat Humidity	P	• Delay (root causes) • Unusual conditions • Included in schedule • Directed acceleration in inclement weather
Field Interferences	P	• Defective drawings • Stacking of crews • Out-of-sequence work • Failure to coordinate crafts • Changed conditions
Loss of Normal Learning Curve	P	• Stop-start, leapfrogging • Excessive terminations • Excessive changes • Out-of-sequence work • Multiple shifts
Limited Qualified Work Force, Work Force Morale	P	• Competition for labor force in area • Poor pay/job conditions • Remote area • Poor supervision and training • Bad crew

overmanning, or multiple shifts, all arising from directed or constructive acceleration. Is not the root cause of the delay a key proof issue also? Should it not be addressed with the same care and scrutiny as the calculation of impact? Absolutely!

All three types of causal factors may be reasonable requirements for proof of damages and the analyst should look for and deal with all reasonable possible explanations for the claimed damages costs. Nothing should be left to inference because someone, at sometime, is sure to dig down beneath the analyst's well-documented impact factor and challenge its clay-footed root cause. Just as sure as the contractor claims late approvals or late deliveries, the owner will claim that the contractor failed either to staff the job timely or to provide competent workers in accordance with the contract, or will make some allegation equally damaging to the proof theory. Such attacks are better defended when foreseen and disposed of in advance.

Moreover, litigation is far too expensive for claims analysts to delude themselves or their clients. Objective assessment of damages is the best service an analyst can provide. That process is aided substantially when the analysis is structured to seek out not only the primary factors but the underlying and root causes as well.

§ 19.5 —Reasonable Proof of Damages from Lost Productivity

Proof of damages resulting from productivity loss, although not requiring precision, should survive four tests of reasonableness:

1. The incurrence of loss (additional costs) should be conclusively established
2. Reasonableness of the contractor's plan should be established; typical contractor-caused factors should be examined and either included or eliminated as part of the attribution analyses
3. Specific factors causing the loss should be identified
4. A reasonable quantitative link should be established between causal factors and claimed damage amounts.

These are all important elements in prevailing in claim situations, but the first two are critical. The loss itself is the one element a contractor should be able to establish conclusively, without question. Establishing that loss puts everyone on notice that the contractor has been harmed. Demonstrating the reasonableness of the plan (or bid) is also essential to blocking a principal defense contention. Showing historical ability to perform at the planned rate conveys that something out of the ordinary happened to the contractor.

There is perhaps a fifth test that should be applied whenever major productivity losses are claimed: common sense. That test asks the question, "If the contractor really lost 50 percent productivity because of owner disruptions, where are all the complaints the contractor registered with the owner, documenting the problem and demanding relief?" Their existence does not necessarily prove the disruption or the productivity loss, but their absence raises a difficult common sense hurdle.

Most lost productivity claims often fail, or should fail, on one or more of the reasonableness tests, particularly the quantification of causal impacts and the related tying of responsibility for those impacts. Problems seem to stem not so much from a lack of available information or proof methods and techniques as from a lack of understanding of productivity basics and applied logic.

§ 19.6 —Other Factors Affecting Labor Costs and Entitlement

The determination of a labor overrun does not, in and of itself, establish lost productivity or that lost productivity accounted entirely for the identified overrun. Several other potential explanations should be examined before advancing or accepting such a claim. First consider contractor errors or changes in the contractor's planned approach:

Quantities and specifications. Were there changes to either that affected cost? If so, were the changes in the plan the result of estimating errors by the contractor or changes in the contract scope? Were job activities and related costs overlooked in the estimate? Are costs covered by change orders?

Cost and mix of labor. Did labor rates or the mix of journeymen and apprentice labor change? Did the cost increase because of the change in labor mix rather than increased hours?

Once satisfied that changes to quantities, specifications, or labor rates did not account for any increased labor costs, the analyst may conclude that a loss of planned productivity has occurred. However, the question of why the loss occurred remains unanswered. The first place to look in search of that answer should be inward. Is there a self-inflicted wound? The owner is sure to look first at:

Planned production rates. Are the rates in the estimate or budget unreasonable, unsupportable by past performance or industry standards?

Labor and equipment mix. Was there a change in the planned use of equipment or type of equipment that affected labor productivity? Were overall costs affected? Did equipment cost savings offset labor productivity losses to any extent?

Supervision and personnel. Was there a change from the plan in the amount and composition of supervisory and support personnel? Did supervisory span of control increase or did the contractor change the anticipated experience levels of supervisors? Is the management team experienced in the type of construction on the job? Does the team have a history of unsuccessful performance? Did a change in journeymen and apprentice mix result in lower productivity? Were production decreases (units/hour) offset by hourly rate savings?

Size of job and availability of craft work force. Was local craft availability low in relation to job requirements? Some experts[1] estimate productivity losses as high as 20 percent when local craft availability matches the peak job requirement. Losses of 15 to 25 percent are attributed to jobs having peak work force requirements ranging from 200 to 500 workers.[2] Do estimate calculations allow for such factors?

Absenteeism and turnover. Were rates significantly greater than allowed for in plans (industry or historical norms included in estimating productivity standards)? Studies attribute added costs of 12 paid hours for every 8-hour absence and 24 hours for every termination.[3] What standards are incorporated in the bid?

Local work force characteristics. Does the estimate allow for local work force productivity characteristics as might be evidenced in various publications?

Once all these factors have been evaluated and their impact either accounted for or affirmatively eliminated, the analysis can move on to identifying and calculating compensable damages resulting from productivity losses.

§ 19.7 Selecting a General Approach

The general approach and analytical techniques used in preparing a claim are usually determined by the quality of the contractor's job records. The better the accounting records and job documentation, the more straight-

---

[1] Neil *et al., Predicting Productivity,* 1984 AACE Transactions.

[2] *Id.*

[3] *Absenteeism and Turnover, Construction Industry Cost Effectiveness Project,* 1982 Bus. Roundtable (New York, NY).

forward and detailed the damage claim is likely to be. Most often, the claims analyst is left with something between minimal and optimal information and is faced with finding one or a combination of approaches and techniques that best match available data, make sense, and present a convincing case of damages incurred.

One of the first decisions is whether to use a "top-down" or a "bottom-up" general approach. As their names suggest, the two methodologies approach damages from opposite directions. Of the two, the top-down approach usually is less time-consuming, can be accomplished with less information, tends to be the more general in its presentation, and is most commonly encountered (in some variation).

§ 19.8 —Top-down Approach

Table 19–2 illustrates a simple *top-down* concept. The approach starts from a recognized outcome (for example, total labor costs) and works downward (or backward), identifying causes of lost productivity and calculating the costs attributed to each, usually as a percentage of the total cost. The concept works best when an entire job is impacted and there are multiple factors that have compounding impacts on productivity.

Table 19–2

Top-down Claim

Total Hours Incurred	10,000	
Budgeted Hours	5,000	
Overrun	5,000	
Impacts	Hours	Cost
Overtime @ 5% of total	500	$ 20,000
Overmanning at 30% of 9,500 hours	2,850	114,000
Restricted access at 10% of 6,540 hours	665	26,600
Weather at 15% of 5,985 hours	898	35,920
Other impacts	87	3,480
TOTAL	5,000	$200,000

Top-down calculations and concepts appear deceptively simple. For example, a disputed job might have incurred 1,000 hours of labor, as we have depicted in **Table 19–2**. Using a top-down approach, an analyst might assert from other analyses that 10 percent of those hours resulted from overmanning inefficiencies. One hundred hours at appropriate labor rates would be claimed as damages resulting from that productivity impact factor.

The amount attributed to overmanning would then be deducted from the total hours worked before calculating another impact category (for example, overtime inefficiency) in order to avoid double counting impacts. The process would then continue, working down through the various impacts until the costs of all identified impacts were calculated and set aside.

§ 19.9 —Problems with Top-down Approach

Top-down damage analyses can provide acceptable damage calculations, depending on the nature of the disruption and on the care and accuracy of the analyses. There are, however, several potential problems and pitfalls often seen with top-down presentations:

1. Top-down analyses tend to mask actual causes of costs by focusing on outcomes and ignoring or circumventing the chronology and impact of specific events and circumstances, for example, focusing on overmanning or overtime rather than events that necessitated increased manning or overtime
2. By failing to identify and link production losses to root causes, top-down claims often take on the basic concept of a total cost claim, asking the trier of fact to believe that all costs calculated for the impacts (outcomes) were the fault of the defendant
3. Top-down damage calculations always present a high potential for double counting of impacts by failing to exclude from further calculations those hours and costs already claimed as damages or by mixing calculation methods (for example, claiming inefficiency percentages and costs for specific work, such as repairs)
4. Top-down analyses may overstate damages when multiple impacts are not compounding or do not impact the entire job or activity under analysis.

§ 19.10 —Bottom-up Analysis

The bottom-up approach usually begins with the budget as the starting point of its analysis and works forward, typically in chronological fashion, identifying impacts and the costs of each. Each causal factor is assessed as encountered in the examination, including responsibility for the event and condition, and a revised worker-hour base, cost, and claimed damages are calculated following completion of each component.

Although more difficult, the approach is generally superior to the top-down method because it forces the examination of specific events and conditions and their linkage to costs incurred as the analysis moves forward through execution of the project. Properly applied, the approach provides a well-reasoned and clearly articulated assessment of impacts and resultant damages. And because of its building-block or stair-step approach to revising the base budget as impacts are identified, the bottom-up method is particularly suitable to capturing the increasing magnitude of impacts (the ripple effect) as they continue.

A bottom-up claim approach can take a number of forms or be presented in various levels of detail. **Table 19–3** is a simple example of one summary claim format that demonstrates the general concept.

Starting with the budget, or a specific portion of the budget, we can see in Section I that the sample job was planned to be completed in 50 days, with a total expenditure of 2,000 hours, or an average daily crew of five workmen, with a labor rate of $40 an hour. Approved changes added 250 hours and two days to the schedule, establishing an approved revised budget of 2,250 hours.

Section II summarizes the additional compensable work requirements and days of extension, if any, granted by the owner. Ideally, these would obtain from a chronological analysis of events and conditions on the job. Included in this section are nonproductive hours paid but lost because of owner-caused problems, nonproduction days lost to delay, and disputed extra work items. The lost hours paid in this section demonstrate that unproductive hours not only result in costs for idle workers but also constitute lost production that must be recaptured in the project schedule. Days lost to delay highlight the overall compaction of the work and the compounding impact of added work requirements.

Sections I and II are then combined to establish the total work requirement and allowed workdays before productivity impacts are calculated. In our constructed scenario, Sections I and II depict a revised work requirement of 3,310 hours to be accomplished in 52 days. Daily work force requirements have been increased by 60 percent over plan because of the approved changes and the specific items identified in Section II.

Section III displays the expected inefficiency from increased crewing, estimated at 11 percent based on industry productivity curves, and yielding an anticipated impact of 409 hours (3,310 divided by 89 percent). In addition, the contractor worked 300 hours of extended overtime at the owner's direction, impacting some 1500 worker hours at 5 percent. The overall analysis supports a total expected work requirement of 3,794 hours, with approximately 1,544 hours of disputed extra work and lost productivity.

Table 19–3

Bottom-up Claim

	Base Hours Required	Cost @ $40/Hr.	Approved Work Days
Section I—Budget			
Original Budget	2,000	$ 80,000	50
Approved Changes	250	10,000	4
Revised Budget	2,250	$ 90,000	54
Section II—Claims Before Impact			
A. Lost/Paid Hours			
—Defective Drawings—Bldg. 3	200	$ 8,000	
—Flooding—Bldg. 5	160	6,400	
—Damage to Concrete—Bldg. 2	300	12,000	
B. Nonproductive Delay Days (Backup Detail)	0		(2)
C. Disputed Extra Work			
—Hopper and Apron	400	16,000	
Total Budget and Claims Before Impact	3,310	$132,400	52
Section III—Productivity Impacts			
—Average Daily Manning—8			
—Increase Over Plan—60%			
A. Increased crew @ 11% Impact	409	$ 16,360	6
B. Overtime 300 Hours Worked 1,500 Impacted @ 5%	75	3,000	1
Section IV—Total Revised Cost	3,794	$151,760	59
Less Revised Budget	2,250	90,000	
CLAIM	1,544	$ 61,760	

Section IV simply totals all costs (assume overtime premium was paid) and subtracts the revised budget to arrive at the claimed damages.

The bottom up approach appears to present a much clearer presentation of events and their relationship to impacts and costs and is much less subject to error or obfuscation than a top-down presentation. Although preparation costs typically exceed those of a top-down analysis, the added value of the resulting product usually justifies the added expenditure. The author recommends its use whenever sufficient information exists to support the analysis.

§ 19.11 Developing the Claim: Variance Analysis

The analyst should begin claim development with a simple total cost variance analysis, similar to **Table 19–4**, which compares the budgeted and actual labor costs by job area or activity. The analysis, conducted early in the project, provides the analyst with an overview of the job performance and a readily understandable snapshot of the magnitude of the problem and the overall performance in specific job areas. It is extremely useful because:

1. As an analytical tool, the variance analysis highlights significant areas and focuses on areas warranting greatest attention
2. As a presentation tool, the total cost presentation demonstrates the extent to which the contractor has been harmed (expenditure of 200,000 hours over a budget of 100,000 hours is an obvious fact not easily swept under a rug or attributed to contractor oversight)
3. It establishes for jurors a perspective of the value of the work performed and creates a foundation of understanding needed to move on to more complex analyses
4. When all is said and done, the total cost presentation may well be the single element of the dispute that is understood during deliberations.

Table 19–4

Total Cost Variance Analysis

Labor Hours:	Budget	Actual	Variance
Area 1	$ 100	$ 100	$ --
Area 2	150	475	325
Area 3	200	350	150
Area 4	200	600	400
	$ 650	$ 1,525	$ 875

Labor Cost:	Budget	Actual	Variance
Area 1	$ 4,000	$ 4,000	$ --
Area 2	6,000	21,375	15,375
Area 3	8,000	14,700	6,700
Area 4	8,000	27,000	19,000
	$26,000	$67,075	$41,075

Concurrent to, or immediately following, preparation of the variance analysis, project background information and information related to events affecting performance of the project should be collected. Activities in this phase are normally of two types: (1) interviews with project personnel to gain their insight into problems and perceived impacts; and (2) review and analysis of various project source documents, including:

1. Bid estimate file
2. Project contract
3. Contract schedule, manloading and equipment schedules, planned and actual
4. Job cost reports, productivity reports, craft hour reports, and other management reports
5. Contract drawings
6. Certified payroll, payroll registers, and time cards
7. Material, equipment, and subcontractor invoices
8. Equipment time cards/logs
9. Daily logs and reports, meeting notes, transmittal logs
10. Project correspondence, including internal memos
11. Requests for information, extra work requests
12. Authorizations, change order requests, approved change orders
13. Claims submitted by and to contractor.

Principal products from this phase of work consist of as-built and as-planned documents, developed and prepared on timelines, which overlay key aspects of the job by area and time period; for example:

1. Production units completed
2. Daily manloading and period labor costs
3. Equipment use and costs
4. Impact events and conditions affecting the job (including changes)
5. Payment requests and revenues received
6. Notices, communications, and other records documenting actions taken or positions stated.

As the analyst works through the phase, ideally a chronology of the project will unfold and significant impacts can be identified and traced to causal events and circumstances in specific job areas and during specific time periods, thus allowing the analyst to develop preliminary damage packages. From these the analyst usually is able to determine where productivity losses likely occurred, the various entitlement theories potentially applicable and their requirements, alternative methods for quantifying the damage, and the reasonableness of potential approaches, given the information and resources available.

§ 19.12 Quantifying Productivity Losses

Some techniques commonly used to quantify productivity losses in construction claims are preferable to others, but all have distinct advantages and disadvantages. Some are far simpler; others present more convincing results. All share a common weakness—lack of precision. None precisely measures claimed productivity damages. Rather, each provides supporting evidence of the reasonableness of the claimed damage and a reasonable explanation for the documented hard money loss incurred on planned labor.

§ 19.13 Documenting Disruption

Documenting disruptive events and activities at the time of occurrence can be critical to proving both entitlement and damages. Unfortunately, such occurrences and their impacts often go unrecorded, or recordings reflect only minimal information contained in a notice or logging. All such disruptions should be systematically documented in detail, including a description of the disruption and responsibility for its cause, the activities, area, and crews impacted, any mitigating actions taken, and the estimated production losses experienced by the crew on the date of the recording. Continued collection of ongoing costs can be simplified by creating cost accounting systems, similar to extra work accounts, in which categories of disruptions are coded and sequentially subcoded to create running accounts of specific disruptions. Examples of such accounts include:

- Defective drawings
- Access restrictions
- Out-of-sequence work
- Relocation of crews, equipment, and scaffolding
- Repairing damage by others
- Field interferences, crowding, stacking of crews
- Over-inspection
- Out-of-scope work
- Late deliveries, owner-caused delays.

Information of this type is somewhat difficult to obtain because it falls outside the expertise and mindset of most construction supervisors and is not as important to them as the principal concerns of getting the job done. However, such information is attainable with crews trained to recognize claim situations and with appropriate cost accounting systems and controls at the jobsite. Capturing the data will not guarantee compensation, but a detailed costing under a few disruption codes can certainly provide more convincing chronology of damages than a laundry list of general accusations supported only by an expert's opinion of what might be expected when such things happen.

§ 19.14 Measured Mile Approach

Measured mile methods are used to determine productivity losses by comparing production rates achieved in unimpacted work periods to production rates experienced during periods of claimed impact. **Figure 19–1** illustrates a typical measured mile concept.

Underlying the measured mile methodology are the assumption and assertion that productivity rates achieved during the unimpacted period would have been achieved in the impacted period(s) (or bettered with learning curve efficiencies) *but for* the owner-caused factors that impacted production. Claimed damages are based on measured rate and cost differences in the two periods, which are applied to impacted production units and extended to arrive at claimed impact amounts.

Generally, analysts using a measured mile approach eliminate from consideration the first and last 10 percent of a job because those periods usually are not representative of the project as a whole. The analyst then seeks

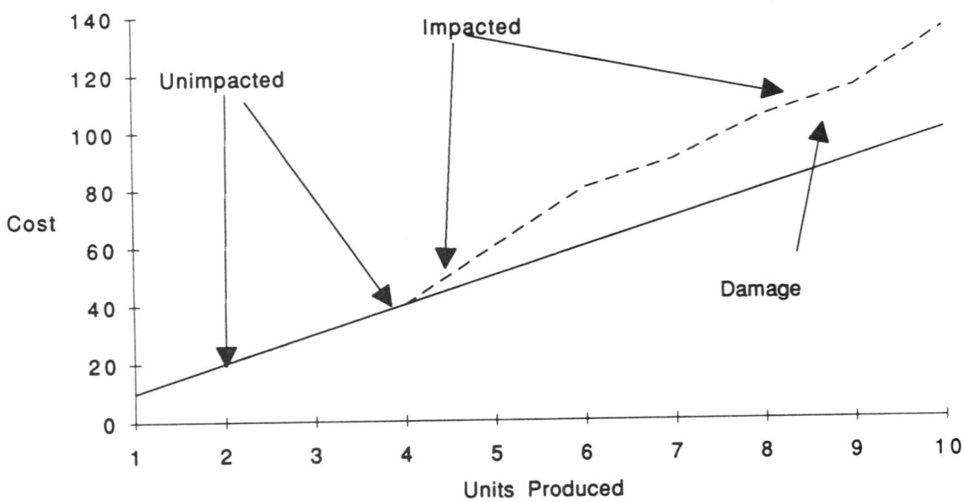

Figure 19–1. Measured mile technique.

a representative period of unimpacted work, that is, a period when (1) the work performed was similar in all aspects to work performed during periods of claimed impact, and (2) a sufficient amount was performed to demonstrate the contractor's ability to perform at the observed rate over an extended period.

When possible, the unimpacted period is selected from the same job as the impacted periods against which production rates will be compared. Obviously, similar work done on the same job is less susceptible to criticisms of differing conditions and noncomparability than work selected from another job, no matter how similar. Nevertheless, there are instances when an unimpacted period on the disputed job simply cannot be found, forcing the analyst either to substitute unimpacted production rates from other similar jobs (essentially prove the reasonableness of the bid from prior experience) or to move to another method of proof.

The measured mile approach requires two measures during specific time periods of the job: production cost (for example, craft hours), and units of physical production (for example, square feet formed, units installed, cubic yards poured). Properly applied, comparisons of these costs can be a key element in establishing reasonableness of the contractor's planned productivity and can be one of the more convincing proofs of damages. In many cases, however, the approach as applied represents little more than an unsupported disguised total cost methodology or a meaningless comparison of unreliable or noncomparable data.

How can a discrete costing of lost productivity be a total cost approach? In its simplest form, the measured mile is nothing more than, or at least no more than one step removed from, pure total cost. It has merely shown that a certain budget was reasonable (either the bid budget or budget revised by actual production) and that a loss of that productivity occurred, causing a loss equal to the total cost of the difference.

The methodology, in and of itself, neither links the loss incurred to specific causation factors nor establishes responsibility for the loss incurred. Causation factors and their linkage to productivity losses must be established independently to provide a discrete damage claim.

Moreover, the data used in the unimpacted baseline and that used in the impacted periods warrant careful scrutiny because they are often misleading. As an initial test, asserted production in the baseline period should be checked against the bid estimate and the manloading schedules to see whether production is well above the original plan, possibly an indication of misrepresentation or a biased sampling. A second test of reasonableness should focus on the number of observations included in the baseline and on the reliability of any conclusions reached based on that number and the dispersion of observations.

Also, a thorough analysis of measured mile data often reveals that work and the conditions under which it was performed in the comparison periods were not comparable for reasons having nothing whatsoever to do with alleged impacts. Production losses, rather than resulting from claimed impacts, instead are often shown to be losses that reasonably should have been expected once normal differences in the work or working conditions are fully understood. For example, demonstrating that work in the impacted period was more complex or difficult than in the baseline (performed at higher elevations, or under predictably restricted access) could render measured mile comparisons virtually useless unless reasonable allowances for such conditions have been made by the analyst.

Beyond the work itself, there are important considerations of measurement standards, methods, and policies employed in the separate measurement periods. Did the unimpacted period have different measures of production than impacted periods? For example, did the unimpacted period measure production on the basis of units installed, but a higher standard used in the impacted period (for example, units turned over and accepted)? Were the production amounts in each period independently confirmed, or did the high production rates in unimpacted periods merely represent self-serving, overreported production in the contractor's own job cost system? Was confirmation of reported progress more lax in earlier periods than later periods? Are the units of production truly comparable in both periods, or do the impacted periods contain additional work or hidden work actually part of but not completed in the unimpacted period (stripping forms, point and patch, grouting, or rework of unimpacted period defective construction)?

Flaws such as those described are usually present in measured mile claims of lost productivity, thus substantially diminishing their integrity and value. In some instances, the methodology is so flawed as to be of more value to the defense than to the contractor attempting to use it.

§ 19.15 Dallavia Method

The *Dallavia method,* shown in **Table 19–5** utilizes as performance predictors eight elements believed to impact construction productivity, with three subcategories included in each of the eight elements. As with many methods used for productivity evaluation, the Dallavia system is intended primarily for purposes of prediction rather than retrospective analyses. However, if the system is a valid predictor, it follows that the system also should be an accurate measurement device in its reverse application.

Each Dallavia element and subcategory is broken into three ranges of expected productivity: low—below 55 percent; average—56 to 85 percent; and high—86 to 100 percent. Each element specifies the conditions expected to produce a given range of production efficiency.

Table 19–5

Dallavia Production Range Indices

DALLAVIA PRODUCTION RANGE INDICES

	Production efficiency, percent		
PRODUCTION	25 35 45 55	65 75 85	95 100
ELEMENTS	Low	Average	High
1. General economy	prosperous	normal	hard times
local business trend	stimulated	normal	depressed
construction volume	high	normal	low
unemployment	low	normal	high
2. Amount of work	limited	average	extensive
design areas	unfavorable	average	favorable
manual operations	limited	average	extensive
mechanized operations	limited	average	extensive
3. Labor	poor	average	good
training	poor	average	good
pay	low	average	good
supply	scarce	average	surplus
4. Supervision	poor	average	good
training	poor	average	good
pay	low	average	good
supply	scarce	average	surplus
5. Job conditions	poor	average	good
management	poor	average	good
site and materials	unfavorable	average	favorable
workmanship required	first rate	regular	passable
length of operations	short	average	long
6. Weather	bad	fair	good
precipitation	much	some	occasional
cold	bitter	moderate	occasional
heat	oppressive	moderate	occasional
7. Equipment	poor	normal	good
applicability	poor	normal	good
condition	poor	fair	good
maintenance, repairs	slow	average	quick
8. Delay	numerous	some	minimum
job flexibility	poor	average	good
delivery	slow	normal	prompt
expediting	poor	average	good

The analyst using Dallavia evaluates each element with respect to conditions on the job (expected or experienced) as measured against the productivity factors contained in the Dallavia table. Poor labor, for example, might receive a rating falling anywhere between 25 and 55 percent. After each element is evaluated and rated, the analyst averages the percentages to estimate average productivity achieved. Each category is assumed to have equal weight in determining the overall impact.

As an example, assume that the first seven elements all rate in the top productivity range, 100 percent. Now assume that delay conditions are so severe throughout the job that a 25 percent productivity rating is warranted. Is the expected productivity over 90 percent as the averaging method would indicate? Should we ignore the 100 percent ratings and use common sense? Make some adjustments?

Let's take another example. Assume that labor, supervision, and equipment all receive 25 percent productivity ratings, a pretty severe impact by any standard. Everything else receives 100 percent. Is it reasonable to think that labor productivity under this scenario is likely to reach or exceed 70 percent? What does common sense tell us?

The Dallavia technique has very limited value in claim situations. Most elements in the Dallavia model address elements that should be known going into the bidding of the job, and most (except No. 8, and in some instances Nos. 5, 6, and 7) tend to favor the owner in explaining costs. Moreover, even when there is an assertion that Dallavia elements are applicable to a specific case, there remains the problem of demonstrating true comparability of Dallavia productivity and the productivity standards assumed in the bid. Did anyone expect 100 percent productivity as defined by Dallavia? Was the bid prepared using Dallavia adjustments?

§ 19.16 —Modified Dallavia

The term "modified Dallavia" can be a general description of any productivity measurement system that employs a set of working conditions set forth as factors affecting productivity and then seeks to estimate productivity losses according to the presence of those factors on the job. Similar to Dallavia, such systems typically use a matrix with defined impact factors and a percentage range of impact for each factor (for example, 3 to 10 percent), depending on the severity of impact presence (low, moderate, or severe).[4] Although impact factors and impact ranges may differ according to whose modified Dallavia method is used, the general approach remains similar.

---

[4] MCAA Bull. No. 58 (Mechanical Contractors Ass'n of America).

The impact factors may be overlapping or additive, depending largely on the subjective opinion of the analyst and her powers of persuasion. The factors represent the total range of potential impacts considered. Impacts are usually measured against the budget; however, some apply them to total hours worked. There are sufficient impact items and ranges to arrive at practically any answer the analyst desires, especially if the methodology is simply applied to the project as a whole.

Most modified Dallavia methods employ impact factors that are widely recognized as having adverse effects on labor productivity. The principal weakness of the techniques lies in the totally subjective nature of the analysis, the general absence of application rules, and what amounts to an open invitation to double-count various related impacts. Total reliance is placed on the integrity and ability of the expert to pick and choose from a market basket of impact items and quantitative ranges. The end result is an appearance of quantitative objectivity and precision, but one that defies verification.

How, for example, can an expert reasonably select impact categories from 10 to 30 related classifications, determine which of the nearly indistinguishable factors are separate, distinct, and additive, then select the correct impact for each from a range of up to 20 points in a single category, then apply all those separate findings to an entire project, and arrive at an answer that even approximates actual productivity loss?

Consider some of the minor complexities. Were trade stacking, crowding, and out-of-sequence work really separate impact factors, or did the trade stacking occur because of out-of-sequence work? Did out-of-sequence work result from crowding or restricted access, or were crowding and out-of-sequence work problems separate and apart from restricted access? Were the defective drawings really the impact or were the field interferences they created?

Obviously, the expert arrives at a reasonable answer by knowing the reasonable answer from the start, picking and choosing and applying her judgment in a manner that provides the most reasonable support for her assertions, all of which may be done entirely in good faith. The point, however, is that the process tends to be the most subjective of the productivity impact analyses.

There is nothing wrong with an expert's stating her opinion of what impact one might expect, given a certain set of events and conditions. The problem with modified Dallavia methods is the appearance that some form of scientific structure and quantitative precision has been brought to the process.

Although not a proponent of modified Dallavia methods, the author has used some variations on occasion and no doubt will continue to use them. It is recommended to use the impact categories individually, and generally as secondary or tertiary support for findings resulting from other analyses.

One should also apply the methodology to specific segments of the job during specified periods so that impact categories can be isolated and limited to as few as possible. This approach is helpful in eliminating duplications that usually result from broadbrush applications.

For example, a specific time period involving 1,000 craft hours may have been found to be overmanned by 30 percent and to have suffered a 10-percent loss in productivity, as determined from a measured mile analysis. As support for the causal relationship, an expert might reasonably offer the findings from various overmanning productivity curves and a modified Dallavia chart showing an expected impact range from moderate overmanning.

§ 19.17 Using Productivity Curves to Calculate Damages

Productivity curves are often used to support damage claims arising from acceleration (including losses from crew increases, crowding, and extended overtime) and from losses caused by inclement weather. Curves from numerous studies have been developed by various industry associations, the Department of Labor, the Department of the Army, and various private consultants to the construction industry.

§ 19.18 —Productivity Losses from Acceleration

Acceleration or *compaction* occurs whenever a contractor is forced to perform a greater amount of work in a period than originally planned. Acceleration itself is an entitlement issue, with damages generally obtaining from overtime premium costs and inefficiency costs resulting from extended overtime, increased manning, crowding/stacking, and out-of-sequence work.

Technically, acceleration typically occurs in one of two circumstances: (1) a delay period in which production falls below plan and lost production must be recaptured either within the original schedule or within a schedule wherein full extension has not been granted; (2) the owner orders a reduction, or compaction, to the contractual schedule. Some states require proof of an order by the owner to accelerate the job; others view denial of a justified extension as constructive acceleration.

In practice, acceleration and resulting impacts may occur whenever there is a delay or schedule reduction, whenever the scope of work is increased, or whenever any combination of the three occurs to the extent that contractors are forced to increase their daily production in order to satisfy the owner's schedule. Calculating acceleration damages involves two basic steps: quantifying acceleration requirements (justification), and quantifying damages.

§ 19.19 —Acceleration Requirements

To calculate acceleration needed to meet increased work requirements, the analyst first recognizes that increased production, rather than reduced time, is the issue. This is an important distinction when the amount of acceleration will be expressed as a percentage of plan.

The Army Corps of Engineers *Modification Impact Evaluation Guide* (MIEG) provides a simple method to calculate acceleration needed when production requirements are increased. Reduced to its simplest form, the method simply identifies the average work force originally planned for the accelerated period and the "new" average resulting from the revised work load or schedule. The increased amount is divided by the planned amount, identifying the amount of acceleration needed.

For example, a job is planned to be completed in 15 days with a crew of 10. Because of subsequent owner-caused events, the work must be completed in 10 days, requiring a crew of 15, or the same 150 productive hours as planned, excluding supervision. The work has been accelerated by 50 percent, as follows:

$$\frac{15 \text{ craftspersons/day}}{10 \text{ craftspersons/day}} = 1.50 = (1.50 - 1) = 50\% \text{ acceleration}$$

Had work requirements also increased by 10 crew days during the same period, then acceleration during the 10-day schedule would have required 16 persons/day, or a 60 percent acceleration of daily production.

Having identified the acceleration needed to meet the owner's schedule, the next task is to determine what impact that acceleration might have on production efficiency. Four basic alternatives are available to the contractor to increase production: overtime, increased crewing, multiple shifts, or some combination of the three. All have recognized impacts on productivity.

§ 19.20 —Inefficiency from Crew Increases and Overmanning

Numerous studies have been conducted to determine the relationship between increasing the work force and productivity losses resulting from attendant problems, for example, out-of-sequence work, restricted access, dilution of supervision, and so forth. Typically, results of the studies are reflected in productivity curves that plot average percentage reductions in productivity for a given percentage of increased manning above optimum, or planned, levels.

Of the curves developed, those encountered most frequently fall into two classes: (1) increased crewing curves, such as those published by the Army Corps of Engineers[5]; (2) overmanning/crowding curves, such as the charts developed by the Contractors Consulting Corporation[6] and the crowding curve published by the Army Corps of Engineers.[7] All the curves predict productivity loss amounts experienced when crews are increased or when crowding and stacking occurs.

The advantage of such curves is in the similarity of their findings (all predict losses) and the relatively conceptual simplicity embodied in the overmanning curves: they concern themselves with one principal causation factor that embodies a multitude of others that are reasonable outgrowths of overmanning.

On the other hand, there are typically several weaknesses associated with the use of overmanning curves. First, of course, is the absence of any assurance that curves used for comparison purposes were based on work and conditions similar to the job under dispute. Second is the typical absence of available data supporting the study methodology and findings. And there always will be the "chicken and the egg" question. Did the inefficiencies reflected in study data result from overmanning, or was overmanning simply the method used to overcome an inability (for any number of reasons) to meet production objectives?

On balance, the problems of overmanning curves can be overcome to a large extent by the similarity of results from diverse studies, and the credentials of those individuals and entities producing the curves. The Department of the Army, Corps of Engineers, as an owner and the largest contractor in the world, lends exceptionally strong credence to impacts depicted in crowding curves published in its *Modification Impact Evaluation Guide,* at least as a representation of minimum impacts that should be expected.

§ 19.21 —Productivity Loss from Increased Crewing (Without Crowding)

Inefficiency resulting from increasing crew sizes will vary depending on a number of factors, including supervision and equipment availability, and

---

[5] Dep't of the Army, Corps of Engineers, Modification Impact Evaluation Guide (1979).

[6] Contractors Consulting Corp., *The Productivity Survey,* Specialized Management Seminars (1981).

[7] Dep't of the Army, Corps of Engineers, Modification Impact Evaluation Guide (1979).

the extent to which crowding and overmanning of the job occurs. Several productivity curves are available to predict the impact of overmanning, but few deal only with increased crews. Of those that do, the most definitive are those of the Army Corps of Engineers. Although considerably more conservative than most overmanning curves, they serve as a very useful starting point and add credence to the concept of lost productivity both because of the extensive construction experience of the Corps and because they were developed by the owner for use in negotiating changes with contractors.

Figures 19–2 and **19–3** are two curves taken from the MIEG manual. The first projects the incremental crewing increase needed to achieve a given level of increased production on the project. The second shows the overall efficiency of an entire crew given certain increases to crew size.

For example, **Figure 19–2** shows that achieving a 50-percent increase in production (vertical axis) typically would require an 80-percent increase

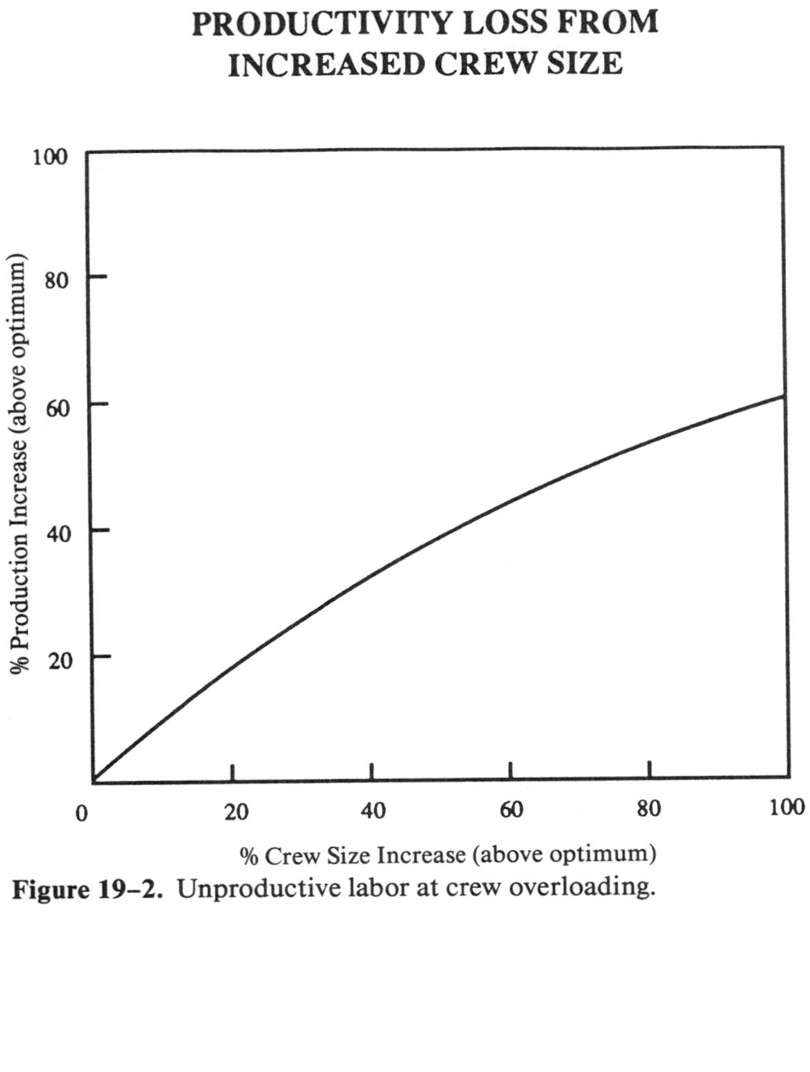

Figure 19–2. Unproductive labor at crew overloading.

(horizontal axis) in the size of the crew. **Figure 19–3** effectively translates that calculation to overall crew impact:

$$\frac{\text{150 percent (Production increase)}}{\text{180 percent (Crew increase)}} = 83.33\% \text{ productivity}$$

Thus we can see that an 80-percent crew increase, without crowding, typically would result in a 16.67 percent expected loss of worker productivity, or 30 crew days in our original example.

$$18 - 15 = 3 \times 10 = 30, \text{ or}$$
$$180 \times .1667 = 30$$

Aware of relationships reflected in **Figure 19–2**, one can approximate that once planned crew size is exceeded by more than 20 percent, each additional craftsperson increases productivity at about 50 percent of the added cost, up to a doubling of the crews. No information is provided beyond a 100-percent increase, but we can reasonably assume conditions will deteriorate rather than improve as crews increase.

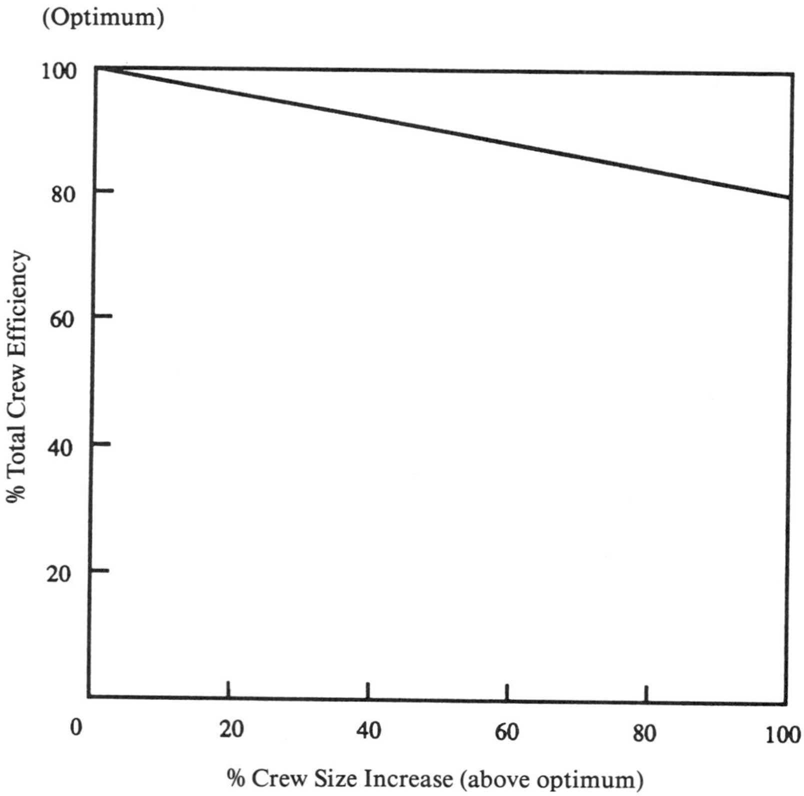

Figure 19–3. Efficiency of crew overloading.

§ 19.22 —Overmanning/Crowding

Section 19.21 assumes that increased crewing has occurred without crowding. That distinction is apparent from separate curves established for the two circumstances by the Army Corps of Engineers. *Crowding* exists when available crewing exceeds the demand of work available to be done, the capacity of support resources, such as equipment, or the space available to perform the work. These are also the conditions assumed to be present in various overmanning curves. The result is that production rates decline further below planned levels and the cost per output of production increases, an all too common problem on construction jobs.

Most overmanning curves, including the MIEG crowding curve (**Figure 19–4**), reflect strikingly similar impacts for overmanning up to 100 percent. Although some provide for impact differences based on the size of the work force, most report fairly modest impacts (about 2 to 3 percent for

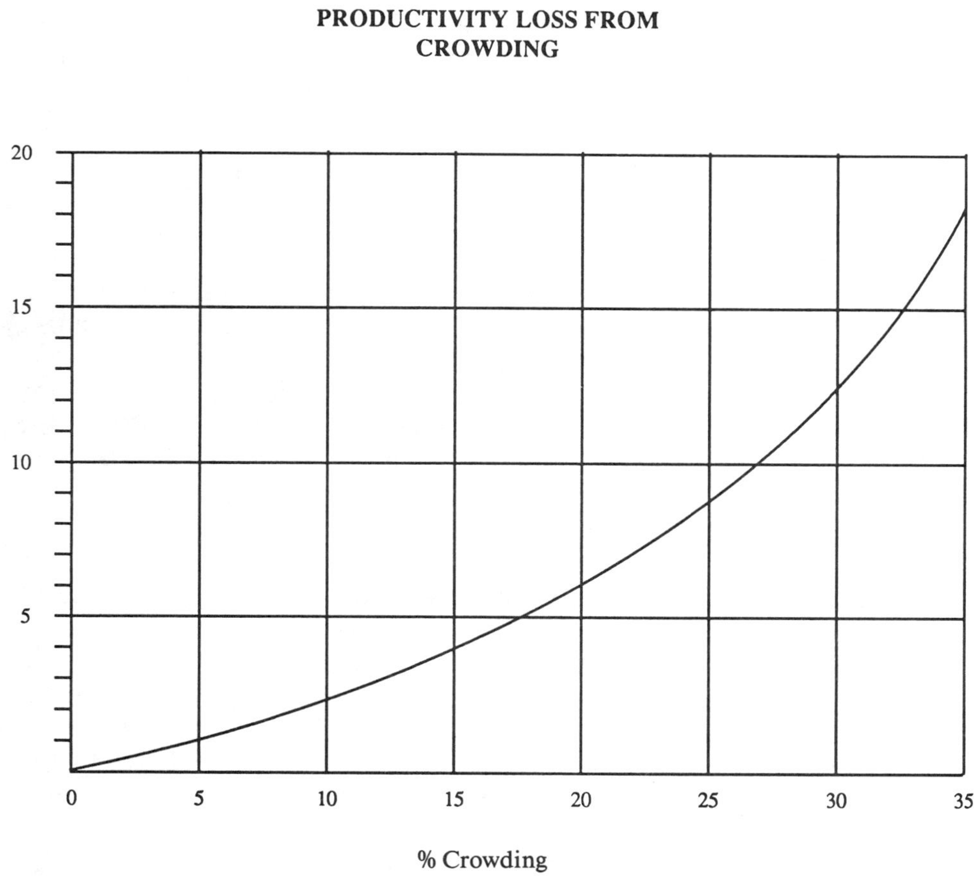

Figure 19–4. Effect of crowding on labor efficiency.

each 10-percent increase) for increases up to 30 or 40 percent. Thereafter, the impact becomes more pronounced, with each additional percent providing about 1/2 percent of increased productivity. At an overmanning level of 100 percent, the curves typically show a productivity loss of 40 to 50 percent (assumes a straight line extrapolation of MIEG rates to 100 percent crowding).

Calculating productivity loss predicted by one or more of the curves is simple. In retrospective calculations, the total hours worked under a given level of overmanning are multiplied by the predicted amount of inefficiency, say 50 percent, providing the amount of expected inefficiency supported by the curve. Looking forward, the productive hours required of a given crew would be divided by the expected productivity level, thus projecting the total hours needed to complete the activity. Inefficiency would be the difference between the total and the productive hours needed.

Overmanning curves pertain to the number of workers on a single shift. That is, the number of workers on multiple shifts should not be lumped together to create an impression of huge increases over plan or to calculate percentage increases to be applied against productivity curves. Multiple shifts usually result in worker inefficiencies also, however those inefficiencies must be determined as separate and distinct calculations.

§ 19.23 —Extended Overtime Inefficiency

The concept of productivity loss from extended overtime is widely, but not universally, accepted throughout the construction industry. Curves reflecting expected losses are available from a variety of sources, including the Department of Labor, National Electrical Contractors Association (NECA), Business Roundtable Committee on Construction, and the Army Corps of Engineers *Modification Impact Evaluation Guide.*[8] All are readily available and commonly used. Our discussion, however, is limited to those published by the Business Roundtable and the Army Corps of Engineers.

Table 19–6 reflects the two charts published by Business Roundtable, one depicting the cumulative impact of a 50-hour week and another depicting the impact experienced with 60-hour workweeks. Each depicts a sliding range of impact, with some overlap projected at various points. Both curves assume extended use of overtime by the entire work shift.

Figure 19–5 is the array of overtime productivity impacts reflected in the Army Corps of Engineers MIEG manual. The chart includes a much wider range of work shifts than does the Business Roundtable study, but considers the impact only over a duration of four weeks. In some instances (the 50-hour week), the charts level off rapidly, and in others (70-hour week), the charts suggest continued deterioration beyond the four-week

[8] Dep't of the Army, Corps of Engineers, Modification Impact Evaluation Guide (1979).

Table 19–6

Relationships of Hours Worked, Productivity, and Costs

Relationships of Hours Worked, Productivity, and Costs
(40 Hours vs. 60 Hours)

1	2	3	4	5	6	7	8
	Productivity Rate				Hour Loss		Hour Cost
60 Hour Overtime Work Weeks	40 Hr. Week	60 Hr. Week	Actual Hour Output for 60 Hr. Week	Hour Gain Over 40 Hr. Week	Due to Productivity Drop	Premium Hours	to Overtime Operation (at 2x)
0-1-2	1.00	.90	54.0	14.0	6.0	20.0	26.0
2-3-4		.86	51.6	11.6	8.4	20.0	28.4
4-5-6		.80	48.0	8.0	12.0	20.0	32.0
6-7-8		.71	42.6	2.6	17.4	20.0	37.4
8-9-10		.66	39.6	.04	20.4	20.0	40.4

Relationships of Hours Worked, Productivity, and Costs
(40 Hours vs. 50 Hours)

1	2	3	4	5	6	7	8
	Productivity Rate				Hour Loss		Hour Cost
60 Hour Overtime Work Weeks	40 Hr. Week	50 Hr. Week	Actual Hour Output for 50 Hr. Week	Hour Gain Over 40 Hr. Week	Due to Productivity Drop	Premium Hours	to Overtime Operation (at 2x)
0-1-2	1.00	.926	46.3	6.3	3.7	10.0	13.7
2-3-4		.90	45.0	5.0	5.0	10.0	15.0
4-5-6		.87	43.5	3.5	6.5	10.0	16.5
6-7-8		.80	40.0	0.0	10.0	10.0	20.0
8-9-10		.752	37.6	-2.4	12.4	10.0	22.4

Reproduced with permission of The Business Roundtable, *CICE Report C-2, Scheduled Overtime Effect on Construction Projects.*

period. Obviously, the projected results are subject to interpretation and considerable argument.

Within the time periods reflected on the charts and curves, interpretation of projected impacts is relatively straightforward and should result in a weighted average calculation of impact. For example, one week worked at 100-percent productivity, two weeks at 95-percent productivity, and 3 weeks at 90-percent productivity would represent six weeks of work at an average productivity of 93 percent, or:

Weeks	Productivity	Weight
1	100	100
2	95	190
3	90	270
6		560

$$\text{Average} = \frac{560}{6} = 93.33$$

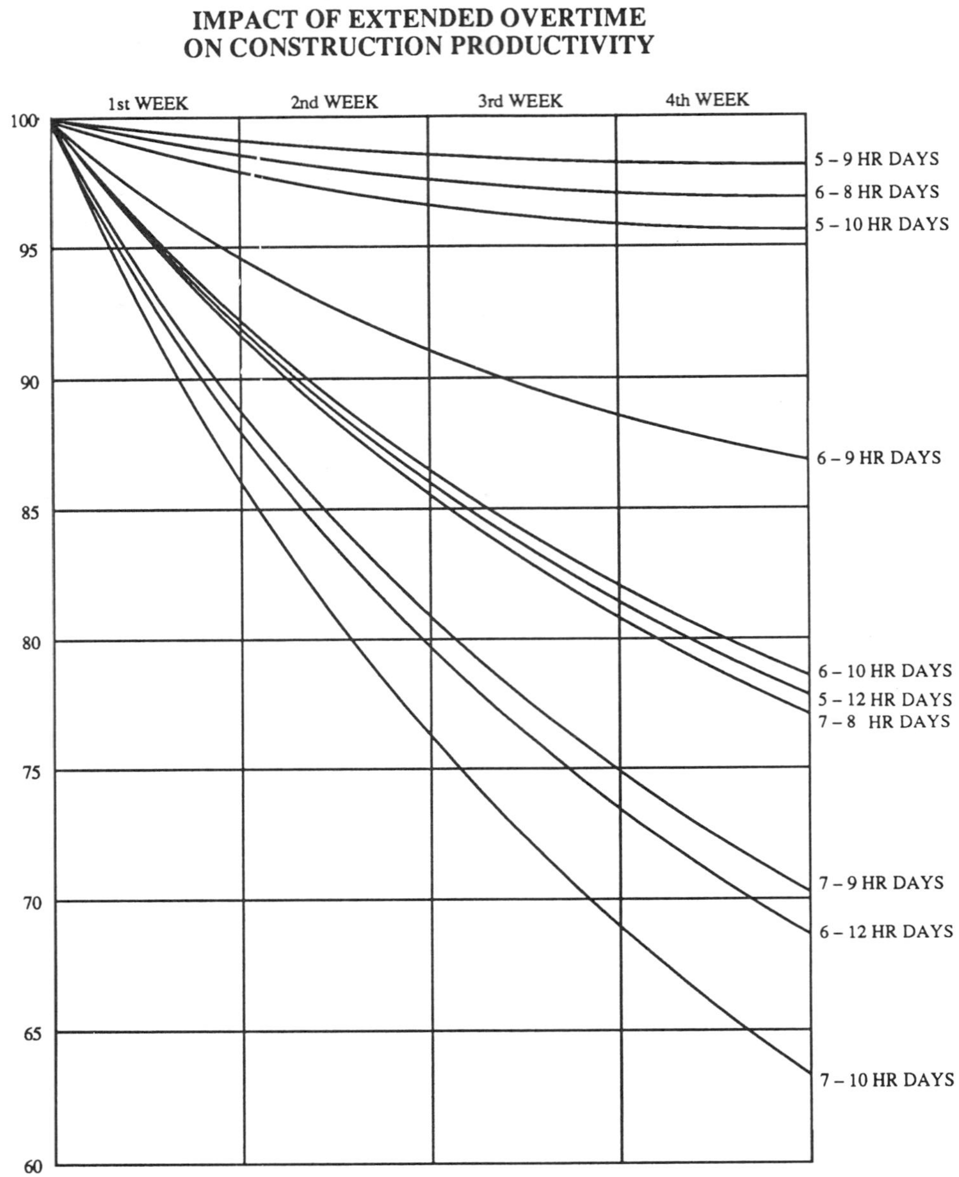

Figure 19–5. Effect of work schedule on efficiency.

Most important is to understand that the productivity loss is applied to all hours worked by the individual(s) working the extended overtime: for example, all 60 hours of the 60-hour week, all 50 of the 50-hour week, and so forth. Extended overtime impacts do not apply in the amounts shown, however, when the shifts are not continuous for extended periods, such as when overtime is rotated among individuals.

§ 19.24 Calculating Lost Productivity from Inclement Weather

Inclement weather (excessive heat, cold, or humidity) is recognized throughout the construction industry as having an adverse impact on productivity. Numerous studies may be obtained from industry associations or from public libraries citing the effects of climatic conditions on construction industry work.[9]

Figure 19–6 compares the productivity rates of the two studies at temperatures between − 10 degrees and 40 degrees. The differences are substantial at lower temperatures, but the general trends are similar.

Most studies conclude that productivity is unimpacted by weather when temperatures are between 40 and 70 degrees and humidity remains below 80 percent. When any of the three falls outside those respective ranges, impact will occur, with humidity having greatest individual impact at higher temperatures and severe cold being a significant factor regardless of humidity.

Wind velocity, in conjunction with cold weather, exacerbates cold temperatures by creating effective temperatures potentially much colder than

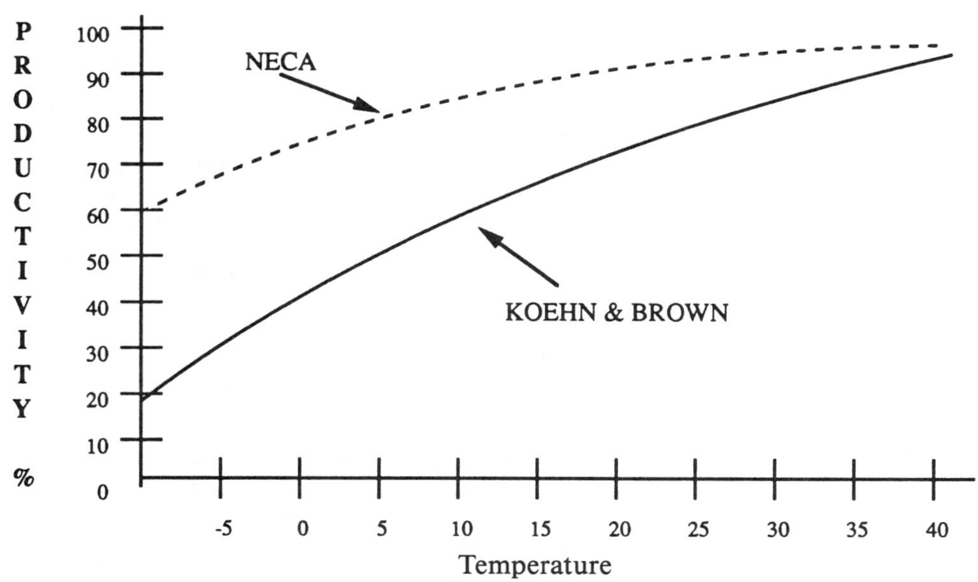

Figure 19–6. Construction productivity as function of temperature and 75% humidity.

[9] National Electrical Contractors Ass'n, The Effect of Temperature on Productivity (NECA) (pertains to light construction work); Koehn & Brown, Climatic Effects on Construction (1985) (pertains to more strenuous activities).

WIND SPEED MPH	ACTUAL THERMOMETER READING °F									
	50	40	30	20	10	0	-10	-20	-30	-40
Calm	50	40	30	20	10	0	-10	-20	-30	-40
5	48	37	27	16	6	-5	-15	-26	-36	-47
10	40	28	16	4	-9	-21	-33	-46	-58	-70
15	36	22	9	-5	-18	-36	-45	-58	-72	-85
20	32	18	4	-10	-25	-39	-53	-67	-82	-96
25	50	16	0	-15	-29	-44	-59	-74	-88	-104
30	28	13	-2	-18	-33	-48	-63	-79	-94	-109
35	27	11	-4	-20	-35	-49	-67	-82	-98	-113
40	26	10	-6	-21	-37	-53	-69	-85	-100	-116

Figure 19–7. Wind chill factor effective or equivalent temperatures °F. *Source:* National Safety Council.

those contained in official temperature recordings. **Figure 19–7** is a National Safety Council chart providing detailed information on the impact of various wind velocities on a wide range of actual temperature readings. As is readily apparent, wind velocity can be extremely important to the analyst when temperatures fall below 20 degrees or when velocities exceed 15 miles per hour.

§ 19.25 Calculating Compounding Impacts

Productivity impacts from overmanning, overtime, and weather usually are considered to be compounding whenever they occur concurrently. Although reasoning supports this concept, there is little documentation to support this position. The problem lies in the uncertainty of the amount of impact that should be allocable to each factor. Would it be the same as the impact attributable in isolated conditions, a little less, or a little more?

Most experts representing the contractor assert the compounded effects at those rates found under isolated impact conditions. Those representing the owner challenge the entire concept. The author believes that compounding may or may not occur. Moreover, the measures should not be considered precise determinants of impact, only measures of reasonable expectations. In some instances, impacts may exceed the amounts predicted even with compounding, and in others, impacts may actually be less than predicted even without compounding. Each circumstance must be viewed in relation to the actual outcome and the range of reasonable explanations accounting for those outcomes.

In any event, if the impacts are calculated assuming a compounding effect, the order of calculation will have no impact on overall results. It will, however, affect individual category amounts.

§ 19.26 Learning Curve Claims

Many claims involving disruptive activities contain assertions regarding productivity losses incurred because the contractor was unable to achieve the benefit of normal experience, or learning curve efficiencies. Some actually present a calculated loss, but many simply refer to the loss in general terms, often in support of measured mile findings: "expected productivity in impacted period should have exceeded baseline productivity had normal learning curve efficiencies occurred."

Some efficiencies should accrue from undisrupted repetition of construction tasks; however, most construction tasks do not typically fall within the pure concepts of experience curve efficiencies. True experience curve gains (for example, 15 to 20 percent increased efficiency for every doubling of production), as depicted in **Figure 19–8**, typically are found in manufacturing, where tasks are truly repetitive and the production environments are more systematic and controlled.

In construction claims asserted along learning curve concepts, the author prefers the *start-stop orientation analysis* published by the Army Corps of Engineers, and shown in **Figure 19–9**. This technique measures the impact of unplanned stops and starts on the premise that skilled craftsmen will require some orientation time whenever a new job is started, but that orientation should not exceed 8 hours so long as the task remains within the craftsman's trade. Within this framework, some simple jobs are started with a high degree of productivity and full productivity is achieved rapidly. Complex jobs are begun with low productivity and greater orientation is needed to reach full productivity.

Application of the method requires either a detailed study of orientation times for specific jobs or, more likely, the subjective judgment of experienced personnel. Events causing new and unscheduled starts must be identified, along with the type and number of craftsmen involved and the type and complexity of the jobs involved.

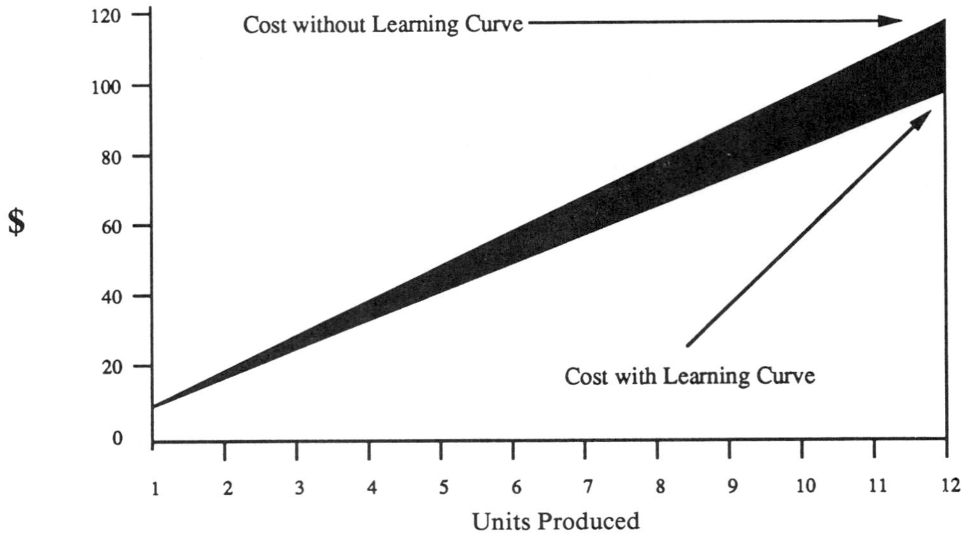

Figure 19–8. Learning curve affect on costs.

Figure 19–9 is the theoretical productivity scale taken from the MIEG and **Figure 19–10** is its accompanying chart, which is used to measure hours lost by each worker each time a job experiences an unexpected start. That amount is determined by the estimated orientation starting point of the particular activity.

The calculation is as accurate as the identified unscheduled starts and crews affected, the estimated starting point, and orientation time required to achieve full productivity. Most likely, it will be an imprecise measure. It does, however, provide a structured approach to developing a measure of reasonableness and a conceptual framework for explaining disruptive impacts. Applied with care and restraint, it can be a significant piece of evidence with which the defense must reckon. It is also an effective means of setting forth all the disruptive actions of the adverse party and reinforcing that each caused a disruption to labor productivity.

§ 19.27 Ratio Delay Studies

A jobsite survey method may be used to identify causes of lost productivity and to quantify inefficiency costs as a percentage of total costs incurred. The methodology consists of a series of timed observations over a number of time intervals. Observers record all activities taking place within their assigned observation area, noting activities and classifying them either as productive or nonproductive. Causes for nonproductive activities are then identified by questioning workers and recorded into causal categories, for

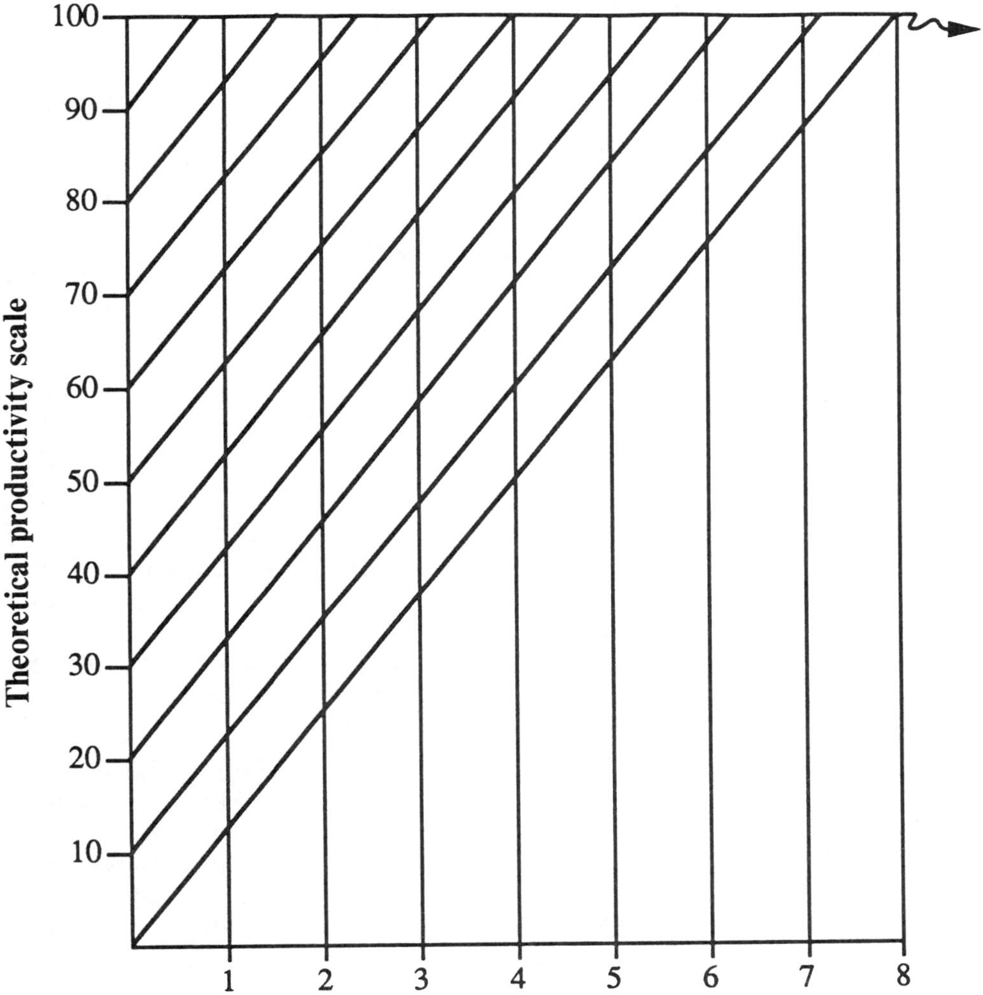

Figure 19–9. Start-stop productivity loss.

example, waiting for materials or equipment, waiting for instructions, and so forth.

The completed study is totalled, and the relative proportion of productive and nonproductive activities is determined from recorded observations. Percentages applied against labor costs provide a detailed allocation of cost by activity.

Ratio delay studies can be an effective method of evaluating productivity and factors affecting jobsite production at a given time. They can also be

(Based on Construction Operations Orientation/Learning Chart)

Productivity Starting Point	*Duration (HR)*	*Average Loss (HR)*
100	0	0
90	0.8	0.4
80	1.6	0.8
70	2.4	1.2
60	3.2	1.6
50	4.0	2.0
40	4.8	2.4
30	5.6	2.8
20	6.4	3.2
10	7.2	3.6
0	8.0	4.0

Figure 19–10. Productivity losses derived from MIEG figures.

useful in establishing baseline productivity characteristics for use in later measured mile studies. And they can be used to identify the cost of nonproductive activities during periods of disruption.

As "stand alone" studies of disrupted work and resultant damages, ratio delay studies are of limited value in claim situations. That is, the studies require some form of valid comparison data in order to show true impact and establish entitlement. For example, a good jobsite sampling study might establish that, because of various documented nonproductive activities, a jobsite was operating at only 30-percent productivity during a disrupted period. However, without comparative data, the study has provided no evidence that 30-percent productivity is out of the ordinary nor that all the nonproductive activities recorded are anything more than one would expect to find on any construction job. As with all other proof techniques, the ratio delay must show that a higher level of productivity was reasonably attainable but for the disruptive acts, errors, or omissions of the other party.

CHAPTER 20

DEFENDING AGAINST OWNER CLAIMS

Mark L. Fleder
Peter J. Smith

Mark L. Fleder is a partner in the Roseland, New Jersey, law firm of Connell, Foley & Geiser, Esqs. He specializes in construction matters, principally in the negotiation, litigation, and arbitration of complex technical disputes. A graduate of Princeton University and the Rutgers University School of Law, he is a member of the American Bar Association's Forum Committee on the Construction Industry as well as the Public Contract Law Section. Mr. Fleder also lectures widely to attorney and non-attorney audiences on various subjects in construction law, and he has authored recent publications on selected topics.

Peter J. Smith is a partner at the Roseland, New Jersey, law firm of Connell, Foley & Geiser, Esqs. He graduated from the University of Notre Dame and from the Rutgers University School of Law. He specializes in the litigation of construction and related commercial matters and is a member of the Public Contract Law Sections of the New Jersey American Bar Associations.

§ 20.1 Available Defenses

§ 20.2 Compliance with Plans and Specifications

§ 20.3 Waiver

§ 20.4 Statutes of Limitations

§ 20.5 Supervening Impracticability
§ 20.6 Pre-existing Impracticability
§ 20.7 Warranties and their Limitations
§ 20.8 Damages
§ 20.9 When Owner Retains Duty to Coordinate
§ 20.10 Liquidated Damages
§ 20.11 Substantial Performance
§ 20.12 Accord and Satisfaction
§ 20.13 Arbitration Defense
§ 20.14 Termination Defense
§ 20.15 Other Contractual Remedy Limitations
§ 20.16 Other Owner Claims and Contractor Defenses

§ 20.1 Available Defenses

Regardless of the size of the project and dollar amount of a contractor's agreement with an owner, a contractor is always vulnerable to owner claims for a multitude of problems that may afflict the project. Most of the rights and duties with which the law is concerned and about which the contractor should be concerned may be classified generally as arising either out of contract or tort. Contract rights and duties are voluntarily assumed by agreement of the parties and are specially tailored for the particular owner, contractor, and project. Assuming that the terms of the contract are not violative of public policy, each party is entitled to performance by the other, and if one party's breach causes damage to the other, the law provides a remedy.

A *tort* is a civil wrong committed by one to the damage of another, arising not from any contract between them, but rather by reason of their relationship in society.[1] Thus, for example, the driver of an automobile has a duty to exercise reasonable care in the operation of the automobile so as not to interfere unreasonably with the right of another to operate a car or to walk across the street. The important consideration is always the relationship between the parties, because rights and duties spring only from that relationship.

---

[1] Purchasers of a structure from an original owner frequently choose to sue the contractor in tort because they have no direct contractual relationship. The courts are split in such cases on whether the lack of contractual privity ought to bar such tort actions. *See, e.g.,* Wells v. Clowers Constr. Co., 476 So. 2d 105 (Ala. 1985) (holding that lack of privity is a bar); Sewell v. Gregory, 371 S.E.2d 82 (W. Va. 1988) (privity not required in negligence actions).

This chapter gives an overview of the defenses available to a contractor.[2] Legal principles set forth herein are for general reference and should be considered in light of any applicable local, state, or federal statute or regulation, as well as the terms of any contract between the contractor and the owner.

This general review of the defenses available to a contractor against the claims of an owner deals with the primary (and most common) owner's claims: claims of defective construction; claims of delay in completion of the project; and claims in connection with the termination of a contractor prior to completion of the project.[3]

§ 20.2 Compliance with Plans and Specifications

The rule is well settled in nearly every jurisdiction that when a contractor is hired to build according to plans or specifications furnished by the owner and those plans are followed, the contractor will not be responsible for damages resulting solely from defects in the plans or specifications themselves, absent any negligence on the contractor's part or any express warranty by the contractor that the plans and specifications are free from defects.[4] This is true whether the plans were actually furnished by the owner itself or by an architect employed by the owner.[5] The rule has been noted by

---

[2] Corporate contractors, of course, have an ultimate defense of limited liability stemming from their legal entity. Occasionally, however, owners are able to pierce the corporate veil in order to hold the individual owners of the contractor liable. *See, e.g.,* Jablonsky v. Klemm, 377 N.W.2d 560 (N.D. 1985); Welch v. Fuhrnan, 496 So. 2d 484 (La. Ct. App. 1986). When the owner can sue the contractor's surety as well, the individual owners of the incorporated contractor may also ultimately be liable personally through the operation of their agreements to indemnify the surety. See **Ch. 12**.

[3] For additional discussion of these issues from the perspective of the owner, *see* Cox, Tiede & Denton, *Owner Damages,* Construction Briefings No. 83-3 (1983).

[4] 13 Am. Jur. 2d *Building and Construction Contracts* § 28 (1964); Annotation, *Construction Contractor's Liability to Contractee for Defects or Insufficiency of Work Attributable to the Latter's Plans and Specifications,* 6 A.L.R.3d 1389, 1394, 1397 (1966) [hereinafter *Contractor's Liability*]; United States v. Spearin, 248 U.S. 132 (1918); Reiman Constr. Co. v. Jerry Hiller Co., 709 P.2d 1271 (Wyo. 1985). *See, e.g.,* Theisse-Nonnemache, Inc. v. Duff, 393 N.W.2d 397 (Minn. Ct. App. 1986) (roofer's warranty was not exclusively owner's remedy for failure of roof to conform with plans; prime contractor was also liable). *See also* F.A. Gray, Inc. v. Weiss, 519 A.2d 716 (Me. 1986) (painter had no liability for using specified but unsuitable stain, even though owner claimed that painter should have known better). Of course, the contractor is responsible not only for failing to comply with the specifications itself, but also if its subcontractors fail to comply.

[5] 13 Am. Jur. 2d *Building and Construction Contracts* § 28 (1964); Staley v. New, 56 N.M. 745, 250 P.2d 893 (1952) (plans furnished by owner's architect); United States v. Spearin, 248 U.S. 132 (1918) (plans furnished by United States government/owner).

courts as particularly applicable when a contractor becomes aware of defects in plans and warns the owner of the defects, but the owner refuses to make any changes.[6]

One typical fact pattern in which defects are held not chargeable to the contractor occurs when the owner's specifications call for a product by name. The contractor is deemed in compliance with the contract if he supplies that brand, even though it turns out to be defective.[7] Owner's counsel must be acutely aware that the burden of proving the existence and cause of the defect, by a preponderance of the evidence, is normally on the owner. That burden is not always an easy one to carry.[8] In addition, the owner must prove either that the cause of the defect was a breach of the contractor's obligation or that the risk was one the contractor had agreed to shoulder. If the contract does not clearly address the issue of responsibility, that proof too can be very difficult. For example, in *Marshall County Redi-Mix, Inc. v. Matthew*[9] the floor slab being poured by the contractor froze. The owner refused to pay the contractor, who then filed a mechanics' lien and sued to foreclose. The owner counterclaimed for the damages suffered on account of the defective slab. The trial court found for the owner. On appeal, the trial court's judgment dismissing the contractor's claim was affirmed, but the judgment on the owner's counterclaim was reversed. Because neither party could prove that the cause of the defect (the freezing) was a risk or responsibility assumed by the other party, both were left with their respective losses. In that case, counsel for the owner should probably have come to trial prepared to prove that it was customary for contractors to take responsibility to provide winter protection to curing concrete. Such gaps in the contract can sometimes be filled in by other means.[10]

In the typical case, proof of the cause and effect of the defect, as well as proof of responsibility, will require expert testimony.[11] Of course, whether the work complied with the contract requirements cannot always be

---

[6] Ridley Inv. Co. v. Croll, 56 Del. 208, 192 A.2d 925 (1963) (cited in *Contractor's Liability* at 1394; Passaic Valley Sewerage Comm'rs v. Tierney, 1 F.2d 304 (3d Cir. 1924). *Accord* Ellis Millwork, Inc. v. Frees, Inc., 493 So. 2d 696 (La. Ct. App. 1986).

[7] *See, e.g.,* City of Covington v. Heard, 428 So. 2d 1132 (La. Ct. App. 1983).

[8] *See, e.g.,* Melder v. Gassiott, 436 So. 2d 628 (La. Ct. App. 1983); Chandler v. Fuqua, 420 So. 2d 1348 (La. Ct. App. 1982).

[9] 447 N.E.2d 1165 (Ind. Ct. App. 1983).

[10] *See, e.g.,* Quedding v. Arisumi Bros., Inc., 66 Haw. 335, 661 P.2d 706 (1983), involving the collapse of a wall caused by the failure to install steel reinforcing bars. Although the bars were not shown in the plans, the court found them to be required by Maui's uniform building code.

[11] *See, e.g.,* Ozark Skyways, Inc. v. Bomark Steel Structures, Inc., 647 S.W.2d 170 (Mo. Ct. App. 1983), holding that the expert had established that the contractor's deviation from the specifications made the structure vulnerable to frost heave, that frost heave had actually occurred, and that it was the cause of the failure of the doors of the airplane hangar to operate properly.

definitely proved, leaving potential jury questions. Evidence of compliance can take the form of inferences from the parties' behavior during the course of the job, however.[12]

Although it is probably not a reliable precedent today, one case went so far as to hold that even when the contractor drew up the plans, which were subsequently accepted and adopted by the owner after review, the contractor was not liable for damages arising solely from defects in the plans.[13] There is, however, some authority for the proposition that the contractor is liable for damages resulting from defective plans furnished by the owner if the damage occurs prior to completion of the contractor's performance.[14] These cases were decided on the theory that if one contracts to build a building according to plans that are open to inspection, one cannot be relieved of one's contractual duty in the absence of fraud or duress. The cases that stand for this proposition, however, are not recent, and their rationale was particularly appropriate to a time when construction design was simpler. Even in jurisdictions adhering to this theory, contractors have been held not liable when the owner impliedly or expressly warranted the plans as free from defect.[15]

Generally, there are two situations in which a contractor may be held liable for damages caused by defects in the plans and specifications furnished by an owner. One occurs when the contractor makes significant

---

[12] *See, e.g.,* Alquire v. Walker, 154 Ill. App. 3d 438, 506 N.E.2d 1334 (1987) (owner's failure to complain during course of work was evidence that project had been completed within reasonable time); Sweeny Co. v. Engineers-Constructors, Inc., 823 F.2d 805 (4th Cir. 1987) (payments, certified by the architect, provided evidence, but not conclusive evidence, that quality of work met contract requirements).

[13] Roberts v. Sinnot, 55 Mont. 369, 177 P. 252 (1918).

[14] Lonergan v. San Antonio Loan & Trust Co., 101 Tex. 63, 104 S.W. 1061 (1907), *motion for reh'g overruled,* 101 Tex. 81, 106 S.W. 876 (1908); Brasher v. Alexandria, 215 La. 887, 41 So. 2d 819 (1949); N.J. Magnam Co. v. Fuller, 222 Mass. 530, 111 N.E. 399 (1916). *But see* Konyar v. Jonsson, 184 Ill. App. 3d 865, 540 N.E.2d 944 (1989), which found a contractor not liable for damage that occurred prior to completion of a false floor. The contractor could not complete his work until an electrician performed his work. The owner's employees were moved back into the room and one of them tripped over an open trough. The contractor was found not liable because there was nothing inherently dangerous about the specifications to which the contractor had adhered and, anyway, he had no reason to know the employees would be moved back into the room before the contractor had completed his work.

[15] Pittman Constr. Co. v. Housing Auth., 169 So. 2d 122 (La. Ct. App. 1964), *writ refused,* 237 La. 343, 170 So. 2d 865, (Lt. Ct. App.), *writ refused,* 247 La. 346, 170 So. 2d 866 (La. Ct. App. 1965); Penn Bridge Co. v. New Orleans, 222 F. 737 (5th Cir. 1915). *But see* Davidson v. Burns, 749 S.W.2d 446 (Mo. Ct. App. 1988). Despite the fact that the owner warranted the adequacy and the accuracy of plans and specifications provided to the contractor, the contractor was found liable when the sea wall it had constructed collapsed. The court found that the contractor had a duty to warn the owner of the deficiencies in the plans and specifications.

departures from the plans or specifications.[16] Notwithstanding this, if the contractor deviates from the plans with the owner's knowledge and the owner does not object, the contractor will not be held liable unless the consequences of such deviation are so well known that the contractor should have been aware of the danger.[17] When the contractor originally deviated from the plans, but made corrections pursuant to directions from the owner's architect, the contractor was also found to be not liable.[18] In another case, when the contractor deviated from plans and failed to correct deviations despite the owner's protest, the contractor was found liable.[19]

The second situation in which a contractor may be held liable for damages caused by defects in plans furnished by the owner occurs when the contractor expressly or impliedly warrants the sufficiency of the owner's plans or clearly contracts to erect a building free of defect.[20] The existence of this warranty should be determined from close examination of both the contract and the relationship of the contractor and the owner on the project. Notwithstanding boilerplate warnings and disclaimers in bidding documents with regard to plans and specifications, the very limited time available to bidders to estimate cost does not permit substantial investment in thorough independent studies of site conditions. The contractor should thus be careful not to sign a contract expressing any warranty of site conditions without the opportunity to inspect those conditions thoroughly.

Based on the conventional wisdom that the best defense is a good offense, the contractor should consider the potential liability of the design professional for design shortcomings. The *Restatement (Second) of Torts* provides that:

> (1) One who, in the course of his business, profession or employment, or in any other transaction in which he has a pecuniary interest, supplies false information for the guidance of others in their business transactions, is subject to liability for pecuniary loss caused to them by their justifiable reliance upon the information, if he fails to exercise reasonable care or competence in obtaining or communicating the information.

---

[16] Drummond v. Hughes, 91 N.J.L. 563, 104 A. 137 (1918); Filbert v. Philadelphia, 181 Pa. 530, 37 A. 545 (1897); 13 Am. Jur. 2d *Building and Construction Contracts* § 28 (1964).

[17] Mann v. Clowser, 190 Va. 887, 59 S.E.2d 78 (1950).

[18] Fuchs v. Parsons Constr. Co., 172 Neb. 719, 111 N.W.2d 727 (1961).

[19] Otto Misch Co. v. E.E. Davis Co., 241 Mich. 285, 217 N.W. 38 (1928).

[20] 13 Am. Jur. 2d *Building and Construction Contracts* § 28 (1964); Cameron-Hawn Realty Co. v. Albany, 207 N.Y. 377, 101 N.E. 162 (1913); Miller v. City of Broken Arrow, 660 F.2d 450 (10th Cir.), *cert. denied,* 455 U.S. 1020 (1982); Southern New England Contracting Co. v. State, 165 Conn. 644, 345 A.2d 550 (1974); Mayville-Portland Sch. Dist. v. C.I. Linfoot Co., 261 N.W.2d 907 (N.D. 1978).

(2) Except as stated in Subsection (3), the liability stated in Subsection (1) is limited to loss suffered

(a) by the person or one of a limited group of persons for whose benefit and guidance he intends to supply the information or knows that the recipient intends to supply it; and

(b) through reliance upon it in a transaction that he intends the information to influence or knows that the recipient so intends or in a substantially similar transaction.

(3) The liability of one who is under a public duty to give the information extends to loss suffered by any of the class of persons for whose benefit the duty is created, in any of the transactions in which it is intended to protect them.[21]

Although this is not necessarily representative of the law in any given state, it appears to be the general direction in which the law is moving in this field. It has been held that a design professional is answerable in tort to a contractor who claims damage as the result of reliance upon plans prepared by that professional, even in the absence of privity of contract.[22] In a Texas case, however, the court of appeals for that jurisdiction reached a different conclusion, holding that a contractor could not maintain a suit against an architect/engineer charging negligence in failing to supervise and administer the project properly.[23] There was a vigorous dissent by the chief justice, who announced that he would have followed the view just discussed and allowed the suit.

Although the Texas decision is probably inconsistent with the law in most other jurisdictions, it is possible to reconcile the case. The Texas case alleged negligence only in the performance of duty during the construction phase, as opposed to negligent design. Construction supervision duties spring entirely from the contract between the architect/engineer and the owner, and thus it can be argued that the contractor, who is a stranger to that agreement, should not be permitted to complain if the architect/engineer breaches its contract with the owner.

§ 20.3 Waiver

Generally, when a contract is breached in a material respect, the injured party is accorded a choice of remedies for damage incurred. However, when the injured party treats the contract as still in effect after knowledge of the

---

[21] Restatement (Second) of Torts § 552 (1977).

[22] Conforti & Eisele, Inc. v. John C. Morris Assocs., 175 N.J. Super. 341, 418 A.2d 1290 (1981).

[23] Bernard Johnson, Inc. v. Continental Constructors, Inc., 630 S.W.2d 365 (Tex. Civ. App. 1982).

breach by the other party, its conduct is incompatible with an intention to consider the contract ended. Therefore, the otherwise injured party is deemed to have elected not to assert the breach as a cause for refusing to continue the contract.[24] This is the legal doctrine of *waiver.*[25]

In the context of a construction project, the concept of waiver is no different in principle from dealing with a claimed defect under a contract for the sale of goods. Generally, if a defect in the work is or ought to be known, its acceptance imposes a duty to pay for it, and if no protest or complaint about the quality of work is promptly made, any right to claim damages for defects in performance is also discharged.[26] For example, it has been held that the supervision of an entire sidewalk construction project and the acceptance of the sidewalk upon completion of the project amounted to waiver.[27] Even though knowledge of the defects was not expressly found, such knowledge was imputed. Likewise, it has been held that daily inspections of a road under construction, and acceptance of the road upon completion, amounted to waiver of a claim against the contractor.[28]

The waiver rule is often invoked when the defective performance is a failure to complete construction in accordance with contract requirements, followed by acceptance of the late performance by the owner. In such cases, the defect is obvious and the only question is whether acceptance was intended by the owner. A number of cases have held that waiver as to the time of performance was an effective defense available to the contractor.[29]

There are, however, two major exceptions in the construction contract context in which there can be no waiver by an owner of the right to remedy for defective performance. The first such situation is when the defects are

---

[24] 5 S. Williston, A Treatise on the Law of Contracts § 700 (3d ed. 1961) [hereinafter Williston].

[25] Of course the contract itself may waive rights that would have existed but for the contract, although in such cases the waiver is not of a breach but rather of a contract standard that establishes that no breach occurred. *See* Blue Cross v. McDevitt & Street Co., 234 Va. 191, 360 S.E.2d 825 (1987) (owner's claim for property damage against contractor and architect barred by contractual waiver of claims for losses covered by insurance).

[26] Williston § 724; 13 Am. Jur. 2d *Building and Construction Contracts* § 55 (1964). *See also* Johnson v. Fenestra, Inc., 305 F.2d 179 (3d Cir. 1962).

[27] Katz v. Bedford, 77 Cal. 319, 19 P. 523 (1888).

[28] City of St. Claire Shores v. L.&L. Constr. Co., 363 Mich. 518, 109 N.W.2d 802 (1961). *See also* K&G Constr. Co. v. Harris, 223 Md. 305, 164 A.2d 451 (1960); Kandalis v. Paul Pet Constr. Co., 210 Md. 319, 123 A.2d 345 (1956).

[29] *See, e.g.,* Phillips & Colby Constr. Co. v. Seymour, 91 U.S. 646 (1875); Smither & Co. v. Calvin Humphrey Corp., 232 F. Supp. 204 (D.D.C. 1964); Commercial Contractor, Inc. v. United States Fidelity & Guar. Co., 524 F.2d 944 (5th Cir. 1975). *See also* Marathon Oil Co. v. Hollis, 167 Ga. App. 48, 305 S.E.2d 864 (1983) (agreement to revisions in project schedules modifies contract completion date).

latent and are thus unknown and unknowable by the owner at the time of acceptance. Acceptance by the owner in such situations has been held not to amount to waiver.[30] The other significant exception to the waiver doctrine in the construction contract context occurs when the contractee/employer is the owner of the land upon which the building or construction work is to be done. In this case, the owner may be obliged to accept the work in order to take or retain possession of his land. Accordingly, there "is no legal presumption in this type of contract that acceptance will discharge any right of damages for defects in performance, unless a length of time

---

[30] 13 Am. Jur. 2d *Building and Construction Contracts* § 55 (1964). *See also* Clear v. Patterson, 80 N.M. 654, 459 P.2d 358 (1969); Salem Realty Co. v. Batson, 256 N.C. 298, 123 S.E.2d 744 (1962); Cantrell v. Woodhill Enters., Inc., 273 N.C. 490, 160 S.E.2d 476 (1968).

Making final payment with knowledge of the defect may also release the contractor. Renown, Inc. v. Hensel Phelps Constr. Co., 154 Cal. App. 3d 413, 201 Cal. Rptr. 242 (1984); Kennemore v. Bennett, 740 S.W.2d 39 (Tex. Civ. App. 1987) (owner's forcible taking of possession accompanied by tender of final payment estops him from claiming that work was incomplete); All Seasons' Water Users Ass'n, Inc. v. Northern Improvement Co., 399 N.W.2d 278 (N.D. 1987) (acceptance of pipeline leaves only remedy under one-year contractual warranty for latent defects); E.G. Schafer Constr. Co. v. Gallagher Transfer & Storage Co., 495 So. 2d 348 (La. Ct. App. 1986) (owner's signing of "acceptance" supports finding that work was not defective). Merely taking occupancy with such knowledge, however, when the project is not substantially complete does not operate as an acceptance or waiver. J.R. Sinnott Carpentry, Inc. v. Phillips, 110 Ill. App. 3d 632, 66 Ill. Dec. 671, 443 N.E.2d 597 (1983); and even an architect's certification of completion will not operate to waive or bar claims for defects that were latent at the time the certification was issued. Trenton Constr. Co. v. Straub, 310 S.E.2d 496 (W. Va. 1984).

Circumstances may negate a waiver claim in similar cases, however. *See, e.g.,* Perry Roofing Co. v. Olcott, 722 S.W.2d 538 (Tex. Civ. App. 1986) (homeowner's mistaken belief that cause of roof problem was hail damage did not estop him from making claim for roof defects); Bonstaff v. Jefferson United Enters., Inc., 501 So. 2d 874 (La. Ct. App. 1987) (new home buyer's failure to detect one-inch tilt in kitchen slab does not bar claim for defect; buyers of new homes should not be charged with making detailed inspections).

Although most contract forms and court decisions give significant protection against inadvertent waivers or releases, it is not uncommon that when the parties dispute with each other during the course of construction, they will often compromise and settle with each other. The documentation executed by the parties, when settling interim disputes, frequently will turn out to have broadly phrased language of release, including release of all present and future claims. When later defects become apparent or complaints develop, owners find that legal actions on those accounts are barred by the previous releases. Cases illustrating this circumstance are: Grimm v. F.D. Borkholder, Inc., 454 N.E.2d 84 (Ind. Ct. App. 1983); State Distrib. Corp. v. G.E. Bobbitt & Assocs., Inc., 62 N.C. App. 530, 303 S.E.2d 349 (1983); Alabama Power Co. v. Blount Bros. Corp., 445 So. 2d 250 (Ala. 1984); Gus T. Hange & Son Painting Co. v. Tri-State Constr. Co., 662 S.W.2d 928 (Mo. Ct. App. 1984); Shaw v. Bridges Gallagher, Inc., 174 Ill. App. 3d 680, 528 N.E.2d 1349 (1988).

unreasonable under the circumstances lapses without complaint."[31] The question is one of fact: in some cases, acceptance and occupancy without objection, under circumstances making it clear that the owner accepts the building as is, will amount to waiver.

When the owner had use of a building long enough to discover defects, the waiver doctrine was held to apply.[32] Payment, whether partial or in full, is merely one fact to be considered in determining whether an owner has accepted the building as is and waived exception. Payment is not in itself conclusive on the issue of waiver.[33]

§ 20.4 Statutes of Limitations

Statutes of limitation govern the time period within which a contractor may be held accountable for its activity in relation to a project. An action against a contractor may be based on any number of theories, all of which may have distinct statutes of limitation.

Generally, statutes of limitation for actions based in contract are longer than those for actions based in tort. Typically, an owner's claims against a contractor include counts based on tort theory and separate counts based on allegations of breach of contract. Apart from the distinction between contract and tort actions, some jurisdictions have separate statutes of limitation covering actions for injuries to real property[34] and actions on unwritten contracts.[35] Some jurisdictions even have a statute of limitation

---

[31] Williston § 724. *See also* Restatement (Second) of Contracts § 246(d) illus. 6 & 7 (1981); Aubrey v. Helton, 276 Ala. 134, 159 So. 2d 837 (1964); Weinberg v. Wilensky, 26 N.J. Super. 301, 97 A.2d 707 (App. Div. 1953); 13 Am. Jur. 2d *Building and Construction Contracts* § 56 (1964).

A similar situation occurs when the owner is obligated to accept the work because the owner needs the facilities constructed. In Castille v. 3-D Chems., Inc., 520 So. 2d 1002 (La. Ct. App. 1987), a farmer had storage bins constructed but realized later that defective materials were used. By that time, however, the facility was necessary to hold the farmer's harvest. The court held that the farmer did not waive his claim against the contractor by accepting the work.

[32] Steltz v. Armory Co., 15 Idaho 551, 99 P. 98 (1908). *See* 13 Am. Jur. 2d *Building and Construction Contracts* § 56 (1964); Restatement (Second) of Contracts § 246(d) illus. 9 (1981).

[33] 13 Am. Jur. 2d *Building and Construction Contracts* §§ 58–59 (1964). Claims may also be (but rarely are) barred by laches prior to the expiration of any limitation statute. *See, e.g.*, Axia, Inc. v. I.C. Harbour Constr. Co., 150 Ill. App. 3d 645, 103 Ill. Dec. 801, 501 N.E.2d 1339 (1986) (10-month wait to sue after contractor ceased repair effort does not bar suit).

[34] *See* 34 Am. Jur. *Limitation of Actions* § 73 (1941).

[35] *See id.* §§ 92–94. An analogous problem arises when there are two different contract limitation statutes, one for ordinary contracts and another for contracts under seal. *See* Square D Co. v. C.J. Kern Contractors, Inc., 314 N.C. 423, 334 S.E.2d 63 (1985).

applying specifically to actions brought against contractors, engineers, architects, builders, and developers for inadequate performance under a construction contract; some such statutes apply to both contract and tort actions.[36]

Statutes of limitation typically provide a limited time for bringing suit after the cause of action accrues or arises. There is another variety of limitation statute running from fixed times or dates, whether or a not a cognizable claim existed at that time, thus fixing absolute outside limits on the time in which actions may be brought. These statutes are sometimes called *statutes of repose,* and they typically begin running at the date of substantial completion or final payment.[37]

There is an enormous amount of litigation concerning statutes of limitation on the question of when an owner's cause of action accrues or arises so as to commence the running of the limitation period. In some states, the focus of the decision on this question seems to turn on when the contract breach or tort occurred during the construction period, typically dating the running of the statute from an event such as completion or final payment, on the theory that failure to resolve the problem at that point is the latest breach.[38] Other states tend to be influenced by versions of the malpractice "discovery rule" theory, holding that the statute does not begin to run until the owner was on some sort of notice of the problem.[39]

---

[36] *See, e.g.,* N.J. Stat. Ann. § 2A:14-1.1 (West 1952).

[37] For a general commentary on these statutes, see Comment, *Limitation of Action Statutes for Architects and Engineers—Blueprints for Non-Action,* 18 Cath. U.L. Rev. 361 (1969); Heller, *The District of Columbia's Architects' and Builders' Statutes of Repose; Its Application and the Need for Amendment,* 34 Cath. U.L. Rev. 919 (1985); Comment, *The Kentucky Statute of Repose for Improvements to Real Property,* 73 Ky. L.J. 1143 (1985); Note, *Oklahoma's Statute of Repose Limits Liability of Architects and Engineers for Negligence: A Potential Nightmare,* 22 Tulsa L. Rev. 85 (1986); Note, *The Decline and Rise of Statutes of Repose,* 19 Creighton L. Rev. 509 (1987).

[38] *See, e.g.,* State v. Lundin, 91 A.D.2d 343, 459 N.Y.S.2d 904 (1983) (statute runs from date construction was completed rather than date of owner's acceptance by final payment); Phillips Constr. Co. v. City of N.Y., 61 N.Y.2d 949, 463 N.E.2d 585, 475 N.Y.S.2d 244 (1984) (substantial completion); Antoniou v. Kenick, 124 N.H. 606, 474 A.2d 566 (1984) (when work is completed).

[39] For recent examples of cases decided on that basis, *see* Filcek v. Utica Bldg. Co., 131 Mich. App. 396, 345 N.W.2d 707 (1984); Criswell v. M.J. Brock & Sons, 681 P.2d 495 (Colo. 1984) (statute runs from when owner discovers cause of defect); Lumberman's Mut. Casualty Co. v. Patillo Constr. Co., 254 Ga. 461, 330 S.E.2d 344 (1985) (when owner discovered or should have discovered damages); Linn Reorg. Sch. Dist. No. 2 v. Butler Mfg. Co., 672 S.W.2d 340 (Mo. 1984) (when damage is capable of ascertainment); Pembee Mfg. Corp. v. Cape Fear Constr. Co., 313 N.C. 488, 329 S.E.2d 350 (1985) (when defect first becomes noticeable); Dillon County Sch. Dist. No. 2 v. Lewis Sheet Metal Works, Inc., 286 S.C. 207, 332 S.E.2d 555 (Ct. App. 1985) (same); Dubin v. Dow Corning Corp., 478 So. 2d 71 (Fla. Dist. Ct. App. 1985) (same).

There are, of course, a number of theories available to owners whose claims may appear to be barred by the statute to claim that its operation has been tolled.[40]

A Colorado case construed the four-year statute of limitations imposed in sales of goods cases under Article 2 of the Uniform Commercial Code (UCC) using a similar theory.[41] This case involved a guarantee of a leaking roof. Because the guarantee was for future performance, the court held it was not breached (and, therefore, the cause of action did not accrue) until the roofing contractor rejected the owner's demand to make good on the guaranty by recoating the roof, even though the defects (leaks) had become apparent more than four years prior to the institution of the suit.

Statutes of repose, no less than statutes of limitations, raise questions of interpretation. One type of problem arises when such statutes are first adopted—claimants believing that they still have time to sue (because, for example, the preexisting statutes, although containing short periods of limitation, did not commence running until late discovery of an ancient defect)—can be trapped into having their claims wiped out on the date the new statute of repose becomes effective. Two Illinois courts handled cases with such circumstances. Both held that such claimants should have an additional reasonable period in which to bring their actions, but held that waits of 21 months and 9 months, respectively, were in excess of such a reasonable, additional time.[42] Claimants with newly discovered damages from old defects also argue that because their actions are still timely under conflicting conventional statutes of limitations, such statutes should be regarded as relieving them from the bar of the repose acts. In two states, courts have rejected such claims.[43]

Also, it is not always clear just which possible defendants fall into the classes protected by any particular state's statute. For example, Virginia was recently forced to decide whether material suppliers were protected in

[40] For some examples, see Bethesda Lutheran Church v. Twin City Constr. Co., 356 N.W.2d 344 (Minn. 1984) (promises to cure toll statute); Dillon County Sch. Dist. No. 2 v. Lewis Sheet Metal Works, Inc., 286 S.C. 207, 332 S.E.2d 555 (Ct. App. 1985) (same); Board of Educ. v. Thompson Constr. Corp., 111 A.D.2d 497, 488 N.Y.S.2d 880 (1985) (continuing confidential relationship with architect tolls statute against him but not against contractor); Kulpinski v. City of Tarpon Springs, 473 So. 2d 813 (Fla. Dist. Ct. App. 1985) (continuing flooding renews running of statute for damages caused by each flood).

[41] Smith v. Union Supply Co., 675 P.2d 333 (Colo. Ct. App. 1984).

[42] Champaign County Nursing Home v. Petry Roofing, Inc., 117 Ill. App. 3d 76, 72 Ill. Dec. 594, 452 N.E.2d 847 (1983); Matayka v. Mella, 119 Ill. App. 3d 221, 74 Ill. Dec. 851, 456 N.E.2d 353 (1984).

[43] Stephens v. Creel, 429 So. 2d 278 (Ala. 1983); Okla Homer Smith Furniture Mfg. Co. v. Larson & Wear, Inc., 278 Ark. 467, 646 S.W.2d 696 (1983).

the face of language indicating that material manufacturers were not intended to be covered.[44]

Finally, problems can arise as to when the repose statute commences running. If, for example, the statute runs only from the completion of the entire project, the excavator will normally have a longer exposure than the painter. In a suit against a design-build contractor, one court held that a suit brought within the repose period for substantial completion of the whole project was timely, even though it was filed more than the permitted statutory number of years after completion of work on the leaky roof that was the subject of the complaint.[45]

When a reviewing court is faced with a choice between a statute of limitation for a contract action and a statute of limitation for a tort action, the cases generally hold that the longer contract statute applies.[46] Notwithstanding this general rule, if the action sounds only tort, a court will of course limit the action to the shorter tort limitation period.

For example, in *Lexington Insurance Co. v. Abarca Warehouses Corp.*,[47] the court held that an owner of property that had suffered serious damage in a fire was bound by a one-year tort limitation statute rather than a 15-year contract limitation statute. The court found the action to be based upon the negligence of the contractor's employee and not upon the failure to install a cooling tower that apparently could have prevented the fire.

Accordingly, counsel defending a contractor from the claim of an owner should carefully examine the allegations of the complaint and, if appropriate, raise the defense that the action is barred by the applicable statute of limitation.

---

[44] Cape Henry Towers, Inc. v. National Gypsum Co., 229 Va. 596, 331 S.E.2d 476 (1985).

[45] Mahoney-Troast Constr. Co. v. Supermarkets Gen. Corp., 183 N.J. Super. 325, 460 A.2d 149 (1983).

[46] *See* Annotation, *What Statute of Limitations Governs Actions by Contractor for Defective or Improper Performance of Work by Private Building Contractor,* 1 A.L.R.3d 914 (1965).

When an owner sues a contractor for breach of implied warranty or workmanlike construction, an Ohio appellate court has held the action to be limited by the statute of limitations applicable to tort, not contract actions. Kirk v. Jim Walter Homes, Inc., 41 Ohio App. 3d 128, 534 N.E.2d 1235 (1987). *See generally* Annotation, *What Statute of Limitations Governs Action by Contractee for Defective or Improper Performance of Work by Private Building Contractor,* 1 A.L.R.3d 914 (1965). *Accord* Northern Ind. Pub. Serv. Co. v. Fattore Constr. Co., 468 N.E.2d 633 (Ind. Ct. App. 1985). On the other hand, if the shorter statute is one of those specifically drafted to govern construction disputes and the longer one is a more general statute governing a large number of contract or tort claims, courts will sometimes choose the shorter on the grounds that the legislature intended to preempt the general statute by passing the specific one. *See, e.g.,* Dubin v. Dow Corning Corp., 478 So. 2d 71 (Fla. Dist. Ct. App. 1985); Mohawk Green Apartments v. Kramer, 709 P.2d 955 (Colo. Ct. App. 1985).

[47] 337 F. Supp. 902 (D.P.R. 1971), *aff'd,* 476 F.2d 44 (1st Cir. 1973).

Of course, one way to avoid all the above uncertainty is to incorporate contractual clauses limiting the right of the parties to assert claims to a short but reasonable period. Such clauses are generally enforceable.[48]

§ 20.5 Supervening Impracticability

The doctrine of supervening impracticability is set forth in the *Restatement (Second) of Contracts* as follows:

> Where, after a contract is made, a party's performance is made impracticable without his fault by the occurrence of an event the non-occurrence of which was a basic assumption on which the contract was made, his duty to render that performance is discharged, unless the language or the circumstances indicate the contrary.[49]

It has been held that when a contractor contracts to repair an owner's building, but before the contractor has finished repair to the building it is destroyed by causes outside the responsibility of the contractor, the contractor's performance is discharged.[50] If the contractor had begun repairs before the building was destroyed, the contractor may recover the value of the services already rendered, again assuming that the building was destroyed through no fault of the contractor.[51] Should the parties contractually allocate the risk to the contractor, however, the allocation of that responsibility will be given effect;[52] that is, a contractor may not be able to recover in quantum meruit for services and materials rendered when it retains control over the materials used in the construction.[53]

In a contract for construction of a building, in general, impossibility of performance due to an unanticipated supervening event is the only excuse upon which a contractor may rely to excuse nonperformance of its contractual obligations. Mere impracticability in terms of hardship to the

---

[48] *See, e.g.,* Wayne Drilling & Blasting, Inc. v. Felix Indus., Inc., 129 A.D.2d 633, 514 N.Y.S.2d 114 (1987).

[49] Restatement (Second) of Contracts § 261 (1981).

[50] *Id.* §§ 263, 261 cmt. d, illus. 6; 13 Am. Jur. 2d *Building and Construction Contracts* § 68 (1964). *See also* Annotation, *Liabilities or risks of loss arising out of contract for repairs or additions to, or installations in, existing building which, without fault of either party, is destroyed pending performance,* 28 A.L.R.3d 788, 792 (1969) [hereinafter *Liabilities or risks*].

[51] *Liabilities or risks* at 795; 13 Am. Jur. 2d *Building and Construction Contracts* § 68 (1964). *See also* Bell v. Carver, 245 Ark. 30, 431 S.W.2d 452 (1968) (cited in Annotation, 28 A.L.R.3d 781 (1969); Trip v. Henderson, 158 Fla. 442, 28 So. 2d 857 (1947); Matthews Constr. Co. v. Brady, 104 N.J.L. 438, 140 A. 433 (1928).

[52] *Liabilities or risks* at 809.

[53] Schaeffer Piano Mfg. Co. v. National Fire Extinguisher Co., 148 F. 159 (7th Cir. 1907).

contractor in performing its obligations due to adverse weather[54] or higher than anticipated construction costs[55] will not excuse performance. It has been held that the risk of abnormal weather is assumed by the construction contractor unless a provision in the contract states otherwise.[56] Likewise, a mere change in the degree of difficulty or expense due to such causes as increased wages, prices of raw materials, or costs of construction, unless well beyond normal range, do not amount to impracticability because this is the sort of risk that a fixed-price contract is intended to cover.[57]

The impracticability that excuses nonperformance must be due to an act of God or other unforeseeable, drastic change in a material condition upon which the contract is made. It is not enough that the change only makes it impracticable for the particular contractor to perform; performance itself must be impossible.[58] Notwithstanding this, a drastic change in economic conditions may be an excuse for nonperformance when caused by the occurrence of an event the nonoccurrence of which was a fundamental assumption of the contract.[59] Likewise, when an unanticipated supervening event makes construction difficult, for example, when zoning laws change after a contract to build is entered into, the contractor is obliged to "use reasonable efforts to surmount obstacles to performance and a performance is impracticable only if it is so in spite of such efforts."[60] It has been held that the rule excusing a contractor from performance of a contract for impracticability when performance will violate zoning regulations is not applicable if the zoning laws permit a variance and the contractor has not made a bona fide attempt to obtain a variance.[61]

As can be seen, the doctrine of supervening impracticability, in effect, affords a contractor a very narrow defense in only the most unusual of

---

[54] 18 S. Williston, A Treatise on the Law of Contracts § 1964 (3d ed. 1978); White v. Mitchell, 123 Wash. 630, 213 P. 10 (1923).

[55] Restatement (Second) of Contracts § 261 cmt. b (1981). *See also* Chouteau v. United States, 95 U.S. 61 (1877); Frank T. Hickey, Inc. v. Los Angeles Jewish Community Council, 128 Cal. App. 2d 676, 276 P.2d 52 (1954); Barnard-Curtis Co. v. United States, 301 F.2d 909 (Ct. Cl. 1962).

[56] Associated Eng'rs & Contractors, Inc. v. State, 58 Haw. 322, 568 P.2d 512 (1977).

[57] Restatement (Second) of Contracts § 261 cmt. d (1981). *But see* Florida Power & Light Co. v. Westinghouse Elec. Corp., 826 F.2d 239 (4th Cir. 1987) (contractor excused from duty to dispose of spent nuclear fuel when government discontinued reprocessing of fuel after contract had been entered into); Blount Bros. Corp. v. United States, 872 F.2d 1003 (Fed. Cir. 1989) (contractor not liable for failure to meet contract's stone color requirements because of government's failure to locate sample that would meet its specifications and contractor's repeated efforts to do so).

[58] Restatement (Second) of Contracts § 261 cmt. e, illus. 14.

[59] *Id.* § 261 cmt. d.

[60] *Id.* § 261.

[61] Pennsylvania State Shopping Plazas, Inc. v. Olive, 202 Va. 862, 120 S.E.2d 372 (1961).

circumstances. It can be anticipated that these circumstances will be viewed strictly by any reviewing body.

§ 20.6 Pre-existing Impracticability

If, subsequent to entering into a contract, the contractor and the owner become aware of facts that render performance impracticable (or substantially frustrate the principle purpose of the contractor) and of which neither party knew or had reason to know at the time of making of the contract, then discovery of such facts is treated as if it were a supervening event rendered the contract impractical to perform.[62] For example, in *Boston Plate & Window Glass Co. v. John Bowen Co.,*[63] a contractor that won a public bid entered into a subcontract with the plaintiff. Before the subcontractor began work, a court declared the general contractor's contracts with the state void for reasons of which the contractor had no knowledge. The court ruled that the contractor was not liable to its subcontractor for breach of contract because its performance was impossible because of pre-existing impossibility. Likewise, in *Partridge v. Presley,*[64] a contract for the sale of real estate included a provision that the seller would deliver a permit allowing a modification of the structure to become a two-family house. Because the zoning laws prohibit such a modification, the court declared the contract void due to pre-existing impossibility.

Some authorities state that the defense of pre-existing impossibility/impracticability, if proven, renders a contract void ab initio, rather than discharging the duty of the contractor to perform.[65]

As with supervening impracticability, the pre-existing fact rendering performance impracticable must be a fact the nonexistence of which was a basic assumption of the contract. Whether something was a basic assumption of the contract is a question of fact and depends upon all circumstances surrounding the contract.[66] Occasionally, for instance, a court will find that soil conditions suitable to the intended purpose of the contract are a basic assumption of the contract. This assumption is usually made, however, in

---

[62] Restatement (Second) of Contracts § 266(1), (2) (1981); 18 S. Williston, A Treatise on the Law of Contracts § 1933 (3d ed. 1978). *See also* Annotation, *Modern Status of the Rules Regarding Impossibility of Performance as Defense in Action for Breach of Contract,* 84 A.L.R.2d 12, 32 (1962) [hereinafter *Modern Status*].

[63] 335 Mass. 697, 141 N.E.2d 715 (1957).

[64] 189 F.2d 645 (D.C. Cir.), *cert. denied,* 342 U.S. 850 (1951).

[65] Restatement (Second) of Contracts § 266(1), (2) (1981). *See also Modern Status* at 32; Varia v. Southwick, 81 Idaho 68, 337 P.2d 374 (1959).

[66] *See* Restatement (Second) of Contracts §§ 261 cmt. b, 266 cmt. a (1981).

mining cases. For example, in *Mineral Park Land Co. v. Howard,*[67] the court held that when soil conditions under a contract to remove dirt made the contract impracticable of performance (performance would cost 10 times as much as anticipated), the contract was held to be void.[68]

In construction contracts, it is generally held that the contractor agrees unconditionally to perform in building a house, building, or road, laying pipe, and so on, and unanticipated conditions of the soil or other factors rendering performance impracticable are no excuse. It has been held, for instance, that when soil conditions made building a house on a proposed site impracticable, the contractor failing to build the house was liable for breach of contract.[69] Also, when a contractor could not lay water mains under a river according to the terms of the contract, it was held liable for breach of contract after another contractor subsequently did the job.[70] Subjective impossibility is no excuse.

However, if the owner prepares the plans, chooses the site, or does other acts amounting to a warranty that the plans for the building on that site are sound, the builder may be excused from performance.[71] Of course, the contract itself may either explicitly or by inference allocate the risk of impracticability, in which case the terms of the contract control.[72]

If only part of the contractor's performance is impracticable, its duty to render the remaining part is unaffected if it can render substantial performance of the contract, or if the owner agrees to accept the partial performance in full satisfaction of the contract.[73] If the contractor renders partial substantial performance according to the terms of the contract, it must render substitute performance for the part that is impracticable to the extent that such substitute performance is a reasonable alternative.[74] When the contractor has rendered in good faith a performance that does not strictly comply with the contract requirements but amounts to substantial performance,

---

[67] 172 Cal. 289, 156 P. 458 (1916).

[68] *See also* Virginia Iron, Coal & Coke v. Graham, 124 Va. 692, 98 S.E. 659 (1919).

[69] Stees v. Leonard, 20 Minn. 494 (1874).

[70] B's Co. v. B.T. Barber & Assocs., Inc., 391 F.2d 130 (4th Cir. 1968). *See* 13 Am. Jur. 2d *Building and Construction Contracts* § 1964 (3d ed. 1978).

[71] *Contractor's Liability* at 1409–12. *See also* Ridley Inv. Co. v. Croll, 56 Del. 208, 192 A.2d 925 (1963); Miller v. City of Broken Arrow, 660 F.2d 450 (10th Cir. 1981), *cert. denied,* 455 U.S. 1020 (1982).

[72] Restatement (Second) of Contracts § 265 cmt. c (1981). *See also* Philadelphia Hous. Auth. v. Turner Constr. Co., 343 Pa. 512, 23 A.2d 426 (1942) (contractor warranted sufficiency of plans supplied by owner, and thereby assumed risk of impracticability).

[73] Restatement (Second) of Contracts § 270 cmt. b (1981). *See also* Grenier v. Compratt Constr. Co., 189 Conn. 144, 454 A.2d 1289 (1983).

[74] Restatement (Second) of Contracts § 270(a) (1981).

the contractor is entitled to recovery on a quantum meruit basis.[75] In determining what amounts to substantial performance, it is helpful to consider the following definition:

> In the common case where performances are to be exchanged under an exchange of promises, performance would be substantial if the failure of performance would not be material . . . . [B]oth parties then remain bound to complete the exchange, subject to discharge of the duty to perform the impracticable part and a compensatory claim for restitution.[76]

The same rule applies when, instead of a part of the contractor's performance being impracticable, a condition of the contract does not occur. That is, "[I]mpracticability excuses the non-occurrence of a condition if the occurrence of the condition is not a material part of the agreed exchange and forfeiture would otherwise result."[77] For example, in *Greiner v. Comporait Construction Co.,*[78] the contractor completed road construction but the city engineer refused to exercise his judgment as to the adequacy of the work. Because the contractor could not obtain a letter of certification from the city engineer as required by the contract, the court held for the contractor, noting that the failure to obtain the letter of certification did not materially affect the bargain because the contractor had fulfilled the purpose of the condition by another device.

§ 20.7 Warranties and their Limitations

Although the Uniform Commercial Code (UCC) provides an effective body of law for construing contracts for the sale of goods, in general, the provisions of the UCC covering warranties and limitations of warranties do not apply, except by analogy, to construction contracts, insofar as the latter deal exclusively with supplying labor, design, or other services on the construction project. It is not surprising, therefore, that courts have held that a contract for the waterproofing of a basement, for example, is not a sale of goods;[79] neither is a contract to build a house[80] or construct a swimming pool.[81]

---

[75] 13 Am. Jur. 2d *Building and Construction Contracts* §§ 41–42 (1964).

[76] Restatement (Second) of Contracts § 270 cmt. B (1981).

[77] *Id.* § 271.

[78] 189 Conn. 144, 454 A.2d 1289, 1292 (1983).

[79] Peltz Constr. Co. v. Dunham, 436 N.E.2d 892 (Ind. Ct. App. 1982).

[80] G-W-L, Inc. v. Robichaux, 643 S.W.2d 392 (Tex. 1982).

[81] Chlan v. K.D.I. Sylvan Pools, Inc., 53 Md. App. 236, 452 A.2d 1259 (1982).

However, the provisions of the UCC relating to expressed warranties,[82] implied warranties,[83] and the limitations thereof[84] will apply when construction, design, or installation services provided with materials are merely incidental. Thus, a subcontract for the supply and installation of an air-conditioning unit has been held to be a sale of goods[85] supporting the application of the UCC; a contract to supply and pour concrete has also been held to be a sale of goods.[86]

Even though building and the like are generally not considered goods, if the finished product itself is found to be a good, in many instances the courts will find construction contracts to be, in reality, contracts for the sale of goods. For instance, a grain silo[87] and a diving board installed with a built-in pool[88] were both held to be goods; the sale of prefabricated modular buildings,[89] the sale and installation of an electrical floor,[90] the sale and construction of a one-million-gallon water tank,[91] the design, construction, and delivery of a sewage processing plant,[92] and the installation of a pulp mill boiler and equipment[93] were all held to be sales of goods. In each case, whether the end product involves a sale of goods under the UCC is a question of fact.[94]

Separate and apart from the application of the UCC, in general, building contractors impliedly warrant that work will be done in a skillful manner

---

[82] U.C.C. § 2-313 (1983) provides that an affirmation of fact or any promise constitutes an express warranty.

[83] U.C.C. § 2-314 (1983) provides an implied warranty of merchantability; U.C.C. § 2-315 provides an implied warranty of fitness for the intended purpose.

[84] *Id.* § 2-316 provides that implied warranties may be excluded or modified, but only if the exclusion is conspicuous and all rules are complied with strictly. *Id.* § 2-319 deals with limitation of remedies. *Id.* § 2-207 relates to the "battle of the forms."

[85] Howard Dodge & Sons, Inc. v. Finn, 391 N.E.2d 638 (Ind. Ct. App. 1979).

[86] S.J. Groves & Son v. Warner Co., 576 F.2d 524 (3d Cir. 1978).

[87] Clevenger & Wright Co. v. A.O. Smith Harverstore Prods., Inc., 625 S.W.2d 906 (Mo. Ct. App. 1981).

[88] Anthony Pools v. Sheehan, 295 Md. 285, 455 A.2d 434 (1983).

[89] Cates v. Morgan Portable Bldg. Corp., 591 F.2d 17 (7th Cir. 1979).

[90] Aluminum Co. of Am. v. Electro-Flo Corp., 451 F.2d 1115 (10th Cir. 1971).

[91] Pittsburgh-Des Moines Steel Co. v. Brookhaven Manor Water Co., 532 F.2d 572 (7th Cir. 1976).

[92] Omaha Pollution Control Corp. v. Carver-Greenfield Corp., 413 F. Supp. 1069 (D. Neb. 1976).

[93] Lincoln Pump & Paper Co. v. Dravo Corp., 436 F. Supp. 262 (D. Me. 1977).

[94] *See* U.C.C. § 2-105 (1983). *See also* Space Leasing Assocs. v. Atlantic Bldg. Sys., Inc., 144 Ga. App. 320, 241 S.E.2d 438 (1977). *See generally* Annotation, *What Constitutes "goods" within the Scope of UCC Article 2,* 4 A.L.R.4th 912 (1981); Annotation, *Applicability of Warranty of Fitness under UCC § 2-315 to Supplies or Equipment Used in Performance of Service Contract,* 47 A.L.R.4th 238 (1986).

and in accordance with good usage and accepted practices in the community in which the work is done.[95] Additionally, virtually all jurisdictions recognize the existence of implied warranties of skillful performance and of habitability made by builder/vendors of new residential homes.[96] Most jurisdictions imply these warranties as a matter of common law, but some have statutes fixing them.[97] Some jurisdictions limit this warranty either by

---

[95] *13 Am. Jur. 2d Building and Construction Contracts* § 27 (1964). *See also* Henggler v. Gindra, 191 Neb. 317, 214 N.W.2d 925 (1974); Hodgson v. Chin, 168 N.J. Super. 549, 403 A.2d 942 (App. Div. 1979); Caceci v. DiCanio Constr. Corp., 72 N.Y.2d 52, 526 N.E.2d 266, 530 N.Y.S.2d 771 (1988).

[96] Annotation, *Liability of Builder-Vendor or Other Vendor of New Dwelling for Loss, Injury, or Damage Occasioned by Defective Condition Thereof,* 25 A.L.R.3d 383, 413 (1969). *See generally* Spragens, *Builders' New Home Warranties,* Construction Briefings No. 81-3 (1981). Recent cases involving this warranty obligation include: Gadbois v. Leb-Co Builders, Inc., 312 Pa. Super. 144, 458 A.2d 555 (1983) (septic tank backups justify damage verdict of $18,000 based on evidence that problem lowered value of home by that amount); George v. Veach, 67 N.C. App. 674, 313 S.E.2d 920 (1984) (warranty covers defective septic system); Dillig v. Fisher, 142 Ariz. 47, 688 P.2d 693 (1984) (warranty applies to roof leaks even though home in question was not initially built for resale). For discussion of a related issue, see Annotation, *Real Estate Broker's Liability to Purchaser for Misrepresentation or Nondisclosure of Physical Defects in Property Sold,* 46 A.L.R.4th 546 (1986).

The warranty of habitability will extend in many cases to purchasers from the initial owner. *See* Redarowicz v. Ohlendorf, 92 Ill. App. 2d 171, 441 N.E.2d 324 (1982) (chimney separation, wall cracks, and leakage); Gupta v. Ritter Homes, Inc., 646 S.W.2d 168 (Tex. Ct. App. 1983) (wall and driveway cracks); Keyes v. Guy Bailey Homes, Inc., 439 So. 2d 670 (Miss. 1983) (cracks); Degnan v. Executive Homes, Inc., 215 Mont. 162, 696 P.2d 431 (1985). *But see* Clark v. Landelco, Inc., 657 S.W.2d 634 (Mo. Ct. App. 1984) (holding warranty extends to initial purchaser only); San Francisco Real Estate Investors v. J.A. Jones Constr. Co., 703 F.2d 976 (6th Cir. 1983) (applying Ohio law to bar warranty claim by subsequent purchaser of commercial as opposed to residential property).

Doing minimal rehabilitative work in the course of converting an existing apartment building into a condominium, however, does not give rise to a habitability warranty. *See* Kelley v. Astor Investors, Inc., 123 Ill. App. 3d 593, 462 N.E.2d 996 (1984). Although the warranty may not be disclaimable in a consumer context, the result may be otherwise when the project is commercial. *See* Frickil v. Sunnyside Enters., Inc., 106 Wash. 2d 714, 725 P.2d 422 (1986) (disclaimer valid against owner of apartment complex). It is not breached by the builder's mere failure to obtain or deliver a certificate of occupancy (which has the effect of barring the owner from renting out the premises). *See* Dann v. Perrotti & Hauptman Dev. Co., 670 P.2d 448 (Colo. Ct. App. 1983). Also, the warranty may be deemed to have been given only by commercial builders. *See* Siders v. School, 188 Cal. App. 3d 1217, 233 Cal. Rptr. 906 (1986), rejecting homebuyer's warranty claim for house built by and purchased from a do-it-yourself owner. *See also* Levinson & Silver, *Do Commercial Property Tenants Possess Warranties of Habitability?* 14 Real Est. L.J. 59 (1985); McKie, *Liability of Construction Professionals Under Implied Warranty of Habitability,* 5 Miss. C.L. Rev. 135 (1986).

[97] *See* D.C. Code Ann. § 45-1801 (1981) (especially § 45-1847(b)); La. Civ. Code Ann. art. 2762 (West 1952); Md. Real Prop. Code Ann. § 10-201(c)–203 (1981).

providing that it applies only as between the builder/vendor and the original purchaser of the residential home,[98] or by limiting the applicability of the implied warranty of habitability to contracts by builders/vendors for construction of a new dwelling.[99]

Although the implied warranty of skillful performance applies to building contracts in most jurisdictions,[100] the warranty does not guarantee that work will be perfect forever; rather, the builder impliedly warrants that what it builds will be constructed in a reasonably skillful manner.[101] The warranty does not expire after a set time but, as time goes on, it becomes more likely that defects that arise are not due to the builder's breach of the implied warranty of skillful performance.[102] Many jurisdictions hold that implied warranties extend from the builder to all subsequent purchasers, subject to the limitations imposed by time and other defenses such as waiver. However, it has been held that the reasonable time limitation on bringing a suit for implied breach of warranty is tolled when builders fraudulently conceal defects.[103]

The primary limitations on implied warranties available to construction contractors as defenses, other than the reasonable time limitation described above, are contractual. The contractor may, by contract, limit or exclude the implied warranties of skillful performance or habitability. In order to do so, though, the exclusion must not have the appearance of a contract of adhesion. Although the contractor may express a limit or exclude such warranties, it must do so clearly. Clauses excluding implied warranties will be strictly construed against the drafter.[104]

When a contract for construction contains express warranties relating to the same subject matter the implied warranties normally covered (the quality of work or habitability of the building), the express warranties control. It has been held that when express warranties as to the details of construction

---

[98] *See, e.g.,* Sousa v. Albino, 120 R.I. 461, 388 A.2d 804 (1978).

[99] Groover v. Magnavox, 71 F.R.D. 638 (D. Pa. 1976).

[100] Whirlpool Corp. v. Morse, 222 F. Supp. 645 (D. Minn. 1963), *aff'd,* 332 F.2d 901 (8th Cir. 1964); Kubbe v. Crescent Steel, 105 Ariz. 459, 466 P.2d 753 (1970); Aced v. Hobbs-Sesack Plumbing Co., 55 Cal. 2d 573, 360 P.2d 897, 12 Cal. Rptr. 257 (1961); Vernali v. Centrali, 28 Conn. Supp. 476, 266 A.2d 200 (Super. Ct. 1970); Mann v. Clowser, 190 Va. 887, 59 S.E.2d 78 (1950); Gosselin v. Better Homes, Inc., 256 A.2d 629 (Me. 1969).

[101] Parsons v. Beaulieu, 429 A.2d 214 (Me. 1981). *See also* Lempke v. Dagenais, 130 N.H. 782, 547 A.2d 290 (1988) (privity of contract was not required to maintain action for implied warranty of workmanlike quality; purely economic harm could be recovered under such a theory).

[102] Parsons v. Beaulieu, 429 A.2d 214 (Me. 1981).

[103] Reichelet v. Urban Inv. & Dev. Co., 577 F. Supp. 971 (N.D. Ill. 1984).

[104] Cavasant v. Campopiano, 114 R.I. 24, 327 A.2d 831 (1974). Dewberry v. Maddox, 755 S.W.2d 50 (Tenn. Ct. App. 1988).

of a home excluded implied warranties on the same subject matter, the express warranties did not also eliminate implied warranties relating to soil conditions.[105]

Express warranties are common in construction contracts, usually representing an agreement by the parties as to the quality of the work the contractor is to perform.[106] Such warranties are given effect as they are written. For example, a warranty by a builder that its work would be free of defects in labor and materials for one year has been given effect.[107]

Express warranties may be a part of a written contract, or may be made orally subsequent to the making of the contract. One court held that "certification" of steelwork in a building constituted a warranty that the building was designed to carry the required loads.[108] Also, oral assurances made by a contractor subsequent to the written agreement between the parties that defects would be cured or warranties supplied was given effect by the court.[109]

A contractor faced with allegations of breach of express warranties in a contract with an owner should consider using the contractual defenses discussed in this chapter, depending on the facts of the case.

§ 20.8 Damages

Although the formula for recovery of damages differs in construction defect cases and in delay cases, the theory for an award of damages remains

---

[105] F.&S. Constr. Co. v. Berube, 322 F.2d 782 (10th Cir. 1963). *See also* Twenty-First Century Properties Co. v. Carpenter Insulation & Coatings Co., 694 F. Supp. 148 (D. Md. 1988) (contractor's disclaimer of implied warranty did not cover implied warranty of fitness of end product, but covered only ingredient products used during installation process).

[106] AIA Doc. A201, General Conditions of the Contract for Construction, Art. 3.5 (1987) contains such a warranty.

[107] Austin Co. v. Vaughn Bldg. Corp., 643 S.W.2d 113 (Tex. 1982); Fidelity & Casualty Co. v. J.A. Jones Constr. Co., 200 F. Supp. 264 (D. Ark. 1961), *aff'd,* 325 F.2d 605 (8th Cir. 1963).

[108] Industrial Dev. Bd. v. Fequa Indus., Inc., 523 F.2d 1226 (5th Cir. 1975). *See also* Herman v. Bonanza Bldgs., Inc., 233 Neb. 474, 390 N.W.2d 536 (1986) (holding that by furnishing manufacturer's brochure, contractor gave express warranty).

[109] Salem Towne Apartments, Inc. v. McDaniel & Sons Roofing Co., 330 F. Supp. 906 (E.D.N.C. 1970). *Accord* S.S. Steele & Co. v. Pugh, 473 S.E.2d 978 (Ala. 1985), in which the owner claimed he had refrained from rejecting a slab on the contractor's assurance that it was sound and that he would guarantee it for 25 years. When the slab subsequently failed, the owner prevailed on a warranty theory as well as on the theory that the contractor had misrepresented the true condition of the slab. *See generally* Annotation, *Affirmations or Representations Made after the Sale is Closed as Basis of Warranty under UCC § 2-313(1)(a),* 47 A.L.R.4th 200 (1986).

the same—to put the nonbreaching party where it would have been had the promise been performed.[110] There are two components in the practical application of this theory: (1) the cost of substitute performance; and (2) any further losses resulting from the breach that any reasonable person, at the time of entry into a contract, would have foreseen would occur from a breach.

The cost of substitute performance, or the standard measure of damages when an owner alleges breach of contract by a contractor, pertains also to the owner's allegations of delay and defect. Generally, in determining the measure of damages, it is appropriate to consider the time of the alleged breach. If the contractor's breach is proven before construction begins, the owner's measure of damages is the cost of completion of work, together with reasonable compensation for unavoidable delay. If the owner proves a contractor's breach during construction, damages include the cost of completing the project, assuming there is no undue economic waste,[111] and reasonable compensation for unavoidable delay. The contractor, in turn, may be able to claim recovery in quasi-contract for its partial performance. When the contractor completes its performance, but is late, the owner can claim damages for the loss incurred by not being able to use the property on the contractually scheduled completion date. If the damages for this lost

---

[110] *See, e.g.,* 525 Main St. Corp. v. Eagle Roofing Co., 34 N.J. 251, 254, 168 A.2d 33 (1961).
Occasionally, however, the owner will claim that the appropriate remedy is not damages, but rescission, in which case the remedy is to get his money back, or otherwise be restored to the status quo ante. *See, e.g.,* Hallmark of Farmington, Inc. v. Roy, 1 Conn. App. 278, 471 A.2d 651 (1984) (owner was given all his money back when swimming pool completed by contractor turned out to be unusable). The owner also got his money back in Yurchak v. Jack Boiman Constr. Co., 3 Ohio App. 3d 15, 443 N.E.2d 526 (1983), when, after the basement waterproofing contractor had completed his work, the basement continued to leak. In Coubarreaux v. Hines, 442 So. 2d 898 (La. Ct. App. 1984), the owner not only got back what he had paid for a worthless swimming pool, but also recovered the cost to remove the pool and restore the premises to their precontract condition. *See also* Ed Hackstaff Concrete, Inc. v. Power Ridge Condominium "A" Owners Ass'n, Inc., 679 P.2d 1112 (Colo. Ct. App. 1984). Cases that forgive owners the duty to make final payment to the contractor without requiring them to prove the costs to complete, such as Jackson v. Spurlock, 424 So. 2d 1088 (La. Ct. App. 1983), represent a partial application of this restitution theory.

[111] Restatement (Second) of Contracts § 348(2) (1981). Nisbet v. Yellownick, 124 Ill. App. 3d 466, 464 N.E.2d 781 (1984) (damages equal cost to repair plus loss of rental value for period during which project was uninhabitable); Ralph D. Nelson Co. v. Beil, 671 P.2d 85 (Okla. Ct. App. 1983) (delay damages recoverable in addition to completion costs). Note that if the owner's claim is not for noncompletion but rather for defects alone, his right to recover may be contingent on his first offering the contractor the opportunity to cure the defects. Zobel & Dahl Constr. v. Crotty, 356 N.W.2d 42 (Minn. 1984). *See also* Shaw v. Bridges Gallagher, Inc., 174 Ill. App. 3d 680, 528 N.E.2d 1349 (1988).

use were not foreseeable at the time the contract was entered into, the owner's delay damages are severely limited.[112]

When there has been substantial performance of the construction contract, the contractor has a widely recognized claim for the contract price, less the cost of remedying defects or omissions. Although this is a deviation from the general rule that absolute completion of performance must be proved before the right to payment can be enforced, it has been justified by one court on the basis that when the labor and materials of the contractor go to form an addition affixed to lands, the right of the owner of the land to refuse to accept the work cannot be exercised without doing an injustice to one party or the other.[113]

Lacking substantial performance, an owner's damages for breach by a contractor are limited to the cost of completion, provided there is no undue

---

[112] Restatement (Second) of Contracts § 348(1). A variant of this rule is found in states that do not recognize claims for purely economic losses when the owner's action is grounded exclusively in tort. *See, e.g.,* D.&A. Dev. Corp. v. Butler, 367 N.W.2d 156 (Minn. Ct. App. 1984).

[113] Palmieri v. Albanese, 12 N.J. Super. 338, 79 A.2d 699 (App. Div. 1951). *See also* Salard v. Jim Walter Homes, Inc., 563 So. 2d 1327 (La. Ct. App. 1990) (owner entitled to cost of repair after contractor substantially performed; owner not entitled to rescind contract and have improvement removed).

When the owner sues to recover the repair or completion costs, a number of minor complications arise. In some cases, courts award the actual costs to repair or complete. Kirkpatrick v. Temme, 98 Nev. 523, 654 P.2d 1011 (1983). Other courts phrase the formula in terms of reasonable completion costs. Marshall v. Karl F. Schultz, Inc., 428 So. 2d 533 (Fla. Dist. Ct. App. 1983). In any case, the owner may not recover the costs of putting the project in better condition than it would have been had there been no breach. Fortier v. Sessum, 441 So. 2d 1238 (La. Ct. App. 1984).

Once the contractor proves that the project is substantially complete, the burden of proof is normally shifted to the owner to establish the costs of completion or repair. Jackson v. Spurlock, 424 So. 2d 1088 (La. Ct. App. 1983). The cost rule is a derivative of the substantial performance doctrine, which has historically been applied to construction contracts. Under that doctrine, the contractor is entitled to the contract price less the cost of curing minor deficiencies. When the owner sues to recover those costs, the burden of proving the amount due is normally on him. In a decision regulating the quality of that proof, the Florida District Court of Appeal reversed a judgment in favor of an owner based on evidence of the estimated cost of repair. Because the repairs had actually been made, the court remanded for a new hearing on what the actual costs were. Barile Excavating & Pipeline Co. v. Kendall Properties, Inc., 462 So. 2d 1129 (Fla. Dist. Ct. App. 1984). The normal case, however, does not cast the owner in the role of plaintiff. The issue usually arises in the contractor's suit for recovery of the contract price. A few states apply their substantial performance doctrine in such cases to place the burden of showing what the repair costs are on the contractor, who, incidentally, will nearly always have to rely on cost estimates rather than actual costs. For a recent example in Texas of this twist of the damage proof burdens, see Shaddock v. Storm King Window Co., 696 S.W.2d 271 (Tex. Ct. App. 1985).

economic waste. Examples of this principle in operation are best set forth in the *Restatement (Second) of Contracts.*[114]

In addition to a contractor's potential defense that a particular remedy may involve undue economic waste, an owner must also prove that the losses it allegedly suffered as a result of the contractor's breach were certain in their nature and not speculative. It has been held that in determining the "consequences" of a breach, damages "must be reasonably certain and definite . . . as distinguished from the mere quantitative uncertainty."[115] Applying this rule to a claim of delay damage, the fact of delay in completion of the project must be clearly established, although the value of that delay need not be proved with such certainty. Of course, without certain proofs of the value of the delay, an owner may limit its damage recovery.[116]

Likewise, an owner confronted with a breach by a contractor is under a duty to mitigate damages by reasonable efforts.[117] The term "reasonable" is overriding in the sense that an owner must make all reasonable attempts to mitigate its damages. The evaluation of that duty is measured by whether or not the plaintiff acted reasonably under the circumstances.[118] The burden of proof, however, is on the defendant/contractor to show actual or potential mitigation and the amount of damages for which the owner itself must account.[119]

---

[114] § 348 illus. 2, 3, and 4 (1981). *See generally* Annotation, *Modern Status of Rule as to Whether Cost of Correction or Difference in Value of Structure Is Proper Measure of Damages for Breach of Construction Contract,* 41 A.L.R.4th 110 (1985); Bruner, *Construction Claim Recovery Measures,* 20 Forum 278 (1985). For some recent cases applying the diminution in value measure, *see* Hortman v. Cantrell, 173 Ga. App. 429, 326 S.E.2d 779 (1985); Johnston v. Garages Etc., Inc., 367 N.W.2d 85 (Minn. Ct. App. 1985); Gadbois v. Leb-Co Builders, Inc., 312 Pa. Super. 144, 458 A.2d 555 (1983).

[115] Tessmar v. Grosner, 23 N.J. 193, 203, 128 A.2d 467 (1957); LeGare, Inc. v. Brookhaven Residential Sales, 337 Pa. Super. 478, 487 A.2d 360 (1985).

[116] Restatement (Second) of Contracts § 348(1) (1981).

[117] McGraw v. Johnson, 42 N.J. Super. 267, 273, 126 A.2d 203 (App. Div. 1956); Leto v. Cypress Builders, Inc., 428 So. 2d 819 (La. Ct. App. 1983). An interesting Iowa case recently considered whether, in such an action for negligence, the defense of contributory negligence should be permitted. The court held that the owner's failure to repair the defects promptly (which repairs might have averted the financial failure of the apartment complex in question) would not constitute contributory negligence inasmuch as it did not occur prior to or at the time of the contractor's improper work. R.E.T. Corp. v. Frank Paxton Co., 329 N.W.2d 416 (Iowa 1983). Presumably, proof of that sort would operate—if not to bar an owner's claim, at least to reduce it—on the theory that even victims of negligence are obliged to mitigate their damages.

[118] McDonald v. Mianecki, 79 N.J. 275, 299, 398 A.2d 1283 (1979).

[119] Sandler v. Lawn-A-Mat, 141 N.J. Super. 437, 455, 358 A.2d 805 (App. Div.), *cert. denied,* 71 N.J. 503, 366 A.2d 658 (1976).

§ 20.9 When Owner Retains Duty to Coordinate

At common law, an owner is charged with certain coordinating responsibilities as a result of its duty to finish access to the construction site. This duty in turn arises from the implied provision in every contract that the other party promises to cooperate and that failure to do so is a breach.[120]

A restatement of these principles as they stand today was presented by the New Jersey Supreme Court in *Broadway Maintenance Corp. v. Rutgers:*

> If no one were designated to carry on the overall supervision, the reasonable implication would be that the owner would perform those duties. In so doing the owner impliedly assumes the duty to coordinate the various contractors to prevent unreasonable delays on the project. That is a reasonable assumption because the contracting authority has the power to use its superior position and to invoke its contractual rights to compel cooperation among contractors. The owner is impliedly obligated to act in good faith and to do that which it reasonably can to ensure that the other contractors adhere to the time schedules established for the project. An owner's failure to take action in the face of unnecessary and unreasonable delays by one of the contracting parties would ordinarily evidence bad faith and constitute a breach of its implied duty to coordinate.[121]

Consequently, in the absence of a contractual provision to the contrary, an owner is assumed to have retained its duty to coordinate the construction project among the primes.

This duty is expressly noted in American Institute of Architects (AIA) Document A201.[122] That portion of the AIA contract operates to allow multiple prime contractors at the owner's option.

It is frequently difficult in a multiple prime construction project, however, to determine when an owner has retained the duty to coordinate, in the absence of an express provision such as that in the AIA contract.

In *Broadway Maintenance* the electrical and plumbing prime contractors brought actions against Rutgers for damages caused by delays in construction of the defendant's medical school. The prime contractor for general construction, Briscoe, was brought in as a third-party defendant by Rutgers and settled prior to trial. Each of the contracts between Rutgers and the

---

[120] 11 S. Williston, A Treatise on the Law of Contracts §§ 1296, 1316 (3d ed. 1968). *See also* Glassman Constr. Co., Inc. v. Maryland City Plaza, Inc., 371 F. Supp. 1154 (D. Md. 1974), *aff'd,* 530 F.2d 968 (4th Cir. 1975); George A. Fuller Co. v. United States, 69 F. Supp. 409 (Ct. Cl. 1947).

[121] 90 N.J. 253, 265, 447 A.2d 907 (1982).

[122] AIA Doc. A201, General Conditions of the Contract for Construction, Art. 6.1.1 (1987).

individual primes contained the following language with respect to the coordinating responsibilities of the general contractor, Briscoe:

G-4-N.1 UNIQUE ROLE OF RESPONSIBILITY: STAFFING:

The General Contractor has the responsibility for being the supervisor, manager, overseer, coordinator and expediter of all the Contractors and of the total construction process and all of its parts in accordance with the Contract. In executing the duties incurred by these responsibilities, the General Contractor shall provide sufficient executive and supervisory staff in the field to enable efficient and expeditious handling of these matters. There shall be at least one full-time project Manager assigned by the General Contractor to his home office, as well as the field staff referred to above; the Project Manager shall attend each Progress Meeting at the site.

G-4-N.2 OWNER'S RELIANCE UPON GENERAL CONTRACTOR:

The Owner relies upon the organization, management, skill, cooperation and efficiency of the General Contractor to supervise, direct, control and manage the General Construction work and the efforts of the other Contractors so as to deliver the intended building conforming to the Contract and within the scheduled time.

G-4-N.3 OTHER CONTRACTORS' RELIANCE UPON GENERAL CONTRACTOR:

All other Contractors shall rely upon the organization, management, skill, cooperation and efficiency of the General Contractor to supervise, direct, control and manage the general construction work and the efforts of the other Contractor so as to deliver the intended building conforming to the Contract and within the scheduled time.

G-4-F.4 PROJECT PLANNING, SCHEDULING AND CONTROL:

("CRITICAL PATH METHOD"): As an aid to the General Contractor, and all other Contractors, to bring the completion of the project within the time allocated, the Owner has contracted the services of a Critical Plan Method Scheduling Consultant for project planning, scheduling, and control, and the General Contractor shall incorporate and enforce the combined schedule as his own. Each Contractor agrees to cooperate and coordinate his own operations in order to meet effectively all scheduled task deadlines.[123]

[123] Edwin J. Dobson, Jr., Inc. v. Rutgers State Univ., 157 N.J. Super. 357, 384 A.2d 1121 (1978).

Despite this language delegating coordination responsibilities to Briscoe, the main means of enforcing coordination remained with the owner, pursuant to the following contract provision, also contained in each of the separate prime contracts:

> f. In case the Contractor, by his own acts or the acts of any person or persons in his employ, shall unnecessarily delay, in the opinion of the Architect, the work of the Owner or other Contractors, by not properly cooperating with them or by not affording them efficient opportunity of facility to perform work as may be specified, the Contractor shall, in that case, pay all costs and expenses incurred by such parties due to any such delays and he hereby authorizes the Owner to deduct the amount of such costs and expenses from any monies due or to become due the Contractor under this Contract, based on the investigations and recommendations of the Architect.[124]

The heart of the court's opinion rejecting any cause of action by the primes against Rutgers for failure to coordinate the work was the reasoning that the power to impose sanctions and the duty to coordinate were distinct.[125]

In contrast to *Broadway Maintenance,* other courts have found the right to impose sanctions on a delaying contractor so significant as to become tantamount to a duty to coordinate. By way of example, in *Tippets-Abbett-McCarthy-Stratton v. New York State Thruway Authority*[126] an engineer sought compensation from the state for additional supervision services extended because of a contractor's delay. The New York Court of Claims stated:

> The Attorney General further argues that it was the [engineer]'s duty to insure that the job progressed satisfactorily. But the real power to impose sanctions upon an inefficient or dilatory contractors was retained by the Thruway Authority. [The engineer] could not remove the contractor from the job; could not hold up payment; could not cancel the contractor nor avail itself of any penalty for the contractor's delay.

As can be readily seen from *Broadway Maintenance* and *Tippets,* the courts will use a factual balancing process in determining whether an owner in a multiple prime construction contract has retained its common law duty to coordinate. The balance is delicate and consideration of who has the power to impose sanctions is a factor to be considered. More

---

[124] 384 A.2d at 1126 n.4.

[125] Broadway Maintenance Corp. v. Rutgers, 90 N.J. 253, 266–68, 447 A.2d 907 (1982).

[126] 27 Misc. 2d 522, 523, 212 N.Y.S.2d 263 (Ct. Cl. 1961), *rev'd on other grounds,* 18 A.D.2d 402, 239 N.Y.S.2d 732, *aff'd,* 13 N.Y.2d 1091, 196 N.E.2d 64, 246 N.Y.S.2d 409 (1963).

important, however, may be the actual conduct of the owner throughout the project; whether, for instance, the owner has exercised the power to terminate a prime contractor or has taken over the work of any prime. In those instances, although the owner may have expressed its intent in the contract to have someone else supervise the work, conduct in the field may have altered the expressed intent.[127]

Of course, an owner who has retained the duty to coordinate shares in the responsibility to see that the project is completed on time. Its failure to do so could support not only an affirmative defense but perhaps a counterclaim by the contractor against the owner for delay damages.

§ 20.10 Liquidated Damages

In general, damages for breach of contract by either an owner or a contractor may be liquidated in an agreement between them, but only at an amount that is reasonable in light of the anticipated or actual damages caused by the breach, and considering the difficulty of proof of the loss.[128] If the amount fixed by the contractor as liquidated damages is unreasonably large in light of the anticipated or actual damages, a liquidated damages provision is unenforceable because it is regarded as a penalty.[129] Whether an amount fixed by a contract as damages is a valid liquidated damages clause or an invalid penalty is a question of law.[130]

Reasonableness of the amount fixed as damages is determined as of the time of the contract. The question to be determined by the court is: what damages were contemplated as likely by the parties at the time in the event of delay in completion of the project?[131] Thus, if the contractor promises to complete performance by a specified date or to pay $1,000 a day for every day's delay in completing it, and the contractor takes 10 days beyond the date stipulated to complete the project, then the contractor must pay the

---

[127] *See, e.g.,* Natkin & Co. v. George A. Fuller Co., 347 F. Supp. 17, 35–36 (W.D. Mo. 1972).

[128] Restatement (Second) of Contracts § 356(1) (1981); 5 S. Williston, A Treatise on the Law of Contracts § 775A (3d ed. 1961); Leasing Serv. Corp. v. Justice, 673 F.2d 70 (2d Cir. 1982); Wilson v. Clarke, 470 F.2d 1218 (1st Cir. 1972); Ray Sumlin Constr. Co. v. City of Mobile, 519 So. 2d 511 (Ala. 1988); Dairy Farm Leasing Co. v. Hartley, 395 A.2d 1135 (Me. 1978).

[129] Restatement (Second) of Contracts § 356(1) (1981); 5 S. Williston, A Treatise on the Law of Contracts § 776 (3d ed. 1961).

[130] 5 S. Williston, A Treatise on the Law of Contracts § 778 (3d ed. 1961).

[131] *Id.* § 777; E.C. Ernst, Inc. v. Manhattan Constr. Co., 551 F.2d 1026 (5th Cir. 1977) (subsequent history omitted); United Order of Am. Bricklayers & Stone Masons Union No. 21 v. Thorlief Larsen & Son, Inc., 519 F.2d 331 (7th Cir. 1975); Osceola County v. Bumble Bee Constr., Inc., 479 So. 2d 310 (Fla. Dist. Ct. App. 1985).

$10,000 if $1,000 a day is not unreasonable in the light of the anticipated loss. Additionally, the actual loss to the owner must be difficult to prove. In these circumstances, the amount fixed is not a penalty.[132]

With regard to particular liquidated damages clauses, it has been held that a contract's liquidated damages clause is not to be considered a penalty simply because the amount of damages assessed by the contract escalates with the period of delay.[133] However, when the amount fixed by the liquidated damages clause is not reasonably proportionate to the damages actually sustained, the courts may refuse to enforce the clause as being against public policy.[134] Also, a court may refuse to enforce such a clause if it determines that the amount fixed could not have been based upon the damages that would likely have resulted from breach of the contract.[135]

After satisfying the court that the liquidated damages are not a penalty, a party seeking to enforce a liquidated damages clause must show that the contract was actually breached and, more importantly, that it itself strictly complied with the terms of the contract.[136] Courts following this rule in effect place the burden of proof upon the party (usually the owner) seeking to enforce a liquidated damages clause automatically upon delayed completion of the project. In this respect, liquidated damages claims are similar to suits for actual damages; that is, the party seeking recovery by way of a contract provision must still prove that it is entitled to recover. If a party seeking to enforce a clause that fixes damages for delay has itself contributed to that delay, there is some authority for the proposition that it cannot enforce a liquidated damages clause at all.[137]

The better view, though, is that the person seeking recovery by way of a clause allotting damages for delay on a per diem basis can recover only such

---

[132] Restatement (Second) of Contracts § 356 cmt. b, illus. 3 (1981); United States v. Bethlehem Steel Co., 205 U.S. 105 (1907); Dahlstrom Corp. v. State Highway Comm'n, 590 F.2d 614 (5th Cir. 1979); Gustav Hirsch Org., Inc. v. East Ky. Rival Elec. Co-op Corp., 201 F. Supp. 809 (D. Ky. 1962).

[133] Grenier v. Compratt Constr. Co., 189 Conn. 144, 454 A.2d 1289 (1983).

[134] San Ore-Gradner v. Missouri Pac. R.R. Co., 496 F. Supp. 1337 (E.D. Ark. 1980); Hungerford Constr. Co. v. Florida Citrus Exposition, Inc., 410 F.2d 1229 (5th Cir.), *cert. denied,* 396 U.S. 928 (1969).

[135] Hammaker v. Schleigh, 157 Md. 652, 147 A. 790 (1929); 218–220 Market St. Corp. v. Krich-Radisco, Inc., 124 N.J.L. 302, 11 A.2d 109 (1940); Rye v. Public Serv. Mut. Ins. Co., 34 N.Y.2d 470, 315 N.E.2d 458, 358 N.Y.S.2d 391 (1974); Muller v. Light, 538 S.W.2d 487 (Tex. Civ. App. 1976).

[136] Utica Mut. Co. v. DiDonato, 187 N.J. Super. 30, 453 A.2d 559 (App. Div. 1982); Vines v. Orchard Hills, Inc., 181 Conn. 501, 435 A.2d 1022 (1980); Dairy Farm Leasing Co., Inc. v. Hartley, 395 A.2d 1135 (Me. 1978); Wilson v. Clarke, 470 F.2d 1218 (1st Cir. 1972); General Ins. Co. of Am. v. Commerce Hyatt House, 5 Cal. App. 3d 460, 85 Cal. Rptr. 317 (1970).

[137] Gillioz v. State Highway Comm'n, 348 Mo. 211, 153 S.W.2d 18 (1941); Psaty & Fuhrman, Inc. v. Housing Auth., 76 R.I. 87, 68 A.2d 32 (1949).

damages that are not attributable to its own acts.[138] Only delay attributable to a contractor's fault can be the subject of recovery under a liquidated damages clause.[139] It would be inherently unfair to impose liquidated damages upon a contractor for a period of time during which delay was in fact caused by another contractor or the owner.

The contractor must remember, therefore, in defending damages against the claim of an owner seeking to enforce a liquidated damages clause, that the owner has the burden of proving in most instances that:

1. The amount of damages fixed is a reasonable estimate of the harm caused by the alleged breach
2. The harm caused by the alleged breach is one incapable or very difficult to estimate accurately
3. The delay was not attributable to the owner or another contractor.

Absent proof of these three elements, any liquidated damages assessed should be deemed a penalty and unenforceable.

After the question of enforceability of the liquidated damages clause is answered, the next problem arises in attempting to apply it. The principal difficulties arise in determining when the damages start running and when they should be deemed to have stopped. The general rule is that the damages start running on the date the contract time (as extended for excusable delays) expires. For example, when the government terminated a contractor for default on the original contract completion date, it sought to assess liquidated damages from the date of termination. The board of contract appeals held, however, that the damages should be assessed only from the extended completion date.[140] The board further held that the damages would be thereafter assessed only for a reasonable time, reversing a determination that the contractor should pay them for a period of time during which the government's completing contractor unreasonably delayed the completion of the project.

Likewise, the rule is that the liquidated damages normally run only until the project is substantially completed. Some cases have made harsh-sounding exceptions to the rule, however. In *Sutter Corp. v. Tri-Boro Municipal Authority*[141] the contract required the job to be complete by October 1975, with liquidated damages charged for delay thereafter. The punch list was actually issued in December 1975, but the job was not certified complete by the engineer until December 1976. The court held

---

[138] 13 Am. Jur. 2d *Building and Construction Contracts* § 87 (1964).

[139] City of Houma v. C-Well Ltd., 515 So. 2d 646 (La. Ct. App. 1987); Bedford-Carthage Stone Co. v. Ranney, 34 S.W.2d 387 (Tex. Civ. App. 1930).

[140] Globe Eng'g Corp., ASBCA No. 28832, 85-3 B.C.A. (CCH) ¶ 18,436 (1985).

[141] 338 Pa. Super. 217, 487 A.2d 933 (1985).

the owner to be entitled to the liquidated damages for the entire period prior to the engineer's certification, even though the project, a sewage plant, had been in operation for most of the period.[142]

§ 20.11 Substantial Performance

When a contractor has, in good faith, rendered performance that turns out to be defective or incomplete, it may not be a breach of its contract if it has substantially performed the terms of the contract.[143] If the owner sues the contractor for breach based on an allegation of defective performance by the contractor, the contractor may plead substantial performance as a defense. If the contractor is successful in establishing the defense, the owner may recover only the difference between the contract price paid to the contractor and the value of the work as is, or the cost of repairing the defect, if such cost would not be too great.[144] Absent substantial performance, a breach by the contractor may result in complete forfeiture of the unpaid contract price, or the owner may recover in full the costs of remedying the defective performance in order to make it comply with the contract specifications.

Thus, when a subcontractor's performance under a contract is grossly incomplete or ineffective, it will probably be liable to the owner for the full cost of repair.[145] The same rule of damages applies when the contractor renders defective, though possibly substantial, performance in bad faith.[146]

The rule of payment to the contractor upon substantial performance is based upon quantum meruit principles: if the owner has received something of value, he must pay for it according to its value, whether it was what the owner contracted for or not.[147] The following definition of *substantial performance* may be helpful: "There is substantial performance of

---

[142] For an excellent summary of the law of liquidated damages, see Barbara & Kozek, *Liquidated Damages,* Construction Briefings No. 84-4 (1984).

[143] 13 Am. Jur. 2d *Building and Construction Contracts* § 41 (1964); Williston § 805. The question of how much either the cost to fix or the reduction in value amounts to frequently requires expert testimony. *See, e.g.,* Ellis Millwork, Inc. v. Frees, Inc., 493 So. 2d 696 (La. Ct. App. 1986). See also the discussion of the substantial performance rule in **§ 20.8**.

[144] 13 Am. Jur. 2d *Building and Construction Contracts* §§ 42, 81 (1964); Williston § 805.

[145] 13 Am. Jur. 2d *Building and Construction Contracts* § 41 (1964); Tolstoy Constr. Co. v. Minter, 78 Cal. App. 3d 665, 143 Cal. Rptr. 570 (1978).

[146] Fidelity & Deposit Co. v. Steel, 607 S.W.2d 17 (Tex. Civ. App. 1980). The question of how much either the cost to fix or the reduction in value amounts to frequently requires expert testimony. *See, e.g.,* Ellis Millwork, Inc. v. Frees, Inc., 493 So. 2d 696 (La. Ct. App. 1986). See also the discussion of the substantial performance rule in **§ 20.8**.

[147] 13 Am. Jur. 2d *Building and Construction Contracts* § 41 (1964); Williston § 805.

a contract where all the essentials necessary to the full accomplishment of the purposes for which the thing contracted for has been constructed are performed with such approximation to complete performance that the Owner obtains substantially what is called for by the Contract."[148] Nonetheless, substantial completion does not apply if the deviations from the contract are such that an allowance out of the contract price would not give the other party essentially what it contracted for.[149]

A well-known case involved a contractor whose construction of a house called for a certain brand of pipe. The builder built the house exactly according to specifications except that he used a different brand of pipe, essentially equal in quality to the brand specified in the contract. The court held that the doctrine of substantial performance limited the owner's possible recovery to the difference in value of the two kinds of pipe, rather than the full cost of tearing out the old pipe and putting in new pipe.[150] Another court held that a slight deviation in the color of brick siding on a house did not amount to a failure to comply with the substantial provisions of a contract to apply the siding.[151] Even if there are significant deviations from plans, the courts have found substantial performance when the plans or other circumstances indicated that such deviations were of a nonessential character.[152]

Notwithstanding this, one court has held that a failure to install a roof of uniform color under a roofing contract rendered performance not substantial.[153] It has also been said that in construction contracts there can be no substantial performance if the defect is "structural," in the sense that it affects the soundness of the building.[154]

Sometimes the courts measure substantial performance in terms of the cost required to remedy the defect relative to the entire contract price. If the cost of remedy is great compared to the contract price, the courts are hesitant to find that there has been substantial performance.[155] More recently, however, one court noted that "the question whether the building contract has been substantially performed is not to be decided upon a percentage

---

[148] 13 Am. Jur. 2d *Building and Construction Contracts* § 43 (1964); Jardine Estates, Inc. v. Donna Brook Corp., 42 N.J. Super. 332, 126 A.2d 372 (App. Div. 1956); Foeller v. Heintz, 137 Wis. 169, 118 N.W. 543 (1908).

[149] Williston § 805.

[150] Jacob & Youngs v. Kent, 230 N.Y. 239, 129 N.E. 889 (1921).

[151] S.D. & D.L. Cota Plastering Co. v. Moore, 247 Iowa 972, 77 N.W.2d 475 (1956).

[152] Plante v. Jacobs, 10 Wis. 2d 567, 103 N.W.2d 296 (1960); Dixon v. Nelson, 79 S.D. 44, 107 N.W.2d 505 (1961).

[153] D.W. Grun Roofing & Constr. Co. v. Lope, 529 S.W.2d 258 (Tex. Civ. App. 1975).

[154] Spence v. Harm, 163 N.Y. 220, 57 N.E. 412 (1900).

[155] Nees v. Weaver, 222 Wis. 492, 269 N.W. 266 (1936); Manthey v. Stock, 133 Wis. 197, 113 N.W. 443 (1907).

basis . . . ."[156] In the end, as Justice Holmes said, "the question is one of degree, to be answered, if there is doubt, by the triers of fact."[157]

§ 20.12 Accord and Satisfaction

By definition, an accord and satisfaction consists of two elements. First is the *accord,* or agreement, whereby one of the parties undertakes to give or perform, and the other to accept, in satisfaction of a claim, something other than or different from that to which the second party is or considers itself to be entitled. Second is the *satisfaction:* the execution or performance of the accord or agreement.[158] Until performance of the accord, the original duty is suspended unless there is such a breach of the accord as to discharge a new duty of the obligee to accept the performance in satisfaction. If there is such a breach, the obligee may enforce either the original duty or any duty under the accord.[159]

The accord entitles the obligor to a chance to render the substitute performance in satisfaction of the original duty. Under the rules set forth in the *Restatement (Second) of Contracts,* the obligee's right to enforce that duty is suspended subject to the terms of the accord until the obligor has had that chance.[160]

An accord is like the making of a new contract. Generally, there is no accord and satisfaction without offer by one party and acceptance by the other of substituted performance in full settlement.[161] Thus, it was held

---

[156] Jardine Estates, Inc. v. Donna Brook Corp., 42 N.J. Super. 332, 126 A.2d 372 (App. Div. 1956); *accord* Plante v. Jacobs, 10 Wis. 2d 567, 103 N.W.2d 296 (1960).

[157] Jacob & Youngs v. Kent, 230 N.Y. 239, 243, 129 N.E. 889 (1921).

[158] Restatement (Second) of Contracts § 281(1) (1981); Long v. Weiler, 395 S.W.2d 234 (Mo. Ct. App. 1965); 15 S. Williston, A Treatise on the Law of Contracts § 1838 (3d ed. 1972).

[159] Restatement (Second) of Contracts § 281(2) (1981); W.F. Constr. Co. v. Kalik, 103 Idaho 713, 652 P.2d 661 (Ct. App. 1982). Original contract called for plaintiff to be paid 15% of the direct construction costs; the defendant refused to pay, claiming that the plaintiff rendered defective performance. The parties agreed that the plaintiff would remedy the defects and that the defendant would pay the plaintiff 10% of the direct costs. After the plaintiff performed according to the new contract, the defendant still refused to pay. The court held for the plaintiff in the amount stated in the original contract (15%). *See* Stinson v. Mueller, 449 A.2d 329 (D.C. 1982) (document, signed by contractor, promising repayment of money owed as refund on renovation project, did not constitute accord and satisfaction barring suit by owner against contractor for breach of original renovation contract, because contractor failed to perform fully repayment required by document).

[160] Restatement (Second) of Contracts § 281 cmt. b (1981).

[161] *Id.* § 281 cmt. A; Laganas v. Installation Specialists, Inc., 291 A.2d 187 (D.C. 1972).

that a contractor and a homeowner did not reach accord and satisfaction regarding a damage claim for defects in a garage floor when there was evidence that the homeowners were aware of the cracks around the time they paid for the garage and no evidence indicated that they communicated this knowledge to the contractor.[162] Further, neither the original bill nor the reduced bill, which the homeowners paid, referred on its face to the claim for damages.

It is sometimes said that determining whether accord and satisfaction has been reached between the parties turns on the intent of the parties.[163] One case held that mutual assent of the parties to settlement of the dispute was a requirement for accord and satisfaction, and that the creditor must fully understand that the amount tendered was conditioned upon its being accepted as a full disposition of the underlying obligation.[164]

The contractor/defendant should be aware, when considering raising the defense of accord and satisfaction, that it is an affirmative defense on which the defendant bears the burden of proof.[165]

§ 20.13 Arbitration Defense

A contract between an owner and a contractor often contains an agreement to arbitrate some or all of the disputes arising between the parties (see **Chapter 14**); an owner, however, may bring a claim against a contractor in a court of law. Prior to answering the owner's complaint in that forum, the contractor should consider raising as a defense the agreement to arbitrate.

Arbitration is a remedy favored by the courts, and they will look to enforce any such agreements to arbitrate that can be read to govern a particular dispute.[166] Many jurisdictions now have statutory schemes whereby a party to an action brought in any court and arising out of an agreement providing for arbitration may obtain a stay of the action pending

---

[162] Parsons v. Beaulieu, 429 A.2d 214 (Me. 1981). *See also* Mahler v. Bellis, 231 Neb. 161, 435 N.W.2d 661 (1989) (accord and satisfaction is effective only as to damages known at time of accord).

[163] Publicker Indus., Inc. v. Romar Ceramics Corp., 603 F.2d 1065 (3d Cir. 1979); Tuskegee Alumni Hous. Found., Inc. v. National Homes Constr. Corp., 450 F. Supp. 714 (S.D. Ohio 1978), *aff'd,* 624 F.2d 1101 (5th Cir. 1980).

[164] Flowers v. Diamond Shamrock Corp., 693 F.2d 1146 (5th Cir. 1982).

[165] Delhomme Indus., Inc. v. Houston Beechcraft, Inc., 669 F.2d 1049 (5th Cir. 1982); Larson v. Erickson, 549 F.2d 1136 (8th Cir. 1977); Studiengesellschaft Kohle MbH v. Novamont Corp., 485 F. Supp. 471 (S.D.N.Y. 1980).

[166] Keppler v. Terhune, 88 N.J. Super. 455, 212 A.2d 683 (App. Div. 1965); Ench Equip. Corp. v. N.K. Foods, Inc. 43 N.J. Super. 500, 503, 129 A.2d 313 (App. Div. 1957); Collingswood Hosiery Mills v. American Fed. Hosiery Works, 28 N.J. Super. 605, 101 A.2d 372 (Ch. Div. 1953).

arbitration.[167] Those same statutory schemes often include other provisions for enforcement of an agreement to arbitrate, including procedures for confirmation of an arbitration award, allowing the award the force and effect of a judgment rendered by a court of law.[168]

Even if the contractor answers a complaint in an action filed in a court of law, an owner's allegation that the contractor has thereby waived its right to arbitration will not be readily acknowledged by the courts.[169] Likewise, an owner's allegation that a contractor is guilty of laches by answering a complaint filed in a court of law, notwithstanding an agreement to arbitrate, is also subject to challenge by the contractor. To constitute a valid defense of laches, generally the delay must not only be unexplained and inexcusable, but must have visited prejudice upon the party asserting the delay.[170]

An example of an arbitration clause clearly setting forth arbitration as a remedy for all disputes between an owner and a contractor appears in AIA Document A201. The AIA provision does not refer to the location of the arbitration or the law to be applied, but it is often wise for contractors to consider, at the time of agreement with the owner, whether to add specific provisions providing for arbitration to take place at a convenient location pursuant to the rules of a friendly jurisdiction. Contractors may also wish to preserve legal remedies in certain areas and provide for a particular means of arbitrator selection.

Most arbitration clauses in construction contracts provide for arbitration pursuant to the Construction Industry Arbitration Rules.[171] In general, those rules generate a more loosely structured and faster dispute resolution process than can be obtained in the courts. For example, they do not provide for any discovery (deposition of witnesses prior to the hearings, or interrogatories that could be served on a party prior to the hearing). Additionally the rules provide that "conformity to legal rules of evidence shall not be necessary."

In addition to these considerations, lawyers and contractors look to arbitration for dispute resolution because the arbitrators (either one or a panel

---

[167] United States Arbitration Act, 9 U.S.C. § 1 (1988); Cal. Civ. Proc. Code § 1208 (West 1982); Fla. Stat. Ann. § 682.01 (West 1966); Ind. Code Ann. § 34-4-2-1 (West 1983); Mo. Ann. Stat. § 435.350 (Vernon 1952); N.J. Stat. Ann. § 2A:24-1 (West 1953); N.Y. Civ. Prac. L.&R. § 7501 (1978); Ohio Rev. Code Ann. § 2711.01 (Page 1981); Pa. Stat. Ann. tit. 5, § 161 (Purdon 1963).

[168] *Id.*

[169] *See, e.g.,* Hilti v. Oldach, 392 F.2d 368 (1st Cir. 1968).

[170] *See, e.g.,* Mitchell v. Alfred Hoffman, 48 N.J. Super. 396, 137 A.2d 569 (App. Div. 1958) (citing Stroebel v. Jefferson Trucking & Rigging Co., 125 N.J.L. 484, 487, 15 A.2d 805 (1940)).

[171] American Arbitration Association, Construction Industry Arbitration Rules, Rule 31. Copies of these rules may be obtained from the American Arbitration Association, 140 West 51st Street, New York, NY 10020.

of three) are from within the construction industry and have a greater knowledge of that industry than does the average judge. This is particularly important, considering that the arbitrator comes to the hearing with a background in the construction industry. As can be seen from a review of the various statutory schemes for arbitration in different jurisdictions, one disadvantage of arbitration is that an award based upon an error in fact or law cannot be overturned.[172]

Careful consideration should be given to all these factors as applied to the particular facts at hand before determining to seek relief through arbitration, if it is provided for in the contract. In any event, if a contractor has entered into an arbitration agreement with the owner in any form, but is sued by an owner in a court of law, it should assert the arbitration clause as a defense in its answer to the complaint.

§ 20.14 Termination Defense

In the absence of a provision clearly delineating procedures and conditions for terminating a contractor during the course of a construction project, an owner can terminate only a contractor that has materially breached the terms of the contract between them. What constitutes a material breach of the contract or a material failure understandably varies from one situation to the next. However, a *material breach* is fairly characterized as a substantial failure of the agreement between the parties that justifies the other party's not performing its obligations under the agreement any further.[173] A contractor's failure to provide labor forces for the project may amount to a material breach, depending upon several variable factors, including the time period that labor forces were not available to the project, the extent of the work remaining on the project, the effect of the lack of labor forces on other phases of the work, and other considerations, such as whether the owner was making timely payments under the contract for the contract work completed.

---

[172] *See* United States Arbitration Act, 9 U.S.C. § 1 (1988); Cal. Civ. Proc. Code § 1208 (West 1982); Fla. Stat. Ann. § 682.01 (West 1966); Ind. Code Ann. § 34-4-2-1 (West 1983); Mo. Ann. Stat. § 435.350 (Vernon 1952); N.J. Stat. Ann. § 2A:24-1 (West 1953); N.Y. Civ. Prac. L.&R. § 7501 (1978); Ohio Rev. Code Ann. § 2711.01 (Page 1981); Pa. Stat. Ann. tit. 5, § 161 (Purdon 1963). *See also* City of College Park v. Batson-Cook Co., 196 Ga. App. 138, 395 S.E.2d 385 (1990) (dispute between parties involving meaning, interpretation, and application of contract terms was properly within powers at arbitrators).

[173] *See, e.g.,* Gradco, Inc. v. St. Clair County Bd. of Educ., 477 So. 2d 365 (Ala. 1985) (once contractor's breach determined to be material, mitigation of damages doctrine does not require owner to accept further performance from him).

The *Restatement (Second) of Contracts* sets forth the following rule addressing the contractor's primary defense to termination by an owner—failure of an owner to satisfy a material requirement of the agreement between the parties. It provides, in pertinent part: "[I]t is a condition of each party's remaining duties to render performances to be exchanged under an exchange of promises that there be no uncured material failure by the other party to render any such performance due at an earlier time."[174]

An illustration in the *Restatement* describes the operation of this principle when a contractor would typically have a defense to termination by the owner:

1. A contracts to build a house for B for $50,000.00, progress payments to be made monthly in an amount equal to eighty-five percent of the price of the work performed during the preceding month, the balance to be paid on the architect's certificate of satisfactory completion of the house. Without justification, B fails to make a $5,000.00 progress payment. A thereupon stops work on the house and a week goes by. A's failure to continue the work is not a breach and B has no claim against A. B's failure to make the progress payment is an uncured material failure of performance which operates as a non-occurrence of a condition of A's remaining duties of performance under the exchange. If B offers to make the delayed payment and in all the circumstances, it is not too late to cure the material breach, A's duties to continue the work are not discharged. A has a claim against B for damages for partial breach because of the delay.[175]

In this instance, if contractor A were terminated by owner B, the contractor would have a defense that the prior material breach by the owner excused any further performance of the contractor. If this were found to be a material breach, the contractor would have been wrongfully terminated and would not only have a defense to the termination by the owner, but also an affirmative claim against the owner. Generally, the failure of an owner to make a progress payment within the time set forth in the contract is an uncured material failure of performance excusing the contractor that stops work on the project. As can be seen from the illustration, it is critical to determine which party caused the first material breach. Obviously, if the contractor stops work and then the owner fails in making a progress payment, the contractor will not be protected by the law.

A contractor may have a separate defense after termination by an owner: that the owner may be deemed to have waived a material failure on the part of the contractor. For instance, if a contractor is terminated by an owner

---

[174] Restatement (Second) of Contracts § 237 (1981).

[175] *Id.* § 237 illus. 1.

based upon the material failure to use equipment conforming to the specifications of the owner, the contractor may claim that the owner waived this material failure. In order to claim this waiver defense properly, the contractor must show that the owner was aware of the material failure at some earlier point and that the contractor was allowed to continue despite this failure.

Contract language often provides the contractor with relatively clear guidance as to what specific acts on its part will entitle the owner to terminate it. For example, the widely used AIA Document A201 clearly establishes conditions and procedures for termination of a contractor. Nonetheless, contractors can utilize a variety of defenses.

§ 20.15 Other Contractual Remedy Limitations

The parties may, of course, have further agreed in their contracts to other limitations on the assertion of claims among themselves. Owners, for example, are sometimes surprised to find that a liquidated damages clause operates as a limitation on the contractor's liability (as when the liquidated damage sum provided in the contract is vastly undercompensatory).[176] The courts will generally treat clauses providing only limited remedies as intended to be merely cumulative with whatever remedies are available. It follows that in order to bar an owner's claim effectively, the limitation clause must clearly express the intent that it be exclusive of other remedies.[177]

§ 20.16 Other Owner Claims and Contractor Defenses

This section points out additional matters of possible concern to contractors defending against construction claims. In large part, recovery of these types of damages has not been allowed as a matter of law.

Claims for mental anguish and emotional distress. These claims tend to be asserted mainly by homeowners, as a way to gain compensation for the day-to-day disruptions that follow the defective construction or late delivery of what was expected to be a dream house. To date, the courts have

[176] For such a recent case, see Burns v. Hanover Ins. Co., 454 A.2d 325 (D.C. 1983). For a contrary interpretation, see East Larimer County Water Dist. v. Centric Corp., 693 P.2d 1019 (Colo. Ct. App. 1984).

[177] *See, e.g.,* City of Jacksonville v. Orr Constr. Co., 427 So. 2d 237 (Fla. Dist. Ct. App. 1983).

been unsympathetic to claimants seeking relief for such sufferings.[178] However a recent case may show the way toward an exception to the no mental anguish damage rule. In *B&B Cut Stone Co. v. Jack C. Resneck,*[179] the contract called for construction of a marble fireplace. The owner refused to pay the contractor, offsetting his "moral damages" for defects in the work. The court held that the fireplace was not intended to be useful, but instead was a work of art for which "moral damages" were appropriately awarded.

Punitive damages. These damages are rarely awarded except in unusual cases. The general rule is that the behavior complained of must amount to a separate tort, which itself is of the sort that would justify such relief.[180]

Prejudgment interest. In most cases, the quantum of recovery to which the owner is entitled will not be a fixed sum. The issue of quantum, like the question of liability, will be one of decision by the fact finder at trial. Accordingly, claims for prejudgment interest are rarely honored.[181] When the owner's claim arises from a repudiation of the entire contract, on the other hand, the damages are easily liquidated at the amount of the difference between the contract price and the price offered by the second lowest bidder, in which case prejudgment interest should be recoverable, computed from the dates at which the owner is actually obligated to pay out sums in excess of the original contract price.[182] Even when the damage sum can be liquidated, the owner may be holding retained sums or offset sums from the contract price, which means that the contractor has not unlawfully withheld the sums necessary to compensate for its breach. In such circumstances,

---

[178] *See, e.g.,* Groh v. Broadland Builders, Inc., 120 Mich. App. 214, 327 N.W.2d 443 (1983) (held that such recovery not available in suit grounded in breach of contract and breach of warranty because those theories are contractual and, under the rule of *Hadley v. Baxendale,* not within contemplation of underlying contract); Maltzahn v. Roch, 427 So. 2d 586 (La. Ct. App. 1983) (held that damages for anguish or inconvenience available only if principal object of contract was one of intellectual enjoyment); Cooper v. Superior Court, 153 Cal. App. 3d 1008, 200 Cal. Rptr. 746 (1984) (dismissing tort suit by homeowner whose house, adjacent to construction site, had been damaged by contractor's equipment; holding that emotional distress not within reasonably foreseeable scope of risk of injury). *But see* B&M Homes v. Hogan, 376 So. 2d 667 (Ala. 1981).

[179] 465 So. 2d 851 (La. Ct. App. 1985).

[180] *See* Quedding v. Arisumi Bros., Inc., 66 Haw. 335, 661 P.2d 706 (1983) (holding that an owner had failed to show the required wanton or reckless behavior). *See generally* Annotation, *Punitive Damages for Breach of Building or Construction Contract,* A.L.R.4th 110 (1985). As to whether the contractor's insurance coverage will pay any judgment for punitive damages, *see* J. Morrison, The Insurability of Punitive Damages: A Current and Jurisdictional Analysis (1985).

[181] *See* Adler v. Seligman, 438 So. 2d 1963 (Fla. Dist. Ct. App. 1983). *See also* Marathon Oil Co. v. Hollis, 167 Ga. App. 48, 305 S.E.2d 864 (1983).

[182] East Larimer County Water Dist. v. Centric Corp., 693 P.2d 1019 (Colo. Ct. App. 1984).

prejudgment interest will not be awarded.[183] When it is the contractor or architect claiming prejudgment interest, the problem is frequently not so much the uncertainty of the amount owed, but rather the dates upon which it could be said to have been due. Construction contracts usually call for payments to be made as work is completed. Computation of prejudgment interest when the contractor has been wrongfully terminated thus requires proof of when work would have reached the stages at which the payments lost in the termination would have become due.[184]

Attorneys' fees. These are sometimes recoverable under a specific provision of the construction contract.[185] In a few states, attorneys' fees can also be recovered pursuant to special statutes, such as a deceptive and unfair trade practices act. A 1985 Texas case involved such a statute.[186] Finally, hold harmless clauses in construction contracts frequently call for the indemnitor to pay the indemnitee's attorneys' fees. Absent such clauses, the right to indemnification for attorney's fees may turn on whether the claimant's suit against the indemnitee is based only on theories that the indemnitee is vicariously responsible for the indemnitor's action. If any of the plaintiff's pleaded and proved theories make the indemnitee independently responsible for the plaintiff's losses, no attorneys' fees are recoverable.[187]

Statutory penalties or enhanced damages. Sometimes local pressure groups (or larger political movements) succeed in obtaining passage of special statutes that penalize sellers for wrongful dealings with consumers.[188] Contractors who seek to charge owners with usurious interest may similarly face liability for penalties.[189]

Joint and severally liable defendants. Construction projects usually involve multiple parties. As a result, situations when two or more parties may

---

[183] Subsurfco, Inc. v. B-Y Water Dist., 369 N.W.2d 129 (S.D. 1985).

[184] *See, e.g.,* Metropolitan Dade County v. Bouterse, Perez & Fabregas Architects, Planners, Inc., 463 So. 2d 526 (Fla. Dist. Ct. App. 1985).

[185] For example of such a contract (but a case in which the fees were nonetheless held not to be recoverable by a contractor suing an owner), *see* National Roofing & Siding Co. v. Giaise, 434 So. 2d 85 (La. Ct. App. 1983).

[186] Mathews v. Candlewood Builders, Inc. 685 S.W.2d 649 (Tex. 1985).

[187] *See, e.g.,* JKT Co. v. Hardwick, 284 S.C. 110, 335 S.E.2d 329 (Ct. App. 1984).

[188] For an illustration about how an owner might recover treble damages against the contractor under such a statute, *see* Birds Constr., Inc. v. McKay, 657 S.W.2d 514 (Tex. Ct. App. 1983).

[189] *See, e.g.,* Amarillo Equity Investors, Inc. v. Craycroft Lacy Partners, 654 S.W.2d 28 (Tex. Ct. App. 1983); Mathews v. Candlewood Builders, Inc., 685 S.W.2d 649 (Tex. 1985) (attorneys' fees).

share liability abound. Care must be taken in settling claims with fewer than all of them lest the case against the remaining nonsettling parties be jeopardized.[190]

Specific performance or equitable relief. In a limited number of circumstances, the courts will order work to be done and payments to be made on pain of contempt.[191] Likewise, when the contractor's obligations are intermeshed with a contractual requirement to convey real estate, specific performance may be available.[192]

---

[190] *See, e.g.,* Perlmutter v. Harmony Homes, Inc., 677 P.2d 381 (Colo. Ct. App. 1984).

[191] *See, e.g.,* Walters v. Campeau, 205 Mont. 448, 668 P.2d 1054 (1983).

[192] *See, e.g.,* Schimmer v. H.W. Freeman Constr. Co., 643 S.W.2d 621 (Mo. Ct. App. 1983).

CHAPTER 21

TAX CONSIDERATIONS OF CONSTRUCTION LITIGATION

Richard Hawkins
James R. Puetz

Richard Hawkins is a partner with Arthur Andersen & Company in Portland, Oregon. He is the author of numerous professional articles dealing with the construction industry. Mr. Hawkins has over 20 years of public accounting experience, both as an auditor and tax consultant, with a concentration in the construction and real estate industries. He is a member of the Tax and Fiscal Affairs Committee of the Associated General Contractors of America.

James R. Puetz is a member of the Oregon Bar Association and a tax senior in the International Tax Services Group of Price Waterhouse in Portland, Oregon. Mr. Puetz's responsibilities include monitoring tax rules and case law relating to the construction industry. In addition, he performs engagement responsibilities for a number of domestic and international tax clients. Mr. Puetz received his B.S. degree in accounting from North Dakota State University, his Masters of Accountancy from the University of North Dakota, and his law degree from Northwestern School of Law of Lewis and Clark College.

§ 21.1 Introduction

HOW PROCEEDS FROM SETTLEMENTS OR JUDGMENTS ARE TAXED

§ 21.2 Treatment of Proceeds

§ 21.3 —Proceeds Treated as Ordinary Income

§ 21.4 —Proceeds Treated as Return of Capital

§ 21.5 —Proceeds Treated as Nontaxable

HOW PAYMENT OF SETTLEMENTS AND JUDGMENTS IS TREATED FOR TAX PURPOSES

§ 21.6 Introduction

§ 21.7 General Principles

§ 21.8 Payments Treated as Deductible Expenses

§ 21.9 Payments Treated as Capital Expenditures

§ 21.10 Expenses That May Not Be Deducted or Capitalized

TIMING OF INCOME RECOGNITION AND EXPENSE DEDUCTION

§ 21.11 Introduction

§ 21.12 Cash and Accrual Methods

§ 21.13 Long-Term Contract Methods of Accounting

§ 21.14 —Percentage-of-Completion

§ 21.15 —Completed Contract Method

SUBSTANTIATING THE DESIRED TAX TREATMENT

§ 21.16 Introduction

§ 21.17 Written Documentation

§ 21.18 Actions of the Parties

TAX PLANNING

§ 21.19 Timing of Tax Planning

§ 21.20 Choice of Claims

§ 21.1 Introduction

Generally, the greatest concern of a contractor involved in a lawsuit is how to maximize its recovery or minimize its liability. One of the last things a contractor thinks of when in a litigation posture is the tax consequence related to the outcome of the litigation. Proper tax planning at the beginning of the litigation process may enhance the benefits or mitigate the consequences of a judgment or settlement.

This chapter discusses the income tax consequences that a contractor may face in a lawsuit. The chapter focuses on the tax treatment of proceeds received from—as well as the expenditures paid—in a lawsuit. In addition, the timing of income recognition and expense deduction is addressed. Finally, the chapter discusses the various tax planning opportunities that are available to structure the judgment or settlement to achieve the most beneficial tax treatment.

HOW PROCEEDS FROM SETTLEMENTS OR JUDGMENTS ARE TAXED

§ 21.2 Treatment of Proceeds

For tax purposes the characterization of the proceeds received from a settlement or judgment of a construction dispute depends on the nature and origin of the claim.[1] Generally, proceeds received from a construction claim are treated as:

1. Ordinary income
2. A return of capital
3. Nontaxable.

§ 21.3 —Proceeds Treated as Ordinary Income

Lost Profits

The general rule is that damages awarded or payments received in settlement of a claim for loss of profits are taxed as ordinary income.[2] The theory behind this treatment is that the recovery represents the profits that the plaintiff would have earned had the defendant not interfered with the plaintiff's operations.

Tax Benefit Doctrine

When a contractor has previously taken a tax deduction for costs incurred, which it later seeks to recover in a lawsuit, the proceeds received for such costs are taxed as ordinary income pursuant to the tax benefit doctrine.[3]

---

[1] United States v. Gilmore, 372 U.S. 39 (1963).

[2] Swastika Oil & Gas Co. v. Commissioner, 123 F.2d 382 (6th Cir. 1941); *see also* Collins v. Commissioner, 18 T.C.M. (CCH) 756 (1959).

[3] I.R.C. § 111 (1988) and the Treas. Regs. thereto.

The *tax benefit doctrine* is a judicial creation[4] that states that the subsequent recovery of previously incurred costs is taxable to the extent that the costs yielded a tax benefit (deduction) to the taxpayer.

Therefore, when a contractor is suing for reimbursement from another party because that party caused the contractor to incur cost overruns, the proceeds received would be taxed as ordinary income to the extent that the cost overruns were deducted on the contractor's tax return. Likewise, amounts received representing additional contract proceeds for change orders or amounts recovered that were paid to subcontractors for their portion of the work done on the construction contract will also be taxed as ordinary income.[5]

Harm to Business Reputation Resulting in Lost Profits

Not all construction litigation is related to a breach of the construction contract. Contractors often find themselves embroiled in litigation over business and personal torts such as slander and libel. Proceeds received for harm to business reputation or product may be treated as taxable or nontaxable depending on the allegations in the complaint. When a contractor files a slander or libel lawsuit alleging that the defendant's tortious actions caused the contractor to lose future business profits, the proceeds received for that claim generally are treated as ordinary income.[6] When the complaint, however, alleges that the defendant's actions impaired the contractor's goodwill, the proceeds generally are treated as a return of capital.[7]

Punitive Damages

Determining the characterization of proceeds received as punitive damages is one of the least settled issues in this area of tax law. Both the IRS and the courts have vacillated on the issue of whether punitive damages should be taxed as ordinary income or be considered as nontaxable.[8]

---

[4] The tax benefit doctrine has its roots in judicial decisions. However, due to its longstanding support, it was enacted as part of the IRC.

[5] The examples used here to describe the application of the tax benefit doctrine are taken from Construction Litigation: Representing the Contractor ch. 17 (R. Cushman, J. Carter & A. Silverman, eds., John Wiley & Sons 1989).

[6] Wolfson, 45 T.C.M. (CCH) 297 (1982); *see also* Agar v. Commissioner, 290 F.2d 283 (2d Cir. 1961); Rev. Rul. 58-418, 1958-2 C.B. 18.

[7] Impairment of goodwill is discussed in §§ **21.4** and **21.20**. In addition, a discussion of the tax strategies involved in a harm to business reputation case is discussed in § **21.20**.

[8] Rev. Rul. 58-418, 1958-2 C.B. 18 (IRS ruled that punitive damages were ordinary income); Rev. Rul. 75-45, 1975-1 C.B. 45 (IRS ruled that punitive damages received from insurance company on wrongful death claim were nontaxable under § 104); Rev.

In the 1989 Revenue Reconciliation Act, however, Congress attempted to provide some guidance on this matter. Congress amended I.R.C. § 104 so that punitive damages received after July 10, 1989, that are in connection with a personal injury claim for nonphysical injuries are taxable as ordinary income. Alternatively, punitive damages received on a personal injury claim for physical injuries are nontaxable.[9]

The 1989 Act is not a panacea with respect to characterizing the tax effect of receiving punitive damages. The 1989 Act is limited to personal injury actions only; the Act does not provide any guidance on how to classify punitive damages received in nonpersonal injury cases such as contract claims, fraud claims, or antitrust claims. The greater weight of judicial and administrative authority, however, treats recoveries of punitive damages from nonpersonal injury claims as ordinary income.[10]

§ 21.4 —Proceeds Treated as Return of Capital

In a claim for damage to tangible capital assets (for example, machinery and equipment) or intangible goodwill, the damages received on a judgment or in settlement of the claim are generally treated as a *return of capital.*[11] Return of capital treatment is a two-part analysis. First, recoveries are applied to reduce a capital asset's basis. Therefore, in a lawsuit in which capital assets have a basis in excess of the damages received, no tax is realized. Instead, the asset's basis is reduced by the amount of the recovery, thus contributing to a greater capital gain on the eventual sale of the asset sometime in the future.

Second, to the extent that a recovery exceeds the basis of a capital asset or goodwill, the excess will be treated as either ordinary income or capital gain. Ordinary income treatment is prescribed when the excess is attributed to depreciation recapture.[12] Consequently, if a contractor sues for injury to machinery and equipment and the machinery and equipment is fully depreciated, the damages received would be treated as ordinary income to the extent of the depreciation recapture.

Capital gain treatment is prescribed when the excess is not attributed to depreciation recapture but to market appreciation of the asset or some

---

Rul. 84-108, 1984-2 C.B. 32 (IRS revoked its prior ruling in Rev. Rul. 75-45 and ruled that punitive damages received in wrongful death action were taxable as ordinary income).

[9] *See* 1989 Revenue Reconciliation Act § 7641(a); *see also* I.R.C. § 104(a).

[10] *See* Commissioner v. Glenshaw Glass Co., 348 U.S. 426 (1955).

[11] Raytheon Prod. Corp. v. Commissioner, 144 F.2d 110 (1st Cir. 1944); *see also* Bresler v. Commissioner, 65 T.C. 182 (1975); *see generally* 5 Mertens Law of Federal Income Taxation § 24A (1991) [hereinafter Mertens].

[12] Rev. Rul. 68-378, 1968-2 C.B. 335.

other factor.[13] In *Raytheon Production Corp.,* the First Circuit provided the following example:

> A buys Blackacre for $5,000. It appreciates in value to $50,000. B tortiously destroys it by fire. A sues and recovers $50,000 in tort damages from B.[14]

The court stated that although no gain was derived by A from the lawsuit, $45,000 of the market appreciation was realized as gain on the conversion of Blackacre into money damages.[15]

As the example indicates, capital gain treatment will generally be applicable only if the claim involves an asset whose market appreciation exceeds its potential depreciation recapture. This situation typically involves assets such as real estate and acquired goodwill (that is, goodwill in which the contractor has basis).

§ 21.5 —Proceeds Treated as Nontaxable

Section 104(a)(2) of the Internal Revenue Code provides that "gross income does not include the amount of any damages received (whether by suit or agreement . . .) on account of personal injuries . . . .[16] This exclusionary treatment would apply to damages received in tort actions for emotional distress, injury to personal reputation as a result of defamation, slander, or libel,[17] and assault or battery. Therefore, to be nontaxable, the damages received must be for harm to the reputation of the contractor itself, as distinguished from harm to the reputation of the contractor's business.[18]

---

[13] *See* Bresler v. Commissioner, 65 T.C. 182, 184; *see also* Raytheon Prod. Corp. v. Commissioner, 144 F.2d 110, 114; *see generally* Mertens § 24A.

[14] Raytheon Prod. Corp. v. Commissioner, 144 F.2d 110, 114.

[15] *Id.*

[16] I.R.C. § 104(a)(2) (emphasis added).

[17] Slander and libel were discussed in § **21.3** in a harm to business reputation context. To the extent that the reputation of a contractor's business is harmed, the damages will be taxable as ordinary income, unless the contractor can establish that the goodwill of the business was impaired, in which case capital gain treatment may be applicable.

[18] In the harm to business reputation context, damages are generally taxable if the damages represent lost profits. However, if the claim is for harm to goodwill, the damages are taxable only to the extent that they exceed the contractor's basis in the goodwill.

HOW PAYMENT OF SETTLEMENTS AND JUDGMENTS IS TREATED FOR TAX PURPOSES

§ 21.6 Introduction

Like the taxation of litigation proceeds, the tax treatment of litigation payments depends on the nature of the claim. In general, litigation payments fall into three categories:

1. Deductible expenses of conducting a trade or business or related income-producing activities (I.R.C. §§ 162, 212)
2. Capital expenses that may be added to the basis or
3. Nondeductible personal expenses or fines.

The origin of the claim rule governs the characterization of payments arising from litigation and will determine the category into which the payment will fall. Because the defendant may be unaware of a pending lawsuit until the complaint is filed, the defendant has less opportunity and time to influence the characterization of the payment than the plaintiff does. Therefore the defendant's tax planning should start when the defendant prepares to answer the plaintiff's complaint. This section examines each of the broad categories of payments arising from litigation and the rules governing the tax characterization of the payments.

§ 21.7 General Principles

The nature of the underlying claim determines the character of both proceeds received and payments made during a lawsuit.[19] Though settlements, releases, and other agreements reached in litigation may seem like "deals," a lawsuit is not, in itself, considered a sale or exchange requiring capital treatment of expense or income items.[20] However, if the dispute concerns the sale of a capital asset, a payment to settle the suit should be treated as a

---

[19] *See* United States v. Gilmore, 372 U.S. 39 (1963); Anchor Coupling Co., Inc. v. United States, 427 F.2d 429 (7th Cir. 1970), *cert. denied,* 401 U.S. 908 (1971); Arthur H. DuGrenier, Inc. v. Commissioner, 58 T.C. 931 (1972).

[20] Rev. Rul. 74-251, 1974-1 C.B. 234.

capital expenditure.[21] If the payment relates to a negligence claim asserted against a business, it will likely be a deductible business expense.[22]

The importance of income and expense characterization has diminished since the 1986 Tax Reform Act,[23] which applies similar tax rates to ordinary income and capital gain. Nevertheless, capital losses may be carried over to reduce future income and capital expenses may be added to the basis; therefore, future characterization should remain an important issue in litigation strategy concerning payments.

The potential payor should also consider whether a seemingly nondeductible claim may be separated into parts, some of which may be deducted or capitalized.[24] Documentation is important in this area. *GC Services Corp. v. Commissioner*[25] involved a dispute over a sale of stock in which the seller (taxpayer) combined the stock sale with a release of pending legal actions. The court disallowed the deduction for the taxpayer's release of claims because the sale agreement did not make any specific allocation to the noncapital expense.

The form of payment does not determine the character of the payment. In *DeVito v. Commissioner,*[26] for example, the court held damages for breach of contract to be a deductible business expense even though the taxpayer paid in stock rather than cash. In the same way, *Camloc Fastener Co. v. Commissioner*[27] involved a termination of a sales contract. The parties drew up a settlement in the form of a patent sale to create a lien to guarantee the payments. Nevertheless, the court held the required payments to be deductible because they did not relate to a capital exchange between the parties.

The IRS may argue that the recipient's characterization of litigation proceeds should govern the payor's characterization of the expense.[28] This emphasizes the importance of prejudgment consideration of tax consequences and negotiation with the opposing party. The issue may also arise as to which entity or person, within a group of related defendants, is entitled to a deduction.[29]

---

[21] *Id. See also* Woodward v. Commissioner, 410 F.2d 313 (8th Cir. 1969), *aff'd,* 397 U.S. 572 (1970).

[22] *E.g.,* Eisler v. Commissioner, 59 T.C. 634 (1973), *acq.,* 1973-2 C.B. 1.

[23] Pub. L. No. 99-514, 99th Cong., 2d Sess. (1986).

[24] Tech. Adv. Mem. 85-04-004 (Oct. 15, 1984) (portion of payment personal, not deductible).

[25] 73 T.C. 406 (1979).

[26] 39 T.C.M. (CCH) 152 (1972).

[27] 10 T.C. 1024 (1948), *acq.,* 1948-2 C.B. 1.

[28] Kimbell v. United States, 490 F.2d 203 (5th Cir.), *cert. denied,* 419 U.S. 833 (1974).

[29] Independent Oil v. Commissioner, 4 T.C.M. 36 (1945) (corporation denied deduction because not the party liable). Interstate Transit Lines v. Commissioner, 319 U.S. 590 (1943).

§ 21.8 Payments Treated as Deductible Expenses

Deductible under § 162

Ordinary and necessary expenses of carrying on a trade or business are deductible under I.R.C. § 162. An expense is *ordinary* and *necessary* if it is reasonably related to a taxpayer's business and is helpful and appropriate to that business. Accordingly, the payment of any expense that would have been deductible if the defendant had paid it without litigation, is deductible if paid in the form of damages pursuant to a lawsuit.[30] Expenses such as back wages, compensation for services, contract service fees, and payments for noninventory supplies and materials are examples of deductible litigation payments.

Under § 162, a taxpayer may deduct an ordinary and necessary expense that is normally expected in a situation even if the situation rarely arises. Under Treasury Regulation § 1.162-1, an expense payment need not be frequent or regularly occurring to be "ordinary." Therefore, the requirement to pay general damages or settlement fees may qualify as an ordinary business expense despite the infrequency of litigation.

Deductible under § 212

Litigation payments may also qualify as an itemized deduction for an individual under § 212 of the Code, although cases when construction litigants would use this section rather than § 162 would be rare. Section 212 grants a deduction, subject to 2 percent of adjustsed gross income (AGI) floor, for certain expenses incurred in the production of income. Miscellaneous deductions for unreimbursed job expenses and expenses for the production and collection of taxable income are equal to the amount by which the total amount of all these types of miscellaneous expenses exceeds 2 percent of adjusted gross income. Section 212 expenses are ordinary and necessary expenses paid or incurred during the tax year for the production or collection of income or for the management, conservation, or maintenance of property held for the production of income.[31]

The key issue under § 212 is whether the expense can be linked directly to an income-producing activity.[32] In *Delp v. Commissioner*[33] the taxpayers

---

[30] *See, e.g.,* Sanders v. Commissioner, 225 F.2d 629 (10th Cir. 1955), *cert. denied,* 350 U.S. 967 (1956).

[31] I.R.C. § 212; Treas. Reg. § 1.212-1(a) (1990).

[32] *See, e.g.,* Delp v. Commissioner, 30 T.C. 1230 (1958); McCaa v. Commissioner, 26 T.C.M. (CCH) 711 (1967); United States v. Gilmore, 372 U.S. 39 (1963).

[33] 30 T.C. 1230 (1958).

failed to prove that contract payments to their brother were related to any income-producing activity. The fact that the payments were to compensate the brother for loss of income from a partnership was not sufficient to link the payment with income-producing activities.

Another consideration under § 212 is whether a payment is related to producing, collecting, or conserving income, or whether it is in defense of title to income-producing property.[34] The former type of payment is deductible under § 212, but the latter is generally a capital expense.

§ 21.9 Payments Treated as Capital Expenditures

Expenses related to the acquisition of capital assets generally are not deducted, but are capitalized as additions to the basis of the property. These costs would then be recovered over the life of the equipment through annual depreciation deductions. Therefore, if a contractor incurs litigation costs in a claim for breach of contract to purchase equipment, the litigation costs should be added to the equipment's basis.

§ 21.10 Expenses That May Not Be Deducted or Capitalized

A taxpayer may not deduct the amount of any fine or penalty paid to a federal, state, or foreign government entity for the violation of any law.[35] A fine or penalty for this purpose includes civil and criminal penalties, and payments to settle actual or potential civil or criminal liabilities prior to imposition of a fine or penalty. Two-thirds of treble damages paid pursuant to antitrust claims are not deductible if there is a conviction or plea of guilty or nolo contendere in a criminal proceeding.[36]

In general, if litigation payments cannot be characterized as deductible or capital expenses under a specific provision of the Code, they will be deemed to be personal. In *United States v. Gilmore*[37] the Supreme Court held that the taxpayer's payments related to a divorce settlement were nondeductible personal expenses. The Court rejected the taxpayer's claim that the divorce settlement expense was necessary to protect the taxpayer's

---

[34] *E.g.*, Turzillo v. Commissioner, 346 F.2d 884 (6th Cir. 1965).

[35] I.R.C. § 162(f); Treas. Reg. § 1.162-21(a) (1990).

[36] I.R.C. § 162(g); Treas. Reg. § 1.162-22 (1990).

[37] 372 U.S. 39 (1963).

business reputation and controlling stock interest. A personal expense does not become a business expense simply because it may also help one's business in some incidental fashion.

TIMING OF INCOME RECOGNITION AND EXPENSE DEDUCTION

§ 21.11 Introduction

Once the contractor has determined how to classify litigation proceeds and expenses for tax purposes, the contractor must determine when to report them on the tax return. The timing of recognition of income and expenses from litigation depends on the tax accounting method elected by the contractor.[38] The two basic tax accounting methods are the cash receipts and disbursements method and the accrual method. In addition, the contractor may elect to use one of the long-term contract methods of accounting: percentage-of-completion method; or completed contract method.[39]

§ 21.12 Cash and Accrual Methods

Under the *cash method* of accounting, income is recognized when received, or "constructively" received, and expenses are recognized when they are paid.[40] Therefore, under the cash method, a contractor would not recognize any income upon prevailing in a lawsuit until the contractor actually or constructively receives the litigation proceeds.

Under the *accrual method* of accounting, income and expenses are recognized when: all the events have occurred that fix the right to receive income or to establish the fact of the liability; and the amount can be determined with reasonable accuracy.[41] Therefore, under this "all events test," litigation proceeds would be recognized as income in the year the suit is settled or judgment is rendered.

---

[38] I.R.C. §§ 446, 451, 460, and 461.

[39] *Id.* §§ 446, 451, and 460; *see also* Treas. Reg. §§ 1.446-1, 1.451-3 (1990).

[40] Treas. Reg. § 1.446-1(c) (1990).

[41] *Id.*

§ 21.13 Long-Term Contract Methods of Accounting

The tax consequences of disputes and claims on a contractor will depend in part on the long-term contract method the contractor employs. *Long-term contract methods* determine when the taxpayer must report contract revenues and expenses. In the wake of the Tax Reform Act of 1986, most contractors must now use the percentage-of-completion method.[42] Under the new § 460, contractors must also apply a look-back method upon contract completion. Under the *look-back rule,* a taxpayer must redetermine tax liability for previous years based on actual contract costs and revenues and pay interest on any additional tax due. Although mandatory for most contractors, percentage-of-completion and look-back rules can be avoided by certain small contractors who may use other methods, such as the more advantageous completed contract method.

§ 21.14 —Percentage-of-Completion

Most taxpayers performing contracts after July of 1989 must use the *percentage-of-completion method.*[43] This method compares actual contract cost to total estimated contract costs to arrive at a percent of the contract revenue or loss that must be included in income each year.[44] The key difficulty for the taxpayer is to estimate contract costs and revenues accurately. If disputes or claims relating to cost and revenue items cause them to change, the taxpayer must adjust these estimates as the contract progresses. Since the 1986 Act, percentage-of-completion rules have focused on the accuracy of the taxpayer's cost and revenue estimates. The look-back rules, for example, operate as a penalty for inaccurate estimation of contract revenue and costs. The focus on accurate reporting makes it essential that the construction contractor attempt to resolve and account for disputed items early in the course of the contract so that estimates may be revised.

The percentage-of-completion formula is presented in terms of the amount of revenue the contractor must recognize after all costs are accounted for under the taxpayer's regular method of accounting.[45] The

---

[42] I.R.C. § 460.

[43] *Id.*

[44] I.R.S. Notice 89-15, 1989-1 C.B. 634.

[45] *Id.* The percentage of completion formula is described as follows:

> Under the percentage of completion method, the taxpayer must include in gross income in each taxable year ending after the date that the contract is entered into an amount equal to the excess of (1) the product of (a) the total amount of revenue

formula may be better understood if stated in terms of gross profit. Under the percentage-of-completion method, the gross profit to be recognized on any contract during a taxable year is the estimated gross profit at contract completion times the percentage-of-completion at year end, minus any portion of the total estimated gross profit that was recognized in prior years. The gross profit formula is stated as follows:[46]

PCGP = (TGP × PC) – PYGP
PCGP = current year percentage-of-completion gross profit
TGP = total gross profit (TCP = TCC)
TCP = total estimated contract price
TCC = total estimated contract cost
PC = percentage-of-completion ratio, computed by the cost-to-cost method
PYGP = prior years' cumulative percentage-of-completion gross profit

The total gross profit (TGP) and percentage-of-completion (PC) are the two key components of this formula that the contractor must compute. A brief discussion of the rules and principles the contractor must follow to determine these amounts follows. Unfortunately, neither the Code nor the IRS provide much guidance on the treatment of disputes, claims, and litigation in applying this formula.

Total Gross Profit

Total gross profit is the total estimated contract price less the total estimated contract cost. The total contract price is the amount the contractor

---

that the taxpayer estimates it will receive with respect to the contract, multiplied by (b) the cumulative percentage of the contract that has been completed as of the end of the taxable year, over (2) the total cumulative amount of contract revenue required to be included in gross income in all preceding taxable years. This amount may be expressed by the following formula:

CCR = (TCR × PC) – I

where:

CCR = current year contract revenue included in gross income

TCR = the total amount of revenue that the taxpayer expects to receive with respect to the contract

PC = the cumulative percentage of the contract that has been completed as of the end of the taxable year

I = the total cumulative amount of contract revenue required to be included in gross income in all preceding taxable years

[46] For more information on the formula and its components, see D. Meals et al., 1 Guide to Construction Contractors ch. 4 (Practitioner's Publishing Co.).

expects to realize from the contract. The total contract cost is the estimate of the costs the taxpayer expects to incur in performing the contract. Both of these components are estimates that may require adjustment during the life of the contract. For example, the cost-plus, time-and-material, and change order pricing mechanisms of various types of contracts cause the total contract price to fluctuate from year to year. Likewise, costs will often fluctuate due to overruns, supply shortages, and the like.

The general rule governing cost and revenue estimation is that the contractor must adjust the estimate whenever changing circumstances can be reasonably predicted and measured. If a revenue item is not reasonably predictable or measurable, the IRC provides only that the contractor must report any income not previously includable in gross income in the first taxable year following the taxable year the contract was completed.[47] This rule does not provide guidance on the tax treatment of proceeds received, or damages paid, as a result of litigation being settled following the year the contract is completed.[48]

At least on the cost side of the total gross profit equation there is one settled rule concerning litigation. The cost estimate should not include any general contingency allowance that would cover the possible expenses of litigation, abnormal weather, or strikes, unless those expenses are reasonably expected to be incurred and measurable as of the taxpayer's year end. Even if the costs of such events become measurable after the year end but before filing a return, the estimated cost should not change because the amount of the adjustment was not foreseeable at year's end. By contrast, a measurable but not yet incurred cost must be included in the cost estimate. For example, all payments withheld from subcontractors pending acceptance of the subcontractors' work should be included.

Percentage-of-Completion

Once the contractor estimates the total gross profit, it must determine what percent of that profit to recognize in the current taxable year. The formula taxpayers must use to compute percentage-of-completion is called the *cost-to-cost method,* and it may be stated as follows:

PC = ACC / TCC
PC = percentage-of-completion

---

[47] I.R.C. § 460(b)(1). This rule specifically does not apply to the look-back rules set forth at *id.* 460(b)(2).

[48] One can speculate that this is a rule of convenience for the taxpayer. That is, the income or loss attributable to the contract, but becoming reasonably measurable only after the contract is completed, must be carried to the first year after contract completion, but should not affect all of the years in the life of the contract.

ACC = actual contract cost incurred since inception of the contract
TCC = total contract cost

The determination of actual contract cost is subject to the principles already discussed. The most controversial issue in this formula concerns the timing of recognition of the cost. The IRS provides specific guidance concerning direct material costs as follows: "The cost of direct materials and supplies that are purchased specifically for a particular long-term contract are allocable to the contract in the taxable year in which such costs are incurred."[49] If this principle governs the treatment of costs generally, then the actual costs resulting from litigation or settlement would also be allocable to the contract in the year incurred. In any case, for planning purposes it is important to remember that as actual costs increase within a taxable year, the percentage-of-completion ratio also increases, thus increasing the amount of gross profit the contractor must include in income.

In applying the cost-to-cost method, a contractor must include almost all types of costs in the actual and total contract cost figures. This includes direct materials and labor and most indirect costs. However, a simplified cost-to-cost method is available to certain qualifying contractors.[50] Under the simplified method, the only costs attributable to the contract for purposes of computing the actual and total contract costs are direct material, direct labor, and tax return depreciation, amortization, and cost recovery allowances on equipment or facilities directly associated with the contract.

§ 21.15 —Completed Contract Method

Certain small contractors are exempt from the mandatory use of the percentage-of-completion method for regular tax purposes.[51] Two types of contractors may use the completed contract method instead of the percentage-of-completion method: (1) home construction contractors; and (2) construction contractors who estimate that the contract will be complete within two years from commencement, and whose average annual gross receipts for the three taxable years preceding the taxable year in which the contract is entered into do not exceed $10 million.[52]

---

[49] I.R.S. Notice 89-15 at A-35, 1989-1 C.B. 634.

[50] I.R.C. § 460(b)(4)(A). Only taxpayers using the percentage-of-completion method for all items under all long-term contracts, or cash-basis homebuilders using the percentage-of-completion capitalized cost method may use this simplified method.

[51] I.R.C. § 460(e)(1). Contractors exempt from percentage-of-completion rules must nevertheless use the percentage-of-completion method for alternative minimum tax purposes. *See* I.R.C. 56(a)(3).

[52] *Id.* § 460(e)(1).

The *completed contract method* is advantageous from a tax standpoint because it permits the taxpayer to defer the reporting of net income from the contract until the taxable year in which the contract is complete.[53] The IRC defines the completed contract method as follows:

> [U]nder the completed contract method, gross income derived from long-term contracts must be reported by including the gross contract price of each contract in gross income for the taxable year in which such contract is completed . . . . All costs properly allocable to a long-term contract . . . must be deducted from gross income for the taxable year in which the contract is completed.[54]

Under this method, therefore, the key issue for the contractor is the allocation of actual income and expense items to a particular contract in question. Whereas the IRC focuses on accurate estimates under the percentage-of-completion method, under the completed contract method it emphasizes proper allocation of expenses and income among contracts[55] and defines when a contract may be considered complete.[56]

In accounting for claims and disputes under the completed contract method, the significant questions involve the time of completion. A long-term contract is not considered completed until final completion and acceptance have occurred.[57] A taxpayer may not delay the completion of a contract for the principal purpose of deferring income tax.

Unlike the percentage-of-completion regulation rules, the completed contract regulations address in greater detail how disputed contracts are to be treated.[58] With respect to a disputed contract, the regulations provide rules for three basic categories of disputes:

1. When the party contracting with the taxpayer demands a reduction in contract price or additional work[59]
2. When the taxpayer demands an increase in contract price[60]

---

[53] Treas. Reg. § 1.451-3 (1990).

[54] *Id.* § 1.451-3(d)(1).

[55] *Id.* § 1.451-3(a)(4). When the taxpayer has attempted to distort income and expenses through the use of an aggregate contract or a series of contracts, the commissioner may treat one agreement as several contracts or treat several agreements as one contract to reflect income clearly.

[56] *Id.* § 1.451-3(b)(1).

[57] *Id.* § 1.451-3(b)(2)(i). For a thorough discussion of the completeness issue see Ball, Ball & Brosamer, Inc. v. Commissioner, 60 T.C.M. (CCH) 587 (1990).

[58] Treas. Reg. § 1.451-3(d)(2), (3), (4).

[59] *Id.* § 1.451-3(d)(2)(i).

[60] *Id.* § 1.451-3(d)(3).

3. When both the taxpayer and the contracting party demand either concessions in price or additional work.[61]

A discussion of these rules is beyond the scope of this chapter, however, the following examples are provided for general reference:

Contracting Party Disputes Taxpayer Performance:

X, a calendar year taxpayer utilizing the completed contract method of accounting, constructs a building for Y pursuant to a long-term contract. According to the terms of the contract, the gross contract price is $2,000,000. X finishes construction of the building in 1972 at a cost of $1,900,000. Y examines the building and is dissatisfied with the construction. He demands either alterations or a reduction in the gross contract. The amount reasonably in dispute is $500,000. This dispute affects so much of the contract price that X is unable to determine whether a profit or a loss will ultimately be realized on such contract. Accordingly . . . X does not include any portion of the gross contract price in gross income and does not deduct any costs which are properly allocable to the contract until the taxable year in which the dispute is resolved.

Taxpayer Disputes Contracting Party Performance:

S, a calendar year taxpayer utilizing the completed contract method of accounting, constructs a building for T pursuant to a long-term contract. Under the terms of the contract, S is entitled to receive $100,000 upon completion of the building. S finishes construction of the building in 1974 at a cost of $105,000. T examines the building in 1974 and agrees that it meets his specifications; however, as of the end of 1974, S and T are unable to agree as to the merits of S's claim for an additional $10,000 for certain items which S alleges are changes in contract specifications and T alleges are within the scope of the contract's original specifications. Under these circumstances, S must include in income in 1974 the gross contract price of $100,000 and must deduct from gross income in such year the $105,000 of costs. In 1975 the dispute is resolved by a payment to S of $2,000 with respect to his claim. S must include this $2,000 in gross income in 1975.

Taxpayer and Contracting Party Dispute Each Other's Performance:

W, a calendar year taxpayer utilizing the completed contract method of accounting, constructs a factory for Z pursuant to a long-term contract. Under the terms of the contract, Z agrees to pay W a total of $100,000 for construction of the factory. W finishes construction of the factory in December 1974 at a cost of $110,000. When Z examines the factory in December 1974, Z is dissatisfied with the location and workmanship of certain heating ducts. As of the end of 1974, W contends that the heating

[61] *Id.* § 1.451-3(d)(4).

ducts as constructed are in accordance with contract specifications. The amount reasonably in dispute with respect to the heating ducts is $6,000. As of this time, W is claiming $14,000 in addition to the original contract price for certain changes in contract specifications which W alleges have increased his costs. Z denies that such changes have increased W's costs. In 1975 the disputes between W and Z are resolved by performance of additional work by W at a cost of $1,000 and by an agreement that the contract price would be revised downward to $96,000. Under these circumstances, W must include in his gross income for 1974, $94,000 (the gross contract price less the amount reasonably in dispute because of Z's claim, or $100,000 – $6,000). In 1974, W must also deduct $104,000 (his costs incurred of $110,000 less $6,000, an amount equal to the amount in dispute). In 1975, W must include in gross income an additional $2,000 ($96,000 – $94,000) and must deduct $7,000 (the $1,000 of costs W incurs in such year plus the $6,000 of previously undeducted costs.)[62]

SUBSTANTIATING THE DESIRED TAX TREATMENT

§ 21.16 Introduction

The tax consequences of a lawsuit depend on the nature of the lawsuit. The manner in which the claim is pleaded, argued, and resolved will determine how the proceeds received, expenses incurred, and damages paid are treated for tax purposes.

Upon settlement of or judgment in a lawsuit, a contractor must look at the outcome of the litigation and determine how to treat the proceeds received and/or expenses incurred on its income tax return. Should the IRS challenge the contractor's return position, the taxpayer has the burden of proving that its position is tenable within the purview of the IRC, Treasury Regulations, and judicial decisions.

The taxpayer will meet the burden of proof only if the written documentation, testimony, and other relevant facts and circumstances produced at the trial level substantiate the taxpayer's return. Consequently, the method in which the contractor decides to pursue its claim will define the parameters within which the IRS and the Tax Court will analyze any tax dispute. Therefore, adequate tax planning at the outset of the litigation should prove to be useful if a tax dispute arises at a later time.

[62] *Id.* § 1.451-3(d).

§ 21.17 Written Documentation

The Complaint

The starting point for determining how litigation proceeds received or expenses incurred are taxed is the complaint. A contractor trying to argue that the proceeds received are nontaxable as damages for personal injuries is likely not to prevail when the complaint alleges breach of contract.[63]

The complaint is a persuasive piece of evidence in determining how litigation proceeds should be taxed because in it the litigant sets forth the allegations forming the underlying claim and makes the prayer for relief.[64] Because the complaint describes the nature of the claim, it is a major determinant of the tax character of the proceeds received or expenses incurred.

Although the complaint is important, it does not always control the tax result of litigation. The facts and circumstances surrounding the receipt of the proceeds or payment of the expenses may govern their tax treatment. In *Phoenix Coal Co. v. Commissioner*[65] the complaint alleged that the defendant injured the taxpayer's goodwill. Nevertheless, the taxpayer failed to prove at the trial that any goodwill existed at the time of the defendant's actions. Moreover, the evidence revealed that the damages received were for lost profits. As a result, the Second Circuit upheld the Tax Court's decision that the damages received should be taxable as ordinary income.

In *W. Walley, Inc. v. Commissioner*[66] the taxpayer alleged in its complaint that the defendant's breach of contract impaired the taxpayer's goodwill and caused it to lose profits. Upon settlement of the claim, the taxpayer treated the proceeds as compensation for damage to goodwill (return of capital treatment). The Tax Court upheld the IRS's claim that the recovery was for lost profits. The Tax Court reached this decision because the taxpayer did not prove, either in the lawsuit or in the Tax Court, that any goodwill existed.

These cases emphasize that the complaint is an important starting point for determining the nature and character of the proceeds received and expenses incurred in litigation. The complaint alone, however, cannot control the tax consequences of a lawsuit if the evidence produced either at trial or before the Tax Court does not support the allegations in the complaint. Therefore, the tax planning involved with litigation of claims does not end with drafting the complaint; instead, it continues throughout the litigation process.

---

[63] *See* Gunderson v. Commissioner, 38 T.C.M. (CCH) 464 (1979).

[64] *See* Rev. Rul. 85-98, 1985-2 C.B. 51.

[65] 231 F.2d 420, 422–23 (2d Cir. 1956).

[66] 7 T.C.M. (CCH) 137 (1948).

Release Agreement upon Settlement

Construction litigation often ends by the parties settling the claim. When the release agreement between the parties allocates proceeds in a rational manner among the various claims, the proceeds will generally be taxed in accordance with the release. As with the complaint, however, there is no guarantee that the proceeds will be taxed according to the method provided in the release if evidence points to a different, more appropriate tax treatment.[67]

The Judgment

In the event a court resolves the lawsuit, the court's order may specifically allocate which proceeds apply to which claims. The order will not specify the tax treatment to be applied to the proceeds. However, should the IRS dispute the taxpayer's return treatment of the proceeds, the allocation in the court's order will be considered in determining the dollar amount to be allocated to the disputed claims.

§ 21.18 Actions of the Parties

The written documentation generated by a lawsuit provides a good starting point for determining the tax treatment of litigation proceeds and expenses. Nevertheless, the actions of the litigating parties may be the best indicator of how proceeds and expenses should be treated for tax purposes.

Assume a contractor sues for lost profits and impairment of goodwill. The contractor receives $100,000 in settlement of these two claims. The contractor reports only $30,000 as ordinary income on its tax return and claims that the remaining $70,000 is a nontaxable return of capital. For financial and tax reporting purposes, the contractor does not have a separately stated goodwill account.

If a tax dispute arises over the contractor's treatment of the $70,000 as nontaxable return of capital, the IRS is likely to look at the contractor's financial reporting procedures. Because the contractor's actions tend to indicate that it did not have any basis in its goodwill, the IRS is likely to reclassify the nontaxable return of capital as capital gain.[68]

---

[67] Wood & Noel, *Tax Aspects of Settlements, Judgments, Antitrust Payments and Recoveries, in* Tax Management Portfolios, No. 121 at A-13 (BNA 1990).

[68] This example is oversimplified in that the IRS would likely argue a number of issues, one being that none of the proceeds apply to goodwill and all of the proceeds were for lost profits. For an example of this situation, see generally Raytheon Prod. Corp. v. Commissioner, 144 F.2d 110 (1st Cir. 1944).

TAX PLANNING

§ 21.19 Timing of Tax Planning

The tax consequences of a particular lawsuit will depend on the nature of the legal claim. Therefore, the framing of the complaint, the wording of the pleadings, the presentation of the evidence, and the ultimate settlement or judgment of the claim will contribute to determining how the damages received, or expenses incurred, will be treated for tax purposes. Therefore, to achieve favorable tax consequences, it is important to start the tax planning at the same time the litigation strategy is initiated. By waiting until the lawsuit is resolved the litigant forgoes the opportunity to plan a meaningful tax strategy.

§ 21.20 Choice of Claims

The newly enacted capital gains rate reduction[69] and the income exclusion provided in I.R.C. § 104(a)(2) for damages received for personal injuries[70] provide significant tax planning opportunities for the construction contractor involved in litigation.

Loss of Profits versus Impairment to Goodwill

When the contractor alleges that a party destroyed all or a portion of the contractor's business enterprise, the contractor could sue on a loss of profits theory, an impairment of goodwill theory, or both. As noted in **§ 21.3**, damages received for loss of profits would be taxable as ordinary income, but damages received for impairment of goodwill would be taxed in accordance with return of capital principles.

Noting at the outset of the litigation the differences in the tax consequences between pursuing a loss of profits claim over an impairment of goodwill claim is critical. The number of judicial decisions in this area suggests that the two theories are very similar.[71] When the legal outcome of pursuing one theory over the other is the same, it may make sense to pursue an impairment of goodwill claim over a loss of profits claim because of the

---

[69] Revenue Reconciliation Act of 1990. The RRA of 1990 enacted a preferential capital gains tax for individuals of 28%.

[70] See **§ 21.5**.

[71] *See* Raytheon Prod. Corp. v. Commissioner, 144 F.2d 110 (1st Cir. 1944); Phoenix Coal Co. v. Commissioner, 231 F.2d 420 (2d Cir. 1956); W. Walley, Inc. v. Commissioner, 7 T.C.M. (CCH) 137 (1948).

favorable capital recovery tax treatment accorded to damages received for impairment of goodwill.

In *Raytheon Production Corp.* the taxpayer corporation alleged that the defendant destroyed the taxpayer's business enterprise and goodwill in interstate commerce. To prove that it had goodwill amounting to $3 million, the taxpayer provided evidence of the number of customers it had prior to the defendant's actions and the potential profits to be derived therefrom. The parties settled the suit in the taxpayer's favor prior to trial, and the taxpayer treated the settlement proceeds as a nontaxable return of capital. The IRS challenged this position, arguing that the settlement recovery was for lost profits. The First Circuit determined that the recovery was for impairment of goodwill, not for lost profits, even though the plaintiff provided significant evidence of lost profits to prove the value of its goodwill. On this issue, the court stated that "allegations and evidence as to the amount of profits were necessary in order to establish the value of the goodwill and business since it is derived by a capitalization of profits."[72]

Although the court held that capital recovery treatment should apply, it did not agree with the taxpayer that the entire amount of proceeds was a nontaxable recovery of basis. Rather, the court required the taxpayer to apply capital gain treatment to the extent that the proceeds exceeded the taxpayer's basis in the goodwill. The court based its decision on the fact that although the plaintiff established that its goodwill was worth $3 million, it did not establish that it had a cost basis in its goodwill sufficient to absorb the total recovery.

The *Raytheon* decision is instructive on how the courts will resolve the lost profits versus impairment of goodwill issue. It also illustrates the similarity between claims for impairment of goodwill and lost profits. Based on this decision, a litigating contractor pursuing an impairment of goodwill theory should draft the allegations and produce sufficient evidence to prove that goodwill exists. Moreover, the prayer for relief should seek recovery for the impairment of such goodwill.

Goodwill may be established by presenting evidence of what a company is worth over its historical cost in its assets. Under the *Raytheon* line of reasoning, this may be accomplished by showing the present value of the company's lost future profits. However, although a contractor may be able to establish impairment of goodwill and obtain relief on that theory, nontaxable return of basis will not be prescribed unless the contractor can establish that it has a cost or other basis in the goodwill.

[72] Raytheon Prod. Corp. v. Commissioner, 144 F.2d 110, 113.

Personal Reputation versus Business Reputation

Damages for injury to personal reputation are completely nontaxable,[73] whereas damages to compensate for injury to business reputation are generally taxed as ordinary income.[74] In the small contractor situation involving a sole proprietorship or small partnership, a claim for harm to business reputation may often be indistinguishable from a claim for harm to personal reputation because the contractor and its business are one and the same.[75]

For example, A makes a slanderous comment about B's contracting business and B goes out of business. B could likely sue for harm to personal reputation and/or harm to business reputation. The suit would likely be framed in terms of lost profits or impairment of goodwill. Before preparing the claim, B would be wise to consult with both its litigation and tax counsel to determine which legal theory would provide the best overall legal and tax outcome.

---

[73] I.R.C. § 104(a)(2); Treas. Reg. § 1.104-1(c) (1990). The income exclusion provided by I.R.C. § 104(a)(2) includes compensation for tort or tort-type rights, which include slander, libel, and emotional distress claims. For a discussion of taxation of damages received to compensate for personal injuries, see **§ 21.5**.

[74] See **§ 21.3**. However, when the harm to business reputation resulted in impairment of goodwill, return of capital treatment would be applicable.

[75] A good example of a lawsuit that depicts the close relationship between a claim for injury to personal reputation and injury to business reputation is Agar v. Commissioner, 290 F.2d 283 (2d Cir. 1961).

CHAPTER 22

TRIAL AND APPEAL

William G. Schaefer
Langley R. Shook

William G. Schaefer is a partner in the firm of Sidley & Austin in Washington, D.C. He has a litigation and general business practice that involves various aspects of construction litigation, including private and government contracts, antitrust, safety, and employment matters. Mr. Schaefer was formerly vice president and general counsel of DeKalb AgResearch Inc. He is a member of the bars of the District of Columbia, Maryland, and Illinois.

Langley R. Shook is a partner with Sidley & Austin in Washington, D.C. His practice concentrates on complex litigation, including commercial and contract disputes, environmental law and employment issues. Mr. Shook is admitted to practice in the District of Columbia and Illinois.

§ 22.1 **Overview**

INITIAL ASSESSMENT

§ 22.2 **Why an Assessment?**

§ 22.3 **What Facts Are Most Important to the Case?**

§ 22.4 **What Are the Parties' Key Legal Arguments?**

§ 22.5 What Are the Equities of the Case?
§ 22.6 What Are the Client's Objectives?
§ 22.7 How Can Damages Be Measured?
§ 22.8 What Are the Potential Conflicts of Interest?
§ 22.9 What Is the Purpose of a Trial Plan?
§ 22.10 Should Alternatives to Litigation Be Pursued?

TRIAL PREPARATION

§ 22.11 What Constitutes Trial Preparation?
§ 22.12 What Picture Should the Judge and Jury See?
§ 22.13 Can a Jury Handle a Complex Construction Case?
§ 22.14 How Can Documents Be Managed Effectively?
§ 22.15 How Should Witnesses for Trial Be Selected?
§ 22.16 When and How Should Expert Witnesses Be Used?

MOTIONS AND FILINGS BEFORE TRIAL

§ 22.17 Pretrial Motions
§ 22.18 Pretrial Conferences
§ 22.19 Pretrial Filings

TRIAL

§ 22.20 Opening Statement
§ 22.21 Presentation of Evidence
§ 22.22 Cross-Examination
§ 22.23 Closing Argument

APPEAL

§ 22.24 Planning an Appeal
§ 22.25 Reassessment of the Case
§ 22.26 Appellate Brief
§ 22.27 Oral Argument

§ 22.1 Overview

The construction litigator today faces unprecedented challenges. The size and complexity of projects continue to increase, while the relationships among the parties responsible for planning and construction become more and more complicated. Trial lawyers handling construction disputes must therefore understand relationships that do not fit traditional patterns, and master and apply new legal theories to cases that often involve complex fact situations, while operating within increasingly tight budgets.

This chapter provides guidance for the attorney and client with some experience in construction law or litigation, but who are not experienced in developing the strategy and focus necessary for the effective trial of complex construction cases.

INITIAL ASSESSMENT

§ 22.2 Why an Assessment?

The initial assessment of the case is among the most important steps in managing any complex construction dispute. When faced with litigation, both lawyers and clients make some assessments, but they are likely to differ substantially. Habits of a routine practice or the pressures of a difficult one may cause the lawyer to fail to make the kind of rigorous assessment that larger cases require. Judgments based on inadequate or incorrect information may leave the client in much the same situation. As a result, many lawyers and clients lose control of complex cases and end up merely reacting, ineffectively and inefficiently, to the adversary's more focused initiatives or to the deadlines imposed by the court.

To take the initiative and avoid this pattern of reaction, the lawyer and client together should make a detailed assessment of the case as soon as possible. The assessment is most useful of the case as soon as possible. The assessment is most useful if it is set out in writing. In a large, complex case, if the lawyer does not prepare an assessment, the client should demand one. When counsel is retained by an insurer to represent the insured, the assessment should be prepared for both the insurer and the insured.

The form of assessment will vary according to the nature of the dispute, but a few simple questions should be asked at the start of every case. The following questions give both lawyer and client a framework for efficient and effective trial preparation.

§ 22.3 What Facts Are Most Important to the Case?

Almost no construction case is as simple as it first appears. Consequently, there are substantial risks in approaching a trial, or even discovery or settlement negotiations, without having gathered and critically examined the available facts.

The first step in thoroughly examining the facts is typically the same for all cases—an extended interview with the client. The lawyer should begin by having the client identify the parties and relate the facts with as little prompting as possible. At the same time, the lawyer should ask the client to include his opinions of the legal issues involved. These discussions will bring to the surface any misperceptions of fact the lawyer may have and any legal misunderstandings the client may have.

The lawyer can then focus on the relevant facts in more detail and obtain from the client the names of other individuals who may be able to provide more complete information and later testify at trial, if necessary. Significant issues that deserve consideration at this point include relevant contract provisions and their background, applicable professional standards, and identification of all potential parties. Weaker points in the case must also be discussed, and the lawyer should obtain the names of individuals who can provide further information concerning them. Finally, the lawyer should ask the client for all documents relevant to the claim. If the client does not already have a reliable system for organizing and preserving key documents, it will be important to establish a proper system immediately.

It is often useful, after the first interview, for the client to prepare for counsel a detailed written account of the facts. This written account will ensure that important facts are not lost as the client's memory fades over the extended period it may take to resolve the dispute. Concentrating more closely on relevant events and reviewing backup documents in more detail may also help the client to remember significant but otherwise elusive details. The client's written account, and all other writings prepared in anticipation of trial, should be marked to indicate clearly that they are privileged and confidential.

Soon after interviewing the client, counsel should visit the jobsite. Making this visit early—as close to the time the dispute arose as possible—gives the lawyer a feel for the job that will provide an invaluable base for developing the client's case and conveying an accurate picture to the judge and jury. The lawyer's site visit may also be a good time to arrange for jobsite photographs for later use in trial. In addition, the lawyer may take advantage of the visit to conduct preliminary interviews of the client's key employees. Beginning these interviews early insures that valuable information is not lost and contributes substantially to the lawyer's understanding of the case.

§ 22.4 What Are the Parties' Key Legal Arguments?

Close scrutiny of relevant contract provisions is usually the first step in determining the parties' respective legal rights and duties. Most lawyers with construction law experience will have little difficulty in assessing the strengths and weaknesses of the various contract claims presented. Relevant legal doctrines are not always flagged by the terms of the contract, however, and the lawyer must also consider other possible sources of liability,[1] including:

1. Whether any parties may have been negligent
2. Whether any parties may be liable under strict liability tort theories
3. Whether any parties may be liable under third-party beneficiary theories
4. Whether any express warranties were made
5. Whether the court might find implied warranties, such as the judicially created warranty of good workmanship, or the Uniform Commercial Code (UCC) warranty of merchantability or fitness
6. Whether there has been misrepresentation or fraud
7. Whether a theory of tortious interference with contractual duties might apply
8. Whether the owner is liable for improperly accelerating the contract or changing the specifications
9. Whether violations of statutes may have created liability
10. Whether any insurers or sureties might be held liable.

When identifying applicable legal theories, it is important to consider how various potential claims conflict with one another. The prudent litigator will focus on whether possible success on one legal position might jeopardize more important client interests. For example, in representing a contractor, it may be possible to win a dispute with a subcontractor by proving that the subcontractor acted negligently, only to have the owner use that very evidence to obtain a larger judgment against the contractor under a negligent entrustment theory.

§ 22.5 What Are the Equities of the Case?

In complex construction cases, the lawyer must go beyond articulating technical legal principles and strive to portray the case in terms of equitable considerations that demonstrate why the client should prevail. If these considerations are identified and developed early, they can provide strong leverage during settlement negotiations, facilitating speedy and economical resolution of the case. Moreover, even if settlement is not possible, a refined view of the equities can be used profitably to influence the judge during pretrial proceedings. Finally, during trial, the equities become critical

---

[1] For more detailed information on noncontractual theories of liability, see Grandoff, *Step Three: Consider Theories of Legal Liability Apart from the Contract, in* Seven Steps to Resolving Construction Claims 3-1 (ABA Litigation Section 1983).

themes, and in a complex case they may provide the most important basis for the judge or jury's decision. The effective lawyer will capitalize on this potential, using the equities as recurring themes and supporting them with evidence throughout the trial.

With equities, as with all issues in litigation, it is important that the lawyer examine both sides of the case. The client's position cannot be developed and presented effectively unless counsel sees clearly the equitable appeal of the opposing case and works from the outset to deflect or minimize that appeal.

§ 22.6 What Are the Client's Objectives?

Because construction litigation typically involves disputes over large amounts of money, maximizing or minimizing the amount paid is the most obvious objective. Nonetheless, monetary objectives may not be paramount and are not the only ones to be identified. For one client, the most important goal may be avoiding adverse publicity. Another may be concerned about harmful precedent or even collateral estoppel. The insurer, for example, may be less concerned about the amount of the award than about litigation expenses or how the outcome of a case will affect other contractors it insures.

Counsel must also remember that not all litigants, even in major cases, are intractable enemies. Owners, for example, may have financial or political obligations that require them to pursue a claim. In such a context, the primary goal of a contractor-defendant may be preserving its goodwill with the owner or its general reputation for competence and fair dealing. The lawyer in such a case might determine that an informal mini-trial or other alternative form of dispute resolution would be more likely to produce a desirable result than litigation.[2]

§ 22.7 How Can Damages Be Measured?

Establishing the amount of damages in construction cases is complicated by the difficulties of selecting the damage theories that best fit the client's objective, and by the frequent necessity of sifting through massive accounting and progress records to support the amounts claimed. The lawyer must promptly identify all possible damage theories and establish an organized method for calculating the amount sought. Such early organization will guarantee that the best possible damage evidence is available for trial. If the client wishes to pursue settlement, solid damage figures established early in the case will also act as a strong catalyst for successful negotiations.

---

[2] See § **22.10**.

A number of traditional damage theories may apply in construction litigation, including the basic theories of expectancy and quantum meruit. The lawyer should begin the evaluation by analyzing the traditional theories against the facts. The creative lawyer, however, will then determine whether any newer theories might permit recovery of such items as indirect expenses, consequential damages or economic losses, litigation expenses, or even punitive damages.[3]

After identifying applicable damage theories, the attorney must select a means for calculating the amounts due. In some instances, it will be possible to establish an accounting system that permits maintenance of separate records for dispute-related costs. If such a damage account can be set up immediately after the damages begin to accrue, it will provide a convenient means of proving damages at trial.

In many instances, however, establishing separate contemporaneous accounting is not practical; either the dispute is not recognized early enough to establish an account that completely measures damages, or the damages involve a complex variety of expenses that cannot be accurately or conveniently grouped into appropriate accounts. In larger cases involving such difficulties, it will often be necessary to consult accounting experts who can do the auditing work necessary to reach a reasonable damage figure. Obtaining such expertise early may be extremely beneficial in several ways.

1. The expert often can develop damage theories at the outset of the case
2. The expert can identify the documents and testimony that must be preserved or discovered to measure damages
3. The expert can help analyze the other side's evidence while preparing his own side's affirmative proofs
4. The expert can help establish solid damage figures for use in settlement or alternative dispute resolution.

§ 22.8 What Are the Potential Conflicts of Interest?

Unfortunately for all concerned, conflicts of interest are increasingly present in construction litigation. For example, as more projects use multiple contractors, the lawyer is more frequently faced with the potential

---

[3] Construction damage theories are treated more thoroughly in **Ch. 16**. *See also* Construction Litigation: Strategies and Techniques, (B. Bramble & A. Phillips eds., John Wiley & Sons 1989); Martell & Brenner, *Engineering Trends in Construction Damages: Direct, Indirect, Consequential and Punitive, and "No Damage for Delay" Clauses and Legislative History, in* Emerging Trends in Construction Law (ABA Forum Comm. on Construction Industry 1984); Bruner, *Construction Damages, in* Construction Litigation 251 (N.Y.L.J. Seminars—Press 1979); Currie, *Winning Strategies in Construction Negotiations, Arbitration and Litigation, in* Construction Contracts 1984, at 737, 819–25 (J. Pierce ed. 1984).

conflict of defending several contractors who may be jointly and severally liable.[4] Insurance policies may entail similar conflicts, involving insurers that are bound under such plans to represent all defendants on one project claim.[5] Finally, particularly because of legal theories that allow contractor suits directly against architects, conflicts may pose serious problems for attorneys who represent both contractors and architects.[6]

Because these conflicts are increasingly common and not always obvious, the lawyer and the client should make a special effort to evaluate potential conflicts in the initial assessment. Continued attention to potential conflicts throughout the representation is essential because conflicts are likely to become more apparent as the facts of the case develop.

§ 22.9 What Is the Purpose of a Trial Plan?

Because modern construction cases typically involve complex facts and large numbers of documents, it is essential that the lawyer develop a written plan. This plan will provide focus for the necessary trial preparation. See **Chapter 15**. In its most rudimentary form, the preliminary plan should be included in the written assessment and discussed carefully with the client.

A successful plan is an evolving document that facilitates identifying and obtaining the basic evidence necessary to prosecute or defend each issue in the case. But preparation should not be focused so narrowly that counsel will not discover other valuable evidence. In particular, the context or background of a dispute may provide critical information and evidence. For

---

[4] The lawyer representing more than one defendant may not have adequate incentive to press the defenses of each defendant against the others. The problem is exacerbated when joint tortfeasors have a statutory right of contribution against one another. In such circumstances the potential conflict must be fully disclosed to the clients. *See* Aetna Casualty & Sur. Co. v. United States, 570 F.2d 1197, 1200–02 (4th Cir.), *cert. denied,* 439 U.S. 821 (1978); Kerry Coal Co. v. United Mine Workers, 470 F. Supp. 1032 (W.D. Pa. 1979); Model Rules of Professional Conduct and Code of Judicial Conduct DR 5-105(B) (1989).

[5] In this connection, however, it should also be noted that the comprehensive general liability insurance policy usually contains complex coverage exemptions that increase the chances that insured and insurer will disagree over the actual coverage of the policy. When these conflicts are not resolved, the insurance company is increasingly required to pay for separate counsel chosen by the insured to conduct the defense. United States Fidelity & Guar. Co. v. Louis A. Roser Co., 585 F.2d 932 (8th Cir. 1978); Storm Drilling Co. v. Atlantic Richfield Corp., 386 F. Supp. 830 (E.D. Cal. 1974).

[6] As the traditional roles of architect and contractor have changed, the law has shifted an increasing share of liability to architects. Most prominent has been the courts' abandoning the privity requirement for suits by contractors against architects. Note, *Architectural Malpractice: A Contra-Based Approach,* 92 Harv. L. Rev. 1075, 1081–83 (1979); Gilbane Bldg. Co. v. Nemours Found., 606 F. Supp. 995, 1004 (D. Del. 1985); Donnelly Constr. Co. v. Oberg/Hunt/Gilleland, 139 Ariz. 184, 677 P.2d 1292 (1984).

example, if the claim is for a subcontractor's delay due to lack of diligence, the subcontractor's general incompetence or disguised inexperience may be as important to the case as the fact of its absence from the job at key times.

Planning the case also requires eliminating claims that are not necessary or valuable to the client's case. For example, a contractor may decide against pursuing an attractive negligence claim against a subcontractor that would encourage the owner to pursue a claim against the contractor. If this possibility is not flagged early in the case, valuable time and money will be wasted.

The lawyer should also make an assessment of which parties are able to compensate the injured party. Even the best case or claim is useless against an uninsured party who cannot pay a judgment. Therefore, although keeping litigation options open may require assessing a laundry list of allegations or defenses against every potential party, counsel and the client must both be able to keep their focus on those allegations and defenses—and those parties—most likely to produce a successful prosecution or defense.

Focused preparation also avoids overpreparation, which few clients can afford, or underpreparation, which no client should tolerate. If, for example, eventual trial of the case requires several experts on different issues, counsel who has assessed the case may be able to involve one key expert at the outset and leave the others to a later, more cursory role. The client who understands the case may itself be able to do much of the early analysis more efficiently and economically than the expert. In some instances, if the case is resolved through settlement, early involvement of the client or a single expert may be all that is necessary.

The traditional trial notebook is particularly useful in focusing trial preparation in complex cases. Its initial preparation and continual development by the trial lawyer imposes an invaluable discipline. The notebook can be divided into sections reflecting each major aspect of the case. As additional information is acquired, and as the trial strategy grows more refined, the notebook is continually updated. Ultimately, it becomes a comprehensive guidebook for the trial, with all the key exhibits and anticipated questions for each witness.

§ 22.10 Should Alternatives to Litigation Be Pursued?

Although arbitration may be specified in the construction contract or the dispute may require special government administrative procedures, other means of dispute resolution may also be more appropriate than traditional litigation. In some cases, clients simply cannot afford the money and management time required for a full trial. In other cases, the client may be too concerned about preserving a valuable business relationship to risk the pressures created by full discovery and trial. On overseas projects, the parties may want to avoid litigation in a foreign court. Finally, the client may be involved in other related disputes that may affect trial of the current dispute through collateral estoppel. In these, and many other situations, both lawyer and client should give special attention to the potential for settling the dispute or deciding it by some alternative form of dispute resolution.

Simple settlement negotiations should always be considered. There are numerous times during the course of a case when settlement may be profitably discussed, and trial counsel should identify those times for the client as part of the initial assessment. In many instances, the optimal time will be before the complaint has been filed. At this early stage, the parties' views have not yet been polarized by public confrontation and flexible agreements can be reached privately. There is also a strong motivation to settle at this early stage in order to avoid the expense and time associated with filing a claim and conducting discovery. By settling early, however, each party may run the risk of an unbalanced settlement based on insufficient knowledge.

In some cases, a settlement may best be obtained after suit has commenced and a portion of discovery is completed. At this point, the parties will have a better developed knowledge of the case, and may want to settle to avoid the burdens or embarrassment of further discovery. In still other cases, the parties may settle just before or during trial, either with or without the judge's assistance. Pursuing or deflecting such settlement attempts is an important part of the trial of complex construction cases.

When parties who want to settle are unable to reach agreement without assistance, they may consider using an alternative means of dispute resolution. Often parties who want to settle are unable to focus on central issues or reconcile radically different views of the facts. In such cases, the presence of a mediator, arbitrator, or some figure combining the roles of both mediator and arbitrator may be the best way to reach an accord.[7] The procedures involving mediation or arbitration can be tailored to the circumstances to maximize the potential for agreement.

Some lawyers have been creative in settling disputes through procedures that do not fit the traditional mediation/arbitration models. The mini-trial is one example. In the mini-trial, the lawyers make abbreviated presentations of the case to a small group of key client personnel either alone or in

---

[7] For further information on mediation and noncontractual arbitration of construction disputes, see M. Callahan, B. Bramble & P. Lurie, Arbitration of Construction Disputes (John Wiley & Sons 1990); Alternative Dispute Resolution in the Construction Industry (R. Cushman, G. Hedemann & A. Tucker eds., John Wiley & Sons 1990); Howell, *Putting Arbitration in Perspective,* 5 Construction Litig. Rep. 314 (1984); Olsen, *Dispute Resolution: An Alternative for Large Case Litigation,* 6 Litigation 22 (1980).

the presence of a neutral advisor. The client personnel then meet and try to hammer out an agreement. If they are unsuccessful, the neutral advisor can draft a recommended agreement that is submitted to the parties as a catalyst for further negotiations.[8]

Where alternative dispute resolution is pursued, the role of trial counsel will change, but will not be diminished. Counsel's careful assessment, thorough investigation, and concentrated effort to focus the case, document the facts, and develop the equities remain key to a successful presentation.

TRIAL PREPARATION

§ 22.11 What Constitutes Trial Preparation?

There is no formal demarcation between the initial assessment and trial preparation. Generally, however, it is useful to consider trial preparation as encompassing primarily those activities undertaken with a specific view to what will happen in the courtroom. See **Chapter 15**. As with the initial assessment, trial preparation will vary with the dispute, but answering a few basic questions can be useful.

§ 22.12 What Picture Should the Judge and Jury See?

The first principle of effective trial preparation was articulated effectively by a project manager who was meeting with his company's attorneys prior to a major trial. Exhibits were reviewed, expected testimony of expert and fact witnesses was discussed in detail, and the prospects for success were evaluated. The project manager's response was simple and straightforward: "What is our case?" He understood the evidence and the anticipated legal issues, but he also saw the potentially fatal flaw in counsel's preparation: the evidence would not present a clear picture that would engage and convince the judge and the jury that the contractor had in fact acted with appropriate care.

---

[8] Additional information on the mini-trial may be found in Olsen, *Dispute Resolution: An Alternative for Large Case Litigation,* 6 Litigation 22 (1980); *see also* Green, *Growth of the Mini-Trial,* 9 Litigation 12 (1982); Franklin, *The Mini-Trial: What It Is and What It Isn't and What It Can Do,* Construction L. 1 (Fall 1983). For a discussion of alternative dispute resolution under a court's auspices, including use of a mini-trial to a real jury, see *The Summary Jury Trial and Other Alternative Methods of Dispute Resolution,* 103 F.R.D. 461 (1984).

A successful case is made up of clear pictures. The trial lawyer must distill the complex facts and intricate legal arguments into a focused, integrated, and compelling presentation. If simple and clear enough, the lawyer's presentation and the trial evidence will convey pictures that allow the judge or jury to decide the case confidently, even without full knowledge or understanding of every underlying complexity.

§ 22.13 Can a Jury Handle a Complex Construction Case?

Much attention has been given to the difficulties juries face in deciding complex cases.[9] The length of the trial, the number of parties, the number of claims and crossclaims, witnesses, and documents, combined with unfamiliar factual and legal settings, may make a complex case incomprehensible to lay juries. As a result, at least one court held that the Fifth Amendment due process requirement supersedes the Seventh Amendment right to a jury trial in exceptionally complex cases.[10]

Much of the concern over a jury's inability to handle complex cases is certainly justified. Accordingly, there will be some instances when the lawyer should try to reach an agreement with opposing counsel to permit a bench trial. This is especially true if the lawyer knows the judge is competent and conscientious. Prior to making a final decision to seek a bench trial, however, the lawyer should consider a few of the less obvious drawbacks of such trials. First, a judge sitting without a jury may be willing to apply a more expanded concept of liability than he would incorporate in a jury charge, thinking that he can later limit damages to an amount that seems appropriate. Second, judges, who hear evidence to pass on its admissibility, may be influenced by material they would not allow to go to a jury.[11] They are also generally more willing to admit arguably inadmissible

---

[9] *See, e.g.,* Redish, *Seventh Amendment Right to a Jury Trial, A Study in the Irrationality of Rational Decision Making,* 70 Nw. U. L. Rev. 486 (1975); Note, *Unfit for Jury Determination, Complex Civil Litigation and the Seventh Amendment Right of Trial by Jury,* 20 B.C. L. Rev. 511 (1979); Note, *The Right to a Jury Trial in Complex Civil Litigation,* 92 Harv. L. Rev. 898 (1979); Luneburg & Nordenberg, *Specially Qualified Juries and Expert Non-Jury Tribunals: Alternatives for Coping with the Complexities of Modern Civil Litigation,* 67 U. Va. L.R. 887 (1981).

[10] *In re* Japanese Elecs. Prods. Antitrust Litig., 631 F.2d 1069 (3d Cir. 1980). *Cf. In re* Financial Sec. Litig., 609 F.2d 411 (9th Cir. 1979), *cert. denied sub nom.* Grant v. Union Bank, 446 U.S. 929 (1980); Davis & Cox v. Summa Corp. 751 F.2d 1507, 1516 (9th Cir. 1985); Brisk v. City of Miami Beach, 726 F. Supp. 1305, 1314 (S.D. Fla. 1989).

[11] Lempert, *Civil Juries and Complex Cases: Let's Not Rush to Judgment,* 80 Mich. L. Rev. 68, 94 (1981).

evidence.[12] Finally, judges may organize a jury trial better to avoid undue protraction.[13]

If the lawyer is unable to avoid a jury, or decides that a jury would be a better arbiter of the client's case than a particular judge, there remain a variety of techniques that may be used to assist the jury:

1. Ask that the trial be severed into smaller, more manageable sets of issues. Even the division of liability and damages may result in substantially clearer cases for the jury to decide.
2. Ask the judge to use special verdicts to simplify issues.
3. Use pretrial conferences to limit the testimonial and documentary evidence that will be admitted at trial.
4. Ask the judge to provide the jury with preliminary jury instructions at the start of the trial.[14] The jury can use these instructions to help focus and remember the most relevant evidence.
5. Seek jury instructions that are in plain language and understandable to the jury. Too often, instructions are copied from form books and are plagued with arcane language unintelligible to the jury.[15]
6. Use summaries, charts, or calculations that reduce voluminous evidence to an understandable form.[16]
7. Ask the judge to allow the jurors to take notes or to review the trial transcripts periodically.[17] This increases both the jurors' sense of participation in the trial and their ability to remember key facts.

---

[12] Appellate courts are less likely to reverse a trial judge for admission of incompetent evidence than for exclusion of proper evidence. C. McCormick, Evidence § 60, at 153 (3d ed. 1984).

[13]

> [A] jury trial creates an urgency about deadlines that may be absent when a judge sits alone, and there is strong pressure to minimize interruptions in the presentation of evidence to a jury. While an efficient and energetic judge might be able to accomplish more in less time if unconstrained by a jury, judges who are not outstanding in these respects may benefit from the discipline that a jury imposes.

Lempert, *Civil Juries and Complex Cases: Let's Not Rush to Judgment,* 80 Mich. L. Rev. 68, 93 (1981).

[14] A number of cases have upheld the use of preliminary jury instructions. *See, e.g.,* Stonehocker v. General Motors Corp., 587 F.2d 151, 157 (4th Cir. 1978); Cavendish v. Sunoco Serv., 541 F.2d 1360, 1364–66 (7th Cir. 1971).

[15] Research has shown that traditional jury instructions are difficult for jurors to comprehend and can be rephrased to increase their clarity. A. Elwork, B. Sales & J. Alfini, Making Jury Instructions Understandable (1982).

[16] Fed. R. Evid. 1006 provides in part: "The contents of voluminous writings, recordings, or photographs which cannot conveniently be examined in court may be presented in the form of a chart, summary or calculation."

[17] An increasing number of courts allow jurors to take notes in appropriate cases. *See, e.g.,* United States v. Braverman, 522 F.2d 218, 224 (7th Cir.), *cert. denied,* 423 U.S. 985

8. Ask the judge to allow the jury to question the witnesses. The questions may be in written form and submitted to the judge, who may decide which questions do not call for inadmissible evidence.

Few judges would permit use of all these techniques, but even if only a few are used, the jury is likely to comprehend the case more clearly and reach a more rational verdict.

§ 22.14 How Can Documents Be Managed Effectively?

The complexity of construction litigation makes it imperative for the attorney to use pretrial discovery tools for systematic investigation and development of trial evidence on key issues. Commercial arbitration and administrative proceedings demand similar investigation, although the formal procedures differ. Whatever the dispute or forum, however, many of the relevant facts will be set out or reflected in documents and, as a result, much of the most important evidence may be documents.

Comprehensive review of the multitude of documents involved in most large construction cases requires thorough planning and organization. Initially, a list of the various types of documents available should be prepared. Typical construction projects involve the following types of documents:

1. Contracts between the respective parties (including the owner, the contractor, the architect, and various subcontractors)
2. Insurance policies
3. Specifications and drawings, including addenda and engineering change notices
4. Correspondence and internal memoranda
5. Bid estimates of the contractor, subcontractors and, possibly, budget estimates by the designer
6. Daily work reports and payroll records
7. Progress payment requests and related payment orders
8. Change orders and related documentation
9. Progress schedules (including construction project management charts, bar charts, and updates to such charts)

(1975) (jurors allowed to take notes while jury instructions were being played back to them from tape recording); SCM Corp. v. Xerox Corp., 77 F.R.D. 10, 15 (D. Conn. 1977) (jurors allowed to take notes during trial). *See also* United States v. Marquez, 449 F.2d 89 (2d Cir. 1971), *cert. denied,* 405 U.S. 963 (1972).

10. Equipment use logs
11. Job meeting notes
12. Private or governmental inspection reports
13. Accounting records.

Prior to submitting a document request, the lawyer must narrow this list to the key documents necessary for supporting the client's case. In most instances, these will be the documents specifying what standards the parties were obligated to meet, how the parties actually performed, and what damages resulted from any breaches. Identifying these key documents should progress naturally from the work done in preparing the initial assessment. Consultation with the client and experts may also be required, however, and in some cases the lawyer may even serve a preliminary set of interrogatories to obtain the information necessary to narrow discovery appropriately.

Before actually reviewing any significant number of documents, it is also critical to develop a plan for managing the documents and insuring that they remain accessible before and during trial. For the very large case, a computer data base may be the only practical way to achieve the necessary organization. A data base is often used for access to documents through the recording of such basic data as subject, date, author, and address; including a summary of the text of important documents is also possible and may be useful. Numerous professional services are available to provide the necessary classification, software or hardware systems, and the manpower to run them. In some instances, clients themselves may have the required capability. Finally, there are a growing number of document organization software programs that can be used economically in conjunction with personal computers already owned by the lawyer's firm.

Whether it is desirable to create a computer data base of document information or only a careful index, a few basic principles should be applied to any document management plan:

Organization. No one system will fit all or even most cases. Documents can be coded or filed by site, by chronology, or by subject matter. The paramount purpose of organization is to permit attorney access during discovery, trial preparation, and trial.

Numbering. Individual documents or groups of documents should be numbered for future reference. A document left unnumbered may be lost forever. Numbering codes can be developed to help identify the significance, source, and original file location of documents.

Summaries. Key documents often must be summarized for ease of reference, but selecting competent personnel to prepare the summaries is vital.

Lawyer control. No document organization scheme is a substitute for trial counsel's personal review of documents. Similarly, no document organization scheme is appropriate unless trial counsel understands it and feels completely comfortable with it.

Use at trial. The mechanics of rapid document retrieval must be both planned and tested prior to trial. Locating documents, especially for effective cross-examination, can be a nightmare for the unprepared.

While documents are being reviewed, the lawyer should also be utilizing interrogatories and depositions to gain further information in preparation for trial.[18]

§ 22.15 How Should Witnesses for Trial Be Selected?

The lawyer preparing for trial should use both interviews and depositions to locate and test potential witnesses. During the interview or deposition, counsel has the unique opportunity of probing the limits of the witness's knowledge, veracity, and effectiveness without the risks inherent in courtroom testimony. Fully capitalizing on this opportunity, however, requires careful planning.

Counsel must begin by identifying the witnesses likely to be called by any party; ideally, each one should either be interviewed or deposed prior to trial, although budgetary constraints may prevent this. Normally, witnesses represented by counsel, of course, cannot be contacted directly without their counsel's permission.[19] Although former employees of an adverse party often are approached informally for ex parte interviews, at least one court has held that it is improper to do so.[20] Thus, it is always important to determine the jurisdiction's controlling ethics rules before proceeding with ex parte interviews. All documents relating to each witness's potential testimony must be thoroughly reviewed, both to insure that counsel obtains any possibly relevant information the potential witness can provide, and so that counsel has the background necessary to evaluate and test the potential witness's knowledge and veracity. Finally, it is advisable to mix formal and informal approaches in both interviews and depositions. Interviews should be planned as methodically as depositions and, where

---

[18] See **Ch. 15**.

[19] Model Code of Professional Responsibility DR 7-104(A)(1) (1989); *see also* Model Rules of Professional Conduct Rule 4.2 (1989).

[20] Public Serv. Elec. & Gas Co. v. Associated Elec. & Gas Ins. Servs., Ltd., 745 F. Supp. 1037 (D.N.J. 1990); *but see* Curley v. Cumberland Farms, 134 F.R.D. 77 (D.N.J. 1991).

possible, deposition witnesses should be engaged with the same informal tactics used in interviews.

After depositions and interviews, the universe of potential witnesses will generally be clear, but actual selection of witnesses to testify at trial will require additional consideration. Final selection is commonly based not only on knowledge but also on such subjective factors as demeanor and vulnerability to cross-examination. It is also important to select witnesses capable of explaining technically complex matters in plain and clear language. Lower-level workers directly involved in the project are frequently better witnesses in this respect than more articulate management personnel who are too distant from the job to be able to explain the facts in detail. In other cases, however, the reverse may be true.

§ 22.16 When and How Should Expert Witnesses Be Used?

Most complex construction cases require both expert assistance and expert testimony.[21] There are a variety of contexts in which such expertise may be necessary. For example, a challenge to the adequacy of job specifications may require engineering and architectural experts to evaluate the sufficiency of the design, a metallurgist to testify to the adequacy of the specified steel supports, and geologists or hydrologists to assess whether the specifications reasonably accounted for jobsite soil conditions. Usually, it is wise to begin searching for the proper experts early. Particularly in complex cases, the expert will need time to develop an opinion and prepare for trial. The expert is also likely to be of assistance in discovery and initial investigation of the case. Finally, the expert who is contacted early will be able to develop preliminary conclusions useful during any settlement negotiations.

Before interviewing and selecting experts, counsel must understand the technical dispute. Gaining this understanding should be part of the initial assessment and requires assistance from the client. It may also be necessary to consult secondary sources that provide basic information on the construction technology involved in the dispute. From this, counsel can judge what type of expert and what level of expertise will be necessary to convince the trier of fact.

In some instances, when only limited formal expertise is necessary, it may be possible to use someone from the client's own in-house staff. For example, when a contractor's field inspector has sufficient expertise to identify errors in certain engineering work, a highly trained, highly paid engineering consultant may not be required. The lawyer should exercise

---

[21] See generally **Ch. 16** regarding the use of experts.

caution, however, to avoid in-house experts who have anything in their background that might detract from their stature or objectivity.

If greater expertise is required, the lawyer should consider a number of factors in selecting a suitable expert. If the expert seems generally suitable and does not hold views adverse to the client's position, counsel should begin by carefully scrutinizing the expert's credentials. Obviously, the expert should be formally trained in the substantive area on which he will testify, but it is not always best to select the expert with the best-appearing credentials. For example, training at a school well known in the forum state may impress the judge or jury more than a degree from an institution with a more prestigious national reputation. Likewise, an expert with impeccable academic credentials may suffer from having little practical experience to back them up.

In addition to educational background, counsel should consider the expert's memberships in professional societies and organizations. Membership in such organizations is not merely another credential with which to impress the jury; it is an indication to the lawyer that the expert is likely to be well versed in recent developments in the field. Much information on changes in construction related technology is disseminated primarily through these organizations, and in some cases it is essential that the expert be familiar with the most current developments and practices. In addition, membership in professional organizations may convey to the judge or jury that the expert is well recognized in the field.

Experts who have testified frequently in other cases often perform well on the stand because of their experience. The trial lawyer, however, may sometimes shy away from using such a professional witness out of fear that the judge or jury may consider the witness to be a hired gun. In all cases, before retaining an expert it is absolutely essential to review all of his writings and prior testimony to make certain that they do not conflict with the client's case. All too many trial lawyers and expert witnesses have been red-faced when prior inconsistencies are brought out for the first time during cross-examination. It is usually devastating when one party actually can help prove its case through the other side's expert.

The expert's experience in analyzing related situations is also vital. The lawyer should seek experts familiar with other projects of the same type and size as the one involved in the dispute, both to insure complete understanding and to show the judge or jury that the expert's opinion is well grounded in experience.

Finally, the expert must be able to speak clearly. In particular, the expert must avoid unnecessary technical jargon and testify in plain and simple terms that are understandable to the jury. Academic experts are frequently the best experts in this respect. Years of simplifying complexities for their students, combined with frequent public speaking, often make them excellent communicators. It is important, however, that a professor have practical as well as academic experience. In addition, a professor must be capable of handling the type of hostile and domineering cross-examination common in the courtroom.

There are a number of ways to locate an appropriate expert. Counsel should begin by consulting with the client, and then talking to other lawyers who have handled similar disputes requiring similarly qualified experts. Other lawyers can be a particularly valuable source of information because they can provide a candid evaluation of the expert's courtroom performance and basic knowledge.

Once selected, the expert must be prepared for deposition or trial testimony. In particular, counsel must insure that the expert's opinion is grounded on a thorough examination of all appropriate data and is solid enough to withstand vigorous cross-examination. The lawyer should also familiarize the expert with the rules of evidence, both with regard to testimony and in relation to authentication of any exhibits the expert has prepared. Finally, to insure that the expert is fully prepared, the lawyer should conduct thorough mock direct and cross-examination.

MOTIONS AND FILINGS BEFORE TRIAL

§ 22.17 Pretrial Motions

Lawyers often fail to pay sufficient attention to pretrial motions, viewing them as irritating encumbrances. In fact, carefully prepared pretrial motions may be vehicles for substantial advantage.

Motions to dismiss or strike can be an important tactic in the construction case. Issues of indemnity, punitive damages, or even general liability are among the matters that often can be resolved before trial, frequently even before discovery and other trial preparation. For example, an owner may be able to strike a contractor's delay claims based upon a contract containing a no damages for delay clause.[22] Likewise, any claims brought after a relevant statute of limitations has run may be dismissed peremptorily. The lawyer must exercise some caution in filing such early motions, however, because they may precipitate adverse decisions before the judge fully understands the case.

Motions for summary judgment can also be an effective method for disposing of a case, narrowing the issues, or educating the judge. Many cases

---

[22] *See* Unicon Management Corp. v. City of Chicago, 404 F.2d 627 (7th Cir. 1968); Peter Kiewit Sons' Co. v. Iowa S. Utils. Co., 355 F. Supp. 376 (S.D. Iowa 1973).

can be fully presented on uncontested facts or simply do not have enough substance to justify trial. Judges also recognize that summary disposition of appropriate cases or issues reduces court backlogs and permits others to have their timely day in court. Finally, even if the court denies summary judgment, it may grant partial judgment or at least give the parties guidance as to what issues it believes are significant for trial. In ruling on summary judgment motions, judges often indicate preliminarily their biases and what they consider to be the strengths and weaknesses of each side's case. Similarly, they frequently identify what questions they feel need to be answered at trial. Especially if the motions judge will also be the trial judge, pretrial motions practice can be an invaluable tool to educate both the court and counsel.

Requests for admissions can be used to lay the groundwork for pretrial motions by narrowing the legal issues to be tried. See **Chapter 15**. They are also a powerful tool for simplifying presentation of a case by limiting the amount of evidence required at trial. Finally, they can facilitate admission of documentary evidence by allowing counsel to circumvent tedious authentication procedures.

All of these advantages would be significant in normal litigation, but they are especially important in complex construction cases where simplification usually is so important. But requests for admissions followed by thorough summary judgment motions are often not used, perhaps because counsel have come to expect routine denial of admissions requests arising from a general reluctance to resolve disputed issues prior to completing discovery. Unfortunately, such reluctance may also reflect counsel's failure to develop the clear focus that is necessary to determine what admissions would be significant, and to prepare requests that cannot easily be evaded.

§ 22.18 Pretrial Conferences

Formal pretrial procedures are provided in the rules of virtually every court, government board, or arbitration body. Each judge or presiding officer usually has an additional set of formal and informal procedures for bringing a case to trial.

The most important aspect of pretrial procedure may be the pretrial conference. Although such conferences vary widely in form and substance, most judges use initial and final conferences to identify and narrow the issues for discovery and trial. In these conferences, aggressive and prepared counsel have available formal and informal procedures that may be used to significant advantage. In addition, counsel may use the pretrial conference to educate the judge in a setting less formal than argument on motions and far less constrained than the trial.

§ 22.19 Pretrial Filings

As the final pretrial conference approaches, trial counsel should give particular attention to the following major filings: pretrial or trial briefs, proposed findings, jury instructions, motions to exclude or limit evidence, and lists of witnesses and exhibits.

The pretrial or trial brief requires the most sophisticated advocacy. Its form may be dictated by local rule or practice, but whatever the form, it should probably be counsel's most comprehensive and incisive statement of the case. At its best, the trial brief is a favorable and complete presentation of all the significant issues, assertions of fact, legal arguments, and anticipated evidence. However, it must remain simple and compelling and must portray the equities so as to create the appropriate sympathetic appeal. Finally, it should provide the judge with a road map for favorably deciding critical issues both prior to and during trial.

Special attention should be paid to the choice and balance of trial brief subjects. Because the complexity of modern construction cases can so easily lead either to misunderstanding or to overwhelmed inattention, the trial brief must include clear explanations of the relevant facts. If one or more parties are seeking damages for delay, for example, the trial brief may have to explain the relevant aspects of contract administration, the significance of arcane contract provisions, and the implications of critical path scheduling. Similarly, the trial brief may have to explain pedestrian realities of the jobsite, even if they do not appear complex. For example, if safety is an issue, the brief must explain who had responsibility for that safety, what was the scope of responsibility, and what was the practical chain of command. When explaining such details, however, the trial brief must remain simple and clear. In particular, care should be taken not to let explanation of details become so protracted that it detracts from the main issues.

The jury instructions and the proposed findings of fact and conclusions of law, if they are submitted prior to trial, flow naturally from the trial brief. Again, the practice varies from judge to judge, but the objective is universal: the judge should be offered a set of instructions or findings and conclusions that are comprehensive and compelling. Counsel can start with a conservatively worded set, most likely to be adopted if the judge is at all sympathetic, and then weave in paragraphs reaching for the limits of the law and facts. Merely seeking the findings formally sufficient to uphold a judgment on appeal is not sufficient; the lawyer should try to obtain findings that will assure appellate sympathy and account for the appellate prerogative to expand or change the law.

For example, consider a case involving design problems with structural steel on a project. It might be sufficient for the judge to make a simple finding that the architect/engineer exercised due care in preparation of the drawings and specifications, but why should the advocate stop there? If the evidence shows that the plans were reviewed by three senior engineers, each with 30 years of experience in structural steel design of large-scale commercial projects, why not also ask for a specific finding setting out those facts in detail?

Jury instructions provide fewer opportunities for advocacy on the facts, but they are a useful vehicle for focus and emphasis. This is especially true, as already noted, when judges permit a copy of the instructions to be given to the jury for use during its deliberations. Counsel should also consider the desirability of requesting special interrogatories to the jury. In addition to their role in providing structure for the jury's thinking, special interrogatories can also play a significant role on appeal by exposing irrational verdicts and supporting proper verdicts.

Other seemingly commonplace steps in conjunction with the final pretrial conference also offer important opportunities. For example, exhibit and witness lists should be scrutinized with care. Successful motions to limit evidence can avoid courtroom controversy over unduly prejudicial testimony. In addition, they can eliminate entire areas of evidence that may be only marginally relevant, but would consume substantial trial time, require extensive rebuttal, and unduly confuse the jury.

Optional trial procedures should also be considered for recommendation at the pretrial conference, even if they go beyond normal practice in the jurisdiction. Complex construction litigation may benefit materially from such techniques as notetaking by jurors, creative use of site models, site visits, or videotaped exhibits, and submission of technical testimony in written form. Written testimony can be particularly useful in expediting bench trials and in presenting complex engineering information in a clear form. Controversial procedures such as permitting jurors to ask questions during the trial may also be useful if there is risk of jury confusion. Counsel should request these innovative procedures at the pretrial conference, when judges are often more flexible than they will be once the trial has begun.

Finally, the pretrial conference presents an excellent opportunity to press for settlement. While focusing on the details of the anticipated trial, the judge can be engaged as an individual ally in either supporting bona fide demands or attacking inflated ones.

TRIAL

§ 22.20 Opening Statement

The opening statement is particularly important in complex construction trials. The effective opening statement presents a simple and compelling picture of the facts and law that triers of fact can use to organize their view of the entire trial. To achieve this level of effectiveness, however, the opening statement must be rooted in a clear understanding of the case and a well-defined trial plan. It requires careful preparation and, in a case of any substance, it should be reviewed in advance with the client. The statement may be pitched differently for a judge than for a jury, but the framework it provides remains important and counsel normally should not forgo making a statement in a bench trial unless required to do so. This is particularly true when the judge may have prior experience with the construction industry that leaves him with either outdated ideas or dangerous prejudices.

Much has been written on what should be included in the opening statement.[23] Most commentators agree, however, that the overall goal should be to provide a brief road map explaining how the client's case will be proved, including what witnesses will be called and what their testimony will be. Counsel should refrain from including excess detail that might detract from the clarity and simplicity of this outline. Facts should be explained in a brief and logical manner. Visual aids, especially photographs, should be used to give the trier of fact a feel for the overall project and to convey necessary background information more quickly and compellingly.[24] The bases for significant equitable considerations should be woven in throughout the statement to invoke sympathy and emotional appeal, although counsel must obviously avoid making overstatements that the evidence will not support.

§ 22.21 Presentation of Evidence

Effective presentation of the evidence requires blending traditional principles of trial advocacy with the special demands of complex construction cases. Because every case has its own group of strategical problems requiring individual analysis, this chapter merely identifies some of the recurring considerations that should be part of presenting the evidence in any complex construction case.

Start slowly. Traditional wisdom calls for presenting the strongest witness first. In complex litigation, however, counsel may wish to compromise this principle and select a first witness who is not substantively important

---

[23] For a conventional viewpoint on what should be included in the opening statement, see J. Appleman, Preparation & Trial 189 (1967); I.S. Schweitzer, Cyclopedia of Trial Practice § 172, at 474 (1970).

[24] Counsel must remember, however, that in most jurisdictions photographs, maps, diagrams, and other exhibits may not be used in the opening statement without prior approval of the court. R. Figg, R. McCollough & J. Underwood, Civil Trial Manual (1980).

but capable of clearly describing the parties and the basic facts. Proving liability in complex trials cannot even begin until counsel has educated the trier of fact in the intricacies of the dispute, and this should normally be the function of the first witness.

Present the case in practical terms. The complexities of large construction trials, especially those involving multiple expert witnesses, make it easy to lose the trier of fact in a maze of technological details. Trial counsel must recognize that no matter how many experts testify, judges and juries will base their decisions on whatever practical understanding they can form from the evidence. Counsel must therefore continually refocus on the most relevant and important facts to insure that they will be plainly understood.

Emphasize people. The competent completion of a construction contract depends on people, not just engineering and management. The trier of fact will know this—and treat the contractor sympathetically—only if the people on the job explain what they did and why they did it. In this respect, the inarticulate practical witness is often more effective than the glib manager.

Use construction jargon only if its meaning is clear. Terms of art and professional jargon tend most often to obscure the facts. For example, consider the many meanings of apparently simple terms like "inspection" or "engineering" or "overhead." Accordingly, such terms should be explained and used only when they are clearly understood.

Consider submitting complex testimony in written form. Courts are increasingly experimenting with written direct testimony for complex matters.[25] There are obvious limitations and complications, but they can be reduced by carefully considered procedures. The testimony can be reviewed in advance for objections by opposing counsel. After objections are resolved, the testimony can be admitted and given to the judge or jury for review. The witness can then be made available for additional direct testimony and cross-examination. The practice has most obvious appeal in bench trials, but it has been suggested for jury trials as well. If written testimony is appropriate in jury trials, the witness might read the prepared testimony to the jury. Written testimony has been used for years in administrative proceedings. Experience suggests that there are often substantial benefits to be gained from counsel and the witness working together to formulate a clear and comprehensive statement.

---

[25] *See* Richey, *A Modern Management Technique for Trial Courts to Improve the Quality of Justice: Requiring Direct Testimony to be Submitted in Written Form Prior to Trial,* 72 Geo. L.J. 73 (1983); *see also* Local Rule 9.11.2 of the United States District Court for the Central District of California.

Make clear the significance of each piece of evidence. No document or fact that the lawyer presents at trial is without some connection to the overall understanding of the dispute. For counsel, who has studied the dispute extensively, these connections are obvious, but for the uninitiated judge or jury member, the connection may be clouded unless it is revealed by the lawyer.

Make sure the trier of fact understands everything about key documents. Key documents—contract clauses, inspection reports, memoranda, and so on—inevitably get special attention from the judge and jury, even though the actual practice of construction contracting seldom comports with the documents. Counsel must ensure that nothing in the key documents remain unexplained. The record, for the trier of fact and for the appeal, must be complete.

Select the best possible company representative to sit at counsel table. The assistance of someone who can understand the facts and the issues is essential. Any individual selected for this purpose must also make a good impression in the courtroom and should be coached on appropriate conduct.

§ 22.22 Cross-Examination

The basic cross-examination techniques for attacking and impeaching a witness's testimony are as applicable in construction cases as in any type of litigation. There are, however, a few aspects of cross-examination that are especially important in the construction setting. First, extra care should be taken in deciding whether to cross-examine each witness. In large construction cases there will be many opposing witnesses who do not present any real threat to the client's case. If the trier of fact is likely to recognize the partisan role of these witnesses and not place great reliance upon their testimony, the lawyer may not be prejudiced by failing to cross-examine them. And, of course, cross-examination can backfire if a witness antagonized by cross-examination makes a damaging remark. The lawyer also risks detracting from the power of his cross-examination of more important witnesses.

Second, the lawyer should be particularly careful to use clear language in framing questions. Once again, although counsel is likely to have become versed in relevant construction terminology while preparing the case, the judge or jury is not likely to understand or appreciate the significance of lines of questioning couched in technical jargon.

Counsel should also take into account some of the special considerations involved in cross-examining expert witnesses. It is most important that the lawyer research both the expert's particular views and more general authorities relating to the issues in questions. With this background information, the lawyer may be able to impeach the expert's opinion, either by showing that it is contrary to the general weight of authority, or that it contradicts the expert's own published statements. Counsel may also attack the expert's testimony by revealing that the expert's conclusions are based on improper testing or lack of detailed knowledge of the actual construction methods used. To aid in detecting such deficiencies, the lawyer may wish to have the client's own expert present during direct examination of the opposing expert.

§ 22.23 Closing Argument

Closing arguments are so much a part of the lore and art of trial practice that little can be added to the volumes of available advice. A few points, however, cannot be overemphasized. It is vital that the closing argument do more than summarize the evidence and law relating to the case; it must tell a story. The lawyer must gather up the facts and equitable consideration of the case and paint a picture that compels the trier of fact to reach the desired conclusions.

Unfortunately, creating such a clear image of the case demands a level of preparation that lawyers frequently cannot, or are not willing to, attain. In the most complex cases, such as large construction cases, the burdens of preparation may be particularly onerous, but it is in just such complex cases that a clear picture of the case is most essential. If the underlying dispute is too difficult for the judge or jury to comprehend adequately, the closing argument may provide the only real basis for the ultimate decision. Therefore, before the trial even starts, counsel should prepare a detailed written outline of the closing argument. In some bench trials it may be possible to include a list of principal cases and offer the outline to the court and opposing counsel just prior to the argument. Such an outline can be a compelling road map for both the judge and the law clerk, and the time spent preparing it will insure a clearer argument.

APPEAL

§ 22.24 Planning an Appeal

The appeal can best be considered in three parts: reassessment of the case, briefing, and oral argument. Each of these steps must reflect a recognition that in some respects a case on appeal is closed (for example, some findings of fact may be virtually irreversible), and in some respects it is entirely new (for example, the appellate court may reverse on grounds not ruled on by the trial court), but in most respects the door is open only a crack. However, so long as the door is open at all, counsel and client must again collaborate to focus and present the case.

§ 22.25 Reassessment of the Case

In many ways, reassessment at the start of an appeal is easier than the assessment made at the start of the case. The factual universe is defined by the record in the lower court. The issues are generally defined as they have been preserved for appeal. Also, because during the appeal there will be no discovery, few motions, and no cumbersome trial preparation, the legal fees and associated costs are easier to estimate.

In other respects, the appellate reassessment is very difficult. First, the same questions must be asked about the claims, interests, objectives, facts, equities, and focus.[26] They must be asked with the record in mind, but counsel must recognize that the record will look very different to appellate judges than it did to the trial court. Counsel's most important task may be developing the appellate court's understanding of what is in the record and what its significance is. Once again, the context and the equities can be as important as the evidence specifically related to liability.

The most difficult part of the reassessment may be presented by the wide range of possible results. Each must be identified and evaluated by counsel and client. The difficulty of this process is illustrated by the case on appeal from a trial court's granting of a motion for summary judgment. On large projects with recurring litigation, such dismissals may become almost routine, and often no appeal is taken, especially when other deep-pocket defendants are available. But if the plaintiff does pursue an appeal, it may result in unforeseen consequences. Even though the record is likely to be skimpy and the equities undeveloped, the appellate court may overstep its traditionally limited role and interpret the contract out of context. The result may be a serious misinterpretation of the parties' relationships.

As with the trial, the assessment should have a clear focus. Lawyers who fail to develop a focus often find irresistible the temptation to brief and argue every possible issue. Of course, the risk of exhaustive argument is exhausted judges (or their overworked clerks) who miss the best points and are alienated by the worst.

§ 22.26 Appellate Brief

Preparing the appellate brief starts with research encompassing both the law and the record. The same basic considerations that apply to developing

---

[26] See §§ **22.2–22.10, 22.12.**

the issues at the trial level also apply to an appeal. Thus, attention should be centered on those arguments that best serve the client's overall objectives. This focus allows the lawyer to keep control of the appeal and avoid needless overpreparation.

Rules of the specific appellate court may cause the form of the brief to vary, but the basic format is similar in almost every appellate forum. For example, most appellate courts require a statement of each issue presented for review. The statement must be clear and it should be worded to suggest the desired resolution.

A statement of the case is also generally required. It is essential to the judge's understanding of the basic issues. The statement must show how the controversy arose, what roles the parties played in the construction work at issue, and how the trial court incorporated these facts into its decision. Because encompassing all of these details may require that the lawyer make the statement longer than otherwise appropriate, in particularly complex cases the lawyer may break down various areas of the statement into different sections. For example, a jobsite safety case in which relationships and duties are important might contain a statement of the case organized under the following subheadings:

1. Overall organization of the project
2. The relationship between the contractor and the owner
3. Safety responsibilities on the project
4. The decision of the district court.

The statement of the case should not be an argument, but, like the statement of the issues, its wording and focus should clearly and persuasively suggest the desired result.

The core of the brief is, of course, the argument. Each argument will be developed differently, with the emphasis reflecting the overall position counsel wishes to convey to the judges. The argument section should be organized with headings and subheadings that state succinctly but positively the points being made. The argument section is and should appear entirely different from the statement of the case, where an appearance of objectivity is important.

It is often useful to organize the argument section of an appellate brief into two major parts: the contractor's arguments, and the contractor's answers to the opponent's arguments. The major headings may simply be, "The District Court Correctly Found That . . ." and "Appellant's Arguments that . . . Are Without Merit." The subheadings can then be one-sentence summaries of the argument made in each subsection. A carefully organized argument with effective captions should always result in a table of contents that is itself readable and persuasive.

It is easy to overlook the importance of record excerpts and appendices. In addition to the formal record on appeal, the Federal Rules of Appellate Procedure and many state appellate rules require an appendix to the briefs.[27] The appendix includes any parts of the record to which the parties wish to direct the attention of the court. Although the filing of an appendix does not preclude reliance on parts of the record not included, it typically becomes the handbook for the judges and their clerks, both when the briefs are being considered and during oral argument. Selection of its contents is therefore is very important piece of counsel's advocacy.

§ 22.27 Oral Argument

Oral argument to the appellate court parallels both the opening statement and the closing argument at the trial level. The judges must be oriented to the contractor's case and then must be convinced that the facts and the law support a decision for the contractor. As part of planning the argument, it is important to find out as much as possible about the judges. What are their biases? How carefully will they prepare? How have they decided similar cases or issues? What types of questions do they typically raise during argument?

Oral argument is often interrupted by questions from the judges. Sometimes the questions are so numerous or so insistent that virtually none of the planned argument is delivered. If this happens, counsel should be delighted, not dismayed. The most effective oral arguments can be those that become a dialogue between counsel and the court. Confusion may be distressing, but it is better elicited during argument than left to surface in a misinformed adverse opinion.

To handle such a dialogue, counsel must know both the record and the law. In addition, counsel will occasionally be called on for facts that are not in the record, especially when the case is before the court on a pretrial appeal. An informed answer that includes all the facts important to the client's position is the best response to such a question. Counsel's informed representation is entirely appropriate in such instances, so long as the judges are informed that the facts are not in the record.

Because questioning is likely, preparation for it is essential. At the least, counsel must think through the probable questions from the court and then consider how to answer them, from the perspective of both providing the desired information and furthering the overall argument. Mock questioning by a colleague is especially useful. It counsel has not previously argued before the court, an hour spent observing in the courtroom during preparation is time well spent.

---

[27] *See, e.g.*, Fed. R. App. P. 30.

At the oral argument, the complexity of construction litigation once again influences the strategy. It is especially important to use the argument as a time to identify and correct any misperceptions. It can be especially useful to tell the court at the outset what will be covered in the oral argument. This permits the judges to indicate particular areas of interest, matters they do not fully understand, or areas in which they have no further interest.

Finally, counsel should recall that post-argument filings may be possible, even if only with special leave of the court. An error, a missing record citation, a new relevant decision, or failure to have briefed a case, or an issue raised during the argument may make it necessary for counsel to request leave to make a supplemental filing. If this is done, local rules and informal procedures should be carefully reviewed, the motion for leave should be made promptly, and the filing should normally accompany it.

TABLE OF CASES

Case	*Book §*
A&A Elec., Inc. v. City of King, 54 Cal. App. 3d 457, 126 Cal. Rptr. 585 (1976)	§ 4.29
Abco Tank & Mfg. Co. v. Federal Ins. Co., 550 S.W.2d 193 (Mo. 1977)	§ 11.17
Acchione & Canuso, Inc. v. Commonwealth, 501 Pa. 377, 461 A.2d 765 (1983)	§ 5.3
Aced v. Hobbs-Sesack Plumbing Co., 55 Cal.2d 573, 360 P.2d 897, 12 Cal. Rptr. 257 (1961)	§§ 2.21, 20.7
Acme Process Equip. Co. v. United States, 347 F.2d 509, 171 Ct. Cl. 324 (1965)	§ 10.7
Acquisition Corp. v. American Cast Iron Pipe Co., 543 So. 2d 878 (Fla. Dist. Ct. App. 1989)	§ 2.29
Active Fire Sprinkler Corp. v. United States Postal Serv., 811 F.2d 747 (2d Cir. 1987)	§ 13.18
Adams v. Bryant, 274 S.W.2d 791 (Ky. 1954)	§ 11.5
Adkins v. La Terre Dev. Corp., 387 So. 2d 652 (La. Ct. App. 1980)	§ 11.17
Adler v. Seligman, 438 So. 2d 1963 (Fla. Dist. Ct. App. 1983)	§ 20.16
Admiral Oriental Lines, Inc. v. United States, 86 F.2d 201 (2d Cir. 1936)	§ 12.30
A.E. Inv. Corp. v. Link Builders, Inc., 214 N.W.2d 764 (Wis. 1974)	§ 8.2
Aetna Casualty & Sur. Co. v. United States, 570 F.2d 1197 (4th Cir.), *cert. denied,* 439 U.S. 821 (1978)	§ 22.8
Aetna Ins. Co. v. Hellmuth, Obata & Kassabaum, Inc., 392 F.2d 472 (8th Cir. 1968)	§ 12.33
Affholder, Inc. v. Southern Rock, Inc., 736 F.2d 1007 (5th Cir. 1984)	§ 5.13
Agar v. Commissioner, 290 F.2d 283 (2d Cir. 1961)	§§ 21.3, 21.20
Aid Ins. Servs., Inc. v. Geiger, 294 N.W.2d 411 (N.D. 1980)	§ 11.10
Airco, Inc. v. Energy Research & Dev. Admin., 528 F.2d 1294 (7th Cir. 1975)	§ 6.6
AIU Ins. Co. v. Superior Court (FMC Corp.), 51 Cal. 3d 807, 799 P.2d 1253, 274 Cal. Rptr. 820 (1990)	§ 11.2
A.J. Colella, Inc. v. County of Allegheny, 391 Pa. 103, 173 A.2d 265 (1957)	§ 4.30
Alabama Power Co. v. Blount Bros. Corp., 445 So. 2d 250 (Ala. 1984)	§ 20.3
Alan J Haynes Constr. v. United States, 10 Cl. Ct. 526 (1986)	§ 6.5

Case	*Book §*
Alaska Statebank v. Kirschbaum, 662 P.2d 939 (Alaska 1983)	§ 9.12
Alaska State Bank v. Town of Malvern, 270 N.W.2d 818 (Iowa 1978)	§ 12.31
Alfieri v. Butler, 38 A.D.2d 672, 327 N.Y.S.2d 108 (1971)	§ 7.16
Alger v. United States, 741 F.2d 391 (Fed. Cir. 1984)	§ 6.5
Alguire v. Walker, 154 Ill. App. 3d 438, 506 N.E.2d 1334 (1987)	§ 20.2
Al Johnson Constr. Co. v. United States, 19 Cl. Ct. 732 (1990)	§ 6.5
Allan S. Mead & Assocs., Inc. v. McGarry, 68 N.C. App. 467, 315 S.E.2d 69 (1984)	§ 2.18
Allen Engr. Corp. v. Lattimore, 201 A.2d 13 (Md. Ct. Spec. App. 1964)	§ 5.16
Allen M. Campbell Co. v. Virginia Metal Indus., 708 F.2d 930 (4th Cir. 1983)	§ 2.26
Allied Properties v. John A. Blume & Assocs., Eng'rs, 25 Cal. App. 3d 848, 102 Cal. Rptr. 259 (1972)	§§ 7.6, 8.5
All Seasons' Water Users Ass'n, Inc. v. Northern Improvement Co., 399 N.W.2d 278 (N.D. 1987)	§ 20.3
Alley v. Courtney, 448 So. 2d 858 (La. Ct. App. 1984)	§ 12.33
Aluminum Co. of Am. v. Electro-Flo Corp., 451 F.2d 1115 (10th Cir. 1971)	§ 20.7
Alvarez v. Insurance Co. of N. Am., 667 F. Supp. 689 (N.D. Cal. 1987)	§ 12.27
Alyeska Pipeline Serv. v. Aurora Air Serv., Inc., 604 P.2d 1090 (Alaska 1979)	§ 12.17
Amarillo Equity Investors, Inc. v. Craycroft Lacy Partners, 654 S.W.2d 28 (Tex. Ct. App. 1983)	§ 20.16
Amelco Window Corp. v. Federal Ins. Co., 127 N.J. Super. 342, 317 A.2d 398 (1974)	§ 12.15
American Auto Ins. Co. v. United States *ex rel.* Luce, 269 F.2d 406 (1st Cir. 1959)	§ 13.10
American Bridge Co. v. State, 245 A.D. 535, 283 N.Y.S. 577 (1935)	§ 7.33
American Casualty Co. v. Coastal Caisson Drill Co., 542 So. 2d 957 (Fla. 1989)	§ 13.2
American Casualty Co. v. Irvin, 426 F.2d 647 (5th Cir. 1970)	§ 13.5
American Casualty Co. v. Shattuck, 228 F. Supp. 834 (W.D. Okla. 1964)	§ 12.24
American Casualty Co. v. Southern Materials Co., 261 F.2d 197 (4th Cir. 1958)	§ 13.12
American Casualty Co. v. Timmons, 352 F.2d 563 (6th Cir. 1968)	§ 11.10
American Fid. Fire Ins. Co. v. Construcciones Werl, 407 F. Supp. 164 (D.V.I. 1975)	§ 12.31
American Fid. Fire Ins. Co. v. Pavia-Byrne Eng'g Corp., 393 So. 2d 830 (La. Ct. App.), *cert. denied,* 397 So. 2d 1362 (La. 1981)	§§ 12.24, 12.33

Case	*Book §*
American Home Prods. v. Liberty Mut. Ins. Co., 565 F. Supp. 1485 (S.D.N.Y. 1983), *modified,* 748 F.2d 760 (2d Cir. 1984)	§§ 11.2, 11.6
American Sur. Co. v. Westinghouse Elec. Mfg. Co., 296 U.S. 133 (1935)	§ 13.18
American Sur. Co. v. Wheeling Structural Steel Co., 114 F.2d 237 (4th Cir. 1940)	§ 12.23
Anahuac, Inc. v. Wilkes, 622 S.W.2d 634 (Tex. Civ. App. 1981)	§ 10.9
Anchor Coupling Co. v. United States, 427 F.2d 429 (7th Cir. 1970), *cert. denied,* 401 U.S. 908 (1971)	§ 21.7
Anderson Constr. Co. v. Lyon Metal Prods., Inc., 370 So. 2d 935 (Miss. 1979)	§ 10.2
Anderson Elec., Inc. v. Ledbetter Erection Corp., 115 Ill. 2d 146, 503 N.E.2d 246 (1986)	§ 7.41
Anthony Pools v. Sheehan, 295 Md. 285, 455 A.2d 434 (Ct. App. 1983)	§ 20.7
Antoniou v. Kenick, 124 N.H. 606, 474 A.2d 566 (1984)	§ 20.4
Apache Powder Co. v. Ashton Co., 264 F.2d 417 (9th Cir. 1959)	§ 13.11
Apex Siding Roofing Co. v. First Fed. Sav. & Loan Ass'n, 301 P.2d 352 (Okla. 1956)	§§ 9.9, 9.14
Appalachian Ins. Co. v. Superior Court (Union Carbide Corp.), 162 Cal. App. 3d 427, 208 Cal. Rptr. 627 (1984)	§ 11.2
Applegren v. Milbank Mut. Ins. Co., 268 N.W.2d 114 (N.D. 1978)	§ 11.11
Arc Elec. Constr. Co. v. George A. Fuller Co., 24 N.Y.2d 99, 247 N.E.2d 111, 299 N.Y.S.2d (1969)	§ 15.16
Arcon Constr. Co. v. South Dakota Cement Plant, 349 N.W.2d 407 (S.D. 1984)	§ 5.13
Argonaut Ins. Co. v. Commercial Standard Ins. Co., 380 So. 2d 1066 (Fla. Dist. Ct. App.), *review denied,* 389 So. 2d 1108 (Fla. 1980)	§ 12.33
Arkansas Rice Growers Coop. Assoc. v. Alchemy Indus., Inc., 797 F.2d 565 (8th Cir. 1986)	§ 8.4
A.R. Moyer, Inc. v. Graham, 285 So. 2d 397 (Fla. 1977)	§§ 7.17, 7.22, 8.2
Armstrong & Armstrong, Inc. v. United States, 514 F.2d 402 (9th Cir. 1975)	§ 6.6
Arthur A. Johnson Corp. v. Indemnity Ins., 6 A.D.2d 97, 175 N.Y.S.2d 414 (1958), *aff'd,* 7 N.Y.2d 222, 164 N.E.2d 704, 196 N.Y.S.2d 678 (1959)	§ 11.5
Arthur H. DuGrenier, Inc. v. Commissioner, 58 T.C. 931 (1972)	§ 21.7
Atlas Corp. v. United States, 895 F.2d 745 (Fed. Cir.), *cert. denied,* 111 S. Ct. 46 (1990)	§ 6.5
Attlin Constr., Inc. v. Muncie Community Schs., 413 N.E.2d 281 (Ind. Ct. App. 1980)	§ 7.9
A.R. Moyer, Inc. v. Graham, 295 So. 2d 397 (Fla. 1973)	§ 7.16
Arnold v. United States *ex rel.* Bowman Mech. Contractors, 470 F.2d 243 (10th Cir. 1972)	§ 13.10

Case	*Book §*
Arthur N. Olice Co. v. United States *ex rel.* Marino, 297 F.2d 70 (1st Cir. 1961)	§ 13.9
Associated Eng'rs & Contractors, Inc. v. State, 58 Haw. 322, 568 P.2d 512 (1977)	§ 20.5
Aubrey v. Helton, 276 Ala. 134, 159 So. 2d 837 (1964)	§§ 12.34, 20.3
Auburn, City of v. Nash, 34 A.D.2d 345, 312 N.Y.S.2d 700 (1970)	§ 6.8
Austin v. Parker, 672 F.2d 508 (5th Cir. 1982)	§ 12.37
Austin Co. v. Vaughn Bldg. Corp., 643 S.W.2d 113 (Tex. 1982)	§ 20.7
Autrey v. Willians & Dunlap, 343 F.2d 730 (5th Cir. 1965)	§ 12.34
Avis v. Hartford Fire Ins. Co., 283 N.C. 142, 195 S.E.2d 545 (1973)	§§ 11.20, 11.21
Axia, Inc. v. I.C. Harbour Constr. Co., 150 Ill. App. 3d 645, 103 Ill. Dec. 801, 501 N.E.2d 1339 (1986)	§ 20.3
Bacco Constr. Co. v. American Colloid Co., 148 Mich. App. 397, 384 N.W.2d 427 (1986)	§ 7.41
Bagwell Coatings, Inc. v. Middle S. Energy, Inc., 797 F.2d 1298 (5th Cir. 1986)	§§ 7.11, 7.27, 7.39
Bailey v. Faux, 704 F. Supp. 1051 (D. Utah 1989)	§ 13.14
Bailey v. Meister Brau, Inc., 535 F.2d 982 (7th Cir. 1976)	§ 12.27
Baker v. American Ins. Co., 324 F.2d 748 (4th Cir. 1963)	§ 11.5
Baker & Ford Co. v. United States *ex rel.* Urban Plumbing & Heating Co., 363 F.2d 605 (9th Cir. 1966)	§ 13.10
Balboa Ins. Co. v. Southern Distrib. Corp., 710 P.2d 725 (Nev. 1985)	§ 13.7
Balboa Ins. Co. v. W.C.B. Assocs., Inc., 390 So. 2d 172 (Fla. Dist. Ct. App. 1980)	§ 12.36
Baldwin v. Auto-Owners Ins. Co., 5 Ill. App. 3d 300, 282 N.E.2d 204 (1972)	§ 11.11
Baldwin-Lima-Hamilton Corp. v. Superior Court, 208 Cal. App. 2d 803, 25 Cal. Rptr. 789 (1962)	§ 4.24
Ball, Ball & Brosamer, Inc. v. Commissioner, 60 T.C.M. (CCH) 587 (1990)	§ 21.15
Ball, Ball & Brosamer, Inc. v. United States, 878 F.2d 1426 (Fed. Cir. 1989)	§ 6.5
Baltimore v. Clarke, 97 A. 911 (Md. Ct. App. 1916)	§ 2.28
Baltimore, City of v. De Luca-Davis Constr. Co., 210 Md. 518, 124 A.2d 557 (1956)	§ 5.14
Baltimore Gas & Elec. Co. v. State Roads Comm'n, 214 Md. 266, 134 A.2d 312 (1957)	§ 6.11
Barile Excavating & Pipeline Co. v. Kendall Properties, Inc., 462 So. 2d 1129 (Fla. Dist. Ct. App. 1984)	§ 20.8
Barnard-Curtis Co. v. United States, 301 F.2d 909 (Ct. Cl. 1962)	§ 20.5
Baron Oil Co. v. National Mut. Fire Ins. Co., 470 So. 2d 810 (Fla. Dist. Ct. App. 1985)	§ 11.16

Case	*Book §*
Barre, City of v. New Hampshire Ins. Co., 136 Vt. 484, 396 A.2d 121 (1978)	§ 11.21
Barreto Granite Corp. v. State, 147 Vt. 148, 513 A.2d 608 (1986)	§ 13.5
Bartholomew v. Appalachian Ins. Co., 655 F.2d 27 (1st Cir. 1981)	§ 11.5
Bates & Rogers Constr. Corp. v. Greeley & Hansen, 109 Ill. 2d 225, 486 N.E.2d 902 (1985)	§ 8.2
Bates & Rogers Constr. Corp. v. North Shore Sanitary Dist., 128 Ill. App. 3d 962, 471 N.E.2d 915 (1984), *aff'd on other grounds sub nom.* Bates & Rogers Constr. Corp. v. Greeley & Hansen, 109 Ill. 2d 225, 486 N.E.2d 902 (1985)	§ 8.2
Bates & Rogers Constr. Corp. v. North Shore Sanitary Dist., 92 Ill. App. 3d 90, 414 N.E.2d 1274 (1980)	§§ 7.11, 7.26, 7.31
Baybutt Constr. Co. v. Commercial Union Ins. Co., 678 F. Supp. 562 (W.D. Pa. 1988)	§ 11.10
Bay State Ins. Co. v. Wilson, 96 Ill. 2d 487, 451 N.E.2d 880 (1983)	§ 11.5
Bedford-Carthage Stone Co. v. Ranney, 34 S.W.2d 387 (Tex. Civ. App. 1930)	§ 20.10
Bell v. Carver, 245 Ark. 30, 431 S.W.2d 452 (1968)	§ 20.5
Bell v. Jones, 523 A.2d 982 (D.C. 1986)	§ 8.5
Bell v. United States, 404 F.2d 975 (Ct. Cl. 1968)	§ 16.41
Berley Indus., Inc. v. City of N.Y., 45 N.Y.2d 683, 385 N.E.2d 281, 412 N.Y.S.2d 589 (1978)	§§ 5.13, 16.40
Berkel & Co. Contractors, Inc. v. Providence Hosp., 454 So. 2d 496 (Ala. 1984)	§ 5.10
Bernard Johnson, Inc. v. Continental Constructors, Inc., 630 S.W.2d 365 (Tex. Ct. App. 1982)	§§ 8.2, 20.2
Bescor, Inc. v. Chicago Title & Trust Co., 113 Ill. App. 3d 65, 446 N.E.2d 1209 (1983)	§ 9.21
Bethesda Lutheran Church v. Twin City Constr. Co., 356 N.W.2d 344 (Minn. 1984)	§ 20.4
Biebel Bros. v. USF&G, 522 F.2d 1207 (8th Cir. 1975)	§ 11.10
Bigelow-Liptak Corp. v. Continental Ins. Co., 417 F. Supp. 1276 (E.D. Mich. 1976)	§ 11.11
Bird v. Pan W. Corp., 261 Ark. 56, 546 S.W.2d 417 (1977)	§ 7.7
Birds Constr., Inc. v. McKay, 657 S.W.2d 514 (Tex. Ct. App. 1983)	§ 20.16
B.K. Instrument, Inc. v. United States, 715 F.2d 713 (2d Cir. 1983)	§ 6.6
Blackfield v. Underwriters at Lloyd's, London, 245 Cal. App. 2d 271, 53 Cal. Rptr. 838 (1966)	§ 11.14
Blackhawk Heating & Plumbing Co. v. Seaboard Sur. Co., 534 F. Supp. 309 (N.D. Ill. 1982)	§ 12.35
Blake Constr. v. Alley, 233 Va. 31, 353 S.E.2d 724 (1987)	§ 7.41
Blake Constr. Co. v. C.J. Coakley Co., 431 A.2d 569 (D.C. 1981)	§§ 5.8, 7.35, 10.4

Case	*Book §*
Blinderman Constr. Co. v. United States, 695 F.2d 552 (Fed. Cir. 1982)	§ 2.28
Bloomsburg Mills, Inc. v. Sordoni Constr. Co., 401 Pa. 337, 164 A.2d 201 (1960)	§§ 7.6, 7.19, 8.4
Blosam Constr., Inc. v. Republic Mortgage Inv., 353 So. 2d 1225 (Fla. Dist. Ct. App. 1977), *cert. denied,* 359 So. 2d 1218 (Fla. Dist. Ct. App. 1978)	§ 9.18
Blount Bros. Corp. v. United States, 872 F.2d 1003 (Fed. Cir. 1989)	§ 20.5
Blue Cross v. McDevitt & Street Co., 234 Va. 191, 360 S.E.2d 825 (1987)	§ 20.3
B&M Homes v. Hogan, 376 So. 2d 667 (Ala. 1981)	§ 20.16
Board of Directors v. Regency Tower Venture, 2 Haw. App. 506, 635 P.2d 224 (1981)	§ 7.44
Board of Educ. v. Alcrymat Corp., 258 Md. 508, 266 A.2d 349 (1970)	§ 6.8
Board of Educ. v. Hartford Accident & Indem. Co., 152 Ill. App. 3d 745, 504 N.E.2d 1000 (1987)	§ 13.2
Board of Educ. v. Sever-Williams Co. 22 Ohio St. 2d 107, 258 N.E.2d 605, *cert. denied,* 400 U.S. 916 (1970)	§ 4.30
Board of Educ. v. Thompson Constr. Corp., 111 A.D.2d 497, 488 N.Y.S.2d 880 (1985)	§ 20.4
Board of Trustees v. Kennerly, Slomanson & Smith, 167 N.J. Super. 311, 400 A.2d 850 (Law Div. 1979)	§ 8.4
Boise Jr. College Dist. v. Mattefs Constr. Co. 92 Idaho 757, 450 P2d 604 (1969)	§ 4.30
Bolton Corp. v. T.A. Loving Co., 94 N.C. App. 392, 380 S.E.2d 796 (1989)	§ 7.15
Bond Bros., Inc. v. Robinson, 393 Mass. 546, 471 N.E.2d 1332 (1984)	§ 11.10
Bondumin-McClure, Inc. v. Snow, 183 Cal. App. 2d 58, 6 Cal. Rptr. 52 (1960)	§ 7.6
Bonebreak v. Corx, 499 F.2d 951 (8th Cir. 1974)	§ 2.21
Bonstaff v. Jefferson United Enters., Inc., 501 So. 2d 874 (La. Ct. App. 1987)	§ 20.3
Boomer v. Abbett, 121 Cal. App. 2d 449, 263 P.2d 476 (1953)	§ 5.2
Borell v. Municipality of Metro. Seattle, 698 F.2d 1229 (9th Cir. 1983)	§ 16.29
Borman's, Inc. v. Lake State Dev. Co., 60 Mich. App. 175, 230 N.W.2d 363 (1975)	§§ 7.6, 8.4
Bor-Son Bldg. Corp. v. Employees Commercial Union Ins. Co., 323 N.W.2d 58 (Minn. 1982)	§§ 11.11, 11.14
Boston Ins. Co. v. Grable, 352 F.2d 368 (5th Cir. 1965)	§ 11.11
Boston Plate & Window Glass Co. v. John Bowen Co., 335 Mass. 697, 141 N.E.2d 715 (1957)	§ 20.6
Bowden v. United States *ex rel.* Malloy, 239 F.2d 572 (9th Cir. 1956), *cert. denied,* 353 U.S. 957 (1957)	§ 13.11
Bradley Envtl. Contractors v. Village of Sylvan Beach, 98 A.D.2d 973, 470 N.Y.S.2d 214 (1983)	§ 16.17

Case	*Book §*
Brady v. Board of Educ., 222 A.D. 504, 226 N.Y.S. 707 (1926)	§ 7.33
Brady v. Ralph Parsons Co., 308 Md. 486, 520 A.2d 717 (1987), *aff'd,* 82 Md. App. 519, 572 A.2d 1115 (1990)	§§ 7.2, 7.40
Brady Brick & Supply Co. v. Lotito, 43 Ill. App. 3d 62, 356 N.E.2d 1126 (1976)	§ 5.14
Brasher v. Alexandria, 215 La. 887, 41 So. 2d 819 (1949)	§ 20.2
Bresler v. Commissioner, 65 T.C. 182 (1975)	§ 21.4
Briar Contracting Corp. v. State, 156 A.D.2d 628, 550 N.Y.S.2d 717 (1989)	§ 8.2
Broadway Maintenance Corp. v. Rutgers, 108 N.J. Super. 350, 434 A.2d 1125 (1981)	§§ 7.17, 7.37, 20.9
Broce-O'Dell Concrete Prods., Inc. v. Mel Jarvis Constr. Co., 6 Kan. App. 2d 757, 634 P.2d 1142 (1981)	§ 10.7
Brogan v. National Sur. Co. 246 U.S. 257 (1918)	§ 13.7
Brookhaven Landscape & Grading Co. v. J.F. Barton Contracting Co., 676 F.2d 516 (11th Cir. 1982)	§ 12.28
Brooks Toeers Corp. v. Hunkin-Conkey Constr. Co., 454 F.2d 1203 (10th Cir. 1973)	§ 16.10
Broome, County of v. Aetna Casualty & Sur., 146 A.D.2d 337, 540 N.Y.S.2d 620 (1989)	§ 11.5
Brown v. East Carolina R.R., 54 N.C. 300, 70 S.E. 625 (1911)	§ 2.28
Brown v. Safeway Stores, Inc., 94 Wash. 2d 359, 671 P.2d 704 (1980)	§ 10.27
Brown & Son Elec. Co. v. United States, 163 Ct. Cl. 465 (1963)	§ 4.13
Broyles v. Brown Eng'g Co., 275 Ala. 35, 151 So. 2d 767 (1963)	§§ 7.6, 7.19, 8.4
Bryant Elec. Co. v. City of Fredericksburg, 762 F.2d 1192 (4th Cir. 1985)	§ 8.2
B's Co. v. B.T. Barber & Assocs., Inc., 391 F.2d 130 (4th Cir. 1968)	§ 20.6
B7B Cut Stone Co. v. Jack C. Resneck, 465 So. 2d 851 (La. Ct. App. 1985)	§ 20.16
Buchman Plumbing Co. v. Regents of Univ. of Minn., 298 Minn. 328, 215 N.W.2d 479 (1974)	§ 7.17
Buckley & Co. v. State, 140 N.J. Super. 289, 356 A.2d 56 (1975)	§ 7.32
Building Maintenance Co., ENGBCA No. 4115, 83-2 B.C.A. (CCH) ¶ 16,629 (1983)	§ 5.9
Bulen v. West Bend Mut. Ins. Co., 125 Wis. 259, 371 N.W.2d 392 (1985)	§ 11.10
Burgess Constr. v. M. Marrin & Son Co., 526 F.2d 108 (10th Cir. 1976)	§ 16.5
Burns v. Hanover Ins. Co. 454 A.2d 325 (D.C. 1983)	§ 20.15
Burns v. Washington Sav. & Loan Ass'n, 251 Miss. 789, 421 S.W.2d 332 (1965)	§ 9.9
Burran v. Dambold, 422 F.2d 133 (10th Cir. 1970)	§ 8.5

Case	*Book §*
Burras v. Canal Constr. & Design Co., 470 N.E.2d 1362 (Ind. Ct. App. 1984)	§ 5.9
Burroughs Corp., *In re,* 56 Comp. Gen. 142 (1976)	§ 6.10
Burton-Dixie Corp. v. Timothy McCarthy Constr. Co., 436 F.2d 405 (5th Cir. 1971)	§§ 10.8, 14.12
Busby Sch. of N. Cheyenne Tribe v. United States, 8 Cl. Ct. 596 (1985)	§ 6.5
Caceci v. DiCanio Constr. Corp., 72 N.Y.2d 52, 526 N.E.2d 266, 530 N.Y.S.2d 771 (1988)	§ 20.7
Calandro Dev., Inc. v. R.M. Butler Contractors, Inc., 249 So. 2d 254 (La. Ct. App. 1971)	§ 12.33
Caldwell v. Bechtel, 631 F.2d 989 (D.C. Cir. 1980)	§ 7.14
California Union Ins. Co. v. Landmark Ins. Co., 145 Cal. App. 3d 462, 193 Cal. Rptr. 461 (1983)	§ 11.6
Cameron-Hawn Realty Co. v. Albany, 207 N.Y. 377, 101 N.E. 162 (1913)	§ 20.2
Camloc Fastener Co. v. Commissioner 10 T.C. 1024 (1948)	§ 21.7
Canadian Radium Uranium Corp. v. Indemnity Ins. Co., 411 Ill. 325, 104 N.E.2d 250 (1952)	§ 11.5
Canter v. Schlager, 358 Mass. 789, 267 N.E.2d 492 (1971)	§ 12.24
Cantrel v. Woodhill Enters., Inc., 273 N.C. 490, 160 S.E.2d 476 (1968)	§ 20.3
Cape Henry Towers, Inc. v. National Gypsum Co., 229 Va. 596, 331 S.E.2d 476 (1985)	§ 20.4
Capital Elec. Co., 65 B.C.A. (CCH) Nos. 5313, 5316 (1965)	§§ 16.40, 18.23
Capital Elec. Co. v. United States, 729 F.2d 743 (Fed. Cir. 1984)	§ 5.13
Carnicle v. Swann, 314 N.W.2d 311 (S.D. 1982)	§ 5.14
Carol C. Gelardi Corp. v. Miller Brewing Co., 502 F. Supp. 637 (D.N.J. 1980)	§ 12.27
Caron v. Andrews, 133 Cal. App. 2d 402, 284 P.2d 544 (1955)	§ 12.22
Carpenter v. Suffolk Franklin Sav. Bank, 370 Mass. 314, 346 N.E.2d 892 (1976)	§ 12.37
Carrabine Constr. Co. v. Chrysler Realty Corp., 25 Ohio St. 3d 22, 495 N.E.2d 952 (1986)	§ 7.32
Carrington v. W.A. Soefker & Sons, Inc., 624 S.W.2d 894 (Tenn. Ct. App. 1981)	§ 10.7
Carroll-Boone Water Dist. v. M.&P. Equip. Co., 280 Ark. 560, 661 S.W.2d 560 (1984)	§ 7.6
Carter Lake, City of v. Aetna Casualty & Sur. Co., 604 F.2d 1052 (8th Cir. 1979)	§ 11.5
Case Prestressing Corp. v. Chicago College of Osteopathic Medicine, 118 Ill. App. 3d 782, 455 N.E.2d 811 (1983)	§§ 7.15, 7.27
Casey v. Employers Nat'l Ins. Co., 539 S.W.2d 181 (Tex. Ct. App. 1976)	§ 11.17

Case	*Book §*
Casson Constr., Inc., GSBCA Nos. 4884 *et al.,* 83-1 B.C.A. (CCH) ¶ 16,523	§ 7.27
Castaldo v. Pittsburgh-Des Moines Steel Co., 376 A.2d 88 (Del. 1977)	§ 8.4
Castille v. 3-D Chems., Inc., 520 So. 2d 1002 (La. Ct. App. 1987)	§ 20.3
Cates v. Morgan Portable Bldg. Corp., 591 F.2d 17 (7th Cir. (1979)	§ 20.7
Cavasant v. Campopiano, 114 R.I. 24, 327 A.2d 831 (1974)	§ 20.7
Cavendish v. Sunoco Serv., 541 F.2d 1360 (7th Cir. 1971)	§ 22.13
C.E. Frazier Constr. Co. v. Campbell Roofing & Metal Works, Inc., 373 So. 2d 1036 (Miss. 1979)	§§ 2.26, 10.2
Central Mut. Ins. Co. v. Del Mar Beach Club Owners Ass'n, 123 Cal. App. 3d 916, 176 Cal. Rptr. 895 (1981)	§ 11.1
Century 1 Joint Venture v. USF&G, 63 Md. App. 545, 493 A.2d 370, *cert. denied,* 304 Md. 297, 498 A.2d 1183 (1985)	§§ 11.10, 11.13
Ceramic Tiles Inc. v. Aetna Casualty & Sur. Co., 39 Conn. Supp. 477, 466 A.2d 348 (1983)	§ 11.11
CFS Air Cargo, Inc. B-238698.4, 90-1 CPD ¶ 315 (1990)	§ 4.14
Champaign County Nursing Home v. Petry Roofing, Inc., 117 Ill. App. 3d 76, 452 N.E.2d 847 (1983)	§ 20.4
Chandler v. Fugua, 420 So. 2d 1348 (La. Ct. App. 1982)	§ 20.2
Chariot Textiles Corp. v. Wannalancit Textile Co., 18 N.Y.2d 793, 221 N.E.2d 913, 275 N.Y.S.2d 382 (1966)	§ 10.11
Charles E. Brohawn & Bros., Inc. v. Board of Trustees, 269 Md. 164, 304 A.2d 819 (1973)	§§ 6.8, 6.11
Charles H. Siever, PSBCA No. 460, 80-2 B.C.A. (CCH) ¶ 14,740 (1980)	§ 5.4
Chevron Chem. Corp. v. United States, 5 Cl. Ct. 807 (1984)	§ 6.5
Chicago Bonding & Sur. Co. v. Augusta Savannah Navigation Co., 250 F. 616 (7th Cir.), *cert. denied,* 247 U.S. 509 (1918)	§ 12.23
Chicago College of Osteopathic Medicine v. George A. Fuller Co., 719 F.2d 1335 (7th Cir. 1983)	§ 5.8
Chlan v. K.D.I. Sylvan Pools, Inc., 53 Md. App. 236, 452 A.2d 1259 (1982)	§ 20.7
C.H. Leavell & Co. v. Fireman's Fund Ins. Co., 372 F.2d 784 (9th Cir. 1967)	§§ 10.3, 11.20
Chouteau v. United States, 95 U.S. 61 (1877)	§ 20.5
Christensen v. Idaho Land Developers, Inc., 104 Idaho 458, 660 P.2d 70 (1983)	§ 12.28
C.H. Sanders Co. v. BHAP Hous. Dev. Fund Co., 903 F.2d 114 (2d Cir. 1990)	§ 9.7
Chu v. Canadian Indem. Co., 224 Cal. App. 3d 86, 274 Cal. Rptr. 20 (1990)	§ 11.5
Cincinnati Elecs. Corp. v. Kleppe, 509 F.2d 1080 (6th Cir. 1975)	§ 6.6

Case	*Book §*
Cipriani v. Sun Pipe Line Co., 393 Pa. Super. 471, 574 A.2d 706 (1990)	§ 7.16
C&K Eng'g Contractors v. Amber Steel Co., 23 Cal. 3d 1, 587 P.2d 1136, 151 Cal. Rptr. 323 (1978)	§ 10.2
Claiborne Parish Sch. Bd. v. Fidelity & Deposit Co., 40 F.2d 577 (5th Cir. 1980)	§ 12.31
Clardy v. Barco Constr. Co., 205 Pa. Super. 218, 208 A.2d 793 (1965)	§ 9.9
Clark v. Landelco, Inc., 657 S.W.2d 634 (Mo. Ct. App. 1984)	§ 20.7
Claude E. Atkins Enters. v. United States, 899 F.2d 1180 (Fed. Cir. 1990)	§ 6.5
Claussen v. Aetna Casualty, 259 Ga. 333, 380 S.E.2d 686 (1989)	§ 11.2
Clear v. Patterson, 80 N.M. 654, 459 P.2d 358 (1969)	§ 20.3
Clemens v. Benzinger, 211 A.D. 586, 207 N.Y.S. 539 (1925)	§ 8.6
Clevenger & Wright Co. v. A.O. Smith Harverstore Prods., Inc., 625 S.W.2d 906 (Mo. Ct. App. 1981)	§ 20.7
Clifford MacEvoy Co. v. United States *ex rel.* Calvin Tomkins Co., 332 102 (1944)	§§ 12.37, 13.6
CNA Casualty v. Seaboard Sur. Co., 176 Cal. App. 3d 598, 22 Cal. Rptr. 276 (1986)	§ 11.4
C. Norman Peterson Co. v. Container Corp., 172 Cal. App. 3d 628, 218 Cal. Rptr. 592 (1985)	§§ 5.3, 5.13
COAC, Inc. v. Kennedy Eng'rs, 67 Cal. App. 3d 916, 136 Cal. Rptr. 890 (1977)	§§ 8.2, 8.7
Coalition for United Community Action, Inc., 88-1 B.C.A. (CCH) ¶ 20,290 (LBCA 1987)	§ 6.13
Cobb-Strecker-Dumphy & Zimmerman v. M.A. Mortenson Co., 706 F. Supp. 685 (D. Minn. 1989)	§ 13.7
Cochran v. Ozark Country Club, Inc., 339 So. 2d 1023 (Ala. 1976)	§ 7.7
Coco Bros., Inc. v. Pierce, 741 F.2d 675 (3d Cir. 1984)	§§ 4.16, 6.6
College Park, City of v. Batson-Cook Co., 196 Ga. App. 138, 395 S.E.2d 385 (1990)	§ 20.13
Collingswood Hosiery Mills v. American Fed. Hosiery Works, 28 N.J. Super. 605, 101 A.2d 372 (Ch. Div. 1953)	§ 20.13
Collins v. Commissioner, 18 T.C.M. (CCH) 756 (1959)	§ 21.3
Colonial Refrigerated Transp., Inc. v. Worsham, 705 F.2d 821 (6th Cir. 1983)	§ 11.10
Columbus, City of v. Clark-Dietz & Assocs.-Eng'rs, Inc., 550 F. Supp. 610 (N.D. Miss. 1982)	§§ 8.2, 8.9
Commerce Int'l Co. v. United States, 167 Ct. Cl. 529 (1964)	§ 17.2
Commercial Contractor, Inc. v. United States Fidelity & Guar. Co., 524 F.2d 944 (5th Cir. 1975)	§ 20.3
Commercial Standard Ins. Co. v. Bank of Am., 57 Cal. App. 3d 241, 129 Cal. Rptr. 91 (1976)	§ 9.21

Case	*Book §*
Commercial Union Assurance Cos. v. Gollan, 118 N.H. 744, 394 A.2d 839 (1978)	§ 11.10
Commissioner v. Glenshaw Glass Co., 348 U.S. 426 (1955)	§ 2.13
Commonwealth v. Eastern Paving Co., 288 Pa. 571, 136 A. 853 (1927)	§ 6.8
Comptroller of Treasury v. Panitz, 267 Md. 296, 297 A.2d 289 (1972)	§ 6.11
Concrete Sys., Inc. v. Florida Elec. Co., 425 So. 2d 632 (Fla. Dist. Ct. App. 1983)	§ 10.7
Condenser Serv. & Eng'g Co. v. American Mut. Liab. Ins. Co., 58 N.J. Super. 179, 155 A.2d 789 (1959)	§ 11.11
Conforti & Eisele, Inc. v. John C. Morris Assocs., 175 N.J. Super. 341, 418 A.2d 1290 (1981), *aff'd,* 199 N.J. Super. 498, 489 A.2d 1233 (1985)	§§ 7.16, 7.22, 8.2, 20.2
Connie's Constr. Co. v. Continental Ins. Co., 227 N.W.2d 204 (Iowa 1978)	§ 11.21
Connor v. Great W. Sav. & Loan Ass'n, 69 Cal. 2d 850, 73 Cal. Rptr. 369 (1969)	§ 9.7
Consolidated Aluminum Corp. v. C.F. Bean Corp., 639 F. Supp. 1173 (W.D. La. 1986), *aff'd,* 833 F.2d 65 (5th Cir. 1987), *reh'g denied en banc,* 837 F.2d 1090 (5th Cir.), *cert. denied,* 486 U.S. 1055 (1988)	§ 12.27
Consolidated Fed. Corp. v. Cain, 196 Ga. App. 671, 394 S.E.2d 605 (1990)	§ 2.29
Continental Casualty Co. v. Gilborne Bldg. Co., 391 Mass. 143, 461 N.E.2d 209 (1984)	§ 11.11
Continental Casualty Co. v. Hartford Accident & Indem. Co., 243 Cal. App. 2d 565, 52 Cal. Rptr. 533 (1966)	§ 12.16
Continental Heller Corp., GSBCA No. 6812, 84-2 B.C.A. (CCH) ¶ 17,275 (1984)	§ 5.7
Continental Heller Constr. v. United States, 21 Cl. Ct. 471 (1990)	§ 6.5
Continental Realty Corp. v. Andrew J. Crevolin Co., 380 F. Supp. 246 (S.D. W. Va. 1974)	§ 12.23
Contracting & Material Co. v. City of Chicago, 20 Ill. App. 3d 684, 314 N.E.2d 598 (1974), *rev'd on other grounds,* 64 Ill. 2d 21, 349 N.E.2d 389 (1976)	§§ 16.26, 16.27
Cook v. Citizens Sav. & Loan Ass'n, 346 So. 2d 370 (Miss. 1977)	§ 9.21
Coombs v. Beede, 89 Me. 187, 36 A. 104 (1896)	§ 12.33
Cooper v. Jevne, 56 Cal. App. 3d 860, 129 Cal. Rptr. 724 (1976)	§ 8.2
Cooper v. Superior Court, 153 Cal. App. 3d 1008, 200 Cal. Rptr. 746 (1984)	§ 20.16
Corinno Civetta Constr Corp. v. City of N.Y., 67 N.Y.2d 297, 493 N.E.2d 905, 502 N.Y.S.2d 681 (1986)	§§ 7.32, 16.17, 16.18
Cosmic Constr. Co. v. United States, 697 F.2d 1389 (Fed. Cir. 1982)	§ 6.5

Case	*Book §*
Coubarreaux v. Hines, 442 So. 2d 898 (La. Ct. App. 1984)	§ 20.8
County Asphalt, Inc. v. State, 40 A.D.2d 26, 337 N.Y.S.2d 415 (1972)	§ 16.20
COVCO-Haw. Corp., 83-2 B.C.A. (CCH) ¶ 15,554 (ASBCA 1983)	§ 6.5
Covington, City of v. Heard, 428 So. 2d 1132 (La. Ct. App. 1983)	§ 20.2
Cowles v. City of Minneapolis, 128 Minn. 452, 151 N.W. 184 (1915)	§ 8.4
Craig v. Everett M. Brooks Co., 351 Mass. 497, 222 N.E.2d 752 (1967)	§ 7.11
Craviolini v. Scholer & Fuller Associated Architects, 89 Ariz. 24, 357 P.2d 611 (1961)	§ 8.10
Credit Alliance Corp. v. Andersen & Co., 65 N.Y.2d 536, 483 N.E.2d 110, 493 N.Y.S.2d 435 (1985)	§ 7.41
Creely v. Leisure Living, Inc., 437 So. 2d 816 (La. 1983)	§ 12.28
Criswell v. M.J. Brock & Sons, 681 P.2d 495 (Colo. 1984)	§ 20.4
Cunningham v. Cunningham, 157 F.2d 859 (D.C. Cir. 1946)	§ 12.23
Cunningham Bros., Inc. v. City of Waterloo, 254 Iowa 659, 117 N.W.2d 46 (1962)	§§ 7.35, 16.13
Curley v. Cumberland Farms, 134 F.R.D. 77 (D.N.J. 1991)	§ 22.15
Cuthrell v. Milwaukee Mechanics Ins. Co., 234 N.C. 137, 66 S.E.2d 649 (1951)	§ 11.19
D.&A. Dev. Corp. v. Butler, 367 N.W.2d 156 (Minn. Ct. App. 1984)	§ 20.8
D.A. Hill Co. v. Clevetrust Realty Investors, 524 Pa. 425, 573 A.2d 1005 (1990)	§§ 9.19, 9.20
Dahlstrom Corp. v. State Highway Comm'n, 590 F.2d 614 (5th Cir. 1979)	§ 20.10
Dairy Farm Leasing Co. v. Hartley, 395 A.2d 1135 (Me. 1978)	§ 20.10
Dakota Block Co. v. Western Casualty & Sur. Co., 81 S.D. 213, 132 N.W.2d 826 (1965)	§ 11.8
Dale Benz, Inc., Contractors v. American Casualty Co., 303 F.2d 80 (9th Cir.), *reh'g denied,* 305 F.2d 641 (9th Cir. 1962)	§ 13.10
D'Angelo v. State, 41 A.D.2d 77, 341 N.Y.S.2d 84 (1973), *modified,* 46 A.D.2d 983, 355 N.Y.S.2d 377 (1974)	§ 16.42
Daniels v. Big Horn Fed. Sav. & Loan Ass'n, 604 P.2d 1046 (Wyo. 1980)	§ 9.21
Dann v. Perrotti & Hauptman Dev. Co., 670 P.2d 448 (Colo. Ct. App. 1983)	§ 20.7
Darner Motor Sales, Inc. v. Universal Underwriters Ins. Co., 140 Ariz. 383, 682 P.2d 388 (1984)	§ 12.37
Data Gen. Corp. v. United States, 915 F.2d 1544 (Fed. Cir. 1990)	§ 4.1

Case	*Book §*
Daugherty Co. v. Kimberly-Clark Corp., 14 Cal. App. 3d 151, 92 Cal. Rptr. 120 (1971)	§§ 5.2, 5.3
Davenport & Co. v. Spieker, 197 Cal. App. 3d 566, 242 Cal. Rptr. 911 (1988)	§ 5.4
Davidson v. Burns, 749 S.W.2d 446 (Mo. Ct. App. 1988)	§ 20.2
Davidson & Jones, Inc. v. County of New Hanover, 41 N.C. App. 661, 255 S.E.2d 580 (1979)	§§ 8.2, 8.8
Dawco Constr., Inc. v. United States, 18 Cl. Ct. 682 (1989), *aff'd,* 930 F.2d 872 (Fed. Cir. 1991)	§ 6.5
Deer Park Bank v. Aetna Ins. Co. v. Western Ga. Nat'l Bank, 387 F. Supp. 1090 (N.D. Ga, 1974)	§ 12.24
Degnan v. Executive Homes, Inc., 215 Mont. 162, 696 P.2d 431 (1985)	§ 20.7
Dehnert v. Arrow Sprinklers, Inc., 705 P.2d 846 (Wyo. 1985)	§ 7.18
DeKonty Corp., ASBCA No. 32140, 89-2 B.C.A. ¶ 21,586	§ 6.12
Delancey v. Insurance Co., 52 N.H. 581 (1873)	§ 11.2
Delaware Dredging Co. v. Tucker Stevedoring Co., 25 F.2d 44 (3d Cir. 1928)	§ 13.7
Delhomme Indus., Inc. v. Houston Beechcraft, Inc., 669 F.2d 1049 (5th Cir. 1982)	§ 20.12
Della Ratta, Inc. v. American Better Community Developers, Inc., 38 Md. App. 119, 380 A.2d 627 (1977)	§ 5.12
Del Mar Beach Club Owners Ass'n v. Imperial Contracting Co., 123 Cal. App. 3d 898, 176 Cal. Rptr. 886 (1981)	§ 8.4
Delp v. Commissioner, 30 T.C. 1230 (1958)	§ 21.8
Demharter v. First Fed. Sav. & Loan Ass'n, 194 A.2d 214 (Pa. 1963)	§ 9.9
Department of Transp. v. Arapaho Constr., Inc., 257 Ga. 269, 357 S.E.2d 593 (1987)	§ 7.32
Department of Transp. v. Moseman Constr. Co., 260 Ga. 369, 393 S.E.2d 258 (1990)	§ 2.18
Depot Constr. Corp. v. State, 19 N.Y.2d 109, 224 N.E.2d 866, 278 N.Y.S.2d 363 (1969)	§ 16.29
Detweiler Bros., Inc. v. John Graham Co., 412 F. Supp. 416 (E.D. Wash. 1976)	§§ 7.22, 8.2, 8.10
DeVito v. Commissioner, 39 T.C.M. 152 (1972)	§ 21.7
Dewberry v. Maddox, 755 S.W.2d 50 (Tenn. Ct. App. 1988)	§ 20.7
Dewey Jordan, Inc. v. Maryland-National Capitol Park & Planning Comm'n, 258 Md. 490, 265 A.2d 892 (1970)	§ 2.28
Dickerson Co. v. Iowa State Dep't of Transp., 300 N.W.2d 112 (Iowa 1981)	§ 7.33
Dickerson Constr. Co. v. Process Eng'g Co., 341 So. 2d 646 (Miss. 1977)	§ 8.6
Dillig v. Fisher, 142 Ariz. 47, 688 P.2d 693 (1984)	§ 20.7
Dillingham Shipyard, 84-1 B.C.A. (CCH) ¶ 16,984 (ASBCA 1983)	§ 6.5

Case	*Book §*
Dillon County Sch. Dist. No. 2 v. Lewis Sheet Metal Works, Inc., 286 S.C. 207, 332 S.E.2d 555 (Ct. App. 1985)	§ 20.4
Dillon Properties, Inc. v. Minmar Builders, Inc., 257 Md. 274, 262 A.2d 740 (1970)	§ 7.16
District Concrete Co. v. Bernstein Concrete Corp., 418 A.2d 1030 (D.C. 1980)	§ 5.13
District of Columbia v. Aetna Ins. Co., 462 A.2d 428 (D.C. 1983)	§ 12.31
Diverco, Inc. v. Cheney, 745 F. Supp. 739 (D.D.C. 1990)	§ 6.6
Division of Employment Sec. v. Trice Constr. Co., 555 S.W.2d 65 (Mo. Ct. App. 1977)	§ 12.31
Dixon v. Nelson, 79 S.D. 44, 107 N.W.2d 505 (1961)	§ 20.10
D.K. Meyer Corp. v. Bevco, Inc., 206 Neb. 318, 297 N.W. 2d 773 (1980)	§ 12.38
D&L Constr. Co. v. Triangle Elec. Supply Co., 332 F.2d 1009 (8th Cir. 1964)	§ 13.10
Dobson v. State, 218 N.J. Super. 123, 526 A.2d 1150 (1987)	§ 7.35
D-1 Constructors, Ltd. v. Unified Sch. Dist., 14 Kan. App. 2d 245, 788 P.2d 289 (1990)	§ 7.9
Donnelly Constr. Co. v. Oberg/Hunt/Gilleland, 139 Ariz. 579, 667 P.2d 1298 (1984)	§§ 7.16, 8.2
Donnybrook Bldg. Supply Co. v. Alaska Nat'l Bank, 736 P.2d 1147 (Alaska 1987)	§§ 9.2, 9.4
Dormitory Auth., *In re,* 218 N.Y.2d 114, 218 N.E.2d 693, 271 N.Y.S.2d 983 (1966)	§ 6.8
Dorthy L. Draper v. Airco, Inc., 580 F.2d 91 (3d Cir. 1979)	§ 12.34
Doud Lumber Co. v. Guaranty Sav. & Loan Ass'n, 254 Cal. App. 2d 585, 60 Cal. Rptr. 94 (1967)	§ 9.14
Dougherty v. Parsec, Inc., 872 F.2d 766 (6th Cir. 1989)	§ 12.27
Doundoulakis v. Town of Hempstead, 42 N.Y.2d 440, 368 N.E.2d 24, 398 N.Y.S.2d 401 (1977)	§ 8.4
Dour v. Village of Port Jefferson, 89 Misc. 2d 146, 390 N.Y.S.2d 965 (1941)	§ 6.14
Dow Chem. Co. v. Royal Indem. Co., 635 F.2d 379 (5th Cir. 1981)	§ 11.22
Downey v. United Weatherproofing, Inc., 363 Mo. 582, 253 S.W.2d 976 (1953)	§ 7.18
Downey Sav. & Loan Ass'n v. Ohio Casualty Co., 189 Cal. App. 3d 1072, 234 Cal. Rptr. 835 (1987), *cert. denied,* 486 U.S. 1036 (1988)	§ 12.27
Dravo Corp. v. United States, 594 F.2d 842 (Ct. Cl. 1979)	§ 16.41
Drennan v. Star Paving Co., 51 Cal. 2d 409, 333 P.2d 757 (1958)	§ 2.26
Drummond v. Hughes, 91 N.J.L. 563, 104 A. 137 (1918)	§ 20.2
Dubay v. Trans-America Ins. Co., 75 A.D.2d 312, 429 N.Y.S.2d 449 (1980)	§ 11.11
Dubin v. Dow Corning Corp., 478 So. 2d 71 (Fla. Dist. Ct. App. 1985)	§ 20.4

Case	*Book §*
Dubuque Fire & Marine Ins. Co. v. Caylor, 249 F.2d 162 (10th Cir. 1957)	§ 11.21
D.W. Grun Roofing & Constr. Co. v. Lope, 529 S.W.2d 258 (Tex. Civ. App. 1975)	§ 20.11
D.W. Segars v. Reaves, 567 So. 2d 249 (Ala. 1990)	§ 2.28
E.A. Coronis Assocs. v. M. Gordon Constr. Co., 90 N.J. Super. 69, 216 A.2d 246 (1966)	§ 2.26
Eagle-Picher Indus., Inc. v. Liberty Mut. Ins. Co., 682 F.2d 12 (1st Cir. 1982), *cert. denied sub nom.* Froude v. Eagle-Picher Indus., 460 U.S. 1028 (1983)	§ 11.6
Eagle's Nest. Ltd. Partnership v. Brunzell, 99 Nev. 710, 669 P.2d 714 (1983)	§ 5.7
Earthbank Co. v. City of N.Y., 78 N.Y.2d 855, 598 N.E.2d 443, 549 N.Y.S.2d 314 (1989)	§ 16.20
East Larimer County Water Dist. v. Centric Corp., 693 P.2d 1019 (Colo. Ct. App. 1984)	§§ 20.15, 20.16
East River S.S. Corp. v. Transamerica Delaval, 106 S. Ct. 2295 (1986)	§ 8.2
E.C. Ernst, Inc. v. Koppers Co., 626 F.2d 324 (3d Cir. 1980)	§§ 16.5, 16.35
E.C. Ernst, Inc. v. Manhattan Constr. Co., 551 F.2d 1026 (5th Cir.), *cert. denied,* 434 U.S. 1067 (1977)	§§ 17.33, 8.2, 8.9, 6.15, 16.21, 20.10
E.C. Ernst, Inc. v. City of Tallahassee, 527 F. Supp. 1141 (D. Fla. 1981)	§ 14.5
Ecko Enters., Inc. v. Remi Fortin Constr., Inc., 118 N.H. 37, 382 N.W.2d 773 (1980)	§ 12.38
Economy Lumber Co. v. Insurance Co. of N. Am., 157 Cal. App. 3d 641, 203 Cal. Rptr. 135 (1984)	§ 11.8
Ed Hackstaff Concrete, Inc. v. Power Ridge Condominium "A" Owners Ass'n, Inc., 679 P.2d 1112 (Colo. Ct. App. 1984)	§ 20.8
Ed Helms Elec. Contracting, Inc. v. Barnett Bank, 531 So. 2d 238 (Fla. Dist. Ct. App. 1988)	§§ 9.18, 9.20
Ed Sparks & Sons v. Joe Campbell Constr. Co., 99 Idaho 139, 578 P.2d 681 (1978)	§ 5.15
Edward Joy Co. v. Noise Control Prods., Inc., 111 Misc. 2d 64, 443 N.Y.S.2d 361 (1981)	§ 10.2
Edwin J. Dobson, Jr., Inc. v. Rutgers State Univ., 157 N.J. Super. 357, 384 A.2d 1121 (1978)	§§ 7.37, 20.9
Edwin J. Dobson, Jr., Inc. v. State. 218 N.J. Super. 123, 526 A.2d 1150 (App. Div. 1987)	§ 16.20
Eggers Partnership, 82-1 B.C.A. (CCH) ¶ 15,630 (IBCA 1982)	§ 8.6
E.G. Schafer Constr. Co. v. Gallagher Transfer & Storage Co., 495 So. 2d 348 (La. Ct. App. 1986)	§ 20.3
E.H. Leavell & Co. v. Glantz Contracting Corp., 322 F. Supp. 779 (E.D. La. 1971)	§ 12.33
E.H. Morrill Co. v. State, 65 Cal. 2d 787, 423 P.2d 551, 56 Cal. Rptr. 479 (1967)	§§ 5.5, 5.18

Case	*Book §*
Eichleay Corp., ASBCA No. 5183, 60-2 B.C.A. (CCH) ¶ 2688 (1960)	§§ 5.13, 16.40, 18.23
Eichler Homes, Inc. v. Underwriters at Lloyd's, London, 245 Cal. App. 2d 532, 47 Cal. Rptr. 843 (1965)	§ 11.14
Eisler v. Commissioner, 59 T.C. 634 (1973), *acq.*, 1983-2 C.B. 1	§ 21.7
Ekco Enters., Inc. v. Remi Fortin Constr., Inc., 118 N.H. 37, 382 A.2d 368 (1978)	§ 12.38
Elcar Mobil Home, Inc. v. D.K. Baxter, Inc., 66 N.J. Super. 478, 169 A.2d 509 (1961)	§ 11.11
Electronic Data Sys. Fed. Corp. v. General Servs. Admin. Bd. of Contract Appeals, 792 F.2d 1569 (Fed. Cir. 1986)	§ 4.16
Eliel v. United States, 18 Cl. Ct. 461 (1989)	§ 6.12
Ell-Dorer Contracting Co. v. State, 197 N.J. Super. 175, 484 A,2d 356 (App. Div. 1984)	§§ 5.5, 5.17
Ellis Millwork, Inc. v. Frees, Inc., 493 So. 2d 696 (La. Ct. App. 1986)	§§ 20.2, 20.11
Ely v. Bottini, 179 Cal. App. 2d 287, 3 Cal. Rptr. 756 (1960)	§ 5.12
Embree Constr. Group v. Rafcor, Inc. 97 N.C. App. 418, 388 S.E.2d 604 (1990)	§§ 9.20, 9.23
Emond v. Tyler Bldg. & Constr. Co., 438 So. 2d 681 (La. Ct. App. 1983)	§ 12.33
Empire Constr. Co., ASBCA No. 27540, 84-3 B.C.A. (CCH) ¶ 17,531 (1984)	§ 5.5
Employers Casualty Co. v. Holm, 393 S.W.2d 363 (Tex. Ct. App. 1965)	§ 11.22
Employers Ins. v. Cajun Contractors & Eng'rs, Inc., 459 So. 2d 610 (La. Ct. App. 1984)	§ 12.34
Ench Equip. Corp. v. N.K. Foods, Inc., 43 N.J. Super. 500, 129 A.2d 313 (App. Div. 1957)	§ 20.13
Endres Plumbing Corp. v. State, 198 Misc. 546, 95 N.Y.S. 574 (1950)	§ 7.33
Engineered Prods., Inc. v. Aetna Casualty & Sur. Co., 295 S.C. 375, 368 S.E.2d 674 (1988)	§ 11.10
Episcopal Hous. Corp. v. Federal Ins. Co., 273 S.C. 181, 255 S.E.2d 451 (1979)	§ 10.11
Equitable Casualty & Sur. Co. v. Helena Wholesale Grocery Co., 60 F.2d 380 (8th Cir. 1932)	§ 13.7
Equitable Fire & Marine Ins. Co. v. Allied Steel Constr. Co., 421 F.2d 512 (10th Cir, 1970)	§ 11.22
Eric A. Carlstrom Constr. Co. v. Independent Sch. Dist. No. 77, 256 N.W.2d 479 (Minn. 1977)	§§ 2.13, 2.28
Erwin v. United States, 19 Cl. Ct. 47 (1989)	§ 6.5
Essex House v. St. Paul Fire & Marine Ins. Co., 404 F. Supp. 978 (S.D. Ohio 1975)	§§ 11.18, 11.22
Estrin Constr. Co. v. Aetna Casualty & Sur. Co., 612 S.W.2d 413 (Mo. Ct. App. 1981)	§ 11.11

Case	*Book §*
Evans v. Howard R. Green Co., 231 N.W.2d 907 (Iowa 1975)	§ 8.5
Executive Aviation, Inc. v. National Ins. Underwriters, 16 Cal. App. 3d 789, 94 Cal. Rptr. 347 (1971)	§§ 11.1, 11.23
F.A. Gray, Inc. v. Weiss, 519 A.2d 716 (Me. 1986)	§ 20.2
Fairbanks N. Star Borough v. Rosen Design Assocs., 727 P.2d 758 (Alaska 1986)	§ 8.3
Farm Bureau Town & Country Ins. Co., v. Tumbo, 740 S.W.2d 232 (Mo. Ct. App. 1987)	§ 11.5
Fattore Co. v. Metropolitan Sewerage Comm'n Co., 505 F.2d 1 (7th Cir. 1974)	§§ 16.29, 16.36
F.D. Rich Co. v. United States *ex rel.* Industrial Lumber Co., 417 U.S. 116 (1974)	§§ 13.1, 13.6, 13.10
F.D. Rich Co. v. Wilmington Hous. Auth., 392 F.2d 841 (3d Cir. 1968)	§ 7.33
Federal Crop Ins. Corp. v. Merrill, 332 U.S. 389 (1947)	§ 6.12
Federal Ins. Co. v. Community State Bank, 905 S.2d (5th Cir. 1990)	§ 12.27
Federal Ins. Co. v. P.A.T. Homes, Inc., 113 Ariz. 135, 547 P.2d 1050 (1976), *overruled in part by* State Farm Mut. Ins. Co. v. Wilson, 162 Ariz. 251, 782 P.2d 727 (1989)	§ 11.10
Federal Mongul Corp. v. Universal Constr. Co., 376 So. 2d 716 (Ala. Civ. App. 1979)	§ 8.4
Federated Mut. Ins. Co. v. Concrete Units, 363 N.W.2d 751 (Minn. 1985)	§§ 11.8, 11.13
Fehlhaber Corp. v. State, 69 A.D.2d 362, 419 N.Y.S.2d 773 (1979)	§ 16.40
Ferrell Constr. Co. v. Russell Creek Coal Co., 645 P.2d 1005 (Okla. 1982)	§ 16.43
F.H. McGraw & Co. v. United States, 130 F. Supp. 394 (Ct. Cl. 1955)	§ 16.36
Fidelity & Casualty Co. v. Central Bank, 409 So. 2d 788 (Ala. 1982)	§ 12.31
Fidelity & Casualty Co. v. J.A. Jones Constr. Co., 200 F. Supp. 264 (D. Ark. 1961), *aff'd,* 325 F.2d 605 (8th Cir. 1963)	§ 20.7
Fidelity & Deposit Co. v. Parsons & Whittemore Contracting Corp. 48 N.Y.2d 127, 397 N.E.2d 380, 421 N.Y.S.2d 869 (1979)	§ 13.17
Fidelity & Deposit Co. v. Steel, 607 S.W.2d 17 (Tex. Civ. App. 1980)	§ 20.11
Fidelity Dep't Stores v. Moite, 452 U.S. 392 (1981)	§ 12.27
Filbert v. Philadelphia, 181 Pa. 530, 37 A. 545 (1897)	§ 20.2
Fileck v. Utica Bldg. Co., 131 Mich. App. 396, 345 N.W.2d 707 (1984)	§ 20.4
Filer v. Shapiro, 633 F.2d 139 (2d Cir. 1980)	§ 12.27
Finance Co. of Am. v. United States Fid. & Guar. Co., 277 Md. 177, 353 A.2d 249 (1976)	§ 12.31

Case	*Book §*
Financial Indem. Co. v. Steele & Sons, Inc., 403 So. 2d 600 (Fla. Dist. Ct. App. 1981)	§ 12.33
Financial Sec. Litig., *In re,* 609 F.2d 411 (9th Cir. 1979), *cert. denied sub nom.* Grant v. Union Bank, 446 U.S. 929 (1980)	§ 22.13
Findlen v. Winchendon Hous. Auth., 28 Mass. App. Ct. 977, 553 N.E.2d 554 (1990)	§§ 2.23, 2.28
Fireguard Sprinkler Sys., Inc. v. Scottsdale Ins. Co., 864 F.2d 648 (9th Cir. 1988)	§ 11.14
Fireman's Fund Ins. Co. v. Aetna Casualty & Sur. Co., 223 Cal. App. 3d 1621, 273 Cal. Rptr. 431 (1990)	§ 11.6
Fireman's Fund Ins. Co. v. Fiberboard Corp., 182 Cal. App. 3d 462, 227 Cal. Rptr. 203 (1986)	§ 11.2
Fireman's Fund Ins. Co. v. Millers' Mut. Ins. Ass'n, 451 F.2d 1140 (10th Cir. 1971)	§ 11.19
Fireman's Fund Ins. Co. v. Turlock, 170 Cal. App. 3d 988, 216 Cal. Rptr. 796 (1985)	§ 11.10
First Atl. Bldg. Corp. v. Neubauser Constr. Co., 352 So. 2d 103 (Fla. Dist. Ct. App. 1977)	§ 5.12
First Fed. Sav. Bank v. Fretthold, 195 Ga. App. 482, 394 S.E.2d 128 (1990)	§ 9.21
First Fed. State Bank v. Town of Malvern, 270 N.W.2d 818 (Iowa 1978)	§ 12.31
First Nat'l Bank v. William F. Cann, 503 F. Supp. 419 (W.D. Ohio 1980)	§ 7.22
First Nat'l State Bank v. Carlyle House, Inc., 102 N.J. Super. 300, 246 A.2d 22 (1968), *aff'd,* 107 N.J. Super. 359, 258 A.2d 545 (1969)	§§ 9.9, 9.15, 9.21
Fisher v. Fidelity & Deposit Co., 145 Ill. App. 3d 362, 466 N.E.2d 332 (1984)	§ 12.27
Fisher & Carozza Bros. Co. v. Mackall, 138 Md. 586, 114 A. 580 (1921)	§ 6.11
525 Main St. Corp. v. Eagle Roofing Co., 34 N.J. 251, 168 A.2d 33 (1961)	§ 20.8
Fleisher Eng'g & Constr. Co. v. United States *ex rel.* Hallenbeck, 311 U.S. 15 (1940)	§ 13.11
Flintridge Station Assoc. v. American Fletcher Mortgage Co., 761 F.2d 434 (7th Cir. 1985)	§ 12.27
Floor Craft Floor Covering, Inc. v. Parma Community Gen. Hosp., 54 Ohio St. 3d 1, 560 N.E.3d 206 (1990)	§ 7.41
Florida *ex rel.* Consolidated Pipe & Supply Co. v. Houdaille Indus., 372 So. 2d 1177 (Fla. Dist. Ct. App. 1979)	§ 12.37
Florida Power & Light Co. v. Westinghouse Elec. Corp., 826 F.2d 239 (4th Cir. 1987)	§ 20.5
Flowers v. Diamond Shamrock Corp., 693 F.2d 1146 (5th Cir. 1982)	§ 20.12
Foeller v. Heintz, 137 Wis. 169, 118 N.W. 543 (1908)	§ 20.11
Forman v. Jordan, 131 So. 2d 796 (La. Ct. App. 1961)	§ 11.5
Forte Bros., Inc, v. National Amusements, Inc., 525 A.2d 1301 (R.I. 1987)	§ 8.2

Case	*Book §*
Fortier v. Sessum, 441 So. 2d 1238 (La. Ct. App. 1984)	§ 20.8
Foster Constr. C.A. v. United States, 435 F.2d 873 (Ct. Cl. 1970)	§ 5.5
Fostic v. United Home Improvement Co., 428 N.E.2d 1351 (Ind. Ct. App. 1981)	§ 16.43
Fountainebleau Hotel Corp. v. United Filigree Corp., 298 So. 2d 455 (Fla. Dist. Ct. App. 1974)	§ 11.10
Framington Plumbing & Heating Co. v. Fischer Sand & Aggregate, Inc., 281 N.W.2d 838 (Minn. 1980)	§ 12.34
Framlau Corp. v. United States, 568 F.2d 687 (Ct. Cl. 1977)	§ 16.41
Frank Briscoe Co. v. Georgia Sprinkler Co., 713 F.2d 1500 (11th Cir. 1983)	§ 11.25
Frank Corrente v. Conforti & Eisele Co., 468 A.2d 920 (R.I. 1984)	§ 12.34
Franklin Contracting Co. v. State, 144 N.J. Super. 402, 365 A.2d 952 (1976)	§ 7.32
Frank T. Hickey, Inc. v. Los Angeles Jewish Community Council, 128 Cal. App. 2d 676, 276 P.2d 52 (1954)	§ 20.5
Frederick v. Electro-Coal Transfer Corp., 548 F. Supp. 83 (E.D. La. 1982)	§ 12.37
Freidman v. Edward L. Bakewell, Inc., 654 S.W.2d 367 (Mo. Ct. App. 1983)	§ 12.27
Fresand v. Michigan Mut. Ins. Co., 414 Mich. 686, 327 N.W.2d 286, *aff'd but overruling as to this issue,* 97 Mich. App. 584, 296 N.W.2d 112 (1982)	§ 11.10
Fresno Economy Import Used Cars, Inc. v. USF&G, 76 Cal. App. 3d 272, 142 Cal. Rptr. 681 (1977)	§ 11.14
Fretz Constr. Co. v. Southern Nat'l Bank, 626 S.W.2d 478 (Tex. 1982)	§§ 9.11, 9.14
Frickil v. Sunnyside Enters., Inc., 106 Wash. 2d 714, 725 P.2d 422 (1986)	§ 20.7
Friedman v. Hampden County, 204 Mass. 494, 90 N.E. 851 (1910)	§ 12.1
Friestad v. Travelers Indem. Co., 260 Pa. Super. 178, 393 A.2d 1212 (1978)	§ 11.17
Frischhertz Elec. Co. v. Housing Auth., 534 So. 2d 1310 (La. Ct, App. 1988)	§ 2.19
Fritz-Rumer Cooke Co. v. United States, 279 F.2d 200 (6th Cir. 1960)	§ 16.25
F.&S. Constr. Co. v. Berube, 322 F.2d 782 (10th Cir. 1963)	§ 20.7
Fuchs v. Parsons Constr. Co., 172 Neb. 719, 111 N.W.2d 727 (1961)	§ 20.2
Gadbois v. Leb-Co Builders, Inc., 312 Pa. Super. 144, 458 A.2d 555 (1983)	§§ 20.7, 20.8
Garcia v. Truck Ins. Exch., 36 Cal. 3d 426, 682 P.2d 1100, 204 Cal. Rptr. 435 (1984)	§ 11.2
Garco Indus. Equip. Co. v. Mallory, 485 N.E.2d 652 (Ind. Ct. App. 1985)	§ 13.7

Case	*Book §*
Garden Manor Condominium Assoc., Inc. v. James D. Marks Assocs., Inc., 576 So. 2d 744 (Fla. Dist. Ct. App. 1991)	§ 8.2
Gardner Displays Co. v. United States, 346 F.2d 585 (Ct. Cl. 1965)	§ 16.42
Garvey v. State Farm & Casualty Co., 48 Cal. 3d 395, 770 P.2d 704, 257 Cal. Rptr. 292 (1989)	§ 11.22
Gary L. Shaw Builders, Inc. v. State Auto. Mut. Ins. Co., 229 Mont. 34, 744 P.2d 892 (1987)	§§ 11.10, 11.13
Gateway Co. v. Charlotte Theatres, Inc., 297 F.2d 483 (1st Cir. 1961)	§ 10.2
Gateway Erectors v. Lutheran Gen. Hosp., 102 Ill. App. 3d 300, 430 N.E.2d 20 (1981)	§§ 7.16, 7.17, 7.23, 7.28
Gavlik Constr. Co. v. H.F. Campbell Co., 526 F.2d 777 (3d Cir. 1975)	§ 10.11
G.C. Servs. Corp. v. Commissioner, 73 T.C. 406 (1979)	§ 21.7
Gebco Inv. Corp., *In re,* 641 F.2d 143 (3d Cir. 1981)	§§ 9.8, 9.9
Geddes & Smith, Inc. v. St. Paul-Mercury Indem. Co., 51 Cal. 2d 558, 344 P.2d 881 (1959)	§§ 11.8, 11.14
Gee v. Eberle, 279 Pa. Super. 101, 420 A.2d 1050 (1980)	§§ 9.8, 9.14, 9.16, 9.18, 9.19, 9.20
General Am. Transp. Corp. v. Sun Ins. Office Ltd., 369 F.2d 906 (6th Cir. 1966)	§§ 11.20, 11.22
General Bldg. Contractors v. County of Onieda, 54 Misc. 2d 260, 282 N.Y.S.2d 385 (1967)	§ 7.12
General Contracting Co. v. United States, 287 F.2d 411 (Ct. Cl. 1961)	§ 5.2
General Fed. Constr., Inc. v. D.R. Thomas, Inc., 52 Md. App. 700, A.2d 1250 (1982)	§ 13.9
General Ins. Co. v. Commerce Hyatt House, 5 Cal. App. 3d 460, 85 Cal. Rptr. 317 (1970)	§ 5.4
General Ins. Co. v. Hercules Constr. Co., 385 F.2d 13 (8th Cir. 1967)	§§ 5.13, 16.34
General Ins. Co. of Am. v. Commerce Hyatt House, 5 Cal. App. 3d 460, 85 Cal. Rptr. 317 (1970)	§ 20.10
General Ins. Co. of Am. v. Mammoth Vista Owners Ass'n, Inc., 174 Cal. App. 3d 810, 220 Cal. Rptr. 291 (1985)	§ 12.27
General Ins. Co. of Am. v United States *ex rel.* Audrey Moore & Son, 406 F.2d 442 (5th Cir.), *on reh'g,* 409 F.2d 1326 (5th Cir.), *cert. denied,* 396 U.S, 902 (1969)	§ 13.14
General Mut. Ins. Co. v. Wright, 7 Misc. 2d 331, 161 N.Y.S.2d 974 (Sup. Ct. 1957)	§ 11.11
General Tel. Co., *In re,* 57 Comp. Gen. 89 (1977)	§ 6.10
General Trading Corp. v. Burnup & Sims, Inc., 523 F.2d 98 (3d Cir. 1975)	§ 12.33
George v. Veach, 67 N.C. App. 674, 313 S.E.2d 920 (1984)	§ 20.7

Case	*Book §*
George A. Fuller Co. v. United States, 104 Ct. Cl. 176 (1945)	§ 5.4
George A. Fuller Co. v. United States, 69 F. Supp. 409 (Ct. Cl. 1947)	§§ 16.3, 20.9
Geremia v. Boyarsky, 107 Conn. 387, 140 A. 749 (1928)	§ 4.31
GF Business Equip., Inc. v. Tennessee Valley Auth., 430 F. Supp. 699 (E.D. Tenn. 1975), *aff'd mem.,* 556 F.2d 581 (6th Cir. 1977)	§ 6.6
Gherardi v. Board of Educ., 53 N.J. Super. 349, 147 A.2d 535 (1958)	§ 7.35
Giammetta Assocs., Inc. v. J.J. White, Inc., 573 F. Supp. 112 (E.D. Pa. 1983)	§ 5.8
Gillioz v. State Highway Comm'n, 348 Mo. 211, 153 S.W.2d 18 (141)	§ 20.10
Gilmore v. Century Bank & Trust Co., 20 Mass. App. 49, 477 N.E.2d 1069 (1985)	§§ 9.7, 9.9
Givoh Assocs. v. American Druggist Ins. Co., 562 F. Supp. 1346 (E.D.N.Y. 1983)	§ 12.33
Glades County v. Detroit Fid. & Sur. Co., 57 F.2d 449 (5th Cir. 1932)	§ 12.30
Glassell-Taylor Co. v. Magnolia Petroleum Co., 153 F.2d 527 (5th Cir. 1946)	§ 13.7
Glassman Constr. Co. v. Maryland City Plaza, Inc., 371 F. Supp. 1154 (D. Md. 1974), *aff'd,* 530 F.2d 968 (4th Cir. 1975)	§§ 16.3, 20.9
G.L. Christian & Assocs. v. United States, 312 F.2d 418 (Ct. Cl.), *cert. denied,* 375 U.S. 954 (1963)	§ 12.4
Glen Falls Ins. Co. v. Fields, 181 So. 2d 187 (Fla. Dist. Ct. App. 1965)	§ 11.11
Glen Falls Ins. Co. v. Globe Indem. Co., 214 La. 467, 38 So. 2d 139 (1948)	§ 11.25
Globe Eng'g Corp., ASBCA No. 28832, 85-B.N.A. (CCH) ¶ 18,436 (1985)	§ 20.10
Goesseling v. Better Homes, Inc., 256 A.2d 629 (Me. 1969)	§ 20.7
Goldberry Operating Co. v. Cassity, Inc., 367 So. 2d 133 (La. Ct. App. 1979)	§ 11.11
Golomore Assocs. v. New Jersey State Highway Auth., 173 N.J. Super. 55, 413 A.2d 361 (1980)	§ 5.5
Gon v. First State Ins. Co., 871 F.2d 863 (9th Cir. 1989)	§ 11.1
Gonzales Custom Painting, Inc., ASBCA Nos. 39527, 90-3 B.C.A. ¶ 22,950	§ 6.12
Gorrell v. Fowler, 248 Ga. 801, 286 S.E.2d 13 (1982)	§ 7.7
Governor v. Madrazo, 26 U.S. (1 Pet.) 110 (1828)	§ 12.31
Gradco, Inc. v. St. Clair County Bd. of Educ., 477 So. 2d 365 (Ala. 1985)	§ 20.14
Granite Constr. Co., IBCA No. 1-1442-3-81, 82-2 B.C.A. (CCH) ¶ 15,975	§ 7.30
Grant Constr. Co. v. Burns, 92 Idaho 408, 443 P.2d 1005 (1968)	§ 16.16

Case	*Book §*
Gravely v. Providence Partners, 549 F.2d 958 (4th Cir. 1977)	§ 7.6
Graves Constr. Co. v. Rockingham Nat'l Bank, 220 Va. 844, 263 S.E.2d 408 (1980)	§ 12.31
Gray v. Zurich Ins. Co., 65 Cal. 2d 263, 419 P.2d 168, 54 Cal. Rptr. 104 (1986)	§§ 11.1, 11.4
Great Am. Ins. Co. v. United States, 492 F.2d 821 (Ct. Cl. 1974)	§ 12.31
Great Lakes Constr. Co. v. Republic Creosoting Co., 139 F.2d 456 (8th Cir. 1943)	§ 2.13
Great W. Sav. Bank v. George W. Easley Co., 778 P.2d 569 (Alaska 1989)	§§ 9.2, 9.14, 9.15, 9.16
Green Constr. Co. v. Kansas Power & Light Co., 717 F. Supp. 738 (D. Kan. 1989)	§ 2.23
Green Constr. Co. v. William Form Eng'g Corp., 506 F. Supp. 173 (W.D. Mich. 1980)	§ 7.6
Greenville Indep. Sch. Dist. v. B.&J. Excavating, Inc., 694 S.W.2d 410 (Tex. Civ. App. 1989)	§ 13.18
Grenier v. Compratt Constr. Co., 189 Conn. 144, 454 A.2d 1289 (1983)	§§ 20.6, 20.10
Gribaldo, Jacobs, Jones & Assocs. v. Agrippina Vesicherunges, A.G., 3 Cal. 3d 434, 476 P.2d 406, 91 Cal. Rptr. 6 (1970)	§ 11.1
Gricoski Detective Agency, GSBCA Nos. 8901, 8922, 8923, 8924, 8925, 8926, 90-3 B.C.A. (CCH) ¶ 23,131	§§ 6.12, 6.13
Grimm v. F.D. Borkholder, Inc., 454 N.E.2d 84 (Ind. Ct. App. 1983)	§ 20.3
Griners & Shaw, Inc. v. Federal Ins. Co., 234 F. Supp. 753 (D.S.C. 1964)	§ 13.16
Groh v. Broadland Builders, Inc., 120 Mich. App. 214, 327 N.W.2d 443 (1983)	§ 20.16
Groover v. Magnavox, 71 F.R.D. 638 (D. Pa. 1976)	§ 20.7
Gruman Ecosys. Corp. v. Gainesville-Alachua, 402 F. Supp. 582 (N.D. Fla. 1975)	§ 4.21
Guarantee Elec. Co. v. Big River Elec. Corp., 669 F. Supp. 1371 (W.D. Ky. 1987)	§§ 7.2, 7.11, 7.17, 7.27
Guardian Constr. Co. v. Tetra Tech Richardson, Inc., 583 A.2d 1378 (Del. Super. Ct. 1990)	§ 8.2
Gulf Contracting v. Bibb County, 795 F.2d 980 (11th Cir. 1986)	§§ 7.41, 8.8
Gulf M.&.O. Ry. v. Illinois Cent. R.R., 128 F. Supp. 311 (N.D. Ala. 1954), *aff'd,* 225 F.2d 816 (5th Cir. 1955)	§ 2.19
Gunderson v. Commissioner, 38 T.C.M. (CCH) 464 (1979)	§ 21.17
Gundersons, Inc. v. Tull, 678 P.2d 1061 (Colo. Ct. App. 1984), *modified on other grounds,* 709 P.2d 940 (Colo. 1985)	§ 5.12
Gupta v. Ritter Homes, Inc., 646 S.W.2d 168 (Tex. Ct. App. 1983)	§ 20.7
Gurtler, Hebert & Co. v. Weyland Mach. Shop, Inc., 450 So. 2d 660 (La. Ct. App. 1981)	§§ 8.2, 8.11, 12.33

Case	*Book §*
Gustav Hirsh Org., Inc. v. East Ky. Rival Elec. Co-op Corp., 210 F. Supp. 809 (D. Ky. 1962)	§ 20.10
Gus T. Hange & Son Painting Co. v. Tri-State Constr. Co., 662 S.W.2d 928 (Mo. Ct. App. 1984)	§ 20.3
Guy James Constr. Co. v. Trinity Indus., Inc., 644 F.2d 525 (5th Cir. 1981)	§ 5.13
G-W-L, Inc. v. Robichaux, 643 S.W.2d 392 (Tex. 1982)	§ 20.7
Hackley v. Waldorf-Hoerner Paper Prods. Co., 149 Mont. 286, 425 P.2d 712 (1967)	§ 8.5
Hadley v. Baxendale, 9 Ex. Ch. 341, 156 Eng. Rep. 145 (1854)	§§ 5.12, 16.35
Haerens v. Commercial Casualty Ins. Co., 30 Cal. App. 2d 892, 279 P.2d 211 (1955)	§ 11.11
Hainnes-LaBar Ins. v. Julien Constr. Co., 743 P.2d 1262 (Wyo. 1987)	§ 13.18
Hallmark Ins. Co. v. Superior Court, 201 Cal. App. 3d 1041, 247 Cal. Rptr. 638 (1988)	§§ 11.2, 11.6
Hallmark of Farmington, Inc. v. Roy, 1 Conn. App. 278, 471 A.2d 651 (1984)	§ 20.8
Hammaker v. Schleigh, 157 Md. 652, 147 A. 790 (1929)	§ 20.10
Hans v. Louisiana, 134 U.S. 1 (1890)	§ 12.31
Harbor Ins. Co. v. City of Ontario, 231 Cal. App. 3d 927, 282 Cal. Rptr. 701 (1991)	§ 11.1
Harrington v. Oliver, 459 So. 2d 111 (La. Ct. App.), *cert. denied,* 462 So. 2d 198 (La. 1984)	§ 12.28
Harry Harris, Inc. v. Quality Constr. Co., 593 S.W.2d 872 (Ky. Ct. App. 1979)	§ 10.2
Hartford Accident & Indem., Co. v. Boise Cascade Corp., 489 F. Supp. 855 (N.D. Ill. 1980)	§ 12.31
Hartford Accident & Indem. Co. v. Millis Roofing & Sheet Metal, Inc., 11 Mass. App. Ct. 998, 418 N.E.2d 645 (1981)	§ 12.27
Hartford Accident & Indem. Co. v. Pacific Mut. Life Ins. Co., 861 F.2d 250 (10th Cir. 1988)	§ 11.8
Hartford Accident & Indem. Co. v. Shelby Mut. Ins. Co., 208 So. 2d 465 (Fla. Dist. Ct. App. 1968)	§ 11.11
Harvey's Wagon Wheel, Inc. v. MacSween, 96 Nev. 215, 606 P.2d 1095 (1980)	§ 11.25
Hauenstein v. Saint Paul-Mercury Indem. Co., 242 Minn. 354, 65 N.W.2d 122 (1954)	§ 11.8
Haugan v. Home Indem. Co., 86 S.D. 406, 197 N.W.2d 18 (1972)	§ 11.10
Havens Steel Co. v. Randolph Eng'g Co., 813 F.2d 186 (8th Cir. 1987)	§ 16.41
Hawthorne v. Kober Constr. Co., 196 Mont. 519, 640 P.2d 467 (1982)	§ 7.6
Hayes Int'l Corp. v. McLucas, 509 F.2d 247 (5th Cir.), *cert. denied,* 423 U.S. 864 (1975)	§ 6.6
Helfeldt v. Robinson, 20 S.E.2d 896 (W. Va. 1981)	§ 11.10

Case	*Book §*
Hendrix v. New Amsterdam Casualty, 390 F.2d 299 (10th Cir. 1968)	§ 11.19
Hendrix Elec. Co. v. Casualty Reciprocal Exch., 297 So. 2d 470 (La. Ct. App. 1974)	§ 11.11
Henggler v. Gindra, 191 Neb. 317, 214 N.W.2d 925 (1974)	§ 20.7
Henningsen v. United States Fidelity & Guar. Co., 208 U.S. 404 (1908)	§ 12.31
Hensler v. City of Los Angeles, 124 Cal. App. 2d 71, 268 P.2d 12 (1954)	§ 5.2
Herbison v. Employers Ins. Co., 593 S.W.2d 923 (Tenn. Ct. App. 1979)	§ 11.11
Herman v. Bananza Bldgs., Inc., 233 Neb. 474, 390 N.W.2d 536 (1986)	§ 20.7
Herman H. Neumann, 70-1 B.C.A. (CCH) ¶ 8216 (1970)	§ 16.24
H.E. Wiese, Inc. v. Western Stress, Inc., 407 So. 2d 464 (La. Ct. App. 1981)	§ 11.11
Higgins v. City of Fillmore, 639 P.2d 192 (Utah 1981)	§§ 2.28, 5.13
Highland Constr. Co. v. Union Pac. R.R., 683 P.2d 1042 (Utah 1984)	§ 5.13
Hill v. Polar Pantries, 219 S.C 263, 64 S.E.2d 885 (1951)	§ 7.6
Hilti v. Oldach, 392 F.2d 368 (1st Cir. 1968)	§ 20.13
Himmel Corp. v. Stade, 52 Ill. App. 3d 294, 367 N.E.2d 411 (1977)	§ 7.13
Hionis v. Northern Mut. Ins. Co., 230 Pa. Super. 511, 327 A.2d 363 (1974)	§ 11.2
H.O. Bragg Roofing, Inc. v. First Fed. Sav. & Loan Ass'n, 226 Cal. App. 2d 24, 37 Cal. Rptr. 775 (1964)	§§ 9.14, 9.15
Hodgins v. Marquette Iron Mining Co., 503 F. Supp. 88 (W.D. Mich. 1980)	§ 5.17
Hodgson v. Chin, 168 N.J. Super. 549, 403 A.2d 942 (App. Div. 1979)	§ 20.7
Hogan v. Postin, 695 P.2d 1042 (Wyo. 1985)	§ 8.2
Holman v. Sorenson, 556 P.2d 499 (Utah 1976)	§ 5.12
Home Elec. Co. v. Hall & Underdown Heating & Air Conditioning Co., 86 N.C. App. 540, 358 S.E.2d 539 (1987)	§ 2.26
Home Indem. Co. v. Avol, 706 F. Supp. 728 (C.D. Cal. 1989), *aff'd,* 912 f.2d 469 (9th Cir. 1990)	§ 11.10
Home Indem. Co. v. Leo Davis, Inc., 79 Cal. App. 3d 863, 145 Cal. Rptr. 158 (1978)	§ 11.11
Home Indem. Co. v. United States, 313 F. Supp. 212 (W.D. Mo. 1970)	§ 12.31
Home Ins. Co. v. Landmark Ins. Co., 205 Cal. App. 3d 1388, 253 Cal. Rptr. 277 (1988)	§ 11.6
Home Mut. Fire Ins. Co. v. Hosfelt, 233 F. Supp. 360 (D. Conn. 1962)	§ 11.6
Honeycomb Sys., Inc. v. Admiral Ins. Co., 567 F. Supp. 1400 (D. Me. 1983)	§ 11.13
Hooks v. Southeast Constr. Corp., 538 F.2d 431 (D.C. Cir. Cir. 1976)	§§ 10.2, 10.10

Case	*Book §*
Hoover Groups, Inc. v. Probala & Assocs., 710 F. Supp. 677 (N.D. Ohio 1989)	§ 2.34
Hortman v. Cantrell, 173 Ga. App. 429, 326 S.E.2d 770 (1985)	§ 20.8
Houma, City of v. C-Well Ltd., 515 So. 2d 646 (La. Ct. App. 1987)	§ 20.10
Housing Auth. v. Hubbell, 325 S.W.2d 880 (Tex. Ct. App. 1959)	§ 7.34
Houston, City of v. R.F. Ball Constr. Co., 570 S.W.2d 75 (Tex. Ct. App. 1978)	§ 7.32
Houston Fire & Casualty Ins. Co. v. Riesel Indep. Sch. Dist., 375 S.W.2d 323 (Tex. Civ. App. 1964)	§ 10.8
Howard Dodge & Sons, Inc. v. Finn, 391 N.E.2d 638 (Ind. Ct. App. 1979)	§§ 12.31, 20.7
Howard S. Wright Constr. Co. v. F.E. DeBeer Mechanical Constr. Co., 185 Mont. 47, 604 P.2d 323 (1979)	§ 10.10
Howell v. State Farm Fire & Casualty Co., 218 Cal. App. 3d 1446, 267 Cal. Rptr. 708 (1990)	§ 11.22
Hudik-Ross, Inc. v. 1530 Palisade Ave. Corp., 131 N.J. Super. 159, 329 A.2d 70 (1974)	§ 14.5
Hughes Masonry v. Greater Clark County Sch. Bldg. Corp., 659 F.2d 836 (7th Cir. 1981)	§§ 7.29, 7.38
Hungerford Constr. Co. v. Florida Citrus Exposition, Inc., 410 F.2d 1229 (5th Cir.), *cert. denied,* 396 U.S. 928 (1969)	§ 20.10
Hurst v. Town of Shelburn, 422 N.E.2d 322 (Ind. Ct. App. 1981)	§ 12.27
Hutchens v. McClure, 176 Kan. 43, 296 P.2d 473 (1954)	§ 11.5
Hyman v. Cohen, 73 So. 2d 393 (Fla. 1954)	§ 12.34
Ibex Indus., Inc. v. Coastline Waterproofing, 563 F. Supp. 1142 (D.D.C. 1983)	§§ 13.7, 13.10
Illinois Sur. Co. v. John Davis Co., 244 U.S. 276 (1917)	§ 13.7
Illinois Valley Asphalt, Inc. v. J.F. Edwards Constr. Co., 90 Ill. App. 3d 768, 413 N.E.2d 209	§ 10.2
INA v. Forty-Eight Insulations, 145 Cal. App. 3d 462, 193 Cal. Rptr. 461 (1983)	§ 11.6
INA v. Forty-Eight Insulations, 633 F.2d 1212 (6th Cir.), *reh'g granted in part & denied in part,* 657 F.2d 814 (6th Cir. 1980), *cert. denied,* 454 U.S. 1109 (1981)	§ 11.6
INA v. Northhampton Nat'l Bank, 708 F.2d 13 (1st Cir. 1983)	§ 12.31
INA v. Sam Harris Constr. Co., 22 Cal. 3d 409, 583 P.2d 1335, 149 Cal. Rptr. 292 (1978)	§ 11.6
Independent Oil v. Commissioner, 4 T.C.M. 36 (1945)	§ 21.7
Indiana v. Omega Painting, Inc. 463 N.E.2d 287 (Ind. Ct. App. 1984)	§§ 5.4, 16.10
Indiana Ins. Co. v. DeZutti, 408 N.E.2d 1275 (Ind. 1980)	§ 11.10

Case	*Book §*
Indiana Mortgage & Realty Inv. v. Peacock Constr., 348 So. 2d 59 (Fla. Dist. Ct. App.), *cert. denied,* 353 So. 2d 677 (Fla. Dist. Ct. App. 1977)	§§ 9.14, 9.22
Industrial Dev. Bd. v. Fegua Indus., Inc., 523 F.2d 1226 (5th Cir. 1975)	§ 20.7
Industrial Research Assocs., Inc., DCAB No. WB-5, 68-1 B.C.A.(CCH) ¶ 70.69	§ 6.12
Ingle v. Jones, 69 U.S. (2 Wall.) 762 (1865)	§ 11.18
Inglewood, City of-Los Angeles County Civic Ctr. Auth. v. Superior Court, 7 Cal. 3d 861, 500 P.2d 601, 103 Cal. Rptr. 689 (1972)	§§ 4.8, 7.9
Insurance Co., (INA) v. Forty-Eight Insulations, 633 F.2d 1212 (6th Cir. 1980), *reh'g granted in part & denied in part,* 657 F.2d 814 (6th Cir.), *cert. denied,* 454 U.S. 1109 (1981)	§ 11.6
Insurance Co. of N. Am. v. Citizenbank, 491 So. 2d 880 (Ala. 1986)	§ 12.27
Insurance Co. of N. Am. v. Radiant Elec. Co., 55 Mich. App. 410, 222 N.W.2d 323 (1974)	§ 10.8
Integrated, Inc. v. Alec Fergusson Elec. Contractor, 250 Cal. App. 2d 287, 58 Cal. Rptr. 503 (1967)	§§ 5.9, 5.14
International Derrick & Equip. Co. v. Buxbaum, 240 F.2d 536 (3d Cir. 1956)	§ 11.11
International Eng'g Co. v. Richardson, 512 F.2d 573 (D.C. Cir. 1975), *cert. denied,* 423 U.S. 1048 (1976)	§ 6.5
International Hormones, Inc. v. Safeco, Inc., 57 A.D.2d 857, 394 N.Y.S.2d 260 (1977)	§ 11.13
International Surplus Lines, Inc. v. Devonshire Coverage Corp., 93 Cal. App. 3d 601, 155 Cal. Rptr. 654 (1979)	§ 11.10
Interstate Transit Lines v. Commissioner, 319 U.S. 590 (1943)	§ 21.7
Jablonsky v. Klemm, 377 N.W.2d 560 (N.D. 1985)	§ 20.1
Jackson v. Spurlock, 424 So. 2d 1088 (La. Ct. App. 1983)	§ 20.8
Jackson Township v. Hartford Accident & Indem. Co., 186 N.J. Super. 156, 451 A.2d 990 (1982)	§ 11.2
Jacksonville, City of v. Orr Constr. Co., 427 So. 2d 237 (Fla. Dist. Ct. App. 1983)	§ 20.15
Jacobson & Co., GSBCA No. 5605, 80-2 B.C.A. (CCH) ¶ 14,521	§ 7.37
Jacob & Youngs v. Kent, 230 N.Y. 239, 129 N.E. 889 (1921)	§ 20.11
J.A. Jones Constr. Co. v. Greenbriar Shopping Center, 332 F. Supp. 1336 (N.D. Ga. 1971), *aff'd,* 461 F.2d 1269 (5th Cir. 1972)	§ 16.21
James King & Sons, Inc. v. DeSantis Constr. No. 2 Corp., 97 Misc. 2d 1063, 413 N.Y.S.2d 78 (1977)	§ 10.2
James McKinney & Son, Inc. v. Lake Placid 1980 Olympic Games, 92 A.D.2d 991, 461 N.Y.S.2d 483	

Case	*Book §*
(1983), *modified on other grounds,* 61 N.Y.2d, 462 N.E.2d 137, 473 N.Y.S.2d 960 (1984)	§§ 7.16, 7.19, 8.2
Japanese Elecs. Prods. Antitrust Litig., *In re,* 632 F.2d 1069 (3d Cir. 1980)	§ 22.13
Jardine Estates, Inc. v. Donna Brook Corp., 42 N.J. Super. 332, 126 A.2d 372 (App. Div. 1956)	§ 20.11
J.A. Ross & Co. v. United States, 115 F. Supp. 187 (Ct. Cl. 1953)	§ 16.10
Jasper Constr. v. Foothill Junior College Dist., 91 Cal. App. 3d 1, 153 Cal. Rptr. 767 (1979)	§ 16.4
Jenkins v. Krebs & Sons, Inc., 322 So. 2d 426 (La. Ct. App. 1975)	§ 12.33
J.G. Plumbing Serv., Inc. v. Costal Mortgage Co., 329 So. 2d 393 (Fla. Dist. Ct. App.), *cert. denied,* 339 So. 2d 1169 (Fla. Dist. Ct. App. 1976)	§§ 9.18, 9.22
JKT Co. v. Hardwick, 284 S.C. 10, 335 S.E.2d 329 (Ct. App. 1984)	§ 20.16
Joba Constr. Co. v. Burns & Roe, Inc., 121 Mich. 615, 329 N.W.2d 760 (1982)	§§ 7.18, 12.27
John Burns Constr. Co. v. Interlake, Inc., 105 Ill. App. 3d 19, 433 N.E.2d 1126 (1982)	§ 5.14
John E. Green Plumbing & Heating Co. v. Turner Constr. Co., 742 F.2d 965 (6th Cir. 1984), *cert. denied,* 471 U.S. 1102 (1985)	§§ 7.24, 7.25, 7.26, 8.2, 8.7, 16.35
John E. Green Plumbing & Heating Co. v. Turner Constr. Co., 500 F. Supp. 910 (E.D. Mich. 1980)	§§ 7.18, 7.21, 7.31
John E. Gregory & Son, Inc. v. A. Guenther & Sons Co., 147 Wis. 2d 298, 432 N.W.2d 584 (1988)	§ 7.32
John F. Harkins Co. v. School Dist., 313 Pa. Super. 425, 460 A.2d 260 (1983)	§ 5.13
John J. Calnan Co. v. Talsma Builders, Inc., 67 Ill. 2d 213, 367 N.E.2d 695 (1977)	§ 5.14
Johns-Manville Sales Corp. v. Reliance Ins. Co., 410 F.2d 277 (9th Cir. 1969)	§ 13.18
Johnson v. Fenestra, Inc., 305 F.2d 179 (3d Cir. 1962)	§§ 2.13, 20.3
Johnson v. McGough Constr. Co., 294 N.W.2d 286 (Minn. 1980)	§ 10.10
Johnson v. City of N.Y., 191 A.D. 205, 181 N.Y.S. 137 (1920)	§ 16.18
Johnson v. Salem Title Co., 246 Or. 409, 425 P.2d 519 (1967)	§ 8.5
Johnson v. State, 24 N.Y.2d 958, 250 N.E.2d 75, 302 N.Y.S.2d 489 (1969)	§ 16.16
Johnson Controls, Inc. v. National Valve & Mfg. Co., 569 F. Supp. 758 (E.D. Okla. 1983)	§ 16.28
Johnston v. Garages Etc., Inc., 367 N.W.2d 85 (Minn. Ct. App. 1985)	§ 20.8
Johnstown, City of v. Bankers Standard Ins., 877 F.2d 1146 (2d Cir. 1989)	§ 11.5

Case	*Book §*
John T. Brady & Co. v. Board of Educ., 222 A.D. 504, 226 N.Y.S. 707 (1928)	§ 16.19
Jones v. J.H. Hiser Constr., Inc., 60 Md. App. 671, 484 A.2d 302 (1984), *cert. denied,* 303 Md. 114, 492 A.2d 616 (1985)	§ 12.28
Jones v. Scofield Bros., Inc., 73 F. Supp. 395 (D. Md. 1947)	§ 6.8
Joseph F. Hughes & Co. v. George H. Robinson Corp., 211 Va. 4, 175 S.E.2d 413 (1970)	§ 13.5
Joseph Pickard's Sons Co. v. United States, 532 F.2d 739 (Ct. Cl. 1946)	§ 16.36
J.&R. Elec. Div. of J.O. Mory Stores, Inc. v. Skoog Constr. Co., 38 Ill. App. 3d 747, 348 N.E.2d 474 (1976)	§ 10.2
J.R. Sinnott Carpentry, Inc. v. Phillips, 110 Ill. App. 3d 632, 443 N.E.2d 597 (1983)	§ 20.3
J.W. Bateson Co. v. United States *ex rel.* Board of Trustees, 434 U.S. 586 (1978)	§§ 13.6, 13.7
J.W. Cooper Constr. Co. v. Public Hous. Admin. *ex rel.* Rio Grande Steel Prods. Co., 390 F.2d 175 (10th Cir. 1968)	§ 13.6
Kalisch-Jarcho, Inc. v. City of N.Y., 58 N.Y.2d 377, 448 N.E.2d 413, 461 N.Y.S.2d 476 (1983)	§§ 5.8, 7.32, 7.35, 16.17
Kanters v. Kotick, 102 Wash. 523, 173 P.2d 329 (1918)	§ 12.21
Katz v. Bedford, 77 Cal. 319, 19 P. 523 (1888)	§ 20.3
Keco Indus., Inc. v. United States, 492 F.2d 1200 (Ct. Cl. 1974)	§ 16.30
Keco Indus., Inc. v. United States, 428 F.2d 1233 (Ct. Cl. 714 (1965)	§ 4.16
Keene Corp. v. INA, 667 F.2d 1034 (D.C. Cir. 1981), *cert. denied,* 455 U.S. 1007 (1982)	§ 11.6
Kelley v. Astor Investors, Inc., 123 Ill. App. 3d 593, 462 N.E.2d 996 (1984)	§ 20.7
Kennecott Corp. v. Union Oil, 196 Cal. App. 3d 1179, 242 Cal. Rptr. 403 (1987)	§ 11.2
Kennedy Elec. Co. v. United States Postal Serv., 508 F.2d 954 (10th Cir. 1974)	§ 13.18
Kennemore v. Bennett, 740 S.W.2d 39 (Tex. Civ. App. 1987)	§ 20.3
Keppler v. Terhune, 88 N.J. Super. 455, 212 A.2d 683 (App. Div. 1965)	§ 20.13
Kerry Coal Co. v. United Mine Workers, 470 F. Supp. 1032 (W.D. Pa. 1979)	§ 22.8
Kessler v. Peck, 266 Ala. 669, 98 So. 2d 606 (1957)	§ 7.44
Keyes v. Guy Bailey Homes, Inc., 439 So. 2d 670 (Miss. 1983)	§ 20.7
K&G Constr. Co. v. Harris, 223 Md. 305, 164 A.2d 451 (1960)	§ 20.3
Khabbas v. Swartz, 319 N.W.2d 279 (Iowa 1982)	§ 9.8
Kimbell v. United States, 490 F.2d 203 (5th Cir.), *cert. denied,* 419 U.S. 833 (1974)	§ 21.7

Case	*Book §*
Kinchen v. Gilworth, 454 So. 2d 1130 (La. Ct. App. 1984)	§ 12.28
King Enters., *In re,* 678 F.2d 73 (8th Cir. 1982)	§ 5.13
Kinlau Sheet Metal Works, Inc. v. Great Am. Ins. Co., 537 F.2d 222 (5th Cir. 1976)	§ 13.11
Kirk v. Jim Walte Homes, Inc., 41 Ohio App. 3d 128, 534 N.E.2d 1235 (1987)	§ 20.4
Kirkpatrick v. Temme, 98 Nev. 523, 654 P.2d 1011 (1983)	§ 20.8
Klapper v. Hanover Ins. Co., 39 Misc. 2d 215, 240 N.Y.S.2d 284 (1963)	§ 11.11
Klein-Dickert Oshkosh, Inc. v. Frontier Mortgage Corp., 93 Wis. 2d 660, 287 N.W.2d 742 (1980)	§ 9.22
Knight Constr. Co. v. Barnett Mortgage Trust, 572 S.W.2d 381 (Tex. Ct. App. 1978), *writ refused,* n.r.e.	§§ 9.8, 9.9
Knoell Constr. Co. v. Hanson, 205 Neb. 305, 287 N.W.2d 435 (1980)	§ 5.17
Knutson Constr. Co. v. St. Paul Fire & Marine Ins. Co., 396 N.W.2d 229 (Minn. 1986)	§ 11.14
Konyar v. Jonsson, 184 Ill. App. 3d 865, 540 N.E.2d 944 (1989)	§ 20.2
Koppers Co. v. Garling & Langlois, 594 F.2d 1094 (6th Cir. 1979)	§ 9.23
Korea Dev. Corp. v. United States, 9 Cl. Ct. 167 (1985)	§ 9.7
Kosanovich v. Mead, 463 N.E.2d 257 (Ind. 1984)	§ 12.35
Kraemer Bros., Inc. v. Pulaski State Bank, 138 Wis. 2d 395, 406 N.W.2d 379 (1987)	§ 12.31
Kraemer Bros., Inc. v. United States Fire Ins. Co., 89 Wis. 2d 555, 278 N.W.2d 857 (1979)	§ 11.22
Kreimer v. Second Fed. Sav. & Loan Ass'n, 196 Pa. Super. 644, 176 A.2d 132 (1961)	§ 9.9
Krichner v. Hartford Accident & Indem. Co., 440 S.W.2d 751 (Mo. Ct. App. 1969)	§ 11.11
Krieger v. S.E. Griner Co., 282 Md. 50, 832 A.2d 1069 (1978)	§§ 7.10, 7.11
Kubbe v. Crescent Steel, 105 Ariz. 459, 466 P.2d 753 (1970)	§ 20.7
Kuchenski v. Kramer Sheet Metal, Inc., 377 N.W.2d 133 (N.D. 1985)	§ 13.14
Kulpinski v. City of Tarpon Springs, 473 So. 2d 813 (Fla. Dist. Ct. App. 1985)	§ 20.4
Kvenild v. Taylor, 594 P.2d 972 (Wyo. 1979)	§ 12.27
K-W Indus. v. National Sur. Corp., 855 F.2d 640 (9th Cir. 1988)	§ 13.10
K-W Indus. v. National Sur. Corp., 231 Mont. 461, 754 P.2d 502 (1988)	§ 12.27
Laburnum Constr. Corp., United States, 325 F.2d 451 (Ct. Cl. 1963)	§ 16.4
Laclede Inv. Corp. v. Kaiser, 596 S.W.2d 36 (Mo. Ct. App. 1980)	§ 9.8

Case	*Book §*
Laganas v. Installation Specialists, Inc., 291 A.2d 187 (D.C. 1972)	§ 20.12
LaMarche v. Shelby Mut. Ins. Co., 390 So. 2d 325 (Fla. 1980)	§ 11.10
Lamberg v. Maryland Casualty Co., 418 So. 2d 553 (La. 1982)	§ 12.27
Lane v. Geiger-Berger Assocs., P.C., 608 F.2d 1148 (8th Cir. 1979)	§§ 8.2, 8.8
Langvin v. United States, 100 Ct. Cl. 15 (1943)	§ 2.28
La Rossa v. Scientific Design Co., 402 F.2d 937 (3d Cir. 1968)	§ 7.6
Larson v. Erickson, 549 F.2d 1136 (8th Cir. 1977)	§ 20.12
Latite Roofing Co. v. Urbanek, 528 So. 2d 1381 (Fla. Dist. Ct. App. 1988)	§ 7.41
Lavalleur v. State Auto & Casualty, 208 Neb. 82, 302 N.W.2d 362 (1981)	§ 11.17
La Vine v. Clear Creek Skiing Corp., 557 F.2d 730 (10th Cir. 1977)	§ 7.6
L.B. Herbst Corp. v. Northern Ill. Corp., 99 Ill. App. 2d 101, 241 N.E.2d 125 (1968)	§§ 9.10, 9.14
Leaseway Warehouses, Inc. v. Carlton, 568 F. Supp. 1041 (N.D. Ill 1983)	§ 10.10
Leasing Serv. Corp. v. Justice, 673 F.2d 70 (2d Cir. 1982)	§ 20.10
LeGare, Inc. v. Brookhaven Residential Sales, 337 Pa. Super. 478, 487 A.2d 360 (1985)	§ 20.8
Leigh Furniature & Carpet Co. v. Isom, 657 P.2d 293 (Utah 1982)	§ 12.27
Leiter v. United States, 271 U.S. 204 (1926)	§ 6.10
Leiter Elec. Co. v. Bituminous Casualty Corp., 99 Ill. App. 2d 386, 241 N.E.2d 325 (1968)	§ 11.11
Lemke v. Dagenais, 130 N.H. 782, 547 A.2d 290 (1988)	§ 20.7
Lemoge Elec. v. County of San Mateo, 46 Cal. 2d 659, 297 P.2d 638 (1956)	§ 4.29
Leto v. Cypress Builders, Inc., 428 So. 2d 819 (La. Ct. App. 1983)	§ 20.8
Lewis v. Erie Ins. Exch., 281 Pa. Super. 193, 421 A.2d 1214 (1980)	§ 14.4
Lexington Ins. Co. v. Abarca Warehouse Corp., 337 F. Supp. 902 (D.P.R. 1971) *aff'd,* 476 F.2d 44 (1st Cir. 1973)	§ 20.4
L.F. Pace & Co. v. Travelers Ins. Co., 9 Conn. App. 30, 514 A.2d 766 (1986)	§ 12.27
L.G. DeFelice & Sons, Inc. v. State, 63 Misc. 2d 357, 313 N.Y.S.2d 21 (Ct. Cl. 1962)	§ 16.6
Liberty Bldg. Co. v. Royal Indem Co., 177 Cal. App. 2d 583, 2 Cal. Rptr. 329 (1960)	§ 11.14
Lichter v. Mellon-Stuart Co., 305 F.2d 216 (3d Cir. 1962)	§ 16.7
Lillards, ASBCA No. 6630, 61-1 B.C.A. (CCH) ¶ 3053 (1961)	§ 6.12

Case	*Book §*
Lincoln Pump & Paper Co. v. Dravo Corp., 436 F. Supp. 262 (D. Me. 1977)	§ 20.7
Lincoln Welding Works, Inc. v. Ramierez, 98 Nev. 342, 647 P.2d 381 (1982)	§ 10.4
Lincor Contractors, Ltd. v. Hyskell, 39 Wash. App. 317, 692 P.2d 903 (1984), *review denied,* 103 Wash. 2d 1036 (1985)	§ 9.23
Linn Reorg. Sch. Dist. No. 2 v. Butler Mfg. Co., 672 S.W.2d 340 (Mo. 1984)	§ 20.4
Liptak v. Diane Apartments, Inc., 109 Cal. App. 3d 762, 167 Cal. Rptr. 440 (1980)	§ 7.42
Little Judy Indus., Inc. v. Federal Ins. Co., 280 So. 2d 14 (Fla. Dist. Ct. App.), *cert. denied,* 284 So. 2d 220 (Fla. 1973)	§ 11.22
L.K. Comstock & Co. v. Morse/UBM Joint Venture, 153 Ill. App. 3d 475, 505 N.E.2d 1253 (1987)	§§ 7.2, 7.31
L.L. Jarrell Constr. Co. v. Columbia Casualty Co., 130 F. Supp. 436 (S.D. Ala. 1955)	§ 11.11
Local Joint Executive Bd. v. Stern, 98 Nev. 409, 651 P.2d 637 (1982)	§ 7.41
Lonergan v. San Antonio Loan & Trust Co., 101 Tex. 63, 104 S.W. 1061 (1907), *motion for reh'g overruled,* 101 Tex. 81, 106 S.W. 876 (1908)	§ 20.2
Long v. City of Midway, 169 Ga. App. 72, 311 S.E.2d 508 (1983)	§ 12.34
Long v. Weiler, 395 S.W.2d 234 (Mo. Ct. App. 1965)	§ 20.12
Los Angeles Memorial Coliseum Comm. NFL, 791 F.2d 1356 (9th Cir. 1986)	§ 12.27
Louisiana Fire Ins. Co. v. Royal Indem. Co., 38 So. 2d 807 (La. 1949)	§ 11.25
Lowell v. Maryland Casualty Co., 65 Cal. 2d 298, 419 P.2d 180, 54 Cal. Rptr. 116 (1966)	§ 11.4
Lumberman's Mut. Casualty Co. v. Patillo Constr. Co., 254 Ga. 461, 330 S.E.2d 344 (1985)	§ 20.4
Lumbermen's Mut. Casualty Co. v. Town of Pound Ridge, 362 F.2d 430 (2d Cir. 1966)	§ 11.10
Lutz Eng'g Co. v. Industrial Louvers, Inc., 585 A.2d 631 (R.I. 1991)	§ 8.9
Magnolia Constr. v. Mississipppi Gulf S. Eng'rs, Inc., 518 So. 2d 1194 (Miss. 1988)	§§ 7.27, 8.9
Mahler v. Bellis, 231 Neb. 161, 435 N.W.2d 661 (1989)	§ 20.12
Mahoney-Troast Constr. Co. v. Supermarkets Gen. Corp., 183 N.J. Super. 325, 460 A.2d 149 (1983)	§ 2.4
Mall Properties v. United States, 21 Cl. Ct. 430 (1990)	§ 6.12
Maltzahn v. Roach, 427 So. 2d 586 (La. Ct. App. 1983)	§ 20.16
Manchester Bank v. Connecticut Bank & Trust Co., 497 F. Supp. 1304 (D.N.H. 1980)	§ 12.27
Mann v. Clowser, 190 Va. 887, 59 S.E.2d 78 (1950)	§§ 20.2, 20.7
Mannella v. Pittsburgh, 334 Pa. 396, 6 A.2d 70 (1939)	§ 12.38

Case	*Book §*
Manos v. Degen, 203 Cal. App. 3d 1237, 250 Cal. Rptr. 493 (1988)	§ 9.4
Manshul Constr. Corp. v. Dormitory Auth., 111 Misc. 2d 209, 444 N.Y.S.2d 792 (1981)	§ 16.43
Manshul Constr. Co. v. Dormitory Auth., 79 A.D.2d 383, 436 N.Y.S.2d 724 (1981)	§§ 16.35, 16.40, 16.43
Manthey v. Stock, 133 Wis. 197, 113 N.W. 443 (1907)	§ 20.11
Marathon Oil Co. v. Hollis, 167 Ga. App. 48, 305 S.E.2d 864 (1983)	§§ 20.3, 20.16
Marshall v. Karl F. Schultz, Inc., 428 So. 2d 533 (Fla. Dist. Ct. App. 1983)	§ 20.8
Marshall v. Port Auth., 524 Pa. 1, 568 A.2d 931 (1960)	§ 7.14
Marshall County Redi-Mix, Inc. v. Matthew, 447 N.E.2d 1165 (Ind. Ct. App. 1983)	§ 20.2
Martin v. National Sur. Co., 300 U.S. 588 (1937)	§ 12.31
Martinez v. Hawkeye-Sec. Ins. Co., 196 Colo. 184, 576 P.2d 1017 (1978)	§ 11.17
Martin Fireproofing Corp. v. Aetna Ins. Co., 346 Mass. 498, 194 N.E.2d 1010 (1963)	§ 12.4
Maryland Casualty Co. v. Cunningham, 234 Ala. 80, 173 So. 2d 506 (1937)	§ 12.23
Maryland Casualty Co. v. Farmers Alliance Mut. Ins. Co., 566 F.2d 168 (Okla. Ct. App. 1977)	§ 11.11
Maryland Casualty Co. v. Imperial Contracting Co., 212 Cal. App. 3d 712, 260 Cal. Rptr. 797 (1989)	§ 11.14
Maryland Casualty Co. v. Reeder, 221 Cal. App. 3d 961, 270 Cal. Rptr. 719 (1990)	§§ 11.3, 11.8, 11.12, 11.14
Masson v. Reindollar, 193 Md. 683, 69 A.2d 482 (1949)	§ 6.11
Matayka v. Mella, 119 Ill. App. 3d 221, 456 N.E.2d 353 (1984)	§ 20.4
Matthews v. Candlewood Builders, Inc., 685 S.W.2d 649 (Tex. 1985)	§ 20.16
Matthews Constr. Co. v. Brady, 104 N.J.L. 438, 140 A. 433 (1928)	§ 20.5
Mattingly v. Anthony Indus., Inc., 109 Cal. App. 3d 413, 167 Cal. Rptr. 292 (1980)	§ 12.34
Maurice Pincoffs Co. v. St. Paul Fire & Marine Ins. Co., 447 F.2d 204 (5th Cir. 1971)	§ 11.5
Maxfield v. Simmons, 96 Ill. 2d 81, 449 N.E.2d 110 (1983)	§ 10.10
Maxwell v. Anderson, 181 Mont. 215, 593 P.2d 29 (1979)	§ 5.17
Mayor of Baltimore v. Fidelity & Deposit Co., 282 Md. 432, 386 A.2d 749 (1978)	§ 13.4
Mayville-Portland Sch. Dist. v. C.I. Linfoot Co., 261 N.W.2d 907 (N.D. 1978)	§ 20.2
McCaa v. Commissioner, 26 T.C.M. (CCH) 711 (1967)	§ 21.8
McCarty Corp. v. United States, 499 F.2d 633 (Ct. Cl. 1974)	§ 16.30

Case	*Book §*
McCloskey & Co. v. Wright, 363 F. Supp. 223 (E.D. Va. 1973)	§ 7.42
McCord, Conderon & McDonald, Inc. v. Twin City Fire Ins. Co., 607 S.W.2d 956 (Tex. Ct. App. 1980)	§ 11.11
McCorkle v. Fireman's Ins. Co., 678 F. Supp. 562 (W.D. Pa. 1988)	§ 11.10
McCoy v. Nelson Utils. Servs., 736 S.W.2d 160 (Tex. Civ. App. 1987)	§ 13.18
McCreary Roofing Co., Inc. v. Northern Ins. Co., 218 Pa. Super, 193, 275 A.2d 388 (1971)	§ 11.11
McDaniel v. Ashton-Mardian Co., 357 F.2d 511 (9th Cir. 1966)	§§ 13.9, 16.14
McDonald v. Mianecki, 79 N.J. 275, 398 A.2d 1283 (1979)	§ 20.8
McGann v. Hobbs Lumber Co., 150 W. Va. 364, 145 S.E.2d 476 (1965)	§ 11.2
McGrath v. American Sur. Co., 307 N.Y. 552, 122 N.E.2d 906 (1954)	§ 12.12
McGraw v. Johnson, 42 N.J. Super. 267, 126 A.2d 203 (App. Div. 1956)	§ 20.8
McGuire & Hester v. City & County of S.F., 113 Cal. App. 186, 247 P.2d 934 (1952)	§ 7.32
McLouth Steel Corp. v. Mesta Mach. Co., 214 F.2d 608 (3d Cir. 1954)	§ 11.11
McRaven v. F-Stop Photo Labs, Inc., 660 S.W.2d 459 (Mo. Ct. App. 1983)	§ 11.10
McWaters & Bartlett v. United States *ex rel.* Wilson, 272 F.2d 291 (10th Cir. 1959)	§§ 12.22, 12.23, 13.14
Meadows v. Lee, 175 Cal. App. 3d 475, 221 Cal. Rptr. 22 (1985)	§ 11.2
Meier v. Hardware Mut. Casualty Co., 281 So. 2d 793 (La. Ct. App. 1973)	§ 11.17
Meiser v. Aetna Casualty & Sur. Co., 8 Wis. 2d 233, 98 N.W.2d 919 (1959)	§ 11.11
Melder v. Gassiott, 436 So. 2d 628 (La. Ct. App. 1983)	§ 20.2
Melwin Constr. v. Stonewall Constr. Co., 113 A.2d 108 (D.C. 1955)	§ 2.13
Meng v. Bituminous Casualty Corp., 626 F. Supp. 1237 (S.D. Miss. 1986)	§ 11.13
Meridian Corp. v. McGlynn/Garmaker Co., 567 P.2d 1110 (Utah 1977)	§ 7.7
Merriam v. Kunzig, 476 F.2d 1233 (3d Cir.), *cert. denied,* 414 U.S. 911 (1973)	§ 6.6
Merrick Constr. Co. v. Hartford Fire Ins. Co., 449 So. 2d 85 (La. Ct. App.), *writ denied,* 450 So. 2d 958 (La. 1984)	§§ 12.29, 12.30
Merrill & Seeley v. Admiral Ins. Co., 225 Cal. App. 3d 624, 275 Cal. Rptr. 280 (1990)	§ 11.7

Case	*Book §*
Mervin L. Blades & Son, Inc. v. Lighthouse Sound Marina & Country Club, 37 Md. App. 265, 377 A.2d 523 (1977)	§ 5.17
Metropolitan Dade County v. Bouterse, Perez & Fabregas Architects, Planners, Inc., 463 So. 2d 526 (Fla. Dist. Ct. App. 1985)	§ 20.16
Metropolitan Paving Co. v. United States, 325 F.2d 241 (Ct. Cl. 1963)	§ 16.42
Metropolitan Pipe & Supply Co. v. D'Amore Constr. Co., 309 Mass. 380, 35 N.E.2d 211 (1941)	§ 12.4
Meyers Plumbing & Heating v. West End Fed. Sav. & Loan, 345 Pa. Super. 559, 498 A.2d 966 (1985)	§ 9.18
M.F. Kemper Constr. v. City of Los Angeles, 37 Cal. 2d 696, 235 P.2d 7 (1951)	§ 4.29
Mid Seven Transp. v. Blinderman Constr. Co., 735 F. Supp. 272 (N.D. Ill. 1990)	§ 13.10
Mid-United Contractors, Inc. v. Providence Lloyd's Ins. Co., 754 S.W.2d 824 (Tex. Ct. App. 1988)	§ 11.11
Mike Bradford & Co. v. F.A. Chastain Constr., Inc., 387 F.2d 942 (5th Cir. 1968)	§ 13.14
Miller v. City of Broken Arrow, 660 F.2d 450 (10th Cir. 1981), *cert. denied,* 455 U.S. 1020 (1982)	§§ 8.3, 20.2, 20.6
Miller v. DeWitt, 37 Ill. 2d 273, 226 N.E.2d 630 (1967)	§ 7.14
Miller v. Mountain View Sav. & Loan Ass'n, 238 Cal. App. 2d 644, 48 Cal. Rptr. 278 (1965)	§§ 9.18, 9.19
Milton v. Hudson Sales Corp., 152 Cal. App. 2d 418, 313 P.2d 936 (1957)	§ 4.27
Milton J. Womack, Inc. v. House of Representatives, 509 So. 2d 62 (La. Ct. App. 1987)	§§ 8.2, 8.5, 8.8
Mineral Park Land Co. v. Howard, 172 Cal. 289, 156 P. 458 (1916)	§ 20.6
Mingledorff's, Inc. v. Hicks, 13 Ga. App. 27, 209 S.E.2d 661 (1974)	§ 10.2
Minmar Builders, Inc., GSBCA No. 3430, 72-2 B.C.A. (CCH) ¶ 9599 (1972)	§ 17.2
Minnesota v. McGuire Architects-Planners, 245 N.W.2d 218 (Minn. 1976)	§ 6.8
Minton Constr. Corp. v. Commonwealth, 397 Mass. 879, 494 N.E.2d 1031 (1986)	§ 6.8
Miracle Mile Shopping Center v. National Union Indem. Co., 299 F.2d 780 (7th Cir. 1962)	§ 12.23
Mitchell v. Alfred, 48 N.J. Super. 396, 137 A.2d 569 (App. Div. 1958)	§ 20.13
Mitchell v. Siqueiros, 99 Idaho 396, 582 P.2d 1074 (1978)	§ 10.2
M.J. McGough Co. v. Jane Lamb Memorial Hosp., 302 F. Supp. 482 (S.D. Iowa 1969)	§ 12.7
Mobil Chem. Co. v. Blount Bros., 809 F.2d 1175 (5th Cir. 1987)	§§ 7.15, 16.27

Case	*Book §*
Modany v State Pub. Sch. Bldg. Auth., 417 Pa. 39, 208 A.2d 276 (1965)	§ 4.30
Mogil v. California Physicians Corp., 218 Cal. App. 3d 1030, 267 Cal. Rptr. 487 (1990)	§ 11.5
Mohawk Green Apartments v. Kramer, 709 P.2d 955 (Colo. Ct. App. 1985)	§ 20.4
Mongiovi v. Doerner, 24 Or. App. 639, 546 P.2d 1110 (1976)	§§ 7.8, 7.9
Montgomery County Bd. of Educ. v. Glassman Constr. Co., 245 Md. 192, 225 A.2d 448 (1967)	§ 13.4
Montgomery Indus. Int'l, Inc. v. Thomas Constr. Co., 620 F.2d 91 (5th Cir. 1980)	§§ 2.26, 10.2, 10.10
Montes v. Naismith & Trevino Constr. Co., 459 S.W.2d 691 (Tex. Ct. App. 1970)	§ 12.28
Moore v. Pavex, Inc., No. 2843 S 1984, slip op. (C.P. Dauphin County, Pa., Oct 4, 1985)	§ 8.2
Moore v. PRC Eng'g., Inc., 565 So. 2d 817 (Fla. Dist. Ct. App. 1990)	§ 7.14
Moorehead Constr. Co. v. City of Grand Fortis, 508 F.2d 1008 (8th Cir. 1973)	§ 16.36
Morrison v. MacNamara, 407 A.2d 555 (D.C. 1979)	§ 7.16
Morrison Grain Co. v. Utica Mut. Ins. Co., 632 F.2d 424 (5th Cir. 1980)	§§ 11.21, 11.23
Morrison-Knudsen Co., ASBCA No. 16483, 72-2 B.C.A. (CCH) ¶ 9733	§ 6.12
Mortgage Assocs., Inc. v. Monona Shores, Inc., 47 Wis. 2d 171, 177 N.W.2d 340 (1970)	§§ 9.7, 9.14
Mounds View, City of v. Wallijarvi, 263 N.W.2d 420 (Minn. 1978)	§§ 7.6, 8.4
Moundsview Indep. Sch. Dist. No. 621 v. Buetow & Assocs., Inc., 253 N.W.2d 836 (Minn. 1977)	§ 8.6
Mraz v. Canadian Universal Ins. Co., 804 F.2d 1325 (4th Cir. 1986)	§ 11.6
M&R Contractors & Builders v. Michael, 215 Md. 340, 138 A.2d 350 (1958)	§ 16.35
M. Steinthal & Co. v. Seamans, 455 F.2d 1289 (D.C. Cir. 1971)	§ 6.6
Muller v. Light, 538 S.W.2d 487 (Tex. Civ. App. 1976)	§ 20.10
Murray First Thrift & Loan Co. v. N-C Paving, 576 P.2d 455 (Wyo. 1978)	§ 10.12
Nanuet Nat'l Bank v. Eckerson Terrance, Inc., 47 N.Y.2d 243, 391 N.E.2d 983, 417 N.Y.S.2d 901 (1979)	§ 9.5
Nardi & Co. v. Allabastro, 20 Ill. App. 3d 323, 314 N.E.2d 367 (1974)	§ 12.28
Nat Harrison Assocs., Inc. v. Gulf States Utils. Co., 491 F.2d 578 (5th Cir. 1974)	§ 16.27
National Coop. Refinery Ass'n v. Northern Ordnance, Inc., 238 F.2d 803 (10th Cir. 1956)	§ 12.34

Case	*Book §*
National Hills Shopping Ctr., Inc. v. Insurance Co. of N. Am., 320 F. Supp. 1146 (S.D. Ga. 1970)	§ 10.8
National Investors Fire & Casualty Co. v. Preddy, 248 Ark. 320, 451 S.W.2d 457 (1970)	§ 11.22
National Roofing & Siding Co. v. Giaise, 434 So. 2d 85 (La. Ct. App. 1983)	§ 20.16
National Sand, Inc. v. Nagel Constr. Inc., 182 Mich. App. 327, 451 N.W.2d 618 (1990)	§ 8.2
National Shawmut Bank v. New Amsterdam Casualty Co., 411 F.2d 843 (1st Cir. 1969)	§§ 12.24, 12.31
National Sur. Corp. v. United States, 319 F. Supp. 45 (N.D. Ala. 1970)	§ 12.31
National Sur. Co. v. United States *ex rel.* Way Panama, S.A., 378 F.2d 294 (5th Cir.), *cert. denied,* 389 U.S. 1004 (1967)	§ 13.12
Nationwide Mut. Ins. Co. v. Wenger, 222 Va. 263, 278 S.E.2d 874 (1981)	§ 11.10
Natkin & Co. v. George A. Fuller Co., 347 F. Supp. 17 (W.D. Mo. 1972)	§§ 5.13, 16.27, 20.9
Nees v. Weaver, 222 Wis. 492, 269 N.W. 266 (1936)	§ 20.11
Nelse Mortensen v. Group Health, Inc., 17 Wash. 703, 566 P.2d 560 (1977)	§ 7.32
Nelson v. Commonwealth, 235 Va. 228, 368 S.E.2d 239 (1988)	§ 7.16
Nether Providence Township Sch. Auth. v. Thomas M. Durkin & Sons, Inc., 505 Pa. 42, 476 A.2d 904 (1984)	§§ 5.4, 16.10
New Amsterdam Casualty Co. v. Lundquist, 293 Minn. 274, 198 N.W.2d 543 (1972)	§ 12.30
Newberg v. Illinois State Toll Highway Auth., 153 Ill. App. 3d 918, 506 N.E.2d 658 (1987)	§ 7.32
New Castle County v. Continental Casualty Co., 725 F. Supp. 800 (D. Del.), *motion for reconsideration denied,* 728 F. Supp. 340 (D. Del. 1989), *aff'd in part & reversed in part,* 1991 U.S. App. LEXIS 7849 (3d Cir. Apr. 30, 1991)	§ 11.6
New Hampshire Ins. Co. v. Vieira, 930 F.2d 696 (9th Cir. 1981)	§ 11.8
Newman v. National Fire Ins. Co., 152 Miss. 344, 118 So. 295 (1928)	§ 11.19
Newport News, City of v. Doyle & Russel, Inc., 211 Va. 603, 179 S.E.2d 493 (1971)	§ 4.30
Niagara Mohawk Power Corp. v. Bankers Trust Co., 791 F.2d 242 (2d Cir. 1986)	§ 9.7
Nibbi Bros., Inc. v. Brannan St. Investors, 205 Cal. App. 3d 1415, 253 Cal. Rptr. 289 (1988)	§ 9.22
Nisbet v. Yellownick, 124 Ill. App. 3d 466, 464 N.E.2d 781 (1984)	§ 20.8
N.J. Magnam Co. v. Fuller, 222 Mass. 530, 111 N.E. 399 (1916)	§ 20.2

Case	*Book §*
Noce v. Morgan, 106 F.2d 746 (8th Cir. 1939)	§ 4.16
Nolan Bros., Inc. v. United States, 405 F.2d 1250 (Ct. Cl. 1969)	§ 5.16
Noland Co. v. Allied Contractors, Inc., 273 F.2d 917 (4th Cir. 1959)	§ 13.12
Norair Eng'g Corp. v. United States, 666 F.2d 546 (Ct. Cl. 1981)	§ 16.28
Normoyle-Berg Assocs. v. Village of Deer Creek, 39 Ill. App. 3d 744, 350 N.E.2d 559 (1976)	§§ 7.6, 7.25, 7.27
North Am. Iron & Steel Co., v. Isaacson Steel Erectors, Inc., 36 A.D.2d 770, 321 N.Y.S.2d 254 (1971), *aff'd mem.,* 30 N.Y.2d 640, 282 N.E.2d 621, 331 N.Y.S.2d 667 (1972)	§ 11.11
North Denver Bank v. United States, 432 F.2d 466 (Ct. Cl. 1970)	§ 13.18
Northern Ind. Pub. Serv. Co. v. Fattore Constr. Co., 468 N.E.2d 633 (Ind. Ct. App. 1985)	§ 20.4
Northwestern Mut. Ins. Co. v. Bland, Cave & Dew, 345 Mo. 391, 189 S.W.2d 542 (1945)	§ 11.2
Northwest Fixture Co. v. Kilbourne & Clark Co., 234 U.S. 236 (1913)	§ 12.34
Nowak v. Smith & Mahoney, 110 A.D.2d 288, 494 N.Y.S.2d 449 (1985)	§ 7.14
N.S. Elec. Corp. v. Procida Constr. Corp., N.Y.L.J., Dec. 13, 1989 (N.Y. Sup. Ct., Kings County) 11 CLR 78	§ 7.18
Office of Personnel Management v. Richmond, 110 S. Ct. 2465 (1990)	§ 6.12
Ohio Casualty Ins. Co. v. Terrace Enters., Inc., 260 N.W.2d 450 (Minn. 1977)	§ 11.15
Okla Homer Smith Furniture Mfg. Co. v. Larsen & Wear, Inc., 278 Ark. 467, 646 S.W.2d 696 (1983)	§ 20.4
Oliver B. Cannon & Son, Inc. v. Fidelity & Casualty Co., 484 F. Supp. 1375 (D. Del. 1980)	§ 11.10
Oliver-Finnie Co. v. United States, 279 F.2d 498 (Ct. Cl. 1960)	§ 16.36
Ollice v. Alyeska Pipeline Serv., 659 P.2d 1182 (Alaska 1983)	§ 12.27
Omaha Pollution Control Corp. v. Carver-Greenfield Corp., 413 F. Supp. 1069 (D. Nev. 1976)	§§ 2.21, 20.7
Osceola, City of v. Ghellefald Constr. Co., 225 Iowa 215, 279 N.W. 590 (1938)	§ 12.34
Osceola, County v. Bumble Bee Constr., Inc., 479 So. 2d 310 (Fla. Dist. Ct. App. 1985)	§ 20.10
Ossining Union Free Sch. Dist. v. Anderson La Rocca Anderson, 73 N.Y.2d 417, 539 N.E.2d 91, 541 N.Y.S.2d 335 (1989)	§ 7.41
Otto Misch Co. v. E.E. Davis Co., 241 Mich. 285, 217 N.W. 38 (1928)	§ 20.2

Case	*Book §*
Overall Roofing & Constr., Inc. v. United States, 929 F.2d 687 (Fed. Cir. 1991)	§ 6.5
Overland Constructors, Inc. v. Millard Sch. Dist., 220 Neb. 220, 369 N.W.2d 69 (1985)	§ 8.5
Owen v. Dodd, 431 F. Supp. 1239 (N.D. Miss. 1977)	§ 8.2
Owings v. Western Casualty & Sur. Co., 237 Kan. 89, 697 P.2d 865 (1985)	§ 11.10
Ownes Pac. Marine, Inc. v. Insurance Co. of N. Am., 12 Cal. App. 3d 661, 90 Cal. Rptr. 826 (1970)	§ 11.14
Ozark Dam Constructors v. United States, 127 F. Supp. 187 (Ct. Cl. 1985)	§§ 7.34, 16.20
Ozark Skyways, Inc. v. Bomark Steel Structures, Inc., 647 S.W.2d 170 (Mo. Ct. App. 1983)	§ 20.2
Pacific Employers Ins. Co. v. Superior Court, 221 Cal. App. 3d 1348, 270 Cal. Rptr. 179 (1990)	§ 11.7
Padbloc Co. v. United States, 161 Ct. Cl. 369 (1963)	§ 2.21
Paint Prods. Co. v. AA-1 Steel Equip. Co., 35 Conn. Supp. 52, 393 A.2d 1317 (1977)	§ 10.8
Palmieri v. Alvanese, 12 N.J. Super. 338, 79 A.2d 699 (App. Div. 1951)	§ 20.8
Pankow Constr. Co. v. Advance Mortgage Corp., 618 F.2d 611 (9th Cir. 1980)	§§ 9.2, 9.20, 9.23
Parent v. Stone & Webster Eng'g, 408 Mass. 108, 556 N.E.2d 1009 (1990)	§ 7.11
Parkway Windows, Inc. v. River Tower Assocs., 108 A.D.2d 660, 485 N.Y.S.2d 755 (1985)	§ 7.39
Parsa v. State, 64 N.Y.2d 143, 474 N.E.2d 235, 485 N.Y.S.2d 27 (1984)	§ 6.14
Parsons v. Beaulieu, 429 A.2d 214 (Me. 1981)	§§ 20.7, 20.12
Partridge v. Presley, 189 F.2d 645 (D.C. Cir.), *cert, denied,* 342 U.S. 850 (1951)	§ 20.6
Passaic Valley Sewerage Comm'rs v. Tierney, 1 F.2d 304 (3d Cir. 1924)	§ 20.2
Pastorelli v. Associated Eng'rs, Inc., 176 F. Supp. 159 (D.R.I. 1959)	§§ 8.4, 8.6
Paterson v. Board of Trustees, 157 Cal. App. 2d 811, 321 P.2d 825 (1958)	§ 5.15
Paterson-Leitch Co. v. Massachusetts Wholesale Elec. Co., 840 F.2d 985 (1st Cir. 1988)	§§ 7.2, 7.38
Pathman Constr. Co., ASBCA No. 22,343, 81-1 B.C.A. (CCH) ¶ 15,010 (1981)	§ 2.28
Pathman Constr. Co. v. Hi-way Elec. Co., 65 Ill. 2d 480, 382 N.E.2d 453 (1978)	§§ 5.7, 5.16, 10.10
Paxton v. County of Alameda, 119 Cal. App. 2d 393, 259 P.2d 934 (1953)	§ 8.5
PDM Plumbing & Heating, Inc. v. Findlan, 13 Mass. App. 950, 431 N.E.2d 594 (1982)	§ 5.13
Peach State Uniform Serv., Inc. v. Amerucan Ins. Co., 507 F.2d 996 (5th Cir. 1975)	§ 11.22

Case	*Book §*
Pearlman v. Reliance Ins. Co., 371 U.S. 132 (1962)	§§ 12.31, 13.3, 13.18
Peerless Ins. Co. v. Cerny & Assocs., Inc., 199 F. Supp. 951 (D. Minn. 1961)	§ 12.33
Peerless Ins. Co. v. Wells, 580 A.2d 485 (Vt. 1990)	§ 11.10
Peltz Constr. Co. v. Durham, 436 N.E.2d 892 (Ind. Ct. App. 1982)	§ 20.7
Pembee Mfg. Corp. v. Cape Fear Constr. Co., 313 N.C. 488, 329 S.E.2d 350 (1985)	§ 20.4
Peninsular Supply Co. v. C.B. Day Realty, 423 So. 2d 500 (Fla. Dist. Ct. App. 1982)	§ 5.17
Penn Bridge Co. v. New Orleans, 222 F. 737 (5th Cir. 1915)	§ 20.2
Pennsylvania State Shopping Plazas, Inc. v. Olive, 202 Va. 862, 120 S.E.2d 372 (1961)	§ 20.5
Penn Towne Builders, Inc. v. United States, 4 Cl. Ct. 677 (1984)	§ 9.7
People v. Craig City, 232 N.Y. 125, 133 N.E.2d 419 (1921)	§ 7.33
People *ex rel.* Wells & Newton Co. v. Craig, 232 N.Y. 125, 133 N.E. 419 (1921)	§ 16.19
People's Gas, Light & Coke Co. v. United States Postal Serv., 658 F.2d 1182 (7th Cir. 1981)	§ 6.6
Perlmutter v. Harmony Homes, Inc., 677 P.2d 381 (Colo. Ct. App. 1984)	§ 20.16
Perry Roofing Co. v. Olcott, 722 S.W.2d 538 (Tex. Civ. App. 1986)	§ 20.3
Peter Kiewit Sons' Co. v. Iowa S. Utils. Co., 355 F. Supp. 376 (S.D. Iowa 1973)	§§ 7.31, 7.35, 8.2, 8.4, 8.11, 16.16, 22.17
Peter Kiewit Sons' Co. v. Summit Constr. Co., 422 F.2d 242 (8th Cir. 1969)	§ 16.7
Peters Township Sch. Auth v. United States Fidelity & Guar. Co., 73 Pa. Commw. 365, 467 A.2d 904 (1983)	§ 12.36
Petrol Indus., Inc. v. Gearhart-Owen Indus., Inc., 424 So. 2d 1059 (La. Ct. App. 1982)	§ 11.11
Peyronnin Constr. Co. v. Weiss, 208 N.E.2d 489 (Ind. Ct. App. 1965)	§ 8.2
P.H.A.C. Servs. v. Seaways Int'l, Inc., 403 So. 2d 1199 (La. 1981)	§ 12.28
Philadelphia Facilities Management Corp. v. St. Paul Fire & Marine Ins. Co., 379 F. Supp. 780 (E.D. Pa. 1974)	§ 11.19
Philadelphia Hous. Auth. v. Turner Constr. Co., 343 Pa. 512, 23 A.2d 426 (1942)	§ 20.6
Phil Crowley Steel Corp. v. Sharon Steel Corp., 536 F. Supp. 429 (E.D. Mo. 1982), *rev'd on other grounds,* 702 F.2d 719 (8th Cir. 1983)	§ 12.27
Phillips v. United Eng'rs & Constructors, Inc., 500 N.E.2d 1265 (Ind. Ct. App. 1986)	§ 7.14

Case	*Book §*
Phillips & Colby Constr. Co. v. Seymour, 91 U.S. 646 (1875)	§ 20.3
Phillips Constr. Co. v. City of N.Y., 61 N.Y.2d 949, 463 N.E.2d 585, 475 N.Y.S.2d 244 (1984)	§ 20.4
Phoenix Coal Co. v. Commissioner, 231 F.2d 420 (2d Cir. 1956)	§§ 21.17, 21.20
Phoenix Contractors, Inc. v. General Motors Corp., 135 Mich. App. 787, 355 N.W.2d 673 (1984)	§ 10.6
Phoenix of Hartford v. Holloway Corp., 268 So. 2d 195 (Fla. Dist. Ct. App. 1972)	§ 11.11
Pickeys v. Brown, 431 So. 2d 880 (La. Ct. App. 1983)	§ 12.34
Pierce Assocs., Inc., GSBCA No. 4163, 77-2 B.C.A. (CCH) ¶ 12,746	§ 7.35
Pierce Assocs., Inc. v. Nemours Found., 865 F.2d 530 (3d Cir. 1989)	§§ 5.10, 10.11
Pioneer Plumbing Supply Co. v. Southwest Sav. & Loan Ass'n, 102 Ariz. 258, 428 P.2d 115 (1967)	§§ 9.9, 9.14
Pittman Constr. Co. v. Housing Auth., 169 So. 2d 122 (La. Ct. App. 1964), *writ refused,* 237 La. 343, 170 So. 2d 865 (La. Ct. App.), *writ refused,* 247 La. 346, 170 So. 2d 866 (La. Ct. App. 1965)	§ 20.2
Pittsburgh Bridge & Iron Works v. Liberty Mut. Ins. Co., 444 F.2d 1286 (3d Cir. 1971)	§ 11.14
Pittsburgh-Des Moines Steel Co. v. Brookhaven Manor Water Co., 532 F.2d 572 (7th Cir. 1976)	§§ 2.21, 20.7
Pittsburgh Plate Glass Co., 311 F.2d 410 (10th Cir. 1962)	§ 13.10
P.J. Maffel Bldg. Wrecking Corp. v. United States, 732 F.2d 913 (Fed. Cir. 1984)	§ 16.29
Planning Research Corp., GSBCA No. 10697-P, 1990 BPD ¶ 224 (1990)	§ 4.14
Plante v. Jacobs, 10 Wis. 2d 567, 103 N.W.2d 296 (1960)	§ 20.11
Plan-Tec v. Wiggins, 443 N.E.2d 1212 (Ind. 1983)	§§ 7.10, 7.14
Play Sys., Inc. v. American Druggists Ins. Co., 176 Ga. App. 372, 336 S.E.2d 308 (1985)	§ 13.12
Port City Constr. Co. v. Henderson, 266 So. 2d 896 (Ala. Ct. App. 1972)	§ 2.21
Port Liberty Partnership v. Strober Bros, 228 N.J. Super. 155, 549 A.2d 72 (1988)	§ 7.2
Portland, City of v. G.D. Ward & Assocs., Inc., 89 Or. App. 452, 750 P.2d 171, *review denied,* 305 Or. 672, 757 P.2d 422 (1988)	§ 12.27
Powers Regulator Co. v. United States Fidelity & Guar. Co., 7 Mass. App. Ct. 913, 388 N.E.2d 1205 (1978)	§ 13.17
P.P.G. Indus., Inc. v. Bean Dredging Corp., 447 So. 2d 1058 (La. 1984)	§ 12.27
Prager v. City of N.Y. Hous. Auth., 112 Misc. 2d 1034, 447 N.Y.S.2d 1013 (1982)	§ 7.40
Prairie State Bank v. United States, 164 U.S. 227 (1869)	§ 12.31
Prashker v. United States Guar. Co., 1 N.Y.2d 584, 136 N.E.2d 871, 154 N.Y.S.2d 910 (1956)	§ 11.1

Case	*Book §*
President & Directors v. Madden, 660 F.2d 91 (4th Cir. 1981)	§§ 7.42, 12.36
Prichard Bros., Inc. v. Grady Co., 428 N.W.2d 391 (Minn. 1988)	§§ 7.41, 8.2
Prier v. Refrigeration Eng'g Co., 74 Wash. 2d 25, 442 P.2d 621 (1968)	§ 7.6
Prieto v. Continental Ins. Co., 358 So. 2d 851 (Fla. Dist. Ct. App. 1978)	§ 11.17
Producers Daily Delivery Co. v. Sentry Ins. Co., 41 Cal. 3d 903, 718 P.2d 920, 226 Cal. Rptr. 558 (1986)	§ 11.2
Professional Answering Serv., Inc. v. Central La. Elec. Co., 521 So. 2d 549 (La. Ct. App. 1988)	§ 12.27
Prudential-LMI Commercial Ins. v. Superior Court, 51 Cal. 3d 674, 728 P.2d 1230, 274 Cal. Rptr. 387, *modified,* 52 Cal. 3d 517a (1990)	§ 11.6
Psaty & Fuhrman, Inc. v. Housing Auth., 76 R.I. 87, 68 A.2d 32 (1949)	§§ 7.34, 16.13, 20.10
Public Serv. Elec. & Gas Co. v. Associated Elec. & Gas Ins. Servs., Ltd., 745 F. Supp. 1037 (D.N.J. 1990)	§ 22.15
Public Water Supply Dist. No. 3 v. Reliance Ins. Co., 708 S.W.2d 190 (Mo. Ct. App. 1986)	§ 13.7
Publicker Indus., Inc. v. Romar Ceramics Corp., 603 F.2d 1065 (3d Cir. 1979)	§ 20.12
Pyco Supply Co. v. American Centennial Ins. Co., 85 N.C. App. 253, 354 S.E.2d 360 (1987)	§ 13.5
Pytko v. Connecticut, 28 Conn. Supp. 173, 255 A.2d 640 (1969)	§ 6.8
Qualls v. Country Mut. Ins. Co., 123 Ill. App. 3d 831, 462 N.E.2d 1288 (1984)	§ 11.10
Quedding v. Arisumi Bros., Inc., 66 Haw. 335, 661 P.2d 706 (1983)	§§ 20.2, 20.16
Queensbury Union v. Jim Walter Corp., 91 Misc. 2d 804, 398 N.Y.S.2d 832 (1977)	§ 7.6
Rafeiro v. American Employers' Ins. Co., 5 Cal. App. 3d 799, 85 Cal. Rptr. 701 (1970)	§ 11.3
Ralph C. Sutro Co. v. Paramount Plastering, Inc., 216 Cal. App. 2d 433, 31 Cal. Rptr. 174 (1963)	§ 9.16
Ralph D. Nelson Co. v. Beil, 671 P.2d 85 (Okla. Ct. App. 1983)	§ 20.8
Ranier Credit Co. v. Western Alliance Corp., 171 Cal. App. 3d 255, 217 Cal. Rptr. 291 (1985)	§ 11.2
R.A. Peck, Inc. v. Liberty Fed. Sav. Bank, 108 N.M. 84, 766 P.2d 928 (1988)	§§ 9.21, 9.22
Ray Sumlin Constr. Co. v. City of Mobile, 519 So. 2d 511 (Ala. 1988)	§ 20.10
Raytheon Prod. Corp. v. Commissioner, 144 F.2d 110 (1st Cir. 1944)	§§ 21.14, 21.18, 21.20

Case	*Book §*
R.C. Stanhope, Inc. v. Roanoke Constr. Co., 539 F.2d 992 (4th Cir. 1976)	§ 13.1
ReCon Paving, Inc. v. United States, 745 F.2d 34 (Fed. Cir. 1984)	§ 6.5
Redarowicz v. Ohlendorf, 92 Ill. App. 2d 171, 441 N.E.2d 324 (1982)	§ 20.7
Redman Dev. Corp. v. Piedmont Heating & Air Conditioning Co., 128 Ga. App. 447, 197 S.E.2d 167 (1974)	§ 2.21
Redna Marine Corp. v. Poland, 46 F.R.D. 81 (S.D.N.Y. 1969)	§ 11.23
Reichelet v. Urban Inv. & Dev. Co., 577 F. Supp. 971 (N.D. Ill. 1984)	§ 20.7
Reiman Constr Co. v. Jerry Hiller Co., 709 P.2d 1271 (Wyo. 1985)	§ 20.2
Reliance Ins. Co. v. Jones, 296 F.2d 71 (10th Cir. 1961)	§ 11.19
Remmer v. Glens Falls Indem. Co., 140 Cal. App. 2d 84, 295 P.2d 19 (1956)	§ 11.6
Renown, Inc. v. Hensel Phelps Constr. Co., 154 Cal. App. 3d 413, 201 Cal. Rptr. 242 (1984)	§§ 12.34, 20.3
Reserve Ins. Co. v. Pisciotta, 30 Cal. 3d 800, 640 P.2d 764, 180 Cal. Rptr. 628 (1982)	§ 11.2
R.E.T. Corp. v. Frank Paxton Co., 329 N.W.2d 416 (Iowa 1983)	§ 20.8
Rex Sys., Inc. v. Holiday, 814 F.2d 994 (4th Cir. 1987)	§ 6.6
R.G. Woods & Assocs. Ltd., 85-1 B.C.A. (CCH) ¶ 17,898 (PSBCA 1985)	§ 8.5
Rickel v. Schwinn Bicycle Co., 144 Cal. App. 3d 648, 192 Cal. Rptr. 732 (1983)	§ 12.27
Rider v. United States, 7 Cl. Ct. 770 (1985)	§ 6.5
Ridley v. Pipe Maintenance Servs., Inc., 68 Pa. Commw. 16, 477 A.2d 610 (1984)	§ 6.14
Ridley Inv. Co. v. Croll, 56 Del. 208, 192 A.2d 925 (1963)	§§ 20.2, 20.6
Ridley, Township of v. Haulaway Trash Removal, Inc., 68 Pa. Commw. 16, 448 A.2d 654 (1982)	§ 6.14
Rienharcz v. Chrysler Motors Corp., 514 F. Supp. 1141 (C.D. Cal. 1981)	§ 12.27
Riggins v. Bechtel Power Corp., 44 Wash. App. 244, 722 P.2d 819 (1986)	§§ 7.11, 7.14
Riley Bldg. Supplies, Inc. v. First Citizens Nat'l Bank, 510 So. 2d 506 (Miss. 1987)	§ 9.21
Ringer v. Graham, 293 S.C. 238, 359 S.E.2d 523 (Ct. App. 1987)	§ 7.2
River Valley, Inc. v. American States Ins. Co., 297 Ark. 386, 699 S.W.2d 745 (1985)	§ 13.7
Robberson Steel, Inc. v. J.D. Abrams, Inc., 582 S.W.2d 558 (Tex. Civ. App. 1979)	§ 10.7
Robert Gordon, Inc. v. Ingersoll-Rand Co., 117 F.2d 654 (7th Cir. 1941)	§ 10.3

Case	*Book §*
Roberts v. Sinnot, 55 Mont. 369, 177 P. 252 (1918)	§ 20.2
Roberts Constr. Co., *In re,* 172 Neb. 819, 111 N.W.2d 767 (1961)	§ 2.28
Rockhill v. United States, 288 Md. 237, 418 A.2d 197 (1980)	§ 9.21
Ronald Adams, Contractor, Inc. v. Louisiana, 457 So. 2d 778 (La. Ct. App. 1984)	§ 5.3
Royal Indem. Co. v. T.B. Smith, 121 Ga. App. 272, 173 S.E.2d 738 (1970)	§ 11.11
Royal Indem. Co. v. United States, 371 F.2d 463 (Ct. Cl.), *cert. denied,* 389 U.S. 833 (1967)	§ 12.31
R.P. Russo Contractors v. C.J. Pettinato Realty, 334 Pa. Super. 72, 482 A.2d 1086 (1984)	§§ 9.9, 9.10, 9.23
R.S. Noonan, Inc. v. Morrison-Knudsen Co., 522 F. Supp. 1186 (E.D. La. 1981)	§ 7.23
Rushlight Auto Sprinkler Co. v. City of Portland, 189 Or. 194, 219 P.2d 732 (1950)	§ 4.30
Rush Presbyterian St. Luke's Medical Ctr. v. Safeco Ins. Co., 712 F. Supp. 1344 (N.D. Ill. 1989)	§ 12.27
R.W, Indus. v. National Sur. Corp., 754 P.2d 502 (Mont. 1988)	§ 12.27
Ryan v. Morgan Spear Assocs., Inc., 546 S.W.2d 678 (Tex. Ct. App. 1977)	§ 7.6
Rye v. Public Serv. Mut. Ins. Co., 34 N.Y.2d 470, 315 N.E.2d 458, 358 N.Y.S.2d 391 (1974)	§ 20.10
Sabella v. Wisler, 59 Cal. 2d 21, 377 P.2d 889, 27 Cal. Rptr. 689 (1963)	§ 11.22
Saddler v. United States, 287 F.2d 411 (Ct. Cl. 570 (1937)	§ 5.2
Safeco Ins. Co. v. J.L. Henson, Inc., 601 S.W.2d 183 (Tex. Ct. App. 1980)	§ 12.30
St. Clair Shores v. L.&L. Constr. Co., 363 Mich. 518, 109 N.E.2d 802 (1961)	§ 20.3
St. Paul Fire & Marine Ins. Co. v. Coss, 80 Cal. App. 3d 888, 145 Cal. Rptr. 836 (1978)	§§ 11.8, 11.10
St. Paul Fire & Marine Ins. Co. v. Murray Plumbing & Heating Corp., 65 Cal. App. 3d 66, 135 Cal. Rptr. 120 (1976)	§ 11.22
St. Paul Fire & Marine Ins. Co. v. Sears, Roebuck & Co., 603 F.2d 780 (9th Cir. 1979)	§ 11.1
St. Paul Surplus Lines v. Diversified Athletic Servs., 707 F. Supp. 1506 (N.D. Ill. 1989)	§ 11.10
Salard v. Jim Walter Homes, Inc., 563 So. 2d 1327 (La. Ct. App. 1990)	§ 20.8
Salem Realty Co. v. Batson, 256 N.C. 298, 123 S.E.2d 744 (1962)	§ 20.3
Salem Towne Apartments, Inc. v. McDaniel & Sons Roofing Co., 330 F. Supp. 906 (E.D.N.C. 1970)	§§ 12.34, 20.7
Sample v. Morgan, 311 N.C. App. 717, 319 S.E.2d 607 (1984)	§ 2.18

Case	*Book §*
Sampley Enter., Inc. v. Laurilla, 494 So. 2d 841 (Fla. Dist. Ct. App. 1981)	§ 16.43
Sanders v. Commissioner, 225 F.2d 629 (10th Cir. 1955), *cert. denied,* 350 U.S. 967 (1956)	§ 21.8
San Diego Navy Fed. Credit Union v. Cumis Ins. Soc'y, Inc., 162 Cal. App. 3d 358, 208 Cal. Rptr. 494 (1984)	§ 11.1
Sandler v. Lawn-A-Mat, 141 N.J. Super. 437, 358 A.2d 805 (App. Div.), *cert. denied,* 71 N.J. 503, 366 A.2d 658 (1976)	§ 20.8
Sandolph v. P&L Hauling Contractors, Inc., 430 So. 2d 102 (La. Ct. App. 1983)	§ 12.27
San Francisco Real Estate Investors v. J.A. Jones Constr. Co., 524 F. Supp. 768 (S.D. Ohio 1981). *aff'd,* 703 F.2d 976 (6th Cir. 1983)	§§ 8.2, 20.7
San Jose Prod. Credit Ass'n v. Old Republic Life Ins. Co., 723 F.2d 700 (9th Cir. 1984)	§ 12.27
San Ore-Gradner v. Missouri Pac. R.R. 496 F. Supp. 1337 (E.D. Ark. 1980)	§ 20.10
Santa Fe, Inc. v. United States, 13 Cl. Ct. 464 (1987)	§ 4.16
Santucci Constr. Co. v. Baxter & Woodman, Inc., 151 Ill. App. 3d 547, 502 N.E.2d 1134 (1986)	§§ 7.17, 7.18, 7.27, 7.41
Sasso Contracting Co. v. State, 173 N.J. Super. 486, 414 A.2d 603 (1980)	§ 5.5
Savoy Constr. Co. v. United States, 80-1 B.C.A. (CCH) ¶ 392 (ASBCA), *motion for reconsideration denied,* 80-1 B.C.A. (CCH) ¶ 14,724 (ASBCA 1980)	§ 16.40
Scanwell Lab. v. Shaffer, 424 F.2d 859 (D.C. Cir. 1970)	§§ 6.6, 6.7
Scanwell Lab., Inc. v. Thomas, 521 F.2d 941 (D.C. Cir. 1975), *cert. denied,* 425 U.S. 910 (1976)	§ 16.30
Scarano v. Board of Regents of Univ., 57 A.D.2d 991, 394 N.Y.S.2d 322 (1977)	§ 10.2
Schaeffer Piano Mfg. Co. v. National Fire Extinguisher Co., 148 F. 159 (7th Cir. 1907)	§ 20.5
Schimmer v. H.W. Freeman Constr. Co., 643 S.W.2d 621 (Mo. Ct. App. 1983)	§ 20.16
Schneider Fuel & Supply Co. v. West Allis State Bank, 70 Wis. 2d 1041, 236 N.W.2d 266 (1975)	§ 12.31
Schoffner Indus., Inc. v. W.B. Lloyd Constr. Co., 42 N.C. App. 259, 257 S.E.2d 50 (1978)	§ 8.9
School Bd. v. St. Paul Fire & Marine Ins. Co., 449 So. 2d 872 (Fla. Dist. Ct. App. 1984)	§ 12.34
Scott v. Potomac Ins. Co., 217 Or. 323, 341 P.2d 1083 (1959)	§ 8.6
Scott Elec. Co. v. Industrial Indem. Co., 30 Cal. App. 3d 797, 106 Cal. Rptr. 710 (1973)	§ 11.2
Scottish Union Nat'l. Ins. Co. v. Encampment Smelting Co., 166 F. 231 (8th Cir. 1908), *dissapproved on other grounds* by Concordia Ins. Co. v. School Dist. No. 98, 282 U.S. 545 (1931)	§ 11.19
S.D. & D.L. Cota Plastering Co. v. Moore, 247 Iowa 972, 77 N.W.2d 475 (1956)	§ 20.11

Case	*Book §*
Seaboard Sur. Co. v. Dale Constr. Co., 230 F.2d 625 (1st Cir. 1956)	§ 12.19
Sears, Roebuck & Co. v. Enco Assocs., Inc., 43 N.Y.2d 389, 372 N.E.2d 555, 401 N.Y.S.2d 767 (1977)	§ 8.4
Sears, Roebuck & Co. v. Shamrock Constr. Co., 441 So. 2d 379 (La. Ct. App. 1983)	§ 12.28
Seattle, City of v. Dyad Constr., Inc., 17 Wash. App. 501, 565 P.2d 423 (1972)	§ 7.31
Seattle W. Indus., Inc. v. David A. Mowat Co., 110 Wash. 2d 1, 750 P.2d 245 (1988)	§§ 8.1, 8.2, 8.8
Security Ins. Co. v. Kaye Milling Supply, Inc., 297 Minn. 348, 211 N.W.2d 519 (1973)	§ 11.17
Security Ins. Co. v. United States *ex rel.* Haydis, 338 F.2d 444 (9th Cir. 1964)	§ 13.14
Segovia Dev. Corp. v. Constructora Maza, Inc., 628 F.2d 724 (1st Cir. 1980)	§ 12.25
Seif v. Long Beach, 286 N.Y. 382, 36 N.E.2d 630 (1941)	§ 6.14
Seminole Sheet Metal Co., 828 F.2d 671 (11th Cir. 1987)	§ 8.2
Seretto v. Rockland, S.T.&O.H. Ry., 101 Me. 140, 63 A. 651 (1906)	§ 2.28
Sewell v. Gregory, 371 S.E.2d 82 (W. Va. 1988)	§ 20.1
Shaddock v. Storm King Window Co., 696 S.W.2d 271 (Tex. Ct. App. 1985)	§ 20.8
Shakin v. Buskirk, 454 Mich. 490, 93 N.W.2d 293 (1958)	§ 16.35
Shaw v. Bridges Gallagher, Inc., 174 Ill. App. 3d 680, 528 N.E.2d 1349 (1988)	§§ 20.3, 20.8
Shoffner Indus. v. W.B. Lloyd Constr. Co., 42 N.C. App. 259, 257 S.E.2d 50 (1979)	§ 8.2
Shop & Stop Cos. v. Gilbane Bldg. Co., 364 Mass. 325, 304 N.E.2d 429 (1973)	§ 10.11
Siders v. School, 188 Cal. App. 3d 1217, 233 Cal. Rptr. 906 (1986)	§ 20.7
Sides v. Richard Mach. Works, Inc., 406 F.2d 445 (4th Cir. 1969)	§ 7.16
Siefford v. Housing Auth., 192 Neb. 643, 223 N.W.2d 816 (1974)	§ 16.28
Silverdale Hotel v. Lomas & Nettleton Co., 36 Wash. App. 762, 677 P.2d 773, *review denied,* 101 Wash. 2d 1021 (1984)	§§ 9.9, 9.14
Singsass v. Diederich, 307 Minn. 153, 238 N.W.2d 878 (1976)	§ 11.17
1616 Remine Ltd. Partnership v. Atchinson & Keller Co., 14 Bankr. 484 (E.D. Va. 1981)	§ 12.36
S.J. Groves & Son v. Warner Co., 576 F,2d 524 (3d Cir. 1978)	§ 20.7
S.K. Whitty & Co. v. Laurence L. Lambert & Assoc., 576 So. 2d 599 (La. Ct. App. 1991)	§ 8.2
Slater v. Lawyers Mut. Ins. Co., 227 Cal. App. 3d 1415, 278 Cal. Rptr. 479 (1991)	§ 11.7

Case	Book §
Slattery Assocs. v. City of N.Y., 98 A.D.2d 686, 469 N.Y.S.2d 758 (1983)	§ 16.17
Sloane v. Malcolm Price, Inc., 339 A.2d 43 (D.C. 1975)	§ 5.17
S.L. Rowland Constr. Co. v. St. Paul Fire & Marine Ins. Co., 72 Wash. 2d 682, 434 P.2d 725 (1967)	§ 11.14
Slutsky-Peltz v. Vincennes Community Sch., 556 N.E.2d 344 (Ind. Ct. App. 1990)	§ 2.34
SMC Corp. v. Xerox Corp., 77 F.R.D. 10 (D. Conn. 1977)	§ 22.13
SMC Info. Sys., Inc., 85-3 B.C.A. (CCH) ¶ 18, 388 (GSBCA 1985)	§ 4.16
Smith v. Union Supply Co., 675 P.2d 333 (Colo. Ct. App. 1984)	§ 20.4
Smither & Co. v. Calvin Humphrey Corp., 232 F. Supp. 204 (D.D.C. 1964)	§ 20.3
Smith & Lowe Constr. Co. v. Herrera, 79 N.M. 239, 442 P.2d 197 (1968)	§§ 4.30, 5.14
Smith & Wesson, *In re,* 757 F.2d 431 (1st 1985)	§§ 4.16, 6.6
Sofias v. Bank of Am. Nat'l Trust & Sav. Ass'n, 172 Cal. App. 3d 583, 218 Cal. Rptr. 388 (1985)	§§ 9.4, 9.9
Solite Masonry Units Corp. v. Piland Constr. Co., 217 Va. 727, 232 S.E.2d 759 (1977)	§ 13.4
Son-Shone Grading, Inc. v. ADC Constr. Co., 68 N.C. App. 417, 315 S.E.2d 346, *review denied,* 312 N.C. 85, 321 S.E.2d 900 (1984)	§ 12.38
Sorenson v. City of N.Y., 202 F.2d 857 (2d Cir. 1953), *cert. denied,* 347 U.S. 951 (1954)	§ 6.14
Sousa v. Albino, 120 R.I. 461, 388 A.2d 804 (1978)	§ 20.7
Southeastern Sales & Serv. Co. v. T.T. Watson, Inc., 172 So. 2d 239 (Fla. Dist. Ct. App. 1965)	§§ 2.26, 10.3
Southern Bell Tel. & Tel. Co. v. Acme Elec. Contractors, Inc., 418 So. 2d 1187 (Fla. 1983)	§ 5.13
Southern Cal. Edison Co. v. Harbor Ins. Co., 83 Cal. App. 3d 747, 148 Cal. Rptr. 106 (1978)	§ 11.24
Southern Gulf Utils., Inc. v. Boca Ciega Sanitary Dist., 238 So. 2d 458 (Fla. Dist. Ct. App. 1970)	§ 7.34
Southern New England Contracting Co. v. State, 165 Conn. 644, 345 A.2d 550 (1974)	§ 20.2
Space Leasing Assocs. v. Atlantic Bldg. Sys., Inc., 144 Ga. App. 320, 241 S.E.2d 438 (1977)	§ 20.7
Spang Indus., Inc., Fort Pitt Bridge Div. v. Aetna Casualty & Sur. Co., 512 F.2d 365 (2d Cir. 1975)	§ 5.12
Sparks v. St. Paul Ins. Co., 495 A.2d 406, 100 N.J. 325 (1985)	§ 11.7
Spearin, Preston & Burrows, Inc. v. City of N.Y., 160 A.D.2d 263, 553 N.Y.S.2d 372 (1990)	§ 16.18
Spence v. Harm, 163 N.Y. 220, 57 N.E. 412 (1900)	§ 20.11
Sprayregen v. American Airlines, Inc., 570 F. Supp. 16 (S.D.N.Y. 1983)	§ 7.40
Square D Co. v. C.J. Kern Contractors, Inc., 314 N.C. 423, 334 S.E.2d 63 (1985)	§ 20.4

Case	*Book §*
S.S. Silberblatt, Inc. v. East Harlem Pilot Block, 608 F.2d 28 (2d Cir. 1979)	§§ 9.7, 9.16, 9.18
S.S. Steele & Co. v. Pugh, 473 S.E.2d 978 (Ala. 1985)	§ 20.7
Standard Accident Ins. Co. v. United States *ex rel.* Powell, 302 U.S. 442 (1938)	§ 13.7
Standard Oil Co. v. United States, 340 U.S. 54 (1950)	§ 11.2
Standard Structural Steel Co. v. Bethlehem Steel Corp., 597 F. Supp. 164 (D. Conn. 1984)	§ 11.21
Standard Venetian Blind Co. v. American Empire Ins. Co., 503 Pa. 300, 469 A.2d 563 (1983), (1985)	§ 11.2
State v. Lundin, 91 A.D.2d 343, 459 N.Y.S.2d 904 (1983)	§ 20.4
State Constr. Co. v. Bituminous Casualty Corp., 228 Pa. Super. 1, 323 A.2d 141 (1973)	§ 11.11
State *ex rel.* Fisher Constr. Co. v. Linzell Constr. Co., 101 Ohio App. 219, 137 N.E.2d 427 (1955)	§ 4.23
State *ex rel.* Lane v. Dashiell, 195 Md. 667, 75 A.2d 348 (1950)	§ 6.11
State *ex rel.* National Sur. Corp. v. Malvaney, 221 Miss. 190, 72 So. 2d (1954)	§ 12.33
State Distrib. Corp. v. G.E. Bobbitt & Assocs., Inc., 62 N.C. App. 530, 303 S.E.2d 349 (1983)	§ 20.3
State Farm Fire & Casualty Co. v. Martin, 872 F.2d 319 (9th Cir. 1989)	§ 11.22
State Farm Mut. Auto. Ins. Co. v. Longden, 197 Cal. App. 3d 226, 242 Cal. Rptr. 726 (1987)	§ 11.6
State Farm Mut. Ins. Co. v. Wilson, 162 Ariz. 251, 782 P.2d 727 1989)	§ 11.10
State Highway Admin. v. Greiner Eng'g Sciences, Inc., 83 Md. App. 621, 577 A.2d 363 (1990)	§ 7.32
State Highway Admin. v. Transamerica Ins. Co., 278 Md. 690, 367 A.2d 509 (1976)	§ 13.3
State Sur. Co. v. Lamv Constr. Co., 625 P.2d 184 (Wyo. 1981)	§ 12.34
Stauffer Constr. Co. v. Tate Eng'g, Inc., 44 Md. App. 240, 407 A.2d 1191 (1979)	§ 13.1
Stearns Constr. Corp. v. Carolina Corp., 63 Wis. 2d 342, 217 N.W.2d 291 (1974)	§ 12.34
Steckmar Nat'l Realty & Inv. Corp., Ltd. v. J.I. Case Co., 99 Misc. 2d 212, 415 N.Y.S.2d 946 (1979)	§ 7.41
Stees v. Leonard, 20 Minn. 494 (1874)	§ 20.6
Stehlin-Muller Henes Co. v. City of Bridgeport, 97 Conn. 657, 117 A. 811 (1922)	§§ 2.13, 2.28
Steltz v. Armory Co., 15 Idaho 551, 99 P. 98 (1908)	§ 20.3
Stenerson v. City of Kalispell, 629 P.2d 773 (Mont. 1981)	§ 5.18
Stephens v. Creel, 429 So. 2d 278 (Ala. 1983)	§ 20.4
Stephens v. Great S. Sav. & Loan Ass'n, 421 S.W.2d 332 (Mo. Ct. App. 1967)	§§ 9.9, 9.10
Sterilite Corp. v. Continental Casualty Co., 17 Mass. App. Ct. 316, 458 N.E.2d 338 (1983)	§ 11.13

Case	*Book §*
Stewart v. Estate of Bohnert, 101 Cal. App. 3d 978, 162 Cal. Rptr. 126 (1980)	§ 11.2
Stillwater Condominium Ass'n v. American Home Assurance Co., 508 F. Supp. 1075 (D. Mont. 1981), *aff'd,* 688 F.2d 848 (9th Cir. 1982), *cert. denied,* 460 U.S. 1038 (1983)	§ 11.10
Stinson v. Mueller, 449 A.2d 329 (D.C. 1982)	§ 20.12
Stonehocker v. General Motors Corp., 587 F.2d 151 (4th Cir. 1978)	§ 22.13
Storm Drilling Co. v. Atlantic Richfield Corp., 386 F. Supp. 830 (E.D. Cal. 1974)	§ 22.8
Storms v. United States Fidelity & Guar. Co., 388 A.2d 578 (N.H. 1978)	§§ 11.2, 11.17
Stroebel v. Jefferson Trucking & Rigging Co., 125 N.J.L. 484, 15 A.2d 805 (1940)	§ 20.13
Strouss v. Simmons, 666 Haw. 32, 657 P.2d 1004 (1982)	§§ 9.11, 9.14, 9.15
Strubble v. United Servs. Auto Assocs., 35 Cal. App. 3d 498, 110 Cal. Rptr. 828 (1973)	§ 11.23
Structural Sales, Inc. v. Vavrus, 132 Ill. App. 3d 718, 477 N.E.2d 745 (1985)	§ 10.7
Studiengesellschaft Kohle mbH v. Novomont Corp., 485 F. Supp. 471 (S.D.N.Y. 1980)	§ 20.12
Stura, Inc. v. Fireman's Fund Ins. Co., 67 Haw. 203, 684 P.2d 960 (1984)	§ 11.10
Sturges Mfg. Co. v. Utica Mut. Ins. Co., 37 N.Y.2d 69, 332 N.E.2d 319, 371 N.Y.S.2d 444 (1975)	§ 11.13
Subsurfco, Inc. v. B-Y Water Dist., 369 N.W.2d 129 (S.D. 1985)	§ 20.16
Superior Glass Co. v. First Bristol County Nat'l Bank, 380 Mass. 829, 567 N.E.2d 1244 (1991)	§ 9.20
Superior Glass Co. v. First Bristol County Nat'l Bank, 8 Mass. App. 356, 294 N.E.2d 972 (1979), *aff'd,* 380 Mass. 829, 406 N.E.2d 1209 (1980)	§ 9.21
Sutter Corp. v. Tri-Boro Mun. Auth., 338 Pa. Super. 217, 487 A.2d 933 (1985)	§ 20.10
Suver v. Personal Serv. Ins. Co., 11 Ohio St. 6, 462 N.E.2d 415 (1984)	§ 12.27
Swarthaut v. Beard, 33 Mich. App. 395, 90 N.W.2d 373 (1971), *rev'd on other grounds,* 388 Mich. 637, 202 N.W.2d 300 (1972)	§ 7.14
Swastika Oil & Gas v. Commissioner, 123 F.2d 382 (6th Cir. 1941)	§ 21.3
Sweeney Co. v. Engineers-Constructors, Inc., 823 F.2d 805 (4th Cir. 1987)	§ 20.2
Swinertpm & Walberg Co. v. Inglewood, 40 Cal. App. 3d 98, 114 Cal. Rptr. 834 (1974)	§ 4.27
Sylla v. United States Fidelity & Guar. Co., 54 Cal. App. 3d 895, 127 Cal. Rptr. 38 (1978)	§ 11.6
Symons Corp. v. Insurance Co. of N. Am., 94 N.C. App. 541, 380 S.E.2d 550 (1989)	§ 13.7

Case	*Book §*
Sysorex Info. Sys., GSBCA Nos. 10642-P, 10644-P, 10656-P, 1990 BPD ¶ 224 (1990)	§ 4.14
Szarkowski v. Reliance Ins. Co., 404 N.W.2d 502 (N.D. 1987)	§ 12.27
Taramac Dev. Co. v. Delmater Fround & Assocs., 234 Kan. 618, 675 P.2d 361 (1984)	§ 7.19
Taylor-McDonnell Constr. Co. v. Commercial Union Ins. Co., 229 Mont. 34, 744 P.2d 892 (1987)	§ 11.10
Taylor-Morley-Simons, Inc. v. Michigan Mut. Ins. Co., 645 F. Supp. 596 (E.D. Mo. 1986), *aff'd,* 822 F.2d 1093 (8th Cir. 1987)	§ 11.10
Taylor, Thon, Thompson & Peterson v. Cannaday, 749 P.2d 63 (Mont. 1987)	§ 8.5
T.C. Bateson Constr. Co. v. Lumberman's Mut. Ins. Co., 784 S.W.2d 692 (Tex. Ct. App. 1989)	§§ 11.10, 11.14
Teeples v. Tolson, 207 F. Supp. 212 (D. Or. 1962)	§ 11.18
Tennessee Corp. v. Lamb Bros. Constr. Co., 265 So. 2d 533 (Fla. Dist. Ct. App. 1972)	§ 11.16
Terry v. United States Fidelity & Guar. Co., 196 Wash. 206, 82 P.2d 532 (1938)	§ 12.23
Tessmar v. Grosner, 23 N.J. 193, 128 A.2d 467 (1957)	§ 20.8
Texas E. Transmission Corp. v. Marine Office-Appleton & Cox Corp., 579 F.2d 561 (10th Cir. 1978)	§§ 11.20, 11.21, 11.23
Theisse-Nonnemache, Inc. v. Duff, 393 N.W.2d 397 (Minn. Ct. App. 1986)	§ 20.2
Thermal Reduction Co., B-236724, 89-2 CPD ¶ 527 (1989)	§ 4.14
The T.J. Hooper, 60 F.2d 737 (2d Cir.), *cert. denied,* 287 U.S. 662 (1932)	§ 8.5
Third Nat'l Bank v. Highlands Ins. Co., 603 S.W.2d 730 (Tenn. 1980)	§ 12.31
Thomas W. Hooley & Sons v. Zurich Gen. Accident & Liab. Ins. Co., 235 La. 289, 103 So. 2d 449 (1958)	§ 11.11
Tiano v. Aetna Casulaty & Sur. Co., 102 Mich. App. 177, 301 N.W.2d 476 (1980)	§ 11.17
Tippets-Abbett-McCarthy-Stratton v. New York State Thruway Auth., 27 Misc. 2d 522, 212 N.Y.S.2d 263 (Ct. Cl. 1961), *rev'd on other grounds,* 18 A.D.2d 402, 239 N.Y.S.2d 732, *aff'd,* 13 N.Y.2d 1091, 196 N.E.2d 64, 246 N.Y.S.2d 409 (1963)	§ 20.9
Todd Shipyards Corp. v. Turbine Serv., Inc., 674 F.2d 401 (5th Cir.), *cert. denied sub nom.* Sentry Ins. v. Todd Shipyards Corp., 459 U.S. 1036 (1982)	§ 11.14
Tolstoy Constr. Co. v. Minter, 78 Cal. App. 3d 665, 143 Cal. Rptr. 570 (1978)	§ 20.11
Tonawanda, Town of v. Stapell, Mumm & Beals Corp., 240 App. Div. 472, 270 N.Y.S. 377, *aff'd,* 265 N.Y. 630, 193 N.E. 419 (1934)	§ 12.34
Toombs & Co. v. United States, 4 Ct. Cl. 535 (1984)	§ 17.2

Case	*Book §*
Torrey v. Simon-Torrey, Inc., 307 So. 2d 569 (La. 1974)	§ 12.38
Town Concrete Pipe, Inc. v. Redford, 43 Wash. App. 493, 717 P.2d 1384 (1986)	§§ 9.4, 9.20
T.P.M.P.T. Employees Credit Union v. Charpentier, 376 So. 2d 592 (La. Ct. App. 1979)	§ 12.30
Trans-Bay Eng'rs & Builders, Inc. v. Hills, 551 F.2d 370 (D.C. Cir. 1976)	§ 9.19
Transport Inde. Co. v. Teter, 575 S.W.2d 780 (Mo. Ct. App. 1978)	§ 11.10
Traylor v. Henkels & McCoy, Inc., 99 Idaho 560, 585 P.2d 970 (1979)	§ 5.12
Triax Co. v. United States, 20 Cl. Ct. 507 (1990)	§ 6.5
Trinity Universal Ins. Co. v. United States, 382 F.2d 317 (5th Cir.), *cert. denied,* 389 U.S. 833 (1967)	§ 12.31
Triple A Contractors, Inc. v. Rural Water Dist., 226 Kan. 626, 603 P.2d 184 (1979)	§ 4.30
Transamerica Ins. Co. v. Gage Plumbing & Heating Co., 433 F.2d 1051 (10th Cir. 1970)	§ 11.25
Trans-Bay Eng'rs & Builders, Inc. v. Hills, 551 F.2d 370 (D.C. Cir. 1976)	§ 9.7
Travelers v. Humming Bird Coal Co., 371 S.W.2d 35 (Ky. Ct. App. 1963)	§ 11.5
Travelers Indem. Co. v. United States *ex rel.* Construction Specialities Co., 382 F.2d 103 (10th Cir. 1967)	§ 13.14
Travelers Indem. Co. v. United States *ex rel.* Western Steel Co., 362 F.2d 896 (9th Cir. 1966)	§§ 10.66, 13.10
Treasure State Indus., Inc. v. Welsh, 173 Mont. 403, 567 P.2d 947 (1977)	§ 12.12
Trenton Constr. Co. v. Straub, 310 S.E.2d 496 (W. Va. 1984)	§ 20.3
Tri-Cor, Inc. v. United States, 458 F.2d 112 (Ct. Cl. 1972)	§ 16.28
Trinity Indus., Inc. v. INA, 916 F.2d 267 (5th Cir. 1990), *reh'g denied,* 923 F.2d 851 (5th Cir. 1991)	§ 11.20
Trip v. Henderson, 158 Fla. 442, 28 So. 2d 857 (1947)	§ 20.5
Tull v. Gundersons, Inc., 707 P.2d 940 (Colo. 1985)	§ 5.12
Turner Constr. Co., ASBCA Nos. 25447, 29472, 29591, 29592, 29593, 29830, 29851, 29852, 90-2 B.C.A. (CCH) ¶ 22,649	§ 7.22
Turner Constr. Co. v. John B. Kelly Co., 442 F. Supp. 551 (E.D. Pa. 1976)	§ 11.25
Turzillo v. Commissioner, 346 F.2d 884 (6th Cir. 1965)	§ 21.8
Tuskegee Alumni Hous. Found., Inc. v. National Homes Constr. Corp., 450 F. Supp. 714 (S.D. Ohio 1978), *aff'd,* 624 F.2d 1101 (5th Cir. 1980)	§ 20.12
Twenty-First Century Properties Co. v. Carpenter Insulation & Coatings Co., 694 F. Supp. 148 (D. Md. 1988)	§ 20.7

Case	*Book §*
Twin City Constr. Co. v. ITT Indus. Credit Co., 358 N.W.2d 716 (Minn. Ct. App. 1984)	§§ 9.8, 9.16
218–220 Market St. Corp. v. Krich-Radisco, Inc., 124 N.L.J. 302, 11 A.2d 109 (1940)	§ 20.10
Ulstein Maritime, Ltd. v. United States, 833 F.2d 1052 (1st Cir. 1987)	§ 6.6
Unicon Management Corp. v. City of Chicago, 404 F.2d 627 (7th Cir. 1968)	§ 22.17
Union Bldg. Corp. v. J&J Bldg. & Maintenance Contractors, Inc., 578 S.W.2d 519 (Tex. Civ. App. 1979)	§ 5.13
Unit Data Serv. Corp., GSBCA No. 10775-P, 1990 BPD ¶ 281 (1990)	§ 4.14
United Bonding Ins. Co. v. Stein, 273 F. Supp. 929 (E.D. Pa. 1967)	§ 12.30
United Elec. Corp. v. United States, 647 F.2d 1082 (Ct. Cl. 1981)	§ 13.18
United Order of Am. Bricklayers & Stone Masons Union No. 21 v. Thorleif Larsen & Son, Inc., 519 F.2d 331 (7th Cir. 1975)	§ 20.10
United Stage Equip., Inc. v. Charles Carter & Co., 342 So. 2d 1153 (La. Ct. App. 1977)	§ 7.7
United States v. Ames, 24 F. Cas. 784 (C.C.D. Mass. 1845)	§ 6.8
United States v. Bellard, 674 F.2d 330 (5th Cir. 1982)	§ 12.30
United States v. Bethlehem Steel Co., 205 U.S, 105 (1907)	§ 20.10
United States v. Braverman, 522 F.2d 218 (7th Cir.), *cert. denied,* 423 U.S. 985 (1975)	§ 22.13
United States v. Brooks-Calloway Co., 318 U.S. 120 (1943)	§ 6.23
United States v. Citizens & Southern Nat'l Bank, 889 F.2d 1067 (Fed. Cir. 1989)	§ 4.16
United States v. Citizens & Southern Nat'l Bank, 367 F.2d 473 (4th Cir. 1966)	§ 2.13
United States v. Commonwealth of Pa. Dep't of Highways, 349 F. Supp. 1370 (E.D. Pa. 1972)	§ 13.7
United States v. Crosland Constr. Co., 217 F.2d 275 (4th Cir. 1954)	§ 13.7
United States v. Electronic Data Sys. Fed. Corp., 857 F.2d 1444 (Fed. Cir. 1988)	§ 4.16
United States v. Gilmore, 372 U.S. 39 (1963)	§§ 21.2, 21.5, 21.8
United States v. International Business Machs. Corp., 892 F.2d 1006 (Fed. Cir. 1989), *reh'g denied* (Jan. 17, 1990)	§ 4.14
United States v. John C. Grimberg Co., 702 F.2d 1362 (Fed. Cir. 1983)	§§ 4.16, 6.6
United States v. John Kerns Constr. Co., 140 F.2d 792 (8th Cir. 1944)	§ 10.7

Case	*Book §*
United States v. Johnson Controls, Inc., 2 FPD ¶ 15 (Fed. Cir. 1983)	§ 7.1
United States v. King, 395 U.S. 1 (1969)	§ 6.5
United States v. Maryland Casualty Co., 323 F.2d 473 (5th Cir. 1963)	§ 13.7
United States v. Marquez, 449 F.2d 89 (2d Cir. 1971), *cert. denied,* 405 U.S. 963 (1972)	§ 22.13
United States v. Rogers & Rogers, 161 F. Supp. 132 (S.D. Cal. 1958)	§§ 7.22, 12.33
United States v. Skidmore, Owings & Merrill, 505 F. Supp. 1101 (S.D.N.Y. 1981)	§ 8.3
United States v. Spearin, 248 U.S. 132 (1918)	§§ 2.12, 16.12, 20.2
United States v. United Eng'g & Contracting Co., 234 U.S. 236 (1913)	§ 12.34
United States v. William F. Klingensmith, Inc., 670 F.2d 1227 (D.C. Cir. 1982)	§ 16.21
United States *ex rel.* Altman v. Young Lumber Co., 376 F. Supp. 1290 (D.S.C. 1974)	§ 13.14
United States *ex rel.* A&M Petroleum, Inc. v. Santa Fe Eng'rs, Inc., 660 F. Supp. 111 (S.D. Miss. 1987)	§ 13.12
United States *ex rel.* Angell Bros., Inc. v. Cave Constr., Inc., 250 F. Supp. 873 (D. Mont. 1966)	§ 13.16
United States *ex rel.* Astro Cleaning & Packaging Corp. v. Jamison Co., 425 F.2d 1281 (6th Cir. 1970)	§ 13.10
United States *ex rel.* Aurora Painting, Inc. v. Fireman's Fund Ins. Co., 832 F.2d 1150 (9th Cir. 1987)	§ 13.17
United States *ex rel.* A.V. DeBlasio Constr., Inc. v. Mountain States Constr. Co., 588 F.2d 259 (9th Cir. 1978)	§ 13.10
United States *ex rel.* Bailey v. Freethy, 469 F.2d 1348 (9th Cir. 1972)	§ 13.11
United States *ex rel.* Bailey-Lewis-Williams, Inc. v. Peter Kiewit Sons Co., 195 F. Supp. 752 (D.D.C. 1961), *aff'd,* 299 F.2d 930 (D.C. Cir. 1962)	§ 13.16
United States *ex rel.* B&B Welding, Inc. v. Reliance Ins. Co., 743 F. Supp. 129 (E.D.N.Y. 1990)	§ 13.15
United States *ex rel.* Benkart Co. v. John A. Johnson & Sons, Inc., 236 F.2d 864 (3d Cir. 1956)	§ 13.6
United States *ex rel.* Billows Elec. Supply Co. v. E.J.T. Constr. Co., 517 F. Supp. 1178 (E.D. Pa. 1981), *aff'd,* 688 F.2d 827 (3d Cir.), *cert. denied,* 103 S. Ct. 126 (1982)	§§ 13.10, 13.12, 13.14
United States *ex rel.* Blazer Pac. Equip. Co. v. Fidelity & Deposit Co., 895 F.2d 546 (9th Cir. 1990)	§ 13.7
United States *ex rel.* Board of Trustees v. J.W. Bateson Co., 551 F.2d 1284 (D.C. Cir. 1977)	§ 13.6
United States *ex rel.* Bordallo Consol., Inc. v. Markowitz Bros. (Del.), Inc., 249 F. Supp. 610 (D. Guam 1966)	§ 13.7

Case	*Book §*
United States *ex rel.* Bros. Builders Supply Co. v. Old World Artisans, Inc., 702 F. Supp. 1561 (N.D. Ga. 1988)	§ 13.7
United States *ex rel.* Bryant v. Lembke Constr. Co., 370 F.2d 293 (10th Cir. 1966)	§ 13.6
United States *ex rel.* Bryant Elec. Co. v. Aetna Casualty & Sur. Co., 297 F.2d 665 (2d Cir. 1962)	§ 13.16
United States *ex rel.* Caldwell Foundry & Mach. Co. v. Texas Constr. Co., 237 F.2d 705 (5th Cir. 1955)	§ 13.10
United States *ex rel.* Capitol Elec. Supply Co. v. C.J. Elec. Contractors, Inc., 535 F.2d 1326 (1st Cir. 1976)	§ 13.14
United States *ex rel.* Capolino Sons, Inc. v. Electronic & Missile Facilities, Inc., 364 F.2d 705 (2d Cir.), *cert. denied,* 385 U.S. 924 (1966)	§ 13.16
United States *ex rel.* Carlisle Constr. Co. v. Coastal Structures, Inc., 689 F. Supp. 1092 (M.D. Fla. 1988)	§ 13.7
United States *ex rel.* Carlson v. Continental Casualty Co. 414 F.2d 431 (5th Cir. 1969)	§ 13.7
United States *ex rel.* Carter Equip. Co. v. H.R. Morgan, Inc., 544 F.2d 1271 (5th Cir.), *reh'g granted,* 554 F.2d 164 (5th Cir. 1977)	§ 13.10
United States *ex rel.* Caswell Equip. Co. v. Fidelity & Deposit Co., 494 F. Supp. 354 (D. Minn. 1980)	§ 13.16
United States *ex rel.* Celanese Coatings Co. v. Gullard, 504 F.2d 466 (9th Cir. 1974)	§ 13.13
United States *ex rel.* Charles R. Joyce & Son, Inc. v. F.A. Baehner, Inc., 326 F.2d 556 (2d Cir. 1964)	§ 13.11
United States *ex rel.* C.J.I., Inc. v. Western States Mechanical Contractors, Inc., 834 F.2d 1534 (10th Cir. 1987)	§ 13.10
United Stats *ex rel.* Coffey v. William R. Austin Constr. Co., 436 F. Supp. 626 (W.D. Okla. 1977)	§ 13.16
United States *ex rel.* Eastern Gulf, Inc. v. Metzger Towing, Inc., 910 F.2d 775 (11th Cir. 1990)	§ 13.1
United States *ex rel.* Eddie's Sales & Leasing, Inc. v. Federal Ins. Co., 634 F.2d 1050 (10th Cir. 1980)	§ 13.7
United States *ex rel.* E.E. Black, Ltd, v. Price-McNemar Constr. Co., 320 F.2d 663 (9th Cir. 1963)	§ 13.15
United States *ex rel.* Empire Plastics Corp. v. Western Casualty & Sur. Co., 429 F.2d 905 (10th Cir. 1970)	§§ 12.6, 13.18
United States *ex rel.* E&R Constr. Co. v. Guy H. James Constr. Co., 390 F. Supp. 1193 (M.D. Tenn. 1972), *aff'd,* 489 F.2d 756 (6th Cir. 1974)	§ 13.9
United States *ex rel.* Essex Mach. Works, Inc. v. Rondout Marine, Inc., 312 F. Supp. 846 (S.D.N.Y. 1970)	§ 13.16
United States *ex rel.* Fireman's Fund Ins. Co. v. Frank Briscoe Co., 462 F. Supp. 114 (E.D. La. 1978)	§ 13.16

Case	*Book §*
United States *ex rel.* First Nat'l Bank v. United States Fidelity & Guar. Co., 240 F. Supp. 316 (N.D. Okla. 1965)	§ 13.14
United States *ex rel.* Fordham v. P.W. Parker, Inc., 504 F. Supp. 1066 (D. Md. 1980)	§ 13.12
United States *ex rel.* Franklin Paint Co. v. Kagan, 129 F. Supp. 331 (D. Mass. 1955)	§ 13.12
United States *ex rel.* General Elec. Supply Co. v. Minority Elec. Co., 537 F. Supp. 1018 (S.D. Ga. 1982)	§ 13.10
United States *ex rel.* Getz Bros. & Co. v. Markowitz Bros. (Del.) Inc., 383 F.2d 595 (9th Cir. 1967)	§ 13.3
United States *ex rel.* Greenwald-Supon, Inc. v. Gramercy Contractors, Inc., 433 F. Supp. 156 (S.D.N.Y. 1977)	§§ 13.12, 13.14
United States *ex rel.* Harris Paint Co. v. Seaboard Sur. Co., 437 F.2d 37 (5th Cir. 1971)	§ 13.12
United States *ex rel.* Harvey Gulf Int'l Marine, Inc. v. Maryland Casulaty Co., 573 F.2d 245 (5th Cir. 1978)	§ 13.16
United States *ex rel.* Hasco Elec. Corp. v. Reliance Ins. Co., 390 F. Supp. 158 (E.D.N.Y. 1975)	§ 13.6
United States *ex rel.* Heller Elec. Co. v. William F. Klingensmith, Inc., 670 F.2d 1227 (D.C. Cir. 1982)	§ 13.9
United States *ex rel.* Hillsdale Rock Co. v. Cortelyou & Cole, Inc., 581 F.2d 239 (9th Cir. 1978)	§ 13.11
United States *ex rel.* Honeywell v. A&L Mechanical Contractors, Inc., 677 F.2d 383 (4th Cir. 1982)	§ 13.11
United States *ex rel.* H.T. Sweeney & Son, Inc. v. E.J.T. Constr. Co., 415 F. Supp. 1328 (D. Del. 1976)	§ 13.14
United States *ex rel.* Humble Oil & Ref. Co, v. Fidelity & Casualty Co., 402 F.2d 893 (4th Cir. 1968)	§ 13.15
United States *ex rel.* I. Burack, Inc. v. Sovereign Constr. Co., 338 F. Supp. 657 (S.D.N.Y. 1972)	§ 13.12
United States *ex rel.* J.A. Edwards & Co. v. Peter Reiss Constr. Co., 273 F.2d 880 (2d Cir. 1959), *cert. denied,* 362 U.S. 951 (1960)	§ 13.12
United States *ex rel.* Jinks Lumber Co. v. Federal Ins. Co., 452 F.2d 485 (5th Cir. 1971)	§ 13.11
United States *ex rel.* Joseph I. Richardson, Inc. v. E.J.T. Constr. Co., 453 F. Supp. 435 (D. Del. 1978)	§ 13.14
United States *ex rel.* J.P. Byrne & Co., v. Fire Ass'n, 260 F.2d 541 (2d Cir. 1958)	§ 13.7
United States *ex rel.* Kelly-Mohrusen Co. v. Merle A. Patnode Co., 457 F.2d 116 (7th Cir. 1972)	§ 13.11
United States *ex rel.* Krupp Steel Prods., Inc. v. Aetna Ins. Co., 831 F.2d 938 (11th Cir. 1987)	§ 13.7
United States *ex rel.* Lank Woodwork Co. v. CSH Contractors, Inc., 452 F. Supp. 922 (D.D.C. 1978)	§ 13.14

Case	*Book §*
United States *ex rel.* Los Angeles Testing Lab. v. Rogers & Rogers, 161 F. Supp. 132 (S.D. Cal. 1958)	§§ 8.1, 8.9
United States *ex rel.* Magna Masonry v. R.T. Woodfield, 709 F.2d 249 (4th Cir. 1983)	§ 13.14
United States *ex rel.* Mariana v. Piracci Constr. Co., 405 F. Supp. 904 (D.D.C. 1975)	§ 13.9
United States *ex rel.* Mid-Seven Transp. v. Blinderman Constr. Co., 735 F. Supp. 272 (N.D. Ill. 1990)	§ 13.7
United States *ex rel.* Mississippi Rd. Supply Co. v. H.R. Morgan, Inc., 542 F.2d 262 (5th Cir. 1976), *cert. denied,* 434 U.S. 828 (1977)	§§ 13.1, 13.7
United States *ex rel.* Nelson v. Reliance Ins. Co., 436 F.2d 1366 (10th Cir. 1971)	§ 13.15
United States *ex rel.* Olmsted Elec., Inc. v. Neosho Constr. Co., 599 F.2d 930 (10th Cir. 1979)	§ 13.12
United States *ex rel.* Pensacola Constr. Co. v. St. Paul Fire & Marine Ins. Co., 705 F. Supp. 306 (W.D. La. 1988)	§ 13.17
United States *ex rel.* Pertun Constr. Co. v. Harvesters Group, Inc., 918 F.2d 915 (11th Cir. 1990)	§ 13.9
United States *ex rel.* Pittsburgh-Des Moines Steel Co. v. MacDonald Constr. Co., 281 F. Supp. 1010 (E.D. Mo. 1968)	§§ 13.9, 13.14
United States *ex rel.* Pool Constr. Co. v. Smith Rd. Constr. Co., 227 F. Supp. 315 (D. Okla. 1964)	§ 13.11
United States *ex rel.* Powers Regulator Co. v. Hartford Accident & Indem. Co., 376 F.2d 811 (1st Cir. 1967)	§ 13.6
United States *ex rel.* Pre-Fab Erectors, Inc. v. A.B.C. Roofing & Siding, Inc., 193 F. Supp. 465 (S.D. Cal. 1961)	§ 13.14
United States *ex rel.* Soda v. Montgomery, 253 F.2d 509 (3d Cir. 1958)	§ 13.13
United States *ex rel.* Schaefer Elec., Inc. v. O. Frank Heinz Constr. Co., 300 F. Supp. 396 (S.D. Ill. 1969)	§ 13.10
United States *ex rel.* Sherman v. Carter, 353 U.S. 210 (1957)	§§ 13.7, 13.10
United States *ex rel.* State Elec. Supply Co. v. Hesselden Constr. Co., 404 F.2d 774 (10th Cir. 1068)	§ 13.12
United States *ex rel.* Statham Instruments, Inc. v. Western Casualty & Sur. Co., 359 F.2d 521 (6th Cir. 1966)	§§ 13.13, 13.14
United States *ex rel.* Sunbelt Pipe Corp. v. United States Fidelity & Guar. Co., 785 F.2d 468 (4th Cir. 1986)	§ 13.7
United States *ex rel.* T. Square Equip. Corp. v. Gregor J. Schaefer Sons, Inc., 272 F. Supp. 962 (E.D.N.Y. 1967)	§ 13.14
United States *ex rel.* Vermont Marble Co. v. Roscoe-Ajax Constr. Co., 246 F. Supp. 439 (N.D. Cal. 1965)	§ 13.16
United States *ex rel.* Victor Elec. Corp. v. Maryland Casualty Co., 213 F. Supp. 800 (E.D.N.Y.), *further proceedings,* 215 F. Supp. 700 (E.D.N.Y. 1963)	§ 13.18

Case	*Book §*
United States *ex rel.* Warren v. Kimrey, 489 F.2d 339 (8th Cir. 1974)	§ 12.15
United States *ex rel.* Wellman Eng'g Co. v. MSI Corp., 350 F.2d 285 (2d Cir. 1965)	§ 13.6
United States *ex rel.* West v. Peter Kiewit & Sons' Co., 235 F. Supp. 500 (D. Alaska 1964)	§ 13.7
United States *ex rel.* Westinghouse Elec. Supply Co. v. Endebrock-White Co., 275 F.2d 57 (4th Cir. 1960)	§ 13.7
United States *ex rel.* Wheeling-Pittsburgh Steel Corp. v. Algernon Blair, Inc., 329 F. Supp. 1360 (D.S.C. 1971)	§ 12.36
United States *ex rel.* Witt v. JP, Inc., 655 F. Supp. 480 (D. Alaska 1987)	§ 13.15
United States Fed. Eng'g & Mfg., ASBCA No. 19909, 75-2 B.C.A. (CCH) ¶ 11,578	§ 6.13
United States Fidelity & Guar. Co. v. Hendry Corp., 391 F.2d 13 (5th Cir. 1968)	§ 13.17
United States Fidelity & Guar. Co. v. Louis A. Roser Co., 585 F.2d 932 (8th Cir. 1978)	§ 22.8
United States Fidelity & Guar. Co. v. Nevada Cement Co., 93 Nev. 179, 561 P.2d 1335 (1977)	§ 11.8
United States Fidelity & Guar. Co. v. Orlando Utils. Comm'n, 564 F. Supp. 962 (M.D. Fla. 1983)	§§ 12.31, 12.35
United States Fidelity & Guar. Co. v. Triborough Bridge Auth., 297 N.Y. 31, 74 N.E.2d 226, *reh'g denied,* 297 N.Y. 694, 77 N.E.2d 9 (1947)	§ 12.31
United States Fidelity & Guar. Co. v. United States, 676 F.2d 622 (Ct. Cl. 1982)	§ 12.35
United States Fidelity & Guar. Co. v. United States, 475 F.2d 1377 (Ct. Cl. 1973)	§ 13.18
United States Fidelity & Guar. Co. v. Virginia Eng'g Co., 213 F.2d 109 (4th Cir. 1954)	§ 11.10
United States Fire Ins. Co. v. Colver, 600 P.2d 1 (Alaska 1979)	§ 11.10
United States Propellers v. Zenith Plastics Co., 187 Cal. App. 2d 780, 10 Cal. Rptr. 137 (1960)	§ 5.16
United States Steel Corp. v. Missouri Pac. R.R., 668 F.2d 435 (8th Cir.), *cert. denied,* 459 U.S. 836 (1982)	§§ 7.35, 16.16
Unity Tel. Co. v. Design Serv. Co., 160 Me. 188, 201 A.2d 177 (1964)	§ 12.33
Universal By-Prods., Inc. v. City of Modesto, 43 Cal. App. 3d 145, 117 Cal. Rptr. 535 (1974)	§ 4.27
University of Md. v. Maas, 173 Md. 554, 197 A. 123 (1938)	§ 6.11
Uptagraff v. United States, 315 F.2d 200 (4th Cir.), *cert. denied,* 375 U.S. 818 (1963)	§ 12.24
Usemco, Inc. v. Marbro Co., 60 Md. App. 351, 483 A.2d 88 (1984)	§ 10.7
U.S. Indus., Inc. v. Aetna Casualty & Sur. Co., 690 F.2d 459 (5th Cir. 1982)	§ 11.22
U.S. Indus., Inc. v. Blake Constr. Co., 671 F.2d 539 (D.C. Cir. 1982)	§§ 5.8, 16.18

Case	*Book §*
U.S. Steel v. Construction Aggregates Corp., 559 F. Supp. 414 (E.D. Mich. 1983)	§ 16.36
Utica Mut. Co. v. DiDonato, 187 N.J. Super. 30, 453 A.2d 559 (App. Div. 1982)	§ 20.10
Valley Landscape Co. v. Rollander, 218 Va. 257, 237 S.E.2d 120 (1977)	§ 7.17
Vanasik v. Hirsch & Stevens, 65 Wis. 2d 1, 221 N.W.2d 815 (1974)	§ 7.11
Vari Builders, Inc. v. USF&G, 523 A.2d 549 (Del. Super. Ct. 1986)	§ 11.10
Varia v. Southwick, 81 Idaho 68, 337 P.2d 374 (1959)	§ 20.6
Vernail v. Centrali, 28 Conn. Supp. 476, 266 A.2d 200 (1970)	§ 20.7
Vernon Williams & Sons Constr., Inc. v. Continental Ins. Co., 591 S.W.2d 760 (Tenn. 1979)	§ 11.10
Vey v. Port Auth., 445 N.Y.S.2d 84, 54 N.Y.2d 221, 429 N.E.2d 762 (1981)	§ 10.10
Vines v. Orchard Hills, Inc., 181 Pa. Commw. 501, 435 A.2d 1022 (1980)	§ 20.10
Virginia Iron, Coal & Coke v. Graham, 124 Va. 692, 98 S.E. 659 (1919)	§ 20.6
Visant Elec. Contractors v. Aetna Casualty & Sur. Co., 530 S.W.2d 76 (Tenn. 1975)	§ 11.11
Volf v. Ocean Accident & Guar. Corp., 50 Cal. 2d 373, 325 P.2d 987 (1958)	§ 11.14
Volpe Constr. v. First Nat'l Bank, 30 Mass. App. Ct. 249, 567 N.E.2d 1244 (1991)	§§ 9.9, 9.19, 9.20
Waldinger Corp. v. Ashbrook-Simon-Hartley, Inc., 564 F. Supp. 970 (C.D. Ill. 1983), *aff'd in part & remanded in part sub nom.* Waldinger Corp. v. CRS Group Eng'rs, Inc., 775 F.2d 781 (7th Cir. 1985)	§§ 7.15, 7.18, 7.24, 8.10
Waldinger Corp. v. CRS Group Eng'rs, Inc., 775 F.2d 781 (7th Cir. 1985)	§§ 7.15, 7.18, 7.41, 8.2, 8.10
Waldor Pump & Equip. Co. v. Orr-Schelen-Mayerson & Assocs., 386 N.W.2d 375 (Minn. Ct. App. 1986)	§§ 7.41, 8.10
Wallace Process Piping Co. v. Martin-Marietta Corp., 251 F. Supp. 411 (E.D. Va. 1965)	§ 16.27
Walters v. Campeau, 205 Mont. 448, 668 P.2d 1054 (1983)	§ 20.16
Warner v. Cox, 487 F.2d 1301 (5th Cir. 1974)	§ 6.5
Warner Constr Corp. v. City of Los Angeles, 2 Cal. 3d 285, 466 P.2d 996, 85 Cal. Rptr. 44 (1970)	§ 16.20
Warren Bros. Rds. Co. v. United States, 173 Ct. Cl. 714 (1965)	§ 4.16
Warrior, Hinkle, Inc. v. Andalusia City Sch. Bd., 469 So. 2d 1285 (Ala. 1985)	§ 13.18
Waukesha Concrete Prods. Corp. v. Capitol Indem. Co., 127 Wis. 2d 332, 379 N.W.2d 333 (Ct. App. 1985)	§§ 13.7, 13.10

Case	*Book §*
Wayne Drilling & Blasting, Inc. v. Felix Indus., Inc., 129 A.D.2d 633, 514 N.Y.S.2d 114 (1987)	§ 20.4
Weaver-Bailey Contractors, Inc. v. United States, 19 Cl. Ct. 474 (1990)	§ 2.19
Weedo v. Stone-E-Brick, Inc., 81 N.J. 233, 405 A.2d 788 (1979)	§ 11.10
Weeshoff Constr. Co. v. Los Angeles County Flood Control Dist., 88 Cal. App. 3d 579, 152 Cal. Rptr. 19 (1979)	§ 5.6
W.E. Garrison Grading Co. v. Piracci Constr. Co., 27 N.C. App. 725, 221 S.E.2d 512 (1975), *cert. denied,* 289 N.C. 296, 222 S.E.2d 695 (1976)	§ 12.38
W.E. Gilbert & Assocs. v. South Carolina Nat'l Bank, 285 S.C. 421, 330 S.E.2d 307 (1985)	§ 7.10
Weill Constr. Co. v. Thibodeaux, 491 So. 2d 166 (La. Ct. App. 1986)	§ 8.6
Weinberg v. Wilensky, 26 N.J. Super. 301, 97 A.2d 707 (App. Div. 1953)	§ 20.3
Wellons v. T.E. Ibberson Co., 896 F.2d 1166 (8th Cir. 1989)	§ 7.2
Wells v. Clowers Constr. Co., 476 So. 2d 105 (Ala. 1985)	§ 20.1
Wes-Julian Constr. Corp. v. Commonwealth, 351 Mass. 588, 223 N.E.2d 72 (1967)	§ 16.14
Westates Constr. Co. v. City of Cheyenne, 775 P.2d 502 (Wyo. 1985)	§ 2.29
West Bank Oil, Inc. v. Hartford Accident & Indem. Co., 205 N.J Super. 56, 500 A.2d 32 (1985)	§ 13.6
Westerhold v. Carroll, 419 S.W.2d 73 (Mo. 1967)	§ 12.33
Western Casualty & Sur. Co. v. Biggs, 217 F.2d 163 (7th Cir. 1954)	§ 12.30
Western Empire Constructors, Inc. v. United States, 20 Cl. Ct. 668 (1990)	§ 6.5
Western Employers Ins. Co. v. Arciero & Sons, 145 Cal. App. 3d 1027, 194 Cal. Rptr. 688 (1983)	§ 11.14
Western Eng'rs, Inc. v. State Rd. Comm'n, 20 Utah 2d 294, 437 P.2d 216 (1968)	§§ 7.32, 16.14
Western Waterproofing, Inc. v. Springfield Hous. Auth., 669 F. Supp. 901 (C.D. Ill. 1987)	§ 13.2
Western World Ins. Co. v. Travelers Indem. Co., 358 So. 2d 602 (Fla. Dist. Ct. App. 1978)	§ 12.33
W.F. Constr. Vo. v. Kalik, 103 Idaho 713, 652 P.2d 661 (Ct. App. 1982)	§ 20.12
Wheelabrator Corp. v. Chafee, 455 F.2d 1306 (D.C. Cir. 1971)	§ 4.16
Wheeler & Lewis v. Slifer, 195 Colo. 291, 577 P.2d 1092 (1978)	§ 7.14
Whirlpool Corp. v. Morse, 222 F. Supp. 645 (D. Minn. 1963), *aff'd,* 332 F.2d 901 (8th Cir. 1964)	§ 20.7
White v. Berenda Mesa Water Dist., 7 Cal. App. 3d 894, 87 Cal. Rptr. 388 (1970)	§ 4.29

Case	*Book §*
White v. Mitchell, 123 Wash. 630, 213 P. 10 (1923)	§ 20.5
W.H. Lyman Constr. Co. v. Village of Gurnes, 84 Ill. App. 3d 28, 403 N.E.2d 1325 (1980)	§ 8.10
Wichita Sheet Metal Supply, Inc. v. Dahlstrom & Ferrell Constr. Co., 792 P.2d 1043 (Kan. 1990)	§ 13.6
Wickham Contracting Co., ASBCA No. 19069, 75-1 B.C.A. (CCH) ¶ 11,248	§ 6.12
Wickman v. Northwestern Nat'l Life, 908 F.2d 1077 (1st Cir.), *cert. denied,* 111 S. Ct. 581 (1990)	§ 11.5
Widett v. United States Fidelity & Guar. Co., 815 F.2d 885 (2d Cir. 1987)	§ 7.15
Wierzbicki v. Alaska Mut. Sav. Bank, 630 P.2d 998 (Alaska 1981)	§ 9.7
William F. Wilke, Inc. v. Department of Army, 485 F.2d 180 (4th Cir. 1973)	§ 6.6
William Moors, Inc. v. Pine Lake Shopping Ctr., Inc., 74 Mich. App. 12, 253 N.W.2d 658 (1977)	§ 5.17
Williams v. Aetna Casualty & Sur. Co., 151 N.J. Super. 68, 376 A.2d 562 (App. Div. 1977)	§ 11.17
Williams v. Kerns, 153 Ga. App. 259, 265 S.E.2d 605 (1980)	§ 5.12
Wilson v. Clarke, 470 F.2d 1218 (1st Cir. 1972)	§ 20.10
Wingler v. Niblack, 58 Ill. App. 3d 287, 374 N.E.2d 252 (1978)	§ 5.17
Winnebago Homes, Inc. v. Sheldon, 29 Wis. 2d 692, 139 N.W.2d 606 (1966)	§ 9.9
W.M. Schlosser Co. v. United States, 705 F.2d 1336 (Fed. Cir. 1983)	§ 6.5
W.N. Leslie, Inc. v. Travelers Ins. Co., 264 S.C. 408, 215 S.E.2d 448 (1975)	§ 11.17
Wolfson, 45 T.C.M. (CCH) 297 (1982)	§ 21.13
Woodard v. North Carolina Farm Bureau Mut. Ins. Co., 44 N.C. App. 282, 261 S.E.2d 43 (1979), *cert. denied,* 299 N.C. 546, 265 S.E.2d 406 (1980)	§ 11.17
Woodward v. Commissioner, 410 F.2d 313 (8th Cir. 1969), *aff'd*, 397 U.S. 572 (1970)	§ 21.7
Worsham Constr. Co. v. Reliance Ins. Co., 687 P.2d 988 (Colo. Ct. App. 1984)	§ 11.10
Wright v. Heizer Corp., 560 F.2d 236 (7th Cir. 1977)	§ 12.27
W. Southward Jones, Inc., ASBCA No. 6321, 61-2 B.C.A. (CCH) ¶ 3182	§ 6.13
Wunderlich v. State, 65 Cal. 777, 423 P.2d 545, 56 Cal. Rptr. 473 (1967)	§§ 5.5, 5.18
W. Walley, Inc. v. Commissioner, 7 T.C.M. (CCH) 137 (1948)	§§ 21.17, 21.20
Wyatt v. Ruck Constr. Co., 117 Ariz. 186, 571 P.2d 638 (Ct. App. 1977)	§ 12.27
Wyoming Sawmills v. Halls Transp. Ins. Co., 282 Or. 401, 578 P.2d 1253 (1978)	§ 11.8

Case	*Book §*
Yakima Cement Prods, Co. v. Great Am. Ins. Co., 22 Wash. App. 536, 590 P.2d 371, *rev'd on other grounds,* 93 Wash. 2d 210, 608 P.2d 254 (1979)	§ 11.15
Yarborough Realty Co. v. Barar, 37 Ala. App. 342, 67 So. 2d 853 (1953)	§ 12.34
Yellow Pine Lumber Co. v. Insurance Co. of N. Am., 882 F.2d 470 (10th Cir. 1989)	§ 13.6
Young v. Eastern Eng'g, 381 Pa. Super. 428, 554 A.2d 77 (1989)	§ 7.14
Yurchak v. Jack Boiman Constr. Co., 3 Ohio App. 3d 15, 443 N.E.2d 526 (1983)	§ 20.8
Zanii Constr. Co. v. Fireman's Ins. Co., 81 A.D.2d 106, 440 N.Y.2d 353, *aff'd,* 54 N.Y.2d 999, 430 N.E.2d 922, 446 N.Y.S.2d 45 (1981)	§ 11.10
Zimmerman v. Allstate Ins. Co., 179 Cal. App. 3d 840, 224 Cal. Rptr. 917 (1986)	§ 11.2
Zirin Lab. Int'l v. Mead-Johnson & Co., 208 F. Supp. 633 (E.D. Mich. 1962)	§ 16.35
Zito v. Fireman's Ins. Co., 36 Cal. App. 3d 277, 111 Cal. Rptr. 392 (1973)	§ 11.2
Zobel & Dahl Constr. v. Crotty, 356 N.W.2d 42 (Minn. 1984)	§§ 5.9, 5.12, 20.8

INDEX

ABANDONMENT OF CONTRACT
Suing construction managers § 7.33
Unreasonable or excessive period of delay, proving liability to recover damages § 16.19
ABSENTEEISM AND TURNOVER
Labor productivity § 19.6
ACCELERATION
Productivity losses, labor productivity § 19.18
ACCELERATION CLAIMS
Proving liability to recover damages. See PROVING LIABILITY TO RECOVER DAMAGES
ACCELERATION REQUIREMENTS
Productivity losses, labor productivity § 19.19
ACCEPTANCE
Defending against owner claims, waiver § 20.3
ACCESS TO SITE
Suing private owner, delay § 5.7
ACCORD AND SATISFACTION
Defending against owner claims § 20.12
ACCOUNTING EXPERTS
Initial assessment, trial and appeal § 22.7
ACCRUAL
Defenses, suing construction managers § 7.43
ACCRUAL METHOD ACCOUNTING
Income recognition and expense deduction, timing of § 21.12
ACQUIESCENCE
Suing a government, ratification by contracting officer § 6.13
ACTIONABLE REPRESENTATIONS
Rights based on estoppel, suing construction lenders § 9.14
ACTION OF PARTIES
Tax considerations § 21.18
ACTIVE INTERFERENCE
Defenses, suing construction managers § 7.35
Delay claims §§ 16.16, 16.17
Suing private owner, delay exception § 5.8
ACTS OF GOD
Defending against owner claims, supervening impracticability § 20.5
Proving liability to recover damages §§ 16.22, 16.24
ACTS OF NATURE
Contractor's builder's risk policy, exclusions § 11.22
ACTUAL ACCELERATION
Proving liability to recover damages § 16.27
ACTUAL DAMAGES
Proof of damages. See PROOF OF DAMAGES
ADEQUACY OF APPROPRIATION ACT
Suing a government, federal fiscal restrictions § 6.10
ADMINISTRATION
Suing design professionals, administrative negligence § 8.10
Suing design professionals, liability to contractor § 8.7
ADMINISTRATION OF DRAWINGS
Bases for liability, suing construction managers § 7.24
ADMINISTRATIVE PROCEDURE ACT
Suing a government § 6.4
ADMINISTRATIVE PROCEEDINGS
Trial preparation, trial and appeal § 22.14
ADMISSION REQUESTS
Preparing case for litigation, written requests § 15.18

ADVANCE PAYMENT STATUTE
Suing a government, federal fiscal restrictions § 6.10
ADVERSARY'S CLAIM, KNOWLEDGE OF
Arbitration § 14.3
ADVERSE PUBLICITY
Initial assessment, trial and appeal § 22.6
AFFIDAVITS
Arbitration § 14.25
AFFIRMANCE
Suing a government, authority to act for state § 6.14
AFFIRMATIVE ACTS
Owner's failure to perform, delay claims § 16.3
AFFIRMATIVE DECEPTIONS
Negligent misrepresentation, suing construction lenders § 9.22
AGENCY CONSTRUCTION MANAGEMENT
Suing construction managers §§ 7.3, 7.39
AIA DOCUMENT A201
Defending against owner claims
–Arbitration § 20.13
–Owner's duty to coordinate § 20.9
Suing private owner §§ 5.2, 5.16
AIA DOCUMENT A311
Payment bond claims
–Generally § 13.3
AIA DOCUMENT A312
Payment bond claims
–Limitation period § 13.13
–Notice § 13.11
ALLOCATION OF LIABILITY
Suing design professionals, economic loss limitation § 8.2
ALTERNATIVE DISPUTE RESOLUTION
Initial assessment, trial and appeal §§ 22.6, 22.7, 22.10
ALTERNATIVES TO LITIGATION
Initial assessment, trial and appeal § 22.10
AMBIGUITY
Bid protests and mistakes, bid requirements § 4.7
Contractor's insurance coverage § 11.2
AMERICAN ARBITRATION ASSOCIATION
Application, arbitration § 14.18
AMERICAN RULE
Payment bond claims, attorneys' fees and interest § 13.10
AMOUNTS DUE
Initial assessment, trial and appeal § 22.7
ANALYSIS
Delay. See CRITICAL PATH ANALYSIS TO PROVE DELAY
ANNULMENT
Liquidated damages, suing subcontractors and material suppliers § 10.7
ANTICIPATED BENEFITS
Risk management, litigation and alternatives § 2.9
ANTI-DEFICIENCY ACT
Suing a government, federal fiscal restrictions § 6.10
ANTI-INDEMNITY STATUTES
Indemnification, suing subcontractors and material suppliers § 10.10
APPARENT AUTHORITY
Suing a government, authority to act § 6.12
APPARENT LOW BIDDER
Bid protests and mistakes § 4.3
APPEAL
Federal waiver of contract controversies § 6.5
Litigation management, litigation and alternatives § 2.40
Payment bond claims, limitation period § 13.13
Trial and appeal. See TRIAL AND APPEAL
APPELLATE BRIEF
Appeal, trial and appeal § 22.26
APPENDICES TO BRIEFS
Appeal, trial and appeal § 22.26
APPLICABLE LEGAL THEORIES
Initial assessment, trial and appeal § 22.4
APPLICATION TO AMERICAN ARBITRATION ASSOCIATION
Arbitration § 14.11
APPLICATION TO COURT
Disclosure, arbitration § 14.12

APPORTIONMENT OF DAMAGES
Mutual delay, suing subcontractors and material suppliers § 10.7
ARBITRATION
Adversary's claim, knowledge of § 14.3
Affidavits § 14.25
Application to American Arbitration Association § 14.18
Application to court § 14.19
Arbitration vs. litigation § 14.2
Contract price/payment analysis § 14.16
Creative evidence § 14.26
Defending against owner claims § 20.13
Description of project § 14.14
Description of project time frame § 14.22
Expert testimony § 14.23
Informality § 14.3
Initial presentation § 14.20
Overview of claims § 14.19
Pass-through claims, suing subcontractors and material supplier § 10.11
Payment bond claims § 13.17
Prehearing written submission § 14.20
Preparing exhibits § 14.24
Preparing for hearings § 14.21
Schedule § 14.18
Scheduling hearings § 14.9
Scope of work § 14.17
Sovereign immunity applicability § 6.8
Suing construction managers § 7.38
Suing private owner § 5.1
Trial preparation, trial and appeal § 22.14
Who will tell the story § 14.22
ARBITRATION AWARDS
Arbitration § 14.8
ARBITRATION VS. LITIGATION
Arbitration § 14.2
Dispute management, litigation and alternatives § 2.34
ARBITRATORS
Initial assessment, trial and appeal § 22.10
ARCHITECTS
Litigation and alternatives § 2.12
ARCHITECTS *(Continued)*
Suing. See SUING DESIGN PROFESSIONALS
ARCHITECTURAL MALPRACTICE
Suing design professionals, liability to contractor § 8.1
ARGUMENT
Appeal, trial and appeal § 22.26
ASBESTOS CASES
Contractor's insurance coverage, liability policy, trigger of coverage § 11.6
AS-BUILT CRITICAL PATH SCHEDULE
Critical path analysis to prove delay § 17.8
AS-BUILT DOCUMENTS
Labor productivity § 19.11
AS-BUILT SCHEDULE
Litigation team § 3.10
AS-PLANNED/AS-BUILT COMPARATIVE CHART
Arbitration § 14.18
AS-PLANNED CRITICAL PATH SCHEDULE
Critical path analysis to prove delay § 17.8
AS-PLANNED DOCUMENTS
Labor productivity § 19.11
AS-PLANNED SCHEDULE
Litigation team § 3.10
ASSERTING DAMAGE CLAIMS
Proving liability to recover damages. See PROVING LIABILITY TO RECOVER DAMAGES
ASSOCIATED GENERAL CONTRACTORS (AGC) FORM
Suing construction managers § 7.4
ATTORNEYS' FEES
Arbitration § 14.16
Contractor's insurance coverage § 11.1
Defending against owner claims § 20.16
Payment bonds claims
–Coverage § 13.10
–Taxes § 13.8
ATTORNEY WORK-PRODUCT PRIVILEGE
Trial preparation, experts § 15.11
AUDIT
Trial preparation, discovery § 15.12

AUTHENTICITY OF DOCUMENTS
Trial preparation, document production § 15.18
AUTHORITY
Suing a government §§ 6.12, 6.14
AUTOMATED DATE PROCESSING EQUIPMENT
Bid protests, federal contracts § 4.16
AVAILABLE DEFENSES
Role of surety § 12.20
AWARD
Bid protests, state and local contracts § 4.26

BACK WAGES
Payment bond claims, parties who may make claim § 13.6
BACKWARD PASS
Critical path analysis to prove delay § 17.7
BAD FAITH
Defenses, suing construction managers § 7.34
Delay claims § 16.20
See also GOOD FAITH
BANKING PRACTICE
Failure to observe, suing construction lenders § 9.21
BANKRUPTCY REFORM ACT OF 1978
Parties and causes of action, sureties § 12.32
BARGAINING ROOM
Dispute management, litigation and alternatives § 2.33
BASES FOR ALLOCATING OVERHEAD
Table 18–9, pricing damages § 18.25
BASES FOR LIABILITY
Suing construction managers. See SUING CONSTRUCTION MANAGERS
BASIC PROVISIONS
Risk management, litigation and alternatives § 2.22
BATTLE OF FORMS
Risk management, litigation and alternatives § 2.21
BEHIND SCHEDULE PERFORMANCE
Disallowance of acceleration claims, proving liability to recover damages § 16.28
BENCH TRIALS
Trial preparation, trial and appeal § 22.13
BFCGL ENDORSEMENT
Contractor's insurance coverage, care, custody or control exclusion § 11.11
BFPD ENDORSEMENT
Contractor's insurance coverage, completed operations hazard § 11.17
Contractor's insurance coverage, work or product exclusion § 11.14
BID BONDS
Types of surety bonds. See TYPES OF SURETY BONDS
BIDDING
Suing subcontractors and material suppliers § 10.2
BIDDING REQUIREMENTS
Standard of care, suing construction managers § 7.9
BID DISPUTES
Dispute management,litigation and alternatives § 2.26
BID PREPARATION COST RECOVERY
Proving liability to recover damages § 16.30
BID PROTESTS AND MISTAKES
Generally §§ 4.1, 4.2
Bid bonds, sureties § 12.7
Bid requirements generally § 4.5
Competitive bidding process § 4.3
Considerations for protests § 4.4
Contract award criteria
–Generally § 4.6
–Minority business requirements § 4.10
–Responsibility § 4.8
–Responsiveness § 4.7
–Subcontractor listing requirements § 4.9
Dispute management, litigation and alternatives § 2.26
Federal contracts
–Generally § 4.12
–Grounds for protests § 4.13
–Protest procedure § 4.15
–Relief available § 4.16
–Standing to protest § 4.14
Federally funded grant projects
–Generally § 4.17

BID PROTESTS AND MISTAKES (Continued)
–Grounds for protest § 4.18
–Procedure for protest § 4.20
–Relief available § 4.21
–Standing to protest § 4.19
Grounds for protest § 4.11
Mistakes
–Generally § 4.28
–Equitable principles, jurisdictions following § 4.30
–Federal law § 4.31
–Private owners § 4.32
–State law remedies § 4.29
Private contracts § 4.27
State and local contracts
–Generally § 4.22
–Grounds for protest § 4.23
–Protest procedure § 4.25
–Relief available § 4.26
–Standing to protest § 4.24
Suing a government, judicial review § 6.6
Suing subcontractors and material suppliers § 10.3
BID SHOPPING
Bid protests and mistakes, subcontractor listing requirement § 4.9
BINDING MEDIATION
Dispute management, litigation and alternatives § 2.35
BLANK PURCHASE ORDERS
Documentation, suing subcontractors and material suppliers § 10.13
BOILERPLATE PROVISIONS
Documentation, suing subcontractors and material suppliers § 10.13
Trial preparation, discovery § 15.15
BONA FIDE NEEDS RULE
Suing a government, federal fiscal restrictions § 6.10
BONDS
Payment bond claims. See PAYMENT BOND CLAIMS
Performance. See PERFORMANCE BONDS
Standard of care, suing construction managers § 7.8
Sureties. See SURETIES
BOTTOM-UP ANALYSIS
Labor productivity § 19.10
BRAND NAME PRODUCTS
Defending against owner claims, substantial performance § 20.11
BREACH OF CONTRACT
Contractor's insurance coverage § 11.10
Suing. See SUING PRIVATE OWNER
Suing a government, state fiscal restrictions § 6.11
BREACH OF GOOD FAITH
Parties and causes of action, sureties § 12.27
BROAD INDEMNITY
Indemnification, suing subcontractors and material suppliers § 10.10
BROOKS ACT
Bid protests, federal contracts § 4.16
BUDGET ESTIMATES
Factors affecting project results § 1.4
BUDGETS
Litigation team § 3.2
BUILDER-DEVELOPERS
Contractor's insurance coverage, premises alienated exclusion § 11.12
BUILDER'S RISK POLICY
Contractor's insurance coverage. See CONTRACTOR'S INSURANCE COVERAGE
BUILDING CODES
Legal parameters, litigation and alternatives § 2.18
Suing construction managers § 7.13
Violation of code, suing design professionals, proof of negligence § 8.5
BUILDING REQUIREMENTS
Suing construction managers § 7.9
BURDEN OF PROOF
Bid mistakes § 4.29
Contractor's insurance coverage, builder's risk policy § 11.23
Defending against owner claims
–Accord and satisfaction § 20.12
–Damages § 20.8
–Liquidated damages § 20.10
Mutual delay, suing subcontractors and material suppliers § 10.7
BUSINESS RISKS
Contractor's insurance coverage § 11.3

BUSINESS RISKS *(Continued)*
Contractor's insurance coverage, liability policy exclusions § 11.13
BUSINESS ROUNDTABLE
Factors affecting project results § 1.1

CALCULATING AMOUNTS DUE
Initial assessment, trial and appeal § 22.7
CALCULATING COMPOUNDING IMPACTS
Labor productivity § 19.25
CALCULATING DAMAGES
Litigation management, litigation and alternatives § 2.39
Pricing damages. See PRICING DAMAGES
CANCELLATION OF BID
Bid mistakes, federal law § 4.31
CAPITAL ASSET ACQUISITION
Tax considerations § 21.9
CAPITAL ASSET SALES
Tax considerations § 21.7
CAPITAL EXPENDITURES
Payment of settlements and judgments, tax considerations § 21.9
CAPITAL GAINS
Tax considerations § 21.4
CARE
Contractor's insurance coverage, liability policy exclusions § 11.11
CASE REASSESSMENT
Appeal, trial and appeal § 22.25
CASE STUDY
Industrial construction, factors affecting project results § 1.6
CASE THEORY
Preparing case for litigation § 15.4
CASH METHOD ACCOUNTING
Income recognition and expense deduction, timing of § 21.12
CATEGORIES OF CONTRACT DAMAGES
Pricing damages. See PRICING DAMAGES
CATEGORIES OF DISRUPTIONS
Labor productivity § 19.13
CAUSES OF ACTION
Parties and causes of action. See SURETIES
CERTAINTY RULE
Proving liability to recover damages § 16.35
CHANGE CLAUSE
Delay claims. See DELAY CLAIMS
CHANGED CONDITIONS
Bid bonds, sureties § 10.7
Calculating damages, pricing damages § 18.17
Categories of contract damages, pricing damages § 18.5
Consulting engineer, litigation team § 3.11
Proving liability to recover damages § 16.29
CHANGED PHYSICAL CONDITIONS
Changes, breaches of contract by owner § 5.5
CHANGE ORDERS
Suing private owner, breaches of contract by owner § 5.4
Suing subcontractors and material suppliers § 10.5
CHANGE ORDER SYSTEM
Factors affecting project results § 1.12
CHANGES CLAUSE
Risk management, litigation and alternatives § 2.22
Strictly construed, delay claims § 16.11
Suing private owner § 5.2
CHANGES IN SCOPE
Calculating damages, pricing damages § 18.18
Categories of contract damages, pricing damages § 18.6
Factors affecting project results § 1.7
CHANGES IN WORK
Advanced notice of, suing construction managers § 7.25
CHARACTERISTICS OF EXPERT WITNESSES
Litigation team §§ 3.7–3.12
CHARACTERIZATION OF CONSTRUCTION MANAGER
Suing construction managers § 7.2
CHOICE OF CLAIMS
Tax considerations § 21.20
CHOOSING LAWYERS
Organization, litigation team § 3.5

CHRISTIAN DOCTRINE
Sureties § 12.4
CHRONOLOGICAL ORDER OF CONSTRUCTION PROJECT
Suing construction managers § 7.21
CIVIL PENALTIES
Tax considerations § 21.10
CIVIL SANCTIONS
Licensing requirements, suing construction managers § 7.7
CLAIMANTS
Definition, sureties § 12.2
CLAIMANTS TO CONSTRUCTION FUNDS
Parties and causes of action, sureties §§ 12.23, 12.31
CLAIM BRIEFS
Litigation management, litigation and alternatives § 2.38
CLAIM CONSULTANT
Expert witnesses, litigation team § 3.9
CLAIM PREPARATION COST
Pricing damages § 18.21
CLAIM PRESENTATION
Dispute management, litigation and alternatives § 2.32
CLAIMS
Owner claims. See DEFENDING AGAINST OWNER CLAIMS
Payment bond claims. See PAYMENT BOND CLAIMS
Preservation, litigation and alternatives § 2.29
CLAIMS CONSULTANTS
Arbitration § 14.23
CLAIMS ELIMINATION
Initial assessment, trial and appeal § 22.9
CLAIMS-MADE POLICIES
Contractor's insurance coverage, liability policy insuring agreement § 11.7
CLARIFICATION OF DRAWINGS
Suing construction managers § 7.25
CLARITY OF COMMUNICATION
Trial preparation, trial and appeal § 22.16
CLEARLY ERRONEOUS STANDARD
Federal waiver of contract controversies § 6.5
CLERICAL ERRORS
Bid mistakes. See BID MISTAKES AND PROTESTS
CLERK OF WORK
Arbitration § 14.22
CLIENT INTERVIEW
Initial assessment, trial and appeal § 22.3
CLIENT'S OBJECTIVES
Initial assessment, trial and appeal § 22.6
CLOSING ARGUMENT
Trial and appeal § 22.23
COLLAPSE
Contractor's insurance coverage, liability policy exclusions § 11.16
COLLATERAL ESTOPPEL
Initial assessment, trial and appeal § 22.6
Payment bond claims, jurisdiction and venue § 13.17
COLLEGE-EDUCATED SUPERVISORS
Arbitration § 14.22
COLLUSION
Bid protests and mistakes, bid requirements § 4.5
COMBINATION PAYMENT AND PERFORMANCE BOND FORMS
Sureties § 12.10
COMFORMING TO PRIOR PLANS AND SPECIFICATIONS
Suing construction managers § 7.30
COMMENCEMENT
Defending against owner claims, statutes of limitations § 20.4
Payment bond claims, notice requirements § 13.14
COMMERCIAL ARBITRATION
Trial preparation, trial and appeal § 22.14
COMMERCIAL GENERAL LIABILITY POLICY
Contractor's insurance coverage § 11.4
COMMON CAUSES OF LOST PRODUCTIVITY
Table 19-1, labor productivity § 19.4
COMMON LAW BONDS
Sureties § 12.3

COMMON LAW DUTY TO COORDINATE
Defending against owner claims, owner's duty to coordinate § 20.9
COMMON LAW INDEMNITY
Suing design professionals, indemnity § 8.3
COMMON SENSE
Labor productivity § 19.5
COMPACTION
Labor productivity § 19.17
COMPARATIVE NEGLIGENCE
Defenses, suing construction managers § 7.40
Suing subcontractors and material suppliers § 10.7
COMPARATIVE SCHEDULES
Arbitration § 14.18
COMPARISON OF BID VS. ACTUAL BY CONTRACT WORK ITEM
Table 18–4, pricing damages § 18.12
COMPENSABLE DELAY
Critical path analysis to prove delay § 17.2
COMPENSABLE DELAYS
Dispute management, litigation and alternatives § 2.27
COMPETITION IN CONTRACTING ACT
Suing a government §§ 6.4, 6.7
COMPLAINT PREPARATION
Litigation management, litigation and alternatives § 2.38
COMPLAINTS
Tax considerations § 21.17
COMPLETED CONTRACT METHOD
Income recognition and expense deduction, timing of § 21.15
COMPLETED OPERATIONS HAZARD
Contractor's insurance coverage, liability policy exclusions § 11.17
COMPLETED VS. UNCOMPLETED PROJECTS
Unjust enrichment theories, suing construction lenders § 9.18
COMPLETION
Contractor's insurance coverage, builder's risk policy § 11.19
Defending against owner claims, damages § 20.8
COMPLETION *(Continued)*
Payment bond claims, commencement of limitation period § 13.14
Prevention of completion, suing private owner § 5.12
COMPLETION BOND
Types of surety bonds § 12.9
COMPLETION OF PROJECT
Default, role of surety § 12.22
COMPLEX CONSTRUCTION CASES AND THE JURY
Trial preparation, trial and appeal § 22.13
COMPLEXITY
Liability and alternatives § 2.6
COMPOUNDING IMPACTS, CALCULATION OF
Labor productivity § 19.25
COMPREHENSIVE GENERAL LIABILITY POLICY
Contractor's insurance coverage § 11.3
COMPUTER DATA BASES
Trial preparation, trial and appeal § 22.14
CONCEALED CONDITIONS
Suing private owner, changes § 5.5
CONCEALMENT
Suing construction managers § 7.34
CONCESSIONS
Dispute management, litigation and alternatives § 2.33
CONCURRENT CAUSES
Contractor's builder's risk policy, exclusions § 11.22
Critical path analysis to prove delay § 17.2
CONCURRENT DELAYS
Delay claims § 16.21
CONCURRENT USAGE
Suing construction managers § 7.27
CONDITIONS PRECEDENT
Default, sureties § 12.21
CONDUCT
Negligence, conduct constituting negligence in design professionals § 8.6
CONDUIT CLAUSE
Suing subcontractors and material suppliers § 10.4

CONFERENCE WITH ARBITRATORS
Disclosure, arbitration § 14.11
CONFLICT OF INTEREST
Initial assessment, trial and appeal § 22.8
Suing construction managers § 7.4
CONSOLIDATED ARBITRATION PROCEEDINGS
Pass-through claims, suing subcontractors and material supplier § 10.11
CONSOLIDATION OF COMMON ISSUES OF LAW AND FACT
Pass-through claims, suing subcontractors and material supplier § 10.11
CONSTRAINTS
Influence factors, factors affecting results § 1.5
Phases I and II, factors affecting project results § 1.4
CONSTRUCTABILITY ISSUES
Scope changes, factors affecting project results § 1.10
CONSTRUCTION ARBITRATION
Arbitration. See CONSTRUCTION ARBITRATION
CONSTRUCTION CLAIM INFORMATION DOCUMENTS
Labor productivity § 19.11
CONSTRUCTION CONSULTANT
Expert witnesses, litigation team § 3.12
CONSTRUCTION DISPUTES
Construction risks and rewards. See CONSTRUCTION RISKS AND REWARDS
CONSTRUCTION INDUSTRY COST EFFECTIVENESS STUDY
Factors affecting project results § 1.1
CONSTRUCTION INDUSTRY INSTITUTE
Factors affecting project results § 1.2
CONSTRUCTION LENDERS
Litigation and alternatives § 2.13
Suing construction lenders. See SUING CONSTRUCTION LENDERS
CONSTRUCTION MANAGER
De facto rule, suing construction managers § 7.14
CONSTRUCTION MANAGER *(Continued)*
Litigation and alternatives § 2.13
Suing construction manager. See SUING CONSTRUCTION MANAGER
CONSTRUCTION METHODS
Construction consultant, litigation team § 3.12
CONSTRUCTION OF CONTRACTS
Construction of documents and parol evidence § 12.37
CONSTRUCTION OF DOCUMENTS AND PAROL EVIDENCE
Sureties. See SURETIES
CONSTRUCTION PROJECTS
Major influences, factors affecting project results § 1.8
Scope changes, factors affecting project results § 1.7
CONSTRUCTION RISKS AND REWARDS
Construction disputes
–Generally § 2.5
–Complexity § 2.6
–Contract structures § 2.7
–Sources § 2.8
Need for effective risk, dispute, and litigation management § 2.9
Not for the timid
–Generally § 2.1
–Inherent risk factors § 2.2
–Legislated risks § 2.3
–Risk management § 2.4
CONSTRUCTION SCHEDULE
Dispute management, litigation and alternatives § 2.29
Suing construction managers § 7.27
CONSTRUCTION SUPPORT SERVICES
Failure to provide, suing construction managers § 7.26
CONSTRUCTIVE CHANGES
Breaches of contract by owner, suing private owner § 5.6
Delay claims § 16.12
CONSTRUCTIVE KNOWLEDGE
Suing a government, ratification by contracting officer § 6.13
CONSTRUCTIVE TRUST
Unjust enrichment theories, suing construction lenders § 9.16

CONSULTING ENGINEER
Expert witnesses, litigation team § 3.11
CONSUMED TANGIBLE GOODS
Payment bond claims, parties who may make claim § 13.7
CONTEMPLATED DELAYS
Delay changes § 16.14
CONTINGENT LIABILITY
Pass-through claims, suing subcontractors and material supplier § 10.11
CONTINUED CONDUCT
Defending against owner claims, waiver § 20.3
CONTINUING DAMAGE
Contractor's insurance coverage, liability policy, trigger of coverage § 11.6
CONTINUOUS INSPECTION
Suing design professionals, inspection negligence § 8.9
CONTRACT AUDIT
Pricing damages § 18.13
CONTRACT AWARD CRITERIA
Bid protests and mistakes. See BID PROTESTS AND MISTAKES
CONTRACT DISPUTES ACT
Bid protests, federal contracts § 4.16
Suing a government §§ 6.4, 6.5
CONTRACT DOCUMENTS
Bid protests and mistakes, bid requirments § 4.5
Labor productivity § 19.3
Risk management. See RISK MANAGEMENT
CONTRACT FORMATION
Suing subcontractors and material suppliers § 10.2
CONTRACT FUNDS
Parties and causes of action, sureties § 12.31
Surety's right to, rule of surety § 12.24
CONTRACTING OFFICER
Suing a government, authority to act § 6.12
CONTRACTING PARTY DISPUTES TAXPAYER PERFORMANCE
Tax considerations § 21.15
CONTRACT OBLIGATIONS
Suing construction managers § 5.11
CONTRACTOR
Vs. surety, parties and causes of action, sureties § 12.27
CONTRACTOR-CONSTRUCTION MANAGER
Risk management, litigation and alternatives § 2.13
CONTRACTORS
Insurance coverage. See CONTRACTOR'S INSURANCE COVERAGE
Sureties. See SURETIES
Vs. owner, parties and causes of action, sureties § 12.28
CONTRACTOR'S ANSWERS TO OPPONENT'S ARGUMENTS
Appeal, trial and appeal § 22.26
CONTRACTOR'S ARGUMENTS
Appeal, trial and appeal § 22.26
CONTRACTOR SELECTION
Phase III, factors affecting project results § 1.3
CONTRACTOR'S IMPROVEMENT
Unjust enrichment theories, suing construction lenders § 9.19
CONTRACTOR'S INSURANCE COVERAGE
Generally § 11.1
Builder's risk policy
–Generally § 11.18
–Burden of proof § 11.23
–Future practice § 11.26
–Limitations, see Builder's risk policy limitations, this heading
–Period of coverage § 11.18
–Subrogation § 11.25
–Sue and labor clause § 11.24
Builder's risk policy limitations
–Exclusions § 11.22
–External causes § 11.21
–Fortuitous losses § 11.20
Contra proferentem and reasonable expectations doctrine § 11.2
Liability policy
–Generally § 11.3
–Exclusions, see Liability policy exclusions, this heading
–Insuring agreement, see Liability policy insuring agreement, this heading
Liability policy exclusions
–Generally § 11.9

CONTRACTOR'S INSURANCE COVERAGE *(Continued)*
–Care, custody, or control § 11.11
–Completed operations hazard § 11.17
–Contractually assumed liability § 11.10
–Damage to insured's product or work § 11.14
–Explosion, collapse, or underground property damage § 11.16
–Performance or business risk § 11.13
–Premises alienated § 11.12
–Sistership or recall § 11.15
Liability policy insuring agreement
–Generally § 11.4
–Claims-made policies § 11.7
–Occurrence requirement § 11.5
–Property damage definition § 11.8
–Triggering event under occurrence-based policies § 11.6
CONTRACTOR'S REPRESENTATIVES
Preparing case for litigation, litigation plan § 15.3
CONTRACTOR'S RIGHT OF ACTION
Suing design professional. See SUING DESIGN PROFESSIONAL
CONTRACTOR VS. MISCELLANEOUS PARTIES
Parties and causes of action, sureties § 12.29
CONTRACT PRICE/PAYMENT ANALYSIS
Arbitration § 14.16
CONTRACT STRUCTURES
Liability and alternatives § 2.7
CONTRACT THEORIES
Generally § 9.6
Lender and borrower as single entity § 9.7
Third-party beneficiary status
–Generally § 9.8
–Enforcing rights § 9.10
–Establishing status § 9.9
CONTRACTUAL INTEGRATION
Contract theories, suing construction lenders § 9.7
CONTRACTUALLY ASSUMED LIABILITY
Contractor's insurance coverage, liability policy exclusions § 11.10
CONTRACTUAL RIGHTS
Contract theories, suing construction lenders § 9.6
CONTRA PROFERENTEM
Contractor's insurance coverage § 11.2
CONTRIBUTIONS
Payment bonds, claims covered § 13.8
CONTRIBUTORY NEGLIGENCE
Defenses, suing construction managers § 7.40
CONTROL
Contractor's insurance coverage, liability policy exclusions § 11.11
CONTROLLABILITY
Factors affecting project results § 1.6
CONVENIENCE
Default and termination, suing subcontractors and material suppliers § 10.12
Suing private owner, termination of contract § 5.16
CONVEYING A CLEAR PICTURE
Trial preparation, trial and appeal § 22.12
COORDINATED PERFORMANCE
Suing subcontractors and material suppliers § 10.6
COORDINATING CONSULTANTS AND EXPERTS
Litigation team § 3.13
COORDINATION
Failure. suing construction managers § 7.27
Suing design professionals, liability to contractor §§ 8.7, 8.11
CO-PARTIES
Trial preparation, discovery § 15.12
CORRECTIONS
Defective work, suing subcontractors and material suppliers § 10.9
COST AND MIX OF LABOR
Labor productivity § 19.6
COST AND REVENUE ESTIMATION
Tax considerations § 21.14
COST-BENEFIT ANALYSIS
Risk management, litigation and alternatives § 2.9

COST INFLUENCE AND PROJECT COST VERSUS PROJECT TIME
Figure 1–1, factors affecting project results § 1.2
COST OF CAPITAL
Pricing damages § 18.20
COST OVERRUNS
Contractor's insurance coverage § 11.3
Critical path analysis to prove delay § 17.1
Factors affecting project results § 1.7
COST-PLUS CONTRACT
Suing private owner, liens § 5.17
COST-PLUS FEE PROJECTS
Suing construction managers § 7.3
COST-REIMBURSABLE CONTRACTS
Scope changes, factors affecting project results § 1.10
COST SAVING INCENTIVE
Suing construction managers § 7.4
COST/SCHEDULE CONTROL
Constraints, factors affecting projects results § 1.4
COST SCHEDULES
Pricing damages § 18.12
COST SECURITY
Suing construction managers § 7.4
COSTS RECOVERY
Litigation management, litigation and alternatives § 2.39
COST-TO-COST METHOD
Tax considerations § 21.14
COUNTER OFFERS
Dispute management, litigation and alternatives § 2.33
COURT ORDERS
Parties and causes of action, sureties § 12.30
COURT REFORM ACT
Judicial review of bid protests § 6.6
COURTS, APPLICATION TO
Arbitration § 14.19
COVERAGE
Role of surety § 12.15
CREATIVE EVIDENCE
Arbitration § 14.26
CREDENTIALS EXAMINATION
Trial preparation, trial and appeal § 22.16
CREW INCREASES
Inefficiency, labor productivity § 19.20
Productivity loss, labor productivity § 19.21
CRIMINAL PENALTIES
Tax considerations § 21.10
CRIMINAL SANCTIONS
Licensing requirements, suing construction managers § 7.7
CRITICAL PATH ANALYSIS TO PROVE DELAY
Generally § 17.1
Elements of proof § 17.2
Overview §§ 17.7, 17.8
Strengthening CPM proof strategy § 17.9
Techniques
–Generally § 17.3
–Critical path method § 17.6
–Owner-caused events § 17.4
–Work force schedules compared to revenue received § 17.5
CRITICAL PATH CONSULTANT
Expert witnesses, litigation team § 3.10
CRITICAL PATH NEEDS
Suing construction managers § 7.27
CROSS-EXAMINATION
Arbitration § 14.25
Trial and appeal § 22.22
CUSTODY
Contractor's insurance coverage, liability policy exclusions § 11.11

DALLAVIA METHOD
Labor productivity. See LABOR PRODUCTIVITY
DALLAVIA PRODUCTION RANGE INDICES
Table 19–5 § 19.15
DAMAGES
Checklist Table 18–9
Defending against owner claims §§ 20.8, 20.16
Delay. See DELAY DAMAGES
Pricing. See PRICING DAMAGES
Proving liability to recover damages. See PROVING LIABILITY TO RECOVER DAMAGES
Recovery from performance bond surety § 12.23

DAMAGES *(Continued)*
Suing a government, state fiscal restrictions § 6.11
Suing private owner, delay § 5.7
Suing private owner, remedies § 5.11
Trial preparation, interrogatories § 15.16
DAMAGES ACCOUNT
Initial assessment, trial and appeal § 22.7
DAMAGES CALCULATION
Productivity curves and damages calculation. See PRODUCTIVITY CURVES AND DAMAGES CALCULATION
DAMAGES EXPERT
Expert witnesses, litigation team § 3.8
DAMAGES MEASUREMENT
Initial assessment, trial and appeal § 22.7
DAMAGE SPECIALIST
Pricing damages § 18.13
DAMAGE THEORIES
Initial assessment, trial and appeal § 22.7
DAMAGE TO INSURED'S PRODUCT OR WORK
Contractor's insurance coverage, liability policy exclusions § 11.14
DAMAGE TO OTHER'S PROPERTY
Contractor's insurance coverage, contractually assumed liability exclusion § 11.10
DEADLINE CLAUSES
Proving liability to recover damages § 16.33
DEADLINES
Bid protests, federal contracts § 4.15
DECISION FLOW FOR ENGINEERING BASIS PHASE
Figure 1-3, factors affecting project results § 1.4
DECISION FLOW FOR PRELIMINARY STUDY PHASE
Figure 1-2, factors affecting project results § 1.4
DECLARATORY RELIEF
Bid protests, federal contracts § 4.16
Bid protests, state and local contracts § 4.26
Federal waiver of contract controversies § 6.5
DECLINE IN LABOR PRODUCTIVITY
Disruption. See DISRUPTION
DEDUCTIBLE EXPENSES
Payment of settlements and judgments, tax considerations § 21.8
DEDUCTIBLE UNDER § 212
Tax considerations § 21.8
DE FACTO DEFAULT
Parties and causes of action, sureties § 12.31
DEFAULT
Defective work correction, suing subcontractors and material suppliers § 10.9
Principals, role of surety § 12.16
Suing private owner, termination of contract § 5.16
Suing subcontractors and material suppliers § 10.12
Surety's rights and obligations, role of surety §§ 12.17–12.21
DEFECTIVE DESIGN SPECIFICATIONS
Suing private owner, changes § 5.6
DEFECTIVE MATERIAL
Payment bond claims, commencement of limitation period § 13.14
DEFECTIVE PLAN AND SPECIFICATIONS
Proving liability to recover damages § 16.12
DEFECTIVE PLANS AND SPECIFICATIONS
Defending against owner claims § 20.2
Delay claims § 16.4
DEFECTIVE PRODUCTS
Contractor's insurance coverage, product exclusion § 11.14
Contractor's insurance coverage, property damage defined § 11.8
DEFECTIVE WORK
Contractor's builder's risk policy, exclusions § 11.21
Contractor's builder's risk policy, fortuitous loss § 11.20
Contractor's insurance coverage, work exclusion § 11.14

DEFECTIVE WORK *(Continued)*
Correction, suing subcontractors and material suppliers § 10.9
Warranties, suing subcontractors and material suppliers § 10.8
DEFECTS
Latent. See LATENT DEFECTS
Plans and specifications, bid protest grounds § 4.11
DEFENDING AGAINST OWNER CLAIMS
Accord and satisfaction § 20.12
Arbitration defense § 20.13
Available defenses § 20.1
Coordination, when owner retains duty of § 20.9
Damages § 20.8
–Generally § 20.8
–Liquidated § 20.10
Impracticality
–Pre-existing § 20.6
–Supervening § 20.5
Limitations imposed by contract provisions § 20.15
Other owner claims and defenses § 20.16
Plans and specifications compliance § 20.2
Statutes of limitations § 20.4
Substantial performance § 20.11
Termination defense § 20.14
Waiver, continued performance as § 20.3
Warranties and limitations § 20.7
DEFENSE COSTS
Contractor's insurance coverage § 11.1
DEFENSE OF TITLE
Tax considerations § 21.8
DEFENSES
Claims. See DEFENDING AGAINST OWNER CLAIMS
DEFINITE OFFERS TO PERFORM
Suing subcontractors and material suppliers § 10.2
DEFINITION OF UNJUST DEFINITION
Unjust enrichment theories. SEE UNJUST ENRICHMENT THEORIES
DELAY
Damages. See DELAY DAMAGES
Excusable. See EXCUSABLE DELAY
DELAY CLAIMS
Generally § 16.2
Changes
–Generally § 16.9
–Changes clause strictly construed § 16.11
–Constructive changes § 16.12
–Directed changes § 16.10
Defective plans and specification § 16.4
Disruptions and delays, suing subcontractors and material suppliers § 10.6
Exceptions to no damage for delay clauses
–Generally § 16.15
–Active interference § 16.16
–Active interference not sufficient § 16.17
–Bad faith or fraud § 16.20
–Concurrent delays § 16.21
–Delays not contemplated § 16.18
–Unreasonable or excessive period of delay § 16.19
Excusable contractor delays
–Generally § 16.22
–Labor disputes § 16.25
–Unforeseeability § 16.23
–Unusually severe weather § 16.24
Extension of time clauses § 16.8
Owner's failure to perform affirmative act § 16.3
Owner's failure to provide access to site § 16.5
Restriction on contractor's recovery
–Generally § 16.13
–Contemplated delays § 16.14
Substantial changes in contract scope § 16.7
Unforeseeable subsurface conditions § 16.6
DELAY CLAUSES
Proving liability to recover damages § 16.32
DELAY DAMAGES
Categories of contract damages, pricing damages § 18.3
Defending against owner claims, liquidated damages § 20.10
Defending against owner claims, owner's duty to coordinate § 20.9
Parties and causes of action, sureties §§ 12.28, 12.34

DELAY DAMAGES *(Continued)*
Payment bonds, claims covered § 13.9
Suing design professionals, indemnity § 8.3
DELAYED SITE ACCESS
Bases for liability, suing construction managers § 7.23
DELAY NOT CONTEMPLATED
Defenses, suing construction managers § 7.32
DELAYS
Breaches of contract by owner, suing private owner § 5.7
Calculating damages, pricing damages § 18.15
Contractor's insurance coverage, performance or business risk exclusion § 11.13
Dispute management, litigation and alternatives § 2.27
Disruptions and delays, suing subcontractors and material suppliers § 10.6
Proof. See CRITICAL PATH ANALYSIS TO PROVE DELAY
Suing design professionals, scheduling and coordination negligence § 8.11
DELAYS NOT CONTEMPLATED
Delay claims § 16.18
DELEGATION
Scheduling functions to contractor, suing construction managers § 7.37
DELETION OF WORK
Suing private owner § 5.2
DEMOBILIZATION COSTS
Termination, pricing damages § 18.7
DEMOBILIZATION OF CONSTRUCTION CONTRACTOR
Phase VI, factors affecting project results § 1.3
DEMONSTRATIVE EVIDENCE
Litigation management, litigation and alternatives § 2.39
Trial preparation § 15.24
DE NOVO HEARING
Federal waiver of contract controversies § 6.5
DEPOSITIONS
Preparing case for litigation, discovery §§ 15.21, 15.22
Trial preparation, trial and appeal §§ 22.15, 22.16
DEPRECIATION DEDUCTIONS
Tax considerations § 21.9
DESCRIPTION OF MATERIALS
Suing subcontractors and material suppliers § 10.5
DESCRIPTION OF PROJECT
Arbitration § 14.14
DESCRIPTION OF PROJECT TIME FRAME
Arbitration § 14.22
DESCRIPTION OF WORK
Suing subcontractors and material suppliers § 10.5
DESIGN DEFECTS
Bases for liability, suing construction managers § 7.22
Contractor's builder's risk policy, exclusions § 11.22
Defending against owner claims § 20.2
DESIGN PROFESSIONALS
Defending against owner claims, defective plans and specifications § 20.2
Suing. See SUING DESIGN PROFESSIONALS
DESIGN REVIEWS
Scope changes, factors affecting project results § 1.10
DETAILED ENGINEERING
Phase IV, factors affecting project results § 1.3
DEVELOPING INFORMATION FOR CONSTRUCTION
Factors affecting project results § 1.3
DEVELOPING THE CLAIM
Variance analysis, labor productivity § 19.11
DEVIATION FROM PLANS
Defending against owner claims, defective plans and specifications § 20.2
DIFFERING SITE CONDITIONS
Exculpatory clause, litigation and alternatives § 2.23
Suing private owner, changes § 5.5
DIMINUTION IN VALUE
Contractor's insurance coverage
–Property damage defined § 11.8
DIMINUTION OF VALUE
Contractor's insurance coverage
–Care, custody or control exclusion § 11.11

DIRECT COST OF CHANGE
Changes in scope, pricing damages § 18.18
DIRECT DEALINGS WITH SENDER
Contract theories, suing construction lenders § 9.9
DIRECTED CHANGES
Delay claims § 16.10
DIRECT LABOR COST METHOD
Table 18–10, pricing damages § 18.25
DISALLOWANCE OF ACCELERATION DAMAGE CLAIMS
Proving liability to recover damages § 16.28
DISCHARGE TO MECHANIC
Lien bonds, sureties § 12.11
DISCLOSURE OF CLAIMS
Disclosure, arbitration §§ 14.11, 14.12
DISCOVERY
Arbitration § 14.6
Federal waiver of contract controversies § 6.5
Initial assessment, trial and appeal § 22.10
Preparing case. See PREPARING CASE FOR LITIGATION
Trial preparation, trial and appeal § 22.14
DISCOVERY RULE
Defending against owner claims, statutes of limitations § 20.4
DISCRETE APPROACH
Pricing damages § 18.11
DISCRETE APPROACH, CLAIM SUMMARY
Table 18–3, pricing damages § 18.11
DISPUTED WORK
Suing subcontractors and material suppliers § 10.5
DISPUTE MANAGEMENT
Dispute recognition and reaction
–Generally § 2.28
–Early expert use § 2.30
–Preservation of evidence and claims § 2.29
Settling disputes
–Generally § 2.31
–Arbitration vs. litigation § 2.34
–Negotiation strategies § 2.33
DISPUTE MANAGEMENT *(Continued)*
–Other alternatives § 2.35
–Settlement techniques § 2.32
Types and causes
–Generally § 2.25
–Bid disputes § 2.26
–Performance disputes § 2.27
DISPUTE RECOGNITION
Dispute management, litigation and alternatives § 2.28
DISPUTE RESOLUTION
Risk management, litigation and alternatives § 2.10
DISRUPTION
Calculating damages, pricing damages § 18.16
Categories of contract damages, pricing damages § 18.4
Dispute management, litigation and alternatives § 2.27
DISRUPTION DAMAGES
Proof of damages § 16.42
DIVISION OF LIABILITY AND DAMAGES
Trial preparation, trial and appeal § 22.13
DOCUMENTARY EVIDENCE
Arbitration § 14.9
DOCUMENTATION
Critical path analysis to prove delay § 17.9
DOCUMENTATION SYSTEM
Dispute management, litigation and alternatives § 2.29
DOCUMENTING CONTRACTOR'S CLAIM
Suing subcontractors and material suppliers § 10.13
DOCUMENTING DISRUPTION
Labor productivity § 19.13
DOCUMENTS
Preparing case. See PREPARING CASE FOR LITIGATION
DRAWINGS
Administration, suing construction managers § 7.24
Arbitration § 14.17
Duty to review, suing construction managers § 7.30
Phase IV, factors affecting project results § 1.3

DUAL NOTICE MECHANISM
Suing construction managers § 7.38
DUE PROCESS VS RIGHT TO JURY TRIAL
Trial preparation, trial and appeal § 22.13
DUMMY SUBCONTRACTOR
Payment bond claims, notice § 13.12
DUTY
Negligence theories, suing construction lenders § 9.21
DUTY OF CARE
Suing construction managers § 7.14
DUTY OWED BY CONSTRUCTION MANAGER
Suing construction managers. See SUING CONSTRUCTION MANAGERS
DUTY TO DEFEND
Contractor's insurance coverage §§ 11.1, 11.4
DUTY TO MITIGATE
Defending against owner claims, damages § 20.8
DUTY TO REVIEW
Drawings and prior work, suing construction managers § 7.30

EARLY DECISIONS
Factors affecting project results § 1.2
EARLY SETTLEMENTS
Initial assessment, trial and appeal § 22.10
EARNED CONTRACT BALANCE
Surety's right to contract funds § 12.24
EARTH MOVEMENT
Contractor's builder's risk policy, exclusions § 11.22
EARTH SUBSIDENCE
Contractor's builder's risk policy, exclusions § 11.22
ECONOMIC DAMAGES
Disruptions and delays, suing subcontractors and material suppliers § 10.6
ECONOMIC INABILITY TO PERFORM
Suing subcontractors and material suppliers § 10.12
ECONOMIC LOSS
Design professionals, suing construction managers § 7.41
Limitation, suing design professionals, contractor's right of action § 8.2
No recovery, suing construction managers § 7.41
EDUCATIONAL BACKGROUND
Trial preparation, trial and appeal § 22.16
EFFECTIVE DOCUMENTS MANAGEMENT
Trial preparation, trial and appeal § 22.14
EFFECTIVE LITIGATION STRATEGY
Litigation management, litigation and alternatives § 2.38
EFFECTIVE PREPARATION FOR A CONSTRUCTION ARBITRATION
Arbitration. See ARBITRATION
EFFECTIVE TRIAL PRESENTATION
Litigation management, litigation and alternatives § 2.39
EFFICIENCY OF CREW OVERLOADING
Figure 19–3 § 19.22
EICHLEAY FORMULA
Home office overhead, pricing damages § 18.23
Suing private owner, damages for extra costs § 5.13
Table 18–7 § 18.23
ELEMENTS OF PROOF
Critical path analysis to prove delay § 17.2
ENFORCING THIRD-PARTY RIGHTS
Contract theories, suing construction lenders § 9.10
ENGINEERING DESIGN BASIS
Phase II, factors affecting project results §§ 1.3, 1.4
ENGINEERING DESIGN CONTRACTOR
Factors affecting project results § 1.3
ENGINEERING REQUIREMENTS
Constraints, factors affecting projects results § 1.4

ENGINEERS
  Litigation and alternatives § 2.12
  Suing. See SUING DESIGN PROFESSIONALS
ENHANCED DAMAGES
  Defending against owner claims § 20.16
ENTITLEMENT TO CREDITS
  Arbitration § 14.16
ENVIRONMENTAL PROTECTION AGENCY
  Bid protests and mistakes
  –Listing requirement § 4.9
  –Minority business enterprise requirements § 4.10
  Bid protests and mistakes, listing requirement § 4.9
  Federally funded grant projects § 4.18
ENVIRONMENTAL STANDARDS
  Major influences, factors affecting project results § 1.8
EQUIPMENT BREAKDOWN
  Contractor's builder's risk policy, exclusions § 11.22
EQUIPMENT RENTAL
  Suing private owner, damages for extra costs § 5.13
EQUIPMENT SALES
  Defending against owner claims, warranties and UCC § 20.7
EQUITABLE ESTOPPEL
  Suing construction lender §§ 9.9, 9.12, 9.14
EQUITABLE LIEN
  Suing private owner, liens § 5.17
  Unjust enrichment theories, suing construction lenders §§ 9.16, 9.20
EQUITABLE PRINCIPLES
  Bid protests and mistakes § 4.30
EQUITABLE RELIEF
  Bid protests, federal contracts § 4.16
  Defending against owner claims § 20.16
  Federal waiver of contract controversies § 6.5
EQUITIES OF CASE
  Initial assessment, trial and appeal § 22.5
ERRORS
  Suing a government, authority to act § 6.12
  See also MISTAKES
ERRORS AND OMISSIONS
  Contractor's builder's risk policy, exclusions § 11.22
  Insurance, suing construction managers § 7.8
  Suing design professionals, liability to contractor § 8.7
ESTABLISHING NEGOTIATION STRATEGY
  Dispute management, litigation and alternatives § 2.33
ESTABLISHING THIRD-PARTY BENEFICIARY STATUS
  Contract theories, suing construction linders § 9.9
ESTIMATING
  Productivity and estimating. See LABOR PRODUCTIVITY
ESTOPPEL
  Collateral. See COLLATERAL ESTOPPEL
  Contract theories, suing construction lenders § 9.6
  Equitable estoppel, suing construction lenders § 9.9
  Payment bond claims, notice § 13.12
  Payment bond claims, notice requirements § 13.15
  Promissory. See PROMISSORY ESTOPPEL
  Rights based on. See RIGHTS BASED ON ESTOPPEL
  Suing a government
  –Authority to act § 6.12
  –Authority to act for state § 6.14
  Suing private owner, notice of changes § 5.4
EVALUATIONS
  Deficiencies as bid protest grounds §§ 4.11, 4.13
EVENTS OF DEFAULT
  Role of surety § 12.18
EVENTS THAT CAUSE CLAIMS
  Table 18–1, pricing damages § 18.2
EVER-CHANGING SCOPE
  See FACTORS AFFECTING PROJECT RESULTS
EVIDENCE
  Presentation, trial and appeal § 22.21
  Preservation, litigation and alternatives § 2.29
  Trial preparation § 15.4

EVIDENTIARY HEARINGS
Disclosure, arbitration § 14.11
EXCEPTIONS
No damage for delay clauses, sureties § 12.28
No damages for delay clauses, proving liability to recover damages §§ 15.15, 15.17
No damages for delay clauses, suing construction managers § 7.31
EXCESSIVE DELAY
Suing construction managers § 7.33
EXCESSIVE LITIGATION
Major influences, factors affecting project results § 1.8
EXCULPATORY CLAUSES
Risk management, litigation and alternatives § 2.23
Suing construction managers § 7.32
Suing design professionals, liability to contractor § 8.8
Suing private owner, remedies § 5.18
EXCUSABLE CONTRACTOR DELAYS
Delay claims. See DELAY CLAIMS
EXCUSABLE DELAY
Critical path analysis to prove delay § 17.2
Dispute management, litigation and alternatives § 2.27
Proving liability to recover damages § 16.32
EXCUSES
Bid bonds, types of surety bonds § 12.7
EXHAUSTION OF STATUTORY REMEDIES
Unjust enrichment, suing construction lenders § 9.20
EXONERATION REMEDY
Parties and causes of action, sureties § 12.30
EX PARTE INTERVIEWS
Trial preparation, trial and appeal § 22.15
EXPECTANCY
Initial assessment, trial and appeal § 22.7
EXPECTATION OF CONTRACTOR AND OWNER
Labor productivity § 19.3
EXPECTED PRODUCTIVITY
Figure 19–1, labor productivity § 19.15
EXPECTED PROFITS
Factors affecting project results § 1.7
EXPENSE DEDUCTION
Income recognition and expense deduction, timing of. See INCOME RECOGNITION AND EXPENSE DEDUCTION, TIMING OF
EXPENSES
Payment of settlements and judgments, tax considerations § 21.10
EXPERIENCE CURVES
Disruption, pricing damages § 18.16
EXPERT LISTS
Motions and filings before trial, trial and appeal § 22.19
EXPERT OPINION TESTIMONY
Litigation management, litigation and alternatives § 2.38
Suing construction managers §§ 7.6, 7.16
EXPERTS
Early use, litigation and alternatives § 2.30
Preparing case for litigation, collecting information § 15.11
EXPERTS VS. CONSULTANTS
Arbitration § 14.23
EXPERT TESTIMONY
Arbitration § 14.23
Suing design professionals, proof of negligence § 8.5
EXPERT WITNESSES
Defending against owner claims, defective plans and specifications § 20.2
Litigation team. See LITIGATION TEAM
Trial preparation, depositions § 15.22
EXPLOSION
Contractor's insurance coverage, liability policy exclusions § 11.16
EXPRESS DISCLAIMERS
Third-party rights, suing construction lenders § 9.9
EXPRESS WARRANTIES
Defending against owner claims, defective plans and specifications § 20.2

EXPRESS WARRANTIES *(Continued)*
Defending against owner claims, warranties § 20.7
Suing subcontractors and material suppliers § 10.8
EXTENDED OVERTIME INEFFICIENCY
Labor productivity § 19.23
EXTENDED SERVICE CONSTRUCTION MANAGEMENT
Suing construction managers § 7.5
EXTENSION OF TIME CLAUSES
Delay claims § 16.8
EXTENSION OF TIME OF PERFORMANCE
Proving liability to recover damages § 16.7
EXTENSIONS
Bid protests, federal contracts § 4.15
EXTRA WORK
Claims, proving liability to recover damages § 16.12
Dispute management, litigation and alternatives § 2.27
Suing private owner, remedies § 5.13
EXTREME NEGLIGENCE
Suing construction managers § 7.34

FACT-FINDING CONFERENCE
Bid protests, federal contracts § 4.15
FACTORS AFFECTING PRODUCTIVITY
Labor productivity §§ 19.4, 19.6
FACTORS AFFECTING PROJECT RESULTS
Generally § 1.1
Construction project scope changes § 1.7
Early decisions § 1.2
Ever-changing scope
–Generally § 1.10
–Change order system § 1.12
–Managing change control § 1.11
Factors influencing early decisions § 1.5
Industrial construction: case study § 1.6
Major influences on construction projects
–Generally § 1.8
–Typical project problems § 1.9
FACTORS AFFECTING PROJECT RESULTS *(Continued)*
Project life cycle
–Generally § 1.3
–Phases I and II § 1.4
FACTORS INFLUENCING DECISIONS IN SCOPE DEFINITION PHASE
Figure 1–4 § 1.5
FACTORS INFLUENCING EARLY DECISIONS
Factors affecting project results § 1.5
FACTS
Initial assessment, trial and appeal § 22.3
FACTUAL TESTIMONY
Arbitration § 14.23
FAILURE TO PROVIDE CONSTRUCTION SUPPORT SERVICES
Bases for liability, suing construction managers § 7.26
FAILURE TO PROVIDE TIMELY INFORMATION
Bases for liability, suing construction managers § 7.25
FAILURE TO SCHEDULE AND COORDINATE
Bases for liability, suing construction managers § 7.27
FAIR DEALING
Parties and causes of action, sureties § 12.27
FAST-TRACK CONSTRUCTION
Suing construction managers §§ 7.2, 7.12
FAST-TRACK CONTRACT
Suing design professionals, scheduling and coordination negligence § 8.11
FATAL DEFECTS
Bid protests and mistakes, bid requirements § 4.7
FAULTY PERFORMANCE
Contractor's insurance coverage, performance or business risk exclusion § 11.13
FEDERAL ACQUISITION REGULATION
Suing a government § 6.2

FEDERAL ARBITRATION ACT AND LOCAL ARBITRATION STATUTES
Arbitration § 14.15
FEDERAL CONTRACTS
Bid protests and mistakes. See BID PROTESTS AND MISTAKES
FEDERAL COURT IMPROVEMENT ACT
Bid protests, federal contracts § 4.16
FEDERAL COURTS
Payment bond claims, jurisdiction and venue § 13.16
FEDERAL COURTS IMPROVEMENT ACT
Suing a government § 6.4
FEDERAL DISTRICT COURT
Bid protests, federal contracts § 4.15
FEDERAL LAW
Bid protests and mistakes § 4.31
FEDERALLY FUNDED GRANT PROJECTS
Bid protests and mistakes. See BID PROTESTS AND MISTAKES
FEDERAL PROCUREMENT SYSTEM
Federally funded grant projects § 4.18
FEES
Application to american arbitration association § 14.11
FEMALE EMPLOYMENT REQUIREMENTS
Risk management, litigation and alternatives § 2.18
FIELD CONSTRUCTION
Phase V, factors affecting project results § 1.3
FIELD REPRESENTATIVES
Suing a government, authority to act § 6.12
FIELD WORKERS
Arbitration § 14.22
FIFTH AMENDMENT
Due process vs seventh amendment right to jury trial § 22.13
FILING CLAIMS
Payment bond claims, practice notes § 13.19
FILINGS
Motions and filings before trail. See TRIAL AND APPEAL
FINANCE COSTS
Proof of damages § 16.41
FINANCIAL FEASIBILITY
Phase I, factors affecting project results § 1.3
FINANCIAL RESOURCES
Phase IV, factors affecting project results § 1.3
FINANCIAL STRENGTH OF PRINCIPAL
Default, sureties § 12.16
FINANCING
National housing act, suing construction lenders § 9.7
FINANCING EXISTING CONTRACTOR
Default, role of surety § 12.22
FINES
Tax considerations § 21.10
FIRE DAMAGE
Contractor's builder's risk policy, exclusions § 11.22
FIRM OFFERS
Bids, suing subcontractors and material suppliers § 10.2
FITNESS
Bid protests and mistakes, responsibility § 4.8
FIXED FEE PROJECTS
Suing construction managers § 7.3
FIXED-PRICE CONTRACT
Into cost-plus contracts, total cost approach, pricing damages § 18.9
Suing private owner, liens § 5.17
FIXING INTERNAL RESPONSIBILITY
Organization, litigation team § 3.4
FLOAT
Critical path analysis to prove delay § 17.7
FLOW-DOWN CLAUSE
Defective work correction, suing subcontractors and material suppliers § 10.9
Parties and causes of action, sureties § 12.29
Risk management, litigation and alternatives § 2.22
Suing subcontractors and material suppliers § 10.4

FOCUSED PREPARATION
Initial assessment, trial and appeal § 22.9
FOLLOW-UP NOTICE CLAUSES
Proving liability to recover damages § 16.33
FORESEEABILITY
Defending against owner claims, damages § 20.8
Suing design professionals
–Administrative negligence § 8.10
–Economic loss limitation § 8.2
–Liability to contractor §§ 8.1, 8.7
Suing private owner, damages for prevention of completion § 5.12
FORFEITURE
Defending against owner claims, substantial performance § 20.11
FORM
Bid bonds, types of surety bonds § 12.8
FORMS OF CONSTRUCTION MANAGEMENT PRACTICE
Suing construction managers. See SUING CONSTRUCTION MANAGERS
FORTUITOUS LOSSES
Contractor's insurance coverage, builder's risk policy limitations § 11.20
FORTUITY
Contractor's builder's risk policy, burden of proof § 11.23
Contractor's insurance coverage, liability policy insuring agreement § 11.5
FORUM
Bid protests, federal contracts §§ 4.15, 4.16
Litigation management, litigation and alternatives § 2.37
Selection, suing construction managers § 7.38
FORUM SHOPPING
Contractor's insurance coverage § 11.2
FORWARD PASS
Critical path analysis to prove delay § 17.7
FOUR CORNERS RULE
Sureties § 12.27
FOUR-WAY TEST
Total cost approach, pricing damages § 18.10
FRAUD
Defenses, suing construction managers § 7.34
Delay claims § 16.20
FREEDOM OF INFORMATION ACT
Bid protests, federal contracts § 4.15
Payment bond claims, attorneys' fees and interest § 13.10
FREE FLOAT
Critical path analysis to prove delay § 17.7
FREEZING ASSETS
Stop-notice provisions, suing construction lenders § 9.4
FRONT-COSTS
Termination, pricing damages §§ 18.7, 18.19

GENERAL ACCOUNTING OFFICE
Bid protest grounds § 4.13
Bid protests, federal contracts § 4.15
Recommendations, administrative forum for bid protests § 6.7
GENERAL CONTRACTOR-OWNER RELATIONSHIP
Suing construction managers § 7.4
GENERAL CONTRACTORS
Litigation and alternatives § 2.14
Standard of care, suing construction managers § 7.6
GENERAL PRINCIPLES
Payment of settlements and judgments, tax considerations § 21.7
GENERAL SERVICES ADMINISTRATION BOARD OF CONTRACT APPEALS
Bid protests, federal contracts § 4.15
GOOD FAITH
Parties and causes of action, sureties §§ 12.27, 12.30
See also BAD FAITH
GOVERNMENTS
Suing. See SUING A GOVERNMENT
GROUNDS FOR CHALLENGE
Bid protests and mistakes § 4.4

GUARANTEED MAXIMUM (GMP) PRICE CONSTRUCTION MANAGEMENT
Suing construction managers §§ 7.4, 7.6

HANDSHAKE AGREEMENTS
Documentation, suing subcontractors and material suppliers § 10.13
HARMFUL PRECEDENT
Initial assessment, trial and appeal § 22.6
HARM TO BUSINESS REPUTATION
Tax considerations § 21.3
HEARING PREPARATION
Arbitration § 14.21
HEARINGS
Protest procedure, federally funded grant projects § 4.20
HISTORICAL OVERHEAD ANALYSIS
Table 18–7, pricing damages § 18.12
HISTORICAL PROFIT ANALYSIS
Table 18–8, pricing damages § 18.12
HOLD HARMLESS CLAUSES
Defending against owner claims § 20.16
HOME OFFICE OVERHEAD
Pricing damages. See PRICING DAMAGES
Proof of damages § 16.40
Suing private owner, damages for extra costs § 5.13
HOURS WORKED, PRODUCTIVITY, AND COSTS, RELATIONSHIPS OF
Table 19–6, labor productivity § 19.23
HUD-FINANCED PROJECTS
Unjust enrichment, suing construction lenders § 9.20

IMPACTED PERIODS
Labor productivity § 19.14
IMPACT OF EXTENDED OVERTIME PRODUCTIVITY
Figure 19–5, labor productivity § 19.23
IMPLIED INDEMNIFICATION
Indemnification, suing subcontractors and material suppliers § 10.10
IMPLIED-IN-FACT WAIVER
Federal waiver of contract controversies § 6.5
IMPLIED OBLIGATIONS
Legal parameters, litigation and alternatives § 2.19
IMPLIED PROMISE OF PAYMENT
Suing a government, authority to act for state § 6.14
IMPLIED WAIVERS
Suing private owner, notice of changes § 5.4
IMPLIED WARRANTIES
Defective work correction, suing subcontractors and material suppliers § 10.9
Defending against owner claims, defective plans and specifications § 20.2
Defending against owner claims, warranties § 20.7
Suing construction managers § 7.16
Suing design professionals, negligence § 8.4
Suing subcontractors and material suppliers § 10.8
Theories of recovery, suing construction managers § 7.19
Workmanship, suing subcontractors and material suppliers § 10.8
IMPLIED WARRANTY OF HABITUALITY
Risk management, litigation and alternatives § 2.19
IMPORTANCE OF STATUTORY REMEDIES
Statutory remedies, suing construction lenders §§ 9.2–9.5
IMPRACTICALITY
Defending against owner claims §§ 20.5, 20.6
IMPROPER SUPERVISION
Suing construction managers § 7.27
IMPUTATION OF KNOWLEDGE
Suing a government, ratification by contracting officer § 6.13
INADEQUATE ACCOUNTING PRACTICES
Typical project problems, factors affecting project results § 1.9

INADEQUATE COST CONTROL
Typical project problems, factors affecting project results § 1.9
INCIDENTAL EXPENSES
Suing private owner, damages for prevention of completion § 5.12
INCLEMENT WEATHER
Labor productivity § 19.24
INCOME-PRODUCING ACTIVITY
Tax considerations § 21.8
INCOME RECOGNITION
Income recognition and expense deduction, timing of. See INCOME RECOGNITION AND EXPENSE DEDUCTION, TIMING OF
INCOME RECOGNITION AND EXPENSE DEDUCTION, TIMING OF
Generally § 21.11
Cash and accruel methods § 21.12
Long-term contract methods of accounting
–Generally § 21.13
–Completed contract method § 21.15
–Percentage-of-completion § 21.14
INCREASE IN VALUE OF IMPROVEMENT
Unjust enrichment theories, suing construction lenders § 9.19
INDEMNIFICATION
Defending against owner claims § 20.16
Suing subcontractors and material suppliers § 9.10
INDEMNIFICATION AGREEMENTS
Parties and causes of action, sureties § 12.34
INDEMNITY
Design professional's liability to owner for § 8.3
INDEMNITY AGAINST MECHANICS' LIENS
Lien bonds, sureties § 12.11
INDEMNITY ISSUES
Motions and filings before trial, trial and appeal § 22.17
INDEMNITY RIGHTS
Risk management, litigation and alternatives § 2.15
INDEX
Trial preparation, document management § 15.7
INDUSTRIAL CONSTRUCTION
Case study, factors affecting project results § 1.6
INDUSTRY CUSTOM
Contract theories, suing construction lenders § 9.9
Duty, suing construction lenders § 9.21
INDUSTRY STANDARDS
Suing construction managers § 7.13
INEFFICIENCY
Labor productivity §§ 19.20, 19.23
INFLUENCE FACTORS
Factors affecting project results §§ 1.2, 1.5
Organizational groups, factors affecting project results § 1.5
INHERENT RISK FACTORS
Liability and alternatives § 2.2
INHERENT VICE
Contractor's builder's risk policy, exclusions § 11.22
INITIAL PRESENTATION
Arbitration § 14.20
INJUNCTIVE RELIEF
Bid protests, federal contracts § 4.16
INJURIES TO REAL PROPERTY
Defending against owner claims, statutes of limitations § 20.4
INJURY IN FACT
Contractor's insurance coverage, liability policy, trigger of coverage § 11.6
INSOLVENT CONTRACTOR
Payment bond claims, remedies if payment bond not available § 13.18
INSPECTION
Design professional's liability, negligent supervision and inspection § 8.9
Suing design professionals, conduct constituting negligence § 8.7
Suing design professionals, inspection negligence § 8.9
Suing private owner, delay § 5.7
Trial preparation, discovery § 15.23
INSPECTOR GENERALS
Suing a government § 6.2
INSPECTORS
Suing a government, authority to act § 6.12

INSUFFICIENT WORK DEFINITION
Typical project problems, factors affecting project results § 1.9
INSURANCE
Payment bonds, claims covered § 13.8
INSURANCE CONSIDERATIONS
Standard of care, suing construction managers § 7.8
INSURANCE PREMIUMS
Payment bond claims, taxes § 13.8
INSURED CONTRACT
Contractor's insurance coverage, contractually assumed liability exclusion § 11.10
INTENDED VS. INCIDENTAL BENEFICIARY
Suing construction managers § 7.17
INTENTIONAL INTERFERENCE
Design professional's liability to contractor § 8.10
INTENTIONAL TORT
Risk management, litigation and alternatives §§ 2.12, 2.19
INTENT TO BENEFIT THIRD PARTIES
Contract theories, suing construction lenders § 7.8
Express disclaimers, suing construction lenders § 7.8
INTEREST
Defending against owner claims § 20.16
Payment bonds, claims covered § 13.10
INTERESTED PARTIES
Bid protests § 4.14
INTEREST PARTY
Administrative forum for bid protests § 6.7
INTERFERENCE WITH BIDS
Bases for liability, suing construction managers § 7.21
INTERFERENCE WITH CONTRACT
Suing construction managers § 7.16
Theories of recovery, suing construction managers § 7.18
Tort theories, suing construction lenders § 9.23
INTERFERENCE WITH CONTRACT PERFORMANCE
Parties and causes of action, sureties § 12.27
INTERMEDIATE COVERAGE
Indemnification, suing subcontractors and material suppliers § 10.10
INTERNAL POLICY MANUALS
Duty, suing construction lenders § 9.21
INTERROGATORIES
Litigation management, litigation and alternatives § 2.38
Preparing case for litigation, written requests § 15.16
INTERVIEWS
Trial preparation, trial and appeal § 22.15
Trial preparation, witnesses § 15.10
INVESTIGATION
Preparing case. See PREPARING CASE FOR LITIGATION
Role of surety § 12.19
INVITATION FOR BIDS
Bid protests and mistakes § 4.3
INVOICES
Payment bond claims, commencement of limitation period § 13.14

JOB SITE
See SITE ACCESS; SITE VISITS
JOBSITE INDIRECT COSTS
Proof of damages § 16.39
JOINDER OF ARBITRATION PROCEEDINGS
Pass-through claims, suing subcontractors and material supplier § 10.11
JOINT AND SEVERALLY LIABLE DEFENDANTS
Defending against owner claims § 20.16
JOINT DESIGNATION NUMBERS
Arbitration § 14.9
JOINT VENTURERS
Contract theories, suing construction lenders § 9.7
JUDGMENT
Tax considerations § 21.17
JUDGMENT PROCEEDS
Taxation of settlement or judgment proceeds. See TAXATION OF SETTLEMENT OR JUDGMENT PROCEEDS

JUDICIAL REVIEW
Bid protests, federal contracts § 4.21
Suing a government, bid protests § 6.6
JURISDICTION
Arbitration § 14.22
Payment bond claims § 13.16
JURY ASSISTANCE TECHNIQUES
Trial preparation, trial and appeal
JURY INSTRUCTIONS
Motions and filings before trial, trial and appeal § 22.19
JURY VERDICT APPROACH
Changed conditions, pricing damages § 18.5
JUSTIFIABLE RELIANCE
Bids, suing subcontractors and material suppliers § 10.2

KEY DOCUMENT IDENTIFICATION
Trial preparation, trial and appeal § 22.14
KEY LEGAL ARGUMENTS
Initial assessment, trial and appeal § 22.4
KNOWN DEFICIENCY
Contractor's insurance coverage, sistership or recall exclusion § 11.15

LABOR AND EQUIPMENT MIX
Labor productivity § 19.6
LABOR COSTS
Proof of damages § 16.37
LABOR DISPUTES
Delay claims § 16.25
LABOR ORGANIZATIONS
Major influences, factors affecting project results § 1.8
LABOR PRODUCTIVITY
Generally § 19.1
Calculating compounding impacts § 19.25
Dallavia method
–Generally § 19.15
–Modified dallavia § 19.16
Developing the claim: variance analysis § 19.11
Documenting disruption § 19.13
Inclement weather § 19.24
Learning curve claims § 19.26
LABOR PRODUCTIVITY *(Continued)*
Measured mile approach § 19.14
Productivity and estimating
–Generally § 19.2
–Factors affecting labor productivity § 19.4
Productivity curves and damages calculation
–Generally § 19.17
–Acceleration requirements § 19.19
–Extended overtime inefficiency § 19.23
–Innefficiency from crew increases and overmanning § 19.20
–Overmanning/crowding § 19.22
–Productivity losses from acceleration § 19.18
–Productivity loss from increased crewing § 19.21
Quantifying productivity losses § 19.12
Ratio delay studies § 19.27
Selecting a general approach
–Generally § 19.7
–Bottom-up analysis § 19.10
–Problems with top-down approach § 19.9
–Top-down approach § 19.8
LAND
Trial preparation, discovery § 15.23
LATENT CONDITIONS
Exculpatory clause, litigation and alternatives § 2.23
LATENT DEFECTS
Contractor's builder's risk policy, exclusions § 11.22
Defending against owner claims, waiver § 20.3
LATE PERFORMANCE
Defending against owner claims, waiver § 20.3
LAW OF PROOF OF DAMAGES
Proving liability to recover damages § 16.35
LAWYER CONTROL
Trial preparation, trial and appeal § 22.14
LAWYERS
Arbitration, role in § 14.5
Fees. See ATTORNEYS' FEES

LEARNING CURVE
Affect on costs, Figure 19–8, labor productivity § 19.26
Analysis, disruption, pricing damages § 18.16
Claims, labor productivity § 19.26
LEGAL PARAMETERS
Risk management. See RISK MANAGEMENT
LEGAL THEORIES OF DAMAGES
Proving liability to recover damages § 16.35
LEGISLATED RISKS
Liability and alternatives § 2.3
LENDER AND BORROWER AS SINGLE ENTITY
Contract theories, suing construction lenders § 9.7
LESSEES
Parties and causes of action, sureties § 12.28
LIABILITY
Bases of liability. See SUING CONSTRUCTION MANAGERS
Design professional's liability to owner for § 8.3
Exculpatory clause, litigation and alternatives § 2.23
Suing design professional. See SUING DESIGN PROFESSIONAL
LIABILITY POLICY
Contractor's insurance coverage. See CONTRACTOR'S INSURANCE COVERAGE
LICENSING REQUIREMENTS
Risk management, litigation and alternatives § 2.18
Standard of care, suing construction managers § 7.7
LIEN BOND
Types of surety bonds § 12.11
LIEN RIGHTS
Risk management, litigation and alternatives § 2.15
LIENS
Suing private owner, remedies § 5.17
Sureties § 12.1
LIFE CYCLE OF INDUSTRIAL PROJECT
Figure 1–2, factors affecting project results § 1.3
LIMITATION OF ACTIONS
Notice and limitation of actions. See SURETIES
LIMITATION PERIODS
Notice and limitation of actions, sureties § 12.36
Payment bond claims, notice requirements § 13.14
LIMITED PARTNERSHIP THEORIES
Contract theories, suing construction lenders § 9.7
LIQUIDATED DAMAGES
Defending against owner claims §§ 20.10, 20.15
LIQUIDATED DAMAGES CLAUSE
Disruptions and delays, suing subcontractors and material suppliers § 10.6
Parties and causes of action, sureties § 12.34
Suing subcontractors and material suppliers § 10.7
LIQUIDATION AGREEMENTS
Pass-through claims, suing subcontractors and material supplier § 10.11
LISTS OF WITNESSES AND EXHIBITS
Motions and filings before trial, trial and appeal § 22.19
LITIGATION
Preparing case. See PREPARING CASE FOR LITIGATION
Tax considerations. See TAX CONSIDERATIONS
LITIGATION AND ALTERNATIVES
Construction risks and rewards. See CONSTRUCTION RISKS AND REWARDS
Litigation management
–Appeal § 2.40
–Effective strategy § 2.38
–Effective trial presentation § 2.39
–Objectives § 2.36
–Selection of parties, remedies, and claims § 2.37
Risk management. See RISK MANAGEMENT
LITIGATION EXPENSES
Initial assessment, trial and appeal § 22.6

LITIGATION MANAGEMENT
Litigation and alternatives. See LITIGATION AND ALTERNATIVES
LITIGATION OBJECTIVES
Litigation management, litigation and alternatives § 2.36
LITIGATIONS AND ALTERNATIVES
Dispute management. See DISPUTE MANAGEMENT
LITIGATION STRATEGY
Litigation management, litigation and alternatives § 2.38
LITIGATION SUPPORT GROUP
Trial preparation, discovery § 15.13
LITIGATION TEAM
Generally § 3.1
Coordinating consultants and experts § 3.13
Expert witnesses
–Generally § 3.7
–Claim consultant § 3.7
–Construction consultant § 3.12
–Consulting engineer § 3.11
–Critical path consultant § 3.10
–Damages expert § 3.7
Locating witnesses and consultants § 3.14
Organization
–Generally § 3.3
–Choosing lawyers § 3.5
–Fixing internal responsibility § 3.4
–Selecting other members § 3.6
Planning § 3.2
LITIGATION TRAPS
Parties and causes of action, sureties § 12.28
LITTLE MILLER ACTS
Sureties § 12.4
LOAN AGREEMENTS
Recording requirements, suing construction lenders § 9.5
LOAN DISBURSEMENT PATTERS
Rights based on estoppel § 9.14
LOCAL CODES
Risk management, litigation and alternatives § 2.18
LOCAL GOVERNMENT
Sovereign immunity applicability § 6.8
LOCAL WORK FORCE CHARACTERISTICS
Labor productivity § 19.6
LOCATING WITNESSES AND CONSULTANTS
Litigation team § 3.14
LONG-TERM CONTRACT METHODS OF ACCOUNTING
Income recognition and expense deduction, timing of §§ 21.13–21.15
LOOK-BACK RULE
Tax considerations § 21.13
LOSSES
Disruptions and delays, suing subcontractors and material suppliers § 10.6
LOSS OF PROFITS VS. IMPAIRMENT TO GOODWILL
Tax considerations § 21.20
LOST PROFITS
Payment bonds, claims covered § 13.9
Proof of damages § 16.42
Suing private owner, damages for prevention of completion § 5.12
Tax considerations § 21.3
LOW BIDDER CLAIMS
Proving liability to recover damages § 16.30

MAINTENANCE CONCERNS
Scope changes, factors affecting project results § 1.10
MAJOR INFLUENCES
Construction projects, factors affecting project results § 1.8
MALICIOUS INTERFERENCE
Suing construction managers § 7.18
MALPRACTICE INSURANCE
Suing construction managers § 7.8
MANAGING CHANGE CONTROL
Factors affecting project results § 1.11
MANPOWER RESOURCES
Phase IV, factors affecting project results § 1.3
MANUFACTURERS AND CONTRACTORS LIABILITY
Contractor's insurance coverage, completed operations hazard § 11.17
MANUFACTURER'S DESCRIPTION
Suing design professionals, conduct constituting negligence § 8.6

MARKET PRESSURE
Factors affecting project results § 1.7
MARKUPS IN CHANGE ORDERS
Changes in scope, pricing damages § 18.18
MATERIAL
Payment bond claims, commencement of limitation period § 13.14
MATERIAL AND EQUIPMENT DELIVERIES
Suing construction managers § 7.27
MATERIAL BREACH
Defending against owner claims, termination defense § 20.14
MATERIAL COSTS
Proof of damages § 16.38
MATERIAL DEVIATIONS FROM IFB
Bid protest grounds § 4.11
MATERIAL ELEMENTS
Bid protests and mistakes, bid requirements § 4.7
MATERIAL FAILURE OF PERFORMANCE
Third-party rights, suing construction lenders § 9.9
MATERIAL MISTAKE
Bid mistakes § 4.28
MATERIAL PAYMENT BOND
Payment bond claims § 13.1
MATERIAL SUPPLIERS
Bid protests and mistakes, listing requirement § 4.9
Payment bond claims, notice § 13.11
Payment bond claims, parties who may make claim § 13.6
Suing construction lenders §§ 9.4, 9.5
Suing subcontractors and material suppliers. See SUING SUBCONTRACTORS AND MATERIAL SUPPLIERS
MAXIMIZING SUBSTANTIVE HEARING TIME
Arbitration § 14.9
MEASURED MILE APPROACH
Labor productivity § 19.14
MEASURED MILE TECHNIQUE
Disruption, pricing damages § 18.16
Figure 19–1, labor productivity § 19.14
MEASUREMENT OF DAMAGES
Initial assessment, trial and appeal § 22.7
MEASUREMENT STANDARDS, METHODS, AND POLICIES
Figure 19–1, labor productivity § 19.14
MEASURING UNJUST ENRICHMENT
Unjust enrichment theories, suing construction lenders § 9.19
MECHANICS' LIENS
Payment bond claims § 13.2
Statutory remedies, suing construction lenders § 9.3
Suing private owner, liens § 5.17
Unjust enrichment, suing construction lenders § 9.20
MEDIATION
Suing private owner § 5.1
MEDIATORS
Initial assessment, trial and appeal § 22.10
MEMBERSHIPS IN PROFESSIONAL SOCIETIES AND ORGANIZATIONS
Trial preparation, trial and appeal § 22.16
MENTAL ANGUISH
Defending against owner claims § 20.16
MERCHANTABLE MATERIALS AND EQUIPMENT
Implied warranty suing subcontractors and material suppliers § 10.9
MERELY INCIDENTAL ITEMS
Contractor's insurance coverage, care, custody or control exclusion § 11.11
METHOD OF PERFORMANCE
Risk management, litigation and alternatives § 2.8
Suing private owner, changes § 5.6
MICROFILMS
Trial preparation, document management § 15.8
MILLER ACT
Payment bond claims § 13.4
Payment bond claims, attorneys' fees and interest § 13.10

MILLER ACT *(Continued)*
Payment bond claims, jurisdiction and venue § 13.16
Payment bond claims, limitation period § 13.13
Payment bond claims, notice §§ 13.11, 13.12
Payment bond claims, taxes § 13.8
MINI-TRIALS
Dispute management, litigation and alternatives § 2.35
Initial assessment, trial and appeal § 22.10
MINOR IRREGULARITIES
Bid protests and mistakes, bid requirements § 4.7
MINORITY BUSINESS ENTERPRISE REQUIREMENTS
Bid protests and mistakes, contract award criteria § 4.10
MINORITY EMPLOYMENT REQUIREMENTS
Risk management, litigation and alternatives § 2.18
MIRROR IMAGE RULE
Risk management, litigation and alternatives § 2.21
MISREPRESENTATION
Payment bond claims, estoppel § 13.15
Suing design professionals, liability to contractor § 8.8
Suing private owner § 5.3
Tort theories, suing construction lenders § 9.22
MISTAKES
Bid mistakes. See BID PROTESTS AND MISTAKES
Payment bond claims § 13.5
Suing private owner, rescission § 5.14
MITIGATION
Suing private owner, damages for prevention of completion § 5.12
MODIFICATION IMPACT EVALUATION GUIDE (MIEG)
Labor productivity §§ 19.19, 19.23
MODIFICATIONS
Risk management, litigation and alternatives § 2.24
MODIFIED DALLAVIA METHOD
Labor productivity § 19.16
MONETARY OBJECTIVES
Initial assessment, trial and appeal § 22.6
MORAL DAMAGES
Defending against owner claims § 20.16
MOTIONS AND FILINGS BEFORE TRIAL
Trial and appeal. See TRIAL AND APPEAL
MOTIONS TO COMPEL
Trial preparation, document production request § 15.19
MOTIONS TO DISMISS OR STRIKE
Motions and filings before trial, trial and appeal § 22.17
MOTIONS TO EXCLUDE OR LIMIT EVIDENCE
Motions and filings before trial, trial and appeal § 22.19
MOVABLE GOODS, SALE OF
Risk management, litigation and alternatives § 2.21
MULTI-PARTY ARBITRATION
Pass-through claims, suing subcontractors and material supplier § 10.11
MULTIPLE PRIME CONTRACT
Defending against owner claims, owner's duty to coordinate § 20.9
Suing design professionals, scheduling and coordination negligence § 8.11
MULTIPLE PRIME CONTRACTORS
Risk management, litigation and alternatives § 2.13
MUTUAL DELAY
Suing subcontractors and material suppliers § 10.7
MUTUAL MISTAKE
Suing private owner, rescission § 5.14

NAME BRAND PRODUCT
Defending against owner claims § 20.2
NARROW COVERAGE
Indemnification, suing subcontractors and material suppliers § 10.10
NATIONAL HOUSING ACT
Financing, suing construction lenders § 9.7

NATURE OF DISPUTE
Disclosure, arbitration § 14.11
NECESSARY EXPENSES
Suing a government, federal fiscal restrictions § 6.10
Tax considerations § 21.8
NEED FOR EFFECTIVE MANAGEMENT
Liability and alternatives § 2.9
NEGATIVE CASH FLOW
Cost of capital, pricing damages § 18.20
NEGLIGENCE
Contractor's builder's risk policy
–Exclusions § 11.22
–Fortuitous loss § 11.20
Contractor's insurance coverage, contractually assumed liaiblity exclusion § 11.10
Contributory and comparative, suing construction managers § 7.40
Risk management, litigation and alternatives § 2.12
Suing construction managers §§ 7.16, 7.19, 7.27, 7.29
Suing design professional. See SUING DESIGN PROFESSIONAL
Theories of recovery, suing construction managers § 7.16
Tort theories, suing construction lenders § 9.21
NEGLIGENT DISBURSEMENT OF LOAN FUNDS
Third-party rights, suing construction lenders § 9.9
Tort theories, suing construction lenders § 9.21
NEGLIGENT INTERFERENCE
Suing design professionals, economic loss limitation § 8.2
NEGLIGENT INTERFERENCE WITH CONTRACT
Parties and causes of action, sureties § 12.27
NEGLIGENT MISREPRESENTATION
Tort theories, suing construction lenders § 9.22
NEGOTIATION STRATEGIES
Dispute management, litigation and alternatives § 2.33
NETWORK ANALYSIS
Litigation team § 3.10
NEW CONTRACTOR AND CONTRACT
Default, role of surety § 12.22
NEW TECHNOLOGY
Suing design professionals, proof of negligence § 8.5
NO DAMAGE FOR DELAY CLAUSES
Chapter 16 generally
Defenses, suing construction managers §§ 7.31–7.37
Disruptions and delays, suing subcontractors and material suppliers § 10.6
Exceptions to no damage for delay clauses. See DELAY CLAIMS
Exculpatory clause, litigation and alternatives § 2.23
Parties and causes of action, sureties § 12.28
Proving liability to recover damages § 16.13
Suing private owner, breaches of contract by owner § 5.8
NONARGUMENTATIVE EVIDENCE
Arbitration § 14.9
NONBINDING MEDIATION
Dispute management, litigation and alternatives § 2.35
NONCONTROLLING DELAYS
Litigation team § 3.10
NONDEDUCTIBLE OR NONCAPITALIZABLE EXPENSES
Payment of settlements and judgments, tax considerations
NONDISCLOSING DEMANDS OR COUNTERCLAIMS
Arbitration § 14.11
NONECONOMIC DAMAGES
Suing construction managers § 7.11
NONPAYMENT
Breaches of contract by owner § 5.9
NONPERFORMANCE
Contractor's insurance coverage, performance or business risk exclusion § 11.13
Defending against owner claims, supervening impracticability § 20.5
NONPROFIT ENTITIES
National housing act, suing construction lenders § 9.7

NONREVOCABLE OFFERS
Bids, suing subcontractors and material suppliers § 10.2
NONTAXABLE PROCEEDS
Treatment of proceeds, tax considerations § 21.5
NO RECOVERY FOR ECONOMIC LOSS
Defenses, suing construction managers § 7.41
NO RELIEF FOR DELAY
Proving liability to recover damages § 16.7
NOTICE
Bid protests and mistakes §§ 4.4, 4.29
Changes, breaches of contract by owner § 5.4
Default and termination, suing subcontractors and material suppliers § 10.12
Notice and limitation of actions, sureties § 12.35
Payment bond claims, parties who may make claim § 13.6
Role of surety § 12.19
Suing private owner, delay § 5.7
NOTICE AND LIMITATION OF ACTION
Sureties. See SURETIES
NOTICE CLAUSES
Proving liability to recover damages § 16.33
NOTICE REQUIREMENTS
Dispute management, litigation and alternatives § 2.29
Risk management, litigation and alternatives § 2.18
NUMBERING
Trial preparation, trial and appeal § 22.14

OBJECTION
Trial preparation, document production request § 15.19
OBLIGATIONS
Role of surety §§ 12.17–12.21
OBLIGEE
Definition, sureties § 12.2
OBLIGEE'S CONDUCT
Role of surety § 12.21
OCCUPANCY
Home office overhead, pricing damages § 18.26
OCCUPIED BUILDING
Contractor's insurance coverage, builder's risk policy § 11.19
OCCURRENCE
Contractor's insurance coverage
–Completed operations hazard § 11.17
–Liability policy insuring agreement § 11.5
–Performance or business risk exclusion § 11.13
OCCURRENCE OF UNJUST ENRICHMENT
Suing construction lenders § 9.18
"OF GOOD QUALITY" WORK
Suing construction managers § 7.13
OMISSIONS
Bid protests and mistakes, bid requirments § 4.5
ONE-YEAR RULE
Suing a government, federal fiscal restrictions § 6.10
OPENING STATEMENT
Trial and appeal § 22.20
OPERABILITY CHECKS
Phase VI, factors affecting project results § 1.3
OPERATING PLANT RESPONSIBILITIES
Factors affecting project results § 1.5
OPERATIONS CONCERNS
Scope changes, factors affecting project results § 1.10
OPINIONS
Trial preparation, experts § 15.11
OPTIONAL TRIAL PROCEDURES
Motions and filings before trial, trial and appeal § 22.19
OPTIONS
Default of performance bond principal, role of surety § 12.22
ORAL ARGUMENT
Appeal, trial and appeal § 22.27
ORAL CHANGE ORDERS
Parol evidence, sureties § 12.38
ORAL PROPOSALS
Bids, suing subcontractors and material suppliers § 10.2

ORDINANCES
Legal parameters, litigation and alternatives § 2.18
ORDINARY EXPENSES
Tax considerations § 21.8
ORDINARY INCOME
Treatment of proceeds, tax considerations § 21.3
ORGANIZATION
Litigation team. See LITIGATION TEAM
Trial preparation, trial and appeal § 22.14
ORGANIZATIONAL GROUPS
Influence factors, factors affecting results § 1.5
ORGANIZATIONAL RELATIONSHIPS
Constraints, factors affecting project results § 1.4
ORIGIN OF CLAIMS
Tax considerations § 21.2
OTHER ALTERNATIVES
Dispute management, litigation and alternatives § 2.35
OTHER DAMAGE CLAIMS
Proving liability to recover damages. See PROVING LIABILITY TO RECOVER DAMAGES
OTHER TEAM MEMBERS
Organization, litigation team § 3.6
OTHER TORT THEORIES
Tort theories, suing construction lenders § 9.23
OUTRAGEOUS CONDUCT
Tort theories, suing construction lenders § 9.23
OUTSIDE VENDORS
New technological processes, factors affecting project results § 1.5
OVERHEAD
Suing private owner, damages for extra costs § 5.13
OVERHEAD COST ELEMENTS
Specific base allocation method, pricing damages § 18.25
OVERMANNING
Inefficiency, labor productivity §§ 19.20, 19.22
OVERVIEW OF CLAIMS
Arbitration § 14.19
OWNER CAUSE DELAYS
Parties and causes of action, sureties § 12.28
OWNER-CONSTRUCTION MANAGER CONTRACT
Defenses, suing construction managers § 7.28
OWNER-PRIME CONTRACT
Defenses, suing construction managers § 7.29
OWNER RESPONSIBILITIES
Factors affecting project results § 1.5
Project scope, factors affecting project results § 1.10
OWNERS
Claims. See DEFENDING AGAINST OWNER CLAIMS
Public and private, litigation and alternatives § 2.11
Solvency, risk management, litigation and alternatives § 2.15
Vs. contractor and/or surety § 12.23
OWNER'S AGENT
Defenses, suing construction managers § 7.39
OWNER'S DECISION TO MODIFY
Factors affecting project results § 1.7

PAROL EVIDENCE
Construction of documents and parol evidence. See SURETIES
PARTIAL IMPRACTICABILITY
Defending against owner claims, supervening impracticability § 20.6
PARTIAL PERFORMANCE
Defending against owner claims, damages § 20.8
PARTIES
Complexity, risk management § 2.7
Duty to whom owed, suing construction managers § 7.15
Parties and causes of action. See SURETIES
Surety bonds § 12.2
PARTIES AND RELATIONSHIPS
Risk management. See RISK MANAGEMENT
PARTIES MAKING BOND CLAIMS
Payment bond claims § 13.6

PARTNERSHIP THEORIES
Contract theories, suing construction lenders § 9.7
PASS-THROUGH CLAIMS
Suing subcontractors and material suppliers § 9.11
PAST EXPERIENCES OF PROJECT MANAGEMENT
Factors affecting project results § 1.5
PAST PROJECTS
Disruption, pricing damages § 18.16
PATENT VS. LATENT DEFECTS
Parties and causes of action, sureties § 12.34
PAYMENT
Defending against owner claims, waiver § 20.3
Payment bond claims. See PAYMENT BOND CLAIMS
PAYMENT ANALYSIS
Arbitration § 14.16
PAYMENT BOND CLAIMS
Generally § 13.1
Arbitration and surety § 13.17
Claims covered
–Generally § 13.7
–Attorney's fees and interest § 13.10
–Taxes, contributions, and insurance § 13.8
Jurisdiction and venue § 13.16
Notice requirements
–Generally § 13.11
–Commencement of limitation period § 13.14
–Estoppel § 13.15
–Suit limitations § 13.13
–Time period § 13.12
Parties making bond claims § 13.6
Practice notes § 13.19
Purpose of payment bond § 13.2
Remedies if payment bond claim unavailable § 13.18
Resolving conflicts between bond and statute § 13.5
Statutory requirements § 13.4
Typical provisions § 13.3
PAYMENT BONDS
Default, sureties § 12.17
Risk management, litigation and alternatives § 2.15
Sureties § 12.5
Types of surety bonds § 12.10
PAYMENT OF DAMAGES
Default, role of surety § 12.22
PAYMENT OF SETTLEMENTS AND JUDGMENTS
Tax considerations. See TAX CONSIDERATIONS
PENAL SUM
Damages recoverable, role of surety § 12.23
Default, role of surety § 12.22
PENALTIES
Tax considerations § 21.10
PERCENTAGE-OF-COMPLETION FORMULA
Tax considerations § 21.14
PERFORMANCE BONDS
Damages recoverable, role of surety § 12.23
Default, sureties § 12.17
Default of principle, role of surety § 12.22
Risk management, litigation and alternatives § 2.15
Role of surety § 12.14
Sureties § 12.5
PERFORMANCE DISPUTES
Dispute management, litigation and alternatives § 2.27
PERFORMANCE RISK
Contractor's insurance coverage, liability policy exclusions § 11.13
PERFORMED IN A GOOD AND WORKMANLIKE MANNER
Suing construction managers § 7.13
PERIOD OF COVERAGE
Contractor's insurance coverage, builder's risk policy § 11.18
PERIODS OF DELAY, UNREASONABLE OR EXCESSIVE
Delay claims § 16.19
PERSONAL INJURIES
Tax considerations § 21.5
PERSONALITY STYLES
Litigation team § 3.5
PERSONAL REPUTATION VS. BUSINESS REPUTATION
Tax considerations § 21.20
PHASED CONSTRUCTION
Suing construction managers § 7.2
PHASE I
Preliminary studies §§ 1.3, 1.4

PHASE II
Engineering design basis, factors affecting project results § 1.3
PHASE III
Contractor selection, factors affecting project results § 1.3
PHASE IV
Detailed engineering and procurement, factors affecting project results § 1.3
Financial and manpower resources, factors affecting project results § 1.3
PHASES I AND II: PROJECT LIFE CYCLE
Factors affecting project results § 1.4
PHASE V
Field construction, factors affecting project results § 1.3
PHASE VI
Plant start-up, factors affecting project results § 1.3
PHOTOGRAPHIC EVIDENCE
Arbitration § 14.26
PHOTOGRAPHS OF JOBSITE
Initial assessment, trial and appeal § 22.3
PHYSICAL INJURIES
Suing design professionals, economic loss limitation § 8.2
PLANNED PRODUCTION RATES
Labor productivity § 19.6
PLANNING
Appeal, trial and appeal § 22.24
Litigation team § 3.2
PLANS
Clean set, arbitration § 14.17
Consulting engineer, litigation team § 3.11
PLANS AND SPECIFICATIONS
Defending against owner claims, compliance with plans § 20.2
Suing design professionals, conduct constituting negligence § 8.6
Suing private owner, breaches of contract by owner § 5.3
PLANT START-UP
Phase VI, factors affecting project results § 1.3
PLEADING ALTERATION
Economic loss doctrine, suing construction managers § 7.41
POLITICAL-SOCIAL PRIORITIES
Major influences, factors affecting project results § 1.8
POSSIBLE SOURCES OF LIABILITY
Initial assessment, trial and appeal § 22.4
POST-ARGUMENT FILINGS
Appeal, trial and appeal § 22.27
POTENTIAL CLAIMS CONFLICTS
Initial assessment, trial and appeal § 22.4
POTENTIAL CONFLICTS OF INTEREST
Initial assessment, trial and appeal § 22.8
POTENTIAL LIMITATIONS
Unjust enrichment theories, suing construction lenders § 9.20
PRECLUSION
Payment bond claims, jurisdiction and venue § 13.17
PREDICTION
Figure 19–1, labor productivity § 19.15
PRE-EXISTING IMPRACTICALITY
Defending against owner claims § 20.6
PREHEARING CONFERENCES
Disclosure, arbitration § 14.11
PREHEARING DISCOVERY
Arbitration § 14.6
PREHEARING WRITTEN SUBMISSION
Arbitration § 14.20
PREJUDGMENT INTEREST
Defending against owner claims § 20.16
Payment bond claims, attorneys' fees and interest § 13.10
PRELIMINARY CONSIDERATIONS
Litigation team § 3.1
PRELIMINARY ENGINEERING DESIGN TASKS
Factors affecting project results § 1.3
PRELIMINARY STUDIES
Technical and financial feasibility, factors affecting project results §§ 1.3, 1.4
PRE-MARKING OF DOCUMENTS
Arbitration § 14.9

PREMISES ALIENATED
Contractor's insurance coverage, liability policy exclusions § 11.12
PREPARING CASE FOR LITIGATION
Generally § 15.1
Collecting information
–Experts § 15.11
–Initial plan § 15.6
–Witnesses § 15.10
Depositions §§ 15.21, 15.22
Discovery
–Depositions §§ 15.21, 15.22
–Litigation support group § 15.13
–Obtaining request responses § 15.19
–Plan § 15.12
–Responding to requests § 15.20
Documents
–Generally § 15.7
–Review § 15.9
–Selection, form and numbering § 15.8
Investigation
–Contractor's representatives § 15.3
–Early start § 15.2
Litigation plan
–Developing case theory and plan § 15.4
–Trial book § 15.5
Trial preparation
–General preparation § 15.24
–Other discovery devices § 15.23
Written requests
–Generally § 15.14
–Admission requests § 15.18
–Drafting requests § 15.15
–Interrogatories § 15.16
–Production of documents § 15.17
PREPARING EXHIBITS
Arbitration § 14.24
PREPARING FOR HEARINGS
Arbitration § 14.21
PREQUALIFICATION
Role of surety § 12.13
PRESENTATION FORMAT
Arbitration § 14.19
PRESENTATION OF EVIDENCE
Trial and appeal § 22.21
PRESERVATION
Evidence and claims, litigation and alternatives § 2.29
PRETRIAL BRIEFS
Motions and filings before trial, trial and appeal § 22.19
PRETRIAL DISCOVERY PROCEDURES
Litigation management, litigation and alternatives § 2.38
PRETRIAL FILINGS
Motions and filings before trial, trial and appeal § 22.19
PRETRIAL MOTIONS
Motions and filings before trial, trial and appeal §§ 22.17, 22.18
PRICE ADJUSTMENTS
Changed condition clauses, proving liability to recover damages § 16.29
PRICE CEILING GUARANTEE
Suing construction managers § 7.4
PRICE-PAYMENT ANALYSIS
Arbitration § 14.16
PRICING DAMAGES
Generally §§ 18.1, 18.8
Calculating damages
–Generally § 18.14
–Changed conditions § 18.17
–Changes in scope § 18.18
–Delay § 18.15
–Disruption § 18.16
–Termination § 18.19
Categories of contract damages
–Generally § 18.2
–Changed conditions § 18.5
–Changes in scope § 18.6
–Delay damages § 18.3
–Disruptions § 18.4
–Terminations § 18.7
Claim preparation costs § 18.21
Contract audit § 18.13
Cost of capital § 18.20
Cost schedules § 18.12
Discrete approach § 18.11
Home office overhead
–Generally § 18.22
–*Eichleay* formula § 18.23
–Occupancy § 18.26
–Specific base allocation method § 18.25
–Total direct cost allocation § 18.24
Profit recovery § 18.27
Total cost approach
–Generally § 18.9
–Four-way test § 18.10

PRIMARY CAUSAL FACTOR
Owner interference § 19.4
PRIME CONTRACT SPECIFICATIONS
Suing subcontractors and material suppliers § 10.5
PRINCIPAL
Definition, sureties § 12.2
PRIOR CONTRACTOR'S WORK
Conformance to plans and specifications, suing construction managers § 7.30
PRIOR TESTIMONY
Trial preparation, trial and appeal § 22.16
PRIOR WORK
Duty to review, suing construction managers § 7.30
PRIVATE ATTORNEY GENERAL EXCEPTION
Payment bond claims, attorneys' fees and interest § 13.10
PRIVATE COMMON LAW BONDS
Sureties § 12.3
PRIVATE CONSTRUCTION CONTRACTS
Parties and causes of action, sureties § 12.28
PRIVATE CONTRACTS
Bid protests and mistakes § 4.27
PRIVATE OWNERS
Bid protests and mistakes § 4.32
Suing. See SUING PRIVATE OWNER
PRIVILEGE
Trial preparation, document production § 15.17
PRIVITY
Contract theories, suing construction lenders § 9.7
Defending against owner claims, defective plans and specifications § 20.2
Pass-through claims, suing subcontractors and material supplier § 10.11
Risk management, litigation and alternatives § 2.13
Suing design professionals
–Liability to contractor § 8.1
–Negligence § 8.4
PRIVITY *(Continued)*
Suing private owner, subcontractors § 5.10
PROBLEMS WITH TOP-DOWN APPROACH
Labor productivity § 19.9
PROCEDURES
Arbitration § 14.7
PROCEEDS
Taxation of settlement or judgment proceeds. See TAXATION OF SETTLEMENT OR JUDGMENT PROCEEDS
PROCESS MANAGEMENT
Litigation team § 3.3
PROCUREMENT
Phase IV, factors affecting project results § 1.3
PROCUREMENT CODES
Suing construction managers §§ 7.9, 7.12
PROCUREMENT INTEGRITY
Suing a government § 6.2
PRODUCT
Contractor's insurance coverage, product exclusion § 11.14
PRODUCTION COSTS
Figure 19–1, labor productivity § 19.14
PRODUCTION OF DOCUMENTS
Preparing case for litigation, written discovery requests § 15.17
PRODUCTIVITY AND ESTIMATING
Labor productivity. See LABOR PRODUCTIVITY
Productivity and estimating
–Expectations of owner and contractor § 19.3
–Other factors § 19.6
–Reasonable proof of damages § 19.5
PRODUCTIVITY AS FUNCTION TEMPERATURE AND 75% HUMIDITY
Figure 19–6, labor productivity § 19.24
PRODUCTIVITY CURVES AND DAMAGES CALCULATION
Labor productivity. See LABOR PRODUCTIVITY
PRODUCTIVITY LOSS
Form crowding, Figure 19–4 § 19.22

PRODUCTIVITY LOSS *(Continued)*
Increased crew size, Figure 19-2, labor productivity § 19.22
Mieg figures, Figure 19-10, labor productivity § 19.26
PROFESSIONAL CONSTRUCTION MANAGER
Risk management, litigation and alternatives § 2.13
PROFESSIONALS
Standard of care, suing construction managers § 7.6
PROFESSIONAL VS. GENERAL CONTRACTOR
Suing construction managers §§ 7.2, 7.6, 7.8, 7.9, 7.16
PROFESSIONAL WITNESS
Trial preparation, trial and appeal § 22.16
PROFIT RECOVERY
Pricing damages § 18.27
PROGRESS PAYMENTS
Suing private owner, nonpayment § 5.9
PROJECT CONSTRAINTS
Factors affecting project results § 1.7
PROJECT COST REPORT
Table 18-6, pricing damages § 18.12
PROJECT LIFE CYCLE
See FACTORS AFFECTING PROJECT RESULTS
PROJECT MANAGEMENT CONTROLS
Typical project problems, factors affecting project results § 1.9
PROJECT MANAGEMENT PERSONNEL RESPONSIBILITIES
Factors affecting project results § 1.5
PROJECT OWNER DESIRES
Scope changes, factors affecting project results § 1.10
PROJECT POLICIES
Constraints, factors affecting project results § 1.4
PROJECT PROBLEMS, TYPICAL
Major influences, factors influencing project results § 1.9
PROJECT SCHEDULE
Factors affecting project results § 1.8
PROJECT TIME FRAME
Arbitration § 14.22
PROMISES
Rights based on estoppel § 9.13
PROMISSORY ESTOPPEL
Bid mistakes, private owners § 4.32
Bid protests, private contracts § 4.27
Bids, suing subcontractors and material suppliers § 10.2
Suing construction lenders §§ 9.12, 9.14
PROOF
Defending against owner claims, defective plans and specifications § 20.2
Delay. See CRITICAL PATH ANALYSIS TO PROVE DELAY
Negligence
–Conduct constituting negligence in design professionals § 8.6
–Design professionals § 8.5
Suing private owner, damages for extra costs § 5.13
PROOF OF DAMAGES
Actual damages
–Generally § 16.35
–Finance costs § 16.41
–Home office overhead § 16.40
–Jobsite indirect costs § 16.39
–Labor costs § 16.37
–Material costs § 16.38
–Total cost method § 16.36
Disruption damages § 16.42
Litigation management, litigation and alternatives § 2.39
Lost profits § 16.42
PROPERTY CONCEPTS
Unjust enrichment theories, suing construction lenders § 9.16
PROPERTY DAMAGE
Contractor's insurance coverage, liability policy insuring agreement § 11.8
PROPOSAL BOND
Bid bonds. See BID BONDS
PROPOSED FINDINGS
Motions and filings before trial, trial and appeal § 22.19
PROTESTS
Bid protests. See BID PROTESTS AND MISTAKES
PROVING LIABILITY TO RECOVER DAMAGES
Generally § 16.1
Acceleration claims
–Actual and constructive acceleration § 16.27

PROVING LIABILITY TO RECOVER DAMAGES *(Continued)*
-Definition § 16.26
-Disallowance of acceleration damage claims § 16.28
Asserting damage claims
-Delay and time extension clauses § 16.32
-Notice and deadline clauses § 16.33
-Strict adherence to contract provisions § 16.31
-When time is of the essence § 16.34
Delay claims. See DELAY CLAIMS
Other damage claims
-Changed conditions § 16.29
-Low bidder claims § 16.30
Proof of damages. See PROOF OF DAMAGES
PROXIMATE CAUSE
Contractor's builder's risk policy, exclusions § 11.22
Damages, suing construction managers § 7.16
PSYCHOLOGICAL CONSULTING FIRMS
Litigation team § 3.7
PUBLIC RECORDING STATUTES
Statutory remedies, suing construction lenders § 9.5
PUBLIC WORKS PROJECTS
Federally funded. See FEDERALLY FUNDED GRANT PROJECTS
PUNITIVE DAMAGES
Defending against owner claims § 20.16
Federal waiver of contract controversies § 6.5
Motions and filings before trial, trial and appeal § 22.17
Payment bond claims, attorneys' fees and interest § 13.10
Tax considerations § 21.3
PURPOSE OF TRIAL PLAN
Initial assessment, trial and appeal § 22.9

QUALITY
Bid protests and mistakes, responsibility § 4.8
QUALITY OF WORK
Risk management, litigation and alternatives § 2.8
QUANTIFYING PRODUCTIVITY LOSSES
Labor productivity § 19.12
QUANTITIES AND SPECIFICATION
Labor productivity § 19.6
QUANTITY OF WORK
Risk management, litigation and alternatives § 2.8
QUANTUM MERUIT
Bid mistakes, federal law § 4.31
Initial assessment, trial and appeal § 22.7
Litigation management, litigation and alternatives § 2.37
Parties and causes of action, sureties § 12.28
Suing a government, authority to act for state § 6.14
Suing private owner, breaches of contract by owner § 5.3
QUANTUM VALEBANT
Bid mistakes, federal law § 4.31
QUASI-CONTRACT
Suing a government, authority to act for state § 6.14
QUASI-ESTOPPEL
Suing construction lenders § 9.12
QUIA TIMET SUITS
Parties and causes of action, sureties § 12.30

RATIFICATION
Suing a government, authority to act § 6.13
Suing a government, ratification by contracting officer § 6.13
RATIO DELAY STUDIES
Labor productivity § 19.27
REACTION TO DISPUTES
Dispute management, litigation and alternatives § 2.28
REASONABLE CARE
Risk management, litigation and alternatives § 2.19
REASONABLE CERTAINTY
Proving liability to recover damages § 16.35
REASONABLE EXPECTATIONS
Contractor's insurance coverage § 11.2
REASONABLENESS
Defending against owner claims, liquidated damages § 20.10
Labor productivity, tests § 19.5

REASONABLE PROOF OF DAMAGES
Labor productivity § 19.5
REASONS FOR LACK OF SCOPE DEFINITION
Figure 1–7, factors affecting project results § 1.6
REASSESSMENT OF CASE
Appeal, trial and appeal § 22.25
RECALL
Contractor's insurance coverage, liability policy exclusions § 11.15
RECOGNITION OF DISPUTES
Disputes, litigation and alternatives § 2.28
RECOMMENDED AGREEMENTS
Initial assessment, trial and appeal § 22.10
RECONCILIATION OF ORIGINAL CONTRACT PRICE WITH FINAL REVENUE
Table 18–5, pricing damages § 18.12
RECORD EXCERPTS
Appeal, trial and appeal § 22.26
RECORDING AGREEMENTS
Loan agreements, suing construction lenders § 9.5
RECORD KEEPING REQUIREMENTS
Risk management, litigation and alternatives § 2.18
RECOVERY
Risk management, litigation and alternatives § 2.12
Suing construction lenders § 9.1
RECOVERY IN TORT
Suing design professionals, economic loss limitation § 8.2
RECOVERY OF DAMAGES IN TORT
Suing construction managers § 7.11
REDUCTION OF BUILDING COST AND TIME
Suing construction managers § 7.3
REFORMATION
Bid mistakes § 4.29
Suing private owner, remedies § 5.15
REFUSAL TO HONOR BID
Dispute management, litigation and alternatives § 2.26
REGULATIONS
Legal parameters, litigation and alternatives § 2.18
REIMBURSEMENT
Contractor's builder's risk policy, sue and labor clause § 11.24
REJECTION OF ALL BIDS
Bid protests, federal contracts § 4.16
REJECTION OF WORK
Defective work correction, suing subcontractors and material suppliers § 10.9
RELATIONSHIPS
Risk management. See RISK MANAGEMENT, Parties and relationships
RELEASE AGREEMENT UPON SETTLEMENT
Tax considerations § 21.17
RELIANCE
Bids, suing subcontractors and material suppliers § 10.3
Labor productivity § 19.3
Rights based on estoppel, suing construction lenders §§ 9.12, 9.15
Suing private owner, exculpatory clauses § 5.18
RELIEF
Bid protests and mistakes, state and local contracts § 4.26
REMEDIES
Bid protests, private contracts § 4.27
Default and termination, suing subcontractors and material suppliers § 10.12
Litigation management, litigation and alternatives § 2.37
Payment bond claims, remedies if claim unavailable § 13.18
Suing. See SUING PRIVATE OWNER
REPAIR
Contractor's insurance coverage, builder's risk policy § 11.19
Defending against owner claims, substantial performance § 20.11
Defending against owner claims, supervening impracticability § 20.5
REPORT
Bid protests, federal contracts § 4.15
REPORTING PERIOD
Contractor's insurance coverage, claims-made liability policy § 11.7

REPORTING REQUIREMENTS
Risk management, litigation and alternatives § 2.18
REPRESENTATIONS
Labor productivity § 19.3
Rights based on estoppel §§ 9.13, 9.14
REQUEST FOR ADMISSIONS
Motions and filings before trial, trial and appeal § 22.17
REQUEST FOR ADMISSIONS OF FACT
Litigation management, litigation and alternatives § 2.38
REQUEST FOR PRODUCTION
Documents, interrogatories, and depositions, litigation and alternatives § 2.38
REQUEST FOR PROPOSAL
Bid protests and mistakes § 4.3
REQUESTS
Preparing case for litigation, written discovery requests §§ 15.14–15.18
REQUEST TO INSPECT OR TEST SAMPLES
Trial preparation, discovery § 15.23
REQUEST TO MEASURE, TEST OR SURVEY LAND
Trial preparation, discovery § 15.23
RESALE VALUE
Unjust enrichment theories, suing construction lenders § 9.19
RESCISSION
Bid mistakes §§ 4.29, 4.32
Suing private owner, remedies § 5.14
RESPONSIBILITY
Bid protests and mistakes §§ 4.3, 4.6, 4.8, 4.23
RESPONSIBILITY ASSESSMENT
Critical path analysis to prove delay § 17.2
RESPONSIVENESS
Bid protests and mistakes §§ 4.3, 4.7, 4.23
RESTITUTION
Suing private owner, remedies § 5.14
RESTRICTION ON CONTRACTOR'S RECOVER
Delay claims. See DELAY CLAIMS
RETAINAGE
Parties and causes of action, sureties §§ 12.31–12.33
RETURN OR CAPITAL
Treatment of proceeds, tax considerations § 21.4
REVERSE PRODUCTIVITY MEASURE
Labor productivity § 19.02
RIGHT OF AUDIT
Trial preparation, discovery § 15.12
RIGHTS
Role of surety §§ 12.17–12.21
RIGHTS BASED ON ESTOPPEL
Generally § 9.11
Estoppel theories § 9.12
Successful estoppel claims
–Generally § 9.13
–Actionable representations § 9.14
–Reliance § 9.15
RISK MANAGEMENT
Contract documents: a beginning
–Generally § 2.20
–Basic provisions § 2.22
–Exculpatory and special clauses § 2.23
–Modifications § 2.24
–Uniform Commercial Code applicability § 2.21
Legal parameters
–Generally § 2.17
–Building codes, ordinances, and regulations § 2.18
–Trade usage and implied obligations § 2.19
Liability and alternatives § 2.4
Parties and relationships
–Generally § 2.10
–Architect-engineers § 2.12
–Construction lenders § 2.16
–Construction managers § 2.13
–General contractors, subcontractors, and suppliers § 2.14
–Owners: public and private § 2.11
–Sureties § 2.15
RISK-SHIFTING TERMINOLOGY
Suing subcontractors and material suppliers § 10.4
ROLE OF LAW
Arbitration § 14.4
ROLE OF LAWYERS
Arbitration § 14.5
ROLE OF SURETY
Generally § 12.13
Coverage § 12.15

ROLE OF SURETY *(Continued)*
Default by principal § 12.16
Performance bond § 12.14
Subrogation § 12.25
Surety's options upon default of performance bond principal § 12.22
Surety's rights and obligations upon default
–Generally § 12.17
–Available defenses § 12.20
–Events of default § 12.18
–Notice and investigation § 12.19
–Obligee's conduct § 12.21
Surety's right to contract funds § 12.24
ROOT CAUSE
Owner interference § 19.4

SAFETY
Suing construction managers § 7.14
SAFETY CHECKS
Phase VI, factors affecting project results § 1.3
SAFETY HAZARDS
Suing design professionals, scheduling and coordination negligence § 8.11
SALE OF GOODS
Defending against owner claims, warranties and UCC § 20.7
SCHEDULE
Arbitration § 14.18
Labor productivity § 19.3
SCHEDULE ESTIMATES
Factors affecting project results § 1.4
SCHEDULES OF OTHER CONTRACTORS
Suing construction managers § 7.25
SCHEDULING
Delegation of functions to contractor, suing construction managers § 7.37
Failure, suing construction managers § 7.27
Suing design professionals, liability to contractor §§ 8.7, 8.11
SCHEDULING HEARINGS
Arbitration § 14.9
SCOPE CHANGES
Construction project, factors affecting project results § 1.7
Factors affecting project results § 1.10
SCOPE DECISIONS
Poor definition and loss of control, factors affecting project results § 1.2
SCOPE DEFINITION
Factors affecting project results § 1.6
SCOPE OF DUTY
Suing design professionals, liability to contractor § 8.1
SCOPE OF SUBCONTRACTOR'S WORK
Risk management, litigation and alternatives § 2.22
Suing subcontractors and material suppliers § 10.5
SCOPE OF WORK
Arbitration § 14.17
SECONDARY CAUSES
Owner interference § 19.4
SELECTING A GENERAL APPROACH
Labor productivity. See LABOR PRODUCTIVITY
SELECTION OF ARBITRATORS
Arbitration § 14.7
SELECTION OF PARTIES
Litigation management, litigation and alternatives § 2.37
SELECTION OF WITNESSES
Trial preparation, trial and appeal § 22.15
SELF-INFLICTED WOUNDS
Labor productivity § 19.6
SERVICE
Trial preparation, document production request § 15.19
SETTLEMENT PROCEEDS
Taxation of settlement or judgment proceeds. See TAXATION OF SETTLEMENT OR JUDGMENT PROCEEDS
SETTLEMENTS
Motions and filings before trial, trial and appeal § 22.19
SETTLEMENT TECHNIQUES
Dispute management, litigation and alternatives § 2.32
SETTLING DISPUTES
Dispute management. See DISPUTE MANAGEMENT
SHOP DRAWING APPROVAL
Suing design professionals, administrative negligence § 8.10

SHOP DRAWINGS
Review, suing construction managers § 7.27
Suing construction managers § 7.24
SIGNATURES
Bid protests and mistakes, bid requirments § 4.5
SIGNIFICANT PROBLEM IMPACT VS. OCCURRENCE
Factors affecting project results § 1.6
SIMPLE SETTLEMENT NEGOTIATIONS
Initial assessment, trial and appeal § 22.10
SINGLE PENAL SUMS
Payment plus performance bond, sureties § 12.10
SISTERSHIP
Contractor's insurance coverage, liability policy exclusions § 11.15
SITE ACCESS
Owner's failure to provide, delay claims § 16.5
Suing construction managers § 7.27
SITE VISITS
Arbitration § 14.26
Initial assessment, trial and appeal § 22.3
SIZE OF JOB AND AVAILABILITY OF CRAFT WORK FORCE
Labor productivity § 19.6
SKILLFUL PERFORMANCE
Defending against owner claims, warranties § 20.7
SOFTWARE PROGRAMS
Trial preparation, trial and appeal § 22.14
SOIL CONDITIONS
Defending against owner claims, supervening impracticability § 20.6
SOLICITATION IMPROPRIETIES
Bid protest grounds § 4.11
SOLVENCY
Suing construction lenders § 9.1
SOURCES OF DISPUTES
Liability and alternatives § 2.8
SOVEREIGN IMMUNITY
Risk management, litigation and alternatives § 2.11
Suing a government § 6.3
SPEARIN DOCTRINE
Risk management, litigation and alternatives § 2.12
SPECIAL CLAUSES
Risk management, litigation and alternatives § 2.23
SPECIFICATION DEFECTS
Bid protest grounds §§ 4.11, 4.13
SPECIFICATIONS
Arbitration § 14.17
Labor productivity § 19.3
Phase IV, factors affecting project results § 1.3
Plans. See PLANS AND SPECIFICATIONS
Suing private owner, changes § 5.6
SPECIFIC BASE ALLOCATION METHOD
Home office overhead, pricing damages § 18.25
SPECIFIC PERFORMANCE OR EQUITABLE RELIEF
Defending against owner claims § 20.16
STAFF ENGINEERS
Arbitration § 14.22
STANDARD OF CARE
Suing construction managers § 7.16
Suing construction managers. See SUING CONSTRUCTION MANAGERS
Suing design professionals, negligence § 8.4
STANDING TO CHALLENGE
Bid protests and mistakes § 4.4
STANDING TO PROTEST
Bid protests, state and local contracts § 4.24
Bid protests and mistakes, state and local contracts § 4.24
STANDING TO SUE
Judicial review of bid protests § 6.6
START-STOP ORIENTATION ANALYSIS
Labor productivity § 19.26
START-STOP PRODUCTION LOSS
Figure 19–9 § 19.26
STATE CONTRACTS
Bid protests and mistakes. See BID PROTESTS AND MISTAKES
STATEMENT OF CASE
Appeal, trial and appeal § 22.26
STATEMENTS
Trial preparation, witnesses § 15.10

STATUS
Third-party beneficiary. suing construction lenders §§ 9.8–9.10
STATUTE OF FRAUDS
Bids, suing subcontractors and material suppliers § 10.2
STATUTES OF LIMITATIONS
Contract breach, suing subcontractors and material suppliers § 10.8
Defending against owner claims § 20.4
Defenses, suing construction managers §§ 7.42–7.44
Payment bond claims § 13.13
STATUTES OF REPOSE
Defending against owner claims, statutes of limitations § 20.4
STATUTORY EXCEPTIONS
Defenses, suing construction managers § 7.36
STATUTORY PAYMENT BONDS
Sureties § 12.4
STATUTORY PENALTIES
Defending against owner claims § 20.16
STATUTORY PROVISIONS
Sureties § 12.4
STATUTORY REMEDIES
Importance
–Generally § 9.2
–Loan agreement recording requirements § 9.5
–Mechanics' lien statutes § 9.3
–Stop-notice provisions § 9.4
STATUTORY REQUIREMENTS
Payment bond claims § 13.4
STENOGRAPHIC RECORDS
Arbitration § 14.9
STOP-NOTICE PROVISIONS
Statutory remedies, suing construction lenders § 9.4
STRAW SUBCONTRACTOR
Payment bond claims, notice § 13.12
STRICT ADHERENCE TO CONTRACT PROVISIONS
Proving liability to recover damages § 16.31
STRICT LIABILITY
Suing design professionals, negligence § 8.4
SUBCONTRACTOR LISTING
Bid protests
–Generally § 4.9
–Federal contracts § 4.13
SUBCONTRACTOR PROTECTION
Suing construction lenders §§ 9.4, 9.5
SUBCONTRACTORS
Bid protests and mistakes, contract award criteria § 4.9
Bid protests and mistakes, responsibility § 4.8
Contractor's builder's risk policy, exclusions § 11.22
Contractor's builder's risk policy, subrogation § 11.25
Contractor's insurance coverage, care, custody or control exclusion § 11.11
Contractor's insurance coverage, property damage defined § 11.8
Contractor's insurance coverage, work or product exclusion § 11.14
Disputes involving subcontractors, breaches of contract by owner § 5.10
Litigation and alternatives § 2.14
Payment bond claims, parties who may make claim § 13.6
Standing to protest, federally funded grant projects § 4.19
Suing design professionals, administrative negligence § 8.10
Suing subcontractors and material suppliers. See SUING SUBCONTRATORS AND MATERIAL SUPPLIERS
SUBCONTRACTOR'S BOND
Types of surety bonds § 12.12
SUBORDINATION
Unjust enrichment theories, suing construction lenders § 9.16
SUBPOENA DUCES TECUM
Trial preparation, document production § 15.17
SUBPOENAS
Federal waiver of contract controversies § 6.5
SUBROGATION
Contractor's insurance coverage, builder's risk policy § 11.25

SUBROGATION *(Continued)*
Parties and causes of action, sureties §§ 12.31, 12.33
Role of surety § 12.25
SUBSTANTIAL CHANGES IN CONTRACT SCOPE
Delay claims § 16.7
SUBSTANTIAL COMPLETION
Defending against owner claims, substantial performance § 20.11
SUBSTANTIAL PERFORMANCE
Defending against owner claims § 20.11
SUBSTANTIATING DESIRED TAX TREATMENT
Tax considerations. See TAX CONSIDERATIONS
SUBSTITUTE PERFORMANCE
Defending against owner claims, damages § 20.8
SUBSTITUTION
Suing design professionals, conduct constituting negligence § 8.6
SUB-SUBCONTRACTORS
Payment bond claims, notice § 13.11
Payment bond claims, parties who may make claim § 13.6
SUBSURFACE CONDITIONS
Suing private owner, changes § 5.5
SUCCESSFUL ESTOPPEL CLAIMS
Rights based on estoppel, suing construction lenders § 9.13
SUE AND LABOR CLAUSE
Contractor's insurance coverage, builder's risk policy § 11.24
SUING A GOVERNMENT
Generally § 6.1
Authority to act § 6.12
Authority to act for state § 6.14
Federal government waivers
–Generally § 6.4
–Administrative forum for bid protests § 6.7
–Contract controversies § 6.5
–Judicial review of bid protests § 6.6
Funding and fiscal restrictions
–Generally §§ 6.8, 6.9
–States, fiscal restrictions on § 6.11
Ratification by contrcting officer § 6.13
Sovereign immunity § 6.3
Special problems § 6.2
SUING A GOVERNMENT *(Continued)*
Waivers
–Federal government, see Federal government waivers, this heading
–Sovereign immunity § 6.3
–State and state agency waivers § 6.8
SUING CONSTRUCTION LENDERS
Generally § 9.1
Contract theories. See CONTRACT THEORIES
Rights based on estoppel. See RIGHTS BASED ON ESTOPPEL
Statutory remedies. See STATUTORY REMEDIES
Tort theories
–Misrepresentation § 9.22
–Negligence § 9.21
–Other tort theories § 9.23
Unjust enrichment theories. See UNJUST ENRICHMENT THEORIES
SUING CONSTRUCTION MANAGERS
Bases for liability
–Generally § 7.20
–Administration of drawings § 7.24
–Delayed site access § 7.23
–Design defects § 7.22
–Failure to provide construction support services § 7.26
–Failure to provide timely information § 7.25
–Failure to schedule and coordinate § 7.27
–Interference with bids § 7.21
Construction manager defenses
–Accrual § 7.43
–Active interference § 7.35
–Bad faith or fraud § 7.34
–Contributory and comparative negligence § 7.40
–Delay not contemplated by parties § 7.32
–Delegation of scheduling to contractors § 7.37
–Duty to review drawings and prior work § 7.30
–Forum selection § 7.38
–No damages for delay clauses § 7.31
–No recovery for economic loss § 7.41

SUING CONSTRUCTION MANAGERS *(Continued)*
-Owner/construction manager contract § 7.28
-Owner/prime contract § 7.29
-Owner's agent § 7.39
-Statutes of limitations § 7.42
-Statutory exceptions § 7.36
-Tolling § 7.44
-Unreasonable delay § 7.33
Duty owed by construction manager
-Generally § 7.10
-Building codes and industry standards § 7.13
-Construction manager de facto rule § 7.14
-Contract obligations § 7.11
-Parties to whom duty owed § 7.15
-Procurement codes § 7.12
Forms of construction management practice
-Agency construction management § 7.3
-Extended service § 7.5
-Guaranteed maximum price § 7.4
Introduction
-Role of construction manager § 7.1
Standard of care
-Bidding requirements § 7.9
-Bond and insurance requirements § 7.8
-Licensing requirements § 7.7
-Professional or contractor § 7.6
Suing construction managers
-Construction management defined § 7.2
Theories of recovery
-Implied warranty § 7.19
-Interference with contract § 7.18
-Negligence § 7.16
-Third-party beneficiary § 5.17
SUING DESIGN PROFESSIONALS
Contractor's right of action, bases
-Generally § 8.1
Indemnity, design professional's liability to owner for § 8.3
Liability to contractor
-Generally § 8.7
-Contract administration, negligence or intentional interference § 8.10
-Defective design § 8.8
-Negligent supervision and inspection § 8.9

SUING DESIGN PROFESSIONALS *(Continued)*
-Scheduling and coordination § 8.11
Negligence
-Conduct constituting negligence § 8.6
-Design professional's liability § 8.4
-Liability to contractor § 8.10
-Proof of § 8.5
-Supervision and inspection, negligent § 8.9
SUING PRIVATE OWNER
Generally § 5.1
Breaches of contract by owner
-Changed physical conditions § 5.5
-Changes, generally § 5.2
-Constructive changes § 5.6
-Delay § 5.7
-Disputes involving subcontractors § 5.10
-No damages for delay clauses § 5.8
-Nonpayment § 5.9
-Notice of changes § 5.4
-Scope of work, changes § 5.3
Remedies
-Damages § 5.11
-Exculpatory clauses § 5.18
-Extra work § 5.13
-Liens § 5.17
-Prevention of completion § 5.12
-Reformation § 5.15
-Rescission and restitution § 5.14
-Termination § 5.16
SUING SUBCONTRACTORS AND MATERIAL SUPPLIERS
Generally § 10.1
Bidding and contract formation § 10.2
Bid mistakes § 10.3
Coordinated and timely performance § 10.6
Correcting defective work § 10.9
Default and termination § 10.12
Description of materials § 10.5
Description of work and materials § 10.5
Documemting contractor's claim § 10.13
Flow-down clause § 10.4
Indemnification § 10.10
Pass-through claims § 10.11
Warranties relating to defective work § 10.8

SUIT LIMITATIONS
Payment bond claims, notice requirements § 13.13
SUMMARIES
Trial preparation, trial and appeal § 22.14
SUMMARY JUDGMENT
Motions and filings before trial, trial and appeal § 22.17
Parties and causes of action, sureties § 12.30
SUPERVENING IMPRACTICALITY
Defending against owner claims § 20.5
SUPERVISION
Design professional's liability, negligent supervision and inspection § 8.9
Suing design professionals, conduct constituting negligence §§ 8.6, 8.7
SUPERVISION AND PERSONNEL
Labor productivity § 19.6
SUPPLIERS
Litigation and alternatives § 2.14
SUPPORTIVE COURT CASES
Arbitration § 14.4
SUPPORT SERVICES
Failure to provide, suing construction managers § 7.26
SURETIES
Generally § 12.1
Construction of documents and parol evidence §§ 12.37, 12.38
Litigation and alternatives § 2.15
Notice and limitation of actions
–Limitation periods § 12.36
–Notice periods § 12.35
Parties and causes of action
–Generally § 12.26
–Contractor vs. miscellaneous parties § 12.29
–Contractor vs. owner § 12.28
–Contractor vs. surety § 12.27
–Owner vs. contractor and/or surety § 12.34
–Surety vs. bank § 12.31
–Surety vs. contractor § 12.30
–Surety vs. miscellaneous parties § 12.33
–Surety vs. owner § 12.32
Parties to surety bonds § 12.2
Payment bond claims § 13.17
Payment bond claims, taxes § 13.8
SURETIES *(Continued)*
Private (common law) bonds § 12.3
Role of surety. See ROLE OF SURETY
Statutory payment bonds § 12.4
Types of surety bonds. See TYPES OF SURETY BONDS
SURETY'S LIABILITY
Damages recoverable, role of surety § 12.23
SURETY'S ROLE
See ROLE OF SURETY
SURETY VS. BANK
Parties and causes of action, sureties § 12.31
SURETY VS. CONTRACTOR
Parties and causes of action, sureties § 12.30
SURETY VS. MISCELLANEOUS PARTIES
Parties and causes of action, sureties § 12.33
SURETY VS. OWNER
Parties and causes of action, sureties § 12.32
SUSPECTED DEFICIENCY
Contractor's insurance coverage, sistership or recall exclusion § 11.15
SUSPENDING AWARD
Bid protests, federal contracts § 4.15
SUSPENSION OF CONTRACT
Suing private owner, termination of contract § 5.16
SUSPENSION OF WORK
Suing private owner, delay § 5.7

TAKEOVER AGREEMENTS
Default, role of surety § 12.22
TAX ACCOUNTING METHODS
Tax considerations §§ 21.11–21.15
TAXATION OF SETTLEMENT OR JUDGMENT PROCEEDS
Treatment of proceeds
–Generally § 21.2
–Nontaxable treatment § 21.5
–Ordinary income § 21.3
–Return of capital § 21.4
TAX BENEFIT DOCTRINE
Tax considerations § 21.3
TAX CONSIDERATIONS
Generally § 21.1
Income recognition and expense deduction, timing of. See INCOME

TAX CONSIDERATIONS *(Continued)*
RECOGNITION AND EXPENSE DEDUCTION, TIMING OF
Payment of settlements and judgments
–Generally § 21.6
–Capital expenditures § 21.9
–Deductible expenses § 21.8
–General principles § 21.7
–Nondeductible or capitalized expenses § 21.10
Substantiating desired tax treatment
–Generally § 21.16
–Actions of parties § 21.18
–Choice of claims § 21.20
–Timing of tax planning § 21.19
–Written documentation § 21.17
Taxation of settlement or judgment proceeds. See TAXATION OF SETTLEMENT OR JUDGMENT PROCEEDS
TAXES
Payment bonds, claims covered § 13.8
TAXPAYER AND CONTRACTING PARTY DISPUTE EACH OTHER'S PERFORMANCE
Tax considerations § 21.15
TAXPAYER DISPUTES CONTRACTING PARTY PERFORMANCE
Tax considerations § 21.15
TAX PLANNING
Timing, tax considerations § 21.19
TEAM LEADER
Litigation team § 3.5
TECHNICAL DISPUTE UNDERSTANDING
Trial preparation, trial and appeal § 22.16
TECHNICAL FEASIBILITY
Phase I, factors affecting project results § 1.3
TECHNIQUES TO ASSIST JURY
Trial preparation, trial and appeal § 22.13
TELEPHONE CONVERSATIONS
Documentation, suing subcontractors and material suppliers § 10.13
TEMPERATURE VS. 75% HUMIDITY
Figure 19–6, labor productivity § 19.24
TERMINATION
Calculating damages, pricing damages § 18.19
Categories of contract damages, pricing damages § 18.2
For convenience, suing subcontractors and material suppliers § 10.12
Defending against owner claims § 20.14
Suing private owner, remedies § 5.16
Suing subcontractors and material suppliers § 10.12
TERMINATION OF CONTRACT FOR CONVENIENCE
Bid protests, federal contracts § 4.16
TERMS OF LOAN AGREEMENT
Contract theories, suing construction lenders § 9.9
TESTS OF REASONABLENESS
Labor productivity § 19.5
THEORIES OF RECOVERY
Suing construction managers. See SUING CONSTRUCTION MANAGERS
THIRD PARTIES
Trial preparation, discovery § 15.12
THIRD-PARTY BENEFICIARY
Parties and causes of action, sureties § 12.33
Pass-through claims, suing subcontractors and material supplier § 10.11
Payment bond claims, remedies if payment bond not available § 13.18
Performance bonds, sureties § 12.15
Risk management, litigation and alternatives § 2.12
Status. See CONTRACT THEORIES
Suing construction managers §§ 7.16, 7.19, 7.28
Suing private owner, subcontractors § 5.10
Theories of recovery, suing construction managers § 7.17
THIRD-PARTY LIABILITY POLICIES
Contractor's insurance coverage, liability policy, trigger of coverage § 11.6

THIRD-PARTY PRACTICE
Pass-through claims, suing subcontractors and material supplier § 10.11
TIME EXTENSION CLAUSES
Changed condition clauses, proving liability to recover damages § 16.29
Proving liability to recover damages §§ 16.7, 16.32
TIME LIMITS
Protest procedure, federally funded grant projects § 4.20
TIMELY INFORMATION
Failure to provide, suing construction managers § 7.25
TIMELY PERFORMANCE
Suing subcontractors and material suppliers § 10.6
TIME OF COMPLETION
Tax considerations § 21.15
TIME OF PERFORMANCE
Proving liability to recover damages § 16.1
TIME PERIOD
Payment bond claims, notice requirements § 13.12
TIME-RELATED COSTS
Delay damages, pricing damages § 18.3
TIME-SENSITIVITY
Construction costs, litigation and alternatives § 2.2
TIME VALUE OF MONEY
Risk management, litigation and alternatives § 2.9
TIMING OF TAX PLANNING
Tax considerations § 21.19
TOLLING
Defenses, suing construction managers § 7.44
TOP-DOWN APPROACH
Labor productivity § 19.8
TOP-DOWN CLAIM
Table 19–2, labor productivity § 19.8
TORT
Suing construction managers § 7.15
TORT, ELEMENTS OF
Parties and causes of action, sureties § 12.27
TORT ACTION
Tax considerations § 21.5
TORT CLAIMS
Suing construction managers § 7.11
TORTIOUS INTERFERENCE
Suing construction managers § 7.18
TORTIOUS INTERFERENCE WITH BUSINESS EXPECTANCY
Parties and causes of action, sureties § 12.27
TORT RIGHTS
Risk management, litigation and alternatives § 2.19
TORT THEORIES
Suing construction lenders. See SUING CONSTRUCTION LENDERS
TOTAL COST APPROACH
Changed conditions, pricing damages §§ 18, 18.14.12
TOTAL COST METHOD
Pricing damages. See PRICING DAMAGES
Proof of damages § 16.36
Suing private owner, damages for extra costs § 5.13
Table 18–2, pricing damages § 18.9
TOTAL DIRECT COST ALLOCATION
Home office overhead, pricing damages § 18.24
TOTAL DIRECT COST METHOD
Table 18–8, pricing damages § 18.24
TOTAL FLOAT
Critical path analysis to prove delay § 17.7
TOTAL GROSS PROFIT
Tax considerations § 21.14
TRADE SECRETS
Trial preparation, discovery § 15.12
TRADE USAGE
Legal parameters, litigation and alternatives § 2.19
TREATMENT OF PROCEEDS
Taxation of settlement or judgment proceeds. See TAXATION OF SETTLEMENT OR JUDGMENT PROCEEDS
TREBLE DAMAGES
Tax considerations § 21.10
TRIAL
Preparing case. See PREPARING CASE FOR LITIGATION
Trial and appeal. See TRIAL AND APPEAL

TRIAL AND APPEAL
Generally § 21.2
Appeal
–Appellate brief § 22.26
–Oral argument § 22.27
–Planning § 22.24
–Reassessment of case § 22.25
Initial assessment
–Generally § 22.2
–Alternatives to litigation § 21.10
–Client's objectives § 22.6
–Damages measurement § 21.7
–Equities of case § 22.5
–Facts § 22.3
–Key legal arguments § 22.4
–Potential conflicts of interest § 21.8
–Purpose of trial plan § 21.9
Motions and filing before trial
–Pretiral motions § 22.17
–Pretrial conferences § 22.18
–Pretrial filings § 22.19
Trial
–Closing argument § 22.23
–Cross-examination § 22.22
–Opening statement § 22.20
–Presentation of evidence § 22.21
Trial preparation
–Generally § 22.11
–Complex construction cases and the jury § 22.16
–Conveying a clear picture § 21.12
–Effective documents management § 22.14
–Witness selection § 22.15
–Witness use § 22.16
TRIAL BOOK
Preparing case for litigation, litigation plan § 15.5
Trial preparation § 15.5
TRIAL BRIEFS
Motions and filings before trial, trial and appeal § 22.19
TRIAL NOTEBOOK
Initial assessment, trial and appeal § 22.9
TRIAL PLAN PURPOSE
Initial assessment, trial and appeal § 22.9
TRIAL PREPARATION
Trial and appeal. See TRIAL AND PREPARATION
TRIAL PRESENTATION
Litigation management, litigation and alternatives § 2.39
TRUSTWORTHINESS
Bid protests and mistakes, responsibility § 4.8
TRUTH IN NEGOTIATION ACT
Suing a government § 6.2
TUCKER ACT
Federal waiver of contract controversies § 6.5
TURN-KEY CONSTRUCTION
Contractor's insurance coverage, premises alienated exclusion § 11.12
TYPES AND CAUSES OF DISPUTES
Dispute management. See DISPUTE MANAGEMENT
TYPES OF CONSTRUCTION DOCUMENTS
Trial preparation, trial and appeal § 22.14
TYPES OF SURETY BONDS
Bid bonds
–Generally § 12.5
–Excuses § 12.7
–Form of bid or proposal bond § 12.8
–Voiding § 12.6
Completion bond § 12.9
Lien bond § 12.11
Payment bond § 12.10
Subcontractor's bond § 12.12

UNANTICIPATED IDLE RESOURCES
Termination, pricing damages § 18.7
UNANTICIPATED SUBSURFACE CONDITIONS
Exculpatory clause, litigation and alternatives § 2.23
UNAPPROVED CHANGE ORDERS
Changes in scope, pricing damages § 18.6
UNAUTHORIZED CONTRACT
Suing a government, authority to act for state § 6.14
UNCONSCIONABILITY
Bid mistakes § 4.29
UNCONTEMPLATED DELAYS
Delay claims § 16.18
Suing construction managers § 7.32

UNCONTESTED MATTER
Arbitration § 14.16
UNDERESTIMATED COSTS
Typical project problems, factors affecting project results § 1.9
UNDERGROUND PROPERTY DAMAGE
Contractor's insurance coverage, liability policy exclusions § 11.16
UNDISTRIBUTED CONSTRUCTION LOAN FUNDS
Unjust enrichment theories, suing construction lenders §§ 9.19, 9.20
UNDUE ECONOMIC WASTE
Defending against owner claims, damages § 20.8
UNFORESEEABILITY
Delay claims § 16.23
UNFORESEEABLE CAUSES
No damages for delay, suing construction managers § 7.32
UNFORESEEABLE SUBSURFACE CONDITIONS
Delay claims § 16.6
UNIFORM COMMERCIAL CODE
Bids, suing subcontractors and material suppliers § 10.2
Defending against owner claims, warranties § 20.7
Implied warrantym suing subcontractors and material suppliers § 10.9
Surety's right to contract funds § 12.24
UNIFORM COMMERCIAL CODE APPLICABILITY
Risk management, litigation and alternatives § 2.21
UNILATERAL MISTAKE
Bid mistakes § 4.29
Suing private owner, rescission § 5.14
UNIMPACTED PERIODS
Labor productivity § 19.14
UNIT PRICE BASIS PRICING
Termination, pricing damages § 18.7
UNITS OF PHYSICAL PRODUCTION
Figure 19–1, labor productivity § 19.14
UNIT SPECIFICATION
Factors affecting project results § 1.4
UNJUST ENRICHMENT THEORIES
Generally § 9.16
Definition in construction
–Generally § 9.17
–Measurement § 9.19
–Occurrence § 9.18
Litigation management, litigation and alternatives § 2.37
Potential limitations § 9.20
UNLAWFUL CONVERSION OF FUNDS
Parties and causes of action, sureties § 12.32
UNREALISTIC SCHEDULES
Typical project problems, factors affecting project results § 1.9
UNREASONABLE DELAYS
Defenses, suing construction managers § 7.33
Owner interference § 19.3
UNREASONABLE OR EXCESSIVE PERIODS OF DELAY
Delay claims § 16.19
UNUSUALLY SEVERE WEATHER
Delay claims § 16.24
U.S. ARMY CORPS OF ENGINEERS MANUAL
Dispute management, litigation and alternatives § 2.33
U.S. CLAIMS COURT
Bid protests, federal contracts § 4.15
Federal waiver of contract controversies § 6.5
USE OF WITNESSES
Trial preparation, trial and appeal § 22.15

VARIANCE ANALYSIS
Developing the claim, labor productivity § 19.11
Table 19–4, labor productivity § 19.11
VENUE
Payment bond claims § 13.16
VERIFICATION
Bid mistakes, federal law § 4.31
VIDEO PRESENTATIONS
Arbitration § 14.26
VIDEOTAPE DEPOSITIONS
Trial preparation, depositions § 15.21

VOIDING
Bid bonds, types of surety bonds § 12.6

WAGE STANDARDS
Risk management, litigation and alternatives § 2.18
WAIVER
Defending against owner claims, continued performance as waiver § 20.3
Defending against owner claims, termination defense § 20.14
Payment bond claims, notice § 13.12
Suing a government. See SUING A GOVERNMENT
Suing private owner, notice of changes § 5.4
WAR DAMAGE
Contractor's builder's risk policy, exclusions § 11.22
WARRANTIES
Defective work, suing subcontractors and material suppliers § 10.8
Express. See EXPRESS WARRANTIES
Implied. See IMPLIED WARRANTIES
Warranties and limitations § 20.7
WARRANTY
Defending against owner claims, defective plans and specifications § 20.2
WARRANTY CLAIMS
Contractor's insurance coverage, property damage defined § 11.8
WHEN TIME IS OF THE ESSENCE
Proving liability to recover damages § 16.34
WHO WILL TELL THE STORY
Arbitration § 14.22
WILLFUL MISREPRESENTATION
Suing construction managers § 7.34
WIND CHILL FACTOR
Figure 19–7 § 19.24
WIN-WIN APPROACH
Dispute management, litigation and alternatives § 2.33
WITHDRAWAL OF BID
Bid mistakes, federal law § 4.31
WITHDRAWAL OF BIDS
Suing subcontractors and material suppliers §§ 10.2, 10.3
WITHHOLDING AWARD
Bid protests, federal contracts § 4.15
WITHHOLDING TAX
Payment bond claims, taxes § 13.8
WITNESSES
Arbitration § 14.22
Preparing case for litigation, collecting information § 15.10
Trial preparation, interogatories § 15.16
WITNESS LISTS
Motions and filings before trial, trial and appeal § 22.19
WITNESS PREPARATION
Trial preparation, depositions § 15.22
WITNESS SELECTION
Trial preparation, trial and appeal § 22.15
WITNESS USE
Trial preparation, trial and appeal § 22.15
WORK
Contractor's insurance coverage, work exclusion § 11.14
WORKER'S COMPENSATION INSURANCE
Payment bond claims, taxes § 13.8
WORK FORCE SCHEDULES
Critical path analysis to prove delay, schedules and revenues compared § 17.5
WORKOUT AGREEMENTS
Contract theories, suing construction lenders § 9.7
WRIT OF MANDAMUS
Bid protests, state and local contracts §§ 4.24, 4.26
WRITTEN ACCOUNTS OF FACTS
Initial assessment, trial and appeal § 22.3
WRITTEN DOCUMENTATION
Tax considerations § 21.17
WRITTEN SUBMISSIONS
Prehearings, arbitration § 14.20
WRONGFUL INTENT
Unjust enrichment theories, suing construction lenders § 9.20

ZONING LAW CHANGES
Defending against owner claims, supervening impracticability § 20.6